TRAVEL GUIDE

BEAUTIFUL BRITISH COLUMBIA®
Magazine

BEAUTIFUL BRITISH COLUMBIA®
Magazine

Editor-in-Chief: Bryan McGill
Executive Editor: Cheryl Coull
Art Director: Ken Seabrook
Editorial Assistant: Joel Schaefer
Copy Editor: Anita Willis
Graphic Designer: Noreen Dennis

Writers and Researchers:
Lynn Atkinson, Cheryl Coull, Doug Leighton,
John Lutz, Bruce Obee, Anne Mayhew,
Bryan McGill, Rosemary Neering,
Joel Schaefer, Andrew Scott, Jim Stirling.

Special Thanks To:
April L. Mol, B.C. Wildlife Watch,
Ministry of Environment, Lands, and Parks;
BC Parks; Regional Roadside Development staff,
Ministry of Transportation and Highways.

Regional and Route Maps: Rob Struthers/
Dennis & Struthers Communications.

Gateway and City Maps:
ptc phototype composing ltd, Victoria.

Photography: Gunter Marx Photography

Published by
Beautiful British Columbia,
a Division of Great Pacific Industries Inc.,
929 Ellery Street, Victoria, British Columbia, Canada
V9A 7B4.
Phone: 250-384-5456.
Website: www.beautifulbc.ca

President
Robert Hunt

Director, Publishing and Manufacturing
Tony Owen

Managing Director,
Attractions and Corporate Development
Ruth Heyes

To order the *Beautiful British Columbia*
Travel Guide, call toll-free in Canada and the USA
1-800-663-7611, or from Victoria and
elsewhere 250-384-5456. Weekdays
8 a.m.-5 p.m. Pacific Time. Fax: 1-800-308-4533
toll-free in Canada and USA, or 250-384-2812
from Victoria and elsewhere.
E-mail: orders@beautifulbc.ca

Canadian Cataloguing in Publication Data
Main entry under title:
Beautiful British Columbia Travel Guide
ISSN 1485-0915
1. British Columbia – Guidebooks. I.
Beautiful British Columbia Magazine (Firm)
FC3807.C68 917.11
C98-300911-2
F1087.7.C68
ISBN 1-894226-01-1 (Paperback)
ISBN 1-894226-02-X (Spiral bound)

Prepress
by WYSIWYG

Printed in Canada
by FRIESENS

Front photo: Approaching the southwest coast of
Vancouver Island by land.

Sunset over the Gulf Islands.

BEAUTIFUL BRITISH COLUMBIA

TRAVEL GUIDE

A GUIDE
TO THE TRAVEL GUIDE

This guidebook is designed to help you have the best imaginable touring experience within British Columbia and the Alberta Rockies – the richest, most interesting, most rewarding, even the funniest. The essence of this guidebook lies in the *Logs*, with their item-by-item coverage of highways and byroads, with all the bits of local gossip and tips that come with the meal. Like *Ship's Logs* or *Pilot's Logs*, our *Travellers' Logs* go from Here-to-There. They're capsule journals to adventure.

All you have to know is which Here-to-There you want to "do," so this book is designed to be used at home first (or in the hotel, or at the campsite with a Coleman lantern). That is where you take a broad look at what you might want to explore, read introductions to the regions, check opening remarks that introduce each *Log*, see if it's the kind of road you want to travel, if you have the right vehicle, if it's what you feel like.

When you have pinpointed your trek, and chosen your route maps, then the book goes "on the road" right beside you.

ALL DISTANCES ARE NOT EQUAL! We admit right up front that our distances are only reasonably accurate. We found a welter of contradictions among current official and unofficial sources on distances between towns, cities, and other points on the maps. This was largely due to varying starting points, such as town borders (often unclear) and town centres. Whenever possible, we measured from city or town halls, or village offices, to gauge distances from town to town.

Also note that all odometers are not equal. It may be worthwhile to check yours out. And tire pressure influences the readings: low tire pressure makes for longer kilometres. With all these factors, the best we can say is that our distances are "approximately exact," but probably more exact over all than any other single source.

With minor variations, we have stayed with the six new tourism regions created by the BC government: British Columbia Rockies, Thompson-Okanagan, and so on. These regions can feel arbitrary when, on the road, you must refer to yet another chapter, but for the most part, they provide a useful reflection the province's major geographic and cultural differences.

If at any time you become lost while travelling within BC, well, what a great opportunity – just collar the nearest resident. Locals are likely to be friendly and may know some good stories.

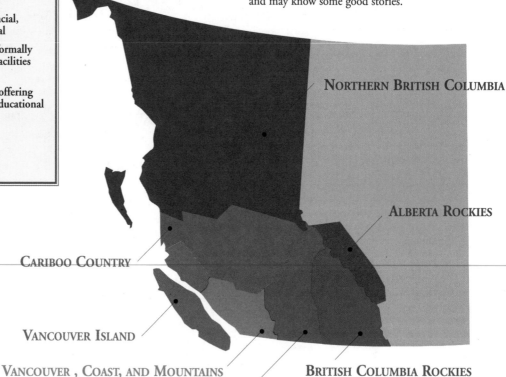

Legend:

- Towns and cities
- Information centres
- Jet service
- Airstrips
- Ferry terminals
- Campgrounds: tent and trailer
- Campgrounds: tent only
- Important junctions
- Rest Areas
- Points of interest
- Historic sites
- Hostels
- Parks: national, provincial, municipal, and regional
- Recreation areas: not formally parks - may not have facilities
- Sites identified by BC Wildlife Watch as offering wildlife-viewing and educational opportunities.
- Bus stations
- Train stations

Map labels:
NORTHERN BRITISH COLUMBIA
ALBERTA ROCKIES
CARIBOO COUNTRY
VANCOUVER ISLAND
VANCOUVER, COAST, AND MOUNTAINS
BRITISH COLUMBIA ROCKIES
THOMPSON OKANAGAN

The Route Maps

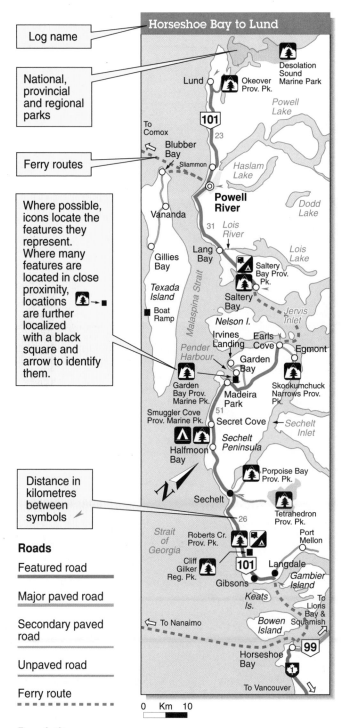

Log name → Horseshoe Bay to Lund

National, provincial and regional parks

Ferry routes

Where possible, icons locate the features they represent. Where many features are located in close proximity, locations are further localized with a black square and arrow to identify them.

Distance in kilometres between symbols

Map labels: Lund, Okeover Prov. Pk., Desolation Sound Marine Park, Powell Lake, 101, To Comox, 23, Blubber Bay, Sliammon, Haslam Lake, Powell River, Dodd Lake, Vananda, 31, Lois River, Gillies Bay, Lang Bay, Lois Lake, Texada Island, Saltery Bay Prov. Pk., Boat Ramp, Saltery Bay, Malaspina Strait, Jervis Inlet, Nelson I., Irvines Landing, Earls Cove, Egmont, Pender Harbour, Garden Bay, Garden Bay Prov. Marine Pk., Skookumchuck Narrows Prov. Pk., Madeira Park, Smuggler Cove Prov. Marine Pk., 51, Secret Cove, Sechelt Inlet, Sechelt Peninsula, Halfmoon Bay, Porpoise Bay Prov. Pk., Sechelt, 26, Tetrahedron Prov. Pk., Strait of Georgia, Roberts Cr. Prov. Pk., Port Mellon, Cliff Gilker Reg. Pk., 101, Langdale, Gibsons, Gambier Island, Keats Is., To Lions Bay & Squamish, To Nanaimo, Bowen Island, Horseshoe Bay, 99, 1, To Vancouver

0   Km   10

Roads

Featured road

Major paved road

Secondary paved road

Unpaved road

Ferry route

Population

◉ 25,000+

◎ 5,000 – 25,000

● 1,000 – 5,000

○ Under 1,000

Deeper, broader, bigger, better

In this, our 6th edition of the *Beautiful British Columbia Travel Guide*, we introduce a new section. "What is BC?" provides a thousand facts and more, about BC's coast and Interior, its lakes and rivers, its forests and mountains, and its people. When fitted together, these puzzle pieces profile an amazing province and add up to a single, irrefutable fact: BC is BIG.

BC is big, and as it continues to develop, so does our *Travel Guide*, now eight pages thicker. Since the last edition, there is more parkland (nearly 11 percent of the province), there are more wildlife watch sites (now 346), more highways, more ways for travellers to experience the history and geography of this vast region. And, if BC weren't big enough, the *Travel Guide* has swept into the southern Yukon Territory, annexing the Alaska Highway from Watson Lake to Whitehorse, including routes to Skagway, Alaska, as well as to Atlin and Tatshenshini-Alsek Wilderness Park in BC's remote northeast corner.

The *Travel Guide* is growing in depth as well as breadth. While we remain strictly committed to our founding principle — to guide you with clear directions through the biggest cities to the wildest places, to country festivals, fruit stands, and rest areas — we also strive to take you beneath the surface. What lies under the asphalt and irrigated desert? Who lived here a century ago? What would you have found here 1,000 years ago, or even 515 million years ago? And where are we headed, not just on today's road trip, but in the grand scheme of things?

BC is big, and so is the *Travel Guide* — by no means a "pocket guidebook." It has taken us 350,000 meticulously chosen words to tell this epic story, to travel down 40,000 kilometres of highways and byroads. More than 5,000 detailed entries have been incorporated into six fat new regions, in keeping with Tourism BC's simpler approach to the province's cultural geography.

We have filled the *Travel Guide*'s 316 pages with 85 maps and more than 100 colour photographs — glimpses of some of the places you might not get to this summer, simply because BC is so big. But there are other seasons.

With all it contains, the *Travel Guide* is much more than just a travel guide. It is an indispensable reference book. An entertaining campfire read. Or, for those rainy days at home, a journey of the mind.

— *Cheryl Coull*

Route Finder: Route Maps at a Glance

Boxes identify specific route descriptions or *Logs*, the regions, and the pages where they are to be found.

Dawson Creek

Grande Pairie

Hinton

Jasper

Tête Jaune Cache

Houston

Vanderhoof

Prince George

Quesnel

Williams Lake

100 Mile House

Bella Coola

Port Hardy

Powell River

Lund

Campbell River

Courtenay
Comox

Nanaimo

Port Alberni

Lake Louise
Banff

Radium Hot Springs
Invermere

Golden

Revelstoke

Sicamous
Salmon Arm

Nakusp

Kamloops

Vernon

Kelowna
Peachland

Merritt

Penticton

Princeton

Lytton

Hope

Chilliwack

Abbotsford

Kimberley

Cranbrook

Castlegar

Nelson

Trail

Grand Forks

Osoyoos

Squamish

Horseshoe Bay

Vancouver

Victoria

Fernie

Creston

Tumbler Ridge

287

284

265

266

251

247

243

176

234

221

218

207

203

229

205

200

197

194

215

192

189

187

212

166

163

169

158

153

147

176

180

135

172

129

124

108

137

117

122

167

57

52

39

48

64

80

66

111

73

83

Haida
Gwaii

Pacific
Ocean

Vancouver
Island

7

WHAT IS BC?

What is this place, BC, you ask. On the verge of an adventure, you want to know what you're getting into. How big, how wide, how many rivers will you have to cross, will you need an umbrella, how wild is the wildlife, how tall the trees? Are there people there? Do they live in igloos? Read on, and be prepared. There is no place like BC.

BC IS A PROVINCE

• Canada's third largest. At 947,796 sq km, it takes up 9.5 percent of the world's second-largest country – 0.64 percent of the world's land surface.
• BC is four times bigger than Great Britain, 2.5 times bigger than Japan. Only about 30 nations are larger than BC.

• To BC's west: the largest body of water on Earth – the Pacific Ocean. Japan lies 7,456km west of Vancouver Island. BC's true westernmost point is actually not on the coast, but inland, on the BC/Alaska border, at Boundary Peak, in an unnamed snowfield.
• East of BC: the Prairie province of Alberta. To the north: Canada's remote, sparsely populated Yukon Territory and Northwest Territories, and the American state of Alaska. Southward: the main body of the world's fourth-largest country, the US. BC shares this boundary with the states of Washington, Idaho, and Montana.
• Shaped like a rhomboid, BC stretches from the sea to the Rocky Mountains, 901km along the 49th Parallel. It runs 1,467km from the southeast corner to the northeast: this border with Alberta follows the height of land in the Rocky Mountains, then contrives a straight line north. From the northeast corner, BC's border traces the 60th Parallel 816km west to the Haines Triangle. Finally, the western boundary: washed by sea and tides and rain, a phenomenally convoluted coastline estimated to be 27,000km long.
• Victoria, on Vancouver Island, is BC's capital. The Rand McNally International Atlas lists 70 other cities, counties, states, lakes, rivers, falls, mountains, and stations, including one other island capital, in the Seychelles, all named after Victoria, Queen of Great Britain, 1837-1901.

BC IS MANY PLACES

• BC is 18 percent rock, ice, and tundra; 62.9 percent forest; 3.8 percent lake, river, and swamp. Only 3 percent of BC has soil suitable for agriculture.
• There is no other place in the world with BC's diversity of landscape and climate: here are sea coast, mountains, valleys, glaciers, plateaus, tundra, prairie, and a "pocket desert" – all together eight regional micro-climates, three of four continental climatic zones, and 14 local biogeoclimatic zones (see below).

BC IS FORESTS

• BC's 14 biogeoclimatic zones range from treeless Alpine Tundra (18 percent of BC) to Bunchgrass (0.3 percent of BC), to Spruce-Willow-Birch (8 percent of BC) and Coastal Douglas fir (0.2 percent of BC).
• One of the planet's most biologically "productive" environments is the Coastal Western Hemlock biogeoclimatic zone (11 percent of BC, stretching 900km along the Pacific coast). This coastal temperate rainforest supports five million species of animals, insects, and plants, including 3,000 species of mushroom, and some of the oldest and largest trees in the world – yellow cedars that live to be more than 1,000 years old, and 90m Sitka spruce. Intense environmental battles are waged over this forest: 53 percent of BC's original temperate rainforest has been logged. What remains in BC is 25 percent of all the temperate rainforest anywhere in the world. Clearcutting continues: 123ha per day. The world's largest unlogged coastal temperate rainforest is the 4,050-sq-km Kitlope Valley, now a heritage conservancy.
• BC's largest biogeoclimatic zone is the Boreal White and Black Spruce zone (16 percent of BC). The boreal forests of northern BC – part of a 1,000km-wide belt that stretches across Canada – behave like a natural thermostat, absorbing poisonous carbon dioxide from the atmosphere.
• Of the 62.9 percent of BC that is forested, 43 percent is old growth (coastal trees more than 250 years old; Interior trees more than 120 years old). Most of this remaining old growth is in small, fragmented stands, and does not reflect the grandeur of what stood up to the mid-19th century.
• The official estimate of BC's remaining old-growth

forest that stands in protected areas is 13 percent (some environmentalists say it is only about 6 percent). Protected areas now make up 11 percent of BC (see BC's Parks).

• On the coast, half of all trees ever cut have been logged since 1967; in the Interior, half of all trees cut have been logged since 1977.

• Trees most harvested are hemlock, cedar, balsam, and Douglas fir on the coast; and spruce and lodgepole pine in the Interior.

• The largest silviculture plantation (i.e. replanted clearcut) in the world is in the upper Bowron River Valley: 53,000ha.

BC IS A SHANGRI-LA OF MOUNTAINS

• 75 percent of BC is 1,000m or more above sea level. The province is ribbed by the Canadian Cordillera, one of the world's major mountain systems. Its parallel mountain ranges, plateaus, and highlands – 725km wide – run southeast to northwest from the 49th parallel to the 60th parallel. The Cordillera includes the ranges of Vancouver Island (which rival the Rockies when you consider the vertical distance from the sea bottom to the highest peak) and the Coast Mountains, North America's highest and third highest in the world after the Himalayas and Andes. The rich prairie farmland of the Peace River region, east of the Rockies in BC's northeast corner, is the only part of BC outside the Cordillera.

• BC's highest point is Fairweather Mountain, 4,633m, on the BC/Alaska border in the Coast Mountains. Just north, Canada's highest point, at 5,951m, is the Yukon's Mount Logan. Near the northwest end of the Coast Mountains is Alaska's Mount McKinley, at 6,194m, North America's highest peak. The highest peak entirely in BC is Mount Waddington, 4,016m. The highest peak in the Rocky Mountains is Mount Robson, 3,954m. Compare all this with the world's highest, Mount Everest in the Himalayas, 8,846m. A number of other Himalayan peaks are well over 8,000m; next highest are the Andes – with Cerro Aconcagua in Argentina the highest among them at 6,960m.

• Birch Mountain, 2,060m, on Theresa Island in Atlin Lake on the lee side of the Coast Mountains, is the highest mountain on a lake island in the world.

• BC's highest city – Kimberley, 1,120m – is in the Purcell Mountains.

• Canada's highest major lake, at 1,171m, is Chilko Lake in Ts'yl-os Provincial Park.

• North America's longest valley is the Rocky Mountain Trench, extending 1,600km from BC's northern border to Montana in the US, and ranging 3-16km wide. It is the birthplace of BC's most important rivers, including the Peace, Columbia, and Fraser.

• BC's highest highway pass is the Salmo-Creston Skyway, 1,774m, in the Selkirk Mountains. The lowest point on a public road anywhere in Canada is the George Massey Tunnel near Vancouver. It runs under the Fraser River, 20m below sea level.

• As much as 7 percent of BC's land surface is covered by glaciers – ice and snow that stays more than a year.

During the Pleistocene Age, nearly all of BC, but only about 30 percent of the planet, was blanketed with ice. Today, glaciers cover about 10 percent of the world's land area: with the greatest proportion being in the Antarctic and Greenland. The largest of BC's thousands of glaciers are along the Northwest coast, where glaciers run one after the other, broken only by rivers. Among them is the Forest Kerr Glacier in the Coast Mountains, near the Iskut River. Weighing some 10,000 metric tons, it is 90 sq km in area and 20km long. BC's glaciers are retreating, or shrinking, at an average rate of 1m a year.

BC IS LONG LAKES AND RIVERS

• BC is one of the world's most water-rich areas, with about 24,000 lakes, rivers, and streams.

• 37 major river systems flow through BC. The longest river entirely within BC is the mighty, muddy Fraser, 1,368km long. The Fraser, Columbia (North America's fifth longest river, at 2,000km), and Thompson, drain 70 percent of BC.

• The longest river in North America is the Mackenzie-Peace River system, born in northern BC and flowing 4,241km to the Beaufort Sea. The Nile is the world's longest: 6,670km.

• BC's shortest river is the Powell River – at 500m, it is the second shortest in the world. The shortest of all is the D River, in Lincoln City, Oregon, 37m long.

• Della Falls, at 440m, are Canada's highest waterfalls, nearly eight times as high as Niagara, and exceeded in the world by only 10 others. Venezuela's Angel Falls, 979m, are the world's highest.

• BC's largest lakes are in the north. The largest of all is manmade – the Williston Reservoir covers 1,658 sq km. The second largest is manmade too – the Nechako Reservoir covers 847 sq km. Atlin Lake, BC's third largest at 743 sq km (140km long), is natural. But the next two largest after that are, once again, manmade – these are the Kinbasket and Arrow reservoirs (an enlargement of the Upper and Lower Arrow lakes).

• BC's deepest lake is Quesnel Lake. At 530m, it's the world's deepest glacier-carved lake. BC's longest natural lake is Babine Lake, 177km.

• Scientists come from all over the world to study tiny Mahoney Lake in the Okanagan. At its deepest levels, this small lake is saltier than the sea, and supports only high densities of purple sulphur bacteria that, miraculously, can live without oxygen.

• There are more than 60 hydroelectric dams and some 35 hydroelectric facilities on BC's rivers, delivering power to 1.5 million British Columbians via 73,000km of transmission and distribution lines.

• North America's most dammed river is the Columbia. In the 2,000km from its headwaters in BC's Rockies, to its mouth on the Oregon Coast, and along its man tributaries, are more than 45 major hydroelectric dams. Of those, at least 18 are in BC. More than 80 percent of BC's electricity comes from the Columbia and Peace rivers.

BC IS PACIFIC ISLANDS

• There are 6,000 islands and islets off the mainland coast of BC: Vancouver Island, at 32,261 sq km, is the largest North American island in the Pacific. It is 451km long and 65-97km wide, with 3,440km of coastline. BC's second-largest island is Graham Island (6,436 sq km), in the Haida Gwaii (Queen Charlotte Islands) archipelago of some 200 islands.

BC IS PEOPLE

• BC's total population – 3.987 million. That's an average of four people per sq km. In Macau, the world's most densely populated country, there are 25,841 people per sq km; in Europe,150 people per sq km. Half of BC's population, however, is concentrated on the Lower Mainland. In Northern BC, excluding Prince George, there are an average of 1.8 people per sq km. In Greater Vancouver, there are 649.4 people per sq km.

• In BC, there are 160 incorporated municipalities, including 41 cities, 50 districts, 14 towns, 44 villages, and one Indian Government District.

• Some 6,000 sq km of BC are taken up by cities, towns, and transportation corridors.

• Like continental landforms, Canada's population (28.8 million) is shifting west. BC is the country's fastest-growing province: our 2 percent growth rate is twice the national average. The mountain resort town of Whistler is the country's fastest-growing community. It is estimated BC's population will reach 5.8 million by 2022.

• BC's biggest cities: Greater Vancouver (1.82 million), Greater Victoria (317,989), Kelowna (89,442), Kamloops (77,421), Prince George (75,150), and Nanaimo (70,130).

• BC's smallest city is Greenwood (784). When incorporated in 1897, its population was about 3,000.

• The longest continuously occupied non-native settlement in BC is McLeod Lake, established in 1805.

• 3.8 percent of BC's population (139,655 people) are aboriginal. There are 197 Indian bands with 1,650 Indian reserves totalling 3,440 sq km (0.37 of BC's total land base). The Nisga'a people of the Nass Valley have negotiated the first treaty between a BC First Nation and the BC and Canadian governments: they will gain control of 1,930 sq km, about one-tenth of their traditional territories.

• About 40 percent of British Columbians are of British descent; 30 percent are descendants of people from other European countries. The largest group of non-Europeans are of Chinese descent: about 9 percent of BC's population. East Indian descendants make up 4.4 percent; other Asian groups make up 5.5 percent. Immigration trends have changed, however; in Vancouver, four of five recent immigrants were born in Asia (Hong Kong, China, and Taiwan); only one in 10 was born in Europe.

• BC's political parties are the New Democratic Party (NDP), Liberal Party, Reform Party, and Green Party (following, for the most part, platforms of their national counterparts), and the Progressive Democratic Alliance. Traditionally, BC politics have been characterized by a strong polarization of left- and right-wing ideologies – the left drawing support of unionized forest workers, and in more recent times, environmentalists.

• No one lives in igloos.

WE ARE LOGGERS, FISHERFOLK, EMU FARMERS

• 1.8 million people work in BC: 113,000 in tourism (not including those self-employed or indirectly employed in tourism). The number is rising. There are 92,000 loggers, mill workers, and silvicultural workers. This number is dropping. About 18,000 people worked in the commercial and recreational fishing industries in 1997, down from 26,000 in 1990. There are 32,950 farmers. Salmon farming employs 2,000 people. Mining directly employs 8,500 people, and a further 4,200 indirectly. BC's public sector – the smallest per capita in Canada – employs 350,550 people.

• Lumber and pulp remain BC's biggest exports, almost half the province's total. Four percent of BC's logs are exported raw.

• Fish harvesters haul in more than 80 species of fin fish, shellfish, and sea plants. Salmon make up 93 percent of that harvest.

• In BC there are eight coal mines, 14 major metal mines, and five smelters. BC is Canada's largest coal-exporting province. Canada's most productive coal mine is southeastern BC's Fording River Mine – processing more than 45 million tonnes a year. The Interior's Highland Valley Copper mine is North America's largest open-pit copper mine. Trail's Cominco smelter is the world's largest zinc and lead smelting complex, processing 300,000 tonnes of zinc and 135,000 tonnes of lead. The Island Copper Mine, on northern Vancouver Island, was the largest open-pit mine in BC until it closed, in 1996. In its day, it was the lowest manmade hole on earth (not including mine shafts), spiralling 396m below sea level.

• BC's 21,835 farms occupy 24,000 sq km. Half are in the Fraser Valley. The Okanagan Valley produces more than 96 percent of BC's tree-fruit crops and wine grapes. 85 percent of BC's wheat is grown in the Peace River Valley. BC's central Interior is cattle country.

• Cranberries, ginseng, and mushrooms are new up-and-comers, representing $26 million, $10 million, and $22 million respectively in 1996 exports. BC is western North America's largest producer of fresh mushrooms, processing 15 million kilograms a year. Since the Canadian Government withdrew its 60-year ban on the production of industrial hemp in the late 1990s, BC has become the North American leader in the development of a crop more versatile than the soybean, cotton plant, and Douglas fir tree combined. Hemp has more than 25,000 uses.

• 180 BC farms raise ostrich-like emus. Emu oil is hailed as a pain reliever and anti-inflammatory.

BC IS LOTUS LAND

• Nearly one in three Canadians say they would pack their bags and move to BC if they could – Vancouver is the most popular choice. Climate, scenery, and access to nature are the reasons. British Columbians are also less inclined to move from their home province than other Canadians – even for a better job.

• Of all Canadians, British Columbians have the highest average incomes ($44,741 for men, $33,008 for women). We live longer than other Canadians: fewer British Columbians die from heart disease, fewer smoke. We are less inclined to be overweight. We drink more than other Canadians: 110 litres of alcohol a year on average, while the national average is 102 litres (only Yukoners out-drink us, 183 litres a year).

BC IS ON SHAKY GROUND

• Every day in BC there is an earthquake, but most days there are two, or three. Of these, few are felt. Most occur along the coast.

• BC's populated Lower Mainland and all of Vancouver Island form the northern reaches of a geologically intense region scientists call Cascadia. From here south to Medocino, California, a sleeping Godzilla stirs: a gargantuan piece of the Earth's crust called the North American Plate is moving west toward Japan at a rate of 2cm a year. Offshore – beneath, and forming the bottom of the Pacific

• The largest on land earthquake in recorded Canada's history struck central Vancouver Island in 1946: with a magnitude of 7.3, it cracked roads and toppled chimneys as far away as Victoria. On man died when his dinghy overturned near Comox; another, in distant Seattle, died of a heart attack. A 5.4 magnitude quake under Pender Island in 1976 broke windows.

• The most severe seabed quake in Canadian history was Aug. 22, 1949, off Haida Gwaii. With a surface wave magnitude of 8.1, it rattled chandeliers in Jasper, Alberta.

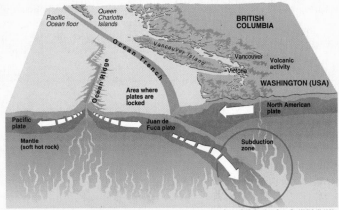

Sources: Pacific Geoscience Centre, Rand McNally World Atlas

Ocean – is the 25km-thick Juan de Fuca Plate, moving (or subducting) east and under the North American plate at a rate of 2.5cm a year. Things, geologically, have been relatively quiet for three centuries. Not good, say scientists, who believe the two opposing plates are jammed, and will, eventually, break free: the Big One, they warn us, will strike again.

New paleo-seismic evidence says that once every 300-600 years on average, a colossal subduction quake hits Cascadia. The last time Godzilla woke: 9pm, January 26, 1700 (prior to the arrival of Europeans here). The earthquake was 9 or more on the Richter scale; the resulting tsunami (meaning "harbour wave" in Japanese) changed the coastal profile, washed away one village that we know of, and, on January 27 and 28, reached the shores of Japan. Geologists estimate the chance of another such event occurring before 2050 is 5-10 percent. The quake that struck Kobe, Japan, in 1995, killing 6,000 people, was 6.9 on the Richter scale.

• The most recent tsunami to affect BC residents occurred Good Friday, March 27, 1964. An 8.5 magnitude quake, centred some 100km east of Anchorage, Alaska, delivered a series of waves to Port Alberni at the head of a 40km inlet. The seas rose 3m above high water: 58 buildings were destroyed, boats were capsized, no one died.

• Volcanic eruptions, in active subduction zones such as Cascadia, are inevitable. As the Juan de Fuca Plate slides beneath North America, deep-seated rocks melt into magma, which rises upward to form volcanoes. Most of Cascadia's volcanoes simmer south of the Canada/US border (Mt St Helens, the most intensely and most recently active, erupted May 18, 1980). Mt Garibaldi and Mt Meager, northeast of Vancouver, are the northernmost Cascadian volcanoes. There are some 30 volcanic cones along a 120km stretch of the Garibaldi-Bridge River area.

• BCs most recent volcanic eruption occurred far north of Cascadia, in the Nass Valley. In about 1750, a river of lava dammed the Tseax River, rerouted the Nass River, and buried two Nisga'a villages.

• The cost of living in Vancouver is 12 percent higher than "typical cities" elsewhere in Canada or the US. House prices on the Lower Mainland are almost $58,000 above the national average of $150,664.

BC IS HOT, COLD, WET, AND DRY

• BC – noted for its moderate climate – has some of the most extreme weather in Canada.
• The most rain in Canada in any given year fell at Henderson Lake on Vancouver Island – 8,123mm (27 feet) in 1931 (North America's record). The wettest place in the world, Mt Waialeale, Hawaii, gets 11,680mm a year. The Canadian city with the highest average annual precipitation is Prince Rupert – 2,552mm (8.5 feet). It also has the lowest average in days of sunshine. Langara Island, on northern Haida Gwaii (Queen Charlotte Islands), holds BC's record for ducky weather – 300 wet days in 1939. BC's greatest 24-hour deluge was at Ucluelet – 489.2mm (19.5 inches – knee deep on a tall man) fell on October 6, 1967.
• Vancouver gets 1,068mm (42.7 inches) of rain each year and 1,931 hours of sunshine. Victoria, just across the strait on Vancouver Island, gets only 700-800mm (28-32 inches) of rain, and an average of 2,082 hours of sunshine.

BC IS SPLENDOUR, WITHOUT DIMINISHMENT

• BC's official shield was designed by Rev Arthur Beanlands in 1906. The Union Jack on the upper third symbolizes the province's origin as a British colony. The gold half-sun on the bottom, imposed upon three wavy blue bars representing the Pacific, symbolizes BC as Canada's most westerly province. The shield is supported by a ram and a stag. BC's motto, engraved on the shield, is Splendour sine occasu (Splendour Without Diminishment). Beneath this are blossoms of the Pacific Dogwood, BC's emblem. The provincial flag, duplicating the shield was adopted in 1960.

• BC's official bird is the brazen Steller's jay.

• BC's official tree: the Western red cedar, valued for its many uses, lives as long as a millennium.

• BC's official stone is BC jade, a nephrite jade, usually dark green.

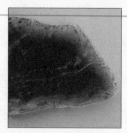

• Some 5,500 to 6,000 umbrellas are left on BC Transit buses each year.
• BC's sunniest place is Cranbrook, with 2,244 hours a year. Estevan, Saskatchewan, holds the Canadian record, with 2,537 hours.
• BC's "pocket desert," in the Okanagan Valley, with its annual average precipitation of 300mm (one foot) receives a scant 50mm (two inches) more rain a year than true deserts. Ashcroft in BC's Interior received only 71mm (2.8 inches) of rain in 1938.
• BC gets record snowfalls – the most in any one day in Canada – 118.1cm (3.8 feet) at Lakelse Lake, Jan 17, 1974. The most in any recorded Canadian winter fell on Mt Copeland, near Revelstoke – 2,446.5cm (79.5 feet) in 1971-72. Canada's highest annual average, 1,433cm (46.5 feet), falls at Glacier National Park, east of Revelstoke. The Canadian city least likely to experience a white Christmas is Victoria, BC.
• BC enjoys Canada's most frost-free days: some 220 days a year along the coast. Victoria holds the record: 685 days, in 1925-1926.
• Kamloops holds Canada's record for the longest heat wave – 24 days in 1958 were 35C (95F) and hotter. Lytton and Lillooet share BC's record for the hottest day: 44.4C (111.9F) on July 16, 1941.
• BC's coldest day: in Smith River, just south of the BC/Yukon border, on Jan 31, 1947, the mercury plunged to -58.9C (-74F).
• BC's windiest place: at Cape St James, at the southern tip of Haida Gwaii, the wind blows 99 percent of the time, and every third day there are gales.

BC IS ROADS, RAILS, FERRIES

• There are 42,500km of public highway in BC – 22,053km are paved. Of this, BC's portion of the Trans-Canada Highway – the world's longest national highway at 8,047km – takes up 993km. An additional 42,459km of logging roads slice through the province.
• There are an average of three road kills per km of BC highway per year. This includes bear, moose, deer, skunks, badgers, and porcupines, but not salamanders, newts, and frogs. On Vancouver Island highways alone, 735 deer were killed in 1997.
• There are an estimated one million cars operating in the Vancouver area (pop. 1.82 million) – more per capita than in Los Angeles.
• There are 6,800km of railway track in BC. The Canadian Pacific Railway (CPR), completed in 1885-86, maintains 2,414km of steel. The Canadian National Railway, maintains 1,894km of track in BC. Canada's smallest official railway is the 2km Fort George Railway, in Prince George.
• The longest railway tunnel in the western hemisphere is the CPR's Mt Macdonald Tunnel built between 1984 and 1988. It cuts 14.6km through Mt Macdonald and Cheops Mountain in the Selkirk Mountains.
• BC Ferries, one of the world's largest ferry fleets, operates 40 ships and carries 22 million passengers a year to 47 ports of call. The two most mammoth ferries each carry 2,000 passengers and 470 vehicles at a time.
• The Vancouver International Airport is Canada's largest after Toronto's: 80,000 people a day flood through its gates. At the international terminal, the world's largest baggage carousels can deliver a 747's cargo to passengers in 27 minutes.
• Prince Rupert's is the third-deepest natural harbour in the world (only Buenos Aires, Argentina, and Sydney, Australia, have deeper harbours).

WHAT TO KNOW

CROSSING THE BORDER

There are 16 points of entry for motorists travelling across the Canada/US boundary into BC. These are indicated on the regional maps. Details are also in the *Logs*. When crossing the border into Canada, US citizens should carry identification. People from other countries need passports. For info on Canada Customs regulations, contact: General Inquiries, First Floor, 333 Dunsmuir St, Vancouver, BC, V6B 5R3. Call 604-666-0545 or 1-800-461-9999; after 4:30pm and weekends or holidays, 604-666-0272; or 604-538-3610 for 24-hour information. For info on US customs regulations, travellers in BC can call 604-278-1825 or 1-800-529-4410.

The CANPASS program provides time-saving lanes and pre-authorized clearance to frequent cross-border travellers at the busy Douglas/Blaine crossing south of Vancouver, and at Boundary Bay, Huntingdon, and Pacific Highway crossings. For info: 604-535-9346.

By Boat

If non-residents are entering BC by boat, there are many marine customs ports. Victoria and Vancouver are the largest, but Nanaimo, Courtenay/Comox, Campbell River, Sidney, Port Alberni, Powell River, Kitimat, Ucluelet, White Rock, Prince Rupert, Bedwell Harbour, and Stewart all have customs facilities. Waneta, on the Columbia River near Trail, can also process visitors arriving by boat.

Declaring Goods

Laws concerning the amount of duty-free goods foreigners can take back to their home countries from Canada vary with each country. Americans returning home after more than 48 hours in Canada can take back $400 US worth of goods, including 1.1 litres of alcohol without paying duty. If you've been in Canada less than 48 hours, the maximum duty-free amount is $200 US.

Sporting and outdoors gear, tape recorders, optical items, stereos, radios, musical instruments, laptops, and other equipment for personal use should be declared when entering Canada.

Guns and Other Other Weapons

Canada has strict laws concerning firearms and restricted weapons. In recent years BC provincial courts have imposed fines and ordered the confiscation of guns illegally carried into Canada from the US. Restricted weapons in Canada include revolvers, pistols, and fully automatic firearms. Rifles and shotguns normally used for hunting may not be brought into Canada, unless the owner intends to hunt.

Motorists who drive into Canada with guns are usually sent back to the US, where they can store their firearms with gun dealers in border towns. Those who arrive on Vancouver Island aboard ferries from the US must declare their guns, which are then sent back on the next US-bound ferry. Those failing to declare firearms are usually charged under Canadian law if a customs search turns up a weapon.

Natural Bridge on the Kicking Horse river in Yoho National park.

Liquor

The legal drinking age in BC is 19. People crossing the BC/US border can carry up to 1.1 litres of spirits or wine, or 8.1 litres of beer or ale. Drinking alcohol in public places is prohibited in BC. Drinking is permitted in provincial campgrounds at your campsite, which is considered private. Impaired driving is a criminal offence.

Pets

Dogs and cats older than three months coming from the US must be accompanied by a veterinary certificate stating the animal has been vaccinated for rabies during the previous three years. The certificate, which should describe the animal, must state the date of vaccination.

Travellers from the US may bring two pet birds into Canada, along with a written declaration that the birds have been in the owner's possession for the previous three months, and have not been in contact with other birds. Parrots require export permits before they can be taken out of the US. Any birds from countries other than the US will be destroyed at the border.

Plants

The import of plants, including soil, is heavily regulated. All plants must be declared at the time of entry.

TOURIST INFORMATION

British Columbia in General: For free BC travel information and reservations call Super, Natural British Columbia toll-free from anywhere in North America at 1-800-663-6000. International visitors may call 250-387-1642 and those in BC's Lower Mainland, 604-663-6000. From within the UK, prospective travellers to BC can call 0891 715000 (premium rate line), and from Germany the number is 06181-45178. Reservations can also be accessed through the Internet at www.snbc-res.com. In Canada and the US, information can be obtained by writing Tourism British Columbia, PO Box 9830 Stn Prov Govt, Victoria, BC, V8W 9W5. In England, write: 1 Regent St, London, England, SW1Y 4NS.

Tourism Regions: BC's six official tourism regions are each administered by a tourism association. The *Travel Guide* has based its regions upon these. Tourism association addresses and phone numbers are provided in the introduction to each region.

Visitor Info Centres: More than 100 communities throughout BC operate official Visitor Info Centres as members of the Visitor InfoNetwork. They provide information about their areas as well as the entire province. Most Info Centres are conspicuous, displaying a distinctive Visitor Info Centre logo: they are often located on main routes into towns. Info Centres operate a minimum of 9am-5pm in July and Aug and most operate year-round. To complement the Visitor InfoNetwork, many small communities operate seasonal information booths. Info Centres and booths are listed in the *Log* after details on the community. Mailing addresses and telephone numbers of Info Centres, Chambers of Commerce, or local government offices are also listed. Some key Visitor Info Centres include the Peace Arch Provincial Visitor Info Centre at 356 King George Hwy located immediately north of the Blaine Canada/US border; the Mount Robson Provincial Visitor Info Centre in Mount Robson Provincial Park, 61km west of the BC/Alberta border; the Yoho Provincial Visitor Info Centre, 15km west of the BC/Alberta border; and the Vancouver and Victoria Info Centres, below.

- **Vancouver:** Info Centre, Plaza level, 200 Burrard St, Vancouver, BC, V6C 3L6. 604-683-2000.
- **Victoria (Vancouver Island):** Info Centre, 812 Wharf St, Victoria, BC, V8W 1T3. 250-953-2033.
- **BC Provincial Parks in General:** BC Parks, 800 Johnson St, Victoria, BC, V8V 1X4. 250-387-5002.
- **National Parks in General:** Canadian Heritage, Parks Canada, Information Services, Western Regional Office, Room 552, 220-4th Ave SE, Calgary, Alberta, T2G 4X3. 403-292-4401. Fax: 403-292-4408.
- **Canada in General:** Tourism Canada, 235 Queen St, Ottawa, Ontario, K1A 0H6. 613-946-1000. Or 250-710-1175 Douglas St, Victoria, BC, V8W 2E1.
- **Yukon Territories:** Tourism Yukon, Box 2703, Whitehorse, YT, Y1A 2C6. 867-667-5340.
- **Alberta:** Travel Alberta, Box 2500, Edmonton, AB, T5J 2Z4. Local calls: 780-427-4321. From across Canada and the US: 1-800-661-8888. At Commerce Place, 10155-102 St, Edmonton, AB, T5J 4L6.

ACCOMMODATION AND CAMPING

Throughout BC there's accommodation to suit every traveller. There are resort lodges with fireplaces and hot tubs or just the basic skier's room. There are hotels, motels, hostels, and family inns offering bed and breakfast (B&Bs). Even the campgrounds range from luxurious to rustic. Many facilities cater to specific activities, such as fishing or horseback riding.

Visit or write specific information centres or regional tourist associations for listings and brochures, and for a free copy of the tourism ministry's BC *Accommodations* guide, listing locations, phone numbers, and prices of hotels, motels, and campgrounds throughout the province. Whatever the season, whatever the region, it is wise to make reservations, especially with campgrounds in popular areas.

For the Hosteller

Hostelling International (HI) Canada, BC Region, offers inexpensive year-round accommodation for individuals and families at 17 locations throughout the province. Reservations are recommended. Memberships offering preferential rates are available at hostels; non-members are welcome. Contact the hostels listed at left, or Hostelling International, BC Region, 402-134 Abbott St, Vancouver, BC, V6B 2K4. 604-684-7101 or 1-800-661-0020. Fax: 604-684-7181. Website: www.hihostels.bc.ca.

Hostel-style accommodation is also available at the **Vancouver YMCA**, 955 Burrard St., Vancouver, BC, V6Z 1Y2. 604-681-0221. The **YWCA** is at 580 Burrard St, V6C 2K9. 604-683-2351. **The University of British Columbia** has summer housing May-Aug. During the school year, a few one-bedroom suites are also available. Contact UBC Conference Centre, 5959 Student Union Boulevard, Vancouver, BC, V6T 2C9. 604-822-1010. In Victoria, the **University of Victoria** has low-budget

---

HOSTELLING INTERNATIONAL - BC REGION

HI-Vancouver Downtown:
1114 Burnaby St. 604-684-4564. Fax: 604-684-4540.
HI-Vancouver Jericho Beach:
1515 Discovery St. 604-224-3208. Fax: 604-224-4852.
HI-Whistler: 5678 Alta Lake Rd 604-932-5492. Fax: 604-932-4687.
HI-Victoria: 516 Yates St. 250-385-4511. Fax: 250-385-3232.
HI-Salt Spring Island: 640 Cusheon Lake Rd. Tel/fax: 250-537-4149.
HI-Pender Island: 250-629-6133 or 1-888-931-3111. Fax: 250-629-3649.
HI-Tofino: Whalers on the Point Guesthouse. 604-684-7101. Fax: 604-684-7181.
HI-Penticton: 464 Ellis St. 250-492-3992. Fax: 250-492-8755.
HI-Kamloops: 7 W Seymour St. 250-828-7991. Fax: 250-828-2442.
HI-Kelowna: 245 Harvey Ave. Tel/fax: 250-763-9814.

HI-Big White: 7650 Porcupine Rd. Tel/fax: 250-765-7050.
HI-Shuswap: Squilax General Store and Hostel. Tel/fax: 250-675-2977.
HI-Nelson: Dancing Bear Inn, 171 Baker St. 250-352-7573. Fax: 250-352-9818.
HI-Rossland: Mountain Shadow Hostel. 250-362-7160 or 1888-393-7180. Fax: 250-362-7150.
HI-Fernie: Raging Elk Hostel. 892 6th Ave. 250-423-6811. Fax: 250-423-6812.
HI- Revelstoke: Revelstoke Traveller's Hostel & Guesthouse. 250-837-4050. Fax: 250-837-6410.
HI-Yoho National Park: Whiskey Jack Hostel, Banff. 403-762-4122. Fax: 403-762-3441.
HI-Powell River: Fiddlehead Farm. 604-483-3018. Fax: 604-485-3832.

| A BRIEF HISTORY OF BRITISH COLUMBIA | **515 Million Years Ago:** *North America lies to the east, but there is no BC – only the sea. And in that sea, a limestone reef, and in that reef, a profusion of the Earth's newest life forms – worm-like critters, Opabinias, with five eyes, creatures whose evolution* | *halts in the mists of time – they have no descendants. And other creatures, who continue. Like the Earth's oldest known chordate, Pikaia graciens. Our ancestor.* | *(Full circle to the present: that limestone reef now sits in BC's Rocky Mountains above the little town of Field. We call it the Burgess Shale – one of the world's scientific wonders.)* | **181 Million Years Ago:** *A dramatic 30-million-year journey begins: North America moves west, sliding into the Intermontane Superterrane, a cluster of underwater land forms, pushing up what are now BC's Interior highlands and mountains.* |

MAJOR BRITISH COLUMBIA EVENTS

Local events are listed alphabetically by town or city in the introduction to each region. Do check them out. They offer the flavour of an area, a glimpse of local life . . . from horse racing at Kamloops' Sagebrush Downs to Lumby's Chicken Flying Contest. There's an Annual Ice Cream Social at McBride, tipi creeping at Moberly Lake, cow-chip bingo in Rock Creek, and an Eagle Count in Squamish. Everywhere, there are rodeos, regattas, sea queens, snowfests, loggers' sports days. Everything has a festival: strawberries, blueberries, blossoms, and borscht. Anything that can move is raced: bicycles, horses, skis, dogs, rafts, mini-sternwheelers, Canada geese (wooden ones), bathtubs, and outhouses.

All these community events give you a chance to stop, have some fun, get to know the locals, and see what they do for work and pleasure. It's a wonderfully rich and colourful array of festivities.

Listed below are some of the major annual events that attract people from all over BC and North America:

- **Abbotsford International Airshow:** Mid-Aug. Abbotsford Airport. Over 300,000 people.
- **Brant Wildlife Festival:** Mid-April. Celebrating the return of the small black goose. Thousands return, thousands celebrate. Many activities, including a Wild Goose Chase. Parksville.
- **Canadian International Dragon Boat Festival:** June. Racing on the waters of Vancouver's False Creek, with multi-cultural entertainment at Pacific Place Plaza of Nations. Attracts 2,000 paddlers, over 100,000 spectators.
- **Cariboo Cross-Country Ski Marathon:** Feb. 100 Mile House. Competitors from Canada and US.
- **Cloverdale Rodeo:** May. The Big One. Rated No. 1 in North America.

- **Coombs Country and Bluegrass Festival:** Early Aug.
- **First Peoples Festival:** Early Aug. Royal BC Museum, Victoria. One of the only exclusively native-run arts and cultural events in Canada.
- **Ironman Canada Triathlon:** Penticton. International qualifier. Late Aug.
- **Kamloopa Indian Powwow:** Mid-Aug. Kamloops. Traditional dances, food.
- **Kelowna Apple Triathlon:** Late summer.
- **Whistler's Classic Music Festival:** Aug. Traditional music in non-traditional settings.
- **Mission Indian Friendship Centre Powwow:** Early July. Mission. Native Indian dances draw participants from all over North America.

- **Nanaimo Marine Festival:** Late-July. It's famous and fun. Bathtubs are raced from Nanaimo, Vancouver Island, to Vancouver.
- **Pacific National Exhibition (PNE):** Two weeks, late Aug-Labour Day. Vancouver. Street shows, rides, and agricultural booths.
- **Harrison Hot Springs World Championship Sand Sculpture Competition:** Early Sept. Sculptures stay till Oct.
- **Swiftsure Sailing Race:** Late May. Victoria. Some 350 sailboats participate.
- **Vancouver Folk Music Festival:** Mid-July. At Jericho

Beach. Music from Latin America, Asia, England, Eastern Europe. Ethnic food.
- **Vancouver Symphony of Fire:** Late July-Aug. Fireworks, over English Bay, to music.
- **Victoria Folkfest:** Late June-early July. Ethnic performances, food booths. Over 150,000 visitors!
- **Williams Lake Stampede:** Early July. Cariboo Country's big stampede. Brahma bull riding, calf roping.
- **Yukon Quest Dogsled Race:** Mid-Feb. 1,600km from Fairbanks, Alaska to Whitehorse, Yukon Territory.

HOLIDAYS IN BRITISH COLUMBIA

There are nine statutory holidays in BC. Many restaurants, shops, pubs, and other businesses, along with airlines, ferry, and transportation companies remain open on holidays. Banks, liquor stores, most offices, and some stores are closed. Boxing Day, Dec 26, is a recognized, but not a statutory holiday.

- New Year's Day: Jan 1.
- Good Friday: Late March, mid-April.
- Victoria Day: May 24 weekend (or close).
- Canada Day: July 1.
- BC Day: Early Aug.
- Labour Day: First Mon in Sept.
- Thanksgiving: Early Oct.
- Remembrance Day: Nov 11.
- Christmas: Dec 25.
- Boxing Day: Dec 26.

125 Million Years Ago: *Dinosaurs roam what is now the east arm of Williston Lake.*

120 Million Years Ago: *The Rocky Mountains throw themselves skyward: it takes 60 million years.*

100 Million Years Ago: *Smaller eastbound continents – Wrangellia and the Alexander Terrane – nudge up against the big continent's shores, adding Vancouver Island, Haida Gwaii (Queen Charlotte Islands), and thousands of other islands to what is now BC's northwest coast.*

50 Million Years Ago: *"Dawn salmon" appear (another species, 10-15 million years later, weighs 500 pounds and bears fangs).*

15-2 Million Years Ago: *From beneath the central Interior, lava gushes up, filling in hollows, levelling 50,000 sq km of Cariboo and Chilcotin plateau; other volcanoes give birth to mountain ranges.*

B&B accommodation early May-Aug. Write: University of Victoria, Housing, Food, and Conference Services, Box 1700, Victoria, BC, V8W 2Y2. 250-721-8395. The **YWCA** in downtown Victoria offers year-round accommodation for women. Write 880 Courtenay St. Victoria, BC, V8W 1C4. 250-386-7511. In Nanaimo, **Malaspina College** has accommodation May-Aug. Write Western Student Housing Ltd, 750 Fourth St, Nanaimo, BC, V9R 6C5. 250-754-6338.

For information on **Elderhostel** programs, see *Educational Holidays,* p.22.

Whistler Resort offers the comforts of a home away from home.

Bed and Breakfast

B&B accommodation in private homes is available in most centres, and some lovely rural spots, too. Contact the British Columbia Bed and Breakfast Association, 604-734-3486. Local listings and information centres can help with specific communities.

Commercial Campgrounds

Many commercial tent, trailer, and RV parks are located in or near communities, or outside populated areas. Some are adjacent First Nations communities, and most are in scenic settings such as on lake or ocean shores. Amenities vary from simple campsites with outhouses to full-service campgrounds with flush toilets and showers, electricity, laundries, sani-stations, stores, playgrounds, and games rooms. Check with information centres or the BC *Accommodations* guide.

Camping in BC's National Parks

There are 11,544 campsites in 175 BC provincial parks, usually in forests or on lakes, rivers, or occasionally on ocean beaches. A small number have wilderness shelters or lodges; some have showers. But generally facilities are basic: flush or pit toilets, fireplaces, picnic tables, wood supply, water. In summer many offer nature walks and talks. Some offer wilderness walk-in camping only. Provincial marine parks are mainly accessible by boat.

The **Discover Camping Campground Reservation Service** is in place for 63 of BC's busiest provincial park campgrounds, to reduce lineups and overnight waits. As little as two days and up to three months in advance, campers can reserve a site for up to 14 nights (some of the busier parks limit stays to 7 nights during the summer). Both the non-refundable reservation fee ($6 per night for a maximum of $18 plus tax) and camping fees for nights reserved, are payable by VISA or MasterCard at the time of booking. **For bookings from anywhere in North America, call the Discover Camping Campground Reservation Service, 1-800-689-9025; from the Lower Mainland or overseas, 604-689-9025.** *Logs* indicate which campgrounds are on the reservation system. At most parks, campsites are also available on a first-come, first-served basis. It is wise to select your site early in the day. Overnight fees range up to $15.50 (and an increase is being considered). They are generally collected between late spring and early fall. Some provincial campgrounds are open year-round, but access in winter may be blocked by snow. Check with district offices (numbers are included in the *Logs*). BC residents who possess a BC Parks Disabled Access Card are permitted to camp free in BC Parks' frontcountry campsites. BC seniors may camp before June 15 and after Labour Day for a 50 percent discount; otherwise the regular fee applies. A few campgrounds have group campsites, for which reservations are required and can be made through the district offices. For more info: BC Parks web site: http://www.elp.gov.bc.ca/ bcparks. Also see BC's Parks, p. 21, in this guide.

There are four national parks in BC with camping facilities for RV and rustic campers. These are Pacific Rim, Kootenay, Yoho, and Glacier. Mt Revelstoke Park and Gwaii Haanas National Park Reserve and Haida Heritage Site have only backcountry camping facilities. Banff and Jasper parks in Alberta have RV and backcountry campgrounds. Overnight fees range from $10 to $22, depending on time of year and type of campsite. Some are open year-round. Backcountry campers in national parks are required to obtain special wilderness passes (annual passes are also available). In addition, a park pass is required for anyone wishing to visit a national park for day activities. See *Logs* or contact Canadian Heritage, Parks Canada, Information Services, Western Regional Office, Room 552, 220-4th Ave SE, Calgary, AB, T2G 4X3. 403-292-4401. Check the Web: http://parkscanada.pch.gc.ca.

2 Million Years Ago:	**34,000 Years Ago:**	**20,000 Years Ago:**	**18,000 Years Ago:**	**13,000-9,000 Years Ago:**
Everything cools. The Pleistocene Epoch – the age of great glaciers – begins.	*A woolly mammoth dies in a sticky pond near present-day Granisle. (It is unearthed in 1971, by workers in an open-pit mine.)*	*As the Pleistocene begins to wane, the peak of Mount Garibaldi bursts through the ice.*	*Salmon swim in what is now Kamloops Lake. (Scientists examining their fossils in the mid-1990s are confounded: wasn't the Thompson Valley, like most of the rest of BC, under a mile of ice? If the valley was habitable to salmon, why not people?)*	*Ice retreats. Forests of lodgepole pine advance, then come Douglas firs, then other familiar foliage. Giant bison, mammoths, and mastodons roam the land. Sea levels fluctuate. Land – and land bridges – appear, and disappear.*

Backcountry Camping

In BC it is legal to camp on Crown land as long as you are not in violation of any permit or lease and no special restrictions or fire closures are in effect. Off the beaten track, are little-known campsites, some set aside by the BC Forest Service or forest companies. In some outback areas of provincial parks, wilderness camping is allowed, but open fires are prohibited.

Anyone is welcome to use these backwoods sites and simple respect for those who follow is expected. **Fire is a serious threat throughout BC** in summer, particularly in these outback sites; ensure that campfires are completely extinguished before going to bed or leaving a campsite for any period of time.

For information and maps of Forest Service recreation sites, write: Forest Practices, Box 9513, Stn Prov Govt, Victoria, BC, V8W 9C2. 250-387-1946. Or contact the Forest Service regional and district offices listed below.

Vancouver Forest Region: 2100 Labieux Rd, Nanaimo, BC, V9T 6E9. 250-751-7001. District offices are in Campbell River, Chilliwack, Port Alberni, Port McNeill, Powell River, Rosedale, Hagensborg, Squamish, and Queen Charlotte City.

Cariboo Forest Region: Suite 200, 640 Borland St, Williams Lake, BC, V2G 4T1. 250-398-4345. District offices in Alexis Creek, Horsefly, 100 Mile House, Quesnel, Williams Lake.

Kamloops Forest Region: 515 Columbia St, Kamloops, BC, V2C 2T7. 250-828-4131. Offices in Clearwater, Kamloops, Merritt, Penticton, Lillooet, Salmon Arm, Vernon.

Nelson Forest Region: 518 Lake St, Nelson, BC, V1L 4C6. 250-354-6200. Offices in Castlegar, Grand Forks, Cranbrook, Golden, Invermere, Nelson, and Revelstoke.

Prince George Forest Region: 1011-4th Ave, Prince George, BC, V2L 3H9. 250-565-6100. Offices in Dawson Creek, McBride, Fort Nelson, Mackenzie, Fort St James, Prince George, Fort St John, and Vanderhoof.

Prince Rupert Forest Region: 3726 Alfred Ave, Bag 5000, Smithers, BC, V0J 2N0. 250-847-7500. District offices in Smithers, Dease Lake, Terrace, Hazelton, Burns Lake, Houston, and Prince Rupert.

TRANSPORTATION

Detailed information on how to get around and between BC's tourism regions — on coastal and inland ferries, airlines, buses, railways, by car or urban transit — can be found in the *Transportation* sections for each specific region. Many of these transportation systems are trans-regional. So, for example, information on mainland to Vancouver Island ferry routes appears under *Vancouver Island, Vancouver, Coast, and Mountains*, and *Northern BC* regions. Information on BC Rail's service from Vancouver to Prince George appears under the regions through which the railway passes — *Vancouver, Coast, and Mountains, Thompson Okanagan, Northern BC,* and *Alberta Rockies.*

Several bus (coach) lines link communities and regions of the province — so look in the *Transportation* section in the region you think you would like to start from, and go from there. Likewise with airlines. *Bon voyage.*

Some Transportation Highlights

■ **BC Ferries:** BC Ferries started out in 1960 with two vessels. Today this government-owned vehicle and passenger fleet is one of the world's largest and most modern with 40 ships serving 47 ports of call on the BC coast. It carries more than 22 million passengers a year, sailing 24 routes year-round. The fleet links BC's mainland to Vancouver Island, the Gulf Islands, the Sechelt Peninsula, and the Queen Charlotte Islands.

■ **VIA Rail:** Canada's national rail service, linking Vancouver to Alberta to the rest of Canada. Includes the E&N (Esquimalt and Nanaimo Railway) linking Victoria, on southern Vancouver Island, to mid-island communities, and terminating in Courtenay.

■ **BC Rail:** A very scenic excursion from North Vancouver to Prince George in Northern BC. From here it's possible to link up with VIA Rail's train west to Prince Rupert, or east to Jasper. See appropriate regions.

■ **Rocky Mountaineer Railtours:** Another very scenic excursion from Vancouver to Jasper, Banff, or Calgary in Alberta. Two days, with an overnight stay in Kamloops. See *Vancouver, Coast, and Mountains* region, also *Thompson Okanagan, Northern BC,* and *Alberta Rockies.*

MOTORING

In many ways, driving is one of the easiest ways to travel in BC, especially if exploring beyond the Lower Mainland or Victoria on Vancouver Island.

While most BC residents are familiar with provincial and Canadian vehicle laws, visitors must make themselves aware of, and follow these regulations. Canadians drive on the right side of the road, as in the US, but use the metric system for distances and speed (see *Metric System,* inside back cover). The speed limit on highways is usually 80-100 kilometres an hour, and in cities and towns, 50 km/h or less. Vans equipped with radar guns and cameras catch speeders in the act. They may be situated in city or highway locations. Once photos have been cross-checked with registration and licence information, speeding tickets are sent in the mail.

Drivers using industrial roads must remember that logging trucks and other working vehicles have the right-of-way. Restrictions may apply on industrial roads: some stipulate hours of use. Companies that maintain industrial roads usually post signs explaining regulations.

TIME ZONES

Like other Canadian provinces, most of BC switches to daylight-saving time from the first Sunday in April to the last Sunday in October. There are also two time zones in BC. Most of the province is on Pacific Time, but as you move east toward the Rockies, time moves an hour ahead to Mountain Time. Alberta is also on Mountain Time. Specific points for time zone changes on major highways are indicated in the appropriate *Logs.*

There are also two maverick areas in BC — the area from Creston to Yahk in southeastern BC, and the Peace River area in the northeast — do not change to daylight-saving time. They hold to Mountain Standard Time all the time.

10,500 Years Ago: *The human occupants of a sandstone cave at the edge of a glacial lake near present-day Fort St John leave behind stone tools. (Of this, BC's oldest known archaeological site, scientists theorize: BC's first people journeyed here from Asia via a land bridge across the Bering Sea. Others postulate that some coastal peoples came by sea: many sites, underwater, await discovery. Some posit migration north into BC from what is now the US.)*

2,000 Years Ago: *A major landslide backs up the Fraser River at Texas Creek, south of Lillooet, flooding villages, blocking salmon, causing famine.*

1,000 Years Ago: *In coastal rainforests, tender Western red cedar seedlings take root: they will grow tall, and stand witness to the following events.*

1579: *Searching for the Northwest Passage, English explorer Francis Drake traces the Pacific coast of America perhaps as far north as the Strait of Juan de Fuca. (Spaniard Juan Perez is more widely accepted as the first European to navigate these waters:*

Getting to Lund, on the Sunshine Coast, is half the fun.

Licences and Insurance

Foreign driver's licences are legal in Canada, but motorists coming from the US should check with their insurance companies about liability insurance for non-residents in Canada. If a car from outside BC is involved in an accident, call the nearest office of the Insurance Corporation of BC (ICBC).

Fuels and Laws

All common fuels, including diesel, leaded and unleaded gasoline, are available and sold in litres. Propane is also available. Motorcyclists must wear helmets, and seat belts must be worn in vehicles. Impaired driving is a criminal offence in Canada, punishable by heavy fines, jail terms, and automatic driving suspensions. Refusing to take a breathalyzer test is also an offence. The impairment level is .08 percent (80mg of alcohol in 100mL of blood).

Maps and Road Conditions

Up-to-date road maps of BC are available from information centres. For information on road conditions, call:
■ **Ministry of Transport and Highways InfoLine:** 1-900-451-4997. (The charge for calls is 75 cents.) To speak with a ministry representative: 604-660-9770.

BC FOR DISABLED TRAVELLERS

Among travellers with disabilities, Vancouver enjoys a reputation as one of the most accessible cities in the world.

Whether it's accessible transportation, progressive building codes, accessible leisure and recreation opportunities, or innovative housing, the province and its two major cities, Vancouver and Victoria, lead the way in making BC a more livable place for people with disabilities, whether they use a wheelchair, a white cane, or a hearing aid.

Transportation

In 1990, Vancouver became the first city in Canada to provide scheduled bus service to people with disabilities. Over 50 percent of all Lower Mainland buses are accessible, with plans to have all routes covered by 2007. All rapid transit SkyTrain stations except Granville Street are also accessible. (For Victoria accessible bus routes, call 250-382-6161.)

Custom door-to-door transportation is provided in most of the province's larger communities. Non-residents may also use the service by registering in advance of travel. (Not worthwhile unless staying more than two

historical revisionists claim Queen Elizabeth suppressed news of Drake's success for strategic reasons.)

1650: *The Little Ice Age of southeastern BC begins. (As recalled by the Ktunaxa people of the Rockies, it will last about 200 years.)*

1700: *A 1,000km-long megathrust earthquake, magnitude 9-plus, strikes BC's coast. The land plunges a metre: at least one village is washed away.*

About 1750: *A mountain in the Nass Valley explodes in a fury of fire and lava. Two Nisga'a villages are buried under molten rock.*

1774: *Stormy weather keeps Juan Perez from setting foot on BC's coast. BC's aboriginal population: possibly 300,000. In the straits near Prince Rupert alone are some 60 Tsimshian villages: perhaps the greatest concentration of people in North America north of Mexico.*

weeks, as rides must be booked four days in advance.) In Vancouver, call 604-430-2742.

Vancouver, Victoria, Kelowna, and many other large BC centres have accessible taxi services. Call Vancouver Taxi, 604-255-5111 or 604-871-1111. For airport service in Vancouver, call the Airporter bus. 604-273-8436. For accessible taxi service in Victoria, call Custom Cabs, 250-744-1230 or Empress Taxi, 250-381-2222.

The BC Paraplegic Association has lift-equipped vans for rent, for use only within a certain radius of the city. 604-324-3611.

BC Ferries offers discounts. 604-669-1211. Wheelchair users should request parking near the elevator at the time of ticket purchase. All washrooms and deck areas are accessible. The ferry route up the Inside Passage to Prince Rupert also has accessible staterooms.

Greyhound Bus Lines has lift-equipped service from Vancouver to Kelowna, Calgary, and Prince George, with stops in major centres along these routes. Book 24 hours in advance. 1-800-661-8747.

Rocky Mountaineer Railtours offers a two-day trip from Vancouver to Jasper or Banff with an overnight stay in an accessible hotel in Kamloops. 604-606-7245.

Accommodation

Under the *Access Canada* program, hotels in BC are using four rating levels that address the needs of people with minor to severe disabilities. See the BC *Accommodations* guide for details, although, currently, very few properties displaying these access ratings are listed in the guide. Call ahead to ensure your requirements can be met. For a list of hotels with wheel-in showers, contact *We're Accessible*, below.

BC residents who possess a BC Parks' Disabled Access Pass are permitted to camp for free in BC Parks' frontcountry campsites. 250-356-8794.

Recreation

Here are just a few of the recreation opportunities available. For a more complete list, contact We're Accessible, below.

In Vancouver, the Grouse Mountain Skyride offers accessibility on the blue gondola with 24-hours' notice: 604-984-0661, ask for the sales department.

The horse-drawn tours of Stanley Park are also accessible to wheelchair users.

The BC Sport and Fitness Council for the Disabled in Vancouver is a group of associations offering competitive and recreational opportunities for disabled skiing, horseback riding, sailing, sledge hockey, ice picking, and track and field. 604-737-3039. The Mobility Opportunities Society also offers disabled sailing and other recreational opportunities. 604-688-6464.

Columbia S.O.I.L., south of Golden, is a non-profit group dedicated to making wilderness parks in BC more accessible. Their two cabins, complete with wheel-in showers, are located in Spillimacheen. 250-346-3276.

The Inland Lake site-and-trail system near Powell River, operated by the Ministry of Forests, provides accessible campsites, fishing wharves, and trails. 604-485-9831.

On Vancouver Island, there are beach access ramps at Parksville, 250-248-3252, and at Miracle Beach in Campbell River.

More Information

■ *BC Accessibility Advisor*: Accessibility Program, Ministry of Municipal Affairs, Box 9490 Stn Prov Govt, Victoria, BC, V8W 9N7. 250-387-7908.

■ *We're Accessible*: Quarterly newsletter for disabled and elderly travellers. For a subscription, call or fax Lynn Atkinson, 604-731-2197, or write 32-1675 Cypress St, Vancouver, BC, V6J 3L4. E-mail: lynna@istar.ca.

■ **Coalition of People With Disabilities**: 604-875-0188; fax 604-875-9227; TDD: 604-875-8835.

■ **Office for Disability Issues**: 100-333 Quebec St, Victoria, BC, V8V 1X4. 250-387-3813; fax 250-387-3114; TDD: 250-387-3555.

■ **BC Paraplegic Association**: 604-324-3611.

■ **CNIB**: 604-4314-2121.

■ **Western Institute for the Deaf and Hard of Hearing**: Contact TDD 604-736-2527 or 604-736-7391.

WEATHER AND WHAT TO WEAR

Hot, cold, dry, wet: the weather in BC is as varied as the geography. Rule of thumb: the farther you are from the western side of a mountain range, the drier it will be. In general, the farther from the ocean, the greater the difference between high summer and low winter temperatures. The time you choose to travel, like the clothes you'll need to wear, depends on what you want to do. There is no wrong time to come – in each season there is something special to do. (See *Outdoor Activities, p.26*.)

On the west coast of Vancouver Island, wet-weather gear is always in style.

1778: *Britain's great navigator, Captain James Cook, is piloted into the village of Yuquot off the west coast of Vancouver Island. The Mowachaht, "people of the deer," have received many visitors over the millennia. Their chief, Maquinna, is one of many hereditary chiefs along this coast. In exchange for European goods, he offers his guests the otter furs they prize.*

1789: *Britain and Spain dispute ownership of North America's northwest coast. By this time, a deadly virus, smallpox, delivered to Mexico by the Spaniards in the early 1500s, has reached the adjacent mainland via overland trails.*

1792: *In the Nootka Accord, Spain and Britain agree the Northwest coast should be open to trading ships of all nations.*

1793: *Scottish explorer and fur trader, Alexander Mackenzie, travelling from the northeast via the Peace and Fraser rivers, becomes the first white man to cross North America by land. He writes of a country so crowded with wild animals it looks like a stall-yard.*

The Wet Coast?

Despite BC's reputation for record rainfalls (see *What is BC,* p.12), annual precipitation on parts of BC's populated coast is substantially lower than much of Canada.

In Victoria, the umbrella is a mandatory item of executive fashion, just as gumboots are traditional for Gulf Islanders. But the truth of the matter is, here, on the leeward side of the Vancouver Island Mountains, one can only expect some 700-800mm of precipitation in a year. Victoria celebrates spring in late February, with a week-long flower count.

BC's gentle year-round climate is one of the main reasons why people from Canada's cold and blustery east move here to what they call "Lotus Land." Parts of the southern coast , including Vancouver, might get damp (mainly in fall and winter), but they'll be neither hot and sticky, nor cold and snowbound. Winter weather, with an average high of 5C, rarely calls for more than a medium overcoat.

Snow may fall on coastal towns and cities a few times a year, but it doesn't remain on the ground for long. Where it does stick is up in the mountains, making for some of North America's finest skiing conditions.

Along BC's northern coast, winter and summer temperatures are cooler than in the south, but the climate can still be characterized as mild. It is wet, though. Prince Rupert gets roughly twice as much rain as Vancouver, and half the sunshine.

Yak Peak, on the Coquihalla Highway. A general rule of travel: higher means cooler.

To wear: most people come for the outdoors and it's advisable to carry wet-weather gear year-round, particularly on the west coast. Hiking boots or high-topped rubber boots tend to get a lot of use at all elevations, and rubber beach shoes are handy for wading near rocky shores in summer. Bring your bathing suit. And, even in summer, a windbreaker. Also binoculars and day-pack.

BC's Desert

As you move farther from the coast and into the Interior valleys of southern BC, the seasons become more "defined." Hotter summers, colder winters. July and August temperatures average in the low 30s Centigrade, and occasionally rise above 40C. Mid-winter temperatures drop below -9 or -10C. (That is still mild by most standards – Winnipeg averages -24C.)

But, it's dry – scanty precipitation is the outstanding characteristic of the Okanagan, Similkameen, and Thompson river valleys.

Don't forget your bathing suit – beaches will beckon.

The Unpredictable Mountains

Southeastern BC is dominated by the Monashees, Selkirks, Purcells, Rockies. A general rule: the higher you go, the cooler it gets.

In summer, the valleys (where you'll find most of the towns and cities) are comfortable, in the mid-30s C and lower. The lakes and rivers offer refreshing breezes, and if that isn't enough, a dip in their glacier-fed waters should be.

Weather can be quite localized and unpredictable in mountain country. Evening temperatures can drop up to 15 degrees below daytime levels, so even in summer warm clothing should be kept on hand. In summer, too, dramatic and wet lightning storms are not uncommon. Strong winds often come with them – don't be out in the middle of a lake.

Most places you'll be, midwinter temperatures won't fall below 7C. Precipitation falls mostly as snow. Mountain highways are constantly maintained: ploughed, sanded, and salted when necessary. A number of the highest highway passes, such as the Salmo-Creston Skyway (el 1,774m), are occasionally deemed avalanche-hazard zones. In such cases they will be closed to traffic while avalanche control measures are taken. Closures may last a few minutes or a few days, and alternate routes, where possible, are suggested.

The Great White? North

From central BC north, summers are short, winters long, and precipitation mostly light. The weather in any season gets cooler as you go north. Summers are mild – highs average 30C around Prince George but drop to below 15C by the time you get to the Peace River Valley. There are occasional sunbursts shooting temperatures 10-15 degrees higher. With or without heat waves, summer days may seem endless: there are 17 hours of daylight at summer solstice in Prince George; 19 hours in Atlin near the Yukon. Indian summers are some of the loveliest times of the year. Misty mornings give way to golden days and crisp evenings. In most northern areas, snow usually falls from September or October through April. In the high Rocky Mountain passes, a light snowfall in early August is not unusual. Winter nights are as long as summer days. And very cold temperatures drop to below -12C in the province's centre; below -25 in the northern corners.

To wear: a bathing suit for heat waves and hot springs; clothing that puts a layer between you and the mosquitoes that can be a nuisance anytime except mid-winter; and for winter you'll need heavy coats, scarves, warm gloves or mitts, and boots. Always bring an extra sweater.

Weather Check

For a recorded daily report on Lower Mainland weather, call 604-664-9010 or 604-664-9032. Call 250-656-3978 for Victoria's weather recording, and for Nanaimo, 250-245-8877. Or call weather stations in Castlegar,

1800: *The population of prairie bison about this time was an estimated 50-60 million.)*

1805: *Simon Fraser, on behalf of Britain's North West Company, establishes Fort McLeod (now BC's oldest continuously inhabited non-native settlement).*

1808: *Fraser traces the river that would later bear his name. David Thompson, explorer and trader for the Hudson's Bay Company, begins charting the Columbia River.*

1843: *On March 15, the Songhees people of southern Vancouver Island observe a brilliant comet arcing across the sky. Its appearance coincides with the arrival of the first European steamship on the Pacific Northwest coast. The comet dominates the sky, night and day, for two months,*

then vanishes: steamship passenger James Douglas of the Hudson's Bay Company never leaves. With 50 employees, he establishes Fort Victoria: a base for trade and the protection from American encroachment, and the future capital of British Columbia.

Dease Lake, Hope, Kamloops, Kelowna, Penticton, Port Alberni, Port Hardy, Prince George, Revelstoke, Terrace, Victoria International Airport. See the phone book's blue pages under Government of Canada, Weather Information.

Winter Weather Warnings

Warnings will be issued if the following conditions are expected:
- **Heavy Snow:** 5cm on the coast, or 10cm in the Interior, or more, expected within 24 hours.
- **Heavy Rain:** 50mm on the inner coast, 100mm on the west coast of Vancouver Island and the north coast, 25mm in the Interior, or more within 24 hours.
- **Winds:** Over 65km/h or gusts over 90km/h expected.
- **Freezing Rain or Drizzle:** Ice-storm warnings will be given if conditions are expected to last more than two hours.

BC'S PARKS

Getting to know BC means getting to know its parks. Between 1992 and 1999, the BC government announced the creation of more than 230 new parks. They range in size from a single hectare at Monte Creek, southeast of Kamloops, to 4.4 million hectares in the northern Rockies. Provincial protected areas now total 654. More than eight million hectares and 9 percent of the province's total land area – has now been safeguarded as provincial Class A parks, wilderness and heritage conservancies, ecological reserves, and recreation areas. Five national parks and hundreds of regional parks, bring the total area protected in BC to well over 10 million hectares: 11 percent of BC.

This is just partway on a difficult journey. Banff Springs, Canada's first national park, was set aside in 1885 with trainloads of wealthy European travellers and cities full of future Canadians in mind. Yoho and Glacier parks soon followed on the BC side of the Rockies. BC's first provincial park, Strathcona, on Vancouver Island, was set aside in 1911 "to preserve a territory as nature made it," and offer a "playground to tourists from around the world." But few people truly believed that BC might one day run out of wilderness.

Where First Nations left only a trace of their existence, those who followed have, in just two short centuries, managed to leave only a trace of the land as it was. Two-thirds of the old-growth forest on Vancouver Island is gone. Every year, another river, threatened by damming, logging, or urban development, is added to the endangered list. Salmon runs are diminishing; there are no more indigenous sea otters, no more Dawson woodland caribou.

In 1987, the United Nations' World Commission on Environment and Development decreed that protecting less than 12 percent of the Earth's surface was unacceptable. The eyes of the world focused upon places like BC, where any wilderness might still be found. Five years

Long Beach, in Pacific Rim National Park Reserve, offers 30 kilometres of sand and pounding surf.

later the BC government drafted its Protected Areas Strategy, vowing to work toward the "12-percent solution" – to double the province's provincial parkland by the year 2000.

The first park created under this strategy was Nisga'a Memorial Lava Bed Park, north of Terrace. It was also the first Class A provincial park to be co-managed by the BC government and a First Nation government.

On other fronts, the province has allied itself with federal, regional, and municipal governments. The Lower Mainland Nature Legacy is a collection of new provincial, regional, and city parks that more than quadruples the region's parkland to nearly 14 percent of the province's most populous region. Southern Vancouver Island's Commonwealth Nature Legacy takes in everything from sea-sprayed hiking trails to inner-city woods. The federal-provincial Pacific Marine Heritage Legacy is a commitment to the creation of a new national park and a series of provincial parks and ecological reserves in the Strait of Georgia.

These new parks are no longer being created strictly as playgrounds for people. We have learned from experience that even parks can be overdeveloped; their roads and services a threat to wildlife habitats. Yet, as our appreciation of the value and fragility of nature increases, people are flocking to parks in increasing numbers.

1846: *The Oregon Treaty establishes the 49th parallel as the boundary between British and American territories.*

1849: *Vancouver Island is declared a British colony. The Hudson's Bay Company can keep its monopoly and stay in charge, if it encourages colonization.*

1850-54: *James Douglas concludes 14 land purchases with a handful of Island leaders. Soon, all but a few small reserves will be the Crown's land. Contrary to British law which states treaties must be made with aboriginal peoples before lands are colonized, no fur-* *ther purchases will be made west of the Rockies for another 145 years.*

1858: *The Fraser River gold rush begins. Thirty thousand prospectors pour through Victoria on Vancouver Island en route to the mainland. The mainland is declared a British colony, and named British Columbia, after a river that was named after*

Altogether, 24 million people are year visit BC's parks. Banff National Park, attracting some 4.5 million visitors annually, has seen massive destruction of animal habitat. Nearly one million people a year come to celebrate the beaches of Pacific Rim National Park. Foot traffic on the park's West Coast Trail has become so heavy that a quota has been instituted.

Among BC's new parks, there may be places where people rarely, if ever, step foot: Khutzeymateen Grizzly Bear Sanctuary on the north coast, will remain for the grizzlies. Scott Islands Marine Park, off the northern tip of Vancouver Island, exists as a living laboratory, only to be observed so that we may gain understanding – and avoid repeating our mistakes. There will be no roads, no signs, campgrounds, trails, or washrooms. Some new parks, on the other hand, will be developed as people places: offering nature programs, weekend excursions, a place to gather. Even before its designation as a provincial park, the Stawamus Chief Rock, north of Vancouver, received thousands of climbers and hikers in a year. The Juan de Fuca Marine Trail northwest of Victoria is in an attempt to satisfy the hunger for wilderness adventure close to home.

At Harrison Hot Springs Sand Sculpture Competition, the artistic spirit meets no limits.

Still other parks, such as Cariboo Country's Churn Creek and Junction Sheep Range, offering limited backcountry access, may serve as classrooms. Here, people might discover nature is not something separate from themselves.

In the pages to follow, the *Travel Guide* leads the way to nearly 1,000 national, provincial, and regional parks – visitors are invited to soak in hot springs, sit under a waterfall, listen to nature talks, watch salmon spawn, birdwatch, camp, walk for days along wild shores. There is also a description of park highlights in the introduction to most regions, and a few glimpses offered of those parks that will be visited only rarely, by humans.

Tread lightly, for in the best of all worlds, there would be no need for parks. For more information:
■ **BC Parks,** 800 Johnson St, Victoria, BC, V8V 1X4. 250-387-5002.
■ **Canadian Heritage, Parks Canada, Information Services,** Western Regional Office, Room 552, 220-4th Ave SE, Calgary, AB, T2G 4X3. 403-492-4401.

EDUCATIONAL HOLIDAYS

Here are opportunities to stop for a few days or longer and sink into the arts, culture, and nature of a place. Several colleges, cultural centres, and other institutions offer courses or experiences in subjects ranging from sketching to native history. You might be able to sign up on the spot, but it's recommended to call or write in advance.

■ **Atlin Arts Centre:** Mid-June to late Sept. Apply up to a year in advance: Monarch Mountain, Atlin, BC, V0W 1A0. Tel/fax: 1-800-651-8882. Three-week multidisciplinary workshops. Beautiful northern summer setting draws students "ready for risk taking" from all over the world. Art programs, 8-10 day wilderness adventures.

■ **Elderhostel Canada:** For anyone who is retired or contemplating retirement. For a brochure of one-week programs offered in some 50 BC communities: Elderhostel Canada, 308 Wellington St, Kingston Ont, K7K 7A7. 613-530-2222. A detailed seasonal catalogue is available free on request (it's also in many libraries). BC locations include Victoria, Kaslo, Galiano Island, Bamfield, Alert Bay, and Haida Gwaii (Queen Charlotte Islands).

■ **Emily Carr Institute of Art and Design Summer Program:** July-mid-Aug. Apply in advance to Part-time Studies, Emily Carr Institute of Art and Design, 1399 Johnston St, Vancouver, BC, V6H 3R9. 604-844-3810. Three-week intensive beginner-advanced courses in visual arts, workshop weekends.

■ **Hollyhock Retreat:** May-Oct. Box 127, Mansons Landing, Cortes Island, BC, V0P 1K0. 1-800-933-6339. Rest and relaxation retreats, workshops in the practical, creative, and healing arts.

■ **Island Mountain Arts (Summer School):** Late July-early Aug. Box 65, Wells, BC, V0K 2R0. 250-994-3466. Courses in visual and musical performing, and literary arts for children and adults.

■ **Kaslo on the Lake Summer Festival of the Arts:** Late July-Aug. Kaslo. Through the Langham Cultural Centre. Box 1000, Kaslo, BC, V0G 1M0. 250-353-2661. Some 30 classes in visual, performing, and healing arts for people of all ages.

■ **Kootenay School of the Arts:** Early July-early Aug. 606 Victoria St, Nelson, BC, V1L 4K9. 250-352-2821. Visual arts and crafts, writing classes.

■ **Malaspina College:** Fall courses. 900 Fifth St, Nanaimo, BC, V9R 5S5. 250-753-3245. From etching on glass to soapmaking, or an introduction to birds of Vancouver Island.

■ **Metchosin Summer School of the Arts:** Mid-July-Aug. 250-391-2420. RR1, Pearson College, Victoria, BC, V9B 5T7. Lester B. Pearson College Campus at Pedder Bay. Intensive weekend and one- and two-week workshops. Writing, ceramics, sculptural basketry, drawing. Also lectures, films, concerts. Lovely natural setting.

■ **Naramata Centre for Continuing Education:** Box 68, Naramata, BC, V0H 1N0. 250-496-5751. Week-long and weekend courses year-round. Self development, spiritual development, children, youth, young adult programs, and creative arts.

■ **Nechako Valley Summer School of the Arts:** Box 1438, Vanderhoof, BC, V0J 3A0. 250-567-3030. Day and week-long art courses, late July-Aug.

■ **Okanagan Summer School of the Arts:** Three weeks in July. School running for over three decades. Box 22037, Penticton, BC, V2A 8L1. 250-493-0390. More

---

an American ship, that was named after a 17th-century Italian explorer, Christopher Columbus. Four years later, the Cariboo gold rush draws thousands more fortune seekers along the same route: one among them carries smallpox. (As a result of this and previous sweeps of

deadly viruses, nine of ten aboriginal people on Vancouver Island and the mainland will die.)

1863: *On southeastern Vancouver Island, Hul'qumi'num (Coast Salish) resistance to colonization is quashed by naval cannon power. Seven men are executed in Victoria's Bastion Square. The following year, five Tsilhqot'in are executed for*

their violent resistance to a road through their mainland territories: but they did narrow a potential floodgate to settlement of their lands.

1866: *The Vancouver Island and mainland colonies form a united British Columbia. BC's first salmon cannery opens on the Fraser River.*

than 80 courses and nearly as many instructors, including world-class performers and artists. Mostly one-week courses, 15-25 hours per week in music, visual and literary arts, theatre, dance, children's programs, fibre arts, computers. Day starts with tai chi. For all ages, all abilities.

■ **Outward Bound Western Canada:** 411-1367 W Broadway, Vancouver, BC, V6H 4A9, 604-737-3093. Programs promote personal growth through a shared wilderness adventure. Mountaineering courses of 9-36 days in the Coast Mountains north of Whistler. For ages 15-adult.

■ **Royal British Columbia Museum:** 675 Belleville St, Victoria. 250-387-5745. Environmentally oriented excursions, April-Oct. From spelunking at Horne Lake Caves to archaeological expeditions; also children's tours.

■ **Strathcona Park Lodge and Outdoor Education Centre:** Box 2160, Campbell River, BC, V9W 5C9. 250-286-3122. Outdoor summer camps, family excursions. For everyone. Also the COLT (Canadian Outdoor Leadership Training) Centre, with 100-day intensive programs developing water- and land-based outdoor skills, environmental awareness, and teaching ability in experiential education. For adults 19 and over. Call 250-286-3122.

■ **University of BC Museum of Anthropology:** See *Vancouver*, p.98. Native cultural workshops and excursions.

■ **University of Victoria:** Division of Continuing Studies, Box 3030, Stn CSC. Victoria, BC, V8W 3N6. 250-721-8481. Nature courses, seniors programs, BC heritage.

■ **West Kootenay Women's Festival:** Mid-Aug. Vallican. 250-352-9916. Workshops, arts and crafts bazaar, music, children's activities.

THE ROAD TO ABORIGINAL BC

Within this province's geometric boundaries are the boundaries of 40 major cultural groups – distinctive peoples, living according to their own time-tested laws, systems of resource management, and profound spiritualities. Little understood by newcomers, they have been collectively referred to as Indians or natives, but know themselves by such names as Nlaka'pamux, "people of the canyon," Gitxsan, "people of the river of mists," Dakelh, "people who travel on the water." Within the larger groups are tribes, clans, families, each too with its own name and boundaries. Rooted within them are eight of the 11 aboriginal language families found in all of Canada: any two as different from one another as English is from Bengali. Within these are dozens of languages, hundreds of dialects.

Their oral histories, if recorded, would fill libraries, as would the events carved in wood and painted on stone throughout the province. They tell us how these societies have survived ice ages, floods, rivers changing course, famines, wars. But the greatest single threat to their complex web, and to their very existence, has been the arrival of Europeans. See *A Brief History of BC*, pp.14-25.

The current treaty process between First Nations, and the BC and Canadian governments, though fraught

with obstacles and opposition, is helping to increase awareness of the aboriginal landscape, histories, and issues. More and more First Nations communities are opening their doors, inviting visitors to learn from them. Each day, the number of cultural centres, interpretive sites, tours, events, and art galleries grows. On Haida Gwaii, Watchmen greet visitors at ancient villages emptied by smallpox over a century ago. At Xa:ytem National Historic Site east of Vancouver, Sto:lo guides share lessons taught by the Transformer, Xexa:ls. At Duncan's Cowichan Native Village, visitors are treated to a feast of salmon, clams, venison, songs, dances, and stories. Vancouver's UBC Museum of Anthropology, the Royal BC Museum in Victoria, and other community museums, also work closely with First Nations to offer lively presentations from enduring cultures. Many of these opportunities are described in the *Logs* to follow.

For a complete immersion into the ancient and contemporary landscapes of aboriginal BC, *A Traveller's Guide to Aboriginal B.C.*, published by *Beautiful British Columbia Magazine* and Whitecap Books, is highly recommended. This 254-page book, written by Cheryl Coull, in consultation with hundreds of First Nation elders and leaders, guides travellers through traditional territories, boundary by boundary, community by community, offering protocols for visiting, and sharing a wealth of stories that reach back to the beginning of time.

WILDLIFE

BC has more resident wild animal species than anywhere in Canada. Three-quarters of Canada's wildlife species – 120 mammals and nearly 300 birds – actually breed here. In total, 143 mammal species, 454 bird species, 19 reptiles and 20 amphibians can be found living in or passing through BC.

Most conspicuous are the birds, from tiny chickadees and kinglets to eagles and ospreys. More than a million birds migrate on the Pacific flyway and hundreds of thousands stop to nest. The province's wetlands are inhabited by countless waterfowl divers and dabblers, trumpeter and whistling swans, snow geese, Canada geese, and pelicans.

Off the coast, more than two dozen marine mammal species – sea lions, dolphins, seals, killer whales, humpback whales, porpoises – are seen regularly by beachcombers, boaters, and seashore hikers. Nearly all of the world's 24,000 Pacific grey whales swim past the length of BC's coast in the spring and fall.

Inland, BC is home to more big-game species than any other place on Earth: mountain goats, moose, caribou, bighorn sheep, deer, and elk can be seen browsing by the highway's edge in less central parts of the province. Wolves, cougars, black bears, and North America's second largest land animals – the grizzly bears – are less frequently seen.

Oft seen and equally intriguing are the little critters – fishers, badgers, porcupines, skunks, otters, mink, weasels, squirrels, chipmunks, turtles, toads, and shrews.

The stories of many coastal peoples are carved into poles at Vancouver's Stanley Park.

1871: *BC's 12,000 non-native residents agree to enter Canadian Confederation on the condition a transcontinental railway is built.*

1876: *Aboriginal peoples are made subject to the federal Indian Act, which regulates every aspect of their lives.*

1877: *A BC/Canada Indian Reserve Commission begins marking out Indian reserves. Altogether, the Indians will get 0.34% of the province. Meanwhile, the government grants railway companies 8% of BC's most valuable and arable land (75,685 sq km in total).*

1881: *BC's first census: 26,849 aboriginal people, 19,069 whites, 4,195 Chinese, 274 blacks.*

1886: *The first transcontinental Canadian Pacific Railway train steams into what will become BC's largest city, Vancouver. Aboriginal people are outnumbered in the wave of new settlement. Prairie bison are extinct.*

The depths of BC's waters are well known to divers from around the world. Visibility can be phenomenal, rendering colours and seascapes of startling clarity. Gigantism is common in many species: mussels so huge that one will make a chowder, and the world's largest sea urchin, the giant red, with a diameter over 18cm. The diver faces few dangers from the sea creatures themselves. Only one common jellyfish is poisonous, the lion's mane of Sherlock Holmes' notoriety. Wolf eels can be dangerous, but only if pestered; they can be quite gent*eel* if treated with TLC. There are many shark species in BC waters, including the large (up to 6m) primitive sixgill, but no recorded shark attacks. The theory is that cold water makes them more docile.

WILDLIFE VIEWING

British Columbia Wildlife Watch, a provincial wildlife viewing program, has identified viewing sites throughout the province. These are places where people may observe wildlife in their natural habitats: migrating birds along the Pacific flyway; spawning salmon in Goldstream River north of Victoria; mountain goats on the rocky hillsides near Hedley; butterflies in many habitats from wild places to city parks. These and many other viewing opportunities are indicated in the *Logs* by the binoculars icon, or in listings under communites, with the words "BC Wildlife Watch viewing site." For more information write: BC Wildlife Watch, Box 7394 Stn Prov Govt, Victoria, BC, V8W 9M4. Call 250-387-9737.

Many animals will be visible only if they wish to be. It's a privilege to capture these animals on film and, while most are harmless, a few mishaps involving wild animals and humans occur each year. Common sense and caution should be exercised when trespassing into a wild animal's domain.

Other opportunities to witness, or even help wildlife, are at wildlife recovery centres, such as the North Island Wildlife Recovery Centre, near Parksville on Vancouver Island, where humans can adopt (contribute to the cost of caring for) orphaned and injured animals so they can be returned to the wild. There are also recovery centres at Burnaby Lake Regional Park, and in Delta (the OWL – Orphaned Wildlife Rehabilitation Society).

All five Pacific salmon species migrate far into the province's Interior. The Fraser, with its many tributaries, has the largest salmon runs in the world. As many as 300 million young salmon may migrate out of the river some years, and up to 18 million, in the most exceptional of years, may return to spawn.

It is not surprising then that British Columbians take their wildlife seriously. A federal survey found that nearly 91 percent – the highest figure in Canada – support conservation of abundant wildlife. What's more, 2.3 million BC residents spend an estimated $622 million a year to study, photographs, and feed animals.

Beware the Bear and Cougar

Both bears and cougars, found in most parts of BC, normally avoid confrontation with humans. Make these animals aware of your presence by singing, shouting, or shaking a tin of pebbles. Remember, bears (black and grizzly) are everywhere. Respect all bears – they can be dangerous. Never approach a bear; never attempt to feed a bear; be defensive – never surprise a bear. Cook and eat well away from your tent. Lock your food in the trunk of a car. In the backcountry, food should be strung high in a tree a good distance from camp. Properly store and pack out all garbage. Many parks provide information on how to avoid unfortunate encounters with bears.

Cougars, more timid than bears, are rarely seen by campers. But some, particularly old or sick animals, view small children and dogs as easy prey. Having said this, it is only fair to add that, while your chances of seeing a cougar in the wilderness are slight, come winter, cougars sometimes start moving around, especially south into Victoria. Usually a cougar or three per winter finds itself loping about the residential streets of that proverbially civilized town, and one winter, one made its way into the parkade of the venerable Empress Hotel.

Rattlers are Rare

The northern Pacific rattlesnake, BC's only venomous snake, occurs in the desert-like south Okanagan Valley, and in the Interior dry belt as far north as Cache Creek. Unless you step on a rattlesnake, you're not likely to get bitten, but if you see one, give it a wide berth and keep your pets away from it.

Bugs and Buzzers

Mosquitoes and blackflies, particularly in northern BC, are numerous in spring and summer when they breed. Your best defences are fly swatters and insect repellents.

Bees, hornets, and wasps usually sting only in self-defence. The pain and itching of a sting can be relieved by applying an ice pack or a paste of baking soda and cold cream.

Ticks are a hazard to people and pets, especially in dry areas. They attach themselves to the skin and draw blood through sharp beaks. Applying gasoline, kerosene, alcohol, or a hot match to a tick will force it to relax its jaws. Then you can gently lift it out.

Paralytic Shellfish Poisoning

Shellfish collectors should be wary of red tides. This deadly phenomenon is caused by microscopic algae ingested by filter-feeding shellfish, such as mussels, oysters, or clams. These algae bloom in the sunlight, often giving the sea a tomato-soup appearance. Although harmless to shellfish, they produce some of the most toxic natural poisons on Earth, causing muscular paralysis and possible death by asphyxiation in warm-blooded animals. If you eat contaminated shellfish you may feel a tingling in your lips and tongue, followed by a numb-

---

1913: *Construction of the Canadian National Railway along the Fraser River at Hells Gate triggers a landslide: in one of BC's worst environmental disasters, millions of salmon fail to reach their spawning grounds. Fisheries never recover.*

1920s: *The peak of BC's salmon-fishing industry: there are 70 salmon canneries along BC's coast.*

1947: *Aboriginal peoples are granted the vote in BC provincial elections (they must wait until 1960 to vote in federal elections).*

1950s-60s: *Man reshapes BC. The largest dams on Earth transform rivers into the province's biggest lakes; giant turbines power dozens of new pulp mills and smelters fed by forests and mines. Ripple Rock, an obstacle to shipping, is obliterated in the world's largest manmade non-atomic explosion. The Trans-Canada Highway is completed, asphalt reaches every corner of the province; new bridges, railways, BC Ferries, and Beautiful British Columbia Magazine, founded in 1959, signal this an era of boundless optimism.*

ness in your toes and fingertips. Induce vomiting and call a doctor. Federal fisheries authorities monitor the coast areas and post warnings in contaminated areas. It is dangerous and illegal to harvest shellfish from these areas.

KEEPING BC BEAUTIFUL

Take nothing more than photographs, leave only footprints.

This old nature lover's motto is still valid, although, with the increasing volume of traffic through many of the province's wilderness areas, even footprints can be too much to leave behind. They cause erosion, damage fragile plants and tree roots. The motto reminds us, nonetheless, that if there is to be any wilderness left for us to enjoy, each of us must take seriously our responsibility to tread lightly, and keep to a minimum our impact on the world around us.

The Outdoor Recreation Council of BC has published "A Wilderness Code of Ethics," a brochure to guide us on our individual journeys. It offers advice on safety and preparedness, for our own sakes, then asks us to take precautions for the sake of the land and all who travel behind us. Stick to the trail, travel single file, avoid the temptation to detour muddy sections. When your party has to cross a meadow, spread out, then rejoin later at the trail.

Choose your campsite carefully: a spot with little or no vegetation well away from the trail and at least 60m from water. If a heavily used or damaged site is found, use it rather than damage another spot. Around camp, wear light sneakers to avoid excessive trampling of the campsite. Carry a camp stove: fires are not allowed everywhere. Treat all water (use boiling, filter, or iodine). Leave Fido at home.

And remember, if you can pack it in, you can pack it out.

For the brochure or more information about intelligent use and management of outdoor places, contact the Outdoor Recreation Council of BC, 604-737-3058, or e-mail: orcbc@istar.ca. Also see *Outdoor Activities*.

The Council is just one of many organizations dedicated to the enjoyment and preservation of the province's natural resources. For more information about these organizations, or what you can do to help keep BC beautiful, contact:

■ **The Nature Trust of British Columbia:** 808-100 Park Royal South, West Vancouver, BC, V7T 1A2. 604-925-1128. Since 1971 this charitable corporation, created by the Government of Canada, has secured the acquisition of more than 200 areas of ecological significance. These cover more than 13,000ha, creating a legacy of grasslands, marshes, forests and mountains, and plant and wildlife species.

■ **Sierra Club of Western Canada:** 1525 Amelia St, Victoria, BC, V8W 2K1. 250-386-5255. This first chapter of the Sierra Club in Canada was opened in Victoria in 1969. Goals are to help save wilderness areas and salmon, and change forest practices. Publishes *Sierra* magazine, and calendar.

ENDANGERED SPECIES

Sea otter populations are expanding in B.C.

Now on the red list – either threatened, endangered, or candidates for these designations – are more than 77 species of vertebrate animals, and 193 plant species. Four animal species are officially listed as endangered under BC's Wildlife Act — the Vancouver Island marmot, the burrowing owl, the sea otter, and the American white pelican.

The chocolate-coloured Vancouver Island marmot, which inhabits logged and alpine areas of the south island, faces a dangerous precipice. Only about 100 remain in the wild. A captive breeding program is being developed, but with each passing month their chances of survival shrink. Captive breeding is the best chance for the pigeon-sized burrowing owl that has nearly vanished from the south Okanagan. Numbers have climbed from only 50 a few years ago.

Sea otters, numbering now about 2,500 in BC, were re-introduced from Alaska in the late 1960s and early '70s. Sea otters can be seen in a large area of the northwest coast of Vancouver Island and the Hakai Wilderness Area on the mainland coast. They reach their highest densities at Checleset Bay, an ecological reserve off northwest Vancouver Island.

BC's white pelican population remains small, but stable. The number of breeding pairs rose to about 400 by the early 1980s, from only about 100 a decade earlier. There is a breeding colony west of Williams Lake, and the birds are often seen feeding on lakes in the area.

■ **Western Canada Wilderness Committee:** 20 Water St, Vancouver, BC, V6B 1A4. 604-683-8220. Operating out of Vancouver with a Victoria chapter. Calendar, books on alternative forest practices, field guides, T-shirts, posters, newsletter.

■ **Greenpeace:** 1726 Commercial Dr., Vancouver, BC, V5N 4A3. 604-253-7701. This international organization originated in Vancouver.

■ **Friends of Ecological Reserves:** Box 8477, Victoria, BC, V8W 3S1. 250-595-4813. Working province-wide to protect reserves already established, and to propose new ones. Reserves are unique ecosystems established by orders-in-council for study purposes, or to preserve rare or endangered plants, animals, and land formations. Some are listed in the *Travel Guide*, others are better kept as secrets. More than 100 reserves to date.

1993: *The forests of Clayoquot Sound become a symbol of all that has been lost. Sea otters, whales, salmon, jobs. Environmentalists, aboriginal peoples, loggers, and multi-national logging companies fight over what's left: 800 logging protesters are arrested in the largest act of civil disobedience in Canada's history. Meanwhile, the BC government is pressed to begin the process of negotiating treaties with First Nations.*

1999: *In the St Elias Mountains of the north, the Yakutat Terrane is colliding into the Chugach Terrane, forcing North America's highest mountains upward – 4cm a year. On the south coast, converging Juan de Fuca and North American plates are jammed. Sooner or later, they'll shake loose. Glaciers continue to retreat: perhaps it's global warming caused by human events. Or perhaps something much larger, for, as Richard and Sydney Cannings remind us in* British Columbia: A Natural History:

"We may only be living in a short interval of warmth amid a long period of ice."

Outdoor Activities

The following is a list of BC's best-loved outdoor activities. More information can often be found in the *Logs*. Check the *Index* for communities, parks, lakes, rivers, and other places listed below.

The Outdoor Recreation Council of BC was established in 1976 to provide a central resource and information centre on outdoor recreation and education in BC. More than 50 associations and groups are involved in the activities listed below, and a few others are Outdoor Recreation Council of BC members. The council has published eight regional maps showing where to hike, horseback ride, launch boats, mountain climb, camp, view wildlife, and take advantage of BC's other recreational opportunities. Contact Suite 334, 1367 W Broadway St, Vancouver, BC, V6H 4A9. 604-737-3058. Website: www.bcadventure.com. The council also publishes a brochure entitled *A Wilderness Code of Ethics*, describing how travellers can minimize their impact on wilderness areas.

Rentals: For camping, climbing, boating, horseback riding, skiing, gold panning – you name it – look in the classified section of the telephone book, or ask at information centres.

Boating
BC has more than 27,000km of ocean coastline and 18,000 sq km of inland waters. There are more than 6,000 islands and islets. Season is basically year-round. Thousands of charter companies and rental outlets can recommend the best places to go. Ask at information centres, or check phone books for listings.

Transporting Boats into Canada: Contact Canada Customs, 333 Dunsmuir St, First Floor, Vancouver, BC, V6B 5R3. Or call 604-666-3228.

Best Sailing and Cruising Places: Inside Passage, Jervis Inlet, Desolation Sound, Princess Louisa Inlet, Gulf Islands, Howe Sound, Queen Charlotte Islands. For instruction info, phone the Sailing Association of BC at 604-737-3113.

Best Canoeing and Kayaking Places: Bowron Lake Provincial Park and Tweedsmuir Provincial Park in the Cariboo; Broken Group Islands, Nitinat Lakes,

Burrard Inlet offers sailing against a backdrop of North Shore Mountains.

Nootka Sound, Upper Campbell and Buttle lakes on Vancouver Island; Wells Gray Provincial Park in the Thompson Okanagan; Powell River canoe route in southwestern BC; Queen Charlotte Islands. For flatwater, whitewater, and recreational canoeing information, contact the Recreational Canoeing Association of BC, 604-437-1140 or 604-853-9320. Also, the Whitewater Kayaking Association of BC, c/o Sport BC, 1367 W Broadway St, Vancouver, BC, V3H 4E9. 604-515-6379. Website: www.white water.org. For sea kayaking

contact the Sea Kayak Association of BC, PO Box 751 Postal Station A, Vancouver, BC, V6C 2N6, or call 604-228-1450.

River Rafting: Some 35 outfitters are ready to take groups or individuals along BC's watery pathways. Some of the best rivers: Fraser, Thompson, Tatshenshini-Alsek, Chilcotin, Chilliwack, Kootenay, Skeena, and in the Northwest Territories, the Nahanni River. Contact BC Parks, 800 Johnson St, Victoria, BC, V8V 1X4. 250-387-4550.

Houseboating: On Shuswap Lake (more than

300 houseboats for charter and 1,000km of navigable waterways) in Thompson Okanagan, also Okanagan Lake, Kootenay Lake.

Bungy Jumping
A relatively new sport from Down Under, bungy jumping is plunging off a 50m bridge with just an elastic bungy cord tied to your ankles. It traces back to simple transportation – swinging off vines in the South Pacific. The Bungy Zone in Nanaimo on Vancouver Island, the first legal bungy jumping organization in North America, is famous for its "Naked Day" event. Contact the Bungy Zone, Box 399, Stn A, Nanaimo, BC, V9R 5L3. 250-753-5867.

Caving
About 1,000 of BC's thousands of caves have been charted and explored. The caves of Vancouver Island rank among the most significant and spectacular systems of the world. Most are undeveloped, and subject to everything from flash floods to mud slides.

Helmets, lights, appropriate footwear, and extreme caution are required. The best way to start is on a tour guided by an experienced operator or caving club.

Most Popular Caves: Nakimu Caves in Glacier National Park; in the Rockies, Arctomys Cave near Mt Robson is -536m, the second deepest cave system north of Mexico (the deepest, at -614m, is in the Quatsino Master System, in BC's new White Ridge Provincial Park). The Yorkshire Pot complex at Crowsnest, almost 10km long. Cody Cave Provincial Park, near Ainsworth. On Vancouver Island: Horne Lake Cave Provincial Park, Little Hustan Lake Caves Regional Park, Upana Caves Recreation Site.

Tours: At Horne Lake Caves Provincial Park and out of Gold River, Port McNeill, on Vancouver Island, and at Ainsworth, in the BC Rockies region.

Recreational Caving: Contact BC Speleological Federation, 544 Springbok Rd, Campbell River, BC, V9W 8A2. 250-283-CAVE for info on federation members throughout BC. Also North Vancouver Island Regional District, 250-956-3301.

Commercial Caving: Cave Guiding Association of BC, Box 431, Gold River, BC, V0P 1G0. 250-956-4827.

Cycling
In BC, cyclists are required by law to wear a helmet. Almost all cycling shops and major department stores carry a range of helmets that meet national safety standards.

Cycling BC: Suite 332-1367 W Broadway St, Vancouver, BC, V6H 4A9, 604-737-3034 for info on routes, safety, and equipment.

Popular and Not-So-Hilly Routes: Check Logs for the Gulf Islands, Saanich Peninsula (Vancouver Island), Fraser

Valley, Sunshine Coast, Okanagan Valley; Kettle Valley Railway (see p.143).

Popular Mountain Routes: Check Logs for BC Rockies region.

Popular Urban Routes: Galloping Goose Trail, Victoria; Stanley Park Seawall, Vancouver.

Tours: Companies in Vancouver and New Westminster, Victoria on Vancouver Island, Nelson in the Kootenays, and Banff, Alberta. Write the Bicycling Association, and check with information centres.

Diving

BC's waters are said by National Geographic magazine to be the finest in the world second to the Red Sea. Best months for visibility are July/Aug–March. Prime time is Oct–Jan.

Popular Diving Spots: In southwestern BC – Sunshine Coast, North Vancouver, Powell River. Around Vancouver Island – Barkley Sound, Race Rocks near Victoria, Saanich Inlet, Discovery Passage.

Artificial Reefs: Ships scuttled to become full-scale marine ecosystems include HMCS Mackenzie near Sidney, the freighter GB Church off Portland Island near Sidney, the destroyer Chaudiere north of Sechelt, and the Columbia near Campbell River.

Fishing and Fish Watching

BC's five salmon species, giant halibut, and lingcod are found along thousands of fishable kilometres of coastline; freshwater trout are found in the province's 2,200 lakes and 37 river systems. In 1998, the federal Department of Fisheries and Oceans announced sportfishing restrictions, particularly on coho salmon, as part of efforts to conserve stocks. Be sure to contact the department for information before setting out.

Blackcomb Mountain draws daredevil skiers.

Best Saltwater Fishing: In the chuck around Campbell River. The tyee (trophy-sized chinook salmon) is the prize, often weighing more than 22kg. Also spring salmon, lingcod and halibut. Best in spring, summer, fall.

Best Freshwater Fishing: Steelhead (feisty sea-run rainbow trout) at 3-10kg. Also cutthroat, Dolly Varden, kokanee (land-locked sockeye) and a number of varieties of trout, especially rainbow. Anywhere there's a lake or river. North of Kamloops, bellyboating features fishing from a float tube.

What Tackle Where: Ask Department of Fisheries and Oceans Canada, Recreational Fisheries Branch, marina and sporting goods store operators, or anyone you see carrying a fish. Check the bookstore too.

Regulations: Licences are required for anyone sport-fishing in tidal waters. Freshwater angling licences are required for all persons aged 16 or over. Licences are sold in many sporting goods stores, department stores, marinas and government agencies. For spe-

cific info about tidal-water fishing regulations and conditions, contact the Department of Fisheries and Oceans Canada, 555 W Hastings St, Vancouver, BC, V6B 5G3. Call 604-666-6331 or 604-666-2826 for a 24-hour taped message of tidal water openings and closures, or call 1-888-997-7997. Website: http://www.pac.dfo-mpo.gc.ca. For non-tidal water fishing, contact the Ministry of Fisheries, Sport Fisheries, 780 Blanshard St, Victoria, BC, V8V 1X4. 250-356-5908.

Fishing Camps: Throughout province. Ranging from rustic to luxurious. Check information centres, and Tourism BC's Accommodations guide.

Fish Hatcheries and Spawning Rivers: Listed in the Logs, are more than 50 hatcheries, spawning channels, and major spawning rivers, throughout BC where salmon, sea-run trout, and freshwater trout can be viewed at various stages of their life cycle. The federal Ministry of Fisheries and Oceans publishes a brochure, "Where and

When to See Salmon." Contact the Department of Fisheries and Oceans, Station 321, 400-555 W Hastings St, Vancouver, BC, V6B 5G3. 604-666-6614. BC's ministry of Environment, Lands and Parks has "Fish Viewing in Urban Streams – Lower Mainland Region." Contact them at 10470-152nd St, Surrey, BC, V3R 0Y3. 604-582-5200. BC Wildlife Watch viewing sites also include fish-viewing opportunities.

Loggers' sports events are held throughout B.C.

Some of the best places to see late summer or early fall salmon runs are the Adams River, Hells Gate Fishways on the Fraser River, Fulton River Spawning Channels, Goldstream and Stamp Falls provincial parks on Vancouver Island, and the Weaver Creek Spawning Channel, east of Mission.

Trout hatcheries come under BC Ministry of Fisheries, 780 Blanshard St, Victoria, BC, V8V 1X4.

Gold Panning

You might find gold in many of BC's creeks and rivers. In the Cariboo area, try Emory Bar at Emory Creek Provincial Park near Yale, the Gold Panning Recreational Reserve near Lytton, Lillooet; in Northern BC there's Kleanza Creek Provincial Park, Telegraph Creek, and

Spruce Creek near Atlin; the Princeton area of the Similkameen Valley; and Goldstream River in Goldstream Provincial Park on Vancouver Island; at Atlin in BC's northwest corner.

Regulations: Hand-panning for gold is permitted everywhere in BC except placer (staked) claims or leases and most parks and aboriginal reserves. For info: Chief Gold Commissioner, Mineral Titles Branch, Box 9322, 3rd Floor, 1810 Blanshard St, Victoria, BC, V8W 9N3. 250-952-0542. Or drop in on the gold commissioner for the mining division where you wish to pan.

Golfing

BC is a golfer's paradise, and among the few places on the continent to be selected by the Professional Golf Association as a golf tour destination. There are more than 200 golf courses ranging from par 3s to challenging 18-hole championship courses.

Best Places: Fairmont and Radium Hot Springs, BC Rockies, the Okanagan Valley, Whistler, Vancouver, and Victoria. Because of the mild climates, you can golf year-round in Vancouver, Coast, and Mountains and Vancouver Island regions. Contact information centres. Write Tourism British

Columbia, Box 9830 Stn Prov Govt, 1117 Wharf St, Victoria, BC, V8W 9W5. Call 1-800-663-6000 or 604-663-6000 in Vancouver.

Hang-Gliding

The closest thing to a bird's-eye view of BC.
Best time: Spring to early summer.
Best Places: Grouse Mountain, Saltspring Island, Duncan, Pemberton, Ashcroft, Cache Creek, Kamloops and Clinton in and around the Cariboo, Vernon, Falkland, and Sicamous in the Thompson-Okanagan, and Golden, in the BC Rockies. Many qualified instructors in these areas offer instruction and professional-assisted tandem rides. Various competitions. Contact the Hang-Gliding Association of BC, RR 1, S4-C46, Peachland, BC, V0H 1X0. Call 250-470-8674. Website: Http: bchpa@simplenet.com.

some popular trails have quota registration systems to reduce foot traffic. Maps are usually available in parks, also from Provincial Parks offices, national parks, information centres, outdoor stores.

BC's Most Popular:
■ **West Coast (Historic Lifesaving) Trail:** 5-7 days, Vancouver Island. Trail open April-Sept. Reservations must be made. Full details, p.52.
■ **Cape Scott Trail:** To tip of North Vancouver Island, beaches, lighthouse, history; one long day in. See p.79.
■ **Nuxalk-Carrier Heritage Trail:** Cariboo Country. Trace aboriginal footsteps 420km; 25 days. See p.248.
■ **Naikoon Provincial Park East Beach Trail:** Queen Charlotte Islands, 5-7 days of beach walking. See p.279.
■ Juan de Fuca Marine Trail: 47km of west-coast hiking and beachcombing

Lussier Hot Springs add a luxurious element to the mountain wilderness.

Horseback Riding

Best Places:
Cariboo Country, Cascade Mountains (Manning and Cathedral provincial parks are just a few hours from Vancouver), northern wilderness parks, BC Rockies, Thompson-Okanagan. Ask at information centres for list of stables, outfitters, riding camps. There are also more than a dozen guest ranches in BC; some offer a rustic ranch setting, others are full-facility resorts. Contact the BC Guest Ranchers' Association, Box 4501, Williams Lake, BC, V26 2V8, or the Cariboo Chilcotin Coast Tourist Association, 250-392-2226.

Hot-Air Ballooning

Passengers have exchanged wedding vows, held company picnics, filmed music videos, even shot a TV scene in a hot-air balloon – others just enjoy the view hundreds of metres up. Conditions are best between spring and early fall. There are two outfits in the Vancouver, Coast, and Mountains region: Fantasy Balloon Charters in Langley, 604-530-1974; Pegasus Ballooning in Surrey, 604-533-2071. As well, Stardust Ballooning in Kelowna hosts the Balloon Rendezvous every Thanksgiving weekend. 250-868-8382 for more info.

Hot Spring Soaking

Famous Resorts and Developed Springs:
Ainsworth, Nakusp, Albert Canyon, Fairmont, Radium, and Halcyon in the BC Rockies; Harrison in Vancouver, Coast, and Mountains; Lakelse, Liard River, Alaska Highway in Northern BC.
Undeveloped for the Adventurous:
Hot Springs Cove on Vancouver Island, Halfway River and Lussier in the BC Rockies, the Pemberton area in Vancouver, Coast, and Mountains. Be forewarned: bathing suits are optional.

Mountaineering and Rock Climbing

Though BC is one of the world's best climbing locations, there is as yet no central source of information on where, when, and how to go, or on all the types of mountaineering and climbing possible.
Federation of Mountain Clubs: Suite 47 W Broadway St, Vancouver, BC, V5Y 1P1. Call 604-878-7007 for info on hiking, mountaineering, and climbing courses. These can be holidays in themselves. The Federation can also provide a list of mountain-oriented clubs. Visitors are welcome to join these groups for hiking, ski-mountaineering, climbing, and other excursions geared to mountain enthusiasts of all ages and abilities.

Best Places:
Provincial and national parks in the Rockies, Selkirks, Purcells, Monashees, and Coast Mountains. The Rocky Mountains currently provide the most accessible high-peak climbing, but other ranges, such as the Coast Mountains, offer fantastic fly-in wilderness climbing opportunities. The Mt Waddington area on the central coast is very popular for ski mountaineering.
Famous Rocks to Climb:
The Stawamus Chief and other peaks in Tantalus Range near Squamish, a short distance from Vancouver; Zopkios Ridge (Coquihalla Highway); Bugaboo Provincial Park and Alpine Recreation Area in the BC Rockies.
For More Information:
Write provincial parks listed here. Check bookstores. Write the Federation of Mountain Clubs (above) for lists of local organizations.

Skiing

BC lies within Canada's Cordilleran region, one of the major mountain systems of the world. The entire province consists of ranges, subranges, and high-elevation plateaus. Downhill, cross-country, helicopter, and powdercat skiing are well established. There are 35 full-facility downhill ski areas in BC, plus a few family-oriented hills with limited facilities. There are also some 30 cross-country or Nordic skiing destinations, plus countless local areas – anywhere where there's fresh air, scenery, snow, and enough space between the trees.
Most Popular Downhill Ski Areas: Whistler/Blackcomb and Grouse in Vancouver, Coast, and Mountains; Red Mountain and Whitewater in the BC Rockies region; Big White and Silver Star in the Okanagan; Mt Washington, Vancouver Island.

Para-gliding from The Peak in North Vancouver.

Hiking and Walking

Provincial and National Parks: Some of the province's best hiking. Within BC Parks alone are some 3,500km of trails. Treks for the fit and experienced that take days or weeks to complete; yet often, in the same park, there are easy walking trails taking just minutes or a few hours. Plan early –

within an hour's drive of Victoria. See p.51.
■ **Local Trails:** Information centres often have detailed maps for nearby trails.
■ **Beaches, Deer Trails:** On your own – watch for high tides and headlands, try not to get lost in the forest. Write Outdoor Recreation Council for safety info. See p.26.

Horses graze on the tall grass of the Nicola Valley's Douglas Lake Ranch.

Greenhorns and cowgirls ride together at the Douglas Lake Ranch.

Most Popular Cross-country Ski Areas: Mt Washington on Vancouver Island; Whistler Mountain and Manning Park, Vancouver, Coast, and Mountains; 108 Mile and The Hills, in the Cariboo. For downhill and cross-country, see Ski Index and Logs. Or write Tourism British Columbia, Box 9830, Stn Prov Govt, Victoria, BC, V8W 9W5.

Surfing

Best Places: On Vancouver Island's west coast, at Jordan River, Sombrio Beach, and Long Beach. Coastal water temperatures range from 4C in Jan to 13C in Aug. Come prepared with a full wet suit, including hood, gloves, and booties. Rentals in Victoria, Vancouver, Tofino.

Whale Watching – Grey Whales

Best Places From Land: Pacific Rim National Park on Vancouver Island. Some 24,000 grey whales travel north along BC's west coast Feb-April on their annual migration from Baja California to the Bering Sea. They pass by again, heading south, Sept-Oct. On clear, calm days you may see tails and flippers. On stormy days, you may see spume. Use binoculars. Some grey whales remain resident year-round. Visit Wickaninnish Centre for excellent displays. Park naturalists also on hand. Whales can also be seen from North Beach on Graham Island in the Queen Charlotte Islands.
From Sea: Charters and tours depart from Vancouver and North Vancouver; and from Tofino and Ucluelet on Vancouver Island. Ask at information centres.

Whale Watching – Killer Whales

Best Places From Land: Serendipity helps. Best time is mid-April to late Oct, from shores in Haro and Johnstone straits, near Vancouver Island. About 30 pods, with a total population of some 300 whales, live year-round in waters between BC and Washington State.
From Sea: Pods of killer whales, also Dall's porpoises, are occasionally spotted from BC Ferries in Active Pass through the Gulf Islands and more often through the Inside Passage. Charter operators offer very good chance of sighting. Ask at information centres in Vancouver and North Vancouver, and on Vancouver Island at Victoria, Nanaimo, Port McNeill, Alert Bay, Port Hardy, Tofino, and Ucluelet. In Telegraph Cove, ask anyone there (or call Stubbs Island Charters, 250-928-3117 or 1-800-665-3066) – it's one of the best spots.

Windsurfing

Best Places: Squamish and the Sunshine Coast, north of Vancouver, Jericho Beach in Vancouver and White Rock, all in the Vancouver, Coast, and Mountains region Okanagan, Kalamalka, and Shuswap lakes in the Thompson-Okanagan, and Elk and Nitinat lakes on Vancouver Island. Rentals available. For instruction, try Windsure Windsurfing School in Vancouver, 604-224-0615. Experts flock to the prime locale of Squamish.

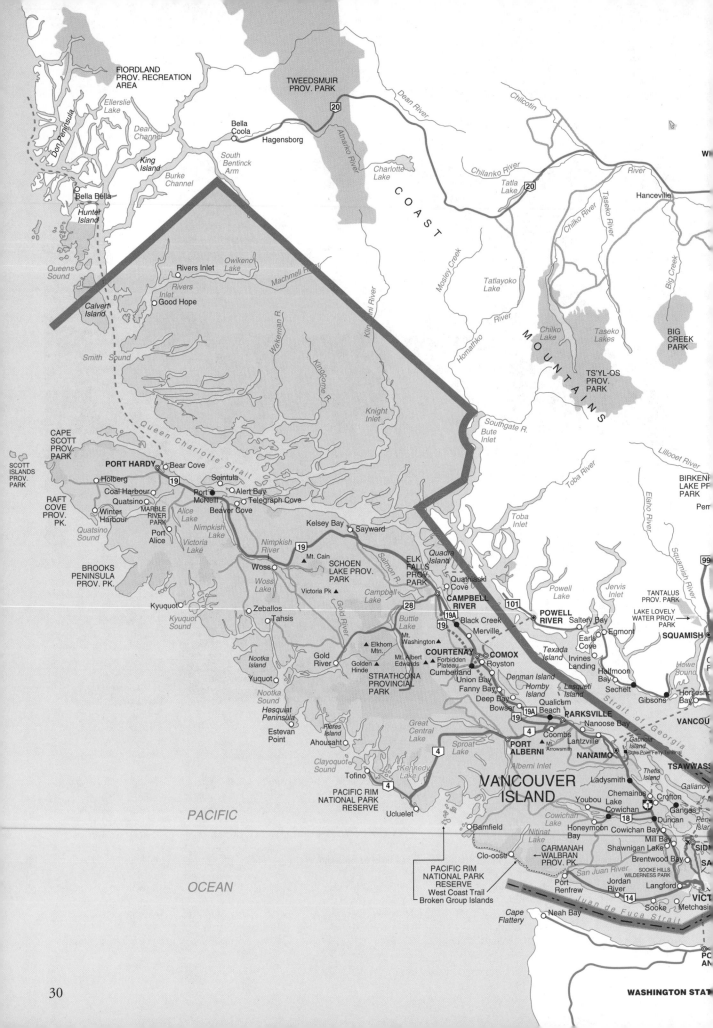

FIORDLAND
PROV. RECREATION
AREA

Ellerslie
Lake

Dean
Channel

Don Peninsula

King
Island

Burke
Channel

Bella Bella

Hunter
Island

Queens
Sound

Calvert
Island

Smith Sound

TWEEDSMUIR
PROV. PARK

20

Bella
Coola

Hagensborg

South
Bentinck
Arm

Rivers Inlet

Owikeno
Lake

Rivers
Inlet

Good Hope

Machmell River

Wakeman R.

Klinaklini River

Dean River

COAST

Chilcotin

Charlotte
Lake

Chilanko River

Tatla
Lake

20

River

Hanceville

Mosley Creek

Tatlayoko
Lake

Chilko River

Taseko River

Chilko
Lake

Homathko
River

Taseko
Lakes

BIG
CREEK
PARK

TS'YL-OS
PROV.
PARK

MOUNTAINS

Big Creek

Kingcome R.

Knight
Inlet

Southgate R.
Bute
Inlet

Lillooet River

Queen Charlotte Strait

CAPE
SCOTT
PROV.
PARK

SCOTT
ISLANDS
PROV.
PARK

RAFT
COVE
PROV.
PK.

BROOKS
PENINSULA
PROV. PK.

PORT HARDY
Bear Cove

Holberg

Coal Harbour

Quatsino

Winter
Harbour

Quatsino
Sound

MARBLE
RIVER
PARK

Port Alice

Port
McNeill

Sointula

Alert Bay

Telegraph Cove

Beaver Cove

19

Alice
Lake

Nimpkish
Lake

Victoria
Lake

Kelsey Bay

Sayward

Nimpkish
River

19

Mt. Cain

Woss

Woss
Lake

Victoria Pk.

SCHOEN
LAKE PROV.
PARK

Salmon R.

Campbell
Lake

ELK
FALLS
PROV.
PARK

Quadra
Island

Quathiaski
Cove

CAMPBELL
RIVER

28

19A

Black Creek

Merville

BIRKENHEAD
LAKE PROV.
PARK

Toba River

Toba
Inlet

Powell
Lake

Jervis
Inlet

Elaho River

Squamish River

99

TANTALUS
PROV. PARK

LAKE LOVELY
WATER PROV.
PARK

SQUAMISH

POWELL
RIVER

Saltery Bay

Earls
Cove

Egmont

Kyuquot

Zeballos

Tahsis

Kyuquot
Sound

Gold River

19

Elkhorn
Mtn.

Golden
Hinde

Mt.
Washington

Mt. Albert
Edwards

STRATHCONA
PROVINCIAL
PARK

Buttle
Lake

Gold River

COURTENAY

Forbidden
Plateau

Cumberland

COMOX

Royston

Union Bay

Fanny Bay

Denman Island

Hornby
Island

Texada
Island

Lasqueti
Island

Irvines
Landing

Halfmoon
Bay

Sechelt

Gibsons

Horseshoe
Bay

Howe
Sound

VANCOUVER

Nootka
Island

Yuquot

Nootka
Sound

Hesquiat
Peninsula

Estevan
Point

Ahousaht

Flores
Island

Clayoquot
Sound

Tofino

Great
Central
Lake

Sproat
Lake

Kennedy
Lake

Deep Bay

Bowser

Qualicum
Beach

19A

PARKSVILLE

4

Coombs

Mt.
Arrowsmith

Lantzville

PORT
ALBERNI

Alberni Inlet

Nanoose Bay

Gabriola
Island

NANAIMO

Duke Point Ferry Terminal

Thetis
Island

Ladysmith

Chemainus

Crofton

Ganges

Galiano I.

TSAWWASSEN

VICTORIA

PACIFIC

4

PACIFIC RIM
NATIONAL PARK
RESERVE

Ucluelet

Bamfield

Clo-oose

CARMANAH
WALBRAN
PROV. PK.

PACIFIC RIM
NATIONAL PARK
RESERVE
West Coast Trail
Broken Group Islands

OCEAN

Cape
Flattery

Neah Bay

VANCOUVER
ISLAND

Cowichan
Lake

Youbou

Nitinat
Lake

San Juan River

Port
Renfrew

Honeymoon
Bay

Lake
Cowichan

18

Cowichan Bay

Duncan

Mill Bay

Shawnigan Lake

Jordan
River

Sooke Hills
Wilderness Park

Brentwood Bay

SIDNEY

San Juan de Fuca Strait

14

Sooke

Langford

Pender
Island

SAANICH

PORT
ANGELES

WASHINGTON STATE

30

VANCOUVER ISLAND

BIG, BEAUTIFUL, INCOMPARABLE

> **"** *To describe the beauties of this region, will, on some future occasion be a grateful task to the pen of a skillful panegyrist. The serenity of the climate, the innumerable pleasing landscapes, and the abundant fertility that nature puts forth, require only to be enriched by the industry of man with villages, mansions, cottages and other buildings, to render it the most lovely country that can be imagined.* **"**
>
> Captain George Vancouver (1757 – 1798)

Captain Vancouver's favourable description of the island that bears his name is not surprising. For natives and newcomers alike, the "serenity of the climate, the ... pleasing landscapes" that so impressed Vancouver two centuries ago, are still the island's most attractive attributes. What's interesting, however, is that this admiring portrayal was written by a man who for two decades had explored the shores of some of the world's most beautiful islands – Tahiti, New Guinea, the Canary Islands, Hawaii, New Zealand, the Solomon Islands, and West Indies. Yet it was the wild and intricate coast of Vancouver Island, the rainforests, rivers, and mountains, that stirred his imagination.

The immensity of this island must soon have become apparent to the young captain as he explored the inside waters – between Vancouver Island and the mainland – in the spring and summer of 1792. At the end of summer he returned to Nootka Island, off Vancouver Island's west coast, where he'd landed 14 years earlier as a crewman with Captain James Cook. Neither Cook nor Vancouver at that time realized they'd come upon the largest North American island in the Pacific.

Vancouver's journey focused on the mainland shore, so he didn't travel every inch of the island's 3,440km coastline. But certainly he saw many of the harbours and headlands, the estuaries, islands, and inlets that today's sailors encounter as they circumnavigate Vancouver Island.

It would have been difficult for Vancouver to appreciate the incredible diversity of his newfound island without exploring the dense virgin forests. The mountains that form the backbone of Vancouver Island rival the Rockies when the vertical distance between peaks and foothills is considered. Mt Golden Hinde, at 2,200m the highest point, stands at the island's centre. High in these mountains, above forests of western red cedar and hemlock, Douglas fir and Sitka spruce, profusions of wildflowers embellish alpine meadows. The glaciers and frigid lakes surrounding these meadows form the headwaters of countless watersheds, streams, and tributaries that flow through some 2,000 island lakes before reaching the sea. Not far from Mt Golden Hinde, in Strathcona Provincial Park, is Della Falls, 440m high, Canada's highest falls tumbling in three cascades from the cold, clear waters of a mountain lake.

Geographically, the differences between the east and west sides of the island are profound. While the western side of the mountains is penetrated by more than two dozen long, meandering inlets, the low-lying eastern side has only one – the famous Saanich Inlet. The west coast is the wild side of Vancouver Island, a rugged, often inhospitable place inhabited by the hale and the dauntless west-coast settlements – Bamfield, Ucluelet, Tofino, Tahsis, Zeballos – small compared to those on the other side. Almost all of the island's major centres are spread along the east coast.

Strathcona Park Lodge beckons adventurers to the mountainous heart of Vancouver Island.

Thirty-three mammal species, from bats to beavers, inhabit the island. There are thousands of black bears, black-tailed deer, and Roosevelt elk, as well as cougars and timber wolves. At some higher elevations are small colonies of Vancouver Island marmots, an endangered subspecies – more rare than the giant panda – unique to the island.

More conspicuous are the birds, hundreds of thousands that migrate on the Pacific flyway in spring and fall. One hundred and fifty species stop here each spring to breed, thousands of birds remain through winter. The seas surrounding Vancouver Island are home for 28 marine mammal species. Blubbery Steller's sea lions, sea otters, and playful dolphins patrol these waters with harbour and fur seals, porpoises, whales, and others.

Sailing around the island, touching upon its shores here and there, Vancouver could not realize the diversity of landscapes and creatures, nor the diversity of peoples. Here "since time began," were three major cultural groups, speaking languages as varied as any in Europe, managing a wealth of resources within boundaries as clearly defined as any in Europe.

On the island's storm-swept west coast – the many Nuu-chah-nulth tribes, the only northwest coast people to hunt whales in the open sea. Of these, it was the Mowachaht tribe that guided lost captains Cook and Vancouver into their sheltered bay at Yuquot on Nootka Island. The thick sea otter furs they received as gifts drew others, and Yuquot was soon an international trading centre. Claims to this coast brought Spain, England, and their allies to the brink of war – unbeknown to the chiefs who already owned these territories.

East of Nuu-chah-nulth territories, across the Vancouver Island Range, were 30 tribes of Kwakwaka'wakw peoples: they owned rivers silver with eulachon. To the south and east, the Hul'qumi'num-speaking (Coast Salish) peoples: their seas were the gentler straits travelled by millions of migrating sockeye salmon. On sun-baked shores they carefully tended their crop – the tasty bulb of the blue camas flower.

"The industry of man" that Vancouver longed for, was, of course European, in style. The British Colony of Vancouver Island was established in 1849. The entire island, a total of 32,261 sq km, was leased by the British Crown to the Hudson's Bay Company for seven shillings a year on the condition lands would be opened for colonization. The trading company was permitted to sell land and mineral rights to prospective settlers.

From its precarious beginning in 1843 with just 50 Europeans at Fort Victoria, Vancouver Island has become home to more than half a million relative newcomers. Well aware that their home is like few other places in the world, more and more islanders are becoming environmentally conscious and active – hoping that the forests and the fish that Captain Vancouver celebrated will endure more than two centuries of the "industry of man."

VANCOUVER ISLAND'S VITAL STATISTICS

Vancouver Island's Measurements:
- Total area: 32,261 sq km
- Distance north to south: 451km from BC capital of Victoria to Cape Scott
- Average width: 80 to 100km
- Coastline length: 3,440km

Vancouver Island's Population:
- Total: 671,844
- Long Island, New York, nine times smaller than Vancouver Island, has a population density 135 times as high.
- Vancouver Island comprises 18 percent of BC's total population.
- There are an average of 21.3 people per sq km on Vancouver Island.
- The entire northern half of Vancouver Island is inhabited by less than three percent of the island's total population – 97 percent live between Campbell River and Victoria. Well over half live in and around Victoria.

Where the People Are:

Greater Victoria   317,989

Includes the cities of Victoria and Colwood, the district municipalities of Oak Bay, Esquimalt, Saanich, Central Saanich, North Saanich, Metchosin, and the townships of Sidney and View Royal.

Other Large Centres:

Nanaimo	70,130
Campbell River	28, 851
North Cowichan	25, 305
Courtenay	19,592
Port Alberni	18,468
Comox	11,847
Port Hardy	5,283

INFORMATION

Tourism Vancouver Island: 302-45 Bastion Square, Victoria, BC, V8W 1J1. 250-382-3551; fax: 250-382-3523 for info about Vancouver Island and the Gulf Islands. E-mail: tavi@island.bc.ca. Addresses and phone numbers of local information centres are in the traveller's logs with write-ups on each community.

TRANSPORTATION

Getting to and around Vancouver Island is simple. The island is well served by ferries, airlines, buses, a railway, rental vehicles, and taxis. Paved highways lead to all major population centres, and much in between is accessible by logging roads, most of which are open to the public. Information centres can provide info on major airlines and ferry operators as well as on small airlines and boat companies offering scheduled or charter services. They can also help with water taxis, bicycle and moped rentals, city bus routes and schedules.

Airlines

Victoria International is the island's largest airport. Many Gulf Island and west-coast points are served by small airlines with scheduled and charter flights. Usually, travel agents can provide the most up-to-date information on Vancouver Island flights.

- **Air BC:** 1-800-667-3721. (From the US: 1-800-776-3000. From Victoria: 250-360-9074). Victoria Harbour and Victoria International Airport, Nanaimo, Comox, Campbell River, Seattle-Tacoma International Airport, Calgary, Edmonton, Winnipeg.
- **Air Canada:** 1-800-663-3721. (US: 1-800-776-3000. Victoria: 250-360-9074). Departures from Victoria to connect with flights to national and international destinations.
- **Air Nootka:** 250-283-2255. Central and north coast.
- **Air Rainbow:** 1-888-287-8371 or 250-287-8371. Vancouver, Campbell River, Discovery Islands, North Coast.
- **Airspeed Aviation:** 250-655-4300. Victoria-Abbotsford.
- **Av West Charters:** 1-800-463-5946. Out of Victoria, Vancouver.
- **Awood Air Ltd:** 250-656-5521. Victoria-Vancouver airports.
- **Baxter Aviation:** 1-800-661-5599. Nanaimo-Vancouver.
- **Canadian Airlines International:** 1-800-665-1177 or 604-279-6611. Victoria, Nanaimo, Comox, Campbell River, Sandspit on Queen Charlotte Islands, and major national and international destinations.
- **Harbour Air:** 1-800-665-0212. Vancouver, Victoria, Gulf Islands, Duncan.
- **Helijet Airways:** 1-800-665-4354 or 250-382-6222. From Ogden Point near Victoria Harbour. Downtown Victoria - downtown Vancouver or Vancouver International Airport; Victoria - Seattle; charters.

■ **Horizon Air:** 1-800-547-9308. Connects Victoria with Vancouver, Kelowna and major international flights at Seattle-Tacoma, Calgary, and Edmonton.

■ **Island Hopper:** 250-753-2020. Sunshine Coast-Nanaimo-Vancouver.

■ **Island Valley Airways:** 1-877-533-7555. Langley to Victoria to Nanaimo and Comox.

■ **KD Air:** 1-800-665-4244. Charters: Vancouver, Qualicum Beach, Port Alberni, Texada Island.

■ **Kenmore Air:** 1-800-543-9595. Victoria Harbour-Seattle Harbour, north island fish camps, Inside Passage, and Gulf Islands.

■ **Klitsa Air:** 250-723-2375. Charters from Port Alberni.

■ **Long Beach Helicopter Ltd:** 250-758-0024. Charters from Nanaimo, Campbell River.

■ **North Vancouver Air:** 604-278-1608 or 1-800-228-6608. Vancouver, Victoria, Tofino, Ucluelet, Port Alberni, Nanaimo, Nelson, Creston.

■ **Pacific Coastal Airlines:** 1-800-663-2872. Vancouver to Anahim Lake, Bella Bella, Bella Coola, Port Hardy, Powell River, Campbell River. Floatplane service to north-central coast.

■ **Vancouver Island Air:** 250-287-2433 or 250-949-6800. Serving the island's north coast from Campbell River.

■ **Vancouver Island Helicopters:** 250-656-3987. Charters from Sidney.

■ **West Coast Air:** 1-800-347-2222 or 250-388-4521. Victoria-Vancouver, Victoria Harbour-Coal Harbour.

■ **West Jet:** 1-800-538-5696. Departs Victoria daily for Vancouver, Kelowna, Calgary, Edmonton, Regina, Saskatoon, and Winnipeg.

BC Ferries

BC Ferries link Vancouver Island to the Lower Mainland, Gulf Islands, and north coast, sailing 24 routes year-round. The fleet's two super-ferries seat 2,000 passengers and carry 470 vehicles. *The Spirit of British Columbia* and the *Spirit of Vancouver Island* on the Swartz Bay-Tsawwassen run offer what their older sisters do, but they're bigger, and have more: restaurant, cafeteria, and snack bar, two video arcades, study and work cubicles with computer hookups, complete wheelchair accessibility, and a bridge bristling with high-tech gear. The fleet's first new catamaran – the Pacificat fast ferry carrying 1,000 passengers and 250 cars at 68km/h – was tested in 1998. It will zip from Nanaimo's Departure Bay to Vancouver's Horseshoe Bay in 65 minutes, shaving 30 minutes off the trip. Two more catamarans are planned.

Call Victoria at 250-386-3431 or toll-free in BC at 1-888-223-3779, 7am-10pm daily for general information on any route or schedule, or for reservations, taken on some routes. Write: BC Ferries Corporation, 1112 Fort St, Victoria, BC, V8V 4V2. Or, check the Internet: www.bcferries.bc.ca.

Vancouver to Victoria

BC Ferries sail from Tsawwassen, on the mainland 30km south of Vancouver, to Swartz Bay, 32km north of Victoria on Vancouver Island. Hourly sailings June (7am-7pm, plus 9pm), July-Aug (7am-10pm). Other seasons, every two hours on the odd hour, 7am-9pm, sometimes sailing hourly during peak times and holidays. The 44km trip is one hour and 35 minutes. Reservations are available. Call toll-free in BC: 1-888-724-5223. Outside BC: 604-444-2890.

Bus services link Tsawwassen, Horseshoe Bay, and Swartz Bay ferry terminals to Vancouver and Victoria. There are pickup and drop-off locations en route, and tickets can be purchased on the ferry. There are also regularly scheduled city buses to and from the ferry terminals, but the service between Victoria and Swartz Bay is particularly circuitous and time consuming. See *Bus Lines* below.

Vancouver to Nanaimo

Vancouver Island's second major BC Ferries terminal is at Nanaimo. **Departure Bay**, near the city centre, receives ships from **Horseshoe Bay** in West Vancouver. From Horseshoe Bay, the trip is 50km, 95 minutes by regular ferry; 65 minutes on the new Pacificat. The year-round schedule, as posted, offers sailings every two hours, departing either on the hour or half-hour. Call BC Ferries for exact times. Travellers also have the option of crossing from Tsawwassen to the new **Duke Point** ferry terminal, about 11km south of Nanaimo. The Mid-Island Express to Duke Point from Tsawwassen offers eight round trips daily from 5:15am to 10:45pm. The trip is 60km, two hours. Call BC Ferries for schedule. 1-888-223-3779.

Mammoth ferries squeeze between Gulf Islands in Active Pass.

Gulf Islands and Points North

BC Ferries from both Tsawwassen and Swartz Bay also serve the southern Gulf Islands – Saltspring, the Penders, Galiano, Mayne, and Saturna. Reservations are not taken for Gulf Island sailings from Swartz Bay, or for inter-island travel, but vehicle reservations are recommended for sailings from Tsawwassen to the islands, and back. It is possible to "cruise" the southern Gulf Islands aboard BC Ferries: each morning ferries depart from Swartz Bay, navigating the scenic island channels, and return three to four hours later. Call BC Ferries for exact schedule.

Between Victoria and Nanaimo, BC Ferries run across Saanich Inlet from **Mill Bay** to **Brentwood Bay**, from **Crofton** to **Saltspring Island**, and from **Chemainus** to **Kuper** and **Thetis islands**. Downtown Nanaimo is terminus for BC Ferries to **Gabriola Island**. South of Courtenay, BC Ferries run from **Buckley Bay** to **Denman Island** and from Denman to **Hornby Island**. Regular daily runs are made between **Comox** and **Powell River** and from Powell River to **Texada Island**. Ferries from **Campbell River**, 44km north of Comox, serve **Quadra Island**, and ferries run from **Quadra** to **Cortes Island**.

On northern Vancouver Island, BC Ferries run from **Port McNeill** to **Alert Bay**, on Cormorant Island, and **Sointula**, on Malcolm Island. **Bear Cove**, near **Port Hardy**, is the southern terminus for BC Ferries' "liner," *Queen of the North*. The ship, equipped for longer cruises, makes a 491km journey through the scenic Inside Passage to **Prince Rupert**, BC's most northerly coastal city. Late May-Sept, it's a 15-hour, one-way day cruise. The ship leaves Bear Cove one day, Prince Rupert the next. October-April there is one sailing weekly; from early May there are two sailings weekly. Reservations for passengers and vehicles should be made well in advance. Cabins are available. Travellers who need overnight accommodation at Port Hardy should book rooms when making ferry reservations. Travel counsellors are aboard ferries on the northern run to help with accommodation reservations and information. (See *Northern BC*, p.260, for Alaska Marine Highway ferry linking Prince Rupert to Alaska).

Also departing from Port Hardy is the *Queen of Chilliwack,* carrying 115 cars and 389 passengers on the **Discovery Coast Passage** route to Bella Coola. Sails July-Sept. Reservations required. Trips vary from 14-hour nonstop run between Port Hardy and Bella Coola to a 33-hour run that stops at McLoughlin Bay, Shearwater, Klemtu, and Ocean Falls. No run stops at all the ports in daylight. Along the route, travellers can disembark to make shoreside excursions – as short as the one to four hours the ship is in port, or until the ship's eventual return. Tourist operators at Port Hardy, Shearwater, Klemtu, Ocean Falls, and Bella Coola offer two- to seven-day packages that include accommodation, food, and/or activities such as fishing, kayaking, or boat trips. Passengers can also disembark with their own kayaks, to be picked up elsewhere. Travellers can also make the round trip by ferry between Port Hardy and Bella Coola, or take their car to Bella Coola, and disembark for points elsewhere in the province. There are no staterooms, but the ferry is comfortably refitted with reclining seats, showers, expanded cafeteria, licenced lounge, and video arcade.

The new Sunshine Coast CirclePac offers discounts for travellers making any combination of two Sunshine Coast crossings and two Georgia Strait crossings. Inquire with first ferry ticket purchase at Comox, Nanaimo, Swartz Bay, Horseshoe Bay, Sunshine Coast, or Tsawwassen.

Other Ferry Services

■ **Alberni Marine Transportation Company:** Box 188, Port Alberni, BC, V9Y 7M7. 250-723-8313 or toll-free April-Sept, 1-800-663-7192. Based in Port Alberni, the MV *Lady Rose*, a 31m passenger and cargo ship and the MV *Francis Barkley*, serve communities of Barkley Sound. Year-round, links **Port Alberni** to **Bamfield** via **Kildonan** and way points; sails Tues, Thurs, Sat only. June 1-Sept 25: also sails Mon, Wed, Fri to **Ucluelet** and **Broken Group Islands.** July 1-Labour Day, sails Fri to Bamfield and Kildonan, sails Sun to Bamfield and Broken Group. Canoe and kayak rentals available.

■ **Black Ball Transport Inc:** 250-386-2202 in Victoria, 360-457-4491 in Port Angeles, Washington. The MV *Coho* sails daily year-round between **Port Angeles,** Washington, and **Victoria Harbour.** During summer the ship sails from Victoria four times daily from 6:10am. Return trips from Port Angeles begin at 8:20am. One hour and 35 minutes. No

A lighthouse stands guard at Georgina Point on Mayne Island.

reservations taken. Fewer sailings during off-season. It's advisable to call for info on line-ups in summer and on holidays.

■ **Clipper Navigation Ltd:** 250-382-8100 in Victoria; 206-448-5000 in Seattle. Fleet of catamarans offers year-round, daily service between **Victoria Harbour** and **Seattle's Pier 69.** Four daily sailings in summer, leaving Seattle at 7:30am, 8am, 8:30am and 4pm; leaving Victoria 11:45am, 1pm, 5:30pm, and 7pm. Other seasons, one sailing, leaving Seattle at 8:30am, leaving Victoria 6pm or 7pm. Two and a half to three hours. Wise to make reservations at least 24 hours in advance. Daily, mid-May to late Sept, the *Princess Marguerite III,* (200 vehicles, 900 passengers) leaves Victoria's Ogden Point, 7:30am for 4.5-hour sailing; leaves Seattle's Pier 48 at 1pm.

■ **Marine Link Tours:** 250-286-3347. Box 451, Campbell River, BC, V9W 5C1. Mid-March to mid-Oct, the *Aurora Explorer,* a 27m freight boat invites passengers on its working tour of BC mainland inlets northeast of Campbell River.

■ **Nootka Sound Service Ltd:** 250-283-2325 or 250-283-2515. *Uchuck III* provides year-round freight and passenger service for coastal communities in Nootka Sound. Departs from **Gold River.** Sails to **Tahsis** and back on Tues. To **Kyuquot** Thurs and back to Gold River on Fri. On Wed and Sat, July to mid-Sept only, sails to **Friendly Cove** and back.

■ **Victoria Rapid Transit Inc:** 250-361-9144 in BC; 360-452-8088 in Port Angeles, Washington; 1-800-633-1589 (in Washington) for reservations. Victoria Express passenger ferry offers one-hour crossing to 148 walk-on passengers travelling between **Victoria Harbour** and **Port Angeles.** Two sailings daily each way in spring and fall; three from late June to early Sept.

■ **Victoria-San Juan Cruises:** 1-800-443-4552. 355 Harris Ave, Suite 104, Bellingham, Washington, USA, 98225. *Victoria Star II* carries 150 passengers between **Bellingham** and **Victoria,** once daily May-Oct, departing 9am to arrive in Victoria at 2pm; departing Victoria 5pm to arrive in Bellingham 8pm.

■ **Washington State Ferries:** In BC call 250-381-1551 or 250-656-1531; in Washington 1-800-84-FERRY; outside Washington State, 206-464-6400. Ferries run from **Anacortes,** Washington, through San Juan Islands to **Sidney,** on the Saanich Peninsula 5km south of BC Ferry terminal at Swartz Bay. In summer, two sailings a day. First one from Anacortes leaves 7:30am, second leaves 2:20pm; first one from Sidney, 11:15am, second leaves 6pm. In winter one daily sailing from each side. Journey varies, about three hours depending on number of San Juan Island stops. Vehicle reservations recommended in summer.

Bus Lines

■ **Azure Transport Ltd:** 1-888-537-4737 or 250-537-4737. Saltspring Island: Fulford Harbour, Ganges, Long Harbour, Vesuvius. Charter bus service and package tours from Victoria and Vancouver.

■ **Gray Line of Seattle:** 206-626-6090. Seattle, Victoria, Vancouver.

■ **Island Coach Lines:** 250-385-4411. City-

The Causeway in downtown Victoria is meant to be savoured.

to-city service from Victoria to Port Hardy. Reservations not taken. Connects in Port Alberni with Orient Stage Lines, serving west-coast villages of Ucluelet and Tofino near Long Beach. Info Centres can help arrange bus and van charters.

■ **Knight Limousine Service:** 250-477-8700. City and airport limo service, charter bus service all over Vancouver Island.

■ **Maverick Coachlines:** 604-662-8051. Vancouver to Nanaimo and Whistler.

■ **Pacific Coach Lines:** 1-800-661-1725. Between Victoria and Vancouver, leaving city bus terminals about 75 minutes before each BC Ferries sailing.

■ **West Coast Trail Express:** 250-477-8700. Victoria to Juan de Fuca Marine Trail heads; Victoria and Nanaimo to West Coast Trail heads.

Railway

■ **Esquimalt and Nanaimo Railway:** 250-383-4324 in Victoria, 1-800-561-8630 outside Victoria. For a behind-the-scenes look at southern Vancouver Island, make a reservation on the E&N Railway, running between Victoria and Courtenay since before 1900. Now operated by VIA Rail Canada. Victoria's station is downtown next to the Johnson St Bridge, with parking nearby. Passenger dayliner leaves Victoria Mon-Sat at 8:15am and makes up to 19 stops by the time it reaches Courtenay at 12:50pm. It returns to Victoria at 5:45pm. It's a fascinating trip that crosses deep canyons and passes waterfalls, salmon rivers, beaches, ghost towns, and historic sites. Schedule subject to change.

Car and RV Rentals

Highway travellers can rent cars from several agencies with offices at airports and downtown locations in island cities. Also RVs from some island companies.

Vancouver Island Highway Project

Over 450km of island highway – from Victoria in the south to Port Hardy in the north – connect the unexpected and incongruous. Most of Vancouver Island's cities, towns, and villages are along this long and scenic east-coast road; most others are linked to it either by logging roads or paved arteries that flow to the west, between island mountains.

In the past two decades, there have been dramatic increases in traffic, and the winding highway has been described as "an overworked blood vessel burdened by a flow it can no longer handle." The Vancouver Island Highway Project, announced in 1988 and scheduled to be completed by 2002, will relieve congestion and improve safety by adding lanes and medians, upgrading traffic lights, building expressways, bypasses, and interchanges. Portions of the project are complete; in sections, work is ongoing, and island travellers may encounter delays or detours. Route maps accompanying logs indicate the original island highway. They also show new routes and routes yet to be completed. Parts of the project include:

■ The Nanaimo Parkway (Hwy 19), a 21km expressway hugging Nanaimo's western edge. Highway 1 – the Trans-Canada – through Nanaimo has 19 stoplights, and without an alternative, was a major bottleneck. The new expressway is now complete. See p. 63.

■ The 128km Inland Island Highway, bypassing coastal communities from Parksville to Campbell River. The first 45km section from Craig's Crossing to Mud Bay (Fanny Bay) is now complete. See p. 66.

■ The Trans-Canada Hwy (Hwy 1) just north of Victoria. This has been upgraded to freeway standards.

■ An expressway standard to allow 3m shoulder for bicycle traffic. When this is complete, by 2004, cyclists should be able to ride comfortably and safely from Campbell River to downtown Victoria.

These changes will save time and lives. Some travellers will, of course, prefer to stick to the old, meandering coastal routes. See *Logs* for new routes and old. For more information on the Vancouver Island Highway Project, call 250-953-4949 and, please, drive carefully.

City Travel

Taxis are plentiful. City bus services are available in Greater Victoria and Saanich Peninsula, Duncan-Lake Cowichan-Cobble Hill-Cowichan Bay-Mill Bay, Nanaimo, Parksville, Campbell River, Comox-Courtenay-Cumberland, and Port Alberni. Info Centres have bus information.

VANCOUVER ISLAND EVENTS

Alert Bay
- **Sports Weekend:** Mid-June.
- **Sea Festival:** Mid-Aug.

Campbell River
- **Daiwa Fishing Derby:** Late May-Sept.
- **Children's Festival:** July 1.
- **Driftwood Carving Contest:** Early July.
- **Summer Festival:** Early Aug.

Chemainus
- **Chemainus Daze:** Early July.
- **Teddy Bear Picnic:** Early July.

Colwood
- **Luxton Rodeo:** Mid-May.
- **Gllangcolme Days:** June.
- **Luxton Fall Fair:** Mid-Sept.

Comox Valley
- **Trumpeter Swan Festival:** Feb.
- **Courtenay Youth Music Camp:** Early July-early Aug. Indoor and outdoor concerts.
- **Filberg Festival:** Early Aug.
- **CFB Comox Air Show:** Aug (alternate years).
- **Fall Fair:** Mid-Sept.

Coombs
- **Coombs Country and Bluegrass Festival:** Early Aug.
- **Coombs Rodeo:** Late July. Cowboys from all over BC.
- **Old Time Fiddlers Championships:** Early July.

Cowichan Bay
- **Boat Festival:** Early June. At Maritime Centre. Classic boats, the Fast-and-Furious Boat Building Contest (build a boat and race it within four hours), boat-building house for children, folk singers, dancing.

Cumberland
- **Empire Days:** Victoria Day weekend.
- **Miners' Memorial Day:** Late June.

Duncan
- **Regional Heritage Days:** Mid-May.
- **Cowichan Tribes Canoe Races:** May.
- **Summer Festival:** Mid-July.
- **Island's Folk Festival:** Mid-July.
- **Cowichan Exhibition:** Early Sept.
- **Christmas Chaos:** Nov.

Esquimalt
- **Buccaneer Days:** Late May.
- **CFB Esquimalt Armed Forces Open House:** Late May.

Galiano Island
- **Artist Guild Summer Sale:** Mid-July.
- **Galiano Wine Festival:** Mid-Aug.
- **Blackberry Festival:** Thanksgiving Sat.
- **Galiano Weavers Exhibit and Sale:** July and Nov.

Gold River
- **The Great Walk:** Early June. 67km from Gold River to Tahsis.
- **Loggers' Sports:** Late June.

Jordan River
- **Surf Slalom Social:** Late April. Windsurfers' gathering.

Ladysmith
- **Celebration Days:** Late July.
- **Fall Fair:** Mid-Sept.
- **Festival of Lights and Christmas Light Cruise:** Late Nov-early Dec.

Lake Cowichan Area
- **Heritage Days:** May.
- **Lake Days:** June.
- **Honeymoon Bay Summer Festival:** July.
- **Youbou Regatta:** Aug.

Langford
- **Luxton Rodeo:** Mid-May.
- **Luxton Fall Fair:** Mid-Sept.

Mayne Island
- **Summer Mania Fair:** July.
- **Springwater Lodge Salmon Derby:** July.
- **Mayne Island Fall Fair:** Aug.
- **Lions' Salmon Bake:** Early Sept.

Metchosin
- **Metchosin International Summer School of the Arts:** Late June-early July. Lester B Pearson College Campus.
- **Metchosin Sheep Dog Trials:** Late July.
- **Gift Show and Studio Tour:** Nov.

Mill Bay
- **Country Music Jamboree:** Late May, early June.

Royal Canadian Mounted Police add to the colour of the Indigenous Games in Victoria's Inner Harbour.

- **Malahat First Nations Canoe Races:** June.
- **Fishing Derby:** Mid-Aug.

Nanaimo
- **Empire Days:** Mid-May.
- **Nanaimo Marine Festival:** Late July. Culminating in famous Bathtub Race between Nanaimo and Vancouver's Kitsilano Beach.
- **Nanaimo Festival:** May-July. Theatrical performances based on area's history.
- **Salmon Festival:** Early Aug.
- **Vancouver Island Exhibition:** Mid-Aug.
- **Dixieland Jazz Festival and Vintage Car Rally:** Early Sept. Two-day celebration ending with antique car parade from Nanaimo to Victoria.

Parksville
- **Brant Wildlife Festival:** Mid-April. Organized by the Mid-Island Wildlife Watch Society, offers goose viewing stations, birding competition, nature talks by international experts, wildlife art, carving, photography, stories, children's activities.
- **World Croquet Championship:** Mid-Aug.

Pender Island
- **Solstice Theatre:** March.
- **Around Pender Yacht Race:** Late Aug.
- **Annual Fall Fair:** Late Aug.

Port Alberni
- **Golden Oldies Car Show:** Mid-July and mid-Aug.
- **Forestry Week:** Mid-May.
- **Salmon Festival:** Labour Day weekend.
- **Fall Fair:** Weekend after Labour Day.

Port Hardy
- **Filomi Days:** Mid-July. (Fishing, Logging, Mining Days.)
- **Regional Fall Fair:** Early Sept.

Port McNeill
- **Port McNeill Daze:** Mid-May.
- **North Island Loggers' Sports:** Early July.

Qualicum Beach
- **Fire and Ice:** Early May. Chili and ice carvings.
- **Art in Action:** Early July.

Saltspring Island
- **Spring Festival:** March/April.
- **Market in the Park:** April-Oct.
- **Sea Capers:** Mid-June.
- **Festival of Performing Arts:** July.
- **Fall Fair:** Mid-Sept.
- **Guild Christmas Show and Sale:** Mid-Nov to mid-Dec. Jewellers, painters, potters, weavers, woodworkers.
- **Christmas Ship:** Early Dec.

Classic Boat Festival, Victoria's Inner Harbour.

Saturna Island
- **Canada Day Lamb Bake:** Held every July 1 weekend since 1949 on a farm below Mt Warburton Pike. Most celebrated annual event in the Gulf Islands.

Sayward-Kelsey Bay
- **Loggers' Sports:** Early July.
- **Oscar Daze:** Early Aug.
- **Salmon Derby:** Labour Day weekend.

Sidney and Saanich Peninsula
- **Sidney Days and Jazz Festival:** Late June-early July.
- **Saanich Fall Fair:** Early Sept. The oldest agricultural fair west of the Great Lakes. Livestock, sheep shearing, show jumping, crafts, produce, home baking, fiddle competition, kids' rides. It's all here, from little piggies and giant pumpkins to the best baron of beef anywhere. At Saanichton Fair Grounds.
- **Saltwater:** Mid-Sept. An new annual festival celebrating maritime arts and music.

Sointula (Malcolm Island)
- **Harmony Hike:** 25km tour. Late June.
- **Winter Festival:** Late Nov. Local artists and musicians.

Sooke
- **Sooke Region Museum Open House and Salmon BBQ:** Late June.
- **All Sooke Day and Annual Festival of History:** Third Sat in July. Loggers' sports on Sat. Festival through to next weekend – fishing derby, heritage events, and pioneer fashion shows, tea parties, excursions.
- **Fine Arts Festival:** Early Aug. Sooke Arena, adjacent museum. Week-long event is one of BC's largest juried art shows.

Telegraph Cove
- **Boardwalk Craft Fair:** Early Aug.

Tofino
- **Whale Festival:** Mid-March to mid-April. Celebrating annual migration of some 20,000 Pacific grey whales.

Ucluelet
- **Whale Festival:** Mid-March to mid-April.
- **Salmon Derbies:** July and Aug.
- **Pacific Rim Summer Festival:** Mid-late July.
- **Ukee Days:** Late July.

Victoria
- **TerrifVic Dixieland Jazz Party:** Late April.
- **Victoria Days and Parade:** May Day.
- **Harbour Fest:** Mid-May.
- **Swiftsure Sailing Race:** Late May.
- **Oak Bay Tea Party:** Early June.
- **Jazz Fest International:** Late June-early July.
- **Victoria Folkfest:** Late June-early July.
- **Canada Day Celebrations:** July 1.
- **Victoria Shakespeare Festival:** July-Aug.
- **First People's Festival:** Early Aug.
- **Sun Fest:** Mid-Aug.
- **Classic Boat Festival:** Late Aug, early Sept.
- **Fringe Festival:** Aug to early Sept.
- **Christmas Festival:** Dec to early Jan.
- **First Night:** New Year's Eve.

Zeballos
- **Fall Fair:** Sept. Firemen display 1947 La France fire truck.

Alert Bay on Cormorant Island is home to world–renowned Kwakwaka'wakw carvers.

VANCOUVER ISLAND ROUTES AND HIGHLIGHTS

TRAVELLER'S LOGS

HIGHLIGHTS

SWARTZ BAY TO VICTORIA

PATRICIA BAY HIGHWAY (HIGHWAY 17)

For travellers arriving on Vancouver Island at BC Ferries' Swartz Bay terminal this is the most direct route to Victoria. Swartz Bay is the province's third largest and busiest ferry terminal after Tsawwassen and Duke Point. Each year, some seven million passengers walk, bus, or drive through the Swartz Bay terminal on their way to or from the mainland and Gulf Islands.

Hwy 17 from the ferry terminal is an increasingly busy route, though much of the old charm of this four-lane 80km/h path down the Saanich Peninsula remains. It leads through rolling farmland, past glimpses of Haro Strait, and occasionally, Washington State's Mt Baker is visible, shimmering to the east. But, when off-loading ferry traffic is bumper-to-bumper, you'll need to keep your eyes on the road.

If you're not in a hurry, a quieter, even more scenic alternate to Hwy 17 is Hwy 17A, the old Pat Bay Hwy, skirting the western shores of Saanich Peninsula. This road, offering views of the Saanich Inlet, winds through pastoral countryside where wild deer often roam the same farmyards as sheep. Flowers, vegetables, eggs, and other produce are sold at roadside stands. Potters sell their wares. Hwy 17A, known as West Saanich Rd, is a route to **Patricia Bay**, **Brentwood Bay**, **Butchart Gardens**, and the **Dominion Astrophysical Observatory**. The *Log* covers Hwy 17 first, then Hwy 17A.

Highway 17

Swartz Bay Ferry Terminal: At north tip of Saanich Peninsula, 32km north of Victoria. A pleasant place to watch ferries, massive and small, weave between islands, arriving from and departing to Tsawwassen or Gulf Islands. Coffee shop. Local arts and crafts for sale in summer.

McDonald Park-Wain Rds: Second traffic light after ferry terminal. Turn west (right) on Wain Rd to get to Hwy 17A. Turn east 2km to reach McDonald Provincial Park and the backdoor route to Sidney.

Horth Hill Regional Park: West on Wain Rd, then north on Tatlow Rd. 40-minute hike to summit and views of peninsula, channels, and islands. Spring wildflowers and fall mushrooms.

Sandown Harness Raceway: Via McDonald Park turnoff, at 1810 Glamorgan Rd. 250-656-1631. Harness racing with full wagering facilities.

McDonald Provincial Park: 20ha; 28 campsites. 250-391-2300. Good overnighter for campers arriving on a late ferry.

Sidney: (Pop. 10,701). 5km from ferry terminal, left off Hwy 17 onto Beacon Ave. Named after Frederick Sidney, a 19th-century Royal Navy man and colleague of surveyor Captain George Richards, who completed mapping of the area in 1859. The town itself is on former farmland acquired by early settlers from the Hudson's Bay Company. Sidney was founded in the 1890s at the terminus of the Victoria and Sidney Railway. Today, with a high ratio of retirees, it is the downtown of the Saanich Peninsula – although with nary a parking meter in sight, it has a small-town feel. The main street, Beacon Ave, leading down to the wharf and the fresh fish market, is a pleasant place to lollygag. There are cafes, bakeries, restaurants, hotels, marinas, diving facilities, and the new Port of Sidney development, with breakwater, marina, specialty shops, pub, waterfront park, and promenade. Some people visit Sidney just to browse the bookstores: there are five wonderfully eclectic shops along Beacon Ave or Third St.

Mid-Sept, Sidney hosts **Saltwater**, a new annual festival celebrating maritime arts and music.

Sidney Information: Two Info Centres are run by the Saanich Peninsula Chamber of Commerce, Box 2014, Sidney, BC, V8L 3A3. 250-656-3616. They provide information on Sidney and the entire Saanich Peninsula, beach walks, horseback and bike riding, whale-watching tours, diving around artificial reefs, fishing charters. The main Info Centre is on the west side of Hwy 17, halfway between the BC Ferries terminal and Sidney. March-Nov: 250-656-0525 or 250-656-3260. The second is in Sidney on 5th St and Ocean Ave. Open when ferries arrive and depart.

Washington State Ferries: In Sidney at 2499 Ocean Ave (5km south of BC Ferries Terminal). Follow signs. Sails to San Juan Islands and Anacortes, Washington State. See *Transportation*, p.35.

■ **Sidney Marine Mammal and Historical Museum:** 9801 Seaport Pl, near Sidney wharf. 250-656-1322. Daily in summer. Winter hours variable, please call. Pioneer artifacts and photos; exhibits on the ecology of whales, sea lions, seals, and sea otters.

■ **Sidney Harbour Cruises:** 250-655-5211. Connects Port of Sidney to marinas and pubs at Tsehum Harbour and Canoe Cove, near Swartz Bay.

■ **Lochside Trail:** Favoured by cyclists and walkers, it starts at Beacon Ave and Lochside Dr and joins up with the **Galloping Goose Trail** at Quadra St (near Greenridge Cr) in Victoria – about a two-hour cycle one way. Except where it follows quiet neighbourhood streets, the trail is often dirt, cutting through forests, passing beaches, parks, farmers' fields, hobby farms with pigs and turkeys, and a field for flying model airplanes. Start heading south on Lochside Dr, along the Sidney waterfront, above the walkway that starts at Tulista Park. Route continues past Bazan Bay Park to Mt Newton Rd, then onto a new section to the side of the Pat Bay Hwy (Hwy 17) for about 1km. After passing Cordova Bay Golf Course and a number of small parks, trail passes through the Blenkinsop Valley to Blenkinsop Lake. Blenkinsop Rd links trail to Galloping Goose at Quadra St.

■ **Nilltu,o:** (pronounced Neeckth twa). Mural on BC Tel building at corner of Beacon and Resthaven avenues. It means "at the very beginning" and depicts Coast Salish aboriginal paddlers in stormy seas.

■ **24 Carrot Country Market:** Sanscha Hall

grounds. Sun, 10-2, mid-June to late Sept.

■ **Golfing on the Saanich Peninsula: Glen Meadows Golf and Country Club** at 1050 McTavish Rd, 250-656-3921, offers 18 holes, electric golf carts, cafe, and restaurant. The **Ardmore** Golf Course, at the corner of W Saanich Rd and Ardmore Dr, 250-656-4621, offers nine holes. The **Sunshine Hills Golf Course**, just off Hwy 17 at 7081 Central Saanich Rd, offers 18 holes.

■ **Mineral World and the Scratch Patch:** 9891 Seaport Pl. 250-655-4367. Daily, year-round. Gallery of sculptures, stone gifts, jewelry. Nature section has interactive displays. In the Scratch Patch rockhounds can gather semi-precious stones and shells, or pan for gold.

Sidney Spit Provincial Marine Park: 177ha; 20 campsites. 250-391-2300. On Sidney Island, 3km east of Sidney. Foot-passenger ferry from marina at end of Beacon Ave in Sidney. Mid-May to late Sept. Beautiful sandy beaches, lagoon, open meadows, and forests. Eagles, herons, waterfowl, large herds of fallow deer. A pleasant day trip.

Princess Margaret Provincial Marine Park: 194ha; primitive camping in three areas. 250-391-2300. On Portland Island, 8km northeast of Sidney. By private boat or Scenic Ferries of Sidney: 250-655-4465. Boaters can anchor safely and come ashore for picnics and day excursions; kayakers and canoeists are rewarded for their efforts with campsites set in shoreline groves of arbutus and Douglas fir. Main anchorage, with dock, barbecue and pits toilets is at Princess Bay on island's south end. Basic facilities at Arbutus Point and Shell Beach. Royal Cove, the old farmsite, also has a dock. Hiking trails circle and crisscross the island. Substantial middens suggest Portland Island was a summer fishing camp for Coast Salish people. The first non-native settlers here were Kanakas – people from the Sandwich Islands, as Hawaii was known in the 19th century. The island was tenanted and farmed through the first half of the 20th century, and was acquired by the BC government in 1958. Fires are not permitted.

McTavish Rd: West off Hwy 17, 7.5km south of Swartz Bay. Route to International Airport and Hwy 17A.

Victoria International Airport: 7.5km south of Swartz Bay, head west on McTavish Rd. Then 2km to Vancouver Island's main airport served by major airlines. (It's about 3.5km on McTavish to Hwy 17A.)

■ **BC Aviation Museum:** At airport on Norseman Rd. 250-655-3300. Daily. Showcases history of flight in Canada. Exhibits include replica of Gibson Twin Plane built by Victoria's William Gibson in 1910. It flew 60m before crashing into an oak tree, beating the Wright brothers' 1903 record 36m "flight."

John Dean Provincial Park: 155ha. Day use. West off Hwy 17A onto McTavish, then north on East Saanich Rd about 2km to Dean Park Rd. West to park

and Mt Newton, or Lauwelnew, as the Wsanec (Saanich) people have long known it. Its name means "the place of refuge." The Wsanec people found safety here when the Great Flood washed over these lands. Views of Saanich Peninsula, Gulf Islands, Cascade Mountains. Hiking trails.

Mount Newton Cross Rd: 11km south of Swartz Bay. West for 5km to Hwy 17A.

Island View Rd: 14km south of Swartz Bay. West to Butchart Gardens (see below). East for 3km past farm land to **Island View Beach Regional Park** (25.5ha). Long, sandy beach, upland meadows, dunes, views of the Gulf Islands, and sometimes even the BC mainland. Good bird-watching, too. Righteous nudists occasionally sun themselves here.

Saanich Historical Artifacts Society: 7321 Lochside Rd. 250-652-5522. Daily. Mornings in winter, all day early June-Sept. Group tours by arrangement. East off Hwy 17 on Island View Rd, follow signs. 12ha site with small lake, forest trails, nature pond, and working artifacts: farming equipment, model railroad, sawmill, planer mill. At Summer Fair in late June everything that works is turned on. Wagon rides, food, fun.

Sayward Rd: 18km south of Swartz Bay. East to Victoria's Marine Scenic Dr, Cordova Bay, and Mt Douglas Park (see *Victoria* for details).

Elk/Beaver Lake Regional Park: About 100m beyond Sayward Rd. 411ha. Greater Victoria's most popular park with two lakes joined by a narrow channel and extensive network of trails. Four beaches, swimming, canoeing, rowing, waterskiing, windsurfing,

15km walking, biking, and bridle trails. Check for summer programs. The Elk Lake Rowing Centre is home of the Victoria Rowing Society which includes the Canadian National Rowing Team and University of Victoria rowers. The society has turned out such national and international champions as 1996 Olympic medal-lists Derek Porter and Silken Laumann.

Royal Oak Dr: 22km south of Swartz Bay. Exit leads to Broadmead and Royal Oak shopping area and Hwy 17A.

McKenzie Ave: 26km south of Swartz Bay. Downtown Victoria starts here. West for about 2km leads to Hwy 1 (Trans-Canada Hwy). East to Swan Lake and University of Victoria.

Swan Lake-Christmas Hill Nature Sanctuary: 46ha. Access from McKenzie Ave, then Rainbow Rd. 250-479-0211. Year-round, nature house and programs for nature study. Floating boardwalk, trails, ponds, bird blinds. Excellent family day trip.

University of Victoria: 4.5km east of Hwy 17 via McKenzie Ave. 162ha campus for over 17,500 students. Individual or group tours by arrangement: 250-721-6248 or 250-721-7211. One of BC's four universities. Centre of activity with many public events often listed in local newspapers. Pleasant grounds with chapel, walking/jogging trails, flower gardens – springtime rhododendron gardens are a very worthwhile stroll.

Victoria: (Greater Victoria pop. 317,989). 6km south of McKenzie Ave. Encompasses southern knob of Vancouver Island and is home to more than half of island's residents. See *City of Sea and Gardens*, p.42.

SCENIC ALTERNATE

Trial Island is a backdrop for golfers at one of Victoria's most scenic courses.

HIGHWAY 17A
(Swartz Bay to Victoria)

Highway 17A, or West Saanich Rd, can be reached by turning west on Wain Rd at second traffic light south of Swartz Bay ferry terminal, and driving 2.5km to Hwy 17A. It is 24km from junction of Hwy 17A and Wain Rd to Royal Oak Dr, just north of Victoria, where Hwy 17A joins Hwy 17.

Also many access points to the Saanich Inlet.

Saanich Inlet: While Vancouver Island's storm-thrashed west coast is gouged by five great sounds full of inlets, the gentle east coast is indented by only one relatively small fiord. From Goldstream Provincial Park at its steep-sided head, to its island-clogged mouth at the Strait of Georgia, the inlet offers 25km of sheltered, navigable waters. Regular ferries link idyllic communities – Brentwood Bay on the east shore, Mill Bay on the west. Pastoral homesteads look out to a paradise for kayakers and sailors. This has long been the waterway and harvesting grounds of the Wsanec, or Saanich people, who still live in villages on the Saanich Peninsula, and are closely related to the Malahat First Nation on the opposite shores.

The Saanich Inlet distinguishes itself with qualities shared by only three other water bodies in the world. The Black Sea, a fiord in Venezuela, BC's Nitinat Lake, and this inlet are all shallower at their mouths than their main bodies, creating unusual circumstances for the circulation of water. The maximum depth of the Saanich Inlet's entrance is 75m; then the ocean floor plunges to depths of as much as 225m. The upper levels in this bowl circulate with changing tides, but the deeper waters, heavier with salt and lower in oxygen, tend to stagnate. Only with the highest mid-winter tides is there enough force from the straits to push fresh water in and old water out.

This wonder of nature is posing a conundrum for humankind as the population increases on both sides of the inlet, threatening a back-yard wilderness where pods of killer whales still visit, eagles and ospreys fish from trees over the water, and mink and river otters forage the shores. There are now 35,000 people on the Saanich Peninsula, and major new developments promise to add tremendously to the amount of effluent being poured into the inlet. Already, clam beds are contaminated; sportfishermen are catching a tiny fraction of the 25,000 salmon they took annually two and three decades ago. Hope lies in controlling development in a place where so many would live, and in the creation of parkland. Toward this, Goldstream Provincial Park at the inlet's head, has been expanded, and with the newly designated 1,221ha Gowlland Tod Provincial Park straddling the waterway, 8km of this remarkable and fragile shoreline will remain for all creatures to enjoy.

Patricia Bay: 1km south of Wain Rd on Hwy 17A. Gravel and sand beach with warm summer swimming. Wintering grounds for sea lions and waterfowl. Year-round for harbour seals, river otters. Holy Trinity Anglican Church, built 1885, overlooks bay. Federal

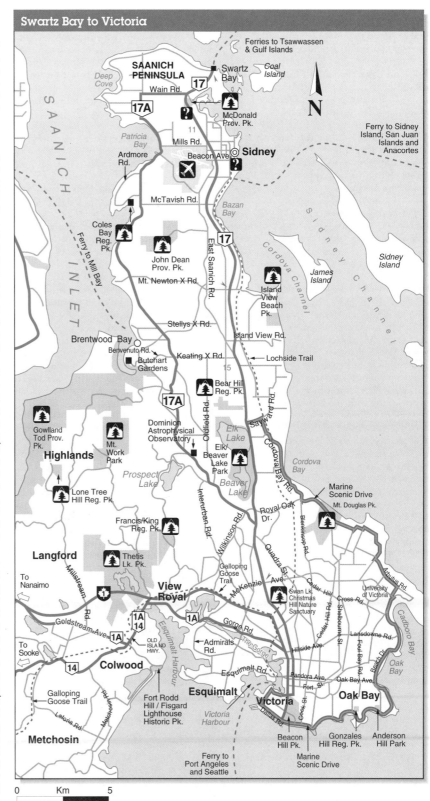

Swartz Bay to Victoria

Institute of Ocean Sciences on south side, offers tours by appointment only, Mon and Wed. 250-363-6518. Geographical centre seismographs monitor Juan de Fuca fault line.

Mills Rd: East off Hwy 17A, 2km south of Wain Rd. 3km to Sidney and Hwy 17.

Coles Bay Regional Park: 4ha. West off Hwy 17A on Ardmore Rd, 3.5km south of Wain Rd. (Ardmore Rd is a horseshoe that intersects Hwy 17A at two points. Take the most southerly turn onto Ardmore). A quiet refuge on the west side of the peninsula. Twisty creekside trails for wandering, waterfowl viewing, beachcombing, and picnicking.

McTavish Rd: East off Hwy 17A, 6.5km south of Wain Rd. 3km to Victoria International Airport turnoff and Hwy 17.

John Dean Provincial Park: 155ha. East off Hwy 17A onto McTavish, then north on East Saanich Rd 2km to Dean Park Rd. West to park. For details, see below.

Mt Newton Cross Rd: East off Hwy 17A, 10.5km south of Wain Rd. About 800m to **St Stephen's Church**, built in 1862, oldest church in BC still on original site. About 5km to Hwy 17.

Brentwood Bay: (Pop. 3,200). 12.5km south of Wain Rd. Part of Central Saanich municipality and home to world-famous Butchart Gardens (below), this village on Saanich Inlet takes its name from Brentwood, Essex, in England. The original part of this community is at the bottom of Verdier Ave, in and around the ferry dock. Here are weathered wharves (some with cafes on them), marinas, and lanes and pathways winding past pleasing cottages. Brentwood Bay was once noted for its salmon fishing, but those days are long gone. Now it is becoming more of a jumping-off point for recreationists, such as kayakers, canoeists, and mountain bikers, especially with the creation of new parkland on Saanich and Tod inlets (see *Gowlland Tod Provincial Park*). Brentwood Bay, like other rural areas on the Saanich Peninsula, is seeing its bucolic charm eaten away by developmental pressures. A sign of the future is much-maligned Port Royale, a California-style condominium complex containing 146 units terracing the scalped shores overlooking the bay.

Brentwood-Mill Bay Ferry: 13.5km south of Wain Rd turn west on Verdier Ave in Brentwood Bay. 250-386-3431. Small car and passenger ferry crosses Saanich Inlet, bypassing Victoria. Road from terminal on Mill Bay side of inlet leads to Hwy 1. Ferry runs approximately every hour and 10 minutes from either side, morning until early evening. Crossing takes 25 minutes. Cyclists cross here for day trips in Shawnigan Lake area. See p.58.
■ **Saanich Pioneer Museum:** On East Saanich Rd, south of Mt Newton Cross Rd. Mon, 9:30-1:30. Photos and documents of the Peninsula's past.
■ **Farmer's Market:** Agricultural Fairgrounds on Stelly's Cross Rd. Sat, June-Oct.

Keating Cross Rd and Benvenuto Ave: 15.5km south of Wain Rd. East for 3km to Hwy 17. West 2km to **Butchart Gardens**.

Victoria Butterfly Gardens: 1461 Benvenuto Ave. Corner of W Saanich Rd and Keating-Cross Rd. 250-652-3822. Daily. Call for seasonal hours. Folklore says it's good luck to have a butterfly land on you. Here, with hundreds of live butterflies fluttering through lush tropical gardens, the odds are good. Life cycle from eggs to cocoons. Restaurant and deli.

Butchart Gardens: 800 Benvenuto Ave, Brentwood Bay. 250-652-5256. Open

daily. What was a limestone quarry, became, in 1904, gardens of delight, drawing over one million visitors a year. The 20ha estate overlooking Tod Inlet includes Sunken Garden, Japanese Garden, rose, and Italian gardens. A variety of entertainment is offered daily, May 15-Sept 30; "Night Illuminations," displays subtly coloured lights June 15-Sept 30; fireworks set to music Sat nights, July-Aug (come early to avoid disappointing lineups); Christmas lights and carollers, early Dec-early Jan. Restaurants and coffee bars.

Gowlland Tod Provincial Park: 1,221ha. Day use. 250-391-2300. Three main vehicle access points. The Wallace Dr access is via Wallace Dr off Benvenuto Rd just before Butchart Gardens. The McKenzie Bight access follows Wallace Dr south to Willis Point Rd, then to Durrance Rd. The Caleb Pike access follows Durrance Rd south until it becomes Millstream Lake Rd and meets Millstream Rd, then follows Millstream Rd to Caleb Pike Rd. Established in 1994 as part of Commonwealth Nature Legacy (p.46), this park embraces much that is both rare and representative of the Saanich Inlet. The northernmost section takes in the western banks of Tod Inlet. 15,000 years ago, glaciers sculpted a fiord deeper at its foot than its mouth. The Wsanec (Saanich) people of the Peninsula came to know the inlet as Snictel, "place of the blue grouse." These sunny and warm slopes provided a nursery for the birds until this century when development drove them away. Further south, the Gowlland Range rises 430m from the deep waters of Finlayson Arm. Douglas-fir forest, grassy meadows, arbutus, and manzanita are home for deer, cougars, black bears, over 100 species of birds. More than 20 percent of BC's rare plants grow here. Finlayson Arm provides habitat for giant cloud sponge, anemones, and lamp shells. Extensive network of hiking trails and horse trails on old logging and mining roads. Boaters can anchor overnight: there is excellent diving. Fires not permitted.

Mount Work Regional Park: 536ha. 15.5km south of Wain Rd, turn right off Hwy 17A onto Wallace Dr, then immediately onto Willis Point Rd. 11km hiking trail leads to mountain summit. Durrance, Fork, and Pease lakes are popular swimming spots.

Dominion Astrophysical Observatory: 21km south of Wain Rd, on Little Saanich Mountain, east side of Hwy 17A (5071 W Saanich Rd). Open daily May-Aug. Mon-Fri in winter. Also Sat nights early April-late Oct. 250-363-0001. A stargazer's delight, visited every clear night by astronomers from across Canada and around the world. Here is what was, in 1918, the world's largest telescope, at 1.82m. It was used to determine the size, structure, and rotation of the galaxy.

Bear Hill Regional Park: 49ha. About 1km beyond observatory, onto Old West Saanich Rd, then Bear Hill Rd. Trails for hikers and horseback riding lead to views and wildflowers.

Royal Oak Dr: East off Hwy 17A, 24km south of Wain Rd. Short distance to Hwy 17. West onto Wilkinson Rd, leads about 5km to Hwy 1.

Victoria: (Greater Victoria pop. 330,806). See *Victoria, City of Sea and Gardens*, below. Hwy 1, the Trans-Canada, which leaves Vancouver Island at Nanaimo, begins in Victoria. Hwy 14 runs from Colwood, a Greater Victoria municipality, to Port Renfrew on the island's southwest coast (p.48).

VICTORIA

CITY OF SEA AND GARDENS

Victorians are a fortunate lot, for they live in one of the world's most idyllic settings. Bounded by ocean on three sides, Victoria is a city of the sea. This is BC's provincial capital, set on the extreme southern tip of Vancouver Island, where the Canadian-American border has been stretched below the 49th parallel to keep all of the island in Canada. Not far from Victoria's harbour, Race Rocks lighthouse, the most southerly point in western Canada, is only 8km from the international boundary. Washington State's Olympic Mountains, 20km across Juan de Fuca Strait, form a dramatic backdrop to Victoria. On clear days the steel-blue slopes and wintry peaks seem as if they're standing in the city's back yard.

Victoria's mild climate and seaside location have always made it a place where people want to live. When the first European ships sailed through these straits, there were 10 Lekwammen villages along the shores of what is now Greater Victoria, looking out from favoured bays now named Cadboro, Oak, McNeill. The straits were their salmon river: the Lekwammen devised an elaborate technology, setting reef nets where the fish migrated closest to shore. On sun-baked slopes, such as Meeqan, now called Beacon Hill Park, they "warmed their bellies," played summer games, and carefully tended crops of camas bulbs vital to their diet and economy.

In 1842, James Douglas of the British Hudson's Bay Company, searching the Pacific coast north of the Columbia River for new headquarters, came upon these seaside gardens. In his eyes, this was God's work – "a perfect Eden." The Lekwammen people welcomed Douglas and his small entourage as new trading partners, and helped them to build a trading post on their land. Fort Camouson was named for a sacred Lekwammen landmark. Later, the name was changed to honor Victoria, Queen of Great Britain, 1837-1901. The Lekwammen – today's Songhees and Esquimalt First Nations – moved in closer to the trading centre at the foot of today's Johnson St, and to a site nearby, where the Parliament Buildings now preside.

Thousands of aboriginal peoples from nations up and down BC's coast also converged, seeking their own opportunities to trade with the newcomers.

As gold seekers and merchants traded along the western edge of North America in the late 1800s and early 1900s, they drastically shifted the population balance in favour of non-aboriginal peoples. Victoria soon became the busiest seaport north of San Francisco, with nearly a thousand ships a year sailing between Victoria and the Orient, California, Australia, New Zealand, and Panama.

Today, Victoria remains a busy seaport with a Canadian Coast Guard station, regular visits by cruise ships, military ships, tall ships,

and freighters. There are tour boats, fishboats, houseboats, sailboats, cruisers. Floatplanes and helicopters make some 16,000 takeoffs and landings a year. The Inner Harbour receives ships with names like the *Princess Marguerite*, *Victoria Star*, and *Coho*, dropping throngs of travellers from Seattle, Port Angeles, and Bellingham, and jet-propelled catamarans carry still more from Seattle.

On the streets above the harbour, summer tourists, cameras dangling, brochures in hand, crowd into double-decker buses and horse-drawn carriages for tours of the city. Pedal-powered kabuki cabs weave through the traffic,

people pose beside a kilted bagpiper playing on a corner.

Recent development has stepped up the tempo and brought a "big city" feel to Victoria. It is no longer the retirement capital of Canada, a place on the coast where Prairie farmers come to live. Victoria, which for years had the country's highest population of senior citizens, has fallen behind other communities as a retirement centre.

While the bustle of downtown Victoria is most noticeable with the annual torrent of tourists – nearly four million a year – recent growth throughout Greater Victoria is obvious year-round. The once pastoral Saanich Peninsula has become built up with new residential and commercial subdivisions. The rural western communities of Colwood, View Royal, and Metchosin have become incorporated as municipalities.

Victoria's population is nearly 320,000, an increase of more than 180,000 since the early '60s. Major expansions of the BC Ferries terminal and the Trans-Canada and Patricia Bay highways – the city's main commuter routes – have brought some relief from bumper-to-bumper rush-hour traffic, something Victorians once believed was only a mainland misfortune.

In the downtown core, new development has sought a marriage with historic design. The city's largest hotel, the landmark Empress, built in 1908, has been restored to reflect its original opulence. Nearby St Ann's Academy, dating back to the city's very beginnings (the chapel was built in 1858) sat in near ruins for decades behind high walls. Its finest features, now revived, St Ann's is a centre for the arts, and the business of government.

The Victoria Conference Centre is a 1,500-seat complex that takes advantage of the grace notes all around it: the Empress, the BC Parliament Buildings, the Crystal Garden, Thunderbird Park.

A few blocks from the conference centre, the 150-store Eaton Centre was built to look old, the centre is a four-story, brick-faced structure with the facade of some heritage buildings that were demolished.

Across Victoria Harbour from the Empress, Songhees First Nation land, sold to the BC government in 1910, has been changed from an industrial eyesore into upscale condominiums (the design and look of which has been a target of criticism) and the 250-room Ocean Pointe resort-hotel. The development includes the portion of the waterfront walkway from the Songhees land to neighbouring West Bay. These developments are adding a new, possibly elitist, dimension to an area that has been considered "on the wrong side of the (Johnson Street) bridge" for years. But now, a 5km seaside promenade joins the two sides of the harbour (see *Windy Fringes*, p.47, for details).

Esquimalt and West Bay are linked to downtown Victoria by the Johnson St Bridge, one of two remaining bascule lift bridges in Canada. Opened in 1924, its 635kg counterweights pivot each span like a massive trap door.

A short distance from the Johnson St Bridge, on Fisgard St, is Chinatown. Small but

significant, Victoria's Asian quarter is the oldest in Canada.

The city's most recent developments, however, might be more aptly called non-developments. As shorelines and meadows vanish, Victorians are more prone to question the need for another shopping centre or upscale housing development. Some precious parcels, such as Mystic Vale near the university, Glencoe Cove, and Panama Hill, will now remain as city refuges for people and wildlife as part of the Commonwealth Nature Legacy. The Nature Legacy also embraces the vast Gowlland Tod Provincial Park and Juan de Fuca Marine Trail, on the city's periphery. In 1997, the Capital Regional District doubled its parkland, creating the 4,107ha Sooke Hills Wilderness Park Reserve, so ecologically precious, it is not even open to the public.

And, despite its growth, Victoria has managed to retain an Old-World charm that distinguishes it from other cities. Certainly on Vancouver Island, where the history and present-day economy are based on forestry and other resource industries, Victoria's gentility would seem an incongruity. Resource industries employ less than four percent of Victoria's work force; service industries employ nearly 40 percent. With Victoria being BC's capital and numerous federal workers employed at CFB Esquimalt and other federal institutions, more than 17 percent of Victorians are public servants. Fifteen percent are involved in trade businesses, mainly because of tourism and the high number of retired people.

Victoria's gentility is also reflected in a passion for gardens. There are dozens of parks and public gardens, from Beacon Hill to Butchart, and more than 1,000 hanging flower baskets throughout the downtown core. This is a city where even apartment dwellers keep a flower garden. It's a city of geranium, gladiola, dahlia, and orchid societies. Enthusiasts flaunt their nearly year-round growing season with a flower count in late February, after the snowdrops have already come and gone. Annual counts surpass four billion blossoms – cherry blossoms, plum blossoms, heather, crocuses, daisies, polyanthus. Some Februarys bring tulips. But even without the green thumbs, this sun-drenched southern knob of Vancouver Island would be a garden, saturated with the amber of arbutus trees, pinks from wild roses, and blue from the camas meadows that moved James Douglas, almost 160 years ago, to call this place Eden.

Victoria is perceived as having only one major flaw: it dumps its raw sewage (though screened) into Juan de Fuca Strait. This has created an international controversy, angering US communities across the strait. Although some experts maintain that the sewage is immediately dissolved by the strait's strong currents, mounting pressure and tourist convention boycotts may force Victoria to opt for sewage treatment quicker than it now plans.

? **Victoria Information:** Victoria Visitor Info Centre, 812 Wharf St, Victoria, BC, V8W 1T3. 250-953-2033. Internet: http://travelvictoria.bc.ca. On the harbour front. Daily. A one-stop shopping centre for tourists. Licenced to carry out some travel agency functions: staff help book hotel and B&B accommodation, tours and charters, restaurant meals, transportation, and entertainment.

✈ **Victoria International Airport:** On the Saanich Peninsula north of Victoria via Hwy 17. It is 25km to airport turnoff at McTavish Rd, then 2km to Vancouver Island's main airport, served by major airlines. (For airlines, see p.32.)

🚌 **Victoria Bus Depot:** 700 Douglas St, at Belleville St, downtown. Buses to and from Seattle, Vancouver, all of Vancouver Island. Lockers. (See Bus Lines, p.35.)

🚆 **VIA Rail Station:** At Pandora and Store streets, next to Johnson St Bridge. Terminus for E&N Railway's passenger dayliner making 224km journey along Vancouver Island's east coast, to Courtenay. (For details, see *Railway*, p.35.)

City Fare

Although Victoria's climate and scenery may entice people outdoors, it is also a place for indoors lovers. Besides its parks and pathways there are neighbourhood pubs, many decorated in keeping with the city's early history, some serving their own home brews. Entertainment is provided in some pubs and lounges. Unlimited types of cuisine are served in restaurants, cafes, and takeouts. Victoria has its own symphony and opera company, as well as several theatre groups. Art shows, films, lectures, plays, concerts, and other performances are held throughout the year at theatres and galleries. The **McPherson Playhouse**, adjacent City Hall, is one of the most exquisite Edwardian-type performance venues in Canada. The **Belfry Theatre** company, at the heart of the old Fernwood district, performs in what was the Emmanuel Baptist Church, built in 1892.

Most events are advertised in the *Times-Colonist*, Victoria's daily newspaper, and in other local publications. *Monday Magazine*, a Victoria weekly, *The Martlet*, University of Victoria newspaper, and *Focus on Women* magazine carry extensive calendars of arts events. Other events calendars are available at the Info Centre.

■ **Afternoon Teas:** That hint of old England that for some defines a visit to Victoria. Wee sandwiches, pastries, scones, and cream in just the right surroundings – (it can be pricey, so be prepared). Most popular is the Empress Hotel,1-800-441-1414: they serve an average of 100,000 teas a year – at about $34 per person. Other venues: Oak Bay Beach Hotel, 250-598-1134; Butchart Gardens, 250-652-5256; Blethering Place Tearoom and Restaurant, 250-598-1413; Adriennes Tea Garden, 250-658-1535; Four Mile House Tearoom and Restaurant, 250-479-2514.

Architectural Wonders

■ **BC Parliament Buildings:** On Belleville St above Victoria Harbour. 250-387-3046. Daily, June-Labour Day, tours every 20 minutes. Weekdays in winter, several tours daily. Public galleries open when legislature in session. Buildings were constructed for $923,000 and completed in 1897, in time for the diamond jubilee of Queen Victoria. Gilded statue of Captain George Vancouver, first European to circumnavigate this vast island, stands atop the highest copper dome.

■ **Empress Hotel:** 721 Government St, overlooking the Inner Harbour. 250-384-8111. The ivy-coated Empress, designed to reflect the grand chateaus of Europe, has watched over the harbour since 1908. Many visitors regard staying at the Empress and having a drink in the Bengal Lounge as must entries in their travel diaries. The hotel's elegant Edwardian-Victorian interior has recently been refurbished. Its 475 rooms – including eight in the Romantic Attic, accessible by a private staircase – range from $135 to a luxurious $1,700. Some guests drop by simply for Afternoon Tea. Visiting Royals and celebrities are sometimes glimpsed in the lobby. The Empress Room is known for its fine West-Coast cuisine. Also a buffet-style restaurant and a dozen shops to browse for tartans, jewelry, gift wear.

■ **St Ann's Academy:** Humboldt St, off Blanshard. 250-386-1428. Wed-Sun, 10-4. Four Catholic nuns, Sisters of St Ann's, arrived in what was a frontier outpost in 1858. In a log school, they taught the children of Victoria's Hudson's Bay employees. That year, St Ann's chapel, Victoria's first Roman Catholic cathedral was built. Then, in 1871, the grander vision – the academy, an elegant structure in French provincial tradition – was realized a short distance away on Humboldt St, and the chapel was moved to join it. East and west wings were added in 1886 and 1910, and the school thrived until 1973 when it succumbed to declining enrollments. In 1998, after a $16.2-million restoration, St Ann's is open again, now an arts and government complex surrounded by elegant gardens. An interpretive centre in the main foyer explains the academy's past.

■ **Ogden Point Breakwater:** Ship watchers often bring binoculars here to the eastern entrance of Victoria Harbour. The breakwater, with a navigational light at the end, stretches 750m out to sea, providing partial protection for the harbour. Built of 18t blocks of granite, it was completed in 1917 at a cost of $1.8 million, nearly twice as much as the BC Legislative Buildings. Its ledges and concrete surface are a favourite spot for fishermen and joggers. The Ogden Point Marine Reserve here is one of the most spectacular shore-diving sites in Canada. In the kelp forest beneath the waves off the breakwater, divers may encounter resident wolf eels, giant Pacific Octopus, crabs, harbour seals, and anemones. The Ogden point Dive Centre has rentals, certified instruction, charters, hot showers. 250-380-9119. Upstairs, is the Ogden Point Cafe, for landlubbers too.

■ **Crystal Garden:** 713 Douglas St. 250-381-1213. Daily. Glass-roofed Crystal Garden opened 1925. Originally a social centre with ballroom and British Empire's largest saltwater swimming pool, it was closed in 1971 because of soaring maintenance costs. Renovated and reopened in 1980, again as a social centre, with tea room, ballroom, and luxuriant tropical gardens with exotic plants and caged animals: miniature monkeys, fish, macaws, parrots, flamingoes, bats and butterflies, but no swimming anymore, for people.

The Parliament Buildings in Victoria, British Columbia's capital.

■ **Victoria Conference Centre:** 720 Douglas St. 250-361-1000. Behind the Empress Hotel and across from Crystal Garden, grand-scale modern-day architecture has recently joined that of past. Opened in 1989, it can host up to 1,500 delegates in the largest of its 15 meeting rooms. Lecture theatre seats 400. Totem pole and fountains in plaza and foyer.

■ **Craigdarroch Castle:** 1050 Joan Cres. 250-592-5323. Daily. Castle built shortly before turn of the century for Robert Dunsmuir, the Scottish-born entrepreneur who founded the coal mines in Nanaimo, and earned a reputation as a strike breaker and robber baron. The castle's conspicuous stone towers rise from a hilltop in Victoria's prestigious Rockland neighbourhood, near Government House. Granites, marbles, and sandstone of the highest quality were used for the exterior. Inside, every piece of wood and stone was meticulously tooled. Intricate panelling adorns walls and ceiling of the main hall and follows the main staircase 87 steps into a dancing hall and main tower. Dunsmuir died before the castle was finished, but his widow remained there until her death in 1908. It was later used as a hospital for soldiers, a college, school board offices, and music conservatory. The castle is now a museum.

■ **Christ Church Cathedral:** At Quadra and Courtenay streets. 250-383-2714. Self-guided tour brochures available at front of church; guided tours by arrangement. Built 1929, Christ Church Cathedral is one of few remaining Canadian churches with real bells. One pillar was named Robin Pillar after construction was delayed because a robin had built a nest on it. Inside, the choir screen and massive organ, with 3,000 pipes, are from Westminster Abbey. Pulpit is made from a 500-year-old oak tree.

Museums , Galleries, Arts

■ **Royal BC Museum:** 675 Belleville St. 250-387-3014 or 1-800-661-5411. Daily. With some 10 million items in its collections, this is one of Canada's finest museums, renowned for its presentation of First Nations history and culture. Also a pioneer town, sawmill, fish cannery, coal mine, train station, and theatre. You can board Captain George Vancouver's ship, the *Discovery*, saunter through woods or along seashore, or take an undersea journey in a submarine. Guided eco-tours to whales, salmon, forests, caves. New here: the **National Geographic Theatre** featuring an **Imax** projector showing regularly scheduled films on a screen six storeys high and eight storeys wide. Excellent bookstore and gift shop.

■ **Art Gallery of Greater Victoria:** 1040 Moss St, just off Fort St. 250-384-4101. Daily. Mondays by donation. Gallery occupies Spencer Mansion, built 1890. Works of Emily Carr and only entire Shinto shrine outside Japan on display. Tours. Architectural Bike Tour, late Sept-early Oct.

■ **Maritime Museum of BC:** 28 Bastion Sq. 250-385-4222. Daily. In Victoria's first courthouse (1899). Vice Admiralty Court room, models, west-coast lighthouses, the dugout canoe that circumnavigated the world. New Passenger Travel Gallery presents ferry travel from early in the century to the present.

■ **Emily Carr House:** 207 Government St. 250-387-4697. Mid-May to mid-Oct, daily. Italianate-style home of Victoria's best-known artist, Emily Carr, who died in 1945. Furnished rooms and exhibit about her.

■ **Maltwood Art Museum and Gallery:** University Centre, University of Victoria. 250-721-8298. Mon-Fri. Collection of late sculptor Katherine Maltwood was donated to University of Victoria in 1964. Pieces from collection, comprised of decorative arts, paintings, furniture, and other items, are often incorporated into gallery's changing exhibits.

■ **Point Ellice House:** 2616 Pleasant St. 250-387-4697. Daily, mid-May to mid-Sept. Built as private home in 1861, now contains collection of Victoriana. Special events in summer.

■ **Craigflower Farm and School House:** At corner of Craigflower and Admirals. 250-383-4627 or 250-387-4697. Daily, July-Sept, 12-4; Thurs-Mon, 12-4, late May 27 to late June and Sept-early Oct. Built in 1856 on one of Victoria's first farms. On same site is one of western Canada's oldest schoolhouses. Special events, summer, harvest time, and other times. Canadiana Costume Museum Archives of BC is also here. Site overlooks Portage Inlet, nearly 9km from the head of Victoria Harbour, a familiar sight to people commuting to Victoria on the Trans-Canada Hwy.

■ **Helmcken House:** Behind Thunderbird Park next to Royal BC Museum. 250-361-0021 or 250-387-4697. Daily, 11-5, May-Sept. Daily 12-4, Feb-April and Oct to mid-Nov. Christmas programs late Dec. Built 1852, BC's oldest standing home. Special Christmas events.

■ **Starfish Glassworks:** 630 Yates St. 250-388-7828. From gallery filled with glass vases, bowls, and sculptures, visitors can view studio where artists turn scorching hot blobs of glass into exquisite forms.

Squares and Alleys

■ **Bastion Square:** The heart of Victoria's Old Town and site of original Fort Victoria, where former saloons, hotels, bordellos, and warehouses have become restaurants, offices, and art galleries.

■ **Market Square:** Lower Johnson, Store, and Pandora streets. This is the heart of Victoria's Old Town – its story begins with the gold rush, in 1858. On lower Johnson St thousands of white immigrants found cheap housing, restaurants, saloons, opium, prospecting supplies. The Pandora side, separated by a ravine, was home to the Chinese community until the 1880s, when Chinatown shifted to Fisgard St. A depression followed the gold rush, but the Old Town was revived, in the 1880s, by a world demand for lumber, sealskins, coal, salmon, and other resources funnelled through Victoria's port. Buildings constructed then – the Italianate-style Grand Pacific Hotel, the Strand, and the Senator hotels, merchant houses – served Klondike gold rushers, and the working classes of Victoria through to the 1950s. Today, these heritage buildings form three sides of Market Square, a 1970s revival of the Old Town, with more than 65 cafes, restaurants, and specialty stores. The courtyard, once the ravine separating Chinese and white communities, is now a centre for events and festivals that bring the community together.

■ **Chinatown and Fan Tan Alley:** Today a centre of commerce and culture for many Chinese Canadians, Victoria's Chinatown is the oldest on the west coast of North America. In the late 1800s, after the gold rush and completion of the railway, Chinese labourers, not welcome elsewhere, congregated here. With 3,000 residents in 1858, it was the largest Chinatown in Canada. They were mostly men, who came with the dream of saving money and returning home to China. They worked in laundries, restaurants, shops; enjoyed their own temples, operas, and theatres. Fan Tan Alley's nooks and crannies were once occupied by gambling houses offering mah jong, fan-tan, dominoes, and the numbers game. Around the turn of the century, production of opium in Chinatown was one of BC's largest industries. It's believed more than a dozen major opium dealers had thriving businesses based in Victoria, just blocks from the northwest coast's largest red-light district.

The entrance to today's Chinatown, at Government and Fisgard streets, was marked conspicuously in 1981 by the Gate of Harmonious Interest, with two hand-carved stone lions from Suchow, China, Victoria's twin city. Restaurants and shops sell food, art, herbs, and other items from China.

■ **Centennial Square:** Douglas and Pandora streets. Here is Victoria's City Hall, built 1897 and one of the first major downtown buildings to be refurbished in an effort to preserve the city's architectural heritage. 250-385-5711 for tours by arrangement. There are plans afoot for major redevelopment of the square.

■ **Antique Row:** Up from the waterfront along Fort St, more Olde England is visible along this street, where Tudor-style buildings house several antique stores.

■ **Oak Bay:** More English than England. To arrive in this municipality is to step behind the "Tweed Curtain" where afternoon tea is served according to tradition, and the local gentry slip into the Oak Bay Beach Hotel's Snug pub for a quiet drink. In prohibition days, amaretto and apricot brandy, called Snug Tea, were concealed in brown betty puddings. There's a real tea party here, too, a big annual event, early June, on the sandy shores of Willows Beach.

■ **Uplands Estates:** Beyond Willows Beach the Marine Scenic Drive (see below) carries on past posh homes and gardens of Uplands Estates. Many of these homes look toward Chatham and Discovery islands, named for Captain Vancouver's ships. Uplands was originally the site of the Hudson's Bay Company's sheep farm, which supplied early colonists.

Gardens and Parks

With such a multitude of historic sites and a high population of retired people, Victoria is sometimes mistakenly viewed as a salty home for contented laggards and remittance men. But the city is anything but stodgy. Anyone arriving at Victoria Harbour on the sunny days of spring and summer is enveloped in the city's vivacity. Thousands of flowers on the harbour's Causeway spell "Welcome to Victoria." Bells ring in the Netherlands Carillon Tower, in front of the Royal BC Museum, and street performers add to the ambience. Up from the harbour,

fiddlers, folksingers, and classical ensembles busk on downtown streets. Known as the "City of Gardens," an annual average of 2,200 hours of sunshine here helps the flowers and blossoms bloom before any other city in Canada.

■ **Hanging Baskets:** Spring to fall, Victoria's streets are colourfully embellished by more than 1,000 hanging baskets, each with 25 flowering plants adorning antique-style lamps.

■ **Beacon Hill Park:** Each spring hundreds of thousands of daffodils and blue camas flowers blanket the slopes of Beacon Hill, site of a 74ha city park overlooking Juan de Fuca Strait and the Olympic Mountains of Washington State. Another 30,000 flowers are planted in the park twice a year. With its streams and duck ponds, peacocks, aviary, shrubs, oak trees and firs, play-

Victoria's incomparable Butchart Gardens.

grounds, paths, flower gardens, and lovers' lane, the park is a quiet getaway in the midst of downtown Victoria. Rare in a city park, much of Beacon Hill is left wild (tended, but wild), and this is precisely what is most refreshing. Beacon Drive-In across from the park on Douglas St is a popular stop for soft ice cream.

■ **Butchart Gardens:** Brentwood Bay. See *Swartz Bay to Victoria*, p.42.

■ **Thunderbird Park:** Corner of Belleville and Douglas streets. A longhouse, carved poles, and other works of the northwest coast's native culture are on outdoor display. Haida, Tsimshian, Nuu-chah-nulth, Coast Salish, Kwakwaka'wakw, and Nuxalk people are represented, and carvers can often be observed at work.

■ **Government House:** 1401 Rockland Ave. 250-387-2080. Grounds open daily. Meticulously maintained lawns and gardens are a delight for flower lovers. Much of the grounds have been restored to display Victoria's native flora, including Garry oaks and camas flowers. The lordly mansion is home of BC's lieutenant-governor and is often used to accommodate visiting royalty.

■ **Horticultural Centre of the Pacific:** On Beaver Lake Rd, west of West Saanich Rd. 250-479-6162. Daily, dawn to dusk; 8-8 in summer. A 44.5ha gardeners' haven, where flowers are blooming every month.

■ **University of Victoria:** 14ha of parklike grounds on campus with jogging trails, and in spring, a blazing glory of rhododendrons. Duck ponds, woods, and benches. See *Swartz Bay to Victoria*, p.40.

■ **Ross Bay Cemetery:** Fairfield Rd and Memorial Cr, near start of Marine Scenic Dr, just beyond Clover Point. Some 27,000 graves on 11ha site. This is the final resting place of such notable British Columbians as Robert Dunsmuir, Emily Carr, Sir James Douglas, and Sir Matthew Baillie Begbie, BC's first magistrate. Because little burial space is left, this cemetery is becoming more and more an historic park, invaded by strollers, joggers, artists, tourists, and scholars. A cemetery for the living, one might say. **Old Cemeteries Society:** Box 50004, 15-1594 Fairfield Rd, Victoria, BC, V8S 1G1, 250-598-8870, offers fascinating tours of Ross Bay and other city cemeteries, including the Old Quadra Street Burying Ground, Chinese Cemetery, Jewish Cemetery.

■ **Commonwealth Nature Legacy:** A "living heritage of green space" within arm's reach of Victoria. This collection of provincial, municipal, and regional parks, named for the Commonwealth Games hosted here in 1994, includes the forests, meadows, and waterways of **Gowlland Tod Provincial Park** (p.42), just 20 minutes from downtown. The **Juan de Fuca Marine Trail** offers up to 47km of west-coast hiking and beachcombing within an hour's drive of the city (p. 51). Also protected within the Legacy are the shores of **Glencoe Cove**, at the eastern edge of Victoria, looking out to Haro Strait. This is the site of aboriginal middens and home to rare oceanfront plant species. Nearby, the **Haro Woods**, adjacent the University of Victoria, protect Douglas-fir forest, eagles, owls, and hawks. At **Panama Hill**, 12.5ha of Garry-oak meadow will become an important "green link" in the **Colquitz Linear Park** system – 7km of hiking and cycling trails connecting the Gorge waterway to Elk and Beaver lakes. The Legacy parks will link with existing parks to form green corridors stretching north and west.

■ **Capital Regional District (CRD) Parks:** 24 parks, protecting 8,000ha of magical spots from Mount Parke in the Gulf Islands, to the open seas of East Sooke Park on southern Vancouver Island. The recent acquisition of Sooke Hills Regional Wilderness Park, an important watershed not open to the public, has doubled the CRD's parks base. There are 300km of hiking trails and nature walks, including the 60km Galloping Goose Trail (below). Natural and cultural history programs include birdwatching, wild-plant gathering, outdoor survival, and Nightwalkers – out in the woods on Halloween night. There is a nature information centre at Witty's Lagoon Park, and a nature house at Francis/King Park. See immediately below, and *Logs* and *Index* for other parks. For info: Capital Regional District Parks, 490 Atkins Ave, Victoria, BC, V9B 2Z8. 250-478-3344 or 250-474-PARK.

■ **Galloping Goose Regional Trail:** Winds 60km through urban, suburban, and rural landscapes, following an abandoned Canadian National Railway line from Saanich to downtown Victoria, through the Western Communities all the way to the abandoned gold-mining town, Leechtown, bigger than Victoria in the 1860s. The trail, named after historic gas-powered rail bus that carried passengers to Leechtown, is for cyclists, pedestrians, riders on horseback, even rollerbladers (some sections are paved). The trail intersects with streets, passes over the Trans-Canada Hwy via a special $1.1-million bridge with wheelchair access and rest areas, crosses creeks and inlets via three trestles (including the old Selkirk railway trestle crossing the Gorge waterway), and cuts through forests. Official trailhead is at west end of Johnson St Bridge, but there are many access points, including Atkins Rd, Luxton Fair Grounds, Happy Valley Rd, and Roche Cove Regional Park. Also, the Saanich Municipal Hall on Vernon Ave off W Saanich Rd, and at Quadra St just south of Greenridge Cr (parking is limited here). One day the trail will link Swartz Bay and Port Renfrew. For map and trail etiquette, call CRD Parks (above). Most bike shops also have info.

■ **Gonzales Hill Regional Park:** 1.8ha. Denison Rd in Victoria. Stunning views from site of observatory built in 1914.

■ **Mount Douglas Park:** Summit of Mt Douglas provides beautiful views over city. Beaches below forests of fir and cedar are a favourite family picnicking place. Marine Scenic Dr continues through park, beyond Cordova Bay toward Hwy 17 on Saanich Peninsula.

■ **Mt Work-Hartland Mountain Biking Park:** 210ha. At the end of Hartland Ave off W Saanich Rd. 250-477-2455 for info or ask

Wee ferries whiz passengers around Victoria's Inner Harbour.

at bike stores. The first mountain-biking area in a public park on Vancouver Island. Old fire roads are now trails for beginner to advanced bikers. Hoses for washing bikes; washrooms.

■ **Anderson Hill Park:** Off Newport Ave to Island Rd. A quiet spot with views across the strait to islands; camas flowers in spring.

■ **The Gorge Waterway:** Victoria's Outer and Inner harbours narrow to form the Gorge, a long fiord meandering northwest through the city, widening at its end as Portage Inlet. So strong are the tides at certain times that kayakers run them for white-water paddling practice. Kinsmen Gorge Park and the Gorge-side promenade are favourite spots for herring fishing, particularly for children, in late winter and early spring. BC Wildlife Watch viewing site.

■ **Saxe Point Park:** At south end of Fraser St, in Esquimalt. Sea breezes, waves, views of the Olympic Mountains, walking trails.

■ **Garry Oak Meadows:** Some best places to see are UVic campus, Beacon Hill Park, Mt Tolmie, Government House. Garry oaks are the largest and longest-lived deciduous trees in Western Canada, dating back as far as 8,000 years in Victoria. *Quercus garryana* is found from California's Santa Cruz Mountains through western reaches of Oregon and Washington, the southeastern portion of Vancouver Island up to Courtenay, on Gulf Islands, and parts of the Lower Mainland. Garry oak meadows are endangered: contact Garry Oak Meadow Preservation Society, c/o 3873 Swan Lake Rd, Victoria, BC, V8X 3W1. 250-479-0211.

Windy Fringes

The main similarity between Victoria and other Vancouver Island communities is the variety of outdoors opportunities available. Attractions, both manmade and natural, in and around the city provide activities for cyclists, hikers, sightseers, canoeists and kayakers, sailors and boaters, joggers, naturalists, photographers, anglers, and general outdoors enthusiasts.

■ **Harbour Walkway and Victoria Harbour Ferries:** A close-up perspective of Victoria's raggedy shores via footpath and wee ferries. It's 10km or so from West Bay in Esquimalt to Ross Bay beyond downtown Victoria; most of the route is boardwalk and pathway. The first 2km stretch from the West Bay Marina, called Westsongway, passes the new Songhees hotel-condo site, and ends up at the Johnson St Bridge. The next 3km offer a slight detour around some of Victoria's oldest architecture, then connect with the Inner Harbour walkway, or another detour up onto Belleville St, and more walkway to Fisherman's Wharf. The next 6km skirt by the Canadian Coast Guard, Ogden Point, cruise ships, the breakwater, Dallas Rd, Beacon Hill Park, hang-gliders, kite flyers, windsurfers, sea gulls, Olympic Mt views, Clover Point.

Victoria Harbour Ferries connect points along the first 5km, picking up and dropping off at West Bay Marina (near Spinnaker's Pub – home brew, halibut and chips), Songhees (Ocean Pointe Resort is here), Inner Harbour (the Empress for tea), Coast Harbourside, Fisherman's Wharf (Barb's Place fish and chips). And they scoot up the Gorge, stopping at Point Ellice House.

■ **Mile Zero and Marine Scenic Dr:** At the foot of Douglas St on the waterfront at Dallas Rd. Start of the Trans-Canada Hwy (Hwy 1). Also start of Marine Scenic Dr that traces shore for about 30km to south end of Saanich Peninsula. A relaxing drive or bicycle ride with constant views of sea and Olympic Mountains.

■ **Victoria Beaches:** The beaches along Marine Scenic Dr are pleasant places to bask in summer sun or cool off with a dip in the chilly sea. Popular sunbathing beaches are Gonzales Bay, Shoal Bay, Willows Beach, Cadboro Bay, Mt Douglas Beach, and Cordova Bay. On the other side of Victoria: sandy shores at Esquimalt Lagoon, Witty's Lagoon, and Weirs Beach. But summer swimmers beware: BC's capital city, in spite of its recent rapid growth, continues to dump raw sewage into the sea – waters are tested and warnings posted when fecal coliform counts become dangerously high for swimming.

Victoria is hit by an average of eight winter gales a year, and these same balmy sunbathing beaches become particularly invigorating for beach walkers in a pitiless winter downpour and howling wind.

■ **Victoria's Golf Courses:** There are 14 public and semi-private courses in and around Greater Victoria. Visitors are welcome at the semi-private clubs, though reservations should be made. Courses are situated in some of city's most scenic locations: ask at Info Centre.

■ **Strategic Esquimalt:** 4km west of Victoria Harbour entrance is Esquimalt Harbour, home of Canada's Pacific naval fleet. Originally the West-Coast base for the British Royal Navy (since 1865), the Canadian Forces Base here today is a large centre with dockyards, moorings, and administrative quarters. During the Cold War a decade ago, Esquimalt was mainly a training base. Today, it has achieved near parity with Halifax as an important base, boasting five new frigates, two renovated destroyers, and a supply ship. Esquimalt also has four new maritime coastal patrol vessels stationed here and will be getting two more. Within the next two years, Esquimalt will also be home for a new submarine and crew. Esquimalt was incorporated as a municipality in 1912. An older section of Greater Victoria, Esquimalt has a number of heritage buildings and beaches with excellent views of Victoria Harbour and Juan de Fuca Strait. Much of Esquimalt's intriguing military history is depicted at the **CFB Esquimalt Naval and Military Museum**, built in 1891 as an annex to the Royal Naval Hospital. The museum is inside the CFB Esquimalt gates, Buildings 20, 37 and 39; open Mon-Fri. 250-363-4312. Also HMCS Naden Heritage Walking Tours (Mon-Fri, year-round) and HMC Dockyard Historic Bus Tours (June-Aug).

■ **Race Rocks/Marine Ecological Reserve:** Visible from Beacon Hill Park on a clear day. On the southwestern horizon, they look like a submarine, with their lighthouse sticking up. Race Rocks is the most southerly point in western Canada. The island-rocks, in Juan de Fuca Strait only 8km from the Canada-US boundary, are named for the tides that swirl around them. Before the "light" was put in, in Dec 1860, some three dozen ships met disaster here; but even since the lighthouse there have been tragedies. The infamous currents that plague boaters support some of the most prolific marine life on the BC coast, including as many as 1,000 California and Steller's sea lions that use the rocks as a winter haulout Oct-April. In 1980, after an intense campaign conducted by students and teachers from the nearby Pearson College of the Pacific, a 220ha ecological reserve was established here. The college (see p. 49) continues as a steward of the reserve, conducting research and assisting hundreds of biology and marine science students from around the world. The lighthouse was to become fully automated in March 1997, but a two-year reprieve has been negotiated by the college and the Canadian Coast Guard.

■ **Whale-Watching Tours:** Ask at Info Centre about excursions in search of killer whales, porpoises, sea lions, seals, and marine birds in waters around Victoria.

■ **Sea-Monster Spotting:** Cadborosaurus is said to have a horselike head and dragonlike tail, and bears a resemblance to the West Coast native people's Huyitliik, "who moves by wiggling back and forth." Scientists believe in him ... her. The best evidence so far is a photo of a half-digested infant serpent found in the stomach of a whale at a Queen Charlotte Islands whaling station in 1937. Statistics over the last century average one (reported) sighting a year. A relatively high proportion of these have been made in waters in and around Cadboro Bay. Saanich Inlet is the major breeding ground, according to one biologist and cryptozoologist.

Victoria Attractions

■ **Anne Hathaway's Cottage:** 429 Lampson St. 250-388-4353. Daily tours. Outside downtown Victoria, in Esquimalt, Olde England Inn and Anne Hathaway's Cottage are part of a re-created 16th-century English village.

■ **Miniature World:** 649 Humboldt St. 250-385-9731. Daily. Displays in miniature, with figurines hand-carved by Canadian artists, depicting historic events, nursery rhymes,

industry. A must for model-train and toy-soldier buffs.

■ **Royal London Wax Museum:** 470 Belleville St. 250-388-4461. Daily. Queen Victoria and Princess Di are among more than 200 wax figures on display.

■ **Undersea Gardens:** 490 Belleville St. 250-382-5717. Daily. Next to Wax Museum below harbour's Causeway. Descend beneath the sea for a look at native marine life.

■ **Victoria Bug Zoo:** 1107 Wharf St. 250-384-2847. Tues-Sun, year-round.

VICTORIA TO PORT RENFREW

SOOKE ROAD
(Highway 14)

Highway 14, known as Sooke Road (into Sooke village and points west), is also known locally as the West Coast Road. It begins at Colwood Corners, just west of Victoria, and runs 95km to the village of Port Renfrew. To reach the start of Hwy 14, head north on Hwy 1 from Victoria – then, 7km from the city core, take the Colwood Interchange (Hwy 1A/14 exit). This is also the best access for the West Shore Communities of Colwood, Langford, and Metchosin. Until the last few decades, these were the countryside, home to real farmers and back to the landers. In the last decade, Colwood and Langford particularly, have expanded to become bedroom communities for Victoria, and now, are shamelessly open to commercial development of the strip mall variety.

Hwy 14 leads to destinations along the southwestern side of Vancouver Island. The seashore here is exposed to weather systems that sweep down Juan de Fuca Strait, giving it a more rugged appearance than the other side of the island. The highway itself reflects that: it can be narrow, and sharp corners often creep up under thick west-coast fog banks. An added danger is the temptation, while taking corners at highway speeds, to scan the shimmering horizon for freighters, pods of killer whales, or whatever other adventures might be out there.

For those who wish to contemplate this landscape at a safer speed, there is every opportunity. The Juan de Fuca Marine Trail parallels 47km of the West Coast Rd. The Galloping Goose Trail offers nearly 50km of hiking, biking or horseback riding in this area. The Kludahk Forest Recreation Trail traces the San Juan Ridge for 30km. And, there's the West Coast Trail, beginning where the West Coast Rd ends, offering another 77km of west coast to walk.

■ **View Royal:** (Pop. 6,441). About 6km west of Victoria city centre via Hwys 1 or 1A. Incorporated 1988, View Royal was settled in the early 1850s by Dr. Helmcken when he purchased 259ha of farmland from the Hudson's Bay Company. Set partially atop a rocky oceanfront outcropping, it's mostly a residential area today. A marker and bronze

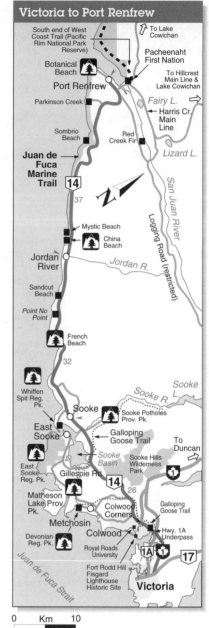

Victoria to Port Renfrew

0   Km   10

plaque at the foot of present-day Helmcken Rd commemorate the days when crews from passing ships replenished their freshwater supply from a spring that flows from property on Bessborough Rd.

■ **Galloping Goose Regional Trail (Western Section):** Access on Atkins Rd, about 100m past the Colwood Interchange. Turn right off Hwy 1A and watch for signs. From here trail runs about 50km through communities of View Royal, Colwood, Langford, Metchosin, and Sooke, all the way to Leechtown, once the site of a gold-mining community. For info on Victoria and Saanich Peninsula sections of trail, see pp.47 and 39.

■ **Fort Rodd Hill National Historic Site and Fisgard Lighthouse:** 42.5ha. 603 Fort Rodd Hill Rd, 250-478-5849. Daily,

10am-5:30pm. Turnoff to Fort Rodd Hill 400m before Colwood Corners. Deer, arbutus, Douglas fir forests, and manicured lawns adorn this historic site at this western entrance to Esquimalt Harbour, once a strategic defense position. The Fisgard Light, built in 1860, and still operational, was the first on BC's coast. Military artifacts and modern exhibits. No pets.

Colwood: (Pop. 13,848). 18km west of Victoria city centre. Incorporated 1985, the city of Colwood has grown out of one of four large farms established outside Fort Victoria by Puget's Sound Agricultural Company. The 243ha farm, partially cleared in the 1850s, was named after a residence of E.E. Langford, who operated the farm. This burgeoning commercial and residential community plans to create a new neighbourhood, Royal Bay, at the site of the local, scenically situated gravel pits.

Colwood Information: Info Centre, West Shore Chamber of Commerce, 697 Goldstream Ave, Victoria, BC, V9B 2X2. 250-478-1130. Chamber of Commerce office and Info Centre at corner of Hwy 1A (Goldstream Ave) and Millstream Rd in municipality of **Langford**, 2km north of Colwood. Open till 5pm in summer.

Colwood Corners: Junction of Hwy 1A (Goldstream Ave) and Hwy 14 (Sooke Rd). Goldstream Ave leads northwest through heartland of Langford municipality, below.

SIDE TRIP

to Langford

Langford: (Pop. 18,060). 2km northwest of Colwood on Goldstream Ave. Named for E.E. Langford, bailiff for the Puget Sound Agricultural Company, the farming arm of the Hudson's Bay Company, in the 1850s. This is the rapidly developing commercial and industrial centre of the West Shore Communities.

Return to Highway 14

From Colwood Corners, heading west on Hwy 14, set your trip gauge now.

Royal Roads University: Sooke Rd, 0.5km west of Colwood Corners. In Hatley Park (National Historic Site), an elaborate estate comprised of luxuriant gardens and Hatley Castle, built in 1908 by James Dunsmuir, industrialist and BC premier, 1900-1902. He was son of Scottish coal baron Robert Dunsmuir who built Victoria's Craigdarroch Castle (p.45). Royal Roads Military College occupied the site until 1994. Two years later, classes began at this new university offering condensed programs in leadership training, entrepreneurial management, and environmental studies. University enquiries: 250-391-2511. Visitors are welcome to visit the gardens, daily until dusk. No charge. No crowds. Friends of Hatley Park conduct tours; campus maps available in castle foyer. 250-391-2551.

The Pacific dogwood tree flourishes on southern Vancouver Island. Its flower is the provincial emblem.

Metchosin Rd: 2km west of Colwood Corners, turn south off Hwy 14. Alternate route to Sooke offering a string of superb nature-viewing spots.

SIDE TRIP

to Metchosin and East Sooke

Metchosin: (Pop. 4,670). District boundaries 10km beyond Colwood on Metchosin Rd; also accessible via Happy Valley Rd off Sooke Rd (Hwy 14), see below. Community centre (church, community and municipal hall) is at Metchosin Corner, junction of Metchosin and Happy Valley roads. Metchosin, or *smets-shosin*, in the native Coast Salish language is said to mean "place smelling of fish oil" – one story suggests the name was bestowed here after a dead whale was cast up on a nearby beach. Much time has passed: Metchosin smells like sea and forest, and it wants to stay that way. Its citizens are staunch in their struggles to avoid being swallowed up by a Victoria megalopolis. My-Chosen Cafe, Metchosin Country Store, and Country Crafters' Giftshop are at the corner of Metchosin and Happy Valley roads.

■ **Metchosin School Museum:** Metchosin and Happy Valley roads. 250-478-3451. Sat-Sun, afternoons, April-Oct. First school in BC after province joined Confederation in 1871. Opened 1872, closed for good 1949. Also here, **Pioneer Implement Museum**, open with Farmer's Market, May-Sept, 11-2.

Albert Head Lagoon Park: 6.9ha. On Metchosin Rd turn south at Far Hill Rd (just past gravel pit), right at Lower Park Dr. Wildlife sanctuary, cobble beach for picnicking and sunbathing. Views of Albert Head, Strait of Juan de Fuca, and Victoria skyline. Lagoon north of beach is home to an abundant wildlife population, including elegant swans.

Witty's Lagoon Regional Park: 56.5ha. Parking 7km from turnoff at Hwy 14. Guided walks, map at parking lot. 250-474-2454 or 250-474-7275. Birdwatcher's paradise. Luxuriant forests of Douglas fir and sword fern, and creeks surround Sitting Lady Falls. Long sandy beach with rocky shore leads to Tower Point. Seals and great blue herons make regular appearances. Marked trails and picnic grounds.

Devonian Regional Park: 13ha. 5km beyond Witty's Lagoon on William Head Rd. 250-478-3344. Nature sanctuary tucked between Metchosin farms. Walking and bridle trails, birdwatching, picnicking, and beachcombing.

Pearson College of the Pacific: Pearson College Dr. Take William Head Rd from end of Metchosin Rd. 250-391-2411. On shore of idyllic Pedder Bay. One of nine United World Colleges. Provides 200 scholarships to students from around the world who complete the equivalent of grade 12 and first-year university. Tours by arrangement Oct-April. Hosts many seasonal programs, including the midsummer Metchosin International Summer School for the Arts, see p.36.

Matheson Lake Regional Park: 162ha. West onto Happy Valley Rd at end of Metchosin Rd, then south onto Rocky Point Rd. 5km to Matheson Lake turnoff. Trail circles lake. Fishing, canoeing, swimming. Galloping Goose Regional Trail passes above lake.

East Sooke Regional Park: 1,4224ha. Just beyond Matheson Lake, take East Sooke Rd. Turn south on Becher Bay Rd or continue to end of East Sooke Rd to park. 250-478-3344. Extensive trail system can be confusing without maps: stop at Regional Parks' office (p.47) for maps. If planning long hike, allow for ample daylight hours. Do not leave valuables in your car.

A major hiking and outdoors destination for both the day-tripper and experienced adventurer. Especially invigorating in howling winter gales (check marine weather by calling 250-656-2714). Beautiful old forests of western red cedar and hemlock, Douglas fir, stately Sitka spruce, stunted shore pine, and twisted arbutus. Bald eagles watch from forest's edge while pelagic cormorants and other divers fish along the rocky shores. River otters and mink scurry between driftwood logs and sea lions are commonly seen swimming offshore Sept-May. Patient nature lovers are occasionally rewarded with a glimpse of willowy mist shooting from the blowholes of passing killer whales.

Here also are good vantage points to watch hundreds of turkey vultures (*Cathartes aura*, "pacifier" or "cleanser") congregating for their annual migration 21km across Juan de Fuca Strait in late summer. Good spots include Creyke Point, a short distance from the Aylard Farm parking lot on the park's east side: from here look east to Rocky Point. Also look from Beechey Head, a 30-minute shoreline hike from the parking lot.

The park's trails range from simple seaside strolls to rugged routes for the hale and hearty. Most challenging is the 10km Coast Trail, a six- or seven-hour trek along entire southern shoreline of the park. Inland trails to Mt Maguire (272m) and Babbington Hill (228m) lead to sweeping views of Juan de Fuca Strait and Washington's Olympic Mountains. Open fields and small beaches, many with offshore isthmuses and islets, make excellent picnic sites. Spin-casting for salmon is particularly good near kelp beds off Creyke Point and Beechey Head, at park's eastern end. On the northeast side, Anderson Cove is a tranquil backwater. Canoeists and kayakers can launch from a trail for an afternoon paddle around the sheltered waters of Sooke Basin and Sooke River estuary.

Return to Highway 14

Jacklin Rd: 4km west of Colwood Corners. Marking Langford District boundary. Leads north to Station and Goldstream avenues – downtown **Langford** (p.49).

Happy Valley Rd: 5km west of Colwood Corners. Leads south through the District of Langford to Metchosin – about 10km to Metchosin Rd and Metchosin Corner, p. 49.

Gillespie Rd: 16km west of Colwood Corners, just beyond 17 Mile House Pub. Connects East Sooke Rd and Hwy 14. From here Hwy 14 skirts Sooke Basin and harbour.

Roche Cove Regional Park: 117ha. South off Gillespie Rd, 3km. 250-478-3344. 7km of trails through cedar forest along Galloping Goose Trail.

Sooke Potholes Provincial Park: 7ha. Day use. 28km from Colwood turn north at Sooke River Rd. Nearly 5km to park. Cool, clear swimming holes. Often packed on hot summer days. Salmon spawning in autumn. It's possible to bike here along the Galloping Goose Trail.

Sooke Region Museum and Art Gallery: 23km from Colwood, Sooke side of Sooke River Bridge on Hwy 14. 250-642-6351. Houses Info Centre. Actors invite guests into Moss Cottage and entertain them as if they were visiting a working family at the turn of the century. Collection includes logging and fishing artifacts, T'Sou-ke First Nation history, and a reconstruction of Sheringham Point Lighthouse. The art gallery features the work of a local artist each month, and annually hosts the **Sooke Fine Arts Festival**, one of BC's largest juried art shows attracting hundreds of artists and thousands of art lovers. Closed winter Mondays.

Sooke: (Pop. 11,500). 24.5km west of Colwood. Bustling community overlooking the sheltered waters of Sooke Harbour, Western Canada's southernmost harbour. In the summer of 1864, this was a daily drop-off point for as many as 100 men who came to work some 40km of gold diggings on the Sooke and Leech rivers, 16km upstream from the sea. In the gold-rush frenzy, politicians predicted the area could employ 4,000 men. But within a year, after $100,000 worth of gold was taken, the rush was over. Sooke now is a logging and fishing community, known for the logging events at its annual All Sooke Day and its excellent year-round salmon fishing. Ask at Info Centre about marinas, boat rentals, fishing charters.

Sooke Harbour is protected from choppy seas of Juan de Fuca Strait by a narrow strip of land known as **Whiffen Spit**. From the spit, the harbour stretches nearly 5km along the shores of downtown Sooke before opening onto Sooke Basin, a sheltered backwater twice the size of the harbour. Excellent paddling territory. Commercial fishermen mooring at government wharf in Sooke Harbour often sell fresh seafood from their boats.

Gourmets who want to sample local seafood and other produce can settle into a seaside seat at the Sooke Harbour House, a hotel and restaurant on Whiffen Spit Rd given top ratings in international gourmet magazines. Only BC cuisine – sea urchins, scallops, shrimp, geoducks, whelks and periwinkles, moon snails, flying squid, a variety of fish, and two dozen types of crab – are served here. Most meats – grass-fed lamb, suckling pig, rabbit, veal – are bought from nearby farms. Herbs

and vegetables are grown on the grounds. Then there's The Good Life, a bookstore and cafe, and Mom's Cafe, wafting the aroma of sticky cinnamon buns.

Sooke is an explorer's haven with dozens of activities organized through Edward Milne Community School. Its new design was inspired by the salvaged skeleton of a grey whale – now suspended from the ceiling. There are boat tours to sea caves, heritage tours by land and sea, lectures on astronomy, modern and natural history. Cruises aboard a classic yacht and helicopter trips to mountaintops, ancient forests, and remote beaches have been offered through the school. Call the school, 250-642-6371, or check with Info Centre.

Sooke now has its own 35-member philharmonic orchestra – conducted by Norman Nelson, retired concertmaster of the Vancouver Symphony Orchestra and co-founder of London's famous St. Martin-in-the-Fields.

Sooke Information: Info Centre operates from Sooke Region Museum, Box 774, 2070 Phillips Rd, Sooke, BC, V0S 1N0. 250-642-6351.

Kludahk Trail: 250-642-3523 for info and maps. BC Forest Service trail running more than 30km along San Juan Ridge, accessible from Sooke by logging roads opened and closed on a varying schedule. Hiking, cross-country skiing, snowshoeing, canoeing, campsites with fire pits and pit toilets. Cabins available to Kludahk Outdoors Club members.

Whiffen Spit Park: 27km west of Colwood, on Whiffen Spit Rd. 1,200m spit with Juan de Fuca Strait on one side, Sooke Harbour on the other. Sooke Harbour House is within spitting distance.

French Beach Provincial Park: 59ha; 69 campsites (reservations taken: call 1-800-689-9025; from the Lower Mainland or overseas, call 604-689-9025). 46km west of Colwood. General info: 250-387-2300. Wooded trail to beach. Good views across Juan de Fuca Strait to Olympic Mountains. Hiking, spin-casting, wildlife, birdwatching.

Point No Point: 50km west of Colwood. Tearoom and cottages. Trails along shore and over headland with twisted trees battered by furious storms. Named for confusion area caused early hydrographers who saw a distinct headland from one viewpoint, but no point at all from another. Don't miss the point of Point No Point, a 400m jutting land and rock mass breaking up ferocious waves. Great beaches. Grey whales delight visitors in spring and autumn; orcas pass by in summer.

Sandcut Beach: 52.5km west of Colwood, sign-posted trail to lovely beach. Walk up Sandcut Creek, which cascades onto beach. Delicious potholes.

Jordan River: (Pop. 284). 57km west of Colwood. A small logging community and home of the Jordan River Surf Club, where heavy surf pounds the shore off the river's mouth. A national magazine described these beaches as the "pumping hypothermic heart of Canadian surfing." Western Forest Products offers guided nature walks and tours of logging operations. 250-646-2017.

Juan de Fuca (Provincial Park) Marine Trail: Camping at trailhead, beach, and forest sites. 250-391-2300. Day- and multi-day hiking, Southernmost trailhead is at China Beach, 61km west of Colwood. From here a corridor traces the coast 47km to Botanical Beach near Port Renfrew. This park was created as part of the Commonwealth Nature Legacy in 1994. It's fast becoming an alternative for hikers turned away at the busy West Coast Trail (below), and for those who would choose a shorter hike, closer to the city – there are several points where hikers can enter and exit this adventure. As with the West Coast Trail, hikers should be well informed and well prepared.

Bald eagle: wildlife within arm's reach of Victoria.

The marine trail links former provincial parks – China Beach, Loss Creek, Parkinson Creek, and Botanical Beach – as well as popular undeveloped beaches, Sombrio and Mystic. Main trailheads and vehicle access points, furnished with information signs and maps, are: China Beach, Sombrio Beach, Parkinson Creek, and Botanical Beach, listed separately below in this *Log*. Overnight camping in vehicles is permitted at China Beach, Sombrio Beach, and Parkinson Creek trailheads, but not Botanical Beach. There is beach camping at Bear Beach (km 8.7), Chin Beach (km 20.6), Sombrio Beach East (km 28), Sombrio Beach West (km 29.6), and Sombrio Beach West-West (km 30.2). At the forest campgrounds – Kuitsche Cove, km 34, and Payzant Creek, km 40, camping is on designated tent pads and camp fires are not permitted.

Hiking is primarily through forest, along beaches, and over rocky headlands where it is possible to see seals, killer whales, and in spring and autumn, grey whales on their annual migrations. Bears and cougars, too, (if you don't have bells or whistles, belt out Broadway tunes). The most difficult passage is between Bear Creek and Loss Creek – lots of muddy ups and downs. Upgrading and further signing is ongoing. Beach access, except at marked points, can be a scramble. Be prepared for rain and high tides cutting beaches off from the trails.

China Beach (Juan de Fuca Provincial Park): Southern terminus of Juan de Fuca Marine Trail. Short walk through forest of giant Douglas firs, hemlocks, and western red cedars to waterfall, tidal pools, sandy beach for wading and picnicking.

Sombrio Beach (Juan de Fuca Provincial Park): About 80km west of Colwood. Access to Juan de Fuca Marine Trail and camping. The 10-minute hike in may be very muddy, but visitors are rewarded with a long surf-battered shore and picturesque creek flowing across one end and sea caves at other. This is a very popular surfing spot. The area's last old-growth forest within a reasonable day-trip of BC's capital city was logged, despite widespread public objection, leaving only a small fringe of trees along the beach. For about two decades, a community of squatters lived here peacefully in elaborate shanties built with materials from the great lumberyard of the sea. When Sombrio was designated parkland in 1994, they were told to find new homes; the last families left in 1998.

Parkinson Creek (Juan de Fuca Provincial Park): South off Hwy 14 about 90km west of Colwood. An official access point to Juan de Fuca Marine Trail. 3km hike east from waterfront to camping at Kuitsche Creek. Day-long hike (10km) to Botanical Beach.

Red Creek Fir: 94.5km west of Colwood. Sign-posted 12km gravel road to trail leading to Canada's biggest Douglas fir, when you combine tree's height with diameter. 73m to its broken top, it has spent over 900 years filling out to its current 4m diameter. The sole survivor of a well-worked industrial forest, it is on a rugged trail, and is hard to find.

Deering Rd: 97km west of Colwood. Leads a short distance to **Pacheenaht First Nation** on San Juan River. Community offers camping, showers, and towels to hikers starting or finishing the **West Coast Trail** (below). This is also start of 54.5km logging road to Lake Cowichan.

Side Trip

to Lake Cowichan

Logging Roads: Right at junction just past wooden bridge. Signs posted. Turn east on Harris Creek Mainline to Lake Cowichan. Groves of second-growth Douglas fir and hemlock along winding, partially paved logging road. Outdoor options abound along rugged route. Swimming, fishing, camping, canoeing; hiking, mountain cycling on rough trails. See also, p.64.

Fairy Lake: 5.5km from Port Renfrew. Follow road past head of Port San Juan, crossing bridges over San Juan River, and turn east to Forest Service campsite. 32ha lake is backwater off San Juan River. 36 basic camping sites accessible by gravel road. Tables, toilets, and fire rings. Excellent fishing, canoeing, and picnicking on sandy beaches.

Lizard Lake: On east side of road, about 16.5km from Port Renfrew, near site where Harris Creek runs into San Juan River. 8ha marshy lake with nine Forest Service camping units. Campground is vehicle accessible by gravel road. Tables, toilets, fire rings. Swimming, canoeing, birdwatching.

Harris Creek Trail: 18km from Port Renfrew, near start of rougher, unpaved road. Trail not posted. Following a 400m treacherous descent, courageous hikers are rewarded with refreshing pools of Harris Creek. In fall, the waters here are full of spring salmon, coho, and steelhead.

Hillcrest Mainline: About 32km from Port Renfrew. Continue northeast to Mesachie and Cowichan lakes on Hillcrest Mainline. Gravel roads are shared with logging trucks here. Use extra caution during weekdays, and drive with headlights on. Road winds above steep canyons and offers pleasing views, except where recent clearcutting has left richly forested mountaintops with stark bald spots. Harris Creek Mainline continues northwest on logging road to Gordon Bay Provincial Park.

Mesachie Lake: End of 54.5km logging road. Small town of Mesachie Lake just east of turnoff. Lake Cowichan, 7km east of turnoff. West to Honeymoon Bay, 5km, and Gordon Bay Provincial Park, 7km from turnoff. See *Lake Cowichan to Bamfield*, p.64.

Return to Highway 14

Port Renfrew: (Pop. 400). 95km west of Colwood on Hwy 14. Scenic village at the mouth of the San Juan River on Port San Juan. Port Renfrew's seafaring heritage is celebrated throughout the community, where garages are painted with murals depicting ships ahoy. This small community serves many purposes. It's the southeast terminus of Pacific Rim National Park's West Coast Trail (below); it's starting point of logging roads to Cowichan Lake (below and p.64); and terminus of the new Juan de Fuca Marine Trail (above). The area is heavily used by hikers, beachcombers, paddlers, anglers, and hunters.

The Port Renfrew Hotel and Pub stands at the foot of the long government wharf, the end of the West Coast Rd – the beginning, and end, of the West Coast Trail. Here, hikers from around the world put up their feet and drink to their adventures, while some locals, at least, look forward to the rainy obscurity of winter, when loggers prevail.

West Coast Trail (Pacific Rim National Park Reserve): In Port Renfrew, follow signs to Parks Canada information centre. A 77km soul-stirring tramp through some of the world's most magnificent scenery begins with a short boat ride from from Pacheenaht First Nation Village. Then it's five to ten days of rain, sun, waterfalls, bogs, bliss, and blisters.

The West Coast Trail was first carved through the rainforest of southwestern Vancouver Island as refuge and a way out for mariners shipwrecked along the "Graveyard of the Pacific." In 1970, the trail was embraced as part of Pacific Rim National Park Reserve.

The trail begins in the traditional territories of the Pacheenaht First Nation, and ends at Pachena Bay, 3km from Bamfield, traditional home of the Huu-ay-aht First Nation. It also transects Ditidaht First Nation territories. The Quu'as West Coast Trail Group, comprised of trail guardians from each of these communities, works with Parks Canada to manage the trail, and look after their ancient fishing, whaling, and village sites.

To reduce the impact of increasing traffic on the trail's fragile environment, Parks Canada has established a quota system for Trail Use Permits. Each day the trail is open, (May 1-Sept 30), 60 hikers are allowed to start out: 26 from the north end and 26 from the south; eight from Nitinat Lake (mid-point trailhead for hiking half the trail). Of those, 20 from each end must have reservations; six each day from the two trailheads may register on a first-come, first-served basis. Reservations are taken beginning March 1 for the upcoming hiking season only. **To reserve permits, call (Discover British Columbia) 604-663-6000 from Vancouver; 1-800-663-6000 from BC, Canada, the US, and 250-387-1642 outside Canada and the US.** The fee to make a reser-

vation is $25 per person. The Trail Use Fee is $70 per person. There are additional fees for short ferry crossings. In addition, the Huu-ay-aht First Nation may levy a voluntary $20 fee for passage over their traditional lands.

For maps and tide tables, information on reservations, and pre- and post-hiking accommodation and transportation contact park information centres in Port Renfrew, 250-647-5434, or Pachena Bay (May-Sept), 250-728-3234. Off-season, contact the Park Administrative Centre in Ucluelet. Write: West Coast Trail, Pacific Rim National Park Reserve, Box 280, Ucluelet, BC, Canada, V0R 3A0.

Because the trail is not a circle, getting home from the terminus can be complicated. The West Coast Trail Express (250-380-0580) travels from Victoria and Nanaimo to Pachena Bay/Bamfield, Port Renfrew and Nitinat (Ditidaht) Village. The Pacheenaht First Nation Bus Service (250-647-5521) also serves Port Renfrew and Bamfield. Transportation from Port Alberni to Bamfield includes Western Bus Lines, 250-723-3341, via logging road, and the Alberni Marine Transport Ltd ferries, via the Alberni Inlet (250-723-8313). Water taxi and air charter services may also be available.

Botanical Beach (Juan de Fuca Provincial Park): 350ha; no camping. 4km beyond Port Renfrew. Follow Hwy 14 to its end. Sign indicates left turn on 3.5km gravel road to Botanical Beach and northern terminus of Juan de Fuca Marine Trail. Botanical Beach, at the entrance to Juan de Fuca Strait, is one of southwest Vancouver Island's most intriguing beaches. Natural amphitheatre for would-be thespians; deep, clear tidal pools, some teeming with marine life, others empty. Odd formations carved in sandstone from tidal erosion. Good viewpoint for Pacific grey whales, especially during spring migration. Toilets, information, picnicking.

Professor Josephine Tilden, University of Minnesota, arrived here by native canoe in 1901. She and her students operated a marine biological station for about five years, but their efforts were inhibited by the lack of a road. Since then, the marine life here has been studied by several universities. If you're travelling to Botanical Beach to see the intertidal life, check local newspaper under Tofino tides: a low tide of 1.2m or less is best for viewing.

THE SOUTHERN GULF ISLANDS

The idyllic Gulf Islands lie in the rain shadow of the Vancouver Island Range, protected from moisture-laden storms that blow from the open Pacific. Rainfall here, in the Strait of Georgia, is about one-third as high as on Vancouver Island's west coast. There are some 200 Gulf Islands, but most are small, uninhabited, and without ferry access. Off the north end of the Saanich Peninsula, however, the larger islands are home to more than 11,400 permanent residents, about one-quarter of them retired. While some workers commute

daily to Vancouver Island and Vancouver, trade among tourists and retired people still supports much of the islands' burgeoning economies.

The people who live here come from widely varied backgrounds, bringing an interesting, and often controversial, mixture of ideas, vocations, avocations. There are farmers and fishermen, bankers and lawyers, sculptors, authors, shipwrights, realtors and land developers, painters, and poets. These islands are one of those rare places where you choose your own lifestyle, set your own pace. More and more people are discovering this; in fact, the islands' population increased by 27 percent in the last decade.

While the lifestyle may appeal to some, it's the mild climate and inviting landscapes that attract the traveller. You can drive through valleys of pastoral farmland surrounded by forested mountains. From peaks of 700m you can watch ferries weave their way through island channels. There are sweeping scenes of woods and water, gravel and shell beaches, cottages clustered around quiet coves, sheep, old farmhouses.

Seaside resorts and bed-and-breakfast homes make the Gulf Islands a good destination any time of year. Information centres carry detailed listings of places to stay and some private cottage owners offer their cabins to visitors through newspaper ads. Although provincial campgrounds are limited, some of the nicest camping spots in southern BC are on the Gulf Islands.

The intricate network of waterways among the islands and islets are usually sheltered enough for canoes, kayaks, and other small boats. A rowboat or car-topper gets a lot of use on any Gulf Island. Hiking boots, gumboots, day packs, and binoculars also come in handy.

The populated islands in southern Georgia Strait – **Saltspring**, the **Penders, Galiano, Mayne**, and **Saturna** – can be reached by vehicle and passenger ferries from Tsawwassen, on the mainland, and from Swartz Bay, on Vancouver Island. Reservations are taken only for vehicles travelling from Tsawwassen, and sailing schedules vary with seasons and destinations. You can call BC Ferries 7am-10pm daily for vehicle reservations and info on any route or schedule. In Victoria: 250-386-3431; for BC, toll-free: 1-888-223-3779. Kayakers or canoeists can carry their boats aboard a ferry as hand luggage and some use the ferries to avoid wide crossings between major islands. The hundreds of cyclists who tour the Gulf Islands each year pay a fare for their bicycles. Viable Marine services also offer water taxi services and marine wildlife tours in the southern Gulf Islands – including Pender, Mayne, Galiano, and Saturna islands. 250-539-3200.

These major islands have services to support their populations – gas stations, stores, restaurants, recycling centres. Other southern Gulf Islands, including **Thetis, Kuper**, and **Gabriola**, are reached from ferry terminals along the eastern side of Vancouver Island, and are covered in the *Log*. The northern Gulf Islands are described in *Victoria to Nanaimo* and *Nanaimo to Campbell River* sections.

The islands' population suddenly explodes during summer. Many accommodations are

booked several months in advance: people who don't book ahead, particularly in summer and on holiday weekends, may find themselves marooned with nowhere to stay. Most provincial campgrounds operate on a first-come, first-served basis, so it's wise to head directly from the ferry to a campsite and leave the exploring until later. Fire is a major hazard on all islands and is prohibited in many areas: extreme caution should be exercised with cigarettes and campfires. Water is often in short supply during summer and should be used sparingly: on islands other than Saltspring, hikers and cyclists would be wise to carry their own water. Not everyone here is on holiday: though highways appear as meandering country roads, they are main thoroughfares for locals going about their daily business. Cyclists should ride with great care, only in single file, and refrain from stopping on tight curves and hillcrests. All beaches are publicly owned, but the privacy of adjacent landowners deserves respect.

Saltspring Island

In early times, the Wsanec (or Saanich) people of the Saanich Peninsula, and the Cowichan people across Sansum Narrows shared the island's beaches and resources. Gleaming white shell middens and maps bearing their place names are evidence of their former camps and villages. Saltspring was the first of the Gulf Islands to be settled, by Black Americans in 1857. European-descended families arrived soon after. The newcomers named the island for the 14 briny pools, ranging in size from 1m to 25m in diameter, situated at the island's north end. Salty water still bubbles up, and the Salty Springs Spa Resort on North Beach Rd treats guests to healing mineral baths.

Saltspring, with more than 180 sq km and almost 10,000 residents, is now the largest and most populated Gulf Island. Because of its proximity to Victoria, this island has the highest number of commuters and the most frequent sailings – the last five years has seen a tripling of traffic to the island. Ferries to Vancouver Island run from Fulford Harbour to Swartz Bay and from Vesuvius to Crofton. Ferries to the mainland at Tsawwassen run from Long Harbour. There is Harbour Air Service from Vancouver (see *Transportation*, p.32). Bus transit is limited: call Info Centre (below) about possible summer service from ferries to Ganges and points en route, or call Azure Transportation Ltd, 250-537-4737. There are also taxis: 250-537-3030, and car rentals: 250-537-4225.

The island is not only the largest, but the most diverse, with the highest peaks in the Gulf Islands and a dozen lakes. St Mary Lake, the largest, has some of BC's finest fishing for smallmouth bass, rainbow and cutthroat trout. Stowell, Weston, Blackburn, and Cusheon lakes also provide excellent trout fishing.

Many of the attractions can be seen in a whirlwind two-hour, 60km drive, but thor-

Montague Harbour on Galiano Island is a popular destination for kayakers.

ough exploration of Saltspring could take weeks. Visitors often complain that they didn't realize the island was so large. They leave inadequate time to see much, then go home disappointed. It would be frustrating to allow less than a full day for a trip to Saltspring.

The island has resorts, hotels, B&B establishments, campgrounds; plus stores to serve a large population. Saltspring is renowned for its community of artists and craftspeople, and often their best work is found only on the island. There are many studios, galleries, and shops in Fulford and Ganges, and along the meandering roads in between. Find them as you explore, or ask at the Info Centre or B&Bs for studio tour map and schedule.

Saltspring Island Information: Info Centre, Saltspring Island Chamber of Commerce, at 121 Lower Ganges Rd in village of Ganges. 250-537-4223. Year-round. Maps, accommodation listings, self-guided studio and nursery tours are available here.

The *Log* describes some of the sights you'd see if you landed at Fulford Harbour and explored the main routes. Please travel with care.

Fulford Harbour: A tiny ferry dock settlement full of island spirit. There are a few small houses perched on the hillside, a grocery store/gas station, post office, restaurant, ice cream, pottery, curios, marina, and a pub farther down the road overlooking the bay. It's the sort of place you don't mind hanging around, should you miss the ferry back to Swartz Bay. Unless it's the *last* ferry of the day. Be sure to check the schedule.

■ **Salt Spring Island Fibre Studios:** Write 121 Mountain Rd, Saltspring Island, BC, V8K 1T8. 250-537-2656 or 250-537-5137. New cooperative brings together island's traditional resources (sheep) and talents (arts and crafts) to produce hand-spun, hand-dyed yarns, and sophisticated designs. Demonstrations, workshops.

■ **Gulf Islands Experience:** 250-537-8895. Write Gulf Islands Experience, 2068 Musgrave Rd, Saltspring Island, BC, V8K 1V5. A chance to meet island artisans, ecologists, organic farmers, historians. Half-day to full weekend experiences include guided visits to historic sites, hiking trips, visits to organic farms and nurseries, workshops in fibre arts or pottery at island studios.

St Paul's Church: Tiny Catholic church overlooking Fulford Harbour. It's a heart-warming sight to travellers approaching the island on the ferry. The church was built between 1880 and 1883. Some building materials used were ferried from Vancouver Island's Cowichan Bay to Burgoyne Bay on Saltspring, then hauled by oxen-drawn stoneboat (a land-going barge) to the Fulford site.

Beaver Point Rd and Fulford-Ganges Rd: At the Y intersection above Fulford Harbour, the sharp right is Beaver Point Rd. The Fulford-Ganges Rd follows the gentle contour of the harbour – look for geese and swans that winter here – before cutting northwest into the heart of Saltspring Island.

The *Log* first follows Beaver Point Rd, then returns, tracing the route into Ganges.

Stowell Lake: About 1km from Fulford ferry terminal. A small trout-fishing and swimming hole on Beaver Point Rd,

Weston Lake: 2km beyond Stowell Lake, Weston is known for its trophy-sized trout. Swimming.

Beaver Point Provincial Park: 16ha. On Beaver Point Rd. This little park is site of the second-oldest school still standing in BC. After educating island youngsters for 66 years, it closed in 1951. Now it's a preschool.

Ruckle Provincial Park: 486ha; 70 walk-in campsites. At end of Beaver Point Rd. 250-391-2300. For group reservations, call 250-539-2115. The largest provincial park in the Gulf Islands. Embraces a working sheep farm, forest, and open, grassy field above a rocky shoreline where BC Ferries pass as they travel to and from Swartz Bay. It's a pleasant place to walk or just sit and watch the birds and marine traffic. The original Ruckle home, erected in 1876, stands near park entrance. Two other homes built around 1904 still house members of the Ruckle family. Another farmhouse was built in the 1940s, and is now park headquarters.

Return via Beaver Point Road to Fulford Harbour

Fulford Sunday Market: At head of Fulford Harbour, adjacent Fulford Inn. Local artists and craftspeople display their stuff, summer, early fall.

Drummond Park: Small park, at head of Fulford Harbour on west side. Site of a petroglyph: a sandstone carving of a seal.

Mill Farm Regional Park: 65ha. Undeveloped/no facilities. At the head of Fulford Harbour, turn left onto Isabella Point Rd, then right onto narrow and very rough Musgrave Rd. Not recommended for low-clearance vehicles or winter travel. Follow Musgrave Rd about 12km to signs. Former cooperative was acquired in 1996 as part of the Pacific Marine Heritage Legacy to protect its 26ha grove of old-growth Douglas fir and increasingly rare wildflower and Garry oak habitat. The park, on the western slopes of Mt Bruce, is home to two endangered species of butterfly and three endangered plants: the phantom orchid, the yellow montane violet, and the scalepod. Mt Bruce, at 698m, is the highest point in the Gulf Islands and a popular jumping-off spot for hang-gliders. Nearby Mt Tuam, 609m, forms the southwestern hump of Saltspring visible from the Saanich Peninsula. Its name comes from the Wsanec native word *cu-an*, "mountains at each end."

Akerman Museum: 2501 Fulford-Ganges Rd, 0.5km from Fulford Harbour. Private museum featuring First Nations' and settlers' artifacts. Call ahead, 250-653-4228.

High Mountain Honey: 2431 Fulford-Ganges Rd, 1km from Fulford Harbour. Honey for sale, and if proprietor is on hand, a hearty intro to local history.

Blackburn Meadows Golf Club: About 8km from Fulford Harbour, left onto Blackburn Rd, about 1km. 250-537-1707. Nine-hole target-style, chemical-free course. Family oriented.

Cusheon Lake Rd: About 9km from Fulford Harbour. Cusheon Lake, a short distance down the road, is a pleasant place for an August plunge.

Cranberry Rd: Turn off Fulford-Ganges Rd 2km beyond Cusheon Lake Rd. About 7km up this winding dirt road is Baynes Peak (595m), third highest peak on the Islands. Within the 197ha Mount Maxwell Provincial Park.

Mount Maxwell Provincial Park: 199ha. Take Cranberry Rd and follow signs. Too rough for RVs and low-slung cars. Breathtaking views of Fulford Harbour and islands beyond, Burgoyne Bay, Maple Bay, and Sansum Narrows between Saltspring and Vancouver Island. Hiking trails.

Mouat Regional Park: 23ha; 15-site campground. At foot of Ganges Hill in the village of Ganges. This small park is a wooded getaway amid the activity of Saltspring's major commercial centre. The Mouats emigrated from Scotland in the 1880s. The family is still a going concern on the island.

Ganges: (Pop. 1,133). This bustling seaside village – the largest in the Gulf Islands – belies the belief that the islands are sleepy hideaways on the edge of civilization. There are banks and shopping malls, supermarkets, liquor store, restaurants, laundromats, public showers, pharmacies, real estate offices, marinas, service stations, the Gulf Islands' Lady Minto Hospital, condominiums and anything else needed by some 10,000 islanders plus visitors. There's an outdoor **Saturday Market**, featuring fresh island produce and local artistry, at Centennial Park in the village centre. A 2km seaside walkway at the park brings harbour bustle and ocean views closer yet. Ganges is an arts centre, with several galleries within walking distance, featuring locally crafted pottery, stained glass, jewelry, basketry, weaving, paintings, and prints. The local Arts Council's summer-long show, Artcraft, representing over 200 Gulf Island artists and craftspeople, is at Mahon Hall, on the corner of Lower Ganges and Rainbow roads. Artspring is the new community arts building.

Upper-Lower Ganges Rd: Both lead northwest out of Ganges, linking up with roads to Vesuvius Bay and Long Harbour for ferries to Crofton on Vancouver Island, or the mainland at Swartz Bay.

Salt Spring Island Golf and Country Club: On Lower Ganges Rd, a short distance beyond Ganges. Nine-hole course open to public every day.

Vesuvius Bay Rd: Just beyond golf course. Northwest to Vesuvius Bay; southwest connects Upper Ganges Rd with Long Harbour Rd and ferries to mainland.

St Mary Lake: At junction of the Upper and Lower Ganges roads and Vesuvius Bay Rd. This is Saltspring's main resort area. Excellent trout and smallmouth bass fishing. Unfortunately there's only a small clearing at the roadside for public swimming and boat launching. Electric motors only.

Vesuvius Bay: At the end of Vesuvius Bay Rd. A handful of unassuming homes bent seaward, a restaurant, store, motel, and pub featuring local brews and enchanted views of Stuart Channel and Crofton on Vancouver Island. BC Ferries sail there from here. This was the home of Saltspring's first settlers in 1857 – nine American Blacks with newly purchased freedom.

Sunset Dr: Leads from Vesuvius to "the north end," the pointy end of Saltspring, eventually joining up with North End Rd, North Beach Rd, Walker's Hook Rd, Stark Rd, and reconnecting with the Upper Ganges Rd. This is a pleasant tour offering rolling farmland, grazing sheep, and sea views across Trincomali Channel to Galiano Island.

Long Harbour: Southeast from Vesuvius Rd and the Upper-Lower Ganges junction. At the end of Long Harbour Rd. BC Ferries terminal for sailings to the mainland and outer Gulf Islands.

The Pender Islands

North and South Pender islands, joined by a bridge, encompass 34 sq km, and are inhabited by about 2,000 permanent residents.

Before the turn of the century the Pender Islands were linked by a wide land neck known as the Indian Portage. The islands were separated in 1903, when a canal was dredged, then rejoined by a highway bridge in 1955. About 90 percent of the Penders' residents live on North Pender, mainly around Magic Lake. The islanders have conspicuously marked many of their public beach accesses and there are several quiet coves and bays to enjoy. Many of these places are sheltered, and a small boat opens lots of areas for exploration. Terminal for ferries from both Swartz Bay and Tsawwassen is at Otter Bay, on North Pender. The *Log* here describes some of the sights you'll find as you travel from Otter Bay.

Pender Islands Information: Info Centre at 2332 Otter Bay Rd, Box 75, Pender Island, BC, V0N 2M0. Located 800m from ferry terminal. Daily, June-Sept. No phone: in off-season call 250-681-6541, or ask at local businesses.

Pender Island Golf and Country Club: A nine-hole course on Otter Bay Rd between ferry terminal and Port Washington. Open to public.

Port Washington: On shores of Grimmer Bay, this is a small community with a government wharf.

South Otter Bay Protected Area: 215ha. From the ferry on Otter Bay Rd, turn right on South Otter Bay Rd, left on Shingle Bay Rd. Park at top of hill. Healthy wildlife habitat offers hiking trails through old-growth forest, along shorelines and ridge tops, and to Roe Lake, a small, warm lake.

Hope Bay: Another charming community with a government wharf.

Driftwood Centre: At intersection of Bedwell Harbour and Razor Point roads. The main commercial centre for the island. Nearby is Browning Harbour with a marina, pub, camping, and accommodation.

Prior Centennial Provincial Park: 16ha; 17-site campground (reservations taken: call 1-800-689-9025; from the Lower Mainland or overseas, call 604-689-9025). Off Canal Rd. General info: 250-391-2300. A nicely wooded provincial park. Hamilton and Medicine beaches within walking distance.

Magic Lake: Down Schooner Way, beyond Prior Centennial Park. Here is a major subdivision which, in the late 1960s and early 1970s, sparked a bitter controversy over

55

development on the Gulf Islands. The debate led to the formation of the Islands Trust, a group of elected representatives who govern the Gulf Islands in much the same manner as a municipal council. Thieves Bay, near the end of Schooner Way, is the location of a private marina.

Mortimer Spit: A sandy shore near the bridge between the two islands with sheltered waters, good swimming beaches.

Mount Norman Regional Park: Off Canal Rd linking North and South Pender islands, to Ainsley Rd, and follow signs to parking lot. Steep paths lead to highest point on the island (244m) for spectacular views of Pender Island and its neighbours.

Bedwell Harbour: At the end of Spalding Rd. In summer there is a Canadian Customs Port of Entry here for air and sea craft. Full-service destination resort and marina offers canoeing, kayaking, whale watching, and swimming. There is also a weekend shuttle to Hope Bay. 1-800-663-2899.

Church of the Good Shepherd: On Gowlland Point Rd, short walk from Bedwell Harbour resort. Rustic, wooden Anglican church built 1938 by Pender Island pioneers. A pleasant place to contemplate. Sunday services.

Beaumont Provincial Marine Park: 58ha; 11 walk-in campsites. North side of Bedwell Harbour, reached by boat or by 40-minute hike from Ainsley Point Rd through Mt Norman Regional Park. 250-391-2300. One of the most popular marine parks in the Gulf Islands. Can be reached by rowboat from Bedwell Harbour Resort. Trail from the park leads to top of Mt Norman (see above).

Galiano Island

Galiano is a long, narrow island on the outer edge of the southern Gulf Islands. It's the second largest of these islands, encompassing 57 sq km, with a population of about 1000. The driest of the Gulf Islands, it gets less than 60cm of rainfall a year. It's an attractive island with secluded beaches, sheltered harbours, and a relaxed pace. Ferries from both the BC mainland and Vancouver Island arrive on Galiano at Sturdies Bay.

Arts and crafts galleries, B&Bs, lodges, cottages, small resorts, seaside restaurants, bakery, pub, massage therapist, trail rides, kayaking tours, bike rentals and tours, fishing, sailing. The *Log* here describes sights you'll see as you travel from Sturdies Bay toward Porlier Pass at the northwest end of the island.

Galiano Island Information: Box 73, Galiano Island, BC, V0N 1P0. 250-539-2233. Information centre on Sturdies Rd near ferry terminal. Daily, July-Aug. Weekends, rest of year.

Sturdies Bay: At eastern end of Galiano Island. This is downtown Galiano, with a lodge, ferry terminal, information centre, and stores.

Bellhouse Provincial Park: 2ha. Day use. On south side of Sturdies Bay at Burrill Point. This rocky, moss-covered peninsula overlooking Active Pass is the busiest waterway in the Gulf Islands. Spincasting from shore for salmon, picnicking.

Galiano Bluffs Park: About 120m above Active Pass, this local park provides spectacular views of eagles, seabirds, sea lions (spring and fall migrants), seals, and other marine life in Active Pass, between Galiano and Mayne islands. Some of the largest ships in BC Ferries' fleet run alongside the bottom of the bluffs.

Winter Cove, Saturna Island.

Galiano Golf and Country Club: On Ellis Rd, off Porlier Pass Dr. Nine-hole course open to public.

Montague Harbour Provincial Marine Park: 97ha; 25 vehicle-access campsites/15 walk-in sites (reservations taken: call 1-800-689-9025; from the Lower Mainland or overseas, call 604-689-9025). 8km from ferry terminal. General info: 250-391-2300. The most popular provincial park in the Gulf Islands, with a campground for boaters and bicyclists, and one for vehicles. Shell beaches, warm summer swimming, and hiking are particularly attractive to families.

Retreat Cove: Turnoff 12km along Porlier Pass Dr from Sturdies Bay. Tiny cove with government wharf.

Bodega Ridge Nature Preserve: 150ha. Via Cottage Hills Way or Cook Rd at northwest end of Galiano. Part of federal-provincial Pacific Marine Heritage Legacy, (see p.21). 4km ridge rises from sea cliffs to island's 328m summit. Well-developed hiking trails wind through grasslands and old-growth Douglas fir, and along waterfront. Spectacular views, wildlife. Trail accesses cross private land, please be respectful. For info: Bodega Resort, 250-539-2677.

Spanish Hills: About 25km from Sturdies Bay on Porlier Pass Dr. Officially North Galiano. A one-store stop for sushi, burgers, and groceries.

Race Point Lighthouse: At the northwest end of Galiano Island, overlooking the turbulent waters of Porlier Pass. **Dionisio Provincial Park** (Coon Bay) here has limited facilities. Open fires not permitted.

Mayne Island

A total of 21 sq km, this island has about 550 permanent residents.

Mayne Island, with its BC Ferry terminal at **Village Bay**, has several late 1800s to 1930s buildings to intrigue the history buff. **Miners Bay**, the island's commerce centre, is a pleasant seaside village overlooking Active Pass. When gold was discovered on the Fraser River in 1858, Miners Bay was inundated with fortune seekers travelling between Vancouver Island and the mainland. The bay is precisely halfway between Vancouver Island and the mouth of the Fraser River, and was a convenient overnight stop for miners planning to row across Georgia Strait. That is comparatively recent history – middens excavated near Active Pass suggest at least 5,000 years of aboriginal occupation.

There are no provincial parks on Mayne Island, but there are nice beaches and sea views at **Village Bay, Miners Bay, Bennett Bay, Horton Bay,** and **Piggott Bay**. Sportfishermen often set up bases on Mayne Island to fish the waters in and around Active Pass, which provide some of the Gulf Islands' best salmon fishing.

Mayne Island Information: Mayne Island Community Chamber of Commerce, Box 2, Mayne Island, BC, V0N 2J0. 1-800-665-8577.

Mayne Island Museum: Opposite the community centre, off Fernhill Rd. Daily in summer. A small museum in a building that was built in 1896 as the Plumper Pass Lockup. It houses a variety of local artifacts providing insight into the island's history from the turn of the century.

St Mary Magdalene Church: Overlooking Miners Bay with a cemetery adjoining. Built in 1898, the church stands in a beautiful setting of arbutus and fir trees.

Active Pass Light Station: This station, on Georgina Point, is a familiar sight to people travelling aboard BC Ferries between Swartz Bay and Tsawwassen. Built in 1885.

Dinner Bay Community Park: Follow signs. Barbecue, washrooms. Great view.

Mount Parke Regional Park: Ask an islander for directions. Hiking trails and spectacular views from 255m peak.

Centennial Well: On Horton Bay Rd is the statue of a bearded angel watching over a well – it was built in 1967, Canada's centennial. The water is cold and clean.

Saturna Island

Although Saturna Island, with a total of 31 sq km, is larger than Mayne Island, its population is only 300.

There are a few B&Bs and cottages available for accommodation. No public campgrounds. It is largely used by day trippers and bicyclists, but check ferry schedules as service is not as frequent as to other islands. A government wharf next to BC Ferries' terminal at **Lyall Harbour** is a good launching point for canoeists or kayakers who want to explore the bays and channels between Boot Cove and Winter Cove.

Saturna Island Information: Info Centres in Vancouver, Victoria, and on Saltspring Island can provide accommodation listings for Saturna, with telephone numbers to call for information. People at the island's two stores and at the Lighthouse Pub are always willing to offer information.

Mount Warburton Pike: At 490m, the highest point on Saturna Island. Reached by a winding gravel road passing a 131ha ecological reserve protecting a typical West Coast forest. Tremendous views from the peak. Named after local pioneer, sportsman, and adventurer Warburton Pike, author of *The Barren Grounds of Northern Canada.*

Winter Cove Provincial Marine Park: 91ha. At end of Winter Cove Rd. This provincial park, established in 1979, is a scenic stretch of beach and rocky shore with small marshes and forests above the tide line. It offers trails, picnic tables and other amenities, but no campground.

East Point Regional Park: 2.5ha. Site of lighthouse built in 1888. It looks toward the Canada/US border from the most easterly point in the Gulf Islands, offering views of the San Juan Islands, the US Coast Guard Station on Patos Island, and Mt Constitution on Orcas Island. East Point, with its strange sandstone formations, is a naturalist's paradise: seals, sea lions, and an endless array of seabirds – harlequin ducks, loons, cormorants, sandpipers – can be seen. This is known to be one of the best places in the Gulf Islands to see killer whales in summer. Much of the marine life is attracted by strong tides that curl around the point, forming back eddies where small fish congregate. Birds and salmon feed on the fish and larger animals prey on the salmon. There's excellent spincasting for salmon here. A trail leads to the beach that can be walked at high tide. Be careful not to trespass onto private land.

VICTORIA TO NANAIMO

TRANS-CANADA HIGHWAY (Highway 1)

This, the westernmost stretch of the Trans-Canada Highway, begins at Mile Zero on Dallas Rd in Victoria, at the edge of Beacon Hill Park. (In downtown Victoria, Hwy 1 is Douglas St.) This is the most direct route to the city of Nanaimo, 113km up Vancouver Island's east coast.

The southern portion of the route passes through old forests, climbing to spectacular viewpoints overlooking Saanich Inlet and the Gulf Islands. Farther north, in the Cowichan and Chemainus valleys, scenery gives way to old bastions of the forest industry, and visitors are invited into the work-a-day world of the present and past. There are museums, log dumps, sawmills, a pulp mill, working boom boats, even a "demonstration" forest. Here, too, First Nations people are inviting visitors to experience the landscape as they know it.

The Trans-Canada Hwy leaves Vancouver Island at Nanaimo where BC Ferries sail to Horseshoe Bay and Tsawwassen, near Vancouver, on the mainland. Just before Nanaimo, the new Nanaimo Parkway (Hwy 19 East) gives travellers bound for points up island the welcome option of bypassing Nanaimo altogether. The 21km expressway hugs Nanaimo's western edge, and is interrupted by five controlled intersections, in contrast to the 19 lights that make for sluggish passage through the heart of the city.

This *Log* begins in downtown Victoria on Douglas St (Hwy 1).

Cloverdale Rd: 2km beyond Victoria City Hall (Pandora St, downtown Victoria). Route to access Hwy 17 for Victoria International Airport and BC Ferries at Swartz Bay. Continue on Douglas St (Hwy 1) for this *Log.*

McKenzie Ave: 3km beyond Cloverdale Rd. Busy route to access Hwy 17 and the University of Victoria (see p.40).

Helmcken Rd: 2km beyond McKenzie Ave. **Victoria General Hospital** is near Hwy 1. **Francis/King Regional Park** is north: left on W. Burnside, right on Prospect Lake Rd, left on Munn Rd. 11km of gentle woodland trails. Elsie King Trail is a cedar boardwalk for those with walking disabilities.

Colwood Interchange (Hwy 1A): 500m beyond Helmcken Rd. Exit to Hwys 1A and 14. See *Victoria to Port Renfrew,* p.48.

Thetis Lake Regional Park: 635ha. Take Hwy 1A/14 exit off Hwy 1; proceed to 6 Mile Rd, then turn right and enter the park. 250-478-3344. (Southbound take Exit 11). A popular swimming spot with sandy beaches and high cliffs. Consists of two lakes, and canoeists can squeeze through a cul-

Victoria to Nanaimo

vert where the lakes are joined. Good trout and bass fishing, ideal paddling with forested shoreline, islands, and no powerboats. Forested trails around lakes. Private campground next to park. 250-478-3845.

Millstream Rd: 12km beyond Victoria city centre. Leads north into the **Highlands** (pop. 1,210), incorporated as a municipality in 1995, and is one access to Gowlland Tod Provincial Park, see p.42. Road leads north and south into bedroom community of **Langford** (pop. 18,060). Connector to Hwy 14 and Western Communities of Colwood and Metchosin will be completed in 2002. (See p.49).

SIDE TRIP

to the Highlands

All Fun Waterslide Park: North at Millstream Rd. June-early Sept. 250-474-3184. Has 16 slides, whitewater river run, bumper boats, go-carts, driving range, mini-golf. 100-site RV park year-round. 250-474-4546.

Caleb Pike Homestead: 6.6km north of Hwy 1, on Millstream Rd. Open in summer. Mr. Pike arrived in 1850 to work for the Hudson's Bay Company. This was the heart of his sheep and cattle ranch.

Lone Tree Hill Regional Park: 31ha. 8km north of Hwy 1 on Millstream Rd. In the Highlands overlooking Finlayson Arm. Named for "heritage tree" at scenic summit – the decaying trunk of a Douglas fir. Bald eagles, red-tailed hawks, deer.

Return to Highway 1

Mill Hill Regional Park: 50ha. South on Millstream Rd to Atkins Rd. Left 1km to park. Mill Hill summit provides sweeping views of Esquimalt Harbour. Hiking trails through forest and wildflowers, wetlands.

Western Communities Information: 17km beyond Victoria city centre. Info Centre, West Shore Chamber of Commerce (representing **Colwood**, **Highlands**, **Langford**, **Metchosin**, and **View Royal**). 697 Goldstream Ave, Langford, BC, V9B 2X2. 250-478-1130. Year-round.

Goldstream Provincial Park: 394ha; 173 campsites (reservations taken: call 1-800-689-9025; from the Lower Mainland or overseas, call 604-689-9025). Sani-station. Turnoff to campground is 18.5km from city centre; turnoff to day-use area is 20km from Victoria city centre. General info: 250-391-2300. Slow highway speed as you pass by giant maples, virgin forests of Douglas fir and 600-year-old western red cedar. Thousands come to watch salmon (mostly chum, also coho and chinook) spawn here in the fall. The biggest run is usually around Remembrance Day weekend (early Nov). Trails along river on both sides of Hwy 1 reveal ferns, mushrooms, wildflowers and flowering dogwood trees. Visitor centre and salt marsh area near estuary. Old mine shafts from late 1800s when miners took small amounts of gold. From parking lot, it's about 200m to Mt Finlayson Trail sign, and start of three-hour steep hike through arbutus and oak groves to views of Finlayson Arm and Victoria.

Malahat Drive: Begins at Goldstream Park. This 16km drive over Malahat Mountain was a livestock track, sliced through rugged terrain in 1861. In 1884 it was upgraded to wagon-road standards, and became a paved road, over a slightly different route, in 1911. It has undergone repeated upgradings.

Spectacular forest-fringed drive offering glimpses of Finlayson Arm.

Shawnigan Lake South Access: West off Hwy 1, 28km north of Victoria. This road follows east shore of lake and rejoins Hwy 1 at Mill Bay. (Also a cutoff directly to north end of the lake, see below.)

SIDE TRIP

to Shawnigan Lake

Shawnigan Lake is a popular summer recreation and cottage area.

Shawnigan Lake: 7km drive through forest to lake. Well-established summer vacation area with old cottages and new houses along the lakeshore. Lake is 8km long and about 1km wide. Offers waterskiing, canoeing, swimming, fishing.

Memory Island Provincial Park: 1ha. Beautiful island with small beaches near south end of lake. The island was purchased by families who lost sons in the Second World War, and presented to the province as a park in their memory. Boat access only.

West Shawnigan Lake Provincial Park: 9ha. On northwest side. Take West Shawnigan Lake Rd at intersection about 6km from Hwy 1. Swimming, boating, family picnics. Safe children's beach.

Return to Highway 1

Spectacle Lake Provincial Park: 65ha. About 1km north of Shawnigan Lake south turnoff, follow signs west off Hwy 1. Good trout fishing. Trail around lake.

Malahat Summit: 31km north of Victoria. At 352m, marked by Salish Bear totem pole. Excellent views of lower Saanich Inlet, eastern Vancouver Island's only inlet. Details on p.41. Access for northbound traffic only.

Arbutus Rest Area: 32km north of Victoria. Try solar-powered composting toilets set amid small grove of large arbutus trees. Stunning views.

Gulf Islands Viewpoint: 33km north of Victoria. A very worthwhile stop. Spectacular views across Saanich Inlet to Saanich Peninsula, southern Gulf Islands, American San Juan Islands. The volcanic peak of Washington State's Mt Baker (3,285m) shimmers in background.

Bamberton Provincial Park: 28ha; 50 campsites (reservations taken: call 1-800-689-9025; from the Lower Mainland or overseas, call 604-689-9025). 36km north of Victoria, east at bottom of Malahat Dr on Mill Bay Rd. Park entrance 1km. General info: 250-391-2300. Oceanfront park with sandy swimming beach on Saanich Inlet, adjacent former cement factory. There's salmon fishing in the

inlet and a public boat launch farther along Mill Bay Rd at the end of Handy Rd.

Brentwood-Mill Bay Ferry: Just beyond Bamberton Park entrance on Mill Bay Rd is turnoff to ferry terminal. 250-386-3431. Car and passenger ferry across Saanich Inlet to Brentwood Bay, near Butchart Gardens. Sailings every hour and 10 minutes from early morning to early evening.

Mill Bay: (Pop. 953). 41km north of Victoria. It's worth a detour off the highway to explore quiet waterfront streets and Gulf Island views. Nearby Satellite Channel good spot to see seals clamouring on floats and docks. Community is expanding, with service stations, shopping centre, marina, and liquor store. Also government wharf, public boat ramp, swimming. Farmers-Flea Market summer weekends.

Mill Bay Information: South Cowichan Chamber of Commerce in Mill Bay Shopping Centre, Deloume Rd, RR 1, Mill Bay, BC, V0R 2P0. 250-743-3566. On Hwy 1 at Shawnigan Lake-Mill Bay Rd. Year-round, self-service, seasonally staffed.

Shawnigan Lake-Mill Bay Rd: North end of Mill Bay. This is the north entrance to the community of Shawnigan Lake. 5km to lake and village.

Shawnigan Lake: (Pop. 1,020). Public beach on Renfrew Rd across from Mason's Store (turn right at village).
■ **Shawnigan Lake Museum:** In old firehall on four-corner stop in village. 250-743-3566. Open afternoons, July-Aug.
■ **Auld Kirk Gallery:** Exhibits work of artists attracted to area. 250-743-4811.

Beyond Mill Bay on Hwy 1, the scenery begins to reflect "up-island" realities. Highwayside businesses advertise their wares: second-hand goods, antiques, used cars, wood and wood stoves, taxidermy.

Vineyard Tours: On the pastoral slopes off Hwy 1 between Mill Bay and Cowichan Bay are four vineyards and a cidery welcoming visitors for tours and tastes. Maps available from Mill Bay Information Centre or Duncan-Cowichan Info Centre (below).
■ **Merridale Cider:** Along Shawnigan-Mill Bay Rd, turn right at Cameron-Taggert Rd, then right onto Merridale. 250-743-4293. Tours and sales, Mon-Sat, year-round.
■ **Vignetta Zanatta:** 5039 Marshall Rd. 250-748-2338. Producing Italian-style wines for four decades. Restaurant. Call for tour and tasting times.
■ **Blue Grouse Vineyards:** 4365 Blue Grouse Rd. 250-743-3834. Traditional German-style wines. Wed, Fri, Sat, Sun, 11-5, year round.
■ **Venturi Schulze Vineyards:** 4235 Trans-Canada Hwy (Hwy 1), Cobble Hill. 250-743-5630. Produces wine and Balsamic vinegar. Accommodation in century-old farmhouse. Tours and tastings by appointment.
■ **Cherry Point Vineyards:** 840 Cherry Point Rd, Cobble Hill. 250-743-1272. Winery and B&B. Tours daily, 11:30-6.

Steam locomotive displayed at the BC Forest Museum near Duncan.

■ **Alderley Vineyards:** 1751 Stamps Rd. 250-746-7122. Thurs-Sun, 1-5 or by appointment. Tours Sat-Sun, 2pm. Distinctly Cowichan Valley dry whites and reds.

Arbutus Ridge: 45km beyond Victoria, follow signs leading east off Hwy 1. An instant utopia: 676 homes planned, most completed on 300-acre development by Canadian Retirement Corporation of Richmond, BC. There are a few arbutus trees near the golf course, but the slope, highly visible from Satellite Channel, has been unsympathetically cleared of vegetation. 18-hole golf course open to public.

Cobble Hill-Cowichan Bay Roads: 48km north of Victoria; 7km north of Shawnigan Lake-Mill Bay Rd on Hwy 1. West to **Cobble Hill** (village and area pop. 3,000) and **Shawnigan Lake**. **Quarry Regional Wilderness Park** offers 2- to 3km hike up Cobble Hill, through mature forest and views over Shawnigan Lake, Gulf Islands, Saanich Peninsula, Cowichan Bay. Cowichan Bay Rd leads east to Cowichan Bay and then reconnects with Hwy 1.

Cowichan Rest Area: East side of Hwy 1 at Cobble Hill-Cowichan Bay roads.

SIDE TRIP

to Cowichan Bay

Cowichan Bay: (Pop. 2,679). At Cowichan River estuary. Sportfishing and forestry village with hotels, pub, restaurants, marinas, charters, fish market. A salty, charming, weathered ambience. Major log dump and sawmill at head of bay. Boom boats operating.

■ **Wooden Boat Society and Cowichan Bay Maritime Centre:** Village centre. 250-746-4955. Write Box 787, Duncan, BC, V9L 3Y1. Daily, 10-dusk, April-Sept. Society, dedicated to preserving traditional skills, offers courses in small-boat building. Centre's maritime memorabilia shows area's development. Hands-on exhibits. Local artists in summer.

■ **Marine Ecology Station:** Pier 66 (1751 Cowichan Bay Rd). 250-748-4522. Daily, 12-5 in summer, otherwise Sat-Sun afternoons. Groups by arrangement. Aquarium exhibits of different BC marine habitats, and unusual mini-aquariums with microscopes for eyeball-to-eyeball encounters with little critters like hermit crabs, fan worms, and starfish. Sailing charters from nearby Pier 66.

■ **South Cowichan Lawn Tennis Club:** Beyond village at intersection of Cowichan Bay and Tzouhalem roads. 250-746-7282. Second oldest tennis club in British Commonwealth after Wimbledon. Now a BC Heritage Site. Annual Grass-Court Championships held since 1887 is now three events, one each in June, July, Aug. Lawn courts a rare pleasure. Open to public.

■ **Hecate Regional Park and Theik Reserve Footpath:** 1.5ha. Off highway in village. Shoreline footpath traverses one of several Cowichan Tribes reserves and offers birdwatching and views of Mt Tzouhalem, or as the Cowichan people know it, S'khowtzun Smend, "warmed by the sun."

Return to Highway 1

Dougan Lake: About 51km north of Victoria. Excellent trout fishing.

Cowichan Station Rd: 52.5km north of Victoria. Leads to Cowichan Station and **Bright Angel Provincial Park** on Koksilah River, with playground, river swimming, picnicking. Lovely cycling territory.

Whippletree Junction: 53.5km north of Victoria; 7km south of Duncan. Daily. Recreated turn-of-the-century village with 14 restored buildings from Duncan's old Chinatown and elsewhere. Specialty shops.

Cowichan Golf and Country Club: 55.5km north of Victoria. 250-746-5333. 18-hole, full-facility course with enchanted views of Mt Tzouhalem.

Cowichan Bay Rd: 56.5km north of Victoria. Northerly turnoff (east) to Cowichan Bay.

Hwy 1 descends into the Cowichan Valley, home of the Cowichan First Nation, and one of two main agricultural valleys on Vancouver Island.

Old Farm Market: 57km north of Victoria. People come all the way from Victoria for local vegetables and fruit in season.

Cowichan River Footpath: 58.5km north of Victoria, Allenby Rd leads west off Hwy 1. 1.5km to stop sign; left on Indian Rd, right onto Glenora Rd, then right on Vaux Rd, and finally onto Robertson Rd. 8km from Allenby turnoff to Cowichan Fish and Game Association parking lot. 250-746-1070. Water, washrooms, phone. Start of 19km anglers' and hikers' trail tracing one of Vancouver Island's most popular recreational rivers. The Cowichan River is known for rainbow and steelhead trout and sizable salmon runs, and is one of only two BC river systems with brown trout, a trophy species introduced to the Cowichan and Qualicum rivers in the 1930s. Trail transects **Cowichan River Provincial Park** and is also accessed from Hwy 18 (see p.64). Shorter loops of trail can be hiked. Maps at Duncan-Cowichan Info Centre (below).

Cowichan River: 59.5km north of Victoria, at southern edge of Duncan, Silver Bridge spans Cowichan River. From its headwaters at Cowichan Lake, river winds 47km through canyons and forests, flows under this bridge, then through Cowichan Tribes reserve and pastoral farmland at its estuary on Cowichan Bay.

Duncan: (Pop. 4,583). 61km north of Victoria. The city of Duncan grew up from a whistle stop at William Duncan's farm in the 1880s. Today, it is the main centre for the Cowichan Valley's 74,000 residents.

The valley is the original home of the Cowichan Tribes, with about 3,000 people living mostly in Duncan and six adjacent reserve communities. The Cowichan people are known today for their heavy, warm woolen sweaters, toques, mitts, and other knitted garments. Their history and culture is shared at the **Cowichan Native Village** (below) and throughout Duncan, which refers to itself as the City of Totems. Since 1985, 41 carved poles have been erected along the highway and in the downtown area. A guidebook, available from the Duncan Info Centre, tells of the carvers, the traditional poles and the non-traditional, such as "Transition," depicting three killer whales and a seal, and the "Rick Hansen Man-in-Motion Pole," featuring the celebrated wheelchair athlete supporting the earth. Another 80 poles, some privately owned, are located throughout the Cowichan Valley.

Duncan is also home of nationally acclaimed artist E.J. Hughes. In 1949, Group of Seven artist Lawren Harris said Hughes was "as distinctive and visionary a painter of the West Coast as Emily Carr." His oil landscapes are realistic, colourful renderings of local beaches, inlets, log booms, ferries gliding into Saltspring Island's Fulford Harbour, views of Shawnigan Lake. Despite, or maybe because of, his national reputation, his work is not easy to find on the West Coast. Try the University of Victoria, Victoria Art Gallery, the Vancouver Art Gallery.

To appreciate browse-worthy Duncan, turn west off Hwy 1 thoroughfare.

Duncan Information: Info Centre, 381 Trans-Canada Hwy, Duncan, BC, V9L 3R5. 250-746-4636. In Overwaitea Centre Mall on Hwy 1. April-Oct.

■ **Cowichan Native Village:** 200 Cowichan Way, Duncan, BC, V9L 4T8. 250-746-8119. Turn left immediately after crossing Cowichan River on Silver Bridge. Excellent multimedia presentation and exhibits tell the history of the Cowichan people from the beginning of time to the present. Artists and elders work on site, and in summer the Feasts and Legends program and the Mid-day Salmon BBQ honour visitors with traditional-style food, storytelling, and dancing. The centre has a large collection of arts and crafts, books, hand-knit Cowichan sweaters, and cafe and restaurant offering native foods. Daily, year-round.

■ **Cowichan Valley Museum:** 120 Canada Ave, Via Rail or Duncan Station. Mon-Sat and some Sundays, 10-4, June-Sept. Wed-Fri, 11-4, Sat 12-4, Oct-May. Call 250-746-6612 or write Cowichan Historical Society, Box 1014, Duncan, BC, V9L 3Y2. In 1912 train station. Domestic artifacts, tools, and medical equipment displayed in period-room settings. Also photo and archival collection and special exhibits.

■ **Freshwater Ecocentre:** 1080 Wharncliffe Rd. East off Hwy 1 onto Trunk Rd, then follow signs. 250-746-6722. Interactive exhibits on wetland wildlife and fisheries; aquarium, theatre. Trout hatchery next door.

■ **Cowichan and Chemainus Valleys Ecomuseum Society:** 160 Jubilee St, Duncan, BC, V9L 3X8. Downtown. 250-746-1611. The ecomuseum, a museum without walls, takes in the two valleys' 1,000 sq km, revealing the legacy of the forest industry that developed this region. Residents are actively involved in showing visitors their heritage, and the value

and beauty of the region. Fascinating information on area sites. Natural history also available here. Daily, April-Oct: woods and mill tours. July-Aug: join in on Skutz Falls walking tours.

■ **Yokum Valley Golf:** 5551 Jordan Lane, off Hwy 18 and follow signs. 250-748-6360. Par 3 golf, night golf, putting green, catch-and-release trout-fishing tournaments, restaurant, RV parking.

■ **Duncan Meadows Golf Course:** 6507 North Rd, off Hwy 18 and follow signs. 250-746-8993.

■ **Fun Pacific:** 2591 Beverley St, off Hwy 1 at north end of town. 250-746-4441. Driving range, mini-golf, go-carts.

■ **World's Largest Hockey Stick:** North end of town, near community centre on Hwy 1. It is 63m high; formerly at Expo 86.

SIDE TRIP

to Maple Bay

From downtown Duncan, turn east onto Trunk Rd.

Quamichan Lake: Follow Trunk Rd to Tzouhalem Rd and take turnoff (left) to Maple Bay Rd. A few metres to Indian Rd leads to **Art Mann Park** on lake. Marshy shoreline and island with otters and abundant waterfowl. Especially good birdwatching during fall migrations and spring nesting. Trout fishing. Launching from shore at park.

Maple Bay: (Pop. 1,098). 6km from start of Maple Bay Rd. Idyllic seaside community overlooking bay and Sansum Narrows, between Vancouver Island and Saltspring Island. Municipal park beach, government wharf, marinas, charters, restaurants, shops, pubs. Kayaking, windsurfing, diving.

Genoa Bay: Sheltered cove off Cowichan Bay about 8km south of Maple Bay. Take Genoa Bay Rd off Maple Bay Rd and drive to end. Marina, restaurant. Hiking on Mt Tzouhalem.

Return to Highway 1

Somenos Marsh Wildlife Refuge: 62km north of Victoria, just north of Duncan. East side of highway. 48ha nesting and wintering habitat for some two dozen waterfowl and several upland bird species. Owned by Nature Trust of BC. View from highway pullout or take short trail about 50m north of pullout to nesting project managed by Ducks Unlimited Canada. Summer viewing for nesting birds, thousands of wintering waterfowl.

BC Forest Museum: 63km north of Victoria. Daily, early May-late Sept. 250-715-1113. On more than 40ha near Somenos Lake. Portrays history of BC's forest industry through indoor and outdoor exhibits. Working sawmill and restored planer mill on the site provide lumber for the museum. Blacksmith's shop, pit saw, and activities such as leaf rubbing, hands-on games, plus aquari-

um and terrarium. Most intriguing feature is a narrow-gauge steam locomotive that travels through a farmstead, logging camp, and forest, and over the Somenos Lake trestle.

Highway 18: Off Hwy 1, 65.5km north of Victoria. West 28km to Lake Cowichan. East onto Herd Rd for Maple Bay. See *Lake Cowichan to Bamfield*, p.64.

Crofton: (Pop. 2,500). 72.5km north of Victoria, turn east off Hwy 1 for 6km drive to hamlet overlooking Osborne Bay. One of BC's first instant towns, Crofton, built in 1902, was a smelter site for copper from Mr Croft's mine on nearby Mt Sicker. The smelter closed in 1908. Since 1957, Crofton has been a pulp-mill town. There are pubs, motels, restaurants, an RV park, fishing off the wharf, swimming at Crofton Beach or **Osborne Bay Regional Park**, or the local pool. Half-hour hike or longer to Maple Mountain Municipal Park. Ask at Info Centre.

Crofton Information: Info Centre, Crofton Museum and Community Centre, Box 128, Crofton, BC, V0R 1R0. 250-246-2456. Next to BC Ferries' terminal at foot of Joan Ave. Daily in summer.

Saltspring Island Ferry: At foot of Joan St in Crofton. Car and passenger ferries to Saltspring's **Vesuvius Bay** leave Crofton regularly from morning until early evening. 250-386-3431. For details on Saltspring Island see *Gulf Islands*, p.52.

■ **Crofton (Old School) Museum:** Next to ferry terminal. Summer. Features local Mt Sicker copper mining and refining industry.

■ **Fletcher Challenge Pulp Mill Tours:** 250-246-6006. Tues and Thurs, 1pm.

Follow sign-posted back roads from Crofton to the small town of Chemainus, or continue on Hwy 1 for 15km, to Chemainus turnoff.

Chemainus: (Pop. 3,900). 77km north of Victoria, then 2km east off Hwy 1. Overlooking Stuart Channel. Canada's largest permanent outdoor art gallery. Chemainus, in the municipality of North Cowichan, faced economic uncertainty in the early 1980s with the closure of the town's sawmill. But an ambitious revitalization program was launched, centred on the work of talented artists who painted murals depicting the area's history on downtown walls. Now as many as 300,000 visitors a year come to see the 33 larger-than-life murals. The newest one, *Memories of a Chinese Boy*, is located near the Info Centre. Chemainus, calling itself "The Little Town That Did," is becoming a Canadian art centre. There are also sculptors, potters, painters, glassworkers and First Nations artists. A new sawmill has opened, and Chemainus is now a two-industry town.

Chemainus Information: Info Centre, Chemainus and District Chamber of Commerce, Box 575, Chemainus, BC, V0R 1K0. 250-246-4701. At 9796 Willow St, across from Waterwheel Park. Year-round. In summer, there is also a Mural Information Kiosk across the street.

■ **Chemainus Theatre:** Corner of Chemainus

Chiefs and elders of Vancouver Island's past are brought to life on a Chemainus mural.

■ **Black Nugget Museum:** 12 Gatacre St, half a block off Hwy 1. May-Sept. 250-245-4846. In a partially restored hotel built in 1881, and moved to Ladysmith from Wellington, another coal mining community north of Nanaimo. Native artifacts, period garments, furniture, household goods.

■ **Transfer Beach:** 5ha. Local park on Ladysmith Harbour at south entrance to town. Warm summer swimming, picnicking. Horseshoe pitch, shelters, wooded waterfront walkway leading to heritage harbour site, and award-winning Kinsmen Kidland Adventure Playground. RV park.

■ **Main Street Ladysmith:** Stroll by restored buildings on 1st Ave, also art gallery, gift shops, antiques and collectibles. Walking-tour map available.

■ **Holland Trail System:** Stroll beach front and wooded hills. Ladysmith Parks, 250-245-6424.

Ivy Green Park and Campground: 93km north of Victoria. 250-741-4985. Late May to mid-Sept. Former provincial park was returned to Chemainus First Nation as part of land claim. Visitors welcome to visit day-use area: swim in Ladysmith Harbour; view first-growth Douglas fir, stroll trails. Overnight camping. The Chemainus First Nation and Vancouver Island Highway Project have cooperated to create an enhanced fish habitat and traditional-use plant garden at nearby Bush Creek, to be completed early 1999.

Cedar Rd-Yellowpoint Rd: 95km north of Victoria. Cedar Rd, which leads to the Nanaimo bedroom community of Cedar, is also the starting point of a pleasant 22km triangular loop tracing Yellow Point Rd to the sea and back, to rejoin Cedar Rd near Nanaimo.

SIDE TRIP

to Cedar and Yellow Point

The Cedar Rd-Yellow Point Rd junction is 3km east of Hwy 1. From here, the road meanders westward and seaward by rolling fields, fir and arbutus groves, phlegmatic sheep, cows and horses at pasture, galleries, guest houses, lodges, and pubs. It is about 8km to Yellow Point and the Yellow Point Lodge, offering Gulf Island views, gravel beaches, and sandstone shores.

Roberts Memorial Provincial Park: 14ha. About 3km beyond Yellow Point. Quiet spot on ocean. Picnicking, swimming, fishing.

Quennell Lake: About 4km beyond Roberts Memorial Park. Interesting 121ha canoeing lake with a number of long arms and narrow channels. Noted for its smallmouth bass and trout fishing.

Hemer Provincial Park: 93ha. On Holden Lake. Follow signs from Yellow Point Rd. Lovely walk through forest along lakeshore. Easy hiking, horseback riding, fishing, and canoeing.

Rd and Victoria St. In the building with the dome. Reservations: 250-246-9820 or 1-800-565-7738. Dinner theatre offers "high cuisine buffet," matinees and evening presentations of popular classics.

■ **Chemainus Valley Museum:** In Waterwheel Park. 250-246-2445.

Thetis and Kuper Islands Ferry: A small car and passenger ferry runs from downtown Chemainus to these two islands. Kuper Island (pop. 271) is home to the Penelakut First Nation. Thetis Island (pop. 235) is an interesting place for a drive or bicycle ride. Its shores are often explored by paddlers. Summer sea is warm for swimming.

Mt Breton Golf Club: On Henry Rd and Hwy 1 (Chemainus turnoff). Box 187, Chemainus, BC, V0R 1K0. 250-246-9322. 18 holes in a pretty setting.

Ladysmith: (Pop. 6,456). 87km north of Victoria. Ladysmith bears a slight resemblance to early San Francisco, with its old houses built on steep slopes above the sea. Overlooking its deepwater harbour, Ladysmith

is the true Vancouver Island location of the 49th Parallel. This Canada/US boundary was extended south of Victoria to keep all of the island in Canada.

The town was first named Oyster Harbour for the abundant oyster beds nearby. During the Boer War, BC coal-mining magnate James Dunsmuir renamed it for Ladysmith, South Africa, and named the streets after Boer War generals. This was a coal mining town, and in 1913 was the scene of one of the most bitter labour disputes in Canadian history as unrest over safety and union issues spread here from Cumberland to the north. Many of Ladysmith's original buildings here were brought by rail from Extension Mines near Nanaimo.

In the 1930s, the local economy turned from mining to forestry. Tourism is increasingly important: there are attractive heritage buildings in the downtown core; new housing developments are swallowing up the peripheries. Boat launch.

Ladysmith Information: Ladysmith Chamber of Commerce, 216 Gatacre St, Box 598, Ladysmith, BC, V0R 2E0. 250-245-Daily, June-Sept.

From here, Yellow Point Rd continues northeast, eventually rejoining Cedar Rd. (The Crow and Gate British-style pub, just before the junction, is a worthwhile stop.)

Cable Bay Trail: Take Cedar Rd to Harmac Junction, near the Millway Store. Turn left onto Holden-Corso Rd. Follow it into the Cedar District, to Barnes Rd, then left onto Nicola Rd. Challenging 1.9km trail leads to Cable Bay Bridge; informal trail continues about 1km to Dodd Narrows. Listen for the sea lions barking.

Brother Twelve: Take Cedar Rd to Harmac Junction, near the Millway Store. Turn left onto Holden-Corso Rd. Follow it into the Cedar District, to Barnes Rd, then Fawcett Rd and Murdoch Rd.

He is long gone, but some of the houses here – now privately owned and renovated – are vestiges of the Twelfth Brother of an occult brotherhood, The Great White Lodge, said to guide the evolution of the human race. A series of remarkable visions led Brother Twelve, a middle-aged English sea captain named Edward Arthur Wilson, to this picturesque knob of land, Cedar-by-the-Sea, in the late 1920s. Here, sounding "the first trumpet blast of the New Age," the prophet shared his visions and accumulated vast sums of money from his thousands of followers. He also sought, and failed to gain, world power by influencing the US presidency. The House of Mystery is on a cliff above the boat ramp at the foot of Nelson Rd. Little remains of another settlement on nearby **Valdes Island**.

Ultimately, Brother Twelve moved his utopia 2km across Stuart Channel, to **De Courcy Island**, only accessible by private boat. At the lagoon on the island's south end, now **Pirate's Cove Provincial Marine Park**, he established headquarters, hoarded gold in mason jars, and drove his followers to the point of revolt in the construction of his bastion against Armageddon. Brother Twelve, and his "bizarre" companion, Madame Zee, disappeared with some $400,000 in bank notes and gold. There's some evidence he died in Switzerland shortly thereafter. There's some evidence he didn't. For more, read *Brother Twelve: The Incredible Story of Canada's False Prophet*, by John Oliphant.

From here Cedar Rd continues north and rejoins Hwy 1 about 11km north of Cedar Rd's south access.

The *Log* proceeds from the south access.

Return to Highway 1

Nanaimo (Cassidy) Airport: Entrance road off Hwy 1, 2.5km north of Cedar Rd's south access. 97.5km north of Victoria. Scheduled and charter flights.

Nanaimo Community Hatchery: Turn onto Beck Rd (at Cassidy Inn), 99km beyond Victoria. Write Nanaimo River Salmonid Enhancement Program, 271 Pine St, Nanaimo, BC, V9R 2B7. 250-245-7780. Follow signs to hatchery: chinook, coho, chum. Open year-round.

Cassidy Rest Area: At turnoff to hatchery. Information board.

Nanaimo River Bridge: 99.5km beyond Victoria. A major recreational fishing stream, Nanaimo River runs more than 60km from its headwaters, west of Green Mountain, through a series of lakes to Nanaimo Harbour.

The Bungy Zone and Nanaimo Lakes: About 100km beyond Victoria, at Nanaimo River Rd. 1-800-668-7771 or 250-753-5867. Daily, hours vary. No reservations required. Road leads to North America's first legal bridge jump site, at the Nanaimo River gorge. Your chance to plunge 50m with just an elastic bungy cord tied to your ankles. The "Ultimate Swing" swings daredevils through canyon at 140km/h. The annual Naked Bungy Weekend is something to see. Tenting, hot tub, volleyball, dining.

Farther on, the Nanaimo River leads to the Nanaimo Lakes for wilderness camping, fishing, and chances to see elk, deer, black bears, maybe even the endangered Vancouver Island marmot. Paved road quickly becomes logging road: visitors must check in at the Fletcher Challenge security gate, about 22km from

Hwy 1. Be well informed about road conditions before you head in: this is a route for "responsible" travellers. Contact Fletcher Challenge, 250-754-3032, and pick up their *Nanaimo Lakes Road Guide*.

Eaglequest Family Golf: 100km beyond Victoria. 1601 Thatcher Rd, Nanaimo, BC, V9R 5X9. 250-754-1325.

Highway 19 East (Duke Point Interchange): 104km north of Victoria; 14km south of Nanaimo. New expressway leads 8.5km off Hwy 1 to **Duke Point Terminal**, opened in 1997 to serve **BC Ferries** traffic between Vancouver's **Tsawwassen** terminal and Nanaimo. Snack bar, play area, video games, and washrooms. A walkway runs the length of the terminal facing out to Northumberland Channel: here are spectacular views of the Coast Mountains, Gabriola Island, and scenes of Nanaimo's bustling forest industry at work.

Biggs and Jack Point Parks: Adjacent Duke Point Ferry Terminal. Access via Hwy 19, 4.5km from Hwy 1. These Nanaimo City parks, linked by a

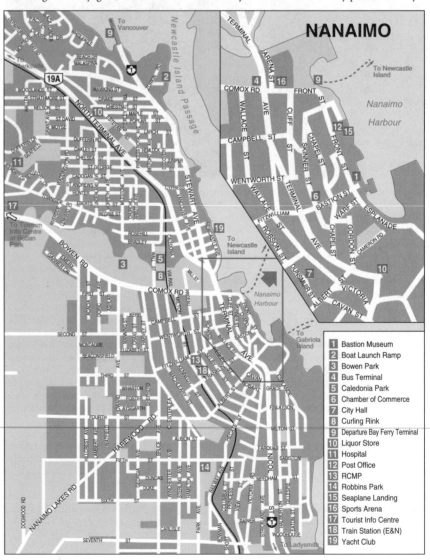

NANAIMO

1	Bastion Museum
2	Boat Launch Ramp
3	Bowen Park
4	Bus Terminal
5	Caledonia Park
6	Chamber of Commerce
7	City Hall
8	Curling Rink
9	Departure Bay Ferry Terminal
10	Liquor Store
11	Hospital
12	Post Office
13	RCMP
14	Robbins Park
15	Seaplane Landing
16	Sports Arena
17	Tourist Info Centre
18	Train Station (E&N)
19	Yacht Club

short trail, offer hiking along shores, tidal pools and bluffs, with opportunities to see forest animals and seabirds, and endless views of Nanaimo Harbour, Nanaimo estuary, and the Strait of Georgia.

Highway 19 West (Nanaimo Parkway): 105.5km north of Victoria, the Nanaimo Parkway, completed in 1997, departs from Hwy 1 on its 21km express route along the western edge of Nanaimo (see below). Five major intersections controlled by lights provide access to Nanaimo. The lights – though a considerable improvement over the 21 possible stops faced by travellers on the highway *through* Nanaimo – are a bane for many who ask: why not interchanges instead? Economic feasibility, replies the Vancouver Island Highway Project. From the start of the Parkway, the lighted intersections are located as follows. 8km: College Dr/Fifth St (to Malaspina College). 10km: Jingle Pot Rd (to downtown and residential areas). 13km: Northfield Rd (to Visitor Info Centre, restaurants, bakery). 16km: Jingle Pot Rd (to commercial/industrial area) and Mostar Rd (to Rutherford Mall). 20km: Aulds Rd (to Woodgrove Shopping Centre). The Parkway rejoins Hwy 1 just beyond the Woodgrove Shopping Centre. For recreational opportunities along **Nanaimo Parkway Trailway**, see below.

Cedar Rd (north access): 106km beyond Victoria on Hwy 1. Another access to the Yellow Point area. (Described above.)

Petroglyph Provincial Park: 2ha. About 108km north of Victoria on Hwy 1. Trails to rock carvings believed to be more than 10,000 years old. Human figures, birds, wolves, lizards, sea monsters, and supernatural creatures are represented. There are other petroglyphs in Nanaimo area. Check with Nanaimo museum.

Nanaimo: (Pop. 70,130). City centre is 3km beyond Petroglyph Park; about 113km north of Victoria. Hwy 1, the Trans-Canada, cuts through the city, leaving Vancouver Island at the Departure Bay ferry terminal. Hwy 19, known as the Island Highway, begins on the north side of the Pearson Bridge, just past Comox Rd and continues north.

The name Nanaimo comes from Sne ney mux – the people who have lived in villages along the Nanaimo River, harbour, and bays since time immemorial, and were here when the first coal mine was developed by the Hudson's Bay Company in 1852. The Sne ney mux worked in the mines alongside European and Chinese labourers until the early 1900s.

The greater demand for oil in the early 1930s spelled the demise of the coal industry, but today the port of Nanaimo, with six deep-sea docks and two major ferry terminals, is Vancouver Island's largest export centre, and one of the fastest growing communities in the province. It is a hub of activity with freighters and fishboats, tugs and barges, yachts and floatplanes coming and going in the harbour.

To appreciate Nanaimo is to get off the highway through its heart – an eyesore of malls and signage that gives the city an understandable but underrated reputation. The city has recently undergone beautification: foundries, mills, and other heavy industries that once dominated the downtown waterfront, though still vital to the city's economy, have found new locations away from downtown in places established specifically for industrial use. Waterfront walkways, gardens, lawns, golf courses, and beaches are taking up the space industrial sites once occupied.

People now can stroll along Nanaimo's 4.4km **Harbourfront Walkway**, past a new seaplane terminal and the Bastion, the city's most notable landmark, to Departure Bay. A footbridge – the Lions Great Bridge – built by the local Lions Club across the Millstone River, links the walkway to the Queen Elizabeth Promenade. Waterfront enhancements emphasize the city's picturesque setting, with the harbour surrounded by wooded islands, the distant peaks of the Coast Mountains rising over Georgia Strait, and at night, the lights of Vancouver.

This city has about two dozen parks totalling 1,100ha. Visiting them could stretch a stay in Nanaimo to several days. Brochure available at Info Centre.

Nanaimo is renowned for its abundance of shopping malls, and despite the new Nanaimo Parkway which diverts much through traffic, Nanaimo's core continues to be very busy, and new malls are under construction.

Nanaimo Information: Info Centre, Nanaimo Tourist and Convention Bureau, Beban House, 2290 Bowen Rd, Nanaimo, BC, V9T 3K7. 250-756-0106.

Departure Bay Ferry Terminal: At the end of the Trans-Canada Hwy on Nanaimo's north side. BC Ferries sail to Horseshoe Bay in West Vancouver (see p.118).

Duke Point Ferry Terminal: 14km south of Nanaimo on Hwy 19 East. BC Ferries sail from here to Tsawwassen, south of Vancouver (see p. 110).

■ **Nanaimo District Museum:** Adjacent Harbour Park Mall at 100 Cameron St. 250-753-1821. Daily, late May to mid-Sept. Tues-Sat, rest of year. Museum has been working closely with the Sne ney mux First Nation to produce *From Our Elders' Elders*, an exhibit which includes artifacts repatriated from museums around the world; other artifacts, an estimated 2,000 years old, were found on Departure Bay beach, a former village site. Also here, a coal mine, pioneer town, and Chinese gallery.

■ **The Bastion:** Corner of Bastion and Front streets. 250-753-1821. Daily July 1-Sept 1. Housed in part of the original Hudson's Bay Fort, the Bastion's collection focuses on the period 1850-1880. Includes insignia, handguns, photographs. Archives of military records, property deeds, and personal documents. Site of Noon Gun ceremony: each day during summer, Bastion guardsmen dressed in colourful naval uniforms of the 1850s, are led to the Bastion by a piper. Under the orders of an officer a cannon is elaborately cleaned, loaded, and fired over the harbour, a salute to visiting ships and an expression of colonial authority.

■ **Historic Buildings:** Include the Nanaimo Courthouse, completed 1896; the Palace Hotel, 1889; and Central Drugs, 1900-style pharmacy opened in 1985 (in the 1911 vintage Dakin Building). Adding to the scenic improvements downtown are old-fashioned lamp standards, brick sidewalks, cobblestone streets. Info Centre has guidebook.

■ **Nanaimo Art Gallery:** At Malaspina University College. 250-755-8790.

■ **Malaspina University College:** 900 5th St, Nanaimo, BC, V9R 5S5. 250-753-3245. A 67ha campus on the lower slopes of Mt Benson with views over Nanaimo Harbour and across Georgia Strait. The university-college features a 276-seat theatre for live performances, the Tamagawa Gardens, and the Museum of Natural History.

■ **Maffeo Sutton Park and Swyalana Lagoon Park:** On downtown waterfront. Site of Canada's first manmade tidal lagoon. Once an abandoned strip of waterfront, lagoon now is a favourite swimming hole and picnic ground. From a bridge across the mouth of the lagoon, people can watch water running through a series of pools and spillways. It's a constant flow that aerates the water for sea cucumbers, starfish, and other subtidal creatures stocked by local scuba divers. Bridge is lighted at night.

■ **Morrell Wildlife Sanctuary:** 111.5ha. Corner of Nanaimo Lakes and Dogwood roads. 11.5km walking trails and self-guided interpretive walks. Beaver habitats, ponds, rocky knolls. Pacific coast forests, displays, films. Interpretive centre open Sundays in summer. 250-753-5811. BC Wildlife Watch viewing site.

■ **Departure Bay:** Next to Departure Bay Ferry Terminal. A major recreational area, heavily used by sunbathers, windsurfers, sailors, and swimmers. Includes a public market with fresh meats, produce, bakery goods, seafood, and gourmet items. Open daily.

■ **Pacific Biological Station:** On Hammond Bay Rd, 2km around the bay from Departure Bay Ferry Terminal. Established in 1908, this federal station is one of the largest fisheries research laboratories in Canada, providing information to help manage and enhance Pacific fisheries. Visitors welcome.

■ **Bowen Park:** On Bowen Rd. Recreation complex, swimming and wading pool, hiking trails, waterfalls, nature centre, and children's barnyard.

■ **Nanaimo Parkway-Trailway:** Tracing the length of the new expressway around Nanaimo. 18km route for walkers, cyclists, wheelchair wheelers, and rollerbladers, offers great views of a growing city, and glimpses of Nanaimo's coal-mining past. Signs along Parkway provide directions to access points. 5km past the Cedar Rd overpass at the Parkway's south end, the trail passes through treed and tranquil Colliery Dam Park, encircling an old mine dam preserved for swimming. 7km farther, the trail travels the old roadbed of coal-baron Robert Dunsmuir's 1875 Wellington Colliery Railway, and wanders along The Bluffs, a plateau overlooking the green patchwork of the Millstone Valley.

■ **Sightseeing Adventures:** At Nanaimo harbour, charters to see seals, herons, cormorants, eagles, sea lions, and killer whales.

■ **The Bungy Zone:** 35 Nanaimo River Rd. 13 km south of Nanaimo. 1-800-668-7771 or 250-753-5867. Daily, hours vary. North America's first legal bridge jump site: people leap, lemminglike, with giant rubber bands attached to their ankles, from a specially designed bridge over the Nanaimo River gorge (see p.62).

■ **Vancouver Island Military Museum:** 5km north of Nanaimo centre, at Rutherford Village Mall. 250-756-2554. Open Mon-Sat.

■ **Karlin Rose Garden:** Corner of Prideaux and Comox streets. Self-guided tour, in spring and summer, of some 800 varieties of roses.

■ **Terra Crystal Galleries:** 557 Terminal Ave S. 250-753-7201. Natural crystal and fossils on display and in gift shop.

■ **Cyber City Adventures:** 1815 Bowen Rd. 250-755-1828. Year-round. Games include laser tag, virtual reality, arcade, go-carts, mini-golf and paint ball.

■ **Golf:** 19 courses within an hour's drive of the city. Ask at Info Centre.

Newcastle Island Provincial Marine Park: 336ha; 18 tent sites. Reached by private boat or foot-passenger ferry that leaves from Maffeo Sutton Park (Nanaimo's downtown waterfront). Ferry runs early May to mid-Oct, every hour on the hour from 10am. Weekends rest of year and by request. 250-391-2300. Canoes, kayaks, and small cartop boats can be launched from ferry wharf or from Brechin Marina, site of a public ramp near Departure Bay ferry terminal (turn toward water on road just before terminal). For overnight parking check with Info Centre.

Beautiful island in Nanaimo Harbour with steep sandstone cliffs and gravel beaches, caves and caverns, forests, native middens. Formerly a coal-mine site and luxury resort. The Pavilion, built in 1931, has been restored and is being used again for dances, theatre productions, and other events, including displays of natural and cultural history. Interpretation programs in summer. Swimming, playground, picnicking, paddling, waterskiing, fishing. And hiking – in about 2.5 hours you can circumnavigate island via a 7.5km trail. Snacks at the Pavilion.

At low tide, mud flats connect Newcastle and Protection islands. Short, mucky crossing to floating Dinghy Dock Pub off opposite shore.

Gabriola Island Ferry: Car and passenger ferry departs from downtown Nanaimo 16 times daily for 20-minute ride.

Gabriola Island

This pretty island totals 50 sq km and has a population of approximately 4,500. There are provincial parks at either end of the island, known for its petroglyphs, the eagles and seabirds that roost and nest on high bluffs, and its many artisans.

There are pubs, restaurants, shops, farmers markets, golf course, tennis courts, and accommodation. Also a museum, art galleries, live theatre, and special summer events.

Drumbeg Provincial Park: 20ha. On island's eastern end. Swimming, fishing, beachcombing.

Gabriola Sands Provincial Park: 6ha. On northwest end of Gabriola Island. Beautiful sand beaches. Near this park is Malaspina Galleries – unusual sandstone galleries created by frost wedging. Picnicking.

Sandwell Provincial Park: 12ha. On northeast tip of island. Sandy beach, lightly forested upland.

OVERLAND TO THE WEST COAST

LAKE COWICHAN TO BAMFIELD (Highway 18)

Truly a side road to adventure: the start of long, unpaved roads cutting right across southern Vancouver Island, from the gentle shores of the east coast to the wave-battered west coast. From cities and retirement communities to logging and fishing villages like Lake Cowichan, Youbou, Bamfield. To ancient forests, like Carmanah, now protected, and others, being logged. From the land of the Coast Salish peoples to where the Nuu-Chah-Nulth people live. Please remember that these are logging roads – the domain of logging trucks: obey signs, turn on your headlights, stay well to the right, keep your eyes on the road no matter how distracting the scenery, and make sure you have a spare tire and the talent to put it on.

Highway 18: Off Hwy 1, 67km north of Victoria, just north of Duncan. See *Victoria to Nanaimo*, p.60, for exact point of departure.

Mount Prevost: 1.5km west of Hwy 1, turn north onto Somenos Rd, then drive slightly more than 1km and turn left onto Mt Prevost Rd. About 8km on rough road to parking lot below 786m summit. Great views of Cowichan and Chemainus valleys, and cairn honouring Second World War veterans. Mountain is known as S'wukus to the Cowichan Tribes, and those who have visited the Cowichan Native Village in Duncan (p.59) will know of its significance.

Chemainus River Provincial Park: 85ha. 6.5km west of Hwy 1, right onto Hillcrest Rd. 5.5km to sign. Parking lot and trail just beyond sign. No facilities. Camping and mountain biking permitted.

Paldi Rest Area: 11.5km west of Hwy 1, overlooking second-growth forest. Named for small settlement nearby, established by Sikh immigrants from India who came to work in logging camps.

Cowichan Valley Demonstration Forest: All along Hwy 18 as far as Lake Cowichan, and around Cowichan Lake's shore.

Trail network includes short nature walk perfect for families. Inquire at the BC Forest Museum, or call 250-715-1113. Signs explain how forest is managed to maintain aesthetic and provide an outdoor classroom of forest management practices.

Cowichan River Provincial Park: 741ha. 20 campsites (reservations taken: call 1-800-689-9025; from the Lower Mainland or overseas, call 604-689-9025). 17.5km west of Hwy 1, Connector Rd leads south off Hwy 1. Follow signs to River Bottom Rd via Cowichan Lake Rd, then turn right on Stoltz Rd for about 1km to stop sign. From stop sign, left 1.5km leads to Stoltz Pool; right 4km leads to Skutz Falls. Park forms corridor tracing the Cowichan River and incorporates a portion of the 19km **Cowichan River Footpath** (see p.59). Park and footpath connect sites such as Stoltz Pool, a popular swimming hole; Marie Canyon, a 2km sheer-sided gap in the bedrock; and Skutz Falls, near the park's western boundary. The name Skutz comes from the Cowichan word, *skwets*, meaning waterfall. Marie Canyon was named for Her Excellency the Viscountess Willingdon in 1930 after her canoe trip downriver from Cowichan Lake to Duncan. Camping, hiking, swimming, rubber rafting, inner tubing, canoeing, kayaking, fishing, fish ladders.

Skutz Falls: 19km west of Hwy 1, Skutz Falls Rd leads south off Hwy, offering a second route (3km) to the falls.

Lake Cowichan: (Pop. 2,856). 28km west of Hwy 1. On Cowichan Lake, one of Vancouver Island's largest lakes, 32km long by 3km wide. Excellent trout fishing, waterskiing, boating. Private and public campsites. 75km drive around lake.

Lake Cowichan Information: Info Centre, Cowichan Lake District Chamber of Commerce, 125C South Shore Rd, Box 540, Lake Cowichan, BC, V0R 2G0. 250-749-3244. Daily, April-Oct. Ask about forestry tours, Wed and Fri in summer, explaining forest practices, sites, history.

■ **Kaatza Station Museum:** 125A South Shore Rd. 250-749-6142. Daily, May-Sept. In 1913 Canadian Pacific Railway station. Features logging and history. Has 1929 Westcan #7 locomotive and #12 Shay locomotive.

North Shore Rd and South Shore Rd: From Lake Cowichan village at the east end of Cowichan Lake, one road skirts the north shore, another the south shore. They meet at the lake's west end, whence a third logging road leads to **Nitinat Lake, Carmanah Walbran Provincial Park,** and **Bamfield.** Below, we follow the North Shore Rd first, then the South Shore Rd. Finally, we continue along that third road toward Nitinat Lake.

North Shore Route

The road skirting the north shore, leading to the community of Youbou, is evident as you enter the village of Lake Cowichan on Hwy 18.

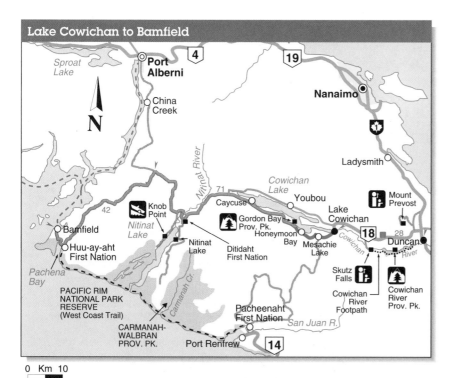

Lake Cowichan to Bamfield

0 Km 10

To Ditidaht First Nation, Nitinat Lake and Carmanah Walbran Park

Ditidaht First Nation: (Pop. 184). On northeast shore of Nitinat Lake, 70km west of Lake Cowichan. 250-745-3333. For some here, Nitinat Lake is ancestral home. Visitor Centre has motel, gas bar, cafe, and laundromat.

Nitinat Lake: Road traces lakeshore. Nitinat Lake is actually something of a tidal inlet, connected to the Pacific Ocean by Nitinat Narrows. This 24km lake smells like the sea, and has tides – "confused sea" conditions – and a pioneering population of sea anemones, jellyfish, and starfish. It is renowned for its constant thermal winds (15-20 knots), providing what windsurfing publications consider to be the best windsurfing conditions in North America. Events include the Nitinat Windsurfing Triathlon, Sail-Ride-Run (late July) and Windsurfing Summer Final (late Aug). Access to Forest Service campground a few kilometres beyond Ditidaht First Nation.

Carmanah Walbran Provincial Park: 16,450ha. About 45km beyond Nitinat Lake campground. 250-391-2300. This extraordinary ancient forest has long been at the heart of industry-vs-environment controversy. With the recent addition of 12,858ha in the Upper Carmanah and Walbran valleys, untouched portions of this major west-coast watershed will remain that way. As you approach the Carmanah, you drive through a vast, dispiriting clearcut. Steep one-hour hiking trail from road leads to the pristine waters of Carmanah Creek. Streamside trails weave through groves of Sitka spruce, some of them believed to be among world's tallest. More than 230 of these spruce stand over 70m high, with trunks 3- to 4m in diameter. Many are 85m tall, and one, the Carmanah Giant, is 95m – thought to be the tallest tree in Canada, and the largest Sitka spruce in the world. There is no public access to lower part of the park surrounding Carmanah Giant – these trails are extremely steep, muddy, and dangerous. Wilderness camping only, at upper section, to avoid the danger of flooding and protect the fragile environment. No access from here to the West Coast Trail. Remember, hikers must be prepared for a wilderness park, not a Sunday stroll. Watch for flash floods, as weather systems approaching Vancouver Island are funnelled into the valley.

Nitinat Triangle: Turn south at junction 2km beyond Nitinat River bridge. About 10km to Knob Point, launching point for paddle down northwest shore of Nitinat Lake to start of Hobiton-Tsusiat watershed. It is a rough, backbreaking 17km canoe route through Nitinat Triangle, part of Pacific Rim National Park.

To West Coast Trail and Bamfield

West Coast Trail (Pacific Rim National Park Reserve) at Pachena Bay: Start

---

Spring Beach Recreation Site: 6km west of Lake Cowichan to Meade Creek Rd (1.5km after road crosses Meade Creek), turn left and drive 0.5km to path. Tenting only at these lakeshore Forest Service sites. Pebbly beach.

Youbou: Lakeside community 15km west of Lake Cowichan on north shore of Cowichan Lake. Pub, restaurants, marina, stores, accommodation. Last chance for gas before 108km logging road to Bamfield.

From here, it's 23km to junction with South Shore Rd. Pleasant campsites.

South Shore Route

Start from southwestern end of village of Lake Cowichan, across the bridge.

Mesachie Lake: 7km beyond Lake Cowichan. This small community is home of the Cowichan Lake BC Forest Research Station, and turning point for 54.5km logging road to Port Renfrew. The road is open during non-working hours. Check at Mesachie Lake store. Good fishing at Lizard Lake, 39km from Mesachie Lake. Fishing and camping at Fairy Lake, 49km from Mesachie Lake. See also *Victoria to Port Renfrew*, p.51.

Honeymoon Bay: Small lakefront community on South Shore Rd, 12km from Lake Cowichan. Post office, stores, camping, boat rentals, neighbourhood pub.

Gordon Bay Provincial Park: 51ha; 126 campsites (reservations taken: call 1-800-689-9025; from the Lower Mainland or overseas, call 604-689-9025). 14km beyond Lake Cowichan. General info: 250-391-2300. A very popular family camping park, with safe sandy beaches, warm swimming. Often full in summer.

Honeymoon Bay Wildflower Ecological Reserve: 15km beyond Lake Cowichan. On flood plain of Sutton Creek. Vancouver Island's largest known concentration of pink easter lilies (*erythronium revolutum*) on display late April. This 7.5ha ecological reserve protects the lilies and two dozen other wildflower species, including wild bleeding heart, smooth wood violet, wild ginger, and white trillium. Area named because local settlers and farmers Henry and Edith March spent their honeymoon here.

Caycuse: 26km beyond Lake Cowichan. Pretty campsite. The surrounding mountains are now lush with second-growth timber, and quiet. But the nearby community of Caycuse was, until recently, the thriving centre of a succession of logging companies that logged these very hills. It is believed to be the longest operating logging camp in Canada, some say in North America. Layoffs and relocations have left Caycuse idle for the first time since 1927. There are hopes Caycuse will be preserved as a heritage site. Ask about it at the **Cowichan and Chemainus Valleys Ecomuseum Society**, 160 Jubilee St, Duncan (see p.60).

To Nitinat Lake, Carmanah Walbran Provincial Park, Bamfield: At west end of Cowichan Lake, where North and South Shore roads meet. 25km west of wildflower reserve. Heather Campground is nearby.

To Nitinat Lake, Carmanah Valley, Bamfield: 19km from end of Cowichan Lake. Well sign-posted. Bridge across Nitinat River on right leads 65km to Bamfield. Left turn leads about 5.5km to Ditidaht First Nation and about 4km farther to campsite on windblown shores of Nitinat Lake.

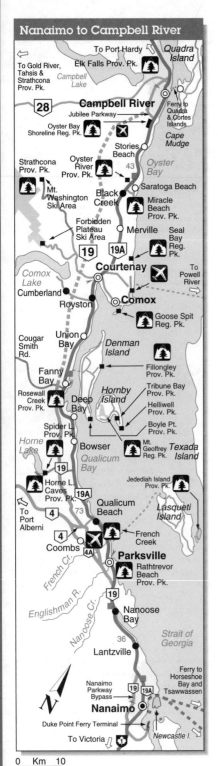

Nanaimo to Campbell River

0   Km   10

NANAIMO TO CAMPBELL RIVER

THE ISLAND HIGHWAY – THE OCEANSIDE ROUTE AND THE INLAND ISLAND HIGHWAY (Highways 19/19A)

And now, for the two types of traveller – two types of highway. There's the original Island Highway: in the 152km between the cities of Nanaimo and Campbell River, its two meandering lanes skirt Vancouver Island's gentle east coast, offering shimmering views of Georgia Strait, the Gulf Islands, and Coast Mountains of mainland BC. Between the "larger" communities of Parksville, Qualicum, Courtenay, Comox, and Campbell River are smaller pockets of civilization: pretty spots – Deep Bay, Oyster Bay, Fanny Bay, Merville – ferry docks, hotels and restaurants with recurring names: Sea Breezes, Sea Views, Bay Views.

Then there's the new 125km expressway, the Inland Island Highway: a four-lane swath through forest, shaving off curves, seaviews, and time. When it's completed – by the year 2001 – the three-hour trip between Nanaimo and Campbell River will be cut in half, leaving the old Island Highway to dedicated plodders. As one mid-island commuter puts it: "The new highway is for *us. The old* highway is for *them* (tourists)."

The new expressway takes the number 19 with it; the older, more scenic alternatives are now Hwy 19A. Hwy 19 now officially begins with the new Nanaimo Parkway just south of Nanaimo: it skirts the city's western edge, merges with a segment of the old Island Highway, then, at Craig's Crossing, 24.5km north of Nanaimo, cuts inland. To date, the Inland Island Hwy has been completed to Fanny Bay, 70.5km north of Nanaimo. Sections to Courtenay and Campbell River will be completed early in the new millennium.

This log begins in Nanaimo. It follows the original Island Highway – the Oceanside Route – with all its delights; and the new expressway is treated as a side trip.

Long Lake: At Jingle Pot Rd, 5km from Nanaimo city centre, turn east to Long Lake and fishing for trout and smallmouth bass. Rest area just beyond Jingle Pot Rd.

Brannen Lake: Continue on Jingle Pot Rd and Biggs Rd. Nearly 110ha. Cutthroat and rainbow trout up to 2.5kg.

Nanaimo Parkway: 9.5km north of Nanaimo, just past Woodgrove Shopping Centre. Northern terminus of 21km expressway bypassing Nanaimo (see p.63).

Lantzville: (Pop. 408). 11.5km north of downtown Nanaimo. Loop road leads east off Hwy 19 to picturesque seaside community. Some years, as many as 400 sea lions winter off the Lantzville waterfront on Ada Islands. Nature cruises from Schooner Cove, 8km to east. Loop road returns to Hwy 19, 5km from the southern turnoff.

Nanoose Bay: Hwy 19 skirts edge of bay just north of Lantzville. Site of the Canadian Forces Maritime Experimental and Test Ranges. Good clam digging if there is no paralytic shellfish ban in effect.

Nanoose Bay Rest Area: 16.5km north of Nanaimo, looking over Nanoose Bay. Only accessible to southbound traffic. Two portable toilets for people, and, for their canine companions, a hydrant with a fence.

Inland Island Hwy (Hwy 19) and Oceanside Route (Hwy 19A): At Craig's Crossing, 24.5km north of Nanaimo. The Inland Island highway cuts away from the coast on its express route to points north as Hwy 19. Hwy 19A continues along the coast, getting you to same places – eventually. Travellers bound for Parksville and Qualicum Beach will find it simplest to stick to the coast and Hwy 19A. Those going beyond may want to fast track via Hwy 19.

It seems simple enough, but the next few kilometres can be confusing even to locals: just north of Parksville on Hwy 19, a third route, Hwy 4A, runs roughly parallel to Hwys 19 and 19A. Hwy 4A provides access to the small communities of Errington and Coombs and merges with Hwy 4 – the Pacific Rim Hwy originating in Qualicum Beach. Hwy 4A can also be accessed from Hwy 19A in downtown Parksville. Hwys 4A/4 – leading to Port Alberni, Tofino, Ucluelet and Pacific Rim National Park – are covered under the *Craig's Crossing to Ucluelet Junction Log*, p.80. Following is a brief description of the Inland Island Hwy (Hwy 19) and its exits, before continuing with detailed coverage of Hwy 19A, the Oceanside Route.

SIDE TRIP

on the Inland Island Highway

It's as though you feel the curve of the Earth's surface: Hwy 19 – plowed through second-growth forest and spanning river canyons – sweeps you away from the convoluted coastline for a journey into another dimension. Here are forest rather than sea views; the green and insular Vancouver Island Mountains rather than the shimmering-in-the-distance Coast Mountains; miles are consumed rather than sampled. This segment of highway begins in the middle of nowhere, and, for now, ends there too: it would be wise to make sure there is enough gas in your tank.

Distances on the Inland Island Hwy are measured from Craig's Crossing, 24.5km north of Nanaimo. Exits from Craig's Crossing are as follows. 5.5km: exit east to **Parksville** (on Hwy 19A) and west to **Errington**, **Coombs** and **Englishman River Falls Provincial Park** (see

---

of the famous trail is 105km by logging road from Youbou, 83km from west end of Cowichan Lake. Road open to public at all times except during extreme fire hazards. Write Pacific Rim National Park Reserve, Box 280, Ucluelet, BC, V0R 3A0. 250-728-3234. (See p.52 for details.)

Bamfield: (Pop. 256). 3km beyond Pachena Bay turnoff, or 108km from Youbou. For details on Bamfield see *Craig's Crossing to Ucluelet Junction*, p.81.

Craig's Crossing to Ucluelet Junction). 14.5km: exit east to **Qualicum Beach**, west to **Port Alberni**, **Bamfield**, **Ucluelet**, **Tofino** and **Pacific Rim Park** (see *Craig's Crossing to Ucluelet Junction*). 29.5km: exit west to **Horne Lake Rd** and west to **Qualicum Bay** or **Bowser** (see below). 42km: exit east to **Deep Bay**. 46km: Inland Island Hwy merges with Oceanside Route (Hwy 19A) at Fanny Bay.

The remainder of the new highway between Fanny Bay and Campbell River will be completed early in the new millennium. Then, travellers will soar over the already completed Tsable River Bridge: just inland from the Buckley Bay ferry terminal, it is the largest single-cell concrete box bridge in North America (this construction technique has only been used once before – at Knight St, in Vancouver). Its four lanes span 400m and rise 20 storeys from the river bed.

Return to Highway 19A

Brant Goose Feeding Area: On Hwy 19A just north of Hwy 19/19A junction at Craig's Crossing. The shores between Parksville and Qualicum Beach, on the Pacific flyway for migratory waterfowl, are part of a wildlife management area. As many as 20,000 elegant black-fronted mallard-sized Brant geese stop to rest and feed here each spring, en route from their winter home in Baja California and other parts of Mexico to summer breeding grounds in Alaska. Over 200 bird species have been recorded. New reserve encompasses 17km of shoreline and 873ha of intertidal flats. It includes the estuaries of Craig and French creeks, the Englishman and Little Qualicum rivers. Parksville-Qualicum Beach's annual three-day **Brant Festival**, mid-April, organized by the Mid-Island Wildlife Watch Society, offers goose viewing stations, birding competition, nature talks, wildlife art, carving, photography, stories, children's activities. 250-248-4117.

Rathtrevor Beach Provincial Park: 347ha; 175 campsites (reservations taken: call 1-800-689-9025; from the Lower Mainland or overseas, call 604-689-9025). Sani-station. General info: 250-954-4600. On southern outskirts of Parksville, 29km north of Nanaimo. More than 2km of sandy shore, 4km of hiking trails, nature house, amphitheatre, summer interpretive programs. One of the most popular family camping spots on Vancouver Island. Full every day in summer.

Englishman River (Orange) Bridge: Just beyond Rathtrevor Provincial Park, highway crosses Englishman River. The river's estuary was saved in 1992 when the Nature Trust of BC emptied its bank account to help other conservation groups rescue an 87ha parcel of land destined to become a 900-site trailer park. The cost: $2.7 million.

Parksville: (Pop. 9,472). On Hwy 19A, 35km north of Nanaimo. Well-established resort community where hundreds of hectares of open sand are exposed at low tides. Ebbing tides leave large shallow pools in the sand, perfect digging spots for young castle builders. Steamy veils of vapour rise from the beach as the summer sun beats down. Water coming in over hot sand warms to comfortable swimming temperatures.

Parksville (named after Nelson Park, first settler and postmaster) and Qualicum Beach (below), are among those North American communities in the midst of a development-versus-environment dilemma. In 1976, 10,000 people lived along this strip of seashore; 25,000 live here now and the population is expected to double again by 2016. Fishing and forestry, the traditional mainstays, have been surpassed by construction and tourism. Much of the highway through Parksville is fronted by strip development. There's an almost continuous string of resorts and tourist facilities between Parksville and Qualicum Beach.

Parksville Information: Info Centre, Parksville and District Chamber of Commerce, Box 99, Parksville, BC, V9P 2G3. 250-248-3613. Fax: 250-248-5210. On Hwy 19 at south entrance to town. Mon-Fri, year-round. Also weekends, June-Sept.

■ **Craig Heritage Park:** About 3km south of town, 1245 E Island Hwy. Daily, mid-May to Labour Day. 250-248-6966 (summer); 250-248-3431 (winter, by appointment). Pioneer and native artifacts, newspaper and photograph archives, and 1946 fire truck in restored 1942 fire hall. Knox United Heritage Church, built 1911-1912, is still open for weddings.

■ **Parksville Community Park:** 6.5ha. Turn off Hwy 19A in city at Corfield Rd. Access to huge, open beach. Swimming, trails, sports field, playground and picnic area, children's waterpark.

■ **Canadian Coast Guard Search and Rescue Station:** At French Creek Marina, 1105 Lee Rd. 250-248-2724. Tours and presentations by arrangement.

■ **North Island Wildlife Recovery Centre and Museum of Nature:** In Errington, off Hwy 4A. See p.80.

■ **St Anne's Anglican Church:** 4km north of Parksville, turn left on Wembley Rd, then left on Church Rd. 250-248-3114. Built 1894, one of the island's oldest churches.

■ **Golf: Morningstar Golf Course**, 525 Lowry's Rd. 250-248-8161, offers 18 holes. **Fairwinds Golf Course**, 3730 Fairwinds Dr, Nanoose Bay, 250-468-7666, 18 holes. **Mulligans Indoor Golf:** 1420 Alberni Hwy, Parksville. 250-954-0307.

■ **Paradise Adventure Mini-golf:** 375 W Island Hwy. 250-248-6612. Two 18-hole mini-golf courses, amusement centre, the Old Woman's Shoe (where kids have birthday parties), and other distractions from sun and sand. Daily, late March to mid-Oct.

Highway 4 Connector: Downtown Parksville. 47km to Port Alberni. Route to the West Coast via Errington and Coombs. See *Craig's Crossing to Ucluelet Junction*, p.80.

French Creek: About 40km north of Nanaimo, east on Lee Rd. Marina, campgrounds, cabins, motels, local park, fishing charters. Seafood sold from commercial fishboats. Good fall fishing from beach at mouth of creek.

Lasqueti Island: East off Hwy 19A at Lee Rd. Foot-passenger ferry only. Ferry has three sailings every day except Tues in summer; no Tues or Wed off-season. Carries 60 passengers for 45-minute, 17km cruise halfway across Georgia Strait. Kayaks, canoes, and bicycles can be carried aboard ferry.

Lasqueti Island

This 68-sq-km island is largely undeveloped, supporting a population of about 300. There are small number of gravel roads, popular among mountain bicyclists who take the ferry to False Bay and ride 15km to Squitty Bay Provincial Park, at the island's eastern end.

Lasqueti's many sheltered coves and bays, offshore reefs, islets, and islands make it fascinating paddling territory. Eagles, turkey vultures, seabirds, river otters, seals, sea lions, and whales are commonly seen. False Bay is "downtown" Lasqueti Island with a general store, marina, and limited accommodation. For information on Lasqueti Island and ferry schedules check at the ferry terminal at French Creek, or at the Parksville Info Centre. Staff at French Creek Marina and Store, 250-248-8912, are helpful.

Jedediah Island Provincial Park: 243ha. By private boat or charter from French Creek or Lasqueti Island. 250-954-4600. Once a private island, now a park for everyone. Old homestead, forest, trails to white-sand beaches, small fiords and bays. Best moorage on northwest coast at Deep Bay, also at Indian Cove and Home Bay. No official campsites; nice spot at Home Bay. Bring drinking water.

Return to Highway 19A

Qualicum Airport: About 44km north of Nanaimo, west off Hwy 19A. Scheduled and charter flights.

Qualicum Beach: (Pop. 6,728). 47km north of Nanaimo on Hwy 19A. One of Vancouver Island's most pleasant and salubrious communities, known largely for good golfing and beachcombing. Enlightened waterfront policies make for easy access to sweeping sandy beaches. The small village, with restaurants, specialty shops, groceries, and galleries, is less than 1km inland from the beach.

Qualicum Beach Information: Info Centre, Qualicum Beach Chamber of Commerce, 2711 W Island Hwy, Qualicum Beach, BC, V9K 2C4. 250-752-9532. Marked by totem pole on Hwy 19A. Daily, year-round.

■ **The Old School House Gallery and Art Centre:** 122 Fern W Rd. Box 791, Qualicum Beach, BC, V9K 1T2. 250-752-6133. Daily, July to mid-Sept. Mon-Sat, rest of year. Non-profit cultural centre. Artists, painters, printmakers, weavers, carvers, jewellers, photographers, crafts makers at work. Each studio offers classes. Also public gallery featuring local, regional, and national artists. Workshops, demonstrations, special events.

■ **Qualicum Beach Historical Museum and Power House Museum:** 587 Beach Rd. 250-752-5533. One focusing on the community, the other on the history of electricity in BC.

■ **Vancouver Island Palaeontology Museum:** 587 Beach Rd. 250-752-9810.

■ **Golf: Eaglecrest Golf Club**, 2.5km south of Qualicum Beach on Island Hwy, 1-800-567-1320 or 250-752-6311, offers 18 holes. **Glengarry Golf Links**,1025 Qualicum Rd, 250-752-8786, offers 18 holes. **Arrowsmith Golf and Country Club**, 2250 Fowler Rd, 250-752-9727, offers 18 holes. **Qualicum Beach Memorial Golf Club**, Crescent Rd, 250-752-6312, has nine holes.

■ **Kayaking:** Ask at Info Centre about rentals and guided outings for beginners. Popular trip is to Little Qualicum River estuary, part of Marshall Stevenson Wildlife Preserve.

Highway 4 (Memorial Ave): West from downtown Qualicum Beach, 4km to Hwy 19 (Inland Island Hwy), then continues to Port Alberni and the West Coast. See *Craig's Crossing to Ucluelet Junction*, p.80.

Little Qualicum River: Mouth of river near Hwy 19A, 51km north of Nanaimo. Qualicum National Wildlife Area. Good birdwatching.

Spider Lake Provincial Park: 65ha. 61km north of Nanaimo, west on Horne Lake Rd. 8km by gravel road off Hwy 19. Long arms and grassy islets. Excellent smallmouth bass fishing. Large but harmless water snakes. Hiking trails, swimming, fishing, and picnicking. No powerboats.

Horne Lake Caves Provincial Park: 123ha. 61km north of Nanaimo, west off Hwy 19A at Horne Lake Rd. 15km to park at lake's western end. Road follows north shore. Two caves open year-round for self-guided tours; three cave tours available in summer and on a more limited basis in winter. Take a spare flashlight and common sense. Most fragile caves are gated, but tours, extremely worthwhile, and stressing conservation, may be available. Check with the Qualicum Beach Info Centre; BC Parks: 250-954-4600; or Horne Lake Cave Tours, 250-248-7829. Horne Lake, headwaters of Qualicum River, is 8km long by 1.5km wide. Good year-round fishing for kokanee, cutthroat and rainbow trout. Caves named after Hudson's Bay Company explorer Adam Grant Horne.

Big Qualicum River Fisheries Project: West at sign just south of Big Qualicum River Bridge, just beyond Horne Lake Park turnoff. More than 100,000 salmon return each year to hatchery, which produces millions of fish. Educational displays and self-guiding paths. Daily, dawn to dusk, year-round. 250-757-8412.

Cola Diner and Qualicum Beaver Resort: 62km north of Nanaimo, at 9338 Island Hwy, Qualicum Bay. 250-757-2029. Cola collectibles from 1905 to the '50s.

Rock formations adorn Tribune Bay on Hornby Island.

Bowser: (Pop. 130). 66km north of Nanaimo on Hwy 19A. Overlooking Georgia Strait. The Bowser Hotel made history in the 1930s by having a dog that served beer to patrons. The community is named for William John Bowser, BC Premier, 1915-16. Services, cottages, boat rentals.

Deep Bay: 70km north of Nanaimo, take Gainsburg Rd. Pleasant fishing resort community. Everything to warm a fisherman's heart.

Rosewall Creek Provincial Park: 54ha. West off Hwy 19A about 76km north of Nanaimo. Fishing.

Fanny Bay Conservation Unit: 80.5km north of Nanaimo, take Ships Point Rd, then follow Tozer Rd to the end. Trail to marshland, tidal mudflats, and forest. Songbirds, woodpeckers, shorebirds, and waterfowl.

Cougar Smith Rd: 82km north of Nanaimo. Named after "Cougar" Cecil Smith, professional cougar hunter, who shot more than 1,000 cougars between 1890 and 1940 when a bounty was offered by the provincial government.

Fanny Bay: (Pop. 110). 83km north of Nanaimo. Tiny seaside community on shores of Baynes Sound. Site of landmark Fanny Bay Inn, known to Vancouver Islanders as the FBI. The name, Fanny Bay, arose from surveys by Captain GH Richards in 1860s. Fanny is an unknown person, enshrined nevertheless for posterity. Just down the highway is the *Brico*, a cable-laying ship hauled ashore to become a restaurant.

Buckley Bay Ferry Terminal: 86km north of Nanaimo. Car and passenger ferries run several times daily to **Denman Island**, and from Denman to **Hornby Island**. Schedule information: 250-335-0323 or 1-888-223-3779. No need to rush: you have 20 minutes to make 11-minute drive across Denman to Hornby Island ferry terminal.

Denman Island

This 50-sq-km island (19km long, 6km wide) has 1,048 year-round residents. There are 48km of public road, about half of that paved. Beautiful sandstone and gravel shores. Oysters, rock crabs, clams. Eagles and seabirds. Black-tailed deer. Good salmon fishing, particularly off south end. Trout fishing in Chickadee and Graham lakes. Limited accommodation and only one small provincial campground. Call ahead or go straight to the campground. Cycle rentals, public art gallery.

This lush, fertile, low-lying paradise has its concerns: in the last decade the island's small population has doubled, and is expected to double again by the end of the decade. Some 97 percent of Denman has now been subdivided, or is available for development, and 25 percent of that is owned by forest companies for potential logging.

Hornby-Denman Tourist Association: c/o Sea Breeze Lodge, Hornby Island, BC, V0R 1Z0. 250-335-2321. Denman Island General Store and Cafe: visitor and accommodation information, food, propane, liquor, fishing licences, and post office. Call 250-335-2293.

Fillongley Provincial Park: 23ha; 10 campsites. 250-954-4600. On Lambert Channel, facing Hornby Island. Small but pleasant park with creek, forest, grassy fields, and several kilometres of gravel and shell beach for walking.

Sandy Island Provincial Marine Park: 18ha; limited camping. 250-954-4600. Water access only. Group of beautiful wooded islands off sandy north end of Denman. Easily reached by small boat. Launching ramp next to ferry terminal on Denman. Accessible by foot from Denman Island at extremely low tides. Swimming, fishing. No fires.

Boyle Point Provincial Park: 125ha. 250-954-4600. Southern tip of Denman, beyond to Hornby Island ferry terminal. Dramatic ocean views from steep escarpment over boulder-strewn beach. Scattered old-growth Douglas fir mingle with second-growth forests. Hiking.

Denman Seniors and Museum Society Activity Centre: 1111 Northwest Rd, in Seniors Community Hall. Daily July-Aug. 250-335-0880. Local natural and human history, shells, fossils, butterflies, northwest-coast native artifacts, European settlement items, work of Denman Lace Club.

Hornby Island

This 30-sq-km island has about 1,000 year-round residents. And many, many more in the summer – on one 1990 summer day, an estimated 10,000 visitors were savouring this wee isle. Ferries run across Lambert Channel from Gravelly Bay, on Denman, to Shingle Spit, on Hornby. Hornby is more mountainous than Denman. The powerful force of the sea has beaten the softer rock faces, leaving dramatic cave formations at Tribune Bay and other sites. Some consider this one of the most appealing islands in Georgia Strait. The primary industry here is crafts – weaving, pottery, art – also some fishing, and farming of cattle and sheep. No provincial campgrounds on Hornby, but there are a number of commercial ones, as well as resort lodges and B&Bs. Kayak rentals seasonally. The Hornby Island Co-op store (a cluster of buildings near Tribune Bay Provincial Park) includes a gas bar, store, restaurants, ice cream bar, bike rentals, and other esoteric shops. Hanging out in the central courtyard is a cultural experience – great for people watching. Some shops are closed in winter.

Hornby is becoming famous as the only place in the world where the primitive, deep-sea, sixgill shark moves into shallow waters (as shallow as 15m), occasionally interfacing with divers. So far, these fearsome-looking sharks have shown themselves to be relatively docile. Opossums have made Hornby their northernmost home in North America.

Hornby-Denman Tourist Association: c/o Sea Breeze Lodge, Hornby Island, BC, V0R 1Z0. 250-335-2321.

Tribune Bay Provincial Park: 95ha. 250-954-4600. At southeast end of Hornby. Beautiful sandy beach. Safe swimming for small children, picnicking, fishing. The only excuse needed to visit Hornby Island.

Helliwell Provincial Park: 2,872ha. 250-954-4600. The other only excuse needed to visit Hornby Island. High cliffs, grassy fields, and forests on St John Point, at the southeast entrance to Tribune Bay. Beachcombing, hiking, spincasting for salmon from shore. Particularly invigorating in winter storms. Park includes underwater area running from St John Point to Lambert Channel – primitive deep-water sharks, underwater caves, shipwreck sites.

Mt Geoffrey Regional Park: 300ha. Follow Shingle Spit Rd, right on Central Rd, and right again on Strachan Rd. Trails to stunning views. Maps available on island: 250-334-6000.

Return to Highway 19A

Baynes Sound Rest Area: 89km north of Nanaimo. Views of eagles, Denman Island, Coast Mountains. Picnic tables. Rest area has been fitted with composting toilet technology. Buildings were carefully designed and constructed to protect the fragile ecology and oyster beds on the sound's pretty foreshore.

Public Shellfish Reserve: 1km stretch of beach adjacent rest area. Managed by Department of Fisheries and Oceans. Pull out your pail and shovel for daily harvesting limit of 15 oysters in the shell or 1/2 litre shucked; 25 butter clams, 12 razor clams, 75 little neck clams.

Union Bay: (Pop. 1,500). 93km north of Nanaimo on Hwy 19. Once a major shipping area for coal from mines at nearby Cumberland: stop-of-interest sign introduces area's tumultuous labour history. For more see below. Boats launch here for 4km cruise to Sandy Island Provincial Park, off north end of Denman Island. Hotel, pub, market, seafood, ice cream. Looking east and slightly north, across the Strait of Georgia: views of **Texada Island**, and beyond to **Powell River** with its steamy pulp and paper mill (see p.116).

Royston: (Pop. 2,125). 101.5km north of Nanaimo, east off Hwy 19. From 1907 to 1947, these waters at the mouth of Comox Harbour served as booming grounds for the busy Comox Logging and Railway Company. The seas could be tempestuous, and in the 1930s, the first of 15 ship's hulls were sunk to create a breakwater. It's all still here to see: the historic hulls still protect logs in adjacent booming grounds. Turn east off Hwy 19 onto Ross Ave. Signs give details of ships sunk. Pleasant picnic stop.

Cumberland Rd: In heart of Royston. West for 6km to Cumberland and beyond to outdoor recreation areas.

SIDE TRIP

to Cumberland

Cumberland: (Pop. 2,548). 6km west of Hwy 19 on Cumberland Rd. Founded in 1888 by coal baron Robert Dunsmuir, and named after the famous English coal-mining district, Cumberland. Here was the heart of a rich coal field that ran along Vancouver Island's east coast. British, Italian, Chinese, and Japanese immigrants, living in segregated neighbourhoods, made this a colourful place in its heyday. The population then was five times

greater than now. There were bars and brothels, gambling houses, fortune tellers, and two 400-seat theatres where touring Chinese singers and acrobats performed. But greed and indifference to safety on the part of the Dunsmuir barons and subsequent mine owners made this a dangerous place to be. In all, 295 miners lost their lives here. Ultimately, wage and safety cuts here and at other mines ignited the bitter Vancouver Island coal miners' strike in 1912. W.J. Bowser, acting premier at the time, sent in 1,000 soldiers to "keep the peace" – i.e. keep the mines running. Four years later, more unrest followed the slaying, just outside Cumberland, of Ginger Goodwin, popular labour leader, pacifist, and "troublemaker" as far as the authorities were concerned. Goodwin had been taking refuge here from a conscription order.

Mine production fell in the late 1920s, the last mine closed in 1966, but much remains of Cumberland's past: piles of slag and sheets of rusted corrugated iron scattered around derelict buildings; remnants of Bonanza Number Four, which in 1912 produced some 2,540 tonnes of coal a day; a downtown mural portraying the community's Chinese heritage. Several buildings – survivors of 1932-33 fires – have been refurbished; one houses an art gallery and several craft stores.

In 1995 the BC Government designated the Cumberland section of the new Inland Island Highway in Goodwin's honour.

For more, read *Ginger: The Life and Death of Albert Goodwin*, by Susan Mayse (Harbour Publishing, 1990).

Cumberland Information: Info Centre, Cumberland Chamber of Commerce, Box 250, Cumberland, BC, V0R 1S0. 250-336-8313. On the main street at 2755 Dunsmuir Ave. Mon-Fri, year-round. Daily, July-Aug.

■ **Cumberland Museum and Archives:** 2680 Dunsmuir Ave. Daily. 250-336-2445. The Cultural Centre, with its historic facades, is reasonably new, and the museum has expanded into it, making room for more of the community's dramatic history – including poignant photographs of the Japanese community developed from a large collection of glass plate negatives rescued from neglect. Heritage tours tell of the buildings and the people who lived in them.

■ **Japanese Cemetery, Chinese Cemetery, Ginger Goodwin's Burial Site:** On Cumberland Rd, east of the village.

■ **Miners' Memorial Day:** Late June. Commemorates miners who lost their lives.

Cumberland Lake Park on Comox Lake: 50-site campground. On south side of lake; trails and lake access 5km west of Cumberland on Comox Lake Rd. North and west sides of lake can also be reached by roads from Cumberland. Major recreation area. Lake, part of Puntledge River system, is 14.5km long by 1.5km wide. Year-round fishing for kokanee, Dolly Varden char, big cutthroat, rainbow trout. Boaters beware of high winds and submerged stumps from raising of lake level.

Lakes Chain: Two small lakes –Willemar and Forbush – reached by logging road from Comox Lake. Wilderness camping, excellent canoeing. Lakes joined by easy-flowing stretch of Puntledge River. Rough trail into Strathcona Provincial Park through old-growth forest from upper end of Forbush Lake. Lots of black bears; wolves may howl at night.

Return to Highway 19A

Courtenay: (Pop.19,592). Outskirts 106.5km north of Nanaimo. In the wide, gently pastoral Comox Valley, the Tsolum and Puntledge rivers merge to become the Courtenay River. The Courtenay River pours into the wide mouth of Comox Harbour, creating a rich tidal estuary teeming with life. Some 80 million years ago, this valley was home to the elasmosaur, a giant long-necked swimming reptile 14m long, weighing as much as 4t. Its fossil, discovered in 1988 along the banks of the Puntledge River, was the first of its kind to be found in Canada west of the Rockies.

The Comox Valley is a rare place. It lies in the rainshadow of the highest peaks of the Vancouver Island Range. Nearby Mt Washington and Forbidden Plateau offer the best downhill and cross-country skiing on Vancouver Island. The valley, with more than its fair share of sunshine, is also one of the island's two main agricultural regions (the second is the Cowichan Valley to the south). This fertile lowland soil drew the first group of settlers in 1862. Many were disgruntled gold-seekers: in farming, their second choice, they found pay dirt. The early elite of Victoria came here, as tourists, to fish for salmon on the banks of the Puntledge River.

The town of Courtenay emerged by the end of the century as a service centre for the valley. Today, Courtenay ranks fourth among Canada's fastest growing urban communities: between the census years of 1991 and 1996, the population increased 48.2 percent, to 17,335 from 11,697, and the numbers are still climbing.

Courtenay–Comox Information: Info Centre, Comox Valley Chamber of Commerce, 2040 Cliffe Ave, Courtenay, BC, V9N 2L3. 250-334-3234. Marked by a black steam locomotive at the south entrance to Courtenay on Hwy 19A. Serves Courtenay and Comox. Daily, year-round. The region is home to several organizations happy to help visitors and residents learn more about their surroundings. For possible tours, presentations, slide shows, books, and pamphlets, call the Strathcona Wilderness Institute, 250-337-8348 or 250-337-8180; Comox-Strathcona Natural History Society, 250-338-6055; Mitlenatch Field Naturalist Society, 250-337-8180 or 250-285-2827.

Courtenay Airstrip: Behind Info Centre off Hwy 19A.

■ **Courtenay and District Museum:** 360 Cliffe Ave. Daily, May-Sept; Tues-Sat, Sept-April. 250-334-3611. In Canada's largest free-span log building. With an 80-million-year-old elasmosaur fossil on display, this is Stop 1 on

Cumberland's Cultural Centre presents the history of a coal-mining town.

the Great Canadian Fossil Trail (other stops include Yoho Burgess Shale Park (p.211) and the Royal Tryell Museum of Paleontology in Alberta. Also First Nations and settlement histories. Guided tours.

■ **Mt Washington Ski Area:** 25km west of Courtenay. Follow signs from town. Write to Mt Washington, Box 3069, Courtenay, BC, V9N 5N3. 250-338-1386. Snow report 250-338-1515. Paved Strathcona Parkway leads 18km up to the mountain. Mt Washington's 1,590m peak looms above the ski area. Spectacular views of surrounding mountains, forests, and glimpses of sea. Vertical drop is 488m. New high-speed detachable quad, regular quad, two triples, a double, and three surface lifts, including the O-Zone snow-tubing park, more than 40 runs, most above 1,200m level. Half-pipe and snowboard park for snowboarders. Full-service day lodge open evenings for dinners and entertainment. There's a ski school, rentals, and facilities for children. Many of the 200 private chalets and condominiums in Mt Washington's village can be rented by skiers; also accommodation in the Deer Lodge. Full-service RV park in the village. Nordic skiing is also extensive: 30km of track-set trails, and accessibility of nearby Strathcona Provincial Park. Lodge, washrooms,

food and beverage areas, retail shops, children's and barbecue areas. In summer, alpine restaurant, camping, mountain biking and rentals, tours, hiking, horseback riding and horse-drawn carriage rides, tours, and Courtenay Youth Music Camp in residence. Summer chairlifts: daily, late July-Thanksgiving.

■ **Forbidden Plateau Ski Area:** On Mt Becher's lower slopes, a 25-minute drive west of Courtenay, in Strathcona Provincial Park. 250-334-4428, 250-334-7944, year-round, or 250-338-1919 for winter conditions. Vertical drop of 366m. Lift up to 1,100m level. Double chairlift, three T-bars, one handle tow; 24 runs and extensive cross-country tracks for intermediate and experienced skiers. Snow-boarder half-pipe to hill facilities. Day skiing: Thurs-Sun, 9am-3:45pm. Night skiing: Wed-Sat, 5pm-10pm. Day lodge with cafeteria, lounge, and other facilities. Accommodation in Courtenay, and RV parking on mountain. Equipment rentals, ski school. Chairlift and restaurant also open late June to early Sept. Summer campground beside lodge. Lodge used for many summer activities. Fishing in alpine lakes, late summer, early fall.

■ **Puntledge River and Hatchery:** Important river for chum, pink, coho, and chinook salmon as well as steelhead trout. 250-338-7444. Year-round. Reached from south entrance to Courtenay by taking Lake Trail Rd, turning right at Powerhouse Rd and following signs. BC Wildlife Watch viewing site.

Comox Rd: East off Hwy 19 at entrance to Courtenay – just past the Courtenay-Comox Info Centre. Scenic route crosses the Courtenay River, then curves southeast along the Comox Peninsula, offering views west across Comox Harbour to Comox Glacier in the distance.

SIDE TRIP

to Comox

Courtenay River Estuary: 1km from Hwy 19. Overlooking breeze-blown grass and sand dunes of the Courtenay River, with dramatic backdrop of Vancouver Island Mountains. Platform for viewing trumpeter swans. Picnic tables, shade trees, and right next door, the Java Junction offering espresso.

Queneesh Native Gift Shop: On Comox Rd, 2km from Hwy 19, on Comox First Nation reserve land. 250-339-7702. Here are the arts of the local Comox First Nation, and outstanding works from all over the Northwest Coast. Adjacent Big House hosts "Sharing the Spirit" Aug 1 weekend: each year the Comox people welcome a cultural group from somewhere in the world, and the public is invited. Pick up the gallery's brochure describing the legend of Queneesh, the aboriginal name of the glacier which dominates the Comox Valley skyline.

Comox: (Pop.11,847). 3.5km from Hwy 19-Comox Rd Junction, on the Comox Peninsula. In the language of the Kwakwaka'wakw aboriginal people who traditionally occupied the shores here and northward, the word Comox means "abundance." The good life here was noted by the earliest of Vancouver Island's non-native settlers too: in the 1860s, '70s, and '80s, before roads, Comox's natural harbour bustled with steam boats bringing supplies and mail to the valley's new settlers and tourists disembarking just for a gander or to fish. During the Second World War, a Canadian Forces Airforce base was established at Comox, and has become the valley's largest employer, specializing in air-sea rescue and long-range maritime patrol. Canadian Forces Base Comox has become a choice posting for airforce personnel from across Canada, and many retire to the valley's sunny sea-and-mountains setting.

Comox's idyllic location is drawing birds of yet another feather. Trumpeter swans, North America's largest and fastest water birds, make the warm and verdant Comox Valley their first major feeding stop on their annual southbound route from Alaska. Ten percent of the world's trumpeter swans – some 2,000 birds – winter here. As many as 500 will congregate in a single field. Each bird (weighing about 12k) may devour 4-5k of grass a day – up to 10 tonnes collectively. To lure them from crop fields, local dairy farmers plant 200ha of oats, barley, winter wheat, fall rye, and ryegrass a year – just for the birds. The swans in turn, draw "avitourists" from around the world early Oct-Feb. During the **Trumpeter Swan Festival** in early Feb, local naturalists take birders on guided tours. For info: Trumpeter Swan Sentinel Society: http://www.vquest.com/swan/ or write the Comox Valley Chamber of Commerce. 250-334-3234.

Comox Information: Info Centre, Comox Valley Chamber of Commerce, 2040 Cliffe Ave, Courtenay, BC, V9N 2L3. 250-334-3234. At the south entrance to Courtenay on Hwy 19A. Also see p. 70.

CFB Comox: Airstrip at the base is used by commercial airlines for scheduled and charter flights. Take Ryan Rd off Hwy 19A from Courtenay bypass.

Powell River Ferry: Take Ryan Rd off Hwy 19A from the Courtenay bypass and follow signs. Car and passenger ferries run 27km, 75 minutes, four sailings daily to Powell River, on mainland north of Vancouver.

■ **Comox Air Force Museum:** At entrance to CFB Comox (above). 250-339-8162. Daily, June-Aug; Sat, Sun, and holidays, Sept-May.

■ **The Beaches:** At Kye Bay, 5km northeast of Comox, are long and sandy beaches, ideal family picnic and swimming spots. Still a bit of a secret, though some families have been summering here for generations. Cottage resort.

■ **Goose Spit Regional Park:** 6ha. South of Comox via Comox Rd, left onto Pritchard Rd, right on Balmoral, cross to Lazlo Rd at which point Balmoral becomes Hawkins Rd. Follow to the spit. 250-334-6000. Sand bar jutting into Comox Harbour offers swimming and windsurfing on harbour and ocean sides.

■ **Seal Bay Regional Nature Park:** 700ha. On coast north of Comox. Follow signs from Island Hwy to Powell River Ferry (Island Hwy, east on Ryan Rd, north on Anderton Rd). Turn north on Waveland Rd, then north on Bates Rd to parking lot and start of over 20km of hiking trails. 250-334-6000. Trail maps available from Comox Valley Info Centre. BC Wildlife Watch viewing site.

■ **Nymph Falls Regional Nature Park:** 55ha. Follow signs to Forbidden Plateau Ski Area, on Forbidden Plateau Rd. 250-334-6000. Located on the Puntledge River, trails lead through second-growth forest to good swimming holes and view of river. Trail maps available from Comox Valley Info Centre.

■ **Stotan Falls:** Comox Logging Rd leads north off Lake Trail Rd to the bridge over the Puntledge River. This popular swimming hole has been a local secret, until now. There are pools carved out of limestone and a waterfall too good to be true.

■ **Mack Laing Nature Park:** End of Comox Ave. Shakesides was private residence of naturalist Mack Laing (1883-1982). Pleasant walks on waterfront and in fir and cedar forest.

Return to Highway 19

Sunnydale Golf and Country Club: 111.5km north of Nanaimo. 5291 North Island Hwy. 250-334-3232. 18 holes.

Courtenay Country Market: 112km north of Nanaimo.

Jupiter Emu Ranch: 118km north of Nanaimo. Store offers meat, oil, gifts.

Merville: (Pop. 865). 119km north of Nanaimo. General store, gas station, and homes along Hwy 19. Named after location in France of Canadians' first field headquarters. This is where BC novelist Jack Hodgins grew up and collected his first impressions for such books as *Spit Delaney's Island*, *Barclay Family Theatre*, and *Broken Ground*.

Black Creek: (Pop. 1,950). 127km north of Nanaimo. Service centre for small Mennonite community and campers at Miracle Beach Provincial Park (below). Country market at outskirts.

Miracle Beach Provincial Park: 137ha. 201 campsites (reservations taken: call 1-800-689-9025; from the Lower Mainland or overseas, call 604-689-9025). 128.5km north of Nanaimo, 24km north of Courtenay. General info: 250-337-2400. One of Vancouver Island's most popular parks. Perfect family camping spot if you don't mind company. Long, safe sandy beach, wooded trails, amphitheatre, visitor centre, interpretive programs.

Mitlenatch Island Provincial Nature Park: 155ha. 13km northeast of Miracle Beach at north end of Georgia Strait. Boat access only. 250-337-2400. Naturalists' paradise. Nesting glaucous-winged gulls, pelagic cormorants, pigeon guillemots. Spring and summer wildflowers. Check with Campbell River Museum, below, for possible naturalist boat tours in summer. No pets.

Saratoga Beach: 130.5km north of Nanaimo. Sandy beach with golf course, commercial campground, marina, boat launch, and other facilities near mouth of Oyster River. Good fishing at Salmon Point.

Oyster River Regional Park: 5ha. 131km north of Nanaimo, just beyond Saratoga Beach, highway crosses Oyster River. Immediately after bridge, turn right onto Glenmore Rd, and travel one block to Regent Rd and parking. 250-334-6000. Trail leads from parking lot through the park and north, past **Woodhus Slough**, to Salmon Point (where there is a good pub and restaurant) along the coast with dramatic views to the Coast Mountains. Over 190 bird species and over 200 plant species have been recorded in slough, marsh, farm-field, beach-plain, and gravel-flats habitats.

Oyster Bay Shoreline Regional Park/Rest Area: 134km north of Nanaimo. Approaching Campbell River, much of the foreshore traced by the highway is seaside park, featuring sparkling views of Quadra Island and the Kwakwaka'wakw First Nations village, Cape Mudge. In the waters of Discovery Pass: seals, herons, and seagulls. Dramatic views of Coast Mountains.

Resort and Park Area: 142km north of Nanaimo. For 8km, beach accesses, bicycle and walking trails, picnic tables, views. Frank James and Ken Ford shoreline parks.

Jubilee Parkway: 143km north of Nanaimo. The Parkway (Hwy 19A) leads west 4.5km to join the northernmost section of the Inland Island Hwy (Hwy 19). It forms the southern leg of a bypass around Campbell River. It also leads to the Campbell River Airport. (The old highway through the heart of Campbell River is also numbered Hwy 19A). From the Parkway's junction with the Inland Island Hwy to the northern outskirts of Campbell River it is 8.5km. There, the new highway merges with the old at its junction with Hwy 28 to points west (see below), and continues north as Hwy 19.

Campbell River: (Pop. 28,851). 152km north of Nanaimo via Hwy 19/19A. Though the major industry is pulp and paper production, and two mines contribute significantly to the area's economy, Campbell River for a full century now, has been better known as a resort and sportfishing centre. The forceful, sometimes treacherous currents of Campbell River's narrow Discovery Passage support a fabulous wealth of marine life, drawing millions of tiny fish that in turn draw multitudes of hungry salmon. Big salmon. Sockeye, coho. And tyees – chinooks over 13kg – that in the past have lured big fishermen, like John Wayne, Bob Hope, Bing Crosby. The famous Tyee Club put sporting men in small rowboats to see who could hook the biggest trophies. The record, in 1968, was a 32kg chinook. Year after year, hundreds of thousands of salmon were proudly taken. Campbell River openly vied with Port Alberni for the title, "Salmon Capital of the World."

"But those days have gone forever," locals say. They're still taking tyees, but not like before, and the coho and sockeye fisheries are closed until stocks, coastwide, recover. People still come to "try" fishing – many hang their rods from the city's Discovery Pier stretching 180m into Discovery Passage. But the real draw now, is not so much what people might take away in their coolers, as what they take away in their hearts: the sight of an orca whale breaching from the deep, the bump of waves beneath a kayak, a face-to-snorkel meeting with a 23kg Pacific octopus, or a glimpse of nature's power as revealed through an exquisite Kwakwaka'wakw native carving.

Campbell River serves as a "metropolitan" gateway to North Island eco-tourism opportunities – with dive shop, charters, arts and entertainment, and accommodation. The city is also a destination in itself: divers come from around the world to explore the sunken HMCS *Columbia* and adjacent waters. And for those still bent on meeting the Big One, Paradise Sound Trekking, 250-830-0662, offers snorkelling trips down the Campbell River to observe salmon spawning. The new Discovery Harbour Shopping Centre at the north edge of downtown is just the start of $44-million plans for the Campbell River Indian Band. Existing shops and the Wei Wai Kum House of Treasures gallery will be accompanied by a hotel, convention centre, casino complex, and a marina expanded to handle cruise ships.

Campbell River Information: Info Centre, Campbell River and District Chamber of Commerce, Box 400, Campbell River, BC, V9W 5B6. 250-287-4636. In Centennial Museum building, 1235 Shoppers Row in Tyee Plaza. Daily, June-Sept. Mon-Sat, rest of year.
■ **Campbell River Museum/Regional Centre of Culture and History:** 470 Island Hwy. 250-287-3103. Daily, in summer. Tues-Sat, 12-5, Oct-April. Overlooking Discovery Passage and Cape Mudge on Quadra Island. First Nations history, European exploration and pioneer history, nature exhibits. Construction of major exhibits in this fairly new museum is ongoing. Contemporary native art and books on history and ethnology. Field trips to historic sites.
■ **Campbell River Optical Marine Museum:** 102-250 Dogwood St. 250-287-2052. Mon-Thurs, year round. Group tours by arrangement. A collection of marine-related artifacts.
■ **Campbell River Public Art Gallery:** 1235 Shoppers Row. 250-287-2261. Tues-Sat, 12-5, July-Aug. Wed-Sat, 12-5, Sept-June.
■ **Haig-Brown House Education Centre:** 2250 Campbell River Rd. 250-286-6646. At former home and grounds of conservationist and writer Roderick Haig-Brown. Programs, tours, workshops, retreats. Includes north island heritage tour, outdoor writers workshop, grandparent and grandchild fly-fishing adventures.
■ **HMCS Columbia:** Former destroyer escort and training ship became, June 22, 1996, the fourth ship scuttled by Artificial Reef Society of BC. Near Maud Island. Ask at Info Centre about charters, rentals. Also see *Outdoor Activities*.
■ **Golf: Sequoia Springs Golf**, 700 Peterson Rd, Campbell River, BC, V9W 3H5, 250-287-4970, offering 18 holes.

Quadra and Cortes Islands: Car and passenger BC Ferries make several sailings daily, 10-minute crossing from downtown Campbell River to Quathiaski Cove on Quadra Island. Ferries from Quadra at Heriot Bay run to Whaletown on Cortes Island. 250-286-1412.

Quadra Island

This 276-sq-km (full-facility) island has a population of 2,627. It has several sheltered harbours. Islands and islets dot its coast. Like Campbell River, it's a good fishing and diving area and also has many lakes. There are communities at Quathiaski Cove and Heriot Bay. No provincial campgrounds, but commercial campsites, lodges, fishing resorts, cottages, and other accommodation, dining.
■ **Kwagiulth Museum:** Cape Mudge Village. Daily, June-Sept. Mon-Sat, Oct-May. 250-285-3733. The building, inspired by the shape of a sea snail, houses part of a potlatch collection. Kwagiulth (Kwakwaka'wakw) artifacts, totem poles, and ceremonial regalia. More than 300 potlatch items were returned here, to their rightful owners, in the early 1980s, after having been seized by the government in 1922 (potlatches were banned in Canada). Some potlatch participants of that time were jailed. In new carving and artists centre, visitors can see works in progress.
■ **Tsa-Kwa-Luten Lodge:** Follow signs from ferry dock. Guided fishing, Kwagiulth Feast and Dance. Box 460 Quathiaski Cove, BC, V0P 1N0. 250-285-2042 or 1-800-665-7745.
■ **Petroglyphs:** Ancient stone drawings in small park across from Kwagiulth Museum. Others at Wa Wa Kie Beach and Francisco Point.

Rebecca Spit Provincial Marine Park: 177ha. Narrow 1.5km spit on east side of Drew Harbour. 250-337-2400. Boat launch, sand beaches, trails, picnicking, swimming, fishing.

Octopus Islands Provincial Marine Park: 109ha. Boat access only. 250-337-2400. Cluster of small islands on northeast side of Quadra Island.

Cortes Island

This 125-sq-km island has a population of 952, and lies at the entrance to Desolation Sound, one of BC's most celebrated cruising areas. Like Quadra Island, Cortes has an intricate shoreline with sheltered harbours, islets, coves. Squirrel Cove, on the east side, is a well-known anchorage with a small tidal waterfall. Gorge Harbour is a large sheltered cove entered through a narrow channel flanked by steep cliffs. Commercial accommodation and a provincial campground.
■ **Hollyhock Retreat:** On Highland Rd, south of Cortes Bay. 1-800-933-6339. A holistic healing centre. Workshops, accommodation, meals, morning yoga, biking, rowing, and a fabulous garden.

Smelt Bay Provincial Park: 16ha. 22 campsites. At southwest end of island. 250-337-2400. Beachcombing, swimming, fishing, paddling, hiking. Known for thousands of spawning smelt here.

Mansons Landing Provincial Marine Park: 100ha. Short distance north of Smelt Bay on island's west side. 250-337-2400. A sheltered cove of the Strait of Georgia to the west, and the west shores of Hague Lake to the east. Nice beaches, swimming, hiking, paddling.

Hague Lake Regional Park: Follow signs to Mansons Landing. Park opposite Cortes Motel for north loop trails or continue on Seaford Rd, left on Bartholomew Rd, left on Hague Rd. Right on Quais Bay Rd for south loop trails. 250-334-6000. Park embraces eastern shores of Hague Lake. Logging here ceased abruptly in the 1920s, when the steam donkey exploded. Its remains remain, along with imposing stands of Douglas fir and cedar, and a spruce "swamp." The place feels wild. Trail maps available on the island.

Von Donop Provincial Marine Park: 1,277ha includes 360ha of foreshore. At Von Donop Inlet. Wilderness camping. 250-954-4600. Klahoose First Nation-BC Parks joint venture protects saltwater lagoons, tidal passes, and old-growth forest of Hathayim, as this place is known to the Coast-Salish-speaking Klahoose people.

CAMPBELL RIVER TO PORT HARDY

NORTH ISLAND HIGHWAY
(Highway 19)

The North Island Highway is the main route to Port Hardy. Bear Cove, near Port Hardy, is terminal for BC Ferries sailings to Prince Rupert and Bella Coola. Ferry travellers planning to stay overnight on the north island should book accommodation at the same time as making reservations for the ferry, to make sure they have somewhere to stay.

Before the opening of the North Island Hwy in 1979, when the area was accessed by logging roads, Campbell River was often mistakenly referred to as "the north island." Campbell River is, in fact, only halfway along the east coast of Vancouver Island, 220km from its northern end, 231km from its southern tip.

A few kilometres from the outskirts of Campbell River, the population thins out considerably. Fewer than 3 percent of the island's residents live on the northern half. The highway narrows to two lanes and moves inland through the forest; the clusters of roadside motels, service stations, eateries, and shopping malls, so noticeable in the south, disappear. And strict regional zoning will prevent them from appearing.

The differences between north and south are profound. There's a frontier feeling on the north island: heavy machinery and logging trucks share the highways with hunters, anglers, campers, canoeists, and sightseers. Ponds and marshlands lie along the roadsides. Fireweed and other spring flowers grow in expansive clearcuts between mountains of replanted timber.

Up here are fishing-logging-milling-mining towns. In the past two decades, recognizing the need to grow beyond resource extraction, they have added tourism to their resumes. North-island towns that have depended on and taken pride in chopping down the biggest trees and hooking the biggest fish share particular affinity for the Tallest, Widest, Longest, and Most Outrageous when advertising their attributes.

Highway 28/19/19A: About 2km north of Campbell River city centre. Hwy 28 leads west 92km to Gold River (and to **Strathcona Provincial Park** and other attractions). There are several wilderness campsites on lakes and streams between Campbell River and Buttle Lake. Hwy 19A through Campbell River merges here with the Inland Island Hwy's Campbell River bypass and continues north as Hwy 19.

SIDE TRIP

to Gold River and Tahsis
(Highway 28)

Quinsam River Hatchery: Take Hwy 28 and watch for hatchery sign on left. Winding road 2.5km to hatchery. 250-287-9564. Self-guided tours. Pink and chinook salmon in Sept, coho in Oct, steelhead in early March. Daily, year-round.

Elk Falls Provincial Park: (Quinsam Campground) 1,086ha; 122 campsites. 250-337-2400. On Hwy 28 just over 1km west of Hwy 19. Confluence of Campbell and Quinsam rivers in park. Swimming, fishing, hiking. John Hart Dam nearby. Tours available. Spawning salmon visible Sept-Dec.

Canyon View Trail: About .5km beyond Elk Falls Park sign, watch for sign to trail. 6km circle route offers splendid views of Campbell River canyon and salmon spawning channels.

Elk Falls: Pullout 3km west of Hwy 19. Sign describes a major forest fire here in 1938.

Elk Falls Viewpoint: 4km west of Hwy 19. Parking and view of Elk Falls.

Loveland Bay Provincial Park and Snowden Demonstration Forest: About 5km west of Hwy 19 (at top of long hill). Go straight through intersection (off Hwy 28), cross the John Hart Dam, then take first left onto Camp 5 Rd (also known as Brewster Rd). About 9km to park with 47 campsites (May-Sept), boat launch, swimming, and canoeing.

It's 1km farther to start of **Snowden Demonstration Forest**. Self-guided tour provides info on replanted clearcuts, managed tree stands, rock formations and the "Suicide Bridge" (a logging trestle built in 1929). Walking trails, picnic tables. Map and brochure available from the Ministry of Forests, Campbell River District: 250-286-9300. Overlapping **Elk Habitat Tour** explains effects of forestry on Roosevelt elk habitat.

Highway 28 and Road to Mine: About 48km west of Campbell River, Hwy 28 slips between Upper Campbell and Buttle lakes, crossing northern Strathcona Provincial Park en route to Gold River. Road south also enters Strathcona Provincial Park, tracing the shores of Buttle Lake to **Boliden/Westmin Resources Mine.** *Log* follows southern route first.

Strathcona Provincial Park: 253,773ha; 161 campsites in two campgrounds plus wilderness camping. 250-337-2400. Vancouver Island's largest provincial park is even larger now with the additions of the Megin Watershed and McBride Creek, totalling over 31,000ha. Strathcona's easternmost point is only 13km from the sea at

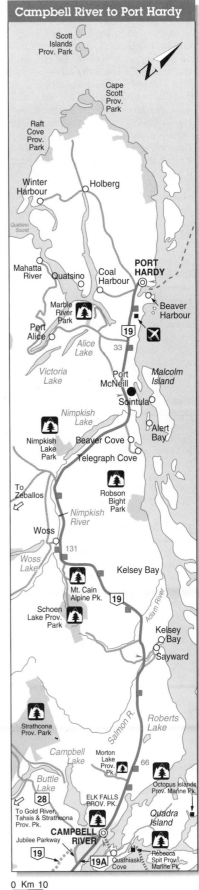

Campbell River to Port Hardy

0 Km 10

Comox Harbour, while its extreme southwest corner reaches tidewater at the head of **Herbert Inlet**, on the opposite side of Vancouver Island. The park is roughly triangular, extending about 65km south from the 50th parallel of latitude. Within its boundaries are Mt Golden Hinde, at 2,200m Vancouver Island's highest peak, and **Della Falls**, at 440m the highest waterfalls in Canada. The Megin River is a popular sport-fishing destination; Megin Lake offers camping, fishing, and canoeing.

Established in 1911, it is the province's first park. With its challenging peaks, alpine meadows, and forests, Strathcona is a hiker's paradise. Its multitude of small lakes attract summer canoeists and anglers. Contact BC Parks (see BC *Introduction,* p. 22) for a brochure and map of trails and facilities.

The main accesses to Strathcona are off Hwy 28 from Campbell River and at Forbidden Plateau outside Courtenay. Della Falls, described in *Craig's Crossing to Ucluelet Junction,* p.82, can be reached by boat and backpack from Great Central Lake near Port Alberni.

■ **Strathcona Park Lodge and Outdoor Education Centre:** Box 2160, Campbell River, BC, V9W 5C5. 250-286-3122. On Upper Campbell Lake along Hwy 28, 38km west of Hwy 19. Well-known for its programs in wilderness skills, outdoor summer camps, family excursions. Provides accommodation and meals. Also the COLT (Canadian Outdoor Leadership Training) Centre, with 105-day intensive programs developing water and land-based outdoor skills, environmental awareness, and teaching ability in experiential education. For adults 19 and over. The Wilderness Youth Leadership Development program has summer camps for 12-18 year olds.

Ralph River: 76 campsites. Reached by driving 45km on Hwy 28 to a bridge between Upper Campbell and Buttle lakes. Don't cross bridge, but continue south along east shore of Buttle Lake for about 25km.

Boliden/Westmin Resources Mine: 12km beyond Ralph River campground and around south end of Buttle Lake. Mainly copper and zinc. Tours: 250-287-9271.

Big Den Rest Area: About 1km beyond Westmin mine.

Buttle Lake: 85 campsites. Drive across bridge between Upper Campbell and Buttle lakes. Turn south after bridge and take short road to campsite.

Gold River: (Pop. 2,041). 89km west of Campbell River. A modern instant town in a wilderness frontier setting. The town, nicely nestled in the Gold River valley, was built in 1965 to support the pulp mill situated 12km downriver, overlooking Muchalat Inlet in Nootka Sound. In 1998, the pulp mill's closure was announced. Gold River's future is uncertain. The river is known for its excellent steelhead fishing. The sound attracts divers and kayakers. In town, there's a nine-hole golf course, and an aquatic and leisure centre.

This region is traditional home to the Mowachaht and Muchalaht tribes of the Nuu-chah-nulth West Coast peoples. The Mowachaht offer tours and visits to their ancient capital, Yuquot, on the southeast tip of Nootka Island, now a national historic site. See *Yuquot*, below.

Pulp Mill Rd leads 12km southwest to the head of Muchalat Inlet and departures for points in Nootka Sound. Unpaved roads lead northwest from Gold River to Tahsis, and to Hwy 19 at Woss.

Gold River Information: Info Centre at Hwy 28 and Scout Lake Rd. c/o Village of Gold River, Box 610, Gold River, BC, V0P 1G0. 250-283-2418 or 250-283-2202. Daily, mid-May to Labour Day. Ask about helicopter tours and fishing and diving charters.

Ahaminaquus Information: Box 459, Gold River, BC, V0P 1G0. 250-283-7464. 12km from Gold River on Pulp Mill Rd. Bookings for water taxis, cabins, and camping at Yuquot.

Nootka Sound Service: MV *Uchuck III* departs from head of Muchalat Inlet, 12km south of Gold River town centre to sail intricate northwest coast. 250-283-2515 or 250-283-2325. Year-round freight and passenger service for west-coast communities in Nootka Sound, Gold River, Yuquot (Friendly Cove), Tahsis, and Kyuquot. See *Transportation,* p.35. Ship is a converted US mine sweeper built in 1943.

Bligh Island Provincial Marine Park: 4,455ha. 250-954-4600. At the entrance to Muchalat Inlet. Reached from Ahaminaquus (Gold River) or Tahsis by boat or plane. This boating, kayaking, and fishing wilderness recreation area embraces a cluster of forested islands called the Spanish Pilot Group. They include the southern portion of Bligh Island, named for Vice-Admiral William Bligh, ship's master aboard Captain James Cook's ship, HMS *Resolution,* which was refitted here in 1778, and for which Resolution Cove is named. Bligh later became famous for his role in the mutiny on the *Bounty,* in the South Seas.

Yuquot (Friendly Cove): (Pop. 3). On southeast corner of Nootka Island, west of Ahaminaquus (Gold River), via Muchalat Inlet. Yuquot is accessible by locally based floatplanes, helicopters, fishing charters, water taxis, and the MV *Uchuck III*. This is traditional territory and ancient summer headquarters of the Mowachaht people. Captain James Cook landed here in 1778 and is credited with being the first European to land on the coast of what later became BC. The British called the people who lived here "Nootka," though the people who live in the area today laugh, and say *nootka* was a warning to the sailors, "circle round," to avoid hitting the rocks. Trade between the Mowachaht and British began immediately – sea otter and other furs for items not available here – and Friendly Cove, or Nootka, became an international trading centre. Today, just one Mowachaht family lives here, though there's still a church and some buildings left from busier times. In summer, **Yuquot Tours** guide visitors to important sites; there is camping, and accommodation in cabins.

Return to Gold River

Upana Caves: About 17km west of Gold River. Take Head Bay Forest Rd west toward Tahsis. Turn at Branch H27 and stop at parking lot short distance up road. Access trail runs 150m to register entrance. Self-guided tours. About one hour through main caves. Several undeveloped caves in one group. 15 known entrances with passages totalling 450m. Caves vary from single rooms to several branching passages. Take reliable flashlight and rubber-soled boots; helmets with lights can be rented at the hardware store in Gold River. For supervised group tours contact Camel Rock Adventures Ltd, Box 711, Gold River, BC, V0P 1G0. 250-283-2332.

Conuma Salmon Hatchery: About midway between Gold River and Tahsis. Look for sign. Write Box 247, Tahsis, BC, V0P 1X0. Fish to see year-round. Steelhead fishing in Conuma River when permitted.

Tahsis: (Pop. 800). 65km west of Gold River. Served by Air Nootka and the MV *Uchuck III*. An ailing forestry community at the head of Tahsis Inlet: closure of the local sawmill places strong hopes for the future on tourism. Sheltered cruising, kayaking and canoeing, eagle watching, caving, fishing, hiking. Marina, fuel dock, public floats, boat launch, charters and rentals, accommodation. Tour bus in summer.

Tahsis Information: Box 278, Tahsis, BC, V0P 1X0. 250-934-6667. July-Aug. Local businesses can provide information other times.

Return to Highway 19

Elk Falls Mill: Turn east off Hwy 19 on Elk Falls Mill Rd, 4km north of Campbell River. Fletcher Challenge Canada Ltd (an amalgamation of BC Forest Products and Crown Forest) pulp and paper mill. For tours: 250-287-5594.

Seymour Narrows and Ripple Rock: Historic site 11km north of Campbell River. 8km round-trip hike. A perilous pass where tides run up to 10 knots: the ominous twin peaks of Ripple Rock once lay just below the surface near the channel's centre. This nautical nuisance is said to have caused two dozen major shipwrecks and claimed more than 100 lives. It was blown out of the water in 1958 with one of the largest non-atomic blasts in history.

Trail to Ripple Rock: Watch for a hiking sign about 6km north of historic site. Two trails to cliffs above Seymour Narrows. About three hours return. See forest birds, seabirds, seals, porpoises and killer whales.

Morton Lake Provincial Park: 67ha; 24 campsites. 250-954-4600. West off Hwy 19 at MacMillan Bloedel, Menzies Bay Division, 20km north of Campbell River. Fishing, windsurfing, hiking, swimming.

Roberts Lake and Rest Area: 32km north of Campbell River, east side of Hwy 19. Kokanee, Dolly Varden char, cutthroat trout. One of dozens of excellent fishing lakes along logging roads on both sides of highway. Detailed maps can be purchased in Campbell River.

McNair Lake: 35.5km north of Campbell River. Hiking Trail.

Rock Bay Rd: 37km north of Campbell River. East on unpaved road, 10km to private campground, launch, and Rock Bay Provincial Marine Park on Johnstone Strait. 4km farther to Chatham Point Lighthouse. Road passes McCreight Lake, another hot fishing spot.

Rock Bay Provincial Marine Park: 525ha. 250-954-4600. Accessible from land via Rock Bay Rd, or by boat. A rocky headland with sheltered bays, walking trails, fishing, diving, camping, boat launch.

Big Tree Creek Rest Area: On Hwy 19, about 47km north of Campbell River.

Salmon Lookout: 52km north of Campbell River.

Dalrymple Creek: 57km north of Campbell River. Hiking trail.

Road to Sayward: 64km north of Campbell River. East on paved road, 10km to village of Sayward and wharf at Kelsey Bay. Turn west to go short distance to information centre.

Here is the southern boundary of the Regional District of Mount Waddington, which encompasses all northern Vancouver Island and a portion of the mainland. Named for **Mt Waddington**, at head of Knight Inlet on the mainland, highest mountain totally within BC. Mt Waddington wasn't mapped until 1925, when its 4,016m peak was spotted from Vancouver Island.

SIDE TRIP

to Sayward-Kelsey Bay

Sayward-Kelsey Bay Information: White River Court, RR 1, Site 11, Box 1, Comp 7, Sayward, BC, V0P 1R0. 250-282-3265. At Sayward Junction, turn west off Hwy 19, and proceed a few hundred metres until you reach service station and coffee bar.

Salmon River: Reputed to hold largest steelhead on island, 74km river empties into Johnstone Strait at Kelsey Bay. Road to Sayward crosses the river twice as river and road wind down the enchanting Salmon River valley. Private campgrounds along lower reaches. The **Salmon River Estuary/Wildlife Reserve** is at the river's mouth. Trumpeter swans, dabbling ducks, ospreys, kestrels, and other hawks thrive here.

Douglas firs, with their thick armour of bark, flourish on northern Vancouver Island.

Hkusam Mountain: El 1,671m. East side of Salmon Valley. Look closely for the steamy ring around its peak – locally it's known as an "Indian blanket." Kwakwaka'wakw people called the mountain Hiatsee Saklekum: "where the breath of the sea lion gathers at the blowhole." A marsh and small lake are said to be the cause of the mysterious fog. Hkusam was the name of a nearby village.

Cable Cafe: About 1km beyond Sayward Junction after you cross the bridge. Cafe is made from 2,500m of used wire rope – 26 tonnes – most of it two-inch skyline logging cable from a method of logging abandoned in the 1950s.

Sayward-Kelsey Bay: (Pop. 440). Service centre for the Salmon River valley area, which has about 1,200 inhabitants, mainly farmers and loggers. First settled in the early 1890s, it is now division headquarters for MacMillan Bloedel forestry operation.

The big wharf at Kelsey Bay was once the southern terminus of BC Ferries Inside Passage sailing to Prince Rupert. Fishboats and charter boats tie up here. Boat launch.

Return to Highway 19

Keta Lake Rest Area: 74km north of Campbell River.

Adam River Bridge: 83km north of Campbell River. Picnic site 2km south of bridge is pleasant place to inhale forest air. To the south are the peaks of Mt Juliet (1,637m) and Mt Romeo (1,661m). These mountains are birthplace of the Adam and Eve rivers, whose courses come together near their estuary, above Johnstone Strait.

Eve River Rest Area: 93km north of Campbell River. Miles and miles of logging-scape: ironically beautiful.

Logging Rd to Schoen Lake: 93km north of Campbell River. The Nimpkish River system, with its headwaters at Mt Alston, about 32km south of this junction, is Vancouver Island's largest watershed. On its 145km journey to the sea, it is joined by the waters of major lakes such as Schoen, Vernon, Woss, and the Klaklakama Lakes.

SIDE TRIP

to Schoen Lake

About 300m from Hwy 19 signs point the way to Schoen Lake, Mt Cain, and Klaklakama Lakes.

Schoen Lake Provincial Park: 8,430ha. 10 campsites. 250-954-4600. South off Hwy 19 and left a short distance from the highway. A stunning wilderness park encompassing mountains, streams, and woodlands. The 1,802m summit of Mt Schoen reflects off the waters of Schoen Lake, a narrow, 5km stretch of canoeing water. Schoen Lake is considered by some to be one of the most scenic lakes on Vancouver Island. Several mountain trails follow water courses around the lake, one leading to Nisnak Meadows, where subalpine wildflowers bloom late spring and summer. Hikers occasionally cross the paths of black bears, beavers, wolves, cougars, black-tailed deer. Also Roosevelt elk, most often seen at twilight. The 13km gravel road is narrow and bumpy in places and goes through active logging areas.

Klaklakama Lakes: On road to Schoen Lake about 7km south of Hwy 19. Two small, lovely campsites, one on each lake. Beautiful canoeing. A nice place to pause for a picnic on the journey up or down island.

Mt Cain Alpine Park: Mt Cain – el 1,646m. On road to Schoen Lake, 16km from Hwy 19. Chains required in winter. Write Mt Cain Alpine Park Society, Box 1225, Port McNeill, BC, V0N 2R0. Access road recently improved, but can still be rough. Vertical drop 450m. Two T-bars, handle-tow. 16 downhill runs. 20km unmarked cross-country trails. Day lodge, rentals, lessons. Limited hostel-style accommodation. Open winter weekends and school holidays. Hiking in summer. Wildflowers and blueberries. The area's fragile ecology features alpine and bog vegetation.

Return to Highway 19

Hoomak Lake Rest Area: About 125km north of Campbell River. Features solar-powered composting toilet technology.

Woss Junction: 130km north of Campbell River. South off Hwy 19, about 2km to community of Woss.

Woss: (Pop. 600). Logging on the north island is not only big business, it's old business. Displayed at this Canadian Forest Products community, is an antique steam locomotive, once used to haul logs. This valley, known for its trout fishing and hunting, has been an important source of timber for several decades; much of it remains accessible by logging roads. Services in this sleepy community include motel, gas station, coffee shop, store. Campgrounds at Woss and Vernon lakes.

Woss Lake Provincial Park: 6,634ha. 250-954-4600. At southeast end of Woss Lake. Reached by boat from Canfor campsite and boat launch at north end of Woss Lake, about 5km south of Woss by logging road. Wilderness camping at edge of steep and forested wilderness.

Return to Highway 19

Eagle's Nest Rest Area: On Hwy 19, about 136km north of Campbell River. River view.

Zeballos Rd: 151km north of Campbell River, west off Hwy 19, 21km on unpaved road to Zeballos.

SIDE TRIP

to Zeballos

Little Hustan Cave Regional Park: Short distance on Zeballos Rd. Not suitable for oversize vehicles. Follow signs. For inexperienced cavers, good caves, with sink holes, canyons, and a cathedral entrance. Large arches and swift-flowing river that disappears and reappears in rock formations.

Zeballos: (Pop. 263). At head of Zeballos Inlet. Pretty village beneath mountains with high cliffs and waterfalls. Once an important gold-mining town with a population over 1,500. Exploration for the mineral is ongoing, but mainstays are logging and fishing. Base for boat trips to the long inlets and waterways around Nootka Island. Though small, the village has campgrounds, a hotel, motel, and other accommodation. Excellent sportfishing.
■ **Zeballos Museum:** On Maquinna Ave. 250-761-4070 or 250-761-4229 in winter. Tues-Sat, July-Aug. By appointment in winter. Gold-mining history.

Fair Harbour: 35km northwest of Zeballos by unpaved road. Launching point for kayakers and boaters exploring Kyuquot Sound, including Brooks Peninsula and Checleset Bay.

Kyuquot: (Pop. 275). At Houpsitas, in Kyuquot Sound. Only accessible by water. Kyuquot Band Office, General Delivery, Kyuquot, BC, V0P 1J0. 250-332-5259. This is the northernmost of 14 Nuu-chah-nulth First Nation tribes. Bed and breakfast, motel and restaurant, boat charters, water taxi.

Brooks Peninsula Provincial Park: 51,631ha. 250-954-4600. Accessible by boat from Fair Harbour and from **Kyuquot** where charters and accommodation are available. 250-332-5259. This mountainous rectangular finger protruding 18km into the Pacific is considered an ecological oddity because it appears to have escaped glaciation during the ice age. Here are white sand and pebble beaches, razorlike peaks, alpine lakes and meadows. The lee side is softer and replete with wildlife. Sheltered fiords, fishing, kayaking.

The peninsula's shores are the home of Canada's only sea otters, endearing, whisker-faced clowns that once thrived along the entire coast of North America. Today, about 2,500 remain in Canada, descendants of Alaskan otters transplanted in late 1960s and early 1970s. The luxurious fur of these marine mammals was not only the cause of their near demise, but one of the main reasons for

European exploration of the BC coast in the late 1700s. The furs were an extremely valuable commodity for merchant seamen eager to satisfy the fashion-conscious mandarins of China. Vancouver Island's last native sea otter was shot dead in 1929 at Kyuquot. After the transplant, they were among that worrisome class of animals known as endangered species, but they are reestablishing themselves now, at an annual growth rate of 12 percent and are starting to disperse themselves up and down the coast, gourmandizing on red sea urchins.

Return to Highway 19

Nimpkish Lake: 11km beyond Zeballos Rd. Gas station, store, and excellent forest-service campground. Early Aug, this is site of annual Nimpkish Speed Slalom Weekend for windsurfers. Accessible by boat from here is **Nimpkish Lake Provincial Park**, 3,950ha, embracing the lake's southwest shores. No facilities. Highway skirts eastern shores of this narrow, 22km-long lake which takes its name from the Nimpkish or 'Namgis people whose place of origin is the Nimpkish River. The 'Namgis now live at Alert Bay on Cormorant Island (below).

Forestry Tours: North Island Forestry Center, operated by five forest companies, near turnoff to Beaver Cove (5000 North Island Hwy). 250-956-3844. Six-hour tours depart weekdays from the forestry centre. Forestry, logging, trail walks, and visits to old-growth forests. Advanced booking required.

Beaver Cove Rd: 187km north of Campbell River. Southeast for 13km to log-sorting grounds at Beaver Cove. Another 2km to Telegraph Cove. (Last 8km is logging road.)

SIDE TRIP

to Telegraph Cove

A good take-off point for whale watching in Johnstone Strait.

Beaver Cove Dryland Sort: About 13km from Hwy 19. Lookout and information sign at east end of sorting grounds. This Canadian Forest Products dryland sort for logs is the largest facility of its kind in Canada. In the past, there was a live-in camp for workers; now everyone commutes – most come from Port McNeill. Each year, some 1.2 million cubic metres of logs are shipped here from the Nimpkish Valley by truck and railcar to be sorted and scaled. Then, tugs sporting 2,000-horsepower engines tow 11 rafts or booms of logs each on a seven-day journey to Vancouver, where they are processed into lumber, hardboard, or pulp and newsprint.

Telegraph Cove: (Pop. 5). Telegraph Cove, on charming boardwalks, was built before the First World War as northern terminus of a telegraph line strung from

Alert Bay on Cormorant Island got its start as a commercial fishing village.

tree to tree along Vancouver Island's coast. After 1922, this was a thriving sawmill community. After the mill closed in the 1980s, Telegraph Cove emerged as major destination for wilderness lovers. Each summer, this teacup of a town is washed by a wave of 100,000 kayakers, fishermen, sightseers. And, mainly, whale watchers – they come to see the killer whales (orcas) that frequent these waters, and rub their bellies on the gravel beaches of Robson Bight at the mouth of the Tsitika River, 20km down Johnstone Strait. **Robson Bight Provincial Park** (6,608ha) embraces the whales' habitat, as well as Mt Derby and Tsitika Mountain ecological reserves, which protect rare alpine forest and bog environments.

Meanwhile, Telegraph Cove's residents feel a mixture of optimism and uneasiness as a $100-million plan to turn the village into a destination community unfolds. A thousand new housing units will surround their houses around the old boardwalk. New is Telegraph Cove's first restaurant and pub – the Killer Whale Cafe and Saltery – into which the sounds of whales will be piped from the new ORCA-FM station near Robson Bight. Fans can tune in to CJKW 88.5 and sing along, as long as they're within 15km of Robson Bight.

Campground, boat launch, boat gas, post office, general store. For bookings and charters: 1-800-200-4665.

Return to Highway 19

Port McNeill: (Pop. 2,925). 194km north of Campbell River, east off Hwy 19 for 2km. Port McNeill, with a sheltered harbour and modern townsite, is home for many who work in the surrounding forests. With two marinas, this is also a launching point for sportfishermen who test their skills in the channels around the many islands between Vancouver Island and the mainland, and in nearby lakes and rivers. The town, built upon a hillside sloping down to its waterfront downtown, provides millionaire views of Broughton Strait for almost everyone who lives there. The town was named for William Henry McNeill (1801-1875), a Boston-born Hudson's Bay Company factor who, in 1849, helped establish the Fort Rupert Coal Mines north of here.

Port McNeill Information: Info Centre, Port McNeill Chamber of Commerce, Box 129, Port McNeill, BC, V0N 2R0. 250-956-3131. On Broughton Blvd, in new museum building (museum is still a work-in-progress). Daily, early June-early Sept.

Regional District of Mount Waddington Information: 2044 McNeill Rd (across from high school). 250-956-3161. Drop in for maps of highways, logging roads, and regional parks. For information by mail, contact information centres in specific north-island communities.

Port McNeill Airstrip: About 2km south of Port McNeill on sign-posted road. Charter flights, private aircraft.

Alert Bay-Sointula: Car and passenger ferries from Port McNeill run across Broughton Strait to Alert Bay, on Cormorant Island, and to Sointula, on Malcolm Island. About nine sailings daily, 20 minutes to Sointula, 40 minutes to Alert Bay. Information: 250-339-0444.

SIDE TRIP

to Alert Bay and Sointula

Alert Bay: On tiny 6.5-sq-km Cormorant Island. (Total pop. 1,267). By ferry from Port McNeill. Alert Bay and Cormorant Island were named for British warships HMS *Alert* and HMS *Cormorant*, which surveyed coastal waters 1846-1861. The 'Namgis people of the Kwakwaka'wakw First Nations moved here on a permanent basis from their place of origin, just across Broughton Strait on the Nimpkish River in the 1870s. They came here to live and work following the establishment of a salmon saltery and church mission. Over the next century and a quarter, native and non-native communities have grown side by side. Alert Bay offers visitors a rare opportunity to explore Kwakwaka'wakw history in depth, and meet some of the people who are keeping this rich and vibrant culture alive.

Alert Bay has nearly 20km of road to roam, nearly all paved. With everything virtually within walking distance, there is, oddly enough, a very active cab fleet ferrying people back and forth along Front and Fir streets. Until 1986, large cruise ships docked at Alert

77

Bay and busloads of sightseers perused the village. Now, only "pocket cruisers" pull in, and vanloads of mostly American travellers tour the cultural centre and stroll the streets.

On the island: accommodation and campgrounds, whale-watching tours, fishing charters, boat launch, moorage, fuel, groceries.

Alert Bay Information: Info Centre, Village of Alert Bay, Box 28, Alert Bay, BC, V0N 1A0. 250-974-5213. On Fir St. Turn right after disembarking from ferry. Mon-Fri, year-round. Daily,July-Aug. Here is an intriguing collection of watercolours by artist Chris Nancarron, who, over a year and a day beginning on a rainy Thanksgiving Day in 1984, painted each section of Fir St, "contriving nothing, observing everything."

Alert Bay Airstrip: About 2km from village centre. Chartered flights.

■ **U'mista Cultural Centre:** Left from ferry dock on Front St. 250-974-5403. Early May-late Sept: daily. Oct-April: Mon-Fri. In modern building modelled after a Kwakwaka'wakw Big House are remarkable ceremonial masks and regalia confiscated by Canadian government in 1921. They were returned in 1979 some 28 years after colonial laws banning potlatch ceremonies had been withdrawn. Also here are baskets, photos, stories from the beginning of time, and videos. Special tours, and in Wed-Sat, July-Aug, see the local 'Na'nakwala Dancers: call 250-974-5501 or 250-974-2626.

■ **Tallest Totem Pole:** Above cultural centre. The Sun Mask on top is visible to all approaching the community. At 52.7m, it held the *Guinness* record from 1972 until 1994 when a pole 2.1m taller was raised in Victoria. Victoria's pole, considered dangerous and not appreciated by Victorians, was brought down in 1997.

■ **'Namgis Burial Grounds:** Right from ferry dock. There's an inexplicable eeriness to carved poles above the beach in this century-old cemetery (please do not trespass).

■ **Other Historic Sites:** Brochures at Info Centre details old shipyard, courthouse, churches, chapel, BC Packers Plant and more.

■ **Gator Gardens:** Trails and boardwalks through an unusual ecological park. Old cedar snags, culturally modified trees, hemlock and pine trees draped with moss. Ravens, eagles, migratory birds.

■ **Alert Bay Library and Museum:** 199 Fir St. 250-974-5721. Mon-Sat, afternoons, July-Aug. Mon, Wed evenings; Fri, Sat afternoons, off-season. Kwakwaka'wakw and local artifacts. Photo/archival collection. St George's Anglican Chapel, built in 1925, open on request.

■ **Alert Bay Art Gallery:** Shares Info Centre complex. Local artists.

Sointula: (Pop. 637). On 83-sq-km Malcolm Island. By ferry from Port McNeill and Alert Bay. A charming fishing village which began as a Finnish cooperative community. Sointula, "A Place of Harmony," was established in 1901 by leader-philosopher-playwright Matti Kurrika. The colonization company he founded collapsed in 1905, but some 100 Finns remained. Just three decades ago, Finnish was the principal language of the island: today, less than 50 percent of the popu-

Beaver Lake, near Port McNeill.

lation is Finnish. The cemetery, burial place for many pioneer Finns, overlooks Broughton Strait (turn right from the ferry).

It's a wonderful place to wander and absorb the maritime atmosphere. There are beaches to walk and logging roads to explore.

Stops include the Hole in the Wall art gallery and traditional co-op general store (c.1909). Whale-watching and fishing charters, kayak and bicycle rentals. Accommodation, campgrounds, including the Bere Point campground on the northern side of the island facing Queen Charlotte Sound, offering about 10 rustic campsites.

■ **Sointula Finnish Museum:** Left on First St immediately after disembarking from ferry. Next to tennis courts. Call 250-973-6353 or 250-973-6764 and someone will come and show you through. No long distance charges from Port McNeill. Artifacts reflect fishing and farming roots of Finnish community.

Return to Highway 19

World's Largest Burl: 1.5km north of Port McNeill turnoff. Burl from a 351-year-old spruce tree. Weighs more than 20t and measures 13.5m around. Was discovered by surveyors near the head of Benson River, 40km south of its current resting place.

Misty Lake Rest Area: About 211km north of Campbell River.

Port Alice Rd: About 214km north of Campbell River, west off Hwy 19 for 58km on paved road to Port Alice. Keep an eye on your picnic basket: black bears, at home along this road, often venture right into Port Alice.

SIDE TRIP

to Port Alice

Beaver Lake: Small shallow lake just off Hwy 19 on Port Alice Rd. Day-use swimming and picnic area. Cutthroat and Dolly Varden.

Seven Hills Golf and Country Club: On Port Alice Hwy, 1km from Hwy 19. 250-949-9818. A shot of civilization in the middle of an absolute wilderness. Nine holes, restaurant, great hazards. Hornsby steam tractor here was built in 1910 in England and used in Dawson City to haul coal. Later brought to Holberg Inlet area to haul logs, but at 40t it got bogged down and was abandoned.

Marble River Recreation Area: About 13km from Hwy 19. Large treed campground. Boat launch, fishing, canoeing, swimming, waterskiing, hiking. Base for north island day trips.

Marble River Provincial Park: 1,512ha. 250-954-4600. Adjacent recreation area. Park embraces both sides of the shallow river canyon, its mouth, and shoreline along Quatsino Narrows, and Varney Bay on Rupert Inlet. Hiking trail provides access to 1.5km of river's south bank. Other areas can be reached only by boat.

Link River Regional Campground: 50km off Hwy 19. Offers 30 campsites. Canoeing and fishing on river, waterskiing on Alice Lake.

Port Alice: (Pop. 1,331). At foot of mountains and at head of Neroutsos Inlet in Quatsino Sound. Bears a remarkable resemblance to the town of Port Annie described by Vancouver Island author Jack Hodgins in one of his best novels, *The Resurrection of Joseph Bourne*. This logging and pulp mill town was actually named after Alice Whalen. In the period after the First World War, the Whalen family operated three pulp mills in the area. In 1965 Port Alice was incorporated as BC's first instant municipality. A new townsite was built to replace the original company town 4km up the inlet, near the pulp mill. The old town closed in 1967.

Full tourist facilities, including accommodation and campgrounds. Boat-launching for exploration and fishing in long inlets of Quatsino Sound. Good fishing and camping at nearby Alice and Victoria lakes.

Port Alice Information: Information centre operates year-round out of Quatsino Chalet, Box 280, Port Alice, BC, V0N 2N0. On the main street at 1061 Marine Dr. Open Mon-Fri. 250-284-3318.

■ **Port Alice Golf and Country Club:** Off Port Alice Hwy, beyond Port Alice townsite and left of the pulp mill. 250-284-3213. Nine holes, nine sand traps, four water hazards.

Logging Rd to Mahatta River: 75km from Port Alice to Side Bay and Klaskino Inlet on the open Pacific. Ribbon-marked trail off Restless Main to beach, and eight-hour serious hike to Lawn Point. No fresh water, no facilities, no signs. Plane wreckage on beach. Consult Western Forest Products maps or ask at Port Alice Information Centre.

Return to Highway 19

Byng Rd: About 225km north of Campbell River, east off Hwy 19. About 1km to Beaver Harbour Rd leading to Fort Rupert First Nation, Storey's Beach, and hiking. 2km on Byng Rd to **Port Hardy Airport**.

SIDE TRIP

to Beaver Harbour

Beaver Harbour: Beaver Harbour Rd leads a short distance to T'sakis Way and Kwakwaka'wakw community of **Kwakiutl** or Fort Rupert, at historic site of **Fort Rupert**, a Hudson's Bay post established in 1849 to take advantage of nearby coal fields. A crumbling chimney is the only remnant of the fort that closed in 1882. The store was taken over by company employee Robert Hunt. Several native artists, including descendants of Hunt, produce outstanding examples of Kwakwaka'wakw art. The Copper Maker gift shop and workshop is open to public. The very end of the road is start of the Tex Lyon Trail to Dillon Point, an arduous trek via headlands and ropes for experienced hikers only.

Return to Highway 19

BC Ferries Terminal: At Bear Cove, about 1km beyond turnoff to airport, Bear Cove Hwy leads east 5km to BC Ferries terminal and Inside Passage departures. Archaeologists have unearthed evidence of human occupation at Bear Cove, suggesting people lived here 12,000 years ago (exhibit at Port Hardy Museum, below). Ferry passengers leaving cars in Port Hardy are advised not to park at terminal: shuttle service is available from hotels, campgrounds, and B&Bs.

Road to Coal Harbour: West off Hwy 19 about 2km beyond airport turnoff, a few metres beyond Quatse River bridge. Hardy Bay Rd leads east: a scenic route along waterfront to Port Hardy.

SIDE TRIP

to Coal Harbour

Island Copper Mine: Visible from the roadside southwest of Port Hardy. The site is closed to visitors. For a short time it was the lowest manmade point on the Earth's surface – the hole reached 396m below sea level when the mine closed in 1996. Under several owners, the mine had operated for a quarter of a century, and at its peak, employed 900 people. The closure was a blow to north island communities. This was Canada's third largest copper mine, also producing molybdenum, silver and gold. Mining and milling techniques pioneered here were adopted by open-pit mines around the world. The former open pit is now a lake, the land around it is covered with young trees.

Coal Harbour: (Pop. 200). 14km southwest of Hwy 19 near mouth of Holberg Inlet. From 1941-1947, this quiet village served as a base for the Royal Canadian Airforce. For two decades after that, Coal Harbour thrived as a whaling station: until recently, the enormous jawbone of a blue whale stood as a reminder (but the bones are away now, for repairs). Cafe. Lots of marine traffic as well as a lovely view from wharf.

Quatsino: (Pop. 100). Accessible from Coal Harbour by water taxi. Fishing for salmon, cod, red snapper. B&B, charters, beachcombing, hiking, berry picking. May see porpoises or whales. For info: call Port Hardy, 250-949-7622.

Return to Highway 19

Port Hardy: (Pop. 5,283). 2km beyond Coal Harbour Rd. 230km north of Campbell River. Port Hardy, the north island's main centre near the edge of the world – a paved seaside path winds along Hardy Bay, a favourite gathering place for bald eagles, Canada geese, and other birds. There are wooden signs, carved by a local artist, depicting fish and wildlife frequently seen by north islanders in their day-to-day travels.

Port Hardy, traditionally, thrived on forestry, mining, and commercial fishing, but with those mainstays withering, there is concern this town and others like it will go the way of Newfoundland outports. Even sportfishing, in this place locally hailed "King Coho Country," is floundering. "Coho salmon are our bread and butter fish," says Ken Jenkin of Cod Father Charters. With government closure of the coho fishery in 1998 to protect dwindling stocks, Jenkin says, "although there appear to be a lot of coho out there, until regulations relax, we may as well call this No Coho Country." Meanwhile, visiting anglers are catching chinook, pink and sockeye salmon, and halibut.

Ask at Info Centre about fishing and kayaking rentals and charters, hiking adventures, and First Nations cultural experiences. Port Hardy is also a take-off point for Cape Scott Provincial Park (below) and Brooks Peninsula Provincial Park (p.76).

Campgrounds are plentiful in and around Port Hardy. But reservations for hotels and motels are absolutely necessary during summer.

Port Hardy Information: Info Centre, Port Hardy and District Chamber of Commerce, Box 249, Port Hardy, BC, V0N 2P0. 250-949-7622. On Market St near ocean. Daily, early June-late Sept. Mon-Fri rest of year.

BC Ferries Terminal: At Bear Cove. From Port Hardy junction take sign-posted route to terminal. Ferries to Prince Rupert and Bella Coola. For details, see *Transportation*, p.34.

■ **Port Hardy Museum and Archives:** 7110 Market St. 250-949-8143. Open afternoons Tues, Thurs, Sat; longer hours in summer. Kwakwaka'wakw history, discovery and exploration of coast, a settler's kitchen. Gift shop.

■ **Quatse River Salmon Hatchery:** Northern Vancouver Island Salmonid Enhancement Assn, Box 1409, Port Hardy, BC, V0N 2P0. 250-949-9022. On Hardy Bay Rd, just off Hwy 19 and across from Pioneer Inn. Coho, chinook, and chum. Campground, picnic areas, nature trails along river, fishing. BC Wildlife Watch viewing site.

■ **God's Pocket Provincial Park:** 2,025 ha. Cluster of small islands at entrance to Queen Charlotte Strait just north of Port Hardy. No facilities, but nearby God's Pocket Resort offers diving and fishing packages and transportation from Port Hardy. The area and particularly the bay on Hurst Island's northwest side have long been known to mariners as God's Pocket. Park protects seabird breeding colony and bald eagle habitat.

Road to Cape Scott: 63km unpaved road leads from Port Hardy to small communities of Holberg and Winter Harbour and endless hiking.

SIDE TRIP

to Cape Scott

Those who want to see the extreme northwest tip of Vancouver Island – the largest North American island in the Pacific – must don backpacks and boots and hike the historic Cape Scott Trail.

Georgie Lake Campground: 6km along road to Cape Scott sign indicates access road leading another 6km to lake. Lakeside trail, great canoeing, spectacular sunsets.

The Shoe Tree: About 13km west of Port Hardy, by Kains Lake. Hundreds of shoes from around the world adorn a 22m cedar snag. Shoes began to appear here in 1990 after a Holberg resident nailed six pairs of her son's old shoes at the tree's base.

Holberg: 42km west of Port Hardy at the head of Holberg Inlet. Groceries and fuel. Once known as world's largest floating logging camp. Cafe, pub.

Raft Cove Provincial Park: 405ha. 250-954-4600. 14km south of Holberg, left at sign to San Josef Bay. 40-minute hike into cove. Wilderness camping, windswept beaches, surfing, kayaking.

Winter Harbour: (Pop. 54). 20km south of Holberg at mouth of Quatsino Sound. Shelter for fishermen from the open waters of the Pacific. Houses along the waterfront joined by boardwalk. Trail leads to rainforest hiking. Campground. Fishing, logging, fish farming are mainstays. Store, marina.

■ **Kwaksistah Regional Park and Campground:** On road into Winter Harbour. 12 campsites.

■ **Botel Trail:** At end of road, past store. 20-minute hike to the next bay.

Cape Scott Provincial Park: 21,849ha. Small campground on San Josef River at trailhead and wilderness camping. 250-954-4600. For experienced and well-equipped hikers. 40-minute hike to sandy beaches of San Josef Bay for hikers unwilling to walk the longer, historic Cape Scott Trail (at least eight

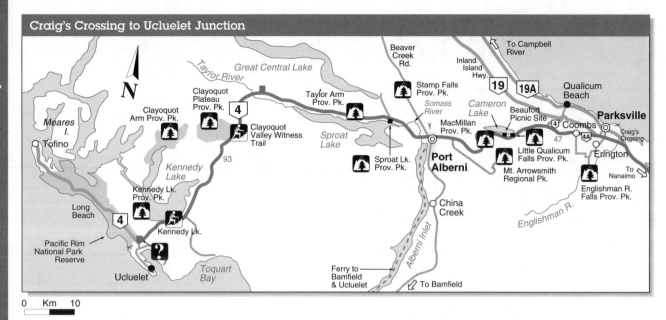

Craig's Crossing to Ucluelet Junction

0   Km   10

hours). Rugged wilderness, covering 64km of extraordinary coastline with 23km of sandy beaches. A network of trails, laboriously carved through the tangled bush by enterprising Danish colonists at the turn of the century, has been rescued from encroaching rainforests, reopening the tortuous 27.5km route to the cape. A few man-made relics, the odd tumbledown cabin, and rows of weather-beaten driftwood fences remain as testimony to efforts defeated when the government broke its promise to provide the settlers with road access to markets.

The Cape Scott Sand Neck is a peculiar bridge of sand that actually joins the cape to the mainland of Vancouver Island. This is the only place where both sides of Vancouver Island can be seen at once. Beyond the sand neck you can climb a wooden plank road to a lighthouse, high above the sea. From here the view is staggering.

Scott Islands Provincial Park: 6,125ha. 250-954-4600. 10km northwest of Vancouver Island's northwestern tip; extremely rough crossing from Cape Scott by private or charter boat. Lanz and Cox islands, totalling 3,500ha, have been combined with three ecological reserves: Anne Valee (Triangle Island), Beresford Island, and Sartine Island. Please respect reserve areas.

CRAIG'S CROSSING TO UCLUELET JUNCTION

HIGHWAY 19, ALBERNI HIGHWAY, AND HIGHWAY 4

This 140km route to the Pacific Rim and the west-coast villages of Tofino and Ucluelet begins at Craig's Crossing, 24.5km north of Nanaimo on Hwy 19. Travellers can remain on the new Inland Island Hwy until reaching the Hwy 4 junction beyond Craig's Crossing. Or, they can detour earlier, onto the Alberni Hwy originating in

Parksville, and enjoy sites around Errington and Coombs.

Immediately as the highway leaves east-coast Vancouver Island seascapes, it cuts into the mountainous heart of Vancouver Island, through dark evergreen forests. Beyond Cameron Lake, Hwy 4 winds between towering 800-year-old Douglas firs of Cathedral Grove, in MacMillan Provincial Park. The city of Port Alberni marks the first third of the journey. From here it is just one hour and a half to the pounding surf of the west coast of North America.

The 42km stretch of Hwy 4 between Ucluelet and Tofino, which includes Long Beach, is under *Ucluelet to Tofino*, p.83.

Errington Rd: 5km west of Parksville. To Errington and Englishman River Falls Provincial Park (below).

Errington: At Errington Rd and Grafton Ave. Small community with general store, post office, restaurant.
■ **North Island Wildlife Recovery Centre and Museum of Nature:** 1240 Leffler Rd. Follow signs. 250-248-8534. Non-profit society nurses injured birds and mammals back to health. Humans can adopt an eagle, a heron, otter, fawn, even a crow, and contribute to the cost of care. Reservations required for guided tours only.

Englishman River Falls Provincial Park: 97ha; 105 campsites (reservations taken: call 1-800-689-9025; from the Lower Mainland or overseas, call 604-689-9025). Follow signs at Errington Rd; 9km to park. General info: 250-954-4600. Take your snorkel and air mattress. Great swimming. Scenic waterfalls and gorge, lush forest, hiking trails. Steelhead, rainbow, and cutthroat trout.

Coombs: (Pop. 840). Just over 9km west of Parksville. Goats chewing sod up on the roof of the Old Country Market were all it took to stop traffic – in simpler times. A taste

of home-grown rooted in the turn of the century, Coombs grew out of the Salvation Army's immigration program that brought nearly a quarter of a million poor English and Welsh to Canada. A handful of families settled here under the Salvation Army's Ensign Crego and the community took its name from the Army's commissioner in Canada, Thomas Coombs.

Coombs remained a refuge for all sorts of folk seeking the simple life. But since the 1980s the roadside has mushroomed with "old-fashioned" ice cream parlours, antique stores, a tattoo studio, and the Coombs Emporium and Frontier Town – three dozen novelty shops around mini-golf and a plastic castle. Some old pleasures remain: the Coombs General Store (serving the community's every need since 1910), summer bluegrass festivals, and goats on the roof.

Vancouver Island Butterfly World: 1km west of Coombs. 250-248-7026. Mid-March-late Oct. Hundreds of live, "free-flying" butterflies from all over the world. And everything you always wanted to know about the personal lives – courtship, egg laying, caterpillar rearing – of butterflies. Second location near Victoria. See *Swartz Bay to Victoria*, p.42.

Alberni Highway: North off Hwy 4, 3km from Coombs. To Qualicum Beach, Inland Island Hwy, and Hwy 19. See *Nanaimo to Campbell River*, p.66.

Little Qualicum Fish Hatchery: 2.5km beyond Hwy 4A junction, turn onto Melrose Rd and follow signs. 250-752-3231. Open 8-4. Best times to visit are Oct-Nov and Feb-June. More than four million chinook reared.

Little Qualicum Falls Provincial Park: 440ha; 91 campsites. 250-954-4600. North off Hwy 4, 4.5km west of Hwy 4A. Beautiful falls and forests. Includes the entire southern shore of Cameron Lake, which feeds Little Qualicum River. Hiking, swimming, snorkelling, paddling, fishing. Only BC river besides the Cowichan to have brown trout. Fish in the dark with big, fuzzy flies.

Cameron Lake Picnic Site: At outlet of lake, 4km west of Little Qualicum Park turnoff. Part of Little Qualicum Park. Cameron Lake, 12km long by 1km wide, can become dangerously choppy with little warning. Boaters: keep an eye on winds. Fishing, swimming, windsurfing. Folklore says it's bottomless.

Angel Rock: About 2km beyond picnic site. Striking rock juts out over highway. Where young Port Albernians sometimes advertise their love for one another in spray paint.

Beaufort Picnic Site: Nearly 3km west of Cameron Lake Picnic Site. Part of the same park.

MacMillan Provincial Park (Cathedral Grove): 136ha. End of Cameron Lake, 31km west of Parksville. Includes lakeshore. Site of Cathedral Grove: some of the largest remaining Douglas fir trees on the island, many up to 800 years old. Trail through magnificent forest remnant. Park donated by Harvey Reginald MacMillan, first provincial chief forester for BC (1909-13). He later headed H.R. MacMillan Export Company (now multinational MacMillan Bloedel). Unintentionally a poignant memorial for what used to be on Vancouver Island, and a dramatic contrast to the clearcuts to be seen farther down the road. Picnicking, fishing, hiking.

The Hump: About 36km west of Parksville, engine test begins. Highway leads 2km to Port Alberni Summit, el 375m.

Mount Arrowsmith Regional Park: 925ha. South off Hwy 4, 41km west of Parksville. Another 27km to facilities. Scenic skiing and hiking. Vertical drop of 183m. Two T-bars, one rope tow, day lodge. Ski facilities open weekends and holidays during season. Downhill and cross-country, snowshoeing, rock and ice climbing. Summer hiking, wildflowers, fishing. Great views from Mt Arrowsmith (1,817m) and Mt Cokely (1,616m). Very wise to carry chains.

Port Alberni Access: 42.5km west of Parksville. Southwest to south Port Alberni, west to continuation of Hwy 4. Info Centre (see below) located here.

Port Alberni: (Pop. 18,468). On Hwy 4, 47km west of Parksville. At the head of Vancouver Island's longest inlet: this is a saltwater town a full 40km from the west coast. The inlet rivals the fiords of Norway with wooded peaks up to 1,300m and dozens of streams running down the mountains. In spite of its distance from the open seas, the city received considerable tsunami damage in 1964 when waters rose nearly 3m above normal high tide levels. Some people looked out windows to see their cars floating by.

From its early days as a copper, gold, and silver mining town, Port Alberni has been largely regarded as an industrial centre. Now with the forest industry in increasing peril here, the town's heavy industry is becoming part of its tourist industry. Visitors take tours of still active logging areas and the pulp mill; people strolling on government docks buy fresh seafood from fishboats; displays in the local museum focus on industries of the Alberni Valley. During provincial Forestry Week in May, trucks and heavy equipment are brought in from the bush, polished and paraded through downtown streets.

The Alberni **Harbour Quay** is in south Port Alberni at the foot of Argyle St. It's home port for the MV *Lady Rose*, a 31m passenger and cargo ship, and the MV *Francis Barkley*, serving the communities of Barkley Sound. It's also a place for people, with stores and restaurants, art galleries, a forestry visitor centre, charter-boat outlets, and picnic grounds. On summer weekends, *Two Spot*, an old steam engine once used to haul lumber, takes passengers along the waterfront.

The city is well known for its salmon fishing: there are marinas, accommodation, tackle and outdoors shops, charters and boat rentals.

Port Alberni Information: Info Centre, Alberni Valley Chamber of Commerce, RR2, Site 215 C10, Port Alberni, BC, V9Y 7L6. 250-724-6535. At 2533 Redford St. Well-posted building at entrance to town. Mon-Fri, year-round. Daily, late spring to early fall.

Alberni Marine Transportation Company: Operators of the *Lady Rose* serving communities of Barkley Sound, Bamfield, Ucluelet, Kildonan, Broken Group Islands. Based at Alberni Harbour Quay. 10-hour cruises between Port Alberni and Ucluelet, through the Broken Group, during summer. See *Transportation*, p.34, for schedule. Ask about canoe and kayak rentals here. The *Lady Rose* was built in 1937 in Glasgow, Scotland. During the Second World War she carried army personnel, mail, and food for 7,000 servicemen.

Port Alberni Airport: About 12km west of city centre on Hwy 4 turn right onto Coleman Rd. Scheduled and charter flights. Another airport is across Somass River Bridge on Hwy 4 about 3km west of city centre. First road on left after crossing bridge. Floatplanes and grass strip.

■ **Alberni Valley Museum:** Echo Recreation Centre, 4255 Wallace St. 250-723-2181. Tues-Sat. Innovative community museum with operating waterwheel electrical generator, visitor-operated steam engine and other working displays. Major collection of Nuu-chah-nulth artifacts.

■ **McLean Mill National Historic Site:** From Hwy 4, turn right onto Beaver Creek Rd, right onto Smith Rd. Go 3km. Info: 250-723-2181. Steam-driven sawmill operated 1925-1965. Officially opens in 2000.

■ **Log Train Trail Regional Park:** Starts at Maebelle Rd, one block north of Info Centre. Follow signs. 20km linear park traces abandoned logging rail right-of-way passing through districts of Cherry Creek, Beaufort, and Beaver Creek, second-growth forests and panoramic views of Alberni Valley. It crosses the original trail into the valley – the Horne Lake Trail –

and passes by the McLean's Mill National Historic Site. Newly developed for hiking, horseback riding, mountain biking. No motorized vehicles. Maps available from Info Centre.

■ **Dry Creek Municipal Park and Campground:** 60 tent/vehicle campsites, sanistation. Hookups, showers. On Napier St, but ask at Info Centre for directions. In a forest beside a lovely creek that often dries up in summer. Pleasant trails, walking distance to Harbour Quay, close to downtown and marina.

■ **Paper Mill Dam Municipal Park:** Via Falls Rd off Hwy 4. A sudden narrowing of the Somass River creates ripples and pools that are perfect for swimming. Picnicking, hiking.

SIDE TRIP

to Bamfield and the West Coast Trail

Port Alberni is starting point of a 102km unpaved road to the village of Bamfield, and the start of the famous West Coast Trail. To find the beginning of the Bamfield Rd, take the south (left) Port Alberni turnoff as you enter town from the Parksville side and follow signs carefully.

China Creek: About 14km south of Port Alberni on Alberni Inlet. Site of marina and campground with boat launch. Windsurfers who come to take advantage of the inlet's strong and steady winds use it as a base. Heavily used by salmon fishermen.

West Coast Trail (Pacific Rim National Park Reserve): 99km from Port Alberni by gravel road to Pachena Bay, Parks Canada information booth and northern terminus of West Coast Trail. 250-728-3234. (For details on trail and transportation, see p. 52) Trailhead camping in park on long, surf-battered sandy shores, and at Huu-ay-aht First Nation Campground.

Bamfield: (Pop. 338). By unpaved road 102km south of Port Alberni or 108km west of Youbou on Cowichan Lake (see *Lake Cowichan to Bamfield*, p.64). Or come via the *Lady Rose* from Port Alberni.

Salmon fishing is one of the main reasons why the population of Bamfield, on the southeast side of Barkley Sound, jumps to more than 2,000 in summer. Sportfishermen use Bamfield as a base to fish the waters of Barkley Sound and Alberni Inlet. The community is also inundated each year by hundreds of hikers, canoeists, scuba divers, kayakers. Despite its small size, the community is well-equipped with general stores, accommodation, charters, boat rentals, galleries, liquor outlets, and other services.

The village itself is an enchanting place with a seaside boardwalk along one side and trails to pretty beaches. Only one side of Bamfield Inlet is accessible by road, so the inlet is the village's highway. You can lean against a rail on the boardwalk and watch a steady stream of boats flowing past the shops and houses that overlook the inlet.

About 12km west of Bamfield, in the centre of Barkley Sound, are the Broken Group Islands. A part of Pacific Rim National Park Reserve, these 100-odd islands and islets lure canoeists, kayakers, cruisers, and sailors. These mariners commonly sight killer whales and grey whales, porpoises, seals, sea lions, river otters, basking sharks, nesting cormorants, and bald eagles.

Bamfield Information: Bamfield Chamber of Commerce, Box 5, Bamfield, BC, V0R 1B0. Brochures available at information centre, stores, restaurants, and businesses.

■ **Bamfield Marine Station:** Near mouth of Bamfield Inlet, accessible by road. Write Bamfield Marine Station, Bamfield, BC, V0R 1B0. 250-728-3301. Was trans-Pacific cable station at turn of century. In 1969 became marine biological research station for the five western Canadian universities and international researchers. Lobby area, with scientific and historical displays, is open year-round. Guided tours: Sat-Sun 1-3, May-Aug.

Return to Port Alberni and Highway 4

Highway 4 to Pacific Rim: As you enter Port Alberni from Parksville, take right fork into town and follow signs. At Somass River turn north toward Pacific Rim Park. Known locally as the Pacific Rim Hwy.

Stamp Falls Provincial Park: 234ha; 22 campsites. 250-954-4600. About 400m after turning toward Pacific Rim Park is the start of a 12km road to Stamp Falls Park. Cool, clear waters ideal for snorkelling and swimming. Pretty falls and fishway to help spawning sockeye, coho, and chinook salmon.

Sproat Lake Provincial Park: 39ha; 59 campsites, sani-station. 250-954-4600. Just off Hwy 4, 10km beyond turnoff to Stamp Falls. Busy in summer. Nice beaches and lots of boating territory. Petroglyphs, hiking, swimming, fishing. The world's largest water bombers, in the lake near the park, are used to fight forest fires. Measuring 36.5m long with a wingspan of 61m, each Martin Mars Bomber can carry 27t of water. Park named for the energetic Gilbert Malcolm Sproat (1834-1913), sawmill manager, Agent General in London, Indian Reserve Commissioner, and Gold Commissioner.

Great Central Lake Rd: North off Hwy 4, opposite Sproat Lake Park turnoff.

SIDE TRIP

to Great Central Lake

Large lake, 34km by 2km. Good fishing. Boat and backpack route to Della Falls.

Robertson Creek Fish Hatchery: Near outlet of Great Central Lake about 7km northwest of Hwy 4. 250-724-6521. One of

The wind-ravaged west coast of Vancouver Island.

main reasons for tremendous sportfishing success in Alberni Inlet and Barkley Sound. Built in 1959 to introduce pink salmon to the Stamp-Somass river system, primary spawning grounds for Alberni Inlet salmon. Expanded in 1980 to produce millions of smolts annually – nine million chinook, one million coho, 200,000 steelhead. See adult coho and chinook Sept-Nov, spawning steelhead in Feb, juvenile coho and steelhead year-round, chinook fry April-May.

Della Falls: Not accessible by road. About 9km northwest of Hwy 4, Great Central Lake Rd ends near the Ark Resort. From here it's 34km along Great Central Lake by boat, then 16 challenging kilometres (seven hours) by foot along historic Drinkwater Creek trail to Canada's highest waterfalls, located in the southeast corner of Strathcona Provincial Park. 250-954-4600. At 440m, the falls, named for wife of pioneer Joe Drinkwater, are nearly eight times as high as Niagara and are exceeded in the world by only 10 others. Hiking season is May-Oct. Shelter and camping at trailhead; wilderness campsites at 7km, 12.5km, 15.2km along trail. Camping, canoe rentals, boat launching, charters and guided trips at Ark Resort, RR 3, Site 306, Comp 1, Port Alberni, BC, V9Y 7L7. 250-723-2657.

Return to Highway 4

Hwy 4 ascends gradually as it skirts the shore of Sproat Lake. Beyond the end of the lake it follows the Taylor River for about 7km before crossing it. From here, road climbs over Sutton Pass in the Mackenzie Range. It then turns south and follows the Kennedy River as it winds through the Mackenzie Range to Kennedy Lake and its final destination, Tofino Inlet.

Taylor Arm Provincial Park: 79ha. About 5km beyond Sproat Lake Park. 250-337-2400. Forested park with hiking trails, fishing, swimming. Undeveloped campsites.

Sproat Lake Pullout: 33km beyond Port Alberni.

Taylor River Rest Area: 37km beyond Port Alberni. Features composting-toilet.

Clayoquot Valley Witness Trail: About 45km west of Port Alberni, right off Hwy 4 on Upper Kennedy logging road (400m past Sutton Pass Rd sign). 7.5km to north trailhead. South trailhead is about 58km west of Port Alberni: right off Hwy 4 onto Kenquot Main logging road, proceed to locked gate; 7km hike to signs. About four days to hike 29km trail built 1994-95 to generate support for protection of forests. Moderate-difficult hiking; some boardwalk and log crossings; wilderness campsites. Boardwalk and benches carved with names of people who worked to protect Clayoquot Sound from logging. For map and info, call Tla-o-qui-aht First Nation in Opitsaht, 250-725-3233. Trail passes between two provincial parks designated after "the summer of discontent" in Clayoquot Sound, when some 800 protesters were arrested for blocking logging trucks (more below). **Clayoquot Plateau Provincial Park**, not easily accessible, stretches from the rapids of the Kennedy River to the high plateau at the headwaters of the Clayoquot River system. **Clayoquot Arm Park** is described below.

Road to Toquart Bay: 81km west of Port Alberni. As Hwy 4 skirts Kennedy Lake, watch for a logging road running parallel to highway, opposite lake. Rough 16km road to hard-packed sandy beach. Boat launching. Good base for fishing and paddling excursions into Barkley Sound. Expect lots of company.

Kennedy Lake Provincial Park: 285ha. About 83km west of Port Alberni. On Vancouver Island's largest lake, 69 sq km. Also one of its nastiest. Although it can be a good fishing and boating lake, it is also hemmed in by steep mountains and subject to sudden, strong winds. About 2km to "secret beach," a favorite gathering place for locals. Boaters can access 1,490ha **Clayoquot Arm Provincial Park**, to the northwest, on Clayoquot Arm of Kennedy Lake. Hiking, fishing, wilderness camping, canoeing, kayaking.

Ucluelet-Tofino-Port Alberni Junction: 89km west of Port Alberni. Hwy leads southeast for 8km to Ucluelet. Northwest for 34km to Tofino. Long Beach, in Pacific Rim National Park Reserve, is between this junction and Tofino. See *Ucluelet to Tofino (Long Beach)*, below. Info Centre open in summer.

UCLUELET TO TOFINO: LONG BEACH

PACIFIC RIM HIGHWAY (Highway 4)

The 41.5km stretch of Hwy 4 between Ucluelet and Tofino provides road access to the Long Beach section of Pacific Rim National Park Reserve. Signs indicate where to find information, where to camp, hike, or stroll on the beach. For the 800,000 visitors a year, there are hotels, motels, resorts, and campgrounds outside the park boundaries. Tourism is a year-round industry here and reservations for accommodation are highly recommended.

This route also traverses or provides access to the traditional territories of five Nuu-chah-nulth First Nations tribes. These communities, including one within the national park boundaries, offer a range of services and opportunities to explore Nuu-chah-nulth history and culture. For information and bookings, see *Tofino*, below.

Ucluelet: (Pop. 1,658). On Ucluth Peninsula, 8km southeast of the Ucluelet-Tofino-Port Alberni junction. Ucluelet is a logging, fishing, and tourist village about a

third of the way up Ucluelet Inlet from Barkley Sound. It's a base for both commercial and pleasure boats, and for operators of nature, kayaking, and whale-watching trips within Barkley Sound and the Broken Group Islands.

The town – with shops, restaurants, and accommodation – has most tourist amenities. Galleries and specialty shops display the work of local artists, including First Nations artists.

The village's name comes from the Nuu-chah-nulth word, *Ucluth,* "wind blowing into the bay." Ucluelet First Nation people live in Ucluelet and in a small community on the eastern shore of the inlet.

Ucluelet Information: Ucluelet Chamber of Commerce, Box 428, Ucluelet, BC, V0R 3A0. 250-726-4641. The main Info Centre is at the foot of Government Wharf on Main St. Daily in summer; rest of year: Mon-Fri.
■ **Canadian Princess:** Downtown. An historic west-coast steamship (built 1932), converted to resort facilities. A former Canadian Hydrographic Service vessel, now the mother ship for motor launch fishing and nature excursions to Barkley Sound. Onboard lounge and restaurant.
■ **Government Dock:** Foot of Main St. Sea lions, seals, and eagles can be viewed from the dock and adjoining seawall promenade. A good place to watch fishing and excursion vessels coming and going.
■ **Big Beach Park:** Reached by boardwalk trail from Bay St, or for beach access only, from the western foot of Matterson Dr. Tide pools and beautiful shoreline flowers.
■ **He-Tin-Kis Park:** About 1km south of downtown. Boardwalk trail through old-growth cedar and spruce, rugged shoreline and views of the open pacific.
■ **Amphitrite Point Lighthouse:** On southern tip of Ucluth Peninsula. The lighthouse, established in 1905, has a commanding view over the open Pacific and Barkley Sound. Stroll around on concrete paths. Lovely sunsets. In March-April, there are excellent views of migrating grey whales; in winter, a stunning spot for storm watching.

Willowbrae Trail – Florencia/Halfmoon Bay:. Access from gravel road on east side of Pacific Rim Hwy and junction of Willowbrae Rd. Little-known boardwalk trail winds through old-growth forest. At trail fork, choose either secluded Half Moon Bay or continue to southern tip of Florencia Beach. Both trails have steep slope access to the beach which may not be suitable for all visitors.

Ucluelet-Tofino-Port Alberni Junction: 8km from Ucluelet. Northeast to Port Alberni, northwest to Pacific Rim National Park Reserve (Long Beach Unit), and Tofino.

Pacific Rim National Park Reserve: Boundary for the Long Beach unit of the park is 1km toward Tofino from junction. This section of the park encompasses 13,765ha of land and water. The entire park, including the West Coast Trail and Broken Group Islands and 49,962ha of ocean, is 84,642ha.

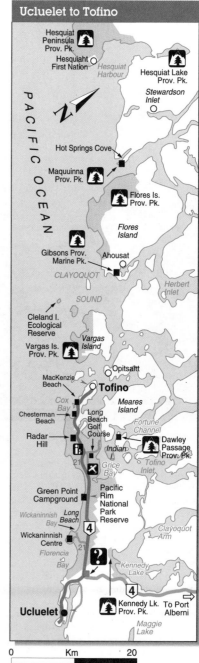

Ucluelet to Tofino (map)

Before the creation of Pacific Rim Park, there was no place on Canada's west coast where representative features of this magnificent coastal environment were preserved.

Long Beach, a long-standing secret among Vancouver Islanders, was accessible by a meandering dirt track from Port Alberni. (It was referred to as "Long Bay" by the first settlers who arrived just after the turn of the century.) The paving of Hwy 4 in the early 1970s brought a never-ending stream of tourists: though some islanders share their secret with reluctance, there has been no effort to stem the flow. In spite of the growing number of visitors, there are still some out-of-the-way places, quiet coves, and deserted beaches, not far from the more crowded, easily accessible areas.

Surf, sand, and sun: Vancouver Island's west coast sets the mood.

More than half of the 30km of shoreline at Long Beach is sand: you can hike the beaches and trails from Schooner Cove to Half Moon Bay. There are parking lots and wheelchair ramps within easy reach of the main beaches. Hiking trails lead to other beaches and enchanting forests throughout the Long Beach area. Park use fees are is effect March 15-Oct 15, at hourly, daily, or seasonal rates. Information about the park and hiking trails is available at park's information centre. Interpretive programs featuring the natural and cultural heritage of the park run through the summer. Tune car radio to 1260 for Long Beach weather and park news.

Pacific Rim National Park Reserve Information Centre: 3km northwest of Ucluelet-Tofino-Port Alberni junction. Info on all three units of the park. Open daily, mid-March to mid-Oct. 250-726-4212. Year-round, call 250-726-7721.

Long Beach Rd: Southwest of Hwy 4, 2km northwest of information centre. To Florencia and Wickaninnish bays.

Florencia Bay: South off Long Beach Rd 1.5km from Hwy 4. 1km to parking and trail. Also known as Wreck Beach. Inhabited by squatters in driftwood shacks before creation of the park. Lovely 5km beach.

Wickaninnish Bay and Centre: At end of Long Beach Rd, beyond park headquarters. Wickaninnish, "having no one in front of him in the canoe," was the leading chief in the Clayoquot Sound area in the 1800s. He played a major role as intermediary between European and First Nations sea-otter fur traders.

Here on this long, sandy, surf-battered shore, from late Feb-May you can look out to sea and catch glimpses of willowy mist shooting high above the waves. It's coming from Pacific grey whales on their northward migration to the Bering Sea. As many as 21,000 pass within sight of Vancouver Island on a 10,000km journey from Baja California, the longest migration of any mammal on earth. Some whales remain as year-round residents, and may be seen by keen observers. Information centres have details on whale-watching tours: some 15,000 people a year are taken out to mingle with the whales. Some experts fear for both the welfare of the whales, and the watchers (the danger, it seems, is spinal injuries from pounding over the waves in rubber dinghies).

The Wickaninnish Centre has observation decks with telescopes for looking out to sea. Films, exhibits, murals inside offer deeper insights into the north Pacific. Restaurant. Open during the day, late spring to fall.

Green Point Campground: Southwest off Hwy 4, 8km northwest of Long Beach Rd. 94 drive-in campsites, also walk-in tent sites on the beach and in the forest. Reservations for drive-in sites are taken after March 1: call 1-800-689-9025. Summer is extremely busy. Presentations at Green Point Theatre in evenings, usually early enough for sleepy children.

Tofino Airport: 4km northwest of Green Point campground.

Long Beach: Southwest off Hwy 4, 4km northwest of Green Point. Surfers, windsurfers, and kayakers test their skills here. The long, sandy beach is a favourite for hikers, joggers, beachcombers. In summer you can kick off your shoes and walk the beach with the pounding surf slurping up the shores, swirling around your bare feet. It's particularly invigorating in winter when furious storms lash the headlands, shaking the trees and spattering salt spray on your face. Bundle up in warm, wet-weather gear and listen to the surf as you brave the elements. But, on headlands, always use caution and obey signs: rogue waves have been known to sweep unwary sea gazers from their rocky roosts, and tragedy is the outcome.

Grice Bay: North off Hwy 4, less than 1km north of Schooner Cove. Boat launch 2km from highway. Large shallow bay near Tofino Inlet. Important wintering area for thousands of birds.

Long Beach Golf Course: At junction of Hwy 4 and Grice Bay Rd. 250-725-3332. Nine holes, driving range, restaurant, and campground.

Radar (Kap'yong) Hill: Southwest turn off Hwy 4, about 3.5km northwest of Schooner Cove. 1.5km to the 96m summit. Spectacular views from site of station constructed in 1952 with US funds as part of Distant Early Warning system. Bring binoculars. Exciting in strong winds. New name, Kap'yong, honours Canada's role in UN intervention in Korea, 1950-53.

Chesterman Beach: Southwest off Hwy 4, 5km northwest of Radar Hill turnoff. 2km beach outside the park with a delightful islet that can be reached at low tides. Don't get marooned. The new Wickaninnish Inn here offers luxurious winter storm watching.

Tofino Mudflats: 1.5km north of Chesterman Beach, turn east (right) onto Sharp Rd. This is currently the best access to one of the most valuable water-bird habitats on Vancouver Island's west coast. The 1,600ha mudflats and 400ha forestland were declared a Wildlife Management Area in 1997. Western sandpipers congregate here in the thousands. Nature watchers may also observe four species of loon, many pelagic birds, herons, porpoises, and seals.

MacKenzie Beach: 1km northwest of Sharp Rd. Sandy beach nearly 1km long. Accommodation and campground.

Tofino: (Pop. 1,170). Just beyond MacKenzie Beach. At end of Hwy 4, 34km northwest of Ucluelet-Tofino-Port Alberni junction. At tip of Esowista Peninsula, a 16km land neck near the entrance to Clayoquot Sound (see below).

Tofino is a pretty fishing and tourist village surrounded by impressive islands forested by impressive trees. It takes its name from Tofino Inlet, named by the Spaniards in 1792, for the hydrographer Vicente Tofino de San Miguel.

This is a bustling supply centre for tourists visiting Pacific Rim National Park as well as the 1,500 residents of five Nuu-chah-nulth communities and a few others who make their homes on the secluded shores and islands of Clayoquot Sound. It's also a gateway to markets where fishermen and oyster farmers sell their wares: salmon, cod, halibut, prawns, crabs, and other seafoods. One of Tofino's government wharves is known locally as the "crab dock" and is used by crab fishermen to store traps and tie up their boats. If you happen to be there when a crab fisherman arrives, you could buy some fresh from the traps.

Docks here are also busy with the comings and goings of tours: hot springs tours (see below), First Nations cultural tours, whale-watching and wildlife tours, sea-kayaking tours.

With the recent influx of tourists to Tofino, residents have learned to fight vigorously to protect their scenic, and fragile, environment from the clearcut logging practiced by multinational companies (see *Clayoquot Sound*, below). They're encouraging eco-tourism as a way to have both jobs and trees.

Tofino Information: Info Centre, Tofino-Long Beach Chamber of Commerce, Box 249, Tofino, BC, V0R 2Z0. 250-725-3414. On Campbell St, main road into town. Open daily July-Aug. Weekends May-June, Sept.

■ **West Coast Maritime Museum/Whale Centre:** In town centre. 250-725-2132. Daily, March-Oct. Maritime and trade history. Artifacts from sunken ships, Nuu-chah-nulth culture, and sea life. Also whale exhibits and marine excursions.

■ **Eagle Aerie Gallery:** 350 Campbell St. Longhouse-style gallery designed by Tsimshian eagle clan artist Roy Vickers. Offers shelter from the rain and warmth for the spirit. Vickers' paintings, mixing elements of traditional native art with colourful modern graphic images, fetch a high price worldwide. *A Meeting of Chiefs* was presented to Queen Elizabeth in 1987.

■ **House of Himwitsa:** 300 Main St. 1-800-889-1974. First Nations art – prints, jewelry, carvings. Lodging with views, restaurant, whale-watching tours, ice cream, and global currency exchange.

■ **Common Loaf Bake Shop:** 180 First St. A favourite hang-out on rainy days. Tasty cinnamon buns; informative notice board.

■ **Coast Guard Station Tours:** Beside government wharf.

■ **Crab for Sale:** Live and cheap, from Crab Dock or Weigh West Resort.

Clayoquot Sound: Stretching 65km southeast from just beyond Kennedy Lake to Hesquiat Peninsula, and embracing the three major islands, Flores, Vargas, and Meares. This is the traditional territory of five Nuu-chah-nulth tribes. The Tla-o-qui-aht people live mainly at Opitsaht, on Meares Island, and at Esowista (within park boundaries just south of Tofino); the Ucluelet and Toquaht tribes live to the east; the Ahousaht and Hesquiaht to the west. Around them are 3,000 sq km of islands, salmon-rich rivers, and forest. This is the largest expanse of low-elevation old-growth temperate rainforest left in North America. In 1993, the BC Government's decision to let logging companies take two-thirds of Clayoquot's old trees sparked Canada's largest civil disobedience action ever. By summer's end, thousands had visited the Peace Camp pitched in a clearcut just east of the Tofino-Ucluelet junction, and over 800 people had been arrested in daily attempts to stop logging trucks from getting through. With a new Interim Measures Agreement in place between the government and the Nuu-chah-nulth, giving local people more say in resource management, the level of conflict has been reduced.

■ **Island Views:** West to east from Tofino, Stubbs and Arnet (or Tibbs) islands. The community of Clayoquot, on Stubbs Island, was settled by Europeans in the 1850s, before Tofino was established. Arnet Island was home of eccentric young Englishman Fred Tibbs. In a 36m fir tree, he built a seat so he could enjoy both his gramophone and the view.

■ **Meares Island:** At 8,600ha it's smaller than Nantucket, larger than Hong Kong or Bermuda, and dominates the intricate waterways around Tofino. The Tla-o-qui-aht village of Opitsaht, visible from the government dock at Tofino, watches over ancient cedar and hemlock forests spared at least for now from the chainsaw. The island was declared a Nuu-chah-nulth tribal park in 1985. The 3km Meares Island Big Cedar Trail leads to the Hanging Garden Cedar, estimated to be over 2,000 years old. Tours depart from Tofino.

■ **Dawley Passage Provincial Park:** 154ha. 15km northwest of Tofino, at south end of Fortune Channel between Meares Island and Vancouver Island. Boat access only. No signs, no facilities. An exceptional diversity of marine species thrives in the fast currents of these tidal narrows. Popular diving area.

■ **Vargas Island:** 5km by boat from Tofino to vast sandy beaches, whale watching, private inn. Accommodation, camping, day trips, swimming, kayaking. Vargas Island Inn: 250-725-3309. Island's west facing shores and adjacent islands now comprise **Vargas Island Provincial Park**, 5,970ha.

■ **Flores Island:** 20km northwest from Tofino by floatplane or water taxi. The Nuu-chah-nulth community of Ahousaht (at Marktosis) is start of 16km **Ahousaht Wild Side Heritage Trail** leading south and west along white sand beaches and through rainforest to views from 886m Mt Flores. Call 250-670-9531 or 250-670-9586 for guided cultural tours or trail info; day trips or camping. Just south of Marktosis is **Gibson Provincial Marine Park**, 142ha. Taking in 7,113ha of the island's southern and western shores is the new **Flores Island Provincial Park**. Kayaking.

■ **Hot Springs Cove:** 37km northwest of Tofino, in 2,299ha **Maquinna Provincial Park**. Reached by boat and floatplane from Tofino. Site of Vancouver Island's only known hot springs. They look much like a typical west-coast creek, but the steaming water is 50 C at its source and it cools as it flows over a waterfall and through a series of pools to the sea. Unforgettable day trip from Long Beach area. Well-maintained campsite in park. Due north 15km by boat is the new **Sydney Inlet Provincial Park**, 2,774ha, embracing west and east shores of steep-sided fiord. No signs, no facilities. Boating, kayaking, chinook fishing at mouth of Sydney River.

■ **Hesquiat Peninsula:** About 40km north of Tofino by boat or floatplane. The northwestern edge of Clayoquot Sound is traditional home of the Hesquiaht people whose main village today is at Refuge Cove in Sydney Inlet. They offer lodging and transportation to area attractions such as hot springs and parks (call 250-670-1106). Two new provincial parks in the area are **Hesquiat Peninsula Provincial Park**, 7,889ha, and **Hesquiat Lake Provincial Park**, 62ha. No signs, no facilities. Boaters must be aware of off-shore reefs which pose navigational hazards. Coastal hiking and kayaking.

■ **Sulphur Passage Provincial Park:** 2,299ha. In the Upper Shelter Inlet north of Flores Island. No signs, no facilities. Most of this park's land base is on an island called Obstruction, sitting at the intersection of three channels – Sulphur Passage, Hayden Passage, and Shelter Inlet. Sulphur Passage is a narrow and very deep fiord, offering little shore access. Shelter Inlet is popular for kayakers.

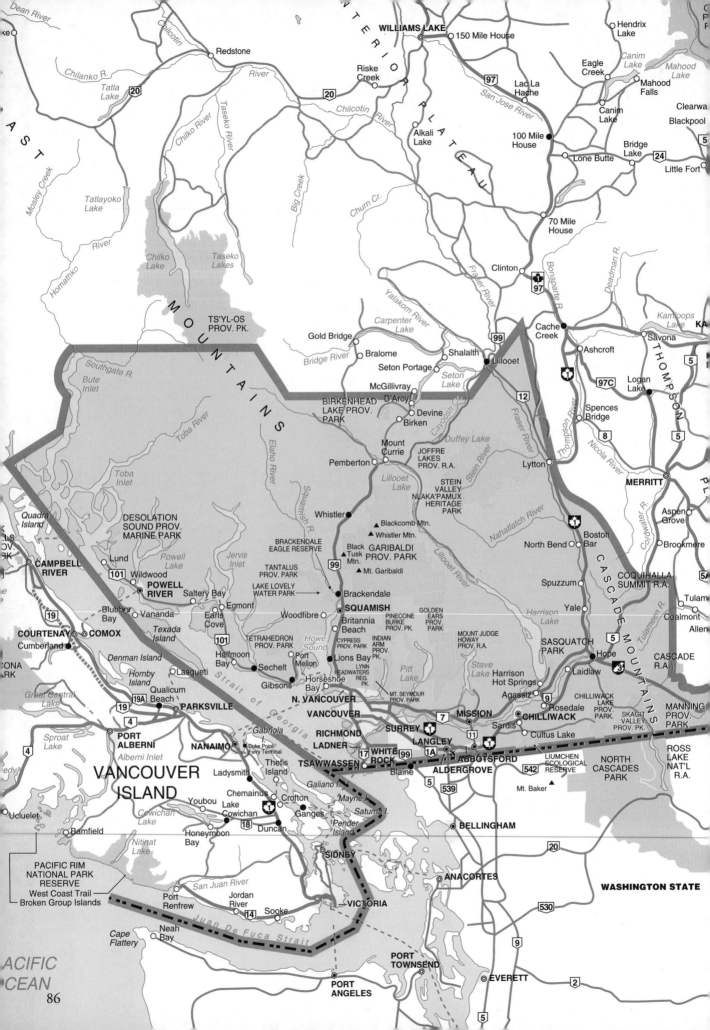

VANCOUVER, COAST, AND MOUNTAINS

CITIES IN THE WILD

> **"***In earlier times, this Fraser River resembled an enormous dish that stored up food for all mankind; for the indians flocked here from every quarter to catch the fish that abounded in its waters.***"**
>
> Old Pierre, Fraser River Katzie First Nation, 1936

In some ways, this southwest corner of BC has remained unchanged "since time began." On a rare coastal lowland facing the protected waters of the Strait of Georgia is the most intense population concentration in the province. Greater Vancouver, with a population of 1.8 million people – half the population of all British Columbia – stretches along the riverbank, snug between sea and snowcapped mountains.

It's a young metropolis – only 113 years old – but an ancient place. For at least 9,000 years, and still now, this valley has belonged to the Musqueam and Tsawwassen peoples, the Semiahmoo, and 20 other First Nations who comprise the Sto:lo Nation, "people of the river"– the one we now call Fraser. The Sto:lo share with us stories that reach back to when their ancestors became the first salmon, giant sturgeon, and cedar trees. Their ancient and populous villages stretched from the mighty river's forked mouth up to its canyons above Hope. Those villages became even more populous when their relatives from Vancouver Island across the strait travelled up the river highway in great flotillas to dipnet for salmon with them, harvest from the marshes, and celebrate their wealth in long winter ceremonies.

But beyond this busy river corridor and its lowland deltas, a vast, nearly trackless, wilderness remains. A look at the map, and the story is told: much of it is blank, no cities, few roads. Much of this region – the size of Vancouver Island – is coast and mountains, still inaccessible except by helicopter, boat, or logging road. It embraces hundreds of kilo-

metres of deeply indented coastline north past Desolation Sound to Bute Inlet, as well as wild mountainous country from Bute Inlet east almost to Lillooet on the fringes of the Cariboo. The eastern boundary cuts through the Stein River valley, curving southeast to include part of the Coquihalla Highway, and Manning Provincial Park.

The south perimeter is a long, roadless stretch neighbouring another country, a segment of the world's longest undefended border. Manning Provincial Park and Skagit Valley Provincial Park, snug against the 49th parallel that separates Canada and the US, offer alpine meadows, waterfalls, forests, and abundant wildlife, very different from the wide, open Fraser Valley.

All this is scarcely more than two hours' drive from downtown Vancouver. One can travel from the silver bridges of a river and seaside metropolis to roadless wilderness, all within the space of a pleasant excursion, a morning away from the river's mouth. North of Vancouver, and connected only by ferry, are the laid-back, salty-dog communities of the Sunshine Coast, populated partly by intrepid commuters who have found a way to keep the natural life. And a mere 60km northeast into the mountains, standing sentinel to the town of Squamish, is the Stawamus Chief, a 652m granite monolith offering ultimate challenges to the mountain climber. Beckoning north along Howe Sound is Garibaldi Provincial Park, and the fabulous resort village of Whistler perched wondrously under the twin peaks of Whistler and Blackcomb.

The Vancouver cityscape, adorned by the "sails" of Canada Place, is a harmonious convergence of land and sea.

The coast and mountain wilderness seems even more remarkable when seen as a backdrop to a metropolis expected to grow in population by as much as 50 percent in the next decade. To protect what's left, the BC government in the mid-1990s embarked on the largest park expansion initiative of its kind in Canadian history, quadrupling the region's parkland to more than 14 percent of its total area. This ensures the future of Vancouver's coast, mountain, and river heritage, not only for people, but for grizzly bears, eagles, migratory salmon, and waterfowl.

The Fraser River is why so many people live in this southwest corner of BC. It's what drew Europeans here in the first place – searching for a way from the west coast to the heart of the continent. It was in 1791 that Jose Maria Narvaez, a pilot in the Spanish Navy, surveying the Strait of Georgia in his tiny ship, the *Santa Saturnina*, spied the mighty river's opening. The next year, the British captain, George Vancouver, surveying the strait from a longboat, dismissed the confluence as too shallow for a useful passage. Just north of the Fraser, he entered a deep inlet, met and traded with the aboriginal inhabitants of the ancient Squamish village X'ay'xi, now part of Stanley Park. He named the inlet Burrard, after a colleague, then continued on his way north toward Howe Sound. He did not record – and probably never knew of – Whul-whul-Lay-ton, "whiteman place," named by the Squamish in commemoration of their first encounter with newcomers near the mouth of the Squamish River.

The British, who claimed these lands, gleaned no more intimate knowledge of the Fraser River until 1808, when the Hudson's Bay Company's fur-trade explorer, Simon Fraser, paddled, portaged, and clawed his way down its 1,368km length from the Rocky Mountains, though its treacherous canyons, to its mouth.

He learned, alas, this was not the coast-interior highway of his dreams. Nevertheless, in 1827, the Hudson's Bay Company established Fort Langley on the Fraser, 48km from the sea. Self-sufficiency was the company goal, but in truth, the fort's few dozen inhabitants depended entirely on the Sto:lo people for their survival. They provided not only furs, but salmon, which the company purchased by the tonne and shipped in barrels to hungry forts throughout the Pacific Rim.

Some of the fort employees became the Lower Mainland's first non-Sto:lo settlers. Among them were Kanakas, Hawaiian natives who married into Sto:lo families and took up farming in the Fraser Valley.

The balance of people and power shifted suddenly in 1858 with just one word: gold. Almost overnight, as many as 20,000-30,000 determined prospectors (many from California where the gold rush of 1849 had petered out) swarmed across the Strait of Georgia from the little Hudson's Bay Company stockade of Fort Victoria. Thousands more came overland from the south across the fledgling Canada/US border. And, in a dramatic move to preserve British interests, the Crown colony of mainland BC was declared, with Fort Langley as its capital.

Within a year gold seekers had dredged the gravelly bars of the lower Fraser, and were inland bound. The first road to the Cariboo gold fields traced aboriginal trails along the Harrison River and Harrison Lake. The 160km Douglas Trail to Lillooet, named for the new colony's governor, James Douglas, was abandoned in 1864 when an alternate route opened from the base of the Fraser Canyon. Steamboats from the coast delivered miners and their followers to new boom towns on the riverbank at Hope and Yale.

Within a decade, the gold rush had all but subsided. But right from the start many a prospector saw more value in land and timber than in gold. Settlement was encouraged. Already, by 1859, Colonel Moody had selected and surveyed the site for New Westminster – the new colony's capital until 1868, when Victoria, on Vancouver Island, became capital for a united island-mainland colony. Logging camps and sawmills sprang up along the forested shores of Burrard Inlet; farms and villages, along the Fraser River from Ladner to Chilliwack.

The city of Vancouver itself was a relative late comer. The seed for Western Canada's metropolis was a saloon – Gassy Jack's – serving Burrard Inlet logging camps and sawmills. Gastown became Granville, then Vancouver – with a little help from the Canadian Pacific Railway. Canada's Prime Minister John A. Macdonald, in 1871, had promised BC a rail link right to the coast as a condition of joining the Canadian Confederation. The promise was 15 years in the keeping, but when the final few kilometres of track were laid west of Port Moody in 1887, the new city of Vancouver, booming with land speculators, was the deep-seaport terminus of a trans-continental railway.

Today, Vancouver's port is North America's busiest. The Vancouver International Airport, facing an ancient Musqueam Village, is the continent's major gateway to the Pacific Rim. At Tsawwassen, the Tsawwassen First Nation looks out to BC's busiest ferry terminal, linking the mainland to Vancouver Island. Inland, tracing both banks of the Fraser – the "enormous dish that stored up food for all mankind" – are freeways linking 20 burgeoning Lower Mainland and Fraser Valley municipalities. Vancouver's rapid transit SkyTrain reaches southeast to Surrey; the new West Coast Express commuter train extends east along the Fraser's north bank all the way to Mission. Meanwhile, to the south, near White Rock and the Semiahmoo First Nation, Highway 99 begins its journey north from BC's busiest border crossing, travelling through the heart of Vancouver, past the glistening seas of Howe Sound and into the magic realm of the Coast Mountains.

Vancouver, coast, mountains: any one of these is extraordinary; to have them altogether makes for a place like none other on Earth.

In the foreground, White Rock's namesake shimmers; to the south is Mount Baker in Washington State.

INFORMATION

Vancouver, Coast, and Mountains Tourism Region: #204-1755 W Broadway, Vancouver, BC, V6J 4S5. 604-739-9011. 1-800-667-3306. Fax: 604-739-0153. E-mail: info@coastandmountains.bc.ca. Addresses and telephone numbers of local information centres are given in the *Logs* under each community.

TRANSPORTATION

Transportation corridors and facilities in the Vancouver, Coast, and Mountains region are extensive, and information centres can provide valuable information on all types of transportation, including boat charters, water taxis, and canoe, kayak, bicycle, and moped rentals. Free Vancouver city bus schedules and specially priced bus tickets are available at the Vancouver Travel Info Centre, Plaza Level, 200 Burrard St Vancouver, BC, V6C 3L6. 604-683-2000 or 1-800-663-6000. Day Pass gives unlimited rides on buses, SkyTrain, and SeaBus.

By Road

Highways and roads in the region are in excellent or good condition. However, there are certain areas where caution is advised. On the Sechelt Peninsula, Hwy 101 narrows at Secret Cove just beyond Sechelt. It's advisable to drive slowly and use pullouts to let faster traffic pass. Hwy 99, known as the Squamish Hwy, can also be a challenge at night, or in rain or snow.

Airlines

Over 11 million passengers a year pass through Vancouver International Airport, off Hwy 99 in Richmond, a 25-minute drive south from downtown Vancouver (see p.98). Downtown, Vancouver Harbour bustles with with floatplanes departing daily to Victoria and other destinations.

■ **Air BC:** 1-800-663-3721. Daily from Vancouver to Vancouver Island and destinations throughout BC; also from Powell River to Comox.

■ **Air Canada:** 1-800-663-3721. Departures from Vancouver to national and international destinations.

■ **Airspeed Aviation:** 604-852-9245. Half-hour flights between Abbotsford and Victoria.

■ **Awood Air Ltd:** 250-656-5521. Vancouver-Nanaimo airports.

■ **Baxter Aviation:** 1-800-661-5599. Vancouver-Nanaimo, harbour to harbour.

■ **Canadian Airlines International:** 1-800-665-1177 or 604-279-6611. From Vancouver to provincial, national, and international destinations.

■ **Rainbow Air:** 1-888-287-8371 or 250-287-8371. From Vancouver to over 170 coastal destinations including Campbell River, Minstrel Island, Qualicum, Stuart Island, Sullivan Bay.

■ **Harbour Air:** 1-800-665-0212. Flights to

Vancouver's SkyTrain arcs over the Fraser River; behind it, stands the Patullo Bridge.

Duncan and southern Gulf Islands – Saltspring, Pender, Saturna, Galiano, Mayne, Thetis. From Vancouver's Coal Harbour Rd, two blocks west of Canada Place.

■ **Helijet Airways:** 1-800-665-4354. Regular flights from Vancouver International Airport and Vancouver Harbour to Whistler. Downtown Vancouver to downtown Victoria, harbour to harbour, several times daily.

■ **Island Hopper:** 250-753-2020. From Coal Harbour's Tradewinds Barge in downtown Vancouver to Nanaimo Harbour and Sechelt Peninsula.

■ **North Vancouver Air:** 604-278-1608 or 1-800-228-6608. From Vancouver, scheduled flights, tours, and charters to Creston, Nelson, Port Alberni, Tofino, Ucluelet, Victoria.

■ **Pacific Coastal Airlines:** 1-800-663-2872. Vancouver to Anahim Lake, Bella Bella, Bella Coola, Port Hardy, Powell River, Campbell River; floatplanes to north-central coast.

■ **Shuswap Air:** 1-800-663-4074. Vancouver to Salmon Arm. To Douglas Lake Ranch on request.

■ **Vancouver Island Air:** 250-287-2433 or 250-949-6800. To many points on northern Vancouver Island and mainland coast.

■ **West Coast Air:** 1-800-347-2222 or 250-388-4521. Regular service between Vancouver's Coal Harbour and Victoria's harbour. Charters.

BC Ferries

BC Ferries link Vancouver and the Lower Mainland with Vancouver Island and the Sunshine Coast. Sailings from Vancouver Island carry passengers to BC's north coast and to the Queen Charlotte Islands. The fleet's largest two super ferries seat 2,000 passengers and carry 470 vehicles. The *Spirit of British Columbia* and the *Spirit of Vancouver Island* on the Swartz Bay-Tsawwassen run offer what their older sisters do, but they're bigger, and

have more: restaurant, cafeteria, and snack bar, two video arcades, study and work cubicles with computer hookups, complete wheelchair accessibility, and a bridge bristling with high-tech gear. The fleet's first new catamaran – the Pacificat fast ferry carrying 1,000 passengers and 250 cars – was tested in 1998 for upcoming operations. At 68km/h, it will zip from Vancouver's Horseshoe Bay to Nanaimo's Departure Bay in 65 minutes, shaving 30 minutes off the trip.

Call toll-free in BC at 1-888-BCFERRY or or Victoria at 250-386-3431, 7am-10pm daily for general information on any route or schedule, or for reservations, which are taken only for mainland-Gulf Islands, the Inside Passage, the Discovery Coast Passage, or Queen Charlotte Islands routes. 24-hour recorded schedule information is also available at the above numbers. Write: BC Ferries Corporation, 1112 Fort St, Victoria, BC, V8V 4V2, or check the Internet: www.bcferries.bc.ca.

Vancouver to Victoria

BC Ferries sail from Tsawwassen, on the mainland 30km south of Vancouver, to Swartz Bay, 32km north of Victoria, on Vancouver Island. Hourly sailings June (7am-7pm and 9pm), July (7am-10pm). Other seasons, every two hours on the odd hour from 7am-9pm, sometimes sailing hourly during peak times and holidays. The 44km trip is one hour and 35 minutes. Reservations are available: in BC call 1-888-724-5223; outside BC, call 604-444-2890. (To reach Tsawwassen direct when driving west on Hwy 1 – that is, bypassing Vancouver – follow signs to ferries via Hwy 10 south through Langley and east 49km to Hwy 17 at Ladner.)

All ships carry cars, campers and RVs, trucks, and buses. Vessels have elevators and special facilities for disabled travellers.

Bus services link Tsawwassen, Horseshoe Bay, and Swartz Bay ferry terminals to Vancouver and Victoria. There are pickup and drop-off locations en route and tickets can be purchased on the ferry. There are also regularly scheduled city buses to and from the ferry terminals. See *Bus Lines*, below.

Vancouver to Nanaimo

BC Ferries from both **Tsawwassen**, south of Vancouver, and **Horseshoe Bay** in West Vancouver serve **Nanaimo** on Vancouver Island. From Horseshoe Bay, the trip is 50km, one hour and 35 minutes. The year-round schedule offers sailings every two hours either on the hour or half hour. Travellers also have the option of crossing from **Tsawwassen** to the **Duke Point** terminal about 11km south of Nanaimo: the Mid-Island Express offers eight round trips daily from 5:15am to 10:45pm. Trip is 60km, two hours. Call BC Ferries for schedule. Reservations are available for these routes: call toll-free in BC 1-888-724-5223. Outside of BC, 604-444-2890.

Gulf Islands and the Sunshine Coast

Ferries from both Tsawwassen on the mainland and Swartz Bay on Vancouver Island serve the southern Gulf Islands – Saltspring, the Penders, Galiano, Mayne, and Saturna. Vehicle reservations are recommended for sailings from Tsawwassen to and from the islands. Please note that reservations are not taken for Gulf Island sailings from Swartz Bay, or for inter-island travel.

Ferries from Horseshoe Bay to Langdale on the Sunshine Coast (40-minute trip) depart eight times daily. In summer, two extra sailings on Sun and holiday Mon. In winter, one extra sailing on long weekends. Ten sailings daily from Powell River to Blubber Bay on Texada Island (35 minutes) – only nine on dangerous-cargo Wednesdays. Four daily sailings in summer (four in winter) from Powell River to Little River, Comox, on Vancouver Island, a 75-minute trip.

The Sunshine Coast CirclePac offers discounts for travellers making any combination of two Sunshine Coast crossings and two Georgia Strait crossings. Inquire with first ferry ticket purchase at Comox, Nanaimo, Swartz Bay, Horseshoe Bay, Sunshine Coast, or Tsawwassen.

Bus Lines

■ **City Link Bus Lines:** 604-878-1290 or 604-793-1290 (recording). Daily service between downtown Vancouver and Chilliwack with stops in New Westminster, Aldergrove, and Abbotsford. Charters.

■ **Greyhound Lines:** 1-800-661-8747. Vancouver to destinations province-wide.

■ **Malaspina Coach Lines:** 1-800-227-8287. Twice daily between Vancouver and Powell River with stops in Gibsons and Sechelt.

■ **Pacific Coach Lines:** 1-800-661-1725. Vancouver to Victoria via BC Ferries with connecting shuttle service from Vancouver International Airport. Connecting service for Tsawwassen and Swartz Bay terminals for Gulf Island foot passengers. Connecting service with Mid-Island Express in Tsawwassen. Daily sightseeing for Victoria and Vancouver.

■ **Perimeter Transportation:** 604-266-5386 or 604-261-2299. Year-round from Vancouver International Airport to Whistler Resort.

■ **Quick Shuttle:** 604-940-4428 or 1-800-665-2122. Up to eight trips daily between Vancouver and SeaTac Airport in Seattle. Departing from Sandman Hotel (and pickups along the way).

Railways

■ **BC Rail:** 604-631-3500. Or within BC, 1-800-339-8752. From the rest of Canada or the US, 1-800-663-8238. Fax: 604-984-5505. Offering service out of North Vancouver to as far north as Prince George. The **Cariboo Prospector** departs 7am from North Vancouver's BC Rail Station. Route traces the shores of sparkling Howe Sound, cuts through coastal forest, skirts mountains, badlands, and rangelands. Arrives in Lillooet daily, 12:35pm. Can be a one-day excursion, with lunch in Lillooet, and back to Vancouver for a late dinner. On Sun, Wed, and Fri, part of the train continues to Prince George, a 745km journey (with stops en route, including at Whistler where there is a free shuttle bus to and from the village during ski season). Reservations required for points beyond Lillooet.

The **Whistler Explorer** operates late May to early Oct. Departs Whistler 8:30am, Mon-Fri for day trip to Kelly Lake in the Fraser Canyon, returning to Whistler 6:10pm.

BC Rail also operates the "Pacific Starlight Dinner Train" – gourmet dining in restored dome and salon cars with names like Stardust and Indigo. May to mid-Oct. Departs North Vancouver, 6:15, Wed-Sun, for Porteau Cove, and is back by 10pm.

The **Royal Hudson Steam Train** travels between North Vancouver and Squamish, from early June to mid-Sept, departing 10am Wed-Sun. For round trip by train, optional Parlour Class includes lunch and afternoon tea. Passengers also have the option of travelling to Squamish by rail, and returning by water aboard MV *Britannia* – two seating levels, sun deck, views of Howe Sound, Burrard Inlet, English Bay, and Vancouver Harbour. Advance bookings recommended for weekends. Call either BC Rail or Harbour Cruises, 604-688-7246, for the train/boat trip.

■ **VIA Rail:** 1-800-561-8630. First-class transcontinental service aboard *The Canadian*: routed from Vancouver through Jasper to Edmonton, and points east to Toronto. These trains, refurbished for vacationers with dining cars, sleeping accommodations, and showers, are reminiscent of the golden days of passenger rail service in Canada. The three-night, three-day trip departs from Vancouver at 7:00pm, to allow daylight travel though the Rocky Mountains.

■ **Rocky Mountaineer Railtours:** 1-800-665-7245. May to mid-Oct. Sublime train trip through the Rockies. Vancouver to Jasper, Vancouver to Banff, optional to Calgary. Travels only in daylight, with dome car. Passengers going east or west spend the night in Kamloops. Continental breakfast, lunch, hotel included.

■ **Amtrak:** 1-800-USA-RAIL, or 604-585-4848. Once daily between downtown Seattle and Vancouver's Pacific Central Station (1150 Station St). Departs Vancouver 6pm; arrives Seattle 9:45pm. Departs Seattle 7:45am, arriving in Vancouver 11:40am.

Car and RV Rentals

Consult the Yellow Pages of Vancouver phone book for complete listings of car and RV rentals. Information centres can also assist.

City Travel

■ **BC Transit:** 604-521-0400. Bus service for Vancouver, Burnaby, New Westminster, Richmond, North Vancouver, Coquitlam, Port Coquitlam, Maple Ridge, Pitt Meadows, Langley, White Rock, Surrey, Delta, South Delta (Ladner), BC Ferries terminal at Tsawwassen, and Vancouver International Airport. Many buses provide wheelchair- and scooter-accessible service; some have racks for bicycles. Information centres carry BC Transit info and schedules; also special rate tickets.

■ **City Link Bus Lines:** 604-878-1290 or 604-793-1290 (recording). Daily service between downtown Vancouver and Chilliwack, with stops in New Westminster, Aldergrove, and Abbotsford. Charters by arrangement.

■ **handyDART:** For info, call 604-430-2892; for bookings, 604-430-2692. Lift-equipped vans carry disabled passengers unable to use public transit. Regular commuting and occasional trips may be booked, at least 24 hours in advance, and up to seven days in advance. Accommodates wheelchairs and scooters.

■ **Langley Greyhound Bus Depot:** 604-534-4737. For points beyond Langley terminus of BC Transit.

■ **Link Bus Service:** Provides connecting service from main BC Transit routes to rural areas of Maple Ridge (Haney) and Pitt Meadows. Call *BC Transit*, above.

■ **SeaBus:** 604-521-0400. Two 400-passenger catamaran ferries, the *Burrard Beaver* and the *Burrard Otter*, link downtown Vancouver to the North Shore. The trip across Burrard Inlet takes about 12 minutes and carries an average of 21,000 passengers on summer weekdays. SeaBus has become a major tourist attraction – offering a sweeping view of the North Shore mountains, Stanley Park, and the city skyline. Buses connect with SeaBus sailings near the SeaBus terminal on the waterfront. Bicycles permitted during off-peak weekday runs, and all day weekends and holidays. SeaBus is wheelchair- and scooter-accessible.

■ **SkyTrain:** 604-521-0400. Introduced 1986, Vancouver's light rapid transit system is North America's longest, completely automated, driverless rapid transit system. Designed to carry 110,000 people a day, at speeds up to 90km/h. Cars have specially designated wheelchair areas and all stations, except Granville Station, have elevators. SkyTrain links 20 stations along the 28.8km route from downtown Vancouver's Waterfront Station to Scott Rd Station, at King George Hwy in Surrey. The 39-minute trip includes a 1.5km haul beneath the city of Vancouver, and generous above-ground views of coastal mountains. In store are plans for 21km, 14-station, $450-million addition to connect New Westminster and Coquitlam to Vancouver via the Lougheed Hwy and Broadway Ave. Bomardier will build it. ETA: 2001.

■ **West Coast Express:** 604-689-3641 or 1-800-570-7245 (Mission). Commuter express train linking Mission and waypoints to Vancouver waterfront. Mon-Fri: five 73-minute westbound trips in the morning starting from Mission at 5:27; five eastbound trips in the afternoon starting at 3:50. Stops at Port Moody, Coquitlam Central, Port Coquitlam, Pitt Meadows, Maple Ridge, Port Haney. No scheduled trips on weekends but there may be advertised special trains. Free transfers to all connecting BC Transit services. Wheelchair- and scooter-accessible. Bicycles welcome.

■ **West Vancouver Transit System:** 604-985-7777. BC Transit bus, SkyTrain, and SeaBus transfers can be used on the West Vancouver Transit System. Blue Buses serve West Vancouver, including British Properties, Horseshoe Bay, and Ambleside. Limited weekday service to Lions Bay.

■ **Taxis:** Consult *Yellow Pages.* Vancouver's award-winning TAXIHOST program, a first for Canada, has trained almost 4,000 drivers in local knowledge, Road Sense traffic skills, and SuperHost Tourism programs. Luxury limousine service available.

■ **City Parking:** Most downtown parking runs $6 to $12 per day. Pay just $6 per day under Library Square (entry on Hamilton, off Georgia): Ford Theatre, Queen Elizabeth Theatre and Playhouse are across the street, an easy stroll to BC Place or GM Place stadiums. Metered parking is expensive.

REGIONAL FEATURE

The Mighty Fraser

The Fraser River delivers 121 billion cubic metres of fresh water to the ocean each year, enough to fill BC's big Okanagan Lake four and a half times. With a catchment basin of 234,000 square kilometres, about a quarter of BC, it is the fifth largest river system in Canada.

Flowing a total of 1,368km from its Rocky Mountains' headwaters to the Pacific, the Fraser is also the nation's fifth longest river. It begins as a trickle in the spruce swamps of Fraser Pass, about 35km southwest of Jasper, Alberta, on the BC side of the Great Divide. It is joined by countless creeks and streams, several of them extensive watersheds themselves.

As it flows northwest toward central BC, it picks up water from the Bowron, McGregor, Willow, and Salmon rivers. It bends south at Prince George, where it meets the Nechako River. With its own catchment area of 42,500 square kilometres, the Nechako drains 10 major lakes. Downstream, beyond the Blackwater River from the west, the Quesnel River, carrying the runoff from the Cariboo River, Quesnel and Horsefly lakes, flows from the east. Fifty kilometres southwest of Williams Lake, the Fraser is met by the Chilcotin, fed by its own rivers and creeks.

Farther down, past the Bridge and Stein rivers, the Thompson, draining 59,000 square kilometres, is the Fraser's largest tributary. The South Thompson flows down from the Monashee Mountains, bringing with it the

A trans continental Canadian Pacific Railway train traces the mighty Fraser River near Saddle Rock.

waters of Adams and Shuswap lakes as it meets the North Thompson at Kamloops. It's interesting that the North Thompson begins only 100km west of the Fraser's birthplace, yet the rivers flow in opposite directions before uniting at Lytton, 1,000km from the headwaters of the Fraser.

As the Fraser begins to level into its estuary below Hope, it is swelled by the runoff from the Chilliwack River, and Lillooet, Harrison, Stave, and Pitt lakes.

For 8,000 years, the Fraser's phenomenal flows have been adding 12 million cubic metres of sediment to its delta each year, creating islands, extending the mainland farther west. Although the flows of tributary systems such as the Nechako, Seton, Bridge, Stave, Alouette, and upper South Thompson are affected by dams, the Fraser's mainstream remains dam-free. Controversial plans to dam the Fraser near Moran Canyon, about 35km upstream from Lillooet, have been discussed in the past. For the moment, however, it seems unlikely the Fraser will be dammed.

More than 1.8 million people, about half of all British Columbians, live along the banks of the Fraser and its tributaries. Human settlement and industry invariably create effluent. Two million cubic metres of waste water are dumped into the Fraser every day, half of it from munic-

ipal sewage plants. More than 580,000 cubic metres are discharged from pulp mills and nearly 400,000 cubic metres come from other industries and miscellaneous sources.

Despite pollution, the Fraser River remains the world's largest salmon producing system, with annual returns of 12 million fish in recent years. Although all five species of salmon spawn in the Fraser watershed, along with 48 other species, including the giant sturgeon, eulachon, and trout, it is largely a sockeye river with 30 distinct runs. The river's rich estuary winters and feeds some 200 species of birds. In 1998, the Fraser River became the 23rd river in Canada to receive Canadian Heritage River status.

In the pages to follow, the Fraser River will appear again and again. Highways and railways travel alongside it. Bridges cross it. Parks offer respite by its ever-flowing waters. People fish. There are places to watch wildlife. Riverboats, tours, and charters make their way upriver – though no further than the canyon above Yale (there is, at Hells Gate, an aerial tram, for a glimpse). River rafting companies run down the Fraser, and do deliver adventurers through its terrific canyon (one busy company is based at Yale, see p.91). First Nations offer educational tours, a chance to see how they have lived along the Fraser's banks since time began. For all this, follow the *Logs.*

VANCOUVER, COAST, AND MOUNTAINS EVENTS

Abbotsford
- **Bradner Flower Show:** Mid-April. Showing off the daffodils: this is BC's largest bulb-growing region.
- **Abbotsford International Music Festival:** April. More than 80 bands.
- **Abbotsford Berry Festival:** Early July.
- **Agrifair:** Late July-Aug. Central Fraser Valley Exhibition Grounds.
- **Abbotsford International Airshow/ Week Festival:** Early-Aug. Abbotsford Airport. Mt Lehman Rd 3km south of Hwy 1. Week-long event, culminating in North America's leading airshow, attracting 300,000 people. Latest in aircraft technology, daredevil aerobatics.

Agassiz
- **Fall Fair and Corn Festival:** Mid-Sept.

Aldergrove
- **Festival Days:** Mid-June. Fireworks, outhouse races.

Boston Bar
- **May Days:** Late May.

Burnaby
- **Burnaby's Birthday Party:** Sept. Burnaby Village Museum.

Chilliwack
- **Chilliwack Native Powwow:** April.
- **Krafty Raft Race:** July. Cultus Lake.
- **Chilliwack Exhibition:** Aug.
- **Country Music Festival:** Aug.
- **Antique Threshing Bee:** Aug.
- **Bluegrass Festival:** Sept.

Coquitlam
- **Festival du Bois (Festival of the Woods):** Early March. In Maillardville. BC's only French-Canadian festival.
- **Coquitlam Festival:** Events all summer. Teddy Bear picnic, model marine boat show, fishing derby.

Delta/Ladner
- **Delta Pioneer Days:** May.
- **Fraser River Festival:** June. Deas Island Regional Park.
- **International Bog Day:** July.
- **Snow Goose Month:** Nov. At Reifel Bird Sanctuary and Alaksen National Wildlife Area.

Fort Langley
- **May Day Celebrations:** Maypole dancing, parade.
- **Fur Brigade Days:** Early Aug.
- **Fort Langley Country Fair and Equestrian Grand Prix:** Mid-Aug.
- **Festival of the Performing Arts:** Aug.
- **Cranberry Festival:** Early Oct.

Gambier Island
- **Arts and Crafts Fair:** Aug.

Gibsons (Sunshine Coast)
- **Sea Cavalcade:** Mid-July. Swimming race from Keats Island to Gibsons, water parade.

Halfmoon Bay (Sunshine Coast)
- **Halfmoon Bay Country Fair:** July. Kids' fishing derby, car rally, crafts.

Harrison Mills
- **Harrison-Chehalis Bald Eagle Festival:** Late Nov.

Harrison Hot Springs
- **Harrison Festival of the Arts:** July. Arts and cultures of the Third World.
- **World Championship Sand Sculpture Competition:** Sept, second weekend. On the beach at Harrison Lake, largest sand sculptures ever produced.

Hope
- **Festival of the Woods:** July 1.
- **Brigade Days:** Weekend after Labour Day, Sept.
- **Manning Park Bird Blitz:** Mid-July. Call 250-840-8836.

Langley
- **Little Britches Rodeo:** Late June.
- **Country Style Days:** June.

Lillooet
- **Only in Lillooet Days:** June. The Old West re-created.
- **Lillooet Fall Fair:** Mid-Sept.

Lund (Sunshine Coast)
- **Lund Days:** Early Aug.

Lytton
- **Lytton Days:** May long weekend.
- **Jelly Roll Days:** Aug. Slowpitch and Jelly Roll entertainment.
- **Remembrance Powwow:** Nov.

Maple Ridge
- **Mountain Festival:** Early May.
- **Ridge Meadows Agricultural Fair:** Late July. Since 1905.
- **Midsummer Festival:** Mid-Aug.
- **Whonnock Lake Day Folk Festival:** Mid-Sept.

Mission
- **BC Vocal Jazz Festival:** March.
- **Annual Mission Indian Friendship Centre Powwow:** 2nd weekend July. Native dancers from all over North America. Buffalo burgers, salmon bake.
- **Folk Music Festival:** July.
- **Stratford-on-the-Fraser Shakespeare Festival:** July.

Mount Currie
- **Lillooet Lake Rodeo:** Long weekends in May and Sept.

New Westminster
- **Chinese New Year:** Jan-Feb.
- **New Westminster Jazz Festival:** March.
- **Hyack Festival:** Week-long festival starting Victoria Day weekend. History of New Westminster celebrated. Highlight is ancient and honourable Hyack Anvil Battery that fires a deafening "21-gun" salute to the Queen each Victoria Day, using explosives under anvils instead of cannons. Longest running annual event of its kind in the Commonwealth.
- **Finnish, Portuguese , Philippine Festivals:** June.
- **Fraser Fest:** July. Westminster Quay. Boat show, tugboat parade.

North and West Vancouver
- **Return of the Osprey Festival:** Mid-May. Maplewood Flats.
- **Wey-ah-wichen Canoe Festival:** Mid-July. Cates Park.
- **Caribbean Festival:** Late July. Waterfront Park.
- **Harmony Arts Festival:** Mid-Aug.
- **Scottish Festival:** Mid-Aug.
- **Grouse Mountain Fly Off:** Mid-Aug. Hang-gliding and paragliding.
- **North Shore Heritage Weekend:** Late Sept.
- **Winterfest:** Dec. On Grouse Mountain. Three-week celebration: Festival of Lights, sleigh rides, snow sculptures, ice skating.

Pemberton
- **Canada Day Celebrations:** July 1. Parades, parties, loggers' sports, canoe races.

Pitt Meadows
- **Pitt Meadows Day:** June.
- **Pitt Meadows Blueberry Festival:** Aug.

Port Coquitlam
- **May Days:** May long weekend.
- **Canada Day Celebrations:** July 1.
- **Music in the Park:** July-Aug, Sundays. Lions Park.

Port Moody
- **Golden Spike Day Fest:** Canada Day.

Powell River
- **Kathaumixw International Choral Festival:** June-July. Biannual: 2000, 2002...
- **Sea Fair:** Mid-Aug. Loggers' sports and Sidewinder Rodeo.

- **Blackberry Festival:** Late Aug.
- **Sunshine Folkfest:** Labour Day Weekend.

Richmond
- **Slugfest:** Early June.
- **South Arm Family Festival:** June.
- **Annual Workboat Parade:** July.
- **Steveston Salmon Festival:** July 1.
- **Multi-fest:** 2nd Sunday in Aug.
- **Cranberry Harvest Festival:** Early Oct.
- **Fraser River Carol Ship:** Dec. Christmas carolling on the water.

Roberts Creek (Sunshine Coast)
- **Creek Daze:** Aug. Talent show, craft fair, the famous Mr Roberts Creek contest.

Seabird Island
- **Seabird Island First Nations Festival:** Late May. Canoe races, native arts, salmon barbecue.

Sechelt (Sunshine Coast)
- **Sandcastle Competition:** Mid-July.
- **Sunshine Coast Arts and Crafts Fair:** Aug.
- **Sunshine Coast Country Music Festival:** Mid-Aug.
- **Festival of the Written Arts:** Mid-Aug. Rockwood Centre. 604-885-9631. Canadian authors, readings, workshops.

Squamish
- **Bald Eagle Count:** Jan.
- **Royal Hudson Steam Train/Britannia Boat Tours Seasonal Launch:** Late May.
- **Squamish Days Loggers' Sports:** Aug (BC Day weekend). World's largest loggers' sports show.
- **Squamish Open Regatta:** Early Aug.
- **Squamish Adventure Festival:** Summer. Mountain-bike race, windsurfing, whitewater competitions.

Surrey
- **Cloverdale Rodeo:** May. The Big One. Rated No. 1 in North America.
- **Colour It Surrey:** Sept. Multicultural festival of visual and performing arts.
- **Surrey Fall Fair:** Mid-Sept.
- **Harness Racing:** Oct-April.

Texada Island
- **Texada Sandcastle Contest:** Aug.

Vancouver
- **Polar Bear Swim:** Jan 1. Jericho Beach.
- **Annual Ice Sculpting Competition:** Jan. Seymour Ski Country. 604-986-2261.
- **Chinese New Year Festival:** Late Jan or early Feb. In Chinatown.
- **Storytelling Festival:** June. West End venues.

Children are front and centre stage at Lower Mainland events.

- **Vancouver International Marathon:** Early May.
- **Vancouver Children's Festival:** Late-May. Vanier Park.
- **Canadian International Dragon Boat Festival:** June. More than 2,000 paddlers. 100,000 spectators line False Creek.
- **International Jazz Festival:** Last two weeks of June.
- **Italian Week:** July.
- **Bard on the Beach Shakespeare Festival:** Nightly, June to Sept. Vanier Park.
- **Vancouver Folk Music Festival:** Mid-July.
- **Vancouver Comedy Festival:** End of July.
- **Vancouver Chamber Music Festival:** Late July or early Aug.
- **Symphony of Fire:** Late July-Aug. English Bay. Fireworks set to music.
- **International Triathlon:** Aug.
- **Powell Street Festival:** First week Aug. A Japanese festival. Oppenheimer Park.
- **Pacific National Exhibition:** Last two weeks of Aug to Labour Day. Happening since 1910, and one of North America's largest fall fairs.
- **Vancouver Fringe Festival:** Mid-Sept.
- **Terry Fox Run:** Sept.
- **Vancouver International Film Festival:** Oct.
- **Vancouver International Writers' Festival:** Late Oct. On Granville Island.

- **Hadassah Bazaar:** Early Nov.
- **Christmas Carol Cruises:** Dec.
- **Festival of Lights:** Early Dec.

Whistler
- **World Ski and Snowboard:** April.
- **Classical Music Festival and Summit Concert Series:** Aug. Traditional music in non-traditional settings, including Brass on a Raft, at Lost Lake.
- **Really Big Street Fest:** Sept. Music, juggling, comedy, magic, clowns.
- **Jazz and Blues Weekend:** Sept.
- **Cornucopia:** Mid-Nov. Food and Wine celebration.
- **Hong Kong Bank Whistler Start:** Dec. World Cup downhill skiing and snowboarding.

White Rock
- **May Fair:** May. Midway, crafts.
- **Tour de White Rock Cycle Race:** Late June.
- **Crescent Beach Triathlon:** Aug.
- **Sea Festival:** First weekend Aug. Torchlight parade, duck race, bathtub race.

Yale
- **Strawberry Social:** June.
- **Gold Rush Days:** July.
- **Annual Fraser River History Conference:** Early Oct.

Gastown's Steam Clock is powered by the heating systems of Vancouver downtown buildings.

VANCOUVER, COAST, AND MOUNTAINS ROUTES AND HIGHLIGHTS

TRAVELLER'S LOGS

HIGHLIGHTS

THE GATEWAY CITIES

Vancouver and its sister cities and municipalities enjoy a sumptuous setting spread across the estuary of the Fraser River, and they offer bounteous food for body and soul, just as the river itself has done for millennia. Today, nearly a dozen communities border the port of Vancouver. The Greater Vancouver Regional District (GVRD), with a total population of 1.8 million, encompasses the cities of Vancouver, New Westminster, North Vancouver, Richmond, Burnaby, Surrey, Coquitlam, Port Coquitlam, White Rock, Langley, and Port Moody; the districts of Delta, North Vancouver (it is both a city and a district), Langley, West Vancouver; villages of Anmore, Belcarra, and Lions Bay; and three electoral areas (University of British Columbia Endowment Lands, Ioco, and Bowen Island).

An intense population core, it embraces half of BC's residents. Industry vies with residential and agricultural demands for coveted land. More than 100,000 people work in shipping and related industries.

Vancouver and its suburban communities form a gateway into the province, welcoming thousands of travellers a year. They come on jets from Europe and the Orient, on liners, yachts, and skiffs from up and down the coast, and in automobiles from everywhere. Greater Vancouver is a gateway, but also a destination in itself. Endless pleasurable days could be spent in "downtown British Columbia." For this reason, and also because of their size and location, **Vancouver**, **The North Shore (North Vancouver and West Vancouver), Burnaby, New Westminster, Surrey**, and **Richmond** have each been given a section in the pages following. Other Gateway cities and municipalities will be found along the appropriate routes.

Transportation corridors are clearly marked on the Gateway map (p.96), and detailed in the appropriate *Log*.

VANCOUVER

CITY OF SALT AIR AND SUCCESS

Vancouver: (Pop. 514,008). A city bounded by water on three sides. To the north, Burrard Inlet separates Vancouver from North and West Vancouver. The inlet is spanned by two major bridges, the Lions Gate Bridge at First Narrows, and the Ironworkers

Memorial Second Narrows Bridge, 9km inland. The Strait of Georgia (Pacific Ocean) is Vancouver's western boundary. To the south, the north arm of the Fraser River separates Vancouver from its southern satellite communities. Five major bridges span this torrent: Oak St, Knight St, Pattullo, Alex Fraser, and Port Mann.

Perhaps it's the ocean salt in the air, or the slowing of the pulse at sea levels. Maybe it's just the constant lapping of water at Vancouver's edges that gives the city its Bank Holiday feeling. Vancouver is a city of and for the water. The Coast Mountains' sharp peaks are reflected in the city's mirrored skyscrapers – but the water has dictated the city's design, and what people do here. On its peninsula between Burrard Inlet and the Fraser River, the city breathes with the ebb and flow of tides.

This is North America's busiest seaport. Each year, Vancouver's port facilities export some 73 million tonnes of cargo. Everything from coal and wheat to forest products and minerals passes through 27 specialized terminals. From the days of its first cargo export in 1864 (pickets to Australia) to today, the port of Vancouver has continuously increased its influence. Its sheltered location is a favourable one, in the lee of Vancouver Island, and about mid-point on North America's west coast. More than 3,000 foreign ships, representing the trade of 90 nations, enter the harbour each year.

It was a short century ago – not much more than the life span of a person – that Musqueam and Squamish villages flourished on the shores of Vancouver's beaches, and harvested at sites where giant freighters now berth. There are few cities on the continent that have undergone so much change in such a short time. Even just a decade ago, this was still a "nice city" where nothing much happened – a "Lotus Land" for those who would choose lifestyle first. Real movers and shakers went east to advance their careers.

In 1986, Vancouver celebrated its 100th birthday with Expo 86 – a world transportation exposition, the largest such event in North America to date. Canada Place. a striking new trade and convention centre and cruise-ship terminal, opened. The SkyTrain, a new-age rapid-transit service, carried its first passengers between downtown Vancouver and New Westminster. On centre stage, before the world, appeared a city to be taken seriously, a city that just happened to enjoy good weather year-round, a vast wilderness playground in its back yard, and in its front yard, the sea, beaches, and access to the burgeoning opportunities of the nations of the Pacific Rim.

Between 1987 and 1992, Vancouver's population grew by more than 17 percent (while populations in most of the rest of BC shrank). Those who moved "back east" to advance their careers began returning home, drawn by the brighter possibilities of Vancouver. By 1990, Vancouver had become North America's third largest film production centre, after Los Angeles and New York. High-tech firms, biomedical, computer, and communications companies started opening branch offices here. Real estate values climbed: Vancouver became more expensive to live in than Toronto, and suburbs mushroomed throughout the Lower Mainland and Fraser Valley. Commuter times stretched to metropolitan proportions. In 1993, the world again focused on Vancouver: host of the Peace Summit between US president Bill Clinton and Russian president Boris Yeltsin.

Vancouver's increasing economic diversity is also reflected in a new diversity in population. The strong majority of British descen-

dants is giving way to emerging communities of Chinese, German, Indo-Pakistani, French, Italian, Dutch, Scandinavian, Ukrainian, Filipino, Aboriginal, Japanese, Jewish and Greek peoples. Almost three-quarters who settle here from outside Canada are Asian in origin – most of these coming from Hong Kong, since the 1984 agreement between Britain and China that returned Hong Kong to China in 1997. Asian investment and immigration have

dramatically changed the face of the city.

Vancouver, unlike so many North American cities, is a people place. Planners have kept the freeway out of downtown, with its residential population that continues to grow. The West End, looking out to English Bay, has one of the country's highest population densities. Downtown itself is shifting dramatically southeast from Granville and Georgia to meet new developments – including a colos-

sal new library and performing arts centre – at False Creek, site of Expo 86. Baby boomers are buying in and near Yaletown, transforming a heritage warehouse district into an ideal place to live, work, and play.

And still, elements of the old Lotus Land remain. Vancouver is clean and relatively safe, important words as we enter a new millennium. In the spring, 60,000 plum and cherry trees blossom. In summer, fleets of windsurfers – their canvases a riot of colour – dart between freighters anchored in the bay. For office workers to enjoy on their lunch breaks, there are nearly a dozen city beaches, including Wreck Beach, where bathing suits are optional. In the fall, the beauty of the 10km seawall walk around Stanley Park is heightened by the gold of autumn leaves. And come December, the Skyride on Grouse Mountain is a silver thread in the distance.

The arts, entertainment, sports and recreation, dining, and shopping have exploded in a rich variety that reflects the city's love for the flamboyant and innovative. There's even an **Arts Hotline** (604-684-2787). Indeed the arts scene is lively, with a public art gallery housed in a heritage courthouse, an opera company, several dozen theatres, and ballet and dance companies. Almost a city in itself is the **University of British Columbia (UBC)**, a

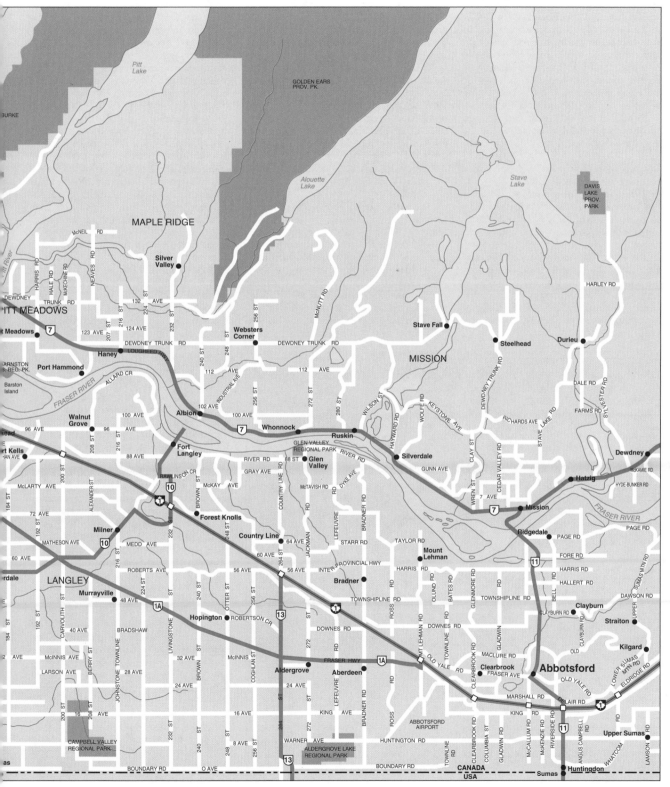

major international university with its own museums, theatres, art gallery, Botanical and Nitobe gardens, music, restaurants, English teas, and wonderful trails on the beach.

Multicultural differences are celebrated. Authentic pockets of Europe and the Far East are open for everyone to explore. Robson Street, a continental shopping thoroughfare once largely German, has been affectionately called "Robsonstrasse" for decades. Vancouver's Chinatown is the third largest in North America (after San Francisco's and New York's).

To everyone's delight, dining out in Vancouver is an ongoing feast with more than 4,000 restaurants, representing the cuisine of more than 25 nationalities. From Chinatown's Sunday morning dim sum, to French cooking and Japanese sushi bars in Gastown, eating well in Vancouver is an international affair.

Eating well can also begin with any one of the fresh produce markets proliferating in the city. The largest and most colourful is on **Granville Island** under the Granville St Bridge, a short hop by car or public transit from the downtown shopping core.

Vancouver Information: Tourism Vancouver, Plaza level, 200 Burrard St, Vancouver, BC, V6C 3L6. 604-683-200 or 1-800-663-6000. Web site: www.tourism-vancouver.org. Daily, Late May-early Sept. Mon-Sat rest of year. At the Reservation Area, travellers can book sightseeing tours, boat cruises, and accommodation. Highly recommended (and sold here): the BC Transit DayPass which allows unlimited rides on buses, the SkyTrain, and SeaBus on day of purchase. Can be purchased in advance.

Vancouver International Airport: On Sea Island in Richmond south of Vancouver. From downtown Vancouver, cross Arthur Laing Bridge at the foot of Granville St; or off Hwy 99 at Bridgeport Rd. For flight info and reservations, call airline companies or travel agencies. Parkade is connected to both Domestic and International Terminal buildings. For airport info, call 604-276-6101.

This is Canada's second largest airport after Toronto's: more than 80,000 people a day (15 million a year), not including meeters and greeters, flood through the airport's gates, going to or coming from elsewhere in Canada, 26 US cities, the Pacific Rim (including daily flights from Beijing, China) and the rest of the world. To handle the increasing traffic, the new International Terminal Building was opened in 1996, offering an additional 105,000 square metres to complement the Domestic Terminal (the old Main Terminal), and the south terminal, serving interior and remote coastal destinations. The airport's third runway opened a few months later, a 15-storey, 398-room Canadian Pacific Hotel in 1999, and upgrading continues.

The International Terminal features the largest baggage carousels in the world – each delivers a 747's cargo full of luggage to passengers in 25 minutes. There are five moving sidewalks and 115 check-in counters, all barrier-free to disabled persons, and the first in North America to use the space-efficient Common Use Terminal Equipment system that allows any airline carrier access to any available terminal. The 26 immigration inspection stations can process up to 2,900 passengers an hour.

Vancouver lies in the traditional territories of the X'muzk'i'um First Nation, and greeting visitors here are two 5.5m "welcome figures," carved by X'muzk'i'um artists. Also on display are a giant cedar sculpture inspired by the spindle-whorl technology of local Salish weaving, and four traditional weavings.

With 54 stores, boutiques, cafes, fast-food outlets and elegant restaurants, the airport has become a destination in itself. Vancouverites can come to the airport to shop, have dinner, watch the planes take off and land. They can come just to ponder the airport's $3-million centrepiece, *Spirit of Haida Gwaii, the Jade Canoe*, a life-sized bronze canoe crowded with larger-than-life passengers: Bear and Bear Mother, Mouse Woman, Beaver, Frog, and Eagle. Raven is steering. Of *their* journey, Haida artist Bill Reid (1920-1998) asks us, "There is certainly no lack of activity in our little boat, but is there any purpose? The boat goes on, forever anchored in the same place." Behind the sculpture, a 40m-wide wall of coloured glass washes a great wave of water into the terminal. The ocean, North Shore mountains and forests, all visible from here, are reflected in the terminal's design: in the support beams that resemble trees, in the sea-blue carpets, and even the light fixtures, designed to resemble log booms floating in the Fraser River.

Pacific Central Station: On Station St at Main and Terminal, overlooking False Creek. VIA Rail, Amtrak, and Pacific Coach Lines buses depart from here. SkyTrain Terminal is adjacent, facing Chinatown. Parking, newspapers and magazines, fast food.

Museums and Attractions

Rain or shine, Vancouver is a family-oriented city with a wealth of activities to enjoy. Easy to get to by car or local transit, the following attractions are highly recommended.

■ **University of British Columbia:** In Point Grey, on a stunning site jutting out into the Strait of Georgia. Famous for its **Museum of Anthropology, Botanical Garden**, and **Nitobe Memorial Garden** (see below), as well as the **M.Y. Williams Geological Museum**, plus an art gallery of its own, theatres, an observatory, aquatic centre, sports facilities. There is even a "Hortline" Tues-Wed afternoons (604-822-5858), in case your plants are acting up. UBC is cultural home to 34,000 students a year, and a major resource and inspiration to 70,000 others a year who visit the campus for non-credit courses, events, lectures.
■ **UBC Museum of Anthropology:** 6393 NW Marine Dr, UBC campus. 604-822-3825. Daily in summer; Sept-June, closed Mon. Designed by BC architect Arthur Erickson, the award-winning glass-and-concrete building was inspired by the west-coast aboriginal longhouse. From the massive front doors carved by northern Gitxsan craftsmen, to the forest of ancient poles in the Great Hall and Haida artist Bill Reid's cedar sculpture, *Raven and the First Men*, this museum is a feast for the soul and must not be missed. There are special exhibits and events, and endless exploring in research collections kept in visible storage. Outside are poles carved more recently, and a

VANCOUVER Downtown

1 Aquarium/Zoo
2 B.C. Place Stadium
3 Vancouver Museum
4 Canada Place
5 Floatplane Base
6 Ford Centre
7 General Motors Place
8 Granville Market
9 Harbour Centre
10 Hospital
11 Marina
12 Maritime Museum
13 Pacific Central Station-Trains/Buses
14 Pacific Centre
15 Pacific Space Centre
16 Park/Beach
17 Post Office
18 Q E Theatre
19 Robson Square
20 Royal Centre
21 Seabus Terminal
22 Visitor Info Centre
23 Vancouver Art Gallery
24 Vancouver City Library

Crab sculpture at H.R. MacMillan Planetarium.

life-sized model Haida village. A three-gallery wing houses a permanent display of European ceramics.

■ **Vancouver Museum:** 1100 Chestnut St, south end of Burrard Bridge, in Vanier Park. 604-736-4431. Daily, July-Aug; Tues-Sun, Oct-April. Canada's largest civic museum. Permanent and visiting exhibits of history and art of Canada's aboriginal people, history of Vancouver, decorative arts. 19th-century period rooms. Special events and children's programs.

■ **Pacific Space Centre:** 1100 Chestnut St (Vanier Park). 604-738-7827. Daily, July-Aug; closed Mon, Sept-June. Journey through galaxies in **H.R. MacMillan Planetarium Star Theatre**, programs from laser/rock concerts to family and children's matinees. GroundStation Canada explores Canada's achievements in space, also Cosmic Gallery and Virtual Voyages. At **Gordon Southam Observatory**, a 0.5m telescope brings the stars to you. Open weekends: 604-738-2855 for hours.

■ **Vancouver Maritime Museum:** 1905 Ogden Ave, at foot of Cypress St (five-minute walk from Vancouver Museum). 604-257-8300. Daily, 10-5, May-Sept; closed Mon, off-season. Vancouver's marine history. Housed here is the *St. Roch*, the first ship to cross the North West Passage from west to east (1942), the first to cross it in both directions (1944) and the first to circumnavigate North America (1950). It is a National Historic Site. Visiting ships moor behind museum at Heritage Harbour. Children's Maritime Discovery Centre features computer games, underwater robot, "fishing for a living," and tugboat wheelhouse displays.

■ **The Vancouver Aquarium:** In Stanley Park. Recording: 604-268-9900, or 604-659-3474. Daily. A chance to learn about the 80 percent of the world's creatures that live in water. Exhibits feature sea otters and killer whales of the Pacific Northwest; beluga whales of the Arctic; scarlet ibis and sloths of the Amazon. The new Ducks Unlimited Wetlands Discovery Centre leads us into BC's wetlands.

■ **CN IMAX Theatre:** 201-999 Canada Place. 604-682-4629. Daily. Specially designed theatre with IMAX technology. Screen is five stories high; film frame is the largest in motion picture history, 10 times larger than conventional 35mm frame. Viewers feel as if they are in the film as the camera travels through space or across the Grand Canyon.

■ **Science World:** 1455 Quebec St, near Main St SkyTrain Station, in geodesic dome at east end of False Creek. 604-268-6363. A $50-million project in former Expo Centre. Dynamic interactive science exhibits and events, live performances. Bytes Cafeteria, gift shop. Also houses **Alcan Omnimax Theatre,** world's largest domed screen, 10 tonnes of sound equipment. Separate admission.

■ **BC Place Stadium:** 777 Pacific Blvd S. Events Info Line: 604-661-7373. Stadium: 604-669-2300. Called the "Giant Pincushion," this is the world's largest air-supported domed stadium: 760m in circumference, 60m high. Canada's first covered stadium, opened June, 1983, is home to the BC Lions football team. The 60,000-seat facility, covering 10ha, is used for sports, concerts, trade shows.

■ **BC Sports Hall of Fame:** 604-669-2300. Gate A, BC Place. Year-round.

■ **The Lookout! At Harbour Centre:** Across from Waterfront SkyTrain Station and SeaBus, at 555 W Hastings St. 604-689-0421. Glass skylift elevators carry visitors 167m to a 360-degree view of Vancouver. Video show, 8:30am-10:30pm, in summer; 9-9 in winter. Guided tours.

■ **Port of Vancouver:** 1300 Stewart St (north foot of Clark Dr). 604-666-6129. Year-round viewing centre at Vanterm Container Terminal. This is Canada's largest port: more than 3,000 vessels call each year with cargo from 90 nations.

■ **General Motors Place:** 604-899-7400. Locally known as "The Garage," new 20,000-seat stadium is home to Vancouver Grizzlies NBA basketball team and Vancouver Canucks hockey team. Venue for big concerts.

■ **Pacific National Exhibition (PNE) Grounds:** On Hastings between Renfrew and Cassiar. 604-253-2311. Mid-Aug to Labour Day. Site of one of Canada's largest and most prestigious fairs. Big-name entertainment, demolition derby, agricultural exhibits, pavilions. Also home of **Playland Entertainment Park**, featuring Canada's largest wooden roller coaster (built of select Douglas fir in 1958, it has thrilled over 10 million riders), rides (up to 50 at PNE time), street entertainment, magic shows, petting zoo. Open weekends and holidays in spring and fall, daily in summer. At McGill and Renfrew is the thoroughbred **Racetrack**, clubhouse, grandstand. Mid-April to mid-Oct. 604-254-1631.

■ **Vintage Interurban Streetcar No. 1207:** Runs along a 1.5km section of rail between Leg-in-Boot Square and Granville Island – the first phase of service that will eventually extend westward to Vanier Park, and eastward to Chinatown, Gastown, Stanley Park and downtown. Weekends and holidays, 1-5pm, June-late Sept. One of three cars built in 1905 to link south Vancouver and Steveston.

■ **The Canadian Craft Museum:** 639 Hornby St. 604-687-8266. Open daily. Formerly the Cartwright Gallery, became "The Canadian Craft Museum" in 1990, reflecting its national stature and backed by a 99-year lease of the new three-level museum building at Cathedral Place in heart of downtown. The first national cultural facility dedicated to craft. Historical and contemporary exhibits, collections, education programs, workshops, travelling exhibitions.

■ **Sunmore Ginseng Tours:** 3418 Main St. 604-873-3918. Year-round. Learn about this healing root.

■ **Vancouver Police Museum:** 240 E Cordova St. 604-665-3346. May-Sept, Mon-Sat; winter, Mon-Fri. In BC Coroner's Court building. Historical police artifacts; jail cell, counterfeiting, crime scene, morgue and coroner's displays. Guided tours, programs.

■ **BC Golf Museum:** 2545 Blanca St. 604-222-4653. BC's only golf museum.

■ **Landmark Clocks International:** 123 Cambie St. Year-round. Largest collection of antique clocks, watches, pocket watches in Canada. Place of the maker of the Gastown Steam Clock (1977) and Otaru Steam Clock (1994).

Parks and Gardens

Vancouver is regarded by many who live here as one big garden. Vast parks surround the city, and almost every yard abounds with foliage and floral colour.

■ **Lower Mainland Nature Legacy:** The largest park expansion initiative of its kind in Canadian history. In 1996, ensuring the future of Vancouver's back-yard wilderness and more than quadrupling the region's parkland to 14 percent, this collection of new provincial, regional, and municipal parks brought the Lower Mainland's total parkland to over 200,000ha. The legacy embraces relatively small areas – popular day-trip recreation sites such as **Barnston Island**, near Langley, and the forests of **Burnaby Mountain** near Simon Fraser University. Also wildernesses such as

Indian Arm (Say-Nuth-Khaw-Yum) Provincial Park (p.104) protecting the east shores of a 30km fiord; Pinecone Burke Provincial Park (p.130), protecting the western shores of Pitt Lake, the largest freshwater tidal lake in North America, and the 60-sq-km Tetrahedron Wilderness Area on the Sechelt Peninsula. The legacy safeguards some of the most significant wildlife habitat in North America, including 11,000ha in the Boundary Bay Wildlife Management Area (p.110), near Delta; the Brackendale Eagle Reserve (p.119), an important wintering site for bald eagles; and the Bishop River wilderness, home to a large population of grizzly bears.

■ Greater Vancouver Regional District (GVRD) Parks: 604-432-6350. 22 parks protect and make accessible more than 11,000ha within and around Canada's third largest metropolis. They include Pacific Spirit Regional Park, forest and foreshore stretching across Point Grey, separating Vancouver from the University of BC. Its thin foreshore wraps around the tip of the peninsula and touches the Fraser River, the Strait of Georgia, and Burrard Inlet. At 809ha, Pacific Spirit Park is larger than Stanley Park, and far less busy, offering more than 35km of multi-purpose trails shared by pedestrians, cyclists, and horseback riders. Camosun Bog (entrance off 19th Ave and Camosun St) is the oldest bog in the Lower Mainland, originating 12,000 years ago. Interesting vegetation, including sphagnum moss, cloudberry, and sundew, can be seen from the boardwalk. Park information centre at 4915 W 16th Ave. For other GVRD parks, see *Logs* and *Index*. Also contact: Greater Vancouver Regional District Parks, 4330 Kingsway, Burnaby, BC, V5H 4G8.

■ Stanley Park: Foot of W Georgia St. On a 405ha peninsula between English Bay and Burrard Inlet. One of North America's largest and most impressive city parks. Dedicated "to the use and enjoyment of people of all colours, creeds and customs for all time" by Lord Stanley, Governor-General of Canada 1888-1893. The Nature House, Children's Farmyard, Miniature Railway, and Vancouver Aquarium are off West Georgia St entrance. Water birds are numerous at Lost Lagoon Oct-April. Spring migration brings songbirds. BC Wildlife Watch viewing site.

■ The Stanley Park Seawall: Along 10km of park perimeter. The dream of Park Commissioner M.S. Logan who began seeking federal grants to extend existing seawalls in 1916. He envisioned a seawall walk devoid of automobiles, passing under shady trees beside sandy beaches and rocky foreshores, with magnificent views of harbour, mountains, and forest. On July 22, 1971, the last granite blocks were put in place. It's now a walkway and bicycle route. The waters along the seawall are visited by large flocks of diving water birds, including scoters, goldeneyes, grebes, cormorants, loons and scaups. A nesting seabird colony is situated on the Prospect Point cliffs. Look for pelagic cormorants plus a few glaucous-winged gulls and pigeon guillemots. BC Wildlife Watch viewing site.

■ Stanley Park Scenic Dr: Begins and ends at W Georgia St. Circles perimeter of park.

Brockton Point offers panorama of Burrard Inlet and North Shore mountains. Road continues to Prospect Point. Siwash Rock can't be seen from road, but footpaths lead to the seawall and this famous landmark. Ferguson Point has view of Third Beach, the Point Grey Peninsula, and Vancouver Island. Road continues past Second Beach and Lost Lagoon. There is good parking within walking distance of most attractions.

■ UBC Botanical Garden and Nitobe Memorial Garden: Both botanical gardens are on the university campus, but Nitobe Memorial Garden is separated from the Main Garden (see below).

UBC Botanical Garden is at 6804 SW Marine Dr (corner of 16th Ave and SW Marine Dr). 604-822-4208 or 604-822-9666. Daily, year-round. One of Canada's oldest botanical gardens: not a show garden, but a 29ha classroom and living museum of plants

Chinese New Year parade, Chinatown, Vancouver.

from around the world. Over 10,000 species in eight separate gardens: Alpine, BC Native, Perennia, Arbour, Physick (16th century herb garden), Food, Asian, and Winter. Over 400 rhododendrons in the Asian Garden, plus giant snow lilies from the Himalayas, and kiwi fruit (Chinese gooseberries) growing naturally like ivy up a Douglas fir. The Physick Garden is laid out around a sundial; collection even includes belladonna. Shop-in-the-Garden: 604-822-4529.

Nitobe Memorial Garden is near Gate Four on NW Marine Dr. 604-822-6038 or 604-822-9666. Daily year-round. An authentic 1.5ha Japanese stroll and tea garden created in 1960 by Dr Kannosuke Mori. A serene place, giving a sense of seasonal change and harmony.

■ Queen Elizabeth Park and Bloedel Floral Conservatory: 33rd Ave and Cambie St. 604-257-8584. Daily. Former site of two stone quarries, now a 53ha park. Little Mountain, city's highest point, stands 152m above sea level. Displays of every major native species of tree and shrub, several foreign specimens, all in as native a habitat as possible. Bloedel Conservatory is Canada's largest single-structure conservatory: it displays more than 500 species of plants from rainforest to desert envi-

ronments; also tropical birds and fish. The Civic Arboretum, Canada's first, is a unique combination of park and botanical garden.

■ VanDusen Botanical Garden: 37th Ave and Oak St. 604-878-9274. Daily, year-round. Tours Easter to Thanksgiving. 22ha of garden with notable fuchsias, roses, hanging baskets, heathers. Oriental displays, international flora and fauna. Many rarities, Elizabethan hedge maze, topiaries, children's garden. Woodland-and-lake paths surround formal gardens.

■ Dr Sun Yat-Sen Classical Chinese Garden: 578 Carrall St (in Chinatown). 604-689-7133 or 604-622-3207. Daily. First authentic classical Chinese garden built outside China. A $5-million Ming Dynasty replica, built by artisans from Suzhou, a Chinese city famous for its gardens. Every pebble has been placed with painstaking awareness of harmony.

Places and Plazas, Streets and Alleys

Vancouver's shopping areas are a mix of retail stores with art galleries and studios, restaurants and cafes, people-watching and window-shopping.

■ Granville Island: South side of False Creek, beneath Granville St Bridge. Access via W 4th Ave. Information Centre at 1592 Johnston St near the Public Market. 604-666-6477. Decaying warehouses and boat sheds transformed into shopping, residential, entertainment complexes. Giant indoor market open daily, except Mon in winter. Galleries, studios, two theatres, a brewery, hotel, restaurants, tennis courts, children's water play area, art school, walkway along False Creek. Sea Village is one of Vancouver's few houseboat communities. Many special events: International Comedy Fest, Jazz Fest, Wooden Boat Festival, Shakespeare Under the Stars (see *Vancouver, Coast, and Mountains, Events*, p.92). Can also be reached by water bus from Beach Ave dock behind Vancouver Aquatic Centre.

■ False Creek: The meandering saltwater inlet that snakes its way into the heart of downtown Vancouver. "False" because it was not the elusive mouth of the Fraser that explorers had hoped for. False Creek was scene of decay and toxic waters for decades, an eyesore impossible to avoid for thousands of motorists crossed it daily via the Burrard, Granville, or Cambie St bridges. Since chosen as site of Expo 86, False Creek has been given miraculous new life, and it is becoming the new heart of downtown Vancouver. First the water's edge was reclaimed for Expo. That area has now become Plaza of Nations, with room enough for more than 100,000 celebrators to cheer on the dragon boats in the mammoth June Dragon Boat Festival. Another Expo legacy: Science World (and Alcan Omnimax Theatre). Nearby is BC Place Stadium.

Renewal has been extended to the north, south, and finally the east shores, with the opening in 1992 of Citygate, a major residential project. The whole area has become an award-winning urban redevelopment project, a blend of residential housing, marinas, parks, and restaurants, linked by a seawall promenade. Vancouver Parks is completing a marine park greenbelt from Vanier Park, at the Planetarium, all the way around False Creek to Wainborne

Park at the foot of Richards St, near the north footings of the Granville St Bridge. And every inch of this greenbelt is waterfront. Moreover, now that industries have been forced to relocate, and sewage, chemicals, and heavy metals are no longer being dumped into the creek, this once toxic sea has become clean again.

■ **Yaletown:** Homer, Hamilton, and Mainland streets from Davie to Smithe. A century ago this district boasted more saloons per acre than anywhere in North America. Then it became a warehouse district. Now its trendy urban lofts are the place to be for baby boomers and empty nesters avoiding the 'burbs. Here are shops and galleries, billiards, pizza, and beer at the Yaletown Brewing Company on Mainland.

■ **Robson Street:** Blend of old and new. From the Vancouver Art Gallery in a 19th-century historic courthouse, to modern gallerias where high-end fashion is sold. Robson St, between Howe and Broughton streets, was, at one time, mainly German, earning it the nickname of "Robsonstrasse." Today, it's known for chic clothing, accessory, and specialty shops and is referred to as Vancouver's Golden Mile.

■ **Robson Square:** Robson St between Hornby and Howe streets. Heart of downtown Vancouver. Parades, marches, speeches, New Year's Eve celebrations all take place here. Some BC government offices. Covered skating rink. Robson Square Media Centre hosts events from lectures to films and premieres.

■ **Granville and Georgia Streets:** Centre of commercial ventures. Six blocks of the Granville St Mall are closed to traffic, except buses and taxis. Major department stores and malls. **SeaBus Terminal** to North Vancouver is located at bottom (north end) of Granville St.

■ **Pacific Centre:** Downtown. 700 W Georgia St. Three levels, two major department stores.

■ **Chinatown:** Between Carrall St and Gore Ave. North America's third largest Chinese community after San Francisco's and New York's. The first Chinese arrived in 1858, during the gold rush, more came later to build the Canadian Pacific Railway. Phone booths are adorned with pagoda-style roofs; street names are in English and Chinese. The aromas of China entice visitors into shops selling herbs and teas, pastries, dim sum, fresh fruits, and vegetables. Other stores tempt with silk, jade, ivory, bamboo, rattan, and brassware. Here, at Keefer and East Pender, is North America's only night market: bustling each weekend night from late spring through early fall, with some 20,000 visitors. Here too, the World's Thinnest Office Building (see *Architectural Points of Interest*, below).

■ **Punjabi Market:** Main St between 49th and 51st. A social, religious, commercial, and cultural centre for BC's 80,000 south Asians from India, Pakistan, Fiji, East Africa, and Sri Lanka. More than 20 percent of shopping clientele are non-Asian, coming to enjoy the music, food, and fashions of ancient cultures. More than 100 businesses flourish.

■ **Gastown:** Carrall, Powell, Water, and Alexander streets meet at Maple Tree Square to form Gastown. Named after "Gassy Jack" Deighton, pioneering tavern keeper whose statue stands in Maple Tree Square. As the city grew, it moved westward and changed its name

Kayakers seek the sandy shores of Vancouver's popular Jericho Beach.

to Vancouver; Gastown became Old Vancouver, and slid into decline. In 1971, it was designated a heritage area, and renewal began. Now a fertile mix of old and new, with the vigour and excitement of one of the world's largest seaports just two blocks away. Water St is noted for period cobblestones and storefronts. Two-tonne 1977 Gastown Steam Clock, at corner of Cambie and Water, is world's first. Operates on steam generated from heating system in nearby buildings. Whistles every 15 minutes, emits bursts of steam on the hour. Walking tours in summer depart 2pm from Gassy Jack Statue: 604-683-5650.

■ **Commercial Drive:** Between Broadway Ave (9th Ave) and Hastings St. Locals call this part of town "The Drive." Coffee bars, Italian restaurants, Santa Barbara Market. Mercato Mall at 1st and Commercial.

■ **Downtown Waterfront and Waterfront Centre:** Downtown shore of Burrard Inlet, including **Canada Place** (see below) and the restored **Canadian Pacific Railway (CPR)**, have undergone dramatic and invigorating changes. New buildings, hotels, shopping corridors and centres, green spaces, waterfalls. Waterfront Centre Hotel, part of **Waterfront Centre**, is one of the new buildings. **CPR Station** is SeaBus and SkyTrain terminal.

■ **Tour of the Port:** Vanterm public viewing area at Vanterm Container Terminal, 1300 Stewart St. 604-666-6129. From an observation deck on 4th floor of terminal's administration building, entire terminal is seen: container cranes and lift trucks. Interactive displays. Unrestricted view of Burrard Inlet from Vancouver wharves on the west to Seaboard Lumber Terminal on the east.

■ **South Granville:** Granville St between 4th Ave and 16th Ave. Largely shopping, with upscale fashion stores, galleries, delis.

The Best of the Beaches

■ **Vancouver Beaches:** They curve 16km along English Bay from Wreck Beach (the city's

unofficial nude beach) to First Narrows beach. There are 11 in all: Wreck Beach, Locarno, Jericho, Point Grey, Kitsilano, Sunset, Second, Third, Ambleside, Spanish Banks, and English Bay. It's possible at low tide, if you're athletic, to walk from Kitsilano Beach along the shoreline to Wreck Beach. June-Sept, outdoor pools at "Kits" Beach and Second Beach are available for use.

■ **Kitsilano Showboat:** 604-734-7332. A tradition since 1935. Open-air amphitheatre on Kitsilano Beach offering unique no-cost outdoor beachside entertainment. Evenings, mid-June to Aug: Mon, Wed, Fri.

Architectural Points of Interest

Vancouver is a modern city, just over a century old. A comparison of old and new architecture – from the mansions of Shaughnessy to highrises of the West End – puts history into perspective.

■ **The Law Courts:** 800 Smythe St between Hornby and Howe. 604-660-2847. Mon-Fri. Designed by city's own Arthur Erickson. Concrete building is enclosed by glass from 4th to 7th floors. Covers a city block.

■ **Canada Place:** 999 Canada Place on Burrard Inlet, at foot of Howe St. 604-775-8687. Daily, in summer; Mon-Fri, off-season. Built as Canada Pavilion for a nautical feel. Its roof looks like a series of sails. Promenade is three city blocks long, excellent views of the port. Cruise-ship terminal, **Vancouver Trade and Convention Centre** (604-641-1987), restaurants, ballrooms, exhibition halls, shops, hotel, **CN IMAX Theatre**.

■ **Sinclair Centre:** Between Granville and Howe, Hastings and Cordova. 604-659-1009. A commercial centre. Four restored buildings cover entire city block, linked together by a two-level glass roofed Heritage Court and Galleria. Heritage buildings (1910-1937) include Old Post Office, R.V. Winch Building, Customs Examining Warehouse, Federal Building.

■ **Dominion Building:** 207 W Hastings St. 13-storey 1908 building was called the most modern office building in Canada and the tallest building in the British Empire.

■ **World's Thinnest Office Building:** At corner of Pender and Carrall streets in Chinatown. A structure 1.8m wide and two stories tall. Won the *Ripley's Believe It or Not* designation first, as "world's thinnest," then achieved a Guinness World Record as "shallowest commercial building in the world," becoming the first and only building in Canada in *The Guinness Book of World Records.* Without really even trying, the Sam Kee Thin Building ("Slender on Pender," "Thin Wins") has become a tourist destination.

■ **The West End:** Some of the highest density housing in Canada. There are still a few samples of the original wood-frame homes (see *Barclay Square,* below). But high and low rises, shops, movie houses, restaurants, cafes, and supermarkets now predominate. Stroll along Denman St from English Bay and enjoy some of the best ice cream in the city.

■ **Barclay Heritage Square:** West End, bounded by Barclay, Nicola, Haro, and Broughton streets. Unique park site developed by Vancouver Board of Parks and Recreation. Includes nine historic West End houses, 1890-1908, in original settings with period landscaping and gardens. Six have been rehabilitated for family accommodation, creating a unique link with the past. Centrepieces are Barclay Manor, a venue for senior citizens' events, and the Roedde family's house, now **Roedde House Museum**, Vancouver's first "house" museum. Roedde House is open for public viewing, and may be rented for small receptions. For information: 604-684-7040.

■ **Shaughnessy:** Above W 16th Ave and Granville St. Here are the imposing homes of Vancouver's elite. In 1907, Canadian Pacific Railway began to transform this former tract of forest into premier residential land when the West End began losing its exclusive character. Note the curving streets, generous lots, porte-cochères for carriages.

■ **Vancouver Public Library:** Between Robson and Georgia (opposite the new Ford Centre for the Performing Arts, below). 604-331-3600. A $100-million project, the largest capital expense in the city's history, opened in 1995. Winning design by team of Moshe Safdie and Downs/Archambault. In an ironic post-modern sort of way, the nine-storey oval library is designed to look like the original Colosseum in Rome. A 22-storey federal tower curves around one corner. Library has 35,100 square metres for books, online catalogues, CD-ROMS, a computer lab, children's library, as well as a gift shop, sushi bar, and shop-lined concourse. Language lab offers self-tutoring in 90 languages. Temporary library cards for visitors.

Arts and Culture

Vancouver offers entertainment from Broadway shows and international entertainers to a fringe theatre festival (every Sept). More than 30 theatre companies and a dozen theatres showcase plays, concerts, and dance; nearly 60 galleries feature everything from Inuit to avant-garde. Call the **Arts Hotline**, 604-684-ARTS, for current information on 3,200 events a year. For tickets to most events, call TicketMaster, 604-280-4444. For arts and entertainment listings also consult the city's two daily newspapers, *The Province*, a morning tabloid, and *The Vancouver Sun. The Georgia Straight* is a free weekly tabloid with extensive listings.

■ **Ford Centre for the Performing Arts:** 777 Homer St, at Robson. 604-602-0616. Vancouver's magnificent new three-level 1,824-seat theatre designed, like the library across the street, by Moshe Safdie.

■ **The Orpheum Theatre:** 884 Granville St at Smithe. 604-665-3050; 604-280-4444 for tickets. Once a chic movie house, now Vancouver's oldest, most dignified concert hall. Home of Vancouver Symphony Orchestra. Refurbished to its original splendor. One-thousand-bulb crystal chandeliers, original Wurlitzer organ.

■ **The Queen Elizabeth Playhouse and Theatre:** 600 Hamilton St (at Georgia). 604-665-3050 for info; 604-280-4444 for tickets. Opera, ballet, live theatre, music.

■ **Other Theatres to Enjoy:** The popular Arts Club Theatre at three venues, including Granville Island; Bard on the Beach, in Vanier Park, mid-June to mid-Sept; Firehall Arts Centre at 280 E Cordova, the original No. 1 Firehall; the Vancouver East Cultural Centre at 1895 Venables, in a turn-of-the-century church; the Vancouver TheatreSports League, offering improv at 2750 Granville; and the Waterfront Theatre on Granville Island.

■ **The Vancouver Art Gallery:** 750 Hornby St, Robson Square. 604-662-4719 or 604-662-4700. Daily. In city's former courthouse, built 1911. Architect Francis Rattenbury also designed Empress Hotel and Legislative Buildings in Victoria. Canadian and international contemporary arts. Permanent collection includes works of Victoria's Emily Carr. Shop and cafe.

■ **Roundhouse Community Centre:** 181 Roundhouse Mews, at Pacific Blvd between Drake and Davie. 604-689-5858 or 604-713-1800. Opened 1997 and built around Canadian Pacific Railway roundhouse turntable dating to 1912, and historic locomotive #374 which ended its cross-Canada journey May 23, 1887. Roundhouse is setting for courses and workshops in martial arts, dance, health and fitness, music, and visual arts. Performance centre, exhibition hall, gymnasium, cafe.

THE NORTH SHORE

NORTH VANCOUVER AND WEST VANCOUVER: A MOUNTAIN PLAYGROUND

Vancouver's North Shore is home to 165,000 people in three municipalities: the City of North Vancouver, the District of North Vancouver, and the District of West Vancouver. While not merging identities, they merge as a geographic and recreational destination. The North Shore we refer to here is the north shore of Burrard Inlet, that long arm of the sea extending 24km west to Port Moody, then north another 23km along Indian Arm. Traditionally the home shores and avenue for three Coast Salish nations, the inlet is now spanned by two dramatic bridges – the Lions Gate at the First Narrows, and the Ironworkers Memorial Bridge at the Second Narrows – linking Vancouver and Burnaby on the south shore, with the North Shore. These are busy bridges, and can be nerve-wracking in heavy traffic, especially to anyone attempting to enjoy the scenery. The North Shore Mountains, the twin peaks of the Lions preside over the lands below, reminding everyone that there's year-round recreation up top, at Cypress Bowl, Grouse Mountain, Mt Seymour. The third inlet crossing allows much more time to enjoy the view: the Seabus is a link in the local transit system: hang on to your transfers. Two catamaran ferries slip back and forth across the inlet carrying 400 passengers at a time on their 12-minute crossings. See p. 90.

North Vancouver

North Vancouver: (Pop. 114,475). This city lies 8km north of downtown Vancouver, on the north shore of Burrard Inlet, east of the Lions Gate Bridge on Marine Dr and Hwy 1/99. The District Municipality of North Vancouver (pop. 81,848) surrounds the city borders except for the waterfront, from Capilano River (and West Vancouver) to the west, and Indian Arm to the east.

This is the contemporary heartland of the Squamish First Nation, whose traditional territories reach up to the headwaters of the Squamish and Cheakamus rivers. Three of seven Squamish communities are situated in North Vancouver. The Park Royal Shopping Mall is on land belonging to the Capilano Reserve. Whu-mul-chits-tun, at the mouth of the Squamish River, was a major salmon-fishing site. Mission, at Esplanade and 3rd St, has the largest marina in BC, and shops selling Coast Salish arts and crafts. Squamish Nation headquarters are at Seymour Creek, just off the Ironworkers Memorial Second Narrows Bridge.

North Vancouver's waterfront was one of the first on the Lower Mainland to be developed by European-descended newcomers and remains one of Greater Vancouver's most active port areas. Early sawmills, including the first built by Philip Hicks in the early 1860s, have given way to shipbuilding and rail-oriented activities. Long ago, Lonsdale Ave was a log-skid for clearing the forests; now it's the main shopping street, and there's also the **Lonsdale Quay Market** with over 80 shops and restaurants.

The area was named Moodyville by lumber entrepreneur Sewell "Sue" Prescott Moody around 1867. He declared it a dry town – which may have been a factor in the establishment of a ferry service across the inlet to the saloons and hotels of Brighton and Gastown. The district was incorporated in 1891, the city in 1907.

North Vancouver overlooks Burrard Inlet and is backed by the Coast Mountain range, offering some of Lower Mainland's finest scenery with an array of natural attractions from alpine wilderness and ski terrain to spectacular canyons and rivers.

North Vancouver Information: Info Centre, 131 East 2nd St, North Vancouver, BC, V7L 1C2. 604-987-4488. E-mail: nvtour@cofcnorthvan.org. Internet: http://www.cofcnorthvan.org. Weekdays 9-5 year-round. Two info booths operate daily in summer, one at junction of Capilano Rd and Marine Dr, other at foot of Lonsdale Ave.

■ **North Vancouver Museum:** 209 W 4th. 604-987-5618. Tues-Sun: 12-5. Domestic exhibits, logging, shipbuilding, farming, small businesses, and Coast Salish artifacts. Photograph gallery. Gift shop.

■ **Presentation House Gallery:** 333 Chesterfield Ave. 604-986-1351. Wed-Sun, 12-5. Photographic exhibits, historic and contemporary.

■ **Lonsdale Quay Market:** At foot of Lonsdale Ave. 604-985-6261. Take the SeaBus direct from Waterfront Station in Vancouver. Lots of excitement under one big roof, plus an observation tower to take in the view.

■ **Pacific Great Eastern Station:** Foot of Lonsdale Ave. 604-987-5618. Wed-Sun, 12-4. Art and rail history displays.

■ **Park and Tilford Gardens:** Adjacent Tilford Shopping Centre at Brooksbank Ave and Main St. 604-984-8200. Wheelchair accessible. Free admission and parking. Series of outdoor rooms: gardens include Asia, herb, west coast, and rhododendron.

■ **Maplewood Farm:** 405 Seymour River Pl. 604-929-5610. Tues-Sun, holiday Mondays, 10-4. 2ha farm with domestic animals and birds. Children's petting areas: Goathill and Rabbitat. Farm Fair mid-Sept.

■ **Capilano Suspension Bridge and Park:** 3735 Capilano Rd. 604-985-7474. Daily. One of Greater Vancouver's earliest tourist attractions, the original bridge was built 1889 by Scotsman George McKay and well-known Squamish figures August Jack and his brother Willie. Current bridge, in place since 1956, is built of wire rope with wood decking and stretches 137m across the canyon and 70m above the river. It is the longest pedestrian suspension bridge at that height in the world. 6ha park with a 60m waterfall, ponds, river, and walking trails. First Nations artists at work in longhouse carving centre. Gift shop features handcrafted Canadian arts. Snack bar and BBQ May-Sept; full-service restaurant year-round.

■ **Cleveland Dam:** North on Capilano Rd to Nancy Greene Way. In northern section of Capilano Canyon Park. Built 1954. Dam created Capilano Lake, which supplies much of Vancouver's drinking water. Hiking trails and picnicking sites.

■ **Capilano River Regional Park:** 163ha. Accessible from Capilano Hatchery turnoff or Cleveland Dam parking lot. 604-432-6350. Extensive trails, whitewater kayaking, picnicking, fishing. 7.5km Capilano Pacific Trail leads from Cleveland Dam through impressive forests of Douglas fir and cedar and follows the bends of Capilano River to its mouth near Ambleside Park in West Vancouver. Large totem collection. BC Wildlife Watch viewing site.

■ **Capilano Salmon Hatchery:** 4500 Capilano Park Rd. 604-666-1790. Daily. Established in 1971 by federal and provincial governments. Walk-through exhibits of salmon in various stages of development. Fish ladders. Working models and diagrams show salmon's life cycle. BC Wildlife Watch viewing site.

■ **Grouse Mountain and Skyride:** 6400 Nancy Greene Way, north along Capilano Lake. 604-984-0661. Snow Phone: 604-986-6262. Named in 1894 by hikers who came upon a blue grouse on the mountain trails, this

The Capilano Suspension Bridge hovers 170 metres above the Capilano River.

is the earliest developed ski area around, and quite a Vancouver institution. About a dozen ski runs, many visible from downtown Vancouver. Night skiing can be gorgeous, and the twinkling lights up the mountain are a part of Vancouver's nightlife. In summer: hang-gliding, hiking, loggers' sports. The **Skyride** (daily year-round) carries passengers in gondola to top of Grouse Mountain for panoramic view of city's skyline and harbour, and the Strait of Georgia. Takes eight minutes, rising from 290m to 1,250m above sea level. Here is the **Theatre in the Sky**, Canada's first high-definition electronic cinema. Near 3-D quality gives viewers the sensation of being in the picture. Now playing: *Born to Fly*, a remarkable aerial overview of BC. Grouse Nest Restaurant, reservations: 604-986-6378 (Skyride ticket included). Chainsaw carvings adorn new chalet.

■ **Lynn Headwaters Regional Park:** 4,685ha. 604-432-6350. From Second Narrows (Ironworkers Memorial) Bridge or Lions Gate Bridge, take Hwy 1 to Lynn Valley Rd (Exit 19) in North Vancouver. Follow Lynn Valley Rd 4km to park entrance. Rugged mountain wilderness at city's edge. 20km of developed forest trails that lead to panoramic vistas, picnicking, and historic BC Mills House built in 1908.

■ **Lynn Canyon Park and Ecological Centre:** 250ha. 3663 Park Rd. 604-981-3103. Daily, Feb-Nov; Sunday, rest of year. Natural park surrounds deep gorge cut into mountains by Lynn Creek. Suspension bridge is 68m long and hovers a thrilling 75m above the waters. Ecological Centre, built in the shape of a dogwood, teaches about interdependence of plants, animals, people. BC Wildlife Watch viewing site.

■ **Seymour Demonstration Forest and Seymour River Fish Hatchery:** 5,600ha. 604-432-6286. Take Lillooet Rd exit from Upper Levels Hwy, go past Capilano College, through cemetery and along gravel road to forest entrance. About 14 times the size of Stanley Park, with 40km of trails, walkways and roads, but not technically a park – the forest is part of the Seymour Watershed, supplying water to Greater Vancouver. There is cycling and rollerblading on weekends; canoeing and kayaking (by permit), some fishing. But education is main thrust: forest interpretive trails, fish watching, Sunday tours (call ahead: 604-987-1273). BC Wildlife Watch viewing site.

■ **Mt Seymour Provincial Park:** 3,508ha. 604-924-2200. On Mt Seymour Rd off Mt Seymour Parkway, eastern region of North Vancouver. Park is named after Frederick Seymour, BC's governor, 1864-1869. The closest provincial park to Vancouver offers mountaineering, challenging hikes, and day trips through terrain that reaches a height of 1,508m at Mt Bishop. Four main trails cut through park. Visit Goldie and Mystery lakes. Mt Seymour Parkway offers spectacular views. BC Wildlife Watch viewing site.

■ **Seymour Ski Country:** In Mt Seymour Provincial Park. 1700 Mt Seymour Rd, North Vancouver, BC, V7G 1L3. 604-986-2261 or Snow Phone: 604-718-7771. Particularly attractive to learners. Mystery Peak chairlift climbs 1,200m. Skiing, snowboarding, snowshoeing, and snow-tubing through park forests. Snowshoeing programs. Three double chairlifts and rope tow for beginners. Ski rentals, ski school, night skiing. Restaurant, cafe.

■ **Maplewood Flats:** Off Dollarton Hwy 2km east of Ironworkers Memorial Second Narrows Bridge. Follow wildlife viewing signs to parking, trails, and viewing area. Wheelchair accessible. Songbirds, water birds, ospreys, harbour seals. BC Wildlife Watch viewing site.

■ **Cates Park:** 24ha. 604-990-3830. On the Dollarton Hwy at Roche Point, jutting out into eastern reaches of Burrard Inlet. On shores of Indian Arm, this is a popular summer picnic spot. Swimming, boat-launch facilities, two play areas. 15m Indian war canoe, built in 1921 by Chief Henry Peter George, is on display.

■ **Murdo Fraser Pitch and Putt Golf Course:** 2700 Pemberton Ave. 604-980-8410. In forested park with ponds, flower beds, walkways, and picnic tables.

Deep Cove: 8.5km east of Dollarton Hwy Interchange. Part of District Municipality of North Vancouver. A charming pocket cove on the west shore of **Indian Arm**, a steep and dramatic fiord extending north 30.5km from Burrard Inlet, and averaging about 1.5km in width. The arm has long been a popular getaway for Greater Vancouver recreational boaters, kayakers, fishermen, and now its northernmost reaches have been set aside as Indian Arm Provincial Park (below). Deep Cove provides the arm's only major moorage, though many boaters anchor at other points along the inlet. With homes clinging to the hills above and Coombe Park and Jug Island across the water, Deep Cove offers some of the most beautiful scenery in the Lower Mainland. Boats can be moored offshore or at the marina; there's scuba diving, boat rentals, swimming, waterskiing, picnicking.

Deep Cove Information: North Vancouver Info Centre, 131 East 2nd St, North Vancouver, BC, V7L 1C2. 604-987-4488. Weekdays, 9-5, year-round.

■ **Indian Arm Provincial Park:** 9,300ha. 604-924-2200. Accessed by boat from Burrard Inlet. Deep Cove, south of the park, on the west bank, has a marina; public wharf at Belcarra Regional Park, on the east bank. Park is jointly managed by the BC Government and the local Tsleil-Waututh First Nation, who know it as Say-Nuth-Khaw-Yum. Wilderness area with no facilities, protecting old-growth forests, alpine lakes, the 50m Granite Falls, and the precious Indian River estuary. Bishop Creek is a popular anchorage on the west shore, and Croker Island is a well-known scuba-diving site. BC Wildlife Watch viewing site.

West Vancouver

West Vancouver: (Pop. 41,778). Just west of Lions Gate Bridge, on Marine Dr. Incorporates four villages (Ambleside, Dundarave, Caulfeild, and Horseshoe Bay) spread loosely along the north shore of Burrard Inlet. Marine Dr and Taylor Way intersection near the Lions Gate Bridge is, in a sense, downtown West Vancouver. The Park Royal Shopping Centre covers both sides of Marine Dr west of Taylor Way.

West Vancouver is one of Canada's most picturesque residential communities. It lies along the lower slope of 1,324m Hollyburn Mountain between the Capilano River valley and Horseshoe Bay, bordered by Burrard Inlet to the south and Howe Sound to the west.

West Vancouver has close to 2,500ha of park and recreation land, and boasts the highest per capita income in Canada. The British Properties, a 1,600ha area, sprawling halfway up Hollyburn Mountain, contains some of Vancouver's most expensive and stately homes. The shoreline is dotted with parks, many kilometres of seawalls and walks, and marina facilities at Fishermans Cove and Horseshoe Bay.

West Vancouver Information: North Vancouver Info Centre, 131 East 2nd St, North Vancouver, BC, V7L 1C2. 604-987-4488. Weekdays, 9-5, year-round. Two info booths daily in summer: one at the junction of Capilano Rd and Marine Dr; the other at the foot of Lonsdale Ave.

■ **Ambleside Park:** 604-925-7200. Off Marine Dr between Capilano River and Keith Rd. On Burrard Inlet across the water from Stanley Park. Sea walks and beaches. BC Wildlife Watch viewing site.

■ **Lighthouse Park:** 604-925-7200. 12km south of Horseshoe Bay. South of Hwy 1/99 via Caulfeild Dr. Turn southwest to park.

Semi-wilderness retreat on the mouth of Burrard Inlet. East from the park, across English Bay, is view of Stanley Park and downtown Vancouver. West is Bowen Island. Hiking trails through some of the Lower Mainland's oldest Douglas fir forest to Point Atkinson Lighthouse, built 1912. No camping. BC Wildlife Watch viewing site.

■ **Cypress Provincial Park:** 3,012ha. Year-round. 604-926-6007. 12km north of Cypress Bowl Rd and Hwy 1/99 junction. Cypress Mountain is part of the North Shore mountain chain overlooking Vancouver. Named for its spectacular western red cedars and yellow cedars, both members of the cypress family, this is one of BC's most visited day-use parks. Mountain meadows, lakes, forests. Vistas of 1,646m Lions Mountain, Howe Sound, Gulf Islands. Excellent hiking trails, including the 3km wheelchair-accessible Yew Lake Trail. This is also a haven for wildlife, including the rare tailed frog, on the endangered species list. Alpine ski area, two chairlifts, double rope tow, a total of 25 runs, 16km of ski touring trails. A snowshoe and winter-hiking trail connects parking lot with Hollyburn Lodge. Ski school and ski rentals. Snowmobiling. Restaurant and licenced sundeck. BC Wildlife Watch viewing site.

■ **Whytecliffe Park:** Off Marine Dr in Horseshoe Bay. Trails, picnics. Departure point for diving excursions.

BURNABY

ROOM WITH A VIEW

Burnaby: (Pop.179,209). 10km east of Vancouver city centre. Main entrances into Burnaby from Hwy 1 are Sprott St, Grandview Hwy, Willingdon Ave, Cariboo Interchange.

The city of Burnaby is bordered by Burrard Inlet to the north, and the north arm of the Fraser River to the south. It is named for Robert Burnaby (1828-1878), British colonist, merchant, and businessman. The trees of **Central Park**, a 90ha area on the western edge of the municipality, were first thinned out in 1863 by Royal Engineers looking for masts for the British Navy's sailing ships.

Incorporated in 1892, Burnaby today carries a mixture of commercial and industrial development, and is second only to Vancouver as a centre of employment. Burnaby offers nearly 4,400ha of parkland within its 96 square kilometres.

Burnaby Information: Metrotown Information Centre, 4600 Kingsway. 604-431-8046. Daily, May 1-Sept 30. City Hall Information Centre, 4949 Canada Way, Burnaby, BC, V5G 1M2. 604-294-7944. Oct 1-April 30, weekdays.

■ **Simon Fraser University:** Atop Burnaby Mountain. From Hastings St (Hwy 7A) take Burnaby Mountain Parkway. Follow signs. 604-291-4323. Established 1965, and notable for its striking architecture by Arthur Erickson and Geoffrey Massey. Museum of Archaeology

and Ethnology, open daily, features Northwest Coast native art, domestic utensils, tools. SFU and **Burnaby Mountain Park** (see below) offer spectacular views of Burrard Inlet, Burnaby, and Vancouver. Wheelchair accessible. Group tours. Horizons Restaurant. There is also Simon Fraser University at Harbour Centre, 515 W Hastings St, Vancouver, BC, V6B 5K3.

■ **Burnaby Mountain Park:** From Lougheed Hwy, turn north on Gaglardi Way to Centennial Way. 604-294-7450. Views from trails. Wheelchair accessible. Playground, rose garden, and the Kamui Mintara (Playground of the Gods), a cluster of carved poles by Japanese sculptor Nuburi Toko and his son, symbolizing goodwill between Burnaby and its sister city, Kushiro, Japan.

■ **Deer Lake, Century Park and Deer Lake Park:** Deer Lake is a small lake in the heart of Burnaby (south of much larger Burnaby Lake), offering two quite different park experiences.

On north shore is **Century Park**, a formal area including gardens, **Burnaby Art Gallery, James Cowan Theatre, Burnaby Arts Centre, and Burnaby Heritage Village** (more below). Century Park is accessed from Gilpin St on the west; or from Canada Way to Sperling Ave to Deer Lake Ave.

Deer Lake Park, accessed from Sperling Ave, offers fishing, boating, jogging, picnicking, and casual strolling. Lake is home to a variety of waterfowl. Wonderful views on a clear day: immediate scenes of the lake, distant glimpses of Vancouver's towered structures, Burnaby Mountain, and North Shore peaks. BC Wildlife Watch viewing site.

■ **Shadbolt Centre for the Arts:** 6450 Deer Lake Ave. 604-291-6864. Mon-Fri. Houses 300-seat James Cowan Centre, 120-seat recital hall, convention facilities, and dance studio.

■ **Burnaby Heritage Village and Carousel:** 6501 Deer Lake Ave. 604-293-6501. Daily, March-Oct. Open Christmas and Thanksgiving. Open-air historical village. More than 30 buildings and outdoor displays depicting life in Lower Mainland from 1890-1925. Guides often wear traditional dress. Vintage carousel operating.

■ **Burnaby Lake Regional Park:** 311ha. 604-432-6350. In the centre of the city, between the Lougheed and Trans-Canada highways – entrance at Piper Ave off Winston and Avalon, off Cariboo. More than 200 species of birds recorded in this urban park, from hummingbirds to bald eagles; mammals include beavers, coyotes, muskrats, and squirrels. Trail system offers hikes in a setting ranging from cool, shady forest to open marshland. Level, soft-surface 11km trail circles the lake (allow about 2.5 hours). For shorter walks, loop trails east and west of the nature house (see below) meander through a variety of habitats. Nature study, canoeing, horseback riding, walking and picnicking, offer hours of relaxation at this calm oasis. Wildlife Rescue Association's wildlife rehabilitation facility (604-526-7275) is located on south shore of lake. Here, at the self-guided wildlife habitat garden, you can find out how to design a wildlife-friendly back yard. BC Wildlife Watch viewing site. **Burnaby Lake Nature House** is at 4519 Piper Ave. 604-432-6350. Programs year-round for children, adults, groups. Phone for brochure.

- **BC Parkway and Highland Park Line:** 19km cycling and pedestrian trail tracing SkyTrain route from Burnaby to Vancouver's False Creek Waterfront and New Westminster Quay in New Westminster.
- **Central Park:** On east boundary of Burnaby, on Boundary Rd between Kingsway and Imperial. 604-294-7450. Take SkyTrain to Patterson Station. Large urban park with exceptional children's playground, pitch-and-putt golf course, trails, stadium.
- **Burnaby Fraser Foreshore Park:** On Burnaby's south shore, at the end of Bryne Rd. 2km trail tracing the bustling Fraser River.
- **Metrotown Centre:** Kingsway, between Boundary Rd and Royal Oak. A massive commercial, residential, and entertainment complex, next to SkyTrain Metrotown Station. Eaton Centre Metrotown has more than 175 shops and services, three major department stores. Linked to SkyTrain by a covered passerelle.
- **Golfing: Central Park Pitch and Putt**, 604-434-2727. **Riverway Public Golf Course**, 18 holes on Burnaby's south shore, 604-280-4653. **Burnaby Mountain Golf Course**, 18 holes at the mountain's base, 604-280-7355. **Kensington Park Pitch and Putt**, north side of Burnaby, 604-291-9525.

NEW WESTMINSTER

THE ROYAL CITY

New Westminster: (Pop. 49,350). 12km southeast of downtown Vancouver, on the north shore of the Fraser River estuary, upstream from delta islands of Lulu and Annacis.

Throughout the 1860s, New Westminster was a Fraser River boom town populated by thousands of gold prospectors. Known as the "Royal City," it was founded in early 1859 by Colonel R.C. Moody of the Royal Engineers, and named by Queen Victoria that same summer. A year later, in July 1860, New Westminster became the first incorporated municipality west of the Great Lakes, and, until 1866, it was capital city of the mainland colony of BC.

About that time, in 1863, Walter B. Cheadle, an early tourist, described the city: "New Westminster stands on rising ground above the river, amidst the densest forest, which has cost fortunes to clear away, averaging $3 a stump.... It is finely placed and will be a pretty place in time."

From 1866 to 1868, New Westminster continued as capital city, now of the joint mainland BC and Vancouver Island colony. But by the late 1860s, the gold rush had ended and the city's population and importance as a commercial centre had declined, at least for the time being. In 1868, title of capital city was transferred to Victoria.

Today, New Westminster is a bustling city in the heart of the Lower Mainland, a large freshwater port, and an important supplement to the port of Vancouver. Cities and municipalities now surround it on all sides. The city used to be known for its **Pattullo Bridge**, not so affectionately called the "Pay-Toll-O Bridge" for its unpopular toll, long since removed. Now "New West" is known for its historic architecture, parks, and innovative development, particularly on the waterfront, with its glittering, bright blue two-storey public market. Columbia St, the main road, was dusty and unused right through the 1970s. Expo year, 1986, marked the opening of the **SkyTrain**, a light rapid-transit system that linked New Westminster easily with Vancouver, and things started to change. There was an invasion of visitors during Expo, and a swelling of population once New West became a viable commuter city for Vancouver workers. Businesses started pulling up their socks, renovating, remodelling. New businesses moved in. New heritage-look structures appeared. No longer a mishmash of decaying buildings, New Westminster in some ways resembles San Francisco, with its hilliness, its waterfront and bridges, even its gold-rush history.

New Westminster's three **SkyTrain** stations are at: 8th St just north of Westminster Quay; 22nd St at 8th Ave; and the Columbia St terminus. Continuous departures for downtown Vancouver; every 27 minutes. A bridge has been built parallel to the Pattullo, and the SkyTrain now extends south into Surrey, to Scott Rd, Surrey Central, and King George stations, along King George Hwy.

New Westminster Information: Info Centre at New Westminster Quay, at foot of 8th St. 810 Quayside Dr. 604-526-1905. Daily, 9:30-5:30.
- **Westminster Quay and Public Market:** On waterfront at foot of 8th St. The heart of New Westminster's waterfront redevelopment. Open daily. Walkway along Fraser River, interpretive signs. Shops, dining, entertainment. The Inn at Westminster Quay is worth a look, excitingly designed on pillars reaching out over the river.
- **Paddlewheeler River Adventures:** 604-525-4465. Tickets by phone or at Westminster Quay. Fraser River cruises aboard *The Native*, a 27m replica of a paddlewheeler, between New Westminster and Fort Langley. Full-day narrated history cruises and special-event cruises. Board next to Westminster Quay Public Market.
- **Starline Tours:** 604-522-3506. Year-round. River tours feature history and ecology of New Westminster, Steveston, Pitt Lake and Harrison Hot Springs. April-May, daily trips to watch sea lions.
- **Irving House Historic Centre:** 302 Royal Ave. 604-527-4640. Tues-Sun, and holiday

High-rise towers in Burnaby's Metrotown.

Mon, May to mid-Sept: weekends, 1-5, mid-Sept to April. Wed-Sun: group tours by appointment. Original residence of Captain William Irving, "King of the River," completed in 1865.

■ **New Westminster Museum and Archives:** 302 Royal Ave. 604-527-4640. Tues-Sun, and holiday Mon, May to mid-Sept; weekends, 1-5, mid-Sept to April. Near Irving House. Artifacts and displays of local history, including an 1876 Dufferin Coach.

■ **Museum of Royal Westminster Regiment:** The Armoury, 530 Queen's Ave. 604-526-5116. Tues and Thurs, 11-3. Collection of military artifacts related to New Westminster dating back to 1863.

■ **SS Samson V Maritime Museum:** Waterfront, between public market and the Inn. 604-522-6894. Sat-Sun. Extended hours in summer. SS *Samson V* was the last sternwheeler on the Fraser River. Built in 1937, she operated until 1980.

■ **Canadian Lacrosse Hall of Fame:** Centennial Centre, 65 E 6th Ave. 604-527-4640. Daily on request. Lacrosse is Canada's national sport.

■ **Queen's Park:** 1st St and 3rd Ave. Wooded areas. Site of **New Westminster Arts Centre** and **Peter Legge Playhouse** (three or four performances a year). Also Rainbow Playland with colourful spray pool, petting farm, adventure playground. May long weekend to Aug.

■ **Canada Games Pool:** 6th Ave and McBride Blvd. 604-526-4281. Daily. Olympic size. 65m warm pool with rope swing, trolley ride, tubes, mats, indoor waterslide. Fitness centre, sauna, whirlpool.

■ **Douglas College (main campus):** 700 Royal Ave. 604-527-5400. (Also campuses in Coquitlam and Maple Ridge.) BC's largest community college, with up to 11,000 students. Performing arts theatre, art gallery, athletic facilities, library.

SURREY

BLENDING OF WORLDS

Surrey: (Pop. 304,477). Sitting nicely between a curve of the Fraser River to the north, and Boundary Bay and the Canada/US Border to the south. BC's second largest city is expected to surpass Vancouver by the year 2021, as the province's most populated city.

James Kennedy was the first British subject to take up land in the area, pre-empting for the price of one dollar an acre in 1861. Surrey incorporated in 1879 when there were fewer than 1,000 residents over approximately 200 square kilometres. The name, Surrey, was offered by H.J. Brewer, one of the all-English founding fathers, noting the site looked across the Fraser River to New Westminster, just as old Westminster lies across the Thames River from the County of Surrey. The first city hall, completed 1881, is now part of the Centennial Museum.

The big push to develop came in 1891 when the first railway, the New Westminster

Southern, passed through. After that, Surrey's growth closely followed the expansion of the railway.

Surrey today incorporates six townships, little pockets of development that grew. They include **Whalley** (pop. 74,100), in the northwest corner, which holds the key to much of the area's history; **Guildford** (pop. 46,800), the business centre; **South Surrey** (pop. 55,700), also known as Sunnyside, which includes Crescent Beach, a hot spot for sun worshippers, and is more like a summer resort; **Newton** (pop. 77,400), started as a stop along the old interurban rail line; **Cloverdale** (pop. 30,800) home of the Surrey Fall Fair and Cloverdale Rodeo, and whose main drag, 176th St, is becoming increasingly popular as a movie set because of its old storefronts; and **Fleetwood**, the newest member of the family.

While the city lacks a thriving, vibrant cultural hub, it does offer an appealing blend of industry, commerce, and agriculture, leaving something of a laid-back country feel. One third of Surrey is protected agricultural land, and development along the 330km of streams and rivers that flow through the city has been strictly monitored. Surrey boasts more per capita green space than any Lower Mainland city, and plans to connect its many parks with green corridors.

The **SkyTrain** extends south into Surrey at Scott Rd Station (Scott Rd and King George Hwy in north Surrey), Gateway Station (108th Ave and King George Hwy), Surrey Central Station (King George Hwy and 102 Ave), and King George Station (King George Hwy and 100 Ave).

Surrey Information: One Info Centre is at 15105A-105th Ave, Surrey, BC, V3R 7G9 (in Guildford). 604-581-7130. Year-round. Also at Surrey Museum, below.

■ **Surrey Museum and Archives:** 6022-176th St (in Cloverdale). 604-502-6456. Tues-Sat, 9-4; also Sundays in Aug. In the oldest remaining log cabin in Surrey, pioneer story is told through farm implements, furniture, household items. Native artifacts.

■ **Self-guided History Tours:** Exploring the town centre on foot: Surrey's first bank, the old municipal hall, and more. Further afield by car: historic churches, barns, schools. Pamphlets and maps at Surrey Museum and Archives, above.

■ **Surrey Arts Centre and Bear Creek Park:** Art in the Park, at 13750-88th Ave (between King George Hwy and 140th, in North Surrey). 604-501-5580. Daily. Arts complex with gallery, theatre, classrooms. Park offers excellent picnic and play facilities for all ages, including Canada's first outdoor climbing wall.

■ **Historic Stewart Farm and Hooser Weaving Centre:** 13723 Crescent Rd (South Surrey), in **Elgin Heritage Park** on the waterfront. 604-502-6456. Victoria-style farmhouse built in 1894 by the Stewart family, who lived in the home and farmed the land for six decades. The Peace Arch Weavers and Spinners Guild operates Hooser Weaving Centre in the farmhouse. Displays of spinning and weaving beginning June.

■ **Cloverdale Fairgrounds and the Cloverdale Rodeo:** 6050-176th St at 60th Ave

in Cloverdale. 604-576-9461. Harness Racing, Oct-April. Home of the Cloverdale Rodeo, May long weekend. The Stetson Bowl seats 5,500. Usually over 500 entries. Claims more cowboys and cowgirls than any other rodeo in Canada. Steer wrestling, wild-horse racing, ladies' barrel racing, wild-cow milking. Pancake breakfasts, midway, saloon, the works.

■ **Tynehead Regional Park:** 261ha. 604-432-6350. Main entrance at **Tynehead Hatchery**, 16585-96 Ave. Scenic trails wind along Serpentine River through mixed forests and meadows. Picnic at Serpentine Hollow and visit the butterfly garden. Hatchery tours by appointment: 604-589-9127. BC Wildlife Watch viewing site.

■ **Surrey Bend Regional Park (Robert Point Rest Area – Barnston Island):** 12.5ha. From Hwy 1 take Exit 53 (176th St) north until 104th Ave. Turn right and follow to parking lot at end of road. Robert Point is only accessible by ferry and a 1.8km walk or cycle (no vehicle parking). 604-432-6350. Picnicking, fishing, viewpoint. BC Wildlife Watch viewing site.

■ **Redwood Park Arboretum:** 20 Ave and 176 St near US Border. A strange and moving story behind the planting of this arboretum. The land was given to twins Peter and David Brown by their father on their 21st birthdays in 1893. Both had become deaf in their teens after bouts with scarlet fever. They systematically began replanting where logging had stripped the hilltop. Over the years, the "Tree Twins" collected seeds and seedlings from all over the world for their arboretum. They also grew solitary, living apart from the world in a two-storey tree house. The park is owned by the city of Surrey.

■ **Semiahmoo Trail:** Begins at 24 Ave west of 152nd St and runs northwest beyond 32nd Ave. Once the overland trading route for the Musqueam, Kwantlen, Semiahmoo, and Lummi peoples, this was the main route between the Semiahmoo Village in White Rock and Klall, a village in what is now South Westminster. The route was built up by the Royal Engineers and used by settlers until the King George Hwy opened in 1940.

■ **Crescent Beach and Blackie Spit:** 3124 McBride Ave. One of the most popular beaches around, and Blackie Spit is *the* sunning spot. Shoreline walk extends to Peace Arch Provincial Park (see p.108). On east side of Boundary Bay Wildlife Management Area. Shorebird diversity is greatest in late summer, early fall. BC Wildlife Watch viewing site. Also check out Ocean Park Rd running south from Crescent Beach; it fronts a rockier beach, interesting for its marine life.

■ **Serpentine Wildlife Area:** King George Hwy near 48th Ave in South Surrey. A natural area for walking. A series of wetlands provide habitat for waterfowl, shorebirds, and hawks. Mallards, teals, pintails, shovelers, wigeons, buffleheads, and mergansers are common during migration and the winter months. BC Wildlife Watch viewing site.

■ **More Surrey Trails and Parks:** Sunnyside Acres Urban Forest, 148 St and 24 Ave; **Green Timbers Park and Urban Forest**, 148 St and 100 Ave; **Bothwell Park**, 96 Ave and 168 St;

The fish boat docks of Steveston have been transformed into people places.

Crescent Park, 28 Ave and Crescent Rd; Hawthorne Park, 10503-144 St; Hazelnut Meadows Park, 140 St between 68 Ave and 70 Ave; Invergarry Park, 14500-block of 116A Ave; Fleetwood Park, 80 Ave and 160 St; Hi-Knoll Park, 196 St and 48 Ave; Ocean Park Shoreline Walk, begins at the foot of 24 Ave.

■ **Cloverdale Walking Tour:** 6022-176 St. 604-502-6456. Visit such enduring sites as the Town Hall, dating to 1881, the Municipal Hall, 1912, and Duckworth's Dry Goods Store, 1929.

■ **Green Timbers Heritage Forestry Tour:** 9800A 140 St. 604-582-7170.

■ **Fraser Downs:** At Cloverdale Fairgrounds, 60th Ave and 176 St. 604-576-9141. Live harness racing and simulcast thoroughbred and harness racing, Wed, Oct-April. 3,300-seat glass-enclosed grandstand.

■ **Guildford Mall:** 104 Ave and 152 St. 604-585-1565. One of BC's largest malls. Two shopping complexes joined by overhead walkways; over 230 shops.

■ **Rainforest Reptile Refuge:** 16 Ave and 176 St. 604-538-1711. Devoted to exotic reptiles and amphibians. Tues-Sun.

■ **Balloons Above the Valley:** 24149-63 Ave, Langley. 604-533-2378. A chance to rise above it all in a hot-air balloon.

■ **Farmers' Market:** Surrey Central Station parking lot. Saturdays.

■ **Newton Wave Pool:** 13730-72nd Ave. 604-501-5540. Daily. A 38m pool with two 60m waterslides, hydro pool, steam room, children's pool, lounge, and concession.

■ **Softball BC Complex (Softball City):** 24th Ave and 148th St in South Surrey. 604-531-3220. A state-of-the-art complex, with four baseball diamonds.

■ **Golf:** 16 world-class courses, including Northview Golf and Country Club (250-878-9600) designed by legendary Arnold Palmer. Site of the annual Greater Vancouver Open Golf Tournament, Sept. Info Centre has details.

RICHMOND

HOME OF VANCOUVER INTERNATIONAL AIRPORT

Richmond: (Pop. 148,867). Immediately north of George Massey Tunnel. Richmond is actually an island city, consisting of a number of silt-formed islands between the north and south arms of the Fraser River where it flows into the Gulf of Georgia. The main part of Richmond is on Lulu, the largest island, named by Royal Engineer Colonel Moody in the 1860s, honouring visiting theatre actress Miss Lulu Sweet. Just north, the Vancouver International Airport is on Sea Island.

Richmond is accessible by the Arthur Laing, Oak St, or Knight St bridges to the north, Hwy 91 to the east, or the George Massey Tunnel (Hwy 99) to the south. Exit Hwy 99 at Steveston Hwy for the Village of Steveston, or at Bridgeport Rd for the airport.

The city received its name from an Australian farming family, the McRoberts. They settled here in the early 1860s (making this one of BC's oldest communities) and nostalgically named the area after Richmond, Australia.

Added to Richmond's original industries – farming, fishing, and waterborne trade – is a balance of major commercial, recreational, and residential developments. Richmond continues to grow: and today is home to 18 percent of the Lower Mainland's Chinese-Canadian community. Other Asian cultures are also represented here. The colour and bustle of Asia can be felt on a stroll along Alexandra Rd with its variety of restaurants, farmers markets, and shops. Adding to the volume of shopping-mall experiences Richmond is growing famous for are six Asian-style shopping malls within a three-block radius. More than 300 shops, taking up more retail space than Vancouver's Chinatown, proffer dim sum and sushi, pastries, jewelry, and the latest designer fashions from Hong Kong, Tokyo, and Taipei.

For seekers of simplicity: there's buying fish on the old Steveston docks, sandbar fishing, taking a meditative stroll on the dikes, or visiting the Buddhist temple (below).

Richmond Information: Info Centre on east side of Hwy 99, just beyond George Massey Tunnel. Daily, year-round. 11980 Deas Thruway, Richmond, BC, V6W 1L1. 604-271-8280.

Vancouver International Airport: On Sea Island. Accessed from the north by the Arthur Laing Bridge at foot of Granville St; or off Hwy 99 at Bridgeport Rd and Sea Island

Way to Sea Island Bridge. Within Richmond, can also be accessed over Dinsmore Bridge north of Westminster Hwy on Gilbert Rd, or via No. 2 Rd Bridge and Russ Baker Way. Details on airport, p.98.

■ **Richmond Art Gallery:** 180-7700 Minoru Gate, in **Richmond Arts Centre.** 604-231-6440. Daily. Local, Canadian, international artists.

■ **Richmond Museum and Archives:** Adjacent to Richmond Art Gallery. 604-231-6440. Daily. Richmond's history. Turn-of-the-century living room, wedding dresses and veil from late 1800s. Lace-making display.

■ **Minoru Park Complex:** Borders Gilbert Rd and Granville Ave. 604-276-4107. Downtown delight. Pierrefonds Gardens, Minoru Lake, Historic Minoru Chapel, an all-weather track, aquatic centre, tennis courts, ice arenas.

■ **Richmond Nature Park and Nature House:** 11851 Westminster Hwy (at corner of No. 5 Rd). 604-273-7015. Daily. Over 80ha of preserved bog environment. Four trails, longest over 1.6km long. Nature house with displays of birds, snakes, frogs, salamanders, and working beehive. Nature games for children. Pond in park. BC Wildlife Watch viewing site.

■ **Bridgepoint Harbour:** 8811 River Rd (in north Richmond, facing Sea Island). Public boardwalk, pier, shops, marina, family restaurant and pub.

■ **London Heritage Farm:** 6511 Dyke Rd on south arm of the Fraser River, near Steveston. 604-271-5220. Former London family farmhouse, restored to 1880-1914 period. Tours and picnics, tea and goodies.

■ **Steveston Heritage Fishing Village:** Southwest corner of Richmond. 8km off Hwy 99 along Steveston Hwy. 604-277-8280. In its heyday at the turn of the century, Steveston was the busiest fishing port in the world, with 14 canneries packing more than 195,000 cases of salmon each year. Today, home to almost 1,000 commercial fishing vessels, Steveston is still the largest commercial fishing harbour in Canada. Here are rustic buildings, old net lofts and sheds that attract artists and photographers. Crafts, antiques, museums, galleries, restaurants. On the wharf visitors can buy fresh salmon, tuna, sole, halibut, shrimp, prawns, and crab directly from fishboats.

The **Gulf of Georgia Cannery National Historic Site** is at 12138 Fourth Ave. 604-664-9009. May to mid-Oct. Wheelchair accessible. Complex of buildings, constructed between 1894 and 1964, was known as "the monster cannery at Steveston." It was the last intact cannery on the Fraser River: as late as 1979 its premises were still being used for herring reduction. Displays include a model of a canning line, fish-processing equipment, archival photos, canning memorabilia, and fishing tools. In 1998, the New York-based World Monument Fund ranked this as one of the world's 100 most endangered cultural sites: the 4,645-square-metre cannery rests upon 600 wooden piles.

The **Steveston Jetty** acts as a dike for the silt-laden waters of the Fraser River. In April and May the end of the rocky dike is visited by hundreds of California sea lions and a few Steller's sea lions. BC Wildlife Watch viewing site. Wildlife tours, see next entry.

■ **Cannery Channel Tours:** 118, 11675-7th Ave. 604-274-9565. On the hour, 11am-sunset, May-Oct. Reservations. *River Queen* leaves Steveston's Fisherman's Wharf. See Canada's largest fishing fleet (learn to tell a purse-seiner from a gillnetter), birdlife, and sunsets. Also nature walking tours.

■ **Steveston Museum:** 3811 Moncton St, Steveston (main street). 604-271-6868. Mon-Sat. Local fishing industry, early settlement.

■ **Britannia Shipyard Park:** 5180 Westwater Dr, Steveston. 604-718-1200. Riverfront site and visitor centre present history of wooden boat building and fishing families in the area.

■ **Chinese Buddhist Temple:** 9160 Steveston Hwy. 604-274-2822. Open daily. Outstanding example of Chinese palatial architecture, bonsai garden, Buddhist museum, exhibits, ceremonies in progress.

■ **Nanaksar Gurdwara Gursikh Temple:** 18691 Westminster Hwy. 604-270-7369. This striking sky-blue onion-topped temple rises from farmlands like a blue vision of the Taj Mahal.

■ **Iona Beach Regional Park:** 114ha. At westerly tip of Sea Island in Fraser River estuary near the Vancouver International Airport. From Hwy 99 take Sea Island Way west and cross Moray Bridge. Turn right immediately to Grauer Rd and follow park signs (about 12km from bridge to park.) 604-432-6350. Extensive mud flats, long jetties, marshes, and nearby sewage lagoons attract rare shorebirds and many waterfowl, as well as international birders throughout the year. A volunteer project has restored a marsh providing habitat for the rare

yellow-headed blackbird. Picnicking, walking, cycling, and horseback riding. BC Wildlife Watch viewing site.

■ **Sturgeon Bank Wildlife Management Area:** 5,152ha of marsh, mud flat, and open water. Stretches from Steveston Jetty (above) to Iona Beach Park. Heavily used by waterbirds, shorebirds, raptors, and songbirds. BC Wildlife Watch viewing site.

■ **Riversports and Entertainment Complex:** #6 Rd and Steveston Hwy. 604-241-0700. To keep youth off the streets: a 12-screen, $12-million movie theatre complex that has topped box office movie totals for North America; a bowling centre, aqua centre, six-rink arena, restaurants, and training facility for the NBA's Vancouver Grizzlies.

■ **Trev Deeley Motorcycle Museum:** 13500 Verdun Pl. 604-273-5421. Mon-Fri, year-round. Free. Over 250 classic and antique motorcycles.

US BORDER TO HORSESHOE BAY

NORTH-SOUTH CORRIDOR (Highways 99 and 99/1)

The route from the Canada/US border to Horseshoe Bay passes through the most populated region of BC, taking in the city of Vancouver itself. It is well served with accommodation and amenities of every kind.

The crisscrossing of freeways and highways can make passage through the city limits and environs bewildering. This section is designed to assist the traveller in getting into or through Vancouver, or to White Rock, Delta, West Vancouver, and so on. It is not intended as a trip in itself. Follow the route map provided here or, for an overview, see the *Gateway map*, p.96.

Hwy 99, four lanes, leaves the Canada/US border and continues through Delta and Richmond into Vancouver. It crosses the Oak St Bridge over the Fraser River, and continues through downtown Vancouver. After passing through 405ha Stanley Park, Hwy 99 crosses the Lions Gate Bridge with its spectacular view of Burrard Inlet.

The route continues as Hwy 1/99 to Horseshoe Bay on Howe Sound. From here, travellers can go north on Hwy 99 (the Squamish Hwy) to Squamish, Whistler, Pemberton, and over the mountains into the Cariboo; or sail via BC Ferries to Vancouver Island, Bowen Island, or the Sunshine Coast. The distance from Peace Arch Provincial Park at the border to Horseshoe Bay is 71km.

Peace Arch Provincial Park: 9ha. At Canada/US border. 604-924-2200. Commemorates the lasting peace between Canada and US. Dedicated in Sept 1921. The park, declared "international territory," straddles both sides of the border and is jointly maintained by BC and Washington State. Visitors from either side of the border may enjoy the park without passing through customs. Formal gardens, rockeries, group picnic sites.

British Columbia Information: Peace Arch Provincial Visitor Info Centre. 200m north of Canada Customs on Hwy 99. Daily, year-round: Mid-May to Sept, 8-8; Sept to Mid-May, 9-5.

Campbell River Rd (8th Ave): West 2.5km to White Rock.

White Rock: (Pop. 17,210). On Boundary Bay, 5km beyond border on Hwy 99. Bordered on the south by the US, north and east by District of Surrey, west by Semiahmoo Bay.

The community is named for the 486t white rock deposited on the beach, by a glacier perhaps, or, according to one legend, the Sea God's son, who threw it from Vancouver Island, and founded a new tribe here with his Cowichan Princess. The rock, still a visible local landmark, has been painted white, but was originally limed white by the guano of thousands of roosting seabirds.

Industrial and residential activity burgeoned here at the turn of the century with the establishment of the Great Northern Railway along the city's waterfront. By 1937, this was a summer seaside resort with a population of more than 1,000. White Rock incorporated as a city in 1957 when it separated from Surrey.

White Rock is picture-perfect, with more than 4.5km of beach front and a warm, dry climate. There is more sunshine in White Rock than anywhere else on the Lower Mainland, and the community is still considered a summer seaside resort. The Peace Arch is visible from White Rock's long, walkable pier. Year-round, in all hours and weather, people will be found strolling along the 2km pedestrian promenade linking West Beach and East Beach. Lots of trendy restaurants and fish-and-chip diners along the waterfront.

White Rock Information: Info Centre, White Rock and South Surrey Chamber of Commerce, 15150 Russel Ave, White Rock, BC, V4B 2P5. 604-536-6844. Weekdays, year-round. Seasonal centre next to Station Museum on Marine Dr, mid-May to Sept.

■ **White Rock Museum and Archives at Station Centre:** 14970 Marine Dr. 604-541-2222. Daily, year-round; closed Christmas-New Year's Day. In restored 1913 Great Northern Railway station.

■ **White Rock Pier:** On west side of museum. A well-known local structure extending .5km out into Semiahmoo Bay. The original pier was built on this site in 1913-14. Open for walking and sightseeing. Wheelchair accessible. BC Wildlife Watch viewing site.

Nicomekl River: Crosses under Hwy 99, 9km beyond border. 25km long. The river flows through the bottomland of Surrey into Mud Bay. Part of an historic portage route. Cutthroats, jacks, and coho.

King George Hwy (Hwy 99A) Interchange: 10km north of Canada/US border. An important interchange. Exit north for Trans-Canada Hwy 1 (via Hwy 10); or for access into Surrey, or through Surrey north to New Westminster. (Note that Hwy 91, coming up to the west, is a better route to New Westminster.)

■ **For connection with Trans-Canada Hwy and points east:** On King George Hwy, 4km north of interchange with Hwy 99, take east exit to Hwy 10. Hwy 10 travels east 20km to join the Trans-Canada Hwy northeast of Langley. In the other direction, it bends north to link up with Hwy 17 as an alternate route to catch the ferry to Vancouver Island (see below).

■ King George Hwy crosses north-south through the city of **Surrey**. It travels l6km north from the interchange with Hwy 99, then over the Pattullo Bridge to **New Westminster**. For details, see *New Westminster*, p.105, and *Surrey*, p.106.

Serpentine River: 2.5km beyond Nicomekl River. Flows through Surrey into Mud Bay. A narrow stream, 32km long. Habitat for cutthroat, Dolly Varden, rainbow, coho, and steelhead.

Highway 91 (Annacis Island Hwy): 8km northwest of King George Hwy Interchange. Exit north to **New Westminster**, over Annacis Island and the Alex Fraser Bridge.

Highway 10 (Ladner Trunk Rd): 4km west of Hwy 91 (22km north of US Border). Exit east, 26km to Langley; about 10km farther to Hwy 1 (Trans-Canada). Exit west to **Ladner** and the **District Municipality of Delta**. (Western portion only of Hwy 10 is called Ladner Trunk Rd.) Details on Langley in *Vancouver to Hope – South Bank*, p.126.

SIDE TRIP

to North Delta and Ladner

Delta: (Pop. 95,411). On Hwy 10, 8km west of junction with Hwy 99 (30km beyond border). Named for the delta on which the community sits – glacial and alluvial silt were delivered here gradually by the Fraser River over the past 10,000 years. Delta's 336 square kilometres are bounded by Fraser River, Surrey, Strait of Georgia, and the Canada/US border at Boundary Bay. The tip of the peninsula drops below the 49th parallel, so there is a small part of America at **Point Roberts**, south of Boundary Bay. Delta is also known as Tunnel Town, for the long George Massey Tunnel that passes *under* the Fraser River. It opened in 1959, replacing Woodward's Landing Ferry linking Delta with Richmond and Vancouver.

Early occupants of the area were Sto:lo and Tsawwassen First Nations – the St Mungo Archaeological Site on the riverbanks is testimony to more than 4,000 years of aboriginal habitation. European settlers began moving here in the late 1860s, and by 1868 land was being claimed for farming. Thomas and William Ladner (also see *Ladner*, p.110) filed for land next to the Chillukthan Slough. By 1877 almost all of the Delta lowlands were settled, and the process of diking and draining water-soaked lowlands began. The Municipality of Delta was incorporated in 1879.

Delta today is comprised of three urban communities: **North Delta** (bordering Surrey), the village of **Ladner** (and Westham Island), at the river mouth, and **Tsawwassen** (to the south), site of the BC Ferries terminal. Dairying

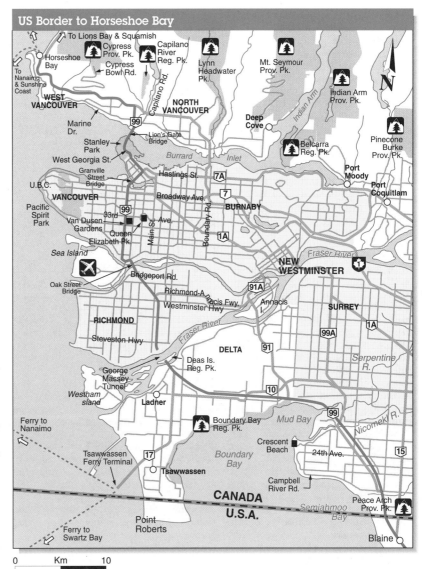

US Border to Horseshoe Bay

continues to be the most important farming in the area. Industry is concentrated in three distinct areas: Tilbury Island, Annacis Island, and the Roberts Bank deep-sea superport. In the centre of it all lies **Burns Bog**, the lungs of the Lower Mainland (see below).

Delta Information: Info Centre, 6201-60th Ave, Delta, BC, V4K 4E2. 604-946-4232. Open daily in summer, weekdays in winter.

■ **Delta Museum and Archives:** 4858 Delta St, in Ladner. 604-946-9322. Tues-Sun. Three floors in 1912 building that once housed municipal offices, courts, and jail. First Nations, settlement, and community's history.

■ **George C. Reifel Migratory Bird Sanctuary:** 5191 Robertson Rd, on north tip of Westham Island, 10km west of Ladner. Part of Alaksen National Wildlife Area. 604-946-6980. Daily. More than 260 species observed here, including the uncommon black-crowned night herons and some 25,000 snow geese on their fall and spring migrations. November is Snow Goose Month with activities most weekends. Gift shop, picnic grounds. Wheelchair accessible. BC Wildlife Watch viewing site.

■ **Burns Bog:** 4,000ha bounded by Fraser River on the north, Boundary Bay on the south, Ladner (or Crescent Slough) on the west, and Hwy 91 on the east. The bog, the largest undeveloped urban land area in Canada, serves a range of essential ecological functions, including "scrubbing" carbon dioxide from the atmosphere, and providing a habitat for 178 species of birds and mammals, including bears and deer. It is a stopover for some 1.5 million migrating waterfowl·on the Pacific flyway, and a refuge for the threatened sandhill crane – the oldest known bird, its ancestors date back 60 million years. Also, rare Mariposa butterflies, and plants commonly found only in alpine areas. Bogs around the world are endangered or have already been destroyed by development, and this is no exception. The bog has already been strip mined for peat, and is a receptacle for tonnes of Lower Mainland garbage. One developer is eyeing the bog for a cranberry farm. For hikes and more information: Burns Bog Conservation Society, 202-11961 88 Ave, Delta, BC, V4C 3C9. 604-572-0373. BC Wildlife Watch viewing site.

■ **Westham Island Pumpkin Frenzy:** A one-lane swinging bridge, built 1917, is gateway to the island farming community. Late Sept-Oct, farm produce stands selling their autumn wares, are elaborately decorated with pumpkin people, jack-o'-lanterns, and gourds.

■ **Boundary Bay Wildlife Management Area:** 11,000ha including Mud Bay. From Tsawwassen to Crescent Beach. Internationally important habitat for waterfowl and shorebirds. This area, including the adjacent farmlands, is home to Canada's largest concentration of wintering raptors. BC Wildlife Watch viewing site.

■ **OWL (Orphaned Wildlife Rehabilitation Society):** 3800-72nd St, Delta, BC, V4K 3N2. 604-946-3171. Tours, Sat-Sun, 10-3. Raptors – hawks, eagles, and owls – are rehabilitated and returned to the wild.

Ladner: (Pop. 1,780). At the mouth of the Fraser River, forming the western terminus of Hwy 10. Southbound on Hwy 99, take first exit south of George Massey Tunnel. A fishing and agricultural village within the municipality of Delta. Cornishmen William Ladner and his brother Thomas were among those seeking their fortune on the Fraser during the 1858 gold rush – they ended up here a decade later, some of the valley's first serious farmers.

Ladner has a pleasant village atmosphere: there's fish for sale at the government wharf, riverfront walks, seafood restaurants. The **Delta Museum**, above, sometimes offers historical and architectural walking tours of Ladner – once known as Ladner's Landing. In Ladner Harbour Park, eagles perch on huge cottonwoods. Dikes, protecting the flat, low-lying land from floods, provide scenic walking and biking routes along wildlife-rich estuary. Ask Delta Info Centre (above) for other opportunities.

Tsawwassen Ferry Terminal: To reach terminal from Ladner, return east on Hwy 10 (Ladner Trunk Rd) to Hwy 17; terminal is about 12km south. (Ferries to Victoria, Nanaimo, Gulf Islands.) Also see below.

■ **South Arm Marshes Wildlife Management Area:** 886ha. Access from River Rd. Islands, freshwater and intertidal marshes. BC Wildlife Watch viewing site.

Return to Highway 99

Highway 17 (Ladner Interchange): 8km beyond junction of Hwys 99 and 10 (30km from US border). Exit southwest, 14km to Tsawwassen Ferry Terminal. Exit northeast to 60th Ave, and Deas Island Regional Park.

SIDE TRIP

to Tsawwassen, Ferry Terminal, and Vancouver Island

Tsawwassen: (Pop. 19,508). On square-bottomed peninsula forming southwestern part of Municipality of Delta (for info, see *Delta*, p.109). The name, in the language of the Tsawwassen First Nation, means "looking toward the sea." Their village – marked by the massive Tsa Tsu Shores condominium development, cafe, and carved poles – faces the sea and the BC Ferries terminal, which was attached to their peninsula by a 2km causeway in 1959. Windsurfing off the causeway spit is very popular.

Tsawwassen Ferry Terminal: On Hwy 17, 14km southwest of junction with Hwy 99. BC Ferries run from Vancouver (Tsawwassen) to Victoria (Swartz Bay) on Vancouver Island. Also, to Nanaimo (Departure Bay and Duke Point) on Vancouver Island, and to the Gulf Islands. Sailing time to Swartz Bay is 95 minutes (then a 30-minute drive to Victoria). Sailing distance is 38.5km. Ferry info: 604-277-0277.

Roberts Bank Superport: Visible to the north of the BC Ferries causeway. Westshore Terminals sits at the end of a 5km causeway jutting into the Strait of Georgia from the tidal flats at Roberts Bank. This major coal exporting facility (now Canada's largest) opened in 1970 to handle coal coming by train from mines in southeastern BC and southwestern Alberta. As much as 22 million tonnes of coal a year is transferred to the world's largest dry-bulk carriers for shipment to 20 countries.

Splashdown Park: On Hwy 17, just north of BC Ferries terminal. May-Sept. 604-943-2251. 13 waterslides, hot tub, video arcade, volleyball, basketball, and other games.

Boundary Bay Regional Park: 182ha. 604-432-6350. From Hwy 17, turn left (east) at 12th Ave, to parking lot at dike, or continue to park entrance. This spectacular ocean beach park has sand dunes, salt marshes, lagoons, and extensive sand and tidal flats. Picnicking, swimming, walking, and wildlife viewing. Start of 16km Boundary Bay dike trail, which is a popular destination for walkers, hikers, cyclists, and equestrians. Unsurpassed area for wintering birds of prey such as hawks and owls. Boundary Bay has Canada's highest number of wintering raptors both in species and number of individuals.

Return to Highway 99

Deas Island Regional Park: 72ha. 604-432-6350. Exit northeast at Hwy 17 (Ladner Interchange). Follow 62B St (River Rd) 4km to park. John Sullivan Deas, the island's first settler, was a freed slave from the US. He arrived in 1873 and established the island's first cannery. This island park is also home to the Delta Agricultural Hall built in 1894; Burrvilla, a Queen Anne style residence built in 1905; and the one-room Inverholme Schoolhouse, built 1909. Burrvilla, furnished with Victorian antiques and collectibles, many for sale, is open daily May to mid-Oct. Walking, picnicking, group camping, rowing and canoeing in Deas Slough; fishing, nature study, and horseback riding. Fraser River Festival is here, early June.

George Massey Tunnel: 2km beyond Hwys 99/17 junction. Completed 1959, 1.6km four-lane tunnel passes under the Fraser River linking Delta to Richmond. Still called the Deas Island Tunnel by diehards.

Steveston Highway Interchange: 1km beyond the George Massey Tunnel. First exit to Richmond and Village of Steveston.

Richmond: (Pop. 148,867). Township of Richmond consists of a number of islands, the main one being **Lulu Island**, cradled between north and south arms of the Fraser River. The **Vancouver International Airport** is on Sea Island, north of Lulu. For more info on Richmond and Village of Steveston, which is part of it, see *Richmond*, pp.107-108.

Richmond East/West Freeway (Hwy 91): 5km beyond the Steveston Hwy Interchange. Exit east, 16km to Annacis Island, where highway divides. Then, either go north on Hwy 91A to New Westminster via the magnificent **Alex Fraser Bridge**; or turn south on Hwy 91, 10km to North Delta. **Note:** To access **Knight St** and **Knight St Bridge** into Vancouver (an alternate route), turn east on Hwy 91, then north on Knight St.

Bridgeport Rd: 1km beyond Cambie Rd. Exit west 2km to Sea Island Bridge which crosses Fraser River to **Vancouver International Airport**. Follow signs.

Vancouver International Airport: On Sea Island, in Richmond, south of Vancouver. Details, p.98.

Oak St Bridge: Cross Oak St Bridge over the north arm of the Fraser River. Continue north on Oak St to Park Rd (just north of 64th St). Jog west (left) on Park, then north (right) onto Granville St (Vancouver's main street). This part of Hwy 99 is now **Granville St**. Continue all the way downtown on Granville St (Hwy 99).

33rd Ave: Turn east to **VanDusen Botanical Garden** at Oak St, and farther east to **Bloedel Conservatory and Queen Elizabeth Park** at Cambie St. For further details, see "Parks and Gardens," *Vancouver*, p.100.

16th Ave: West (left) to **University of British Columbia.** For information on UBC, see *Vancouver*, p.98.

Broadway Ave (Hwy 7): Broadway is 9th Ave, if you're counting, and it does make it easier. West (left) to UBC. East 9km to Burnaby; 9km beyond Burnaby to Coquitlam. See *Vancouver to Hope, North Bank*, p.129.

False Creek and the Granville St Bridge: Six blocks north of Broadway, Granville St Bridge arcs over popular **Granville Island** and its **Public Market** (see p.100). The island sits in False Creek, an inlet of the Pacific Ocean. Captain G.H. Richards sailed up this waterway in the late 1850s hoping it was a stream that might lead to the Fraser River. After finding mud flats instead, he named it False Creek.

Granville and Seymour Streets: To stay on Hwy 99, take the Seymour St ramp just off the Granville St Bridge, and continue along Seymour until Georgia St. Then turn left.

Stanley Park: At foot of W Georgia St. For details on this magnificent natural park, see *Vancouver*, p.100.

Lions Gate Bridge (First Narrows): At north tip of Stanley Park. Bridge spans 842m and arches 60m above the first narrowing of the Burrard Inlet, carrying traffic to West and North Vancouver. Completed in 1938, the bridge was named for the twin peaks of The Lions overlooking Vancouver. It was built by the Guinness family (Irish brewers) to link the North Shore's British Properties with Vancouver. Flanking the bridge are monumental sculpted lions, completed in 1939 by Charles Marega, then considered Western Canada's greatest sculptor. On its first day open, 5,616 vehicles crossed, each paying a 25-cent toll. The bridge became toll-free in 1955 when the BC government paid $6 million for it. Because of the wear and tear of heavy traffic (60,000 vehicles daily) the bridge roadway is to be upgraded, 1999-2000.

Burrard Inlet: Focus of Vancouver's early development. Century-old port bustles with supertankers and freighters from around the world. Inlet extends 24km west to Port Moody, and north another 23km along Indian Arm, past Deep Cove to the Wigwam Inn.

Marine Dr: Exit immediately beyond Lions Gate Bridge. For **Horseshoe Bay** and **West Vancouver**, travel straight and follow the off ramp to Taylor Way. For **North Vancouver** and **Deep Cove**, turn east on Marine Dr. For info on West Vancouver, North Vancouver, Mt Seymour Provincial Park, Cates Park, and Deep Cove, see *North Shore*, p.102.

Taylor Way: Crosses Marine Dr at first set of traffic lights. Taylor Way is basically West Vancouver (for West Van, see *North Shore*, p.102). For Horseshoe Bay and other parts north, travel straight ahead (north) on Taylor Way. At junction with Hwy 1, make a west turn onto Hwy 99/1 for Horseshoe Bay. Turn east on Hwy 1 (here called the Upper Levels Hwy) to **North Vancouver, Mt Seymour Provincial Park, Ironworkers Memorial Second Narrows Bridge**.

Cypress Bowl Rd: 6km west of Taylor Way. Turn north and travel 12km to Cypress Provincial Park. For details, see *North Shore*, p.104.

Caulfeild Dr: 5km beyond exit to Cypress Provincial Park. Exit north then turn south and follow signs to Lighthouse Park in Caulfeild. Details in *North Shore*, p.104.

Highway 99: At this point, Hwy 99 turns north to Lions Bay, Squamish, and Whistler. Details: *Horseshoe Bay to Lillooet*, p.118. For Horseshoe Bay and BC Ferries, exit to Horseshoe Bay, follow signs.

Horseshoe Bay and BC Ferries Terminal: Departures to Nanaimo on Vancouver Island, Bowen Island in Howe Sound, and Langdale on Sunshine Coast. For Bowen Island and Sunshine Coast to Powell River, see *Horseshoe Bay to Lund*, below.

Whytecliffe Park: Off Marine Dr in Horseshoe Bay. Trails, picnics. Departure point for diving excursions.

HORSESHOE BAY TO LUND

THE SUNSHINE COAST (Highway 101)

The Sunshine Coast, though on the mainland and north of Vancouver, is islandlike in its existence, depending largely on car-carrying ferries for its connection to the rest of the world. A main segment, Sechelt Peninsula, is just barely a peninsula. It's also a benchland barricaded from the rest of the mainland by the forbidding Coast Mountains. Much of the peninsula is covered by second-growth western red cedar and Douglas fir. Winters are mild and wet and summers are sunnier and drier than many other coastal areas.

The Sunshine Coast may be close in distance to cosmopolitan action, but to reach its southernmost part requires a 45-minute ferry ride across Howe Sound from Horseshoe Bay. To reach Powell River and Lund – the northernmost terminal for Hwy 101 and the farthest you can go by conventional means – another ferry ride takes 50 minutes, from Earls Cove to Saltery Bay. Other ferries link the Sunshine Coast with Vancouver Island and with the offshore islands of Texada and Savary.

The coastline offers some of the world's best scuba diving, with underwater seascapes that rival the tropics for colour and variety. The 2,400 hours of yearly sun make the maze of inlets, channels, and straits even more attractive. With all its nooks and crannies and its reflective lifestyle, the Sechelt Peninsula boasts a thriving artistic community. Painters, writers, craftspeople, and musicians are as rife as yachtsmen and retired salts.

As you disembark from the ferry at Langdale on Sechelt Peninsula, the two-lane Hwy 101 wanders through Gibsons, a delightful coast town made famous by the long-running and now-cancelled CBC television series, *The Beachcombers*. Beyond Sechelt the highway becomes winding.

There are excellent views of the Strait of Georgia from the town of Sechelt and other points on the highway. Elsewhere, for good water views, locals recommend detours down one of the peninsula's many side roads. Some argue that this 165km drive, together with the scenic ferry rides, is the prettiest in the province. Though not as tourist-oriented and as quaint as the Sechelt Peninsula, Powell River, near the end of this sinuous drive, is worth the effort of taking the second ferry. Some would say that this mill town, enclosed

Horseshoe Bay to Lund

0   Km   10

by ocean and wilderness lakes and clearcut-pocketed forest, is a great place to live.

Visitor Info Centres provide hourly updated information on availability of provincial park and private campsites. Book into a campsite as early in the day as possible. Most BC Parks are on a first-come, first-served basis; most are full by 2:30pm, especially those on the more accessible Sechelt Peninsula. Those BC Parks on the reservations system are indicated in the *Log*. For more info, see p.111. Also, be prepared for ferry lineups and long waits, especially on summer weekends. For easy access to exploring, walking, and picnicking, sites there are, in addition to several excellent provincial parks, Sunshine Coast Regional Parks, also listed in the *Log*. For more general information, call the Sunshine Coast Regional District, 604-885-2261.

Horseshoe Bay: (Pop. 1,037). Junction of Hwys 1 and 99. Terminal for BC Ferries to **Langdale** on Sunshine Coast, Departure Bay in **Nanaimo** on Vancouver Island, and **Snug Cove** on Bowen Island. BC Ferries information: 604-277-0277.

The *Queen of Cowichan* (370 cars, 1,500 passengers) normally sails Howe Sound between Horseshoe Bay and Langdale. The ferry passes between Bowen and Gambier islands on its 15.5km, 35-minute trips. The *Queen of Capilano* (85 cars), built in 1991 and boasting high-tech steering gear, makes the short hop to **Bowen Island**. For description of Horseshoe Bay, a picturesque village, see p.118.

SIDE TRIP

to Bowen Island

The ferry from Horseshoe Bay arrives at Snug Cove on 52-sq-km Bowen Island, a 20-minute, 5km ride. Many of Bowen's 3,000 residents commute daily between Vancouver and this bedroom community named after James Bowen (1751-1835), a British Navy rear-admiral.

Bowen Island was once Vancouver's Coney Island, a resort where residents escaped on weekends to dance, picnic, and play. It's still an excellent place for a refreshing day trip, but without the merry crowds that were brought in by the Union Steamship Company until 1950.

If you don't bring your car, it's a short walk from the ferry to the island's pubs, cafes, restaurants, and shops. At 726m, Mt Gardner is Bowen's highest point and the views are worth the all-day hike. Also, worth a visit: the original orchard (just past Dunfield & Daughters) and two restored classic 1920s Bowen cottages. One is a museum, furnished with Bowen bits of the era; the other houses a seasonal information centre. In fall, one of several local B&Bs, The Lodge at The Old Dorm, hosts Island-Stay Learning Experiences (ISLE), offering programs ranging from romance writing to film appreciation, and portrait painting to gardening (604-947-0947). Creativity is in the air here – it was at the Bowen Island post office that Nick Bantock dreamed up his first best-selling book, *Griffin & Sabine*.

Bowen Island Information: Bowen Island Chamber of Commerce, Box 199, Bowen Island, BC, V0N 1G0. 604-947-2275.

■ **Crippen Regional Park:** 242ha. 604-432-6350. From ferry terminal, 2km trail leads past the Terminal Creek Fishway, to 4km loop trail around Killarney Lake, passing through flooded forests and marshes rich with bird life. See coho; may be cutthroat in fishway. Historic Union Steamship Company store, built 1924, is at park entrance and once served as a post office and general store for thousands of visitors from Vancouver. BC Wildlife Watch viewing site.

■ **Heritage Walking Tour:** 604-947-9146.

Return to Highway 101

Langdale: (Pop. 137). On Howe Sound, opposite Horseshoe Bay. Named after Robinson Henry Langdale (1835-1908), a Yorkshireman who settled here in 1892. Jumping-off point for touring the Sechelt Peninsula. **Earls Cove**, the next ferry landing at peninsula's other end, is 81km away on Hwy 101. Ferry info: 604-886-2242.

■ **Langdale Creek:** Visible along the chain link fence of the ferry terminal. Spawning coho and chum salmon, mid-Oct to mid-Dec. BC Wildlife Watch viewing site.

Port Mellon Rd: Northeast (right) out of Langdale leads 10km to tiny communities of Hillside and Port Mellon, popular destinations for boating excursions. Port Mellon has a state-of-the-art pulp mill founded by Captain H.A. Mellon in 1908; it was upgraded to the tune of $1 billion in recent years. Immediately north of Port Mellon is new 6,164ha **Tetrahedron Provincial Park**. No facilities; restricted access. Park is part of the Lower Mainland Nature Legacy, and encompasses mountains of the Tetrahedron Range, old-growth forest, and the water supply for the lower Sunshine Coast.

Soames Hill Hiking Trail: 3.5km beyond Langdale Ferry Terminal on upper highway (North Rd). Turn left on Chamberlain and left on Bridgeman. It's a 20-minute climb to the top, using steps, hand rails, and cedar walkways. From 243m, great view of Keats Island, Gibsons Harbour, Strait of Georgia, Barfleur Passage. On a clear day, see Vancouver Island, 30km away.

Gibsons: (Pop. 3,732). Veer left westward from Langdale Ferry Terminal on Hwy 101 (Marine Dr) to downtown Gibsons, 4km away and running past the tiny settlements of **Hopkins Landing** and **Granthams Landing**. Go straight ahead on upper highway (North Rd), which skirts fringes of town and rejoins lower highway.

Named for George Gibson who settled in 1886. When he and his two sons were trying to sail a sloop to Oyster Bay on Vancouver Island, a southeaster blew them off course and into Howe Sound. Anchored in the lee of **Keats Island**, they beheld the headland that would become their home. It was originally Gibson's Landing, but in 1947 locals persuaded the post office to drop the "Landing." The old name persists on some travel brochures.

Built on a hillside overlooking Shoal Channel and Howe Sound. Upper Marine Dr leads to shopping area; Lower Marine Dr to waterfront, the tourist precinct, and a cluster of interesting shops along Gower Pt Rd. Until 1991, **Molly's Reach Cafe** was the setting for the internationally popular CBC Television series, *The Beachcombers*, a weekly sit-com about a log-salvaging company. Molly's Reach is now a real cafe. Take a stroll along the sea walk, just down from Molly's Reach.

The Port Mellon Pulp Mill is the area's major employer, but that doesn't take away

from the fact that Gibsons is a bona fide fishing village and now a booming bedroom community for the metropolis of Vancouver. Rapid development here and elsewhere on the Sechelt Peninsula is altering the bucolic lifestyle that has made the Sunshine Coast so attractive to urban refugees and retirees in the first place. New commuter ferry is helping to handle the increasing demand (see below).

Gibsons Information: Info Centre, Box 1190, Gibsons, BC, V0N 1V0. 604-886-2325. Follow signs off Hwy 101 to Lower Marine Dr and Gower Point Rd (kitty-corner from Molly's Reach Cafe). Weekdays in winter, daily in summer. This Info Centre features a burial plot for George Gibson and family members, a somewhat haunting touch that was done as part of a downtown revitalization scheme. You will definitely feel the pull of history as you pose your travelling companions at the tombstones for photos, a step away from the Info Centre's doorstep.

Sunshine Coast Commuter Ferry: Between Gibsons and downtown Vancouver. Regent Navigation: 604-740-1803. 40-passenger *Georgia Master* leaves Gibsons' Government Wharf weekdays 6:30am; leaves downtown Vancouver at 4:50pm. 55 minutes.

■ **Gibsons Sea Walk:** From Government Wharf to Gibsons Marina in Lower Gibsons, a 10-minute walk; lit at night.

■ **Gower Pt Rd and Ocean Beach Esplanade:** If you take Gower Pt Rd west and north out of downtown, you'll be treated to an incomparable drive that turns away from Howe Sound to face the Strait of Georgia. You may also decide to lose yourself in a labyrinth of residential streets called the Bluff. **Chaster Park** at Gower Pt has picnic tables. Captain George Vancouver stopped here in 1792.

■ **Elphinstone Pioneer Museum:** 716 Winn Rd, downtown Gibsons. 604-886-8232. Daily May-Sept, or on request. Regional museum for Sunshine Coast. Bedford Shell Collection is one of Canada's largest.

Whispering Firs Regional Park: About 8km from Langdale. Picnic tables, BBQ cookhouse, playground, fitness and walking trail.

Roberts Creek: (Pop. 2,236). 9km beyond Langdale off Hwy 101 along scenic **Lower Roberts Creek Rd** that eventually loops back to highway. A 6km drive takes you to the library and General Store with its in-the-know bulletin board. Named for Thomas Roberts who settled here in 1889. Natural beauty and quiet surroundings; known for its B&B facilities.

Roberts Creek Information: Gibsons Info Centre.

■ **Cliff Gilker Regional Park:** 65ha. Along Hwy 101 just before Roberts Creek Rd, 16km from Langdale. Nature trails, two creeks (Clack and Roberts), cedar bridges, waterfalls (Leisure and Shadow), picnic site, sports field, children's play area.

■ **Sunshine Coast Golf & Country Club:** Next to Gilker Park. 604-885-9212. Tough 18-hole course, loaded with water hazards and sand traps.

The massive hulks of ships form the breakwater at Powell River on the Sunshine Coast.

■ **Roberts Creek Regional Park/Esplanade:** Bottom of Roberts Creek Rd. Sandy beach, swimming, picnicking, pretty views, along .5km jetty.

Roberts Creek Provincial Park: 40ha; 25 campsites. 604-898-3678. 18km from Langdale off Hwy 101. A separate day-use section is found 1.5km southeast on Beach Rd, or, if you're driving west, off Hwy 101 at Flume Rd, 17km from Langdale. Water is chilly, but people swim here. At low tide, this beach picnic area is a good spot to observe sea stars, mussels, and oysters. Flume Rd marks course of a long-gone 6km flume on which were floated cedar blocks from inland forests to booming grounds at Roberts Creek mouth.

Chapman Creek Hatchery: 21km from Langdale. Signs lead to **Sunshine Coast Salmonid Enhancement Society Hatchery.** 604-885-4136. Tours daily, May-Oct. Viewing platform, trails to see spawning salmon in fall. Fresh trout for sale.

Davis Bay: 22km from Langdale. Hwy 101 swings along the Strait of Georgia. This beautiful sandy beach is one of the most accessible and beautiful in the region. Resort atmosphere. Davis Bay pier good for fishing. Take a walk to **Mission Point** at Chapman Creek's mouth. Watch for sea lions and harbour seals. Leaving Davis Bay, you drive up a hill before entering Sechelt.

Sechelt: (Pop. 7,343). 27km beyond Langdale on Hwy 101. An intriguing, lovely location. Town sits on sand bar barely a kilometre in width. Strait of Georgia to the south, Sechelt Inlet to the north. This land bridge prevents Sechelt Peninsula from being an island.

This isthmus village is base for the Sechelt (or shishalh) First Nation, whose influence on this coast is pervasive. What you first see as you enter Sechelt is an imposing cultural centre – the **House of hewhiwus** (House of Chiefs), containing offices of Sechelt Indian Government District, a museum, 280-seat Raven's Cry Theatre, and gift shop. Behind the centre and facing Trail Bay in neat rows are homes of the Sechelt people. Decimated in the last century by smallpox, the Sechelt Nation is now thriving, and with the Sechelt Act of 1986, has achieved its own particular style of self-government. In 1998, a draft treaty was completed between the Sechelt Nation and BC Government.

Elsewhere, check out downtown Sechelt's **Snickett Park** and **Pebble Beach** for relaxation and swimming. The Boulevard provides a bracing waterfront walk. Ask the locals or the Info Centre how to get to **Kinnikinnick Park**. It's hard to find, but worth the effort. The coastline around Sechelt is accessible for scuba diving, cruising, and salmon fishing.

Sechelt plays host to the internationally acclaimed **Festival of the Written Arts**, mid-Aug, at the Rockwood Lodge (below), a heritage building dating to 1936.

Sechelt Information: Info Centre, Box 360, Sechelt, BC, V0N 3A0. 604-885-0662. In Trail Bay Mall, 5755 Cowrie St. Weekdays in winter, daily in summer.
■ **Sunshine Coast Arts Centre:** Junction of Trail and Medusa roads. 604-885-5412. Tues-Sun, summer; Wed-Sun, off-season.
■ **Sunshine Coast Slipper Factory:** 5685 Cowrie St. 1-800-499-1636. Year-round.
■ **Rockwood Lodge Gardens:** At top of Cowrie St. 604-885-2522. Year-round. Rhododendrons, fuchsias, roses.
■ **Sechelt Golf and Country Club:** East off highway onto Trail Ave, follow signs to 6177

Ripple Way. 604-885-4653. 18 holes, year-round, covered driving range, coffee shop.

Inland Sea: Sechelt town sits at the southern tip of an oceanic waterway with 480km of mountain-sheltered coastline. The main inlet is **Sechelt**, branches of which are Salmon and Narrows inlets. At its far end is foreboding **Skookumchuk Narrows** (see p.115). Except for a few small settlements, the Inland Sea is much the same as it was when gouged out by a wall of ice 10,000 years ago. Eight marine parks are found along the Inland Sea, plus some private marinas and resorts.
■ **HMCS Chaudière:** This 118m Canadian warship, a decommissioned destroyer escort, requires some effort to visit. You have to dive 35m below Sechelt Inlet off Kunechin Point, 6km north of Sechelt. The gutted ship was scuttled Dec 1992 in an ambitious project by the Artificial Reef Society of BC. It thudded into the seabed on a tilt, canting over hard on its port side, the twin barrels of the forward gun jammed into the mud.

East Porpoise Bay Rd: Leads northeast (right) out of Sechelt to Porpoise Bay Provincial Park 4km beyond town. Signs also lead to **Maclean Bay Hatchery** operated by the Sechelt Indian Government District. Tours by arrangement, 604-885-5562. Fishing from the rocks.

Porpoise Bay Provincial Park: 61ha; 84 campsites (reservations taken: call 1-800-689-9025; from the Lower Mainland or overseas, call 604-689-9025). Also six cycle-in campsites and a group campground for 100 that can be reserved. Sani-station. General info: 604-898-3678. Turn northeast at Sechelt, follow road 4km to park. Swimmers enjoy the wide, sandy beach at this park on Sechelt Inlet's east side. Sunbathing and canoeing; fishing in inlet and various rivers and creeks for salmon and cod. In fall, **Angus Creek** features a chum salmon run. Park also provides access to **Sechelt Inlets Marine Recreation Area** for canoeists and car-toppers. Arrive early in the day to get a campsite in summer. Campfires restricted to communal fire pits. Wheelchair accessible.

Redrooffs Rd: Off Hwy 101 at **Sargeant Bay**, just beyond Sechelt's western outskirts, 34km from Langdale. This alternate route into **Halfmoon Bay** follows Strait of Georgia coastline. Twisty, narrow, hilly. RV drivers, proceed with caution.

Sargeant Bay Provincial Park: 57ha. Day use. Mostly undeveloped. Just west of Sechelt, off Hwy 101. Freshwater marsh for birdwatching. Cobble beach and walking trails. Hiking trail to Triangle Lake. Fish ladder to watch spawning salmon. Lots of intertidal life. It's a fragile habitat, so keep dogs leashed.

Halfmoon Bay Lookout: 13km beyond Sechelt on Hwy 101, overlooking Halfmoon Bay, **Welcome Pass**, **Malaspina Strait**, and **Thormanby Islands**. Strait named for Captain Alexandro Malaspina, Spaniard who explored the Pacific Coast from 1789-1794. These are now popular yachting waters.

Halfmoon Bay: A large scoop of a bay protected from open sea by South Thormanby Island. Public wharf, general store, liquor store, post office, low-tide public boat launch. Halfmoon Bay has five regional parks. One is **Coopers Green Regional Park,** on Fisherman Rd, off Redrooffs Rd; picnic area, boat launch. Another, **Redrooffs Trail & Pier,** off Redrooffs Rd, has nature trail, picnic area, and beach walk.

Smuggler Cove Provincial Marine Park: 182ha; 5 wilderness/walk-in campsites. 604-898-3678. 14km beyond Sechelt. Follow Brooks Rd off Hwy 101. Hike in 1km or paddle from Brooks Cove through Welcome Passage. Small, all-weather, protected anchorage. Forested uplands, rocky headlands. Fishing, swimming, hiking. **Frenchman's Cove,** a shallow inlet at park's southeast corner, may be entered by boat from Halfmoon Bay.

Secret Cove: 16.5km beyond Sechelt. Private marine park with year-round fishing for red snapper, salmon, flounder, cod. Three marinas serve private boaters.

The landscape becomes more rugged as you head northward to Pender Harbour away from the shelfland between Gibsons and Sechelt. Hwy 101 winds, climbs, and dips at the base of the **Caren Range**. Spectacular views of ocean and small islands unfold as you enter the Pender Harbour area. Roads curve around gem-like lakes as they dead-end in magical coves and resort enclaves.

Pender Harbour: A beautiful, deep harbour, about halfway between Vancouver and Princess Louisa Inlet (as a boat travels). It incorporates communities of **Madeira Park**, to the south, **Irvines Landing** at the mouth of the harbour on the north side, and **Garden Bay**. Although Madeira Park and Garden Bay have their own post offices, residents here are more likely to consider themselves simply Pender Harbourites – very closely connected by water.

This is a prime sportfishing area, with a dozen resorts and marinas, cabins and campgrounds, moorage, diving facilities. Also, a nine-hole golf course.

Population is still somewhat scarce here, but foreign investment is beginning to pour in, and it remains to be seen how long this splendid labyrinth of delights can escape the pressure of development moving up the peninsula.

Madeira Park Rd: Just past Paq Lake, 29km beyond Sechelt and 59km from Langdale. Turn off Hwy 101 to reach Madeira Park business section.

Madeira Park: (Pop. 1,100). Rural district 29km beyond Sechelt and 59km from Langdale. Named by Joseph Gonsalos who settled here in early 1900s from the Madeira Islands, Portugal. Pender Harbour's largest community, with grocery stores, a post office, pharmacy, bank, liquor store, beauty shop, bingo hall. Just beyond the business section is lovely **Welbourn Cove**. A marina, picnic area, boat launch and cultural centre (library, art gallery and music school).

Madeira Park Information: Pender Harbour and Egmont Info Centre, Box 265, Madeira Park, BC, V0N 2H0. 604-883-2561. Seasonal.

Road to Garden Bay, Garden Bay Provincial Marine Park, and Irvines Landing: 5.5km beyond Madeira Park. Turn west. Both Garden Bay and Irvines Landing are 8km away. Irvines Landing Rd splits off westward from Garden Bay Rd as latter veers southward along **Garden Bay Lake**.

Garden Bay Provincial Marine Park: 163ha. Fronted by 200m of shoreline on Garden Bay. Includes 471m Mt Daniel, known by the Sechelt First Nation as a place of great ceremonial significance: the eastern peak was long ago the setting for puberty rites. The western peak offers view of lakes, inlets, and islands. Summit and cemetery on waterfront are protected archaeology sites. Open anchorage. Dinghy float. Little development.

John Daly Regional Park: 1ha. On Garden Bay Rd just off Hwy 101. Nature trail, picnic site. In fall, salmon spawn in Anderson Creek.

Mt Daniel Hiking Trail: Take Garden Bay Rd from Hwy 101 to first road on left past Oyster Bay Rd (trail not well marked).

Katherine Lake Regional Park: 24 RV sites, 10 tent sites. Showers. On

smallest of the four superb lakes in and around Irvines Landing and Garden Bay. Ideal base from which to hop around the Pender Harbour area. Sandy beach: swimming, picnicking.

Garden Bay: Another spellbinding locale. Shouldn't be missed, especially if you are a hopeless romantic. Hotels, resorts, marinas, restaurants, even a drive-in deli, and a totem pole. Gorgeous views up Pender Harbour.

Irvines Landing: Irvines Landing Rd climbs up from Garden Bay Lake past Mixal and Hotel lakes and down into the landing at the entrance to Pender Harbour. Consists of marina, pub, boat launch, and cold beer and wine store. Picturesque view of harbour. Named after Charles Irving, who started a trading post on this site around 1865. Steve Danes, a Latvian seaman, bought the landing in 1898. With his father-in-law, Joseph Gonsalas of Madeira Island, Danes built the Irvines Landing Hotel and Store. After being a fish-processing centre, the landing has become a popular anchorage and vacation spot.

■ Pender Hill Hiking Trail: Trail starts .25km from Orca Rd with a parking area provided. Fairly steep, 30-minute hike offers spectacular views of Pender Harbour, Texada Island, Vancouver Island, Georgia Strait.

Back on Hwy 101, you take the last leg of your journey up the lower Sunshine Coast, heading 16km for **Earls Cove** and another wondrous ferry ride, or one last side trip to **Egmont** and the trailhead to legendary **Skookumchuck Narrows**.

Sakinaw and Ruby Lakes: Sakinaw Lake Rd is 14km from Madeira Park. Hwy 101 begins to skirt Ruby Lake just beyond. These bigger peninsula lakes draw paddlers and anglers. 1.3km portage between the lakes. Sudden winds can make Sakinaw dangerous. **Dan Bosch Regional Park**, on Ruby Lake, is 1km past Ruby Lake Restaurant on Hwy 101. Swimming, picnicking, 1.5km walking trail.

Ruby Creek: At Ruby Lake, turn onto Halowell Rd. See cutthroat trout spawning in fall.

SIDE TRIP

to Egmont and Skookumchuck Narrows

Egmont Rd: Just south of Earls Cove, turn east 16km beyond Madeira Park on Hwy 101. About 5km, skirting northern tips of North and Waugh lakes.

Egmont: (Pop. 119) Village on Secret Bay offers moorage and supplies as last stop for yachters heading up **Prince of Wales Reach** for incomparable **Princess Louisa Inlet** (see below). It is also the trailhead for **Skookumchuck Narrows** (see below). As you drive into Egmont you will see 1,982m Mt Churchill that overlooks Prince of Wales Reach in the wild beyond.

Starfish cluster on the shoreline at Saltery Bay Provincial Park.

this coast. A ramp for disabled divers and swimmers descends into the water. Swimming, boat launch, hiking, fishing. Two beachfront areas on north shore of Jervis Inlet. Mounds of seashells on the beach reveal that this was originally an aboriginal fishing ground. Killer whales and sea lions can sometimes be seen.

Lois River: 11.5km from Saltery Bay. Flows from 1,414ha Lois Lake (created by a hydro dam) into Malaspina Strait. Start of the Powell Forest Canoe Route (below). Fish for rainbow, kokanee, and Dolly Varden.

Lang Bay: (Pop. 264) 12km beyond Saltery Bay. Small community on Malaspina Strait. Country farmers raise Scottish Highland cattle, sheep, turkeys. Their homes look over the sea. There's a "good mile" of lovely sand; public beach access at north end of this protected bay. Safe swimming. Horseback riding. Eagle photography – the birds swoop down the creek in fall when it's chock-full of spawning chinook. Canoeing: access to first portage of Lois Lake, one of the Powell Lakes chain. (For more details see *Powell Forest Canoe Route,* p.116.) Private campground.

Lang Creek Hatchery and Spawning Channel: 22km beyond Saltery Bay, take Duck Lake Rd, turn right after Duck Lake outlet bridge and follow signs. 604-485-7612. In fall, salmon spawn in creek and manmade channel at the hatchery. Hatchery open July-late Nov; best viewing Sept-Oct. Grounds open year-round for picnics, walks. Watch pink, chum, coho, and giant chinook jump into tanks right below your feet. School tours on egg-taking days. **Lang Creek Estuary** across from hatchery offers waterfowl and bald eagle viewing.

Westview Ferry Terminal: Just as you enter Powell River's downtown in its Westview neighbourhood, 31km from Saltery Bay, turn left (or west) to Wharf or Courtenay streets. 604-485-2943. From here, ferries travel to **Comox** (Little River) on **Vancouver Island** and **Blubber Bay** on **Texada Island**. The *Queen of Sidney,* one of the first two vessels built by BC Ferries, holds 138 cars and 989 passengers and takes 75 minutes to travel the 27km across the Strait of Georgia to Comox. Contrary to the highly busy ferry runs from the Vancouver area to Victoria and Nanaimo on Vancouver Island, this ferry is usually only partly full and makes for a comfortable and scenic trip. Four sailings a day, the last one leaving at 8:45pm. The *North Island Princess* ferry to Texada Island carries 49 cars, 293 passengers. 35 minutes, 7km, 10 daily sailings.

SIDE TRIP

to Texada Island

Texada, known locally as "The Rock," is a mountainous industrial island. At 287 sq km, 43km long and roughly 8km wide, it is the largest in the southern Inside Passage. Part of the Regional District of Powell River, Texada is home to 1,200 people, many of whom com-

Skookumchuck Narrows Provincial Park: 123ha. 604-898-3678. Northeast tip of Sechelt Peninsula overlooking narrows. 4km trail leads from parking lot at Egmont to Roland Pt.

Skookumchuck is Chinook jargon meaning "turbulent waters" or "rapid torrent." As the tides move through the narrows, they form rapids that boil and bubble with an audible roar. In spring, rapids can attain 12-14 knots. Trail network leads to Roland and Narrows points, prime viewing areas for the phenomenon. Explanatory signs. Picnicking and day use. After the 45-minute hike over a reasonable trail, try to time your arrival there with peak tidal flows.

Return to Highway 101 and Earls Cove

Earls Cove: Board BC Ferries from Earls Cove to **Saltery Bay** on north shore of **Jervis Inlet**. The 50-minute ferry ride is a wonderfully scenic respite before you can continue up Hwy 101. The ferry heads northward up **Agamemnon Channel** before rounding the northern tip of sparsely populated **Nelson Island** into Jervis Inlet and southward to Saltery Bay. Rugged Coast Mountains rise over trackless wilderness. For BC Ferries information: Victoria, 250-386-3431; anywhere else in BC, toll-free 1-888-223-3779.

Jervis Inlet: Cuts inland 74km from Malaspina Strait, leads to Hotham Sound, Sechelt Inlet, Prince of Wales Reach, Princess Royal Reach, and Queens Reach. Named by Captain George Vancouver after Rear Admiral Sir John Jervis. Steep mountainous shores and deep water (over 200m).

Princess Louisa Inlet: Off Queens Reach and what at first looks like a large stream is **Malibu Rapids**, a 6km passage that leads to this small fabled inlet hidden in the recesses of the Coast Mountains. The inlet, almost completely closed, is 300m deep and 800m wide. Sailors throttle through this dangerous entrance at the right tidal moments to enjoy this peerless natural paradise. At the inlet's head is **Princess Louisa Provincial Marine Park**, 65ha. A tremendous 1,524m cliff, and spectacular 37m **Chatterbox Falls**, a roar within a vast wild silence. Mountain goats travel the cliff.

Saltery Bay: (Pop. 90). Terminal for ferry to and from Earls Cove (see above). 1-888-223-3779. Limited anchorage for small craft. Log booming ground. From here Hwy 101 winds westward along Jervis Inlet and Malaspina Strait becoming Marine Ave as it turns north into Powell River's downtown 30km away.

■ **Sunshine Coast Trail:** Saltery Bay is southern terminus of new 180km hiking trail that leads northwest past Lois Lake, along Powell Lake and Okeover Inlet to Sarah Point north of Lund. There are many access points, allowing hikers to design their own adventures. Map and info from Powell River Visitors Bureau, 604-485-4701. Informal campsites, B&Bs and Fiddlehead Farm Hostel along the way. A company called Sophisticated Sherpas, 604-483-9565, will pick up and drop off hikers, deliver gear to campsites each night, cook meals.

Saltery Bay Provincial Park: 69ha; 45 campsites (reservations taken: call 1-800-689-9025; from the Lower Mainland or overseas, call 604-689-9025). Sani-station. General info: 604-898-3678. North Shore of Jervis Inlet, 1km beyond Saltery Bay ferry terminal. This is a rare, underused provincial park, and some say it has the most beautiful waterfront in the parks system. A 3m bronze mermaid was placed under 20m of water here, marking just one of several great scuba-diving spots along

mute to Powell River to work. The two main settlements are at **Gillies Bay** and **Van Anda**. Texada has more BC Ferries sailings from the mainland than any of the Gulf Islands to the south (there are 20 daily 35-minute crossings to and from Powell River).

Texada was part of the traditional territories of the Coast Salish speaking Sliammon people. In 1791, the Spanish explorer Jose Maria Narvaez sailed by, and, it is believed, named it after Felix de Tejeda, a Spanish rear-admiral. For nearly a century white whalers rendered whale fat at what became Blubber Bay. Iron, gold, and copper – and the limestone used in making cement, pulp, chemicals (and Rolaids) – have also fuelled Texada's economy for a century (along with illegal liquor and, more recently, discreet crops of marijuana). In the early 1900s, the boomtown Van Anda boasted three hotels, a hospital, newspaper, jail, and saloons. The limestone industry still thrives: the largest of three island quarries ships more than three million tonnes a year to cement plants, pulp mills, and chemical factories.

For visitors, Texada offers hiking, cycling, beachcombing, camping, kayaking, and scuba-diving in some of the clearest waters on the south coast. The island, a BC Wildlife Watch viewing site, is home to a large, easily viewed population of white-tailed deer. Van Anda has a hotel and Gillies Bay a motel and two campgrounds, a general store with liquor outlet, and an art gallery. Boat launches and moorage.

A ridge of rugged mountains runs the island's length, reaching highest elevations in the undeveloped southern end. "Flower rocks," unique to the island, look as if they have white flowers embedded in them, and are used for making jewelry.

Bring your vehicle: there is no public transportation on Texada.

Texada Island Information: Contact Powell River Info Centre, below.

Shelter Point Regional Park: 52 campsites. Sani-station, showers. 604-486-7228. On Texada's west coast, just past Gillies Bay, 19km from Blubber Bay. Year-round. Hiking trails. Boat launch. Wildlife watching.

Return to Highway 101

Powell River: (Pop. 13,131). 31km beyond Saltery Bay. Despite the evidence of clearcut logging that has fuelled the economy of Powell River, the area is still impressive, because of its encircling environment of ocean, lakes, and wilderness, and because of the pleasantness of the town itself.

Powell River was built up around the massive MacMillan Bloedel pulp-and-paper mill after it began operations in 1910. The original neighbourhood, called the Townsite, spread up from the waterfront mill. The 30 commercial buildings and 400 Victorian-style homes comprise BC's only national historic region (see below). It will give you the feeling of being in a time warp.

Powell River has three other neighbourhoods, all distinctive. Westview, the section you encounter entering Powell River from

Saltery Bay, is the main residential and shopping area. Cranberry, which lies farther back from the waterfront than the other neighbourhoods, feels like a separate small town: friendly corner stores, a bird and wildlife sanctuary on Cranberry Lake, and large residential lots. On the other side of the river as you head up Hwy 101 for Lund and the end of the road, you skirt Wildwood, both upscale and pastoral.

Powell River is well known outside Canada for its international choral festival, Kathaumixw, a Coast Salish word for a gathering of different peoples. The biennial event draws choirs from all over the globe. Nicknamed "River City" by the locals, this mill town is also noted for its own musical and dancing talents. Its Boys Choir and its Youth Choir have received international acclaim. Its School of Dance is a source of talent for the prestigious Royal Winnipeg Ballet.

Powell River residents are sensitive to people with disabilities. Streets and buildings have been made easier to use, a wheelchair trail has been built around a nearby wilderness lake.

Powell River is being advertised "The Dive Capital of Canada," because of its clear waters and diverse sea life (including uncommonly large octopuses and wolf eels). There are 20 major dive sites nearby, including Octopus City and The Hulks, a ring of old ships forming a breakwater near the mill.

Year-round salmon fishing: several marinas; close to 30 lakes within easy reach of the city, many have fishing for cutthroat trout.

Powell River Information: Info Centre, 4690 Marine Ave, Powell River, BC, V8A 2L1. 604-485-4701. Four blocks north of BC Ferries terminal. Daily, in summer; weekdays, off-season.

Valentine Mountain Viewpoint: End of Crown St. Panoramic view of Strait of Malaspina from 182m lookout. Reached by 20-minute hike along trail, and rock stairway. Bald eagles year-round. In late fall, dozens of eagles are attracted by salmon spawning.

Willingdon Beach Park: Municipal 70-site campground on Powell River's waterfront, just a few minutes from downtown on Hwy 101. 604-485-2242.

Powell Forest Canoe Route: Begins at Lois Lake, 20km southeast of Powell River. Portages and streams connect 12 lakes over 80km. Suitable for children and adults who are experienced in the outdoors, route has canoe resting racks, 21 campsites, picnic spots.

Inland Lake Site and Trail System: Follow Cranberry St to Haslam, which becomes Inland Lake Rd. Open April 15-Oct 15. The BC Forest Service has encircled Inland Lake with a 13km wheelchair-accessible trail, complete with special cabins and wharves. Camping, fishing, boating. To reserve accessible shelters: 604-485-4701. BC Wildlife Watch viewing site.

Powell River Historic Museum: 4800 Marine Dr. 604-485-2222. Daily, June-Aug; Mon-Fri, Sept-June. Third largest photo archives in BC. Artifacts and displays of area's history include notorious "Billy Goat" Smith's cabin. Smith (d. 1958) was reputed to have been involved in the New York murder of architect Stanford White in 1906.

Powell River Historic Townsite: 5907 Arbutus St. 604-483-3901. One of few places in Canada (all the rest are in the Maritimes) designated a national historic region by the National Historic Sites and Monuments Board. A remarkably preserved example of a single-industry company-built town from the early part of the 20th century. The Powell River Paper Company was incorporated in 1909, and began construction on the mill and the surrounding town, modelled loosely on the British City Garden Movement. Here are more than 400 homes built between 1911 and 1930, and several commercial and institutional buildings. Guided and self-guided tours (ask at Info Centre).

Pacifica Papers Ltd: One of the world's biggest pulp and paper mills, it created Powell River. New owners took over from MacMillan Bloedel in 1998. Summer tours, Mon-Sat, 9:30am; off-season call 604-485-4701.

Powell River and Lake: On Hwy 101, as you leave the Townsite for Lund, you cross Wildwood Bridge over Powell River. Only 500m long, it is the second shortest river in world. The shortest river, according to *Beautiful British Columbia Travel Guide* sleuth, Joel Schaefer, is the humble D River in Lincoln City, Oregon, USA. It flows a mere 37m, give or take a few centimetres. Powell River flows from Powell Lake. Discoveries of trapped salt water 120m below the lake's surface suggest the lake was an inlet until just after the last ice age. Powell River Dam crosses the river, making water available to the mill. Just past the bridge is the turnoff right to **Powell Place**, a marina complex with pub and restaurant, built on the site of an old shingle mill. Charter houseboats here to tour Powell Lake, which recedes 50km into mountainous wilderness. **Fiddlehead Farm**, on Powell Lake, is accessible only by boat from Powell River or by hiking in on the **Sunshine Coast Trail**, (p. 115). Two hours of farm chores a day plus $22 get a traveller a warm bed, hot showers, and three wholesome meals with produce from the organic garden. The meditation hut was designed by a visiting Japanese architect, the barn was built by Mark Vonnegut, hippie son of counterculture literary hero, Kurt Vonnegut.

You are now on the last 30km leg of Hwy 101 as you head to Lund, midway on the west side of Malaspina Peninsula. Landings on the peninsula are jumping-off points to **Savary Island** and **Copeland Islands Marine Park**, off the peninsula's western shores, **Desolation Sound** and **Desolation Sound Marine Park**, off its northern tip, and **Okeover Inlet**, which runs along its eastern shores. This is another paradise for yachtsmen, kayakers, fishermen, and beachcombers. Charters available.

Sliammon: (Pop. 565). 3km beyond Powell River. Road to Sliammon First Nation village is just past bridge over Sliammon Creek, flowing from Sliammon Lake to Malaspina Strait. Community operates Sliammon Hatchery, offering cross-cultural awareness programs for school children. 604-483-4111. Year-round fishing for kokanee and cutthroat. Best salmon fishing end of Sept. Hundreds of bald eagles in the fall. Offshore is Harwood Island, Sliammon reserve land.

Dinner Rock Park: 16.5km northwest of Powell River. Turn west down gravel road. A small, rustic forestry campsite with minimal facilities on Malaspina Strait.

Okeover Arm Provincial Park: 4ha; 18 campsites. 604-898-3678. 17.5km northwest of Powell River, turn east onto paved Malaspina Rd, travel 5km. Park is on east side of the Malaspina Peninsula on Okeover Inlet. Walking through lightly forested upland. Canoeing, kayaking, diving, launching point for Desolation Sound. Observing marine life, fishing. Nearby floats indicate oyster farms.

Lund: (Pop. 204). 27km beyond Powell River at northern end of Hwy 101. Swedish brothers Frederick and Charles Thulin, who settled here 1889, named site after a city in Sweden. The renovated Lund Hotel, its pub now a watering hole for loggers and tourists, was built by the Thulins in 1895. When logging was the main industry of this isolated settlement, it was supplied by steamboat. Ocean laps under the deck of a charming coffeehouse. Salmon sportfishing starts right off Lund breakwater. Marina and public floats, seafood shop, post office, store. Water taxi to **Savary Island** (see below), boat charters. In summertime, this quiet seaside village often becomes a bedlam of vacationers, mainly coming and going from Savary Island, fishing waters, and nearby marine parks.

Lund Information: Powell River Info Centre, 4690 Marine Ave, Powell River, BC, V8A 2L1. 604-485-4701. Weekdays in winter, daily in summer.

Savary Island: 6km offshore from Lund. Only public access is via 12-minute water-taxi ride (604-483-9749) from Lund, or charter airline. About 70 people live year-round on this pearl of an island that looks like it floated up from the South Seas. Unlike most Gulf Islands, Savary runs east-west and is really an 8km clay ridge covered in sand. Two centuries ago, explorer George Vancouver observed Savary, with its white-sand beaches, as having "beauty such as we have seldom enjoyed." Great swimming in clear, warm waters. The north shore has vast sandy beaches. The south shore, facing strait winds, has big rollers and attracts surfers. An oddity is the biggest arbutus tree in BC, on the north shore, a walk across the narrow island. B&Bs but no campgrounds. Many Lower Mainlanders have summer cabins here, and voted against having electricity. Public wharf and floats at **Keefer Bay**.

Copeland Islands Provincial Marine Park: 423ha. Mossy, undeveloped. Also known as "Ragged Islands." An easy day trip for kayakers paddling northward from Lund. Thulin Passage, separating islands from BC mainland, is 137m wide, just enough for boom-toting tugs to squeeze through.

Desolation Sound: Joins Lewis Channel between Cortes and West Redonda islands and joins Homfray Channel along East Redonda Island. So named by Captain George Vancouver in 1792. Wrote the captain in his log: "Our residence here was truly forlorn; an awful silence pervaded the gloomy forests. . . the steep rocky shores prevented the use of the seine, and not a fish at the bottom could be tempted to take the hook." Tell that to the thousands of boaters who come here to play and fish in the summer.

Desolation Sound Provincial Marine Park: 8,256ha. 604-898-3678. BC's largest marine park, and it's a beauty. On north shore of **Gifford Peninsula**. No road access. More than 60km of shoreline, several offshore islands, a gradually rising upland that contains a number of lakes, waterways, and waterfalls. Unwin Lake, a 173ha body of fresh water, is park's largest.

Set back to the north and east, Coast Mountains soar to more than 2,400m. Warm waters surrounding park teem with sea life. Ideal for swimming and scuba-diving. Several safe anchorages: **Prideaux Haven**, **Tenedos Bay**, and **Grace Harbour**. It's busy, though – and BC Parks reminds you take take your garbage with you.

HORSESHOE BAY TO LILLOOET

SQUAMISH HIGHWAY AND DUFFEY LAKE ROAD (Highway 99)

The Squamish Hwy (Hwy 99) from Horseshoe Bay to Pemberton (135km) traces the shores of dramatic Howe Sound to Squamish, continuing north to Whistler and the town of Pemberton. (It's an even 100km from Horseshoe Bay to Whistler, another 35km to Pemberton.)

The next portion of this highway, from Pemberton to Lillooet (about 100km), has only recently become an extension of Hwy 99, with the paving of Duffey Lake Rd (84.5km) through the Cayoosh Range (the Duffey Lake Rd section starts on p.122).

Also called the "Sea to Sky Highway," the Squamish Hwy is a spectacular drive, though not exactly a relaxing one. In the stretch between Horseshoe Bay and Squamish, the highway is often cut out of the cliff, following the scenic shoreline of Howe Sound from on high, and there is the occasional switchback. For the first 20km, there is a sign almost every kilometre warning of rockfall hazard areas. Caution is advised, especially at night or during heavy rains. As one local said, "The road is beautiful. But in the mountains, you drive with care and respect." Watch the signs, take it easy, and don't push it: the two-lane highway widens at regular intervals to allow passing.

There are alternatives to motor travel on this route. BC Rail runs its refurbished passenger service from the North Vancouver station with stops at Whistler Creek (near Whistler Resort) and Pemberton en route north. The

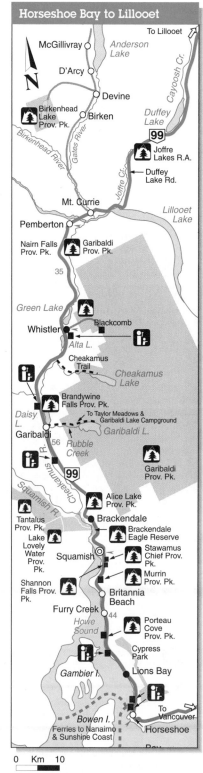

Horseshoe Bay to Lillooet

0 Km 10

Royal Hudson steam train and MV *Britannia* also offer an unusual six-and-a-half-hour train-steamship outing. (For these, see p.90).

The Squamish Highway takes its name from the Squamish First Nation. Its route leads inland from their southern and contemporary headquarters on the North Shore (see p.102), first tracing the Squamish River and then the Cheakamus River, both still vital to the Squamish Nation's traditional salmon-fishing economy.

Horseshoe Bay: (Pop. 1,037). 20km northwest of Vancouver on Hwys 99 and 1. This is terminus for BC Ferries travelling to Departure Bay (Nanaimo) on Vancouver Island; the Sechelt Peninsula (Langdale); and Bowen Island.

Horseshoe Bay lies at the entrance to Howe Sound. It was once used as a camping place for aboriginal peoples travelling between present-day Squamish and Burrard Inlet. The first Europeans, Spaniards under Commander Jose Narvaez, landed here in 1791. One year later, British Captain George Vancouver explored the area, describing Howe Sound as "a solemn inland sea, studded with beautiful forest-clad islands, covered with towering trees whose branches at high tide are lapped by clear waters teeming with fish."

Today's Horseshoe Bay is a charming recreational and bedroom community for the city of Vancouver. Its small village offers shopping, tourist facilities, a marina with boat rentals, and a long-popular fish'n'chips outlet called Trolls.

Horseshoe Bay Information: North Vancouver Info Centre, 131 East 2nd St, North Vancouver, BC, V7L 1C2. 604-987-4488. Open daily in summer, weekdays off-season.

Viewpoint: On Hwy 99, 2km beyond Horseshoe Bay. Watch the ferries make their way through Howe Sound from Vancouver Island, the Sunshine Coast, and Bowen Island. Plus pleasure craft of every size and description.

Viewpoint: 6km beyond Horseshoe Bay. Views of Howe Sound, Queen Charlotte Channel, and nearby Gambier, Bowen, and Anvil islands.

Lions Bay: (Pop. 1,328). 11km beyond Horseshoe Bay on Hwy 99. A quiet residential area overlooking Howe Sound. To the north is 1,646m Lions Mountain.

Lions Bay Information: Lions Bay Municipal Hall (400 Centre Rd), Box 141, Lions Bay, BC, V0N 2E0. 604-921-9333 or 604-921-9811. Open Mon, Tues, Thurs.

Porteau Cove Provincial Park: 50ha; 59 campsites; 15 walk-in sites (reservations taken: call 1-800-689-9025; from the Lower Mainland or overseas, call 604-689-9025). General info: 604-898-3678. 22km north of Horseshoe Bay, on east shore of Howe Sound between Lions Bay and Britannia Beach. Developed park, picnic areas. Great for scuba-diving, windsurfing, snorkeling, swimming, fishing. Boat-launch facilities. Park is set between the Coast Mountains and Howe Sound islands, and the cove itself is a snug haven at park's south end.

Furry Creek Golf and Country Club: 26km north of Horseshoe Bay. Info: 604-896-2226. Tee times: 604-922-9461. 18-hole par 72 championship course. Course climbs to 120m above sea level at the 9th tee, and descends to the shores of Howe Sound at its 14th hole. Named for trapper and prospector Oliver Furry, who in 1898 staked claims to rich copper deposits that were later mined at Britannia Beach. Two restaurants.

Britannia Beach: (Est. pop. 350). 33km beyond Horseshoe Bay on Hwy 99. From 1930 to 1935, Britannia Beach was the British Empire's largest producer of copper. Over its 70 years of operation, the Britannia mine produced some 600 million kilos of copper, employing more than 60,000 people. Permanently closed in 1974, it operates now as the BC Museum of Mining, described below.

Meanwhile, the former mining town is beginning to shine as a stopover on the road to Whistler. The old movie theatre has been turned into a general store; artsy-craftsy galleries, shops, bistros, and restaurants are popping up like mushrooms. Speaking of which, Britannia Beach's newest industry, is Betty's Best Mushrooms. Betty Shore, a.k.a Madam Mushroom, is a pioneer in BC wild mushroom marketing. Her plant processes nearly 2,000kg a day, harvested from forests throughout BC for shipment to Japan and Europe.

■ **BC Museum of Mining:** In Britannia Beach. 604-896-2233, or from Vancouver, 604-688-8735. May-Oct; year-round for pre-booked tours. Dark caves, dramatic rock walls, old buildings: a perfect movie set. Britannia Beach and the BC Museum of Mining, a national historic site, have starred in nearly 80 movie and TV productions. Be there yourself: guided underground tours lead to slushers, muckers, drills and a gravity-fed concentrator building, one of the last standing in the world: at its peak, it processed over 6.4 million kilos of ore daily. Video presentation, museum.

Murrin Provincial Park: 24ha. 3km beyond Britannia Beach, straddling Hwy 99, and featuring tiny, clean Browning Lake. Park was donated by BC Electric Railway and named for company president, 1929-1946. Lake takes its name from the 1919 general superintendent of the Britannia Mining and Smelting Co, who shared his summer cottage here with mine employees. Swimming, fishing, sunbathing, walking trails, picnics. Steep, almost vertical, cliffs – with names like The Shaman, Sugarloaf, and Levitcus – suitable for novice and intermediate rock climbers. Just beyond the parking lot, across the highway, trail leads to pretty Petgill Lake, outside of the park.

Shannon Falls Provincial Park: 28ha. 604-898-3678. East off Hwy 99, 7km beyond Britannia Beach. Picnicking, hiking. Splendid views of 335m Shannon Falls – BC's third largest falls – right from your car. Six times the elevation of Niagara, well worth pulling over for. Viewing platform at base of falls.

Stawamus Chief Provincial Park: 521ha; 40-site walk in campground. Just north of Shannon Falls, east of highway. The 652m Chief is destination each year for thousands of rock climbers and hikers. It offers 180 routes, some a challenge for the novice or intermediate, others strictly for top-ranking climbers. The first of a number of spectacular vantage points offers panoramic views of Howe Sound, the town of Squamish, and the southern Tantalus Mountains. The rock is sacred to Squamish First Nation people. Campground is a good base for mountain bikers and climbers.

Squamish: (Pop. 13,994). 11km beyond Britannia Beach. Squamish is at head of Howe Sound, overlooked by 2,678m Mt Garibaldi and the striking silvery granite cliffs of the Stawamus Chief. European settlers arrived in the area in 1888. By 1891, store and post office had been established, and logging of giant cedar and fir trees was underway. Giant logs are dumped and boomed (gathered together) for towing into Howe Sound.

Funky and unpretentious, Squamish is becoming known throughout North America as premier windsurfing territory. The winds are truly a phenomenon. Situated at the head of the sound in a narrow corridor, the town is surrounded by massive, sheer rock faces that heat up between 10am and 5pm, creating a geothermal effect. Some spots are suitable for beginners, or you can go right up to world championship levels in some particularly windy spots.

As well, Squamish is a rock climber's heaven, not just for the Chief, but for the more varied, and sunnier, Smoke Bluffs that overlook the town.

Diving, horseback riding, glacier-landing tours, hiking, river rafting, canoeing, fishing and llama backpacking are also on the menu; and the golf course gets rave reviews.

Squamish Information: Info Centre, 37950 Cleveland Ave, Squamish, BC, V0N 3G0. 604-892-9244. Daily. In pleasant park offering clear views of the Chief, and featuring sculptures carved from intriguing stone, some found locally. Good picnic and photo stop.

■ **Glacier Tours:** Departing from Squamish Municipal Airport. 1-800-265-0088 in BC. 604-898-9016. May-Nov. Ski planes leave the airport three times daily, flying passengers over some of the largest glaciers and icecaps in North America. The icecaps of the Tantalus Range can be up to 457m thick and several kilometres long.

■ **Sta-wa-mus Native Cultural Centre:** About 1km south of Squamish on Hwy 99. For info on activities: 604-892-5166 or 604-892-5553.

■ **Squamish Estuary:** Excellent birdwatching year-round, but especially during spring and fall migrations. Trails. BC Wildlife Watch viewing site.

■ **Golf: Squamish Valley Golf and Country Club,** just north of town off Hwy 99. 604-898-9336. 18 holes. A prestigious course. Also curling and squash.

■ **West Coast Railway Heritage Park:** Hwy 99 to Centennial Way to Government Rd (watch for signs). 1-800-722-1233 or 604-828-9336. May-Oct. 58 vintage railway cars and locomotives. Nature trail, picnic tables.

■ **Soo Coalition for Sustainable Forests:** 1498 Pemberton Ave. 604-892-9766. Mon-Fri, year-round. Forest-industry advocate offers tours of tree farms and local forest operations; information on area forest practices.

Cheakamus River: Joins with Squamish River 8km beyond Squamish. Cheakamus means "salmon weir place." There were once several Squamish villages in the vicinity of this salmon-rich site. From here, the two rivers flow as one, south into Howe Sound.

Brackendale: 10km beyond downtown Squamish (since 1964 part of Squamish district municipality). A quietly active, arts-minded community that happened to find itself amidst one of North America's largest congregations of eagles. The Brackendale Art Gallery Society here initiated the Brackendale Winter Eagle Festival (see below). Stop in at the Brackendale Art Gallery, Theatre, and Tea House, 604-898-3333.

Brackendale Eagle Reserve: 600ha. In Brackendale, follow Government Rd (the main street). Park at dike, and walk along the dike to viewpoint. A thin fringe along the river's east bank, and more land on the west side, comprise the Brackendale Eagle Reserve. The Squamish River provides a buffer between people and bald eagles, most on the west bank. These are the birds' wintering grounds, and site of the BC Wildlife Service's yearly bald eagle count. Jan-Feb may bring as may as 2,000 eagles to the banks of the Squamish River and its tributaries. In the winter of 1994, the Squamish River had the largest concentration of bald eagles on Earth – 3,769 – 274 more than the world record set in the 1980s at Alaska's Chilkat River. Day after day, each bird devours nearly a tenth of its own weight – as much as half a kilo – in fish. The eagle numbers peak around Christmas. By February, when all the fish have spawned, the avian carnivores again face the hardship of hunting herring, waterfowl, rabbits, and rodents.

Those who come to view the eagles should consider themselves visitors in their domain, and try to minimize disturbance. Wildlife officials have found eagles will stop feeding if people approach within 150m. Dogs are best left at home. Children should be discouraged from throwing sticks or stones, and everyone watching the birds should be reasonably quiet and not make sudden movements.

Maps and information are available from the Squamish Info Centre (above).

Tenderfoot Hatchery: Just outside Brackendale turn onto the Squamish Valley Rd. Travel 3.6km, cross bridge, turn right onto Paradise Valley Rd for 4.3km to Midnight Way. 604-898-3657. Chinook, coho, and steelhead. Year-round.

Lake Lovely Water Provincial Recreation Area: 1,300ha. 604-898-3678. West side of Squamish River across from Brackendale. Access by floatplane, or by boat and trail. Rough gravel road on Squamish First Nation's Cheakamus Reserve leads to Squamish River's east bank; steep trail to lake begins on the west bank – the crossing can be treacherous. Pristine pocket wilderness surrounded by mountains of the recently protected Tantalus Range. Tent site, toilets on southeast side of

Alta Lake is one of five pretty lakes connected by trails near the resort town of Whistler.

Lake Lovely Water; alpine cabin and toilets on northeast side.

Alice Lake Provincial Park: 397ha; 88 campsites. 604-898-3678. 13km beyond Squamish. Dominated by towering Coast Mountains, and surrounded by dense forests and grassy areas. Picnicking, birdwatching, swimming, canoeing. Fish for small cutthroat and rainbow.

Viewpoint: West side of Hwy 99, 25km beyond Squamish. Views of Cheakamus River. Winter fishing for steelhead; in summer, spring salmon; in fall, Dolly Varden.

Garibaldi Provincial Park: 194,650ha; 196 wilderness/walk-in campsites throughout park. 604-898-3678. Signs on Hwy 99 between Squamish and Whistler indicate trails for access to the park. Developed trail systems provide primary entry into the five most popular areas: Diamond Head, Black Tusk/Garibaldi Lake, Cheakamus Lake, Singing Pass, and Wedgemount Lake. Park offers azure-blue lakes, including Garibaldi, Corrie, and Helm; and the Coast Mountain Range including 2,678m Garibaldi Mountain and 2,438m Mt Sir Richard; glaciers, alpine tarns, cascading streams, and rivers, including Tawasus and Iceworm creeks and the Cheakamus and Pitt rivers. Meadows filled with alpine flowers. Many of park's features were formed by volcanic action.

Diamond Head area, often with 5m of snow, is popular with experienced Nordic skiers. Overnight accommodation at Elfin Shelter. The skiing at Diamond Head is challenging and exhilarating.

Garibaldi Lake and Taylor Meadows Campgrounds: Turn off 31km beyond Squamish on east side of Hwy 99. Trail, 9km long, follows Rubble Creek to Garibaldi Lake, major campground in Garibaldi Provincial Park.

Daisy Lake: Off Hwy 99, some 31km beyond Squamish. Small lake formed by dam on the Cheakamus River. Fish for rainbow, Dolly Varden, and kokanee. Boat launching.

Brandywine Falls Provincial Park: 143ha; 15 campsites. 604-898-3678. Off Hwy 99, some 37km beyond Squamish. Picnicking, fishing, hiking trails, and views of the falls, Daisy Lake and mountains of Garibaldi Provincial Park (2,316m Black Tusk). The 66m falls are smooth, wide, and impressive, and less than a 10-minute walk from the highway.

Function Junction: 49km beyond Squamish, west side of Hwy 99. Funky name for an industrial park and mall.

Cheakamus Lake: In Garibaldi Provincial Park. Enter by Cheakamus Trail entrance off Hwy 99, 49km beyond Squamish. Road leads from Hwy 99 to trailhead, an easy 3km hike to spectacular lake. Fish for rainbow and Dolly Varden.

119

Whistler: (Pop. 7,172). 56km beyond Squamish in the Coast Mountains. Whistler is a fabulous, four-seasons world-destination resort community cradled by two magnificent mountains, Whistler (2,182m), and Blackcomb (2,287m). 13 high-speed lifts for the two mountains (the most at a single resort in North America) rise up steps away from accommodation.

The resort – which takes 4,000 people to operate – has been rated "The Number One Resort in North America" by *Mountain Sports and Living Magazine* and *Ski Magazine*, and is considered one of the top five ski resorts in the world.

Centre of everything, and unique in North America, is **Whistler Village,** an intimate European-style village with cobbled streets and plazas, outdoor cafes and bistros, walkways, movie theatre, underground parking, shops, restaurants, lounges, a variety of accommodation, and daily street entertainment from May-Oct.

Whistler Resort is not so much a place as a phenomenon. Now BC's fastest-growing municipality, it was only a few decades ago that the site was a garbage dump prowled by bears.

In the early '70s, Whistler's ski value was becoming recognized, and hasty random building of weekend cabins was going unchecked. The foresight of a few wise people in the early '70s brought a quick halt to this scattered development. In 1975, the government froze development, and established Whistler as the province's first and only Resort Municipality. Controls were established, and a long-range plan carved out. The resort opened Dec 1980, and is already three-quarters of the way to reaching its ceiling of 53,741 beds. Meanwhile, a second village, Whistler North, has been completed.

Whistler Village has an unbelievable quality, enhanced by a knockout palette of pastel colours brushed over the architecture: pale aqua and green metal roofs, rose pink trim, turquoise walls, peach facing. Even the Chateau Whistler is apricot-beige with blue-green turrets and tops. The 3,250-sq-m Whistler Conference Centre is landmarked by an eye-catching tentlike roof in aquamarine. The $8.5 million Roundhouse Lodge, new in 1998 with 1,740 restaurant seats, is the largest conference facility at any resort in North America.

Everyone tries for a bit of history with Whistler, but there isn't much. There's Marvellous Myrtle and her husband Alex Philip, who trekked up the Pemberton Trail in 1911, took a buckboard to Brackendale, and a packhorse beyond. They bought land on the shores of Alta Lake and there, with romance in their hearts that was to last a lifetime, they built their Rainbow Lodge, and named the places here (River of Golden Dreams, for one). The fishing lodge ran until 1948, always to capacity, especially after the PGE Railway came through from Squamish in 1915. Myrtle's 1920s photograph appears everywhere: she graces a beached canoe, with her catch before her, a row of 12 freshly caught silvery trout. But Myrtle and Alex have little to do with Whistler as we know it today.

Whistler is said to be named for the whistling of the little hoary marmot, its mascot. But it could also be the whistling of the winds through Singing Pass between the mountains. The real history of Whistler seems to be geological - the development of the mountains and the glaciers over millennia. Whistler's big problem now is to contain development before it overshadows the natural environment that makes this place appealing.

Outside trail and pedestrian areas, there is occasional congested vehicular traffic, especially on the access roads off Hwy 99 which cuts through the heart of the valley.

Whistler Area Information: Info Centre, Box 181, Whistler, BC, V0N 2B0. 604-932-5528. At junction of Hwy 99 and Lake Placid Rd, at Whistler Creek gondola base. In summer, extra drop-in Info Centres at Village Square and Village Gate. Daily. Information also from the Whistler Resort Association, 4010 Whistler Way, Whistler, BC, V0N 1B4. 604-932-3928. For accommodation reservations: 1-800-944-7853 or direct, 604-664-5625. Whistler Activity and Information Centre: 604-932-2394.

Whistler in Summer

Whistler Resort features an amazing variety of summer activities for all ages and interests. Some of the best bargains are to be found in summer, and you can also pick and choose where to stay, and what to do. Five pretty lakes are strung through the valley, beads on a necklace: Alpha, Nita, Alta, Lost, and Green. They offer six lakeside parks, most with beaches. A scenic 20km valley trail connects all the parks to Whistler Village. Mostly paved, the trail is ideal for strolling, jogging, in-line skating, or biking. There's also, of course, picnicking, swimming, windsurfing, canoeing, fishing, boating.

Both Whistler and Blackcomb mountains operate lifts year-round, except three to four weeks of maintenance in the fall. Blackcomb is the only mountain in North America to offer summer skiing (on Horstman Glacier). Other summer activities: golfing, horseback riding, whitewater rafting, jet-boating, kayaking, guided tours on foot, bicycle, mountain bike, bus, or plane, heli-hiking, helicopter flight-seeing, paragliding, hayrides, ATV tours. A must-do: paddling to the River of Golden Dreams between Alta and Green lakes. Black bears are often seen in the village, along trails, and beneath the chairlifts.

■ **Gondolas and Chairlift Rides:** Whistler Village. For Whistler/Blackcomb: 604-932-3434. Summer hiking, skiing, and exploring; also winter ski access to the mountains.

■ **Golf Courses: The Whistler Golf Course,** next to Whistler Village, is a richly scenic 18-hole course designed by Arnold Palmer. 604-932-4544. The **Chateau Whistler Golf Course,** designed by Robert Trent Jones II, is on the hillside of Blackcomb. Golf carts are mandatory on this strenuous course of rock faces, canyons, and waterfalls. **Nicklaus North,** designed by Jack Nicklaus, is on the shores of Green Lake. 604-938-9898. Twenty-five minutes north of Whistler is the **Big Sky Golf and Country Club,** designed by Robert Cupp. 1-800-668-7900.

Whistler in Winter

For winter, both mountains offer exceptional downhill skiing, with a combined total of more than 200 runs and 32 lifts. Whistler Mountain is the official ski area in the Lower Mainland for the Canadian National Ski Team. It has North America's second longest lift-serviced vertical at 1,530m. Blackcomb is called The Mile-High Mountain, with the longest lift-serviced vertical (1,609m) and longest uninterrupted fall-line skiing in North America. Also cross-country skiing, heli-skiing, snowmobiling, sleigh rides, and snowshoeing.

For current snow conditions on either mountain, call (from Vancouver) 604-687-7507. Locally: 604-932-4211.

■ **Chateau Whistler Resort:** Billed as a "castle in the mountains," the 12-storey, 563-room edifice constructed in 1989 is the largest resort hotel to be built in Canada since the turn of the century. The grandeur of yesteryear is translated through early Canadian pine armoires, Mennonite hooked rugs and quilts, aboriginal twig furniture, and friendly folk art from decoys and rocking horses to birdhouses. Even if you're camping, check out the Great Hall and the Mallard Bar. 604-938-8000.

■ **Whistler Museum and Archives:** 4329 Main St, Whistler Village, next to public library. 604-932-2019. Interesting small museum featuring Whistler and Rainbow Lodge nostalgia, early logging tools, and ski equipment. Slide shows, heritage walks.

Nairn Falls Provincial Park: 171ha; 88 campsites. 604-898-3678. 28km beyond Whistler. 60m Nairn Falls tumble into Green River. Hiking. Rainbow and Dolly Varden.

Pemberton: (Pop. 855). 35km beyond Whistler on Hwy 99. A farming village lying flat in a startling steep-walled alpine setting, Pemberton is proud to call itself "the disease free capital of the world for seed potatoes." Surrounding mountains hide delightful, relatively unknown, hot springs. A host of other outdoor activities: golf, hiking, fishing, llama treks, horseback riding, river rafting, glider tours, jet boating (to Nairn Falls or Skookumchuck Village). Pemberton's sleepiness is ending as more of Whistler's work force seeks cheaper accommodation here. It is also becoming a recreational centre in its own right.

A well-maintained road, paved then gravel, goes northwest to Pemberton Meadows, continuing northeast through to Gold Bridge. Road is paved for only about 23km. Just before pavement ends, road forks. Take right onto Lillooet Forest Rd (north side of Lillooet River). A few kilometres farther, there's a junction: turn right (northeast) over Hurley Pass to hook up with Bridge River Rd along Carpenter Lake. See Side Trip to Gold Bridge and Bralorne, *Lillooet Road,* p.123.

Pemberton Information: Information centre in town centre at junction of Hwy 99 and Portage Rd. Daily, mid-June to Aug. Pemberton Chamber of Commerce, Box 370, Pemberton, BC, V0N 2L0. 604-894-6175.

Golf and ski seasons overlap at Whistler.

■ **Pemberton Museum:** 7424 Prospects St, Pemberton Village. Daily July-Aug, or by appointment. Main buildings focus on two cultures. Settler's house contains Fraser River gold-rush exhibits. Two other houses on site originally belonged to Lil'wat peoples in Mount Currie and D'Arcy, near Pemberton.

■ **Pemberton Soaring Centre:** At Pemberton Airport, 3km east of Pemberton.1-800-831-2611. Daily, April-Sept. Glide over glaciers. 20-minute flights and longer.

■ **Skookumchuck Hot Springs:** 77km south on the Lillooet River, on the original Cariboo Wagon Rd (rougher than a washboard, potholes are deep). One of the springs, **The St Agnes Well,** was named in the 1860s by Judge Matthew Baillie Begbie. Natural and undeveloped. The hot spring and the cold spring intermingle under a cedar A-frame, where taps let bathers adjust the temperatures. On private land, springs are taken care of by users. Very crowded on weekends.

Mount Currie: (Pop. 1,400). 6km east of Pemberton on Hwy 99. Village is the base of the busy Mount Currie Reserve, the Lil'wat group of the St'at'imc Nation. The village, which sits under a mountain of the same name, is noted for its rodeo, held twice a year, on long weekends in May and Sept. Mount Currie was named after a Scot, John Currie, who took up ranching in the area with his Lillooet native wife in 1885 after failing to strike it rich in the California and Cariboo gold rushes.

Southeast of the old village, near Lillooet Lake, is Xitolacw, the newest subdivision of Mount Currie, with a school and community centre. Near the start of the Duffey Lake Rd, take a north turn uphill for 4km.

The Spirit Circle Art, Craft and Tea Company is among a handful of small Mount Currie Mount Currie businesses well worth visiting.

■ **Native Cultural Learning Centre/WD Bar Ranch Lil'wat Adventures:** Box 239, Mount Currie, BC, V0N 2K0. Messages: 604-894-5669. North America's First Nations broncoriding champion introduces visitors to area's landscape and history on guided horse-pack and canoe trips.

Road to D'Arcy: North out of Mount Currie. This is part of the old Douglas Trail, the original (and arduous) route to the Cariboo gold fields in 1858. The trail was actually a series of portages between four big lakes (Harrison, Lillooet, Anderson, and Seton) from the upper Fraser Valley to Lillooet. This section, which follows the Birkenhead River for about its first 15km, was the trail between Lillooet and Anderson lakes. It was abandoned when the Cariboo Road over the Fraser Canyon was completed in 1863. BC Rail tracks between North Vancouver and Lillooet also follows this route, which goes over Pemberton Pass.

SIDE TRIP

to D'Arcy

This paved road has opened up rugged mountain scenery to recreation and tourism. It winds 38km to D'Arcy at the southwestern end of dazzling Anderson Lake. From Mount Currie, turn north, following the Birkenhead River. Two Forest Service campsites are found along the first 10km.

Fee Creek Spawning and Rearing Channel: About 10km north of Mt Currie. Look for BC Wildlife Watch viewing signs. Protected channel, trails, coho salmon Nov-Dec.

Birken: (Pop. 109). 23km from Mount Currie. Just over Pemberton Pass, on Gates Lake. Settlement for logging, farming, and tourism. Camping and cabins at resort across from Gates Lake.

Devine: (Pop. 35). 29km from Mount Currie. Former sawmill site. A smattering of residents remain.

Birkenhead Lake Provincial Park: 9,755ha; 85 campsites plus six walk-in. Turn northwest at Devine. Good gravel road, 18km to park facilities. In snow-topped Coast Mountains, remote 6km-long Birkenhead Lake provides fishing for kokanee, rainbow trout, Dolly Varden, whitefish. In spring, mountain goats may be seen on nearby cliffs. During spring and summer check Phelix Creek for spawning kokanee.

D'Arcy: (Pop. 60). A First Nations community. Great view of an imposing lake. Two private lakeside campgrounds. To go farther up the lake one encounters a challenging 4x4 road, not for faint of heart. It goes up and down mountain to Seton Portage, between Anderson and Seton lakes, and then on to Bridge River Rd into Lillooet. See also *Lillooet Road*, p.123.

■ **Gates Creek Spawning Channel:** Before reaching the end of the road in D'Arcy, turn right at the old church and cross the bridge.

Spawning channel is immediately on the right. The first sockeye begin moving up the fish ladder mid-Aug. BC Wildlife Watch viewing site.

Return to Mount Currie and Highway 99

Start of Duffey Lake Rd (Hwy 99): The Duffey Lake Rd officially begins about 9km past Mount Currie, on the northwestern shore of Lillooet Lake, where the Birkenhead River outflows.

Until recently, this dramatic 84.5km route through the Cayoosh Range to the Cariboo was strictly 4x4 fare. Some $22.5 million later, the Duffey Lake Rd is paved and widened, and it's pavement all the way from Pemberton to Lillooet (100km total). The road opens up the Pemberton area even more for recreation activities, and gives travellers and locals a direct and reliable route into the Cariboo.

It's an exciting route (a magnet for wannabe Hell's Angels), traversing two climactic zones, from the Coast Mountains through to semi-arid ranchlands. This was originally a logging road, not a tourist route, so drive with utmost care and attention. One memorable stretch features a sequence of three double-backed switchbacks. The first half of the road traverses mountains, eventually tracking the south shore of narrow 6.5km-long Duffey Lake to its eastern point.

Joffre Lakes Provincial Park: 1,460ha. About 10km from start of Duffey Lake Rd. 604-898-3678. Features a trail connecting three turquoise lakes with the road. Short walk to the first lake is worthwhile for the view.

Duffey Lake Provincial Park: 2,379ha. About 37km from start of Duffey Lake Rd. 604-898-3678. Former Forest Service recreation site provides basic facilities for camping and boating. Worthwhile stop to stretch legs and view landscape transition from wet coastal forest to dry highland plateau.

Halfway Mark: 42km from start of Duffey Lake Rd. Say goodbye to Duffey Lake. From here, road follows pretty Cayoosh Creek down toward Lillooet. And it will be downhill much of the way: expect a 13 percent grade at some points, one of the steepest grades in BC. The road is very beautiful, with thimbleberries and all, but there are few pullouts, and there can be rocks on the road (lots of rocks).

Seton Lake: About 80km from start of Duffey Lake Rd and 5km from Lillooet. With a whiff of sagebrush in the air, the road opens high on a vista of stunning green Seton Lake. Good picnic area and camping down on lakeshore.

BC Hydro Dam: 1km from Seton Lake (down an 11 percent grade). Left of highway. Dams Seton Creek.

Seton Creek Spawning Channel: Just beyond Hydro Dam, left of highway.

Pink salmon return here to spawn in early Oct, every other year, in the odd years. Displays of life cycle of salmon.

Lillooet: (Pop. 1,988). 84.5km northeast of start of Duffey Lake Rd. From this point, go north on Hwy 99 (formerly Hwy 12) to Hwy 97 just north of Cache Creek; or south on old Hwy 12 to Lytton. See *Lillooet Road,* below.

These limestone formations give Marble Canyon Park its name.

LILLOOET ROAD

HIGHWAYS 99 AND 12

The Lillooet Road loops from a point on the Cariboo Hwy (Hwy 97) 11km north of Cache Creek and leads in a vaguely westerly fashion 75km to Lillooet (this part is an extension of Hwy 99 through from Whistler, and used to be called Hwy 12). Then the Lillooet Rd (here still called Hwy 12) continues southeast from Lillooet along the Fraser River another 64km to Lytton and the Trans-Canada Hwy 1.

In terms of awesome scenery, this is perhaps the most underrated route in BC. As it follows the churning Fraser River, the road twists, climbs, and descends in hair-raising hairpin bends. Often the river is pressed in by mountainsides, with the road carved into the cliffs high above. There are struggling pine trees and sagebrush. Intriguing homesteads appear in gaps between verticals. As you peer down and over the Fraser you might see a bench with an irrigated field on it – a deep green blotch in the vast brown. At one end of the ride, just as you pass the viewpoint where the blue waters of the North Thompson River blast out into the yellow-brown surge of the Fraser, you find yourself suddenly on a quiet residential street in Lytton. It's like being beamed down from the moon into a familiar back yard.

The Lillooet Rd gives access to the largely undeveloped wilderness beyond Bralorne and

Bridge River, at the south end of the Chilcotin. Lillooet itself, the heart of one of the driest regions in BC, offers its Golden Mile of History, a rockhound's paradise, and a healthful, insect-free climate attested to by the advanced ages noted on pioneers' tombstones.

The *Log* begins at the Hwy 99 turnoff from Hwy 97, and proceeds south.

Highways 97 and 99: 11km north of Cache Creek. Hwy 99 travels in a westerly fashion 75km to Lillooet.

Hat Creek Ranch: At junction of Hwys 97 and 99. Details on p.243.

Marble Canyon Provincial Park: 335ha; 26 campsites. 250-851-3000. About 28km west of Hwy 99 junction. June-Sept. The 1,000m limestone cliffs of Marble Canyon give the park its name. Camping, picnicking, paddling, swimming, fishing, hiking. Crown and Turquoise lakes. Trail to waterfall and Teapot Rock formation. Native plants include coyote willow, used by St'at'imc and Secwepemc aboriginal peoples for rope making, and soapberry, the berries whipped with water to make Indian ice cream.

Pavilion Lake: About 30km west of Hwy 97 junction. A car-stopper. (Trout, too.)

Pavilion Rd: About 5km past Pavilion Lake, 35km west of Hwy 97. Leads north 31km to Clinton, over 2,089m Pavilion Mountain. For local First Nations this was an important harvesting place for roots and bulbs and a deer-hunting site. In the early 1860s, the main Cariboo road came through here. It was the first wagon road in BC to be surveyed (in 1863, by Royal Engineer Sgt James McMurphy). Passengers had to push the coaches uphill, and freight wagons dragged logs as brakes on down grades. Spectacular views and the old Carson Ranch as well. The road is part gravel, part paved, and pretty narrow. May be closed in winter; check locally, and if there's been so much as a drop of rain, pass this one by. Muddy curves are treacherous.

Note: About 15km from Hwy 99, Pavilion Rd forks at **Kelly Lake**. Take right (northeast) fork 16km to Clinton; northwest is the Jesmond Rd connecting 39km north with Big Bar Rd. The Cariboo is laced with fascinating back roads like these. Details in *Cariboo Country* p.243.

Fraser Benchlands: For the next 40km, from Marble Canyon south to Lillooet, the highway skirts the upper Fraser Canyon. Semi-desert benchlands high above the river are often irrigated to produce crops or pasture. Benchlands lie at the original level of the land in this region. The deeply incised cliffs that descend to the river are the result of centuries of erosion by water and weather. Here, the highway corkscrews in a long, dazzling descent to Lillooet.

Road to Lillooet: 75km from Hwy 97 junction. West into Lillooet across Bridge of the 23 Camels.

Bridge of the 23 Camels: Built in 1981, crossing the Fraser River at Lillooet. Named for ill-fated beasts brought as freight carriers during Cariboo Gold Rush. In May 1862, the two-humped Bactrian camels arrived at Port Douglas, at the head of Harrison Lake. By 1864 this Dromedary Express had been disbanded. The rocky landscape was too harsh for their large flat feet, but the stubborn camels also made it hard on themselves by refusing to fit in socially. Indiscriminate in their discrimination, they bit and kicked mules, oxen, and men. They ate everything, including laundry, and their potent odour was so offensive that other pack animals bolted in fear. Some camels died in snow storms, others were shot and eaten.

Lillooet: (Pop. 1,988). 86km north and west of Cache Creek; 64km north of Lytton. Community takes its name from the Lil'wat First Nations people to the west across the Coast Mountains, based in Mount Currie. They are closely related to the St'at'imc people who once lived on the site now occupied by Lillooet, and now live just above the town. Some of the most productive aboriginal salmon-fishing sites are on the banks of the Fraser River at Lillooet and at the rapids near Bridge River, 6km upriver by road from the north end of town.

The town of Lillooet, incorporated in 1946, dates back to the Cariboo Gold Rush. It was terminus of the boat route north through Harrison and Anderson lakes, and the beginning of the first Cariboo Road. By 1863, Lillooet had a population of 15,000 and claimed to be the second-largest town north of San Francisco.

As oxen cannot be backed up, Lillooet's main street was made wide enough to turn a double freight wagon hauled by the 10 yoke-spans of oxen required to pull 20t over the 2,000m Pavilion summit.

More recently, resident legend Ma Murray put Lillooet on the map. With her husband, George, Ma founded the *Bridge River-Lillooet News* in 1934, the liveliest weekly in the province. A tough-talking, down-to-earth editor who snorted snuff and smoked hand-rolled cigarettes as she pounded away on her old typewriter, Ma's pungent commentaries on politics and events were quoted across Canada.

In a 1975 interview with *Beautiful British Columbia Magazine*, when she was 88 years old and still living in her big white house on Lillooet's main street, Ma Murray said: "We moved up here in 1933 with the children and everything, and, oh, we've been rewarded. It's like casting your bread on the waters and it comes back with nuts and raisins and cinnamon on it. It's a fabulous country and anybody would be a sap that ever got a chance to get into it that didn't stay. It couldn't help but fascinate anyone who ever came here. Lillooet just couldn't miss." Margaret Lally Murray died in 1982 at age 94.

Lillooet Information: Info Centre, Box 441, Lillooet, BC, V0K 1V0. 250-256-4308. 790 Main St. Shares former Anglican church with village museum. Daily, July-Aug. Afternoons, on shoulder months. Closed winter. Off-season: 250-256-4556.

■ **Mile 0 Cairn:** Main St, in the centre of Lillooet, marks beginning of first Cariboo Road. The towns and villages on the Cariboo Road that incorporate mileages into their names number from this point. Cairn is part of Lillooet's Golden Mile of History, with 15 historic points of interest along the town's main streets.

■ **Hangman's Tree:** On the benchland above Main St. Said to be one of the places where "Hanging" Judge Matthew Baillie Begbie meted out justice in the 1860s: probably a slander on the name of a man strict but fair, who rarely sentenced anyone to die.

■ **Old Newspaper Office:** Main St. Former haunt of famed frontier journalist Ma Murray. Her newspaper guaranteed "a chuckle every week and a belly laugh once a month or your money back." Equipment is now in museum (see below).

■ **Lillooet Museum:** With Info Centre, in former St Mary's Anglican Church. Box 441, Main St, Lillooet, BC, V0K 1V0. 250-256-4308. Daily, July-Aug. Off season: 250-256-4556. Afternoons, on shoulder months. Local pioneer and mining artifacts, First Nations artifacts, Chinese utensils, Ma Murray's printing press, and a Ma Murray family video.

■ **Miyazaki Heritage House:** 6th Ave off Main St. Built in the 1890s, occupied by Dr Masajiro Miyazaki and family after he was interned in wartime evacuation, then sent to provide medical care for Japanese evacuated to the Lillooet area. Recipient of the Order of Canada for his pioneering medical work.

■ **Rockhounding:** This is one of BC's finest rockhounding areas, with jade, agate, and other semi-precious stones. Largest jade boulder found to date weighed more than 16t.

■ **Gold Panning:** Cayoosh Creek Park. Ask at Info Centre.

■ **Golf: Sheep Pasture Golf Course**, On Texas Creek Rd, 8km south of town. Local farmer Dave Jones has converted his 600ha sheep pasture to dual use. Now sheep must share their turf with golfers. "Never a baaaad round," Jones boasts. Fabulous views of Fraser River and mountains, especially from second hole.

■ **Chinese Rock Piles:** Two locations. On Main St below Hangman's Tree Park, and by old suspension bridge. Tailings left by Chinese miners are evidence of their efforts.

■ **Cariboo Chilcotin Helicopters Ltd:** Nugget Rd, Lillooet, BC, V0K 1V0. 250-256-4888. Wilderness adventures, photo safaris.

Bridge River Rd: West from Main St at north end of town.

SIDE TRIP

to Gold Bridge and Bralorne

Bridge River Rd, gravel, leads west 100km to Gold Bridge, 7km further to Bralorne. This is also the route to Tyax Mountain Lake Resort, one of two side trips off this side trip. This is a drive for the adventurous. The first 47km of this precipitous road features hairpin turns as it mainly follows the Bridge River, twisting high above it or dipping down into its

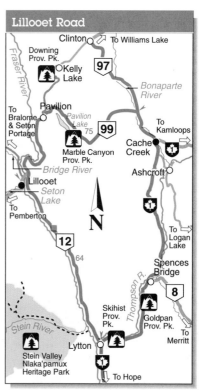

Lillooet Road

eerie canyons. All along the river are old gold claims going back as far as 1859. The first excursion off this road, just as you reach Carpenter Lake, is the thrilling Seton Portage Rd that takes the heroic driver over a mountain to the Shalalth powerhouse and to historic Seton Portage. The last half of the Bridge River Rd skirts the north shores of sinewy Carpenter Lake and allows for more relaxed breathing. For the second excursion off the Gold River Rd, look for Tyaughton Lake Rd to Tyax Resort about 43km along Carpenter Lake.

Terzaghi Dam: 47km from Lillooet, at the base of Mission Mountain near Carpenter Lake, at junction with Seton Portage Rd. Intake structures above the dam divert Bridge River through Mission Mountain via two long tunnels with a vertical drop of 326m down to powerhouses at Shalalth, on Seton Portage Rd.

Seton Portage Rd: 47km from Lillooet, at eastern tip of Carpenter Lake. Goes south 18km over spiralling Mission Pass down to Shalalth (pronounced "shalath") and Seton Portage on Seton Lake. Descent to Seton Lake is a dramatic 1,300m. Road is gravel, safe for most vehicles, but trailers not recommended.

Shalalth: On Seton Portage Rd, 17km south of Hwy 40. Site of Bridge River hydroelectric complex, and powerhouses #1 and #2. Tours on request. Also picnics, boat-launching site.

Seton Portage: (Pop. 96). Just 1km west along the lake from Shalalth, 65km beyond Lillooet. Seton Portage was site of first railway in BC, using wooden rails to portage supplies between Anderson and Seton lakes in gold-rush days. Each lake is some 210m deep. Today, a small spirited community.

■ **Seton Portage Provincial Park:** 1ha. Beside information centre caboose on Seton Portage Rd. May-Oct. Day use.

Carpenter Lake: Hwy 40 follows north shore of Carpenter Lake for 53km west from Seton Portage Rd junction and Terzaghi Dam to Gold Bridge. Several Forest Service recreation sites on Carpenter Lake.

Tyaughton Lake Rd: Turn north 90km beyond Lillooet. Tyaughton means "lake of the jumping fish." This is also home territory of cougars, black bears, mountain goats, and California bighorn sheep.

■ **Tyax Mountain Lake Resort:** 5km north of Hwy 40 on Tyaughton Lake Rd. Tyax Mountain Lake Resort, Tyaughton Lake Rd, Gold Bridge, BC, V0K 1P0. 250-238-2221. Luxury resort includes a stunning lodge, said to be the largest log structure on the West Coast. Heli-skiing, tennis, riding, beach, canoes, sailboats, hot tub, sauna, fitness centre. Shuttle service from Lillooet train station.

Gold Bridge: (Pop. 68). 10km west of Tyaughton Lake Rd, 100km west of Lillooet. Resort community. Fishing, public gold panning on east bank of Hurley River, access to mountain snowmobiling, ski touring, hiking, riding. Guest ranches, lodges, Forest Service recreation sites all nearby.

Bralorne: (Pop. 78). 7km beyond Gold Bridge. Home in 1920s to the Bralorne Pioneer Mine, the richest gold claim in Canada, producing over $145 million worth of gold before it closed in 1970. Historic area is now home to resorts featuring a variety of wilderness activities: fishing, trail riding, sailing, ghost-town tours. Hiking and ski touring on Warner Pass Trail, Chism Pass Trail, and McGillivray Pass Trail, day-use trails near townsite. Cross-country skiing, sleigh rides, snowshoeing.

■ **Bralorne Pioneer Museum:** 250-238-2349. Thurs-Mon, 10-4, July-early Sept. Off-season: 250-238-2240. Mining equipment, photos of miners and families.

Return to Lillooet and Bridge of the 23 Camels

Duffey Lake Rd (Hwy 99): At this point, the Lillooet Road continues south from Lillooet on Hwy 12 along the east bank of the Fraser River, and we leave Hwy 99.

For your information, what Hwy 99 does is cross the Fraser at the Bridge of 23 Camels, and travel south over Cayoosh Creek. From here it continues southwest to Seton Lake, Duffey Lake, Pemberton, and through to Whistler, Squamish, and Horseshoe Bay on the coast. It is an excellent paved road. A circle tour from Vancouver is possible using Hwy 99 (including the Duffey Lake Rd), Hwy 12, and Hwy 1. See *Horseshoe Bay to Lillooet*, p.122.

Lillooet Road (Highway 12)

The following 64km between Lillooet and Lytton are exciting. "You're fine as long as you don't look up," advised the girl in the bakery in Lillooet. Another word of advice: don't look down either. Rocks can skelter down from above, especially in a rainstorm (rain is infrequent), and far below are the yellow-brown swirling waters of the Fraser Canyon. Just keep driving.

Texas Creek Rest Area: 19km south of Lillooet.

Ginseng Farming: 30km south of Lillooet. Stretching out over the Fraser benchlands are endless rows of mysterious crops shaded with black plastic screening. It's ginseng, and this area is the world's largest producer of North American ginseng. There are a total of 1,400ha under cultivation in BC, 70 percent in this region. "So much ginseng, so little time." The screening is polypropylene shade cloth. Ginseng requires deep shade for growth, and its water requirements must be strictly controlled, thus the attraction of this exceedingly dry region (ginseng is also being grown in the Merritt and Kamloops area). Seeds take at least 18 months to germinate. Exported to Asian markets, it is belived to combat weakness and increase energy. Write Chai-Na-Ta Ginseng Products, 5965 205A St, Langley, BC, V3A 8C4.

Lytton Ferry: 61.5km southeast of Lillooet on Hwy 12. To Stein Valley Nlaka'pamux Heritage Park (see p.137). Five-minute crossing. Reaction ferry carries 9t. Two vehicles or 20 passengers.

Lytton: (Pop. 322). 2.5km south of Lytton Ferry, 64km south of Lillooet. For details on Lytton, see p.137.

VANCOUVER TO HOPE SOUTH BANK

TRANS-CANADA HIGHWAY (Highway 1)

The Trans-Canada Hwy starts from Mile Zero in Victoria, travels north up-island to Nanaimo, and crosses from there to the mainland at Horseshoe Bay. Eastbound travellers can pick up Hwy 1 at any spot that is convenient to them (the North Shore; or south across the Second Narrows Bridge into Vancouver or Burnaby; or at any points farther east). Follow the route map provided, and the Gateway map, p.96, which has even more details on web of intersections from Vancouver to just beyond Abbotsford.

The Trans-Canada Hwy between Vancouver and Hope is a direct and efficient route. It leads through Burnaby, skirts New Westminster, and bears east providing access to Langley, Aldergrove, Clearbrook, Abbotsford, and Chilliwack before reaching Hope. It traverses BC's most heavily populated strip. About half of all British Columbians live in Vancouver or the Fraser Valley, on or near this route. Yet it is

attractive, leading not only through densely populated areas and zones of heavy industry, but also through rich agricultural country, with rolling farmlands and historic villages. And all the while, the mountains rise, blue and shadowy on the edges of the valley.

Via Hwy 1, the distance to Hope from downtown Vancouver at the south end of the Second Narrows Bridge (the junction of Hwys 1 and 7A) is 147km.

Ironworkers Memorial Second Narrows Bridge: Hwy 1, spanning Burrard Inlet to link the North Shore with Vancouver and Burnaby. Name commemorates 23 workers who died during the bridge's construction in 1958. BC's worst-ever construction disaster occurred when the nearly completed structure collapsed and hurled several dozen workers into Burrard Inlet. 18 people died; five died in other construction accidents on the bridge. Burrard Inlet was the focus of early development, and today is the city's busy deep-water port. The inlet extends east, past the Reed Point Marina, to Port Moody, and north, beyond Deep Cove, to Wigwam Inn on Indian Arm. For details, see *North Shore*, p.103.

PNE Grounds and Racetrack: Just over the bridge, exit right (west) at Hastings St for Pacific National Exhibition Park. Details under *Vancouver*, p.99.

Boundary Rd: 3km beyond junction of Hwys 1 and 7A. Hwy 1 crosses Boundary Rd which marks the boundary between Vancouver and Burnaby. Exit here for Burnaby, and for further details, see p.104.

Grandview Hwy: Just past Boundary Rd junction, Grandview Hwy (an extension of 12th Ave) comes in from the west and dissolves into Hwy 1.

Willingdon Ave: Just over 1km beyond Grandview Hwy junction. Exit for Burnaby, or for connections with Hwys 1A/99A (south), or Hwys 7 and 7A (north).

Burnaby: (Pop. 179,209). 10km from Vancouver city centre. Exit from Hwy 1 at Willingdon Ave, Sprott St, Cariboo Interchange. Vancouver's immediate eastern neighbour, see p.104.

Sprott St: 3.5km beyond Willingdon Ave Interchange. Exit to Sprott St north, turn east to **Burnaby Lake Regional Park.** Exit at Sprott St south to Canada Way. Follow signs from junction of Sprott St and Canada Way to **Deer Lake and park.** For info on Burnaby Lake and Deer Lake, see p.104.

Cariboo Rd Interchange: 4km beyond Sprott St junction. Exit north, follow road to Gaglardi Way. Gaglardi Way leads 6km to **Simon Fraser University** and **Burnaby Mountain Park.** For info, see *Burnaby*, p.104.

Brunette Ave Interchange: Nearly 3km beyond Cariboo Rd. Exit south and drive 1km to New Westminster.

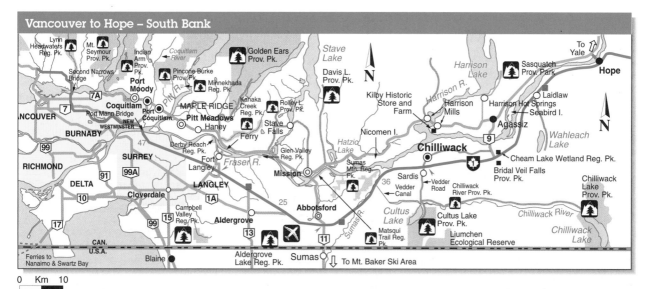

Vancouver to Hope – South Bank

0 Km 10

New Westminster: (Pop: 49,350) Turn south 1km beyond junction of Hwy 1 and Brunette Rd. See p.105.

Lougheed Highway (Hwy 7): 4.5km beyond Brunette Rd Interchange. Exit north to **Coquitlam.** Follow signs to Hwy 7 (Lougheed Hwy) and travel 9km to **Port Coquitlam.** For info on Coquitlam and Port Coquitlam, see *Vancouver to Hope - North Bank,* p.130.

Port Mann Bridge: Crosses Fraser River 2km beyond Lougheed Hwy (Hwy 7) Interchange. Links Coquitlam with Surrey. Bridge is 2,094m long, 16.5m wide.

Fraser River Delta and Estuary: Northwest of Port Mann Bridge, the Pitt and Coquitlam rivers flow into the Fraser River. One of the most productive fish and wildlife areas of the world. As many as 300 million young salmon leave the estuary every year. More than one million migrating waterfowl stop here on their way between Siberia and South America.

Surrey: (Pop: 245,173). Immediately beyond the Port Mann Bridge on Hwy 1. Once BC's largest municipality in terms of area, covering 203 sq km. Now officially a city. For details, see p.106.

152nd St (Johnston Rd): 9km beyond the Lougheed Hwy Interchange. Exit south into the heart of Surrey and its five townships (Whalley, Sunnyside, Newton, Guildford, and Cloverdale); continue farther south to White Rock (22km south of Hwy 1). Details for *Surrey,* p.106; for White Rock, p.108.

Highway 15 (176th St or Pacific Hwy): 6km beyond l52nd St junction. Turn south, through Surrey (and township of Cloverdale), 21km to Douglas Border Crossing (Canada/US).

Carvolth Rd (200th St): 6km beyond Hwy 15 junction. Exit south 8km to city of Langley (first of two main exits off Hwy 1 to the city).

Highway 10: 8km beyond Carvolth Rd junction. Exit south and drive 9km to **Langley.** From there it's 48km southwest to Tsawwassen and BC Ferries Terminal. Exit north on Hwy 10, 1km to **Fort Langley.**

SIDE TRIP

to Fort Langley and Langley

Fort Langley: (Pop. 16,200). 2km beyond southern terminus of Albion Ferry (see below). First European establishment in Fraser Valley, originally part of a network of trading posts established by the Hudson's Bay Company.

The first fort site, built 1827, was about 4km downriver from here. It was abandoned so company employees could be closer to larger tracts of fertile land for farming. The second fort was built in 1838, on an 8,000-year-old archaeological site. In the late 1850s, Fort Langley became a starting-off point for the Fraser gold fields. Today, as well as being a gold mine of history, Fort Langley is a thriving agricultural and residential area with plenty of tourist services.

Fort Langley Information: Info Centre (CN Heritage Station), 23245 Glover Rd, Langley, BC, V1M 2R4. 604-513-8787. Daily, May-Sept. Off-season call: 604-888-1477.

Albion Ferry: 604-467-7298. Free. Daily every 15 minutes from 5am-1am across the Fraser, giving motorists a direct connection between Hwy 1 on the south shore, and Hwy 7 on the north. (See *Vancouver to Hope – Highway 7,* p.132, for connecting points on north shore.)

■ **BC Farm Machinery and Agricultural Museum:** 9131 Kings St. Downtown Fort Langley. 604-888-2273. Daily, April to mid-Oct. Collection of machinery from many areas of BC, notably Fraser Valley. Also, household furnishings, logging and fishing equipment.

■ **Langley Centennial Museum and National Exhibition Centre:** Corner of Mavis and King. 604-888-3922. Daily, summer; Tues-Sun, off-season. Sto:lo First Nation, 19th-century pioneer. Re-created rooms include home-

steader's kitchen, Victorian parlour, and Noel Booth General Store. Year-round exhibits and programs. An active museum!

■ **Fort Langley National Historic Park:** 23433 Mavis St, on banks of Fraser River across from McMillan Island. 604-513-4777. Daily. From the time of its construction in 1827 to its decline in the 1880s, Fort Langley played a major role in the development of what is now the province of BC.

The fort functioned primarily as a provisioning and administrative centre for Hudson's Bay Company operations in the Pacific Northwest. Through its gates passed the adventurers who opened up the mountainous interior: traders travelling the Brigade Trail north in search of furs for "the Company," and later, some 30,000 prospectors heading for the gold fields of the upper Fraser River.

The fort depended on the region's Sto:lo people, who provided a steady supply of furs and salmon, and labour for agricultural pursuits. At its peak, the fort distributed one to two thousand barrels of salmon each year to distant company outposts. Each barrel weighed up to 365kg.

It was in the "big house" at Fort Langley that BC was declared a Crown colony in 1858. Operations ceased here in 1886. The site deteriorated until 1923 when it was declared "of national historic interest," and marked with a commemorative plaque. In May 1955, the fort was established as a national historic park. Careful restoration work has been done on the palisades, buildings, furnishings to create a glimpse of Canada's pioneering past. Costumed staff demonstrate blacksmithing, barrel making, pioneer cooking.

■ **Fraser River Cruises:** 604-525-4465 or fax 604-525-5944 (New Westminster) for info on Paddle Wheeler River Adventures between New Westminster and Fort Langley. Riverside views of Haney, Port Hammond, Surrey, Pitt Meadows, Coquitlam, and Whalley. Boat docks at Fort Pub and Riverside Centre, 9273 Glover Rd, in Fort Langley.

■ **Glen Valley Regional Park:** 112ha. From Fort Langley follow River Rd east tracing the Fraser's south bank. Also accessible from Hwy

1, east of Fort Langley, by taking 264th St north to River Rd, then right (River Rd is marked 88 Ave here). 604-432-6350. Park includes Crescent Island (only accessible by boat) offshore from Poplar Bar. Popular fishing areas are Two-Bit Bar, Poplar Bar, Duncan Bar.

Langley: (Pop. 80,179). Heart is at Carvolth Rd and Hwy 10, 9km south of Hwy 1. There are actually two Langleys – the district municipality, and the city in the middle of that. Each has its own mayor. The District Municipality of Langley stretches from the Canada/US border north to the Fraser River. This is an important farming and residential area.

Langley Information: Info Centre, Unit 1-5761 Glover Rd, Langley, BC, V3A 8M8. 604-530-6656. Weekdays.

■ **Canadian Museum of Flight:** Langley Airport, Hangar 3, 5333-216 St. 604-532-0035. Year-round. One of two places in the world where you can see a Second World War Handley Page Hampden bomber: it was brought up from the bottom of the Strait of Georgia in 1986.

■ **Derby Reach Regional Park:** 304ha. Camping. Near Fort Langley off 200 St on Allard Cres. 604-432-6350. Edgewater Bar is considered one of the finest fishing bars on the Fraser River. Camping, picnicking, walking. Houston Trail, further east, provides 4km of hiking and equestrian use. Park was site of original Fort Langley and the township of Derby, and now houses the historic Karr/Mercer Barn (circa 1878) and Houston House (1909).

■ **Campbell Valley Regional Park:** 533ha. From Hwy 1 eastbound take 200th St exit south for 14.5km. Turn left at 8th Ave, look for park signs. 604-432-6350. Diverse natural habitats created by logging, farming, irrigation. 20km of walking trails, horseback riding, picnics, group camp, and butterfly garden. Annand/Rowlatt Farm, built 1888 and Lochiel School, 1924. Visitor centre programs July-Aug. BC Wildlife Watch viewing site.

■ **Blair Recreation Centre:** 22200 Fraser Hwy. 604-533-6170. Daily, year-round. Wave machine makes bathers feel they're face to face with the Pacific. Volcano erupts, lights flash. Waterfall, fitness centre, sauna.

Return to Highway 1

264th St (Hwy 13): 7km beyond Hwy 10 junction. Exit south 4km to Hwy 1A (Fraser Hwy), Aldergrove, and the Aldergrove/Lynden border crossing.

Aldergrove: (Pop. 9,600). 5km beyond junction of Hwys 1 and 13, on Hwy 1A. On south side of lower Fraser Valley, near Fraser River. Named for abundant second growth of alder trees. Famous for dairy, chicken, raspberry, and strawberry farms.

Aldergrove Information: 27256 Fraser Hwy, Langley. 604-856-8383. Weekdays, summer; Mon, Wed, Fri, 9am-1am, off-season. Or write Langley Info Centre, above.

■ **Greater Vancouver Zoological Centre:**

5048-264th St. 604-856-6825. 48ha. Daily. From Aoudads to Zebras, more than 100 species from around the world, including giraffes, jaguars, hippos, and rhinos. Petting zoo, train rides.

■ **Aldergrove Lake Regional Park:** 250ha. Junction of Hwy 13 and Huntingdon Rd. Enter off 8th Ave, 5km south of Aldergrove and 1.5km east of Hwy 13. 604-432-6350. Small, manmade lake surrounded by gently rolling hills and meadows. Walking, picnicking, swimming, cycling, equestrian trails, dogs off-leash area. Excellent views of Mt Baker (3,285m) just south of the border in Washington State. North America's answer to Mt Fuji, picturesque Mt Baker is one of a chain of volcanoes in the Cascade Range that includes Mt St Helens in Oregon, which erupted catastrophically in 1980.

■ **Aldergrove/Lynden Border Crossing:** Alternate route from Fraser Valley and Hwy 1 to US. Duty Free Shop at border crossing for tourists leaving Canada.

Bradner Rest Area: About 6km east of Hwy 13 junction. For westbound traffic only.

Mt Lehman Rd (Exit 83): 10km east of Hwy 13 junction. South 3km to Abbotsford International Airport/Tradex Conference Centre.

Abbotsford International Airport: On Mt Lehman Rd, 3km south of Hwy 1. 604-855-1001. A regional airport. Contact individual airlines for info on arrivals and departures. Site of the **Abbotsford International Airshow**, biggest in North America attracting 250,000 people every Aug. 604-852-8511 (more info below). For **Tradex Conference Centre**: 604-850-1533.

Clearbrook Rd (Exit 87): 8km beyond Mt Lehman Rd. South 2.5km to Matsqui Recreation Centre.

McCallum Rd (Exit 90): 4km beyond Clearbrook Rd. South 4km to Abbotsford Visitor Info Centre.

Highway 11/Sumas Way (Exit 92): 2.5km beyond McCallum Rd. Exit (north) to enter Abbotsford. Mission, on north bank of Fraser River, is 11km beyond Abbotsford on Hwy 11. For details see *Vancouver to Hope – North Bank*, p.132. Hwy 11 exit south leads 4km to the Sumas (Canada/US) border crossing, and beyond to Mt Baker ski area in Washington State.

Abbotsford: (Pop: 105,403). 25km beyond Langley on Hwy 1. The "City in the Country" covers 357 square kilometres – fertile farmland stretching from the US border north to the Fraser River, west to Langley and east to Chilliwack. And it takes in eight communities – Sumas, Matsqui, Clayburn Village, Mt Lehman, Bradner, Clearbrook, Huntingdon, and the old village of Abbotsford – all now officially Abbotsford, "the largest city in the Fraser Valley." Recent population growth

has blurred the old boundaries somewhat, but each community clings to its own identity.

In the wake of the 1858 gold rush, the cedar forests that once prevailed here were cleared for farmland. Half a dozen new villages emerged and thrived from the fledgling logging industry, and sawmilling. Then farms took root in the region's rich soil. In 1910, this side of the Fraser River was connected to "distant" coastal cities by the BC Electric railway. The service, which became known as the "milk run," delivered people and their produce – fresh milk and cream – to the coast. In 1919, in a hunger for more farmland, a scheme was set in motion to drain and dike Sumas Lake, a vast and shallow lake covering the district's western precincts. This also happened to be the long time "food basket" of the Kw'ekw'i:qw people, more commonly referred to today as the Sumas First Nation. Their main village overlooked marshy shores thriving with migrating waterfowl and rich vegetation. The lake became 6,500ha of farmland, planted with hops and tobacco.

Abbotsford today celebrates itself as "the Raspberry Capital of Canada" – North America's second largest producer of raspberries, with an estimated annual production of 15.5 million kilos. The hop and tobacco farms of Sumas Prairie are now dairy farms – producing famous Fraser Valley dairy products. The village of Bradner is "the Daffodil Capital of Canada." There also are ostrich and llama farms, kiwi and vegetable farms, and apple orchards. Some offer tours; ask at Info Centre. Also check *Events*, p.92, for annual festivals.

Abbotsford might also be called "the Bible Belt of BC" – the city boasts 84 churches, and is home to a large population of Mennonite farmers who arrived in the 1930s, founding communities at Greendale, Yarrow, and Vedder Crossing. There is a Mennonite museum and restaurant at the Clearbrook Centre (see below).

Abbotsford Information: Info Centre, 2462 McCallum Rd, Abbotsford, BC, V2S 3P9. 604-859-9651. Daily July-Aug, weekdays in winter.

■ **Abbotsford International Airshow:** On Mt Lehman Rd, 3km south of Hwy 1. 604-852-8511. Second weekend in Aug. Running for over 35 years and the undisputed king of North American airshows, the 1998 show was cancelled with money problems. Military and civilian precision aerobatic teams, historical and experimental aircraft, stunt flyers from around the world. The Snowbirds and others sign autographs. There are pancake breakfasts, paper-plane competitions, old-fashioned picnics, and socials. Campground. Everyone goes plane crazy.

■ **Matsqui-Sumas-Abbotsford (MSA) Museum, Trethewey House:** 2313 Ware St. 604-853-0313. Daily, 1-5, July-Aug; Mon-Fri, 1-5, Sept-June. Main floor of Trethewey House restored to 1920s period. Visual history of region's first residents, the Sto:lo people, and early pioneers. Tours to Mill Lake-Mill Site, Clayburn Village (see below).

■ **Mill Lake and Centennial Park:** Downtown Abbotsford. Canoeing, picnicking, walking and jogging trails. BC Wildlife Watch viewing site.

Harvest time in the Fraser Valley, food basket of the Lower Mainland.

■ **Fraser Valley Trout Hatchery:** 34345 Vye Rd. 604-852-5388. Visitor Centre: 604-852-5444. Daily in summer. View species of trout at various stages of growth in a living stream, with integrated computer systems. Guided tours. BC Wildlife Watch viewing site.

■ **Matsqui Trail Regional Park:** 117ha. Off Riverside St on south shore of Fraser. 604-432-6350. 10km of dike trail with active farmland on one side and the busy Fraser River on the other is suitable for walking, cycling, or horseback riding. Sportfishing for chinook salmon, as well as steelhead and cutthroat trout. Check regulations for type of licence required. For those fishing, there is limited camping at the Mission Bridge and Page Rd areas.

■ **Barrowtown Pump Station:** 16km east of Abbotsford. Access is from Hwy 1 westbound. Heading east, take No.1 Rd exit to Hwy 1 westbound, then turn onto Quadling Rd. 604-823-4678. Since its construction in 1920, and during its 60 years of operation, the old Sumas station drained some 6,500ha of agricultural land and 2,000ha of steep hillside. The present Barrowtown Pump Station opened in 1985. Call in advance for tours.

■ **Old Clayburn Village:** North of Abbotsford via Abbotsford-Mission Hwy. Right on Clayburn Rd to BC's first company town. The Clayburn brick manufacturing company was incorporated and a village was established in 1905. The clay came from Sumas Mountain to the east (see Sumas Mountain Park, below); bricks fired here were used to build houses in Victoria, Vancouver, the western US, and even the Orient. At Clayburn village are red-brick houses designed by renowned architect, Samuel McLure; also heritage church and school.

■ **Clearbrook Community Centre:** 2825 Clearbrook Rd. 604-853-5532. Mennonite historical society with archives, restaurant featuring ethnic cuisine, gift shop.

■ **Matsqui Recreation Centre:** 3106 Clearbrook Rd. 604-855-0500. Offers a Polynesian swimming experience in BC's largest wave pool; waterslide and swirl pool.

■ **Abbotsford Recreation Centre:** 34690 Old Yale Rd. 604-853-4221. First facility in North America to house both an Olympic-size ice sheet and free-form skating area – the "Ice Experience," is enhanced by lush trees, mountains and clouds, a snow-making machine, and tunnel. Pool, sauna, whirlpool.

■ **Golf:** Ledgeview Golf Club, 35997 McKee Rd, 604-859-8993, offers 18 holes. **Valley Golf Centre,** 4211 Gladwin Rd, 604-853-4653, has nine-hole course and driving range. **Fraserglen,** 35036 S. Parallel Rd, 604-852-3477, has 18-hole course with driving range.

■ **Wonderland Amusement Park:** 36165 N Parallel Rd. 604-850-0411. Features mini-golf, go-carts.

 **Sumas Mountain (Fraser Valley Regional District) Park:** 1,400ha. No facilities. North from Abbotsford on Abbotsford-Mission Hwy, then east on Fore Rd, north on Beharrell Rd, then right (northeast) on Page Rd. Right again on Upper Sumas Mountain Rd to Smith Rd. Centennial Trail starts from end of Smith Rd. About 2.5 hours moderate hike to Chadsey Lake along well-maintained trail, through mixed forest (including Garry oak and Douglas fir), and over log bridge, to great views of Vancouver from 907m Sumas Mountain. Another way: continue driving on Upper Sumas Mountain Rd past

Smith Rd to Batt Rd, which connects to Forest Service Rd leading to hydro tower. Rough but possible by car to reach more stunning views.

Highway 11: Leads south from Abbotsford to **Canada/US Border Crossing at Sumas.** Route to US Hwy I-5. Duty Free Shop at border crossing for tourists leaving Canada.

Whatcom Rd (Exit 95): 5.5km beyond Sumas Route 11, exit Hwy 1 north to Wonderland Amusement Park.

Cole Road Rest Area: Exit after Whatcom Rd.

Vedder Canal: On Hwy 1, about 19km beyond Hwy 11 junction. Constructed in early 1920s to drain Sumas Lake and reclaim 13,355ha in Chilliwack Valley. In 1954, canal was used for rowing races associated with the Commonwealth Games.

Vedder Rd: 17km beyond Vedder Canal. Exit south, 13km to Cultus Lake Provincial Park (see below). Exit north, 1km to Chilliwack.

Chilliwack: (Pop. 60,186). 1km north off Hwy 1 onto Yale Rd. At the centre of a farming and dairy region. The mild climate and fertile soil give it the accolade "Green Heart of British Columbia." Lower Mainlanders make this a destination in late summer, to buy sweet-tasting corn sold by the roadside.

The name Chilliwack comes from the T'selxwiqw (very roughly pronounced Chilliwack) First Nation people whose nine contemporary villages form the city's western perimeter and the heart of Sardis, south across Hwy 1. It means "going back upstream," or "backwaters," referring to their more ancient homeland on the upper reaches of the fast-flowing Chilliwack River.

The area is well known for fishing in nearby lakes and rivers, including Chilliwack and Lindemen lakes, and Chilliwack and Vedder rivers. Also excellent riding trails.

Chilliwack Information: Info Centre, 44150 Luckakuck Way, Sardis, BC, V2R 4A7. 604-858-8121. Daily, summer, Mon-Sat in winter.

Chilliwack Airport: Young Rd South. 604-792-3430. Small, busy airport on southern border of Chilliwack. One paved runway. Operates 24 hours a day and handles a variety of aircraft.

■ **Chilliwack Farm Tours:** Ask for map at Info Centre. 16 local farms produce everything from Arabian horses to herbs; most offer goodies: fresh-baked buns, roasted nuts, flowers, preserves, mile-high pies. **The Apple Farm and Country Store,** 4490 Boundary Rd, 604-823-4311, has farm animals, a playground, 22 kinds of apples, and special events year-round.

■ **Western Canada's First Fruit Winery:** Bertrand Creek Farms, 1386 Frost Rd, Lindell Beach. 604-858-6233. Flavours include raspberry, blueberry, blackberry, red currant, black currant, white currant, and gooseberry.

■ **Chilliwack Museum and Archives:** 45820 Spadina Ave. 604-795-5210. Daily except Sun. In Chilliwack's only national historic site, the old city hall. Artifacts explain history. China, baskets, farm and medical equipment.

■ **Chilliwack River Hatchery:** Off Chilliwack River Crossing at junction of Slesse Creek and Chilliwack River. 604-858-7227. Year-round. Chum, coho, chinook, steelhead. BC Wildlife Watch viewing site.

■ **Atchelitz Threshermen's Antique Powerland:** South from Chilliwack across Hwy 1, in Sardis at 44150 Luckakuck Way (Behind Info Centre). 604-858-2119. June 1-Sept 30. Antique cars, trucks, tractors, wagons. Working blacksmith's shop and sawmill.

■ **Golf:** Cheam Golf Centre, 44610 Luckakuck Way; 604-858-7991; 18 holes. Chilliwack Golf and Country Club, 41894 Yale Rd W; 1-888-757-7222; 18 holes. Kinkora Golf Course, 46050 Higginson Rd, 604-858-8717; 18 holes.

Chilliwack River: 10km along Vedder Rd, then onto Chilliwack Lake Rd. Leads to Chilliwack River and several Forest Service recreation and camp sites. For area map: Chilliwack Forest District, Box 159, 9880 South McGrath Rd, Rosedale, BC, V0X 1X0. 604-794-2100.

Chilliwack Lake Provincial Park: 9,258ha. 155 vehicle/tent campsites. 604-824-2300. 52km southwest of Chilliwack on Chilliwack Lake Rd. Offers all that's expected of a pretty lake. Fishing, swimming, boating. Spawning cutthroat in April. Hiking in area.

Cultus Lake Provincial Park: 656ha; 296 campsites plus group site (reservations taken: call 1-800-689-9025; from the Lower Mainland or overseas, call 604-689-9025). Sani-station. General Info: 604-824-2300. Exit south on Vedder Rd, travel 13km to park. Cultus Lake was known as Th'ewa:li or Soowahlie by the Sto:lo people. Cultus is a Chinook jargon word meaning "worthless" or "bad." A Slellucum or supernatural being in the form of a great bear was said to inhabit the lake area. This being was responsible for fierce storms on the lake, which became a taboo area, and, locals attest, is not without its mysteries even today. Nevertheless, this is one of the Lower Mainland's most popular parks.

Four separate campgrounds: Clear Creek, Delta Grove, Entrance Bay, Maple Bay. Picnicking, swimming, hiking and bridle trails, boat launch. Fishing for rainbow and cutthroat trout, Dolly Varden. July-Aug, park naturalists are on hand. Also, self-guiding interpretive trail.

Cultus Lake Waterpark: 75 Columbia Valley Hwy (Follow signs). 604-858-7241. Mid-May to Sept. Waterslides, boating, golfing, fishing, hiking, horseback riding, camping.

Cultus Golf Park: 4000 Columbia Valley Hwy. 604-858-9902. Full facilities, 18 holes.

Return to Highway 1 and Vedder Road Junction

Highway 9: 16km beyond Vedder Rd junction. Exit south 3km to Bridal Veil Falls Provincial Park and other attractions.

Bridal Veil Falls Provincial Park: 32ha. 25m waterfall cascades down a rocky mountain face. A 15-minute stroll through a forest of cedar and fir leads to a viewpoint at base of the falls.

Trans-Canada Waterslide: Intersection of Hwys 1 and 9. 604-794-7455. Weekends late May to mid-June. Daily mid-June to Sept.

Sandstone Gallery Mineral Museum: At Hwys 1 and 9. 604-794-3003.

Dinotown: Intersection of Hwys 1 and 9. 1-800-491-7627 or 604-794-7410. Daily, early June-Sept. Dinosaur bones; rides, stage show.

SIDE TRIP

to Minter Gardens, Agassiz, and Harrison Hot Springs

Hwy 9 north leads past Minter Gardens turnoff, then over the Fraser River. 10km to Agassiz; 14km beyond Agassiz to Harrison Hot Springs. Details on Agassiz and Harrison in *Vancouver to Hope – North Bank*, p.134.

Minter Gardens: 52892 Bunker Rd, near Hwy 9, just north of Hwy 1. Take Exit 135 off Hwy 1. 604-794-7191 or 1-800-661-3919. Daily April-Oct. 11ha with spectacular views of Cheam Peak. Maze, aviaries, topiary animals, fragrance garden for the blind, colonial floral ladies, rose and fern gardens, Chinese garden with Penjing rock bonsai. Two restaurants, gift and plant shops. Garden's creator, Brian Minter, is a well-known gardening radio commentator.

Bridal Falls Golf Course and Driving Range: Across from Minter Gardens. 604-794-7788. Nine holes, mini-golf.

Cheam Lake Wetlands Regional Park: 93ha. 604-792-0061. Immediately north of Hwy 1 on Hwy 9, turn east and travel about 3km. Habitat restoration project involving the reflooding of Cheam Lake after mining here. New ecosystem is emerging. Trails and boardwalk; interpretive program in summer.

Return to Highway 1

Road to Wahleach (or Jones) Lake (Exit 153): 18km beyond Hwy 9 junction.

Wahleach (or Jones) Lake: On Wahleach Lake logging road 11km south of Hwy 1. 342ha lake offers fishing for rainbow, kokanee, some cutthroat, May-Sept. A glacier-fed hydro reservoir, lake's water level fluctuates through summer months. Areas around the lake offer good examples of the effects of clearcut logging. Camping at BC Hydro recreation site.

Laidlaw Rd: 20km beyond the junction of Hwys 1 and 9. Exit 153 to Laidlaw.

Laidlaw: (Pop. 158). On Laidlaw Rd 20km beyond Hwy 9 junction. Farmer W.F. Laidlaw had insisted a Canadian Northern Railway station be named in his honour when the railroad laid tracks across his farm. Southeast: 2,076m Isolillock Peak.

■ **The Country Stop:** Country store in old gas-station building, year-round.

Hunter Creek Rest Area (Exit 160): 25km beyond junction of Hwys 1 and 9. Left to rest area. Hunter Creek flows north into Fraser River. Named after a storekeeper who acquired land in the area in 1889.

Hope Business Route (Exit 165): 9.5km beyond Laidlaw. Exit south for connection with Flood Hope Rd (old Hwy 1) to reach **Skagit Valley Provincial Park.** Or take Silverhope Creek exit (Exit 168), 5.5km east of Hope Business Route.

SIDE TRIP

to Skagit Valley Provincial Park

Silver Lake Provincial Park: 77ha. 25 campsites. 604-824-2300. On unpaved Silverhope Creek Rd, 6km south of Hwy 1. Fishing and hiking in area.

Skagit Valley Provincial Park: 27,948ha; 131 campsites in two campgrounds plus group site. 604-824-2300. Silverhope Creek Rd leads southeast 35km to park entrance; 26km farther to Ross Lake.

An environmental success story from the 1970s. The beautiful wild Skagit River rises in Manning Park, runs south through its stunning forest valley, and then vanishes south of US border in a reservoir behind a hydro dam. The whole Skagit Valley on the Canadian side was nearly flooded, too, but for the efforts of a handful of early activists. Bravo!

Area is now jointly managed by Canada and US through Skagit Valley Commission. Park extends from Ross Lake on Canada/US border, north to Crowsnest Hwy, its east border running alongside Manning Park. Part of Ross Lake expands into the park in early summer, receding back across border in spring. Within the park, dense vegetation and rushing streams. Boisterous Skagit River cuts through the wide glaciated Skagit Valley, fringed with impressive mountain peaks, including Mt Brice, 2,163m; Shawatum Mountain, 2,158m; Silvertip Mountain, 2,250m; and Whitworth Peak, 2,294m. Campgrounds are Ross Lake and Silvertip. Hiking, canoeing, swimming, boating, fishing, hunting, snowshoeing, cross-country skiing (no set tracks).

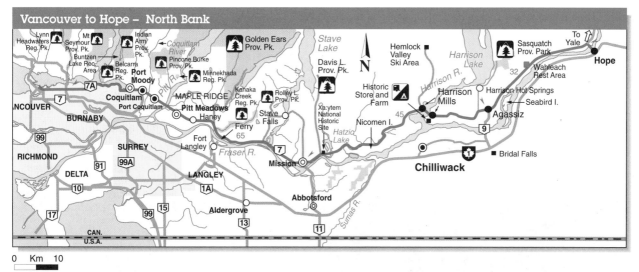

Vancouver to Hope – North Bank

0 Km 10

Return to Highway 1

Highway 3 (the Crowsnest): Leads 7km southeast to junction with Hwy 5 (Coquihalla Hwy). For info on Coquihalla Hwy north to Merritt (115km) and Kamloops (98km beyond Merritt), see *Hope to Kamloops*, p.172. Hwy 3 east leads 20km to Manning Provincial Park. See *Hope to Princeton*, p. 137.

Hope (Exit 170): (Pop. 6,247). 35km beyond junction of Hwys 1 and 9, at junction of Hwys 1, 3, 5, and 7. For details, see p.138.

VANCOUVER TO HOPE NORTH BANK

LOUGHEED HIGHWAY (Highway 7)

Highway 7, the Lougheed, is an older route connecting Vancouver and Hope, separated by a distance of 142.5km. This route follows the north shore of the Fraser River as it moves through the broad Fraser Valley, bound for the imposing peaks of the Coast Mountains. It leads through residential areas, farming regions, and large undeveloped areas.

Information about Greater Vancouver is provided separately, so coverage will begin with the city of Port Moody, at the head of Burrard Inlet. Both Hwy 7A (the Barnet Hwy) and Hwy 7 (the Lougheed) lead there from downtown Vancouver. Follow the route map, above, or for greater detail on the Coquitlam/Maple Ridge districts, see *Gateway map*, p.96, which covers the area from Vancouver to Mission.

Vancouver's Hastings St becomes the Barnet Hwy as it begins to skirt the southern shores of Burrard Inlet. This scenic drive offers stunning views of the mountains layered down the inlet. The distance on this highway (7A) from Boundary Rd in Vancouver to Port Moody is l4.5km. On Hwy 7, slightly to the south, it is 21km from downtown Vancouver to Port Moody. Hwy 7 offers access to Burnaby.

While Hwy 7 offers a few glimpses of the region's busy waterways, the new West Coast Express commuter train, on the CPR line, traces the edges of the broad, earth-brown Fraser and the shores of sparkling blue Burrard Inlet. This is an *express* – designed for commuters, but even people without schedules to keep appreciate the 77-minute trip. The scenic Express also makes special excursions on weekends, just for explorers, linking up with B&Bs, and places to see around Mission. See p.91 for info on where and when to get on and off.

Port Moody: (Pop. 20,847). l4.5km east of downtown Vancouver on Hwy 7A, and 2km west of junction of Hwys 7 and 7A. At the head of Burrard Inlet. Port Moody was named in 1860 for Colonel Richard Moody (1813-1887), commanding officer of the Royal Engineers stationed in BC between 1858 and 1863.

The city was the Canadian Pacific Railway's western terminus. The first train from Montreal arrived here on July 4, 1886. In 1887, the line was extended the extra 20km to Vancouver, and Port Moody's status as a trading centre diminished. It is now an important residential area with a wealth of city parks, five of them overlooking the shores of Burrard Inlet.

Port Moody Information: Coquitlam Info Centre, 3-1180 Pinetree Way, Coquitlam, BC, V3B 7L2. 604-464-2716. In Lincoln Centre Mall. Daily in summer; weekdays in winter.

■ **Port Moody Station Museum:** 2734 Murray St, Willingdon Park. 604-939-1648. Wed-Sun. In a restored 1907 CPR station on site of original western terminus. Pioneer artifacts and railway memorabilia.

■ **Port Moody Parks and the Shoreline Trail:** The head of Burrard Inlet is ringed with five Port Moody city parks. Guildford Way turns into Murray St, on the inlet's south shore. Here, Rocky Point Park and pier mark beginning of 3km pedestrian pathway connecting Rocky Point to Inlet Park, Shoreline Park, Town Centre, Old Mill Park, and Old Orchard Park. Adjacent streets, including Guildford Way, Murray St, Clarke St, Alderside Rd, and Heritage Mountain Blvd, are all marked for

bicycle traffic. Inland, Noons Creek Park has boardwalks and a small hatchery. Port Moody Parks and Recreation: 604-469-4555. BC Wildlife Watch viewing site.

Belcarra Regional Park: 1,116ha. Take Ioco Rd northwest from Port Moody centre, turn north onto 1st Ave, continue until road forks: left to Belcarra Park on Bedwell Bay Rd. Follow signs for 8km to White Pine Beach on Sasamat Lake or continue 4km to Belcarra picnic area on Indian Arm. 604-432-6360. On a handle of land jutting into Indian Arm. One of the GVRD's busiest parks, best times to visit are mid-week or off-season. 9km of shoreline, three beaches, sandy coves, mud flats. Diving and boating. Inland there's hiking, and swimming at Sasamat Lake, reputed to be the warmest in the Lower Mainland. Public wharf, and access to Indian Arm and **Indian Arm Provincial Park**. Also see Deep Cove, p.103.

Buntzen Lake Reservoir Recreation Area: Take Ioco Rd northwest from Port Moody centre, turn north onto 1st Ave, continue until road forks: left to Belcarra Park, right to Buntzen Lake Recreational Area on Sunnyside Rd. Follow signs. 604-528-1801. Two power plants supply 76,700kw of power to Vancouver. Buntzen Lake, formerly called Lake Beautiful, was renamed after Johannes Buntzen, first general manager of BC Electric Company. The Buntzen Lake project was put in service by the Vancouver Power Company in 1903 to provide Vancouver's first hydroelectric power. A 3.6km tunnel carries water from Coquitlam Lake to Buntzen Lake, and then to the power plants on Indian Arm. Boat launch, hiking, equestrian trails, picnic tables.

Highways 7A and 7 (Lougheed Hwy): Junction is 2km east of Port Moody. Hwy 7A continues from here as Hwy 7.

Coquitlam River: Passing under Hwy 7, 1.5km beyond junction of Hwys 7 and 7A. A narrow, winding, 14km river flowing from Coquitlam Lake, through the cities of Coquitlam and Port Coquitlam, into the Fraser River. The river offers 10km of shoreline access, starting from **Coquitlam River Park**

129

(see below). The bad news is, according to the Outdoor Recreation Council of BC, this river is one of the most endangered in BC, and the Fraser, into which it flows, ranks as *the* most endangered. The Coquitlam is said to be "plagued by the collective impact of a rapidly growing society." A dam at the river's head impacts spawning coho salmon; gravel pits, housing developments, and logging upstream affect the quality and patterns of flow.

rivalling any in the Lower Mainland. To the west, north, and east, existing parks – Belcarra Regional Park, Buntzen Lake Reservoir Recreation Area, and Minnekhada Regional Park – have been joined by vast tracts from the new Lower Mainland Nature Legacy – Indian Arm Provincial Park, Pinecone Burke Provincial Park, and wildlife management areas embracing rich river marshes and sloughs. Details following.

facility, the farm provided food and rehabilitative labour for patients of the hospital. The program was phased out in 1983, and now this field is home for many species of birds and animals. Park protects salmon-bearing waterway. No formal facilities, but dikes provide walking and cycling. Excellent birdwatching year-round. BC Wildlife Watch viewing site.

■ **Riverview:** Across the road from Colony Farm Park. Take Cape Horn Ave east to Pine Terrace and look for kiosk with map and brochures for self-guided tour. This is site of original UBC botanical garden established by John Davidson in 1911. Today, there are over 600 heritage trees throughout the grounds.

■ **Minnekhada Regional Park:** 219ha. 604-432-6350. From Lougheed Hwy, turn north on Coast Meridian Rd and travel 2.5km to Apel Dr. Head east to Victoria Dr. Follow Victoria Dr 3.5km to park entrance off Quarry Rd. Marsh with wildlife, rocky knolls overlooking Pitt River flood plain, and Pitt-Addington Marsh Wildlife Management Area (see below). The lodge, built in 1934 to resemble a Scottish hunting retreat, is open to the public on the first Sunday of the month Feb-Dec, 1-4pm and is available for special events year-round. BC Wildlife Watch viewing site.

■ **Pitt-Addington Marsh Wildlife Management Area:** 2,882ha. Three parcels of important habitat, consisting of marsh, wetlands, and upland forest. The Addington Marsh Unit is best accessed through the trails in Minnekhada Regional Park (see above). The Pitt unit is reached from Pitt Meadows off Hwy 7, then Harris Rd. (Follow directions to Grant Narrows Regional Park, below.) Viewing towers and trail around outer dike. More than 230 bird species recorded. Winter highlights include swans, eagles, and waterfowl. In summer, ospreys, songbirds, muskrats, and beavers. BC Wildlife Watch viewing site.

■ **DeBouville Slough:** In northeast Coquitlam with access from the junction of Cedar Dr and Victoria Dr. Birdwatching highlights include nesting great blue herons and green herons. Excellent viewing opportunities from dikes on both sides of the slough. BC Wildlife Watch viewing site.

Great blue herons fish in the shallow sloughs of the Fraser Valley.

Coquitlam: (Pop. 101,820). On Hwy 7 at junction of 7 and 7A, 2km east of Port Moody. The District of Coquitlam, straddling the Coquitlam River, embraces the cities of Coquitlam and Port Coquitlam. It stretches north from industrial lands on the banks of the Fraser River, to the mountain wilderness of Pinecone Burke Provincial Park (below).

River, city, and district take their name from the Kwikwetl'em (roughly pronounced Coquitlam) First Nation people who now live in a small village near the mouth of the Coquitlam River. Sto:lo elders tell us the name means "smell like fish," describing a difficult period in the long history of the river's First People.

The city of Coquitlam, incorporated in 1891, is still searching for an identity of its own. The city started out as a rural centre boosted by the establishment of Canada's then largest sawmill. In 1901 a large number of French-speaking Canadians came to work here and settled in their own village, Maillardville. In 1913 both Fraser Mills, surrounding the sawmill, and Port Coquitlam seceded from Coquitlam, leaving Coquitlam as little more than a bedroom community for Vancouver. With a population that has grown fivefold in the last four decades, Coquitlam is just now developing its own town centre – with a new city hall and library, cultural centre, the David Lam Douglas College campus, school, and recreational complex – just north off Hwy 7 at Pinetree Way. And the city is emerging as the gateway to wilderness recreation opportunities

Coquitlam Information: Coquitlam Info Centre, 3-1180 Pinetree Way, Coquitlam, BC, V3B 7L2. 604-464-2716. In Lincoln Centre Mall. Daily in summer; weekdays in winter.

■ **Maillardville:** The core of old Maillardville occupies six downtown blocks just north of Hwy 7, bordered by Brunette, Schoolhouse, Rochester, and Blue Mountain streets. Now part of Coquitlam, this is the Lower Mainland's oldest francophone community. It was settled, 1901, by French-Canadians who had moved west to work in Fraser Valley mills. Village core is now being upgraded to include an expanded Place des Arts (see below). There's a Society of Maillardville, representing about 14 francophone associations with a combined membership of about 4,000; the *caisse populaire* with bilingual tellers; *foyer Maillard*, a bilingual seniors residence; Our Lady of Lourdes Church and Rectory; and Laval Square, are at Laval just off Brunette. *On parle français*. Overall, the number of francophones is declining, while Coquitlam's Chinese speaking population has tripled in the last 40 years.

■ **Place des Arts:** 1120 Brunette Ave. 604-664-1636. Daily except Sun. Paintings, weaving, quilts, stone carvings, pottery.

■ **Coquitlam River Park:** Turn north off Hwy 7 at Shaughnessy St, 1km to riverside picnic site. Fish for steelhead.

■ **Colony Farm Regional Park:** 262ha. At end of Colony Farm Rd. Take Cape Horn exchange off Hwy 7. 604-432-6350. Established 1904 as the site of a 400ha provincial mental-health

Pinecone Burke Provincial Park: 38,000ha. North of Coquitlam: this largest of the Lower Mainland Nature Legacy parks is undeveloped, with few access points and trails, and no facilities at this time. 604-924-2200. This vast wilderness, named for its inclusion of Pinecone Lake and Burke Mountain, begins in the north, with Pinecone Lake and dozens more alpine lakes feeding into the Pitt River (also see *Pitt River and Pitt Lake*, below). It sweeps south, embracing the western shores of Pitt Lake, the largest freshwater tidal lake in North America.

Other wonders here: Widgeon Slough, the largest freshwater wetland in southwestern BC; Widgeon Lake, one of the largest mountain lakes in the region; and Meslilloet Icefield, Greater Vancouver's closest glacier. Also grizzly bears, mountain goats, even the Pacific jumping mouse. Roads leading northeast from Coquitlam link up to well-established trails: Quarry Rd links to Munro and Dennett lakes;

Harper Rd links to the high plateau of Burke Mountain. The Pitt River provides access to Widgeon Slough. From a campsite there, it's an easy two-hour walk to Widgeon Falls. A strenuous hike, requiring an overnight trip, leads farther up the valley to Widgeon Lake.

From the north end of Pitt Lake (only accessible by boat) a deactivated logging road leads 16km to trailhead for Boise Valley and Cedar Spirit Grove (a group of 1,000-year-old western red cedars). This is a hike for those with good route-finding and wilderness smarts. Pinecone Lake is accessible from Upper Pitt Valley via 30km logging road, or from the Squamish side via logging roads in the Mamquam Valley.

A few tour operators offer guided trips and water-taxi service. Pitt Lake Resort on the Upper Pitt River serves as a base for exploring: 604-520-1796 from Vancouver, or 1-800-665-6206. See Trek Adventures offers guided trips and photography tours: 604-220-5945.

Port Coquitlam: (Pop. 46,682). On Hwy 7, 2km east of Coquitlam. Coquitlam and Pitt rivers run along east and west borders of Port Coquitlam. This major industrial and commercial area seceded from Coquitlam in 1913 after the CPR announced plans to relocate its main railway yards here, from Vancouver.

Port Coquitlam Information: Coquitlam Info Centre, 3-1180 Pinetree Way, Coquitlam, BC, V3B 7L2. 604-464-2716. In Lincoln Centre Mall. Daily in summer; weekdays in winter.

Pitt River and Pitt Lake: Pitt River Bridge on Hwy 7 passes over river 9km east of Port Moody. Pitt River flows south from 7,700ha Pitt Lake. Lakeshore provides natural boat launch. A wonderful area to observe nesting ospreys and Trumpeter swans in the winter months. Fishing for steelhead trout and pink, spring, and sockeye salmon. When boating on lake, stay within navigation markers as it is shallow at the south end. Cold water, logs, debris, and high winds make this a hazardous lake.

Pitt River continues southwest past Hwy 7, 4.5km to Fraser River. 18km of fishable shoreline. Dolly Varden, cutthroat. Spring and fall fishing is best.

Pitt Meadows: (District pop. 13,346). 11km beyond Port Moody. Incorporated in 1914, this district is on north bank of the Fraser between Port Coquitlam and Maple Ridge. Forestry and agriculture play a major role. Dairy, cranberry, blueberry farms. It's also horse country.

Pitt Meadows Information: Contact Chamber of Commerce, 12492 Harris Rd, Pitt Meadows, BC, V3Y 2J4. 604-465-7820.

Pitt Meadows Airport: From downtown Pitt Meadows, Harris Rd leads south 3km to airport. This 278ha airport is one of the few opened by BC Ministry of Transportation solely for use by small planes. Facilities include three paved runways, floatplane dock on north side of the Fraser River, and control tower.

■ **Pitt Meadows Historical Museum:** 12484 Harris Rd. Sat afternoons. Heritage house with photos, paintings, and Sto:lo history.

■**Pitt-Addington Marsh Wildlife Management Area (Pitt Unit):** See p. 130.

■ **Grant Narrows Regional Park:** 6ha. North off Hwy 7 onto Harris Rd, to McNeil, McNeil to Rennie, north on Rennie to park. 604-826-1291. At Pitt Lake's south end where it narrows to become Pitt River. Parking area, floating dock provides boat access to Pitt Lake and Widgeon Slough. Canoe rentals. Trails to Pitt-Addington Marsh Wildlife Management Area begin at park. Provides canoe access to Pinecone Burke Provincial Park trails and campground via adjacent Widgeon Marsh Regional Park Reserve (across the Pitt River from Grant Narrows and otherwise not open to the public).

■ **Golf: Pitt Meadows Golf Club,** 13615 Harris Rd. 604-465-4711. 18 holes, pro shop, driving range.

Laity St: 5km beyond Harris Rd. Exit to Maple Ridge.

Maple Ridge: (Pop. 56,173). 15km beyond Port Moody on Hwy 7. Kanaka Creek tumbles, river-like, down from Blue Mountain to the northeast, through the heart of the district called Maple Ridge. Woven baskets, unearthed where the creek pours into the Fraser River, tell us people have been here for at least 4,000 years – a good place to catch sockeye salmon. By 1827, when Europeans had established Fort Langley on the river's opposite side, smallpox had already swept through, dramatically changing the peoplescape.

Among the first non-natives to settle here were Kanakas – natives of Hawaii working for the Hudson's Bay Company at the fort. They married into local Sto:lo First Nation families, and some in the 1850s took up land beside Kanaka Creek. A Scot, Sam Robertson, planted his orchard nearby. John McIver arrived in 1860 and chose for his farmsite the ridge above the river, forested by broad-leafed western maples. He named his farm Maple Ridge.

On the shores between the Pitt River to the west and Stave River to the east, nine distinctive communities soon emerged: Pitt Meadows, Whonnock, Yennadon, Websters Corners, Ruskin, Port Hammond, Albion, The Ridge, and Port Haney, an early commercial centre with its wharf and railway station. In 1874, to ease the burden of services and road development, they all came together to create a district – Maple Ridge. It was not until nearly a century later, however, with the consolidation of a postal service, that the name came into common use.

Even now, each of the old communities maintains its own character. Haney, the geographic centre and commercial centre in the more recent past, forms what might be called the downtown core of Maple Ridge. On the old agricultural fairgrounds – the intersection of the Lougheed Hwy and 224th St – are the offices of the municipal government, the library, and the biggest mall, Haney Place.

Maple Ridge's history is felt in Kanaka Regional Park, a corridor along the creek, where ancient trees from Sam Robertson's orchard can still be found. Part of John McIver's farm is now the Maple Ridge Golf Course. Agriculture is still important here, as is the forest industry, still pushing log booms around on the riverfront. Port Haney's story is told on the Fraser River Heritage Walk (see below).

Maple Ridge Information: Maple Ridge Chamber of Commerce, 22238 Lougheed Hwy, Maple Ridge, BC, V2X 2T2. 604-463-3366. Daily June-Aug. Weekdays Sept-May.

■ **Fraser River Heritage Walk:** Paved walkway links key heritage sites in Port Haney, from Port Haney Wharf to Haney House, Brickwood Park, and Maple Ridge Museum.

■ **Haney House:** 11612-224th St. 604-463-1377. Wed-Sun afternoons in summer. Groups and afternoon teas by arrangement. Built in 1878 for the Haney family, wood-frame house is located in an attractive garden near the Fraser River. It remained Haney family residence until 1979 when it was restored with three generations of family furnishings.

■ **St John the Divine Anglican Church:** Laity St and River Rd. Daily. The oldest church in BC, built 1859. Was moved here in 1882 from a site 3km up the opposite side of the Fraser.

■ **The Beast:** Don't miss the town clock outside the Municipal Hall and Police Station. Atop the clock tower is a controversial metal horse – something out of the *Wizard of Oz* – that rears up every hour on the hour. Designed by municipal employee Don Brayford to be a symbol of horse country, its cost was a sore point, but The Beast is proving a wonderment.

■ **Maple Ridge Art Gallery:** 11995 Haney Place. 604-467-5855. Tues-Sun, afternoons, year-round.

■ **Maple Ridge Museum:** 22520 16th Ave. 604-463-5311. Wed-sun, afternoons, July-Aug; Wed and Sun, Sept-June. In former 1907 home overlooking historic Port Haney on the Fraser River. First Nations and pioneer artifacts, photo archives, and a 1930 era railway diorama showing the strong influence of the CPR on the area's growth. Tours, research by appointment.

■ **Kanaka Creek Regional Park:** 413ha. 604-432-6350. From 224th St turn right onto Dewdney Trunk Rd, then south onto 256th St. Park protects 12km of a natural stream corridor in Maple Ridge Municipality. Creek begins in headwaters of Blue Mountain, travels through mature second-growth forests, sandstone canyons, meadows and marshes, before joining the Fraser River. Home to salmon, trout, and the tailed frog. Waterfalls, wetlands, and wildlife. Walking, canoeing, kayaking, horseback riding, sportfishing. Note: equestrian trail requires riders to ford Kanaka Creek, hazardous during high-water conditions. BC Wildlife Watch viewing site.

■ **Bell-Irving Hatchery on Kanaka Creek:** 1km south of Dewdney Trunk Rd on 256th St, sign at entrance. 604-462-8643. Year-round. Tours 2-3pm daily. Cliff Falls downstream. BC Wildlife Watch viewing site.

■ **Horseback Riding:** More than 160km of trails through gorgeous country. Riding trail brochure available at chamber of commerce.

■ **Maple Ridge Golf Course:** 20818 Golf Course Lane. South off Lougheed Hwy at 207th St. 604-465-9221. Nine-hole course with putting green, full clubhouse, lounge.

🚏 **232nd St:** Eastern edge of Maple Ridge, turn north, 8km to **Malcolm Knapp Research Forest**; or north 5km to Fern Crescent that leads east 6km to **Golden Ears Provincial Park**.

SIDE TRIP

to Research Forest and Golden Ears

Malcolm Knapp Research Forest: On 232nd St 8km north of Hwy 7. 604-463-8148. Daily. This 5,157ha forest was established in 1949 as a facility for forestry demonstration and instruction. Managed by UBC Faculty of Forestry. Walking and hiking trails. No dogs or bikes.

Golden Ears Provincial Park: 55,590ha; 343 campsites in two large campgrounds (reservations taken: call 1-800-689-9025; from the Lower Mainland or overseas, call 604-689-9025). More than 150 picnic tables. General info: 604-924-2200. A vast park north of Hwy 7. North on 232nd St; 5km to Fern Cres; east 6km on Fern Cres. Once part of Garibaldi Provincial Park, establishment of Golden Ears Provincial Park in 1964 recognized the mountain barrier, including the 2,583m Mamquam Mountain, dividing the two parks. Named after its famous twin peaks.

The 1,055ha Alouette Lake, a 16km lake within the park, was once a traditional native fishing area. People trapped fish in weirs (series of woven enclosures). Swimming, windsurfing, waterskiing, canoeing, boating, hiking, exploring, climbing, and fishing for cutthroat and Dollies.

Through the 1920s until 1931, when a disastrous fire swept through the valley, the forested slopes above Alouette Lake were site of BC's largest railway logging operation. The Abernathy and Lougheed Logging Company laid more than 135km of railway lines to take out harvested fir, hemlock, red cedar, and balsam trees. These abandoned railway grades make up part of the 42km of bridle trails and 80km of hiking trails in the park. Hiking trails vary in difficulty, from **Centennial Trail** (2.5-hour, a good introduction), to a strenuous seven-hour hike to Golden Ears Mountain at an elevation of over 1,700m. Check information boards at parking lots.

Return to Highway 7

🚏 **240th St:** Exit south 0.5km to Albion Ferry.

⛴ **Albion Ferry:** Part of the provincial highway system; enables motorists to make a direct connection between highways 7 and 1. Crosses Fraser River to **Fort Langley** and **Fort**

Langley National Historic Park. Ferry is free, and runs every 15 min, 5am-1am daily. Trip is 5 minutes. Two ferries, 23 cars each. 604-467-7298. For Fort Langley, see *Vancouver to Hope – South Bank*, p. 125.

🚏 **272nd St:** 6.5km east of 240th St. To Rolley Lake Provincial Park.

SIDE TRIP

to Rolley and Stave lakes

Rolley Lake Provincial Park: 115ha; 64 campsites (reservations taken: call 1-800-689-9025; from the Lower Mainland or overseas, call 604-689-9025). General info: 604-924-2200. Turn north on 28th St (it becomes Wilson St), then east on Dewdney Trunk Rd to Bell St. Bell St leads 4.5km to park. 20ha Rolley Lake was named after James and Fanny Rolley who homesteaded here in 1888. In the early 1900s, the lake was used as a holding pond for shingle bolts destined for the Stoltze mill at nearby Ruskin. A wooden flume sped the bolts 5km downhill to the mill. In the 1930s, this area supported a small Japanese-Canadian hand-logging operation typical of many that existed throughout the province.

Today: walking around the lakeshore, picnicking, swimming, canoeing. Visitor programs. Rainbow, cutthroat, Dolly Varden, and brown bullhead fishing best in spring and fall. No powerboats.

Stave Lake Recreation Area: 50ha. Return from Rolley Lake Provincial Park to Dewdney Trunk Rd and follow it northeast for 5km to Stave Lake and falls. Hudson's Bay Company had a cooperage at Fort Langley where BC's first barrels were made. The wood for the staves for these barrels was hewed on the banks of this river, thus its name, Stave River. The lake is the result of a dam built across Stave River. Trails, beach, boat launch, swimming, fishing for cutthroat, Dolly Varden, and rainbow. Stave Falls Dam and Powerhouse was location for Paramount film *We're No Angels*.

Hayward Lake Reservoir Recreation Area: South of Stave Falls Dam. Many trails, swimming, canoeing, picnicking.

Ruskin Recreation Site: On Hayward St just below Hayward Dam. Side channel with spawning chum salmon Oct-Nov. Bald eagles common late winter.

Return to Highway 7

Mission: (Pop. 30,519). On Hwy 7, 26km east of Maple Ridge and 41km east of Port Moody. Mission is terminus of the West Coast Express, offering 77-minute commuter rail service from Vancouver (see p.91 and p.129). The city takes its name from St Mary's Roman Catholic Mission, the dream of French Oblate priest Father Fouquet. In 1861, atop the hill overlooking the river, he founded

the mission to bring Christianity to First Nations people in the area. The mission was also a popular stopping place for trappers, settlers, and other river travellers. Fouquet later opened a residential school for native children, which was a common way throughout BC to subdue vital native cultures.

In 1953, Mission was the site chosen by Benedictine monks for their new monastic retreat centre, the Westminster Abbey Seminary of Christ the King. Their remarkable church, with its tower of 10 bells, and 64 stained-glass windows, was completed in 1982 after nearly three decades of planning and building. Today, about 35 Benedictines sustain themselves through prayer and the fruits of their labour on the land. They include in their daily routine, time to welcome guests who want to spend a few hours or days in meditation and peace (see below).

The District of Mission, incorporated 1892, occupies 24,300ha and includes large portions of agricultural land. There are also about 15 cedar shake and shingle mills within Mission.

❓ **Mission Information:** Info Centre, 34033 Lougheed Hwy, Mission, BC, V2V 5X8. (3km east of Mission on Hwy 7, at St Mary's Park.) 604-826-6914. Daily in summer; weekdays, off-season.

■ **Mission Museum:** 33201 Second Ave. 604-826-1011. Tues-Sun, 12-4, summer; Tues-Fri, 12-4, off-season. In old Bank of Commerce, a 1907 two-storey prefab building. "Rivers, Rails, and Robbers" exhibit traces community's story from prehistoric times to end of Second World War.

■ **Westminster Abbey:** North off Hwy 7 on Dewdney Trunk Rd. 604-826-8975. Benedictine monks welcome visitors 1:30-4pm, Mon-Sat; 2-4:30 Sun, for views from the hill overlooking the river, and a glimpse of life on 80ha abbey, farm, and seminary campus. The church with tall stained-glass windows, glass dome, and bells is a highlight. Visitors may attend liturgies, join midnight mass at Christmas, or make their own contemplative retreat.

■ **Fraser River Heritage Regional Park:** 16.5ha. Off Hwy 7 on Stave Lake St, right on 5th Ave. 604-826-0277. Site of former St Mary's Mission and Indian Residential School. **Norma Kenney House,** two-storey log building, is park's reception centre, also the Blackberry Kitchen, serving light meals.

■ **Toti:lthlet Centre:** 34110 Lougheed Hwy, east of downtown Mission. Sto:lo learning centre and trade school where visitors can enjoy meals prepared by students. Native crafts.

■ **Mission Raceway Park:** 32670 Dyke Rd. 604-826-6315. Feb-Nov. Drag, road, and motocross racing.

■ **U-Fish for Trout:** At Sun Valley Trout Park, 31395 Silverdale Ave. At Trout Creek Farm, 31474 Tounshipline Ave, 604-466-9396.

🚏 **Highway 11:** In Mission. Turn south across the Mission Bridge to **Matsqui Trail Regional Park** on south shore of Fraser; travel 12km to **Abbotsford**; 5km south from Abbotsford to the **Sumas (Canada/US) border crossing**. For info on Abbotsford, see *Vancouver to Hope – South Bank*, p.126.

Neilson Regional Park: 10ha. On east outskirts of Mission, about 2km past info centre, Dewdney Trunk Rd leads north to Park on west side of Hatzic Lake. Magnificent views up the Fraser Valley to Mt Cheam and Cheam Ridge. 2km of walking trails, picnic tables, cookhouse, beach, canoe launch.

Xa:ytem (Hatzic Rock) National Historic Site and Interpretive Centre: On Hwy 7, about 2.5km east of Mission Info Centre. 604-820-9725. Open in summer and available for school tours. On this site is an immense triangular rock held sacred to Sto:lo people for the stories associated with it. Just before the rock was to be destroyed to clear the site for development, researchers pointed to evidence of continuous occupation reaching back some 9,000 years. The village, occupied by ancestors of the Sto:lo Nation, was emptied by smallpox in the mid to late 1800s.

Wagon World: On Hwy 7, about 3km east of Mission. Daily. 604-826-1010. Miniature replicas of wagons from various periods, and three full-sized wagons. Tours.

Cascade Falls Regional Park: 9.5ha nature park. On Hwy 7, 6km east of Mission, turn north on Sylvester Rd, right on Ridgeview Rd. Features a waterfall on Cascade Creek. Upper falls drop 25m to a large pool; series of smaller falls to valley floor.

Dewdney and Hawkins-Pickle Rd: Small community of Dewdney is past the Sylvester Rd junction, about 7km east of Mission, at start of Nicomen Slough.

Inch Creek Hatchery: North on Hawkins-Pickle Rd 0.5km past the dog-leg; pavement leads left, hatchery is on gravel road to right. Write Box 61, 38620 Bell Rd, Dewdney, V0M 1H0. 604-826-0244. Chum, chinook, coho, trout, cutthroat; best times: spring and winter. Sturgeon in display pond.

Dewdney Nature Regional Park: 7ha. Outside the dike on east side of River Rd South. Good river fishing, boat launch.

Nicomen Slough Bridge: The other side of Dewdney (and 9km east of Mission). Highway crosses the slough onto **Nicomen Island**.

Nicomen Island: Highway traverses 15km-long Nicomen Island, one of a series of islands on the Fraser River between Mission and Agassiz. This island is one of the prime farming areas in the Fraser Valley. Nicomen Slough, north of the highway, runs parallel to the Fraser River, along the northern shores of Skumalasph and Nicomen islands. The slough provides important wintering grounds for bald eagles, trumpeter swans, and many waterfowl species. Also this stretch offers 21km of fishable length with steelhead and cutthroat.

Deroche Bridge: Highway crosses the slough north to small community of Deroche, 19km east of Mission.

Harrison Bay: 28km east of Mission. Area is Sasquatch (or Bigfoot) country, so keep a close eye on the tall timbers for BC's version of the abominable snowman. Sasquatches, hairy giants twice the size of humans, supposedly came down from the hills in pre-colonial times, to abduct young women. The beasts sealed the women's eyes with pitch so that they couldn't see where they were being taken. If you do see a Sasquatch in the forest, contact the local authorities. However, you are more likely to see bald eagles, blue herons, or mallards, or catch a glimpse of a black bear or even a cougar. The bay's shores are home to the **Sq'ewlets (Scowlitz) First Nation**, offering historical and archaeological tours of the Harrison River, 604-826-5813.

Harrison Mills: 30km east of Dewdney. Early on, this west-bank settlement was called Chehalis Crossing; Harrison Mills was on the west side of the Harrison River. In the 1960s, a west-side post office adopted the name Harrison Mills, and now both sides share the name. See *Kilby Historic Store*, below.

Morris Valley Rd: Leads north from Harrison Mills (west side of the Harrison River). 14km to Hemlock Valley Ski Area.

SIDE TRIP

to Hemlock Valley

Sandpiper Golf Course: 14282 Morris Valley Rd. 1km north of Harrison Mills. 604-796-1000. 18 holes adjacent Rowena's Inn on the River.

Weaver Creek Spawning Channel: On Morris Valley Rd take right fork about 300m from highway; signs lead 12km to spawning channel. 604-796-9444. Sockeye, some chum and pink salmon. Displays. Look for American dipper and a few bald eagles in winter.

Chehalis River Hatchery: About 10km north of Hwy 7 on Morris Valley Rd. 16250 Morris Valley Rd. 604-796-2281. Chum, coho, chinook, steelhead salmon, and cutthroat trout. Something to see year-round.

Hemlock Valley Ski Area: 14km north of Hwy 7. 1-800-665-7080 or 604-797-4411. Open Dec-March. Located in a natural snow bowl, Hemlock has 365m-vertical drop, one triple chair, two double chairs, and one handle tow. Toboggans for rent. Cafeteria, lounge, ski school, ski patrol, ski rentals, and repair shops.

Return to Highway 7

Harrison River: 32.5km beyond Mission, just beyond Morris Valley Rd, Hwy 7 crosses river feeding into the Fraser River from Harrison Lake. One of the larger tributaries of the Fraser in the Lower Mainland. The slow-flowing river is navigable by canoe, kayak, or other small craft (see *Harrison Hot Springs*, below). All five Pacific salmon species return to the Harrison, including BC's largest chinook run, peaking in Nov. The fish attract up to 1,500 bald eagles each winter. And BC Wildlife Watch hosts the annual Harrison-Chehalis Bald Eagle Festival

In the heart of the Fraser Valley, Harrison Lake and the Coast Mountains.

late Nov-early Dec, focusing on viewing sites between Mission and Harrison Hot Springs. Nov-Jan is the best time to view salmon, eagles and trumpeter swans.

Kilby Historic Store and Farm: 7ha. Immediately on east side of Harrison River, signs lead right off Hwy 7. 1.6km to heritage site and adjacent park. 604-796-9576. Daily, 11-5, April-Nov. Pre-booked tours year-round.

General stores played a crucial role in the province's history. At Kilby, visitors can poke around the store that served the close-knit community of Harrison Mills in the 1920s and 1930s. In a single moment, step back 70 years. Thomas Kilby, and particularly his son Acton who took over in 1928, were pack rats. They saved everything, from the attic to the root cellar, every bill and order form. Long-forgotten brands and types of goods fill the shelves, with sundries hanging from the ceiling. A checkerboard sits by a potbellied stove where local folk once socialized.

Special exhibit focuses on the neighbouring Sto:lo First Nation communities of Sq'ewlets and Sts'a'i:les. Innovative educational programs include a period-complete store in the basement where school children can weigh out bulk foods, measure beans by the quart, crank the old phone, and press apples for cider. Events every weekend throughout summer. Picnic site, gift shop and tea room.

The first non-aboriginal community here, in the 1870s, was called Carnarvon. By the 1890s, it was being called Harrison River, and within another two decades, Harrison Mills, for the busy sawmill situated across the train tracks from the store. It was one of the Fraser Valley's first major sawmills, built in 1870 and powered by a waterwheel. Its hungry saws were fed with Douglas fir cut from virgin forests.

Kilby Provincial Park: 3ha; 38 campsites. 604-824-2300. Just beyond Kilby Store and Farm, on shore of Harrison River looking across Harrison Bay. Picnicking, fishing, boat launch. Excellent eagle and swan watching in winter.

Highway 9: 45km east of Mission. North to Harrison Hot Springs and Sasquatch Provincial Park.

SIDE TRIP

to Sasquatch Provincial Park and Harrison Hot Springs

Harrison Hot Springs: (Pop. 898). On Hwy 9, just 6.5km beyond the junction of Hwys 7 and 9. On the south shores of Harrison Lake. The first stories of warm water in Harrison Lake date back to 1859, when a gold prospector, canoeing on the lake, overturned his boat. Instead of perishing in the cold waters, he found the water warm and comfortable.

There has been a hotel at Harrison Lake since 1886. Harrison Hot Springs is a health and vacation resort with two mineral springs

and a sandy beach on the lakeshore. The source of the hot springs is two sulphur-potash outlets that emerge from mountains on the western shore of the lake. Temperatures from these two springs register 58 C and 62 C. The surrounding area is good for rockhounds. Lucky visitors may find jade, garnets, agates, fossils, or gold.

Harrison Hot Springs Information: Info Centre, 499 Hot Springs Rd, Box 255, Harrison Hot Springs, BC, V0M 1K0. 604-796-3425. May-Oct.

Harrison Public Hot Pool: At Harrison Hot Springs Rd and Esplanade Ave. Daily. More than 204,416 litres of hot spring water is piped from hot spring source, then cooled to a comfortable 39C.

Harrison Lake: North-south oriented lake over 60km long. Lake was part of late 1850s gold-rush route for miners travelling between the Fraser River and gold fields in the Cariboo. Today there is swimming, canoeing, and fishing for cutthroat and steelhead. Boat ramp. Rowboat and sailboat rentals; parasailing, windsurfing. Boat tours of the lake sail twice daily during summer from Harrison Hot Springs Hotel.

Harrison River: Flowing slow and wide from Harrison Lake to the Fraser River. Public beach and ramp at Harrison Hot Springs are launching points for 18km day-trip downriver to Harrison Mills, by canoe, kayak, or other small watercraft. It is also possible to make a 5km side trip up Morris Creek into Morris Lake. May see spawning salmon, eagles feeding (Nov-Feb), Trumpeter swans, ducks, aboriginal pictographs, remnants of early logging, and the wreckage of the *Port Douglas*, a 13m steam-powered tug that sank in 1923.

Hiking Trails: The 6km Campbell Lake Trail begins at the village reservoir and climbs 600m. Other trails lead to viewpoints over Harrison Lake. Sometimes, mountain goats can be spotted on the bluffs over Deer Lake.

World Championship Sand Sculpture Competition: Second weekend of Sept on Harrison Lake. Artists from as far away as Russia and the Netherlands spend days on ambitious creations made from as much as 50 tonnes of sand. Monumental finished sculptures are on exhibition for one month.

Harrison Festival of the Arts: July. 604-796-3664. Celebrating world music, theatre, dance, and visual arts against a backdrop of mountains and lake. Includes Children's Day.

Oaktree Golf Course: Just north of Hwy 7 and Hwy 9 junction, 3890 Hotsprings Rd. 604-796-9009. Nine holes.

Sasquatch Provincial Park: 1,217ha; 177 campsites (reservations taken: call 1-800-689-9025; from the Lower Mainland or overseas, call 604-689-9025). General info: 604-824-2300. 6.5km beyond Harrison Hot Springs on Rockwell Dr. Though the park is named for the legendary Bigfoot, most visitors report seeing the more plentiful deer, squirrels, and beaver. There are four lakes here, including the 112ha Hicks Lake, and forests surrounded by mountains, including the 1,524m Lookout Peak. Camping, canoeing, swimming, fishing, hiking. Lovely evergreen and deciduous forest.

Green Point Picnic Area: In Sasquatch Provincial Park, 8km north of Harrison Hot Springs on Rockwell Rd between Trout and Harrison lakes. The picnic area borders Harrison Lake. Boat launch.

Return to Highway 7

Agassiz: (Pop. 5,000). At junction of Hwys 7 and 9, 45km beyond Mission. Named after Captain Lewis Agassiz, formerly of the Royal Welsh Fusiliers. After working the Cariboo gold fields, he turned to farming in the Fraser Valley, establishing residence in 1867.

Agassiz Information: Contact Harrison Hot Springs Info Centre, Box 255, Harrison Hot Springs, BC, V0K 1K0. 604-796-3425. May-Oct.

Agassiz-Harrison Museum: 6947 Hwy 7, on the grounds of the Federal Research Station. 604-796-3545. Daily, May-early Sept. In CPR station, built 1893. Telegraph office and waiting room restored to original state.

Kalaya Creek Emu Ranch: 7671 McDonald Rd. 604-796-9129. April-Oct. Tours, gift shop.

Seabird Island: (Pop. 496). 3km east of Agassiz, highway crosses Maria Slough to what is almost imperceptibly an island. Seabird was named after an American paddlewheeler that ran aground here in the summer of 1858. In 1879, the Department of Indian Affairs designated this a reserve, urging Sto:lo First Nations families from throughout the area to take up farming here. At north end of island are **Seabird Island Cafe and Truck Stop Inn**, with a store, and Sto:lo arts and crafts. **Seabird Island Festival** is late May: 604-796-2177. In Maria Slough, fish for cutthroat and rainbow trout in spring.

Wahleach Rest Area: About 15km beyond Agassiz. Until 1995, this was Johnsons Slough Rest Area, named for an early settler. To honour this as a site important to the Sto:lo First Nations people, the BC Ministry of Transportation and Highways renamed it Wahleach, or Xwelich, for a former village just upriver from here. At the rest area a lively kiosk with four illustrated panels introduces travellers to the Stol:o people, "people of the river," and their rich history reaching back to the beginning of time, when their ancestors became the first salmon and cedar trees, and these sloughs were inhabited by the supernatural double-headed serpent, Silqhey.

Ruby Creek: Flows under Hwy 7, 18km beyond Agassiz. Named for the rubies and garnets found here. (Would-be rockhounds should note that they are not gem quality, and are of little monetary value.) Fish for cutthroat and steelhead along the creek's 4km of shoreline.

Highway 1: 31km beyond Agassiz. North 22km to Yale. See *Hope to Lytton*, next. Or turn south over the Fraser Bridge 3km to Hope and the junction of Hwys 1 and 3. See *Hope to Princeton*, p. 138.

HOPE TO LYTTON

TRANS-CANADA HIGHWAY (Highway 1)

The 108km from Hope north to Lytton on Hwy 1 (the Trans-Canada) are arguably one of the world's most exciting drives: highway ledged into the steep walls of the Fraser Canyon, the river boiling grey-brown below. In the late '40s this road was just a single track, and if two cars met around a rock, one of them had to back up. It was terrifying. The highway is beautiful now, but the route still makes the stomach tighten, and the tunnels rival anything Disneyland has to offer. There are seven tunnels between Hope and Boston Bar and one has a real twist in it: for a few seconds, there's no light at the end of the tunnel. We're not telling which one of the tunnels it is. Just know it's coming.

Long before dynamite, these canyon walls were traversed by aboriginal peoples. Explorer Simon Fraser dared follow them in 1808: "We had to pass where no human being should venture. Yet in those places there is a regular footpath impressed, or rather indented, by frequent travelling upon the very rocks."

Fifty years later, in the spring of 1858, gold was discovered on the bars of the Fraser River north of Hope. By fall, some 30,000 miners had scrambled or paddled their way up from the river's mouth, or from the south via the Okanagan Valley, across the 12-year-old Canada/US border. In their desperation for gold, few cared that they were trespassing on the traditional territories and fishing grounds of the Nlaka'pamux (Thompson people), "people of the canyon." Both miners and aboriginal people were killed as interests collided, and a full-scale war was narrowly averted by a peace agreement negotiated with Chief Cixpe'ntlam at Nlaka'pamux headquarters in Lytton. By year's end, most of the miners had left, frustrated by the hardships. Today's highway tunnels through the canyon are named for the bars where the miners camped, and reflect the miners' origins and occupations. Other names remind us of the ongoing presence of the Nlaka'pamux people, still centred in Lytton.

Discoveries of gold farther north in the Cariboo in 1860 made a more passable route through the canyon "imperative." Cariboo Road construction between Yale and Lytton started in 1862, and except for the section between Alexandra and Boston Bar, it was completed in 1864.

In 1880, the first dynamite blast set off construction for the Fraser Canyon section of the Canadian Pacific Railway. Some sections cost as much as $200,000 per mile. Four tunnels were drilled and dynamited within less than 1.5km of Yale. The CPR route through the canyon was completed in 1885. (Note that the CP rails run west of the canyon; the more recent Canadian National Railway tracks are along the east bank.)

From Hope, Hwy 1 hugs the west side of the Fraser River, then crosses over just beyond Spuzzum to chase the muddy river's east banks all the way to its confluence with the Thompson River at Lytton. There Hwy 12 picks up the Fraser, going northwest to Lillooet (see p.122). Hwy 1 continues along the Thompson River en route to Spences Bridge, Cache Creek, and Kamloops (see p.167). From Cache Creek, Hwy 97 leads north to the cities of Williams Lake and Prince George.

Hope: (Pop. 6,247). 147km east of Vancouver via Hwy 1. Hope is a crossroads, at the junctions Hwy 1, Hwy 3 (the Crowsnest), Hwy 5 (Coquihalla), and Hwy 7. Details. p.138.

Highway 7: 1km beyond Hope. 33km west to Agassiz and 11km beyond Agassiz to Harrison Hot Springs. See p.134.

Lake of the Woods Rest Area: 5km beyond Hope. A very pretty lake with small public beach, excellent swimming, fishing (and ice fishing), canoeing. No powerboats.

Emory Creek Provincial Park: 15ha; 34 campsites. 15km beyond Hope on Hwy 1. 604-824-2300. Site of former Emory City, a town built for the miners of 1858 who sought their fortunes in Fraser River gold. After the rush, the town was left to Chinese miners. A stop-of-interest plaque here honours the role of Chinese immigrants in building the CPR. From the 1860s to the 1880s their numbers grew from 2,500 to some 17,000. Legend says they produced twice as much gold as the Europeans by working the tailings left behind. In the early 1880s Emory hoped to become Pacific terminus of the CPR, but the dream died when the railway bypassed the town in 1886. Within a few years, the former city of 13 streets, nine saloons, a newspaper, brewery, and sawmill was again a virtual ghost town. Now it is a tranquil, wooded site with riverside trails and good river fishing.

Historic Yale: Southern edge of Yale, 24km beyond Hope. Sign honours head of navigation on the Fraser River. See *Yale*, below.

Yale: (Pop. 169). On Hwy 1, 24km north of Hope. There were once Sto:lo First Nations villages on both sides of the Fraser here. This was an important debarkation point for canoes from as far away as Vancouver Island bound for fishing sites on the rapids just above Yale. In 1848 a Hudson's Bay Company fur-trade post called "The Falls," (after the rapids) was established here; it was renamed in 1847 for James Murray Yale, the officer in charge of the HBC at Fort Langley.

Yale became the head of navigation on the Fraser River largely because of the massive, black Lady Franklin Rock. This boulder in the middle of the Fraser River was so large it blocked travel by steamers upriver past Yale. Goods had to be unloaded from the river steamers at Yale, and carried on by wagon trains to the Fraser Canyon and Cariboo gold fields. Yale became a gold-rush town – starting point of the famous Cariboo Wagon Road – a city of tents, shacks, stores, barrooms, and gambling houses where 30,000 prospectors passed through during the rush of 1858.

By 1886, with completion of the CPR, Yale's glory days as gold-rush town and transportation terminus were over. Today, Yale is a forestry and service centre rich in early pioneering history. The town is also a base for river-raft adventures companies conducting trips along the Fraser and Nahatlatch rivers.

Yale Information: No information centre, but ask at Yale Museum, below.

■ **Yale Museum:** 31179 Douglas St. 604-863-2324. Daily, June-Sept. Wed-Sun, spring and fall. Air-conditioned. In an 1868 house. Video detailing history of the Fraser Canyon's gold-rush period. Gold-panning waterpark and gold-panning instruction, aboriginal artifacts and baskets, memorabilia of the gold rush and CPR. Photos of Yale from 1860 to present. A national monument to contributions made by Chinese railway workers stands in front of the museum, one of the few trilingual signs put out by the federal government. Guided walking tours of Yale, and lantern tours of the pioneer cemetery (July-Aug).

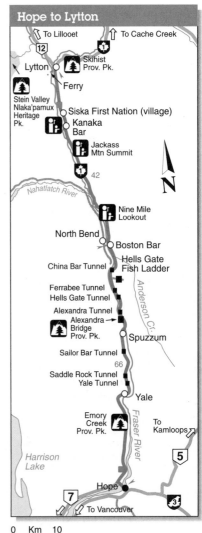

Hope to Lytton

To Lillooet — To Cache Creek
12 — 1
Lytton — Skihist Prov. Pk.
Ferry
Stein Valley Nlaka'pamux Heritage Pk.
Siska First Nation (village)
Kanaka Bar
Jackass Mtn Summit
42
Nahatlatch River
N
Nine Mile Lookout
North Bend
Boston Bar
Hells Gate Fish Ladder
China Bar Tunnel
Anderson Cr.
Ferrabee Tunnel
Hells Gate Tunnel
Alexandra Tunnel
Alexandra Bridge Prov. Pk.
Spuzzum
Sailor Bar Tunnel
66
Saddle Rock Tunnel
Yale Tunnel
Yale
Emory Creek Prov. Pk.
Fraser River
To Kamloops
5
Harrison Lake
Hope
7
To Vancouver
3

0   Km   10

■ **St John the Divine Church:** On Hwy 1 at traffic light. Provincial heritage site. Daily in summer. Oldest church in BC still on its original foundations. Built by Royal Engineers about 1859. Pioneer cemetery tells of tragic losses during gold rush and building of railway.

■ **Lady Franklin Rock:** Ask at the museum for directions to viewing spot. It is said the rock is named to honour Lady Franklin, wife of Sir John Franklin, Arctic explorer last heard from July 26, 1845. Dozens of search expeditions failed to find him. Lady Franklin, while on her own search, visited Yale. The river here is still an important aboriginal fishing site.

■ **Barnards Express Commemorative Plaque and Cariboo Wagon Road National Monument:** On waterfront at Albert St.

■ **Spirit Cave Hiking Trail:** 1km south of Yale on Hwy 1. One-hour hike to spectacular views of Cascade Mountains.

■ **Gold Panning:** On the riverfront. 250-863-2324. There are restrictions.

Yale Tunnel: 1.5km beyond Yale. 286m long. First of seven tunnels along this section of Hwy 1.

Saddle Rock Tunnel: 5.5km beyond Yale. 146m long, 11.5m wide. Named for a saddle-shaped rock visible in river from nearby when water was low. Rock is an important aboriginal fishing site.

Sailor Bar Tunnel: 12km beyond Yale. 292m long, 12m wide. Both this tunnel and Saddle Rock Tunnel cost approximately $5,000 per metre to build.

Spuzzum: (Pop. 33). Roadside township on Hwy 1, 18km beyond Yale. Spuzzum is a Nlaka'pamux native word meaning "little flat." Restaurant, gas.

Alexandra Bridge: 20km beyond Yale, Hwy 1 crosses Fraser on new bridge. Old Alexandra Bridge, about 2km upriver, was built in 1926 to replace original 1863 suspension span that extended Cariboo Wagon Road across the Fraser River on its way to the gold fields at Barkerville. Named after Alexandra, Princess of Wales.

Alexandra Bridge Provincial Park: 55ha. 22km beyond Yale on Hwy 1. Follow old roadbed of first Trans-Canada Hwy down to old Alexandra Bridge. Unforgettable views from the bridge. Picnic areas, with a wheelchair-accessible picnic table.

Historic Alexandra Lodge: On Hwy 1, just beyond park. Built 1862 as roadhouse for travellers on Cariboo Wagon Road. Operated until recently: now closed.

Alexandra Tunnel: 24km beyond Yale. 290m long.

Hells Gate Tunnel: 28.5km beyond Yale. 101m long.

Ferrabee Tunnel: 29km beyond Yale. 100m long.

Lower Mainland adventure seekers have recently discovered the Nahatlatch River near Yale.

Hells Gate – Fishways, Airtram, River Rafting: About 30km north of Yale. This extremely fast and narrow passage in the Fraser Canyon daunted the fur-trade explorer Simon Fraser, little comforted by the ladders and scaffolds set here by his aboriginal hosts. Well into the last century, the Nlaka'pamux, "people of the canyon," maintained fish drying racks here. In 1913, during construction of the Canadian National Railway, a landslide blocked the passage and the route for millions of migrating salmon. Although fishways were constructed in 1945-46 to assist the salmon, runs have never recovered, and there are some who call this one of the worst environmental disasters in BC's history. Daily April-Oct, the airtram descends 153m across Fraser River to this historic site, which includes an education centre on the life cycle of the spawning salmon. Suspension bridge, observations decks, restaurant, shops. 604-867-9277.

River-rafting tours through Hells Gate: several private companies run trips through the 28km/h river churning through the canyon here. Somewhat tamer waters of the Fraser and Thompson rivers are also available for rafting enthusiasts. Ask at Yale Museum and Hope Info Centre.

China Bar Tunnel: About 31km beyond Yale. At 610m, one of North America's longest.

Boston Bar: (Pop. 391). 42km beyond Yale. Aboriginal people referred to Americans, who were among hundreds who panned for gold on the banks of the Fraser River here, as "Boston men" because so many came on ships from Boston.

Cog Harrington Bridge: 1km north of Boston Bar. Crosses to North Bend, a divisional point on the Canadian Pacific Railway. The bridge, built in 1986, replaced the Boston Bar-North Bend Ferry, an aerial ferry that ran from 1940. It was simply a cage running on two 4.5cm cables suspended 9m above high water between a tower on the west bank and an anchor block on the east. Electric winches pulled the cage across, carrying one car or 40 passengers. Remaining cable car on display at CN station in Boston Bar.

Logging Road to Nahatlatch Lake and Mehatl Valley: From bridge on North Bend side, Chaumox Rd leads north 15km to another bridge across Nahatlatch River, popular among river rafters. 10km to lake chain, fishing for cutthroat and Dolly Varden, scenery, primitive Forest Service campsites. This is an active forestry road: logging trucks have right of way. North of the Nahatlatch River, 23,860ha of the Mehatl Creek valley and precious spotted owl habitat have been protected in the new **Nahatlatch/Mehatl Provincial Park.** No development.

Nine Mile Lookout: Near Ainslie Creek Bridge, 9km north of Boston Bar.

Boothroyd Airport: Entrance east off Hwy 1, 14km north of Boston Bar.

Jackass Mountain: On Hwy 1, 25.5km north of Boston Bar. Pullout at summit for southbound traffic. Views. Name is memorial to a weary mule that fell, fully loaded, into the canyon below. The mule was part of a stream of freight animals packing supplies along the Cariboo Rd to Interior gold fields in the 1860s.

Kanaka Bar: A few services about 28km north of Boston Bar. The Hudson's Bay Company employed many Hawaiians, or Kanakas, who arrived with them on ships in the 1830s. Many stayed. Some panned for gold here. This was the first place in BC where alfalfa was grown, in the 1860s. About 1km north, road leads west off Hwy 1 toward Kanaka First Nation community. It's about 250m to historic Anglican Church.

Siska First Nation: (Pop. 135). 30km north of Boston Bar (12km south of Lytton). One of 11 Nlaka'pamux First Nation communities. The Siska Creek valley, like the

Stein River valley to the north, is sacred to the Nlaka'pamux, and is a source of much spiritual and artistic inspiration. Several artists from this community are becoming well known for their sculptures in high-quality soapstone taken from ancient quarries hidden deep in the community's traditional mountain territories. The Museum of Civilization in Ottawa, the UBC Museum of Anthropology, and the Royal BC Museum have or will be exhibiting some of their contemporary pieces reflecting styles born centuries ago. Examples are on display in the log administration building, which houses the **Siska Art Gallery**, just off the highway. Siska Museum, here, open daily, June-Oct, displays basketry, soapstone carvings, a sweat lodge, and period "living" rooms from the 1940s.

Siska Information: Box 519, Lytton BC, V0K 1Z0. 250-455-2219.

Siska (Cisco) Bridges: 31km north of Boston Bar. Pullout on east side of highway for view of twin bridges: the CPR crosses from the east bank of the mighty Fraser to the west; the CNR crosses from the west to the east. Nowhere along the canyon is there enough room to run more than one railroad on each side for any useful distance. During the Second World War, this was considered a crucial national transportation junction, and security guards watched it closely.

Scuppa Rest Area: 36km north of Boston Bar.

Lytton: (Pop. 400). On Hwy 1, 42.5km north of Boston Bar. At the confluence of the Fraser and Thompson rivers, an ideal base for adventurous river rafters. Headquarters of the Lytton First Nation (pop. 1,500) of the Nlaka'pamux people, and site of the ancient Nlaka'pamux village and capital, Kumsheen or Lkamtci'n, meaning "confluence." Explorers referred to it as "The Forks," and established the Hudson's Bay Company's Fort Dallas here. In 1858, it was renamed for Sir Edward Bulwer-Lytton, secretary of state for the colonies.

Lytton today is primarily a logging community. The Lytton First Nation has been central in the struggle to save from logging the forests of the Stein Valley, just north, on the opposite side of the Fraser River. Some of the earliest writings on Nlaka'pamux history, social conduct, and spirituality appear on rocky surfaces throughout the valley, long known as StI'yen, "hidden place." It is now called the **Stein Valley Nlaka'pamux Heritage Park**, jointly managed by the provincial government and the Lytton First Nation (details below).

Info Centre offers maps for self-guided historical tours of Lytton: museum has opened next door. People still come to pan for gold left behind by miners in the 1850s and '60s.

Lytton Information: Info Centre, Lytton and District Chamber of Commerce, Box 460, Lytton, BC, V0K 1Z0. 250-455-2523. In town centre at 400 Fraser St. Daily, June-Sept; Mon-Fri, Oct-May.

Lytton Ferry: On Hwy 12, 2km northwest of Lytton. Crosses Fraser River to farms and camps along west side, and to the Stein Valley Nlaka'pamux Heritage Park. 17m

reaction ferry carries 9t, two vehicles, or 20 passengers. Five minutes. On demand 6:30am-10:15pm. No service during high water. Ferry attached to overhead cables; river current provides the power. Operating since 1894.

■ **Stein Valley Nlaka'pamux Heritage Park:** Cross the Fraser River at Lytton via the reaction ferry. It is 4.5km to parking lot marked by a cairn, and start of trail. (About 2km beyond the parking lot is quick access to the Stein River, walking trails, and pictographs.) This is Lytton First Nation reserve land, and Watchmen may charge a small maintenance fee to hikers who must start from here; they also plan to offer guided tours, to pass on their knowledge "to all who wish to learn about the spiritual values we hold." For information: 250-455-2304.

This is the last unlogged watershed in BC within reasonable driving distance of Vancouver. The Lytton First Nation on the valley's eastern end, the St'at'imc People of Mt Currie on the valley's western end, environmental groups, and concerned people throughout the province fought a hard battle through the 1980s and '90s to save the valley's forest and cultural heritage from obliteration. In 1985, the first of many Voices for the Wilderness Festivals drew thousands of supporters from around the world, and awakened Lower Mainland hikers to the potential here. The 75km trail follows the Stein River from an elevation of 460m toward the Coast Mountains, where the headwaters lie at an elevation of 2,400m. There's good family hiking in the lower valley. Only the hale and hearty should attempt the nine-day trek into the rugged alpine regions. Three cable car crossings. Stunning scenery between Stein Mountain (2,774m) and Skihist Mountain (2,944m). Virgin forests of pine, spruce, cottonwood, cedar. Wildflowers, lakes, and streams. Nlaka'pamux elders say this valley is to them what Rome is to Catholics: young people came here seeking "the power of nature," and recorded their experiences on rock walls with red paint. Check bookstores for excellent maps and guidebooks.

■ **Lytton Museum:** Next to Info Centre. Pioneer and golf-panning samplings. Complete works of town's namesake. Across street, in pretty Caboose Park, is 1918 CNR car. Look for 3m long "jelly roll," a log of clay and sand whipped up and deposited during the last ice age, about 10,000 years ago.

■ **Gold Panning Recreational Reserve:** Runs along Fraser River for 5km. Hand-panning only. Inquire at Info Centre.

■ **Lytton Heritage Park:** On Hwy 12, about 8km north of Lytton. For guided tours, contact Info Centre. Inspiring walk under pines to the banks of the Thompson River, a Nlaka'pamux pit-house, and remnants of rock piles and walls built by Chinese immigrants during the gold rush.

Fraser-Thompson River Confluence: These two rivers, which join at Lytton, are part of one of the largest watersheds in Canada. The Fraser, the longest river in BC, fifth longest in Canada, flows 1,368km from its headwaters in the Rockies, near Mt Robson, into the Strait of Georgia at Vancouver.

Through its long journey it is joined by major rivers – the Thompson, Vedder, Nechako, Bridge, Stave, and others (see p. 91). Its waters are swelled by the Thompson River at Lytton, more than 180km upstream from its mouth.

The Thompson, the heart of Thompson Okanagan Country, begins as two rivers which join at Kamloops. The headwaters of the North Thompson are in the Columbia Mountains, just 50km west of the Rockies. The North Thompson flows southwest 200km from Wells Gray Park to Kamloops where it is joined by the South Thompson coming from Little Shuswap Lake. From Kamloops, the Thompson River flows west 40km through Kamloops Lake, southwest to its confluence with the Fraser, a total of 489km from its source.

The Thompson River was named for David Thompson, a young surveyor and explorer who descended the Columbia River from its headwaters to the sea. Ironically, he never saw the Thompson, which was named after him by explorer Simon Fraser. And it was Thompson who named the Fraser (after Fraser, who had travelled the Fraser River from Prince George to the sea in 1808).

Highway 12: Northwest off Hwy 1 in Lytton, making a loop through Lillooet, to join Hwy 99. Hwy 99 connects with Hwy 97 11km north of Cache Creek. See *Cariboo Country*, p.243. Hwy 99 also leads southwest to Mount Currie, Whistler, and the Lower Mainland, see p.117.

HOPE TO PRINCETON

MANNING PROVINCIAL PARK
(Crowsnest Highway, Highway 3)

Hope is the western terminus of the trans-provincial Hwy 3, the Crowsnest. This 136km portion of the Crowsnest winds its way east and south through lakes-and-mountains country, and through the 65,884ha Manning Provincial Park, before cutting north to Princeton.

People still talk of driving the "Hope-Princeton" as if it were something of a feat. There's even a song about it by Canadian folk singer James Keelaghan: "You said I should buck up and shoulder the load/Those words made some sense on the Hope Princeton Road." Though the road is a good one, there's no doubt this is not an easy stretch. There are dramatic turns and switches, some when you least expect them. So take it easy, heed the signs, and don't expect to make time. There are lots of passing lanes.

The origin of the name Crowsnest here is something of a mystery, though it may have come from the Crow people, a tribe of the Sioux who migrated west from the Missouri River area in the 1700s to settle in the Rockies near today's BC/Alberta border. It has also been suggested the highway was named for a flock of crows that habitually nest along the route. Hmmm.

Highways 3 and 1: North on Hwy 1 leads 32km to Yale. For details on Yale, see *Hope to Lytton*, p.129.

Hope: (Pop. 6,247). 53km beyond Chilliwack on Hwy 1. At junction of Hwys 1, 3, 5 and 7, and three waterways, the mighty Fraser and its two substantial tributaries, the Coquihalla River and Silver Hope Creek. Hope sits below the entrance to the Fraser's steep-walled canyon, nestled in a mountain-ringed valley. This was the site of a major Sto:lo village, Ts'qo:ls. In 1848, Henry Newsham Peers, of the Hudson's Bay Company, established Fort Hope here, in hopes his trail would become an all-British trade route between Fort Kamloops (see p.174) and Fort Langley (p.125). The Sto:lo people moved their village about 1km from the fort's palisades, and later, to make room for this burgeoning city, were dispersed to other villages downriver. With the gold rush, beginning in 1858, Hope boomed, busted, and boomed, competing with Yale as a gold-rush centre. Walter B. Cheadle, a tourist here in l863, observed as he travelled downriver: "We passed Hope, a town of 30 or 40 houses, size of Yale. It is most beautifully situated in a large flat with a magnificent amphitheatre of mountains behind. Prettiest site I have seen in the Colony."

The town came to life again, in 1886, as a station on the new CPR mainline. A century later, Hope, a major highways junction, boasts one and only one set of traffic lights. But, increasingly, the town's dramatic setting is making this a destination in itself. Highway travellers stopping for coffee look out to gliders soaring against a backdrop of mountains and the Fraser River. The Vancouver Soaring Association bases itself here because of the consistent ridge lift – winds from the west, funnelling into the valley, and deflecting up with the mountains. The city is also a base for river rafts and jet boats launching on the Coquihalla, Fraser, Nahatlatch, and Thompson rivers.

Only 15 minutes away on Kawkawa Lake Rd are the Othello-Quintette Tunnels in the Coquihalla Canyon Recreation Area (see below), one of the engineering feats of the world. Many nearby lakes, including Kawkawa, Lake of the Woods, Silver, and Ross, are warm, clear, and inviting, with boating, swimming, fishing, picnicking. Greenwood Island in the Fraser River is a heron sanctuary. Croft Island just behind it attracts gold panners. And local mountains – Mt Ogilvie, Mt Hope, Thacker Mountain, and Holy Cross Mountain – lure hikers, mountain bikers, and picnickers (ask at Info Centre).

"Chainsaw-carving capitals" are popping out of the woodwork throughout BC. Hope, with 22 modern-day totems, joins Chetwynd, Revelstoke, and Grouse Mountain in a celebration of the tree as a monumental medium. Info Centre, below, is start of self-guided chainsaw carving tour, and in summer, an artwalk, featuring local artists.

Hope Information: Info Centre, 919 Water St, Box 370, Hope, BC, V0X 1L0. 604-869-2021. Open weekdays year-round. Excellent map displays detail area hikes.

■ **Hope Museum:** 919 Water St. 604-869-7322. Daily May-early Sept. Restored gold concentrator, a ball mill originating from a gold mill in the Coquihalla River valley, local pioneer and Sto:lo artifacts.

■ **Gold Panning:** On the Fraser and Coquihalla rivers. Info Centre has maps marking possible mother lodes. Local hardware store sells gold pans.

■ **Rainbow Junction Community Arts Centre:** Junction of Hwy 1 and Old Hope Princeton Way. In restored CNR station. Presents works of local artists. Arts and crafts, tearoom.

■ **Christ Church National Historic Site:** Downtown Hope. Anglican church, built in 1861, one of the oldest churches in BC on its original site.

■ **Memorial Park:** Downtown Hope. Musical entertainment at park bandstand throughout summer. Trees in the park developed root rot: local chainsaw carver Pete Ryan has transformed 22 stumps into animal forms. First came an eagle sitting on a stump; next a black bear and her cubs. Playground, picnic tables.

■ **Japanese Gardens:** Next to Memorial Park. Dedicated to Japanese-Canadians placed in Tashme internment camp (24km from Hope on Hwy 3) during Second World War.

■ **Centennial Park:** On Fraser River. Signpost gives names and elevations of surrounding peaks. Jet-boat tours depart from dock.

■ **Fort Hope Cairn:** Hwy 1 and Wallace St. Commemorates Hudson's Bay Company's establishment of Fort Hope in 1848.

■ **Sucker Creek Salmon Enhancement Site:** Left on Kawkawa Lake Rd. Cross bridge and immediately turn left. Take short boardwalk to see spawning coho, chum, and pink salmon (Oct-Nov). BC Wildlife Watch viewing site.

■ **Vancouver Soaring Association:** 604-521-5501. Based at Hope Airport. 100-member club flies mainly on weekends, and to promote the sport of soaring (gliding in planes without engines), offers introductory 20-minute flights; also three-flight instructional packages.

■ **Golf: Hope Golf and Country Club**, from 7th Ave, take Golf Course Rd. 604-869-5881. At the base of Thacker Mountain, at the confluence of the Coquihalla and Fraser rivers. Nine-hole course with 18 tee boxes, putting green, driving range, and clubhouse.

■ **H-Tree:** Near intersection of Hudson's Bay St and Fifth Ave. Two saplings were entwined back in the early days; now they create an H for Hope.

Kawkawa Lake Park: 7ha. 5km beyond Hope on Kawkawa Lake Rd. Can be reached from Hwy 3, but it's trickier. Easiest access is from town: take Wallace St (the main drag) east to 6th Ave; turn right at the bowling alley; then left at the ballpark (which is Kawkawa Lake Rd), and follow signs. Shallow waters, not glacial fed, make this warm lake perfect for swimming and boating. Fish for kokanee, rainbow trout, cutthroat trout, and squawfish.

Coquihalla Canyon Recreation Area and Othello Tunnels: 150 ha. East 10km beyond Kawkawa Lake Provincial Park. Take Kawkawa Lake Rd to turnoff for Othello Rd. Follow Othello Rd to Tunnels Rd. Signs mark route to park. This is where first Rambo movie, *First Blood*, was filmed with Sylvester Stallone. Spectacular scenery in gorge has also brought Hollywood here to film *Fire with Fire*, *Shoot to Kill*, *National Dream*, and *Journey Home: Adventures of the Yellow Dog*. A summer run of steelhead trout may be seen (June-Aug) migrating through the canyon's pools and ripples.

Truly a don't-miss is a stroll through the famous Kettle Valley Railway's Othello Tunnels. Construction began in 1910 on this railway that was to connect the Kootenay region with the coast. 61km of track were routed through the Coquihalla Valley from the Coquihalla Summit to junction of the CPR mainline situated across the Fraser River from Hope. Construction was laborious: one particular mile, built in 1914, cost $300,000 to complete. Greatest challenge was the Coquihalla Gorge, where Coquihalla River cut a 91m-deep channel in solid granite.

Chief engineer Andrew McCulloch surveyed the canyon from the vantage point of a wicker basket hanging over the gorge, and decided that he didn't need to bypass the canyon. Instead, he built right through the gorge, tunnelling through five different rock faces in a series of short tunnels. He named tunnels and stations after his daughters and characters from Shakespeare's plays. The Kettle Valley Railway opened in 1916. After a checkered history of service, and much legend and song, the line was officially closed in 1961. Also see p. 143. Flashlights are a good idea. Closed in winter.

Return to Highway 3

Coquihalla Hwy (Hwy 5): From Hope, northeast 115km to Merritt. For details, see *Hope to Kamloops*, p.173.

Nicolum River Provincial Park: 24ha; 9 campsites. 604-824-2300. 7km beyond Hope on north side of Hwy 3. Camping, picnicking, fishing for cutthroat and squawfish on shores of the clear, cool Nicolum River. The 2,286m Tulameen Mountain and 2,438m Mt Outram overlook the park, cutting off the summer's afternoon sun. Evenings are cool.

Hope Slide Viewpoint: 18km beyond Hope. One of BC's most devastating slides took place here in Jan 1965. 46 million cubic metres of earth, rock, and snow – the entire side of a 1,983m-high and 1km-wide mountain – bore down into the valley at a speed in excess of 160km/h. Four people were killed, two were never found. It took 21 days to build a temporary road through the disaster. **Rest area closed in winter.**

Manning Provincial Park: 65,884ha; 353 campsites in four campgrounds (reservations taken: call 1-800-689-9025; from the Lower Mainland or overseas, call 604-689-9025). Also Manning Park Lodge, cabins, chalets, mountain-bike rentals: 250-840-8822. General info: 250-840-8836. Manning Park, 26km beyond Hope in the Cascade Mountains, was established in 1941. Hwy 3 bisects the park: it is 57km from the West Gate to the East Gate. Park headquarters are at exact midpoint between Hope and Princeton, 68km from each town.

Within the park are forested mountains, deep valleys, alpine meadows, azure-blue lakes. Manning Park is enjoyed year-round.

Four campgrounds include: **Hampton** with 98 campsites, 4km east of park headquarters on Hwy 3; **Mule Deer**, 49 campsites, 8.5km east of park headquarters on Hwy 3; **Coldspring**, 63 campsites, 2km west of headquarters on Hwy 3; and **Lightning Lake/Spruce Bay**, 143 campsites, 6km south of headquarters on Gibson Pass Rd. Wilderness campgrounds are located at Monument 78/Pacific Crest, Frosty Creek, Poland Lake, Mowich, Buckhorn, Kicking Horse, Nicomen Lake, and the south end of Strike Lake.

In the summer, a good paved road leads 9km to the Cascade Lookout for views of valley and surrounding peaks. Gravel road leads 6km to Blackwall Peak subalpine meadows, Alpine Naturalist Hut, and Paintbrush and Heather trails. Horseback riding, concession, canoe rentals. In winter, slopes and trails of Gibson Pass Ski Area here challenge skiers of all abilities. Two chairlifts, a T-bar, and poma lift. At least 150km of cross-country trails. Winter camping in tents and RVs at several locations in park.

The park offers excellent wildlife viewing opportunities. The most easily accessed sites are Lightning Lakes, Blackwall Alpine, and the Beaver Pond. Small mammals to look for include chipmunks, two species of marmots, two species of ground squirrels, and pikas. For birdwatchers, the park's Annual Bird Blitz is in the third week of June: 250-840-8836.

Manning Provincial Park West Gate: 26km beyond Hope. Watch for the wood carving of a hoary marmot that marks park entrance. The marmot is a delightful park resident, and signs throughout the park note the best hoary marmot watching spots. In summer, these quite large rodents (up to 9kg) like sunning themselves on the rocks at Blackwall Peak. They have a piercing whistle.

Sumallo Grove: 35km beyond Hope. 700m self-guided trail to magnificent stands of western red cedar and Douglas fir. Wheelchair accessible.

Rhododendron Flats: 37km from Hope. One of the few places in BC where wild rhododendrons grow in their natural state. The red blossoms of this flowering evergreen are at their best early to mid-June. 2km walking trail.

Cascade Provincial Recreation Area: 16,680ha. 250-840-8836. Adjacent northern boundary of Manning Provincial Park, 38.5km beyond Hope. Access on foot or horseback along sections of three heritage trails, the Dewdney (1860), the Whatcom (1858), and the Hope Pass (1861). These trails are silent reminders of earlier attempts to cross the inhospitable Cascade Mountains. Wilderness camping at Paradise Valley.

■ **Dewdney and Whatcom Trails:** Access at the **Skagit Bluffs** and **Snass Creek**, 3km east of Rhododendron Flats. Parking for your car, hitching post for your horse. Bridle and hiking paths along Snass Creek's old Dewdney Trail, which leads to turnoff to Whatcom Trail.

■ **Hope Pass Trail:** Access at **Skaist River**, 6km from Snass Creek, 44km east of Hope. Park at **Cayuse Flats**, south side of Hwy 3. (Cayuse Flats is 24km west of park headquarters.)

Skagit River: Beyond Rhododendron Flats Hwy 3 traces river and sometimes crosses over it. Coming from Ross Lake south across the Canada/US border, the Skagit cuts north through the **Skagit Valley Provincial Park** on Manning Park's western boundary. A provincial wilderness walk-in campsite is located along the Skagit River. Major part of Skagit Valley Provincial Park is accessed from Silverhope Creek Rd *west* of Hope: see *Vancouver to Hope – South Bank*, p.128.

Allison Pass: 58km east of Hope (10km from park headquarters). El 1,341m. Named after John Fall Allison, an early Princeton rancher with many descendants still in the area.

Similkameen River: About 62km beyond Hope. Winding east and north, Hwy 3 traces this river to Princeton and from there east to the Canada/US border. South of the border, the river joins the Okanagan River. In the late 1850s, before the great Fraser River gold rush, prospectors followed gold traces up the Similkameen.

Manning Park Resort, Ski Area and Cascade Lookout: At 67km east of Hope (9km east of Allison Pass), "the Lodge" is almost halfway between Hope and Princeton on Hwy 3, and a natural stopping place. 250-840-8822. Gibson Pass Rd leads out just behind the lodge to the ski area. Another road leads from opposite (north) side of Hwy 3 to Cascade Lookout and mountain views.

Manning Park Corral: Just behind resort, 0.5km up the road to Lightning Lakes. Horse and pony rides. 250-840-8844.

Park Headquarters and Visitor Centre: 1km east of the lodge, equidistant from Hope and Princeton (68km either way). Open daily in summer, it has displays of area's natural and human history. Naturalists answer questions and conduct morning and afternoon walks in July and Aug. The valley walk reveals everyday things in nature often missed. The alpine-meadows walk takes you up mountain slopes carpeted with flowers. Each summer evening, park naturalists give talks or slide shows at amphitheatre on Gibson Pass Rd south of the Lodge. Check at visitor centre or on information boards for details.

Manning Provincial Park East Gate: 15km beyond park headquarters; 84km beyond Hope. Large wood carving of a black bear marks entrance. Black bears are a chief resident, occasionally seen near park campgrounds. They are wild animals and should not be approached, offered food, or tormented.

Similco Mines: 101km east of Hope. Visible on south side of highway, terracing and gravel from copper mines that, after forestry, were Princeton's economic mainstay for 25 years. The mines closed in 1996 after copper prices plummeted.

Princeton: (Pop. 2,826). At junction of Similkameen and Tulameen rivers, 136km beyond Hope. For details on Princeton, see *Princeton to Christina Lake*, p.147. Hwy 3 (the Crowsnest) continues east beyond Princeton through Osoyoos and Crowsnest Pass into Alberta. From Princeton, Hwy 5A leads north to Merritt, through some of North America's finest rainbow trout country. See *Princeton to Kamloops*, p.180.

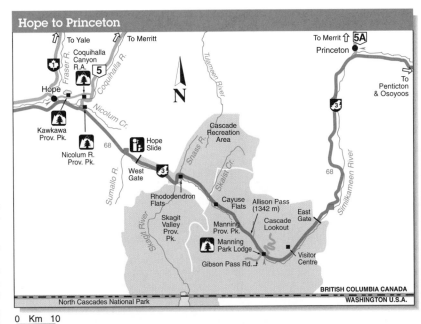

Hope to Princeton

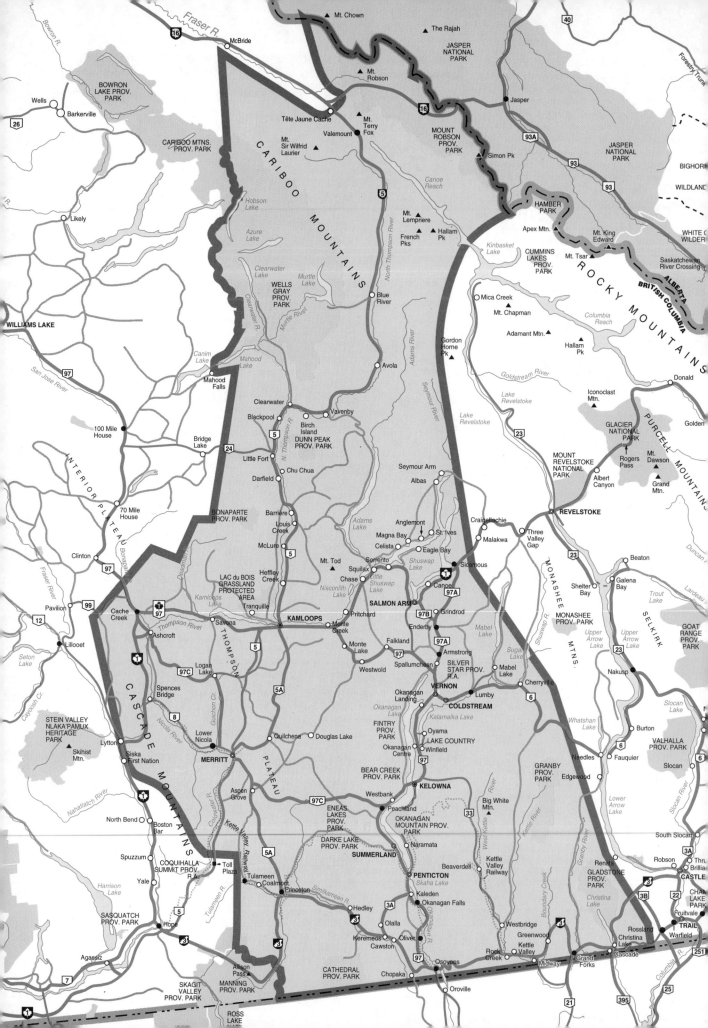

THOMPSON OKANAGAN

AN EDEN OF SUN AND FRUIT GARDENS

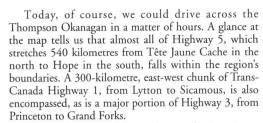

To truly appreciate the moods and seasons of the Thompson Okanagan, one should, by rights, cross the region on foot, or in a canoe, or by horseback. This is how the Interior Salish people – the Nlaka'pamux, Secwepemc and Okanagan – moved through the spectacular landscape, how the first European explorers and settlers ventured over the unfamiliar terrain.

It would have taken a group of early travellers months to traverse this territory from north to south, a distance (for eagles, anyway) of 500 kilometres. Starting at the Alberta border near Mount Robson, the highest peak in the BC Rockies, they would first have had to negotiate a flat-floored rift valley, the Rocky Mountain Trench, where both the Fraser and Columbia rivers rise. As our imaginary wanderers proceeded southward, leaving the glacier-clad Cariboo Mountains and entering the Shuswap Highland, the land would have become less rugged and the montane forests of spruce and fir given way to hemlock and red cedar.

Eventually, they would have emerged onto the Thompson Plateau, which extends from north of Kamloops to the burnt hillsides around Osoyoos. Here, the vegetation changes once again, to Douglas fir and larch and ponderosa pine. At the heart of this vast, arid upland, fragile steppes of bunchgrass offer refuge to bighorn sheep and rattlesnakes. Pocket deserts of sagebrush and prickly pear, home to spadefoot toads, mark its southern edges along the US border.

Despite the name, the Thompson Plateau is not particularly flat. It is a rolling, hilly zone between coastal and interior mountain ranges, incised with valleys and home to some of BC's largest, deepest lakes: Kamloops, Shuswap, Adams and Okanagan (where the Ogopogo serpent is reputed to lurk). Lakes and rivers form natural passageways through the countryside, and old-time travellers followed them. Modern tourists follow them still, as highways run alongside many of the region's rivers, especially the all-important Thompson system.

Today, of course, we could drive across the Thompson Okanagan in a matter of hours. A glance at the map tells us that almost all of Highway 5, which stretches 540 kilometres from Tête Jaune Cache in the north to Hope in the south, falls within the region's boundaries. A 300-kilometre, east-west chunk of Trans-Canada Highway 1, from Lytton to Sicamous, is also encompassed, as is a major portion of Highway 3, from Princeton to Grand Forks.

This is prime ground for outdoors enthusiasts. Large wilderness reserves such as Mount Robson, Cathedral and Wells Gray provincial parks attract hikers and campers. Wells Gray is also known for its superb canoeing, and Echo and Christina lakes are popular with paddlers, too. Houseboats are the lure on Shuswap Lake. Serious whitewater rafters and kayakers head to the Thompson, Clearwater, Granby and Similkameen rivers, windsurfers to Skaha, Okanagan, Kalamalka, Nicola, and Stump lakes. Tire-tube specialists laze down the Okanagan River Channel.

Dozens of provincial parks dot the Thompson Okanagan. Some notable ones are Roderick Haig-Brown near Squilax, where the world-famous Adams River sockeye salmon run; Bonaparte and Dunn Peak, recently established between Kamloops and Clearwater; the desertlike slopes of Okanagan Mountain; Silver Star, with snowmobile and cross-country trails; and Gladstone and Granby east of Okanagan Lake. Shuswap Lake sports 20 small parks, most of which are only accessible by boat. Lac du Bois Grasslands Protected Area, north of Kamloops, preserves a rare, 15,000-hectare bunchgrass ecosystem.

Wildlife viewing is a regional specialty. Black bears are abundant, and moose are often spotted between Merritt and Kamloops. Bighorn sheep peer from the banks of the Thompson River. Birdwatchers spot golden eagles and burrowing owls, hummingbirds and osprey. Some of the best viewing areas include the Robert W. Starratt Wildlife Sanctuary south of Valemount, the Swan Lake Sanctuary, near Vernon, Vaseux Lake, north of Oliver, and Salmon Arm Bay.

Vineyards and wineries are burgeoning along sunny south Okanagan lakeshores.

Winter sports are huge in the Thompson Okanagan. Downhill skiers and snowboarders trek to Apex near Penticton, Kelowna's Big White, Silver Star in Vernon, and Sun Peaks just north of Kamloops. Nordic ski trails abound in the Okanagan Valley, and around Salmon Arm and Merritt, while the Cariboo and Monashee mountains provide world-class heli-skiing. Groomed tracks draw snowmobilers to Graystokes, east of Kelowna, Vernon's Sovereign Lake and the Merritt, Lumby, and Armstrong areas. Even esoteric pursuits such as snowshoeing and dogsledding have enthusiastic followings.

The Kettle Valley Railway (KVR), built at great expense through near-vertical terrain early this century, then torn up when it became unprofitable, is now one of the region's recreational treasures. Much of the track bed, including tunnels and 18 glorious trestle bridges, is publicly owned, open to bikers and horseback riders. Two-wheelers will find a wealth of other trails near Kelowna and Kamloops, at Wildhorse Canyon and Kalamalka Lake. Equestrians head for area guest ranches, or explore the old Brigade Trail above Lake Okanagan and the vastness of Wells Gray Provincial Park.

Sportfishing is a year-round activity in the Thompson Okanagan, which boasts more than 500 lakes and countless streams. Rainbow trout, kokanee, Dolly Varden char, giant lake trout and steelhead are the names of the game; "catch and release" is the preferred method of angling. Golfers can check out more than 50 courses, including some of BC's toughest championship layouts.

Agriculturalists have reason to celebrate the region's outdoors. The Okanagan Valley, with one of the mildest, driest climates in the country, produces bumper harvests of apples, pears, peaches, nectarines, cherries, plums, apricots, and grapes. BC's wineries win awards around the world; winery tours and spring and fall wine festivals give visitors a chance to sample the latest vintages. The north Okanagan is dairy country; Armstrong, in particular, is famous for its cheese. In the Nicola Valley and Kamloops areas, cowboys roam some of BC's oldest, largest cattle ranches, and entrepreneurial farmers raise the province's newest crop: ginseng.

The Thompson Okanagan Region is not all rural. A mild, dry climate suits people as well as fruit, and some of Canada's fastest-growing cities are situated in the Okanagan Valley. Kelowna, with its lakefront parks, sandy beaches, and orchard museum, is now BC's third largest metropolis, its population over 90,000. The cattle centre of Kamloops, located where the North and South Thompson rivers join and noted for its sports facilities, ranks fifth, with more than 75,000 residents. Penticton, Vernon, Salmon Arm, Merritt, and Summerland are the other main towns.

The region's pioneers would be astonished at today's cities and vineyards, and bewildered by the very concept of outdoor recreation. But here and there – at Father Pandosy's Kelowna mission, perhaps, where the Oblate priest first introduced the apple to the Okanagan; at mining ghost towns such as Granite City and Fairview; at Secwepemc Heritage Park, with its archaeology and reconstructed winter village; at the gold-rush inn of Ashcroft Manor and the historic O'Keefe Ranch – they would have felt at home. At these and other rustic sites, and deep in the outback, as well, one gets the feeling that little has changed here in the last century – that in its secret places, the serene and beautiful Thompson Okanagan cannot be touched by time.

INFORMATION

Thompson Okanagan Tourism Association: 1332 Water St, Kelowna, BC, V1Y 9P4. 250-860-5999. Fax: 250-860-9993. E-mail: osta@awinc.com. For accommodation, golf packages and bookings, ski packages, special events: Okanagan Reservations, 1-800-669-1900. Website: http://www.okres.bc.ca. E-mail: sales@okres.bc.ca. Also, in Kamloops: #2-1490 Pearson Pl, Kamloops, BC, V1S 1J9. 250-377-4383 or 1-800-567-2275. Fax: 250-372-2318. E-mail: hcta@sympatico.bc.ca.

Addresses and phone numbers of local information centres are in the Logs with write-ups on each community.

TRANSPORTATION

Moving around the Thompson Okanagan region is as much recreation as destination oriented. Visitor Info Centres have information on everything from two-wheeler and watercraft rentals to hang-gliding clubs, hot-air balloons, and riding stables.

Airlines

The Kelowna International Airport is BC's busiest after Vancouver and Victoria. Airlines serve Kamloops, Kelowna, and Penticton with direct scheduled flights to Vancouver and Calgary. Smaller airline and helicopter companies also serve licenced airstrips in Vernon, Oliver, and Princeton, Revelstoke and Salmon Arm. Check local yellow pages for information about light aircraft and helicopter charters. Summer flight schedules for all airlines are in effect May through Sept.

■ **Air Canada/Air BC:** 1-800-667-3721. (From the US: 1-800-776-3000.) Several flights daily directly to Vancouver; four to Calgary. Air BC and Central Mountain Air are Air Canada's Thompson Okanagan connector. All Air BC and flights are listed in Air Canada's timetable and can be booked through Air Canada.

■ **Canadian Airlines International:** 1-800-665-1177 (Canada) or 1-800-426-7000 (US). Regular connecting flights to Canadian, American, and international destinations. Canadian Airlines offers winter ski tours to Big White and Silver Star out of Kelowna: 1-800-661-8881. Packages include airfare, bus transportation, on-mountain accommodation, and lift tickets.

■ **Canadian Regional Airlines:** Canadian Airlines' commuter partner, serves Penticton, Kelowna, and Kamloops. Contact Canadian Airlines.

■ **Horizon Air:** 1-800-547-9308. Kelowna-Seattle four times daily.

■ **Shuswap Air:** 1-800-663-4074 or 250-832-8830. Vancouver to Salmon Arm.

■ **Wells Gray Air Services:** 1250-674-3115. Sightseeing charters: flights to 100 Mile House, Quesnel Lake, Barkerville.

■ **WestJet Airlines:** 1-800-538-5696. Connects BC's west coast to the Interior, Alberta, Saskatchewan and Manitoba via Kelowna four times daily; Vancouver, Calgary, and Edmonton three times daily; Victoria once a day. Connects to Saskatoon and Regina once a day.

Railways

■ **Rocky Mountaineer Railtours:** Great Canadian Railtour Company, First Floor, 1150 Station St, Vancouver, BC, V6A 2X7. 1-800-665-7245 or 604-606-7200. May to mid-Oct. Sublimely, through the Rockies. Vancouver to Jasper, Vancouver to Banff, optional to Calgary. Travels only in daylight and now has a dome car. Passengers going east or west spend the night in Kamloops (where there is a dinner theatre that highlights the city's history and local fare). Continental breakfast, gourmet lunch, and hotel are included on Railtours.

■ **VIA Rail:** 1-800-561-8630. VIA Rail follows Hwy 1 from the Lower Mainland to Kamloops. Then, it runs northeast along Hwy 5, the Yellowhead, through Valemount and the Rockies to Alberta via Jasper, and continues to Edmonton and Toronto. Departs Vancouver Tues, Fri, Sun, at 7pm.

Bus Lines

■ **Greyhound Canada:** Call Vancouver, 1-800-661-8747, or specific cities: Penticton 250-493-4101; Kelowna 250-860-3835; Vernon 250-545-0527; Kamloops 1-800-661-8747. The only daily motor-coach service in this region. Non-stop express buses run six times daily to and from the Lower Mainland, and offer juice and movies. Buses depart three times daily for Calgary.

■ **City Buses:** BC Transit offers public transportation in Penticton, Kelowna, Vernon, and Kamloops.

By Road

In the Thompson Okanagan, travel is primarily a driving proposition. The main routes – Hwys 1, 3, 5, 97, and 97C – are predominantly two lanes, in excellent condition, with solid paved shoulders, regular passing lanes, and good visibility. Paved secondary roads pose no problem for vehicles from bicycles to motor homes. Back roads are accessible to four-wheel-drive vehicles. Speed limits average between 80 and 90km/h; Hwy 97C, the Coquihalla Connector, bringing the region within easy reach of the Lower Mainland, has limits as high as 110km/h.

The Crowsnest Hwy (Hwy 3) enters the Similkameen Valley from the eastern boundary of Manning Provincial Park. The Hwy 3A cutoff at Keremeos is a popular shortcut to Penticton. Farther east, Hwy 3 climbs nearly 900m in the 32km between Osoyoos and the 1,233m summit of Anarchist Mountain. Highway grades reach 9 percent, and average between 6 and 7 percent. Steep for a long ascent. Hwy 33 north from Rock Creek to Kelowna is a paved, but relatively untravelled, secondary road through open range country and ghost towns.

Hwy 5, north from Hope, transects the entire region diagonally, and is the only avenue through its northernmost reaches.

Hwy 6 enters the Okanagan at Cherryville and ends at Vernon, intersecting Hwy 97. This scenic secondary paved road is most travelled by local farm vehicles and travellers from the Kootenays.

Inland Ferries

The Ministry of Transportation and Highways operates a small fleet of inland ferries to complete the highway system where there are no bridges crossing the Fraser, Thompson, and Upper and Lower Arrow lakes waterways. These ferries are free of charge and carry both passengers and vehicles. Schedule information should be used only as a guideline since times can change on short notice.

■ **Shuswap Lake Ferry Service Ltd:** Box 370, Sicamous, BC, V0E 2V0. 250-836-2200. Boats and a barge for passengers and freight on Shuswap Lake. Various times; $12 per passenger, $27 minimum for car and driver. See *Kamloops to Sicamous*, p. 172.

■ **Adams Lake Ferry:** Southwest end of Adams Lake. Short crossing to cottages on southeast end of lake provides alternative to private road. 24 hours on call.

The provincial government provides ferry service across the Fraser River at Lytton and across the North Thompson River at McClure and Little Fort.

Taxis, Car, and RV Rentals

Taxis can be hired by the kilometre for out-of-town trips. Visitor Info Centres can advise. Auto rental agencies are located at airports and main city centres.

REGIONAL FEATURES

Okanagan Wines

BC's first grape vines were planted near Okanagan Mission, in the 1860s, by Father Charles Pandosy, at least in part for religious reasons. Today, wine is becoming the region's lifeblood: there are 45 wineries in the Okanagan Valley, most of them between Osoyoos and Vernon. In 1990, there were only 18. And wine is now the valley's number one tourist attraction. Visitors come to tour idyllic vineyards looking out over sparkling waters, listen to wine makers trained in California and Europe, and taste a little. BC wines – from Chardonnay to the honey-sweet nectar of Icewine – are winning international awards.

In the desert-cum-orchard lands of the Okanagan, more than 1,200 hectares of grapes are under cultivation. With its northerly latitude, moderate climate, and steep west-facing slopes, this burgeoning grape-growing region is most often compared to Germany's Rhine Valley. Both regions are best known for their white wines; both support a high proportion of small estate or farmgate wineries.

The Kettle Valley Railway bed at Myra Canyon, once for trains, now delights bikers and hikers.

It's a relatively new industry. Jesse Hughes began planting the first extensive vineyards in the Okanagan in 1926 and shipped his grapes to Victoria. In 1931, Guiseppe Ghezzi, along with a syndicate of investors led by Pasquale Capozzi and former BC Premier W.A.C. Bennett, formed what is the province's oldest continuous winery – Calona Wines. By the 1960s, Calona was BC's largest producer of a sweet, fortified drink called wine. The following decades brought more experimentation with European grapes that might be best suited to the valley, consultation with German wine scientists, and the licencing of small estate wineries devoted to quality and precision. In 1988, the Free Trade Agreement eliminated the modest governmental protection Canadian wine makers enjoyed, but compensation payments allowed Okanagan vintners to remove undesirable grape varieties and leap forward. Another boon to the wine boom was the birth of the Vintners Quality Alliance, which insists that bearers of the VQA label use only BC-grown grapes. BC wine makers are not yet through the trial-and-error stage of grape growing: Chardonnay has emerged as the most widely grown, but some 45 wines are being squeezed from such grapes as Johannesburg Reisling, Cabernet Sauvignon, and Pinot Noir.

In a province suffering from the over consumption of non-renewable resources, wine holds much promise. But some people – calling for balance and moderation in all things – want to ensure the Okanagan does not become a California of the North. Already, some of the few wild habitats not suitable for fruit orchards are being eyed for grapes.

Many wineries and vineyards welcome visitors: they are listed in the *Logs* to follow.

The Kettle Valley Railway

If you travel in the Okanagan Valley you will meet it. Once 525km long, this subsidiary of the Canadian Pacific Railway (CPR) ran between Hope and Midway; a long spur line ran north from Coldwater to Spences Bridge. The dream of engineer extraordinaire Andrew McCulloch, it traversed near-impossible terrain, and was said to be the most expensive railway built anywhere in the world.

At first glance, the Okanagan might seem a gentle valley: here are none of the craggy, ice covered peaks of the Rocky or Coast mountains. What we see are soft, brown hills, long, gentle lakes. But, it turns out, the Okanagan Valley offers no easy passage through. Most of the KVR line runs though the Okanagan. To overcome its challenges, the railway travels snakelike, sometimes almost turning back on itself. Its complex route is marked on the Thompson Okanagan regional map, p. 140.

For a whole generation of people – from 1916 to 1949 – this was the only strong link between the Kootenays and BC's Lower Mainland; between the Okanagan and its orchards, and markets east and west. But by 1959, avalanches, mudslides, declining traffic, and alternative routes spelled the demise of the KVR. It was closed down in bits and pieces, from the 1960s on. The tracks have been torn up, but the bed remains. And the KVR is now a railway in our hearts, on our maps, and beneath our feet.

In the *Logs* to follow, the KVR will appear again and again. Highways and back roads trace its flat easy grade. Adventurous drivers may even, on a few occasions find themselves driving on it. Mountain bikers and hikers, riders on horseback celebrate it along mile after wondrous mile of new linear park. Backcountry tour operators take 4x4s on it. KVR stations are now museums and information centres. At the West Summerland station, you can board and ride a steam train. Steam, trestles, tunnels – all put our modern journeys into perspective.

For more, read *McCulloch's Wonder*, by Barrie Sanford, *Exploring the Kettle Valley Railway*, by Beth Hill, and *Cycling the Kettle Valley Railway*, by Dan and Sandra Langford.

THOMPSON OKANAGAN EVENTS

Armstrong
- **Interior Provincial Exhibition and Rodeo:** Early Sept. Four-day agricultural fair.
- **Annual Balloon Rendezvous:** Mid-Oct.

Ashcroft
- **Ashcroft and District Stampede:** Mid-June.

Barrière
- **Squam Bay Fishing Derby:** Early July.
- **North Thompson Fall Fair and Rodeo:** Labour Day weekend.

Beaverdell
- **High Water Days:** Early June.

Bridesville
- **Horse Show:** Late Aug.

Cache Creek
- **Graffiti Days and Old-Time Drags:** Early June.
- **Hat Creek Barn Dance and BBQ:** Aug.
- **Jackpot Team Cattle Penning and Top-Hand Competition:** Mid-Sept. At Hat Creek Ranch. Craft fair.
- **Bonaparte Rodeo:** Sept.

Chase
- **Chase Daze:** Late June.
- **Chase Creek International Equestrian Events:** Sept.

Cherryville
- **Festival of the Arts:** Aug.

Christina Lake
- **Sandcastle Contest:** Early Aug.

Clearwater
- **Wells Gray Loppet:** Feb. Ski race.
- **May Day Parade:** May.
- **Wildflowers Wells Gray:** Late July.

Falkland
- **International Dogsled Races:** Early Jan.
- **Falkland Stampede:** May 24 long weekend. Running since 1919.

Grand Forks
- **Grand Forks International Baseball Tournament:** Teams from as far away as Japan. Five days through Labour Day weekend.
- **Grand Forks Fall Fair & BSHA Horse Show and Rodeo:** Early Sept.

Greenwood
- **Founders Day Celebration:** Mid-July. Family picnic.

Hedley
- **Hedley Heritage Fair:** June.

Kamloops
- **Kamloops Indoor Pro Rodeo:** Late April. At McArthur Island.
- **Sagebrush Downs Horse Racing:** June-Sept.
- **Music in the Park:** July-Aug, evenings.
- **Canada Day Folkfest/Art in the Park:** July 1.
- **Western Festival:** Mid-July. At Sunpeaks.
- **Cattle Drive:** July. Six days, driving cattle along old drovers' trails.
- **Kamloops Rangeland Derby Days:** Late July.
- **Sunpeaks Alpine Blossom Festival:** Late July, early Aug.
- **Kamloops International Air Show:** Early Aug.
- **Kamloopa Indian Powwow:** Mid-Aug. Kamloops Powwow Grounds.
- **Hot Night in the City Car Show:** Late Aug.
- **Provincial Winter Fair:** Late Sept.
- **First Night:** Dec. 31.

Kelowna
- **Snowfest:** Mid-Jan. Parade of lights, bonfire, fishing derby, bed races.
- **Ski-to-Sea Race:** March. Skiing, mountain biking, running, 10-speed biking, and then canoeing. Begins at Big White ski hill, ends in Okanagan Lake.

BLOSSOM TIMES
in the Okanagan Valley
Apricots: Early-mid April.
Cherries: Mid-late April.
Peaches: Mid-late April.
Prunes: Mid-April.
Pears: Mid-April to early May.
Apples: Late April-early May.

HARVEST TIMES
in the Okanagan Valley
Cherries: Late June to early July.
Apricots: Mid-July to mid-Aug.
Peaches: Late July to mid-Aug.
Prunes: Mid-Aug to late-Sept.
Apples: Mid-July to Oct.
Pears: Mid-July to Oct.
Grapes: From mid-Aug.

Okanagan Valley Wine Festivals: Throughout Okanagan Valley. 10-day fall event (early Oct) and a four-day spring event (early May). Call 250-860-5999 or ask at Visitor Info Centres. Events held regionwide: wine auction fund raiser, tastings, gourmet dinners, brunches, tours, wine appreciation seminars, entertainment.

- **Apple Blossom Fair:** May.
- **Knox Mountain Hill Climb:** May long weekend. Motorized madness in specially built cars.
- **Black Mountain Rodeo:** May long weekend.
- **Kelowna Regatta:** Mid-July.
- **Fat Cat Children's Festival:** Late July.
- **Mardi Gras:** Early Aug.
- **Kelowna Apple Triathlon:** Late summer. 1.5km swim, 40km bike, 10km run.

Keremeos
- **Chopaka Rodeo:** Easter Sunday. Real working cowboys .
- **Similkameen Powwow:** Native peoples from BC and Washington State meet for dancing and drumming. May long weekend.
- **Elks Rodeo:** May long weekend. Parade, cowboys, ornery critters.
- **Little Britches Rodeo:** May.
- **Flour and Flower Festival:** July.
- **Bull-A-Rama:** Sept.

Logan Lake
- **Polar Carnival:** Feb.
- **Lobsterfest:** Late May.
- **Rodeo:** Early June.
- **Festival of the Arts:** Late July, early Aug.
- **Little Britches Rodeo:** Mid-Aug.

Lumby
- **BC Open Gold Panning Championships:** Late May.
- **Lumby Snofest:** Jan. Human dogsled race, snogolf, Tacky Tourist contest, ski hill triathlon.
- **Lumby Days:** May/June. Even a Chicken-Flying Contest.

Merritt
- **Children's Festival:** Mid-April.
- **Little Britches Rodeo:** June.
- **Mountain Music Festival:** July.
- **Merritt Rodeo and Fair Days:** Labour Day weekend.
- **Nicola Valley Fall Fair:** Aug.

North Shuswap
- **Adams River Salmon Run:** Oct.

Oliver
- **Sunshine Festival:** Mid-June.
- **Kinsmen Pro Rodeo:** Aug.
- **Festival of the Grape:** Early Oct.

Osoyoos
- **Cherry Festival:** Canada Day long weekend.
- **Kobau Star Gazing Party:** Aug.

Peachland
- **Peachland Fall Fair:** Labour Day Weekend.

Rafters race down the Okanagan River Channel in a Penticton Peach Festival event.

Penticton

- **Mid-Winter Breakout:** Feb. Dance, tricycle races, ice-carving competitions, polar bear dip.
- **Okanagan Fest of Ale:** Early May.
- **Meadowlark Festival:** May 24 weekend. Birdwatching, contests, arts shows throughout Okanagan, but centred in Penticton. 250-492-5275.
- **Peach Festival:** Late July. Half a century old. Raft racing on the Okanagan River Channel, fireworks, big parade, dances.
- **Square Dance Jamboree:** 2nd week Aug.Thousands of dancers.
- **Iron Man Canada:** Late Aug. International qualifier for Hawaii triathlon. Gruelling trials in swimming, running, biking.
- **Pentastic Jazz Festival:** Mid-Sept.

Princeton

- **Annual Pony Express:** June.
- **Princeton Racing Days:** Canada Day long weekend.
- **Princeton Rodeo and Fall Fair:** Mid-Sept.

Rock Creek

- **Rock Creek and Boundary Fall Fair:** Mid-Sept. Cutting horses, bale slinging, cow-chip bingo. The real thing.

Salmon Arm

- **Reino Keski-Salmi Loppet:** Jan. Larch Hills.
- **Sonnet Festival:** Late March.
- **Shuswap Rodeo:** Late June.
- **Strawberry Festival:** July.
- **Bluegrass Festival:** July.
- **Pioneer Days:** Aug.
- **Fall Fair:** Sept.

Sicamous

- **Moose-Mouse Days:** BC Day weekend.
- **Carnival of the Arts:** July 1st weekend.

Sorrento

- **Trappers Landing Days:** July 1. Fireworks, parade, fastball.
- **Shuswap Festival of the Arts:** July.

Squilax

- **Squilax Powwow:** Mid-July.
- **Adams River Salmon Run:** Oct.

Summerland

- **Action Festival:** June, 1st weekend. Festivities and Mud Bog truck race.
- **Festival of Lights:** Late Nov. Christmas merriment.

Tulameen

- **Tulameen Daze:** Early Aug.

Valemount

- **Valemount Days:** Mid-June.

Vernon

- **Winter Carnival:** Early Feb.
- **Cowboy Poetry Roundup and Trappings Show:** Late May. A weekend of pickin' and singin', poetry and art. O'Keefe Ranch.
- **Creative Chaos:** June. Big craft fair.
- **Bella Vista Triathlon:** Early Aug. Bike-run-swim.
- **Oldtime Fiddler's Contest:** Early Aug.
- **Old Fashioned Threshing Bee**: Aug. O'Keefe Ranch.

Westbank

- **Westside Daze:** Late June.
- **Chinook Salmon Run:** Mid-Aug to Sept. Swift Creek.

Mount Robson, the highest peak in BC's Rocky Mountains.

THOMPSON OKANAGAN
ROUTES AND HIGHLIGHTS

TRAVELLER'S LOGS

HIGHLIGHTS

PRINCETON TO CHRISTINA LAKE

CROWSNEST HIGHWAY
(Highway 3)

The Crowsnest Hwy between Princeton and Christina Lake takes us from coast to Kootenays. It takes us from valley to valley, to valley. BC's mountain chains and rivers run, in general, from north to south: eastbound, we are going against the grain. But the upcoming 260km stretch of five valleys is its own world altogether. Between the big, blue snowcapped Cascade Mountains and the big, blue snow-capped ranges of the Kootenays, lies an open landscape characterized by rounded, sun-browned hills, stubby pine forests, and rangeland.

From Princeton, the highway winds gently southeast with the green Similkameen River. In the heart of this valley, the town of Keremeos is the southwestern gateway to orchard country. Fruit stands abound, and if your heart is set on peaches, this is one of the best places to stop. The Crowsnest dips south, almost touching the Canada/US border near Osoyoos, then traverses the Okanagan Valley and the only pocket of desert that exits in Canada. From here, it's up over the Okanagan Highland and down into the quietude of the Kettle River valley. Boundary Creek, a substantial tributary of the Kettle, flows in from the northeast, lending its name to "Boundary Country," a buffer zone between the fertile Okanagan Valley and the craggy peaks to come.

This route also follows the path of much celebrated mining history. The Princeton area was an aboriginal mining mecca in the earliest times. From the 1860s, miners scoured the Similkameen River and its creeks for gold, and later coal, and many settlements in Boundary Country were born as gold and copper boom towns.

Princeton: (Pop. 2,826). 135km east of Hope, el 640m. Turn north off Hwy 3 onto Vermilion St or Bridge St. To the Okanagan First Nations people, this place at the confluence of the Tulameen and Similkameen rivers was Yak Tulameen, "the place where red earth is sold." Red ochre, or vermillion sulphate, prized as a base for paint, was mined from the bluffs along the Tulameen River just west of here, and sold at a marketplace, where the town sits today. There is an ochre mine site right in Princeton too – look for red ochre behind Home Hardware at Bridge St and Fenchurch Ave.

The white fur traders who followed aboriginal trails into the region in the 1800s translated Yak Tulameen into Vermilion Forks. In 1860, James Douglas, governor of the new colony of BC, renamed the junction Princetown, to honour the Prince of Wales' visit to eastern Canada that year.

Princeton served as a centre for some of BC's earliest cattle ranchers for a time. But mining has remained at the heart of this little town's story. Just 19km west of here, a cowboy named Johnny Chance, in 1883, found gold nuggets in Granite Creek, a tributary of the Tulameen River. Granite City in its day was

the third largest city in BC. The ghost towns of Granite City, and Blakeburn, which emerged a few years later as a coal-mining centre, are a short and pleasant drive from Princeton along the Tulameen River. En route is Coalmont: where people still live. Little remains of Allenby, southeast of Princeton on the Coppermine Rd, where ore from Copper Mountain was milled.

It was just two years ago that Similco Mines, just west of town, closed. This major copper mining company was Princeton's second largest employer after forestry. In the face of this, residents are rallying to transform the town's colourful history into a tourism asset. Determined miners are encouraged to visit the gold panning reserve (below).

Other treasures: "a lake a day as long as you stay," – at least 47 good trout lakes (especially Otter, Thynne, Allison, Osprey, and Tepee) within an 80km radius. Secluded sandy beaches along the Tulameen and Similkameen rivers.

Princeton Information: Info Centre on Hwy 3 at eastern outskirts of town. Year-round. Write: Princeton and District Chamber of Commerce, Box 540, Princeton, BC, V0X 1W0. 250-295-3103.

Princeton Airport: 2.5km beyond Princeton on Hwy 5A. 250-492-3001.

■ **Princeton Municipal Campground:** 2km east of town on Hwy 3, on south shore of the Similkameen.

■ **Princeton and District Pioneer Museum and Archives:** 167 Vermilion Ave. 250-295-7588. Daily, July-Aug; rest of year weekdays, by appointment. Understated museum houses one of the best collections of fossils on Earth. They include the earliest history of a number of common species: the first fossilized evidence of a citrus fruit, the first apple, the first salmon. Pioneer furnishings, clothing, mining exhibits.

■ **Gold Panning:** Reserve between Blue Bridge and Pine Trailer Park (near junction of Hwy 3 east and Hwy 3 west at western entrance to Princeton). Check in first with Info Centre or Princeton and District Chamber of Commerce.

■ **Princeton Golf Course:** 3km east of town on Hwy 3. 250-295-6123. Nine holes set in contrasting landscape of green and yellow.

■ **Snowpatch:** West on Tulameen Ave, north on Snowpatch Rd. Family ski hill: three tows.

■ **Castle RV Park:** Northeast outskirts of Princeton, off Hwy 5A. Unusual RV park featuring massive ruins of old cement plant and generating station.

Highway 5A/Coalmont Rd/Old Hedley Rd: At east end of Princeton, turn left onto Bridge St. Follow Hwy 5A sign north. 1km off Hwy 3, the **Old Hedley Rd** leads east. This paved route parallels Hwy 3, the Similkameen River and the Dewdney Trail, completed in 1865 to connect the Kootenay region gold fields to BC's coast. After 27km the Old Hedley Rd rejoins Hwy 3 at the Stirling Creek Bridge, 7km west of Hedley.

Where the Old Hedley Rd heads east, **Coalmont Rd** leads west tracing the winding Tulameen River and offering dramatic views of the vermilion bluffs that lured the first (aboriginal) miners here. It's 18km to the former boomtown of **Coalmont** and nearby ghost towns, Granite City and Blakeburn. It's another 7km to **Tulameen**. From there, the road continues for 45km, toward, but not to Merritt. It rejoins Hwy 5A about 36km south of Merritt.

SIDE TRIP

along Coalmont Road

Coalmont: (Pop. varies – according to sign at entrance to town). 18km west of Princeton via Coalmont Rd. The sign also says: "Women beware, there is a predominance of bachelors living here." During the early 1900s Coalmont boomed. In 1925, with an output of 100,000t of coal, this was the region's largest producer. That title held through 1936, but by 1940, the mines were exhausted, and most of the 250 residents had moved. Today, it's a small, welcoming town with a sense of humour and a well-maintained general store, built 1912. The old **Coalmont Hotel**, established the same year, has a pub, home-style restaurant, and rooms. Ask at store or hotel for info on nearby mine sites.

Granite City: 1.5km southeast of Coalmont on Granite Creek Rd. It's hard to imagine this quiet creekside meadow was a gold-rush boom town. Forest service campsite just past "townsite."

Blakeburn: 10km from Coalmont via Arrasta Creek Rd. 4x4 recommended. Poke around on both sides of the road. An underground mine opened here in the early 1900s and closed in 1940 after 2.5 million tons of coal had been mined; shortly thereafter another 164,000 tons was taken from an open-pit mine. Ghostly remains are easiest to find early spring before the leaves obscure views.

Tulameen: (Pop. 250). 7.5km northwest of Coalmont. On the shores of Otter Lake, this was once called Otter Flats, a getaway for miners seeking R&R. It remains a relaxing summer resort town. General store, boat rentals, restaurant. Tulameen Daze, August long weekend.

Otter Lake Provincial Park: 51ha; 45 campsites/reservations (1-800-689-9025 or 604-689-9025). Info: 250-494-6500. Beach at north end of Tulameen. Campground about 5km farther along lakeshore. Boating, swimming, hiking, gold panning.

Return to Highway 5A

SIDE TRIP

along Princeton-Summerland Road

Highway 5A/Princeton-Summerland Back Road: North of Princeton, just .5km beyond the Hwy 5A/Coalmont Rd/Old Hedley Rd junction, the **Princeton-Summerland Back road** leads east off Hwy 5A.

An adventurous and scenic alternative to Hwy 3A/97 route east, but not a shortcut, no matter what anybody tells you. It's 92km, first half paved, the second half not (with lots of washboard), and very twisty in spots. Best recommended for summer travel. The route traces the old **Kettle Valley Railway**, and while the road map suggests little settlement here, older maps show there were once 11 railway stations between Princeton and Summerland. Back road and railway bed today pass rangeland, tiny lakes, and back-country homes, and provide access to four forest service recreation campgrounds for those escaping the hustle and bustle of mainstream Okanagan campgrounds. Look out for cows on the road.

Forest Service camping at: Chain Lake, 36km (fairly popular); Link Lake, 41km; Osprey Lake, 42km; and Thirsk Lake (or Thirsk Dam), 52.5km. Thirsk Lake is the reservoir for Summerland. At the height of summer, dusty, barren shores and stumps exposed by low water can be quite unappealing. At 82km, the small community of Faulder is a former KVR stop: pavement and a smooth decent into Summerland begins. Also see *Penticton to Kelowna*, p.159. For details on the KVR, see p.143.

Hwy 5A from Princeton continues north beyond the Princeton-Summerland Back Road, 89.5km to Merritt (see p.180 for details).

Return to Highway 3 at Princeton

Bromley Rock Provincial Park: 149ha; 17 campsites. 21km east of Princeton. 250-494-6500. South side of Similkameen River. Park named for large rock bluff. Below it, one gem of a swimming hole.

Stemwinder Provincial Park: 4ha; 27 campsites. 33km east of Princeton. 250-494-6500. Similkameen runs fast here: strong swimmers only. Look out for poison ivy on riverbank.

Nickel Plate and Mascot Mines: 35km east of Princeton on Hwy 3. Remains of cable tramway and wooden ruins (Mascot's bunkhouses) perched at 1,200m on Nickel Plate Mountain cliff. From 1904 to 1955, $47 million in gold was taken from the mountain. The Nickel Plate mine closed in the 1950s and reopened over a decade ago as the Home Stake Nickel Plate Mine. There are long-term plans for an aerial tramway to carry visitors to the site. For now, access is via Nickel Plate-Hedley Rd, below. Check with information centres at Princeton or Keremeos, or at Hedley Heritage Museum, below.

Hedley: (Pop. about 300). 40km beyond Princeton. In 1898 gold miners struck it lucky at nearby Nickel Plate (a mine and a town). So much gold, copper, and silver poured out of the mine that a stamp mill was built, and an aerial tramway 3km long, then the longest in the world, was installed to feed it with ore. Mascot mine also became a bonanza. Hedley

sprang up in the valley. Area population was more than 5,000. At least six hotels gave Hedley an air of prosperity. There were saloons, dancing girls, and fashionable stores selling European lace, Chinese tea, and mink coats.

Starting in 1909, the VV&E Railway stopped at Hedley, shipping ore and carrying passengers, but during a lean spell caused by the First World War, the track was torn up and much of the right-of-way was taken over by what is now Hwy 3. For centuries before, this was the home of aboriginal peoples. At the nearby Okanagan village of Chuchuwayha, people bartered red jasper used for arrowheads.

Today, visitors can still try panning for gold in the Similkameen River or in nearby 20 Mile Creek. Probably better luck with rainbow trout.

With its surrounding (or overhanging) dramatic landscape, and its own beckoning charm, Hedley is worth a stop and a stroll. **Woodley Park**, right downtown behind the 1903 **Grace United Church**, has picnic tables. Sit and soak up the little town's atmosphere.

Hedley Information: Hedley Heritage Museum (below). Or write Hedley Heritage, Arts and Crafts Society, Box 218, Hedley, BC, V0X 1K0.

■ **Hedley Heritage Museum:** Modern cultural centre devoted to Hedley's heritage and arts and crafts. Displays of social and mining history. Artifacts outside include ore car and section of flume. Visitors from as far away as Europe, some of them on genealogical quests, are finding Hedley, and putting down remarks in the guest book to this effect: "I came to see where my grandfather worked."

■ **Hedley Cemetery:** North off Hwy 3. Pioneers buried here include Harry Durnford Barnes, who wrote up Hedley's history until 1948 and recorded that the town was named after Robert Rist Hedley, manager of the Hall Smelter in Nelson.

Mountain Goats: Between Hedley and Keremeos, stop and scan the rocky hillsides on the north side of the highway. About 150 mountain goats live here, and are visible most of the year.

American Railway Rest Area: 62km east of Princeton. A welcoming little rest area, pungent sage to the left, the swirling Similkameen to the right.

Cathedral Provincial Park: 33,272ha; 16 campsites and 70 walk-in sites in three campgrounds, the largest at Quiniscoe Lake, el 2,072m, near Cathedral Lakes Lodge. 1-888-255-4453. Turn south off Hwy 3, 63km beyond Princeton, or 5km west of Keremeos. **Ashnola River Rd** (mostly gravel) leads 21km past small ranches to Cathedral Lakes Lodge base camp. From here, you have two choices. The first is to hike uphill some 16km (6-7 hours rising 1,300m) to campgrounds, Cathedral Lakes Lodge, and start of wilderness trails. The second choice, which BC Parks recommends to first-time visitors, is to call ahead to Cathedral Lakes Lodge (250-226-7560) and reserve 4x4 taxi for ride up Jeep Rd to lodge and campground. The fully-equipped lodge (with cabins) is a com-

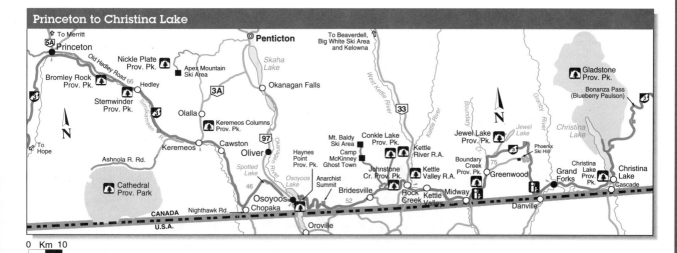

Princeton to Christina Lake

0 Km 10

mercial, private campground within the park. Park offers 50km of wilderness hiking trails, including part of Centennial Trail to Manning Provincial Park. No Sunday strolls: elevation is high, there is snow every month of the year. Dogs not permitted.

The tranquil turquoise Cathedral Lakes are heart of the park: five sparkling pockets of blue nestled below Cathedral Ridge (el 2,400m). The rim trail runs for about 6km along the crest of the ridge, and forms the backbone of an excellent system of well-maintained and easy to follow trails. Hikers will find immense peaks and bizarre mountain forms, including one of BC's most impressive chasms – the vertical sided 300m-deep Giant Cleft in the sheer face of 2,621m Grimface Mountain. Wildlife includes mountain goats, California bighorn sheep, mule deer, squirrels, pikas, golden eagles, hawks. Rainbow, cutthroat trout in lakes and creeks.

Red Bridge: On Ashnola River Rd just off Hwy 3. This covered wooden bridge, three spans across the Similkameen, was built about 1907 by Great Northern Railway for its VV&E spur to Princeton. Deep pools below bridge are a delight for swimming.

Keremeos: (Pop. 1,167). 66km east of Princeton. An irresistible stop. Keremeos sits on a bench where the valley of Keremeos Creek joins the Similkameen River. The Okanagan First Nation people who live in the area, mostly farming and ranching, tell us the name Keremeos means "to cut across the flats, from the creek." All around are mountains (Apex is north, Snowy is south, Kobau is east) rising 1,800m to 2,400m.

The village itself, with wood-fronted buildings dating from the early 1900s, emits an aura of the Old West. Fur trader Alexander Ross was the first white man to show up, in 1813, at what was an ancient native village site. Keremeos started out as a Hudson's Bay Company trading post in 1860, then became a ranching centre; from the 1930s, it also developed into a fruit-growing hub.

The village's present site wasn't its first. It had been located twice elsewhere before settling down. Initially it sprang up on what was known as Coleman's Hay Field up on the bench about a kilometre northwest of the present village. Then, following the water supply, it was moved farther west up the banks of the Similkameen River. When the Keremeos Hotel was built in 1906 (later to burn down) on the present-day site, the village was dismantled again and reconstructed around the hotel.

A long growing season first established fruit growing here by 1910. With perhaps 30 individual stands, this town may be the "Fruit Stand Capital of Canada." Tender spring asparagus; then cherries, apricots, peaches; finally autumn apples and grapes.

Keremeos Information: Information centre, Box 490, Keremeos, V0X 1N0. In Memorial Park town centre, on Hwy 3. 250-499-5225. June-early Sept.

■ **South Similkameen Museum:** 6th Ave and 6th St. 250-499-5445. Tues-Sat, 10-4, June-Aug. By appointment off-season. In former Provincial Police office and jail. Exhibits include police uniforms, pioneer artifacts.

■ **The Grist Mill and Gardens:** Upper Bench Rd, 2.5km from museum. 250-499-2888. May to mid-Oct; informally, rest of year. Beside Keremeos Creek, orchard setting, and heritage gardens: living museum of flowers, plants, and shrubs echoing pioneer past. Built 1877, now restored, is oldest operating water-powered grist mill in BC. Also tea room and hands-on exhibits. This one gets full points.

■ **Vineyards:** St Laszlo Vineyards Ltd, 250-499-2856. Tours and tasting daily, year-round.

■ **Farm Visits: Diggidy Farm & Apiary**, Upper Bench Rd. 250-499-282. Bees and honey year-round. **Bears Farm and Market**, Hwy 3A. 250-499-2814. Daily, May-Oct. **Van Dieman's Turkey Farm & Gobbler Garden**, 10th Ave. 250-499-5890. Turkeys, tours, mini-park.

Highway 3A: Just east of town centre. North 50km to Penticton. Also, south access to Apex Alpine Ski Resort.

SIDE TRIP

on Highway 3A

Keremeos Columns Provincial Park: 20ha; no development. North on Hwy 3A for 4km. East at cemetery. Pavement ends; from here, route is on private property: get permission from residents. Hot, steep 8km hike; take water canteens. 30m-high, 100m-wide columnar basalt cliffs formed by volcanic activity 30 million years ago.

Olalla: (Pop. 341). 6km North of Hwy 3. Community's name is from Chinook jargon (an early Northwest coast trading language): olallie refers to the june berries (also known as service or Saskatoon berries) once plentiful here. William Campbell McDougall chose the name when, as townsite owner and postmaster, he opened the post office here in 1900. Diner, grocery store. Local art in Ken Christmas Art Gallery.

■ **Olalla Rock Giants:** Ask locally for directions to the weird-looking pile of three huge boulders, fallen together perhaps a millennia ago: a kind of prehistoric gigantic sculpture. A group of local artists suggests the Giants are spooky and jinxed, after attempts to photograph and sketch the rocks ended in failure.

Green Mountain Rd: 13.5km. Turn northwest on gravel for Apex Alpine Ski Resort, Apex Mountain Provincial Recreation Area, and Nickel Plate Provincial Park. See *US Border to Penticton*, p.156.

Yellow Lake Rest Area: 17km. Turn south. Cartop launch. Ice fishing.

Another Yellow Lake Rest Area: Other end of 2km Yellow Lake.

Twin Lakes Rd: 20.5 km from Hwy 3. Details on White Lake Valley in *US Border to Penticton*, pp.155-156.

Marron Valley: Hwy 3A cuts through southern tip of Penticton First Nation Reserve 3km beyond White Lake Rd and fringes it again at just before the Hwy 97 junction.

Highway 97: 31.5km beyond Keremeos. Details in *US Border to Penticton*, p.153.

Return to Highway 3 after Keremeos

149

Cawston: (Pop. 843). On Hwy 3, 5km southwest of Keremeos. A quiet town on the banks of the Similkameen River. Local residents have their favorite swimming holes; lots of market and organic gardening. For hiking up Barsello Canyon, ask locally. Cawston was named for Richard Lowe Cawston, pioneer rancher and magistrate credited with with vaccinating native people en masse at nearby Osoyoos during the smallpox epidemic in the late 1800s. The town's fortunes paralleled the Great Northern Railway that ran 1907-1972. (Rail bed is visible from the highway).
■ **Siesta Cactus:** Daly Dr. Daily. 400 varieties of cacti; sales.
■ **Harker's Fruit Ranch:** Agar Rd. 250-499-2751. Country market with organic fruit, snack bar, local crafts, honey, and fresh fruit shakes. Tours in season.
■ **Crowsnest Vineyard:** On Surprise Dr off Lowe Dr. Look for signs. 250-499-5129. Tours daily, year-round.
■ **The Carriage'n'Works:** On Hwy 3, 3km southwest of Keremeos. 250-499-7738. Year-round; call ahead for tours. Historical barn house, horse-drawn wagons and carriages. Wooden wheels constructed.
■ **Ginty's Pond Bird Sanctuary:** Off Main St. BC Wildlife Watch viewing site.

Night Hawk Rd: At beginning of Richter Pass, 24km beyond Keremeos. Leads to Canada-US border crossing.

Richter Pass Summit: (El 2,234m). 33km beyond Keremeos. Local pioneer was Francis Richter (1837-1910), Bohemian immigrant from 1860, and Hudson's Bay Company employee. Later a big rancher in area.

Spotted Lake: 38km beyond Keremeos along Richter Pass, 8km before Osoyoos. Two lakes, first one Spotted Lake. Sometimes spots (called salt plates) not easily identifiable. The 12ha lake's spots are due to deposit of Epsom salts rising to surface. Native people used lake to soak away pain of arthritis and rheumatism. They believed its waters – mainly Epsom and Glauber's salts with small amounts of baking soda, washing soda, salt, and calcium sulphate – also had healing power on the spirit. A soak brought both youth and wisdom. Lake is on private property.

Viewpoint: 41km beyond Keremeos. All of a sudden, Osoyoos, below.

Highway 97: 46km beyond Keremeos. North leads 20km to Oliver and beyond (to Penticton, Kelowna, Vernon).

Osoyoos: (Pop. 3,403). At junction of Hwys 3 and 97. For details see *US Border to Penticton*, p.153.

Osoyoos Viewpoint: 11km east of town. Full panoramic view of Osoyoos Lake and the spit cutting it nearly in two.

Wagon Wheel Ranch: 28.5km east of Osoyoos. 250-446-2466. Daily 10-4,

Beyond the reach of irrigation, a prickly pear cactus blooms.

evenings by reservation. Trout pond and fallow deer farm. Cabin rentals in summer, bakery.

Anarchist Summit: (El 1,233m). 32km east of Osoyoos. Named for settler Richard Sidley who held some "anarchist" views. Still the odd anarchist around. Switchbacks are among province's most memorable. Climb is rewarded with rest area offering views of the oasis and desert around Osoyoos. Your car will need a rest, too.

Bridesville: (Pop. 66). 37km east of Osoyoos. David McBride held water rights to creek from which Great Northern Railway water tanks were supplied. Every third year or so, there's a store or a cafe. Horse Show and Western Games in August.

Mount Baldy Rd: 39km east of Osoyoos, north at **Rock Creek Canyon Bridge** to cross over Rock Creek. Impressive gorge.

SIDE TRIP

to Mt Baldy

Camp McKinney: Ghost town 11.5km northwest of Hwy 3 on Mt Baldy Rd. Amid turn-of-the-century ruins, modern-day prospectors are still looking for the mother lode. Between 1887 and 1903, the Cariboo mine here yielded more than 80,000 ounces of gold, making it one of BC's richest pioneer mines. Buried treasure is said to be in the area still, in the form of two large gold bars taken from a mine official at gunpoint. Use caution in the area, don't venture beyond fenced areas. Wise to stop in at Osoyoos Info Centre.

Mount Baldy Ski Area: 7km beyond Camp McKinney. Also accessible from Oliver (details in US Border to Penticton, p.155).

Continue to Oliver (34.5km along Camp McKinney Rd). Or return with Log to Hwy 3 east.

Return to Highway 3

Conkle Lake Provincial Park: 587ha; 34 campsites. 44km east of Osoyoos, north on Johnstone Creek West Rd. Park is 26km north of Hwy 3 junction. 250-494-6500. Road is extremely rough. But once you get there – a nice spot for a quiet vacation.

Johnstone Creek Provincial Park: 38ha; 16 campsites. 44.5km east of Osoyoos on Hwy 3. 250-494-6500 Waterfall on Johnstone Creek.

Highway 33 North: 51.5km beyond Osoyoos, virtually in Rock Creek (below). North to Westbridge, Beaverdell, Carmi, Kettle River Provincial Recreation Area, Big White, and Kelowna.

SIDE TRIP

along Highway 33

Kettle Valley Railway: From Rock Creek, the old railway bed follows the Kettle River and Hwy 33 north for about 90km before veering west toward Chute Lake, Naramata, and the heart of the Okanagan Valley. From Westbridge north to Hydraulic

Lake (some 77km) the KVR bed is accessible to bikers and hikers for excursions through pastoral countryside and forest land. Info: Okanagan-Similkameen Parks Society, Box 787, Summerland, BC, V0H 1Z0.

Kettle River Provincial Recreation Area: 179ha; 53 campsites. 6.5km north of Rock Creek and Hwy 3 junction. 250-494-6500. KVR right-of-way. Swimming, canoeing (caution advised), fishing. Cross-country skiing.

Westbridge: (Pop. 80). 13.5km north of Rock Creek. Farming community at confluence of Kettle and West Kettle rivers. Post office established in 1900, and bridge across West Kettle River – thus the name. Last gas until Beaverdell.

Rhone Rest Area: 20km north of Rock Creek.

Beaverdell: (Pop. 280). 47.5km north of Rock Creek. Beaver dams still common. Beaverdell Hotel, established 1904, exhibits area artifacts and boasts BC's longest continuously operating pub.

Carmi: (Pop. 44). 56km north of Rock Creek. Mainly abandoned since 1940s, three decades after short heyday. No amenities or facilities.

Road to Big White Ski Area: 96km north of Rock Creek. Turn east, continue for 22km to resort. See *Penticton to Kelowna*, p.162.

Hall Creek Rest Area: 70km north of Rock Creek.

Kelowna: (Pop. 89,442). At the end of Hwy 33, 133km northwest of Hwy 3. See *Penticton to Kelowna*, p.161.

Return to Highway 3

Rock Creek: (Pop. 550 or 142). 52km east of Osoyoos. In 1857, Charlie Dietz started the first rush here, for gold. 5,000 people came, but the mother lode was never found. Copper was, though, and reminders of the 1890s copper mining boom line highway.
■ **Rock Creek Hotel:** Built in 1893, still operating here, with Gold Country Kitchen and Prospector Pub, overlooking Kettle River.

Kettle Valley: Small community just off Hwy 3, 7.5km beyond Rock Creek. A handful of ranchers, one of BC's oldest golf courses, a little church. The church was built in Riverside, a once-upon-a-time mining town 1km east of Rock Creek. The first service was 1912. In 1923, Howard Pannell, carpenter and newspaper editor, accepted an offer of $600 to roll the church, on logs, to Kettle Valley. But he failed to earn the $100 bonus by completing the task in 100 days or less.
■ **Kettle Valley Golf Course:** Along highway. 250-446-2826. Nine-hole course dates

to before First World War; clubhouse is circa 1930.

Sawmill: 15km beyond Rock Creek, 3km east of Midway. Complex operated by Pope and Talbot, major employer.

Kettle Valley Railway Station/Kettle River Museum: 3km beyond sawmill, on Hwy 3 entering Midway. 250-449-2614. Century-old station was terminus of the KVR, which crossed the mountains to Hope. Now a restored railway museum. More below; also more on KVR, p. 143.

Midway: (Pop. 660). Less than 1km past KVR Station, 19km east of Rock Creek and 56km west of Grand Forks. Halfway between the Rockies and the Pacific. Also midway on the old Dewdney Trail that went from Hope to Wild Horse Creek, near Fort Steele. It was midway too, for freight wagons en route from Marcus, Washington, to Fairview near Oliver. They changed horses at Eholt's ranch.

This was first farmland, then a smelter site, now a sawmill town with a penchant for its railway and mining history. It is certainly a town of museums and historic railway stations. Midway has had an airstrip since 1936, unpaved, and right in the town; no commercial flights.
Midway Information: At Midway Village Office, 250-449-2222, or Kettle River Museum, below.
■ **Riverfront Municipal Campground:** 12 formal campsites, lots of flat space; sanistation. Three blocks off Hwy 3 in Midway. Canoeing, swimming.
■ **Kettle River Museum:** Next to the old CPR station, which also houses its own museum, including displays on BC police forces. CPR bunkhouse on site. 250-449-2222 or 250-449-2614 (fax in winter). Daily, mid-May to mid-Sept. Off-season, 250-449-2112. Kettle River history plus 1939 caboose.
■ **Entwined Trees:** Adjacent Medical Clinic. When the boundary between Canada and US was established in 1846 near today's Midway, it separated Okanagan First Nation bands who used to converge here to fish and pick berries. Some say the two sapling pines were entwined to symbolize the bands' spiritual unity.
■ **Kettle River Railway Bed:** If not for erosion and washed-out bridges you could drive it all the way to Penticton. Ask anyone in town where to walk it.
■ **Great Northern Railway:** Drive 2km down Dump Road and walk old rail bed to first tunnel. Built in 1906-1907 as connection to US.

Road to USA: Road through village leads south to border crossing of Midway and a link road via Ferry and Curlew, Washington, to US Hwy 21.

Boundary Creek: Meets Hwy 3 at border. Road follows creek north 16km through Greenwood.

Boundary Falls Park: At Boundary Creek Bridge, 7.5km beyond Midway on

Hwy 3. Undeveloped. Was a smuggling depot, power generation site, and water source for hydraulic mining nearby.

Boundary Creek Provincial Park: 2ha; 18 campsites. 1km beyond falls on Hwy 3, just north of border. 250-825-3500. Camping under cottonwood trees on banks of Boundary Creek. Remnants of stack and slag heap from old BC Copper Company smelter can be seen. Before the First World War, this was North America's largest copper processor. It served some 20 copper and gold mines in the surrounding hills between 1901 and 1919.

Greenwood Smelter Site/Lotzkar Park: 3.5km beyond Boundary Falls, just outside Greenwood city limits. Smelter stack stands 55m high; plaque gives mining history. Industrial ruins on smelter site have now been developed into a park, with hiking trails, picnic area.

Greenwood: (Pop. 784). 16km beyond Midway, at junction of Boundary and Twin creeks. Today, it's the smallest city in BC, though at the turn of century, Greenwood was on its way to becoming one of the West's major centres. In 1895, an optimistic merchant, Robert Wood, surveyed a 3.2km townsite and named it Greenwood. Incorporated in 1897, early in the mining boom, Greenwood had 3,000 residents, three banks, 16 hotels, 15 general stores. This was a wild town with boisterous pianos and night-long gambling parties patronized by such regulars as Pie-Biter Smith, Two-Fingered Jack, and Dirty George. It was the service centre for dozens of mines, including the rich Mother Lode Mine. With the collapse of mining after the First World War, Greenwood became a ghost town. In the early 1940s more than 1,000 Japanese Canadians were sent from the coast, to be interned in Greenwood's empty buildings. Many stayed on.

Twenty turn-of-the-century buildings have been restored; noteworthy, the Courthouse, Post Office, and McArthur Centre. At the information centre, pick up maps of "Outdoor Trails around Historic Greenwood."

Greenwood's City Park offers free camping facilities.
Greenwood Information: Information centre, Greenwood Museum, Copper St (Hwy 3). 250-445-6355.
■ **Greenwood Museum:** Copper St (Hwy 3). 250-445-6355. Daily, mid-June to mid-Sept. Old mining days, people, and their stories of grief and joy, and the Japanese community that began with the internment camps in 1942. Small museum speaks from the heart.
■ **Sacred Heart Catholic Church:** Southeast corner of Wood and Church streets. Built in 1900, still used.
■ **Courthouse:** One block from museum. Built 1905. Wood, with stained-glass windows representing original provinces of Canada. Tours from museum mid-May to mid-Sept.

Jewel Lake Provincial Park: 49ha. 36 campsites. 1km beyond Greenwood, unpaved road off Hwy 3 leads 10km to 3km lake. Fly-casting for rainbow trout in summer, ice fishing and cross-country skiing in winter. In 1913, a record-keeping 17kg rainbow trout was caught in this lake. Facilities include Jewel Lake Resort, open year-round. Trails to remnants of Spotted Horse Mine, Jewel Lake Mine, and ghost town of Eholt.

Wilgress Lake: Small lake 16km beyond Greenwood. Rest area, picnic site, boat launching ramp.

Phoenix Ski Hill: 20km beyond Greenwood, take Phoenix Rd and follow signs for 13km (gravel road). 250-442-2813. Fall-line skiing with 244m vertical drop. Runs named after old copper-mine claims. Day lodge with cafeteria, T-bar, beginners' tow, cross-country trails, rentals shop (rent cross-country skis in Greenwood), and ski school. Same road leads to Phoenix Mine site and signs of open-pit mining.

Phoenix Interpretive Forest: Phoenix Rd is also start of 22km self-guided back road driving tour to Greenwood. Accessible year-round. Takes about two hours. Excellent route description available from Greenwood Museum, above; Boundary Museum, below; or Ministry of Forests, Boundary Forest District, 136 Sagamore Ave, Grand Forks, BC, V0H 1H0. 250-442-5411. 180-sq-km interpretive forest offers insights into area's history and resources from the turn of the century when prospectors sought the mother lode here, to present management of water, timber, wildlife, and mineral resources. Highlights include the Phoenix mine site and cemetery.

Doukhobor Homesteads: Along Hwy 3, en route to Grand Forks, simple two-storey brick houses clustered with barns and workshops are vestiges of the "spirit wrestlers" or Doukhobors. They took refuge in Saskatchewan in the late 1800s, fleeing persecution in Russia for their unorthodox religious beliefs, and arrived here in 1908.

In the 1920s there were about 90 Doukhobor communes in BC, each with about 60 people. They made their own bedding, clothing, and tools, farmed, followed rules based on the Bible. The system began to break down after the death of their leader, Peter Verigin, in 1924, and under pressures of the Depression (also see *BC Rockies, Castlegar,* p.187).

Not to be confused with the main Doukhobor community are the Freedomites, or Sons of Freedom. This radical sect has become well-known for sensational demonstrations (nude parades, fires, and hunger strikes) against what it considers the adoption of impure or materialistic values.

About 5,000 Doukhobor descendants live around Castlegar and the Kootenay-Boundary area, many speaking Russian, and they are still pacifists. Communal homesteads have been abandoned as their inhabitants have become integrated into mainstream BC.

Spencer Hill Viewpoint: On Hwy 3, 13km beyond turnoff to Phoenix Ski Hill. View of Grand Forks and Granby River valley. Also called the Sunshine Valley, beautiful, broad and inviting, with rich, fertile soil.

Highway 41: 2km past viewpoint. 1km to junction for Carson/Danville border.

Grand Forks: (Pop. 4,134). 5km beyond Hwy 41 junction, 40km beyond Greenwood. An attractive valley town with tree-lined streets, named for its location near convergence of Kettle and Granby rivers.

Community owes its existence to the copper mines of Phoenix. The Granby Smelter was built between 1898-1900 and at the time was the largest copper smelter in the British Empire. It closed in 1919: glistening ebony slag is now being used as an abrasive in sandblasting.

Numbers of locals here trace their origins to the Doukhobors; Russian is taught in schools. Check the phone book for names like Abetkoff. The town is well-known for ethnic foods: look for voreniki, pyrahi, galooptsi, and borscht on the menus.

Grand Forks is presided over by wedge-shaped Observation Mountain to the north, and Rattlesnake Mountain to the east (aptly named, they say). About 60km north is the southern boundary of and the only practical access into Granby Provincial Park (see below).

There is a municipal airport within city limits; paved; no commercial flights.

Grand Forks Information: Info Centre, Box 1086, 7362-5th St, Grand Forks, BC, V0H 1H0. Off Hwy 3, next to Boundary Museum. 250-442-2833.

■ **Grand Forks Municipal Park:** End of 5th St, by Kettle River. 250-442-2833. 28 sites with hook-up, unlimited tenting, sani-station, showers, fire pits, playground.

■ **Mountain View Doukhobor Museum:** 3655 Hardy Mountain Rd. North off Hwy 3 (Central Ave) onto 19th St, then follow Hardy Mountain Rd for 5km. Open most days June-Sept. 250-442-8855. In 1912 Doukhobor communal farmhouse. Curator Peter Gritchen shows how his community lived. Beyond, along Hardy Mountain Rd, more Doukhobor architecture.

■ **Grand Forks Milling Cooperative:** Off Hwy 3, just west of city. Mill was built in 1915 to supply flour for Grand Forks' Doukhobor community. Pride of the Valley Flour still made without additives, from locally grown wheat when possible. Call Jack Makortoff, 250-442-8801 or Walter Hoodikoff, 250-442-8570, for tours.

■ **Boundary Museum:** Hwy 3 and 5th St. Daily, mid-May to late Sept. Weekdays in winter. 250-442-3737. Area's rich cultural history.

■ **Downtown Tour:** Soak up mountain-city ambience amid revitalized turn-of-the-century architecture.

■ **Grand Forks Art Gallery:** 7340-5th St, year-round. 250-442-2211. Continuous exhibitions in four galleries. Gift shop.

■ **Fruits and Veggies:** Farmers Market, City Park, Tues, Fri, Sat. Deane Farms, 1275 Carson Rd. 250-442-3400. Daily, April-Oct.

■ **North Fork Scenic Drive:** Loops 30km along Granby River. Info Centre has maps.

■ **Granby Provincial Park:** 40,845ha. No facilities, well-developed trails, or signs. Southern boundary about 65km north of Grand Forks. 250-825-3500. Only access is a 12km route hacked out of wilderness and a forest service campground near trailhead. Must have vehicle with good clearance or 4x4. Follow Granby Rd north 40km, then turn west (left) across a bridge over the Burrell Creek at the Granby-Burrell forest service recreation site. Continue straight on Granby Rd to Km 59, then follow the Bluejoint Lookout Rd. 1km farther, take the spur road to the left to the Traverse Creek campsite, where the Granby River Trail starts. Granby Park is home to rare pockets of old-growth Interior rainforest and a small, threatened population of grizzly bears. For guided hiking tours: Boundary Backcountry Tours, 250-442-3556; for guided horseback trips, 250-442-2849 or 250-265-4539.

Highway 395: 18km east of Grand Forks. Leads southeast 4km to border crossing at Cascade; another 144km to Spokane, Washington.

Christina Lake: (Area pop. 1,100). 21km beyond Grand Forks. Lakeside community swells to 6,000 in summer when travellers converge on "the warmest lake in BC." (There are three "warmest" lakes in BC: Osoyoos and Wasa also make the claim for their lakes.) 19km long and just 55m deep, July water temperature averages 23 C.

Reservations recommended at the eight commercial campgrounds. Back-to-basics camping is available on the north end of the lake, at Forest Service recreation sites accessible only by boat, and at Gladstone Provincial Park, 15km beyond community centre, 6km off Hwy 3 (see below).

Christina Lake Information: Info Centre on Hwy 3. 250-447-6161.

■ **Cascade Gorge:** South on Hwy 395. 300m beyond turnoff, water boils through series of small falls and kettles.

■ **Christina Lake Golf and Country Club:** 18 holes among pines. On Hwy 395, 3km south of community. 250-447-9313.

Christina Lake Provincial Park: 6ha. At southern tip of Christina Lake. Has everything: sand and shade, change rooms, swimming, windsurfing, waterskiing, boat launch, fishing.

Gladstone Provincial Park: 39,322ha. 48 campsites. On east side of Christina Lake, north of the community. 250-825-3500. Beautiful sandy beach. Picnicking, swimming, fishing in former Texas Creek Provincial Park. Recently designated parkland – undeveloped backcountry wilderness – extends northward from the lake's shores. Dry, low-elevation cedar-hemlock forest is important winter range for deer and elk.

From Christina Lake, Hwy 3 climbs east through forests of cedar, hemlock, fir, birch, and pine to the *BC Rockies*. Next centres are Castlegar (73km) and Trail (82km). See p. 187.

US BORDER TO PENTICTON

HIGHWAY 97

Highway 97 begins at the Canada/US border, 4km south of Osoyoos. In the 64km between here and Penticton is a landscape like none other in Canada. Lush orchards, burgeoning vineyards – this is a rare oasis. What we speak of however is not this, but what's beneath it, and around it. And what would be everywhere here if the silent rainbow mist of irrigation ever ceased. Desert. Hot, dry, and mostly brown. Desert plants, desert birds, desert animals, they all make their home in this narrow strip of the Okanagan Valley between Osoyoos and Skaha Lake just south of Penticton. This is the northernmost extension of the Sonoran Desert, reaching here all the way from northern Mexico.

Si. Here, we call it the "pocket desert," because it is a relatively confined and unique area, and because farming and irrigation have left only pockets in a natural desert state. It's also a pocket desert because, experts say, under the strictest definition, it isn't a true desert. It's not dry enough: true deserts get less than 250mm of precipitation a year, while an average of 300mm falls here. And, this desert's too cold: the average annual temperature here of 10C is 2C below what the definition would allow. Strictly speaking, we should call this "mid-latitude steppe."

The sand dunes harbouring cacti and scorpions are natural, but what we see is the verdancy. This is one of the most intensely farmed parts of the Okanagan Valley. The area just south of Oliver is being marketed as the Golden Mile for its volume of high quality wine grapes. Impatient travellers will note that slow-moving trucks and tractors are as common as fruit stands along this two-lane route.

This stretch of valley is also a busy wildlife corridor, and at its narrowest point, around Vaseux Lake, it's more than likely travellers will encounter California bighorn sheep or Trumpeter swans. It's less than an hour's drive from Osoyoos to Penticton, but it could take you much longer to get there.

Haynes Point Provincial Park: 38ha; 41 campsites (reservations taken: call 1-800-689-9025; from the Lower Mainland or overseas, call 604-689-9025). 2km north of border, 2km south of town on Osoyoos Lake. General info: 250-494-6500. 5ha of this park is a distinctive sand spit reaching three-quarters across soupy-warm Osoyoos Lake (just south of the narrowing that carries Hwy 3 across the lake). Wade chest-high across the remaining quarter. This was an original shortcut for horses being herded from the pioneer Haynes Ranch. Look for Canada's tiniest bird, the Calliope hummingbird, plus orioles, Eastern kingbirds, and California quail. Some say this is the most popular park in all of Canada. Most campsites are beachfront, and locals have named them all. Most treasured is the "Corner Suite." Boat launching, wheelchair access.

Highways 3 and 97: 4km north of border. Main St in Osoyoos is Crowsnest Hwy 3, going west over Richter Pass, 36km to Keremeos, and beyond to the Similkameen Valley and Princeton; east leads 46km to Rock Creek, and beyond to Greenwood and Grand Forks. See *Princeton to Christina Lake*, p.150.

Osoyoos: (Pop. 4,021). At Hwy 3/97 junction; 4km north of Canada/US border (Oroville crossing). The town sits midpoint on 19km-long Osoyoos Lake, straddling its west and east shores via a finger of land and a manmade bridge. From BC's earliest days, this was an important junction. Aboriginal trails fanned in four directions from here; fur traders used these routes after the early 1800s; and after 1858, gold seekers from the US bound for BC's Cariboo crossed the new international border via these trails.

Osoyoos takes its name from Soyoos, "gathered together," an aboriginal Okanagan village formerly just south of town. In 1861, during the gold rush, a customs house was established just west of where the bridge is now. In its first three years, nearly 15,000 cattle, horses, sheep, and mules being herded from Washington to the Cariboo gold fields, cleared customs here.

Set on this northern reach of Sonoran Desert, Osoyoos is one of Canada's hot spots, with average daily temperatures in July of 29.1C. The hottest day, since record keeping began in 1954, was July 27, 1998 – the thermometer soared to 42.8C (109F). (The other Canadian hot spots, all just a fraction of a degree hotter than Osoyoos are Ashcroft, Trail, and Lytton).

Beckoning fruit stands and the blue spectre of Osoyoos Lake pull heat-weary travellers off the highway. But Osoyoos, apart from its five small, very busy beaches, isn't highly developed as a lakeside oasis. Businesses and residents pursue a rather contrived Mediterranean architectural theme: red tile, white stucco. The hot afternoon sun here would be better tempered by a judicious planting of shade trees downtown or umbrella-covered cafes.

Water, in this mid-latitude step *is* a problem. Osoyoos sprinkles "reclaimed water," an almost-drinkable sewage effluent on the greens of its 27-hole golf course and the Desert Park Racetrack. Residents voted to stop putting effluent in lake in 1964, opting for sewage lagoons on the West Bench. In 1980, the treated effluent was put to work. Golfers don't notice anything peculiar, though no one is allowed on brilliant green fairways until two hours after sprinkling.

Osoyoos Information: Info Centre at Hwy 3 and 97 junction. Box 227, Osoyoos, BC, V0H 1V0. 1-800-676-9667 or 250-495-7142.

■ **A Pocket of Pocket Desert:** East of the bridge crossing Osoyoos Lake, take the second left onto 45th St. Desert and dunes here are property of the Osoyoos First Nation and visitors are requested to seek permission at the Inkameep Campground here before proceeding. Off-season, call 250-498-3444. Wolf Creek Trail Rides here offers a chance to explore desert life. Whether you call this desert

To Kelowna
To Naramata
Okanagan Lake
Channel Parkway Bypass
Penticton
To Apex Mt. Ski Area & Nickel Plate Prov. Pk.
Skaha Lake
Lakeside Road
Kaleden
Christie Memorial Prov. Pk.
3A
Okanagan Falls Prov. Pk.
Okanagan Falls
40
To Keremeos
White Lake Road
Vaseux Lake Prov. Pk.
Green Lake Road
Vaseux Lake
To Keremeos & Princeton
Tuc-el-nuit Lake
97
Inkaneep Prov. Pk.
Oliver
Fairview
3
Osoyoos Oxbows Reserve
To Mt. Baldy Ski Area
20
Similkameen R.
Osoyoos Lake
Haynes Point Prov. Pk.
Osoyoos
To Rock Creek
0   Km   10
N

or mid-latitude steppe, it is a rare and endangered ecosystem – more at risk than BC's old-growth forests. It's sometimes referred to as the antelope brush ecosystem: this predominant brush, also known as greasewood for the way it crackles and burns, shares the arid landscape with rabbit brush and sage. More than 60 percent has been destroyed; only 9 percent is relatively undisturbed. Found here, and nowhere else in Canada, are the pallid bat (which doesn't hunt with sonar, but uses its ears to hear the delicate rustling of ground-dwelling insects), the shy night snake, and the ground mantis (Canada's only preying mantis, rarely seen because of its resemblance to a sage twig). Missing and feared gone as native residents are the burrowing owl, pygmy short-horned lizard, and white-tailed jack rabbit. Threatened: the western rattlesnake, Great Basin spadefoot toad, white-tailed lizard, and yellow badger.

The Osoyoos Desert Society is planning a reserve and major interpretive centre with boardwalk trails north of Osoyoos. Write them at Box 123, Osoyoos, BC, V0H 1V0. 250-494-2470.

■ **The Beaches:** Gyro Beach and Community Park, right downtown at Park Place and Spartan Dr, and nearby Kinsmen Beach offer the longest stretches of sand, picnicking, and parasailing. The Lions Beach has a playground and picnic tables.

■ **The Kettles:** May be visible from Hwy 97 south of Osoyoos between the Husky gas station and the Canada/US border. Look for them on both sides of the highway near the Sagebrush Lodge. These kettle- or cauldron-like holes, averaging 15-20m across and almost always filled with water, were formed by fragments of glacial ice that penetrated the valley floor, then melted. Such kettles may have lent their name to the Kettle River and valley to the east (see p. 150).

■ **Osoyoos Museum:** In Community Park. Box 791, Osoyoos, BC, V0H 1V0. 250-495-2582. Daily, 10-3, mid-May to early Sept. Bird specimens, Okanagan native artifacts, Inkaneep children's art, history of irrigation, exhibit on BC Provincial Police established in 1858 during gold rush. Original 1891 log schoolhouse.

■ **Osoyoos Art Gallery:** Corner of Main St and 89th. 250-495-2800. Year-round.

■ **The Windmill:** 1km east of bridge on Hwy 3. 250-495-5006. Daily, May-Sept. Tues-Sun, Oct-April. Authentic replica of fully operational stone-grinding flour mill. Tours and demonstrations. Gift shop features Dutch Delft blueware and wooden shoes. Teahouse and tulips in the spring garden.

■ **Golf: Osoyoos Golf and Country Club,** 250-495-7003, 27-hole course: park nine, meadows nine, or desert nine. **Desert Springs,** 250-495-3110, on East Lakeshore Dr, Par 3. **Mini-golf** at several locations.

■ **Wild Rapids Water Slide:** East Lakeshore Dr. 250-495-2621. Daily, July-Aug.

Osoyoos is an oasis in the Pocket Desert.

Inkaneep First Nation (Osoyoos Indian Band): (Pop. 523). Just north of Osoyoos, reserve land stretches north along the east side of Hwy 97, reaching almost to Vaseux Lake. Community operates Canada's second largest vineyard and leases land to Vincore International's winery. Tracts of their land remained undeveloped, and are some of the finest examples of natural "mid-latitude-steppe" ecosystem. Call band office, 250-498-3444, for tour of the reserve and an introduction to Inkaneep people's rich history.

Osoyoos Oxbows Fish and Wildlife Management Reserve: 262ha. Approaching Oliver, 7.5km north of Osoyoos, turn east onto Road 22. 1km to kiosk. Oxbows are bends in the river, and the land between those bends – crucial wildlife refuges. This reserve is one of the last areas in the south Okanagan Valley where water control projects have not transformed the land to the detriment of wildlife. The North Okanagan River Flood Control Project, completed in 1958, turned 58km of meandering river into a 38km channel. The effects are very visible as you wander along the road east of here: compare the oxbows and the channel. The oxbows offer a mixture of open water, marshes, riparian thicket, meadows, grasslands.

Road 22 becomes Black Sage Rd. 2km into scenic vineyard country, a second kiosk focuses on a burrowing owl reestablishment program. The road continues into Inkaneep First Nation reserve land, offering glimpses of real sand dunes and a natural landscape in sharp contrast to surrounding orchards. Please obey signs and stay on the road.

Oliver: (Pop. 4,285). 20km north of Osoyoos. One of the few Okanagan communities not on a lake, Oliver sits along the west bank of the Okanagan River. The town was named for BC Premier "Honest" John Oliver, whose provincial Liberal government in the early 1920s sponsored the Southern Okanagan Lands Project, irrigating land to be settled by soldiers returning from the First World War. In 1923, they built a dam north of town on the Okanagan River, and the irrigation canal still in use today (called "The Ditch"). Oliver lauded itself as the Cantaloupe Capital of Canada. In 1952, to control flooding, 37km of the winding Okanagan river were straightened (see *Oxbows,* above), and between 1963-1973, a 30lb pressure system was installed, taking water to the highest point of every approved orchard and vineyard. There are some 9,000ha of orchard surrounding Oliver today. Along what the town is marketing as "The Golden Mile" of Hwy 97 just south of town, are some of the Okanagan Valley's most productive vineyards. They help supply nine local wineries.

Oliver Information: Info Centre at 36205-93rd St. (Right at 362nd Ave.) Box 460, Oliver, BC, V0H 1T0. 250-498-6321. Housed in 1923 CPR station (moved here from three blocks south). The CPR ran from 1923-1977.

Oliver Airport: East of Hwy 97 entering town. On Airport Rd. 250-498-8971.

■ **Oliver and District Heritage Society Museum and Archives:** 9728-356 Ave. 250-498-4027. Tues-Sun in summer. Call for winter hours. In former headquarters of area BC Provincial Police, built 1924. Exhibits include grassland flora and fauna, early mining artifacts, and the jail from Fairview, now a ghost town (see below). New exhibits feature the construction of the irrigation canal and agriculture that resulted.

■ **Vineyards:** A full day to visit Vincor International, Gehringer, Okanagan, Domaine Combret, Tinhorn Creek, Carriage House, and Gersighel Wineberg, Hester Creek Estate Winery, Inniskillin Okanagan Vineyards. Tastings and some tours offered. Ask at Info Centre.

■ **Fruits or Veggies:** Eagle Bluff Produce, Hwy 97N, just south of Vaseux Lake. 250-498-2531. June to mid-Sept;. Soft fruits. U-Pick Jan Marks, 38063-97th St (4km north of Oliver). 250-498-0761. **Karow Farms,** on Road 15. 250-498-3135. Call ahead for fruit, veggies, U-pick.

■ **Oliver Hiking and Bicycling Trail:** 10km of paved trail; 8km of prepared road bed along Okanagan River from McAlpine Bridge (where Hwy 97 crosses the river just north of Oliver) to Osoyoos Lake. Cycling on dikes, hiking on old railway right of way. Info Centre has map.

■ **Okanagan-Similkameen Cooperative Growers' Association:** 9315-348th Ave. 250-498-3491. Summer tours of Oliver's packing house (operating since 1923).

■ **Golf Courses: Cherry Grove Golf Course,** 250-498-2880, nine holes. **Fairview Mountain Golf Club,** 250-498-6050, 18 holes.

350th Ave and Highway 97: In Oliver, turn west at stoplight onto 350th Ave **(Fairview Rd)**; eventually becomes Oliver-Cawston Rd leaving town.

SIDE TRIP

to Ghost Town

Fairview: 4.5km southwest of Oliver on the steep Fairview Rd (at junction of White Lake Rd). An information kiosk, farmers' fields, and a private residence hidden in the trees, are all that remains of what was, in 1893, the biggest city north of San Francisco. Up to 500 people lived here: the gold was high grade but not plentiful. In 1902 the grand Teepee Hotel burned down; by 1908, Fairview, with it enchanted views of Osoyoos Lake, was a ghost town.

Fairview-White Lake Rd: A pleasant backcountry drive north from Fairview, 6.5km to small community of **Willowbrook.**, and junction with Green Lake Rd.

Green Lake Rd: Leads northeast from Willowbrook, 12.5km to Okanagan Falls, (see below). Leads north as Fairview-White Lake Rd, 7km to **White Lake Valley** and **Dominion Radio Astrophysical Observatory**, and Hwy 97 junction 8km beyond. See *Side Trip to White Lake Valley*, below.

Return to Highway 97 at Oliver

Park Dr (79th St) and Hwy 97: East on 79th St. Cross bridge over Okanagan River, continue past arena, then right onto 362 Ave which becomes **Camp McKinney Rd. Mt Baldy** is 34.5km southeast. South through Camp McKinney to Hwy 3, 11.5km.

Mount Baldy Ski Area: Directions as above. 15 runs over 550m vertical drop accessed by two T-bars. Box 1528, Oliver, BC, V0H 1T0.

Tuc-el-Nuit Dr (71st St): 6km north of Oliver on Hwy 97. Leads to Inkaneep Provincial Park and Tuc-el-Nuit Lake.

Inkaneep Provincial Park: 21ha; 7 campsites. West off Tuc-el-Nuit Dr (71st St) onto Campsite Rd for short distance. 250-494-6500. One of the best, but least-known, birding sites in the Okanagan Valley. Canoeing, fishing.

Tuc-el-Nuit Lake: Return to Tuc-el-Nuit Dr and continue south for 2.5km. Spring-fed lake. Can also access from Oliver, turn right on 79th St, left on 370 Ave to public beach.

Vaseux Lake: 14.5km north of Oliver on Hwy 97. Federal wildlife and migratory bird sanctuary. Shallow, weedy lake – 4km long and 1km wide – bordered by sandy beaches. Powerboats not permitted. One of Canada's foremost birding areas: this narrowing of the Okanagan Valley is a resting point for migrating birds in spring and autumn. Among birds rare or unknown in

other parts of Canada are the canyon wren, white-throated swift, and white-headed woodpecker. Vaseux in French means muddy. Fishing for bass.

McIntyre Bluff: Southwest end of Vaseux Lake, bluff rises straight up 250m from the narrow pass through which Hwy 97 runs. Southbound travellers get the best view: from the rock face emerges the profile of a human face. Some Inkaneep people say it is the face of an old man, others say a young woman, who, before the arrival of Europeans, and during a period of war between Okanagan people and neighbouring Secwepemc people, led the Okanagans to victory by luring a Secwepemc war party over the bluff. Other perspectives: from the east side of Vaseux Lake: the outline in white granite of a native rider and his pony. McIntyre was an 1862 Overlander (see p.177). Four-hour round-trip hike starts at Seacrest Rd (368 Ave): turn off Hwy 97, wind up the hill, turn right into Covert Farms. Stop at office for permission and directions for parking.

Vaseux Lake Provincial Park: 12ha; 12 campsites. 14km north of Oliver. 250-494-6500. Canoeing, ice fishing, wildlife viewing. Drive carefully, there are often California bighorn sheep on highway.

Vaseux Wildlife Centre: 14.5km north of Oliver. North end of Vaseux Lake. Set below dramatic rock cliffs, a kiosk installed by the Vaseux Nature Trust. This is one of the best places in North America to see California bighorn sheep – there are about 350 in the Vaseux band. Signs tell of the host of critters you might see, and of those that you won't anymore. Trails, birdwatching blinds, scientists at work.

Okanagan Falls: (Pop. 1,700). 20km north of Oliver, "OK Falls" to locals. The Okanagan people called this place Kwak-ne-ta, "the little falls." The fast-flowing rapids were a favoured place to catch kokanee, a type of land-locked salmon. In the 1950s, a dam was built to control lake levels south of the rapids, and so diminished the falls. The town today is an orchard and tourist centre. Pleasant sandy beaches at southern end of Skaha Lake.

After running along east side of Vaseux Lake, Hwy 97 cuts through Okanagan Falls before heading up west side of Skaha Lake.

■ **Bassett House and Museum:** South end of Okanagan Falls on Hwy 97. A 1909 T. Eaton Co catalogue home featuring restored residence of the pioneer Bassett family. Mon, Wed, Fri, Sat, May-Sept.

■ **Memorial Rose Garden:** On Hwy 97, in front of library and fire hall. Blooming May-Oct.

■ **Wine Tours: Wild Goose Vineyards and Winery**, Lot 11, Sun Valley Way. 250-479-8919. **Blue Mountain Vineyard and Cellars**, south from Okanagan Falls about 8km, exit east off highway on Oliver Ranch Rd, follow signs. 250-497-8244. **Hawthorne Mountain (LeComte) Vineyards**, 5km off Hwy 97 on west side of town, follow signs from Okanagan Falls Bridge. 250-497-8267. Fabulous valley

views where Hawthorne brothers settled in early 1900s. Daily tours and tasting in settlers' original home. **Stag's Hollow Winery**, 12 Sunvalley Way, 250-497-6162. Wine shop May-Oct; tours year-round by appointment.

■ **Sun Stream Fruit Ltd:** 258 Oliver Ranch Rd. 250-497-5525. Mon-Sat. Dried fruits and veggies, tastings and tours by request.

Green Lake Rd: West from Okanagan Falls. Back road leads south 20km to Oliver, via small community of Willowbrook and Fairview ghost town, see above. First part of road traces Okanagan River and passes vineyards. At 8km, is the Mahoney Lake Ecological Reserve. Scientists come from all over the world to study this small saline lake: its deepest levels, saltier than the sea, support no life except high densities of purple sulphur bacteria that can live without oxygen.

Skaha Lake: Once called Dog Lake, but Skaha is prettier Shuswap native name for same thing. Lake is a beautiful deep blue. Name refers to a hard winter when hungry Hudson's Bay Company traders were reduced to eating dogs. Lake stretches 20km from OK Falls (formerly Dog Town) to Penticton. Skaha was originally part of larger Okanagan Lake until silt deposits created the delta on which Penticton now sits.

Lakeside Rd: Paved 16km secondary highway circling east side of Skaha Lake past Skaha Lake Marina into outskirts of Penticton. Lakeside alternative to Hwy 97.

Christie Memorial Provincial Park: 3ha; day use. At Okanagan Falls town. 200m beach on Skaha Lake. Lots of Canada Geese.

Okanagan Falls Provincial Park: 2ha; 25 campsites. Just past Christie Memorial Park in OK Falls. Turn south. April-Oct. 250-494-6500. Start of deciduous trees above Okanagan River. Fourteen of Canada's 20 species of bat have been recorded here, more than anywhere else is the country. Lots of bugs too. Wheelchair access.

Gillespie House: 3.5km north of Okanagan Falls. **Private residence: not open to the public.** Dugald Gillespie, from Ontario, found his way to the Okanagan Valley in 1894 and took up land. In 1900, he built the first irrigation system in the Kaleden district. He and his son also formed a freight company, carrying supplies, by horse, between Penticton and the new Nickel Plate Mine and the Daly Reduction plant at Hedley. In 1907, the Great Northern Railway made his work redundant; at the same time, land prices around Kaleden were booming (see below). Gillespie sold out and moved to Alberta.

White Lake Rd: 5km north of Okanagan Falls. Turn southwest off Hwy 97 to begin 28.5km loop taking in White Lake Rd, Twin Lakes Rd, and Hwy 3A. **Note: travellers starting out on the other side, i.e. from Hwy 3A, must begin on Twin Lakes Rd (White Lake Rd there is a no-through road).**

SIDE TRIP

to White Lake Valley

An idyllic back-road circle tour within the vee of converging Hwys 97 and 3A. Definitely a route for golfers. About 5km down the road, before the observatory, is the first of two pretty courses: **St Andrew's By-the-Lake**, 250-497-5648. Nine holes, par 36, and replica of stone bridge that spans the Swilican Burn at St. Andrew's, Scotland.

Dominion Radio Astrophysical Observatory: 9km from Kaleden Junction. A startling futuristic contrast to White Lake Valley. Guided tours Sun afternoons, July-Aug. Self-guided tours year-round. 250-490-4355. This wide-bottomed valley surrounded by a ring of low hills, minimizing radio interference, is one of the world's best radio astronomy sites. Visitor centre explains use of radio telescopes for gathering astronomical data. On property is pond-sized White Lake, a haunt for ornithologists viewing sandhill cranes, loggerhead shrikes, long-billed curlews, Brewer's sparrows, sage thrashers.

Just before junction to busy Hwy 3A is **Twin Lakes Golf and Country Club**, a pretty 18 holes. To complete side trip, return to Hwy 97 at Kaleden junction by turning northeast on Hwy 3A through Marron Valley. By turning southwest on Hwy 3A, you head to Hwy 3 junction at Keremeos. From Kaleden junction, it's 2km to pleasant community of Kaleden.

Surprise Ranch: 5km south of observatory. (40448-149th St.) 250-498-2698. Daily, year-round. Call for tours. European wild boar ranch raises boars, sells boar meat.

Return to Highway 97

Highway 3A: 5.5km north of Okanagan Falls; 500m north of White Lake Rd (see above).

Kaleden: (Pop. 1,118). 7km north of Okanagan Falls (1km north of Hwy 3A), take Kaleden turnoff (Lakehill Rd). The village is set on benches over the sparkling waters of Skaha Lake. The KVR traces the shore: a cyclist pedals along it. Just above the railway bed-cum trail, two old structures form the heart of town, and draw us into the dream that put them here. The dreamer was James Ritchie, the Baptist developer who founded West Summerland in 1904. Kaleden – from the Greek *Kalos*, meaning beautiful, and Eden – was born in 1909. Land sales flourished from the start; tens of thousands of fruit trees were planted. Irrigation was expensive, but Ritchie wangled financial support from the British government. The Grand Kaleden Hotel was built in 1912: there were telephones and baths in each of its 28 rooms; French doors opened to an outdoor sleeping balcony, so that brass beds could be rolled out on hot summer evenings. The general store went up across the street the same year.

Then came the First World War and the withdrawal of British financing. Fortunes fizzled; the village survived.

In the early 1930s, residents rejected plans to have the hotel turned into a sanatorium. And so it sits today, a concrete skeleton. In sharp contrast, the general store is now The Historic 1912 Restaurant and Country Inn. Beautifully decorated, offering the best of Okanagan wines, patrons drive all the way from the Lower Mainland.

There's also the Net Cafe (internet that is), on Lakehill Rd, near the entrance to town. Kaleden Pioneer Park has a sandy beach, tennis and volleyball courts, picnic tables, and boat launch.

Stop of Interest: 11km from Okanagan Falls. Viewpoint over Skaha Lake. Picnic table. Sign tells of Okanagan peoples and first white settler, Tom Ellis. More in *Penticton,* below.

Channel Parkway Bypass: 15km from Okanagan Falls. Turn west at light to skirt City of Penticton. Bypass runs 8km adjacent to Okanagan River on west side of town. Turn off on Green Mountain Rd to Apex ski resort 3km north.

SIDE TRIP

to Apex Mountain

Apex Mountain Provincial Recreation Area: 575ha. 32km southwest of Penticton on Green Mountain Rd. No facilities. 250-494-6500. Views of Manning and Cathedral provincial parks from the 2,000m-plus summits of Mt Riordan, Beaconsfield Mountain, and Apex Mountain.

Apex Alpine Mountain Resort: Box 1060, Penticton, BC, V2A 7N7. 250-292-8126 or 1-800-387-2739. Sunniest of Okanagan ski areas, and offering some of BC's best downhill skiing. Four-season holiday destination, in tradition of a western-style guest ranch. Has hotel, and spring, summer, and fall holiday packages, including golf, horseback riding, tennis, nature hikes and outings, mountain biking, and fly-fishing. In winter, skiing: 56 runs over 600m vertical drop. 30km of groomed, track-set cross-country ski trails; 20km backcountry trails; classic and skating trails.

Nickel Plate Provincial Park: 105ha; wilderness camping. 250-494-6500 Park is situated 15km west through Apex resort. Wilderness, sandy beaches on Nickel Plate Lake. Big glacial boulders scattered on north shore. 39km of cross-country trails.

Return to Highway 97

Return to Hwy 97 at Channel Parkway Bypass, enter Penticton, or head north along Okanagan Lake for Kelowna.

Penticton: (Pop. 30,987). 20km north of Okanagan Falls; 60km north of border crossing at Osoyoos. Moonlit beaches, warm night air, restaurants, hotels, the nectars of a dozen vintners: it's a recipe for romance. But Penticton is really a tourist town for families: you can rent bicycles for two, or four or six. There's a water park with giant squirt guns, a peach-shaped concession stand, warm shallow water, and lots of kids burying their parents in the sand.

Penticton lies between two enticing Okanagan lakes. The entire city – the Okanagan Valley's second largest – is squeezed onto a delta only 3.5km-long. At its north end are the soft, pale brown sands of Okanagan Lake; at its south end, the firmer, red, and also said to be warmer, sands of Skaha Lake. A full kilometre of sand at each end. Then, linking the two beaches, is the 7km Okanagan River Channel: sprawled across inner tubes, water babies float from Okanagan Lake to Skaha Lake.

City brochures, offering their own translation for the aboriginal name, Penticton, say this is "a place to live forever." There is no ethnographic evidence to support the translation: but it is the name of the Okanagan First Nation community now situated on the Okanagan Channel's west side.

The first non-native resident was Tom Ellis, who arrived in 1865. When the Penticton people were moved to an Indian reserve in 1877, he preempted their land east of the Okanagan River, and with further acquisitions, became a great cattle baron. It wasn't until the Southern Okanagan Land Company purchased the Ellis Estate in 1905 that Penticton began to grow.

By 1909 when the town was incorporated, a guide to the Okanagan attested to "the extensive planting of fruit trees and their equally prolific growth." Today Penticton is the key packing, processing, and shipping centre for extensive soft-fruit and apple-growing operations in the southern Okanagan. More than 1,000ha of orchards lie within city limits. In April and May, when thousands of fruit trees are in bloom, the city is stunningly beautiful.

Penticton Information: Info Centre at Jubilee Pavilion, 888 Westminster Ave W (at corner of Power St), Penticton, BC, V2A 8R2. 1-800-663-5052 or 250-493-4055. Summer Info Centre on Hwy 97, 5km south of Penticton.

British Columbia Wine Information Centre: At Jubilee Pavilion, 888 Westminster Ave (same building as Penticton information). 250-490-2006. Daily. Information on Okanagan tours, wineries, and events.

■ **The Beaches:** For **Okanagan Lake**, Lakeshore Dr provides access to Okanagan Beach, walking promenade, peach-shaped concession stand, waterslides, bicycle rentals. Next to it is Rotary Park with walking pier, parasailing, waterskiing lessons. Then, Okanagan Lake Park and marina. The Channel Parkway and Lee Ave lead to Skaha Lake Park, slightly more removed from the hubbub of hotels and traffic, with shade trees, concessions, restrooms, and delightful water park for children; boat and jet ski rentals, parasailing, waterskiing lessons, marina.

■ **Okanagan River Channel:** Put into the water at Coyote Cruises, in the big blue building on Riverside Dr, near Riverside Golf. This 7km manmade channel – a straightening of the Okanagan River – flows from Okanagan Lake to Skaha Lake. Perfection: to sunbathe and swim in the morning at Okanagan Beach, then float down the channel (about 2.5 hours) to cap the day at Skaha Lake Beach. (When the waters are lower and slower, rafter's usually stop halfway). Thousands float by on summer weekends. With the Penticton airport to the west, and the busy highway to the east, it's not the most serene setting. Coyote Cruises, 250-492-2115, rents dinghies and tire tubes if you don't bring your own, and provides also transportation back to the starting point. Spawning kokanee may be seen, Sept-Nov. BC Wildlife Watch viewing site.

■ **SS Sicamous:** Beached since 1951 on Okanagan Lake off Lakeshore Dr near exit to Kelowna. 250-492-0403. Daily, mid-June to mid-Sept. Off-season, Mon-Fri. 72m stern-wheeler plied Okanagan Lake between Vernon and Penticton from 1914-1935. Still being restored. It is worth visiting just to see the KVR model, complete with mountain landscapes, trestles, and trains that disappear into tunnels. The SS *Naramata*, a CPR tug also launched in 1914, is being restored.

■ **Rose Gardens:** Next to SS *Sicamous*. Hundreds of varieties.

■ **Penticton (RN Atkinson) Museum and Archives:** Library and museum complex. 785 Main St, Penticton, BC, V2A 5E3. 250-490-2451 for info or group tours. Tues-Sat, 10-5. Okanagan First Nations and pioneer artifacts, natural history, military memorabilia.

■ **Art Gallery of the South Okanagan:** 199 Front St. 250-493-2928. Tues-Fri, also Sat-Sun afternoons. Lectures, workshops, special events, exhibits.

■ **Leir House:** 220 Manor Park Ave. 250-492-7997. Year-round. Home of Penticton and District Community Arts Council, Academy of Music, and a venue for local artists. One of the city's finest historical buildings, built 1927.

■ **Tin Whistle Brewery:** 954 W Eckhardt Ave. 250-770-112. Brewing four types of English Ale, plus special Peaches and Cream brew available only May-Sept. According to some, "the best peach beer you've ever tasted." Drop-in tours and tasting, year-round.

■ **Penticton Trade and Convention Centre:** 273 Power St, Penticton, BC, V2A 7K9. 250-490-2460. Has 4,320 seats. Walking distance to 1,200 motel and hotel rooms. Two blocks from the lake.

■ **Golf: Penticton Golf and Country Club**, 18 holes, W Eckhardt Ave. 250-492-8727. **Pine Hills**, nine holes, 1.5km north of city on Hwy 97. 250-492-5731. **Twin Lake Golf Resort**, 18 holes, 18km southwest of Penticton. 250-497-5359. RV campground, clubhouse, cross-country skiing in winter. **Pleasant Valley**, nine holes, 2.5km east of Main St on Penticton Ave. 250-492-6988. **Riverside Golf**, On Riverside Dr next to Coyote Cruises. 250-492-5847. Mini-golf.

■ **Wonderful Waterworld:** Skaha Lake Rd at Yorkton Ave. 250-493-8121. Late May-Sept. 12 waterslides, hot tub, mini-golf, slot cars, RV park.

■ **Skaha Climbing Bluffs:** Heading south toward Skaha Lake, turn left off South Main onto Crescent Hill Rd. At top of steep hill turn right, continue to dirt road and sign indicating parking lot (about 2.5km from South Main turnoff). Parking fee is $5; lot closed Nov-March. Seasonal passes available. Granite slabs, faces, and jagged overhangs offer vertical challenges to novices and rock monkeys. Hiking trails through sage and ponderosa pine; mountain goats and rattlesnakes. Carry water: noon temperatures can soar above 40C. Be respectful, stick to trails. Info at Ray's Sports Den in Penticton, 250-493-1216 or The Crux Indoor Climbing Centre in Kelowna, 250-860-7325. Also read *Skaha Bluffs*, by Howie Richardson.

■ **Vineyards:** God's Mountain Crest Chalet, East Side Rd (4km south of marina on Skaha Lake, turn left at gazebo), 250-490-4800; organically grown grapes; B&B.

■ **Spawning Kokanee:** In Penticton Creek: view from art gallery to intersection at Eckhardt Ave and Government St. Walkway. BC Wildlife Watch viewing site.

Naramata Rd: Northeast from Penticton via Government St and Haven Hill Rd. Traces east shores of Okanagan Lake to Naramata. Rural homes and lakeside vistas. Look for signs to Hillside Cellars and Lang Vineyards. Lang was BC's first farmgate winery, Hillside was the second. See *Penticton to Kelowna* map, p.159.

SIDE TRIP

to Naramata

Naramata: (Pop. 1,069). 14km north of Penticton via Naramata Rd. Despite what the BC road maps says, Naramata Rd does not continue smoothly north through Naramata and the wilds of Okanagan Mountain

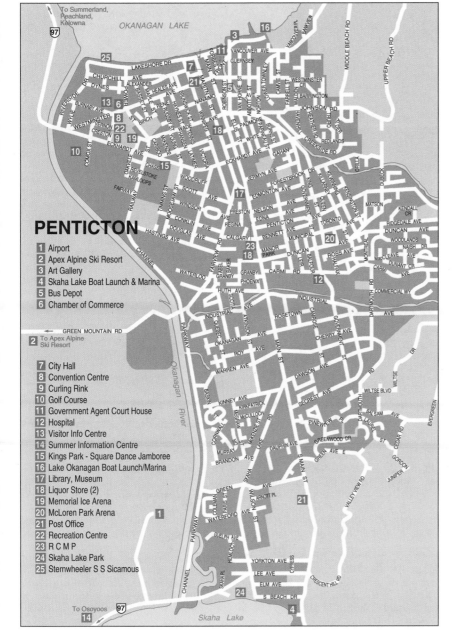

PENTICTON

1 Airport
2 Apex Alpine Ski Resort
3 Art Gallery
4 Skaha Lake Boat Launch & Marina
5 Bus Depot
6 Chamber of Commerce

2 To Apex Alpine Ski Resort

7 City Hall
8 Convention Centre
9 Curling Rink
10 Golf Course
11 Government Agent Court House
12 Hospital
13 Visitor Info Centre
14 Summer Information Centre
15 Kings Park - Square Dance Jamboree
16 Lake Okanagan Boat Launch/Marina
17 Library, Museum
18 Liquor Store (2)
19 Memorial Ice Arena
20 McLoren Park Arena
21 Post Office
22 Recreation Centre
23 R C M P
24 Skaha Lake Park
25 Sternwheeler S S Sicamous

Provincial Park to the Okanagan metropolis of Kelowna. It is possible to get there – if you are determined – via 50km of gravel road, washboard, and the bed of the old Kettle Valley Railway (see below). Naramata is for travellers more than tourists. If you're here, it's because you want to be. Naramata is for painters or poets, who come just to stroll from motels with pleasant courtyards, along lanes shaded by old fruit trees, to quiet sunlit coves.

Naramata means "smile of manitou." (Manitou is an Algonquian word referring to the great and mysterious power of the universe.) This is the name given the town by its founder, John Moore Robinson. This was his third town. The former Wellington County boy, in the new world to get rich, had already established Peachland in 1897, and Summerland, in 1902. In 1907, he bought up the land east of Summerland on Okanagan Lake, and called it East Summerland, but soon determined another name would be less confusing. At a seance held by Mrs. Gillespie, wife of the village postmaster, Robinson listened as the spirit of a great Sioux chief overtook his host and spoke of the chief's beloved wife, Naramata. Robinson liked her name.

In its first days, Naramata was reached by boat or paddlewheeler; by 1910 a horse-and-buggy road linked the village to Penticton. The village drew pioneer orchard growers; in summer, it became a playground. Hundreds converged from towns up the lake to participate in lively regattas: canoe racing, picnics, dancing. In 1910, Robinson built the exclusive Hotel Naramata: hot and cold running water, electricity, gardens, bowling greens, tennis. (The hotel has had many incarnations since then: as a girl's school, then home for Robinson who died in the 1950s, and his descendants. The grand old building, in new hands, is being restored.) In 1915, Naramata became a stop on the new Kettle Valley Railway: with better links to fruit markets, the little town boomed. When the KVR failed and roads again prevailed, Naramata became once again, a destination once chooses deliberately.

Limited, but satisfying choice of places for a quiet supper, including The Country Squire, renowned across Canada for its cuisine: book ahead. At the south edge of town, **Manitou Park** has beaches, boat launch.

Naramata Information: Naramata General Store, on Robinson St (it's also the liquor store, post office, gas station).

■ **Naramata Centre for Continuing Education:** Box 68, Naramata, BC, V0H 1N0. 250-496-5751. A United Church training centre on over 9ha of town and beach. Week-long and weekend courses.

■ **Naramata Museum:** In old firehall on Robinson St. Plans to open in spring 1999. Mural on firehall is a copy of a poster advertising a 1910 regatta.

■ **Kettle Valley Railway:** Traces lakeshore just east of village. Tunnels in mountain cliffs are visible looking northeast from village. From Naramata Rd, turn right onto Smethurst Rd and follow it up the hill until you cross the rail bed. Just past here, you can park, and begin your explorations. The Chute Lake Resort (below), boasts several original KVR buildings

and is a good base for hiking and cycling. Within reach of the Little Tunnel and Adra Tunnel (blocked off and collapsing inside). About 5km east of Naramata is **Rock Oven Park** – ovens were built by railway construction crews nearly a century ago. See Thompson Okanagan regional map, p.140, for the KVR's circuitous route through this area.

■ **Vineyards: Red Rooster Winery**, 910 Debeck Rd. 250-496-4041. Wine shop daily, May-Oct. **Lake Breeze Vineyards**, 930 Sammet Rd. 250-496-5659. Tours daily by request; wine shop hours vary, but daily May-Oct 15. **Lang Vineyard**, 2493 Gammon Rd. 250-496-5987; tours by appointment; wine shop hours vary, but daily May 1-Oct 15. **Kettle Valley Winery**, 2988 Hayman Rd. 250-496-5898. Tours by appointment; wine shop hours vary, but daily, 12-5, May-Nov. **Nichol Vineyard**, 1285 Smethurst Rd. 250-496-5962. Wine shop hours, Tues-Sun, 11-5, summer. **Hillside Estate Winery**, 1350 Naramata Rd. 1-888-923-9463. Daily, tasting and tours.

North Naramata Rd: Leads north from Naramata. 13km to Okanagan Mountain Provincial Park, on loose gravel and washboard. Gravel road continues, skirting east around the park as Chute Lake Rd. Road and rail bed meet 19km from Naramata at Chute Lake, site of a Forest Service Recreation campground and **Chute Lake Resort**. Year-round recreation and accommodation. The resort sits at the site of the Chute Lake Station and a few structural remnants of the station remain. From here, the rail bed is the road: a thrilling drive on easy grade. (Everybody: make train noises.) If you drive to the end (17km from Chute Lake Resort) your front tires will bump into the rim of the long, curved, steel bridge spanning Belleview Creek. This bridge is not for cars. DO NOT CROSS. TURN BACK: follow the Gillard Creek Forest Service Rd into Kelowna. Then loop around from that side for some of the most exciting sites along the KVR, including Myra Canyon (see Kelowna p. 161).

Okanagan Mountain Provincial Park: 10,562ha, 33km of shoreline; 48 walk-in campsites; six marine camping areas. Boat or hike in only. Access to park boundaries on secondary roads from Naramata (to the south) or Kelowna (to the north). Two parking lots, 24km of hiking trails, picnic areas, primitive campsites, and horse-loading ramps are the only development on the last large section of undeveloped shoreline along Okanagan Lake. The park is a mountainous elbow jutting into the east side of the lake: a vast, little-known wilderness harbouring the northernmost examples of "pocket desert" life, as well as plants and animals from wetter northern Okanagan climes. Its westernmost reach, Squally Point, and nearby Rattlesnake Island, are said to be home of Ogopogo.

Return to Penticton

From Penticton, travellers can go north on Hwy 97 to Summerland, Peachland, Kelowna, and beyond. For details see *Penticton to Kelowna*, following.

HIGHWAY 97 NORTH

From Penticton, scenic Hwy 97 traces the shores of Okanagan Lake for 60km to Kelowna, twisting through the heart of the Okanagan Valley. With orchards lining the route, you drive, in spring, through a fairyland of blossoms; in summer and fall, past a continuing array of fruit stands. Vineyards line the scene, and both commercial and estate wineries offer tasting tours. Backcountry parks on both sides of the lake provide a largely untouched wilderness alternative to the busy beach scene along the highway. And this is also Ogopogo Country. The deep 128km Okanagan Lake, carved out by ice-age glaciers, is said to be the home of by Ogopogo, an allegedly friendly prehistoric monster, claimed to have been seen at various times by credible witnesses and now protected under the BC Wildlife Act.

Penticton: (Pop. 30,987). 60km north of border at Osoyoos. See *US Border to Penticton*, p.156.

Hoodoos: Leaving Penticton on Hwy 97, look west for eerie clay formations high up on the benchland. Some 10,000 years ago, the last fragments of glacial ice remained in chunks in the valleys. Lakes formed alongside, them, silt built up at the edges. As the ice chunks melted, the white glacial lacustrine silt lined the valley edges. Streams of spring runoff carried sediment away and left hoodoos.

Kickininee Provincial Park: 49ha; no campsites. Three lakeside locations, from 6-8km north of Penticton. Day use. Beaches at Kickininee, Soorimpt, and Pyramid. Boat launch at Soorimpt.

Sun-Oka Beach Provincial Park: 15ha; no campsites. 10km north of Penticton. Lots of summer fun. Summerland Kinsmen Polar Bear Swim in Jan.

Prairie Valley Rd: 12km north of Penticton. To Darke Lake and Eneas Lakes provincial parks.

SIDE TRIP

to Provincial Parks

Darke Lake Provincial Park: 1,470ha; 5 campsites. 20km northwest on gravel road. 250-494-6500. In pine and fir forest, nice trout.

Eneas Lakes Provincial Park: 1,036ha; no development; limited (four-wheel-drive) access on rough road, 4km past Darke Lake Park. 250-494-6500. Wilderness camping, fishing, and hiking around all four Eneas lakes.

Return to Highway 97

Summerland: (Pop. 10,584). 16km north of Penticton on Hwy 97. At the head of three fertile valleys – Garnett (north), Prairie (centre), Peach (south). The town we see today was born of two spirited entrepreneurs. John Moore Robinson had ventured from his native England to Manitoba, and then BC, set on amassing a quick fortune. It was the taste of Okanagan peaches that first turned the ardent Baptist from floundering mining ventures to land development. Peachland in 1897, was his first Eden. In 1902, Robinson cast his gaze 21km south, and as he had done in Peachland, subdivided the lakeside here into agricultural lots, put in irrigation, and lured long-suffering prairie farmers to paradise and fruit growing: "Heaven on earth with summer weather forever!" His brother, a Baptist minister, drew the new town's name from the Protestant "Summerland Hymn."

His new Eden was already bearing fruit when Manitoba compatriot James Ritchie arrived in 1903. Ritchie set his heart on 150ha just west of Summerland, then an Indian reserve inhabited by the Pierre's, an Okanagan First Nations family. Negotiating with the Indian agent in Vernon, Ritchie got the land; the Pierre's moved farther west. His new development became West Summerland; in 1909 he founded Kaleden (p.156). Meanwhile, in 1907, across the lake, Robinson established East Summerland, later named Naramata.

The promise of the KVR and access to distant markets would have bypassed the folks of Summerland had it not been for their zeal. Told the canyon at Trout Creek, just south of town, was an obstacle too great and another route would be followed, locals demanded what they said would be an "infinitesimal bridge" in the scheme of things. The result: the wondrous McCulloch Trestle, the KVR's largest steel girder bridge, North America's third largest. It's 188m long and 73m high (see it for yourself). On May 31, 1915, the KVR rolled into the West Summerland Station.

Today, the little town of Summerland rivals Kelowna as a major fruit-processing centre. It is home to a fruit-packing house run by BC Fruit Packers, and to Summerland Sweets and the Kettle Valley Dried Fruit Company.

The area is geared for tourists. Lake beaches, two golf courses, one 18 holes. Mutts are even welcomed: Dog Beach, on Lakeshore Dr, has been set aside for man's best friend. The community has taken on a Tudor look, with its wide streets presenting an array of novelty and gift shops. Kayak rentals.

Summerland Information: Info Centre, Summerland Chamber of Commerce, 15600 Hwy 97 (at Thompson Rd), north end of town. Box 1075, Summerland, BC, V0H 1Z0. 250-494-2686.

■ **Summerland Museum:** 9521 Wharton St. Tues-Sat afternoons, year-round; Mon-Sat, 10-4, June-Aug. 250-494-9395. Video presentations of Summerland history, the Kettle Valley Railway, and Okanagan irrigation.

■ **Summerland Art Centre and Gallery:** Main St. 250-494-4494. Mon-Sat, 10-4.

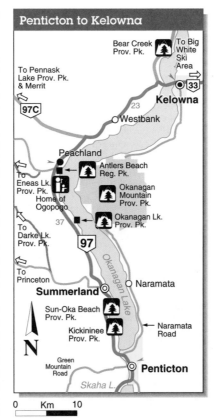

Penticton to Kelowna

■ **Giants Head Park:** On Giants Head Mountain (el 832m), overlooking Summerland. Looking at it from Gartrell Rd, south of downtown, do you think the mountain resembles the profile of a man's head? Drive most of the way up, then it's a worthwhile five-minute walk to views of the valley.

■ **Wineries and Vineyards: Sumac Ridge Estate Winery**, on Hwy 97 north out of town (307 Hwy 97). 250-494-0451. Daily. **Scherzinger Vineyards**, 7311 Fiske Rd. Daily.

■ **Golf:** The **Sumac Ridge Golf Course**, 307 Hwy 97, 250-494-3122. 9-holes, par-3. **Summerland Golf and Country Club**, 2405 Mountain, 250-494-9554. 18 holes.

■ **Pacific Agri-Food Research Centre/Ornamental Gardens and Interpretive Centre:** 4200 Hwy 97 S (across from Sunoka Beach). 250-494-6385. Gardens open daily; interpretive centre, weekday afternoons. Known locally as the Research Station Gardens. The original Dominion experimental farm was established 1914 to research the development of agriculture in the semi-arid Okanagan; the Ornamental Gardens were developed two years later. The properties, now part of Agriculture Canada's Summerland Research Station, are operated by a non-profit organization. The former superintendent's cottage-style home is now the Interpretive Centre surrounded by 6ha of English-style flower beds, lawns, and wooded forest pathways. New Xeriscape (Dryland) Research and Demonstration Garden features water-wise design ideas and plants.

■ **Summerland Trout Hatchery:** 13405 South Lakeshore Dr. 250-494-0491. Daily. Two million rainbow and eastern brook trout raised annually and stocked in 250 lakes. BC Wildlife Watch viewing site.

■ **Fruits and Veggies: Summerland Sweets**, Canyon View Rd. 250-494-0377. Daily, July-Aug, Mon-Sat, rest of year. Fruit candy, syrups, jams, wine pulp. **Kettle Valley Dried Fruits**, 14014 Hwy 97 N. 250-494-0335. Tours and tastings. **Robert's Fruit Market and Orchard**, 13041 Hwy 97. 250-494-5541. May 1-Oct 31. **Bentley Road Fruit and Vegetables**, 16600 Bentley Rd. 250-494-0924;. Seasonal. **Blossom Fruit Stand**, 4km south of Summerland on Hwy 97. 250-494-1111. Fruit stand, orchard visits. **Granny's Fruit Stand**, 13810 Hwy 97. 250-494-7374. Fruits, veggies, baked goods.

■ **Summerland Beaches:** From north to south: Crescent Beach, Peach Orchard Beach, Rotary Beach, Kinsmen Park, S.O.S.A. Rotary Beach, Powell Beach, and Sun-Oka Beach. Boat launches, picnic areas.

■ **George Ryga Centre:** 250-494-1666. Retreat for writers and photographers in heritage house long occupied by writer George Ryga.

■ **Kettle Valley Railway:** Board the **Kettle Valley Steam Train** at Prairie Valley Station, off Prairie Valley Rd, west side of Summerland. 250-494-8422. 90-minute rail tours, May-Oct; days and times vary. Through Okanagan history, flora, fauna, orchards, and vineyards to Canyon View Station at north end of Trout Creek Canyon (train can also be boarded here). Special Great Train Robbery and BBQ, evening runs. The **Trout Creek Canyon Trestle** (described above) is visible from the Agri-Food Research Centre (listed above).

Back Road to Princeton: From downtown Summerland (Wharton St), take Prairie Valley Rd west. An adventurous and scenic alternative to Hwy 97/3A; but not a shortcut, as you may hope. It's 90km, mostly paved, but very twisty in spots, tracing the old KVR route – first visible at small community of Faulder (9.5km). The section from Faulder to Osprey Lake (50km) is rough gravel. Four Forest Service campgrounds (See p.148).

Okanagan Lake Provincial Park: 98ha; 168 campsites (reservations taken: call 1-800-689-9025; from the Lower Mainland or overseas, call 604-689-9025). General info: 250-494-6500. 13km north of Summerland. Sani-station. Boat ramp. International assortment of more than 10,000 trees: Russian olive, China elm, Norway maple, Lombardy poplar. Sandy beaches and views.

Ogopogo's Home: Viewpoint overlooking Rattlesnake Island and Squally Point on the east side of the lake. 6km past Okanagan Lake Park. Ogopogo, or the serpent the Okanagan People call N'xa'xa'etkw, "spiritually powerful in the water," is said to make his/her home in an underwater cave just off the point, and watchers claim repeated sightings here. Good views of both Kelowna and Penticton.

Antlers Beach Regional Park: 2ha; day use. 1.5km past Ogopogo's Viewpoint. Both sides of Hwy 97. Good swimming one side; other has Deep Creek and a waterfall. There is a kokanee spawning run at Deep Creek from mid-Sept.

Peachland: (Pop. 4,524). 21km north of Summerland on the shores of Okanagan Lake. Peachland might be more appropriately named Beachland. You veer down from the highway and end up on Beach Ave. The small town's beachfront runs 6km, all of it public access, most of it skirted by a sunny promenade serviced with docks for diving and sunbathing. Truth is, there are no peaches in Peachland. Area orchards grow them, and a few might sell them along quiet out-of-the-way roadsides: but for visiting peach-seekers, there is no fruit stand (the old stand at the south end of town is closed). If you want a peach, says the Municipal Office, go down to Summerland, or up to Westbank. But, if you want a beach...

It was peaches, nonetheless, that inspired this oasis, in 1897. John Moore Robinson (see p.156 and p.159) planned to make a million in mining. When he tasted the dessert peaches at the Lambly Ranch on Okanagan Lake, he forgot his losses and set about dividing this benchland into 4ha lots, putting in irrigation, and encouraging more settlers. So fruitful were his efforts that he established Summerland in 1902 and Naramata in 1907.

Peachland Information: Peachland Museum, 5890 Beach Ave, Peachland, BC, V0H 1X0. In summer call museum, 250-767-3441, or Municipal Office (5806 Beach Ave). 250-767-2647.

■ **Peachland Museum:** 5890 Beach Ave. Thurs-Tues, July-Aug. 250-767-3441. In former Baptist church, an eight-sided 1910 wood structure. Photos of orchard development.

■ **Wineries: Hainle Vineyards Estate Winery,** Trepanier Bench Rd. 250-767-2525. Summer: Tues-Sun, 10-5. Nov-April: Thurs-Sun, 1-5; specialty wines; lunches daily. **First Estate Cellars,** 5031 Cousins Rd. 250-767-9526. Daily, call for tour times.

■ **Golf: Ponderosa Golf and Country Club,** on Hwy 97, has 18 holes, full dining.

■ **Hardy Falls:** A peaceful nature walk.

Princeton Ave: At Peachland's only stoplight. West to Silver Lake Forestry Centre and Pennask Lake Provincial Park. Pavement peters out into gravel road.

SIDE TRIP

to Pennask Lake

Silver Lake Forestry Centre: 16km west of Peachland off Hwy 97. Well posted. Princeton Ave to fork in road. Take right fork to Brenda Mine. Dawn to dusk, year-round. 250-860-6410. Artifacts from logging, construction, harvesting, and firefighting.

Pennask Lake Provincial Park: 244ha; 28 campsites. 55km northwest of Peachland. As above, head west out of Peachland on Princeton Ave. At fork in road, turn left on rough gravel road. A slow, bumpy drive, but okay in summer with a two-wheel drive. Watch out for logging trucks. Picnicking, fishing, canoeing, birding.

Return to Highway 97

Okanagan Connector (Hwy 97C): At Drought Hill Interchange, just north of Peachland. Terminus of major 108km extension of Coquihalla freeway from Merritt. Connector extends freeway from Lower Mainland into heart of the Okanagan Valley, averting circuitous and slower highway routes that dance by the northern and southern extremities of the valley. This straight and fast shortcut reduces six-hour-or-so trip to just four hours. The Coquihalla Hwy has had a major impact not only on Peachland, which serves as a bedroom community for city workers, but on the entire Okanagan Valley. For details of route, see, p.176.

Okanagan Information: Okanagan Connector Info Centre. On Hwy 97C, 4km from Drought Hill Interchange. April-Nov. Box 26042, Hwy 97C, Westbank, BC, V4T 2G3. 250-767-6677.

Westbank: (Pop. 19,097). 10km north of Peachland on Hwy 97, 2km north of Coquihalla Connector, 12km south of Kelowna. Hwy 97 forks at Paynter's Market. Two lanes running northbound through Westbank are separated by a city block from two lanes southbound. This fast-growing business and residential community on the edge of Kelowna has a history of its own as an important crossroads. In very early times, an Okanagan aboriginal village, Stekatkolxne'ut, overlooked the lake at its narrowest canoe crossing point. Trails (now paved as road) also traced the lakeshore. In the early 1800s fur traders, using these trails, came to know this stopping place as MacDonald's Plain, after a Hudson's Bay Company officer. The Allisons, who settled nearby in 1872, named their local estate Sunnyside. And so this was Sunnyside for a time, as well as Westside (a region stretching halfway up this side of the lake). In 1897, a small wharf, built as a shipping port for grain and named after the first schoolmaster, added another name, Hall's Landing. In 1908, the post office delivered the name Westbank.

Westbank Information: Info Centre, #4-2375 Pamela Rd, Westbank, BC, V4T 2H9 (at fork in Hwy 97 on northbound road). 250-768-3378. Year-round.

■ **Westbank Museum:** On southbound part of Hwy 97. Tues-Sun, June-Aug. 250-768-0110. Travelling north, go one block past fork in highway to Brown St traffic light. Turn left and left again on Hwy 97 southbound for museum and Info Centre.

■ **Wineries: Mission Hill Vineyards,** Mission Hill Rd, overlooking Okanagan Lake. 250-768-7611. Daily tours year-round. Picnic grounds, wheelchair access, tour buses welcome. **Quails' Gate Estate Winery,** 3348 Boucherie. 250-769-3277. Daily, year-round, tours, tasting, picnic tables, wine shop in circa 1873 Allison family homestead cabin. **Slamka Cellars,** 2815 Ourtoland Rd, 250-769-0404. Daily, April-Oct.

■ **Mariners Reef Waterslides:** About 1km east of Westbank on Old Okanagan Hwy.

■ **Old MacDonald's Farm:** 2280 Louie St. Amusements, waterslide, orchard tours.

Westside Rd: 9km north of Westbank, at last light before floating bridge into Kelowna. Paved road winds 67km north along Okanagan Lake's less developed (for now) west shore. It joins up with Hwy 97 about 14km northwest of Vernon. Highlights include Bear Creek Provincial Park, Lake Okanagan Resort, and Fintry Provincial Park. Along the southern portion of the route, a series of new housing "estates," and marina/hotel/resort complexes are springing up. The northern portion includes rangeland for muledeer and California bighorn sheep; the final 22km pass through a refreshingly undeveloped swath of Okanagan First Nations reserve land.

SIDE TRIP

to Bear Creek Park and Fintry

Bear Creek Provincial Park: 178ha. 122 campsites (reservations taken: call 1-800-689-9025; from the Lower Mainland or overseas, call 604-689-9025). Sani-station. 8km north of Hwy 97 junction. General information: 250-494-6500. A delightfully varied park. Some 10km of hiking and easy walking trails through lakeshore delta and uplands plateau. Creek, with waterfall, winds down a canyon to delta and lakeshore.

This is the spot where, a few years ago, salesman Ken Chaplin took controversial video footage of what he thought was Ogopogo. The international furor brought in experts from everywhere, but when the waters cleared, most biologists agreed that this particular monster was actually a beaver.

Full visitor program. Crimson waters mark the onset of kokanee spawning rituals in Bear Creek (officially Lambly Creek), mid-Sept. Boat launch, wheelchair access.

Lake Okanagan Resort: 17km from Hwy 97 junction. Accommodation includes condos, chalets, suites, conference facilities. Riding, tennis, par-3 golf, beach, marina. Casual or gourmet dining, lounge, pub, poolside bar, patio cafe. Kids Kamp activities include "Insanity" obstacle course, and "Backwards Dinner," where children, parents, chefs, waiters, talk, walk, cook, and serve backwards (dessert first, salad last). Year-round. 250-769-3511 or 1-800-663-3273 (BC and AB).

Ridgeview RV Resort and Marina: 30.5km from Hwy 97. Beautiful views from, but not of, this new development. Visible for miles from across the lake, it looks like an open-pit mine.

Fintry: (Pop. 24). 32km from Hwy 97 on Westside Rd. Charming, tiny settlement on Shorts Creek delta. Beach access.

Fintry Provincial Park: 360ha. 50 campsites (reservations taken: call 1-800-689-9025; from the Lower Mainland or overseas, call 604-689-9025). Take Westside Rd to the intersection of Fintry Delta Rd, then follow signs. General information: 250-494-

6500. 2km of sandy beach, hiking on the Shorts Creek Canyon Trail, boat launch 1km outside park. Rustic buildings here are remnants of former Fintry Estate, named in 1909 by James Cameron Dunwaters, after ancestral estate in Scotland.

Newport Beach Recreational Park: 61.5km from Hwy 97. Okanagan First Nations reserve land. Commercial campground features Earthwoman Stage and performances in summer by Okanagan First Nation's Sen Klip Theatre.

Return to Highway 97

Okanagan Lake Floating Bridge: Bisects Okanagan Lake and continues as Hwy 97 through Kelowna. Built in 1958, opened by Princess Margaret, 640m pontoon structure was North America's first and largest floating bridge. Vast improvement over ferry service that dated from 1904 with the *Skookum*, and from 1927, the *Kelowna-Westbank*.

Kelowna: (Pop. 89,442; area pop. about 140,000). 60km north of Penticton, on east shore of Okanagan Lake, just over the Floating Bridge. The city's roots are slightly inland, at L'Anse au Sable or Sandy Cove on Mission Creek, where Father Pandosy's set up his mission in 1859. In 1892, the townsite survey for incorporation shifted the settlement west to the shores of Okanagan Lake, so supplies and people could be easily ferried by steamboat to points north and south. Thus Kelowna's eminently accessible siting.

The city's name comes from the Okanagan First Nation word for grizzly bear. One account says that Okanagan natives were amused by one of the early settlers, a large, rough-hewn and bewhiskered blacksmith named August Gillard. They called him Kim-ach-touch, or "brown bear" – the name soon applied to both the man *and* his land. But Kim-ach-touch, difficult for the white tongue to pronounce, gradually mutated into "Kelowna." It's a good story: but Okanagan elders past have reported there was actually a village named Skela'un.na or "grizzly bear," here long before the arrival of August Gillard.

Soon after Kelowna's incorporation in 1892, the city boasted 11 sawmills, three fruit-packing plants, and two canneries. Tobacco was an original crop (cigars the product), but the slump after the First World War did that one in. This land was destined to yield sweeter things.

Kelowna has long been the Okanagan's largest urban centre, hub of its marketing and distribution activities, focal point of government services. (It also given rise to two BC premiers, W.A.C. Bennett – who founded the Social Credit Party in BC and was premier for 20 years – and his son William R. Bennett, premier, 1975-86.)

But to folks beyond the Peach Curtain, Kelowna has always been the City of Summer. It's one of the prettiest of cities – bright, airy, fresh – a lakeshore community with downtown

lakefront parks and sandy beaches, situated midway along the eastern shores of the beautiful, mysterious, flickering and flashing, 128km-long lake that has slipped itself in between the Interior Plateau and the Okanagan Highland.

Kelowna has always been a juicy, warm, sunny, sailing/swimming/surfing regatta-style hot spot, a family summer place. The stress here is on *summer*. But something is happening. Kelowna is still pretty, sitting in its piece of heaven, but it's no longer small, and it's not just for summer. This long-established vacationland is becoming a rapidly growing tourism and retirement community with its own style of sophistication. People from afar are finding out about Kelowna, they're investing in real estate and businesses, moving here live by the lake year-round.

In the last six years, more than 35,000 people have moved to the city and its suburbs, increasing the area population to more than 140,000. Some 25 percent of the city's population is now senior citizens: there are more than a dozen gated adult communities here. This is juxtaposed with a large transitory population of young people who come to work in orchards and vineyards in summer and fall. The onslaught of development, road congestion, and growing pains are enough to tax the talents of any municipal planner. "It's just like California," sighs one resident. Without skyscrapers and smog.

Partly responsible for this growth spurt was the completion in 1990 of the Peachland Connector from the Coquihalla freeway. Greater Vancouver now lies within four hours of Kelowna. Some families are even commuting,

working four days in Vancouver and returning to the Okanagan for three-day weekends.

Kelowna is surprisingly central. It's 454km from Vancouver, and 623km from Calgary, and Kelowna's airport – third busiest in BC – is less than an hour from either. And Kelowna is activity-oriented: there's access to all water sports, sailing, rowing, canoeing, houseboating, windsurfing, waterskiing, parasailing. Indoor and outdoor racquet courts are located throughout the city. There's a good range of restaurants and nightclubs. For skiers, Big White resort is only 55km from Kelowna on Hwy 33, which follows the old Kettle Valley Railway grade.

One of the biggest attractions now is wine. The verdant rows of at least nine vineyards fringe the city, adding to its cultivated air.

As a complement, theatre, music, ballet, arts and crafts all come under the umbrella of the Kelowna and District Arts Council. The 900-seat Kelowna Community Theatre is home of Sunshine Theatre and the Okanagan Symphony. Kelowna's newspapers are *The Daily Courier* and *Kelowna Capital News*.

Kelowna Information: Info Centre at 544 Harvey Ave (Hwy 97), Kelowna, BC, V1Y 6C9. 1-800-663-4345 (North America), 250-861-1515 (Kelowna). For events, also call Downtown Kelowna: 250-862-3515.

Museums and Galleries

■ **Father Pandosy Mission:** Southeast of city centre at corner of Benvoulin and Casorso roads. Daily, April-Oct. Founded in 1859 by Oblate priest, Father Charles Pandosy, the Immaculate Conception Mission was the first

KELOWNA

1 Art Gallery, Museum
2 Chamber of Commerce
3 City Hall
4 City Park
5 Curling Rink
6 Hospital
7 Liquor Store
8 Memorial Arena
9 Recreation Centre
10 R C M P
11 Strathcona Park
12 Yacht Club

non-native settlement in the Okanagan region, serving both native Okanagan people and white settlers. Restored from original log buildings, the mission, chapel, and schoolhouse provide a vivid illustration of Okanagan Valley life a century ago. Declared an official heritage site in 1983 following discovery of Father Pandosy's grave in abandoned cemetery near his mission.

■ **BC Orchard Industry and Wine Museum:** 1304 Ellis St. 250-763-0433. Tues-Sat, year-round. In Kelowna's first designated heritage building, Laurel packing house, built 1917 for fruit packing. This satellite of Kelowna Museum tells tale of BC's orchard industry. Exhibits deal with all aspects of orchards; also a re-created packing plant and "hands-on" area. The wine museum is actually just a wine sales outlet with a small display. Cherry Fair in July; Apple Fair in Oct.

■ **Kelowna Centennial Museum:** 470 Queensway. 250-763-2417. Variable hours, July-Aug; Sept-June, Tues-Sat. Interior Salish pit dwelling, 1861 trading post, Kelowna's first radio station.

■ **Guisachan Heritage Park:** 1060 Cameron Ave. Part of one of Kelowna's earliest ranches, preempted by John McDougall in 1861; then home of Lord Aberdeen, Governor-General of Canada, 1893-1898. Perennial gardens with plants all labelled. Restaurant.

■ **Benvoulin Heritage Church:** 2279 Benvoulin Rd. 250-762-6911. Presbyterian church built 1892. Open summer afternoons, daily; winter by appointment.

■ **Kelowna Art Gallery:** 1315 Water St. Queensway. 250-762-2226. Daily. International, national, and local art. Growing collection of BC art.

■ **Geert Maas Sculpture Gardens, Gallery and Studio:** 250 Reynolds Rd. 250-860-7012. West of Hwy 97 before the airport on Sexmith Rd, then north onto Reynolds. Mon-Sat, 10-5, May-Oct. Rest of year: varied hours, call ahead. Outdoor "art park," plus gallery.

Beaches, Parks , and Gardens

■ **City Park:** 14.5ha. Along 1km of lakeshore – from foot of floating bridge to large sculpture, *The Sail*, by Dow Reid at foot of Bernard Ave.

■ **Waterfront Park:** At Water St and Cawston. Winding promenade with lagoons and an island amphitheatre.

■ **Lion's Park/Sutherland Hills Nature Walks:** Off Springfield and Benvoulin roads. Pastoral setting. Sept 15-Oct 15 is largest spawning run of local kokanee. Guided tours at this time. BC Wildlife Watch viewing site.

■ **Kasugai Gardens:** Tucked behind Bennett Fountain, on Queen St. Japanese garden complete with boulder-ringed pond, waterfall, stone garden. Kasugai, in Japan, is Kelowna's sister city.

■ **Bertram Creek Regional Park:** End of Lakeshore Rd. Beaches, picnics. Late Oct, spawning kokanee along shoreline. Spring and summer is best time to see waterfowl, song birds, ground squirrels. BC Wildlife Watch viewing site.

■ **Knox Mountain Nature Park:** North end of Ellis St. Hiking and picnicking. At foot of Knox

Mountain is a diving park called **Paul's Tomb**, where a 522kg, 7m-long model of Ogopogo, lurking 8m below the surface, awaits divers. Spring and summer best to see songbirds, marmots. BC Wildlife Watch viewing site.

Tastes of the Land

■ **Vineyards and Wineries:** Most offer tours and tastings year-round. **Summerhill Estate Winery**, 4870 Chute Lake Rd, 1-800-667-3538 or 250-764-8000. BC's first champagne house, specializing in bubblies and Icewines. **Calona Wines**, 1125 Richter St, 1-800-663-5086. Daily tours, year-round. Okanagan's biggest and oldest (est 1932) winery. **St Hubertus Vineyards**, 5225 Lakeshore Rd, 1-800-989-9463. Recently expanded line includes a number of oak-aged wines. **CedarCreek Estate Winery**, 5445 Lakeshore Rd, 250-764-8866. Estate winery in a picture-book setting. Arbour for picnics. **Gray Monk**, 1055 Camp Rd, 250-766-3168. **Mission Hill**, 1730 Mission Hill Rd, 250-768-7611. **Pinot Reach**, 1670 DeHart Rd, 250-764-0078. **House of the Rose**, 2270 Garner Rd, 250-765-0802. **Quail's Gate**, 3303 Boucherie Rd, 769-4451.

■ **Honey Farm Vacation Tours**, 2910 Glenmore Rd, 250-762-8156. Tours daily, 1pm, May-Sept (reservations). Accommodation, honey tasting, birdwatching, canoe trips.

■ **Kelowna Land and Orchard Company Tours:** 2930 Dunster Rd. 250-763-1091. Daily, May-Oct. Tours on antique, tractor-drawn wagons; fresh pressed apple juice, farm animals to visit. This is the first farm to "bag" Fuji apples on the tree: bags go on in June, come off three months later, before shipping. Apples stay green on the tree, then turn bright pink out of the bags, and are shipped to Hong Kong – each apple selling for as much as $15.

■ **Old MacDonald's Farm:** Hwy 97 South at Westbank. 250-768-5167. Orchard tours, petting zoo, amusements. Daily, April-early Sept.

■ **Pioneer Country Market and Museum:** Benvoulin Rd. Daily. 250-762-2544. Where "Onion King" John Casorso produced record-breaking crop in 1909. Grapevine baskets, wonderful jellies.

■ **My Country Garden:** 1760 KLO Rd. 250-769-4799. Daily. Pick a melon and eat it right in the field, with the juice dripping down your chin. Pick herbs and flowers too.

■ **Kelowna Farmers and Crafters Market:** At Springfield and Dilworth. 250-762-5778. Wed and Sat, May-Oct.

■ **Lakeshore Orchards Ltd:** 4719 Lakeshore Rd. 250-764-2930. July-Aug. Cherries: U-pick or they pick.

■ **Paul's Produce:** At Guisachan Dr and Gordon Dr. 250-763-3131.

Kettle Valley Railway

Kelowna, north of, but not on the KVR line, offers recreationists some of the best opportunities to experience its wonders. Myra Canyon is one of the most dramatic moments on the KVR. Ask at Info Centre about hiking, biking, horseback, and 4x4 adventure tours along these routes.

■ **Myra Canyon Access:** In southeast Kelowna, drive along the KLO Rd to McCulloch Rd. About 2km after the pavement ends, you will come to a clearing where the power lines cross above the road. On the right is the Myra Forest Service Rd. Follow this road to the parking lot, about 8km up the hill. The first trestle is a 15-minute walk from here. Allow five hours to see all 18 trestles. Trestles perched from the sheer rock walls of Myra Canyon offer incredible views.

■ **June Springs Access:** Take KLO Rd to McCulloch Rd; McCulloch Rd to June Springs Rd. June Springs will become Little White Forestry Rd – rough, but *usually* passable by *most* vehicles. Drive about 4km, take first left, park. Here is the rail bed; the first trestle is 2km northeast. If mountain biking all 18 trestles and two tunnels, the entire one-way length is 12km.

■ **Chute Lake Access:** From Kelowna's Mission area. Drive south from Kelowna on Lakeshore Rd to Chute Lake Rd. Turn left onto Hedeman Rd and then right onto Gillard Forest Service Rd and proceed for 8.5km (the *No Trespassing* sign beside the road applies to the property it sits on, not the road you'll be travelling). When you arrive at a major intersection, you've reached the KVR. From here, a right turn takes you 12km to the Chute Lake Resort; left leads 4km to tunnels and trestles (see p.158).

Attractions

■ **Scandia:** Amusement park on Hwy 97, about 10km north of floating bridge.

■ **Malibu Grand Prix:** Hwy 97 North at Stremel Rd. 250-765-1434. Go carts, arcade. Year-round.

■ **Mariner's Reef Waterslides:** Old Okanagan Hwy, Westbank. 250-768-5141.

■ **Golf:** Lots of it. **19 Greens**, 2050 Campbell Rd (west side of floating bridge). 250-769-0213. Par 72, 18-hole all-putting course. **Quail Ridge**, Across from Kelowna Airport on Quail Ridge Blvd. 1-800-898-2449. Full facilities and accommodation. **Gallagher's Canyon**, 250-861-4240. Full facilities in canyon setting. **Ponderosa Public Golf**, 250-768-7839. 18 holes. **Sunset Ranch Golf & Country Club**, 4001 Anderson Rd. 250-765-7700. 18 holes; **Kelowna Springs**, 250-765-4653. Around seven spring-fed lakes. **Aspen Grove Golf & Fitness**, 250-766-3933. Nine holes. **Harvest Golf Club**, 250-862-3103. Highly rated in an orchard setting. **Dynamic Golf**, 250-712-1225. **Nevada Bob's Discount Golf and Tennis**, 17-1455 Harvey Ave. 250-762-2111. **Central Park Golf Club**, 250-860-5121. Nine holes. **Eaglequest Kelowna**, 250-860-3850.

Highway 33: Turn off Hwy 97 6.5km after it crosses Kelowna's floating bridge and after it goes through downtown as Harvey Ave. Leads to Big White Ski Resort.

SIDE TRIP

to Big White Ski Resort

Big White Rd: 33km along Hwy 33 (Black Mountain Rd). Turn east 24km for ski resort.

Big White Ski Resort: Box 2039, Stn R, Kelowna, BC, V1X 4K5. Toll-free from BC or AB, 1-800-663-2772, or 250-765-3101. 20km to lower chair. El 2,319m. The highest resort in BC, offering a long season with more than 750cm of light, dry snow. Great when the skies are blue: but up so high, it can get socked in, hence the mountain's nickname, "Big White Out." Skiers may encounter snow ghosts: bizarre shapes formed by snow freezing onto evergreens. This mountain offers an easy, relaxed atmosphere, without the crowds of Whistler/Blackcomb. 92 runs on vertical drop of 710m. More than 25km of cross-country trails. High-speed quad chairlift, warming hut, village mall, outdoor rink; kid's and summer activities (mountain biking, in-line skating, horseback riding, basketball, volleyball, tennis).

Graystokes Recreation Area (Snow-mobiling): 39km from downtown Kelowna to staging area. 18km farther by snowmobile on groomed marked trail to club's chalet. Inquire with Kelowna Info Centre: 1-800-663-4345. Some 120km of trails touring 392 sq km of meadow and alpine. Accommodation: 250-765-8888.

Return to Highway 97

Hwy 97 now proceeds on the east side of Okanagan Lake northward through Vernon to access Trans-Canada Hwy (1) at three locations: Sicamous, Salmon Arm, and Monte Creek. See *Kelowna to Sicamous*, next, or *Index*.

KELOWNA TO SICAMOUS

HIGHWAYS 97 and 97A

The 47km of Hwy 97 between Kelowna and Vernon slices between Okanagan Lake on the west, and a glacial lakes chain – Ellison (or Duck), Wood, Kalamalka, and Swan lakes – on the east. All dazzlers. Beyond Vernon, the highway travels north 75km between the rolling hills of the Thompson Plateau in the west, and Monashee Mountains in the east. Dairy, vegetable, hay, and alfalfa farms begin to dominate the landscape.

Kelowna: (Pop. 89,442). At the junction of Hwys 97 and 33. 60km north of Penticton, 47km south of Vernon. See *Penticton to Kelowna*, p.161.

Kelowna Airport: 8km beyond Hwy 33 junction in Kelowna, east of highway.

Duck Lake Pullout: 4km beyond Kelowna Airport.

Lake Country: (District pop. 9,000). About 10km north of Kelowna. In 1994, the small communities of Winfield, Oyama, Okanagan Centre, Woodsdale and Carr's landing Landing amalgamated to form the District of Lake Country, each to a degree, maintains its own identity.

Lake Country Information: In Lakewood Mall, 1-11852 Highway 97, Winfield, BC. V4V 1E3. 250-766-3876. The only public washrooms between Kelowna and Vernon.

Winfield: Along Hwy 97, 10km north of Kelowna. The southernmost of the Lake Country towns.
■ **Gray Monk Estate Winery & Vineyards:** West off Hwy 97 in Lake Country at Berry Rd (second set of lights), 4km to 1055 Camp Rd. Well-signed. 250-766-3168. Daily, May through Oct. Mon-Sat, Nov-April. Call ahead.
■ **Okanagan Mountain Bike Tours:** 1-888-977-2453 or 250-766-5191. Tours along Kettle Valley Railway beds.

Okanagan Centre Rd E: West from Winfield via Oceola Rd. About 3km west of Hwy 97 Okanagan Centre Rd E becomes Okanagan Centre Rd W, leading south along the shores of Okanagan Lake through the small community of Okanagan Centre. Also, at the point where Okanagan Centre Rd East meets West, Carr's Landing Rd leads north to the very small community of Carr's Landing. From Carr's Landing, Commonage Rd leads northeast, providing rough back-road access to Vernon.

Okanagan Centre: (Pop. 360). On Okanagan Centre Rd about 3km west of Hwy 97. Situated magnificently on hillsides overlooking Okanagan Lake. Perfect orchard and vineyard country.
■ **Lake Country Museum:** Box 25, Okanagan Centre Rd West, Winfield, BC, V0H 2C0. 250-766-2653. May-Sept, Wed-Sun. Displays area history.

Wood Lake: Between Okanagan Centre and Oyama, Hwy 97 hugs this lake named for Thomas Wood who pioneered Okanagan Valley with Cornelius O'Keefe (see p.166 and p.164). This distinctly rectangular lake, 6.5km-by-1.5km, offers good fishing for kokanee and rainbow trout.

Oyama: (Pop. 1,332). On the east side of Hwy 97, 6.5km north of Okanagan Centre Rd. On the land bridge between Wood and Kalamalka lakes. An orchard and fruit-packing community named after Prince Iwao Oyama (1842-1916), a Japanese field marshal.
■ **Gatzke Orchards:** 15686 Hwy 97. 250-548-3444. Fruits and veggies, a museum of farm implements, fresh fruit milkshakes.

Kalamalka Lake Viewpoint: 8km beyond Oyama. Locals call it "Lake of Many Colours." The striking blue-green colour is caused by underground springs pushing glacial silt up from the bottom of the lake. It takes its name for the powerful Okanagan First Nation leader, Kalamalka, who lived at the lake's head. Panoramic view takes in Coldstream Valley and mountains stretching forever eastward. At Kalamalka Lake's north end is a golden sandy shore.

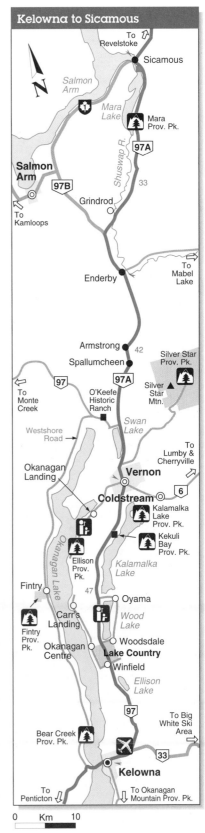

Kelowna to Sicamous

College Way: 1km past viewpoint. Turn east, follow Kickwillie Loop to Westkal Rd, which becomes Kalamalka Rd. Leads to Kalamalka Lake Provincial Park.

Kalamalka Lake Provincial Park: 978ha; day use, no camping. Follow signs. 250-494-6500. Nesting and feeding habitat for a wide variety of birds. Brilliant show of wildflowers. Wheelchair access. Unspoiled swimming beaches. Beware of rattlesnakes!

Predator Ridge Golf Resort: 9km north of Oyama, take **Bailey Rd** exit to Commonage Rd. Follow Commonage Rd past the Vernon Fish and Game Club. 250-542-3436. Also see *Vernon*, below.

Kekuli Bay Provincial Park: 57ha; day use, no camping. One of the best boat launches on Kalamalka Lake. 3km beyond Bailey Rd, take Kalamalka Lakeview Dr, then Highridge Rd. 3km to park. Very busy mid-summer weekends.

Vernon: (Pop. 31,817). 10km north of Kekuli Bay turnoff; 47km north of Kelowna on Hwy 97. The oldest city in the province's Interior has its roots in Nintle-mooschin "jumping over place" – a crossroads of trails from the Kamloops area, Cherry Creek in the Monashee, and Okanagan Mission. The site, at a narrowing of a creek, is still there: at 35th St and 30th Ave. Look for a cairn, and right behind Safeway, a small park with a creek running through it.

During the gold rush, in the 1860s, Cornelius O'Keefe was driving cattle through this region, en route from Oregon in the US, to the Cariboo, providing beef for hungry miners. Here, at the head of Okanagan Lake, where the grass grew higher than a horse's belly,

he paused to wonder why he was driving herds when he could raise fat cattle right where he was. By 1867 O'Keefe had pre-empted land, brought in breeding stock, and was transforming the north Okanagan into cattle country.

By the end of the century, the era of the open range was ending, and a new era was beginning. The region's first commercial orchards were planted in 1891, by Lord Aberdeen. The future governor-general of Canada (1893-1898) bought 5,367ha from Forbes George Vernon, early commissioner of lands and works, and renamed it Coldstream Ranch. At the time a thriving ranch with some 2,000 head of cattle, 80 horses, plus poultry and hogs, Coldstream was to become for many years one of the largest producers of fruit in the British Empire. The lakes here allowed large-scale irrigation which, when introduced in 1908, transformed the region into an agricultural Shangri-la.

In 1917 alone (more than a quarter of a century after Lord and Lady Aberdeen had left the North Okanagan behind) some 800 box-cars of apples and 200 of miscellaneous fruit, valued at $1 million, were shipped. Vernon today is on the northern edge of the Lake District fruit belt, with a climate both cooler and wetter than that of the area to the south. This limits growing to hardier types of apples, prunes, and plums, as well as hay and alfalfa.

Vernon is bounded by three spectacular lakes – Okanagan, Kalamalka, and Swan – with endless sandy beaches. The city has recently become a cool place to visit or live in, attracting yuppies and Generation Xers. Downtown Vernon offers a fine array of coffee-houses, shops, and restaurants. The Vernon

Lodge, at 3914-32nd St, is a major hotel with a real stream, the BX Creek, running though its dining room. The dining room is a tropical forest with two-storey trees. Walking tours include heritage homes on the east hill. Cycling and driving tours are described in the Visitor's Guide at Info Centres.

Adding to the quirky nature of downtown Vernon, just a few blocks away on 24th St, up in the cottonwood trees, are the nests of some 30 breeding pairs of great blue herons. Their favorite fishing spot is a short flight across Hwy 97, at Swan Lake.

Vernon Information: Info Centre at 6326 Hwy 97 N, Box 520, Vernon, BC, V1T 6M4. 250-542-1415. Year-round. Extra seasonal Info Centre, May-Sept.

■ **Greater Vernon Museum and Archives:** Civic Centre Complex, 3009-32nd Ave. Mon-Sat, in summer; Tues-Sat rest of year. 250-542-3142. History of area, plus district archives and research facility.

■ **Historic O'Keefe Ranch:** 12km north of Vernon on Hwy 97. See *Monte Creek to Cherryville*, p.166.

■ **Vernon Art Gallery:** 3228-31st Ave. Mon-Sat. 250-545-3173.

■ **The Floral Clock in Polson Park:** 25th Ave and 32nd St. If you stop and smell these flowers, they'll tell you what time it is. The park's 10m powered floral clock is one of only a few in Canada. It was built in 1958 for the then extravagant sum of $4,500.

■ **Sen Klip Theatre Company:** 250-549-2921 or 250-549-4100. Okanagan First Nation performers gaining appreciation worldwide for their blending of traditional and modern arts. May have summer performances at Newport Beach Recreational Park, off Westside Rd.

■ **Atlantis Waterslides:** 7921 Hwy 97. (5km north of Vernon off Hwy 97.) 250-549-4121. Slides, hot tub, mini-golf. June-early Sept.

■ **Walking Tours:** Buildings date back to the turn of the century. Maps at Info Centre.

■ **Okanagan Spring Brewery:** 2801-27A Ave. 250-542-2337. Housed in a former fruit-packing house. Uses only four ingredients in its brews: water, malted barley, hops, and yeast. Brewing weekdays; tours May-Aug or by arrangement. Call ahead.

■ **Predator Ridge Golf Resort**, 250-542-3436. Part of Vernon's expansion: 2,100 homes, along with a lodging and village complex started in 1998. Rates as one of Canada's best by *Score Magazine*. An extremely challenging, and pricey course. Pro shop, licenced restaurant.

■ **Interior Space and Science Centre:** Next to Polson Park, at Hwy 6 and 25th Ave. 250-545-3644. Tues-Sun, 10-5, year-round. Learning by doing: astronomy, geology, chemistry, biology, electricity, gravity. Thingamajigs Gallery celebrates wacky inventions like the Rock'n'Dry, hair-drying rocking chair.

■ **Fruits and Veggies: Davison Orchards:** 3111 Davison Rd. 250-549-3266. July-Dec. Family farm since 1933 offers fruits and veggies, tours, animals, apple juice. **Bella Vista Farm Market**, 5011 Bella Vista Rd. 250-545-0105. Fruit, veggies, honey, tours. **Aberdeen Farm Market**, 68 North Aberdeen Rd. 250-545-2134. Daily, April-Christmas.

VERNON

1   Civic Centre Ambulance, City Hall, Museum and Library
2   Curling Rink
3   Golf Course
4   Hospital
5   Ice Arena
6   Information Centre
7   Liquor Store
8   Park
9   Post Office
10   Race Track
11   Recreation Centre

Highway 6 East: In Vernon, at 25th Ave, 3km north of College Way junction. Leads 50km east to Cherryville. See *Monte Creek to Cherryville*, below. Heading west 25th Ave, also called Okanagan Landing Rd, leads short distance to Okanagan Landing and Ellison Provincial Park.

Okanagan Landing: (Pop. 1,406). South of downtown Vernon, on Okanagan Lake; officially part of the expanding city of Vernon. Follow 25th Ave about 6km west out of Vernon. Becomes Okanagan Landing Rd.

In 1886, Captain T.D. Shorts launched the area's first steamer here. In 1892, Okanagan Landing became a Canadian Pacific Railway terminus and shipyard, spurring the growth of north Okanagan orchards and towns. The landing remained northern terminus for rail barges and lake steamers until 1936 when roads and rails ended things. The SS *Sicamous*, now beached in Penticton, steamed in here from her last voyage.
■ **Paddlewheel Park:** Commemorating days of steamers and paddlewheelers on Okanagan Lake.

Ellison Provincial Park: 54 campsites (reservations taken: call 1-800-689-9025; from the Lower Mainland or overseas, call 604-689-9025). 9.5km southwest of Okanagan Landing along Okanagan Landing Rd; east shore of Okanagan Lake. General info: 250-494-6500. Visitor programs. In spring and summer, see songbirds and ground squirrels.
■ **Innerspace (Underwater Dive Area):** 4112-25th Ave, Vernon. 250-549-2040. Snorkelling, scuba diving, kayaking. Lessons, rentals, sales.

Silver Star Rd: 2.5km north of Hwy 6 junction in downtown Vernon. Turn east to ski area.

SIDE TRIP

to Silver Star

Silver Star Mountain Resort: On Silver Star Rd, 17.5km east of Hwy 97. Box 3002, Vernon, BC, V1B 3M1. 250-542-0224 or 1-800-663-4431 for reservations year-round. Region's most northerly ski area, with Victorian-style mid-mountain village. Meeting and conference facilities. Offers 84 runs on 485m vertical drop. Full resort facilities with accommodation, restaurants. 37km of groomed cross-country trails (4km lit track) networked with 50km track at adjacent Sovereign Lake area. Tobogganing, skating, tubing, snowmobile tours, snowboard park. Night skiing, après ski, outdoor hot tubs, hotels, and shops. Shuttle service from Kelowna airport. National Altitude Training Centre offers fitness testing, physiotherapy, and sports medicine lab.

In summer, resort features Silver Star, a turn-of-the-century mining town. Chairlift carries sightseers up 300m for views from summit of Silver Star Mountain, mountain biking and hiking in alpine meadows. It's worth a drive anytime of year to view the San Francisco-style "painted ladies" – the eccentric and colourful private houses and cabins surrounding the resort.

Silver Star Provincial Park: 6,092ha. 2km beyond Silver Star Ski Resort on Silver Star Rd. Day use only. **Sovereign Lake Cross Country Ski Area** offers 43km of groomed trails; 25km of snowmobile trails.

Return to Highway 97

Swan Lake: Hwy 97 follows lake for 3km beginning 2.5km north of Silver Star Rd junction. Year-round Info Centre. A fishing and boating lake only (no beach). Public boat launch halfway down east shore. A birding hot spot in the north Okanagan, especially during migrations.
■ **Swan Lake Nurseryland, Fruit Market & Garden Centre:** 6km north of Vernon on west side of Hwy 97. 250-542-7614. Daily, year-round. Fresh fruits, veggies, goodies. Will do picnics for tour buses with a day's notice.

Highway 97 and 97A: Swan Lake Junction is 4km north of Swan Lake, 9km north of Vernon. Hwy 97 turns west for Trans-Canada Hwy 1 and Kamloops via Monte Creek. See *Monte Creek to Cherryville*, following. This *Log* follows Hwy 97A toward Sicamous.

Highway 97A

Spallumcheen: (Pop. 5,322). 4km north of Swan Lake Junction. Spanning the breadth of Spallumcheen Valley surrounding Armstrong: more than 26,000ha of prime mixed agricultural land. Scenic drives, good hiking, snowmobiling.
Spallumcheen Information: Information centre on Smith Dr in Armstrong. Write Box 118, Armstrong, BC, V0E 1B0. 250-546-8616, off-season 250-546-8155.

Armstrong: (Pop. 3,906) On Hwy 97A, 7km north of Swan Lake Junction. Geographic and commercial centre of beautiful Spallumcheen Valley, a rich agricultural area. Named for E.C. Heaton Armstrong, head of the London bank that floated bonds for the Shuswap and Okanagan Railway in 1892. Today known for its cheese (below), and horses. Throughout the year, Armstrong hosts the Riding Club Horse Show, Okanagan Pony Driving Club Horse Show, a Sheep Show, BC Arabian Horse Association Horse Show, 4H Stock Show and Camp, Canadian Icelandic Horse Club Show, BC Peruvian Horse Association Regional Show, Interior Provincial Exhibition and Rodeo, and BC Reigning Association Horse Show, to name a few.

Here also is **Caravan Theatre** – this itinerant band of professional thespians once travelled by horse and wagon to entertain throughout the Okanagan. Now, the Caravan puts on three productions a year, plus workshops and festivals (masking, circus performing, African drumming), from their base on a working, organic farm. Highlight is winter show including a sleigh ride. 250-546-8533.

Armstrong Information: Information centre on Smith Dr. Box 118, Armstrong, BC, V0E 1B0. 250-546-8616. Weekends, June-July; daily, Aug. Or contact Armstrong Chamber of Commerce, 250-546-8155.
■ **Armstrong-Spallumcheen Museum, Archives and Art Gallery:** Pleasant Valley Blvd and Bridge St. Daily, June-Sept. 250-546-8318. Area history exhibits feature railway, agriculture, turn-of-the-century lifestyle.
■ **Armstrong Cheese Factory (Dairyworld Foods):** Two blocks north of museum on Pleasant Valley Rd. 250-546-3084. Processing cheese and milk. Call ahead to visit.
■ **The Village Cheese Company Factory:** 3475 Smith Dr. 1-800-665-0795. Daily, 9-9, May-Sept. Daily, 9-6, Oct-April. Glass-enclosed cheese factory. Watch butter being churned by a steam engine. Cheese, butter, ice cream, bagels and cappuccino for sale.
■ **The Olde School House:** 250-546-9190. May-Sept. Mainland BC's oldest schoolhouse. Lunches and afternoon teas. Fresh strawberries and fruits in season with Devonshire cream. Reservations recommended.
■ **Fruits and Veggies:** Armstrong Farmers' Market, IPE Fairgrounds; Sat, 8-12, April-Dec. **Armstrong Berry Farm**, 1604 Otter Lake X Rd, 250-546-3555. June-Oct; strawberries.

Enderby: (Pop. 2,754). 13km north of Armstrong. At 610m, Enderby Cliffs, on the east shore of the Shuswap River dominate the area. Rock face picks up surprising colour, especially at sunset. Great hiking and views. Slow, shallow Shuswap River meandering from Mabel Lake to Mara Lake is popular route for boaters of all kinds. Wildlife viewing and camping along the way.
Enderby Information: Info Centre on Railway Ave. Write Box 1000, Enderby, BC, V0E 1V0. 250-838-6727.
■ **Enderby and District Museum:** 901 George St, Hwy 97, City Hall complex. 250-838-7170. Mon-Sat. Area history; local art in April.
■ **Riverside RV Park:** On Kildonan Ave, on banks of Shuswap River. 250-838-0155. Some full hook-ups; barbecue, showers, boat launch.

Road to Mabel Lake: Lake can be reached by 35km road east out of Enderby, with gravel roads leading to south and north ends. Area offers camping, RV park, fishing, and hiking. Lake also accessed from south on Hwy 6. See *Monte Creek to Cherryville*, following.

Highway 97B: Hwy 97A forks 6km north of Enderby. Hwy 97B travels northwest 15km to Trans-Canada Hwy junction and Salmon Arm. Hwy 97A continues north, to Sicamous.

Grindrod: (Pop. 421). 4km north of Hwys 97A and 97B junction on the Shuswap River. Named for first inspector of telegraphs on Canadian Pacific Railway in BC.

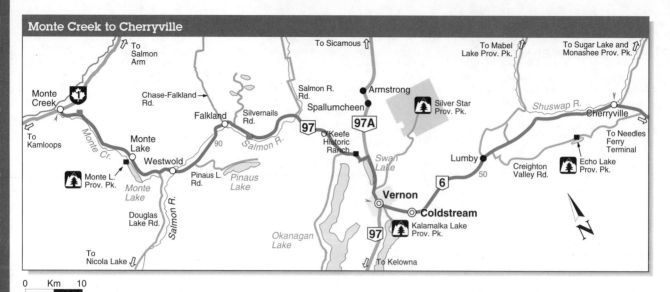

Monte Creek to Cherryville

0   Km   10

Mara Provincial Park: 4ha; day use. On Mara Lake Rd, 13km beyond Grindrod on Hwy 97A, east side of Mara Lake. Green forest and lush cattle pasture herald changing climate at top of Okanagan region. Boat launch.

Mara Lake Rest Area: 7km beyond park. On lakeshore.

Hwy 97A continues 15km to Trans-Canada Hwy 1 junction at Sicamous – 230km north of the Canada/US border.

Sicamous: (Pop. 2,501). About 7km beyond Mara Lake Rest Area. On Hwy 1 at junction of Hwy 97A. For details see p.172.

MONTE CREEK TO CHERRYVILLE

HIGHWAY 97 and HIGHWAY 6 (East)

This short 140km trip juxtaposes two north Okanagan landscapes, the golden hills of ranchland, and the green country beyond. At the outset, Hwy 97 at Monte Creek borders on the landscape of Kamloops and the Thompson River valley. This is horse country: ranching is the mainstay. Cattle ranches dominate all the way to Vernon. The greener landscape on Hwy 6 east of Vernon supports forest and tree-fruit industries. These peter out at the peaks of the Monashee Mountains which form the boundary between the Okanagan Valley and the BC Rockies region.

Monte Creek: (Pop. 65). At the junction of Hwys 1 and 97. 30km east of Kamloops, and 85km northwest of Vernon. Stop of interest near the railway station recalls the infamous "gentleman bandit," Bill Miner, who netted less than $15 in a 1906 Canadian Pacific Railway train hold-up. A feature film, *The Grey Fox*, tells his life story.

Monte Creek Rest Area: 2.5km beyond Monte Creek.

Monte Lake: (Pop. 68). 17km beyond Monte Creek, north end of lake. Farming community with accommodation, and some services.

Douglas Lake Rd: Leads south, 26km beyond Monte Creek. Mostly unpaved road travels 80km through cattle country. Passes by **Douglas Lake Ranch** en route to **Quilchena** on **Nicola Lake**, Hwy 5A. For more than a century, the Douglas Lake Cattle Company has operated its 200,000ha ranch, one of Canada's largest. Many wetlands and lakes throughout the grasslands provide important wildlife habitat. Look for bluebirds, shrikes, bobolinks, waterfowl, ospreys, songbirds, ground squirrels. Some wetlands have nesting black terns. See p.181.

Westwold: (Pop. 369). Small service centre about 1.5km beyond Douglas Lake Rd. First called Grande Prairie, changed to avoid confusion with Alberta town of the same name.

Pinaus Lake: 6km east of Westwold. 8km south on Pinaus Lake Rd. Rainbow trout. Ice fishing. Campground.

Falkland: (Pop. 620). 10km east of Pinaus Lake Rd at junction of Hwy 97 and Chase-Falkland Rd, leading to community of Chase on Hwy 1. The giant Canadian flag above town (lit up at night) is a landmark for truckers, even pilots. Falklanders celebrate their spirited little town as Canada's Most Patriotic Community. The flag, 8.4m high by 16.8m wide and made of metal, rises 150m above the valley. Raised in 1992, it is supported by eight telephone poles, cables, and 18 two-tonne cement blocks.

Falkland grew up around gypsum mining in the early 1900s: the white-coloured mineral is still being trucked out of the surrounding hills. Central and yet on the fringe, Falkland

appeals to new-millennium style home-based entrepreneurs: inventors, publishers, garlic farmers. Farmers and Flea Market, downtown, weekends, May-Sept.

■ **Heritage Park/Museum and Archives:** Eastern edge of town, between Hwy 97 and CNR tracks. 250-379-2435. June to mid-Sept, or by appointment. Mining and CNR history. Main building is the machine shop on original gypsum loading area.

■ **Habitat Farm:** 3548 Shaw Rd (south off Hwy 97, 4km southeast of Falkland). 250-379-2642. Purebred Clun Forest sheep farm with wool studio, art gallery (both in a barn). Salmon habitat restoration can be seen where Salmon River runs through farm. Pasture-raised chickens for sale.

■ **The Pillar:** 15km from Falkland on Falkland-Chase Rd, look east for 30m natural formation of rock and earth.

■ **Manning House:** 19.5km southeast of Falkland via Falkland-Chase Rd, then China Valley Rd. 250-379-2970. "Your day in the country," workshops (making twig chairs, stone planters, wine from berries, rose hips or birch sap).

■ **Hidden Highlands Ranch:** 250-379-2811. Emus, emu oil.

Silvernails Rd: 1.5km east of Falkland. North off Hwy 97. 6km to start of lakes: **Bolean**, **Blair** (or Arthur), and **Spa**. Rainbow trout, ice fishing. Cabins and campground.

Una Rest Area: 10km beyond Silvernails Rd.

Salmon River Rd: 6km east of rest area. Turn north for picturesque 35km route along Salmon River to Hwy 1 at Salmon Arm.

Westside Rd: 13km beyond Salmon River Rd. Travels west shore of **Okanagan Lake**. See *Penticton to Kelowna*, p.160.

Historic O'Keefe Ranch: On Hwy 97, about 1km east of Westside Rd. Near northern tip of Okanagan Lake. Mid-May to

Thanksgiving. 250-542-7868. O'Keefe's ranch was like a small town, with a Roman Catholic church, general store, and post office. (For his story, see Vernon, p.164). Now owned by the city of Vernon. Video, museum, furnished mansion, blacksmith shop, store, model railway, and field exhibits take us back to the beginning of Interior ranching society. This is one of the Thompson Okanagan's most worthwhile visits. Restaurant and gift shop.

Swan Lake Bird Sanctuary: About 4km east of O'Keefe Ranch (just west of Hwy 97A junction). Swampland at north end of lake is protected area for feathered folk. Undeveloped, but fine birding. White geese, swans, herons.

Highway 97A: At Swan Lake – locally "Swan Lake Junction." This *Log* follows Hwy 97 south to Vernon, then Hwy 6 from there. Hwy 97A leads due north from here, to **Armstrong** and **Sicamous**. See *Kelowna to Sicamous*, above.

Highway 97 to Vernon

Vernon: (Pop. 31,817). 9km south of Hwys 97 and 97A junction. Details, p.164.

Highway 6: In downtown Vernon. Leads east 51km to **Cherryville**, and beyond to **Nakusp**.

East on Highway 6

Kalamalka Lake Provincial Park: 978ha; day use, no camping. 1km east of Hwy 97 junction, turn right onto Kalamalka Rd, then right onto Kidston Rd. Follow park signs. Nesting and feeding habitat for a wide variety of birds. Brilliant show of wildflowers. Wheelchair access.

Coldstream: (District Municipality – Pop. 9,422). About 7km east of Vernon on Hwy 6. The Vernon brothers, Forbes and Charles, first ranched here before selling to Lord and Lady Aberdeen during the 1890s. Still one of the biggest ranches, producing beef and tree fruit. Ranch not open to public.

Coldstream was home of naturalist, Anglican priest, and schoolteacher Reverend Austin Mackie (1879-1965). One of his pupils died from a rattlesnake bite in the 1920s, so he waged serious war against the rattlesnake population, killing thousands, bringing them near extinction in some places. He gave names such as Vatican Den to the serpents' lairs.

Lumby: (Pop. 1,689). 17km east of Coldstream, on Hwy 6. A beautiful location at junction of three valleys: the Trinity, Creighton, and Coldstream. Gateway to the **Monashee Mountains** and region's lumber centre – in an area of lakes, streams, and hills. Community is founded on forestry and agriculture, which still play a major role. There are several sawmills and pole plants in Lumby. Potters, weavers, and other artisans have gravitated here.

Lumby Information: Info Centre on Hwy 6. Write Box 534, Lumby, BC, V0E 2G0. Tel/fax: 250-547-2300. July-Aug.

Mabel Lake Provincial Park: 182ha; 81 campsites. Road to Mabel Lake exits north from Lumby. 35km to park. 2,100m developed beach with boat launch. 250-494-6500. A steep, glacier-etched valley. Shuswap Highlands rise to merge with Monashee Mountains to the east. Western view provides a contrast with dry, ponderosa pine and Douglas fir forests of the Thompson Plateau. Rainbow fishing.

Creighton Valley Rd: 4km east of Lumby. South to Echo Lake Provincial Park.

Echo Lake Provincial Park: 154ha. Day use. 4km east of Lumby on Hwy 6, Creighton Valley Rd leads 20km to park. For organized group camping only, reservations through parks' district office. 250-494-0321. For Echo Lake Resort: 250-547-6434; May to mid-Oct, campsites, cabins, boat rentals, store.

Cherryville: (Pop. 500). On Hwy 6, some 22km east of Lumby. From 1876-1890, Cherryville was a placer gold camp in a narrow draw along banks of south fork of Cherry (now Monashee) Creek. In its heyday, it was home to about 200 miners seeking gold and silver-lead.

Monashee Provincial Park: 7,515ha; 12 campsites. Northeast out of Cherryville on Sugar Lake Rd to Spectrum Creek. Parking lot at creek. No further road access. 250-494-6500. Fishing. Details on Sugar Lake and Monashee Provincial Park in *BC Rockies*, p.212.

Hwy 6 continues 84km to Needles Ferry on west side of Lower Arrow Lake in *BC Rockies*. See *BC Rockies* p.212, for details of this route.

LYTTON TO KAMLOOPS

TRANS-CANADA HIGHWAY (Highway 1)

At Lytton, Hwy 1 leaves all the drama of the churning Fraser River, and takes up with the more serene Thompson River. The Thompson River was named for David Thompson, a young surveyor and explorer who descended the Columbia River from its headwaters to the sea (1808-1811). Ironically, he never saw the Thompson, which was named after him by another explorer, Simon Fraser. And it was Thompson who named the Fraser (after Fraser, who had travelled the Fraser River from Prince George to the sea in 1808).

From Lytton, it is 164km to Kamloops. River and highway draw through the arid Thompson Plateau into the heartland of the Secwepemc First Nation and pioneer ranch country.

Lytton: (Pop. 400). On Hwy 1, 108km north of Hope. For details, see *Vancouver, Coast, and Mountains*, p. 137.

Skihist Provincial Park: 33ha; 56 campsites; sani-station. 250-851-3000. On Hwy 1, 8km northeast of Lytton. Views of Thompson Canyon. Water, cutting into the pre-glacial floor of the valley over several centuries, has created almost vertical walls in the mountains. Hiking on old Cariboo Road via two- to three- hour trail circuit. Nov-April, bighorn sheep may be seen along hillsides near park. Wheelchair access.

Goldpan Provincial Park: 5ha; 14 campsites. 250-851-3000. 25km northeast of Lytton on Hwy 1. River-raft stop, steelhead fishing in fall. Limited turning space for big rigs.

The Great Landslide: On western edge of Spences Bridge, on Hwy 1, 35.5km northeast of Lytton. A small Anglican church adjacent land belonging to the Spences Bridge First Nation marks setting for story of tragedy. On August 13, 1905, the lower side of the mountain across the river slid into a small Nlaka'pamux village, burying several people and damming the Thompson River, which drowned 13 more people.

Highway 8: 37km northeast of Lytton, entering Spences Bridge. From here, Hwy 1 continues north, crossing the Thompson River on the Spences Bridge. Hwy 8 leads 1km into downtown Spences Bridge, where there's another bridge across the Thompson.

Spences Bridge: (Pop. 165). On Hwy 8, 37.5km northeast of Lytton. At confluence of the Thompson and Nicola rivers. An important Nlaka'pamux centre. First European community was named for Cook's Ferry that carried passengers across the Thompson River until 1865 when Thomas Spence built the original bridge. Good fishing in Thompson and Nicola rivers. Accommodation and camping. Historic Steelhead Inn, a base for river rafting and fishing, serves meals on the patio and may even offer binoculars to watch nearby nest of ospreys feeding their young. Watch for bighorn sheep.

Highway 8: Just 2km northeast of Spences Bridge, Hwy 8 crosses the Nicola River and makes a sharp turn to the east. Highway follows the northeast side of this scenic river for 65km to Merritt, cutting across the beautiful Nicola Valley. It's a great back road, offering lots of places to stop and sniff the sagebrush or count the black-eyed susans. Here are three villages of the Sce'exmx, the "people of the creeks," who share their language and culture with the Nlaka'pamux to the east. There's a small pleasant, unserviced campground at Shackan, 22.5km east of Spences Bridge. For Merritt, see *Hope to Kamloops*, p.173.

Canadian Northern Pacific's Last Spike: On Hwy 1, about 20km north of Spences Bridge, on Thompson River's east bank.

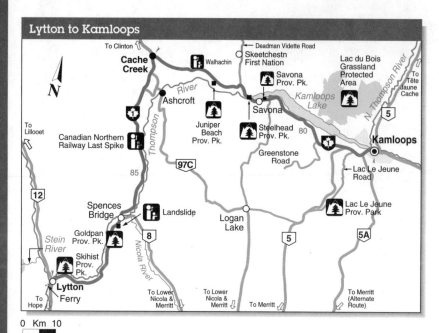

Lytton to Kamloops

0 Km 10

Canada's third transcontinental rail link was completed here, near Basque, on Jan 23, 1915. Rail line later became part of the Canadian National Railways system.

Red Hill Rest Area: 28km beyond Spences Bridge. Red hills stand out against surrounding yellows and greens.

Ashcroft Manor Rd: East off Trans-Canada Hwy, 37.5km north of Spences Bridge. 4km to Ashcroft.

Ashcroft Manor: On Trans-Canada Hwy at turnoff to Ashcroft. 250-453-9983. Daily, 9-9. Built in 1862, Ashcroft Manor was part of a ranch, with grist and sawmills, that supplied Cariboo miners. The manor, one of BC's oldest, served as first courthouse in the area (the famous Judge Begbie himself held court here). Much of the complex was destroyed by fire in 1943, but a roadhouse and log church, with hand-hewn pews, remain. Browse through history, arts and craft store, and art gallery. Tea House Restaurant, gift shop.

Ashcroft: (Pop. 2,028). 4km northeast of Hwy 1, on Ashcroft Manor Rd. Called the "Arizona of Canada," and one of Canada's hot spots. The Ashcroft-Cache Creek area is desert-like, with tumbleweed, cactus, and sage on dry, rolling hills. Real cattle country, ranches for visitors to feel the spirit of the Old West.

Ashcroft Information: Gold Country Communities Society information centre, 301 Brink St. Box 1239, Ashcroft, BC, V0K 1A0. 250-453-9467.

■ **Ashcroft Museum:** 404 Brink St, Box 129, Ashcroft, BC, V0K 1A0. 250-453-9232. In 1916 former federal building. History of Ashcroft, the Cariboo Rd, BC Express Company, main street at the turn of the century, and Nlaka'pamux people.

■ **Heritage Stage Coach Depot:** 6th and Railway. Year-round. Built for BX Stage Coaches, 1911. Now houses shops.

Highway 97C: About 6km north of Ashcroft. Leads 58km east (along what was formerly Highland Valley Rd) to Logan Lake (see p.174), then 42km south (along former Mamit Lake Rd) to Hwy 8, about 5km west of Merritt.

Highway 97: At Cache Creek, 10km north of Ashcroft. Northwest on Hwy 97 to Clinton and Cariboo Country. East on Hwy 1 to Kamloops. The Trans-Canada and Hwy 97 are the same road for the 110km between Cache Creek and Monte Creek, 30km east of Kamloops.

Cache Creek: (Pop. 1,207). At junction of Trans-Canada and Hwy 97, 193km north of Hope. Since the mid-1800s, Cache Creek, in the heart of desert country, has been the halfway point for people travelling between the lower Fraser and Cariboo Country. The historic Fraser Canyon route on Hwy 1 is still known as the "Gold Rush Trail," but visitors today come in search of scenery and outdoor recreation.

Cache Creek is known for its Old West aura, with large cattle ranches, open grasslands, and working cowboys. Also a base for sport-fishermen, and haven for jade hunters. Watch this semi-precious stone being cut, polished, and mounted in Cariboo Jade Shoppe, at 1093 Todd Rd in downtown Cache Creek.

Moving quickly with the times, the community has adopted a "Back to the Fifties" automotive transportation theme – inspired by active drag strip – Nl'ak'apxm Eagle Motorplex – off Hwy 1, 6km south of town. Local shopkeepers drive vintage cars. Graffiti Days is town's big event, mid-June.

Cache Creek Information: Cache Creek Chamber of Commerce, Box 460, Cache Creek, BC, V0K 1H0. 250-457-9566. Also, Village Office, 1389 Quartz St, 250-457-6237, or Copper Canyon Chevron on Hwy 97, two blocks north of the junction of Hwy 1 and Hwy 97.

■ **Historic Hat Creek Ranch:** 11km north of

Cache Creek at junction of Hwys 12 and 97, travel 0.5km west on Hwy 12. 1-800-782-0922 or 250-457-9722. May-late Sept. Interpretive tour of BC's ranching and transportation history, 1860-1915. Last intact stopping house on Old Cariboo Wagon Road. Working ranch also offers history of area's First Nations people, trail rides, snacks, gift shop, wagon tours, blacksmith and farm machinery displays, and special events.

Highways 1 and 97: At Cache Creek, Hwy 97 leads north into the Cariboo. Eastward, Hwys 97 and 1 run together to Monte Creek.

Ghost of Walhachin: South of Hwy 1, 16km east of Cache Creek. In 1908-1909, surveyor, entrepreneur Charles Barnes persuaded a group of English investors to back the purchase of more than 2,000ha of dry Thompson River plateau for conversion into Eden-like orchard lots. An elaborate system of canals and wooden flumes was built to carry water down from higher lands to the north. By 1914, the population of nearly 300 included English farmers, and Canadian and Chinese workers, tradesmen, and merchants. The first trainload of apples had been sent to market. The town, on Canadian National and Canadian Pacific railway main lines, boasted a hotel (proper dress required), school, and post office. There was even promise of a golf course. When the First World War broke out, many settlers returned to the old country, to enlist. A storm ripped out the irrigation flume; the trees were left to die in the desert sun. The few families that did return to Walhachin, turned around and left. A dilapidated irrigation flume is all that remains of the once-flourishing dream. There's now a tiny community called Walhachin, with green and pink clapboard houses, on the Thompson River's south side.

CACHE CREEK

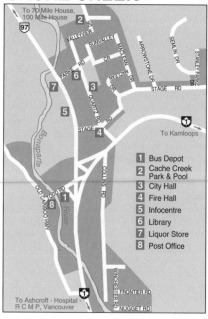

1 Bus Depot
2 Cache Creek Park & Pool
3 City Hall
4 Fire Hall
5 Infocentre
6 Library
7 Liquor Store
8 Post Office

Juniper Beach Provincial Park: 260ha; 30 campsites; sani-station; wheelchair access, showers, some electric hookups. 250-851-3000. South of Hwy 1 on Thompson River, 19km east of Cache Creek. Sagebrush, prickly pear, juniper, cottonwood.

Deadman Vidette Rd: North off Hwy 1, 31km east of Cache Creek. 30km route to start of a lake chain including Mowich, Snohoosh, Skookum, Deadman, and Vidette lakes. Kokanee, rainbow trout. Intriguing river valley with volcanic canyon, rock hoodoos, and waterfalls was traditional gathering place of Secwepemc First Nations people. The Secwepemc village of **Skeetchestn**, 7km from Hwy 1, offers First Nations Cultural Adventure Weekends, including camping kekulis (traditional pit-style winter houses). 250-373-2493. Arts and crafts at convenience store, historic St Mary's Church, in village.

Steelhead Provincial Park: 38ha; 32 campsites. Off Hwy 1, about 35km east of Cache Creek. 250-851-3000. On southwest end of Kamloops Lake. Swimming, fishing, and boating.

Savona Rd: Hwy 1 crosses to south bank of the Thompson at Kamloops Lake, 36km east of Cache Creek. Just across the bridge, a northeast turn off highway leads to lakeshore community of Savona.

Savona: (Pop. 541). On shores of Kamloops Lake. Accommodation, campgrounds. Truck stop here is good place to warm up, or cool down, and learn how to pronounce Savona, named for Francois Saveneaux (Francis Savona) who in 1859 established a ferry service across the Thompson River where it flows out of Kamloops Lake. Meal portions are trucker-sized.

Savona Rd: North off Hwy 1, 4.5km east of bridge, to Savona Provincial Park. South for backcountry route to Logan Lake and Merritt. See *Hope to Kamloops*, p.174.

Savona Provincial Park: 2ha summer swimming spot on Kamloops Lake. A pleasant spot for picnicking.

Kamloops Lake: 4km beyond Savona Rd, 46km from Cache Creek. Viewpoint across lake to reddish-coloured Painted Bluffs. Plaque explains that these large Interior lakes and rivers were highways for stately sternwheelers, vital elements in the settlement of BC.

Greenstone Rd: 63.5km east from Cache Creek. Rough, winding 25km south to Greenstone Mountain. Views from 1,798m peak. Main road and side roads to several lakes (Ned Roberts, Chuwhels, Cornwall, Face, Paska, Roper, Dominic, Andrew, Kwilalkwila, Grace, Dairy, Durand).

Highway 5 (Coquihalla Hwy): South off Hwy 1, 72km beyond Cache Creek. Details in *Hope to Kamloops*, p.172. Hwys 1 and 97 continue east through Kamloops.

Countryside near Kamloops.

Lac Le Jeune Rd: South off Hwy 1, 1.5km east of Hwy 5 junction. Leads to recreation area and three provincial parks. See *Hope to Kamloops*, p.174.

Highway 5A: South off Hwy 1, 6km east of Hwy 5 junction. Alternate route to Merritt. See *Princeton to Kamloops*, p.180.

Kamloops: 80km from Cache Creek. Exit to Columbia St is just over 1km from Hwy 5A junction. For details on Kamloops, see p.174.

KAMLOOPS TO SICAMOUS

TRANS-CANADA HIGHWAY (Highway 1)

From Kamloops, at the eastern end of Kamloops Lake, Highway 1, the Trans-Canada, traces the now placid and pastoral South Thompson River to an oasis of long lakes: Adams, Little Shuswap, and Shuswap. The distance to Sicamous is 131km. It's a landscape worth dallying in: there is more here than meets the eye. The rivers linking the big lakes are home to the most remarkable salmon runs on earth. There are hospitable lakeside towns and wee bays to explore. There's even a hostel in an historic General Store, where you'll hear all about the bats.

Kamloops: 80km from Cache Creek; 205km northeast of Hope. For details on *Kamloops*, see p.174.

Highways 1, 97, and 5: From Kamloops, Hwy 5 (the Yellowhead) runs north along the North Thompson River for 339km to Tête Jaune Cache in the Rockies. Hwys 1 and 97 run east along the south side of the South Thompson River to Monte Creek, and there they split.

Kamloops Wildlife Park: On Hwy 1, 17km east of Kamloops, next to Kamloops Waterslide and RV Park. 250-573-3242. Daily. Some 70 species of native and exotic wildlife – cougars, grizzly bears, moose, elk, bighorn sheep, Siberian tigers, wolves, zebras, squirrel monkeys, donkeys, rabbits, birds. A chance to learn about wildlife rehabilitation, captive breeding and release programs, and species survival programs. A program to breed and rehabilitate the endangered burrowing owl, a robin-sized raptor, is based here. Visitor Centre, concession, gift shop.

Kamloops Waterslide and RV Park: Adjoining wildlife park. 85 RV sites; 19 tenting sites. 250-573-3789. May-Oct. More than 610m of waterslides, hot tubs, wading pool, mini-golf.

Great Train Robbery: On Hwy 1, near Monte Creek train station. 24km from Kamloops. Bill Miner, notorious American stagecoach and train robber, held up a CPR train here in 1906, but made off with only $15. He was caught after an 80km horse chase. Sentenced to life in the BC Penitentiary, he escaped to the US in 1907. Feature film *The Grey Fox* tells the story.

Monte Creek: 31km east of Kamloops. Details on p.166.

Highways 1 and 97: At Monte Creek, 31km east of Kamloops. Hwy 97 runs south to Vernon, see p. 163.

Pritchard: (Area pop. 459). On Hwy 1, 42km from Kamloops. Farming community on South Thompson River.

Chase Creek Rd: South off Hwy 1, 56km east of Kamloops. A 40km mostly paved scenic back road to community of Falkland on Hwy 97. 28km south to Pillar Lake. Cabins, camping. Rainbow trout, ice fishing. For details on Falkland, see p.166.

Chase: (Pop. 2,362). On Trans-Canada Hwy at Little Shuswap Lake, 56km east of Kamloops. Westernmost launching point for intricate waterways of Shuswap Lake system, popular houseboating area. (More on houseboating under *Sicamous*, p.172.) Launching point for 58km canoe journey down Thompson River to Kamloops. Campsite on Banana Island, 13km downstream from Chase.

Beach park, wharf and boat launch, campsites, motels, and resort. In winter, snowmobiling, cross-country skiing, ice fishing.

Town named for Whitfield Chase (1820-96), area's first resident. Chase, a carpenter from New York, was one of those luckless gold seekers who instead found prosperity in ranching. He married a Secwepemc woman and had a large family.

Chase Information: Chase and District Chamber of Commerce Info Centre, 400 Shuswap Ave, Box 592, Chase, BC, V0E 1M0. 250-679-8432. July-Aug: daily; Sept-June: Mon, Wed, Thurs, Fri.

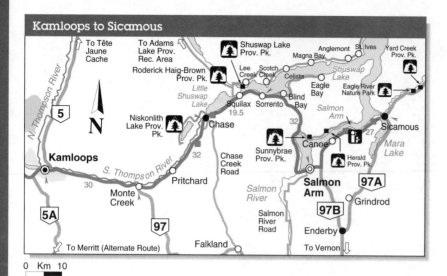

Kamloops to Sicamous

0 Km 10

■ **Chase Museum:** Daily, June-Labour Day.

■ **Sunshore Golf Club:** Nine-hole course on Little Shuswap Lake. Full services.

Niskonlith Lake Provincial Park: 238ha; 30 campsites. 250-851-3000. North off highway onto Pine St in Chase. Cross bridge and travel follow river to a divide in the road. Keep right, follow signs up mountain. About 14km total. Rainbow trout. Hiking, birdwatching, boating, swimming. McGillivray Lake is 15km north.

Chase Creek Falls Rest Area: Off Highway 1, just east of Chase (0.5km west of east entrance to Chase). Shaded creek, waterfall. Bighorn sheep may be visible on the nearby cliffs.

North Shuswap (Squilax) Bridge: About 9km beyond Chase, 67km from Kamloops. Bridge crosses the 4km Little River flowing between Shuswap and Little Shuswap lakes. During the famous Adams River salmon run in times past, this was an important fishing and trading centre for tribes of the Secwepemc First Nation, including the community of Squilax/Little Shuswap Lake (below). July and Aug, there is a booth selling bannock (tasty native-style bread) and salmon just on the north side of the bridge.

SIDE TRIP

to Adams Lake and North Shuswap

Little Shuswap Lake Rd: From bridge, leads west (around north shore of Little Shuswap Lake) 2km to Quaaout Lodge, a $4.5-million recreation resort owned by the Squilax/Little Shuswap Lake First Nation. 1-800-663-4303. Its design was inspired by the kekuli (traditional winter pit-house). Horseback riding, canoeing, and mountain bike rentals. Mid-July, most years, the community hosts the **Squilax Powwow**, drawing dancers, singers, and drummers from all over North America.

Squilax-Anglemont Rd: From Squilax Bridge, leads northwest to turnoff for Adams Lake Provincial Recreation Area; east to Roderick Haig-Brown Provincial Park; and northeast to the north shore of Shuswap Lake's main arm. A 40km drive along the lakeshore takes you through picturesque hamlets – Lee Creek, Scotch Creek, Celista, Magna Bay, and Anglemont, offering services and accommodation, including camping, private cabin rentals, and B&Bs. An attractive bicycling route along the lakeshore complements the plenitude of recreational activities. Beyond Anglemont, a 45km logging road traces the shore to **Seymour Arm**, another pretty village and popular summer vacation spot. For these, see below.

Adams Lake Provincial Recreation Area: 56ha; 32 campsites. 250-851-3000. About 4km from Squilax Bridge, turnoff Squilax-Anglemont Rd onto Holding Rd. It leads northwest 15km to 2,500m shoreline near south end of lake, offering swimming, waterskiing, and fishing.

Roderick Haig-Brown Provincial Park: 988ha. 250-851-3000. Along Squilax-Anglemont Rd, about 5km from Squilax Bridge. Encompasses 11km Adams River from Adams Lake to Shuswap Lake: site of the continent's largest sockeye salmon runs. Every four years (2002, 2006) millions of sockeye return in dominant runs. In the interim, the numbers are smaller but still significant. In early Oct, salmon migrate from the sea, up the Fraser, Thompson, and South Thompson rivers, through Little Shuswap Lake and into the Adams River, a 17-day, 485km odyssey. By spawning time, their silver bodies have turned bright red, with a green head and humped back that is unique to the sockeye. Several thousand chinook and hundreds of coho and pink salmon also spawn here. Observation decks, interpretive signs, and naturalist programs during major sockeye runs. Scenic canyons, forests, wheelchair access. Eagles, gulls, waterfowl; black bears, whitetail and mule deer, beavers, river otters, mink, and lots of Columbia ground squirrels. There's also fish-

ing, canoeing, rafting, cross-country skiing, snowshoeing, hiking.

Lee Creek: (Pop. 650). 8km east of Squilax Bridge along Squilax-Anglemont Rd. Artisan shops.

Scotch Creek: (Pop. 1,100). 17km east of Squilax Bridge along Squilax-Anglemont Rd. Picturesque farming community with old barns and outbuildings near Shuswap Lake Provincial Park. Now the commercial centre for the North Shuswap communities. Inquire at information booth about whitewater raft trips on the Adams River, water recreation, hiking, kayaking. Camping, private cabin accommodation, restaurants and pubs, gas stations, marinas, pharmacy, groceries, bumper boats, and mini-golf.

North Shuswap Information: North Shuswap Chamber of Commerce Travel and Business Information centre, 3871 Squilax-Anglemont Hwy at Scotch Creek. Write Box 101, Celista, BC, V0E 1L0. 250-955-2113 or 1-888-955-1488. Late June-late Aug.

Shuswap Lake Provincial Park: 149ha; 272 campsites (reservations taken: call 1-800-689-9025; from the Lower Mainland or overseas, call 604-689-9025). General info: 250-851-3000. 19km east of Squilax Bridge on Squilax-Anglemont Rd. Favoured family vacation spot. Nature centre, depressions from a 3,000-year-old village, reconstruction of a kekuli, or pit-house, amphitheatre, adventure playground, showers, naturalist programs, boat launching, wheelchair access. Includes Copper Island, 2km offshore. Mule deer often summer on island. Trails, viewpoints.

Celista: (Pop. 950). 26km east of Squilax Bridge, on Squilax-Anglemont Rd. Resort community with accommodation and camping. Named for nearby Celista Creek.

Magna Bay: (Pop. 225). On Squilax-Anglemont Rd, 31km east of Squilax Bridge. Vacation centre. Was called Steamboat Bay when sternwheelers anchored here. Magna is Latin for great, and this bay is a big one. Camping and store.

Anglemont: (Pop. 400). 40km east of Squilax Bridge. Vacation centre with accommodation, camping, and store. Named in 1914 after nearby Angle Mountain.

Horseshoe Bay and St Ives: 4km east of Anglemont. These two beaches are part of **Shuswap Lake Provincial Marine Park.** Undeveloped campsites for boaters. Neighbourhood pub and accommodation.

Albas: 33km northeast of Anglemont. Pretty beach is part of **Shuswap Lake Marine Park.** Small developed campground south of Blueberry Creek; undeveloped site near mouth of Celista Creek. Trail near Steamboat Bay follows Celista Creek, offering waterfalls and remnants of early logging days. Al Bass was an early trapper in this area.

Seymour Arm: (Pop. 100). At head of Shuswap Lake's Seymour Arm, 45km northeast of Anglemont. On the dusty streets a few old cabins remain, remnants from late 1800s when the tiny town was a bustling community of 500 serving miners headed for the Big Bend Gold Rush. The gold disappeared and many of the buildings were destroyed by fire. Today, there's a hotel, restaurant, pub, and general store on the wharf in Bughouse Bay. Store still has old glass hand pump for gas – still working. Village is served by **Shuswap Lake Ferry** service from Sicamous, a vehicle-carrying barge. For details on ferry, see *Sicamous*, p.172.

Silver Beach Provincial Park: 130ha; 35 campsites. 250-851-3000. At Seymour Arm. A popular houseboater destination. Beautiful sandy beaches. Nice paddling at mouth and in lower reaches of Seymour River. Waterfowl watching, trout fishing, windsurfing. See historic townsite and late summer salmon spawning.

Return to Highway 1

Squilax General Store and Travellers Hostel: On north side of Hwy 1, about 1km past turnoff to North Shuswap Bridge. 250-675-2977. A good source of groceries, history, culture, and gossip about the area. Hostel accommodation in 1940s store and in three Canadian National Railway cabooses. A peaceful sojourn on the banks of the Little River. The old store is also home to one of two local colonies of rare Yuma bats. About 600 of the tiny (6g) insectivorous bats migrate to the store's attic each spring to bear young, then leave in the fall to hibernate at an unknown location. A second colony returns in spring to the Little Shuswap Lake First Nation reserve (above). Thousands of bats lived for years in St Peter and Paul Catholic Church, until it burned to the ground in 1994. Local naturalists, teachers, and students built little bat houses, and returning bats numbered about 600 in 1996. The Shuswap region is home to 11 of 16 bat species found in BC, likely because of the area's unique blend of grasslands, arid flatlands, mountains, and forests.

Sorrento: (Pop. 662). On Trans-Canada Hwy, 19.5km east of Chase. Summer cottages and lakeside homes overlook Shuswap Lake for several kilometres on both sides of Sorrento. An established vacation community with area population of more than 4,000 in summer. Motels, resorts, campgrounds, and services. Check at Info Centre for details on Adams River rafting.

Originally called Trapper's Landing, Sorrento is named after the romantic Italian town where early settler J.R. Kinghorn spent his honeymoon. Highlight of town is restored 80-year-old St Mary's Anglican church. It's right on Hwy 1 (also the main street). Caen Rd, north off Hwy 1, leads to Sorrento's old ferry wharf.

Sorrento Information: Info Centre, Sorrento Chamber of Commerce, Box 7, Sorrento, BC, V0E 2W0. 250-675-3515. On Hwy 1 on east side of Sorrento near the Shuswap

Margaret Falls, in Herald Provincial Park.

Estates Golf Course. Daily, July 1-Labour Day.
■ **Pheasant World:** 1280 Trans-Canada Hwy. 250-675-2274. Year-round. Beautiful birds.

Sorrento-Blind Bay Rd: Northeast off Hwy 1, 1km east of Sorrento centre.

SIDE TRIP

to Blind and Eagle Bays

The road to Blind and Eagle bays from eastern outskirts of Sorrento hugs southern shore of Shuswap Lake's main arm. It's 22km to Eagle Bay.

Blind Bay: (Pop. 454). 4km from turnoff at Sorrento. Boat rentals, resorts, campgrounds. Because of the angle at which the bay curves into the lake, it is obscured from sight, thus the name.

Eagle Bay: (Pop. 500). 18km east of Blind Bay. Resorts, campgrounds, and services.

Return to Highway 1

White Lake Rd: Off Hwy 1, about 10km east of Sorrento. Balmoral Rd (north) is another route to Blind Bay. 6km to Little White and White lakes. Cabins and camping. Good hiking, canoeing, and fishing. Also cross-country skiing.

Sunnybrae/Canoe Point Rd: East off Hwy 1, 18km east of Sorrento. Leads to parks on north side of Salmon Arm.

SIDE TRIP

on Sunnybrae/Canoe Pt Rd

Road skirts lakeshore.

Sunnybrae Provincial Park: 25ha. 3km east of Hwy 1. Swimming, boating, fishing, picnicking, wheelchair access.

Sunnybrae: (Pop. 417). 2km east of Sunnybrae Park. Residential centre and holiday spot on lake.

Herald Provincial Park: 79ha; 51 campsites (reservations taken: call 1-800-689-9025; from the Lower Mainland or overseas, call 604-689-9025). General Info: 250-851-3000. 12km east of Hwy 1. Wooded campsites on lakeshore. Good swimming, boating, fishing, hiking, wheelchair access. Spectacular Margaret Falls.

Paradise Point: 2km east of Herald Park. Part of Shuswap Lake Provincial Marine Park, which is divided into several sites around Shuswap Lake. Paradise Point can also be reached by road.

Return to Highway 1

Salmon Arm: (Pop. 14,631). On Hwy 1, 32km east of Sorrento; 111km east of Kamloops. Salmon Arm, largest community in the Shuswap area, lies on the flood plain of the beautiful Salmon River. It's a picturesque setting at the end of one of Shuswap Lake's four long arms. City takes its name from this arm, and the salmon that once swam up the creeks and river in such abundance that the first white settlers used pitchforks to get them, then put them on their fields for fertilizer. After 1913, when a landslide during construction of the Canadian National Railway blocked the Fraser River at Hells Gate, the Salmon River's salmon never returned. However, Friends of the Salmon River have worked to make these waters habitable for salmon of a different stock.

The area was first settled by Europeans after construction of the Canadian Pacific Railway in 1885. Today, Salmon Arm is a centre for fruit and dairy farms. Forestry is also important. Plenty of outdoors activities. The mouth of the Salmon River is an important waterfowl and bird area with at least 150 species, most of which nest here. Of particular interest are the breeding displays of Clark's and western grebes, which come to nest April-June.

Visitors can enjoy the farmer's market at Picadilly Place Mall parking lot, Tues and Fri, May-Oct. There are also summer concerts at the public wharf on Wed nights.

Salmon Arm Information: Salmon Arm and District Chamber of Commerce Info Centre, Box 999, Salmon Arm, BC, V1E 4P2. 751 Marine Park Dr NE. 250-832-2230. Open year-round.

Salmon Arm Airport: On 20th Ave SE, about 5km southeast of town.

■ **R.J. Haney Heritage House and Park:** On Hwy 97B, 4km east of Salmon Arm. May-Aug, Wed-Sun, holiday Mon 10-4. 250-832-5243. Historic schoolhouse, church, farm buildings. Managed by Salmon Arm Museum and Heritage Association.

■ **Larch Hills:** Cross-country ski area. Take Hwy 97B south from city for 6km, turn east on Grandview Bench Rd for 5km, then north on Edgar Rd. 6km to ski area. 150km of trails. El 1,070-1,220m. Rolling terrain of pretty

Larch Hills Forest. Site of annual Reino Keski-Salmi Ski Loppet, a major marathon.

■ **Rotary Peace Park and Public Wharf:** Marine Park Dr, downtown. Dedicated to world peace and understanding. 250m walkway along new pier and marina. Viewing area for shorebirds and waterfowl. Picnic area. BC Wildlife Watch viewing site.

■ **Salmon Arm Golf Course**, 4km east of Salmon Arm on Hwy 97B, 4km south. 18 holes, par 5 professional course.

■ **Fruit and Veggies: Geier's Fruit and Berry Farm**, 3820-40th St, SE. 250-832-8460. Mon-Sun. Berries, fruits and veggies. Call ahead for picking times. **Demille's Fruit & Produce**, Hwy 1 W. 1-888-205-3436. Year-round. Corn, petting zoo, picnic area, seasonal gift shop.

Highway 97B: Just east of Salmon Arm, Leads south, joins Hwy 97A and runs toward Enderby (20km), and Vernon (55km). Details, pp. 163-165.

Canoe: A suburb of Salmon Arm, 6km east. Public beach, picnics. Recreational park with 18-hole, par 3 golf course, driving range, mini-golf, tennis courts, go-carts.

Annis Mountain Rest Area: 15km east of Salmon Arm.

Lake of the Shuswap: 19.5km east of Salmon Arm. Named for the Shuswap or Secwepemc First Nation, northernmost of the great Salishan family comprising 17 contemporary communities. Their 180,000-sq-km traditional territories stretch east to west from Rocky Mountains to the Fraser River, and north to south, approximately from the top of Okanagan Lake to Tête Jaune Cache.

Shuswap Rest Area: 21km east of Salmon Arm. Gorgeous view of Shuswap Lake.

Sicamous: (Pop. 3,088). At junction of Hwy 1 and Hwy 97A, 27km east of Salmon Arm. From Secwepemc word meaning "narrow," or "squeezed in the middle." Sicamous overlooks Sicamous Narrows between Mara and Shuswap lakes. Once a railway construction depot, now known as "the Houseboat Capital of Canada." About eight operators rent some 300 houseboats from Sicamous marinas. Resembling a ragged capital H, Shuswap Lake's four narrow arms are surrounded by the peaks (some higher than 2,200m) and forests of the Monashee Mountains and Shuswap Highland. 1,000km of shoreline, from sheer cliffs to gravel and sandy beaches with gently sloping hills running up into the forests.

Shuswap Lake Provincial Marine Park is divided into a number of popular sites situated around the lake, and offers designated boat/houseboating beaches. Ask at Info Centre about new snowmobile, hiking, and biking trails.

Sicamous Information: Sicamous and District Chamber of Commerce, Travel and Business Info Centre, Box 346, Sicamous, BC, V0E 2V0. 250-836-3313. Downtown at 110 Finlayson St. Year-round.

Shuswap Lake Ferry Service Ltd: Box 370, Sicamous, BC, V0E 2V0. 250-836-2200. Ferry and a barge for passengers and freight. Based in Sicamous, serves lakeside communities year-round, except when there's ice on the lake. MV *Phoebe Ann* is a 15.5m steel-hulled sternwheeler with a snack bar and room for 40 passengers. Some travellers take vehicles to Seymour Arm on the barge, then drive out on Squilax-Anglemont Rd.

■ **Eagle Valley Museum and Heritage Society:** In Finlayson Park. Box 944, Sicamous, BC, V0E 2V0. 250-836-4654. Late June-late Aug. Aboriginal, railway, and settlers' histories are presented here.

■ **D Dutchman Dairy:** 1km east of Sicamous. Free children's zoo with llamas, camels, horses, peacocks. Some say best homemade ice cream in BC. More than 50 flavours.

Highway 97A: Joins Hwy 1 at Sicamous. Hwy 97A runs south 35km to Enderby, 70km to Vernon. Hwy 1 continues northeast along Eagle River. For Sicamous to Lake Louise, see *BC Rockies*, p.207.

HOPE TO KAMLOOPS

COQUIHALLA HIGHWAY (Highway 5)

The Coquihalla, Hwy 5, from Hope to Kamloops, is BC's only toll highway. The toll for cars and RVs is $10. This four-lane, 210km route is 73km shorter than the older Trans-Canada Hwy. The first phase, between Hope and Merritt (115km), was finished in 1986; the second, between Merritt and Kamloops (87km), was completed in 1987. The third and final phase, the "Okanagan Connector," from Merritt to Peachland (108km), was completed in 1990.

Because the Coquihalla has fewer ups, downs, and curves, it saves up to 90 minutes over the older Fraser Canyon route north. There is only one toll gate, between Hope and Merritt; and only one major exit, at Merritt. As the toll gate is south of Merritt, driving is free if you're only going from Merritt north to Kamloops.

There are no restaurants or gas stations on the highway itself, but there are lots of rest areas. You can stop at Hope, Merritt, or Kamloops for gas.

The toll plaza is near the 1,240m summit of the Coquihalla Pass, 55km northeast of Hope. The highway runs through the valleys of the lower Coquihalla River and Boston Bar Creek to the Coquihalla summit, then joins the Coldwater River and follows it to Merritt, where Hwy 5 intersects 5A.

From Merritt, the Coquihalla ascends the Nicola River valley and climbs Clapperton Creek valley to its headwaters, at 1,445m, then goes northeast to Kamloops.

The journey is a two-hour preview of BC's geographic diversity. Travellers from Vancouver move beyond the foothills of the Coast Mountains to be enveloped by the Cascade Mountains. As the highway climbs inland, the scenery changes: the rough peaks are smoother, trees smaller, forests sparser. While the dampness of the coast permeates the west, the semi-arid grasslands of the Fraser Plateau lie high and dry in the sun.

The Coquihalla Hwy is also a short and simple lesson on amazing engineering feats. There are dozens of bridges and overpasses crossing roads, rivers, and railways. Many, in size and design, inspire awe. Snow sheds, diversion trenches, and avalanche-stop dams help hold off the hazards of steep terrain.

The Coquihalla is actually a second effort to provide a transportation route through this formidable terrain. The Kettle Valley Railway operated from 1916 between Vancouver and the West Kootenay, running through the Coquihalla Valley to Hope, where it joined the CPR. Many of its stations were named after characters from Shakespeare's plays – Romeo, Juliet, Othello, Iago. But the railway was doomed from the start. In 1959, after decades of runaway trains, avalanches, derailments, and declining traffic, it was shut down. Tracks were torn up, tunnels filled, trestles blasted out. Remnants can still be seen near Hope in the Coquihalla Canyon Provincial Recreation Area.

The 87km section of the Coquihalla between Merritt and Kamloops is a time saver: it now takes only 45 minutes to whip from city to city, a 15-minute saving from old Hwy 5A. However, for those not in a hurry, the old road remains the scenic one. It's charming and meandering, and thanks to the nearby freeway, free of heavy traffic. It hugs the appealing landscape while the freeway soars over it abstractly. The best part of the freeway is the descent into Kamloops with vistas of giant dry hills. Hwy 5A is a visual treat the whole way.

Summer travellers on the Coquihalla should be careful not to overheat their engines on some of the climbs. It's interesting that it is somewhat easier driving south than north on the Coquihalla. There's a very long 8 percent grade north of the toll booth: going north, it's uphill all the way. Winter travellers should be prepared for snow. The highway is well-maintained and patrolled, and travellers can tune into special radio stations (frequencies posted on signs) for road conditions.

Hope: (Pop. 7,118). For details, see *Vancouver, Coast, and Mountains*, p.138.

Highways 1, 3, and 5: From Hope, Hwy 1, the Trans-Canada, leads north up the Fraser Canyon toward Lytton (p.135), Cache Creek and Kamloops (p.167). Hwy 3, the Hope-Princeton, heads east to Manning Park, Princeton, and the Okanagan Valley (see p. 137). Hwy 5, the Coquihalla, runs northeast to Kamloops.

Coquihalla Canyon Recreation Area: 150ha. 13.5km north of Hope on Hwy 5. If travelling south, take exit on Othello Rd, 42.5km south of toll plaza. 4km to park. Trails, boat launch, viewpoint, abandoned Kettle Valley Railway tunnels. In summer, look for large steelhead trout migrating upstream through the canyon's pools.

🚶 **Coquihalla River Recreation Area:** 100ha. If travelling north, take Carolin Mine exit, 25.5km north of Hope, use the cloverleaf to turn around and head south. If southbound, take exit 32km south of toll plaza. Hiking, fishing.

🛉 **Carolin Mines Exit:** 26km from Hope. See entry above.

🚻 **Zopkios Rest Area:** 40km northeast of Hope. Heated waiting room, hot water.

🛉 **Great Bear Snow Shed:** 42km northeast of Hope. A major engineering task. 300m long, 31m wide. Faced with bear murals.

🚶 **Coquihalla Summit Recreation Area:** 5,750ha. Four accesses. Zopkios viewpoint, 45km north of Hope; Boston Bar Creek, 47.5km north of Hope; Falls Creek, 51km north of Hope; and Coquihalla Lakes, 2km north of toll plaza. Protects an outstanding scenic area in the Cascades. Features Zopkios Ridge, Dry Gulch, Falls Lake, and Coquihalla Lakes.

🚻 **Britton Creek Rest Area:** 51km north of Hope. Heated waiting room, hot water.

🛉🚻 **Toll Plaza and Rest Area:** Near top of Coquihalla Pass, 55km northeast of Hope. 14 lanes and 13 toll booths. Cash goes directly into underground vault, which can be opened only by security. (Toll may also be paid with major credit card.) Heated rest areas for north and southbound travellers.

🌲 **Coldwater River Provincial Park:** 76ha. 67km northeast of Hope. North and south access ramps. Pleasant stroll alongside river. Steelhead fishing.

🛣 **Highways 5, 5A, and 8:** 115km northeast of Hope. Hwy 5 continues through Merritt. Hwy 5A runs south to Princeton (85km), north to Kamloops. Hwy 8 is a 65km back road to Hwy 1 at Spences Bridge, see p.167.

🏛 **Merritt:** (Pop. 7,631). On Hwy 5, 115km northeast of Hope and 108km from Peachland in the Okanagan via the Connector. Merritt, a transportation hub, sits in ranching country at the confluence of the Nicola and Coldwater rivers. The Nicola River, with headwaters only 30km from Okanagan Lake, flows west more than 80km through Douglas and Nicola lakes to Merritt. A particularly attractive river, it continues beyond Merritt for 65km to the Thompson River at Spences Bridge. Merritt is at the junction of territories traditionally belonging to the Nlaka'pamux First Nation people of the Fraser Canyon, the Thompson River and its tributaries, and the Okanagan First Nation people. The city is centre for five aboriginal communities in the valley.

There are about 150 lakes in the area, where anglers catch rainbow and cutthroat trout, kokanee and Dolly Varden char. They say: "A lake a day as long as you stay."

The city spreads out from its most imposing landmark, the Coldwater Hotel, built by Murdoch McIntyre in 1908 for $6,000 just two years after Merritt was established. The previous hotel was too small to handle the coal miners flooding into the new town. When it opened, the Coldwater was considered the finest hotel in BC's Interior: the first to have rooms with attached bathrooms; also five steam-heated sample rooms, where travelling salesmen could lay out their goods for local merchants.

Marie Logan came to Merritt as a youngster in the early 1920s, and she recalls how important the Coldwater was to Merritt's social life. "Couples were married in the hotel and then got a room for $1 and breakfast the next morning for 50 cents."

Saturday was the big night around the hotel when cowboys rode in from the hills to clean up in the hotel before sitting around the balustraded porches to watch "gussied-up" women stroll by. Once, a cowboy rode his horse right into the bar. The grand old hotel still dominates the downtown core. It has a dramatic shrimp-pink exterior with tiered balconies, and a four-storey turret capped with a copper dome. Spacious barroom in brass and oak is well worth a look, a photo, and a long cold one with the locals.

Merritt began when the now-defunct Kettle Valley Railway put a branch line into the coal mines on the town's outskirts. The last mine closed in 1945, but one seam is still burning. Looking out from the Info Centre, puffs of smoke can sometimes be seen.

Today, Merritt, at the junction of Hwys 5, 5A, and 8, offers a full range of travellers' services within easy reach of Vancouver, Kamloops, and Kelowna. The four-day **Merritt Mountain Music Festival** in July is a big draw for country-and-western music lovers. Look for local arts and crafts, award-winning honey.

Fallow deer farming, a tradition in some parts of Europe, was introduced to BC in 1987, and the valley has innovative operations at Canadian Fallow Deer Farms, Douglas Lake Ranch, and Pooley Ranch.

❓ **Merritt Information:** Info Centre, City of Merritt, Box 189, Merritt, BC, V1K 1B8. 250-378-2281. Fax: 250-378-6485. At junction of Hwys 5 and 5A. Daily, all year. A tourist attraction in itself, the huge, two-storey log building sports a brilliant red alpine roof, startling in the burnt sienna landscape. Its dramatic presence arrests the eye of motorists hurtling down the Coquihalla, demanding a stop. Lofty interior features displays of local highlights and a gift shop. Snack shop.

■ **Nicola Valley Museum and Archives:** 2202 Jackson Ave. 250-378-4145. Mon-Fri, 10-3. History of the Nicola Valley, Craigmont Mine, coal mining, ranching, and Nlaka'pamux history. Features the life and times of ethnographer, James Teit (1864-1922), renowned for his detailed records of the history, culture, sciences, and spiritual practices of BC's Interior First Nations.

■ **Merritt City View Point:** Take Juniper Dr and follow signs on gravel road. Views of city and part of Coldwater Valley. Also Queen's Char Trail, a short walk.

■ **Golf: Merritt Golf and Country Club**, Juniper Dr. 250-378-9414. Nine-hole course along the Nicola River. **Nicola Valley Golf Course and RV Park**, Hwy 5A at Quilchena, 18km north of Merritt. Nine-hole course with views of Nicola Lake.

■ **Godey Creek Trail:** Behind Info Centre. Up short hill to an observation lookout.

■ **Kane Valley Cross-country Skiing:** 17km east of Merritt. Once on Hwy 97C, the Okanagan Connector, follow signs. 42km of groomed and marked trails.

■ **Spius Creek Fish Hatchery:** 17km west of Merritt on Hwy 8. Follow signs. BC Wildlife Watch viewing site.

Hope to Kamloops

0   Km   10

Lac Le Jeune-Meadow Creek Rds: 48km north of Merritt. West to Logan Lake. East to Lac Le Jeune.

SIDE TRIP

to Logan Lake

Logan Lake: (Pop. 2,472). On Meadow Creek Rd, 22km west of Hwy 5. Logan Lake, an instant town, incorporated in 1970, is home to 1,100 employees of Highland Valley Copper mining operation, 16km west of community centre. Points of interest include 3200B Wabco ore-haulage truck with a capacity of 235t, and the Bucyrus Erie shovel, housing the Info Centre. For mine tours, see *Highland Valley Copper*, below. Picturesque lakeshore setting, nine-hole golf course. Good fishing in several nearby lakes. Area offers rockhounding, alpine photography, cross-country skiing, snowmobiling, ice fishing. Accommodation and campgrounds. 18km north of town, **Tunkwa Provincial Park** (5,091ha) protects fragile grasslands and wetlands.

Logan Lake Information: Info Centre, District of Logan Lake, Box 190, Logan Lake, BC, V0K 1W0. 250-523-6322. On main road, near recreation centre. Daily, May 15-Oct 15.

Mamit Lake Rd (Hwy 97C): South off Highland Valley Rd, 3km west of Logan Lake. A paved, 40km alternate route to **Merritt** through open cattle country. **Ashcroft** can be reached by continuing west along Highland Valley Rd about 30km.

Highland Valley Copper: On Highland Valley Rd, about 16km west of Logan Lake. Largest open-pit copper mine in North America. Call 250-523-3352 for possible tours.

Return to Highway 5

SIDE TRIP

to Lac Le Jeune

Walloper Lake Provincial Park: 55ha. Wilderness camping only. East off Hwy 5 on Lac Le Jeune Rd. Immediately past turnoff. Rainbow trout fishing, ice fishing, cross-country skiing. Canoe and boat rentals, tackle, accommodation, camping, store.

Lac Le Jeune Provincial Park: 197ha; 144 campsites (reservations taken: call 1-800-689-9025; from the Lower Mainland or overseas, call 604-689-9025). General info: 250-851-3000. East off Lac Le Jeune Rd, 7km northwest of Hwy 5. Good rainbow trout fishing. Visitor programs, wheelchair access, boat launch, sani-station, swimming, cross-country skiing.

Lac Le Jeune Resort: Near provincial park. c/o 650 Victoria St, Kamloops, BC, V2C 2B4. 250-372-2722. Cottages, lodge,

restaurant, convention facilities, nature trails, boating, and fishing.

McConnell Lake Provincial Park: 189ha; 10 campsites. 3km north of turnoff to Lac Le Jeune Park. 250-851-3500. Informal site offers excellent fly-fishing, boating, mountain biking, cross-country skiing, motorcycle ice-racing.

It is possible to reach **Kamloops** by continuing north on Lac Le Jeune Rd for 20km from McConnell Lake. Many lakes and streams.

Return to Highway 5

Highway 1/97: Short distance southwest of Kamloops town centre, 23km north of Lac Le Jeune-Meadow Creek roads junction. West to Cache Creek; east into Kamloops.

Kamloops: (Pop. 77,421). At the end of the Coquihalla Hwy, 200km northeast of Hope. The province's 5th largest city, and its largest in terms of area: Kamloops occupies 31,000ha of Thompson River valley. The old quarter of the city, with its dozen or so well-maintained turn-of-the-century brick buildings, sits on the low banks of the South Thompson River, fronted by a lovely sand-beach park. Greater Kamloops itself is an amalgamation of more than a dozen communities separated from one another by the blue-green waters of the converging North and South Thompson rivers. The city takes its name from this convergence – *Kamloopa* is a Secwepemc native word meaning "where the

rivers meet." This is an ancient Secwepemc gathering place.

Since its establishment as a fur-trading centre in 1812, Kamloops has received travellers coming by packhorse and sternwheeler, by train, truck, and RV. It has always been a junction, an oasis for transient fur traders in the early 1800s, a depot for gold seekers in the 1860s.

As the gold rush faded in the late 1860s, wayworn miners pre-empted farmland and planted the roots of a community. By the time the Canadian Pacific Railway's first transcontinental train passed through in 1886, the government was already building a new courthouse and the locals were lobbying for Kamloops to be the new BC capital. On the old BC Fruitland estates (now North Kamloops), English gentlemen farmers and remittance men raised gamecocks to shoot. Scarlet-coated horsemen galloped about the hills to the sounds of hounds and hunting horns, chasing wild foxes. (In nearby Ashcroft, the quarry was the wily coyote.) By 1893, when the city was incorporated, it was home to 1,000 people. When North Kamloops and Kamloops amalgamated in 1967, there were 20,000 residents.

Today, many of Kamloops' nearly 80,000 residents are employed in the forest industry, in both logging and production of pulp and paper, plywood, and lumber. Large copper mines, south in the Highland Valley, are also major employers. The city is also something of a watering hole for the area's cowboys: the Thompson and nearby Okanagan valleys together support 1,100 ranches, most of them around Kamloops, where BC's cattle industry was born in the 1860s. (See *Index* for historic

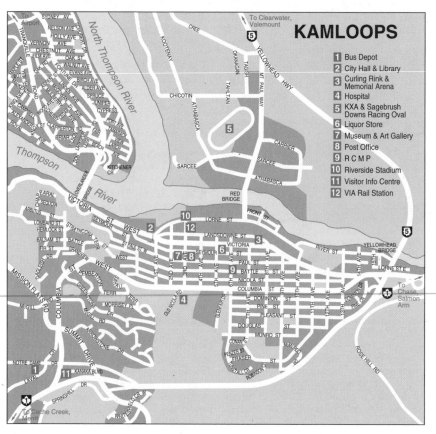

KAMLOOPS

1 Bus Depot
2 City Hall & Library
3 Curling Rink & Memorial Arena
4 Hospital
5 KXA & Sagebrush Downs Racing Oval
6 Liquor Store
7 Museum & Art Gallery
8 Post Office
9 RCMP
10 Riverside Stadium
11 Visitor Info Centre
12 VIA Rail Station

ranches: Harpers, Douglas Lake Cattle Company, Quilchena.) For those who've always dreamed of being a cowboy, the Cattle Drive, in July, has become an annual institution – during six days on old drovers' trails, greenhorns bring the cattle to Kamloops and thus become old hands.

This city, with so much growing space, has ambition. It touts itself both "the Beef Capital" *and* "the Tournament Capital of BC." There are few other towns where you find enough room for 84 baseball diamonds, 73 soccer fields, five ice arenas, 40 gymnasiums, seven golf courses, 53 tennis courts, and the 5,000-seat Riverside Coliseum.

The rolling uplands surrounding the city are a mix of forests and grasslands, with the Coast Mountains in the distant west and the Shuswap Highland in the east. At hand are eerily shaped hills and hoodoos; scorched monoliths convey a feeling of otherworldly beauty.

There are some 300 lakes in the area, reckoned one of BC's best fishing centres, with steelhead, rainbow and eastern brook trout, Dolly Varden char, and kokanee. The most sought-after freshwater fish is named after the city. The Kamloops, a type of rainbow trout, has enticed anglers from around the world. It has been introduced as a sport fish across North America and in New Zealand, Africa, Australia, South America, Japan and southern Asia, Europe, and Hawaii.

Rainbow are stocked in lakes across BC and while the average size is 0.5kg, it is still fairly common for fishermen to land rainbows of about 2.5kg. These feisty fish are taken by all types of anglers, particularly fly-fishermen. There are dozens of lodges and fishing resorts, and many operators belong to the BC Interior Fishing Resort Operators' Association, Box 3301, Kamloops, BC, V2C 6B9. Information centres can help. Or write Thompson Okanagan Tourism Association, p.142.

Skiing is also popular. For info on Sun Peaks Resort, 53km north of Kamloops, see *Kamloops to Jasper National Park*, p.177.

Horseback-riding trips are offered by local stables. Check with info Centre.

Kamloops Information: Info Centre, 1290 W Trans-Canada Hwy (Exit 368), Kamloops, BC, V2C 6R3. 250-374-3377; 1-800-662-1994. Exit 368 off W Trans-Canada Hwy; near Aberdeen Mall. Mon-Fri, early Sept-June 30; daily, July and Aug.

Kamloops Airport: North side of Thompson River, 7km east of town centre. Served by major airlines.

■ **Secwepemc Heritage Park and Museum:** 355 Yellowhead Hwy, Kamloops, BC, V2H 1H1. 250-828-9801. On banks of South Thompson River, on Kamloops Indian Band reserve. 4ha of "living laboratory," museum, university, cultural and public education centre with mandate to bring Secwepemc or Shuswap culture to the world. (Shuswap is an English derivation of Secwepemc, pronounced she-whep-m.) These people have occupied the vast territory from Kamloops north to Soda Creek, east to the Rockies, and west to the Fraser River for thousands of years. The Kamloops Band is one of 17 contemporary Secwepemc bands. The Heritage Park features an archaeo-

logical site – a winter village used by the Secwepemc people 1,200-2,400 years ago, and a reconstructed winter village showing housing over five periods, from 5,000 years ago to the late 19th century. There are also exhibits of native food plants, a salmon-fishing station, native song, dance, storytelling, and theatre; salmon barbecues in a traditional summer lodge; indoor museum exhibits focusing on the Shuswap Nation; Secwepemc arts and crafts sales and demonstrations.

The Kamloops Indian Band, a prosperous community of some 800, supervises industrial parkland, agricultural and grazing lands, historic and archaeological sites extending 11km up the North Thompson and 11km up the South Thompson (13,355ha). The reserve is accessed immediately across the Red Bridge, due north of downtown Kamloops. The Secwepemc language is taught in the local Sek'Lep School. In the new housing development, streets are named Haida Way, Chilcotin Street, Dené Drive. Stop signs say *Esti'l.*

■ **St Joseph's Church:** On Kamloops Indian Band reserve. 250-828-9700. July 1-Labour Day. This little Catholic church was first built in 1846; it has been restored to 1900s period. Cemetery adjacent.

■ **Kamloops Museum and Archives:** 207 Seymour St. 250-828-3576. Tues-Sat, 9:30-4:30, year-round (extended hours in summer). History of the Kamloops region; Secwepemc First Nation culture; fur trade, pioneer, and Victorian life; industry and natural history.

■ **Kamloops Art Gallery:** 101-465 Victoria St. (Same building as library). 250-828-3543. Daily in summer; Tues-Sat off-season. Monthly exhibits, local to international.

■ **Riverside Park:** In town on south side of Thompson River. Tennis, swimming. Walking trails, rose gardens, playground, and water park.

■ **MV Wanda-Sue:** 26m sternwheeler running two-hour narrated cruises on Thompson River. 100 passengers. Licenced galley. Early May-Sept. Daily cruises, charters, group rates. Moored at the foot of 10th Ave. 250-374-7447 or 250-374-1505.

■ **Two River Junction:** At Columbo Lodge on Lorne St and Mt Paul Way. Reservations: 250-314-3939. Frontier dining and musical revue featuring local fare and history. Secwepemc First Nation arts at General Store.

■ **Tranquille Marsh:** West on Tranquille Rd from North Kamloops. 10km to marsh. Very active waterfowl habitat, especially during spring and fall migrations. Hundreds of birds, many species (trumpeter swans, Canada and snow geese, herons). Viewing from road. Short drive beyond marsh, north up Red Lake Rd to see bighorn sheep. BC Wildlife Watch viewing site.

■ **Kamloops Waterslide and RV Park:** 19km east of city on Hwy 1. May long weekend to Labour Day. Slides, hot tubs, wading pool, mini-golf. 85 RV sites, full hook-ups. 250-573-3789.

■ **Kamloops Wildlife Park:** 16km east of city on Hwy 1. 250-573-3242. Year-round. 70 local and endangered species. See p.169.

■ **City of Kamloops Fire Department Museum:** 1205 Summit Dr. 250-372-5131.

Open Mon-Fri. Tours: Tues, Thurs, 11am, noon.

■ **Rocky Mountain Rangers Museum and Archives:** 1221 McGill Rd. 250-372-7424. Inside J.R. Vicars Armoury. Fully operational reserve army regiment.

■ **Kamloops Old Courthouse Hostel:** 7 W Seymour St, Kamloops, BC, V2C 1E4. 250-828-7991. 71-bed international hostel in 1909 courthouse, with Gothic-style arches, stained-glass windows, judge's bench, jury seats, witness box, and prisoner's box. Operated by Canadian Hostelling Association, BC Region.

■ **Canadian Llama Company:** Campbell Creek Rd. 1-888-551-6148. Visit llamas daily, July-Aug.

■ **Golf: Aberdeen Hills Golf Links**, 1185 Links Way. 250-828-1149. **Dunes at Kamloops**, 652 Dunes Dr. 1-888-881-4653. **Eagle Point**, 888 Barnhartvale Rd. 1-888-863-2453. **Kamloops Golf and Country Club**, 3125 Tranquille Rd. 1-888-376-8020. **McArthur Island Golf Course**, 205 Tranquille Rd. 250-554-3211. **Mount Paul Golf Course**, 615 Mount Paul Way. 250-374-4653. **Pineridge Golf Course**, 4725 E Trans Canada Hwy. 250-573-4333. **Rivershore Golf Club**, 250-573-4622. **Wells Gray Golf Course**, 1-888-674-0009. **The Golf Centre**, 2650 Benvoulin Rd. 250-762-4653.

Lac du Bois Grasslands Protected Area: 15,000ha. No facilities (two Forest Service campgrounds just north at Pass and Isobel lakes). Situated northwest of the North Thompson and Thompson river confluence, on the edge of Kamloops. To access **eastern section**, from Hwy 1, at Kamloops take exit 374. Follow Hwy 5 north across the South Thompson River to the second set of traffic lights, turn left on Halston over the North Thompson River. At the traffic light beyond the bridge, take the feeder road on the right up to Westsyde Rd. Immediately cross over to the left-hand lane and turn straight ahead up the hill between subdivisions that soon peter out as the Lac du Bois Rd surface changes to dirt at the cattle guard. To access **western section**, take exit 369 or 374 and follow signs to the airport. From the airport continue west to Tranquille, turn right over the railway tracks, around the Tranquille Sanatorium buildings, and up a long hill. The road to Dewdrop Lake goes straight ahead along the flats, where it makes a sharp, blind, 180-degree turn. The Tranquille River canyon road continues up the hill.

Among BC's largest publicly owned grasslands. Its status as a protected area accommodates established uses – hiking, fishing, mountain biking, motorcycling, dog training, and livestock grazing. Tranquille Canyon forms a natural divide between rolling hills of the eastern section and the Tranquille River valley to the west. Here are all three types of bunch-grass communities found east of the Rockies. Also wildflowers: yellow sagebrush buttercups, biscuit root, and mariposa daisies; birds: sharp-tailed grouse, sapsuckers and hairy woodpeckers; animals: California bighorn sheep, cows. Beware of rattlesnakes. For more information contact BC Parks, Thompson River District, 250-851-3000, Kamloops Info Centre, above, or Thompson Okanagan Tourism, p.142.

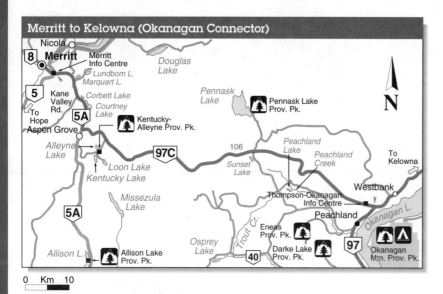

Merritt to Kelowna (Okanagan Connector)

0   Km   10

MERRITT TO KELOWNA

OKANAGAN CONNECTOR
(Highways 5A and 97C)

The 106km Connector between Merritt and Kelowna was the final phase of the Coquihalla freeway. The whole freeway brings the Lower Mainland almost two hours closer to the Okanagan Valley. Greater Vancouver, bustling with its 1.8 million inhabitants, is now less than four hours from Kelowna. The Connector's first 24km trace Hwy 5A south from Merritt. Just before the vale of Aspen Grove, the Connector veers east, tracing Hwy 97C for 82km.

As the landscape unfolds, one thing becomes starkly apparent: this new highway is out of place. It's a long slab of asphalt rolled out over a wild middle of nowhere. It seems nature has lost another battle with the human race, surrendering to $225 million worth of pavement and fences.

This is a road for people with places to go, people to see. Though it is a particularly scenic route, it is not for dawdling sightseers. The speed limit is 110km/h (in winter, heavy snowfalls and fog at higher altitudes will demand caution). Pullouts are scarce: the limited access is designed to minimize damage to the fragile alpine environment. The impact on wildlife has been softened with a $10.5 million protection system, featuring the continent's longest chain-link ungulate fence – 100km. There are 25 wildlife underpasses and an overpass for travelling deer, moose, and cattle. (The fence is expected to pay for itself by cutting insurance claims for accidents involving wildlife.)

From the rolling scrub and grasslands around Merritt, the Connector climbs across Pothole Creek into denser forests. Once over Pennask Summit, now BC's second highest highway pass (highest is Kootenay Pass, Hwy 3), the road follows Trepanier Valley, possibly the most striking vista on the route. As the road descends toward Peachland, Okanagan

Lake beckons, comfortably situated beneath Mt Acland and Okanagan Mountain.

Highways 5 and 5A/Merritt Info Centre: 2.5km south of Merritt. City of Merritt, Box 189, Merritt, BC, V1K 1B8. 250-378-2281. Fax: 250-378-6485. Daily, all year. Info about region, forestry; snack shop, curios.

Kane Valley Cross-country Ski Area: 14km beyond Info Centre. 2km from highway to first parking lot, 2km to more parking. 14 trails totalling 40km. Also self-guided BC Forest Service Demonstration Forest, a 2.5km exploration of trees, plants, undergrowth.

Corbett Lake: 15km beyond Info Centre. This reclaimed lake offers excellent trout fishing. For the Corbett Lake Country Inn: 250-378-4334.

Highway 97C: 24km beyond Info Centre. The Connector continues eastward as 97C. Hwy 5A carries on south. It's a short distance to small community of Aspen Grove, 62km to Princeton.

Loon Lake Rd: 39km beyond Info Centre. 3km to picturesque Loon Lake on good gravel road. This is the way to **Kentucky-Alleyne Provincial Park**, camping, swimming, boating, hiking to Quilchena Falls. See details, *Princeton to Kamloops*, p.180.

Elkhart Rd: 51km beyond Info Centre. Leads to only food and accommodation between Aspen Grove and Hwy 97. Lodge with dining facilities, plus cross-country skiing, snowmobiling. Also a gas station for those who found the uphill climb rather draining.

Sunset Main Rd: 63km beyond Info Centre, take Sunset Main exit. Seasonal road accesses some Thompson Okanagan highlights. Drive with caution, give right of way to logging trucks and forestry vehicles. From start, it is 1.2km to a wide spot in the road and start of a short unmarked path to Sunset Lake.

Farther along, turn left, then cross under Hwy 97C to Pennask and Hatheume lakes, or turn right to reach Peachland Creek (local signage calls it Headwaters) and Peachland Lake. A topographical map, good shock absorbers, and a full day are recommended for the journey.

Pennask Summit: (El 1,728m). 73km beyond Info Centre. BC's 2nd highest highway pass, 46m lower than Hwy 3's Salmo-Creston Skyway.

Brenda Mine: 83km beyond Info Centre. Brenda Mines Ltd operated open-pit copper and molybdenum mine here for 20 years, closing it in 1990. Smooth slope to the right is remains of tailing pond.

Wildlife Overpass: 99km beyond Info Centre. Offering safe passage for pedestrians – mostly deer and moose of Trepanier Creek area. Deer seem to be having an easier time with the concept.

Okanagan Connector Information: Okanagan Connector Info Centre. 102.5km beyond Merritt Info Centre. May to mid-Oct. Box 26042, Westbank, BC, V4T 2G3. 250-767-6677.

Highway 97: 106km beyond Merritt Info centre. South leads to communities of Peachland, Summerland, and Penticton. See p.158. Continuing east leads to Westbank, Kelowna, and Vernon. See p.160.

KAMLOOPS TO JASPER

YELLOWHEAD SOUTH HIGHWAY
(Highways 5 and 16)

The Yellowhead (Hwy 16) is a major Canadian highway beginning far beyond the eastern boundary of BC at Portage la Prairie, Manitoba. It travels west across the Prairies, through Saskatoon, Saskatchewan, and Edmonton, Alberta, entering BC by way of the Yellowhead Pass, 1,600km from its beginning. About 75km west of the pass, at Tête Jaune Cache, the Yellowhead splits, becoming Hwy 16 to the northwest and Hwy 5 southwest. Hwy 16 to the coast is known simply as the Yellowhead; Hwy 5 is the Yellowhead South.

Between Kamloops and Tête Jaune Cache, Hwy 5 runs 340km up the North Thompson River valley, from rolling grasslands through the forests of the Interior wet belt, to the Rockies. It's a long but delightful drive, with many views of the green, swirling North Thompson, one of BC's great rivers. Scenic rest areas, like little parks, are found on the riverbanks, as are hamlets and villages, all worth a stop for local colour.

From the Yellowhead South, this *Log* continues with the 75km segment of Yellowhead 16, eastward from Tête Jaune Cache to the Jasper National Park boundary.

Kamloops: (Pop. 77,421). See *Hope to Kamloops*, p.174.

Hwy 5 skirts Kamloops' core before crossing the South Thompson River about 2km east of its confluence with the North Thompson. It then swings along the western boundary of the Kamloops Indian Reserve before following the North Thompson and CNR tracks upcountry.

Kamloops Indian Reserve: (Pop. 730). Hwy 5 follows reserve's 11km western boundary. This 13,355ha of rugged landscape dominated by the Dome Hills is home of the local Secwepemc (Shuswap) people. The **Secwepemc Heritage Park**, 355 Yellow-head Hwy, offers a fascinating view of Secwepemc history and culture (see p.175).

Paul Lake Rd: East off Hwy 5, some 5.5km north of Kamloops.

SIDE TRIP

to Paul Lake Provincial Park and Harper Mountain

Paul Lake Rd traces Paul Creek through Kamloops Indian Reserve to a provincial park, a ski area, and Pinantan Lake.

Paul Lake Provincial Park: 402ha; 90 campsites, sani-station. 250-851-3000. 18km east of Hwy 5. Popular summer camping spot in forests of Douglas fir and aspen. Wheelchair access. Wildflowers, swimming, cartop-boat launch. Summer is best for squirrels and songbirds.

Harper Mountain: South off Paul Lake Rd 14km east of Hwy 5. Write 2042 Valleyview Dr, Kamloops, BC, V2C 4C5. 250-372-2119. In winter, contact the lodge at 250-573-5115. Downhill and cross-country skiing. Geared to families. 425m vertical drop. 15 runs, triple chair, T-bar, handle tow, tube park, snowboarding Day lodge, ski school. Night skiing.

Pinantan Lake: 7km beyond Paul Lake park. Accommodation, camping, fishing.

Return to Highway 5

Heffley-Louis Creek Rd: 23.5km north of Kamloops, turn east off Hwy 5.

SIDE TRIP

to Heffley Lake and Sun Peaks Resort

Heffley-Louise Creek Rd (formerly Tod Mountain Rd) leads to good fishing spots and resort area.

Heffley Lake: Resort and campground 20km east of Hwy 5. Narrow, 5km lake with island and several small bays. Good rainbow trout fishing. Ice fishing, skating, boat rentals, groceries.

Sun Peaks Resort (Formerly Tod Mountain): 24.5km east of Hwy 5 via Heffley-Louise Creek Rd, then 9km on Sun Peaks Rd. #50-3150 Creekside Way, Sun Peaks Resort, BC, V0E 1Z1. 250-578-7842 or 1-800-807-3257. BC's newest year-round resort. Six new hotels, condos, lodges, restaurants, and shopping. In summer: golf, tennis, mountain biking, horseback riding, hiking, swimming, and music festival and events. In winter: alpine and cross-country skiing, snowboard park. Offers 867m vertical drop, 64 marked trails and eight gladed areas for alpine skiers and snowboarders. Also dogsledding, snowmobiling, ice skating.

Return to Highway 5

McLure Ferry: 43.5km from Kamloops. Road off highway runs west to free reaction ferry. Crosses North Thompson River to Westside Rd which runs south to Kamloops, north to Barrière. Two cars, 12 passengers, 7am to 6:45pm. Doesn't operate in high water (June), when heavy ice flows, or when river is frozen.

McLure: (Pop. 273). 47.5km. Some tourist facilities, campground. Named for rancher John McLure, died 1933, age 84.

Fishtrap Rest Area: 50km from Kamloops. Here at Fishtrap Canyon rapids, native people once trapped spawning salmon.

Overlanders: 54km from Kamloops. Views over North Thompson River where Overlanders of 1862 made their arduous river voyage. This group of some 150 settlers travelled all the way from Ontario by ship, railway, Red River cart, and packhorse, with the assistance of native people over the Rockies, and finally, by perilous river raft. The only woman among these early settlers, Catherine O'Hare Schubert, brought her three children with her, and gave birth to her fourth just hours after reaching Kamloops.

Louis Creek: (Pop. 95). 59km from Kamloops. Lumber mill. Gas and food. Named after Louis Barrie, a prospector who found some gold here in 1860.

Barrière: (Pop. 1,653). A few hundred metres east off Hwy 5, 63km north of Kamloops. Farming and forestry town with nearby fishing, swimming, canoeing, hiking, rockhounding, snowmobiling, and ice fishing. Named in 1828, when French was the language of the fur traders, after rocks in river, which were a barrier to navigation.

Barrière Information: For brochures, write the *Thompson Valley News*, 635 Barrière Town Rd, Barrière, BC, V0E 1E0. 250-672-0013.

■ **North Thompson Museum:** 352 Lilley Rd, Barrière, V0E 1E0. Daily, early May to mid-Sept. 1930s forestry warehouse.

Hwy 5 crosses North Thompson River just north of Barrière, now tracing its west shores.

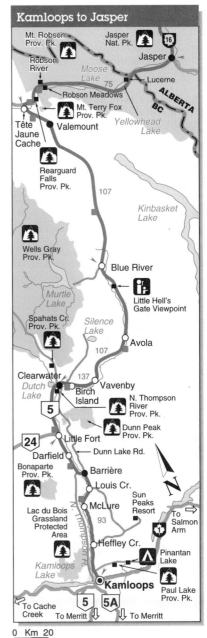

Kamloops to Jasper

0 Km 20

Barrière Lakes: Take Barrière Lakes Rd, east of Barrière. Leads to North, South, and East Barrière lakes. Excellent fishing. Cabins and campgrounds. 16km to fork in road. South leads to South Barrière Lake. Short distance beyond intersection, fork to the north leads to North Barrière Lake; main road continues to East Barrière Lake. All three within 12km of junctions.

Dunn Lake Rd: North from Barrière. A scenic 61km route, mainly gravel, between Barrière and Clearwater. Parallel Hwy 5, but on east side of North Thompson River. Windpass Rd, 33km north of Barrière, is an 8km side road west off Dunn Lake Rd, leading to reaction ferry at Little Fort. Dunn Lake Rd continues 27.5km north of Windpass Rd to Clearwater. Fishing in McTaggart, Dunn, Hallamore, and other lakes along the route.

Dunn Lake has a Forest Service campsite at north end. Dunn Lake Resort is at south end.

Westside Rd: 65km from Kamloops. Secondary route to Kamloops. Unpaved forestry road with several recreation sites.

Chinook Cove Rest Area: 68km from Kamloops. Named for a small community nearby.

Drinking Water Pullout: 73km from Kamloops. Natural spring water piped out of the mountain. Ice cold, pure, delicious.

Darfield: 80km from Kamloops. Farming community. Cattle graze peacefully as you drive by.

Little Fort: (Pop. 175). On Hwy 5, 92km from Kamloops. Accommodation, campground. Hudson's Bay Company trading fort, 1850-52. Crossroads Craft Gallery across from Payless Gas.

Little Fort Ferry: On Hwy 5 at Little Fort. Over North Thompson River to Dunn Lake Rd and Clearwater. On call between 7am-6:45pm. Ferry not in operation 11:45am-1pm or 4:45pm-6pm. Free. Five minutes. One of seven current-propelled ferries still operating in BC. Foot passengers use aerial tramway when ferry is out of service.

Highway 24: West off Hwy 5 at Little Fort. Scenic 97km route through Interlakes District to Hwy 97, 10km south of 100 Mile House. Hwy 24 and side roads lead to dozens of lakes, including Thuya Lakes, Lac Des Roches, Bonaparte, Sheridan, Eagan, Burn, Fawn, Lesser, and Bridge lakes. Fishing resorts, campgrounds; provincial park at Bridge Lake. See details in *Cariboo Country*, p. 245.

Little Fort Rest Area: At north end of the little town.

Blackpool: This hamlet just before Clearwater was named for Blackpool, England. Main attraction is Lacarya Golf Course (par 3/4), clubhouse and lounge. Store, gas, groceries, laundry, and pub.

North Thompson River Provincial Park: 125ha; 61 campsites. 250-851-3000. On Hwy 5, 118km north of Kamloops. Headquarters for Wells Gray Provincial Park. At confluence of North Thompson and Clearwater rivers. Has a children's playground named Poggy Park. Visitor centre, programs, wheelchair access, sani-station.

Clearwater: (Pop. 4,976). On Hwy 5, 122km north of Kamloops. A service centre for an area population of 7,000 and gateway to Wells Gray Provincial Park. Booming these days with new facilities and motels. People seem to have discovered Clearwater: locals moan they used to know everyone here, but not anymore. Though small, the town can be a bit confusing: it has three centres – the old

The Thompson River winds through dry benchlands near Ashcroft.

village on the flats beside the Thompson River; the new townsite on the far side of the Clearwater Bridge; and the cluster of services alongside Hwy 5. See Info Centre about whitewater river rafting, trail rides, canoe trips and rentals, hiking expeditions, backcountry chalets. Good fishing, also snowmobiling, cross-country and backcountry skiing. Plenty of accommodation.

Clearwater Information: Info Centre, Clearwater and District Chamber of Commerce, Box 1988, RR1, Clearwater, BC, V0E 1N0. On Hwy 5 (west side) at Clearwater Valley Rd. Jerry the Moose stands outside. 250-674-2646. Daily, May-Oct. Mon-Sat, Oct-April. This is also information centre for Wells Gray Provincial Park. Gift shop; topographical maps. Two good books: *Exploring Wells Gray Park*, by Roland Neave, and *Nature Wells Gray*, by Cathie Hickson and Trevor Goward.

■ **Clearwater Ski Hill:** On Dunn Lake Rd within town area. Vertical drop more than 300m, five runs, T-bar, night skiing.

■ **Dutch Lake Resort and RV Park:** In town. Swimming, playground, paddling, rainbow trout. Local anglers' club has built trout spawning channel onto the landlocked lake, putting over 100,000 fry back into it. Open for public viewing.

■ **Yellowhead Museum:** From Info Centre turn onto Clearwater Valley Rd (road to Wells Gray). 6km from highway follow sign. RR1, Box 1778, Clearwater, BC, V0E 1N0. 250-674-3660. On one of few original homesteads in area. Open by appointment. Pioneer and native artifacts, natural history displays. Good area information.

■ **Clearwater Trout Hatchery:** 40 Old N. Thompson Hwy. About 1km west of Hwy 5 at Clearwater. 250-674-2580. One of five fisheries operated by the provincial Ministry of Environment. Together, these hatcheries each year stock 1,100-1,200 lakes from southern Vancouver Island to the BC/Yukon border with 10-12 million kokanee salmon and rainbow trout. Ninety-five percent of the stock comes from wild eggs, not brood. Best time

to see fry is Jan-Sept. BC Wildlife Watch Viewing Site.

■ **Wells Gray Adventures:** Several companies offer self-guided to fully-guided adventures. Ask at Info Centre.

Clearwater Valley Rd: North off Hwy 5 at Clearwater. 37km, paved, to main entrance of Wells Gray Provincial Park.

SIDE TRIP

to Wells Gray Provincial Park

After leaving Hwy 5 and Clearwater, road climbs sharply up onto the Spahats Plateau before levelling out.

Wells Gray Park (Spahats Creek Campground): 270ha; 23 campsites. 250-851-3000. 11km north of Clearwater, en route to Wells Gray Park. From road into park you can see where Spahats Creek has carved a 122m deep canyon through layers of lava. Ten-minute walk from parking lot to views of canyon walls and 61m Spahats Falls.

Trophy Mountain Road and Trophy Mountain Recreation Area: 12km from Clearwater turn east. Gravel road with steep grades. Watch for junction 4km from Clearwater Valley Rd. North leads 9km to Trophy Meadows Trail and Trophy Skyline Trail; straight ahead 9km more brings you to start of 52 Ridge Trail. En route, you will pass through a vast clearcut made in the '70s that has failed to regenerate. Trophy Mountain Buffalo Ranch is a real buffalo ranch offering cabins, RV camping, mountain biking, horseback riding, canoe rentals, buffalo meat. 250-674-3095.

Helmcken Falls Lodge: 35km from Clearwater. Just before park entrance. Box 239, Clearwater, BC, V0E 1N0. 250-674-3657. Impressive 1948 lodge is closely identified with park. 21-room hotel, campsites, hook-ups, hiking, horseback riding, cross-country skiing. Dining room.

Wells Gray Provincial Park: 529,748ha; 122 sites in four campgrounds, 25 wilderness camping areas. Campsites are: Pyramid Mountain, 50 sites, 43km from Clearwater; Falls Creek, 41 sites, and Clearwater Lake, 32 sites, 70km from Clearwater; and Mahood Lake, 32 sites, 88km east of 100 Mile House (reached from Hwy 97). Accommodation and services available. Interpretive programs run mid-June to late Aug. Evening programs at the picnic shelter between Clearwater Lake and Falls Creek campgrounds. Boat launch.

A vast wilderness, Wells Gray is one of BC's largest, most spectacular parks. High in the Cariboo Mountains, scenery includes alpine meadows and flowers, snowcapped peaks and glaciers, major lakes, rivers and waterfalls, small lakes and streams, extinct volcanos, lava beds, and mineral springs.

Hiking trails range from half-hour nature walks to week-long backpacking excursions. Extensive canoe trips on Clearwater, Azure, Mahood, and Murtle lakes. This large park is home to many big animals, including moose and mule deer. Osprey are seen at Clearwater Lake, June-Sept. Chinook salmon spawn in the Mahood River, Aug-Oct. More than 40 butterfly species have been recorded.

Wells Gray Provincial Park Information: In Clearwater, or write to BC Parks, Zone Supervisor, Box 4516, RR2, Clearwater, BC, V0E 1N0. 250-587-6150. Topographic map of Wells Gray Provincial Park (PS-WG3) at a scale of 1:125,000 can be purchased at Clearwater Info Centre.

Wells Gray Park Highlights

■ **Dawson Falls:** 5km north of park entrance and information board. Murtle River, here 91m wide, drops 18m, miniature version of Niagara Falls. Short trail to viewpoints.
■ **The Mushbowl:** 6km from park entrance. The Murtle River has carved huge holes in the rock of the narrow gorge: a bridge over the river provides best view of The Mushbowl and Devil's Punch Bowl.
■ **Helmcken Falls:** 10km from park entrance. Fourth largest waterfalls in Canada, park's most famous wonder. Short walk from parking lot to viewpoints. Murtle River plunges over a sheer 137m precipice.
■ **Ray Farm and Mineral Spring:** 19km from park entrance. 15-minute walk to historic homestead created by John Bunyan Ray in the 1920s. Old farmhouse, barns. A 30-minute trail starting to the left of the farm leads to Ray Mineral Spring, a natural cold spring. Bring a cup and juice crystals for a fizzy drink. (Alternate route is to drive 1.7km north to next parking lot and walk 15 minutes to spring). Also, a two-hour loop trail.
■ **Bailey's Chute:** 21km from park entrance. 15-minute trail to chute: a standing wave created by white water crashing into a broad pool. Big chinook salmon jumping late Aug to mid-Sept. Chute named after Jim Bailey, who designed 1949 truss bridge over The

Mushbowl. Bailey drowned in 1952 when his boat overturned in the chute.
■ **Murtle Lake:** Only accessible by vehicle from Blue River, 105.5km northeast of Clearwater on Hwy 5. It's a 26km drive on a rough, narrow gravel road, then a 2.5km portage from parking lot to Murtle Lake Lagoon. This is the largest lake in North America set aside for paddlers only: no motors allowed; no dogs permitted. Sandy beaches, hiking trails, fishing, beautiful sunsets. Canoe permits must be purchased in Blue River.

Return to Highway 5

Silence Lake Rd: Northeast off Hwy 5, just east of Clearwater before Raft River Bridge. Winding 35km logging road along Raft River to Silence Lake.

Birch Island: (Pop. 250). 12km from Clearwater. This small farming and logging village, named after an island in the river, was once the largest community in the North Thompson region. Birch Island was also the site of controversy when a large uranium deposit was discovered, but a moratorium was placed on mining. Dee's General Store, open for 25 years, has gas, groceries, hunting and fishing licences.

Birch Island Rest Area: 12km from Clearwater. Overlooks river valley.

Cross one-way bridge over North Thompson to take secondary route, Lost Creek Rd, on south side of the river. Paved for 14km. Nearing Vavenby, look for Molliet sheep ranch, one of Canada's biggest. Visitors welcome.

Vavenby: (Pop. 396). 26km from Clearwater, then northeast a short distance off Hwy 5. Vavenby General Store – gas, deli, groceries. Tours available at Slocan and Weyerhauser sawmills. Nearby, Vavenby Trail Rides offers horseback riding at Shook Ranch, a real working ranch: 250-676-9598.

Wire Cache Rest Area: 54km from Clearwater. Named because a large amount of telegraph wire was abandoned here around 1874, when a contract to build a telegraph link between Cache Creek and Edmonton was cancelled. Amenities include washroom with running water, parking and roadways accommodating over-length vehicles, children's play structure, picnic area, information kiosk, and riverside walkway.

Avola: (Pop. 160). 68km from Clearwater. Service centre with accommodation. The Log Inn – you can't miss it, it's the only one there – bills itself "The Largest and Friendliest Pub in Avola." Pub is watering hole for loggers, rail workers, and farmers from around the area. A few steps up the street is another log structure, formerly a one-room schoolhouse, which now houses the Avola Library. Main street peters out along banks of North Thompson. Definitely a photogenic stop. Avola is named after a village in Sicily.

Little Hell's Gate Viewpoint: 85km from Clearwater. Follow signs. 3km off Hwy 5 to views of Upper North Thompson River where it narrows to a 4.5m gorge. Open May-Oct. Road *not* accessible to trailers.

Messiter Summit: 86.5km from Clearwater. Views of North Thompson River valley. Highway between Avola and Valemount crosses countryside with a parkland feeling, despite the odd, jarring clearcut to remind you it isn't protected.

Blue River: (Pop. 283). On Hwy 5, 107km from Clearwater. A logging and tourism town and a base for heli-skiers flying into the Cariboo and Monashee mountains. Eleanor Lake, within the town, is site of a campground and Mike Wiegele Heli-Ski Village. Cross-country skiing and ice fishing at Eleanor Lake. Swimming, hiking, and fishing in summer. Offers only road access into Murtle Lake area (above).

Blue River Airport: East off Hwy 5, 1km north of town centre.

Wells Gray Provincial Park (Murtle Lake): 108km from Clearwater (1km north of Blue River), rough gravel road leads 24km (45 minutes) to parking lot at park boundary. Hilly 2.5km trail to Murtle Lake, a hiking and canoeing area (see above).

Thunder River Rest Area: 122km from Clearwater. West into a delightful site: tables beside the rushing Thunder River.

Valemount: (Pop. 1,128). On Hwy 5, 195km from Clearwater. Valemount, where the Cariboo, Monashee, and Rocky mountains meet, is a logging village with good accommodation, campgrounds, and a range of facilities. Nearby is northern end of Kinbasket Lake's Canoe Reach, and start of an extensive boating area (see *BC Rockies*, p.221). Information centre can help with fishing, trail riding, heli-skiing, and snowmobiling trips.

Valemount Information: Information centre, Village of Valemount, Box 168, Valemount, BC, V0E 2Z0. 250-566-4846. On Hwy 5, south side of town. Seasonal.

Valemount Airport: On Hwy 5, about 1km north of village centre.

■ **Robert W. Starratt Wildlife Sanctuary:** On Hwy 5 on south side of town centre. 200ha of marshland. Trails, viewing towers. BC Wildlife Watch viewing site.
■ **George Hicks Regional Park:** On Hwy 5, across from business centre. Parking for RVs, buses, cars. Viewing bridge for chinook salmon run. Trails and picnics. BC Wildlife Watch viewing site.
■ **Robson Helimagic Inc:** Hwy 5 N. Box 18, Valemount, BC, V0E 2Z0. 250-566-4700. Heli-hiking, heli-skiing, heli-sightseeing. Standard or custom tours of Mt Robson, Cariboo Mountains, Robson Valley, and more.

Mt Terry Fox Provincial Park: 1,930ha. East off Hwy 5, 202.5km from Clearwater. Drive 2km to parking area and trailhead for

179

steep, strenuous, but worthwhile 7km hike. Spectacular alpine views. Undeveloped park with 2,650m peak named in honour of one-legged runner who died of bone cancer before completing his historic cross-Canada run.

Mt Terry Fox Viewpoint and Rest Area: 203km from Clearwater, west off Hwy 5.

Jackman Flats: 211km from Clearwater. For botany enthusiasts, signed interpretive trails through area with unusual flora.

Highway 16 (Tête Jaune Cache): At end of Hwy 5, 216km from Clearwater; 338km from Kamloops. *Log* now follows Hwy 16 east to Alberta border, which is also west boundary of Jasper National Park. (Yellowhead continues on to Portage la Prairie, Manitoba, a distance of 1,700km.)

Westward, the Yellowhead (Hwy 16) travels more than 1,000km to its end on the Queen Charlotte Islands (see *Northern BC*).

For details on Tête Jaune Cache, see *Northern BC*, p.266.

The 75km of Hwy 16 from Tête Jaune Cache to Jasper Park's boundary climbs the Rocky Mountain pass for which the highway is named. Although the Yellowhead Pass, 80km east of Tête Jaune Cache, reaches an elevation of 1,131m, the mountains that surround it exceed 3,000m. Scenery is extraordinary, with wintry peaks, glaciers, and cold, turquoise rivers. Journey takes in Mount Robson Provincial Park and Alberta's Jasper National Park.

A powerful visual experience awaits the lucky traveller heading east from Tête Jaune Cache. Around a bend near Mt Terry Fox Provincial Park, suddenly a titanic mountain rises up, blotting out the horizon and dwarfing neighbouring and otherwise impressive peaks. It's Mt Robson, biggest in the Canadian Rockies, and BC's most storied mountain. Often, however, this massif is shrouded by cloud and invisible to travellers going by road or VIA Rail's *Skeena* passenger train.

Tête Jaune Cache Rest Area: 1km east of Tête Jaune Cache junction. Overlooks Fraser River. Interpretive sign commemorating Terry Fox.

Rearguard Falls Provincial Park: 48ha. On Hwy 16, 4km east of Tête Jaune Cache junction. The 10m falls are final obstacle to salmon that migrate about 1,200km up the Fraser River from the sea. Viewpoints, hiking, fishing.

Mt Terry Fox Rest Area: 7.5km east of Tête Jaune Cache junction. Provides telescope to view Mt Terry Fox in Selwyn Range of the Rockies. Some of the best views of Mt Robson. Amenities include washroom with running water, parking and roadway accommodating over-length vehicles, and picnic area. Interpretive sign commemorating Terry Fox.

Mount Robson Provincial Park: 219,829ha; 180 campsites in three campgrounds (reservations taken: call 1-800-689-9025; from the Lower Mainland or overseas, call 604-689-9025). General info: 250-566-4325. The western entrance is on Hwy 16, 14km east of Tête Jaune Cache junction. The eastern entrance is at the BC/Alberta border, 75km east of Tête Jaune Cache junction. Provincial park campsites are: Robson Meadows, 125 sites, and Robson River, 19 sites, both near western entrance, on Hwy 16, 17km east of Tête Jaune Cache; Lucerne, 36 sites, is on Yellowhead Lake about 10km west of Alberta boundary.

Mt Robson, at 3,954m the highest peak in the BC Rockies, dominates the western entrance to the park. The park is bordered on the east by the Continental Divide and Jasper National Park. The rugged snowcapped mountains, wandering valleys, steep-sided canyons, glacier-fed lakes and streams are the birthplace of the Fraser, Canada's third longest river, BC's longest. From its headwaters here the Fraser flows 1,368km to the sea at Vancouver.

Yellowhead Pass, el 1,131m, is the eastern entrance to the park. Much wildlife: moose, mountain goats, mule deer, elk, caribou, grizzly and black bears, pikas, marmots, squirrels, chipmunks, muskrats, beavers, and more than 170 bird species. A hiker's paradise with an extensive network of trails – from a few hours to a few days – to good campsites and viewpoints. Visitor centre, programs, wheelchair access, boat launch, sani-station.

Mount Robson Provincial Park Information: Visitor centre is at Mt Robson Viewpoint 2km from western entrance. Displays on natural and human history, audio-visual programs. Service station, cafe, and store adjacent. Daily mid-May to Sept 30. Write BC Parks, Park Supervisor, Box 579, Valemount, BC, V0E 2Z0. 250-566-4325.

■ **Mount Robson Adventure Holidays:** At Mt Robson Viewpoint. Box 687, Valemount, BC, V0E 2Z0. 250-566-4386. Guided canoeing and hiking, family rafting trips, nature tours, 18-hole nature-themed mini-golf.

Moose Lake and Marsh: Boat launch and picnic facilities at east end, 43.5km from Tête Jaune Cache junction.

Yellowhead Lake: Boat launch, picnic facilities, and viewpoint at east end, 69.5km from junction.

Yellowhead Pass: El 1,131m. 77km from Tête Jaune Cache junction. BC/Alberta border, and division between Jasper National and Mt Robson Provincial parks.

Time Zone: 77km from Tête Jaune Cache junction. As you cross BC/Alberta border, set your time one hour ahead.

Jasper National Park: See *Alberta Rockies*, p.235.

HIGHWAY 5A

Highway 5A, running a total of 183km from Princeton to Kamloops, is often used by travellers from the south Okanagan. Those coming from the Lower Mainland, wanting to save the $10 toll on the Coquihalla Hwy, drive the Hope-Princeton (Hwy 3), then take Hwy 5A north to Kamloops. The route is 118km longer, but avoids the long, steep hills of the Coquihalla.

Princeton: (Pop. 2,796). See details in *Princeton to Christina Lake*, p.147.

Highways 3 and 5A: Hwy 3 (the Crowsnest) from Princeton goes through Manning Provincial Park to Hope, then east to the south Okanagan. Hwy 5A joins Hwy 5, the Coquihalla, at Merritt, 40km north of Princeton. Hwys 5 and 5A continue on their respective journeys from Merritt to Kamloops.

Coalmont Rd: West off Hwy 5A, 1km north of Princeton. Alternate 70km back road toward, but not to, Merritt. Passes community of Coalmont and Otter Lake Provincial Park. Rejoins Hwy 5A about 36km south of Merritt. For details, see *Princeton to Christina Lake*, p.147.

Missezula Lake: East off Hwy 5A onto logging road 4.5km from Princeton. Winding 10km to small lakes and campsite at Missezula Lake. Trout and kokanee.

Five Mile Chain Lakes: East off Hwy 5A, 8km north of Princeton. A 34km back road to chain of excellent trout-fishing lakes, including Chain, Link, Osprey, and Thirsk.

One Mile Chain Lakes: Five-lake chain (McCaffrey, Laird, Dry, Borgeson, and Allison) begins 18km from Princeton. Some have eastern brook trout. Several other small fishing lakes along Hwy 5A.

Allison Lake Provincial Park: 23ha; 24 campsites. 250-494-6500. 28.5km from Princeton.

Gilliford Lake Rest Area: 36km from Princeton. Picnic tables beside the lake, on a bend in the highway.

Coalmont Rd: 52km from Princeton, west off Hwy 5A. Other end of 70km back road mentioned above. To Otter Lake Provincial Park (details, p.148).

Kentucky-Alleyne Provincial Park: 144ha; 63 campsites. 250-494-6500. East off Hwy 5A onto Loon Lake Rd, 55.5km from Princeton. Popular destination. Beautiful blue-green lakes, fishing, boating, hiking, swimming, waterfowl, birdwatching. Hike to Quilchena Falls through open grasslands.

Corbett and Courtney Lakes: 69km from Princeton. Site of 123ha ranch-turned-resort: Corbett Lake Country Inn: 250-378-4334. Fishing, canoeing, hiking, trail riding, cross-country skiing. Boat launch nearby.

Kane Valley: West on Kane Valley Rd, a few hundred metres north of Corbett Lake. One of Interior BC's best cross-country ski areas. 14 trails totalling 40km.

Marquart and Lundbom Lakes: East off Hwy 5A, 77km north of Princeton. Just off highway. Snowmobile reserve with informal trails. Fishing and camping in summer.

Sugarloaf Mountain: East off Hwy 5A, 80km north of Princeton. Superb hiking around 1,364m peak. 4km to Hamilton Lake. For scenic back-road route to western end of Nicola Lake, take northwest turn just over 1km from Hwy 5A and drive about 9km.

Highway 5: Southwest off Hwy 5A, 84km from Princeton, Coquihalla Hwy runs 115km to Hope.

Merritt: (Pop. 6,253). On Hwy 5A, 89.5km from Princeton. See *Hope to Kamloops*, p.173.

Highway 8: 65km route west from Merritt to Hwy 1 at Spences Bridge. See p. 167.

Highway 5 (Coquihalla): 3km north of Merritt, Coquihalla Hwy runs north 80km to Kamloops. Hwy 5A continues past Nicola Lake to Kamloops, 91km.

Nicola Ranch: On Hwy 5A, 7km north of Merritt. 1-888-798-7388. The community of "Nicola on the Lake" was established here in 1864, and by the turn of the century, its population was about 1,000. Today, the historic townsite is part of the Nicola Ranch, one of BC's largest working ranches. It is also home to Canadian Fallow Deer Farms, North America's largest deer farm. For travellers, there is a B&B and accommodation in two historic buildings. Private fishing lakes, horseback riding, the townsite, and deer farm tours. Gift shop and petting zoo.

Nicola Lake Rest Area: About 13km from Merritt. Boat launch.

Monck Provincial Park: 87ha; 71 campsites, sani-station. 250-851-3000. Northeast off Hwy 5A at western side of Nicola Lake, 22km east of Merritt. Family vacation destination. Excellent beaches. Boating, fishing, swimming, paddling, hiking, windsurfing, nature programs, playground, wheelchair access.

Quilchena: (Pop. 24). On Hwy 5A, 23km from Merritt. Overlooking Nicola Lake in the rolling grasslands that were once considered to be Nicola Valley gold. The **Quilchena Cattle Company** is the largest

working ranch in BC still accommodating guests. 250-378-4449. The **Quilchena Hotel**, established 1908 by the Guichon brothers, blends elegance with unpretentious hospitality, maintaining its Old West charm with a saloon (complete with brass foot rails, spittoons, antique cash register, and bullet hole – reputedly placed by a frustrated bar guest in 1912), sitting parlour, iron beds, washstands. General store nearby. Trail rides, hay rides, golf, fishing, hiking. 250-378-2611.

Ranching is still an important part of the local economy. There are dozens of ranches around here, and hundreds of people, real cowboys, who make their living by riding the range. During the summer months some of the cowboys, and most of the cows, are up in higher country taking advantage of the shadier woodlands. They come back down in the fall, and you're more likely to see them then.

Douglas Lake Rd: Southeast off Hwy 5A, 27.5km from Merritt. Leisurely 80km backcountry route from Nicola Lake to tiny community of Westwold (p.166) on Hwy 97. Route passes through grassland and rangeland dotted with lakes, wetlands, and marshes. Many species of waterfowl nest here or migrate through April-Sept. Late spring and summer bring out the songbirds: mountain bluebirds, northern shrike, horned larks, and water pipits. Osprey, eagles, hawks, and falcons are most visible May-Aug. Lots of Columbian ground squirrels. Excellent fishing in Chapperon, Rush, and Salmon lakes.

Douglas Lake Cattle Company: 20km along Douglas Lake Rd, to ranch. Established in 1884, this is Canada's largest cattle company, running up to 20,000 head of cattle over 200,000ha. Offers privately guided day-tours incorporating routine of company into itinerary. Also overview of ranch and exploration of backcountry, cow camps, areas of historic and scenic interest, wildflowers, wildlife. General store, lodge, and resort with boat rentals. Call ahead: 250-350-3344. Call 1-800-663-4838 for fishing resort information.

Peter Hope Lake: East off Hwy 5A, 44km from Merritt. 7km to lake. Hiking, cross-country skiing. Trail circles lake. Accommodation, camping. Named for a prospector and guide of the 1860s.

Stump Lake: Northeast off Hwy 5A, 52km from Merritt. Cross-country skiing at Mineral Hill, overlooking lake. Site of annual Force Ten Summer Classic, a major sailing event. Windsurfing, ice fishing. Migration path: about 20 species of waterfowl, as many as 5,000 birds some days. Access to Stump Lake's northwest shore on Hwy 5A. First in a string of lakes: Tullee, Napier, Richie, Trapp, Shumway. All good fishing spots.

Roche Lake: East off Hwy 5A, 70km from Merritt. 10km to cluster of fishing lakes – Roche, Horseshoe, John Frank, Bulman, Frisken. Accommodation, camping.

Princeton to Kamloops

Kamloops City Limits: 87km from Merritt. Pullout for visitors map, right. Kamloops is a big city; you're still in the southern suburbs – Aberdeen to the west, South Sahali Summit to the east. See city details in *Hope to Kamloops*, p.174

Highway 1/97: 92km from Merritt, west off Hwy 5A. 6km to Hwy 5 (Coquihalla) and fast route south 200km to Hope. 78.5km on Hwy 1/97 to Cache Creek. See *Lytton to Kamloops*, p.167.

Downtown Kamloops: 95km from Merritt. From here, Hwys 1/97 lead east toward Shuswap Lake. See *Kamloops to Sicamous*, p.169. Hwy 5, the Yellowhead, runs north to Tête Jaune Cache. See *Kamloops to Jasper*, p.176.

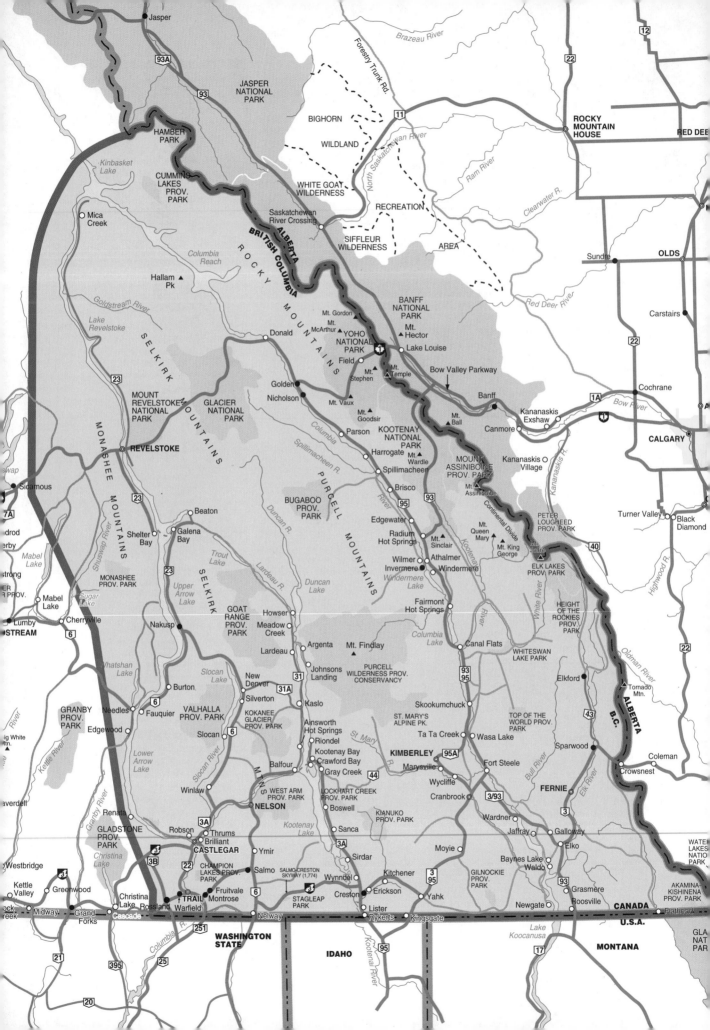

BRITISH COLUMBIA ROCKIES

INSIDE THE MOUNTAIN WALLS

"What is it about the Kootenays that appeals so much to strangers; why do they, like me, feel so at home here? Few people can say. Perhaps it's the land itself: it's so old, and yet parts of it are so young. There are some who say it speaks to people on an unconscious level. I can't tell you – the things that happen in these mountains."

– Wayne Choquette, Archaeologist

The British Columbia Rockies region covers the entire southeast corner of British Columbia, from Hamber Provincial Park in the north to the Arrow lakes and Lake Revelstoke to the west. Technically speaking, the Rocky Mountains themselves are only found east of a great rift valley that runs almost the full length of BC. The Rocky Mountain Trench, in its southern reaches, gives rise to two of the continents great rivers – the Columbia and the Kootenay. And it is for the latter that the region is also often referred to as "the Kootenays."

West of the trench — but part of the BC Rockies region — are the Monashee, Selkirk, and Purcell ranges. This rugged concentration of peaks, known collectively as the Columbia Mountains, would be the glory of most alpine nations. The Rockies, however, are even more glorious. Mount Columbia, straddling the BC/Alberta border at the heart of the Columbia Icefield, soars to 3,747 metres; Mount Clemenceau and Mount Assiniboine both rise above 3,600 metres. (Mount Robson, the highest point in the Canadian Rockies at 3,954 metres, is in the Thompson Okanagan region farther north.)

The BC Rockies region is BC's undisputed mountain playground. Nowhere else in Canada can one find such a concentration of world-famous skiing and snowboarding opportunities. Ski resorts and downhill facilities flourish near the communities of Revelstoke, Golden, Invermere, Fairmont Hot Springs, Nelson, Rossland, Kimberley and Fernie. A dozen helicopter and snowcat operators and lodges offer some of the planet's finest powder skiing at remote hideaways in the Selkirk and Purcell mountains.

But the BC Rockies are more than just a winter wonderland. Maps of the region are richly decorated with green patches, all of which represent parks. Four major national parks — Mount Revelstoke, Glacier, Kootenay, and Yoho — are accessible from Trans-Canada Highway 1 and Highway 93. Other huge preserves cozy up to the border from the Alberta side. Most of the larger BC provincial parks, such as Mount Assiniboine, Height of the Rockies, Elk Lakes, Top of the World, Akamina-Kishinena, Valhalla, Goat Range, Kokanee Glacier, Kianuko, Monashee, Bugaboo Glacier, West Arm, and St Mary's, plus the gigantic Purcell Wilderness Conservancy, are in harder-to-reach areas. Many have been established recently as part of the provincial government's far-sighted Protected Areas Strategy, which aims to set aside 12 percent of BC as parkland and wildlife reserve by the 21st century.

Camping, hiking, canoeing and wildlife viewing are just some of the attractions for

Winding along Highway 3, through the Elk Valley.

park visitors. For those who prefer a little more grooming in their great outdoors, the BC Rockies region also sports 17 full-length golf courses, plus one excellent nine-holer. Many long-established golf clubs, including such championship layouts as Castlegar, Revelstoke, Cranbrook, and the Springs at Radium, have been joined in recent years by a slew of outstanding new designs: Granite Point at Nelson, Kimberley's Trickle Creek, Mountainside at Fairmont, and Greywolf at Panorama.

While tourism has become a major industry in the BC Rockies, the area's fabled mineral resources, which lured early visitors to the mountains, continue to generate a living for many residents. Before the miners opened up the region in the late 1800s, these mountains provided home and livelihood for the Ktunaxa (or Kootenay) aboriginal people. They knew the secret mountain passes; navigated the rivers and the long, narrow lakes; endured winters in deep valleys that rarely saw December sunshine, and survived the "little ice age" of the 17th and 18th centuries, when glaciers returned again.

The region's complex and dramatic river system confused the earliest European explorers. North America's fourth-longest river, the Columbia, rises in Columbia Lake, near Fairmont Hot Springs. From there it flows northwest for 275 kilometres before making a great turn and heading due south through the Arrow lakes and into Washington State on its 2,000-kilometre journey to the Pacific. The Kootenay, meanwhile, a major tributary of the Columbia, rises a mountain away from its parent and flows south, missing Columbia Lake by two scant kilometres, then looping through Montana and Idaho before returning to BC and entering Kootenay Lake. The Kootenay River finally joins the Columbia at Castlegar, just downstream from an old suspension bridge raised by the Doukhobors, Russian pacifists who, in the early 1900s, built dozens of co-operative villages in the region.

David Thompson of the fur-trading North West Company struggled over Howse Pass and down to the Columbia River in 1807 – the first white man to cross the Canadian Rockies. Travelling with eight companions, his aboriginal wife and three small children, he established, with the help of the Ktunaxa people, Kootenae House on Windermere Lake. From this post he set out on the many difficult journeys that would become the basis for his remarkably accurate maps of the Northwest.

In 1863, gold was discovered on Wild Horse Creek, 25 kilometres northeast of Cranbrook. An instant town of 1,500 souls, called Fisherville, soon emerged there — and soon disappeared. The brief gold rush did, however, persuade surveyor Edgar Dewdney to extend a 400-kilometre trail from Hope to the East Kootenays. Not far from Wild Horse, where the St Mary joins the Kootenay River, John Galbraith started a cable ferry service that became the nucleus of the small settlement of Fort Steele. Largely abandoned when the railroad bypassed it in 1898, Fort Steele flourishes today as an historic site – a reconstructed heritage town.

The mineral frenzy in the region continued, but with less glamorous substances than gold. Kimberley's Sullivan Mine, by 1937 the largest zinc-lead-silver operation in the world, continues to produce, but is slated to close in the year 2001. To the northeast, near the Alberta border, the Elk Valley has become BC's most important coal-mining district. In the West Kootenays, major gold, silver, and copper discoveries in the 1880s and 1890s resulted in the appearance of many historic towns, including Nelson, Rossland, Kaslo, and Slocan. Other former bustling communities, though, such as Sandon, Zincton, and Camborne, are now just ghostly presences.

The main urban centres in the BC Rockies today are Cranbrook, population 18,000, and Fernie, Kimberley, Revelstoke, Trail, Nelson, and Castlegar — towns with 5,000 to 10,000 inhabitants. Beyond these and smaller human enclaves, nature still reigns supreme. The Rockies remain a vital sanctuary for such large mammals as elk, mule, and white-tailed deer, moose, black and grizzly bears, coyotes, and wolves. More than 60 percent of BC's avian species can be seen in the open parklands of the Rocky Mountain Trench, an important flyway for migratory birds. The region's mountainsides are coated with larch, aspen, and lodgepole pine, as well as with more familiar trees, such as red cedar, hemlock, subalpine fir, and Engelmann spruce.

Above the forested slopes are the eternal mountains. Some rock formations in the Selkirk and Purcell ranges are 1.6 billion years old, ancient in geographic terms. But the Rockies are young, their wavelike sedimentary layers thrust up a mere 60 million years ago by vast tectonic movements in the earth's crust. Much eroded since then by glaciers, they contain, ironically, some of the oldest known signs of life. Near Field, the remarkable fossils of the Burgess Shale, with imprints of soft-bodied sponges, worms, and multi-eyed and tentacled "sea monsters," date back 515 million years to the Cambrian period. Everywhere in this part of the province, it seems, the snowbound peaks attract the eye, lift the heart, and challenge the imagination.

INFORMATION

Tourism Rockies: Box 10, Kimberley, BC, V1A 2Y5. 250-427-4838 or 1-800-661-6603 Fax: 250-427-3344. At 1905 Warren Ave in Kimberley. E-mail: bcrockies@cyberlink.bc.ca. Addresses and telephone numbers of information centres are in *Logs* with write-ups on each community.

TRANSPORTATION

Getting into, around, and out of the BC Rockies is much easier than it was in the old days. There is an excellent highway system complete with six inland ferries – all of them free – as well as airline and bus service.

Information centres throughout the BC Rockies Region can help with boat, canoe, kayak, bicycle, and moped rentals.

By Road

Most travellers make their way into the BC Rockies region by road. One of BC's most intricate highway systems links major centres and most smaller communities, not to mention several ghost towns. There are no freeways here yet — nothing wider than two lanes, and occasionally just one lane fitted between lake and mountain. Winter snow storms or icey conditions can cause temporary problems; however, roads are promptly plowed and sanded. Much is accessible by logging roads, most of which are open to the public.

The Crowsnest Hwy 3 skirting the US border is one of two major "all-Canadian" routes entering from the east and west. The Trans-Canada Hwy (1) delivers travellers to the region's northern reaches. The BC Rockies Region is within a day's drive from either Vancouver or Calgary. (It is 529km from Creston to Calgary, for example.)

Travellers from the US (via Washington and Idaho) have the following seven entrance points to choose from: Midway, Carson/Grand Forks, Cascade/Christina Lake, Paterson/ Rossland, Waneta/Trail, Nelway/Salmo, and Rykerts. Border crossings are open 8am-midnight, except Midway and Waneta/Trail (9am-5pm). The nearest 24-hour border crossing is Kingsgate, situated at the eastern corner of the region.

Bus Lines

■ **Alpha Omega Tours:** 509-624-4116. Based in Medical Lake, Washington. Charter tours all over southern BC, Alberta.

■ **Dewdney Trail Stages:** 1-800-332-0282. Service daily except Sun. Cranbrook to Golden and return.

■ **Greyhound Bus Lines:** 1-800-661-8747 or specific cities. Daily service begins from Vancouver, entering Kootenay Country via Hwy 3. Coaches stop at waypoints between Castlegar and Nelson, then follow Hwy 6 over the Salmo Skyway and on to Creston before making their way into Alberta. There is also service along Hwy 1 from Calgary through Banff to Radium.

Inland Ferries

The provincial transportation and highways ministry operates a small fleet of inland ferries to complete the highway system where there are no bridges. These ferries are free, and carry passengers and vehicles. Schedules should be used only as a guideline since operating times can change on short notice.

Kootenay Lake
■ **Balfour to Kootenay Bay** (Hwy 3A): Nelson, 250-229-4215. From Balfour hourly 6am-midnight. From Kootenay Bay hourly 7am-1am. 45 minutes. MV *Balfour*: 38 cars, 150 passengers. MV *Anscomb*: 42 cars, 160 passengers. Additional sailings in summer.

Arrow Lakes
■ **Needles to Fauquier** (Hwy 6): New Denver, 250-354-6521; Vernon, 250-549-5440; or Arrow Lakes Marine Office, Ministry of Transportation and Highways, 250-837-7724. From Fauquier every half hour 5am-10pm. From Needles every half hour 5:15am-9:45pm. On call 10pm-5am. 10 minutes. MV *Needles*: 40 cars, 150 passengers.
■ **Shelter Bay to Galena Bay** (Hwy 23): Revelstoke, 250-837-7646; New Denver, 250-358-2212; or Arrow Lakes Marine Office, Ministry of Transportation and Highways, 250-837-7724. From Galena Bay hourly 5:30am-12:30am. From Shelter Bay hourly 5am-midnight. 30 minutes. MV *Galena*: 50 cars, 150 passengers. *MV Shelter Bay* (seasonal) 28 cars, 100 passengers.

Columbia River
■ **Arrow Park** (Hwy 6 – 25.5km south of Nakusp): Shuttle service between 5am-10:55pm. Five minutes. Cable ferry: 8 vehicles, 20 passengers. Service may advance two hours in fire season.

Kootenay River
■ **Glade to Thrums** (22.5km west of Nelson): On demand service. Three minutes. Cable ferry: eight cars, 115 passengers.
■ **Harrop/Procter area to Longbeach** (24km east of Nelson): Crosses the West Arm. On demand 24 hours. Five minutes. Cable ferry: 10 vehicles, 55 passengers.

Airlines

Major airports for the BC Rockies region are at Castlegar and Cranbrook. Airlines offer daily service to Vancouver, Calgary, and Edmonton. Daily flights between Castlegar and Penticton.

■ **Central Mountain Air:** 1-800-663-3721. Links Castlegar and Cranbrook to Vancouver and Calgary.

■ **Canadian Regional Air:** 1-800-665-1177. Serves Castlegar and Cranbrook.

■ **North Vancouver Air:** 1-800-228-6608. Vancouver to Nelson and Creston. Big White Mountain ski packages.

Railway

■ **Rocky Mountaineer Railtours:** 1-800-665-7245. Vancouver to Jasper, Vancouver to Banff, optional to Calgary. Travels only in daylight. Passengers going east or west spend the night in Kamloops. Hotel, continental breakfast, gourmet lunch included. May-early Oct.

Car and RV Rentals

Cars can be rented at the Castlegar airport and downtown locations in most cities. RV rentals are in Penticton, Vernon, and Salmon Arm. Call information centres.

BRITISH COLUMBIA ROCKIES EVENTS

Balfour
- **Fishing Derby:** Thanksgiving weekend.

Boswell
- **Fishing Derby:** Mid-June.
- **East Shore Craft Fair:** Aug long weekend.

Castlegar
- **Doukhobor Music Festival:** May Long weekend.
- **Sunfest:** June.
- **BC Old-time Fiddlers' Contest and Dance:** Mid-Aug.
- **Blueberry Creek Craft Fair:** Early Nov.

Cranbrook
- **Children's Festival:** Mid-May.
- **Rockin' in the Rockies Car Show and Shine:** Early June.
- **Sam Steele Days:** Mid-June. Parade to celebrate Superintendent Sam Steele's arrival in Fort Steele in 1887.
- **Pro Rodeo:** Mid-Aug.

Crawford Bay
- **Fall Fair:** Labour Day weekend. Held since 1910.

Creston
- **Osprey Festival:** Late April.
- **Blossom Festival:** May. Chuckwagon and chariot races, demolition derby, fiddlers, parade, midway, and more.
- **Fall Fair:** Sept.

Elkford
- **Winter in the Wilderness Festival:** Jan. Including sled-dog races.
- **Snowarama:** Feb. Snowmobile fund raiser.
- **WildCat Charlie Days:** Fall. Pays tribute to such pioneers as sometimes cantankerous Charlie Weigert, or Wildcat Charlie.

Fernie
- **Griz Days:** March.
- **Powder, Pedal, Paddle Relay Race:** April. Skiing, biking, canoeing/kayaking.
- **Snow Valley Wranglers Rodeo:** July.
- **The Gathering at Island Lake:** Aug. Folk festival.

Fort Steele Heritage Town
- **Celebration of Horse Power, Halloween, Thanksgiving:** Historic celebrations throughout the year.

Golden
- **Vintage Car Club Show' n' Shine:** July.
- **Golden Rodeo:** Aug long weekend.
- **Hang-gliding and Para-gliding Championships:** Aug.

Horsepower is celebrated at Fort Steele Heritage Town.

Gray Creek
- **Gray Creek Sailing Regatta:** Labour Day weekend.

Invermere
- **Summer Jump Start Festival:** May. Sports tournaments, family events.
- **Visitor Appreciation Day:** July.

Kaslo
- **Kaslo May Days:** May Day weekend, celebrated for 90 years. Longest consecutive yearly Maypole Dance in North America; loggers' sports, parade, May Queen coronation, Cancan girls, childrens events.
- **SS Moyie Family Day:** Mid-June.
- **Kaslo Jazz Etc Festival:** First weekend Aug.
- **Beachcombers' Rainbow Derby:** Nov.

Kimberley
- **Rockin' in the Rockies Fifties Fest:** Early June.
- **Marysville Days:** Early June.
- **International Old-Time Accordion Championship:** July.
- **Julyfest:** July.
- **Alpine Folk Dance Festival:** Sept.

Nakusp
- **Nakusp Fishing Derby:** Early June.
- **Build, Bail, and Sail Race:** Early Aug.
- **Nakusp Fall Fair:** Sept.

Nelson
- **Sno' Fest:** Late Jan.
- **Street Fest:** Late July. Performers and artisans from all over North America.
- **Cyswogn' Fun Triathlon:** Aug.

Radium Hot Springs
- **Wings Over the Rockies:** May. Celebrating the return of the birds. Hikes, speakers, workshops, childrens activities.
- **Sounds Over the Rockies:** July. Gospel music.
- **Classic Car Show and Fall Fair:** Sept.

Revelstoke
- **Snowarama:** 2nd weekend, Feb.
- **Timber Days:** July.
- **Railway Days:** Late Aug.
- **Revelstoke Mountain Arts Festival:** Mid-Sept. Theatre, art, kids events.

Rossland
- **Winter Carnival:** Late Jan. Luge and bobsled races, snowmobile race, bigolfathon (snow golf), saloon, play-money casino.
- **Golden City Days and Fall Fair:** Early Sept. Cancans, saloons, dancing waiters. Plus everything a country fair should offer — competitions in veggie growing, jam making, baking, and brewing.

Slocan Valley
- **New Denver May Days:** Mid-May.
- **Silverton Days:** July 1.
- **Slocan City Logging Show:** Early July.

Sparwood
- **Snowarama:** Late Feb.
- **Coal Miner Days:** June.
- **Coal Mine Tours:** July-Aug.

Trail
- **Silver City Days:** Mid-May. Italian sidewalk cafe, grape stomp, spaghetti-eating contest, midway, jet-boat river racing.

The magnificent Takakkaw Falls, B.C.'s second highest.

BC ROCKIES
ROUTES AND HIGHLIGHTS

TRAVELLER'S LOGS

HIGHLIGHTS

CHRISTINA LAKE TO CASTLEGAR

CROWSNEST HIGHWAY
(Highway 3)

From Christina Lake, Highway 3 traces the southern periphery of a vast wilderness now protected as Gladstone Provincial Park, slices through forests of cedar, hemlock, fir, birch, and pine, to its summit at Bonanza Pass. Here we leave "boundary country," and descend into "the Kootenays" – a region dominated by the meandering and obstreperous waterways of the Kootenay River and Kootenay Lake, and the lofty peaks of the Purcell and Selkirk mountains. It is 73km from Christina Lake to Castlegar.

Christina Lake: (Area pop. 1,100). 21km beyond Grand Forks. For details on this pleasant summer stopover, see *Thompson Okanagan*, p. 152.

McRae Creek: About 11km beyond Christina Lake. Spawning kokanee, early Aug-Sept.

McRae Creek Rest Area: 11km beyond Christina Lake. South side of highway.

Paulson Bridge: 13.5km beyond rest area. Sits 90m over McRae Creek.

Walker Creek Rest Area: 4.5km beyond Paulson Bridge. Footbridges over creek.

Bonanza Pass: 6km beyond rest area. Known locally as the "Blueberry Paulson Summit," el 1,535m.

Big Sheep Creek Rest Area: 6km beyond Bonanza Pass.

Road to Ski Trails: Signs indicate right turn just past rest area. Leads to cross-country skiing.

Nancy Greene Provincial Park: 198ha; 10 parking-lot campsites. 5km beyond road to ski trails, at junction of Hwys 3 and 3B. 250-825-3500. Subalpine lake named for local hero, Nancy Greene of Rossland, who won alpine skiing gold medal for Canada in 1968 Olympics. In all, there are some 45km of trails up and around the lake, including a self-guiding nature trail circling the lake. Great cross-country skiing and hiking. Rainbow trout. Ground squirrels in summer.

Highway 3B: Just beyond the park, 47km from Christina Lake. 28km to Rossland; 38km to Trail.

SIDE TRIP

to Ski Area

Red Mountain Ski Area: On Red Mountain Rd, 25km from Hwy 3/3B junction, 3km north of Rossland Museum on Hwy 3B. Contact Red Mountain, Box 670, Rossland, BC, V0G 1Y0. 250-362-7700 or 1-800-663-0105. For snow report 250-362-5500. First Canadian Downhill Championships were held on Red Mountain in 1897 and Western Canada's first chairlift was installed in 1947. Red and Granite mountains, constituting Red Mountain Ski area, have produced more Canadian National Ski Team members (including 1968 Olympic gold-medal winner Nancy Greene) than any other ski area.

Facilities include Granite's 854m vertical drop, a 7.5km intermediate run, a world-class downhill course, the "powderfields," and over 50km of machine-groomed cross-country ski trails, plus more off the beaten track. Some 77 runs, three triple chairs, two double chairs, one T-bar. Lodge, ski school, and rental shop. Plans are in store for a major new resort-village development at the mountain's base that will see some 1,800 beds in condos, a hotel, townhomes, B&Bs, and single-family homes.

Rossland: (Pop. 3,802). 28km south of Hwy 3 on Hwy 3B. See *Five-town Loop*, p.192.

Return to Highway 3

Castlegar: (Pop. 7,027). 27km beyond Hwy 3B junction; 73km from Christina Lake. Dramatically situated on a strip of benchland on the west bank of the Columbia River, opposite its junction with the Kootenay River. Castlegar is also at junction of Hwy 3 from the west, Hwy 22 coming north from Trail, and Hwy 3A heading north to Nelson.

The Kootenay River flows down from the northeast, and pours into the Columbia River, forming a giant Y. Within a radius of 2.5km of the rivers' confluence, there are, remarkably, seven bridges.

The flatlands on the Columbia's east bank, and between the two rivers, were first occupied in 1908 by the Doukhobors (in Russian: Dukho-borets, "spirit wrestlers") a pacifist group of immigrants who rejected Russia's highly structured state-supported religion, and left their homeland to find freedom from human laws. Here, they constructed some of the earliest bridges. There were at least 24 villages constituting the settlement named Ootischenia or Ootischeniye, "the Valley of Consolation," reflecting the difficulties that

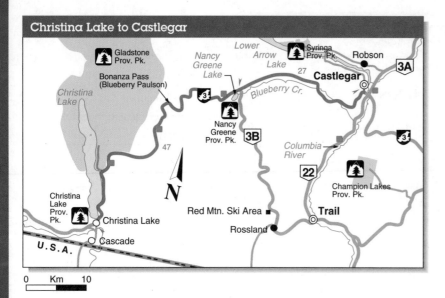

Christina Lake to Castlegar

0 Km 10

Arrow Lakes Waterway: The long and narrow (1- to 2km wide) Arrow lakes reservoir stretches from the Hugh Keenleyside Dam north to Revelstoke, and 230km south to the Grand Coulee Dam, in Washington State. At 500 sq km, it is BC's fifth largest lake. Fishing for kokanee, Gerrard rainbow, Dolly Varden, lingcod and walleye pike. From the "flatlands" of Washington to the cliffs and glaciers of the northern reaches are sandy beaches, creeks, waterfalls, and plenty of places to pull the boat in for back-to-basics camping. Scottie's Marina, 250-365-3267, and Syringa Park Marina, 250-365-5472, in Castlegar, have bait, maps, charts, and all the advice you need.

Water level is controlled by the dam, and can fluctuate 20m from spring through to late summer. The levels can change as much as 30cm in one day.

■ **Castlegar Golf Club:** 18-hole championship course. 250-365-5006. High above Columbia Valley with views of Columbia and Kootenay rivers, and wildlife.

Bridges into the Past

■ **Brilliant Suspension Bridge:** In Brilliant, at bottom of Airport Hill; visible from Hwy 3A. Now a National Historic Site, this 100m steel-and-concrete bridge was built in 1913 on the orders of Doukhobor leader Peter (Lordly) Verigin to connect communal villages to the road to Nelson. When the government denied the Doukhobors' request for a bridge, they raised two-thirds of the required $60,000 (later supplemented by a provincial grant). Men with little education followed an architect's blueprints, worked with handmade tools, and hand-mixed the concrete. A new highway bridge replaced it in 1968.

■ **Columbia River Bridge at Kinnaird:** Carries Hwy 3 across Columbia River. Was largest and longest span of its design in the world when built in the 1950s. Received award of excellence in 1968 for creative use of concrete.

■ **Train Bridge:** Across Columbia River near former ferry crossing at Robson. Once swung parallel to the river to allow sternwheelers passage. Parts of the swing mechanism are still visible.

■ **Zuckerberg Island Bridge:** At the end of 9th St in downtown Castlegar. This 91m, hand-built wooden suspension bridge was built in 1980, for pedestrians only.

■ **Brooklyn Bridge:** Also known as Renata Natural Bridge. 16km upriver from Hugh Keenleyside Dam, on Bulldog Mountain. Accessible only by boat. Trail leads up a bank to what is possibly Canada's largest natural rock bridge. Ask at local marinas for directions. This erosion sculpture, 20m high and 43m long, spans a cascading brook among towering cliffs some 275m above the Lower Arrow Lake and site of early boom town of Brooklyn (now "just a field").

finally brought these refugees here. Six villages were located at Brilliant; others at Raspberry, Robson, Glade, Shoreacres. They all had names in Russian, which meant things like "blessed," "meadowland," "the beautiful," and "the cross." The Doukhobors planted orchards and gardens, built sawmills, pipe works, jam factories. The settlement was one of the more successful communal enterprises attained in North America. The Doukhobors are now an integral part of the Castlegar community. (See *Verigin's Tomb*, below.) Much of this area is now occupied by the Castlegar Airport, golf course, and Hwys 3 and 3A. But some vestiges of this community that thrived under the motto "Toil and a Peaceful Life" have survived. See note on Doukhobor homesteads (previous page).

The newest section of Castlegar sits on the Columbia's west bank, directly opposite the incoming Kootenay River. Hwy 3, with its bridge across the Columbia River, has drawn development toward Trail and Nelson.

In 1988 the Castlegar and District Heritage Society revived the old rail station as a museum, moving it closer to the heart of downtown. It's is now the centrepiece of a revitalized downtown core. Across town: a 25m swimming pool, hot pool, steam room, and gym.

🅿 **Castlegar Information:** Chamber of Commerce and Visitor Info Centre, 1995-6th Ave, Castlegar, BC, V1N 4B7. 250-365-6313. Located off Hwy 3, near Hwy 22 interchange. Year-round. Follow signs.

✈ **Castlegar Airport:** On Airport Rd, off Hwy 3A, 6.5km from city centre. Only air terminal for the Kootenay region. Thrilling landings: wing tips of incoming planes seem almost to touch mountain peaks.

■ **Castlegar Railway Station:** Corner of 13th Ave and 3rd St. Mon-Sat, year-round. 250-365-6440. The unofficial town centre for half a century, built in 1902, rebuilt 1907 after a fire. Declared heritage and now restored as a museum.

■ **Doukhobor Village Museum:** Across from Castlegar Airport. Daily, May 1-Sept 30. 250-365-6622 or 250-365-5327. Descendants of Doukhobors guide visitors through replica of early 1900s communal village. Spinning Wheel

Restaurant offers "good Doukhobor food – no meat, no booze, no smoking."

■ **Kootenay Gallery of Art, History, and Science:** Adjacent Doukhobor Museum. 250-365-3337. Tues-Sun. Local and travelling exhibits of historical, scientific, ethnological, and artistic interest.

■ **Zuckerberg Island Heritage Park:** Near downtown. Turn right at RCMP station on corner of 9th St and proceed to 7th Ave. 250-365-5511 in summer; 250-365-6440 year-round. This 2ha part-time island (sometimes it's a peninsula) born of two rivers offers a microcosm of the area's history. Thousands of years ago, aboriginal peoples built their winter pithouses here; and in 1811, intrepid explorer and mapmaker David Thompson paddled past. A century later, in 1931, Alexander Feodorovitch Zuckerberg arrived to teach the area's Doukhobor children, and settled on this island. His "castle" was an onion-domed **Russian Orthodox Chapel House** that he built himself of mitred logs, with ornate windows, a square rear tower, and carved masks. Bought by the city in 1981, it has been restored from neglect suffered since the gentle Russian's death in 1961. Reached by a 145m pedestrian suspension bridge (90m span). Open daily, June-Sept; call in off-season.

■ **Hugh Keenleyside Dam:** 8km upstream from town centre via Columbia Ave. Informal tours April-Labour Day, on request. 250-365-5299. Completed in 1965, the 50m-high earthfill and concrete structure controls a 3,650,000ha drainage area and holds back the Arrow reservoir (part of the Columbia River system) extending 232km north to Revelstoke.

Several communities were affected by the new lake. Fauquier, Burton, and Edgewood were re-established on higher ground. Others like Needles, now only a ferry dock, were abandoned.

The dam has one of Western Canada's few navigation locks, 15m wide inside and 88m long between gates. It lifts river traffic, including pleasure craft, some 23m to new lake levels. The waterway is also a "logging highway" for tugs and log booms headed for the sawmill and pulp mill downstream.

SIDE TRIP

along Columbia's North Shore

Follow Hwy 3A across the Brilliant Bridge over the Kootenay River, then head east along Broadwater Rd. (Note that a newer bridge, crossing the Columbia River, accesses Broadwater Ave farther east. It can be reached by travelling south on Columbia Ave through downtown Castlegar.)

Verigin's Tomb: On Broadwater Rd, 800m beyond Hwy 3A. Peter (Lordly) Verigin instituted many reforms in the Doukhobor community. In 1924, he was killed by a bomb exploding in his railway coach.

Pass Creek Regional Park: 37 campsites. On Broadwater Rd, 2km beyond Hwy 3A. May-Sept. 250-365-3386. Swimming, hiking to Rosebud Lake, Tulip Creek Falls, and Lions Head.

Robson: 2km beyond park. Residential area for Castlegar; casual fruit farming. Little evidence that this was once a busy rail and barge terminal for ore en route from the Rockies to Trail.

Hugh Keenleyside Dam: About 1km beyond Robson. Road leads across dam, onto Arrow Lakes Dr, past Celgar pulp mill (tours available) and Pope and Talbot sawmill on south bank of Columbia, back to Castlegar (see above).

Syringa Provincial Park: 4,417ha; 60 campsites (reservations taken: call 1-800-689-9025; from the Lower Mainland or overseas, call 604-689-9025); sani-station. General info: 250-825-3500. A few kilometres beyond Robson; 19km northwest of Castlegar, via Broadwater Rd. On east side of Lower Arrow Lake at foot of Columbia Mountains' Norns Range. Recent 4,191ha addition preserves rare low-elevation Interior Douglas-fir forest. Water sports, hiking, outdoor nature displays, interpretive programs. Yellow Pine Trail is a leisurely 45-minute self-guided walk. May see bighorn sheep, deer.

Broadwater Rd ends at Syringa Creek, but the unpaved and rustic Deer Park Rd carries on to a pretty area complete with waterfall, known to locals as Deer Park.

Return to Castlegar

Highway 22: South off Hwy 3, south of downtown Castlegar, Columbia Ave becomes Hwy 22, a two-laner winding south along the west bank of the Columbia River for 26km to Trail. It leads past small bedroom communities with utopian names like China Creek, Blueberry Creek, Genelle, Rivervale, and Oasis. River current too strong for swimming, but good fishing.

Oasis Rest Area: About 21km south of Castlegar.

From Hwy 22/3 junction, Hwy 3 leads northeast 39km to Salmo, and a further 83km to Creston. See *Castlegar to Creston* p.192. Hwy 3A leads northeast 41km to Nelson. See *Five-Town Loop*, following.

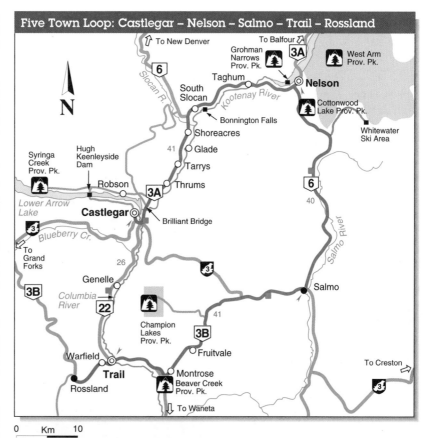

Five Town Loop: Castlegar – Nelson – Salmo – Trail – Rossland

FIVE-TOWN LOOP

CASTLEGAR, NELSON, SALMO, TRAIL, AND ROSSLAND
(Highways 3A, 6, 3B)

The complete circle – Castlegar back to Castlegar – is 148km. Including the 10km on to Rossland, the loop covers 158km of highway, taking in the region's three largest cities (Castlegar, Nelson, and Trail), three of its most important rivers, and three of its highways. Please note that this circle route is not suggested as a trip in itself: this is simply a convenient way to package up this busy part of the BC Rockies region. Where ever you travel in the West Kootenays, you will probably cover some portion of this loop, cross-referenced to other *Logs*.

So read your map carefully to catch all the curves, and welcome to the heart of Kootenay Country. Loop begins at Castlegar, at the junction of the Columbia and Kootenay rivers. It follows Hwy 3A, and the Kootenay River northeast, to Nelson. Then Hwy 6 leads quietly south through the forest along the Salmo River to Salmo. From Salmo, Hwy 3B moves west through Fruitvale and Montrose to Trail and Rossland. Hwy 22 north from Trail returns to Castlegar.

Castlegar: (Pop. 7,027). For details, see *Christina Lake to Castlegar*, p.187

Highway 3A and Broadwater Rd: In Castlegar. Hwy 3 across Kinnaird Bridge leads to Kinnaird Interchange. Here, on the west side of the Columbia River, Hwy 3A leads 3km through Ootischenia to Brilliant, originally Doukhobor settlements, now districts of Castlegar. The highway then crosses the Brilliant Bridge over the Kootenay River. From here Hwy 3A leads northeast 38km to Nelson, and Broadwater Rd leads 5.5km to Robson and beyond to Syringa Creek Provincial Park. See *Christina Lake to Castlegar*, above.

Highway 3A to Nelson

Brilliant Rest Area: Beyond Castlegar, 2.5km northeast of Brilliant Bridge. View of Kootenay River and hydro dams.

Thrums: (Pop. 312). On Hwy 3A, 8km beyond bridge. Some services. Fresh veggies in season. Named after Scottish village in Sir James Barrie's *A Window in Thrums*.

Tarrys: (Area pop. 256). 5km beyond Thrums (13km from Castlegar).

Ferry to Glade: 3km beyond Tarrys (16km from Castlegar), a road leads south 2km to free cable ferry crossing Kootenay River to community of Glade (pop. 351). On-demand service.

Shoreacres: (Pop. 349). 1.5km beyond ferry to Glade. Some services.

Highway 6: 2.5km beyond Shoreacres, 20km beyond Castlegar. Leads north

127km through serene and silvery Slocan Valley to hot-springs resort town of Nakusp. See *Cherryville to Nelson*, p.213. Hwy 6 east joins Hwy 3A as far as Nelson, then veers south to Salmo.

South Slocan: (Pop. 142). On Hwy 3A, 2km beyond Hwy 6 junction.

Bonnington Falls: 3km beyond junction. Series of low falls prevented navigation between the vast Kootenay and Columbia river systems. Today there are four dams in about 5km: South Slocan, Lower Bonnington, Upper Bonnington, and Corra Linn (north of Bonnington Falls). All operated by West Kootenay Power Ltd.

BC Hydro also takes advantage of Bonnington Falls by operating the Kootenay Canal, which diverts water from Kootenay River just above the Corra Linn Dam. The canal carries water along the Kootenay's east side to turbines near the South Slocan Dam. BC's first hydroelectric plant was erected on Cottonwood Creek, just south of Nelson, in 1897.

Bonnington Falls was once a major fishing area for the Lakes Kootenay or Ktunaxa People who caught their salmon in baskets. This was probably a village site as long ago as 4,000 years.

Taghum: (Pop. 142). 11km beyond the falls, 14km beyond the junction. Hwy 3A/6 crosses to south side of Kootenay River. Taghum means "six" in the Chinook trading language (railway siding here was about six miles west of Nelson).

Grohman Narrows Provincial Park: 10ha. 5.5km beyond Taghum, 19.5km beyond the junction, on south shore of Kootenay Lake's west arm. Narrows Island and an abandoned orchard. Picnic site, trails.

Nelson: (Pop. 9,585). 2km from Grohman Narrows Park; 41km northeast of Castlegar on Hwy 3A; 120km northwest of Creston. On the slopes of Selkirk Mountains, overlooking the West Arm of Kootenay Lake.

Nelson's steep streets, clear mountain skies, and turn-of-the-century architecture outshone even Steve Martin who starred in the popular comedy *Roxanne* filmed here. Tourists still circle round the Fire Hall where so much of the story, about lovers of beauty, took place.

When BC's Gold Commissioner, Gilbert Malcom Sproat, in 1887, selected the Toad Mountain silver-mine townsite that later became Nelson, he dreamed "that here, where nature was so bountiful, there might be, could we keep out newspapers and lawyers, the town of all towns for civilized habitation." A century later, Nelson is a town with a genuine atmosphere and more artists and craftspeople per capita than any other city in Canada.

Also more heritage buildings. By the turn of the century, Nelson, by then BC's third largest community, was called the "Queen City." (Now there are at least 25 cities ahead of it, plus several very large "district municipalities.") Today 355 of Nelson's homes, hotels, shops, and office buildings have heritage status. F. M. Rattenbury, famous architect of Victoria's

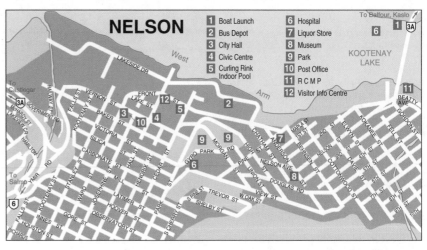

Parliament Buildings and Empress Hotel, also designed Nelson's courthouse and city hall. The ornate and grandiose high-Victorian style of much of the remaining architecture was an anomaly: introduced to Nelson by miners with nouveau-riche tastes, modified by conservative English settlers, and, two or three decades behind the times even during construction.

The first West Kootenay sternwheeler, able to "float on dew," was built here in 1891. Between 1891 and 1957 a fleet of at least 11 of these "graceful white swans" (ranging from 40m-61.5m) operated on Kootenay Lake, connecting rail lines divided by water. Nelson had a speedboat (launch) club, rowing club, and horse racing on Baker St (the main street), plus 23 hotels (each with a bar), and four saloons. The local Dam Busters Diving Club (ask at Info Centre) will give directions to history that has gone under, such as tugboat *Ymir*, in 1929.

Nelson is still the "town of all towns" on Kootenay Lake, with a daily newspaper, the *Nelson Daily News*, and ample niceties for visitors. There is endless hiking, climbing, and huckleberry picking on mountains in summer. In winter, downhill and cross-country skiing are 19km away at Whitewater Ski Area, and only 8km away on the locals' mountain, Morning. Hwy 3A, the "North Shore Highway," leads north over the Nelson Bridge to Hwy 31, to what some consider to be divinely inspired apres-ski, at Ainsworth Hot Springs (46.5km from Nelson). Details in *Balfour to Galena Bay*, p.218.

Nelson Information: Info Centre, Nelson and District Chamber of Commerce, 225 Hall St, Nelson, BC, V1L 5X4. Year-round. 250-352-3433.

Norman Stibbs Airfield: Off Lakeside Dr, 500m from city centre. Air strip, heliport, and floatplane base.

■ **City Tourist Park:** Downtown, corner of High and Willow streets. April-Oct. Reservations: City Hall, 502 Vernon St, Nelson, BC, V1L 4E8. 250-352-9031. 40 campsites. Trailer hook-ups, showers.

■ **Heritage Walking/Motoring Tour and Tour of the Cemetery:** Maps at Info Centre for self-guided tour of heritage buildings. 250-352-3433.

■ **Artwalk:** 75 artists display their work in 12 gallery locations that change monthly. Maps at Info Centre.

■ **Streetcar No. 23 Restored:** By Info Centre. BC's only running historic streetcar. Fare $2. Nelson, in 1899, was probably the smallest city in the world to have its own streetcar. Derailments were frequent on the steep grades, however, and passengers were occasionally delivered through windows of Baker St shops. Not so today. The electric tram with the 11 picture windows runs safely the length of the city along the lakeshore. This car came from Cleveland in 1924. Buses took over from streetcars in 1946.

■ **Capitol Theatre Restored:** On Victoria St, 250-352-6363. In 1927, the Capitol introduced talkies to Nelson. $1 million later: open again for live performances.

■ **Chamber of Mines Eastern BC Museum:** 215 Hall St. 250-352-5242. Year-round. Largest rock collection in BC, mining reference library, historic photos, maps.

■ **Nelson Museum:** Corner of Nelson Ave and Anderson St. 250-352-9813. Afternoons year-round. Nelson and area history, local art displays. Archives on request.

■ **The Murals:** Four of them, on 300 block of Vernon St. Scenes from the movie *Roxanne*; one depicts actor Steve Martin.

■ **Lakeside Park:** Off Nelson Ave, near Nelson Bridge. Lakeshore walkway, picnics, sandy beach, boat rentals, adventure playground, greenhouse, tree tour.

■ **Sculpture for the People:** Lakeside and Gyro parks, Chahko-Mika Mall.

■ **Viewpoint:** At Gyro Park, two blocks from downtown. Trails, gardens, childrens pool, playground, great views of city and lake.

■ **Granite Pointe Golf Course:** On West Richards St. 250-352-5913. Hilly 18-hole course with stunning views of Kokanee Glacier and Kootenay Lake.

■ **Morning Mountain:** Off Granite Rd, 8km west of Nelson on Hwy 3A. 250-352-9969. Day skiing Sat, Sun, Mon, 9:30-3:30. Night skiing Tues-Thurs, 6:30-9:30. Family-oriented. T-bar, 150m vertical drop. Concession, rentals.

■ **Blaylock Estate:** On Hwy 3A, 6km north of Nelson. Eye-stopper of a Tudor mansion built in the late 1930s as a summer cottage for Selwyn G. Blaylock, early president of Cominco. Now condominiums. Garden tours daily, June-Sept. Mansion tours by appointment. 250-825-3454.

Highways 3A and 6: West of downtown Nelson. East on Hwy 3A leads 34km to Balfour and free ferry to Crawford Bay. See *Balfour to Galena Bay*, p.218. Hwy 6 leads south 40km to Salmo.

Highway 6 to Salmo

An impressive stretch of road that skirts the Selkirk Mountains, then cuts right through them.

Cottonwood Lake Regional Park: 8ha. 5km beyond Nelson on Hwy 6. Fishing (no motorboats) on 35ha lake. Hiking, cross-country skiing, roofed shelter.

Nelson Nordic Touring Centre: 6km beyond Nelson, groomed trails developed by Nelson Nordic Ski Club. Night skiing, parking, registration, shelters. Watch for highway signs. Nelson Info Centre has maps.

Whitewater Ski Area: 10km beyond Nelson, then left on Whitewater access road for another 10km. 250-354-4944. Snow report: 250-352-7669.

Whitewater also called "WH$_2$0," the Powder Formula. Considered to have some of the best lift-serviced powder in Canada and the Pacific Northwest. In a natural snow bowl under spire of Mt Ymir. Averages over 13m of light, dry snow annually. 34 runs, two double chairs. Vertical drop 395m. Base lodge with cafeteria, lounge, retail and rental shop, ski school.

Stewart Creek Rest Area: 20km beyond Nelson.

Salmo: (Pop. 1,128). On the Salmo River 40km south of Nelson, at the junction of Hwys 3 and 6. See *Castlegar to Creston*, p.193.

Highway 3 West to 3B

Erie Lake Rest Area: On Hwy 3, 5km west of Salmo. Small roadside lake. Bass and rainbows.

Highway 3 and 3B: 11km west of Salmo. *Log* travels south on 3B to Trail and Rossland.

Champion Lakes Provincial Park: 1,425ha; 95 campsites, sani-station. 250-825-3500. West off Hwy 3B, 7.5km west of Hwy 3 junction. In Bonnington Range, between Columbia River and Beaver Creek, a chain of three lakes connected by trails. Excellent hiking around first and second lakes. Good rainbow trout fishing. Squirrels, chipmunks, porcupines, black bears, deer, coyotes, pikas, beavers, and variety of birds. Adventure playground, amphitheatre for weekend interpretation programs, ramp for manually powered boats. Swimming, snowshoeing, cross-country skiing.

■ **Champion Lakes Golf Course:** On Champion Lakes Rd, just off Hwy 3B. 250-367-7001. A 9-hole course split by Marsh Creek, a natural water hazard, plus three ponds and 41 bunkers, to test the golfer.

Baker Street in downtown Nelson, one of BC's first cities, boasts many fine heritage buildings.

Beaver Valley Family Park: 4km west of Champion Lakes Rd. Situated on Marsh Creek, just off Hwy 3B (2.5km east of Fruitvale). Wheelchair accessible. Tenting, some hook-ups, showers, kitchen, hiking, cross-country skiing. Group picnics and socials. Call Beaver Valley Arena: 250-367-9319 or 250-367-9311.

Fruitvale: (Pop. 2,117). On Hwy 3B, 2.5km west of Beaver Valley Recreation Area. Bedroom community for many of Trail's Cominco employees. Service centre, accommodation, restaurant, pubs. Only 5.5km separate Fruitvale and Montrose (with the small community of Beaver Valley in between), and all share the beautiful Beaver Valley itself, its amenities and attractions.

Beaver Falls: Small community about 2km west of Fruitvale. Main feature is Beaver Falls, one of the highest natural falls in the BC Rockies region. A short walk along the railroad track. Ask locally.

Montrose: (Pop. 1,197). On Hwy 3B, 5.5km west of Fruitvale. Named by Trail lawyer A.G. Cameron, after his hometown in Scotland. Service centre, accommodation.

Waneta Junction (Hwy 22A): 3.5km west of Montrose (34km west of Salmo, 7km east of Trail). Follows Columbia River south for 10.5km to border crossing at Waneta, BC.

SIDE TRIP

on Highway 22A

Beaver Creek Provincial Park: 44ha; 15 campsites. 250-367-7321. On Hwy 22A, 2km south of Waneta Junction. On Columbia River's east side. Fishing, boating, paddling.

Pend-d'Oreille River: The Pend-d'Oreille River flows in a northwesterly direction crossing the international boundary twice. It loops through BC for about 24km; at Waneta, it joins the Columbia River and flows back into the US.

■ **Waneta Electric Power Plant and Dam:** On the Pend-d'Oreille River at its confluence with the Columbia, 10.5km south of Waneta Junction, adjacent the border crossing.

■ **Seven-Mile Dam and Generating Station:** 11km east off Hwy 22A, upstream from the Waneta power plant. Tourist building and viewpoint at top of rock cut above powerhouse access road.

■ **Wildlife Watching:** From Hwy 22A follow paved (Pend-d'Oreille) road to Seven Mile Dam. Best viewing is on north shore of reservoir from the Columbia River to the Salmo River. Highlights: white-tailed deer, mule deer, yellow-bellied marmots, bald eagles, turkey vultures, osprey, and wildflowers. BC Wildlife Watch viewing site.

Return to Highway 3B

Trail: (Pop. 7,696). 7km west of Waneta Junction, on the west and east banks of the Columbia River. Trail is 18km north of the Canada/US border; 26km south of Castlegar via Hwy 22; 108km east of Grand Forks via Hwy 3B. (This *Log* is moving from east to west, an easier entry into Trail, but note that it can be more than exciting coming down into Trail from the west. Down and around on the switchbacks from Rossland to Trail, Hwy 3B descends more than 610m in a distance of only 11km. Check brakes first!)

Trail's beginnings were quiet. It was simply Trail Creek Landing, a cluster of small buildings in a bowl where the old Dewdney Trail forded the Columbia. By 1891, the community was slightly larger, serving as a landing for steamers taking gold, silver, and copper ore to

191

TRAIL

1	Bus Depot	**6**	Liquor Store
2	Chamber of Commerce Visitor Info Centre	**7**	Memorial Arena, Library, Curling Rink
3	City Hall	**8**	Museum
4	Cominco Tours	**9**	Post Office, Customs
5	Hospital	**10**	R C M P

American smelters from nearby booming Rossland.

Now home of Consolidated Mining and Smelting of Canada Ltd, the city is often called "Cominco Ltd with Trail built around it." Trail took firm root as one of BC's key industrial cities. In 1895, American entrepreneur Augustus Heinze had established a smelter here to reduce costs of shipping ore to the US. Now Trail has more than 50 percent of the region's manufacturing.

Though local mines are played out, Cominco's Trail unit today operates the world's largest zinc and lead smelting complex. More than 300,000t of zinc and 135,000t of lead are extracted each year from ores shipped from around the world. Cominco employs more than 2,500 people here.

The town's commercial section is concentrated on a low terrace on the river's west bank, with a retaining wall to protect it from high waters. On the higher levels, Cominco's 120m-tall smokestacks are part of the scenery, along with the surrounding forested mountains, and the wide and soupy Columbia River rushing under the Victoria St Bridge.

West Trail, with steep and narrow streets overlooking the river, and terraced lots lush with vegetables and vineyards, is romantically compared with Italy. About 30 percent of Trail's population is of Italian birth, or descended from "old country" emigrants who began arriving in late 1800s to work the mines, smelters, and railway. Rossland Ave (Hwy 3B in west Trail) is the "Gulch" where the first Italians settled. The best Italian food in BC is said to be in Trail. Daily newspaper is the *Trail Daily Times*.

Trail Information: Info Centre, Trail Chamber of Commerce, 200-1199 Bay Ave, Trail, BC, V1R 4A4. Year-round. 250-368-3144. Summer Info Centre at Nancy Greene Provincial Park (shared by Rossland and Trail), at junction of Hwys 3 and 3B. 250-362-7722. Ask about walking tours.

■ **Cominco Tours:** Trail Chamber of Commerce, 250-368-3144. Call well ahead. Retired company employees show visitors

where ores are melted and separated. They'll also describe the "greening of Trail" over the past seven decades as pollution-control has improved, and waste products have been converted into fertilizer. Visitors must be over 12 years old; wear long pants and sensible shoes.

■ **Italian Community Archives:** In Cristoforo Columbo Lodge (est 1905), 584 Rossland Ave. Call ahead to Chamber of Commerce, 250-368-3144, to arrange visit. The only Italian archives in North America.

■ **City of Trail Museum:** In Trail Memorial Centre (see below). Weekdays, June-Sept.

■ **Gyro Park:** In east Trail. A 3km stretch of riverside park. Stroll, jog, cycle, swim, build sandcastles.

■ **Trail Memorial Centre:** 1051 Victoria St. Daily, year-round. 250-368-6484. Sports Hall of Memories shows that Trail is also "The Home of Champions."

■ **Rock Island:** In east Trail, off Hwy 3B, near Waneta Plaza. Small river island is easily accessible; good for fly, spinner, and bait fishing. Current too rapid for canoes and rowboats.

■ **Golf:** 18-hole **Birchbank Championship Course**, 6km north of Trail on Hwy 22; and Rossland's adventurous nine-hole **Mountain Track** (there's a rope tow from tee to green) 8km west of Trail, or 2km east of Rossland, on Hwy 3B. **Rossland Trail Country Club**, 250-693-2366 or 250-362-5045.

■ **Aquatic and Leisure Centre:** 1875 Columbia Ave. 250-3368-6484.

Highways 3B and 22: In downtown Trail, on the Columbia River's west bank. Hwy 22 leads north, 26km to Castlegar (for details, see *Christina Lake to Castlegar*, p.187), thus completing this circle trip. Hwy 3B leads west 10km in an ascent to Rossland.

Highway 3B to Rossland

Warfield: (Pop. 1,788). 6km west of Trail on Hwy 3B. Home for Cominco workers.

Rossland: (Pop. 3,802). On Hwy 3B, 10km west of Trail. High in the Rossland Mountains (el 1,040m), Rossland sits in the eroded crater of a long-extinct volcano. It is the "Home of Champions" – Olympic champion skiers Nancy Greene and Kerrin Lee-Gartner. Now the town's unique geography has also made it "Mountain Bike Capital of Canada."

From the intersection of Columbia Ave and Washington St look north and a little west to see **Red Mountain** (1,580m), and some of the remains of **Le Roi Gold Mine**, which excited investors around the world after its discovery by itinerant prospectors Moris and Bourgeois in 1890. $30 million came out of this mine in the ancient volcano crater, most famous of some 100 claims in the area. Between 1900-1916, Rossland, the "Golden City," with population of 7,000, produced 50 percent of BC's gold.

Since 1929, Rossland has depended on giant Cominco smelting operations at Trail, though recently there has been a small resurgence of mining for silver and gold.

Rossland Information: Info Centre in Rossland Historical Museum, Box 26,

Rossland, BC, V0G 1Y0. At junction of Hwys 3B and 22. Mid-May to mid-Sept. 250-362-7722. Another Info Centre shared with Trail at Nancy Greene Lake, at junction of Hwys 3 and 3B. Seasonal. 250-362-7722. Or Rossland Chamber of Commerce, Box 1385, 2185 Columbia Ave, Le Roi Mall, Rossland, BC, V0G 1Y0. 250-362-5666.

■ **Rossland Historical Museum:** At junction of Hwys 22 and 3B. Daily mid-May to mid-Sept. 250-362-7722. 2ha museum complex on site of the Black Bear Mine. Tells of geology, gold rush, Cominco Ltd, and Western Canada's famous skiers. Tea room.

■ **Le Roi Gold Mine Tour:** On museum grounds. Daily, mid-May to mid-Sept. 250-362-7722. The only hard-rock gold mine in Canada open to public. Main haulageway leads 267m into Red Mountain to intersection with Le Roi shaft, 100m below surface. A taste of the Rossland mines' 140km of drilled, blasted, and hand-mucked tunnels.

■ **Heritage Walking Tour:** By 1898 Rossland had five banks, seven newspapers, a stock exchange, and 30 saloons doing business 24 hours a day. Today, 30 surviving buildings in the commercial sector have been given heritage status. Info Centre has map.

■ **Rossland Miners Union Hall:** 1854 Columbia Ave. Daily, June-Aug. First union hall in BC, built by Western Federation of Miners in 1897. The hall has recently been restored to its turn-of-the-century appearance. During the summer, the Gold Fever Follies stages performances here, recreating the town's boisterous past. Call 250-362-7191.

Highways 22 and 3B: At Rossland. Hwy 3B leads north 3km to Red Mountain Ski Area, 28km north to junction with Hwy 3. Hwy 22 leads 11.5km to BC/Washington border crossing at Paterson. From Paterson it's another 16km to Northport. **King George VI Provincial Park** is just north of the border. 162ha; 12 campsites. 250-825-3500.

CASTLEGAR TO CRESTON

HIGHWAY 3

This is a route for mountain lovers and mountain climbers. It's 137km of mountains and trees, trees and mountains, an attractive blend of wilderness, wildlife (elk, moose, deer, bear, coyotes, even wolves), and well-spaced humanity. A high point is indeed a high point – 36.5km beyond Salmo is the Skyway, one of Canada's highest highway passes, at 1,774m.

Hwy 3 from Castlegar runs southeast 28km to its junction with Hwy 3B; then 11km beyond to downtown Salmo, where Hwys 3 and 6 become one. At Burnt Flat Junction, about 15km south of Salmo, Hwy 6 continues south to the American border, and Hwy 3 runs east to Creston.

Castlegar: (Pop. 7,027). For details, see *Christina Lake to Castlegar*, p.187.

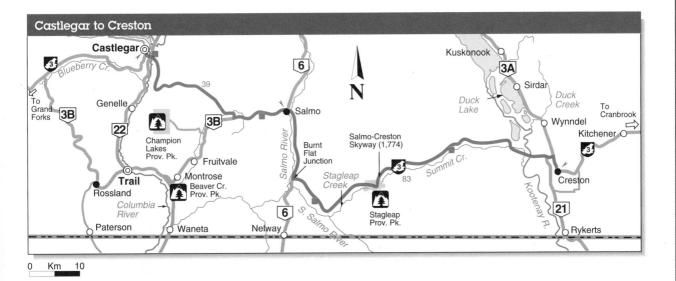

Castlegar to Creston

0 Km 10

Ootischenia Lookout Rest Area: Off Hwy 3, 8km south of Castlegar. Peaceful view of the Kootenay River flowing into the Columbia River. All the turbulence is beneath the surface. The **Mel DeAnna Nature Trail** (2.5km) around Champion Ponds begins at the viewpoint. Ponds were set aside as an environment study area for local schools to research pond life. West Kootenay Naturalist Club, led by the late Mel DeAnna, sponsored the project named in his memory.

Highway 3B: 27km southeast of Castlegar. Leads southwest 27km to Trail. Hwy 3 continues east toward Salmo and Creston.

Erie Lake Rest Area: On Hwy 3, about 6km east of Hwy 3B junction. Small roadside lake. Good spot for children to fish for bass and rainbow trout.

Highway 6: At Salmo, 11km east of Hwy 3B junction. Hwy 6 goes north 40km to Nelson. To the south, Hwys 3 and 6 are the same road as far as Burnt Flat Junction, 15km south of Salmo.

Salmo: (Pop. 1,202). At junction of Hwys 3 and 6, 39km from Castlegar. Salmo is Latin for salmon, and the Salmo River was called the Salmon River as early as the 1850s. In those days, salmon used to run abundantly here, having travelled up the Columbia River. The teeming salmon runs ended with the construction of major dams, but fishing is still good here for the highly prized Dolly Varden.

Salmo started out as Salmon Siding, on the Nelson & Fort Sheppard Railway. The community flourished through the 1950s as both a mining (silver, lead, zinc, and gold) and forestry centre. Today, there are two small sawmills just outside town, and many residents are employed by Cominco in Trail. It is the Burlington Northern Railway that now carries freight, mostly lumber, through the community.

The streets and 1930s architecture of downtown Salmo create a peaceful ambience for visitors. Particularly striking are the series

of stone murals created by students at the school of stone masonry in Salmo. These murals with a difference – made of locally quarried stone – have been mortared onto exterior walls of half a dozen buildings in downtown Salmo. More being added yearly with each class.

There are ample facilities for travellers: accommodation and campgrounds, restaurants, stores, banks, and service stations. Ask for a glass of Salmo's cold, clear water. And check out the great food in the Salmo Hotel.

Salmo Information: Information centre on outskirts of town on Hwy 3, marked by three flag poles. Daily, early May-early Sept.
■ **Salmo Museum:** At corners of Railway Ave and Forest St. 250-357-2200. Daily, May-Sept. Call in off-season.
■ **Kootenay Stone Masonry Training Institution and Kootenay Stone Centre:** Box 486, Salmo, BC, V0G 1Z0. 250-357-9515.
■ **World's Oldest Telephone Booth:** Carved into the trunk of a tree. Log in a few calls home.
■ **Salmo Golf Port:** On Airport Rd, about 5km south of Salmo. A combination airstrip and nine-hole golf course. Planes have priority – but they'll buzz the golf port before landing.
■ **Salmo Ski Hill:** About 1km up Ski Hill Rd on eastern outskirts of town. Vertical drop of 320m. T-bar and rope tow. Downhill, cross-country, and night skiing. Day lodge with restaurant, rental shop, ski school.
■ **Sheep Creek Mines:** About 8km south of Salmo, turn east on gravel Sheep Creek Rd. Along its first 15 to 20km are Kootenay Bell, Reno, Goldbelt, and Queens – abandoned mines. Also opportunities to see yet more wildlife, or cross-country ski. One of several such side roads in area. Ask locals.

Burnt Flat Junction: About 15km south of Salmo. Named for major fire in the area about 1932. Hwy 6 continues south for 10.5km to BC/Washington border crossing at Nelway, BC. Hwy 3 runs east to Creston and Kitchener.

Lost Creek Rest Area: 2km east of Burnt Flat Junction.

Avalanche Zone: About 15km east of Burnt Flat Junction, Kootenay Pass can be seen rising in the distance as this part of the route becomes a roller-coaster ride. There are five cannons positioned to bring down prospective avalanches. In two trouble spots, motorists are requested not to stop.

Stagleap Provincial Park: 1,133ha; day use. On Hwy 3, 21km from Lost Creek Rest Area, 38km southeast of Salmo. At 1,774m Salmo-Creston Summit (Kootenay Pass). Picnic sites near Bridal Lake, at edge of highway. Hiking and cross-country skiing.

Park is named for the large woodland caribou that migrate through area. They are on the US endangered species list, and authorities in both Canada and the US are working to protect and enhance their small population. Look for ground squirrels in summer. Caribou and bighorn sheep may be seen July-Nov.

Salmo-Creston Pass: 38km southeast of Salmo. Often called Mile High Pass, best known as "The Skyway." At 1,774m, this is one of the highest paved roads in Canada (the Highwood Pass, on Alberta's Hwy 40, is higher at 2,206.3m). It is constantly maintained through winter, but subject to occasional avalanche-precaution closures that may last a few minutes or a few days. As an alternate, travel from Salmo north to Nelson, cross the free ferry to Kootenay Bay, and return south on the east shore of Kootenay Lake to Creston. See *Nelson to Creston*, p.215.

Blazed Creek Rest Area: 20km east of Kootenay Pass (58km from Salmo). Old cedar stand by creek.

Creston Valley Wildlife Management Area and Centre: On Hwy 3, 17km from Blazed Creek, 75km east of Salmo (or 10km northwest of Creston). The Creston Valley is one of BC's few generously wide, flat valleys. Here is where the Kootenay River overflows its banks each spring.

The rich silt deposits are valued by farmers, and so some 9,000ha of this floodplain have

193

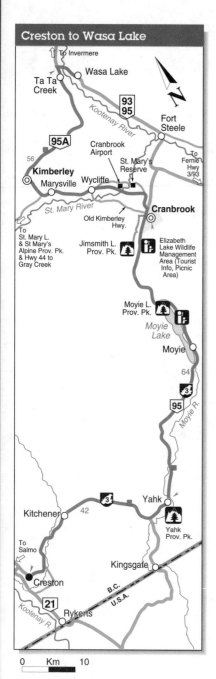

Creston to Wasa Lake

wood, kitchen shelter with electrical outlets. A serviced base for people exploring the marshlands and taking part in the nature programs.

Highway 21: Runs south from Hwy 3 near Creston, about 81km east of Salmo. About 13km to BC/Idaho border crossing at Rykerts, BC.

Highway 3A: On outskirts of Creston. North off Hwy 3 for 79km to Kootenay Bay ferry terminal. Details in *Nelson to Creston*, p. 216.

Creston: (Pop. 4,816). 83km beyond Salmo, on Hwy 3. Details in *Nelson to Creston*, p. 217.

Erickson: (Area pop. 441). 5km beyond Creston on Hwy 3. Farms, orchards, and roadside stands offering fruits and vegetables as they come in season in this lush valley.

Kitchener: (Pop. 218). 13.5km beyond Creston, on Hwy 3. Small service centre with store, pub, and restaurant. Details in *Creston to Wasa Lake, below.*

CRESTON TO WASA LAKE

CROWSNEST HIGHWAY
(Highway 3 and 95A)

This is one of the main corridors for travellers from the coast and the US heading for the Rocky Mountains' national parks. It's a wild and lovely route, much of it following the winding Moyie River as it cuts through the gentler slopes of the Purcell Range.

Hwy 3 (the Crowsnest) traces the Canada/US border from the west. Hwy 95 crosses the US border at Kingsgate. At a junction south of Yahk, these two highways join to become Hwy 3/95, which continues north to Cranbrook. North of Cranbrook, Hwy 95A breaks off from Hwy 3/95, and makes a westerly loop through Kimberley and Ta Ta Creek, north 137km to a junction at Wasa.

The stretch of Hwy 3 between Creston and Yahk is on **Mountain Standard Time** year-round. During summer, when most parts of the province move clocks one hour ahead to daylight-saving time, Creston, Kitchener, and Yahk make no changes. Their Mountain Time is already the same as Pacific daylight-saving time.

Creston: (Pop. 4,816). 122km southeast of Castlegar on Hwy 3, near its intersection with Hwy 3A. 13km north of the BC/Idaho border. For details, see p. 217.

Kitchener: (Pop. 156). 13.5km east of Creston on Hwy 3. Small settlement near the Goat River, with Whistle Stop Inn, store, and restaurant.

Kidd Creek Rest Area: 24.5km east of Creston, on highway's north side.

Highway 95: 38km beyond Creston. South 11km to BC/Idaho border crossing at Kingsgate/Eastport. Customs open 24 hours a day. North, Hwy 95 joins Hwy 3 to become Hwy 3/95.

Yahk Provincial Park: 9ha; 26 campsites. 3.5km north of junction on Hwy 3. A pleasant wooded campsite on the bank of the Moyie River, near services in town of Yahk. Good fishing for dollies May-June.

Yahk: (Pop. 173). 4km beyond Hwy 3/95 junction, bordering the park. A prosperous lumber town with 400 inhabitants in early 1900s. Town's fortunes and population declined during the Depression, but the town has survived. Today, the main export is "I've Been to Yahk and Back" T-shirts, and Ivies Restaurant features Bigyahkattack Burgers. Yahk may be a Ktunaxa word for "bow in the river."

Ryan Rest Area: 7.5km beyond Yahk on Hwy 3/95. Attractive picnic site on the ubiquitous Moyie River.

Hwy 3/95 follows Moyie River north to what else but Moyie Lake. Moose feed along river. Also, mule deer with the giveaway large ears (they're a subspecies of black-tailed deer). Highway follows the east shore of Moyie Lake.

Time Zone: On Hwy 3, 15km east of Yahk. In daylight-saving time (early April to late October) set your watch ahead one hour. You are leaving Mountain Standard Time and entering Mountain daylight-saving time. During Standard Time (the winter months) there is no time change. Yahk is always on Mountain Standard Time.

Highway Pullout: 15.5km beyond Yahk. North side of highway.

Moyie: (Pop. 169). 33km north of Yahk, 31km south of Cranbrook. Exceptionally pretty, on a slight hillside overlooking Moyie Lake, and boasting some character buildings. Name thought to come from the French *mouille,* for "wet or soggy," which is how the early explorers found themselves after dragging through the pass from Cranbrook.

Moyie was for a time site of one of the richest lead-silver mines in the province. The ore body was discovered by Pierre, a Ktunaxa native from the St Eugene Mission near Fort Steele. He guided Father Coccola and miner James Cronin to the location where they staked claims. Pierre and Father Coccola sold their claims to Cronin's mining company, which started the St Eugene Mine. The priest and Pierre used most of their share to build churches in Moyie and at the St Eugene Mission (between Cranbrook and Kimberley).

In 1898 the CPR's Crowsnest line was extended around Moyie Lake, to Kootenay Lake. A steamboat operated on Moyie Lake for two seasons, but the railway took over its job. Moyie's population was more than 800 while the mine operated, but when it closed after 17 years, people moved away.

---

been diked to create fertile farmland. The remaining 6,880ha of wetland has been preserved, thankfully, as a bird and waterfowl refuge and outdoor education centre.

More than 250 bird species call it home. These include swans, Canada and snow geese, scaups, grebes, and many other waterfowl and upland birds. The area between Nelson and the US border has one of the world's highest densities of nesting ospreys. Other area residents are deer, moose, elk, and river otters.

Centre offers guided canoe trips, hikes, meadow walks, marsh crawls, forest walks, and lectures. Binoculars and telescopes are available, and use of a theatre and library is free.

Summit Creek Campground: 50 campsites operated by the wildlife area's management authority. Sani-station, showers, fire-

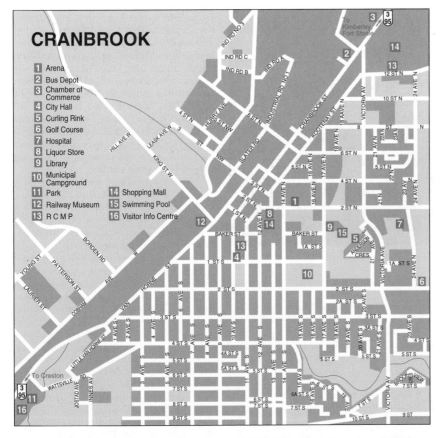

CRANBROOK

1 Arena
2 Bus Depot
3 Chamber of Commerce
4 City Hall
5 Curling Rink
6 Golf Course
7 Hospital
8 Liquor Store
9 Library
10 Municipal Campground
11 Park
12 Railway Museum
13 R C M P
14 Shopping Mall
15 Swimming Pool
16 Visitor Info Centre

South of the present townsite, some of the old mine structures, a slag heap, and an old graveyard, are reminders of town's history. Original fire hall still stands.

Moyie Lake Provincial Park: 90ha; 111 campsites (reservations taken: call 1-800-689-9025; from the Lower Mainland or overseas, call 604-689-9025); sani-station. 46km north of Yahk, 1km off highway. Popular wooded campground on lake's north shore giving good access for water sports. Area used by local sailing club for regattas. Showers, fishing, swimming, boat launch, playground, hiking, picnics, interpretive programs.

On May 29, 1808, explorer David Thompson passed through on his arduous search for a fur-trade route from the Rockies to the Columbia River mouth. Arriving at the peak of spring floods, Thompson found the surging channels of the Moyie River almost impassable. After many attempts to span the river with felled trees (quickly swept away by the torrent), losing valuable furs and goods in the process, they finally advanced.

Jimsmith Lake Provincial Park: 12ha; 29 campsites. 250-422-4200. 62km north of Yahk, 2km west of Cranbrook. West on paved road 4km to park. Wooded campsite on lakeshore. Year-round. Swimming, boating (no powerboats), fishing; cross-country skiing, skating, ice fishing.

Cranbrook: (Pop. 20,000). 64km beyond Yahk on Hwy 3/95. The Rocky Mountain region's major city, sited magnificently on a broad, generous plain with a stunning view of the Rockies east and south, and the Purcells to the west. At this point, the Rocky Mountain Trench is a good 16km wide, and "big sky" is what you see.

Cranbrook sits on what was, before the 1870s, a Ktunaxa camp and pastureland. A group of Ktunaxa people, under the leadership of Chief Joseph, called the place "where two horns lie." The white settlers who eased them out called it Joseph's Prairie. Most of the townsite was purchased originally by the Galbraiths who operated the ferry at Fort Steele. Then Colonel James Baker, member of the BC Legislature, 1886-1900, bought the land and – despite protests of Chief Joseph's adopted son, Chief Isadore – began surveying and fencing. Baker named Cranbrook after his birthplace in England. In 1898, Cranbrook became the divisional point of the CPR, and, therefore, the new capital of the region. (Fort Steele, bypassed, was ruined.) The city was incorporated in 1905.

Cranbrook offers attractions both natural and cultural: 20 parks within the city itself, an 18-hole golf course, the **College of the Rockies**, and a 600-seat performing arts centre called the **Key City Theatre**.

Cranbrook Information: Info Centre, Chamber of Commerce, Box 84, Cranbrook, BC, V1C 4H6. 250-489-5261 or 250-426-5914. Two locations: main office, 2279 Cranbrook St North, on Hwy 3/95, north side of city, year-round; summer office on Hwy 3/95, at Elizabeth Lake Sanctuary, June-Sept.

Cranbrook Airport: Off Hwy 95A, 12km north of Cranbrook. Airport is 3km off Hwy 3/95. (See *Cranbrook Airport Rd*, p.196.)

■ **Canadian Museum of Rail Travel:** 1 Van Horne St North, Cranbrook, BC, V1C 4H9. 250-489-3918. Daily, year-round. Nine original cars from the CPR Trans-Canada Limited of 1929 (which provided luxury service between Montreal and Vancouver). As far as is known, this is the only integrated set in the world, designed at the time as a nine-car travelling hotel. Also a caboose, and CPR station from 1900. The cars, the last of their type built in Canada, represented epitome of railway technology and decor. They are luxurious by any standard, with inlaid Honduran mahogany and black walnut woodwork, brass fixtures, and plush or leather upholstered furniture. Fully restored, the dining car features CPR silverware, glassware, china.

Includes dining car, Argyle (often open for tea); solarium car, River Rouge; deluxe sleeping cars, Rutherglen, Glen Cassie, and Somerset; combination baggage and sleeping car (housing a display on restoration process); day parlour car 6751; baggage car; and superintendent's business car, British Columbia, in completely original condition.

Gift shop, reception area, library, archives, and offices.

■ **Cranbrook Heritage Tour:** Map of heritage buildings at Info Centres or Railway Museum: Imperial Building, City Hall, Fire Hall, Mt Baker Hotel, Masonic Temple, Rotary Clock Tower, Colonel Baker's home.

■ **Cranbrook Golf Club:** 2700 2nd St S. 250-426-6462. Sunny, in-town, 18-hole course with backdrop of stunning Mt Baker.

■ **Elizabeth Lake Sanctuary (Confederation Park):** On Hwy 3/95, south side of Cran-brook. Location of **summer Info Centre**. Also ball fields, and bird sanctuary. This 113ha marsh was preserved in 1972 through the Ministry of Environment and Ducks Unlimited. In the Rocky Mountain Trench migration corridor, the marsh attracts Canada geese, mallard, teal, ringneck, scaup, redhead, goldeneye, bufflehead, and ruddy ducks. Also coots, grebes, black terns, and various songbirds; plus white-tailed deer, moose, muskrats, and painted turtles. Picnic while you watch. BC Wildlife Watch viewing site.

King St West/Wycliffe Rd (the Old Kimberley Hwy): King St W intercepts Van Horne St (Hwy 3/95) in downtown Cranbrook. Take King St W north; it eventually turns into Wycliffe Park Rd, ending at Hwy 95A near Wycliffe Regional Park, 8km north of Hwys 3/95 and 95A junction.

Highways 3/95 and 95A: On north edge of Cranbrook, 4km from city centre, Hwy 95A loops northwest through Kimberley; *Log* follows 95A. For Hwy 3/95 and 3/93 through Fort Steele, see *Elko to Invermere*, p. 200.

Highway 95A

Mission Rd to Kimberley (Old Airport Rd): 1km north of junction with Hwy 3/95. Road, running east of Hwy 95A, is scenic and blacktopped but seldom used. Leads through reserve land at **St Mary's Reserve** and **St Eugene Mission**, past the **Cranbrook Airport**, returning to Hwy 95A 11km north.

St Mary's (Aqam): (Pop. 203). Follow signs a short distance along Mission Rd. After the discovery of gold at Wild Horse Creek in 1863, white miners began flooding into the region. Their presence and new colonial laws began to limit the seasonal movements of the Ktunaxa people. About this time a group of Ktunaxa called the akamnik, under the leadership of Chief Joseph, made their base at present-day Cranbrook (see above), then, in response to white settlement there, moved to the confluence of the St Mary and Kootenay rivers. In 1874, when the Oblates, under Father Fouquet, took up permanent residence here, just a few kilometres upriver, the akamnik moved again, forming the core of a community that became known as the St Mary's Band.

The mission residential school, 1912-1971, is being converted into a four-season resort complex. Planned facilities include a hotel, 18-hole championship golf course, aquatic centre, swimming pools, Ktunaxa interpretive centre, and tipis village. Aqam is also headquarters for the Ktunaxa-Kinbasket Tribal Council.

■ **St Eugene Mission and Church:** The mission was founded by the Oblates in 1855; a resident priest arrived in 1874. Restored church was built in 1897 by Father Coccola and a Ktunaxa man named Pierre from proceeds of their share in St Eugene Mine in Moyie. This is the finest Gothic-style mission church in BC, with hand-painted Italian stained and leaded glass, scalloped louvres, blind windows, and pinnacles and buttresses at each corner. Complete exterior renovation was done in 1985 by the St Mary's Band and East Kootenay Historical Association. Summer tours by reservation: 250-489-2372.

The northern portion of Mission Rd passes by the airport, and continues 3km to junction with Hwy 95A (see below).

Wycliffe Park Rd (Old Kimberley Hwy): 5km north of junction with Hwy 3/95. Road travels west of Hwy 95A (the new Kimberley Hwy) in a loop joining Hwy 95A again at Wycliffe. About 5km along is Bill Dove's **Raptor Rescue and Rehabilitation Society (RRRS)** developed to aid injured or orphaned birds of prey – hawks, falcons, osprey, eagles, and owls. Tours are offered to the public in summer, but by appointment only. Contact Bill Dove, c/o RRRS, at SS3, Site 19-A0, Cranbrook, BC, V1C 6H3. 250-489-2841.

St Mary River: 7km north of 3/95 junction, Hwy 95A crosses this pretty river.

Cranbrook Airport Rd: 12km beyond junction of Hwy 3/95, 16km south of Kimberley. East side of highway. 3km to airport. Daily flights to Vancouver and Calgary.

Wycliffe Regional Park: At junction of Hwy 95A and Airport Rd (see above), west of highway. Small local park with ball park, picnic facilities. Serves farming area of Wycliffe.

Marysville: 21km beyond Hwy 3/95 junction, 7km south of Kimberley. On

Happy Hans in Kimberley, BC's highest city.

southern outskirts of Kimberley, and incorporated into that city. Marysville is site of original smelter built in 1903 for Sullivan Mine. Ore was difficult to process, and the mine and smelter closed after four years.

■ **Marysville Falls:** Sign and parking area in town. It's a short walk along Mark Creek to waterfalls.

Road to St Mary Lake and St Mary's Alpine Provincial Park: On north edge of Marysville, 22km from Hwy 3/95 junction.

SIDE TRIP

to St Mary Lake

St Mary Lake: 17km from junction with Hwy 95A on part-paved, part-gravel road. Fishing. No tourist facilities.

Gray Creek-Kimberley Forestry Rd (Hwy 44): West of St Mary Lake and overland, so to speak, to Kootenay Lake, on top-grade gravel road over Baker Pass. In all, it is 86km from Kimberley to Gray Creek. The road is steep, with some 14 percent grades on the western side. Open seasonally, the route will cut an hour off the journey around. It's scenic, too.

St Mary's Alpine Provincial Park: 9,146ha. Wilderness area, no facilities. 28km north of St Mary Lake on rough gravel logging road. 250-422-4200. Extreme caution: watch for logging trucks. In the Purcell Mountains, a wilderness retreat for the very experienced backcountry traveller. Peaks as high as 2,900m surround the many lakes. Seven main creeks, some with spectacular waterfalls. No designated campsites, no maintained trails.

Return to Highway 95A

Kimberley: (Pop. 6,738). 28km north of Hwy 3/95 junction; 32km north of Cranbrook; 27km south of Wasa. The province's highest town, Kimberley (el. 1,113m) has always been a mining community.

It was named after Kimberley, South Africa, though instead of diamonds, this Kimberley harboured silver, lead, and zinc. In 1892, Joe Bourgeois and James Langill staked the North Star silver-lead claim. Later the same year a second group staked the Shylock and Hamlet claims (which became the Sullivan Mine). The North Star Mine started in 1893, and Kimberley grew up nearby. Ore was hauled by wagon to Fort Steele, then shipped by riverboat to Jennings, Montana. After the Crowsnest Railway was pushed through, the ore was shipped to the smelter at Trail.

Kimberley was always a one-industry town. Everyone worked in the Sullivan Mine. Now, with depleting ore reserves, Cominco has announced permanent closure of the mine by 2001. Like Chemainus, another little BC "town that did," Kimberley is rising high to the occasion. If one mountain can't do it any more, perhaps another can. Hopes are now pinned on North Star Mountain, already becoming a major ski destination. If resourceful Kimberleyites can't work the mines, they'll work the slopes.

In playing upon its status as the second highest city in Canada, Kimberley adopted a Bavarian alpine theme, a sight some travellers may regard as nevertheless peculiar. Stores have gingerbread fronts and bright painted shutters. The pedestrian-only downtown shopping area known as "the Platzl" holds the world's largest operating cuckoo clock. Befitting BC's new Oom-pah-pah capital, a minstrel wanders amidst footbridges, fountains, and flower beds, entertaining on the accordion. For golfers, there are two 18-hole courses.

Kimberley Information: Info Centre, 350 Ross St, Kimberley, BC, V1A 2Z9. 250-427-3666.

■ **Kimberley Heritage Museum:** In the Platzl. Mon-Sat. Winter, afternoons only. 250-427-7510. Historical displays and artifacts.

■ **Cominco Gardens:** Footpath from the Platzl. 250-427-2293. Extensive, beautifully landscaped flower garden. Gift shop, light refreshments.

■ **Bavarian City Mining Railway:** From downtown. Train used in underground mining makes 11km scenic trip. Highlights include 60m trestle, haunted schoolhouse, original Cominco power building, and 24m bridge.

■ **Kimberley Ski and Summer Resort:** 4km from downtown via Gerry Sorenson Way. Info and reservations: 250-427-4881. Summer: chairlift to mountaintop, alpine slide, tennis, mini-golf, bumper boats, go-carts, mountain biking. Winter: vertical 701m; 47 runs, the longest is 6.5km; four chairs, one T-bar, two handle tows. Longest lit run in North America. Nordic skiing. Indoor tennis.

■ **Golf:** Kimberley Golf Club, oldest course in the region, a very playable mountain course just off the cliffs of the St Mary River. Tee times: 250-427-4161 or 1-888-874-2553. **Trickle Creek Golf Resort,** 18-hole course cut into the forested slopes of North Star Mountain. Accommodations adjacent. 250-427-5171.

Cherry Creek Rest Area: 12km beyond Kimberley on Hwy 95A.

Ta Ta Creek: (Pop. 114). 24km beyond Kimberley on Hwy 95A. Stories about how it got its name are legion and lengthy. The one we like involves a bank robber who left the local constable behind, nicely roped up. "Ta ta," was his cheerful farewell.

Highways 93 and 95: 27.5km north of Kimberley, 59.5km north of Cranbrook. North on Hwy 93/95 to Canal Flats, Fairmont Hot Springs, and Invermere. South to Wasa Lake (2km), Fort Steele, Elko, and US Border. See *Elko to Invermere*, p.200.

ROOSVILLE TO CROWSNEST PASS

HIGHWAY 93, CROWSNEST HIGHWAY 3, HIGHWAY 43

Hwy 93 provides easy access to the BC Rockies region from Montana at the Roosville border crossing. The valley in the border area is known as Tobacco Plains, where the Ktunaxa people once cultivated a crop sacred to them. From here it's 36km to the junction at Elko where Hwy 93 veers west toward Kimberley. This *Log* veers east, following the Crowsnest Hwy 3 for 80.5km through the gorgeous Elk River valley to the Crowsnest Pass in the Rockies at the BC/Alberta border.

Crowsnest Pass takes its name from the unusual rounded mountain that stands alone at 2,730m above the rolling hills just into Alberta. Some suggest nomadic Cree peoples passing through the area named the mountain *Kah, Ka-coo-wut-tskis-lun*, meaning "nesting place of the raven." The pass for centuries served as an access route for Ktunaxa people hunting buffalo in the Alberta foothills.

The first white man to traverse the pass, at least from the west, was Michael Phillipps in 1873. Phillipps worked for the Hudson's Bay Company, and was one of the first real settlers in the region. His early efforts to build a trail through the pass were thwarted by Colonel Baker and William Fernie, who were busy sniffing out coal deposits in the Elk Valley and possibly wanted to keep the area under wraps until their claims were staked in the name of the Crow's Nest Coal Company.

Roosville: (Pop. 40). At BC/Montana border. 119km north of Kalispell on US Hwy 93. Customs open 24 hours a day year-round. Fred Roo was postmaster here from 1899. The border town on the US side is called Port of Roosville. Reserve land of Ktunaxa **Tobacco Plains** community extends for 12km north of border. Community operates duty-free shop at border.

Grasmere: (Pop. 147). On Hwy 93, 12km north of border. One-store town named by James Lancaster, an early settler, who was reminded of lovely Grasmere in the English Lake District. Road right off highway at General Store leads to Edwards Lake Campground, operated by Tobacco Plains band. Basic camping, pleasant swimming.

Elk River: 23km north of border, Hwy 93 crosses this beautiful river.

Jaffray-Baynes Lake Rd: 26.5km north of US border. 23km paved back road to the west; rejoins Hwy 3/93 at Jaffray. Road skirts northeast shores of **Lake Koocanusa**, the 110km-long reservoir formed by the Libby Dam on the Kootenay River in Montana. Lake levels fluctuate substantially. Name is combo of Kootenay, Canada, USA.

SIDE TRIP

to Kikomun Creek

Kikomun Creek Provincial Park: 682ha; 135 campsites (reservations taken: call 1-800-689-9025; from the Lower Mainland or overseas, call 604-689-9025), sani-station. 16km off Hwy 93 on Jaffray-Baynes Lake Rd. General info: 250-422-4200. Six warm kettle lakes make this park special. Great beach on Surveyors Lake; hiking/biking, self-guided interpretive trail, boat launch on Lake Koocanusa. Playground, showers, swimming, fishing. Watch for elk and white-tailed deer in winter and early spring. Osprey, loons, turtles. Interpretive programs in summer.

Return to Highway 93

Highway 3: 36km north of US border. Northwest on Hwy 3/93 to Cranbrook (65km), Kimberley, and Fort Steele. Northeast on Hwy 3 (Crowsnest) to Elko, Fernie, Sparwood, and Alberta border (80.5km).

Elko: (Pop. 165). On Hwy 3 just east of junction, 36km north of border. On a bench above the Elk River. Large sawmill is main employer. Before the First World War, Elko, with a population of nearly 1,000, had high hopes of becoming "the Chicago of the Canadian West," even the capital of BC. The flu epidemic of 1918 hit the town hard. Later, a freak hurricane, and then a fire devastated the town. Elko did achieve local fame for its ice cream. Today, it offers limited services.

The Elk Valley: From Elko to Sparwood, Hwy 3 follows the Elk River through the Elk Valley with mountain ranges close on either side. From Sparwood, Hwy 43 follows the river north to Elkford and Elk Lakes Provincial Park.

This beautiful valley was pretty much unsettled until the CPR line was put through the Crowsnest to Cranbrook in 1898. Then the rich coal deposits began to be exploited, people moved into the area, and the *Fernie Free Press* reported in 1901 that the population had reached 3,000. Smaller mining communities such as Hosmer, Michel, Natal, and Corbin sprang up, though most have now disappeared.

Fortunes in the region have fluctuated with the coal markets; mining activity was reduced to almost nil at times. Recently a number of major open-pit mines have been developed, mainly for the export of coking coal to Japan

Roosville to Crowsnest Pass

0 Km 10

and other Asian countries. Mine tours available; contact local information centres.

The Elk Valley was named for the herds of 100 or more elk frequently seen by early explorers. The area is unique in North America in its ability to support large populations of big game. Elk are still the most common large animals, but just from the highway, visitors may also see mule and white-tailed deer, bighorn sheep and black bears. Farther from the beaten track are moose, mountain goats, wolves, grizzlies. Alpine meadows have vivid blue larkspur, red paintbrush, buttercups, and white bunch berry.

The region offers access, mainly by logging roads, to huge unpopulated areas such as the **Flathead Valley** and **Akamina-Kishinena**

Provincial Park, (see p.199). Roads vary greatly: they may be heavily travelled by logging trucks; some are restricted to two-way-radio equipped vehicles. Travellers should gain as much local information as possible and carry topographical maps. (Beware that some of these maps may be quite out of date and roads shown may not be accurate.) The BC Forest Service in Cranbrook can advise on road conditions and restrictions, and has a pamphlet on Forest Service campsites.

Morrissey Provincial Park: 5ha. 16.5km beyond Elko on east side of highway. Picnic area along the Elk River. Fishing.

Highway Pullout: 21km north of Elko, east side of highway.

Fernie Alpine Resort Limited: 25km beyond Elko, west of highway. 250-423-4655. Snow phone: 250-423-3555. Reservations: 1-888-754-7325. Impressive Lizard Range forms backdrop. Nine ski lifts, including double, two triple, and high-speed quad chairlifts, two T-bars, handle tow. Five alpine bowls; cross-country trails. Vertical drop 857m; longest run, 5km. Plenty of on-mountain and off-mountain accommodation.

Mount Fernie Provincial Park: 259ha; 38 campsites (reservations taken: call 1-800-689-9025; from the Lower Mainland or overseas, call 604-689-9025). 28km beyond Elko, west of highway. General info: 250-422-4200. Picnic and day-use area, hiking, self-guided interpretive trail. Lizard Creek, with waterfall, flows through wooded park.

Fernie: (Pop. 5,012). 31.5km north of Elko, 49km east of Alberta border. The community sprang up at the turn of the century along the new railway through the broad, sheltered Elk Valley. Fernie was built in a loop on the Elk River: Hwy 3 enters and exits the town over bridges.

The town was named for William Fernie, instrumental in developing the area's coal mines. Nearby Coal Creek Mine was the economic impetus for a town that suffered serious trials in its early years. The Fernie area was formerly a base for the Ktunaxa community, yakyaqanqat, "way through the mountain." Their descendants now live at Tobacco Plains, and explain how William Fernie wheedled information about a coal deposit from a young yakyaqanqat woman, promising her marriage. Then Fernie spurned her, invoking her mother's wrath. She called upon the spirits to place a curse on the name of Fernie. The events that followed are more than legend.

In 1901, an explosion in the Coal Creek Mine killed at least 128 men. In 1904 there was a fire. Four years later, another fire destroyed whatever was left, killing 10 people and leaving 6,000 homeless. In 1916, a flood occurred. Finally, in 1964, in an elaborate and dramatic ceremony, chiefs Red Eagle and Big Crane of the Tobacco Plains Band held a ceremony to lift the curse on Fernie.

Elk Lake and the Elk Range, just north of Elkford in Elk Lakes Provincial Park.

The saga continues now, some say, high in the Rocky Mountains north of town where the woman, her mother, and Fernie still roam.

Offering skiing in winter (5km west of Fernie off Hwy 3, see above) and fly-fishing in summer on the Elk River and other streams, Fernie is drawing more and more visitors, as well as an influx of escapees from highly commercialized Whistler and big cities such as Calgary. Some are calling it BC's Aspen, for its superb Rocky Mountain setting and the array of intact heritage buildings downtown. In fact, in a recent issrue of New York-based *Men's Journal* magazine profiling "the 20 wildest, tastiest, smartest mountain and beach communities in America," Fernie ranked 7th.

There are a number of bike and hiking trails in, around, and leading out of Fernie. Some 15 bike trails are now listed in a brochure available from the Info Centre. A bike trail leads over the dikes on the Elk River, around part of the city, and through the riverside Mountview Park. An easy bike ride is the Coal Creek Heritage Trail to the old townsite of Coal Creek.

Worth a visit is Fernie's somewhat unkempt pioneer cemetery, which sits atop a hill to the south, overlooking the city. Here, much of Fernie's tragic past is engraved upon headstones. (William Fernie, by the way, moved to Victoria, where he died a bachelor and is buried in the Ross Bay Cemetery. He used his wealth for charitable causes, among which was the Royal Jubilee Hospital.)

Fernie Information: Info Centre, Fernie Chamber of Commerce, Hwy 3 and Dicken Rd, Fernie, BC, V0B 1M0. On north edge of city, beside huge oil derrick. 250-423-6868.

■ **Historic Oil Derrick and Drilling Equipment:** Next to Info Centre. An exact reconstruction of derrick and drilling equipment used 1914-1920 in the Flathead Valley southeast of Fernie.

■ **Fernie and District Historical Museum:** Moved to new location, ask at Info Centre.

■ **Heritage Buildings and Walking Tour:** Map of city available from Info Centre shows heritage building locations including 1911 brick courthouse and 1905 city hall. Some wonderful old stone buildings.

■ **Fernie Golf and Country Club:** 18-hole course flanked by expansive mountains. East end of 2nd Ave. 250-423-7773.

■ **Ghost Rider:** Every summer evening just before sunset, a shadowy ghost rider slides across the slopes of Mt Hosmer (el 2,506m), on Fernie's northern outskirts. The restless soul and steed can be seen at the mouth of a cave as the sun slips behind the rocky cradle of Crowsnest Pass. According to the Ktunaxa of Tobacco Plains, this is the ghost of the woman spurned by William Fernie, with her mother walking behind, the pair in eternal pursuit of the fugitive Fernie.

Road to Mine: Road through town leads 5km to abandoned Coal Creek mine and tonwsite where remnants of the operation still exist. Ask in Fernie for directions.

Highway Pullout: On Hwy 3, 7km past Fernie, east side of highway.

Hosmer: (Pop. 271). On Hwy 3, 11.5km north of Fernie. Former mining town, heritage sites. Charles Rudolph Hosmer was one of Canada's leading industrialists. He was involved with coal mining and controlled Ogilvie Flour Mills. He was also a CPR director. Limited services.

Olson Rest Area: 16km beyond Fernie, on highway's north side. Great view of the Rocky Mountains.

Sparwood: (Pop. 3,982). On Hwy 3, 29km northeast of Fernie; 18km west of Alberta border. Sparwood was incorporated in 1966 to replace the coal-blackened twin towns of Michel and Natal that had existed since the turn of the century. They had reached their peak population of about 2,000 in 1920, but their proximity to the mine, and the amount of coal dust deposited on them, made them look like an environmental nightmare. Residents were moved – many of them reluctantly – to the new town of Sparwood, located about 4.5km from the mine site. Michel and Natal were then bulldozed. In 1968 Kaiser Resources purchased the mine and opened its Balmer open-pit mine at Harmer Ridge across the highway from the old underground mine. In 1991 the operation was sold and is now named the Elkview Coal Corporation.

Tours of the mine operate July-Aug; group tours are available in the off-season. Call the Info Centre. Now on display next to the Info Centre is the mammoth 350t Titan, is the world's largest dump truck.

Sparwood has an impressive leisure centre, golf course, and shopping facilities.

Sparwood Information: Info Centre, Chamber of Commerce, Box 1448, Sparwood, BC, V0B 2G0. Aspen Dr, adjacent Hwy 3, with 3m statue of coal miner in front. Year-round. 250-425-2423.

Elk Valley Regional Airport: North of Sparwood on Hwy 43. Charters.

■ **Sparwood Leisure Centre:** Red Cedar and Pine Ave. 250-425-0552. Pool, whirlpool, sauna, racquetball, weight room, curling, arena, restaurant.

■ **Mountain Shadows Campground:** 30 campsites, sani-station, hook-ups, showers. South entrance to town on Hwy 3, adjacent golf course. 250-425-7815. May-Oct.

■ **Sparwood Golf Club:** On Hwy 3. 250-425-2612. Challenging nine-hole mountain course.

■ **Heritage Murals:** Historic Michel and Natal come to life.

■ **Rocky Mountain High Adventures:** North of Sparwood, just off Hwy 43. 250-425-2399. Horseback riding, hayrides, buggy rides.

Highway 43: Leads north from Sparwood 32km to Elkford, and a further 87km to Elk Lakes Provincial Park.

SIDE TRIP

to Elkford and Park

Hwy 43 follows the Elk River north, and 13km north of Sparwood passes the Line Creek Mine. This open-pit coal mine was developed in 1980.

Elkford: (Pop. 2,729). On Hwy 43, 32km north of Sparwood. Elkford is another new town, incorporated in 1971 shortly after work had started on Fording Coal Mine 29km north of the townsite. In 1982 Westar Mines developed its Greenhills open-pit mine 6km north of town. That mine is also now owned by Fording Coal. Tours of Fording Coal and Greenhills open-pit mines are offered through the chamber of commerce on Saturdays throughout the summer.

Elkford calls itself the "Wilderness Capital of BC," and enjoys a spectacular Rocky Mountain setting. Many wilderness walking trails start just minutes from town. Wildlife is of prime interest: here is one of the largest bighorn sheep populations on the continent. Amenities include a golf course, shopping, parks, aquatic centre, and ski hill.

Elkford Information: Info Centre, Elkford Chamber of Commerce, Box 220, 4A Front St, Elkford, BC, V0B 1H0. 250-865-4614. Year-round.

■ **Elkford Municipal Campground:** 62 RV and tent sites. On Hwy 43 at junction of Michel Rd. 250-865-2241. Full services, hook-ups, sani-station, hiking trails.

■ **Elkford Interpretive Trail System:** More than 40km of trails present hikers and skiers with diverse forest ecosystems. Info Centre has maps and info.

■ **Mountain Meadows Golf Club:** On Hwy 43 in town. 250-865-7413. Nine-hole course, mountain vistas, rentals, restaurant.

■ **Wapiti Ski Hill:** On Natal Rd, very near town. 250-865-2020. Family-oriented, seven runs, T-bar, night skiing, groomed cross-country track, day lodge, ski lessons.

Two adventure roads lead north from Elkford. One is a continuation of Hwy 43, which terminates at the Alberta border. This road is also known as the Elk Lakes Forestry Rd that leads to a magnificent wilderness: **Elk Lakes Provincial Park** and adjacent to it, the new **Height of the Rockies Provincial Park** (see below). This is a secondary gravel road maintained June-Sept for two-wheel-drive access to the park gate. At all other times, this is strictly 4x4 country.

The other road north from Elkford is the Fording Rd. This paved road runs northeast of Elkford along the Fording River to Fording Coal Limited's Greenhills and Fording River mining operations. 5km beyond Elkford a parking lot offers access to the series of hiking trails, including a trail to Josephine Falls.

Some townspeople hope that eventually Hwy 43 will be extended across the border to connect with Alberta's Hwy 40 and Kananaskis country. For now, the area stands in magnificent isolation. Others want to keep it this way.

Elk Lakes Provincial Park: 17,245ha. Backcountry camping. About 47km north of Elkford, the Elk Lakes Forestry Rd crosses the Elk River, joining the Kananaskis Power Line Rd. It is 25km from this crossing to the park. 250-422-4200. Write: BC Parks, Box 118, Wasa, BC, V0B 2H0. Lower Elk Lake campground is about 1km from parking lot; Petain Creek campground is about 1km from south end of Upper Elk Lake. Hikers and cross-country skiers can also enter the park over the West Elk Pass from Alberta's Peter Lougheed Provincial Park.

Subalpine wilderness park with hiking trails leading to Elk Lakes (headwaters of Elk River) and Petain Creek. Another trail leads to Elk Pass over the Continental Divide and into Kananaskis Lakes area in Alberta. The Elk Lakes are surrounded by mountains and glaciers named in honour of French leaders in the First World War: Mt Petain, Mt Nivelle, Mt Joffre, and Mt Foch. Lakes and streams offer fishing for cutthroat, Dolly Varden, and white-

fish. Many mountain goats, elk and moose in summer. Check locally about road conditions before departing. This is a true wilderness area (there are no facilities) for hiking, fishing, mountaineering, horseback riding (Cordona watershed only), and nature appreciation.

Height of the Rockies Provincial Park: 54,208ha. Wilderness camping. No signs, no facilities. Adjacent southern boundary of Elk Lakes Provincial Park. Access to this new park is extremely limited: there are undeveloped trails from Elk Lakes Park and Banff National Park, and logging roads lead in from Canal Flats and along the White River. 250-422-4200. Write BC Parks, Box 118, Wasa, BC, V0B 2H0. Park forms the southern tip of a remarkable stretch of Rocky Mountains national and provincial parkland stretching about 600km northward. It is home to high concentrations of elk, mule deer, bighorn sheep, mountain goats, moose, black and grizzly bears, and cougars. Hiking, mountaineering, horseback riding, fishing. Mechanized access prohibited (including mountain bikes).

Return to Highway 3 at Sparwood

Elkview Coal Corporation: 4km beyond Sparwood Hwy 3 passes through the Elkview mining operation (formerly Westar Mining). The mine is on the west side of the road; office and service buildings on the east. This is the site of former towns of Michel and Natal. One original building remains, the **Michel Hotel** (still in use). Elkview operates one of the largest surface mines in Canada. Its annual output is 3.2 million tonnes.

Just 3km beyond the Michel Hotel, where the railway crosses the highway, a sign points out the road to **Fording Coal Mountain operation.** This mine 29km south of Hwy 3 is just beyond the former mining community of Corbin. The original mine was closed after a strike and riot in 1935. The remains of a few buildings still survive.

Crowsnest Provincial Park: 46ha. 20km east of Sparwood, 400m west of Alberta border. Rest area, picnics, interpretive signs. 250-422-3212. Right in the middle of the Crowsnest Pass.

The Crowsnest Pass is a relatively easy 1,357m pass through the Rockies. It was used for centuries as a travel route by aboriginal peoples. Hwy 3 crosses the BC/Alberta border in the pass, just beyond the park, and carries on through the Alberta coal mining towns of **Coleman** and **Blairmore** to **Fort Macleod**.

Akamina-Kishinena Provincial Park: 10,921ha; backcountry camping only, at Wall Lake and Akamina Meadows. 250-422-3212. Rangers at station below Forum Falls, just before the park boundary at Akamina Pass, mid-June to late Sept. Park, on BC's southeastern border, can be reached through Waterton Lakes National Park in southwest Alberta, or via BC's Flathead River valley (above). The easiest route is this one, via Waterton. Continue on Hwy 3 into Alberta, then take Hwy 6 south from Pincher Creek. Once in the national park, follow Cameron Lake (the Akamina Parkway) Rd for about 14km, watching for the Akamina Pass trailhead on the right, 1km before Cameron Lake. A 1.5km uphill walk leads to Akamina Pass, the boundary between BC and Alberta, and eastern boundary of Akamina-Kishinena Park. This park, created in 1995, borders Alberta's Waterton Lakes National Park and Montana's Glacier National Park. (The same year, UNESCO designated the Waterton-Glacier International Peace Park a World Heritage Site.) Waters from the mountains embraced by these three parks flow into three of the largest river systems in North America – the Saskatchewan, Mississippi, and Columbia.

Akamina-Kishinena itself protects a landscape of international significance. Here are Akamina and Kishinena ridges – made of green and red argillites, sandstones, siltstones, and limestones estimated at 800 million to 1.6 billion years old – offering ridge walking opportunities unmatched in the Canadian Rockies. At the intersection of five major vegetation zones, this is habitat for plants and animals – beargrass, pygmy poppy, and the Yellowstone moose – found nowhere else in BC. Also here, one of North America's densest grizzly bear populations, coyote, deer, moose, mountain goats, and bighorn sheep. Beware of bears.

ELKO TO INVERMERE

HIGHWAY 3/93, HIGHWAY 93, HIGHWAY 93/95

This 176km stretch begins on Hwy 3/93 leading northwest from the Elko junction. The junction is 63.5km east of Cranbrook, 31.5km west of Fernie, and 36km north of the BC/Montana border. Hwy 3/93, which becomes Hwy 93 (just for a short 8km segment west of Fort Steele), and then 93/95, joins the Kootenay River near Wardner and follows its shores closely to Canal Flats. The river flows south, the *Log* flows north. This portion of the Rocky Mountain Trench is quite flat – some woodland, some open grassland – and it is clear why this was used as a transportation corridor by the first travellers. Finally, Hwy 93/95 skirts the long and lovely Columbia and Windermere lakes en route to Invermere.

Jaffray: (Pop. 375). 16.5km beyond Elko. Basic tourist services.

Baynes Lake-Jaffray Rd: At Jaffray. Goes south 11km to Kikomun Creek Provincial Park. Details in *Roosville to Crowsnest Pass*, p.197.

Wardner-Fort Steele Rd: 28km north of Elko, on northeast side of Kootenay River. Alternate (paved) 33km route to Fort Steele via Bull River, Kootenay Trout Hatchery, Norbury Lake Provincial Park.

BACK ROADS TRIP

to Fort Steele

Bull River: (Pop. 18). 5km beyond Hwy 3/93, on Wardner-Fort Steele Rd. The Bull River Inn and a few houses are reminders of its busier days as a lumber town for the CPR. The town shrank after 1900.

Kootenay Trout Hatchery: 8km beyond Hwy 3/93 junction, on Wardner-Fort Steele Rd. Tours: 250-429-3214. Daily, 8-4, year-round. Hatchery raises 6 million trout annually (rainbow, brook, and cutthroat); 75 percent are released in the Kamloops, Cariboo, and Prince George areas, 25 percent in the Kootenays.

Norbury Lake Provincial Park: 97ha; 46 campsites. 16km along Wardner-Fort Steele Rd, 17km south of Fort Steele. 250-422-4200. Below spectacular Steeples Range, includes Peckhams Lake and fronts Norbury Lake. Swimming, fishing, boat launch (no powerboats). Summer's a good time to see ground squirrels and white-tailed deer.

Near Fort Steele junction, road follows, then crosses, **Wildhorse Creek**. This is the creek that precipitated the largest gold rush in the BC Rockies region. See *Introduction to BC Rockies*.

Return to Highway 3/93 and Wardner-Fort Steele Road

Wardner Bridge: Just north of junction with Wardner-Fort Steele Rd, 28km north of Elko, Hwy 3/93 crosses point at which the Kootenay River becomes Lake Koocanusa (Libby Reservoir). Koocanusa is a combo of Kootenay, Canada, and USA.

Wardner Provincial Park: 4ha. South of the highway, across the bridge from the junction. Small park on Lake Koocanusa. Swimming, fishing (no boat launch).

Wardner: (Pop. 195). Off Hwy 3/93 2km beyond Wardner Provincial Park. Founded in 1895, once site of a large sawmill.

Rampart Rest Area: 49km beyond Elko, south of highway.

Highway 3 and Highway 93: A T-intersection 4.5km beyond rest area, 53.5km north of Elko. Here, Hwy 3/93 divides: Hwy 93 leads north 8km to Fort Steele; Hwy 3 leads southwest 6km to Hwy 95, then 4km to downtown Cranbrook. *Log* veers northeast with Hwy 93 to Fort Steele and Invermere.

Fort Steele Heritage Town: 150ha. On Hwy 93, 8km north of Hwy 3/93 junction. 250-489-3351. At the confluence of the Kootenay and St Mary rivers, the former boom town of Fort Steele is very much alive with the presence of the past.

With the gold rush underway about 8km north at Wildhorse Creek in 1864, John Galbraith began a cable ferry service here to help miners get across the Kootenay River. A log store became the centre of the tiny settlement known as Galbraith's Ferry or Galbraith's Landing.

This was a time of great change in the region. White miners were flooding into territories where the Ktunaxa people had moved freely on their seasonal rounds. In about 1884, two miners were murdered, and two years later two Ktunaxa men – Little Isadore and Kapula – were accused, arrested on flimsy evidence, and jailed near Galbraith's Ferry. To their rescue came a Ktunaxa chief, also named Isadore. Confronting colonial laws he believed unjust, he freed the accused, then ejected from his territories the local magistrate's land surveyor (who had been busily fencing off Ktunaxa grazing land). It was now the summer of 1887, and in response to Chief Isadore's actions, local settlers called in the North West Mounted Police – 75 armed men under Inspector Sam Steele. Isadore turned over Little Isadore and Kapula, and though Sam Steele ultimately released them again, white law prevailed. The North West Mounted Police built winter quarters at Galbraith's Ferry (there were no palisades, despite the appearance of today's heritage town), stayed a year, then rode off into the sunset. To honour their heroism, Galbraith's Ferry was renamed Fort Steele.

The dust had barely settled when another mining boom, in 1893, shook the East Kootenay. This time it was hard rock – silver, lead, and zinc – flowing from mines (the North Star and later the Sullivan) to the north near present-day Kimberley. Fort Steele was once again at a nexus: here, ore was transferred from freight wagons to steam-powered riverboats. By 1897, there were more than 4,000 people living in Fort Steele, fuelled on expectations that the railway, too, would soon pass through the Crowsnest Pass and make its divisional point here. The railway came in 1898, but it went to Cranbrook, not Fort Steele. By 1902, the population here had plummeted to 150.

Fort Steele was never completely abandoned: the Kershaw, and Carlin & Durick stores were open until the 1950s. In 1961, the provincial government saw Fort Steele's historic importance, and began reconstruction. More than mere renovation, the town has almost been reborn. There are some 50 buildings, including some from the original town and North West Mounted Police camp, some old buildings moved in from other towns, and some replicas. The Prospector Printing Office prints souvenir copies of old newspapers, Kershaw's Family Store sells pioneer goods once again, and staff and volunteers in costume carry on wheel making, horseshoeing, baking, and quilting.

The town also raises Clydesdale horses, and offers free wagon rides every 20 minutes (horses take time out 1:30-2:30pm). A steam train takes a scenic loop to a lookout over the valley. Special events include the Harvest Festival, Halloween, and Thanksgiving Celebrations, and Wild Horse Theatre productions.

Grounds are open year-round, dawn to dusk; activities are mostly mid-June to early Sept. Admission fee in peak season. Visit the museum, International Hotel Restaurant, Prospector Print Shop, City Bakery, Kershaw's General Store, and Mrs. Sprague's Confectionery.

Wildhorse, Fisherville, and Last Mile of the Dewdney Trail: Just north of Fort Steele on Hwy 93 at junction of Wardner-Fort Steele back road. Two-hour walk up Wildhorse Creek to see remnants of historic gold-rush ghost towns, and the last portion of Dewdney's 1.2m-wide trail that was blazed east from Hope in seven months during 1865.

Campbell-Meyer Rest Area: 3.5km north of Fort Steele, east side of highway. Good place to see western painted turtles.

Bummers Flats: Small pullout 9km north of Fort Steele on Hwy 93, west side of highway. Nesting area in marshes along Kootenay River. Potholes have been created by Ducks Unlimited and provincial government to provide nesting habitat for waterfowl. Also look for mountain bluebirds, pileated woodpeckers, meadowlarks, turkey vultures.

Wasa Slough Wildlife Sanctuary: 14km beyond Fort Steele, northward along Hwy 93 for 4km. Sanctuary borders highway, visible from road. Home to waterfowl, eagles, osprey, herons, turkey vultures. Canada geese nest on top of muskrat houses. (Muskrats don't eat the eggs and would be foolish to try. Geese are fierce.)

Wasa Lake: (Pop. 384). On Hwy 93, 20km beyond Fort Steele. On popular Wasa Lake, shallow and warm for swimming.

Wasa Lake Provincial Park: 144ha; 104 campsites (reservations taken: call 1-800-689-9025; from the Lower Mainland or overseas, call 604-689-9025); sani-station. General info: 250-422-4200. On road that loops around town and lake. Popular for swimming and water sports, less for fishing. Playground, self-guided nature trail, interpretive programs. Good for small mammal spotting: two species of ground squirrel. Gray jays, and Clark's nutcracker. Wasa is a glacier-made kettle lake. Both Osoyoos and Christina lakes have been claimed the warmest, but there are folks who say that Wasa's the winner.

Highway 95A: 2km beyond Wasa. Leads south 27km to Kimberley. Hwy 93 joins up with Hwy 95 north, to become Hwy 93/95.

Wasa Rest Area: About 1.5km north of Hwy 95A.

Skookumchuck: (Pop. 25). On Hwy 93/95, 13km north of Hwy 95A junction, east side of Kootenay River. Crestbrook Forest Industries operates a large pulp mill here. Name is Chinook trading language for "strong water." Restaurant, store, gas.

Premier Lake Provincial Park: 662ha; 56 campsites (reservations taken: call 1-800-689-9025; from the Lower Mainland or overseas, call 604-689-9025). General info: 250-422-4200. Just north of Skookumchuck, gravel road leads 16km east to Premier Lake. Wheelchair accessible campsite and picnic table. Premier and four smaller lakes offer good fishing, summer and winter. Bighorn sheep, elk, and deer. Fish trap display at mouth of Staples Creek shows how eggs are collected for Kootenay Trout Hatchery. Spawning rainbow trout mid-May to mid-June. Swimming, fishing, boat launch, hiking.

Elk Viewing: Cleared hills are good elk-spotting areas, especially in spring. Fence wires are flagged so they are more visible to wildlife when crossing the road.

Whiteswan Lake Rd: 36km beyond Hwy 95A junction. Leads east to Whiteswan Lake and Top of the World provincial parks.

SIDE TRIP

to Provincial Parks

Whiteswan Lake Provincial Park: 1,994ha; 88 campsites in four campgrounds located 17.5-33km off Hwy 93/95 on fairly rough gravel road. 250-422-4200. This logging and mining road occasionally narrows to one lane, edged by cliffs, and drivers must use caution – there's always the chance an ore truck is bearing down around the corner. Trucks have right of way! The experience is worth it: just know what you're facing, and be prepared.

Park is on a scenic plateau in the Kootenay Ranges and includes Whiteswan and Alces (Moose) lakes, part of the White River, and many small creeks. Lakes have been stocked annually since 1961 with rainbow trout. **Alces Lake:** fly-fishing only, no powerboats. Alces is Latin for "moose," seen in and around the lake. These are Shiras moose, a subspecies whose Canadian range is confined to this corner of BC.

Campgrounds are at Alces Lake (one), and Whiteswan Lake (three). **Lussier Hot Springs** (undeveloped natural hot springs) are located at park boundary (at 17.5km). Swimming, fishing, boat launch; winter recreation. 8km hiking trail on north shores of the two lakes.

Lussier River Rd: 22km beyond Hwy 93/95, just inside Whiteswan Lake Park at Alces Lake. Road leads south 31km to Top of the World Provincial Park.

Top of the World Provincial Park: 8,791ha; backcountry camping. 250-422-4200. Write: BC Parks, Box 118, Wasa, BC, V0B 2K0. On Lussier River Rd, 31km south of junction with Whiteswan Lake Rd. Watch for logging and ore trucks. An alpine wilderness park of great beauty. Mt Morro, the highest peak, reaches 3,002m. Trails from the parking area lead to five camping sites. Most popular hike (two-hour) is along Lussier River to Fish Lake;

tent sites and one cabin accommodating up to 24 people on first-come first-served basis. Also, climbing, mountain biking, and horseback riding (designated trails). Good lake fishing for trout. In winter: good fishing, ski touring.

This wilderness has a long history of human use: the Ktunaxa people for millennia mined the area's top-of-the-line chert (a flint-like quartz). Artifacts found on summit of Mt Morro suggest the mountain was an important spiritual destination. Visitors are asked to respect this place as a living museum – take only photographs, leave only footprints.

Elko to Invermere

Return to Highway 93/95

Canal Flats: (Pop. 685). On Hwy 93/95, 41km north of Hwy 95A junction. Between the Kootenay River and the south shore of Columbia Lake. Logging, sawmill.

Canal Flats is centre of one of the continent's most interesting geographical features, sitting on a 2km strip of land separating Columbia Lake (headwaters of the northward-flowing Columbia River), from the southward-flowing Kootenay River. Details on the surprising flow charts of these rivers are in the *Introduction to the British Columbia Rockies*, p.183.

These two river systems have been the focus of much history. David Thompson, the first European to visit, came up the Columbia from the Golden area in 1807, and called the site McGillivray's Portage.

Today's name, Canal Flats, originates from an extraordinary scheme devised in the 1880s by William Adolph Baillie-Grohman, to dig a canal through the portage separating the Kootenay River and Columbia Lake. His stated aim was to drain much of the Kootenay River into the Columbia system, to prevent the annual flooding of valuable farmland along the Kootenay River near today's Creston. There were strong objections from residents of the Columbia Valley, needless to say, and also from the CPR, fearing rail washouts. Undaunted, Baillie-Grohman altered his plans, saying his new purpose was to help navigation through the river systems.

The canal was completed in 1889, but the lock was so narrow and dangerous that only two boats ever passed through it, the *Gwendoline* in 1894, and the *North Star*, in 1902, the latter completely wrecking the locks in the process. (Baillie-Grohman's career was one bizarre disaster after another, often with a silver lining: completing his absurd canal actually netted him a provincial land grant of more than 12,000ha. Not so lucky on a bear hunt, he shot a neighbour's prize boar.)

The idea of a canal or diversion of the Kootenay River at Canal Flats was revived in the 1970s by BC Hydro, planning to generate more electrical capacity in the Columbia River system. The plan met substantial opposition and has not proceeded.

Canal Flats Provincial Park: 6ha. 3km north of Canal Flats. Access from the town (not from Hwy 93/95); take northeast road. On east shore of Columbia Lake. Manicured grounds, picnic, boat launch, windsurfing. Here you may view the remains of the Baillie-Grohman Canal. And, Sept-April, is a good time to see bighorn sheep.

Columbia Wetlands Wildlife Management Area: Along Hwy 93/95 from Canal Flats to Donald. Home to abundant waterfowl, eagles, herons, osprey, deer, and elk. Excellent wildlife viewing opportunities all along the 150km-long management area paralleling the highway.

Coy's Hill Rest Area: 15km beyond Canal Flats.

Dutch Creek Hoodoos: 20km beyond Canal Flats. At the north end of Columbia Lake, near the bridge over Dutch Creek, are strangely shaped formations of earth resulting from erosion. Ktunaxa elders explain that, back in the mists of time, an enormous fish wounded by Coyote tried to make its way along the Rocky Mountain Trench. It was a difficult journey. Finally the fish gave up and died at Canal Flats. As its flesh decomposed, the ribs fell apart. Half became the hoodoos here, the other half are hoodoos farther south, near St Mary's reserve.

West Side Rd: 22km north of Canal Flats, just past the hoodoos, 26km paved back road offers an alternate route to Invermere on the west side of Windermere Lake. Not much traffic: it's a great road for cycling, sometimes used for cycling races.

Columbia River: 23.5km north of Canal Flats, Hwy 93/95 crosses the Columbia as it begins its dramatic 2,000km journey to the Pacific Ocean. Columbia Lake, to the south, forms the headwaters of North America's fourth longest river, and one of its most remarkable in terms of routes. From here, the new river flows due north, but after 300km it turns around its mountain barriers, to flow almost due south to Castlegar, where it is joined by the Kootenay River. From there, it continues southwest, pouring into the Pacific in Oregon, US. This river was called Rio de San Roque by early Spanish explorers. American explorer-trader Capt Robert Gray named it Columbia, after his ship. From this, came the name of our province, British Columbia. The fur trader, David Thompson, first followed the Columbia from its headwaters to its mouth: a task begun in 1808, with the final most difficult kilometres conquered in 1811.

The Columbia, one of the continent's biggest watersheds, is also its most dammed river: from its headwaters to its mouth are at least 45 hydroelectric dams. Of those, about 18 are in BC. More than 80 per cent of BC's electricity comes from either the Columbia River or the Peace Rivers in northern BC. Three major dams (the Duncan, Hugh Keenleyside, and Mica) were built in the 1960s and 1970s to provide power for US generating stations. These and other developments (irrigation projects, stock raising, logging, pollution from cities) have had a major impact on what was was one of the greatest salmon-spawning rivers in the world.

Fairmont Hot Springs: (Pop. 364). On Hwy 93/95, 25km north of Canal Flats. In the shadow of the Rockies, with the Purcells across the valley to the west.

Fairmont Airport: Across the highway from the Fairmont Hot Springs Resort. No scheduled flights.

■ **Fairmont Hot Springs Resort:** Box 10, Fairmont Hot Springs, BC, V0B 1L0. 250-345-6311 or 1-800-663-4979. Established 1922. The Ktunaxa people long ago discovered the curative powers of these waters, odourless and without sulphur. The springs were named in the late 19th century by Sarah Galbraith,

wife of John, first white woman at Galbraith's Ferry. The flowing hot waters have always intrigued. An English manufacturer from Manchester, W. Heap Holland, and then his son, owned the property from the early 1900s, running it as a ranch and resort.

Brothers Lloyd and Earl Wilder, modern pioneers, came out from Saskatchewan after the Second World War and operated a sawmill near Radium. They bought the property in 1957; by the mid-'60s, they had sold the sawmill and begun expansion of the resort. Earl retired, Lloyd carried on. The resort has expanded steadily; with plans projected past the year 2000. Lloyd's great interest was the Charolais cattle from France, the "silver cattle with the golden future." He won the first medal given to a breeder outside France, for the bull "Demos." But finally the ranchland was sacrificed for Fairmont's new jet airstrip. Twenty years of breeding was auctioned off at a World Sale at Fairmont in 1986. A painting of one of the grand silver sires hangs near the resort's lobby.

■ **The Hot Pools:** Resort's 1,000-sq-m swimming and diving pools offer natural mineral waters 35-45C. 8am-10pm daily.

■ **Fairmont Ski Hill:** Vertical drop of 304m; longest run 1.5km; one triple chair, one platter lift. 20km of cross-country trails.

■ **Golf: Mountainside Golf Course at Fairmont Hot Springs Resort**, 250-345-6314 or 1-800-663-4979. 18-hole course with unique crowned greens are a challenge; the scenery is splendid. Packages include unlimited golf on both courses. **Riverside Golf at Fairmont**, 250-345-6346 or 1-800-665-2112. Exciting 18-hole course along 4km of frontage on the Columbia's headwaters. Mediterranean-style clubhouse, with white stucco and red-tile roof. Accommodation packages in cooperation with Fairmont Hot Springs Resort.

Along with golf and skiing, Fairmont offers hiking (ask about Ktunaxa "Spirit Trail" that goes all the way to Canal Flats), trail riding, and plane and helicopter tours to the Bugaboos and Lake of the Hanging Glacier.

Windermere Lake: A few kilometres beyond Fairmont Hot Springs, Hwy 93/95 follows lake's east shore. A popular resort area.

Windermere: (Pop. 1,273). 17km beyond Fairmont. East side of Windermere Lake. Plenty of tourist facilities.

In Windermere, visible for all to see, is loot taken from BC's biggest robbery – the whole of St Peter's Anglican Church. Church is perched where the thieves left it, atop a knoll with views of both the Purcell and Rocky mountains. Back in 1887, St Peter's began life in the railway town of Donald, 209km away. Ten years later, when the CPR moved operations westward, most of Donald's inhabitants trundled off, too, to the burgeoning town of Revelstoke. But Rufus and Celina Kimpton were moving east to Windermere, and they wanted a church. They loaded St Peter's onto a railway flatcar.

Alas, somewhere en route the Kimptons discovered the 270kg bell was gone. While citizens of Revelstoke realized that their church was in Windermere, the Windermerians learned that their bell was in a church steeple in Golden.

■ **St Peter's Church:** Located on Kootenay St. 250-342-6644.

■ **Windermere Valley Golf Course:** An exceptional 18-hole course cut into the mountain's edge. 250-342-3004.

Road to James Chabot Provincial Park, Invermere, and Panorama Resort: 6km beyond Windermere, west off Hwy 93/95.

James Chabot Provincial Park: 13ha. 2km west on road to Invermere. On lake's north shore. Sandy beach, playground. Good swimming, windsurfing, sailing, fishing. Wheelchair ramp into swimming area.

Invermere: (Pop. 2,687). 2km west of the park, 4km off Hwy 93/95 via Athalmer Rd. On the western shores of Windermere Lake. David Thompson, first European into the area, crossed the Rockies in 1807 and travelled up the Columbia River to Windermere Lake. With his aboriginal wife and children, and eight others, he built the region's first trading post, near present-day Invermere, and called it Kootenae House.

Today it's a lively tourist area with Windermere Lake the centre of summer activities, and the ski slopes at Panorama Resort the focus for winter. Sept-Oct, look for spawning kokanee in the Columbia River at the northern end of Windermere Lake.

Established as the shopping centre of the Windermere Valley, Invermere has unique shops, a full range of services, and that special kind of holiday ambience that money can't buy. Just go there.

Invermere Information: Information centre, Columbia Valley Chamber of Commerce, Box 1019, 651 Highway 93/95, Crossroads, Windermere, BC, V0A 1K0. 250-342-6316 or 250-342-2844. Daily.

■ **Windermere Valley Museum:** 622-3rd St. (At the top of the hill and to the right, entering Invermere). 250-342-9769. June-Sept. Winter, by appointment. Pioneer, mining, and railway history: main building is original train station.

■ **Kootenae House Monument:** Right off Wilmer-Panorama Rd onto Westside Rd. A few hundred metres to cairn marking site of trading post built by David Thompson and Ktunaxa people in 1807.

■ **Pynelogs Cultural Centre:** On lakeshore next to Kinsmen Beach Park. Historic building constructed in 1915 by the Lieutenant-Governor of BC, the Honourable Robert Randolph Bruce and his wife, Lady Elizabeth. Now features exhibits, theatre, concerts, workshops, music events.

Panorama Mountain Village: 17.5km west from downtown Invermere, on Toby Creek Rd. Panorama Resort, Panorama, BC, V0A 1T0. 250-342-6941 or 1-800-663-2929. At 1,140m, it's a sky-high resort. All-season, all-family alpine activities. Summer: swimming in pool, tennis, riding, whitewater rafting, hiking, golfing, bicycle touring. Winter: heli-ski-

ing, or simply downhill. Vertical drop is 1,220m; longest run 3.5km. Eight lifts; cross-country trails, hot tubs. Golf course.

Purcell Wilderness Conservancy: 199,683ha; wilderness camping only. 150km of hiking trails. Mechanized access prohibited. For Earl Grey Pass Trail drive 32km on Toby Creek Rd from downtown Invermere. Get directions in Invermere. Gravel road can be busy with logging and ore trucks. Leads to Earl Grey Pass, el 1,070m, maximum el 2,256m; suggested hiking time, three to five days. Also mountaineering and horseback riding (on east side only), fishing, and wildlife viewing. Check Invermere public library for Mary Ann Romback's *With Only the Goosebumps of Gladness Remaining: A Collection of Mountain Hikes.* Earl Grey Pass Trail is also accessible from the town of Argenta on the northeast shore of Kootenay Lake (see p. 220). For more info, write BC Parks, Box 118, Wasa, BC, V0B 2K0. 250-422-4200.

INVERMERE TO GOLDEN

HIGHWAY 93/95 AND HIGHWAY 95

This 117km stretch follows the Columbia River north from Invermere to Golden. Here the Columbia River and Hwy 95 meet the Trans-Canada Hwy (Hwy 1). Beyond Radium, the Rocky Mountain Trench narrows, the mountains become higher and more rugged. To the west, the river winds through extensive marshlands, a superb wildlife habitat. It is interesting to contemplate that little more than 100 years ago, there was no easily passable route through this area at all, though in 1885 the Canadian Pacific Railway had been completed. The railway had reached Golden to the north, and Fort Steele to the south, but there was nothing connecting the two except the Columbia River, and Windermere and Columbia lakes.

There were attempts to provide water links between the rail lines. Frank Armstrong, an enterprising fellow, put the first steamboat on the Columbia one year after the railway came in. He built the *Duchess* out of scrap lumber and began to transport goods and passengers between Golden and Lake Windermere. Low water levels and moving sandbars presented problems. Passengers and crew were frequently required to get into the water and push when the boat ran aground. Passengers were also called upon to go ashore and cut wood to fuel the steam engine.

Problems with the water link farther south, necessitating portages and at one point a horse-drawn tramway, made the dream less than an easy reality. With the building of the Crowsnest Pass Railway in 1898, steamboat service in the south quickly ended. North, on the Columbia River, however, steamers operated until 1914, for a total of 28 years. In all, 15 different boats were used in the Columbia River service. Eventually, completion of the Kootenay Central Railway, and the building of

better highways in the area, spelled the demise of the riverboats.

Hwy 95 may not be as romantic as being right on the river, but no one will be asked to cut wood for the engine, or to get into the water and push.

Invermere to Golden

To Revelstoke
Golden
Nicholson
To Calgary
95
64
Yoho Nat. Pk.
Parson
Columbia River
Harrogate
To Bugaboo Prov. Pk.
Spillimacheen
St. Mark's Church
Brisco
57
95
Edgewater
Radium Hot Springs
93
Dry Gulch Prov. Pk.
Kootenay Nat. Pk.
To Panorama Resort
Athalmer
Invermere
Athalmer Beach Prov. Pk.
To Fairmont Hot Springs
Windermere Lake

0   Km   10

Invermere: (Pop. 2,687). On western shores of Windermere Lake, 4km off Hwy 93/95, on Athalmer Rd. Athalmer Rd junction with Hwy 93/95 is 6km north of Windermere. See p.203.

Dry Gulch Provincial Park: 29ha; 25 campsites. 8km north of Invermere junction, then 1km east off highway on gravel road. 250-422-3212. Wooded site at edge of Stanford Range.

Viewpoint: 11.5km beyond Invermere junction. Panoramic view over the Columbia Valley.

Radium Hot Springs: (Pop. 540). 13km north of Invermere junction, 104km south of Golden. The springs, named for their relatively high radioactivity, surface at 35-47C. Community provides services for visitors to nearby hot pools, campgrounds, and Kootenay National Park. A small Parks Canada book, *Nipika: A Story of Radium Hot Springs*, sells in local stores. A band of well-established Rocky Mountain bighorn sheep are commonly seen near town.

Radium Hot Springs Information: Info Centre, Radium Chamber of Commerce, # 4, 7585 Main St W, Radium Hot Springs, BC, V0A 1M0. 1-800-347-9704 or 250-347-9331.

Radium Hot Springs Airstrip: (El 1,800m). Just west of Radium Hot Springs on Hwy 95. 1-800-347-9704. No scheduled flights.

■ **Radium Hot Springs Pools:** On Hwy 93. Year-round. Operated by Canadian Parks Service, offers both hot (39C) and cool (29C) outdoor pools in a gorgeous mountain setting. A delicious moment in any trip. Year-round.

■ **Radium Hot Springs Resort:** 1.5km south of the town. Box 310, Radium Hot Springs, BC, V0A 1M0. 250-347-9311 or 1-800-667-6444. A complete retreat, with 18-hole showpiece course.

■ **The Springs at Radium Golf Course:** Box 310, Radium Hot Springs, BC, V0A 1M0. 250-347-6444. Golf packages including accommodation and use of other courses: 1-800-667-6200. 18 holes in panoramic setting with views of Columbia River valley, the Purcells, and the Rockies.

Highway 93: In Radium Hot Springs, Hwys 93 and 95 separate. Hwy 93 goes northeast to **Hot Pools**, **Kootenay National Park**, and **Banff National Park**. Details in *Radium Hot Springs and Kootenay National Park*, p.205. Hwy 95 travels north 104km to Golden.

Kootenay National Park: 140,600ha; 401 campsites. **West Gate** is 1km north of Hwy 93/95 junction at Radium. West Gate Information Centre: 250-347-9505 (June-Sept). Year-round: 250-347-9615. Details in *Radium Hot Springs and Kootenay National Park*, p.205.

The next section of the *Log* follows Hwy 95 north along the Columbia River through marshland that is prime wildlife habitat, a breeding and staging area for ducks and geese, as well as for water-dependent birds such as bald eagles, osprey, and herons. More than 270 species of birds have been recorded.

Marshes are also home to aquatic animals such as beaver, muskrat, painted turtles. Also abundant elk and deer, along with smaller populations of bighorn sheep, moose, black bear, cougar, bobcat.

Edgewater: (Pop. 630). 11km beyond Radium. On the "edge" of the Columbia River. Attractive community supported by agriculture and logging. Area is Christmas tree farming land, also excellent grazing range for ungulates (hoofed animals).

The Cauliflower Tree: 21km beyond Radium, on the highway's west side.

Strange-looking Douglas fir may have been afflicted by a virus, causing its deformity. Hard to describe, but you'll know it when you see it. Just beside the road.

Brisco: (Pop. 138). 28km beyond Radium, on Hwy 95. Named for Captain Arthur Brisco who accompanied Captain John Palliser to this area on the Palliser Expedition (1857-60) for the Royal Geographical Society, gathering information on the expanse from Lake Superior to BC's Okanagan Valley.

Brisco Rd: West, unpaved, to the Columbia Wildlife Area and Bugaboo Provincial Park.

SIDE TRIP

to the Bugaboos

Bugaboo Provincial Park: 13,646ha; walk-in camping. 48km west of Hwy 95 at Brisco, on Brisco Rd. Caution: logging trucks. Commercial heli-skiing lodge near park entrance. Write: BC Parks, Box 118, Wasa, BC, V0B 2K0. 250-422-4200. An alpine wilderness park with the largest glaciers in the Purcells, formed long before the Rockies. Erosion has long since worn away the softer rocks leaving exposed the solid granite cores. Ranges should only be climbed by the experienced. Hiking trails to facilities, two tenting grounds, one alpine hut (50 spaces). June-Aug, look for pikas, marmots, ground squirrels, and mountain goats.

Return to Highway 95

The country from here north to Golden is rustic, natural, and not "touristy." Small communities are set with precision in the expanse of valley between mountains and marsh. There are many lovely homesteads on the sloping benchlands. Australian cattle dogs (blue heelers) seem to be popular here and on ranches throughout the area.

Great Blue Heron Rookery: 31.5km beyond Radium on Hwy 95. Look for nests in tall poplars along riverside. The 300 pairs of herons nesting here make it the second largest concentration in Western Canada.

Spillimacheen Rest Area: 34km beyond Radium.

St Mark's Anglican Church: 36km beyond Radium. East of highway, on the hill, old log cabin church is one of province's smallest.

Spillimacheen: (Pop. 77). 40km beyond Radium. An access point to the Columbia River, name comes from word in an aboriginal language meaning "swift running water."

Harrogate: (Pop. 37). 52.5km beyond Radium. Named after a fashionable sum-

The Dutch Creek Hoodoos tower over Columbia Lake's north end.

mer resort in Yorkshire. Before trains, this was a food and rest stop for stagecoaches.

Nesting Platforms and Marshes: Along the way, between 62km and 103km north of Radium. River and marshes are near highway, good viewing. Platforms provide safe nesting sites for Canada geese.

Parson: (Pop. 84). 70km beyond Radium. Logging community, good base for fishing, and there's still gold being panned in Canyon Creek. Town was named after the Parson brothers who owned the hog ranch.

Braisher Creek Rest Area: 75km north of Radium.

Nicholson: (Pop. 1,057). 96km beyond Radium. Named after Swedish homesteaders. Now residential community for Golden, easy access for skiing in Selkirks.

Golden: (Pop. 3,968). 104km beyond Radium. For details see *Sicamous to Lake Louise*, p.210.

Trans-Canada Highway (1): At Golden. Leads west to Revelstoke, east to Yoho and Banff national parks. For continuation of Trans-Canada Hwy, see *Sicamous to Lake Louise*, p.204.

RADIUM HOT SPRINGS AND KOOTENAY NATIONAL PARK

THE BANFF-WINDERMERE PARKWAY (Highway 93)

The Kootenay Parkway offers a leisurely, scenic trip from Radium at the junction of Hwy 95, through Kootenay National Park to Hwy 1 in Banff National Park. It is 94km from the West Gate to the east boundary of Kootenay National Park; it's 10km further to the junction with Hwy 1; and from there, it is an equal 28km on Hwy 1 either north to Lake Louise or south to Banff. Total distance, Radium to Lake Louise or Banff, is 131.5km. This magnificent stretch offers one of the greatest concentrations of stunning scenery in the Rockies parks.

Radium Hot Springs: (Pop. 540). Village lies outside Kootenay National Park gates. See *Invermere to Golden*, p.204.

Highways 93 and 95: In Radium Hot Springs. Hwy goes south as 93/95 to the Invermere junction, 13km, and Cranbrook, 142km. Hwy 95 travels north to Golden, 104km. See *Invermere to Golden*, p.203.

Redstreak Campground: 242 campsites, some hookups, showers, sani-station. Early May to late Sept. 250-347-9615. On a bench above the village of Radium. The campground is actually in Kootenay Park, but vehicle access is only possible from Hwy 93/95 on the south edge of Radium Hot Springs. 30-minute walking trail to hot springs. Interpretive programs.

Kootenay National Park: 140,600ha; 401 campsites. West Gate is 1km out of Radium Hot Springs. It is 94km to the park's East Gate in Vermilion Pass. Any one planning to visit the park for day-use activities or to stay overnight at a lodge or campground must obtain a park pass, available at park gate (see below) or staffed campgrounds. They can also be obtained by calling 1-800-748-7275 and making payment with a VISA or Mastercard. Separate wilderness passes are required for backcountry camping.

What is now Kootenay Park has been used by aboriginal peoples as a travel corridor for thousands of years. Like the travellers of today, they liked to gather at the hot springs. Early European visitors were explorers and fur traders looking for transportation routes through the Rockies. These included Sir George Simpson, governor of the Hudson's Bay Company, who went through in 1841. In the same year, James Sinclair lead a party of settlers from Fort Garry through the canyon that now bears his name. Sir James Hector and the Palliser Expedition were looking for new routes in 1858 when they discovered Vermilion Pass.

In 1920, the parkland was given to the Government of Canada by the Province of BC in return for a road through the central Canadian Rockies. (It was completed in 1923.) In 1985, Kootenay National Park along with Banff, Jasper, and Yoho national parks, and Mt Assiniboine, Mt Robson, and Hamber provincial parks were embraced as a World Heritage Site – a highly significant and valuable representation of the Rocky Mountain landscape. Nearly two million visitors enter Kootenay National Park annually, third in numbers after Banff and Jasper parks.

The park road travels through the Kootenay and Vermilion river valleys, flanked by such peaks as Mount Harkin, 2,982m, Split Peak, 2,926m, Mount Wardle, 2,850m, and Storm Mountain, 3,155m. Milky-green streams and waterfalls tumble from these mountains as the road climbs toward Vermilion Pass, at 1,651m one of BC's highest. Here, on the border between Banff and Kootenay parks, North America splits along the Continental Divide.

Kootenay National Park has more than spectacular mountain scenery: it is extremely varied – the only national park with both cactus and glaciers. There is excellent wildlife viewing. Elk, deer, bighorn sheep, mountain goats, moose, and black bears may be seen along the highway. Wolves, and grizzly bears also inhabit the park, but stick mainly to the park's remote areas. More than 200km of hiking trails offer access to backcountry areas.

Kootenay National Park Information: Write Superintendent, Kootenay National Park, Box 220, Radium Hot Springs, BC, V0A

Radium Hot Springs and Kootenay National Park

1M0. Information centre at pool facility, below. Mid-May to late Sept: 250-347-9505. Year-round: 250-347-9615.

All distances are given from the park's West Gate.

Radium Hot Springs Pools: 3km beyond West Gate. Operated by Parks Canada. Natural hot and cool outdoor pools – temperatures to 40C – in a gorgeous mountain setting. Some 300,000 bathers loll about here every year. Year-round. Cafeteria open May-Oct. Trails from here to Sinclair Canyon Viewpoint and Redstreak Campground.

Bighorn Sheep: 4km beyond West Gate. Seen along road spring and fall.

Sinclair Creek Picnic Site: 9km beyond West Gate. In Sinclair Creek valley.

Olive Lake Picnic Site: 12km beyond West Gate. On shore of unusual, olive-coloured lake. Site of one of the park's first campgrounds: note rustic picnic shelters. 0.5km wheelchair-accessible interpretive trail and boardwalk to the lakeshore. Exhibits feature tactile elements for visually impaired visitors.

Kootenay Valley Viewpoint: 15km beyond West Gate. Sweeping view of valley, and Mitchell and Vermilion mountain ranges. Gray jays and the ubiquitous ground squirrels.

Settlers' Rd: 18km beyond West Gate. Follows Kootenay River south out of park. Caution: logging and ore trucks have right-of-way. Extensive network of logging roads. Get info before venturing forth.

Kootenay River Picnic Site: 22.5km beyond West Gate.

Trail to Nixon Pond: 23km beyond West Gate.

McLeod Meadows Campground: 98 campsites; sani-station. 26.5km beyond West Gate. Mid-May to mid- Sept. On the banks of Kootenay River. Good jumping-off point for experienced canoeists, and a good spot for elk, deer, and coyotes. At least four kinds of orchids bloom here in early summer: calypso, sparrow's egg, white bog, and round-leafed. 2.4km trail leads to Dog Lake.

Dolly Varden Picnic Site: 35km beyond West Gate. Winter camping and fishing.

Kootenay Crossing Bridge: 42.5km beyond West Gate. Warden station. Highway crosses the Kootenay River (6km north it takes up with the Vermilion River). At the crossing, a 12.8km hiking and mountain-biking trail along old fire road leads northwest to park boundary.

Hector Gorge Viewpoint: 46km from West Gate. Named after Dr James Hector of the Palliser Expedition (he whose horse was the Kicking Horse).

Mountain Goats: 47-50km beyond West Gate. Goats are often seen in early summer at the base of Mt Wardle. They come down from the mountain to lick minerals from the banks along the roadside. Please exercise caution when viewing: pull well off the highway and watch for traffic.

Hector Gorge Picnic Site: 48km from West Gate.

Wardle Creek Picnic Area: 52km from West Gate.

Animal Lick: 54.5km beyond West Gate, on the highway's east side. Natural mineral lick. With patience and luck, travellers might see elk, moose, or mule deer.

Simpson Monument and Trail to Mount Assiniboine Provincial Park: 55.5km beyond West Gate. Commemorates journey of Sir George Simpson, governor of the Hudson's Bay Company, who travelled through the area in 1841. Simpson River Trail leads 8km to **Mount Assiniboine Provincial Park** nestled between the southern reaches of Kootenay and Banff national parks, with no road access. Extensive trails, walk-in campsites. In addition to the spectacular scenery, during the summer and early fall, watch for elk, marmots, ground squirrels, deer, moose, bighorn sheep, and mountain goats. This is a special place. Be gentle.

Vermilion River Crossing, Kootenay Park Lodge, Information: 63km from West Gate; 31km from Vermilion Pass, where the highway crosses the Vermilion River. 403-762-9196 or 403-283-7482. Easter to mid-Oct. New visitor centre at the site of a CPR bungalow camp dating back to the 1920s. There is cabin accommodation and a restaurant; new buildings house information centre, gift shop, wheelchair-accessible washrooms, and displays. Trailhead for Verdant Creek and Verendrye Creek trails. Picnicking, fishing.

Floe Lake/Hawk Creek Trailheads: 70km beyond West Gate. Trail leads 10km west to one of the few "berg" lakes in the Rockies, named for the mini-icebergs that break off from Floe Glacier and float on the lake.

Numa Falls Picnic Site: 79km beyond West Gate. Scenic falls on Vermilion River.

Paint Pots: 83km beyond West Gate. Picnics. Self-guiding 0.8km trail to ochre beds and 1.5km to paint pots once a source of vermilion paint used by aboriginal peoples. Cold mineral springs served as a spiritual meeting place for the Stoney and Ktunaxa peoples. Here they processed the red clay or ochre into a powder, later mixed with water and grease.

Paint Pots provide access to major trails in the park's northwest section, and also some of the park's most spectacular sights: Goodsir and Ottertail passes, Tumbling Glacier, Panorama Ridge, the Rock Wall (a towering limestone barrier), 300m Helmet Falls.

Marble Canyon and Tokumm Creek: 85.5km from West Gate. Picnic site. 0.8km trail along rim of extremely narrow canyon cut deep by glacial blue mountain stream. Only 3-18m wide, but in places, the canyon cuts 39m deep into the limestone. The sometimes white dolomite was once mistaken for marble, hence the name. Access to Kaufmann Lake and Tokumm Creek trails.

Marble Canyon Campground: 61 campsites, sani-station. 85.5km from West Gate, 7km from East Gate. Mid-June to early Sept.

Mountains goats pause at a mineral lick in Kootenay National Park.

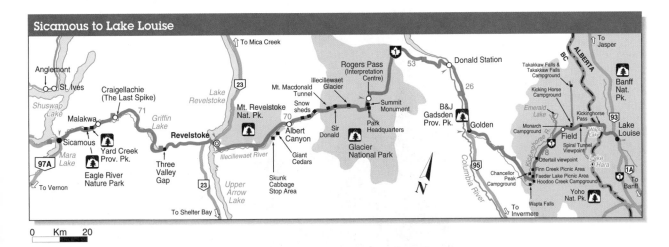

Sicamous to Lake Louise

0   Km   20

Trail to Stanley Glacier: 89km from West Gate. Spectacular four-hour (4.8km) hike to a hanging valley and alpine glacier.

Vermilion Pass and Continental Divide: (El 1,651m). 94km from West Gate. Stop of interest at Continental Divide. To the west, all water flows to the Pacific Ocean; to the east, it flows toward Hudson Bay. The Divide marks the boundary between Alberta and BC, and between Banff and Kootenay national parks. At the Divide, take the **Fireweed Trail**, a short self-guiding nature trail, to see "the Vermilion Pass Burn," result of a 1968 forest fire.

From Vermilion Pass, Hwy 93 descends east 10km to Castle Junction, where it ends in a T-junction with Trans-Canada Hwy 1. (It is picked up by Alberta's Hwy 93 north of Lake Louise.) Following the lovely Bow River, Hwy 1 goes northwest 28km to Lake Louise, or southeast 28km to Banff. Castle Junction is exactly midway. For details, see *Lake Louise to Banff,* p.229.

SICAMOUS TO LAKE LOUISE

TRANS-CANADA HIGHWAY (Highway 1)

This is the easternmost segment, in BC, of the Trans-Canada Highway – the world's longest national highway (totalling 8,047km from St. John's Newfoundland to Victoria, BC). This may also be its most scenic stretch. You decide. From Sicamous to Lake Louise, it's 296km. The Canadian Pacific Railway cut this route first – (completed through here in 1885). Now the Trans-Canada parallels those tracks, which parallel rivers, which have etched themselves between glorious mountains. We are presented with the best of the Selkirks, Purcells, and Rockies.

This is also the birthplace of great rivers. We start out tracing the west-flowing Eagle River, a freshet of the Pacific-bound Fraser River system. Just beyond Three Valley Gap we cross the height of land into the Columbia watershed, and at Revelstoke, make our first encounter with the 2,000km long Columbia River. We take up with its tributary, the Illecillewaet, then, cut through mountains that even the Columbia goes around. We meet the Columbia again at Donald Station, on the southern tip of Kinbasket Lake – a reservoir of the Mica Dam, it is considered BC's fourth largest lake (at 529 sq km). From the city of Golden, the Kicking Horse River guides us to Yoho National Park and another height of land – the Great Divide between Pacific and Arctic watersheds. Here, the Bow River welcomes us to Alberta.

Yoho and Banff are two of Canada's four Rocky Mountain national parks. All four, also including Jasper and Yoho, in 1985 were designated a World Heritage Site by the United Nations Educational, Scientific, and Cultural Organization (UNESCO). The parks are separate, but share common boundaries and appear as one enormous wilderness area.

■ **Time Zone Change**: The transition point from Pacific to Mountain Time occurs 80km east of Revelstoke, within the boundaries of Glacier National Park. Eastbound watches should be set one hour ahead.

Sicamous: (Pop. 2,827). On Hwy 1, 27km east of Salmon Arm. From Secwepemc word meaning "narrow," or "squeezed in the middle." Sicamous overlooks Sicamous Narrows between Mara and Shuswap lakes. Once a railway construction depot, now known as "the Houseboat Capital of Canada." About a dozen operators rent some 300 houseboats from Sicamous marinas. Resembling a ragged capital H, Shuswap Lake's four narrow arms are surrounded by the peaks (some higher than 2,200m) and forests of the Monashee Mountains and Shuswap Highland. Here are 1,000km of shoreline, from sheer cliffs and rock slides to sand and gravel beaches with gently sloping hills running up into the forests.

Shuswap Lake Provincial Marine Park is divided into a number of popular sites situated around the lake, and offers designated boat/houseboating beaches. Events, p.145.

Sicamous Information: Sicamous and District Chamber of Commerce, Travel and Business Info Centre, Box 346, Sicamous, BC, V0E 2V0. 250-836-3313. Downtown at junction of Main and Riverside. Year-round.

Shuswap Lake Ferry Service Ltd: Box 370, Sicamous, BC, V0E 2V0. 250-836-2200. Ferry and a barge for passengers and freight. Based in Sicamous, serves lakeside communities year-round, except when there's ice on the lake. MV *Phoebe Ann* is a 15.5m steel-hulled sternwheeler with a snack bar and room for 40 passengers. Some travellers take vehicles to Seymour Arm on the barge then drive out on Squilax-Anglemont Rd.

■ **Eagle Valley Museum and Heritage Society:** In Finlayson Park. 250-836-4635. Late June-late Aug. Native, railway, and settlers histories are presented here.

■ **D Dutchman Dairy:** 1km east of Sicamous. Free childrens zoo with llamas, camels, horses, peacocks. Some say best homemade ice cream in BC. More than 50 flavours.

■ **Granny's Dollhouse and Collectibles:** 441 Finlayson St. 250-836-3363. Things for sale; dolls, teddy bears, and toys on display.

Highway 97A: Joins Hwy 1 at Sicamous. Hwy 97A runs south 35km to Enderby, 70km to Vernon. Hwy 1 continues northeast along Eagle River.

Eagle River Nature Park: 12km east of Sicamous on Eagle River. Across from KOA. 6km of hiking/cross-country ski trails among ancient cedars. Picnicking.

Yard Creek Provincial Park: 61ha; 65 campsites, sani-station. 250-851-3000. On Hwy 1, 14km east of Sicamous. Interior rain-forest with nature trails and fungi photo ops.

Malakwa: (Pop. 400). 17.5km from Sicamous. Post office, store, fruit stand.

Craigellachie: (Pop. 71). Hwy 1, 25.5km east of Sicamous. Small, unincorporated settlement and historic site where last spike on Canada's first trans-continental railway was driven by Donald Smith, a CPR director, on November 7, 1885. Rest area is a "train station," with caboose, books, calendars, songs on tapes, pop machine. Real freight trains pass by.

Gorge Creek at Craigellachie is a pleasant hour-long round trip stroll beside forested creek. Rainbow trout, Dolly Varden, Rocky Mountain whitefish in nearby Eagle River.

Beardale Castle Miniatureland: On Hwy 1, still at Craigellachie, but now about 30km east of Sicamous. 250-836-2268. May-Sept. Canadian, English, Swiss and German miniature villages with model railways; animated toyland; commemorative large-scale Craigellachie railway display and history. Souvenirs, ice cream.

Eagle River: Last 31km of meandering Eagle River, between Taft and Sicamous. A leisurely canoe trip through forests of spruce, cedar, hemlock, and cottonwood. Water levels best mid-spring and mid-fall. Pleasant camping spots.

Kay Falls: Shady rest stop on Hwy 1, 36km east of Sicamous. Pretty falls.

Enchanted Forest: On Hwy 1, 39km east of Sicamous. 250-837-9477. Mid-May to mid-Sept. 250 figurines, castle, cottage in wooded setting. Food and phone. Access for disabled persons.

Griffin Lake: Southwest of highway, 43km east of Sicamous. First of five fishing lakes along 20km stretch toward Revelstoke. Includes Griffin, Three Valley, Victor, Clanwilliam, and Wetask lakes. All part of Eagle River system. Ice fishing.

Rutherford Beach Rest Area: 45.5km from Sicamous. Overlooking Three Valley Lake.

Three Valley Gap: On Hwy 1 at Three Valley Lake, 47.5km from Sicamous, 75km from Salmon Arm. Unusual resort and pioneer town. Old buildings collected from around BC and reassembled here. Saloon, barber shop, general store, log schoolhouse, blacksmith shop. Arresting alpine setting. Theatre, live entertainment, accommodation, restaurants, gift shop.

Highway 23: South from Hwy 1, just before bridge into Revelstoke, 70km east of Sicamous. 50km to Shelter Bay on Upper Arrow Lake (details p. 221). About 1km farther east on Hwy 1, across the Columbia River Bridge at Revelstoke, Hwy 23 runs north for 134km to Mica Creek (see *Shelter Bay to Mica Creek*, p.221). East of Revelstoke, Hwy 1 follows the Illecillewaet River to Rogers Pass.

Revelstoke: (Pop. 8,047). 71km east of Sicamous on Hwy 1. At the north end of Upper Arrow Lake, the bottom end of Lake Revelstoke; where the Columbia and Illecillewaet rivers meet; at the heart of the Monashee Mountains, and the edge of the Selkirks. For all the natural splendour around it – including two national parks, Mount Revelstoke and Glacier – this pretty city chooses to call itself "Home of the World's Largest Sculpted Grizzly Bears." The two grizzly statues guard the Mackenzie Ave entrance to downtown. Grizzly Plaza here is a friendly place, with gazebo-like bandshell, cobbled street, pleasing turn-of-the-century buildings nearby. And summer evenings, they offer entertainment for visitors.

Alpine meadows, Mount Revelstoke Provincial Park.

All signs of an awakening desire to catch the tourist trade in a community once inward looking, focusing on its railway, logging, and construction industries. The CPR built a small hotel in town as a link to its sternwheeler service south to the Upper and Lower Arrow lakes, but generally railway travellers chose the other CPR hotel at Rogers Pass. Mount Revelstoke National Park opened in 1922, but more often than not, motorists visited the park without even stopping in the city of Revelstoke.

Today, travellers are finding plenty of reasons to make Revelstoke their base for exploring nearby mountain wilderness areas: ask here about snowmobiling, downhill, cross-country, snow-cat, and heli-skiing. Also hiking, canoeing, biking, horseback riding.

While real grizzly bears rarely make their way into Revelstoke, black bears are commonly encountered within city limits.

Revelstoke Information: Info Centre, Revelstoke Chamber of Commerce, Box 490, Revelstoke, BC, V0E 2S0. 250-837-5345 or 250-837-3522. Summer Info Centre at junction of Hwys 1 and 23. Late May-Sept. Chamber of Commerce, 204 Campbell Ave, is open year-round.

Revelstoke Airport: On Airport Way, 5km south of Revelstoke on east side of Upper Arrow Lake.

■ **Revelstoke Museum:** 315 W First St. 250-837-3067. Mon-Sat, June-Aug. Mon-Fri, Sept-May. Local railway, logging, mining, business, and social history.

■ **Revelstoke Courthouse:** 1123 Second St W. 250-837-7636. Mon-Fri. Public access to courtroom is subject to court use and availability of staff. Visitors must be escorted. Excellent restoration of early 20th century courthouse. Has original stained-glass windows, courtroom, marble panelling, furniture.

■ **Revelstoke Piano Museum:** 117 Campbell Ave. 250-837-6554. One of North America's best international piano collections. Call to arrange guided tour. Gift shop.

■ **Revelstoke Railway Museum:** 719 Track St W. 250-837-6060. Daily, 9-8; July-Aug. Reduced hours off-season. In winter, by appointment. The story of the men and women who worked on the railway between Field and Kamloops, emphasizing the great steam era of the 1940s and '50s. Features steam engine 5468, a Mikado P2, and Business Car No. 4, once a Cape Humber solarium car.

■ **Grizzly Gazebo:** Local entertainment Mon-Sat in summer, 7-10pm. Farmer's Market every Sat, spring and summer.

■ **Revelstoke Golf Club:** North side of town with several holes along Columbia River. 18-hole, full-facility course. Used by cross-country skiers in winter.

■ **Mt Macpherson:** Cross-country ski area. South off Hwy 1 onto Hwy 23, on west side of Columbia River Bridge. 5km to parking on Hwy 23. 25km of cross-country trails.

■ **Arrow Lakes:** The Upper and Lower Arrow lakes joined – a reservoir created by the Hugh Keenleyside Dam near Castlegar. It stretches 220km between Revelstoke and Castlegar, 1- to 2km wide. Boating and canoeing, side trips up various creeks; some hiking areas. Informal campsites. Because this is a reservoir, many pullout beaches have been flooded. Canoeists should study topographic maps to see where to land if a wind comes up. Boats can be launched at Revelstoke, below the Revelstoke Dam.

■ **Williamson Lake:** East off Airport Way 4km south of town. Favourite local spot: campground, warm swimming, mini-golf.

■ **Mt Mackenzie Ski Area:** Airport Way from city centre, south for 5km, then east on Westerburg Rd. Box 1000, Revelstoke, BC, V0E 2S0. Fax: 250-837-5224. 610m vertical drop, two chairlifts, a T-bar, handle tow, saloon and cookhouse, ski shop, rentals, ski school, 21 runs. Heli-skiing and snow-cats to 2,380m level of Mt Mackenzie.

■ **Durrand Glacier:** 30km north of Revelstoke. 250-837-2381. Log chalet at 1,935m. Panorama of hanging glaciers, alpine meadows, waterfalls. International mountain school with winter and summer mountaineering, alpine meadow hiking and powder-ski touring camps, mountain rescue courses. Hut-to-hut hiking and skiing, telemark skiing, rock and ice climbing.

■ **Frisby Ridge:** Snowmobiling and cross-country ski area west side of Columbia. North off Hwy 1 on logging road 1km west of Columbia River Bridge. Road skirts Lake Revelstoke for 30km. Frisby Ridge on west side of road.

■ **Revelstoke Dam:** North off Hwy 1 in Revelstoke onto Hwy 23. 4km to Columbia View Provincial Park. Turn west and follow signs. 250-837-6515. Daily, May 1 to mid-Oct. Self-guided, one- or two-hour tours. One of North America's largest and most modern hydroelectric developments. Elevator trip to dam crest lookout at top of 175m concrete dam. Disabled/wheelchair access; wheelchairs available.

■ **Columbia View Provincial Park:** North off Hwy 1 in Revelstoke onto Hwy 23. 4km to park. Picnic area surrounded by Monashee and Selkirk mountains.

■ **Lake Revelstoke:** Widening of the Columbia River north of Revelstoke, created by Revelstoke Dam. 120km of boating water between Revelstoke Dam and Mica Creek. 1km wide. Boats launched above Revelstoke Dam. It's a reservoir, so many beaches are flooded: canoeists should study topographic maps to find places to land in winds.

Soon after leaving Revelstoke, Hwy 1 picks up the Illecillewaet River and follows it to its source, the **Illecillewaet Glacier**, near west side of Rogers Pass.

Illecillewaet Rest Area: 14km east of Revelstoke.

Mount Revelstoke National Park: 26,300ha. No campgrounds within park, but several in Revelstoke. There is also backcountry camping, except in the Miller Lake area and within 5km of Summit Parkway. Park's west gate is 17km from Revelstoke. Information at Rogers Pass, in Glacier National Park, or from Mount Revelstoke Park administration office, Third St and Campbell Ave in Revelstoke. Write to Park Superintendent, Mount Revelstoke and Glacier National Parks, Box 350, Revelstoke, BC, V0E 2S0. 250-837-7500.

There are two main accesses to Mount Revelstoke park. The first is via Summit Rd, north off Hwy 1, 1km east of Revelstoke. This is a winding 26km road to the top of 1,830m Mt Revelstoke. A spectacular alpine area with summer wildflowers, and views of the ice-capped Monashee Mountains and the dramatic Selkirks. In summer, there's a regular shuttle-bus service from Balsam Lake picnic area 2km to summit, in an effort to reduce traffic. The second access, Hwy 1, skirts park's southern boundary. Incredible mountain scenery, centuries-old cedars and hemlocks. Alpine skiing, hiking on trails from short to long, mountaineering, visitor programs. Recommended are the Giant Cedars Trail, a 0.5km boardwalk into a forest of 800-year-old cedars; the Skunk Cabbage Trail, featuring "Naturalist Notebook" signs; and Meadows-in-the-Sky Trail, 1km, featuring the Icebox, a shaded rock cleft where snow persists throughout the summer.

Park has long been a passion of the people of Revelstoke, who were instrumental in its establishment in 1914.

Skunk Cabbage Stop Area: 24km east of Revelstoke. Self-guiding trail. Great bird-watching spot.

Giant Cedars Stop Area: 27km east of Revelstoke. Self-guiding boardwalk trail. Look for bats in the summer months.

Albert Canyon and Hot Springs: On Hwy 1, 35.5km east of Revelstoke. Mineral pool, swimming pool, campground, trading post, coffee shop. Hiking, trail rides, rafting. Completely unrestored ghost town – remnants of cabins and schoolhouse midst forget-me-nots and wild strawberries.

Snow Sheds: On Trans-Canada Hwy, 47km east of Revelstoke. Series of three snow sheds to protect travellers from avalan-ches. More snow sheds ahead in Rogers Pass, notorious for its hazardous snow conditions. Earth dams, dikes, mounds, and catch basins are used in avalanche paths to regulate snowslides.

Glacier National Park: 136,500ha. Hwy 1 enters park 49km east of Revelstoke. Two campgrounds: Loop Brook, on Hwy 1, 14km east of west entrance, 20 campsites; Illecillewaet, turnoff Hwy 1, 3km east of Loop Brook campground, has 58 campsites.

Glacier National Park is in the northern Selkirk Mountains, with the Purcell Mountains near its eastern boundary. Heavy winter snow-falls here maintain more than 400 active glaciers and icefields in the park, nearly 12 percent of its total area. Also features spectacular jagged peaks and alpine scenery with abundant wild-flowers. Mountain goats are the most commonly seen large animal. Here are rainforests, emerald lakes, streams, and waterfalls. 140km of wilderness trails: guided hikes in summer. Check park bulletin boards or Rogers Pass Centre (below).

Many features of the park and its history can be reached easily from the highway corridor. Recommended: the 1.6km Loop Brook trail highlighting the stone pillars that once carried the railway track across the valley; the 1.2km Abandoned Rails Trail, an abandoned rail grade between the Rogers Pass centre; and the Summit Monument.

Slide Path Stop Area: 1km inside park. At bottom of large winter avalanche path.

Hemlock Grove Stop Area: 6km inside park. Boardwalk through old forest.

Mt Macdonald Tunnel: 61km east of Revelstoke, or 13km from Glacier Park west entrance. Visible to eastbound traffic from Hwy 1. Going 14.6km through Mt Macdonald and Cheops Mountain, this is the longest railway tunnel in North America. Part of CPR's $600-million 34km Rogers Pass Project that includes 17km of surface route, six bridges totalling 1.7km, two tunnels. Grade on new line does not exceed 1 percent, compared to old line through Connaught Tunnel, which had a 2.2 percent grade and required six 3,000hp "pusher" locomotives to get westbound trains up the pass. Tunnel construction began from both ends in mid-1984. Laser and satellite surveying techniques ensured both ends met in the middle. Project completed in 1988, on 12th day of 12th month at 12 noon.

Sir Donald Stop Area: 15km inside park. Views of Mount Sir Donald Peak on clear days.

Illecillewaet Glacier: 18km from park's west entrance. "The Great Glacier" is visible from highway, but better seen from entrance to Illecillewaet campground. Network of trails lead from site of former Glacier House, a short walk from the campground.

The Illecillewaet Glacier, one of more than 400 in the park, is an awesome spectacle – a vast sheet of grinding ice that appears, one admirer put it, "to tumble directly out of the sky." The glacier, at its maximum extent in 1886, began retreating until two decades ago. After a brief advance, it's retreating again. From 1886-1925, the CPR's Glacier House and its glacier, "one tremendous dead and silent greatness," drew the goggle-eyed from around the world. Today, the glacier remains great, but Glacier House is a levelled ruin obscured by forest growth.

The best trail to Illecillewaet is the Great Glacier Trail.

Rogers Pass: (El 1,382m). Summit in Glacier National Park, 70km east of Revelstoke (21km from west gate). Site of park interpretation centre (see below), and Glacier Park Lodge, a year-round motel with full dining facilities.

Memorial arch honours completion of the Trans-Canada Hwy over the pass. Pass was located in 1882 by Major A.B. Rogers, a railway engineer. By 1885 the railway through the pass was completed. Construction of the Trans-Canada Hwy through this rugged territory began in 1956, and was completed in 1962. Steep, hazardous terrain and avalanches made construction extremely challenging.

The pass links the Illecillewaet River on the west with Beaver River on the east.

Glacier National Park Information: Centre at Rogers Pass summit. Daily, year-round. 250-814-5233. Park administration office in Revelstoke. Write to Park Superintendent, Mount Revelstoke and Glacier National Parks, Box 350, Revelstoke, BC, V0E 2S0. 250-837-7500.

The Rogers Pass interpretation centre, opened in 1983, is an attraction in itself, drawing as many as 160,000 visitors a year. Same shape as the massive snow sheds, centre houses fascinating displays about Glacier National Park and its history.

A mockup, complete with a running model train, recreates the pass as it was in the 1890s. At that time, the CPR ran its trains right over the pass and through snow sheds now used to protect highway traffic. Between 1885 and 1916, "White Death" (avalanches) killed 250 people – CPR work crews and employees. Worst occurrence was in 1910 when a slide buried 63 people. Other displays illustrate railway tunnels, vegetation zones, the long-gone Glacier House, and the Nakimu Caves – one of the largest cave systems in Canada, opened in 1995 to visitors accompanied by experienced caving guides. Centre has a bookstore operated by Friends of Mt Revelstoke and Glacier national parks. And a colony of ground squirrels entertain visitors around the centre's grounds. Please remember feeding them is dangerous and illegal under park regulations.

Tractor Shed Stop Area: 24km from park's west entrance. Just before a series of five snow sheds.

East Gate of Glacier National Park: 44km from west entrance; 87km from Revelstoke.

Redgrave Rest Area: 24.5km east of Glacier National Park East Gate. Both sides of highway.

Donald Station: (Pop. 101). 36km east of Glacier National Park's East Gate. Named for Donald Smith, CPR director. Town was situated at the CPR's first crossing of the Columbia River.

Doyle Creek Rest Area: Nearly 44km from East Gate, west side of highway.

Burges and James Gadsden Provincial Park: 352ha; day use. 50km from East Gate, west side of highway. Encompasses much of Moberly Marsh along the Columbia River west of Golden. The marsh is an important nesting area and migration stopover. The Gadsdens were a pioneer family in the area.

Highway 95: 61.5km east of Glacier Park, at edge of Golden. Leads south 117km to Invermere. See pp.203-205.

Golden: (Pop. 3,968). At junction of Hwys 1 and 95, 61.5km east of Glacier Park East Gate, 78km west of Lake Louise. A town to delight anybody who has ever counted cars in a train. Golden only began to develop with the coming of the transcontinental CPR in 1884-85. The town then became terminus for steamboat traffic up the Columbia, linking the railway with communities to the south.

Golden epitomizes the region: like many East Kootenay towns, it rose with the boom, then survived the bust because of its breathtaking mountain location, between the massive Rockies and the towering Purcells. And it's not only the mountains, it's the rivers, too.

Golden sits at the mouth of the turbulent Kicking Horse River where it joins the Columbia. Golden today is an outdoor enthusiast's town. There is virtually everything from heli-skiing, ice climbing, hang-gliding, and mountaineering, to horseback riding, river rafting, and kayaking.

Golden Information: Info Centre, Golden Chamber of Commerce, Box 1320, 500-10th Ave N, Golden, BC, V0A 1H0. 1-800-622-4053 or 250-344-7125. Year-round.

■ **Golden Airport:** West side of town. 1220m runway. Flight-seeing tour base.

■ **Golden and District Museum:** 1302-11th Ave, Golden, BC, V0A 1H0. 250-344-5169. Weekdays May, June, Sept. Daily July-Aug. Features area's history, an early log school, and a blacksmith shop.

■ **Golden Municipal Campground:** 70 sites. 250-344-5412 (seasonal). Beside the Kicking Horse River, walking distance from town. Showers, close to outdoor pool. Hook-ups.

■ **Golden Golf and Country Club:** Box 1615, Golden, BC, V0A 1H0. 250-344-2700. 18-hole course on west side of the Columbia amid deer and mountains. Was considered the most extraordinary nine-hole course in BC; now it's doubly wonderful.

■ **Whitetooth Ski Area:** West side of the Columbia River, 13km from Golden. Box 1925, Golden, BC, V0A 1H0. 250-344-6114. Great powder snow. Vertical 530m, 12 runs with the longest 5.5km. Double chair, T-bar, ski school, day lodge. 17km of cross-country ski trails.

■ **Purcell Lodge:** On the eastern border of Glacier National Park. No road in. Accessed by a 15-minute helicopter trip from Golden, or summer hiking trail. Contact Places Less Travelled, Box 1829, Golden, BC, V0A 1H0. 250-344-2639. High comfort level (balconies, showers, flush toilets) at a high altitude (2,195m) amid unspoiled beauty.

■ **Whitewater Adventures:** A number of companies operate in the area. Ask at Info Centre.

The Trans-Canada Hwy (Hwy 1) continues east following the Kicking Horse River for 26km to Yoho National Park West Gate.

Ten Mile Rest Area: 16km east of Golden on Hwy 1.

Mt Hunter Creek Rest Area: 20km east of Golden on Hwy 1.

Yoho National Park: 131,300ha; 262 campsites. In addition to the three road-access campgrounds, Yoho National Park has two easily accessible walk-in campgrounds and a number of primitive backcountry campsites. Western boundary is 26km east of Golden. It is 45km from west to east across the park.

Anyone planning to visit the park for day-use activities or to stay overnight at a lodge or campground must obtain a park pass, available at park gates or staffed campgrounds. They can also be obtained by calling 1-800-748-7275 and making payment with a VISA or Mastercard. Separate wilderness passes are required for backcountry camping and winter camping.

"Yoho" is a Cree word expressing awe. "Kicking Horse" has a longer story behind it. Sir James Hector led the Palliser Expedition through Vermilion Pass in 1858. They continued west to the Kicking Horse River near Wapta Falls. While Hector and his men, starved and sick, rescued a pack horse which had fallen into the river, Hector was kicked in the chest by his own horse. He was knocked senseless, and the other members of his party thought he was dead. They were digging his grave when he revived enough to let them know their actions were premature. Hector's party followed the river east and returned to the Prairies through Kicking Horse Pass.

When the CPR began building its transcontinental line, Major A.B. Rogers surveyed a route through the Kicking Horse Pass, and the railway arrived in 1884.

The new railway's 4.5 percent grade between the pass and the small town of Field was known as the Big Hill, the steepest railway grade in North America. Four extra engines were required to push trains up the hill, and several runaway spur lines were required for downhill traffic. Still, accidents were frequent, and the remains of one wrecked train can be found near the Kicking Horse campground. After 25 years this "temporary" route was replaced by the Spiral Tunnels. From a viewpoint on the highway (see p. 211), visitors can watch trains climbing out of Field disappear into a circular tunnel inside Mt Ogden on the highway's north side. The train emerges from the 890m tunnel, passes under the highway, and circles through a 992m tunnel inside Cathedral Crags on the highway's south side. The tunnels lengthen the route by about 10km, but decrease the grade to about 2.2 percent.

Early tourists came to the Yoho area by rail: the highway wasn't built until 1927.

Yoho offers some 400km of hiking trails, from short walks to day hikes: they are described in the *Backcountry Guide to Yoho National Park*, available at the Visitor Centre. Also ask about guided hikes, fishing, horseback riding, mountaineering and guided mountain adventures, boating, and mountain biking. One of the biggest draws is the Burgess Shale, a fossil bed of soft-bodied marine animals that lived in Cambrian seas 515 million years ago. See p.211.

Yoho Park Information: Information centre at junction of Hwy 1 and Field, 29km beyond park's west boundary; 19km from east boundary or BC/Alberta border (see p.211). Year-round, call 250-343-6783.

All distances within Yoho Park are given from the park's west boundary. Left turns off Trans-Canada Hwy are restricted in the park; some picnic sites and viewpoints are not accessible to eastbound traffic.

Wapta Falls Rd: South off Hwy 1, 4.5km east of west boundary. Gravel road leads 2.5km past Leanchoil Marsh to parking area. At the marsh, watch for muskrats, beavers, elk, moose, and waterfowl. Summer is best. Walk 2.5km to Wapta Falls on Kicking Horse River.

Chancellor Peak Campground: 58 campsites. 5.5km beyond west boundary. North 1km off highway. May to mid-Oct. Great setting on the banks of the Kicking Horse River, with views of Chancellor Peak (el 3,280m), Mt Vaux (el 3,320m), and Mt Ennis (el 3,132m). Watch for parasitic dwarf mistletoe in great bunches in the trees.

Hoodoo Creek Campground: 106 campsites; sani-station. 7km beyond west boundary, just across Kicking Horse River, south of highway. Late June-end of Aug. Steep 3km hiking trail to Leanchoil Hoodoos.

Beyond campground, Hwy 1 follows the Kicking Horse River. Three picnic sites (following) are on river side (north side) of the highway, but restricted left turns limit access for eastbound traffic.

Faeder Lake Picnic Area: 8km beyond west boundary, on highway's north side.

Finn Creek Picnic Area: 13km beyond west boundary, on highway's north side.

Ottertail Viewpoint: 20km beyond west boundary, on highway's north side.

Emerald Lake Lodge, a century-old retreat.

Emerald Lake: 26.5km beyond west boundary, road leads 3km to the **Natural Bridge** eroded out of solid rock by the Kicking Horse River. A short side road leads from the Natural Bridge parking lot past an animal lick to a picnic site on the riverbank. It's 6km beyond the Natural Bridge to stunning Emerald Lake. The lake was discovered in 1882 by CPR packer Tom Wilson who was amazed by the gorgeous colour of the water. (He also named Lake Louise "Emerald Lake," but it was renamed to honour Queen Victoria's daughter.) Moose may appear on the slide areas visible from the lake.

■ **Emerald Lake Lodge:** Original lodge built in 1902 became a tourist destination for the adventurous early in this century. It reopened 1986 with full recreational and conference facilities; 84 rooms in 24 chalets, each with a wood-burning fireplace. 250-343-6321 or 1-800-663-6336.

Parks Canada, BC, Alberta Information: Info Centre, at junction of Hwy 1 and Field, 29km beyond west boundary (19km from east boundary or BC/Alberta border). Year-round. Yoho Park: 250-343-6783. Alberta Tourism: 250-343-6312 (seasonal) or 1-800-661-8888. Tourism BC: 250-343-6783 or 1-800-663-6000.

Field: (Pop. 237). 29km beyond west boundary, just south of Hwy 1, across Kicking Horse River. The town grew during railway construction in 1884, and was for a time an important railway centre because of problems with the Big Hill and subsequent construction of the Spiral Tunnels.

This tiny mountain community promises to be bustling once again, as plans move forward to develop a major museum and research facility to study the rich array of intricate fossils found above the village on the upper slopes of Mt Field. They date back a remarkable 515 million years. **The Burgess Shale** (a UNESCO World Heritage Site declared in 1981) here is one of only three spots in the world where evidence of the strange soft-bodied creatures of the Cambrian period has survived – and this is considered the finest of the three. It will be a while before museum plans are realized, but guided hikes to Walcott's Quarry and the trilobite beds on Mt Stephen are available through Yoho-Burgess Shale Research Foundation (1-800-343-3006). There are also displays at the Field Visitor Centre, Emerald Lake, and the Lake Louise Visitor Centre.

Field is gaining popularity as a base for outdoor adventure: mountain climbing, hiking, ice climbing, and cross-country skiing. Elk appear along the highway mid-Oct to early June. The air is fresh: the elevation here is 1,242m.

Field Information: Information centre, Trans-Canada Hwy, Field, BC, V0A 1G0. 250-343-6783. Year-round.

Yoho Valley Rd: 33km beyond west boundary. Leads north to Monarch Campground, Kicking Horse Campground, Takakkaw Falls, and Takakkaw Falls Campground. June-Aug, keep an eye out for hoary marmots on the rocky slopes. **Warning:** very tight switchbacks on this road (see note below).

SIDE TRIP

to Takakkaw Falls

Monarch Campground: 36 campsites, 8 walk-in. 0.5km beyond Hwy 1 on Yoho Valley Rd. Kitchen shelters, picnic tables, pit toilets, winter camping. Open July-Labour Day weekend.

Kicking Horse Campground: 86 campsites. 1km beyond Hwy 1 on Yoho Valley Rd. Showers, sani-station, interpretive programs. Trails to railway historic sites.

Takakkaw Falls: 15km beyond Hwy 1 on Yoho Valley Rd. Very tight switchbacks prohibit vehicles with trailers or large RVs from using this road. Spectacular 384m falls (second highest in BC) can be viewed from parking lot, or take a short hike to foot of falls. Name is said to be from a Cree word meaning "it is magnificent." Stunning example of hanging valley falls (where falls spill from one slightly higher valley into a deeper one).

Takakkaw Falls Campground: 35 walk-in campsites located a short hike from parking lot.

Return to Highway 1 at Kicking Horse Campground

Spiral Tunnel Viewpoint: 36.5km beyond west boundary. View of famous

Spiral Tunnels built to avoid the treacherous Big Hill. Near viewpoint stands an old bridge that was part of the original track on the Big Hill. The first train attempting to descend the Big Hill plummeted out of control and derailed, killing three men.

Wapta Lake: 40km beyond west boundary. Headwaters of Kicking Horse River. Picnics, waterfowl viewing. Wapta is "running water" in language of the Stoney people.

Highway 1A: 43km beyond west boundary. Leads to Lake O'Hara Rd and Lake O'Hara. Note: the section of Hwy 1A continuing from the Lake O'Hara Rd turnoff to Lake Louise is closed to buses and long vehicles; it is closed entirely in winter, and may soon be decommissioned).

SIDE TRIP

to Lake O'Hara

A beautiful mountain lake with an extensive series of hiking trails. Hwy 1A leads about 200m across railway tracks to junction with Lake O'Hara Rd. Lake O'Hara is 13km southwest. No private vehicles allowed. Walk in, or call Lake O'Hara reservation line for bus service: 250-343-6433, mid-March through Sept. Year-round: (Yoho Park) 250-343-6783. In winter, it is possible to ski in to Lake O'Hara, and camp in the campground: wilderness passes are required. For lodge accommodation, call 250-343-6418, June-Oct, or 403-678-4110 in off-season.

Lake O'Hara Backcountry Campground: 30 walk-in campsites, alpine hut, commercial accommodation.

Gardner Falls, near Nakusp.

13km south of Hwy 1 on Lake O'Hara Rd. Reservations required for bus transportation and overnight stays. June-Sept: 250-343-6433. Year-round: (Yoho Park) 250-343-6783. Reserve three months ahead. Ground squirrels scamper about the northwest end of the lake.

Eastern Boundary of Yoho National Park and the Great Divide: 48km beyond park's west boundary. This is also the Continental Divide, and the boundary between BC and Alberta. Banff National Park begins at this point. See *Alberta Rockies*, p.229.

Return to Highway 1

Lake Louise: (Pop. 355). 52km beyond west boundary; 7km east of BC/Alberta border. Details on p.230. Just west of Lake Louise, turn north onto Hwy 93 for the Icefields Parkway and Jasper (p.234); or take Hwy 1 (p.229) or Hwy 1A, the Bow Valley Parkway (p.233), south to Banff.

CHERRYVILLE TO NELSON

HIGHWAY 6
AND HIGHWAY 23 TO GALENA BAY

Cherryville is a small community on the border between the Thompson Okanagan and BC Rockies regions. Hwy 6 actually begins in Vernon, about 52km west of Cherryville.

It is 290km from Cherryville to Nelson. Hwy 6 leads away from the dry rounded hills of the Okanagan to cross the Monashee Mountains into the moister, greener Kootenay landscape. Between Cherryville and Needles there are steep hills, slow corners, a few backwoods cafes – so little traffic that the highway is sometimes used to herd cattle.

At Needles, a free ferry crosses Lower Arrow Lake to Fauquier. Hwy 6 then runs north to Nakusp, then southeast through the Slocan Valley. South of Slocan, the highway follows the Kootenay River to Nelson.

This *Log* also includes a side trip on Hwy 23 north from Nakusp to Galena Bay and the Galena Bay ferry.

Cherryville: A small centre on Hwy 6, 52km east of Vernon. Cherryville Emporium is store and last gas station before Monashee Pass. Also known for its arts and crafts. Gold Panner Cafe.

Sugar Lake: At Cherryville, turn north off Hwy 6 onto Sugar Lake Rd. 17km to outlet of lake. Gravel roads continue around lakeshores. Crystal-clear lake in the Monashees. Lake was much smaller before 1944 when the dam on the south end was built for irrigation purposes. In spring and fall when the water's low, the foundations of old farmsteads and cottages are visible.

Monashee Provincial Park: 7,513ha. North on Sugar Lake Rd at Cherryville. 35km drive to start of 12km walking trail to park. 250-494-6500. Write BC Parks, Okanagan District, Okanagan Lake Park, Box 399, Summerland, BC, V0H 1Z0.

For topographic map, write: Maps BC, 3rd floor, 1802 Douglas St, Victoria, BC, V8V 1X4. 250-387-1441.

Wilderness park with spectacular mountain views, canyons, river valleys, waterfalls, alpine meadows, wildflowers, lakes, dense forests. Black bears, caribou, mule deer, ground squirrels, many birds.

Kettle River Rd: South off Hwy 6, 36km east of Cherryville. Beautiful back road along Kettle River, between Monashees on the east and Okanagan Highland on the west. 125km to Hwy 33 at Westbridge.

Lost Lake Rest Area: 38km east of Cherryville.

Bench Creek Rest Area: 46km east of Cherryville.

Needles: 86km east of Cherryville. Ferry across Arrow Lake to Fauquier: 5:15am-9:45pm. 10 minutes. 150 passengers, 40 cars. Restrooms.

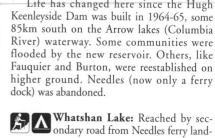

Life has changed here since the Hugh Keenleyside Dam was built in 1964-65, some 85km south on the Arrow lakes (Columbia River) waterway. Some communities were flooded by the new reservoir. Others, like Fauquier and Burton, were reestablished on higher ground. Needles (now only a ferry dock) was abandoned.

Whatshan Lake: Reached by secondary road from Needles ferry land-

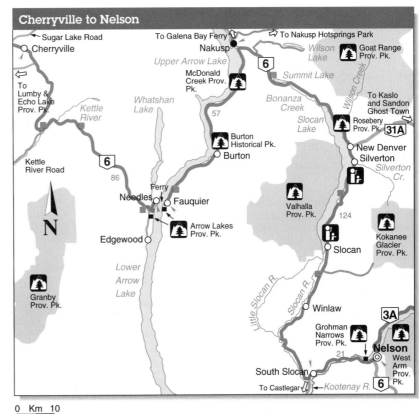

Cherryville to Nelson

ing, 86km east of Cherryville. 7km to outlet of lake. Gravel roads continue around lakeshores. Camping on lakeshore, and fishing.

Fauquier: (Pop. 159). Reestablished after Hugh Keenleyside Dam's waters rose. Named for pioneer rancher and fruit grower who was government agent and Nakusp's first policeman in the 1890s. Some accommodation, camping, fuel, restaurant, store, and golf.

Burton: (Pop. 162). About 21km north of Fauquier. Lakeside community with B&B, camping, store, and fuel.

Burton Historical Park: 22 campsites. About 21km north of Fauquier. Boat ramp, fishing, swimming.

McDonald Creek Provincial Park: 468ha; 38 campsites. 250-825-3500. 46km beyond Fauquier. Camping only on east side of lake. Long beach, boat launching, swimming, fishing.

Nakusp: (Pop. 2,036). 57km north of Fauquier, at junction of Hwys 6 and 23.

Town sits beautifully in a curve of the Upper Arrow Lake, between the Selkirk and Monashee mountains. Tourism is a growing industry. There's a marina, waterfront walk and park, nine-hole golf course, driving range, shops, restaurants, campgrounds, accommodation. Main attraction is the two hot springs, located in the mountains a short distance northeast of town (see below). Old schoolhouse, which houses the museum, library, and village office, is of historic interest; also the Lord Minto Restaurant in former United Church.

Nakusp Information: Info Centre, Nakusp and District Chamber of Commerce, Box 387, Nakusp, BC, V0G 1R0. 250-265-4234 or 1-800-909-8819. At 88-6th St (Hwy 23 in downtown Nakusp). Situated in reproduction of a local sternwheeler's stern.

Nakusp Airport: East off Hwy 23 onto Hot Springs Rd, 3km north of Nakusp.

■ **Nakusp Museum:** On Hwy 23, in Nakusp Village Hall. Daily, 10-5, July-Aug; daily, 12:30-4:30, May-June, Sept-Oct. Tours on request year-round. Displays feature Columbia River steamboats, logging, mining, and aboriginal peoples.

■ **Bonnington Arts Centre:** Corner of Hwy 23 and 4th St. Operated by Arrow Lakes Arts Council, which brings performing artists to Nakusp. Check with Info Centre for events or write to the arts council at Box 895, Nakusp, BC, V0G 1R0.

■ **Kootenay Helicopter Skiing Ltd:** Based in Nakusp. Box 717, Nakusp, BC, V0G 1R0. 250-265-3612 or 1-800-661-0252. Jan to mid-April. Heli-skiing in Selkirks and Monashees with deep powder runs up to 1,525m.

■ **Nakusp Centennial Golf Club:** nine holes. 250-265-4531.

Highway 23: In Nakusp. Hwy 6 continues southeast 46km to New Denver and Slocan Lake. Hwy 23 goes north 49km to Galena Bay ferry.

SIDE TRIP

to Galena Bay

Hwy 23 traces the eastern shore of Upper Arrow Lake to the Galena Bay ferry terminal.

Nakusp Hot Springs: East off Hwy 23 onto Hot Springs Rd, 3km north of Nakusp. Paved 13km road to springs. Owned by village of Nakusp. Daily. Two steaming hot pools, 38-41 C. Particularly invigorating when it's snowing. Change rooms, showers, lockers. Cedar chalets (250-265-4505) and campground.

Ione Rest Area: 18km north of Nakusp. Waterfall on site.

Halfway River Hot Springs: East off Hwy 23, 24km north of Nakusp. Take logging road (just before second bridge) for 10km. Park at skidder trail and follow it about 100m to river. Undeveloped springs are very hot.

Halcyon Hot Springs: On Hwy 23, about 34km north of Nakusp. 1-888-689-4699. Near roadside. Newly developed, open late 1998, and offering camping, cabins, fishing, hiking, horseback riding. Temperatures up to 50C.

Highway 31: 47km north of Nakusp, it intersects with Hwy 23. A 142km alternate route past Trout Lake to Kootenay Lake and Kaslo (see *Balfour to Galena Bay*, p.218). Hwy 23 continues from this junction for 2km to Galena Bay ferry terminal.

Galena Bay: 49km north of Nakusp. Ferry crosses Upper Arrow Lake to Shelter Bay. Free. 20 minutes. Hourly 5:30am-12:30am. 50 vehicles, 150 passengers. For continuation of Hwy 23, see *Shelter Bay to Mica Creek*, p.221.

Return to Highway 6 at Nakusp

Box Lake: South side of Hwy 6, 10km south of Nakusp. Rainbow trout to 2.5kg. Good fly-fishing. Boat launching, camping. Restricted to electric motors.

Summit Lake: North side of Hwy 6, 18km southeast of Nakusp. Resort, camping. Skiing at Summit Peak. T-bar, clubhouse, run by local ski club.

Rosebery Provincial Park: 32ha; 36 campsites. 250-825-3500. On Hwy 6, 40.5km south of Nakusp (5.5km north of New Denver). On Wilson Creek near east shore of Slocan Lake.

New Denver: (Pop. 579). At junction of Hwys 6 and 31A, 46km southeast of Nakusp. See *Balfour to Galena Bay*, p.220.

Highway 31A: East at New Denver. An extremely pleasant 46km route past ghost towns and gold mines to Kaslo on Kootenay Lake. Details in *Balfour to Galena Bay*, p.219.

From New Denver, the lovely Slocan Valley stretches south nearly 80km. Hwy 6 follows the lake, then the river, winding by small farms and homesteads. Because of its light traffic, Hwy 6 has been discovered by the bicycling fraternity as an excellent route for a challenging but quiet pedal.

Slocan Lake: New Denver sits near the northeast shore of Slocan Lake, a narrow 40km jewel in the deep valley between Valhalla and Slocan ranges of the Selkirks. Shores are a rugged combination of bluffs and boulders, with the occasional pebbled or white-sand beach. Native pictographs on shoreline rocks. Rainbow trout to 5kg and Dolly Varden char to 7kg.

Don't be misled by Slocan Lake's postcard-perfect placidness. Strong winds can funnel down between the mountains, whipping waters into frothy, dangerous whitecaps. Winds come with little warning: keep an eye over your shoulder.

Silverton: (Pop. 241). On Hwy 6, 4.5km beyond New Denver. Historic mining town. Community offers campground and other accommodation.

Silverton Information: Village office, 250-358-2472.

■ **Silverton Gallery:** 250-358-7788. July to mid-Sept, Tues-Sun. Summer exhibitions of photography and work of local artists.

■ **Frank Mills Outdoor Mining Exhibit:** Call Village Office, 250-358-2472.

■ **Silverton Resort:** Box 107, Silverton, BC, V0G 2B0. 250-358-7157. Cottages, winter sauna, canoe and kayak rentals on shores of Slocan Lake.

■ **Mistaya Country Inn:** Box 28, Silverton, BC, V0G 2B0. 250-358-7787. Lodge; walking trails, summer trail rides and pack trips through the Selkirks, winter activities.

Slocan Lake Viewpoint: On Hwy 6, 6km beyond New Denver. One of the most spectacular views in the West Kootenays. Fenced path around 120m cliff.

Silverton Lookout Rest Area: 10.5km beyond New Denver.

Kokanee Glacier Provincial Park: See *Nelson to Creston*, p.215. Western edge of the park can be reached from Hwy 6 by turning east onto gravel road, 15km beyond New Denver.

Cape Horn: 26km beyond New Denver. This famous stretch, about 2km long, once narrowed to one lane that clung in white-knuckle curves around a sheer mountainside. A $10-million project completed 1991 took some of the excitement out of the drive. 600,000m of rock were moved about to create a slope angle allowing a regular two-lane highway. The particularly terrifying 1,400m stretch is still quietly missed by some locals. Change comes hard in the Slocan Valley.

Slocan: (Pop. 335). On Hwy 6, 31km beyond New Denver. In the heart of the "Silvery Slocan," this was one of several towns established after prospectors in the 1890s discovered the largest silver-lead deposits in BC.

Mines around Slocan, New Denver, Silverton, and Sandon were worked until high production costs and low ore prices ended the boom. Slocan was incorporated in 1901 when its population was about 2,000 (at one time it reached 6,000). In 1958, Slocan was incorporated again, as a village. Logging and sawmills now the principal industries. Tourism, since establishment of Valhalla Provincial Park in 1983, has become important. Slocan has its own campground. Ask at information centre about adventure tours.

Slocan Information: Information centre, Village of Slocan, 704 Arlington, Box 50, Slocan, BC, V0G 2C0. 250-355-2277, year-round. Off Hwy 6 on Slocan St at Expo Park. Daily, mid-May to mid-Sept. Other times, check with village office located at Delaney Ave and Slocan St.

Valhalla Provincial Park: 49,800ha; wilderness camping. 250-825-3500. Write BC Parks, Nelson Area Office, RR3, S8 C5, Nelson, BC, V1I 5P6. Includes western shore of Slocan Lake and nearly all of the Valhalla Range. Park's Evans Creek-Beatrice Lake Trail can be reached from Slocan by a connecting trail. In Norse mythology, Valhalla

was a palace where slain warriors lived on under the leadership of the god Odin. The splendour of these dramatic peaks fits the heroic legend.

■ **North End of Park:** Turn west off Hwy 6 onto gravel road at Hills, 2km north of Slocan Lake's north end. About 28km on dirt road to start of trails. (Terrain here is rugged; experienced hikers only.)

■ **Southern Part:** Turn into Slocan and cross river. Follow Little Slocan River Rd to Passmore-Hoder Creek junction, then 18.5km to Hoder-Drinnon Creek junction. Also accessible from the village of Slocan, via the Little Slocan Lake Rd. Keep right on rocky spur road to Drinnon Pass trailhead. Boat ramps at Slocan, Silverton, and New Denver. Cartoppers also can be launched at Hills and Rosebery on Hwy 6.

For topographic maps, write Maps BC, 3rd Floor, 1802 Douglas St, Victoria, BC, V8V 1X4. 250-387-1441. For info and a trail guide, write The Valhalla Wilderness Society, Box 224, New Denver, BC, V0G 1S0, or BC Parks, RR 3, Nelson, BC, V1L 5P6.

Peaks of the Valhalla Range dominate the shores of Slocan Lake. On southern boundary is a group of spired and castellated peaks: Mt

Wildflowers on Idaho Peak in the Valhalla Range.

Dag and the Wolfs Ears, both at 2,667m, Gimli and Asgard peaks at 2,758m, and Gladsheim at 2,827m. Among northern peaks is Mt Denver at 2,758m, with New Denver Glacier clinging to its northern slopes.

A park for climbers and hikers, with challenging rock walls and peaks, and trails that take a few hours or a few days. There is rugged terrain, and those venturing in should be in good shape and properly equipped. Maps and compasses a must. It is suggested that anyone considering an extended or overnight hike might register first with the nearest RCMP detachment.

Kokanee Glacier Provincial Park: See *Nelson to Creston*, below. Can be reached from Hwy 6 by turning east onto gravel road at Lemon Creek, 7.5km south of Slocan. 16km to park.

Lemon Creek Rest Area: 7.5km south of Slocan, at Lemon Creek.

Winlaw: (Pop. 180). On Hwy 6, 19.5km south of Slocan on Slocan River. John B. Winlaw built a sawmill here around 1900. Accommodation, campgrounds. As the Slocan River flows through this wide valley, wilderness gives way to farmland.

Highway 3A: Intersects Hwy 6, 46.5km south of Slocan. Hwy 3A goes some 21km south to Castlegar. Hwy 6 continues east 21km to Nelson.

Nelson: (Pop. 9,150). Eastern end of Hwy 6. For details, see *Five-Town Loop*, p.190.

NELSON TO CRESTON

HIGHWAY 3A

Highway 3A between Nelson and Creston is a leisurely, scenic, 113km drive along Kootenay Lake's West Arm and then the main lake's east shores, between the southern Purcell and Selkirk mountains. From Nelson, Hwy 3A goes 34km to Balfour where free car-and-passenger ferry makes a 40-minute trip across Kootenay Lake. From Crawford Bay, a pretty but constantly twisting route hugs the lakeshore 79km to Creston. There are many pleasant stops – beaches, galleries, and second-hand shops – along the way. The ambience is hard to define, but rarified, laid-back, and definitely special.

Nelson: (Pop. 9,585). Details in *Five-Town Loop*, p.190.

To start out, Hwy 3A traces the north bank of the lake's West Arm. The south bank of the West Arm extending east from Nelson remains undeveloped and has been incorporated into the 25,319ha **West Arm Provincial Park**. This protected area provides Nelson's water supply and supports a mountain caribou recovery program. There are no facilities at this time,

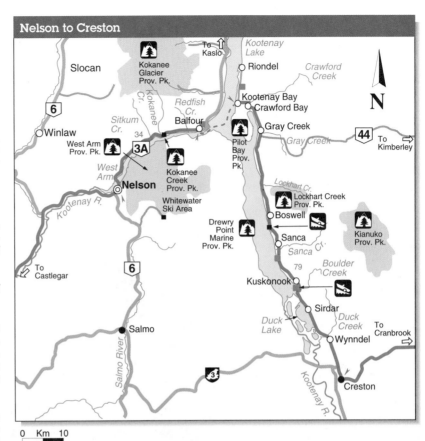

0   Km   10

though the waterway itself is a popular recreation area.

Kokanee Creek Provincial Park: 260ha; 132 campsites in two campgrounds (reservations taken: call 1-800-689-9025; from the Lower Mainland or overseas, call 604-689-9025); sani-station. General info: 250-825-3500. On Hwy 3A, 21km east of Nelson. Excellent family vacation spot with long, sandy beaches, adventure playground, visitor centre. Guided tours of man-made spawning channel for kokanee, which return mid-Aug to mid-Sept. Swimming, fishing, paddling, boating, waterskiing, windsurfing, hiking, visitor programs, photography. Photos especially of ospreys: area has one of the highest osprey (or fish-hawk) populations in North America.

Kokanee Glacier Provincial Park: 32,035ha. For information, write BC Parks, Nelson Area Office, RR3, S8 C5, Nelson, BC, V1I 5P6. 250-825-4421. For topographic map write Maps BC, 3rd Floor, 1802 Douglas St, Victoria, BC, V8V 1X4, 250-387-1441; or Government Agent, 310 Ward St, Nelson, BC, V1L 5S4, 250-354-6104.

Like the centre of a pinwheel, Kokanee Glacier Park can be reached from a circle of access routes, from here near Nelson, also near Ainsworth Hot Springs, Kaslo, and the Slocan Valley (see respective *Logs*). All these routes are limited to appropriate vehicles (see below). Main access is reached by driving north off Hwy 3A from Kokanee Creek Provincial Park. 16km

gravel road, unsuitable for low-slung vehicles, trailers, or RVs. Parking at Gibson Lake where a 2km nature trail encircles the lake. Park is also accessible from Hwys 6, 31, and 31A.

Kokanee Glacier Park, in the Slocan Range of the Selkirk Mountains, is named for the glacier clinging to the eastern and northeastern slopes of 2,774m Kokanee Peak, near the park's centre. It's an undeveloped wilderness with 30 high-elevation lakes, and an extensive network of trails. One of BC's finest hiking locations, it offers designated outback campsites, and a few cabins and shelters. The park embraces a variety of climactic zones, with vegetation ranging from dense forest to alpine grassland. Terrain is rugged and diverse. Wildlife includes mountain goats, deer, hoary marmots, pikas, squirrels, and a variety of birds. Beware of bears.

Prospectors like Dirty Face Johnson and Dutch Charley were drawn to the area more than 100 years ago. Lead, silver, and zinc mines were cut into the rock. The only evidence of this boom left today are ghost towns and abandoned mine shafts.

Balfour: (Pop. 239). On Hwy 3A, 34km east of Nelson. Terminal for ferry across Kootenay Lake to Crawford Bay. Town was originally steamboat terminus for mining activities up and down the lake. A resort community with accommodation, campgrounds, marinas, full range of fishing services. There's a pub right at the ferry dock, and local cafe offers seed to feed the ducks.

■ **Balfour Golf Course:** Nine holes on benchlands above Kootenay Lake. 250-229-4672.

Redfish Creek Spawning Channel: Off Hwy 3A near Balfour. Manmade spawning channel for kokanee. About 3,000 kokanee from mid-Aug to mid-Sept. Interpretive displays, self-guided trails.

Highway 31: From Balfour ferry landing, Hwy 31 runs north to Kaslo, Duncan Lake, Trout Lake, and Galena Bay on Upper Arrow Lake. See *Balfour to Galena Bay*, p.218.

Kootenay Lake: Access at Balfour and other locations along lakeshore. Between the Purcell and Selkirk Mountains. More than 100km long, 2-6km wide. The West Arm runs 30km down to the city of Nelson where it narrows into the Kootenay River, eventually joining the Columbia River at Castlegar.

Fishing on this big lake, which doesn't freeze normally, is a year-round pastime. The lake has been known to yield rainbow trout to 16kg – the world's largest – and Dolly Varden char over 10kg. Kokanee here are also the largest in the world – over 4kg. Kokanee runs in the West Arm peak about the third week in Aug, when they school up at the mouths of creeks. Near the end of July, rainbow trout 1-4kg move into the arm and feed near the surface, an irresistible invitation to fly-fishermen. Rainbow fishing in the West Arm peaks about mid-Sept. Trolling in the main part of Kootenay Lake for huge Dolly Varden and rainbows is good from Oct-June.

At the south end of the lake, Duck Lake, Summit and Corn creeks, and the marshy sloughs of the Creston Valley are good spin-casting waters for largemouth bass, particularly April-May. A hot spot for kids to catch yellow perch with bobbers and worms.

■ **Provincial Marine Parks:** Accessible only by boat. **Midge Creek Park** (158ha; six campsites) is on the west side of Kootenay Lake, 16km north of Creston Valley. **Drewry Point Park** (21ha; two campsites) is also on the west shore, 4km north of Midge Creek. **Pilot Bay Park** (347ha; two campsites) is on the east side near the ferry landing.

Kootenay Lake Ferry: At Balfour, on Hwy 3A, 34km east of Nelson. Car-and-passenger service between Balfour and Kootenay Bay. MV *Anscomb* and MV *Balfour* ply the waters, offering what's billed as the longest free ferry ride in the world. 15-18 runs a day. Begins 6am from Balfour, 6:50am from Kootenay Bay. 40-minute, 9km crossing.

Kootenay Bay: (Pop. 38). 9km across Kootenay Lake from Balfour. Ferry landing has rest area, restaurants, and camping facilities.

Riondel Rd: North off Hwy 3A near Kootenay Bay ferry landing. About 9km to village of Riondel.

Yasodhara Ashram: North on Riondel Rd. Take Walkers Landing turn-off. Box 9, Kootenay Bay, BC, V0B 1X0. 1-800-661-8711. 250-227-9224. Yoga retreat in mountain setting, established more than 30 years ago.

Riondel: (Pop. 350). East side of Kootenay Lake. Village with store, pub, restaurant, and community centre. Nine-hole golf course overlooking lake. Historic walkway through mine site. Public beach. Local Historic Society operates a small museum in Community Centre (former high school). Open on request, call 250-225-3483. Photos of sternwheelers, mining operations, and early history of Riondel, site of the Bluebell Mine, opened 1882, closed 1972. Riondel is now a retirement centre.

Crawford Bay: (Pop. 312). On Hwy 3A, 3.5km southeast of ferry dock. Stores, accommodation, marina. Home to a championship 18-hole golf course, and several unusual cottage industries, such as North Woven

Columbian ground squirrel.

Broom and Kootenay Forge. Forge is a traditional blacksmith shop where visitors can watch craftsmen forge graceful, timeless items. Community named for "White Man Jim" Crawford, a prospector and trapper who died in 1914.

Kootenay Lake Information: Ask at local friendly stores, or write Kootenay Lake Chamber of Commerce, Box 4, Gray Creek, BC, V0B 1S0. 250-227-9315.

Crawford Bay Airstrip: Maintained spring, summer, fall.

■ **Kokanee Springs Golf Resort:** In Crawford Bay. A celebrated 18-hole championship golf course. New luxury E.E. Moore Lodge, where every sun deck faces the Kokanee Glacier. Facilities include airstrip, cottages, campground. Box 96, Crawford Bay, BC, V0B 1E0. 250-227-9226.

■ **Wedgwood Manor:** Victorian-era luxury. Box 135, Crawford Bay, BC, V0B 1E0. 250-227-9233.

Gray Creek: (Pop. 150). On Hwy 3A, 11km south of ferry dock. Beam us down,

Scotty. A time warp here. Gray Creek sets itself up as "metric free." Buy your gas by the gallon, and visit Sharon and Tom Lymbery's Gray Creek Store, where you can also pick up your food, fishing tackle, garden plants, chainsaws, and wood-burning stoves. Also campgrounds, laundromat, boat ramps. Sailing regatta on Labour Day weekend. And underwater, the famous sunken paddlewheeler, *City of Ainsworth*.

Also, "Gentle Adventures" – water taxi across to Pilot Peninsula, sleep in a tipis, enjoy a custom-catered romantic gourmet dinner; or have a seminar or group retreat. Call Guiding Hands Recreation Society, 250-227-9555. Seasonal.

Gray Creek-Kimberley Forestry Rd (Hwy 44): Just south of Gray Creek. Seasonal (June-Oct) gravel road east up Gray Creek and over Baker Pass 86km to Kimberley via St Mary River drainage. Steep, with some 14 percent grades on western side, but passable for RVs and trailers with clearance. East-west, takes an hour off the Calgary to Kootenay Lake trek. Scenic.

Lockhart Creek Provincial Park: 3,751ha; 13 campsites. 250-825-3500. On Hwy 3A, 13.5km south of Gray Creek (24.5km south of ferry). Hiking, fishing, swimming, boat ramp. In a forest of Douglas fir, western red cedar, ponderosa pine. To the east of this small park, the forested headwaters of Lockhart Creek are protected in new addition to this park. Farther west, beyond mountain peaks, is the undeveloped 11,638ha **Kianuko Provincial Park**, protecting the headwaters of Kianuko Creek. Cedar-hemlock and Engelmann spruce forest is home to caribou and moose.

Boswell: (Pop. 200). Lakeside resort 5.5km south of Lockhart Beach (30km beyond ferry). Home of the East Shore Craft Faire, long weekend in Aug. Restaurants, store. Kootenay Lake Adventures, 250-223-8508 or 1-888-293-1598 offers fishing charters and tours.

The Glass House: 7km south of Boswell, 37km south of ferry. 250-223-8372. Circular glass castle 14.5m long by 7.5m wide, with 111.5 sq m floor space. Made in 1955 by retired undertaker David Brown from a stockpile of 150,000 square embalming-fluid bottles. The family lived inside until overwhelmed by curious tourists. Refreshment stand and gift shop May-Oct.

Sanca: (Pop. 33). 41km south of ferry. Once a gold-rush town of 1,500 souls.

Twin Bays Rest Area: 48km south of ferry. Near public beach.

Kuskonook: (Pop. 43). Wee settlement 51km south of ferry.

Kuskonook Rest Area: On Hwy 3A, 56km south of ferry. Pleasant beach with boat ramp, one of many lake accesses on Hwy 3A.

The protected wetlands of the Creston Valley are a refuge for 250 bird species.

Sirdar: (Pop. 50). 58.5 south of ferry, on shores of Duck Lake. Named after Field Marshal Lord Kitchener who was Sirdar, or Commander, of Egyptian army in 1892. Sirdar General Store and Sirdar Pub (with home-made food) are both worth a linger. Southern Purcell Adventures, 250-866-5458, offers "soft" hiking and biking tours.

Wynndel: (Area pop. 723). 8km beyond Sirdar (64.5km south of ferry). Known in the 1890s for its Duck Creek Hotel. Boasts one of the only three grain elevators in southern BC.

Mountain Stream Trout Farm and Recreation Area: 6.5km south of Wynndel (71km south of ferry). Eight trout ponds in woods overlooking Creston Valley. Fishing, hiking, barbecuing, tackle rentals.

Bo-Fjords: Just outside Creston, west side of highway. Breeding ranch of Norwegian fjord horses. Here are North America's tallest draft fjord stallions. Some stand over 15 hands high. Also rare gray fjords: only one in 1,000 born this colour. Manes are black in centre, white outside, bristling upright and cut in traditional crescent. Said to be related to Asian wild horse, the Przewalski. For a tour: 250-428-2181.

Creston: (Pop. 4,816). 79km south of Kootenay Bay ferry, on Hwy 3, near its intersection with Hwy 3A. 13km north of the BC/Idaho border. Creston overlooks a broad, fertile valley where the Kootenay River mean-

ders between the Selkirk and Purcell mountains into Kootenay Lake. Known as the "Valley of the Swans," the area is visited or inhabited by more than 250 bird species. About 12,000ha have been reclaimed by a network of dikes, creating land which has been added to a natural habitat of about 9,000ha. This, and the rolling benchlands above, are important for orchardists, farmers, and hundreds of thousands of waterfowl and other birds that migrate and nest on the Pacific flyway.

Creston has a different history from the rest of the Kootenays, based as it is more on agriculture – dairy farms, orchards – than mining. The area has the mildest climate in southeastern BC, and spring arrives early. May's Blossom Festival celebrates that fact. Fruit stands line Hwy 3A near Creston, and in May, the entire valley is Lilac Heaven. Here are two of only three grain elevators in southern BC (Wynndel has the third). All are on the CPR line. These elevators, and the flat fields of alfalfa, give the place a Prairie feel.

The Creston Valley Wildlife Management Area, about 10km northwest of Creston, is one of the area's highlights. It is covered in *Castlegar to Creston*, p.193.

During the 1860s gold rush, Creston was a major transportation centre on historic Dewdney Trail from Hope to Fort Steele. Hwy 3 from here still follows much the same route. Creston is a service centre for an area population of about 15,000.

Area from Creston east to Yahk is on **Mountain Standard Time** year-round. During summer, when most parts of province move clocks ahead to daylight-saving-time, Creston, Kitchener, and Yahk make no changes. Their mountain time is already the same as daylight saving-time.

Creston Information: Info Centre, Creston and District Chamber of Commerce, Box 268, Creston, BC, V0B 1G0. 250-428-4342. At 1711 Canyon St (Hwy 3). Open daily July-Aug; weekdays year-round. Ask here for brochures on the many trails: biking, hiking, walking, cross-country skiing, birdwatching. Also ask about shopping for treasures by local artisans; bass fishing on Duck Lake; and what's playing at the local drive-in.

Creston Airport: At Lister, about 8km south of Creston. Take Hwy 21 to Mallory Rd and turn east.

■ **Creston Valley Wildlife Management Area and Centre:** On Hwy 3, 10km northwest of Creston. BC Wildlife Watch Viewing Site. Details in *Castlegar to Creston*, p.193.

■ **Creston Valley Museum and Archives (the "Stone House"):** 219 Devon St. 250-428-9262. Daily in summer, by appointment rest of year. Meticulously constructed of local stone (it took 15 years to build), on attractive grounds overlooking the valley. Has replica of world rarity, the Kutenai (Ktunaxa) canoe. "Sturgeon-nosed" canoe points down, under the water, at either end. Only other similar canoe in the world was made by Goldi peoples of Amur River Basin in Russia. Restored 1906 schoolhouse on site.

■ **The Murals:** Now there are nine outdoors, two indoors. The one that began it all is on McDowell's Department Store. Others are around town.

■ **Columbia Brewery:** 1220 Erickson St. 250-428-9344. Brewers of Kokanee beer. Tours, Mon-Fri, Mid-June to early Sept. Gift shop.

■ **Cresteramics:** 921 Railway Ave. 250-428-7412. Mon-Sat, in summer; Mon-Fri, off-season. Ceramics workshop with store. Employment and training for handicapped. Mon-Sat.

■ **The Kootenay Candle Factory:** 1511 Northwest Blvd. 250-428-9785. Daily. Tours weekdays, 10:30am and 1:30pm. Yesteryear candles in wax molds from antique glassware; hand-dipped beeswax candles.

■ **Wayside Garden and Arboretum:** 2915 Hwy 3 at Erickson, eastern outskirts of Creston. Daily May-Oct. Roses, rhododendrons, and others, plus more than 200 trees and shrubs collected from temperate zones of the world. Mountain and orchard views.

■ **Creston Golf Club:** 18-hole course with omnipresent spectacular views of Creston Valley and Selkirk Mountains. 250-428-5515.

■ **Wayside Gardens and Arboretum:** 2915 Hwy 3. 250-428-9785.

■ **The Drive-In:** Just east of town on Hwy 3. One of only six drive-in theatres left in BC. (You might also want to check out the Auto Vue in Trail).

Hwy 3A ends at Creston. From here, Hwy 21 extends south 13km to Rykerts at US border (open 8am-11pm). Hwy 3 extends west and east. Pick up from Creston in *Creston to Wasa Lake*, p.194.

BALFOUR TO GALENA BAY

HIGHWAYS 31 AND 31A

This 178km lakes-and-mountains route from Balfour to Galena Bay first follows Hwy 31 to Kaslo. The highway is just a narrow ledge along the west side of Kootenay Lake. There's a spot or two where curves and bridges and scenery demand fullest attention and braking dexterity.

From Kaslo, there's a choice between continuing on Hwy 31 north past Duncan and Trout lakes to Galena Bay, or switching east on Hwy 31A to New Denver, and on up Hwy 6, then 23, to Galena Bay.

The routes cover the same distance, both 142km. Yet there's a big difference in the experience. Hwy 31, after Kaslo, is more of an adventure: it's rough, somewhat isolated, and portions are unpaved. Hwy 31A offers a totally stunning drive through the Selkirks, skirting ghost towns. Both routes are scenic; both are steeped in gold- and silver-rush history; both are described below. Take your pick.

Balfour: (Area pop. 239). Western terminus for free ferry service across Kootenay Lake. For details of Balfour and east shore, see *Nelson to Creston*, p.215.

All Dressed Up – Nowhere To Go: Between Balfour and Ainsworth Hot Springs, there are about 100 telephone poles wearing neckties. One of BC's wackiest roadside attractions.

Balfour Rest Area: At ferry terminal. Pleasant beach.

Pilot Bay: Road offers view across lake to the smoke stacks of the smelter that treated ore from the Bluebell Mine – the discovery of galena here sparked the Slocan's silver rush.

Coffee Creek: One of five sites in Kootenay Lake Provincial Park. 71ha. On Hwy 31, 10km north of Balfour. Creek boils down a narrow gorge, forcing highway into a very sharp switchback.

Kokanee Glacier Provincial Park: Reached from Hwy 31 by turning west on gravel road at Coffee Creek, 10km north of Balfour. 10km to park boundary. Described in *Nelson to Creston*, p.215.

Ainsworth Hot Springs: (Pop. 89). On Hwy 31, some 15km north of Balfour. Little town features a horseshoe-shaped cave that was a mine shaft, abandoned when drillers discovered more hot water than ore. Highest mineral content of any hot springs in Canada. Pool temperature 45C, and the view is fabulous, too. Year-round. At the turn of the century, Ainsworth supported five hotels: Silver Ledge Hotel remains, now a museum.

Today you can explore a 20m lighted cave to spring's source, a steam bath with stalactites.

Balfour ferry terminal, Kootenay Lake.

■ Ainsworth Hot Springs Resort: Box 1268, Ainsworth Hot Springs, BC, V0G 1A0. 250-229-4212 or 1-800-668-1171.

■ Mountain Trek Fitness Retreat & Health Spa: Box 1352, Ainsworth Hot Springs, BC, V0G 1A0. 1-800-661-5161 or 250-229-5636. 12-room lodge on 14 forested hectares.

Cody Caves Provincial Park: 63ha. West onto gravel road off Hwy 31, 3km north of Ainsworth Hot Springs. 12km to start of 20-minute trail to caves. Road usually passable for high-clearance vehicles June-Oct. GUIDED TOURS ONLY! For tours, contact HiAdventure Corporation: 250-353-7425. For further information, write BC Parks, Nelson Area Office, RR3, S8 C5, Nelson, BC, V1I 5P6. 250-825-3500. Except for a few ladders it's just as Henry Cody found it a century ago. Nearly 1km of passages to explore: stalagmites, stalactites, soda straws, moonmilk, and bacon strips. Helmets, headlamps, and gloves provided, but visitors must wear sturdy, outdoor footwear and warm clothing.

Woodbury Resort and Marina: On Hwy 31, 4km north of Ainsworth Hot Springs. Large resort and marina complex. Motel, chalets, campsites. Box 1262, Ainsworth, BC, V0G 1A0. 250-353-7717.

Woodbury Mining Museum: Across from Woodbury Marina. Box 896, Kaslo, BC, V0G 1M0. 250-354-4470. Daily, early July-early Sept. Tours. Blacksmith shop. Gold panning.

Mirror Lake: A private lake 15.5km beyond Ainsworth Hot Springs. An important shipbuilding site during the mining boom.

Kaslo: (Pop. 1,063). On Hwy 31, 5.5km north of Mirror Lake, 36km north of Balfour. Magnificently set on delta of the Kaslo River, between the Selkirks and the Purcells. Some call this "the Switzerland of the Americas."

As one of the oldest communities in the province, Kaslo celebrated its centenary in 1994. It was forestry, not mining, that encouraged the first settlement here. And although the mining boom of the 1890s played a significant role in the early years, forestry has remained the mainstay of the local economy. Though tranquil today, the town has had its share of disasters. On February 25, 1894, fire broke out at the Bon Ton Restaurant, and swept through the lower half of Front St destroying almost everything. Later that year Kaslo was struck by a hurricane that blew the front out of the Great Northern Hotel and completely swept away the jail; 70 other buildings went, too. During the storm, a bridge and a log jam gave way, and the rising Kaslo River roared through town, destroying even more. Somehow, Kaslo rebuilt over the years.

In recent years, the area has seen significant growth in tourism opportunities. Residents have strived to preserve the many Victorian-era homes, commercial buildings, and heritage sites. The SS *Moyie*, a dry-docked CPR sternwheeler that once plied the waters of Kootenay Lake, is the community's main landmark. There is a mining museum in the old fire hall.

Kaslo is a departure point for hiking, mountain biking, boating, and fishing, and a supply centre for outlying rural communities, with shops selling everything from antiques to logger's equipment. There are gift shops, galleries, a butcher, bakery, and restaurants. Plenty of charming B&Bs. Many fall in love with this little town's beauty and charm.

Kaslo Information: Kaslo Lake Historical Society, Information Centre, Box 537, Kaslo, BC, V0G 1M0. 250-353-2525. In SS *Moyie*, below.

■ SS Moyie: Beached on Front St, the 49m ship was the last commercial sternwheeler to serve in BC. Daily tours mid-May to mid-Sept. 250-353-2525.

Sternwheelers played a major role in opening up the western frontier: their shallow draft and light construction let them nose up on beaches to unload people and freight. In the old days, every wharf on the lake was piled with boxes of apples, waiting for the boat. Life for the lakers beat to the rhythm of the friendly paddlewheel. There are only two dozen sternwheelers left on the continent, six of them in Canada. The oldest is the *Moyie*, the "grand old lady of the lake," launched in Nelson in 1898, retired from service in 1957. Designated an historic site by the Historic Sites and Monuments Board of Canada.

■ Langham Cultural Centre: On A Ave, across from post office. 250-353-2661. Built in 1893 as a hotel for miners (it had a somewhat dubious reputation). Then it was successively occupied by the Bank of British North America, Knapp Bottling Co, a land speculator, and about 80 interned Japanese-Canadians during the Second World War. Now: two galleries, a theatre, studios, arts library, lounge and facilities for artists. Plus newly opened free museum and archival display on Japanese-Canadian internment years.

■ **Kaslo-on-the-Lake Summer School of the Arts:** Contact cultural centre, above, for brochure. Late July-Aug. Course lengths run from an afternoon to five days. Possible subjects are fabric art and design, clay sculpture, tai chi by the lake, healing arts, language arts, mask making, music and dance. An institution now, running for nearly two decades.

■ **Mining Museum:** 402 Front St, in old fire hall. 250-353-7349.

■ **Kaslo Golf and Country Club:** Nine challenging holes. 250-353-2262.

■ **Kaslo Bay:** 2ha. At Kaslo. Part of Kootenay Lake Provincial Park.

Campbell Bay: 25ha. On east side of Kootenay lake, opposite Hwy 31, 4km north of Kaslo. Part of Kootenay Lake Provincial Park. Unorganized camping. Boat access only. Sheltered anchorage. User-maintained trail leads to small mountain lakes.

Highway 31A: Up Main St in Kaslo and northwest, leading 47km to New Denver. Hwy 31 continues north, providing the 142km alternate route to Galena Bay via Trout Lake (see final section of this *Log*).

HIGHWAY 31A TO NEW DENVER

Hwy 31A is brief and beautiful: a 47km link west across the Selkirk Mountains to New Denver. From New Denver, Hwy 6 runs northwest 46km to Nakusp. Last leg is Hwy 23, 49km to Galena Bay ferry terminal, covered in *Cherryville to Nelson*, p.213.

West off Hwy 31 at Kaslo onto Hwy 31A. Road is built on the old roadbed of narrow-gauge Kaslo and Slocan (K&S) Railway. For five years in the 1890s, the K&S carried ore and passengers up and down hair-raising grades on the 45km trip between Sandon and steamboats in Kaslo.

Kokanee Glacier Provincial Park: Described under *Nelson to Creston*, p.215. Can be reached by turning southwest off Hwy 31A onto gravel road 6.5km west of Kaslo. 24km to trails from Joker Millsite.

Fish and Bear Lakes: On Hwy 31A, beginning about 23km west of Kaslo. Rest area at Fish Lake.

Retallack Ghost Town: 27km beyond Kaslo. The area was staked in 1892 for iron, but more valuable galena was found. There was an ore concentrator, hotel, and stores.

Zincton Ghost Town: 32km beyond Kaslo. Zinc was mined here sporadically from the 1892 to early 1950s.

Three Forks Ghost Town: 38km beyond Kaslo, at junction of Kane, Seaton, and Carpenter creeks, named after prospectors. Nothing left of the six hotels.

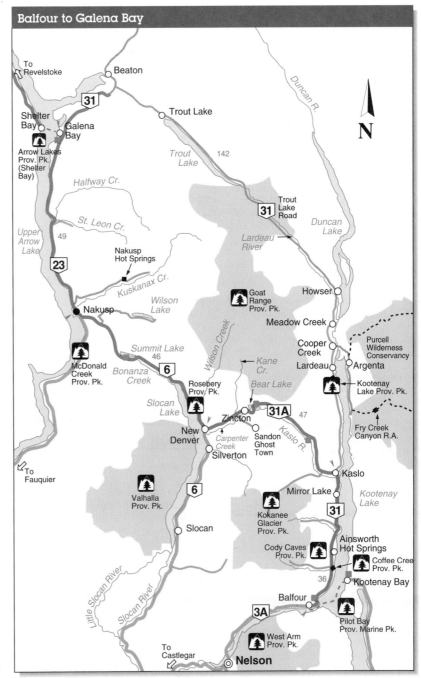

Sandon Ghost Town: South off Hwy 31A on Sandon Rd, just beyond Three Forks. 5km to town. Sandon sits in a valley that is beautiful, but so narrow the towering mountains keep the sun out for much of the day. One of five mining towns in the "Silvery Slocan" that have long been left to the elements. Founded in 1892 and spawned almost overnight by the silver rush, Sandon was a glittering Kootenay mining capital with 29 hotels, 28 saloons, opera house, and red light district. As Colonel Lowery, editor of the *New Denver Ledge*, put it in 1893: "Pumpkins, turnips and townsites are easily grown." Sandon even had electric power (before Vancouver and Victoria). The population was 5,000. During the Second

World War, Sandon served as a detention camp for Japanese-Canadians.

Today, there are just the sounds of Carpenter Creek, a few dilapidated or collapsed buildings from the past, and some historical restoration. Molly Brown's Brothel is being revived by a group of New Denver residents – though it won't be open to the public. Museum is open daily, mid-June to mid-Sept. The Tin Cup Cafe and Prospector's Pick gift shop also welcome summer visitors. A 12km gravel road winds from Sandon to the **Idaho Peak Lookout** parking lot; it's a 1.4km hike from here to lookout, el 2,280m. Or follow 7km of the old K&S Railway bed between Sandon and Three Forks, near Hwy 31A. The ghost town of Cody is an hour's walk east of Sandon. The famous Noble Five mine was situated above Cody.

New Denver: (Pop. 579). At junction of Hwys 31A and 6, 47km northwest of Kaslo. New Denver, idyllically set on the eastern shore of Slocan Lake, is a sleepy mountain town where the odd dog snoozes on the street, and stores have false fronts. But don't be deceived: the town is a busy service centre for hikers, anglers, boaters, skiers, and snowmobilers, with campgrounds, stores, restaurants, accommodation (including the Carpenter Creek Hostel and a golf course. Back in the 1890s, this place was nearly called El Dorado, but New Denver never did produce gold. What it did have, however, was silver, lead, and zinc.

New Denver Information: Write Slocan and District Chamber of Commerce, Box 448, New Denver, BC, V0G 1S0.

■ **Silvery Slocan Museum:** At corner of 6th St and Marine Dr. Late May-early Sept. 250-358-2201. Housed in old Bank of Montreal, BC's oldest wood-frame bank building. Local mining and logging. History of the Japanese in the Slocan Valley.

New Denver Glacier: Across Slocan Lake from New Denver. 6km trail from lakeshore. The only patch of white that remains on surrounding mountains through summer.

Highway 6: In New Denver. South to Silverton and the Slocan Valley. See *Cherryville to Nelson*, p.213. *Log* takes Hwy 6 north to Nakusp.

Return to Kaslo

ALTERNATE ROUTE TO GALENA BAY ON HIGHWAY 31

Hwy 31 between Kaslo and Galena Bay is a 142km alternate route through the once-active Lardeau-Duncan valleys. The landscape is dominated by steep rugged mountains, fast-flowing rivers, and long lakes in narrow forested valleys. The northern section of the highway is gravel, and parts are very narrow (some tight squeezes if trucks come along). At the beginning are old farmsteads on Shutty Bench overlooking Kootenay Lake, lakeside resorts, and camping. Sections of the road, overhung by rocky cliffs, are sometimes closed in winter to clear rock and snowslides.

Grey-green Kootenay argillite, used by aboriginal people for knives, arrowheads, and scrapers, can still be found along creek outwashes.

The towns of Trout Lake City and Ferguson were centres of considerable activity: 200 claims had been staked by 1893. For a while it seemed the Lardeau region might equal the Silvery Slocan, but treacherous terrain made transportation a nightmare. Nevertheless, thousands of miners and others made their way into the northern valleys, and

towns such as Camborne, Poplar Creek, and Goldfields had a brief bloom.

Today, the valleys are quiet. The Kootenay and Arrowhead Railway is gone; so are the sawmills at Gerrard and Howser.

Lost Ledge (Kootenay Lake Provincial Park): 3ha; 10 primitive campsites. On Hwy 31, some 22km north of Kaslo.

Davis Creek (Kootenay Lake Provincial Park): 5ha; 10 simple campsites. On southern outskirts of Lardeau, 30km north of Kaslo.

Lardeau: (Pop. 59). On Hwy 31, 30km north of Kaslo. Logging community on a point on Kootenay Lake's west shore. Gas, fishing licences, cofee, and ice cream at Lardeau Valley Service.

Duncan Dam: East off Hwy 31 at Cooper Creek, 42km north of Kaslo. Road crosses the Duncan River, and runs north to the Duncan Dam. The reservoir can be reached by continuing past the dam. Fishing for Dolly Varden char to 4kg and rainbow trout to 1kg. Camping, boating, paddling, swimming, windsurfing. The west side can be reached from Howser, on Hwy 31, about 7km north of the turnoff to the Duncan Dam Access Rd at Cooper Creek.

SIDE TRIP

to Argenta

Argenta: (Pop. 150). Turn south after crossing the Duncan River and follow road 5km. In 1952, this former mining boom town became a refuge for Quaker families leaving California's growing militarism and materialism. More Quakers joined in the years to come, forming a working cooperative that farmed, logged, landed some building contracts, and experimented with other ventures. Times have changed, but the Quaker spirit persists here. Argenta is a beautiful place, but apart from a B&B, there are no services here. Trails lead from here into the Purcell Wilderness Conservancy and Fry Creek Canyon Provincial Recreation Area (below).

Purcell Wilderness Conservancy: The Earl Grey Pass trailhead is reached by following the main road through Argenta for 4.25km past the post office. This rigorous 61km wilderness trail travels over the Purcell Mountains to the East Kootenay near Invermere. Cable cars cross creeks, and a few kilometres from the Argenta trailhead the route takes hikers past relics of the old mine at Hamill Creek. **Fry Creek Canyon Trail** is reached by driving the narrow and winding road from Argenta 12km south to Johnsons Landing, then following the signs to the trailhead for 4km south. This old mining trail along the creek provides impressive views of the lake and mountains. More details on conservancy on p.203.

Return to Highway 31

Meadow Creek: (Area pop. 300). On Hwy 31, 46km north of Kaslo. Store with post office, service station, cafe, community hall with childrens playground.

■ **Meadow Creek Spawning Channel:** Follow signs from Meadow Creek. Built to compensate for fish lost in construction of Duncan Dam in 1967. Channel is 9m wide and follows wide S-curves for 3.5km. BC's first kokanee spawning channel. Between 500,000 and 1.2 million return each fall. BC Wildlife Watch viewing site.

■ **Selkirk Wilderness Skiing:** Snowcat skiing based at Meadow Mountain Lodge. Runs between 300 to 1,200 vertical metres. Snowcat transportation to 2,440m level. Write to Selkirk Wilderness Skiing Ltd, Meadow Creek, BC, V0G 1N0. 250-366-4424.

Marblehead: Just north of Meadow Creek. Quarry here manufactured tombstones and supplied much of the stone for Nelson's most impressive buildings. Closed about 1940.

Goat Range Provincial Park (Gerrard Campground): 87,947ha; 13 campsites. 250-825-3500. 37km northwest of Meadow Creek at southeast end of Trout Lake. Campground is at the old townsite of Gerrard, terminus of Arrowhead and Kootenay Railway, built 1903. A former CPR branch line connected Trout Lake with steamships at Lardeau on Kootenay Lake; tracks were pulled up in 1942. This campground has been incorporated into Goat Range Provincial Park, created in 1995. The rest of the park consists of an almost roadless Selkirk Mountain wilderness, roughly bordered by Trout Lake to the north, Hwy 31A to the south, and the Lardeau River to the east. This is raw, undeveloped park, with no facilities and only difficult access. BC Parks wishes to minimize the impact of people here. The park's boundaries embrace and protect the 63m Wilson Creek Falls; habitat of mountain goats and grizzly bears, including the rare "white grizzly," with a distinctive blonde colouring; the 3,089m Mt Cooper adorned by the Spokane Glacier; meadows of heather, miniature icebergs drifting in subalpine lakes; and spawning creeks for kokanee salmon and Gerrard rainbow trout. Descriptions of most of the trails leading into the park can be found in *Hiking in the West Kootenay*, by John Carter (out of print, but in most libraries). Getting to trailheads frequently requires a high-clearance, four-wheel drive vehicle. Guide-outfitters offer snowcat skiing, heli-skiing, and summer hiking, adventures. Ask at Nelson and Nakusp Info Centres.

Trout Lake and Lardeau River: Narrow, 28km lake with good fishing for rainbow trout to 2kg. Boat launching at Gerrard or community of Trout Lake, at opposite end of lake. Very large rainbow trout spawn in the Lardeau River at the southern end of Trout Lake. May-June is best. There is a campground (formerly called Trout Lake Provincial Park) near the spawning site.

Trout Lake: (Pop. 56). At northwest end of lake, 65km northwest of Meadow Creek. Views from road high above lake between Gerrard and Trout Lake.

■ **Great Northern Lodge and Great Northern Snow-Cat Skiing Ltd:** Lodge amidst 130 sq km of wilderness ski terrain. Heated snowcats transport 16 passengers at a time from lodge to upper alpine ridges of Great Northern and Thompson mountains. Mid-Dec to mid-April. Box 14, Site 13, RR4, Calgary, AB, T2M 4L4. Call 403-287-2267.

Staubert and Armstrong Lakes: 8km and 13km northwest of Trout Lake. Fishing for rainbow trout and whitefish.

Beaton Rd: North off Hwy 31, 15km northwest of Trout Lake. This is a great road for explorers, and an exciting way to drive back in time. It is certainly off the beaten track. The road goes 5km north to the ghost town of Beaton. Then about 10km farther to Camborne ghost town; and, for the inveterate adventurer, another 10km to Goldfields. Bonus points for getting to Gunterman and Captain Soules falls.

Hill Creek Spawning Channel and Hatchery: West off Hwy 31, 9km west of Beaton Rd turnoff. Manmade 1.5km spawning channel. Mainly for kokanee, but also rainbow. Dolly Varden are raised in the hatchery.

Highway 23: 140km north of Kaslo. Hwy 31 ends at this junction. North onto Hwy 23 for 2km to free **Galena Bay ferry**. Crosses Upper Arrow Lake to Shelter Bay. 30 minutes. Hourly 5:30am-12:30am. (June-Sept: extra sailing at 11:30pm.) 50 vehicles, 150 passengers. For continuation of Hwy 23, see *Shelter Bay to Mica Creek*, following.

SHELTER BAY TO MICA CREEK

HIGHWAY 23

Highway 23 begins at Nakusp and runs north for 48km along the eastern side of Upper Arrow Lake to Galena Bay. There it crosses the lake, by ferry, to Shelter Bay, and continues north on the west side for nearly 50km to Revelstoke. The highway then crosses the Columbia River Bridge, following the east side of Lake Revelstoke for 134km to Mica Creek. The total distance between Shelter Bay and Mica Creek is 190km. For Hwy 23 between Nakusp and Galena Bay see *Cherryville to Nelson*, p.213.

Shelter Bay: The *Galena* ferry to Galena Bay. 30 minutes. 5:30am to 12:30am. Carries 40 vehicles, 200 passengers.

Arrow Lakes Provincial Park (Shelter Bay Site): 93ha; 23 campsites. 250-825-3500. Near Shelter Bay ferry terminal. Boat launches and fishing.

Blanket Creek Provincial Park: 316ha; 64 campsites. 250-825-3500. East off Hwy 23, 25.5km north of Shelter Bay. In forest where Blanket Creek enters Upper Arrow Lake. Kokanee spawn at mouth of creek. Fishing for kokanee, Dolly Varden char, and rainbow trout. Trail to Sutherland Falls, 12m high. Swimming in manmade lake with sandy shore.

Mt Macpherson: Parking on Hwy 23, about 44km north of Shelter Bay. See description in *Sicamous to Lake Louise*, p.208.

Highway 1: At Revelstoke, 49km north of Shelter Bay. West 102km to Salmon Arm. East across Columbia River Bridge, 69km to Rogers Pass. Hwy 23 continues north along east side of Lake Revelstoke for 85km.

Revelstoke: Revelstoke, Columbia View Provincial Park, Revelstoke Dam, and Mount Revelstoke National Park, are described in *Sicamous to Lake Louise*, p.208.

Martha Creek Provincial Park: 71ha; 25 campsites. 250-825-3500. On Hwy 23, 66.5km north of Shelter Bay. Near Lake Revelstoke, reservoir created by Revelstoke Dam on Columbia River. Surrounded by mountains. Fishing, boating, hiking.

Mica Creek: On Hwy 23, 190km north of Shelter Bay. Once a townsite for employees building the Mica Dam 8km north. Today Hydro employees bus in from Revelstoke. Store, gas station, campgrounds.

Mica Dam: At end of Hwy 23, just north of Mica Creek. At 242m, the highest earthfill dam in North America, 11th highest in the world. Began storing water in 1973, flooding Columbia River valley and creating large boating and fishing area.

Kinbasket Lake: This is an extensive reservoir of Mica Dam. Its long arms, less than 2km wide, are surrounded by spectacular mountains. Boaters can launch above the dam and travel in Canoe Reach for 100km along western edge of Rockies, north to Valemount. Or travel south in Columbia Reach for 100km nearly all the way to Donald Station. This point, at the southern end of Columbia Reach, is the termination of a long, leisurely stretch of the Columbia River coming from Canal Flats, in the east Kootenay. This 230km portion of the Columbia is safe canoeing water for families and beginners. Most start at Canal Flats and paddle slowly downstream to Donald Station, or continue about 15km to Kinbasket Lake. It could take an entire summer to paddle it all. The lake borrows its name from the Secwepemc First Nation leader, Kenpesq't, who 100 years ago led his people southeast to their current home on the Columbia River near Invermere.

Shelter Bay to Mica Creek

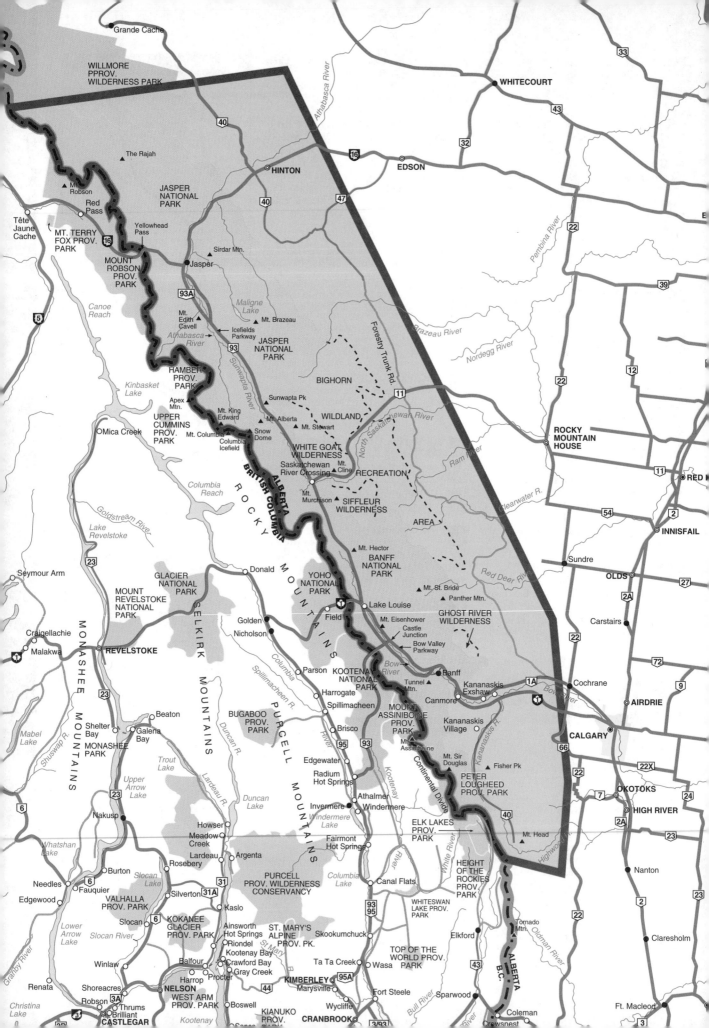

ALBERTA ROCKIES
PINNACLE OF THE WILD ROSE PROVINCE

Lying like a holster along the leg of the Rockies, Alberta, the cowboy province, is two-thirds the size of BC, three times larger than the United Kingdom, and about the same size as the Lone Star state of Texas, with which it is often compared.

Both have cowboy roots and cowboy boots, vast ranches and farms, oil wells, and clusters of glass skyscrapers towering above sprawling young cities. One thing that Texas does not have is the Rockies, and they are the focus of this section.

The scope of this *Travel Guide* does not take us east of the Alberta Rockies, so offered below is only a tantalizing introduction to BC's flamboyant neighbour, Alberta, famed for its stampede and dinosaurs, its oil, and its tremendous hospitality. The *Log* sections of the *Alberta Rockies* will cover in detail Banff National Park and Jasper National Park, ending at the east gates of the two parks. Beyond the mountains, may Alberta unfold for you like a wild prairie rose at dawn.

The Lay of the Land

Alberta sprawls out over 644,390 sq km of land and 16,800 sq km of fresh water, covering a total of 661,190 sq km, making it Canada's fourth largest province. It is 2,400km long, 1,250km wide at the top, narrowing to 600km wide on the US border, giving the province its holster shape. The Continental Divide along the Rocky Mountains is a natural western border. In the south, the 49th parallel forms the boundary with Montana.

From the province's highest point, 3,747m Mt Columbia in Jasper National Park, Alberta rolls east and north from the Rockies, to just 200m above sea level along the Slave River in the far northeast corner. Alberta's river systems go with this flow. The Hay, Peace, and Athabasca river systems of northern Alberta drain north into the Arctic Ocean. Most of southern Alberta is the watershed of the North and South Saskatchewan river systems, flowing east to Hudson Bay. Meltwaters

View from Peyto Lake at Bow Summit in Banff National Park.

from the Columbia Icefields feed, eventually, the Arctic and Atlantic oceans; and the Milk River watershed, in the extreme south, actually drains into the Mississippi River and the Gulf of Mexico.

Badlands, Goodlands, and Others

Alberta offers a rich tapestry of distinct bio-physical regions. The Rockies roll into the foothills, which roll down onto the plains; the north woods – a swath of boreal forest called *taiga* in Russia – thin into aspen parklands; they in turn disappear into semi-arid grasslands of the south. Out into the foothills of southern Alberta is the round northern tip of the Great Plains. Cactus-studded, short-grass prairies cover the driest southeast, with tall-grass prairies farther north and west.

Along the Red Deer River, especially near Drumheller and in Dinosaur Provincial Park, water and wind have carved eerie badlands from the colourful, fossil-filled clay soils. On the Milk River, at Writing-on-Stone Provincial Park, there are sandstone hoodoos etched with the largest collection of native rock "writing" on the North American plains.

Rocky Mountains

Hauntingly beautiful as most of Alberta is, the province's most obvious and famous attraction is the Rocky Mountains. For the last two million years, glaciers and streams and winds have been busy sculpting, slicing, and polishing the Rockies into their present spectacular shape.

Hikers in the Rockies are often astonished to find marine fossils imbedded in peaks now 3,000m above sea level. For most of the past 1.5 billion years, Alberta was at the bottom of shallow seas stretching from the Arctic Ocean to the Gulf of Mexico, steadily blanketed by sinking sediments that in time became layers of sandstone, limestone, shale, and most of Canada's coal, oil, and natural gas.

About 75 million years ago, the North American continental plate, drifting west across the earth's molten basement, collided with the north bound Pacific plate. The Earth's crust buckled where they met, pushing the young Rockies up and a new continental divide farther east. As the land lifted, the sedimentary layers on the eastern slope broke up into massive slabs, which tilted as they were pushed eastward, rippling up foothills in their wake.

So came the Rockies. And since their expansion about 14,000 years ago, the glaciers have retreated to the peaks, and vegetation, wildlife, and people have moved into the landscape.

Albertosaurus and Edmontosaurus

Long known as a rich source of fossil fuels, Alberta has now been recognized as the locale of one of the world's richest deposits of dinosaur fossils. Scientific interest, and the recent dino-craze, have made Alberta, and the Tyrrell Museum of Paleontology near Drumheller, a mecca for both fossil-hunting paleontologists and the tourists sharing their fascination.

Thirty-five different species of dinosaur (the word means "terrible lizard") have been found in Dinosaur Provincial Park, near Brooks, and many other species have been unearthed elsewhere, including a major new find of horned dinosaurs near Grande Prairie. Most of Alberta's dinosaurs lived between 100 and 64 million years ago, when the province was a vast swampy sea. Three local favourites were albertosaurus (a fierce carnivore, cousin to tyrannosaurus), edmontosaurus (a duck-billed plant eater that moved about in herds some 73 million years ago), and edmontonia (a vegetarian protected with armoured plates).

The First Peoples

Alberta was one of the first parts of North America to be inhabited. Crossing the land bridge between Siberia and Alaska 12,000 to 28,000 years ago, the first aboriginal peoples may have moved south through eastern Alberta along the ice-free corridor that ran between the western and eastern continental icecaps. When the ice sheets receded again 14,000 years ago, people we are now calling Paleo-Indians began colonizing the plains. Several sites show evidence of early human activity: artifacts at Vermilion Lakes near Banff; flint quarries at Crowsnest Pass; pictographs near Canmore; ancient campsites in Waterton Lakes National Park.

In the early to mid-1700s, two factors revolutionized Alberta native life. From the southeast came the first horses, traded north from tribe to tribe after being acquired from the Spanish in Mexico in the early 1500s. Horses dramatically transformed the lives of the plains tribes. From the northeast, along the waterways of beaver country, came the fur trade. Long before the first white traders arrived, tribes from the east, primarily the Cree, armed with guns gained through fur trading on their eastern Canadian homelands, began to push west into northern Alberta to exploit the rich furs. The still unarmed Dunne-za (Beaver) and Dene-thah (Slavey) peoples were pushed farther north, the Sarcee farther west, the Blackfoot farther south. But in the late 1700s, the locals finally got their own firearms, held the line, and joined in the lucrative fur trade.

The Banff Springs Hotel in Banff National Park, a landmark amid mountains.

The sky-high Jasper Tramway in Jasper National Park.

The horse and the fur trade brought brief prosperity to the native peoples of Alberta, but in the end, the contact with European civilization proved disastrous. Diseases wiped out healthy tribes, missionary zeal crushed ancient cultures, alcohol destroyed individual and family spirits. The story was far less wild and bloody than in the United States, especially in northern Alberta where the native peoples were partners in the fur trade.

However, nothing can mitigate the over-all tragedy. In 1837, smallpox killed two-thirds of the Blackfoot nation. Today, some reserves have become wealthy from energy and real estate developments, but others are still seeking settlement for outstanding claims.

Fur Traders and Map Makers

In 1754, Hudson's Bay Company explorer Anthony Henday, escorted by Cree traders, ascended the North Saskatchewan and Battle rivers, and became the first white man to see Alberta and the Rockies. He wintered near today's Edmonton and traded with local aboriginal people for the first furs exported from Alberta. In 1792, looking for the legendary river west to the Pacific, "Nor'Wester" Alexander Mackenzie crossed northern Alberta up the Peace River on his way to becoming the first white person to cross North America to the Pacific.

About the same time, Peter Fidler, Hudson's Bay Company scout and surveyor, began 14 years of exploration. Alberta's first mapmaker, he opened up the north. The fur companies raced in to establish trading routes, clients, and posts: at Edmonton in 1795, Rocky Mountain House in 1799, Dunvegan in 1805 (all of which are now fascinating historic sites).

Trains, Grains, Home on the Range

About the time the Mounties were establishing law and order, the first ranchers were eyeing the ocean of grass now all but empty of buffalo, which were slaughtered in the millions by white men. Sir Sanford Fleming began surveying possible routes for the promised transcontinental railway. The CPR finally pushed across southern Alberta to the Rockies below Kicking Horse Pass in 1883, creating Medicine Hat, Calgary and, indirectly, two years later, Canada's first national park, at Banff. Among the first to cash in were the big ranchers who quickly laid claim to the southern foothills. They exported their beef east to market from the Calgary or "Cow Town" railhead.

In 1888, the railway brought the first transcontinental tourists to the Banff Springs Hotel. The fame and fortune of the Canadian Rockies followed.

Buried Treasure

In 1870, a Geological Survey of Canada crew noticed oil and natural gas seeps in what is now Waterton National Park. This went largely ignored amid reports of huge deposits of coal elsewhere. In 1886, local homesteader "Kootenai" Brown reread the old report, began collecting seeping oil, selling it to local ranchers for lamp fuel and lubricant. In 1902, Alberta's first successful oil well was drilled on Cameron Creek, but the deposit was small.

In 1914, oil in quantity was finally found at Turner Valley in the foothills. This first major oil find in the British Empire created great excitement, but didn't pan out. Finally, in 1947, just south of Edmonton at Leduc, patient Imperial Oil drillers finally hit the long-sought black mother lode, and oil began heating up Alberta's economy.

The People Today

More than half of the 2,545,553 Albertans live in the five largest urban centres: Edmonton (884,331), Alberta's capital and gateway to the north; Calgary (840,334), Canada's oil capital; Lethbridge (64,938); Red Deer (60,023); and Medicine Hat (45,892).

Calgary and Edmonton are typical Canadian cities, each with a rich multicultural mix. East of Edmonton is the "Dr Zhivago goes to Quebec" portion of Alberta, punctuated by tall spires of Roman Catholic churches and round domes of Russian Orthodox churches, with coffee shop conversations in English, French, Ukrainian, and Cree. The central parklands were homesteaded by Scandinavians, Icelanders, Germans, Poles. The far south, by Ukrainians, and Mormons from Utah, who brought irrigation to the parched prairies. Canada's only Mormon temple is in Cardston. The mountain parks were developed by British and American interests, and became home to many Swiss, who originally arrived as mountain guides.

The province's economy today is built on fossil fuels, agriculture, and tourism. With 75 percent of Canada's conventional oil, and 86 percent of its natural gas, the "oil-patch" province is in the unique position of having no provincial retail sales tax. Alberta does, however, have a five percent room tax, and, along with the other provinces, enjoys paying the federal seven percent goods and services tax, or GST.

TOURIST INFORMATION

Travel Alberta: Write Box 2500, Edmonton, AB, T5J 2Z4. 403-427-4321. Fax: 403-427-0867. Canada and United States: 1-800-661-8888. Travel Alberta is the central service for all visitor information, and runs a network of information centres province-wide. Centres in Canmore and Edmonton are open year-round. Centres at Lloydminster, Milk River, Oyen, Walsh, Crowsnest Pass, Field (BC), and West Glacier (Montana) are open mid-May to Sept.

Events

For general information on Canada's holidays, see *Introduction to British Columbia, p.15.* The first Monday in August is Alberta Heritage Day, celebrated in almost every community, small and large, and revealing the diverse heritage of the province. Every summer weekend somewhere in Alberta there are ethnic festivals, art and music festivals, regattas, country fairs, First Nations powwows, and *lots* of rodeos, from small town "Howdy neighbour" events to the Big One at Calgary (the Calgary Stampede). It doesn't stop there. Throughout the year there are autumn harvest festivals, winter carnivals, spring ski parties, and "hurray-we-made-it-through-the-winter" parties. Perhaps because of their roots on the big, lonely land, Albertans like to get together and have a good time.

Following are events and programs hosted by Jasper National Park. Contact information centres there for specific times and places.
■ **Jasper...A Walk in the Past:** June-Sept. Nightly, 60- to 90-minute tours. From information centre.
■ **Junior Naturalist:** Late June-Aug. Nightly, for children aged 6-10.
■ **Take a Hike – Parks Day:** Mid-July.
■ **Pocahontas..A Walk in the Past:** July-Aug, Sat. Tours of coal-mining town. From bottom of Miette Hot Springs Rd.
■ **Guest Speaker Series:** July-Aug.
■ **Full Moon Hikes:** May-Aug, on full moon.
■ **Lost in the Woods:** May-July. Children, 6-10, and parents learn survival skills.
■ **Jasper Institute:** Day and weekend courses on birds, flowers, geology, wildlife.
■ **Mountaineering and Interpretive Hiking Program:** Summer. Banff Springs Hotel and Chateau Lake Louise. Jasper Park Lodge offers mountaineering only. Call hotels/lodges. No experience necessary.
■ **Canadian Rockies Experience:** At Banff Springs Hotel. Accommodation, mountaineering, golf, spa, meals. 1-800-441-1414.

Emblems

Alberta's provincial wildflower is the wild rose, and the great horned owl is the provincial bird. The emblem of the Sunshine Province sums it up – snowy mountains, green foothills, golden wheat fields, and evergreen forests under a deep blue sky.

Parks

Alberta has more land in national parks than any other province. Banff, Jasper, and Waterton in the Rockies, Elk Island near

Common red paintbrush.

Edmonton, and Wood Buffalo in the north, together cover more than 20,000 square kilometres. There are two national historic sites: one at Rocky Mountain House, the other is the Bar U Ranch near Longview. Hunting and firearms are not allowed. Contact Parks Canada, Alberta Office, Room 552, 220-4th Ave SE, Calgary, AB, T2G 4X3. 1-800-748-7275 or 403-292-4401.

Currently there are 75 provincial parks and 295 provincial recreation areas representing landscapes and wildlife native to every part of the province. Three wilderness areas – White Goat, Siffleur, and Ghost River – are located in the foothills of Alberta's Rockies. These areas of large undeveloped land provide maximun resource protection – foot travel only; no hunting, fishing, or trapping. Contact Alberta Environmental Protection, Natural Resources Service, Recreation and Protected Areas Division, 2nd Floor, Oxbridge Pl, 9820-106 St, Edmonton, AB, T5K 2J6. 780-427-7009.

Forests

Alberta's forests cover more than half of the province of Alberta – about 350,000 sq km. Most are multi-use areas, managed by the Land and Forest Service to maintain high-quality water, timber, wildlife habitat, recreational, and other resources. Willmore Wilderness Park (accessible by foot or horseback only; fishing and hunting allowed) and Bighorn Wildland Recreation Area offer a wide range of backcountry opportunities. Contact Alberta Environmental Protection (under *Parks*, above) or Forest Management Division, 9th Floor, 9920-108 St, Edmonton, AB, T5K 2M4. 780-427-8474.

Natural Areas

There are more than 150 Natural Areas in Alberta, managed by Alberta Environmental Protection to preserve (usually) small parcels of land with unique, distinctive, or rare flora, fauna, or physical features. Low-impact recreation (hiking, cross-country skiing, birding, photography) is allowed in many, but others have use restrictions to ensure protection of rare or fragile features. Contact Alberta Environmental Protection (under *Parks*, above).

ACCOMMODATION AND CAMPING

Alberta has a complete range of travellers' accommodation: luxurious hotels (including some of the world's most famous mountain resort hotels: Banff Springs, Chateau Lake Louise, Jasper Park Lodge), motels, hostels, ski resorts, guest ranches, vacation farms, fly-in fishing lodges, B&Bs, super-deluxe RV campgrounds, primitive tent sites.

The Alberta Hotel Association annually publishes a campground guide and a comprehensive accommodation guide that includes alternative accommodation (B&Bs, fishing lodges, farms, ranches, hostels) and adventure tours, as well as hotels, motels, and resorts. To get these free, extremely useful publications, contact Travel Alberta, address above.

Hostels

Visitors young and old, single or with family, can enjoy the economy and ambience of hostel accommodation. Open to members and non-members. There are several hostels in Banff, Lake Louise, and in Jasper. Contact: Hostelling International, Southern Alberta, 203-1414 Kensington Rd NW, Calgary, AB, T2N 3P9. 403-283-5551. For hostels within Jasper National Park, contact Hostelling International, Northern Alberta, 10926-88th Ave, Edmonton, AB, T6G 0Z1. 780-432-7798. Internet website: www.hostellingintl. ca/alberta/.

There are YMCA and YWCA hostels in Calgary (YW), Edmonton (YM and YW), Banff (YW), Lethbridge (YW).

For info on their backcountry huts and the Canmore Clubhouse, contact the Alpine Club of Canada, Box 8040, Canmore, AB, T1W 2T8. 403-678-3200.

National Parks

Alberta's five national parks offer a full range of camping opportunities. No reservations. Contact Parks Canada, Alberta Region, Room 552, 220-4th Ave SE, Calgary, AB, T2G 4X3. 1-800-748-7275 or 403-292-4401.

Provincial Parks and Campgrounds

Most provincial parks and recreation areas throughout Alberta offer campground facilities ranging from primitive to fully serviced sites. Many take reservations for individual or group camping. Recreation acitivities include picnicking, fishing, canoeing, hiking, horseback riding, and cross-country skiing. Contact Alberta Environmental Protection, under parks. Natural Resources Service, Recreation and Protected Areas Division, 2nd Floor, Oxbridge Pl, 9820-106 St, Edmonton, AB, T5K 2J6. 780-427-7009.

Back to Basics

Camping is restricted to designated areas to protect adjacent areas from being crushed or trampled. Firewood is provided to save the campground trees. Garbage cans are there to keep the site clean and, in bear country, maintain the peace. Please use the campsites.

TRANSPORTATION

By Road

Thousands of kilometres of highways criss-cross Alberta. The main north-south route (Hwy 2) links the Peace River and Edmonton, to Calgary and Fort Macleod. Most other major roads radiate from it. The most popular scenic route is the Icefields Parkway (Hwy 93) running north-south through Jasper and Banff national parks. Alberta's favourite back-road route, the Forestry Trunk Rd (Hwy 40/734), runs 1,017km along the Rockies from Hwy 3 in Crowsnest Pass to Hwy 2 at Grande Prairie.

The Alberta Motor Association provides travel services to AMA, CAA, AAA, and affiliated overseas auto club members. Head offices are in Calgary (403-240-5300) and Edmonton (780-430-5555). Emergency: 1-800-222-4357 (1-800-AAA-HELP).

Bus Lines

■ **Greyhound Bus Lines:** Across Canada: 1-800-661-8747. Edmonton: 780-421-4211. Calgary: 403-265-9111. Jasper: 403-852-3926. Check phone book for other Alberta communities.

■ **Brewster Transportation and Tours:** Across Canada: 1-800-661-1152.
■ **Red Arrow Express:** Within Alberta: 1-800-232-1958. Serves Edmonton, Calgary, Red Deer, Fort McMurray.
■ **Charters, Tours, Airport Services:** Offered in major cities and tourist centres such as Banff and Jasper. Call Travel Alberta for information: 1-800-661-8888.

Airlines

Major airlines listed below have scheduled flights into Calgary International Airport (403-735-1372), the fourth largest airport in Canada, and/or Edmonton International Airport (780-890-8382 or 1-800-268-7134).

Most other cities and towns in Alberta have scheduled flights or airstrips. No commercial flights to Banff or Jasper. For info on charters, contact local sources or the Alberta Aviation Council, Box 7547 NECSC, Edmonton, AB, T5E 6K1. 780-414-6191.
■ **Air Canada:** 1-800-663-3721.
■ **Canadian Airlines International:** 1-800-665-1177.

Railways

■ **VIA Rail:** 1-800-561-8630. First-class transcontinental service on board The *Canadian*, routed from Vancouver through Jasper to Edmonton, and points east to Toronto. These trains, refurbished for vacationers with dining cars, sleeping accommodation, and showers, are reminiscent of the golden days of passenger rail service in Canada. The three-night, three-day trip departs from Vancouver at 7:00pm, to allow daylight travel though the Rocky Mountains.

■ **Rocky Mountaineer Railtours:** Great Canadian Railtour Company. Canada and US: 1-800-665-7245. May to mid-Oct. Sublime train trip through the Rockies. Vancouver to Jasper, Vancouver to Banff, optional to Calgary. This train travels only in daylight, with dome car, for maximum mountain viewing. Passengers going east or west spend the night in Kamloops, BC. Continental breakfast, lunch, and hotel included.

Car and RV Rentals

Rental cars are available at airports, major hotels, and other agencies in most towns and all cities. RV rentals available in Edmonton and Calgary.

For information on customs, motoring regulations, and emergencies, see appropriate sections in *Introduction to British Columbia*, where the same information applies.

Mount Fitzwilliam is reflected in Jasper National Park's Patricia Lake.

Morraine Lake, in Banff National Park, tucked in the Valley of Ten Peaks.

ALBERTA ROCKIES ROUTES AND HIGHLIGHTS

TRAVELLER'S LOGS

HIGHLIGHTS

LAKE LOUISE TO BANFF

BANFF NATIONAL PARK
(Highway 1)

This 80km section of Hwy 1 passes through arguably the most famous and exciting cluster of mountain landscapes in the world. There surely is more intensity per kilometre here than in any other stretch of the Trans-Canada Highway. This *Log* follows the pearl-blue Bow River from Lake Louise through Banff, but note that Hwy 1 actually follows the river all the way into Calgary, 193km from the BC border. (Sections east of Canmore are not covered in this *Travel Guide*.) Note that recent highway improvements have resulted in the creation of new section of divided highway between Castle Junction and Sunshine Village Rd.

For those seeking a quiet alternative, the original highway, Hwy 1A, parallels the entire route from Lake Louise to Calgary. The section running through Banff National Park is known as the Bow Valley Parkway; see *Log* following. The Canmore to Calgary lap of the old highway is called the Bow Valley Trail.

Much of the divided highway through Banff National Park is lined with fencing to keep wildlife off the road. Watch for animals on the road, particularly at night, along both unfenced and fenced sections.

Great Divide Rd (Hwy 1A): 2km west of BC border, south off Hwy 1. This, the original highway, is now a narrow, less-travelled alternate route to Lake Louise. It is 14km to

Hwy 1 junction at Lake Louise. Road also leads to **Lake O'Hara**. See *Sicamous to Lake Louise*, p.212. **Note: Hwy 1A from the BC border to Lake Louise is closed to buses and long vehicles, is closed in winter, and may soon be decommissioned.**

The Great Divide: Boundary between BC and Alberta, and Yoho and Banff national parks. Also marks the crest of the Rockies, and the continental watershed. All waters west of this point flow into the Pacific Ocean; those east of here empty into the Saskatchewan River system, eventually into Hudson Bay. Views of Bow Range's northern peaks: Mt Niblock (2,976m), Narao Peak (2,913m).

Banff National Park: 6,641 sq km. General info and campgrounds: 403-762-1550. Banff National Park Visitor Centre: 403-762-1550. Write Superintendent, Box 900, Banff, AB, T0L 0C0, or check Internet website: http://parkscanada.pch.gc.ca.

Established in 1885 as an early tourist mecca to help support the new Canadian Pacific Railway, Banff is the oldest and most visited of Canada's national parks. It is also the third oldest national park in the world – named for Banffshire, Scotland, birthplace of two early CPR directors. Banff is the second-largest of the four national parks straddling the Continental Divide. These, along with adjacent BC provincial parks, have been designated the Rocky Mountains World Heritage Site protecting over 20,238 square km of Rocky Mountains. Here are rugged peaks, glaciers and glacial lakes – Louise, Moraine, Bow, Peyto – hoodoos, hot springs, canyons, wild rivers,

wildlife, 1,100km of hiking trails, ski trails and hills, gondolas, accommodation from wilderness huts to palatial hotels. The Icefields Parkway traverses the northern half of the park (see *Lake Louise to Jasper*, p.234); Hwy 1 and Hwy 1A access the south.

Banff National Park attracts over 4 million visitors a year from all over the world (another 4 million pass through the park). They come for the great outdoors, and also the great indoors, the unique combination of natural wilderness and civilized pleasure that dates back to the park's birth over a century ago. The park's popularity, however, is endangering its very existence. The growth in human use of the area and associated development have affected the park's environmental integrity: grizzly bears are threatened, wolves are dying at only slightly slower rates than places where they are hunted. Aquatic ecosystems have been distressed by the introduction of non-native fish; dams control 40 percent of the water flowing into the Bow River watershed. Experts say the environment can be restored, and the park is implementing strategic goals to this end. Recommendations are in place: Banff townsite's population will be limited to 8,000 (it is now 7,615); and future commercial development will be capped.

These days, the busiest times to visit are May to late Sept, long weekends, holidays. The best months for hiking are late June to early Oct when the hiking trails are mostly free of avalanche hazard and snow left over from the previous winter. Feb-April are best for skiing; spring and fall for wildlife viewing.

Banff National Park Campgrounds: 403-762-1550. 13 Parks Canada campgrounds offer about 2,500 sites: three areas with 198 sites on Hwy 93, Icefields Parkway; three areas with 273 sites on Hwy 1A, Bow Valley Parkway; two areas with 405 sites off Hwy 1 near Lake Louise; five areas with 1,594 sites off Hwy 1 near Banff. There is no reservation system. Campgrounds vary in the services provided and fees charged, from the simplest with drinking water and pit toilets, to elaborate grounds with full hook-ups. Most open and close on a staggered schedule from early May-late Sept.

Winter camping is permitted at Lake Louise I, Mosquito Creek, and Tunnel Mountain Village II.

Backcountry camping requires the purchase of a wilderness pass, available from the Banff Infocentre, 224 Banff Ave, or at Lake Louise, in the Samson Mall on Village Dr.

Viewpoint: 5.5km east of BC border on Hwy 1. Overlooks Bath Creek where Major A.B. Rogers, chief CPR surveyor, took an accidental bath while fording the stream on horseback in 1881.

Bow River Bridge: 6km east of border. Bow River is small here, only 32km south of its source in Bow Lake on Hwy 93.

Icefields Parkway (Hwy 93): 7km east of border, leading north along eastern side of Great Divide 230km to Jasper. One of the continent's most spectacular scenic drives.

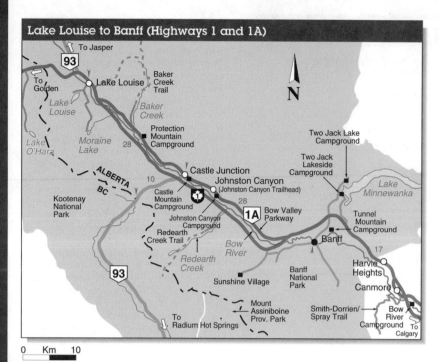

Lake Louise to Banff (Highways 1 and 1A)

Map labels: To Jasper · 93 · To Golden · Lake Louise · Baker Creek Trail · Lake Louise · Baker Creek · Lake O'Hara · Moraine Lake · Protection Mountain Campground · Two Jack Lake Campground · Two Jack Lakeside Campground · Lake Minnewanka · ALBERTA · BC · Castle Junction · Johnston Canyon (Johnston Canyon Trailhead) · 28 · 10 · Castle Mountain Campground · 1 · Bow Valley Parkway · 1A · Tunnel Mountain Campground · Kootenay National Park · Johnston Canyon Campground · Redearth Creek Trail · Bow River · Banff · Redearth Creek · 17 · Harvie Heights · 93 · Sunshine Village · Banff National Park · Canmore · Mount Assiniboine Prov. Park · Smith-Dorrien/Spray Trail · Bow River Campground · To Calgary · To Radium Hot Springs

0 Km 10

Bow Valley Parkway (Hwy 1A): 3km south of Hwy 93 junction; east 500m from Lake Louise exit, then south onto Hwy 1A, an alternate scenic route to Banff along east side of Bow River. See *The Bow Valley Parkway*, following. Turn east here also to Lake Louise Gondola and ski area.

Lake Louise Village: (Pop. 1,500). 10km east of border, 58km west of Banff. CPR reached this point in 1883, at a station called Laggan, where there was a pause before the push westward over Kicking Horse Pass. A trail was cut up the western side of the valley to the just-discovered jewel of the Rockies, Lake Louise, and the railway was soon bringing tourists to this mountain playground, hiring Swiss guides to help the more adventurous climb the local summits. In 1930, skiers built Skoki Lodge east of the village, foreshadowing development of the huge ski area now on the east slope of the Bow Valley.

In the past 15 years, the village of Lake Louise has undergone major expansion (within National Park limits) to handle the expanding influx of both summer and winter tourists.

Lake Louise and Area Information: Parks Canada Visitor Centre (Lake Louise Visitor Reception Centre): 403-522-1200. In the village. Year-round. Hours vary. Park Warden Office in Banff: 403-762-1470 (24 hours). Also, 24-hour emergency: 403-702-4506. Avalanche Report: 403-762-1460.

Canadian Alpine Centre and International Hostel of Lake Louise: In the town site. 403-522-2200. A 150-bed facility built by the Alpine Club of Canada and the Southern Alberta Hostelling Assoc. Includes sauna, reference library, and licenced cafeteria-style Peyto's cafe.

Lake Louise (the lake): 4.5km west of Hwy 1. With a setting that seems too good to be true, the "Mona Lisa of the Mountains" is officially the most famous landmark of the Canadian Rockies. Despite summer crowds, Louise is a "must see." Reflected in the usually calm waters – which change from emerald green to aquamarine – is a spectacular amphitheatre of high peaks, crowned by Mt Victoria (3,464m) and the Victoria Glacier on the crest of the Great Divide. Scenery-stunned visitors are often brought to their senses by the rumbling of ice crashing down the glacier in summer.

Known as the "Lake of Little Fishes" to the local aboriginal people, Louise was discovered for the western world by CPR survey scout Tom Wilson in 1882 when the natives guided him there. (He named it "Emerald Lake." It was later renamed Lake Louise to honour Queen Victoria's daughter.)

■ **Chateau Lake Louise:** 403-522-3511, or for reservations, in North America, call 1-800-441-1414. The year after Wilson found the lake, a trail was cut to it from the railway below, bringing in the first tourists and prompting the CPR to build rough accommodation on the lake's shore in 1890. This burned down, was replaced by a larger, "Swiss style" chalet, then another, until the first two wings of today's Chateau Lake Louise were completed in 1928. It remained largely unchanged, open summers only, until the last decade when the grand hotel's latest chapter began. It opened year-round in 1982, added the third wing in 1988 (from the original plan, complete with copper roofs, giving the hotel 489 rooms). There are a variety of shops and dining rooms; even a special breakfast for early birds to watch the Victoria Glacier blush at dawn.

■ **Lake Louise Trails:** Popular lakeshore trail continues to the Plain of Six Glaciers teahouse, and beyond, if you're a mountaineer, across the divide to Lake O'Hara basin in Yoho National Park. Another charming log teahouse on Lake Agnes trail. Above lake's south shore, Fairview Mountain lookout gives exceptionally fair views.

■ **Moraine Lake:** From a junction 3km up Lake Louise access road, then 12km on Moraine Lake Rd. Panoramic views en route. Set below the **Valley of Ten Peaks**, Moraine Lake rivals Lake Louise in beauty and in fame (it's the scene on the back of the old Canadian $20 bill). Named for the pile of rock which dammed the valley, creating the lake. First thought to be a terminal moraine (rock pushed along by a glacier), but now believed to be debris from a landslide down the Tower of Babel peak to the south; or both. Highly recommended: the short self-guiding interpretive trail to magnificent views at top of the moraine. Golden-mantled ground squirrels (like giant chipmunks); pikas (rock rabbits). Harlequin ducks and dippers along the creek.

■ **Moraine Lake Trails:** Hiking trail along west shore to Valley of the Ten Peaks; Larch Valley trail (popular in autumn when larches turn golden); Paradise Valley loop around Mt Temple and back to a trailhead below on Moraine Lake Rd; a gentle trail south to Consolation Lake.

■ **Moraine Lake Lodge:** Accommodation, restaurant, canoe rentals. Recent major renovation and expansion includes lodge, designed by Arthur Erickson, famed Canadian architect of the UBC Museum of Anthropology, and the new Canadian embassy in Washington, DC.

■ **Lake Louise Ski Area:** East of Lake Louise village exit. 403-522-3555 or 403-256-8473. Or 1-800-258-7669. One of the largest ski areas in Canada: 105 runs, four quad, two double, two triple chairs, one rope tow, one platter, four day lodges. Snow Nov-May.

■ **Cross-country Skiing:** Suitable terrain, popular trails. Easy runs on frozen Lake Louise and on Moraine Lake Rd. Whitehorn and Pipestone (with cosy Skoki Lodge) trail systems are east of the village. For experienced back-country skiers: at times there can be avalanche hazards.

■ **Lake Louise Gondola:** East of Lake Louise village exit (at ski hill). 403-522-3555. The "Friendly Giant" offers panoramic views of Bow Valley. Restaurant, trails on top. Daily, June to mid-Sept.

■ **Lake Louise Campgrounds I and II:** On Fairview Rd SW, 1km from the Lake Louise Visitor Reception Centre. Year-round. 409 sites, winter camping. (Lake Louise I is open year-round, offering 60 sites with electricity; tenters welcome.) Running water; showers available at laundromat in nearby Samson Mall.

■ **Trail Rides:** Brewster Lake Louise Stables, 403-522-3511 or 403-762-5454. Timberline Tours, 403-522-3743.

■ **Alpine Club of Canada:** Box 8040, Canmore, AB, T1W 2T8. 403-678-3200. Huts serving as bases for climbing can be booked by members and non-members. Huts are located at Abbot Pass above Lake Louise, above Moraine Lake, on Castle Mountain, and at other locations.

■ **Parks Canada Shelters:** 403-762-1550. Reservations and backcountry use permits required from Banff Infocentre.

■ **Skoki Lodge:** 14.5km hike/ski from Lake Louise Ski area. 403-522-3555. Beautiful 1930 log lodge and cabins in a legendary retreat. Open Christmas-April, June-Sept.

Return to Highway 1

Mt Temple Viewpoint: 7.5km south of Lake Louise. West, Mt Temple (3,544m) is highest in area, third-highest in Banff Park. Reddish brown Cambrian rocks laid down as sediment in a shallow sea over 500 million years ago. Imposing peak named for British scientist Sir Richard Temple, who came here in 1884. First climbed in 1894.

Taylor Creek Picnic Area: 17.5km south of Lake Louise. Picnic area and angler's trailhead for 7km hike up to Taylor and O'Brien lakes. Forest here, and along highway between Lake Louise and Banff, is mainly even-aged stands of lodgepole pine, result of many fires 100-60 years ago. Spruce will eventually take over as the forest matures.

Highway 93 South (Castle Junction): 28km south of Lake Louise. West on Hwy 93 South (Banff-Windermere Parkway) to Vermilion Pass, BC border, Kootenay National Park, Radium Hot Springs (102.5km). East 500m to Bow River, 1km to Bow Valley Parkway (Hwy 1A).

Divided Highway: At Castle Junction. Divided four-lane highway begins here, and continues beyond Calgary. From here to the park's East Gate, the highway is fenced to keep animals, particularly elk, off the roads. They still cross via a series of specially designed underpasses. Drive with caution, as animals sometimes find their way outside of fenced areas.

Copper Lake: 500m south of Castle Junction. Hidden just west of highway, the little fishing hole is named for Copper Mountain (2,795m) to the south, where copper claims were worked in 1880s. Views of Castle Mountain.

Castle Mountain Viewpoint: 9km south of Castle Junction. One of the best views of Castle Mountain (2,766m), aptly named peak of layered rock weathered into turrets and towers. Named in 1858 by Sir James Hector, geologist of the Palliser Expedition and first white man in area. Castle was renamed Mt Eisenhower after the Second World War, but in 1979, common sense and local pressure prevailed, and the original name was reinstated. First tower is called Eisenhower Peak.

Redearth Creek Trail: 11km south of Castle Junction. Hiking, skiing, backpacking to Shadow Lake (14.5km), and to high alpine meadows around Egypt Lake. Check with park warden office for current regulations for this high-use hiking area.

Bourgeau Lake Trail: Trailhead 18km south of Castle Junction. Classic 8km hike up Wolverine Creek to Bourgeau Lake: forest, waterfalls, high alpine meadow at base of 2,931m Mt Bourgeau.

Sunshine Rd: 21km south of Castle Junction. West 8km to Sunshine Village.

Sunshine Village Ski Resort: Box 1510, Banff, AB, T0L 0C0. 403-762-6500. Alberta: 1-800-372-9583. Canada and US: 1-800-661-1676. 8km west on Sunshine Rd, then 20-minute gondola to village at 2,160m.

The only on-mountain accommodation in the Canadian Rockies. Tonnes of all-natural snow in winter. 12 lifts, 80 runs, 2 high-speed quad chairlifts, gondola, one triple chair, 4 double chairs, 3 T-bars, 2 beginner tows, ski school, groomed trails, lots of untracked powder. Mid-Nov to May 31.

Bow Valley Parkway (Hwy 1A): 24km southeast of Castle Junction. Alternate scenic route along Bow Valley. Seasonal voluntary closures to protect wildlife are in place. See *Bow Valley Parkway*, p. 233.

Vermilion Lakes Viewpoint: 28km south of Castle Junction. Accessible to eastbound traffic only. Three lakes just west of Banff townsite. Archaeological digs nearby revealed that this prime wildlife area first attracted human hunters at least 10,000 years ago.

Rocky Mountain sheep and mule deer often seen above; elk, coyotes, bald eagles, osprey, and waterfowl below.

East to west, dominant landmarks are Tunnel Mountain (1,692m), the low, rounded "mountain" behind Banff (called the "sleeping buffalo" by the aboriginal people, renamed for the tunnel the CPR never built); Mt Rundle (2,949m), an enormous titled chunk of the earth's crust; the "castle," the Banff Springs Hotel, at the bottom of the Spray Valley; pine-carpeted Sulphur Mountain (2,451m), source of Banff's hot sulphur springs.

Banff Townsite West Access: 30km southeast of Castle Junction. South 1km to town. 5km north up steep winding road to views of Banff and Mt Norquay Ski Area.

Banff: (Pop. 7,615). Banff is 38km east of BC border on Hwys 1 and 93; 128km west of Calgary. It's 404km to Edmonton; 848km to Vancouver.

Summer visitors to Banff will agree that the setting is beautiful, but the town is very busy. To the thousands of Japanese who visit each year (10 percent of international visitors are Japanese), it may seem placid, compared to a Tokyo subway, but anyone expecting a rustic, "mountain-town" atmosphere will be very surprised. Banff is an irresistible paradox. In the heart of a national park sits an island of condensed urban civilization, holiday-style. Most visitors love the choices it presents.

It has been this way ever since Banff, the town and the park, was established a century ago. It began in 1883 with the arrival of the CPR. Prospecting on their days off, two railway construction men stumbled upon the hot springs at the base of Sulphur Mountain. They had hoped to stake a claim and eventually create a spa, but the federal government won the option, and in 1885 declared the springs and 16 surrounding kilometres the Hot Springs Reserve. In 1887, the area was enlarged, and the name changed to Rocky Mountains Park.

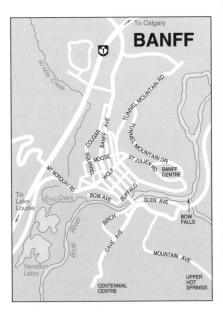

This became Banff National Park in 1930, the start of the Canadian national park system. This was not entirely a noble, far-sighted act to preserve the springs for everyone. The government was then heavily dependent on the financial success of the new railway, and Banff and other parks were created as CPR tourist attractions. (Cars were not allowed in the park until 1916.) The hot springs and the scenery were lures to bring tourists across on the new line (and install them in soon-to-be-built luxury CPR hotels).

Regardless, the tourism-minded planners who laid out the townsite a century ago could hardly have done a nicer job. The town sits beside the Bow River at the base of Sulphur and Tunnel mountains. Towering a vertical mile above the town, Cascade Mountain (2,998m) to the north, Mt Rundle (2,949m) to the east, dominate the views.

No one could have foreseen the numbers of visitors that come here now, filling the compact town to the brim. There are signs in English, French, German, and Japanese. The nearby Parks Canada campgrounds and 3,500 hotel and motel rooms are packed through the summer.

But nature is always close at hand. Elk browse residential shrubbery or graze on the Banff Springs Golf Course. Beavers fell trees along the river, coyotes prowl the alleys at night. Side streets are aptly named: Squirrel, Fox, Beaver, Muskrat.

In 1990, after 105 years of distant government by national parks, Banff became a semi-self-governing municipality (within its mandate as a park service centre). Locals now tackle the problems of parking shortages and winter leftovers, some world-class potholes.

Banff Information: Banff Visitor Centre, 224 Banff Ave. 403-762-1550. Year-round, displays, AV programs. Write Banff National Park, Box 900, Banff, AB, T0L 0C0. Internet website: http://www.world web.com/ ParksCanada-Banff/parks.html. This is an index page for information on many aspects of the Rockies, including Banff, Jasper, Yoho, Kootenay, Waterton national parks and

Rocky Mountain House National Historic Site. There are links from that page to weather reports, road reports, hotels, and the Discover Banff pages. **Banff Park Warden Office:** between Hwy 1 and town site. 403-762-1470. Open Mon-Fri. 24-hour emergency line: 403-762-4506. 24-hour avalanche report: 403-762-1460. **Banff/Lake Louise Tourism Bureau:** also at 224 Banff Ave. Write Box 1298, Banff, AB, T0L 0C0. Daily, 403-762-8421. Administration: 403-762-0270.

■ **Accommodation Reservations/Packages:** Banff Central Reservations, Box 1628, Banff, AB, T0L 0C0. Canada and US: 1-888-661-1676. Reservations can also be made through Good Earth Travel Adventures in Canmore. 1-800-979-9797.

■ **Campgrounds:** 403-762-1550. 1,594 sites in five campgrounds near town, most open mid-May to Sept. (See Tunnel Mountain and Two Jack Lake campgrounds, below.)

■ **Cave and Basin Historic Site:** On Cave Ave. 403-762-1566. Birthplace of Canada's first national park. Hot spring cave, historical and interpretive displays. Short self-guiding Discovery Trail (history and geology); Marsh Trail (plants, wildlife, including the tropical fish which arrived via someone's aquarium in the 1960s). New additions include pool, restaurant, and theatre. Exhibits daily, year-round.

■ **Sundance Canyon:** 3km beyond Cave and Basin, two-hour hike. Lower trail along Bow River is paved and wheelchair accessible.

■ **Upper Hot Springs:** 3km from downtown on Mountain Ave. 403-762-1515. Daily, year-round. If you like it hot, soak in mineral springs up to 43C. Outdoor pool keeps you warm *après ski* even on coldest winter day. Have a massage.

■ **Banff Springs Hotel:** On Spray Ave, 1.5km from downtown Banff (across bridge). Box 960, Banff, AB, T0L 0C0. 403-762-2211. Canada and US: 1-800-441-1414. CPR built its first 250-room hotel here in 1888, above the confluence of the Bow and Spray rivers, and piped in water from the Sulphur Mountain hot springs for their guests. The current "castle," a blend of Scottish baronial and French chateau, was completed in 1928. It was the kind of place "where men would fish and golf, and women would change their clothes." Like who? Winston Churchill, the King of Siam, Paul Newman, Marilyn Monroe, Lassie. Some 50 feature-length motion pictures have been set in the Canadian Rockies, and the Banff Springs Hotel has very often been in the picture, certainly a home for celebrities. Hotel staff claim that ghosts, too, have drifted amid their lovely furniture.

Still owned and operated by Canadian Pacific, the once ultra-exclusive hotel now serves a more "broad-based" clientele, including tour groups from the US and Japan (use of the hotel as a setting for a famous Japanese soap opera has made it something of a mecca), and lots of skiers. The hotel has undergone expansion to 770 rooms to accommodate its growing popularity abroad. The convention centre (with 1,600-person ballroom) was completed in 1992. The Presidential Suite, with private glass elevator, rents for $4,000 a night,

The Post Hotel and Pipestone River at Lake Louise.

Canada's most expensive accommodation. The public is welcome to wander through the parlours, smoking rooms, and lounges, tread on Persian carpets, admire stained-glass windows and gargoyles, recline on Gothic courting chairs or Jacobean hall seats. There are 17 restaurants, sushi bar, coffee shops, lounges, night club, some 50 shops. Also a 27-hole golf course, with sensational new clubhouse, tennis courts, swimming pool, trail rides, bowling alley, and a $12-million European-style spa.

■ **The Banff Centre:** St Julien Rd. For info: 403-762-6100. Tickets: 403-762-6300 or 1-800-413-8368. Unique institute with schools of fine arts, management, and artists' colony. Music, theatre, opera, dance, drama, readings, videos, films. Summer Showcase and Festival of the Arts. Winter film series. Early Nov, Banff Festival of Mountain Films.

■ **Walter Phillips Gallery:** The Banff Centre, St Julien Rd. 403-762-6281. Noon-5, Tues-Sun. Contemporary art exhibitions.

■ **Whyte Museum of the Canadian Rockies:** 110 Bear St. 403-762-2291. Archives of the Canadian Rockies, heritage collection of local human history and galleries with exhibits. Year-round, hours vary with season.

■ **Heritage Tours and Programs:** Guided tours of Banff's heritage homes and galleries. Various times. Contact Whyte Museum, 403-762-2291.

■ **Banff Park Museum National Historic Site:** 91 Banff Ave. 403-762-1558. Declared a National Historic Site in 1985, this unique 1903 "museum of a museum" houses animal exhibits dating back to 1860. Daily, afternoons in winter. Mid-June to Labour day, 10-6.

■ **Luxton Museum:** 1 Birch Ave (just across Banff bridge, then right). 403-762-2388. Fine collections and displays of Plains First Nations artifacts. Summer: 9am-9pm. Winter: 1pm-4:30pm. Guided tours available.

■ **Natural History Museum:** 112 Banff Ave. 403-762-4747. Displays include four dinosaur skulls.

■ **Cascade Gardens:** At south end of Banff Ave, around the stone park administration building. Splendid formal gardens with waterfalls, gazebos. Viewpoint below provides classic Banff Ave/Cascade Mt photo opportunity.

■ **Sulphur Mountain Gondola:** Near Upper Hot Pool, Mountain Ave. 403-762-2523. Eight minutes, great view, restaurant.

■ **Bow Falls:** Short drive along Spray Ave (turn down golf course road just before Banff Springs Hotel), or 30-minute hike along river from the bridge on Banff Ave.

■ **Lake Minnewanka:** Motorboating, fishing for lake trout and whitefish, scuba diving to submerged town, hiking trails, lots of bighorn sheep. Glass-enclosed boats make 90-minute tours to Devil's Gap, late May-Sept. 403-762-3473. Food outlet, boat rentals, fishing tackle and licences.

■ **Bankhead:** 8km from Banff on Lake Minnewanka Rd. Historic site at ruins of early 1900s coal-mining town. 45-minute self-guiding walk. Base of Cascade Mt.

■ **Hoodoos:** Above the Bow River, 4km from Banff on Tunnel Mountain Rd. Pillars of glacial till.

■ **Fenland Trail:** Off Banff west exit road just west of CPR station. Self-guiding trail through wetland and forest. Prime beaver spot.

■ **Banff Mt Norquay Ski Area:** 5km up from Hwy 1, Banff west exit. 403-762-4421. The area's oldest resort, Mt Norquay has been totally redesigned to world-class standards. 25 runs, 2 express quad chairs, 2 double chairs, one surface lift. Great views of Banff. Dec to mid-April; night skiing Fri.

■ **Cross-country Skiing:** Some hiking paths make good ski trails, some don't. Parks brochures and maps help. Every level possible, from a meander around the golf course to a week's camping on a glacier. Close to town: Cascade Fire Rd and Spray River Trail are track set and maintained by Parks Canada. Other routes include Carrot Creek, the golf course, and Tunnel-Hoodoos Loop. For above-tree-line experience without the effort of getting there, take a gondola to Sunshine Village, ski the vast meadows, often into May.

■ **Fishing:** Park licence required. Minnewanka tours: 403-762-3473 for lake trout on Minnewanka; Banff Fishing Unlimited (403-762-4936) for Bow River, mountain lakes. Or go on your own. No fish hogs please.

■ **Boating:** Powerboats allowed only on Lake Minnewanka. Rentals available.

■ **Canoeing:** Rentals on Bow River in townsite.

■ **Windsurfing:** On Vermilion and Two Jack lakes. No rentals.

■ **Float Rafting:** On Bow River. Rocky Mt Raft Tours: 403-762-3632. Gentle rafting for families, children.

■ **Cycling:** Several rental outlets. Mountain bikes restricted to designated trails. Call park infocentre at 403-762-1550 for details, brochures.

■ **Golfing:** 403-762-6801. Challenging and beautiful 27-hole course with clubhouse at the Banff Springs Hotel. Public welcome.

■ **Horseback Riding:** Local outfitters offer short "dude" rides and major pack trips. Brewster Mt Pack Trains: 403-762-5454. Timberline Tours: 403-522-3743. Holiday on Horseback: 403-762-4551. Carriage tours and sleigh rides in season.

■ **Tennis:** Culture and Recreation Dept, Town of Banff, has outdoor courts. 403-762-1200. Summer only. Courts at Banff Springs Hotel.

■ **Banff International Hostel:** On Tunnel Mt Rd 3km southeast. 403-762-4122. Sleeps 216, including families. Cafeteria, kitchen, laundry. Reservations accepted.

■ **Banff YWCA:** 102 Spray Ave. 403-762-3560. 45 rooms (families/doubles) and 13 dormitory rooms sleeping 10-20 people each.

Tunnel Mountain Campgrounds: 3km east of town. Three campgrounds, 1,163 sites including 320 hook-up sites; 200 year-round. Showers, programs. Shuttle from Banff Ave.

Two Jack Lake Campgrounds: 13km northeast of town on Lake Minnewanka Rd. Two campgrounds, 458 sites. Mid-May to Sept.

Highway 1: 2km north of town on Banff Ave. Straight 5.5km to Lake Minnewanka and Two Jack Lake. Turn west to Lake Louise. East 13km to Banff National Park East Gate; 17km to Canmore.

Anthracite Ghost Town: 3km from Banff east access. To the north, outcrops of shale and sandstone containing anthracite coal. Just opposite Cascade Power Plant, and invisible to all but the practiced eye, are remains of a small coal-mining town called Anthracite, which flourished from 1886 till 1904, when Bankhead took prominence.

Cascade Power Plant: 3km from Banff east access. Hydroelectric generator is driven by water channelled down from Lake Minnewanka, leaving the Cascade River, across the railway tracks, usually dry.

Valleyview Picnic Area: 8.5km from Banff east access. Eastbound lane access only. From Banff, the highway sweeps around face of Mt Rundle, which dominates the southern horizon all the way to Canmore.

Banff National Park East Gate: 13km from Banff east access. Congested area.

Canmore West Access: 16.5km from Banff east access.

Canmore: (Pop. 5,681). On Hwy 1, 17km east of Banff. A mountain playground area, boasting a $15 million Olympic Nordic Centre. From here, it is 111km east on Hwy 1 to Calgary.

BOW VALLEY PARKWAY

BANFF NATIONAL PARK (Highway 1A)

Hwy 1A from Lake Louise to Hwy 1, 5.5km west of Banff, is an excellent choice for touring motorists and cyclists. Running parallel to Hwy 1 on the opposite side of the Bow River Valley, Hwy 1A follows the route of the original 1920 road, climbing and winding, allowing views of the peaks at a leisurely pace. There is access back to Hwy 1 at Castle Junction, about midway, if desired. There are campgrounds, commercial bungalow camps, a youth hostel, and picnic areas, plus viewpoints, trails, displays, and an historic site. This is the perfect place to see wildlife – elk, deer, bighorn sheep, coyotes, and, rarely, black bear and wolves. From Lake Louise to Castle Junction, the forests are even-aged stands of lodgepole pine; the southern section has more meadows, aspen groves, riverbottom and mountainside, and is the best area to see wildlife.

Whitehorn Rd: 1km east of Lake Louise. 1km to Lake Louise Gondola and Ski Area. Turn south onto Hwy 1A.

Lake Louise Gondola: 2km east of Lake Louise. 403-522-3555. 3km gondola ride to 2,040m on Whitehorn Mountain. Daily, early-June to late-Sept. Fabulous views of ice-age glaciers, Continental Divide, Lake Louise. At top, hiking trails, restaurant. One of

Canada's largest ski areas. Details in *Lake Louise* section, p.230.

Bow Valley Parkway Exhibit: 1.5km from Lake Louise. Explains the area's history and geology.

Corral Creek Picnic Area: 3.5km from Lake Louise. Quiet spot in forest.

Mt Temple Viewpoint: 5km from Lake Louise. Spectacular Mt Temple (3,544m) is third highest peak in the park, quartzite and limestone formed 500 million years ago.

Baker Creek Picnic Area: 12km from Lake Louise. Panorama Ridge to the west, Protection Mountain to the east. Trail to alpine meadows and good skiing. Resort, bungalows, nearby.

Protection Mountain Campground: 15.5km from Lake Louise. 89 sites. Mid-June to mid-Sept. View of the rugged Bow Range.

Castle Mountain Lookout Trail: 21.5km from Lake Louise. 4km hike through pine forest on fire road to meadow high on side of Castle Mountain. Expansive views.

Storm Mountain Viewpoint: 24km from Lake Louise. This is as far as glacial ice advanced during last major glaciation 8,000 years ago. Look across to Vermilion Pass.

Castle Cliffs Viewpoint: 25.5km from Lake Louise. Look up to red-brown ramparts and turrets of 2,766m Castle Mountain. Named in 1858 by Dr James Hector, surgeon and geologist of Palliser Expedition, first white man to see this natural castle.

Castle Junction: 26.5km from Lake Louise, approximately midway between Lake Louise and Banff. Turn west for 1km to cross Bow River and rejoin Hwy 1.

Castle Mt Village: At Castle Junction. 403-762-3868. Quaint chalet resort with store, service station, accommodation. Open year-round.

Castle Mountain Youth Hostel: Adjacent Castle Junction. Sleeps 36. Reservations: 403-762-4122 or, from Calgary, call 403-237-8282.

Rockbound Lake Trail: Adjacent Castle Junction. 8km hike up to Rockbound and Tower lakes in a hanging valley. 15-minute hike to beautiful Silverton Falls.

Castle Mountain Campground: 0.5km southeast of junction. 44 sites. Mid-May to Sept.

Silver City: 2km southeast of Castle Junction. Site of a mining town that sprang to life in 1883 with arrival of railway. In its two-year lifespan, it boasted a population of 2,000, several hotels and stores. Became a ghost town overnight when copper and lead deposits didn't pan out.

Moose Meadows: 4km southeast of Castle Junction. Open shrub meadows inhabited by everything but moose. They're rarely seen here now due to general habitat changes. View of spiky Pilot Mountain (2,954m).

Johnston Canyon Resort: 7km southeast of junction. Restaurant, store, cozy, old-fashioned cottages. 403-762-2971. May-Sept.

Johnston Canyon Trail: 7km southeast of Castle Junction. One of the most travelled trails of the Rockies snakes up through a spectacular canyon to mountain meadows. 1km to Lower Falls; 3km to Upper Falls; 6km to the Ink Pots. Extraordinarily engineered trails and boardwalks.

Watch for dippers – plump grey birds that can walk underwater along stream bottoms, and nest under waterfalls. Also, the rare black swift: this is one of two nesting colonies in Alberta. The Ink Pots are seven cold-water springs bubbling into clear pools in an open, scenic meadow.

Johnston Canyon Campground: 7.5km southeast of Castle Junction. 140 sites. Mid- May to Sept.

Pilot Pond: 10km southeast of Castle Junction. 400m trail leads down to beautiful hidden lake popular with float-tubing anglers. Formerly called Lizard Lake for the long-toed salamanders that used to breed here in large numbers, until lake was stocked with trout, which ate them!

Hillsdale Meadows Viewpoint: 12km southeast of Castle Junction. Aspen-lined meadows were a traditional native hunting camp at the turn of the century. Grand view of sawtooth peaks of Sawback Range, whose layers were pushed almost vertical by geological mountain building activities. Highest is 2,877m Mt Ishbel, down whose slopes came a gigantic rockslide. Because of divided highway, only westbound travellers can see exhibit at Hillsdale Slide. Trail leads up to top of Johnston Canyon trail.

Tree-in-the-Road: 14km southeast of Castle Junction. This used to be a huge spruce tree in the middle of the road, a famous landmark spared by the earliest road engineers. It blew over in the early 1980s.

Sawback Picnic Area: 15km southeast of Castle junction. Wildlife exhibit, showing bark scars on aspen from hungry elk.

Experimental Range Study Plot: 16km southeast of Castle Junction. Compare vegetation that has been browsed on, to vegetation fenced-off since 1944.

Muleshoe Picnic Area: 21km southeast of Castle Junction. Named for horseshoe-shaped backwater of Bow River. Steep trail east

of road leads to open views. East and 600m up is the **Hole-in-the-Wall Cave** on Mt Cory. Some 30m deep, it was dissolved from bedrock by action of glacial ice and meltwater when glaciers filled the valley. Burned areas on mountain were deliberately set by wardens to re-create natural ecosystem of park that was drastically altered by decades of forest fire control. In doing this, habitat was improved for grazing wildlife.

Backswamp Viewpoint: 24km southeast of Castle Junction. South across valley to Sundance Range; west to 2,931m Mt Bourgeau; farther west to 2,984m Mt Brett, and 2,435m Massive Mountain. River swamp is home to beaver, muskrat, nesting waterfowl, ospreys, songbirds, and a beautiful little carnivorous plant, the purple-flowered common butterwort, which feeds on swamp insects. In winter, this is the best place to watch for wolves. Also bighorn sheep and, in early spring, mountain goats, on Mount Cory above.

Bow Valley Parkway Exhibit: 26km southeast of Castle Junction. Introduces westbound travellers to the Bow Valley.

Fireside Picnic Area: 26.5km southeast of Castle Junction. Just 0.5km east off Hwy 1A to creekside picnic site. Steep trails lead 4.5km to Edith Pass or 6km to Cory Pass; a loop hike if you're energetic. Grand views.

Highway 1: 27km southeast of Castle Junction, 53km from Lake Louise. Hwy 1 leads east 5.5km to Banff.

LAKE LOUISE TO JASPER

ICEFIELDS PARKWAY (Highway 93)

The Icefields Parkway (Hwy 93) provides a direct link from the Trans-Canada Hwy (Hwy 1) near Lake Louise, 229km north to Jasper. It also connects with the David Thompson Hwy (Hwy 11) east to Rocky Mountain House and Red Deer.

For most travellers, however, where Hwy 93 leads is beside the point. The Icefields Parkway is a manmade road following a natural corridor through a vast unspoiled wilderness. Touring here is precisely where they want to be: on a world-famous stretch of spectacular Canadian Rockies scenery with sky-slicing peaks, icefields, glaciers, shockingly blue lakes, forests and wildflower meadows, wilderness, wildlife, and, in summer, *lots* of people! Be prepared: peak season driving and camping can be challenging. Note: few facilities and services. This is also a very popular cycling route.

One pleasant paradox of Hwy 93 is that, although it passes through extremely rugged terrain, the route is an easy drive. It runs through the Main Ranges, with the Front Ranges just to the east. The Main Ranges – the Continental Divide – have most of the glaciers, including the vast Columbia Icefield sprawling

beneath Mt Columbia, at 3,747m, Alberta's highest peak. The Front Ranges in places are tipped like huge dominoes, the result of the earth's forces that formed them.

Hwy 93 traverses two passes, the 2,069m Bow Pass, 44km north up the valley from Hwy 1. Then, following the North Saskatchewan River for 36km, the highway climbs steeply 11km up a side valley to 2,035m Sunwapta Pass near the Columbia Icefield.

Passing through everything from wet and dry valley bottoms to dense mountain forests, from alpine meadows with permafrost, to rock, ice, and lichens, Hwy 93 is a naturalist's dream. Large mammals are often seen early and late in the day. Elk are most common, but moose, mule and white-tailed deer, wolves, coyotes, grizzly and black bears can be seen almost anywhere along the route. Bighorn sheep and mountain goats are found around the icefield; goats are regulars at mineral licks 40km south of Jasper. The rare woodland caribou is occasionally seen in winter north of the icefield near Beauty Creek. Birds to watch for include ptarmigans, rosy finches, and golden eagles above the timberline, boreal owls and white-winged crossbills in high forests, and dippers and harlequin ducks on the streams.

Columbian and golden-mantled ground squirrels ("gophers" and "giant chipmunks") and two grey and black birds – the short-billed gray jay (alias "whiskey jack") and the brash, long-billed Clark's nutcracker – are frequent beggars at roadside stops.

There are 11 Parks Canada campgrounds on the parkway, three in Banff and seven in Jasper. Also, picnic areas, displays, viewpoints, hiking trails. Eight hostels are operated by the Alberta Hostelling Association, five in the Banff National Park section of the parkway, three in Jasper's (see below). Private accommodation and most basic roadside services are available in summer, 39km north of Lake Louise at Bow Lake (no gas); 79km north at Saskatchewan River Crossing; 127km north at Columbia Icefield (no gas); and 176km north at Sunwapta Falls in Jasper National Park. No food or vehicle services in winter.

Icefields Parkway Hostel Information: For hostels south of the Icefields, contact Hostelling International, Southern Alberta, 203-1414 Kensington Rd NW, Calgary, AB, T2N 3P9. 403-283-5551. For hostels within Jasper National Park, contact Hostelling International, Northern Alberta, 10926-88th Ave, Edmonton, AB, T6G 0Z1. 780-432-7798.

Highway 1: Junction of Trans-Canada Hwy and Hwy 93 (Icefields Parkway) 2km north of Lake Louise village overpass. From Lake Louise, drive north 2km to this junction. On Icefields Parkway (Hwy 93), it is 76km to junction of David Thompson Hwy (Hwy 11) at Saskatchewan River Crossing; 121km to the Columbia Icefield; 229km to Jasper.

Herbert Lake: Recreation area is at the north end of lake, 3km north of Hwy 1 on Hwy 93. Picnics, fishing, canoeing, and swimming (this is the only lake around that gets reasonably warm). Superb views south to the cluster of peaks around Lake Louise, crowned by 3,544m Mt Temple.

Hector Lake: 25km north of Hwy 1. Named for Palliser expedition geologist Dr James Hector who found it in 1858. It sparkles below the Waputik (Stoney language for "white goat") Icefield and Range, and 3,246m Mt Balfour. Trail access only.

Mosquito Creek Campground: 25km north of Hwy 1, near Hector Lake. 32 camp-sites, day use, winter camping. Youth Hostel nearby. Along Bow River flats, mosquitoes can be ferocious. 10km trail west to Molar Pass.

Crowfoot Glacier: 34km north of Hwy 1. First glacier on the parkway, named for its distinctive shape. East side of highway, parking lot and trailhead to Dolomite Pass (and Siffleur Wilderness Area), home of Banff Park's only woodland caribou. From here to Bow Summit, watch for grizzlies.

Bow Lake: 36km north of Hwy 1. Source of the Bow River, this very cold, blue lake is fed by the Bow Glacier, a tongue of the Wapta Icefield straddling the Great Divide. Beautiful picnic area on the lake's south shore. The Num-Ti-Jah Lodge, a 1920s, red-roofed log structure on the lake's north shore, was built by pioneer guide and outfitter, Jimmy Simpson. Meals, trail rides, accommodation still offered. A 5km hiking trail leads from north viewpoint parking lot along lakeshore to Bow Glacier Falls (and beyond to an alpine hut below the glacier for serious hikers).

Peyto Lake/Bow Summit: 42km north of Hwy 1. At 2,069m Bow Summit, turn west on access road. 400m walk through fragrant subalpine spruce and fir forest opens to outstanding view over Peyto Lake – maybe the bluest blues in the Rockies – and north down Mistaya River valley. *Mistaya* is Cree for "grizzly bear." Lake was named for Bill Peyto, early guide and outfitter, one of the Rockies' most colourful characters.

Waterfowl Lake Campground: 57km north of Hwy 1. 116 campsites. Day use, wheel-chair facilities, interpretive theatre, canoeing, fishing, trails, birdwatching. In lodgepole pine forest on southeast shore of Lower Waterfowl Lake. 3,307m Mt Chephren to west, 3,290m Howse Peak south, masterworks of glacial sculpting. Migrating and nesting waterfowl.

Mistaya Canyon: 71km north of Hwy 1 on Hwy 93. A short 300m hike to see a slot canyon carved through the limestone.

North Saskatchewan River: 77km north of Hwy 1. A natural path through the mountains, this valley, and Howse Pass just west, was used in 1807 by explorer David Thompson. In 1984, 49km of this river was nominated for inclusion in Canada's Heritage River System. The braided channels and gravel bars mark a young river, shifting each year with spring floods in search of a permanent channel. On south side, water below the bridge is usually green and clear, flowing in from the lake-filtered Mistaya River outlet; on the north, main river runs grey-green, loaded with glacial silt.

Highway 11 (David Thompson Hwy): 79km north of Hwy 1. East 246km on Hwy 11 to Red Deer on Hwy 2. Kootenay Plains Natural Area, Rocky Mountain House National Historic Site, and Sylvan Lake en route.

Saskatchewan River Crossing: At Hwy 11 junction. Services here spring-fall.

Rampart Creek Campground: 12km north of Saskatchewan River Crossing on Hwy 93. 50 campsites. Day use, wheelchair facilities. Mid-June to Sept. Below ramparts of Mt Wilson, a magnificent 3,240m massif topped by quartzite peaks. Some of the best black bear habitat in Banff National Park. Hostel situated below highway.

Weeping Wall: 31km north of Crossing. Viewpoint. Meltwaters spill over a huge, sheer, grey Devonian limestone cliff at base of Cirrus Mountain, freezing in winter to become an international mecca for ice climbers.

The Big Bend: 37km north of Crossing. Source of North Saskatchewan River is the Saskatchewan Glacier, southern toe of the Columbia Icefield, just out of sight but due west. Highway switchbacks east and climbs steeply around Parker Ridge. Gear down!

Parker Ridge: 41km north of Crossing. A short, steep hike (about 5km round trip) leads up onto 2,100m Parker Ridge for a look at life above tree line. Mountain goats and ptarmigan often seen, and despite the Arctic conditions, a host of beautiful flowers and shrubs. Prime spot for winter ski touring, but avalanches are a danger: check with Parks office.

Jasper National Park: 1,087,800ha. Parks Canada in Jasper: 403-852-6176. Jasper National Park, Box 10, Jasper, AB, T0E 1E0. Two infocentres: one in Jasper, on Connaught Dr, across from CNR station, daily year-round; one at Columbia Icefield, Hwy 93, 105km south of Jasper, daily, mid-May to mid-Oct. Interpretive centre, displays, park publications, maps.

Established in 1907. 45km north of Saskatchewan River Crossing on Hwy 93 (108km south of Jasper). Western entrance at BC border, 77km east of Tête Jaune Cache. Eastern entrance 56km northeast of Jasper (306km west of Edmonton). Largest of Canada's four Rocky Mountain national parks. Along with three provincial parks, these parks were declared a World Heritage Site by UNESCO in 1985. Together they enclose a 20,238 sq km wilderness area straddling the Great Continental Divide.

Jasper is a hiker's paradise, from day trails to 10-day wilderness treks. Popular hikes include 45km Skyline Trail from near Jasper to

Lake Louise to Jasper

Maligne Lake and 42km Tonquin Valley loop. Park-use permits are required by backcountry hikers, and the number of hikers for more popular trails is limited by regulations. Reservations can be made for some hikes. Check with park infocentres.

Jasper National Park Campgrounds: 403-852-6176. 10 campgrounds, 1,758 campsites. No reservations.

From the Columbia Icefield, Hwy 93 follows Sunwapta then Athabasca River valleys to Jasper, the park's geographic and cultural centre, 108km north. There are seven Parks Canada campgrounds along the Icefields Parkway.

Wilcox Creek Campground: 2km north of Sunwapta Pass on Hwy 93. 46 campsites, hiking trails. June-Sept.

Columbia Icefield Campground: 4km north of Sunwapta Pass on Hwy 93. 33 campsites (tents only), hiking trails. Mid-May to snowfall.

Columbia Icefield Access: 4.5km north of park boundary (103km south of Jasper) on Hwy 93. A congested area. **Icefield Centre** has parks information and interpretive displays. Here also are Brewster Tours offering 1.5-hour Columbia Icefield Snocoach Tours. Passengers ride onto the Athabasca tongue of icefields in six-wheel-drive snocoaches, then can step onto ice formed from snow that fell 400 years ago. Tickets available in advance: 403-762-6767 or 403-762-6735 or 1-800-350-7433 (groups), or at Icefield Centre. Also food, and lodging. Bighorn sheep, tame to brazen, are often seen here. All services available, May-Oct only.

Road across Hwy 93 from Icefield Centre: 1km to parking lot at Sunwapta Lake, and short trail to toe of Athabasca Glacier. This ice age remnant is receding; note dated posts marking glacier's retreat. **Do not walk on the glacier: it's very dangerous, with many unmarked crevasses.**

Columbia Icefield: 325 sq km. Up to 350m thick. Only the tip of the icefield is visible here: this is the southeast shore of a vast 325 sq km icecap that sprawls 60km north along the Continental Divide. The Athabasca Glacier, beneath 3,491m Mt Athabasca to the west, and the Dome Glacier, spilling down 3,475m Mt Kitchener to the north, are edges of the largest icecap south of the Arctic Circle. They feed river systems flowing to the Pacific, Atlantic, and Arctic oceans. There are dangerous crevasses and the icefields are recommended only for experienced, equipped mountaineers. Most visitors take Sno-Coach tour, above. Professional guided hiking tours available. Contact Peter Lemieux, Athabasca Glacier Icewalks, Box 2067, Banff, AB, T0L 0C0.

Sunwapta Canyon Viewpoint: 6km north of Icefield Centre on Hwy 93. View of 3,475m Mt Athabasca. Mountain sheep and goats. Use caution around this congested viewpoint. Road descends sharply for next 4km north.

Tangle Falls: 7km north of Icefield Centre. A waterfall spills down steps of half-billion-year-old limestone. Another hangout for street-smart bighorn sheep.

Stutfield Glacier Viewpoint: 9km north of Icefield Centre. The Stutfield tongue of the icefield hangs off the northern side of 3,475m Mt Kitchener.

Woodland Caribou: Small herds of this rare animal, depicted on the Canadian 25-cent piece, summer high in the ranges east of Hwy 93, and are often seen along highway in the Beauty Creek area, late fall to spring.

Jonas Creek Campground: 31km north of Icefield Centre (77km south of Jasper). 25 campsites (12 are walk-in sites). Mid-May to snowfall.

Sunwapta Falls: 49km north of Icefield Centre (54km south of Jasper). Turn west 600m to Sunwapta Falls parking lot. Short walk to 9m falls. *Sunwapta* is Stoney word for "roaring river," and it does that. Also trailhead to Fortress Lake in BC's Hamber Provincial Park. Sunwapta Falls Resort on Hwy 93 has restaurant and groceries. Seasonal. 403-852-4852.

Honeymoon Lake Campground: 35 campsites. 53km north of Icefield (50km south of Jasper). Mid-May to snowfall.

Athabasca River: 69km north of Icefield Centre (34km south of Jasper). Viewpoint, picnics. Great views of river valley. Mountain goats along road or river, attracted by minerals in the white glacial soils. Watch for kids on the road! 168km of Athabasca River in Jasper National Park is part of Canadian Heritage Rivers System.

Mt Kerkeslin Campground: 42 campsites. 72km north of Icefield Centre (36km south of Jasper) on Hwy 93. June-early Sept.

Highway 93A: 76km north of Icefield Centre. Access to Athabasca Falls, Wabasso Campground, and famed beauty spot below Mt Edith Cavell. A parallel 24km scenic drive on opposite side of Athabasca River. Rejoins Hwy 93 23km north.

SIDE TRIP

to Athabasca Falls, and Mt Edith Cavell

Athabasca Falls: 400m west on Hwy 93A to parking lot. Short walk to high pressure 12m falls roaring through narrow canyon – awesome with spring runoff.

Wabasso Campground: 228 campsites, sani-station. 14km north of Hwy 93 on Hwy 93A (16km south of Jasper on Hwy 93A). Wheelchair facilities. In lodgepole pine forest along Athabasca River. Late June-Sept.

Mt Edith Cavell Rd: 18km north of Hwy 93 on Hwy 93A. A narrow, winding, 15km road to lake. Be prepared for heavy traffic July-Aug, 10am-3pm. Short hike leads

to classic views of 3,363m **Mt Edith Cavell** reflected in Cavell Lake, Jasper's Lake Louise. Also head of popular hiking and horseback riding trail 20km to Tonquin Valley, one of Jasper's most famous backcountry areas. Road open June-Oct (no bicycles allowed).

Marmot Basin: 20km north of Hwy 93 on Hwy 93A (12km south of Jasper). Jasper's downhill ski area. 403-852-3816. 853m vertical, seven lifts; even mix of novice, intermediate, and expert terrain; the longest run is 5.6km. Snowboard park and telemarking. Dec-April.

Return to Highway 93

Wapiti Campground: 362 campsites, showers, winter camping. 98km north of Columbia Icefield (5km south of Jasper).

Whistlers Rd: 100km north of Icefield Centre (3km south of Jasper) on Hwy 93; to Whistlers Campground and Jasper Tramway. The "whistlers" in question here are hoary marmots, huge alpine woodchucks with loud whistle alarm calls.

Whistlers Campground: 781 campsites. Some fully serviced sites, showers, sani-station. May-Oct. West on Whistler Rd 100m, then south 300m on access.

Jasper International Hostel: On Whistlers Rd, 500m beyond tramway parking lot. 403-852-3215. Sleeps 80. Reservations.

Jasper Tramway: 4km up and west on Whistlers Rd. 403-852-3093. End of March to end of Oct. A reversible tram ride to 2,265m classic alpine meadows, and a fantastic view of the area. Longest and highest tramway in Canada. Treeline Restaurant. Free guided walks to summit.

Jasper: (Pop. 3,269). On Hwy 16 in Jasper National Park, 101km east of Tête Jaune Cache and 1km east of junction of Hwy 93 (Icefields Parkway).

Jasper is a kind of twin sister to Banff. The two used to have a sibling rivalry dating back to the two railways (CNR and CPR) which created the towns (and to a large degree, the parks) and their associated grand resorts, the Jasper Park Lodge and the Banff Springs Hotel. Competition is not so relevant today, especially since the recent acquisition of Jasper Park Lodge by Canadian Pacific Hotels.

Jasper is quieter and more relaxed than Banff, with more original mountain community charm intact than its busy, developed southern sister. This does not reflect on Jasper's relative beauty or attractions, but rather on the simple fact that while Calgary is little more than an hour from Banff on the Trans-Canada Highway, Jasper is a good four hours from Edmonton on a quieter highway. (Note, however, that Hwy 16 to Edmonton has been twinned from Hinton to Edmonton, offering a scenic and safe drive through farmlands, foothills, and forest.) An historical factor is that

Jasper is a major railway town, a third of its residents employed by the CNR. It is not, therefore, as preoccupied with tourism as Banff.

Nevertheless, on a busy summer day in Jasper, the streets are bustling with tourists, shopping for souvenirs or Inuit art, gathering park information and supplies for camping trips, booking raft trips, trail rides, golf games, bus tours, guided tours, or hiking trips (ski trips in winter). With hotels, motels, B&Bs, and campgrounds filled with visitors, plus summer staff to service them, as well as summer cottagers, the town's population seasonally soars to over 20,000. There is a full range of tourist services, but no commercial airport (the nearest is in Hinton, 77km east).

Jasper Information: Write Jasper Tourism and Commerce, Box 98, Jasper, AB, T0E 1E0. Limited info: 403-852-3858. Best to call Parks Canada Infocentre, 500 Connaught Dr. 403-852-6176.

■ **Jasper Walking Tour:** Delightful introduction to Jasper's people, past and present, offered by an innovative, cooperative association called "Friends of Jasper National Park." Guided walks, June-Sept. 403-852-4767. A useful book, *Jasper: a Walk in the Past,* is available in shops and park infocentres. Also free childrens walks, events.

■ **Jasper Yellowhead Museum and Archives:** 400 Pyramid Lake Rd, Box 42, Jasper, AB, T0E 1E0. 403-852-3013. Daily, 10am-9pm, in summer. Winter: varies. Operated by the Jasper Yellowhead Historical Society.

■ **Mt Edith Cavell:** From Hwy 93A about 14km south of Jasper, then up narrow, winding 15km Mt Edith Cavell Rd. Superb views of 3,363m Cavell, self-guided interpretive trail, hiking trail to forefield of Angel Glacier, Cavell Meadows. Mountain named for British nurse executed for helping Allied troops during the First World War.

■ **Mt Edith Cavell Hostel:** Below Angel Glacier. Reservations through Jasper International Hostel: 403-852-3215. Sleeps 32.

■ **Pyramid and Patricia Lakes:** From Connaught Dr in Jasper, turn north on Pine Ave, follow to Pyramid Lake Rd, then 8km of winding road to lakes. Great views of colourful 2,733m Pyramid Mountain. Picnicking, fishing, canoeing, hiking, water sports. Boat rentals: 403-852-3536. Trail rides: 403-852-3562.

■ **The Den Wildlife Museum:** 403-852-3361. Jasper's wildlife museum, downtown in the Whistlers Inn, 105 Miette Ave. Daily. More than 130 specimens in natural settings.

■ **Rafting:** Raft trips down the Athabasca River. Jasper Raft Tours: 403-852-3613. Whitewater Rafting (Jasper) Ltd: 403-852-7238 or 1-800-557-7238. Or down the Maligne River: Rocky Mountain River Guides: 403-852-3777. In winter, Maligne Tours Ltd: 403-852-3370 (visit the ice-covered canyon).

Highway 16 from Jasper

Maligne Lake Rd: 2km northeast of Jasper on Hwy 16. To Lake Annette (2km), Jasper Park Lodge (3km), Maligne Canyon (6km), Medicine Lake (21km), and Maligne Lake (44km).

The Columbia Icefield in Jasper National Park sprawls along the Continental Divide.

SIDE TRIP

on Maligne Lake Road

Lake Annette: Just west of Athabasca River bridge, turn south on Jasper Park Lodge road; 1km to signed access road.

Annette offers beach, picnics, hiking trails, and paved wheelchair path around lake (no bicycles).

Jasper Park Lodge: Just west of Athabasca River Bridge on Maligne Lake Rd, turn south onto 3km access road. 403-852-3301 or 1-800-465-7547 within AB. World-class resort built in Roaring '20s by CNR as an exclusive mountain resort to complement natural surroundings. On beautiful Lac Beauvert, guests stay in bungalows and guest houses arranged on neatly landscaped mini-streets on spacious grounds around the main lodge (built 1953). Unique room service with staff on bicycles. Outstanding 18-hole golf course (the late Bing Crosby's favourite), trail rides, bike, canoe, and paddle-boat rentals, gift shops, restaurants. Cross-country ski trails. Year-round. Now owned by CP Hotels. Beauvert Promenade includes 13 boutiques, nightclub, lounge, dining room.

Maligne Canyon: A steep-walled canyon sliced 50m into limestone by the Maligne River. Self-guiding trail, facilities. Maligne Tours Ltd: 403-852-3370.

Medicine Lake: 6km lake with two picnic areas. Drains into underground channels. Lake levels fluctuate.

Maligne Lake: 403-852-3370. Largest lake in Canadian Rockies, one of the largest glacial lakes in the world. Cruises to Spirit Island in summer. Restaurant, boat rentals, fishing (record 9.3kg rainbow trout caught here in 1980), horseback-riding trails. Premium cross-country skiing: but no services in winter.

Return to Highway 16

Snaring River Campground: 66 sites. Just off Hwy 16, 16km east of Jasper. Mid-May to Sept.

Jasper House: Plaque 34km east of Jasper. Named for Jasper Hawes who arrived in 1817 to take over four-year-old North-West Company fur-trading post across the valley.

Miette Rd: 48km northeast of Jasper. Southeast 2km to **Pocahontas Campground**, 140 sites, wheelchair facilities, self-guided interpretive trail. Punchbowl Falls nearby. Mid-May to mid-Oct.

A farther 15km southeast to Miette Hot Springs, hottest (54C) hot springs in the Canadian Rockies (cooled to 40C for bathers). Scenic pool, picnic area, as well as commercial services. May-Oct. 403-866-3939.

Jasper National Park East Gate: 56km east of Jasper on Hwy 16. From here, it is 306km to Edmonton.

238

CARIBOO COUNTRY

RIDING INTO THE REAL WEST

> *" We have art galleries and museums here, and musical performances and libraries. Please don't write about the Cariboo as the land of the gold pan and the cowboy in the big hat."*
> – Cariboo resident, 1988

Sorry, ma'am. Many a traveller has looked to Cariboo Country for riches or romance, but hardly a one for Shakespeare and sushi. It must be tiring to hear it all over again, but the image of Cariboo Country as a land where cowboys roam the plains, ghosts of gold panners haunt ghost towns, and settlers build dreams of independence and isolation is just too entrancing to abandon. It ain't the Wild West, but it's our West, and we hope it stays that way.

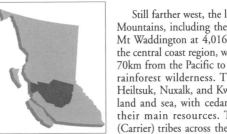

The Cariboo we refer to here is three regions in one, stretching almost from the Alberta border all the way to the Pacific Ocean.

First, there's "the Cariboo" itself, a land of lakes and evergreen forest, spreading west from the foot of the Cariboo Mountains to the Fraser River, north and south across eroded benchlands and deep-cut river canyons.

In the mountains, spruce and fir grow thickly and snow falls some years to a depth that reaches halfway up the houses. Farther west, vegetation is sparser and the climate drier. This is the beginning of cowboy country and home to much of the region's population, grouped in towns and cities along a line midway between the mountains and the Fraser River.

Almost all of the region's industry – mainly logging and sawmilling, mining, and cattle ranching – is also concentrated along this line.

Then, to the west, from the Fraser River to the Coast Mountains, we have the Chilcotin, named for the aboriginal Tsilhqot'in, "people of the young man's river." Their territories, drained by this major tributary of the Fraser River, lie within a landscape of rivers and lakes set in rolling bunchgrass hills. Some of the world's largest cattle ranches are in the Chilcotin, and some of BC's best fresh-water fishing.

Still farther west, the land rises abruptly into the Coast Mountains, including the highest peak totally within BC, Mt Waddington at 4,016m. From the mountains then to the central coast region, where deep fiords cut inland up to 70km from the Pacific to small coastal settlements set in a rainforest wilderness. The coastal First Nations – the Heiltsuk, Nuxalk, and Kwakwaka'wakw – lived from both land and sea, with cedar, salmon, and eulachon among their main resources. They traded with the Dakelh (Carrier) tribes across the Coast Mountains for obsidian, furs, and other goods. On their trading circuit, the Dakelh people walked hundreds of kilometres along routes that became known as grease trails for the eulachon oil that leaked from wooden containers.

The Great Road, or Nuxalk-Carrier Grease Trail, was a major corridor from the Fraser River, across plateaus, to the sea. This was the highway along which North West Company explorer Alexander Mackenzie was led in 1793, to complete his journey from the northeast via the Peace and Fraser rivers, in search of a fur-trade route. He became celebrated as "the first man west," the first white man to cross the North American continent.

Over the next 50 years, fur traders built posts, brought trade goods, and took away beaver and other pelts from the region they named New Caledonia. They suffered mixed emotions, however, when their native acquaintances brought them shiny dust and pebbles from Cariboo rivers. They were delighted to get the gold, but horrified that hundreds of prospectors might invade their carefully guarded trading territory.

By 1857, traders for the Hudson's Bay Company had collected more than 22 kilos of gold, and the company was forced to send it to San Francisco. Reaction was immediate. Thousands booked passage north.

Cowboys ride the range at Hat Creek Ranch.

For five short years, prospectors, merchants, gamblers, farmers, prostitutes, and an assortment of flimflam men rushed from site to site, working their way ever closer to El Dorado, always seeking the mother lode. Creek by creek, instant town to instant town, prospectors worked their way toward the Cariboo Mountains. Finally, in 1861, miners sank shafts through the thick blue clay of an old creek bed, and the wild times on Williams Creek began.

Keithley, Antler, Lightning, Richfield – and finally, Barkerville. The richest vein in the Cariboo had been uncovered. Men dug out some 20 kilos in a single day; some saved their money, some squandered it on liquor and ladies in the growing shantytown of Barkerville. By 1864, Barkerville boasted it was the largest town north of San Francisco.

James Douglas became governor of the new Crown Colony of British Columbia created because of the gold rush. In 1859, he set down-on-their-luck miners to work building a road to the Cariboo. Just as fast, all along this Cariboo Road, roadhouses went up to cater to the needs of travellers. Many of today's village names – from 70 Mile to 150 Mile House – date from that era.

By the 1880s, though, even most of the industrious Chinese miners had abandoned their riverbed workings. Gold continued to be mined, but by hydraulic or deep-pit methods beyond the reach of individual miners, and the yield was low. Prospectors rushed off to other promises of El Dorado; the Cariboo slipped into quieter times.

Some would-be miners, however, looked around at the bunchgrass hills and saw ideal ranching country. They settled in to raise cattle. Others came and saw a place where they could escape from civilization. Eccentric British lords, refugees from smoky cities, European emigrants seeking homesteads, all found a haven in the wide land. They brought with them a desire to do as they pleased, and a determination to live outside the rules that governments imposed. The picture of Cariboo Country as a land with room for every resident to live his or her own life began to grow.

Richmond Hobson, pioneer rancher on the western fringe of the Chilcotin, wrote that the Cariboo was "a land that drew me like a magnet into its soul," echoing and foreshadowing a thousand other settlers who were captured by the magic of Cariboo Country.

Today, Cariboo Country is drawing another breed of adventurer. BC Ferries' Discovery Coast Passage carries sightseers and and kayakers through a landscape and seascape that has changed little in the two centuries since explorer Captain Vancouver approached from the sea and Alexander Mackenzie from the Interior. Just inland from its terminus at Bella Coola is one of BC's oldest and largest provincial parks, Tweedsmuir. The Coast Mountains here are the final challenge for hikers and horseback travellers following Mackenzie's steps seaward along the ancient Nuxalk-Carrier Grease Trail.

Tweedsmuir and other popular wilderness destinations were augmented in the late 1990s by 17 new protected areas – 480,000 hectares of new parks or additions to old ones – bringing the amount of parkland in Cariboo Country to about 12 percent of the region's total land base. Much of the new parkland remains truly protected: barely mapped, with no development and little or no access. Big Creek, Homathko River/Tatlayoko, Nunsti, Marble Range, Edge Hills, and Schoolhouse Lake are parks that will remain the domain of bighorn sheep, moose, cougars, and grizzlies. Likewise, Junction Sheep Range Park, formerly a wildlife management area, protects a herd of California bighorn sheep and 40 species of butterflies. Stum Lake Park has been expanded to protect a crucial breeding colony of endangered white pelicans.

Several relatively new areas, however, await the most intrepid adventure seekers. Kluskoil Lake, Nazko Lakes, and Itcha Ilgachuz parks lie along the grease trails' network. Ts'yl-os Park, embracing a wilderness the size of Prince

The Fraser River cuts through the southern Cariboo.

Edward Island, offers chances to walk through traditional Tsilhqot'in hunting and trapping territories. East across the mighty Fraser River, Cariboo Mountains park links the very busy Bowron Lake and Wells Gray parks to create a 760,000-hectare wilderness. Nearby, the Cariboo River and Moose Valley parks offer moose-viewing opportunities.

Armchair explorers need go no farther than a bookstore or a library to discover this corner of the world. Cariboo Country has inspired works of fiction and non-fiction, settlers stories, tall tales, and biographies that try to capture this spirit, the way more fertile areas produce farm crops. Beware of visiting, however. Once you've been here, it's hard to leave, and it's impossible to stay away.

INFORMATION

Cariboo Chilcotin Coast Tourism Association: 266 Oliver St, Williams Lake, BC, V2G 1M1. 250-392-2226. Toll-free from BC, AB, and US: 1-800-663-5885. Fax: 250-392-2838. E-mail: cta@cariboocountry.org. Or contact the Williams Lake Visitor Info Centre, 1148 S Broadway, Williams Lake, BC, V2G 1A2. 250-392-5025. Fax: 250-392-4214. E-mail: wldcc@stardate.bc.ca. Addresses and telephone numbers of local information centres are provided in the *Logs* under the write-up on each community.

TRANSPORTATION

Getting around in Cariboo Country is a matter of alternatives. If you want to drive paved roads and see the main sites, you can easily do so. If you want back-road adventure, it's there. If you are willing to try walking, horseback riding, flying in small planes, canoeing or rafting, you'll see the same Big Country that locals do. There is also the option of exploring once hard-to-reach destinations on BC Ferries' Discovery Coast Passage route from Port Hardy on Vancouver Island to Bella Coola.

By Road

Cariboo Country is cut into neat packages by its two major roads. The only north-south artery is Hwy 97, the Cariboo Hwy; it runs 441km between Cache Creek and Prince George. A well-maintained, two-lane, paved route, Hwy 97 is the Cariboo lifeline and all the region's major towns are located along it.

To reach Cache Creek from points east, travel west from Alberta on Trans-Canada Hwy 1. Hwy 97 joins the Trans-Canada at Sicamous; continue west to Cache Creek.

Travellers from such northern locales as Edmonton will find it easier to drive south on Hwy 97 from Prince George.

Those on their way to the Cariboo from southern BC can follow several routes: Hwy 1, the Trans-Canada, east and north from Vancouver along the Fraser Canyon to Cache Creek; Hwy 5 (the Coquihalla) north from Hope to Kamloops, then Hwys 1 and 97 west to Cache Creek; or from Osoyoos, Hwy 97 north through the Okanagan, connecting with Hwys 1 and 97 at Monte Creek near Kamloops. Hwy 20 (the Chilcotin or Bella Coola Road) is the other major road in the region. It is two lanes, paved for close to two-thirds of the route, gravel for the remainder. Both are well maintained and usable by any vehicle that can negotiate the climb through the Coast Mountains. To reach Hwy 20, head west at Williams Lake.

Back roads lead to many lakes and ranches and through the scenic backcountry. Almost all of these are gravel or dirt roads. Those described in the *Log* are usually fine for two-wheel-drive vehicles. For large RVs, check

CARIBOO COUNTRY EVENTS

Alkali Lake
- **Rodeo:** Late May.

Alexis Creek
- **Pioneer Days and Fall Fair:** Aug. Parade, ranch games, canoe race, team roping, barbecue.

Anahim Lake
- **Anahim Lake Stampede:** Early Aug. One of the best-known, least-commercialized stampedes in BC.

Barkerville
- **Dominion Day Celebrations:** July 1.
- **Theatre Royal Spring and Summer Shows:** Mid-May to early Sept.
- **Invitational Hose Carriage Races:** Early Sept. Invitational. Local fire departments compete 1870s style.
- **Haunted Tour:** Oct 31.

Bella Bella
- **Waglisla Sports Day:** Late May.
- **Salmon Queen Festival:** July.

Bella Coola
- **Eulachon Fishery:** April.
- **Bella Coola Rodeo:** July.
- **Fall Fair and Loggers Sports:** Labour Day weekend.

Bridge Lake
- **Rodeo:** Late June.

Clinton
- **Clinton Ball:** Late May. Believed to be the oldest annual event in BC. In the 1860s, *the* Cariboo social event. Held in Clinton Hotel (originally 47 Mile House) until it burned down in 1958. Now in Clinton Memorial Hall. Also includes a rodeo, but probably not in the ballroom.
- **Medieval Days:** Early Aug.

Horsefly
- **Horsefly Fall Fair:** Aug.
- **Salmon Run:** Late Aug.

100 Mile House
- **Dogsled Races:** Jan.
- **Cariboo Cross-Country Ski Marathon:** Feb. 50km. Western Canada's largest. Competitors from BC, Canada, US, and Europe.
- **Federation of Canadian Artists Spring Show:** May.
- **Little Britches Rodeo:** May long weekend.
- **Medieval Days:** May and Sept.
- **South Cariboo Childrens Festival:** June.
- **Bridge Lake Amateur Stampede:** Late June.
- **Great Cariboo Ride:** Late July. Six-day, 160km horseback ride.
- **Cariboo Open Golf Tourney:** Early Sept. At 108 Mile Ranch.

Lac la Hache
- **South Cariboo Square Dance Jamboree:** June. (Also 100 Mile House).

Lone Butte
- **Black Powder Shoot:** July.

Likely
- **Black Powder Rendezvous:** July.

Competitors from all over BC in shooting events.

Quesnel
- **Sled Dog Race Championships:** Jan.
- **Billy Barker Days:** Mid-July. Four days. Parade, fireworks, largest amateur rodeo in BC, whitewater raft race.
- **Fall Fair:** Late Aug. Draft horse pulling, dog pulling, agricultural delights, midway.

Riske Creek
- **Frontier Days:** Aug.

Wells
- **Comedy Auction:** Late July. Collectibles auction, hose carriage races in Barkerville.

Williams Lake
- **Williams Lake Stampede:** Four-day event over the July 1 weekend. This is the big one, and the old one (getting on for 70 years), the major stampede of Cariboo cow country, with professional cowboys and cowgirls competing in saddle bronc riding, calf roping, team roping, Brahma bull riding. Native dancing, old-time fiddling, car races, and a parade.
- **Williams Lake Fall Fair:** Late Aug. Stampede Grounds.
- **Wrestling Day:** The day after Boxing Day. At least it is in Williams Lake, where civic employees have been enjoying a paid holiday on Jan 2 since 1959. A day to wrestle with hangovers, it was thought.

locally before setting out.

The Cariboo is also crisscrossed by a fascinating variety of dirt roads, tracks, and trails that can be traversed by some vehicles in some weather. Always check locally on conditions, since bridges may be out or culverts collapsed. Rule of thumb: when you're in the Cariboo, always ask first, and never go in wet weather.

Car and RV Rentals
Cars can be rented at 100 Mile House, Williams Lake, Quesnel, Bella Coola. RVs at Williams Lake: contact Chemo RV, 250-392-4451.

Bus Lines
- **Canim Lake Stage Lines:** Box 415, 100 Mile House, BC, V0K 2E0. 250-397-2562. Service from 100 Mile House to Noranda Mines, Canim Lake South, Hendrix Lake, and waypoints.
- **Greyhound Bus Lines:** 1-800-661-8747. Three times daily between Vancouver and Cache Creek, Williams Lake, Quesnel, Prince George, and points along the Cariboo Hwy.
- **Gold Pan City Stage Lines:** 1471 Quesnel-Hixon Rd, Quesnel. 250-992-6168. Scheduled service: Williams Lake-Bella Coola, Quesnel-Barkerville.

Airlines
Scheduled air service is available in Williams Lake, Quesnel, Anahim Lake, Bella Coola, and Bella Bella.
- **Air BC:** 604-688-5515. Scheduled service to Williams Lake and Quesnel.
- **Harbour Airlines:** 250-627-1341. Coastal flights from Prince Rupert.
- **Pacific Coastal Airlines:** 1-800-663-2872. Vancouver to Anahim Lake, Bella Bella, Bella Coola, Port Hardy, Powell River, Campbell River; floatplanes to north-central coast.

BC Ferries
Departing from Port Hardy is the *Queen of Chilliwack,* carrying 115 cars and 389 passengers on the **Discovery Coast Passage** route to **Bella Coola.** Sails July-Sept. Reservations required. Trips vary from 14-hour nonstop run between Port Hardy and Bella Coola to a 33-hour run that stops at McLoughlin Bay, Shearwater, Klemtu, and Ocean Falls. For more details, see p.255. Call Victoria at 250-386-3431. Or call 1-888-223-3779 for 24-hour general information on any route or schedule. Write: BC Ferries Corporation, 1112 Fort St, Victoria, BC, V8V 4V2. Check the Internet: http://vvv.com/ferries. Or contact the Williams Lake Visitor Info Centre (see p.247).

Railways
Passenger rail service is available from Vancouver to the Cariboo along a highly scenic route.
- **BC Rail:** 604-631-3500. Or within BC: 1-800-339-8752. From the rest of Canada or the US: 1-800-663-8238. Fax: 604-984-5505. Offering service out of North Vancouver to as far north as Prince George. The **Cariboo Prospector** departs 7am from North Vancouver's BC Rail Station. Arrives in Lillooet daily, 12:35pm. On Sun, Wed, and Fri, part of the train continues to Prince George, a 745km journey (with stops en route, including Cariboo destinations of Clinton, Quesnel, Williams Lake, and 100 Mile House). Reservations required for points beyond Lillooet.

Aspen forest shimmers in the autumn light.

CARIBOO COUNTRY
ROUTES AND HIGHLIGHTS

TRAVELLER'S LOGS

HIGHLIGHTS

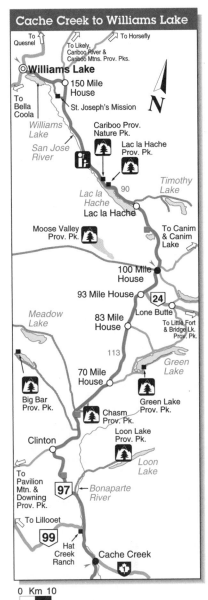

Cache Creek to Williams Lake

To Quesnel · To Likely, Cariboo River & Cariboo Mtns. Prov. Pks. · To Horsefly

◎ Williams Lake
○ 150 Mile House
To Bella Coola
St. Joseph's Mission
Williams Lake
San Jose River
Cariboo Prov. Nature Pk.
Lac la Hache Prov. Pk.
Timothy Lake
Lac la Hache
90
Lac la Hache
Moose Valley Prov. Pk.
To Canim & Canim Lake
100 Mile House
93 Mile House
24
Lone Butte
To Little Fort & Bridge Lk. Prov. Pk.
Meadow Lake
83 Mile House
113
Green Lake
70 Mile House
Big Bar Prov. Pk.
Chasm Prov. Pk.
Green Lake Prov. Pk.
Loon Lake Prov. Pk.
Clinton
Loon Lake
To Pavilion Mtn. & Downing Prov. Pk.
97
Bonaparte River
To Lillooet
99
Hat Creek Ranch
Cache Creek
1

0 Km 10

CACHE CREEK TO WILLIAMS LAKE

THE CARIBOO HIGHWAY (Highway 97)

The Cariboo Hwy, Hwy 97 north, begins in Cache Creek, at the junction of Trans-Canada Hwy 1 and Hwy 97, and runs north 445km to Prince George. The section from Cache Creek to Williams Lake is 203km. To reach the Cariboo Hwy, head west from Kamloops on Hwy 1/97, or north from Hope on Hwy 1.

The Cariboo Hwy snakes through the ranch, plateau, and mountain country of the fabled Cariboo. To the east are the lakes and streams that yielded the gold that sparked the Cariboo Gold Rush.

To the west stretches the Chilcotin, a vast expanse of plain, plateau, and mountain, virtually uninhabited, much of it unreachable, except on foot or horseback, or by boat or plane. Wherever water is available, there are stands of Douglas fir, lodgepole pine, and aspens.

Cache Creek: (Pop. 1,115). For details, see *Thompson Okanagan*, p.168.

Highway 99: 11km north of Cache Creek. Hwy 99 (formerly Hwy 12) comes in from the west, from North Vancouver via Whistler and Lillooet, to end at Hwy 97. It is 75km to Lillooet. For details, see *Vancouver, Coast, and Mountains,* p. 122.

Historic Hat Creek Ranch: At junction of Hwys 97 and 99. Daily, mid-May to mid-Sept. 250-457-9722 or 1-800-782-0922. This 1861 ranch was a roadhouse stop on the original Cariboo Wagon Road. Guided tours include visits with the blacksmith and saddle maker, trail and wagon rides, and First Nations culture. Cafeteria and gift shop.

Loon Lake Rd: 21km north of Cache Creek turn east to Loon Lake. Paved all the way.

SIDE TRIP

to Loon Lake

Loon Lake: A popular family fishing and resort area, 20km northeast of Hwy 97 junction, on Loon Lake Rd. Lake is nearly 12km long, only about 400m wide. Dependable stocks of rainbow trout.

Loon Lake Provincial Park: 3ha; 14 campsites. 250-398-4414. Midway on lake, nestled in a forest of Douglas fir and ponderosa pine.

Return to Highway 97

Carguile Rest Area: 5km beyond Loon Lake Rd turnoff, 26km from Cache Creek.

Cariboo Lakes: Between Loon Lake and Clinton are many small roadside lakes, some fresh, some alkaline. Fed by rainwater and runoff, they have no intakes or outlets, and most shrink to small pools in summer sun.

Clinton: (Pop. 729). 40km beyond Cache Creek. In gold-rush days, Clinton was at the junction of the two wagon roads leading to the gold fields, so it was a major stopping place for merchants, ranchers, and would-be prospectors. Driving into Clinton today involves a time-warp: there's the feeling you have wandered into a Wild West movie set. Clinton residents still seem to be prime examples of the pioneering, individualistic spirit of the Cariboo, routing motorcycle gangs (a famous incident in the '60s) and in general keeping the town the way they want it. Area ranches offer trail riding, hiking, fishing, barbecues. Some are open year-round for cross-country skiing, sleighing. (And hot tubbing.) All ranches have regular guest pickup at BC Rail Station in Clinton.

Clinton Information: Clinton and District Chamber of Commerce, 1522 Cariboo Hwy, Clinton, BC, V0K 1K0. 250-459-2224. Daily, June-Sept. Also Clinton Village Office, 250-459-2261. Or ask local merchants.

■ **South Cariboo Historical Museum:** 1419 Cariboo Hwy. 250-459-2442. June-Aug. Originally an 1890s schoolhouse, built from local, homemade bricks. Now houses native, Chinese, and gold-rush artifacts.

■ **Wolf's Cry Inn:** 250-459-2610. Chef at this restaurant is drawing crowds.

Pavilion Mountain Rd: Southwest as you enter Clinton, leads 16km southwest to **Kelly Lake**. Paved to Kelly Lake, where road forks. **North fork** is the Jesmond Rd through to Jesmond and the Big Bar Ferry (see *Big Bar Rd Side Trip*, p.244). **South fork** leads about 15km over Pavilion Mountain to Pavilion on Hwy 99. Panoramic view of Coast Mountains, alpine flowers, and a cattle ranch perched on the mountaintop. Don't attempt to travel south of Kelly Lake if it has been raining, or even if it looks like rain. Muddy curves are extremely treacherous in this usually bone-dry land. Check locally for conditions. For details from Pavilion on, see *Vancouver, Coast, and Mountains*, p.122.

Downing Provincial Park: 100ha; some RV camping in parking lot; 18 walk-in sites. 16km southwest of Clinton on Pavilion Mountain Rd. 250-398-4414. On shores of mountain-surrounded Kelly Lake.

Big Bar Rd: Off Hwy 97, 9.5km north of Clinton. West to Chilcotin ranch country, gravel back roads, and provincial park.

SIDE TRIP

on Big Bar Road

Cross-country Ski Trails: South off Big Bar Rd, 6km from Hwy 97. 60km of marked trails. Hiking and mountain biking.

Moondance Guest Ranch: 14km west on Big Bar Rd; turn south on Hook Rd for 4km; then west 2km on Isadore Rd, and watch for signs. May-Oct. Box 177, Clinton, BC, V0K 1K0. 1-888-459-7775. Small ranch for dedicated horse people. Lessons for beginners, guided rides along some 300km of pine-forested trails. Private cabins, fabulous food, sauna, and outdoor hot tub.

Big Bar Lake Provincial Park: 332ha; 33 campsites. 250-398-4414. June-Sept. On Big Bar Rd, 34km northwest of Hwy 97. Fraser Plateau landscape, created by glacial action, with Marble Range to south. Glacial rubble formed eskers (long, snaking ridges of gravel), drumlins (tear-shaped hills), and other geological formations. Camping, swimming, fishing, boating (10km/h speed limit), picnicking. Deer, bear, moose, squirrels, marmots.

Road to Meadow Lake Road: 10km north of Big Bar Lake, 44km from Hwy 97. T-junction. Right fork turns sharply northeast, 8km to Meadow Lake where it joins Meadow Lake Rd (see below). Big Bar Rd curves left or southwest toward Jesmond and Big Bar Creek.

Big Bar Guest Ranch: On Big Bar Rd, 4km west of Meadow Lake Rd fork, 48km from Hwy 97. Box 27, Jesmond, Clinton, BC, V0K 1K0. 250-459-2333. Year-round. Has cross-country skiing, skating, sleigh rides, winter riding, dogsledding, snowshoeing, snowmobiling, gold panning, pack trips, riding lessons, river rafting on the Fraser.

Jesmond Rd: 5km from Big Bar Guest Ranch, 53km from Hwy 97. Jesmond Rd comes in from Kelly Lake to the south. Big Bar Rd turns northwest 19km to the **Fraser River** and **Big Bar Ferry**.

Big Bar: 19km from junction with Jesmond Rd. 35km downstream from the **Gang Ranch** (see below). Current-driven ferry crosses the Fraser River. There has been a ferry in continuous operation at this point since 1894. When water is low or icy, an aerial tramway operates for passengers only. At times like this,

At the Hat Creek Ranch, hang on to your hat.

ranchers leave a truck on either side. On demand 7am-7pm (except noon-1pm, 5-6pm). Takes 5 minutes.

Rock piles on the riverbanks show where Chinese miners painstakingly washed the gravel for gold. On the **West Bank**, there's a 4x4 road that goes all the way to **Lillooet**, 64km, three hours. Watch for California bighorn sheep along the roadside.

Jesmond: On Jesmond Rd, 1km south of turnoff to Big Bar Ferry. Behind the lilacs is the original ranch homesteaded by Phil Grinder in 1870. Ranch became an overnight stopping place for the Clinton to 150 Mile stagecoach. Owned by the Coldwell family since 1911, it ran for years as a post office and store. Peter Coldwell wanted to call it "Mountain House," but that was thought too general. The Post Office did approve the name Jesmond, after the town in England. Today a private residence. Post office closed in 1965, store in 1970.

Cougar Point: South on Jesmond Rd 10km from Circle H Mountain Lodge. At fork, take High Bar Rd 8km down in a stunning descent to the Fraser River. Chilcotin Plateau and panorama of ranches stretch out to the north and west. (This back road continues north along the Fraser to Big Bar Creek.)

Return to Highway 97

Clinton Lookout and Big Bar Rest Area: 9.5km north of Clinton on Hwy 97, just north of Big Bar Rd. From here to Prince George, BC Rail tracks parallel the highway. Railway extends 745km from North Vancouver to Prince George. There are several stops throughout the Cariboo. Freight lines carry on 823km to Fort Nelson.

Meadow Lake Rd: West off Hwy 97, 7km north of Big Bar Rd junction, 16.5km north of Clinton.

SIDE TRIP

on Meadow Lake Rd

Meadow Lake Rd offers an adventurous back-road trip through the heart of the western Chilcotin Mountains to Meadow Lake and the famous **Gang Ranch** (see below), where Dog Creek Rd goes north 86km to Hwy 20 and Williams Lake. The whole area is laced with roads, most of them rough, some maintained by the BC Forest Service: going thither and yon, ask as you go. Back-roads maps available at information centres. Also see Cariboo Country regional map, p.238.

Meadow Lake: About 46km west of Hwy 97 on Meadow Lake Rd. Even for locals, the lake is hard to find: it dries up somewhat in summer. But if you can see it, you know you're about halfway to the Gang Ranch.

No-Name Rd: Back road comes in from the south, where it connects 8km away with Big Bar Rd. Once you see this junction, you know you have just passed Meadow Lake (in case you missed it).

Gang Ranch: 100km west of Hwy 97 on Meadow Lake Rd. Travel 46km west of Meadow Lake junction (above) to Churn Creek Bridge, a suspension bridge; cross bridge, take right fork at top of the hill, then drive 4km in to the ranch.

This was the largest cattle ranch in North America, and still is one of the largest working ranches – some 400,000ha, a million acres stretching north to the Chilcotin Mountains and west to the Coast Range. "To ride the summer range took a good week," says Jim Prentice, great grandson of the ranch's second owner, T. D. Galpin. The story Prentice tells is out of the Wild West. Jerome and Thaddeus Harper, real cowboys, drove their herd up from the States during the gold rush in the 1860s – and spotted their fortunes in the grasslands. (It was after their day the ranch got its name – probably because they were the first in BC's Interior to use the multi-bladed gang plough. The JH – Jerome Harper – brand has been passed along to each new owner up to the present day.)

Most of the ranch buildings – cookhouse, bunkhouse, post office, one-room school – are painted a distinctive red. Bed and Breakfast is offered. Gang Ranch Ltd, Gang Ranch PO, BC, V0K 1N0. 250-459-7923.

Churn Creek Provincial Park: 36,100ha. 250-398-4414. No facilities. From the Gang Ranch crossing on the Fraser River, turn south on the Empire Valley Ranch Rd. All roads are gravel and can be extremely slippery during and just after rain. A 4x4 vehicle is a must. Use only designated roads – driving on grasslands is prohibited. Churn Creek park was set aside in 1994 to protect a rare grassland ecosystem. Grasslands comprise only 1.8 percent of BC's land base, and are threatened by overgrazing and development. The park includes 11,000ha of the former Empire

Valley Ranch. Within the rolling hills and serrated river benches of the area live 55 of the province's endangered, threatened, or vulnerable species, including 600 California Bighorn sheep, rare spotted bats, and long-billed curlews. Hiking and horseback riding are good ways to explore.

Dog Creek Rd: At Churn Creek bridge turnoff to the Gang Ranch. Continues north 86km to Hwy 20 (Bella Coola Rd) near Williams Lake. Details in *Williams Lake to Bella Coola*, p.251.

Dog Creek: (Pop. 88). About 10km north of Churn Creek Bridge, on Dog Creek Rd. Secwepemc First Nations community of Dog Creek, or Xqet'em, has general store and gas station. Non-natives arrived in 1856; built the (now gone) Dog Creek Hotel and BC's first flour mill.

Alkali Lake: On Dog Creek Rd, 34km north of Churn Creek bridge. Home to white pelicans during spring and fall migrations. Also to other migrant birds. Indeed, a mecca for birdwatchers. The **Alkali Lake Ranch**, with its distinctive red-roofed log buildings, dates back to the beginnings of colonial BC. Founder, Henry Otto Bowe came to Canada from Germany in 1858. A year later, he had land here; by the next year he had stocked it with 500 head of longhorn cattle driven up from Oregon. He also had 80 brood mares and five stallions. In 1861, he established a public stopping house at the ranch to serve gold seekers following the fur brigade trails that passed through Alkali Lake. The ranch passed out of Bowe family hands in 1910. (In 1912 it was listed as being 25,000 acres, all fenced.) Mario von Riedemann bought the ranch in 1940.

The Secwepemc First Nations community of **Alkali Lake**, a leader in drug and alcohol programs, has cafe and store.

It is 27km farther to the community of Springhouse; 13km south to junction with road from Chimney Lake; a final 12km to connect with Hwy 20.

Return to Highway 97

Chasm Provincial Park: 3,067ha; day use. Year-round. 5.5km north of Meadow Lake Rd, 22km north of Clinton, turn east on gravel road; 4km to park. Painted Chasm is a spectacular cut in lava bedrock, closed on three sides, about 1.5km long and up to 120m deep. Reveals the colours and textures of volcanoes active 12-25 million years ago. The chasm was cut by glacial meltwaters about 10,000 years ago.

70 Mile House: (Pop. 923). On Hwy 97, 9km beyond turnoff to Chasm Park, 31km north of Clinton (71km north of Cache Creek). Historic roadhouse location, one of first stopping places on the Cariboo Wagon Rd. Named because roadhouse was 70 miles on the Cariboo Wagon Road from Lillooet.

Old Bonaparte Rd: At 70 Mile House. Gateway to the South Cariboo lakes, goes east to **Green** and **Watch lakes** and others. 6km from 70 Mile, road forks at North Bonaparte, south fork leading through Bonaparte Valley to Bonaparte Lake. Many delightful smaller lakes within walking distance of Bonaparte Lake. Boating, hunting, fishing, riding, swimming, cross-country skiing. Resorts and guest ranches. North fork is North Green Lake Rd.

Green Lake: At the fork, take North Green Lake Rd. A warm, shallow, turquoise-green lake, 15km long, edged with fir, larch, and whispering aspen. Greenish hue comes from algae and other microorganisms, though some say it's from the reflections of the trees. In any case, there's good swimming, fishing, and birding (particularly osprey and bald eagles). Resorts and lodges.

Flying U Ranch: On north shore of Green Lake, 6km from the fork. Box 69, 70 Mile House, BC, V0K 2K0. 250-456-7717. An historic 18,000ha working ranch. Only resort ranch in BC where guests – provided with maps – can trail ride on their own. Has an airstrip, and its own BC Rail train stop, Flying U.

Green Lake Provincial Park: 347ha; 121 campsites at three campgrounds (reservations taken: call 1-800-689-9025; from the Lower Mainland or overseas, call 604-689-9025). Sani-station. General info: 250-398-4414. May-Sept. 15km northeast of 70 Mile House, on Old Bonaparte Rd (paved). Water activities; picnicking, playground.

Road at 83 Mile House: 18km north of 70 Mile House, 89.5km north of Cache Creek. Leads southeast to Green Lake area.

93 Mile House: (Est. Pop. 91). 103km north of Cache Creek.

Highway 24: Just north of 93 Mile, 103.5km north of Cache Creek. Highway travels east through Lakes Country.

SIDE TRIP

to Lakes Country

Hwy 24 offers a scenic, potentially fishful trip through the south Cariboo, continuing east 97km to the small community of Little Fort on Yellowhead Hwy 5. See *Thompson Okanagan*, p.178, for details on the easterly portions of Hwy 24.

Lone Butte: (Area pop. 1,877). 10km east of Hwy 97 on Hwy 24. Small settlement and BC Railway station. Has the line's last standing wooden water tower, from the age of steam. Named for the large flattop hill to the east. Guest ranches in area.

Interlakes District: Hwy 24 leads to hundreds of lakes offering fishing, mainly

for rainbow trout, also eastern brook trout, lake trout, burbot, and kokanee. Sheridan and Bridge lakes are favourites; Lac des Roches is good for fly-fishing. Resorts throughout area provide facilities ranging from primitive to luxurious. Some stay open through winter for cross-country skiing.

Bridge Lake: (Pop. 278). 51km east of Hwy 97. Tourist services, resorts. Bridge Lake Centennial Park for picnicking.

Bridge Lake Provincial Park: 6ha; 20 vehicle/tent campsites, seven walk-in campsites. At Bridge Lake, off Hwy 24. 250-851-3000. May-Sept. Walking trail around Bridge Lake.

Lac des Roches Rest Area: Just beyond Bridge Lake.

Little Fort: (Pop. 175). 97km east of Hwy 97. See *Thompson Okanagan*, p.178.

Return to Highway 97

100 Mile House: (Pop. 6,325). 113km north of Cache Creek; 90km south of Williams Lake. 100 Mile House was a stopping place on the Cariboo Road as early as 1861. A stagecoach from the 1860s is exhibited at Red Coach Inn, north end of town. In 1930, Lord Martin Cecil (who became the Marquis of Exeter) arrived here to manage his father's property, the Bridge Creek Ranch. 100 Mile House was well known around the world as BC headquarters of the Emissaries of Divine Light, a non-sectarian group headed by Cecil until his death in 1988.

100 Mile House is now a service centre for the central Cariboo, with a trading population of some 20,000. It's a major producer of log homes for North American and Japanese markets. Houses are completely finished, then dismantled and shipped off.

In winter, 100 Mile House is a centre for cross-country skiing and in early Feb hosts the Cariboo Marathon, a 50km race drawing more than 1,000 participants from across the continent.

100 Mile House Information: Info Centre, South Cariboo Chamber of Commerce, Box 2312, 100 Mile House, BC, V0K 2E0. 250-395-5353. Fax: 250-395-4083. E-mail: sccofc@bcinternet.net. Websites: http://www2.bcinternet.net/~100mile/sccofc.html. Also http://cariboolinks.com/visitors-guide/index.html. Daily, July-Aug. Weekdays, 9-5, off-season. On Hwy 97, beside the giant skis: 12m-long replicas of racing cross-country skis, flanked by 9m ski poles – reputed to be world's largest.

■ **100 Mile Marsh:** Behind Info Centre. Trail offers chances to see waterfowl, songbirds, beavers. BC Wildlife Watch viewing site.

Road to Canim Lake: 4km north of 100 Mile House, at top of hill. Stay on paved road. Leads east 36km to Canim Lake, and on to Mahood Falls.

245

SIDE TRIP

to Canim Lake

Forest Grove: (Pop. 837). Small community about 20km east of Hwy 97. Take north fork to **Ruth Lake**.

Ruth Lake Provincial Park: 30ha. 9km north of Forest Grove. April-Oct. 250-398-4414. Day-use area, small beach, picnicking. May-June are great months for visiting.

Canim Lake: (Pop. 494). 16km east of Forest Grove, 36km east of Hwy 97 junction. A large lake – 37km long – surrounded by mountains. Harbours large sport fish, the "laker" or char. Family-oriented resort community. Fishing, horseback riding, water activities, birdwatching. Road forks here, leading north to Eagle Creek and along lake's north shore, or east along south shore toward Mahood Falls. Tourist facilities along both roads.

Canim Beach Provincial Park: 6ha; 7 vehicle/tent campsites. 5km north of Canim Lake community, following north fork. April-Oct. 250-398-4414. Gravel and pebble beach. Moose often seen.

Hathaway, Sulphurous, and Horse Lakes: Take east fork out of Canim Lake community. At 24km east of Canim Lake, turn southwest for these and other resort lakes. Road leads back to Hwy 97 at 100 Mile House.

Canim River Falls, Mahood Lake, Deception Falls: Take east fork out of Canim Lake community (as above). Travel 24km to fork in road. Take northeast fork for 6km. Walk to Canim and Mahood falls, spectacular cascades between Canim and Mahood lakes. Mahood Lake is part of, and a secondary entrance into **Wells Gray Provincial Park**. A store, resorts, and a wilderness campground are located in area. Deception Falls are on Deception Creek just above where it flows into Mahood Lake. See *Thompson Okanagan*, p.178.

Return to Highway 97

Exeter Rd: North end of 100 Mile House. Leads to **Moose Valley Provincial Park**, and joins Dog Creek Rd (see above).

Moose Valley Provincial Park: 2,322ha; rustic camping only. 250-398-4414. From 100 Mile House, turn left onto Exeter Rd. Cross railway tracks and follow signs along active gravel logging road for 28km. Last 10km is extremely rough and not recommended for low-clearance vehicles. Canoeing on chain of small lakes; cross-country skiing and snowshoeing in winter. Moose and other wildlife.

108 Mile Ranch/Rest Area: (Pop. 2,038). 13km north of 100 Mile House on Hwy 97. Once a large cattle operation. Now features history, and fine resorts.

■ **108 Mile House Heritage Site:** Contact 100 Mile House & District Historical Society, Box 225, 108 Mile Ranch, BC, V0K 2Z0. 250-791-5288 or 250-791-1971. Daily, 10-6, late May-late Sept. Late 19th and early 20th century buildings at north entrance to 108 Mile Ranch include rebuilt ranch building from 105 Mile, the telegraph house, post office, and the ice house – a tea house and craft store. The restored Watson Clydesdale Barn, built circa 1908, is one of the largest log barns in Canada. Guided tours.

■ **Best Western 108 Resort:** 260ha all-season recreational resort with airstrip. Comp 2, 108 Mile Ranch, BC, V0K 2Z0. 250-791-5211 or 1-800-667-5233. Spa, heated pool, tennis, trail riding, 200km cross-country trails, snowmobiling, and (believe it!) golf. The **108 Resort Golf Club** offers a demanding, 18-hole championship course.

■ **Hills Health & Guest Ranch:** Box 26, 108 Mile Ranch, BC, V0K 2Z0. 250-791-5225. Pool, spa services, aerobics, horseback riding, cross-country and downhill skiing, and tubing.

Lac la Hache: (Pop. 1,295). 25km beyond 100 Mile House. Called the "Longest Town in the Cariboo," it stretches several kilometres along a beautiful lakeshore. Lac la Hache, which translates as "Lake of the Axe," is, the story goes, named for an axe that an early French Canadian fur trader dropped through a hole in the lake ice. That perhaps wasn't all that he called it. Today, there is still fishing (and ice fishing) – for kokanee, large lake trout. Also resorts, winter sports.

Lac la Hache Information: Contact 100 Mile House Info Centre, south Cariboo Chamber of Commerce, Box 2312, 100 Mile House, BC, V0K 2E0. 250-395-5353.

Road to Timothy Lake: To Timothy and other fishing lakes, east at Lac la Hache. Road partially paved. Many services.

Lac la Hache Provincial Park: 24ha; 83 campsites; sani-station. 250-398-4414. 13.5km north of Lac la Hache, camping area on east side of highway, picnic sites on west beside lake. Beach, forest trails, winter recreation.

Cariboo Provincial Nature Park: 98ha. Year-round. 15km north of Lac la Hache, walk-in only. 250-398-4414. Set aside as a place to study nature. Beaver pond on San Jose River, waterfowl on Frog Lake. Tread carefully; don't disturb the wildlife.

San Jose River: West side of highway, which follows the river almost to Williams Lake. River drains Lac la Hache and winds its way gently, flowing into Williams Lake.

To the Gold Fields: 27km north of Lac la Hache. Sign explains background of the 1860s gold rush.

Mission Rd: 45km north of Lac la Hache. West a short distance to site of **St Joseph's Mission**. A few old farm buildings

and a small cemetery are all that remains of mission established by Oblates of Mary Immaculate in 1866, for the Secwepemc, Dakelh (Carrier), and Tsilhqot'in peoples. Father James Maria McGuckin operated a farm/ranch to provide income. Its OMI cattle brand was the first registered in the Cariboo.

150 Mile House: (Pop. 899). 50km north of Lac la Hache. Once an important junction where passengers changed stagecoaches before going west to the Chilcotin or east to the gold fields. Now a small service centre for surrounding region.

Road to Horsefly: To community of Horsefly and Quesnel Lake. Turn east at 150 Mile House. Paved road to Horsefly. Gravel to lakes beyond. Leads through open pasture and rolling hills with Cariboo Mountains in background.

SIDE TRIP

to Horsefly, Quesnel Lake, and (Eventually) Likely

Horsefly: (Pop. 500). 56km east of Hwy 97 and 150 Mile House. On the banks of the Horsefly River, an important salmon spawning stream. First called Harper's Camp, after one of the brothers who founded the Gang Ranch. Renamed when later settlers discovered one of the drawbacks to its location. Site of first gold discovery in the Cariboo, in 1859. Prospectors, still with stakes in the area, can sometimes be seen washing creek gravel.

■ **Jack Lynn Memorial Museum:** Campbell Ave, one block south of Horsefly town centre. 250-620-3384. July-Aug, Tues-Sat. Horsefly's mining, trapping, logging days.

■ **Horsefly River Spawning Channel:** Across river from town. Spawning sockeye mid-Sept. BC Wildlife Watch viewing site.

Road to Lakes: Bear right in Horsefly on paved road, connects up with gravel roads leading to lakes. 1.5km east, the road splits: north fork to **Horsefly and Quesnel lakes**; south fork to **Black Creek** and **Canim Lake**.

Horsefly Lake Provincial Park: 148ha; 23 campsites. May-Oct. 250-398-4414. 13km northeast of Horsefly. Follow lakes road to Horsefly Lake. Water activities. Salmon run mid-Sept. Good base camp for hiking and exploring.

Quesnel Lake: 36km northeast of Horsefly. Gravel road dead-ends on southern shores of Quesnel Lake. At 530m, Quesnel Lake is the deepest lake in BC, and second deepest in North America. If there are any lake monsters or Ogopogo cousins, they haven't shown up yet. But there are lots of resorts, good fishing, skiing.

Road to Likely: Bear north past the schoolhouse in Horsefly onto Mitchell Bay Rd to Likely. Road passes along west end of

Quesnel Lake, giving fine river and lake views. Resorts, campgrounds. Closed in winter. Check locally for road conditions, especially in wet weather. This is a good gravel road, but not recommended for RVs. A better route, north from 150 Mile House, is cited immediately below.

Continue to Likely on Quesnel Lake road, or return to Hwy 97 at 150 Mile House. A second paved road from 150 Mile House leads north to Big Lake Ranch, and around Morehead Lake, again to Likely.

Quesnel River Hatchery: Chinook salmon hatchery on road to Likely (2km south of Likely). Daily. Adult salmon Aug-late Sept. Fry: Jan to mid-May.

Likely: (Pop. 350). 80km northeast of 150 Mile House. No, it's not named because gold was likely to be found here. John A. ("Plato John") Likely, a 1920s gold miner who liked to consider the meaning of life, gave his name to this pretty community on the Quesnel River at its mouth on Quesnel Lake. The Likely area has witnessed some of the richest gold finds in the district; as late as 1922, some 20kg were taken out from a single mine in one year. Mineral exploration continues to be Likely's most important economic activity, but visitors appreciate its fishing, hunting, hiking, and history.

Likely Information: Information centre, Box 79, Likely, BC, V0L 1N0. 250-790-2422. On Likely St. Late May-Sept. Off-season call 250-790-2557.

■ **Cedar Point Park:** On Cedar Creek Rd in Likely. A pretty day-use park sporting some hefty mining artifacts, including one of the Twin Giants, huge steam shovels weighing 10,000kg each.

Road to Quesnelle Forks: Cross bridge over Quesnel River at Likely, continue for 200m, turn northwest on Quesnelle Forks Rd.

Note: As with other Cariboo back roads, the road to Quesnelle Forks can be difficult in wet weather.

Quesnelle Forks: About 8km beyond Likely. Now a ghost town, in 1859 Quesnelle Forks claimed fame as "the largest city on the mainland." The gold – and the fame – lasted five years, as miners, gamblers, storekeepers, and ladies of the evening crowded into the log buildings hastily built near the gold finds. Once home to 5,000 people, Quesnelle Forks shrank as the gold ran out. Today, greying log buildings are set amidst fields of daisies. The cemetery has been restored, and there is a wheelchair-accessible bathroom.

Bullion Pit: 5km west of Likely, off the road back to Hwy 97. Simply called **Hydraulic** on some area maps. Billed as the world's largest gold-mining pit, the Bullion hydraulic mine pit sinks 90m into the ground, and is more than 3km long. Gold-mining operations took place from 1892-1942. From 1892 to 1898, gold worth $1.25 million was extracted. Abandoned after the original strike, the hydraulic area still produced almost $1

WILLIAMS LAKE

1 Bus Depot	**6** Hospital
2 Cariboo Tourist Association	**7** Liquor Store
3 Chamber of Commerce Infocentre, Museum	**8** Railway Station
4 City Hall	**9** R C M P
5 Fire Hall	**10** Stampede Grounds

million in gold for the Chinese miners who stayed on. Later hydraulic operations drew on water carried in over 65km of canals. In 1938, the mine used more water each day than the city of Vancouver.

Here, in March 1988, pensioner-prospector George Williams unearthed a gold nugget the size of a turkey egg. It weighed 28g, and was worth as much as $10,000. Williams had no plans to sell it.

Return to Highway 97

Williams Lake: (Pop. 10,472). 15km north of 150 Mile House, 203km north of Cache Creek. The only city between Hope and Quesnel, and, it's Stampede Town. The famous Williams Lake Stampede, a four-day event over the July 1 weekend, was officially started in the 1920s, and is now a major professional rodeo.

The community probably takes its name from Secwepemc Chief William, who moved his people here from nearby Chimney Creek in the early 1860s, and was prominent at the Oblates of Mary Immaculate mission established in 1867.

Williams Lake did not share in the Cariboo gold bonanza, all because of a loan that was refused. Tom Manifee owned land now at the heart of the city. Asked by the Cariboo Road contractors for a short-term loan so they could pay their workers, he refused. Refusal led to angry words, and angry words led the contractors to reroute the road through 150 Mile House, where the roadhouse owner was more than pleased to lend them money. Bypassed, Manifee's roadhouse got no more business, and Williams Lake did not come into its own until the Pacific Great Eastern Railway tracks arrived in 1920. In a reversal of fate, the coming of steel did in 150 Mile House, and established Williams Lake as the area's commercial centre.

Williams Lake has a diversified economic base, with forestry, mining, and agriculture; and the most active stockyard in the province. All tourist facilities available.

Williams Lake Information: Info centre, Williams Lake and District Chamber of Commerce, 1148 S Broadway (Hwy 97 at south end of town), Williams Lake, BC, V2G 1A2. 250-392-5025. Daily July-Aug. Weekdays Sept-June.

Williams Lake Airport: East 11km north of Williams Lake. Service to Vancouver, Prince George. Charters.

■ **Williams Lake Museum:** 113 N 4th Ave, Williams Lake, BC, V2G 2C8. 250-392-7404. June-Sept, Mon-Sat 10-4. Off-season, Tues-Sat 11-4.

■ **Stationhouse Gallery:** At the foot of Oliver St. #1 N Mackenzie Ave, BC Rail Station, Williams Lake, BC, V2G 1N4. 250-392-6113. Year-round. In historic passenger train depot. Monthly shows, some local work, crafts.

■ **Scout Island Nature Centre:** On Scout Island at west end of Williams Lake, reached by a causeway. Turn off Hwy 97 east of city centre, follow signs. Centre is only 0.5km from Hwy 97. Area open year-round. Nature house seasonal, May-Aug 9-4. 250-398-8532. Nature house for adults and children, lots of hands-on exhibits. Trails along lakeshore. BC Wildlife Watch viewing site.

■ **Williams Lake River Valley Trail:** Along Williams Lake River in and north of town. Several access ponts. Map at Info Centre. BC Wildlife Watch viewing site.

■ **Golf:** Williams Lake Golf and Tennis Club, 208 Fairview Dr (five minutes from town), 250-392-6026, offers 18-hole championship course, night-lit tennis courts, and restaurant.

Highway 20: Hwy 20 comes into town at the traffic lights at the south end of the lake, goes straight through town to Oliver St, the town's centre. Turn west on Hwy 20 for Bella Coola. For details see *Williams Lake to Bella Coola*, p.251. Or continue north on Hwy 97 to Quesnel.

WILLIAMS LAKE TO PRINCE GEORGE

CARIBOO HIGHWAY (HIGHWAY 97)

From Williams Lake, the Cariboo Hwy (Hwy 97) continues north 238km to Prince George. On the northern fringes of the Cariboo, beyond Quesnel, the landscape changes, as evergreen forest closes in on road and river, and the lakes country is left behind. For the thousands of visitors interested: the turnoff to **Barkerville** is 5km north of downtown Quesnel, on Hwy 26.

Williams Lake: (Pop. 10,472). At Hwys 97 and 20. For details, see *Cache Creek to Williams Lake*, above. From here, it's 119km to Quesnel; and a further 119km from Quesnel to Prince George.

Soda Creek Rd: From main intersection of Hwys 97 and 20 in downtown Williams Lake, head west past the Stampede

Grounds, then turn right at second set of traffic lights on Mackenzie Ave. This becomes Soda Creek Rd which runs, part paved, part gravel, north out of town along the east bank of the Fraser, parallel to Hwy 97. About 20km north of Williams Lake, is **Rudy Johnson's Bridge**, built by an independent and annoyed west-side rancher who resented having to travel west on the Bella Coola Rd, then north up the Fraser west-side road in a time-consuming detour every time he wanted to go to town. The government refused to build a bridge, so in 1968 Johnson had one shipped down in pieces from Alaska. He erected it across the Fraser where government engineers had said a bridge was impossible, and ran it for 15 years as a private toll bridge, heavily used by logging trucks and ranch traffic. The government then took it over. It now operates as a free crossing.

Cross here to **Meldrum Creek Rd** on the west side, and continue north through ranchland and forest, to the Marguerite ferry. Or continue on the Soda Creek Rd.

Hwy 97 from Williams Lake also continues to Soda Creek.

Xats'ull (Soda Creek) First Nation: (Pop. 59). 33km north of Williams Lake, take McAllister Rd off Hwy 97, then travel 2km along Indian Reserve Rd. Archaeologists are unearthing history reaching back at least 2,000 years. And this Secwepemc community is sharing that history at traditional-style pithouse village, where groups are offered salmon cooked over open fires and cultural workshops led by elders. Individual travellers welcome for day visits.

Xats'ull Information: Soda Creek Band, RR4, Site 15, Comp 2, Williams Lake, BC, V2G 4M8. 250-297-6323.

Soda Creek: (Est. pop. 32). 33km north of Williams Lake. Creek bed, carbonate of lime, causes the water to bubble. This is the head of the upper Fraser Canyon, and the beginning of 650km of navigable river waters, which is why the town became the gold-rush road terminus for sternwheelers. They were transported in by road, and reassembled here to carry miners north to Quesnel. When the railway came through in 1920, the steamboats disappeared.

McLeese Lake: (Est. pop. 300). A small community 43.5km north of Williams Lake. Resorts on lake, swimming raft, tourist facilities.

McLeese Lake Rest Area: 44.5km north of Williams Lake, at the north end of McLeese Lake. Haunted by restless loons.

Likely Rd: At north end of McLeese Lake, turn east on gravel road leading to Big Lake Ranch, Horsefly, and, just possibly, Likely. See *Cache Creek to Williams Lake*, p.246.

Marguerite Ferry: 62.5km north of Williams Lake. Usually April-Sept. Stops when the river freezes. Small, passenger-only aerial tram runs when ferry doesn't. One of the

last reaction ferries crossing the Fraser. Runs on an overhead cable; power is supplied by the river current. Holds one RV, one car. Free. On call 7am-6:45pm (except 11:45am-1pm, 4:45pm-6pm.)

Fort Alexandria Monument: 66.5km north of Williams Lake. Was last post established (1821) by the North West Company west of the Rockies, and Alexander Mackenzie's farthest point south in his Fraser River descent, 1793.

Australian Rest Area: 83km north of Williams Lake, west side of highway. This farming area began as the Australian Ranch in 1863, when two wandering Aussies, Andrew Olsen and Stephen Downes, gave up on the gold fields and started a ranch on these rich alluvial benchlands.

Kersley: (Pop. 283). 98km north of Williams Lake. Named for early rancher Charles Kersley, who supplied foodstuffs to men working the gold fields.

Quesnel-Hydraulic Rd: 114km north of Williams Lake. Paved in a loop around Dragon Lake and back to Hwy 97 just south of Quesnel. Dragon is a beautiful fishing lake. Fish here have been used to produce eggs for hatchery stock.

Quesnel: (Pop. 8,468). 119km north of Williams Lake, at the confluence of the Fraser and Quesnel rivers. Fur-trade explorer Alexander Mackenzie, seeking a route west to the Pacific Ocean, stopped here in 1793 on his way down the Fraser River. Counselled by the local Dakelh (Carrier) people to leave the river, he reluctantly set out overland on the Great Road tracing the Blackwater River, just northwest of here. The road he walked is now a 420km-or-so heritage trail – the **Nuxalk-Carrier Grease Trail** – tracing thousands of

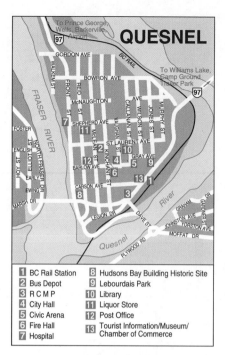

QUESNEL

To Prince George, Wells, Barkerville, Airport

To Williams Lake, Camp Ground Trailer Park

1	BC Rail Station	8	Hudsons Bay Building Historic Site
2	Bus Depot	9	Lebourdais Park
3	R C M P	10	Library
4	City Hall	11	Liquor Store
5	Civic Arena	12	Post Office
6	Fire Hall	13	Tourist Information/Museum/ Chamber of Commerce
7	Hospital		

years of history across the plateaus and the Coast Mountains (see below). Fifteen years later, explorer Simon Fraser, on his quest to reach the sea, also stopped here, but he chose to continue his journey down the river that now bears his name. This town takes its name from a member of his party, Jules Maurice Quesnelle.

Downtown Quesnel is bridge-dependent: it lies on a rounded piece of land held between the Fraser and a great curve of the Quesnel River. This is exactly the point where, in the late 1850s, gold rushers left the Fraser and headed east along muddy trails for Barkerville and Williams Creek.

Today Quesnel is a major lumber, pulp, commercial, and service centre for the north Cariboo. Quesnel is also the turnoff to one of the province's main attractions, the former ghost town of **Barkerville** (see p. 250).

Quesnel Information: Info Centre at south entrance to town opposite BC Rail station (at museum). Seasonal: extended hours May-Sept. 1-800-992-4922 or 250-992-8716.

■ **Gold Panning:** You can't pan or set up your sluice box in staked territory, but you can pick up a map at the Gold Commissioner's Office, Suite 102, 350 Barlow Ave, Quesnel, BC, V2J 2C1, or call 250-992-4301 to find some tiny corner that isn't staked. Or try your hand at panning in the Quesnel River where it joins the Fraser in Quesnel city limits; it's set aside for public hand panning.

■ **Quesnel and District Museum and Archives:** South end of town at **LeBourdais Park** (Hwy 97 and Carson Ave). 250-992-9580. Open year-round with extended hours May-Sept. Historic Cariboo: pioneers' artifacts and a rare collection of Chinese items. Discovery Place for children. LeBourdais Park has an outstanding rose garden (next to Pioneer Cemetery). Gift shop.

■ **Heritage Corner:** At Carson and Front streets, where Hwy 97 turns north for Prince George. Old Fraser bridge, built in 1929, is now a footbridge. New bridge was built in 1970. Remains of the steamer *Enterprise* from gold-rush days. Cornish waterwheel used in sluicing. Cairn commemorating the Overland Telegraph Line, which reached Quesnel in 1865, as part of a grandiose scheme to link North America and Europe via Asia. **Hudson's Bay Company Store**, a log building dating from 1882, is now the Heritage House Restaurant.

■ **Riverfront Trail Park:** Paved trail starts at Fraser River footbridge (Carson and Front streets), goes through the park, then along Quesnel River and past BC Rail yards. **Voyageur Canoe Trips** accessed from Riverfront Park. BC Wildlife Watch viewing site.

■ **Golf: Quesnel Golf Course**, on 6 Mile Rd, 5.5km west of Quesnel across Fraser Bridge; 250-249-5550; 18 holes. **Dragon Lake Golf Course**, 250-747-1358, nine-hole executive course.

■ **Nuxalk-Carrier Grease Trail (Alexander Mackenzie Heritage Trail):** Quesnel is base camp for arduous 420km trek tracing aboriginal route and explorer's footsteps across much of the width of BC. Trip is most often made from east to west, on horseback or by backpacking. Kilometre Zero is 60km northwest of

Quesnel. Take Nazko Rd (described below) to Bouchie Lake; turn right on Blackwater Rd, and continue to Blackwater Bridge. Park here at start of trail. For weekenders, there is a Forest Service campsite just north at Punchaw Lake. For seasoned hikers planning a long walk, the journey can be completed in about 18 days, but arrangements must be made with air charter companies to replenish supplies at least once along the route.

The trail follows the Blackwater River west for 222km, passing Euchiniko, Kluskus, Tsacha, Tsetzi, and Eliguk lakes. A 118km section leading to Hwy 20 then follows parts of the Dean River, Tanya Lakes, and the Mackenzie Valley, and passes the Rainbow Range into Tweedsmuir Provincial Park. The trail ends at Burnt Bridge on Hwy 20, which can be followed into Bella Coola, but the adventure ends at Sir Alexander Mackenzie Provincial Park in the Dean Channel northwest of Bella Coola, where Mackenzie painted a record of his feat on July 22, 1793.

The route crosses through or near 22 Dakelh (Carrier) reserves and hundreds of archaeological sites. It is wise, before starting out, to contact the administration offices of each of the following First Nations: Nazko, for km 0-82 (250-992-9085); Kluskus for km 82-201.5 (250-992-8186); Ulkatcho for km 201.5-347 (250-742-3260). For more details, *In the Steps of Alexander Mackenzie*, a step-by-step guide and maps by John Woodworth, is distributed by the Alexander Mackenzie Trail Association, Box 425, Stn A, Kelowna, BC, V1Y 7P1. Also look for *The Best of B.C. Natural Highs*, by Steve Short and Bernie Palmer. Ask at Quesnel Info Centre for directions to trailhead and exploring opportunities in the area.

There are several side trips from Quesnel leading west or south from West Quesnel over the Moffat Bridge. Cross the bridge from Hwy 97 (Front St). BC Ministry of Forests maps detail roads and campsites.

CIRCLE TRIP

to Bouchie Lake, Puntchesakut Lake, Nazko, Blackwater River, and the Grease Trail

Nazko Rd: Across Moffat Bridge, then north on Elliott St to Bouchie Lake and Nazko. Road forks at **Bouchie Lake**, 11km northwest of Quesnel. The **North fork**, Blackwater Rd, takes the circle counterclockwise. The **South fork**, Nazko Rd, runs clockwise. Either way, the circle trip from Bouchie Lake to Bouchie Lake is 217km. The direction chosen here is the **south fork**.

Puntchesakut Lake Provincial Park: 38ha. 27km west of Bouchie Lake on Nazko Rd. May-Oct. Picnicking, fishing, swimming, boat launch.

Nazko: Small community 58km west of Puntchesakut Lake, 85km west of Bouchie Lake, on the Nazko River.

Nazko River: From Nazko, road follows the Nazko River north 47km to a junction with the Blackwater River (also called the West Road River) and Blackwater Rd.

Nuxalk-Carrier Grease Trail: Access for day trips at several places along Nazko Rd, along the old Blackwater Rd connecting with Nazko Rd, or near Bella Coola (see p.254). Horseback riding, fishing, wildlife viewing, camping, snowshoeing, cross-country skiing.

Kluskoil Lake Provincial Park: 15,584ha; rustic campground. 250-398-4414. Extends west off Nazko Rd at the confluence of the Nazko and Blackwater rivers. Walk in the last 8km from road to park. Access point for Nuxalk-Carrier Grease Trail. Be respectful of privately owned cabins nearby.

Blackwater and Nazko Rds: 47km north of Nazko. Blackwater Rd travels east 19km to Boot Lake, then a final 66km east back to Bouchie Lake, passing Pantage Lake on the way back into Quesnel.

SIDE TRIP

to Pinnacles Provincial Park

Baker Dr: Depart Quesnel travelling west across Moffat Bridge, then north on Baker Dr to Pinnacles Park.

Pinnacles Provincial Park: 124ha. 8km west of Quesnel on Baker Dr. May-Oct. Unusual geological formations (pinnacles or hoodoos) made by glacial erosion and weather. Good viewpoint.

SIDE TRIP

on West Fraser Rd

West Fraser Rd: Depart Quesnel travelling west across Moffat Bridge, then south on Anderson Dr. Paved, then gravel road leads down west side of the river to Marguerite and Meldrum Creek, eventually connecting with Hwy 20 southwest of Williams Lake. For details on **Marguerite Ferry** and **Meldrum Creek Rd**, see above.

Return to Highway 97

Quesnel Forest Industry Observation Tower: 3km north of Quesnel on Hwy 97. Year-round. Observation Tower gives a bird's-eye view of "Two Mile Flat" industrial area: four lumber mills, two pulp mills, related activities. Tours of mills and harvesting areas can be arranged.

Barkerville Hwy (Hwy 26): 5km north of downtown Quesnel. East to Cottonwood House, Wells, the Bowron Lakes, and Barkerville Historic Town. Unofficially known as "the Gold Rush Trail."

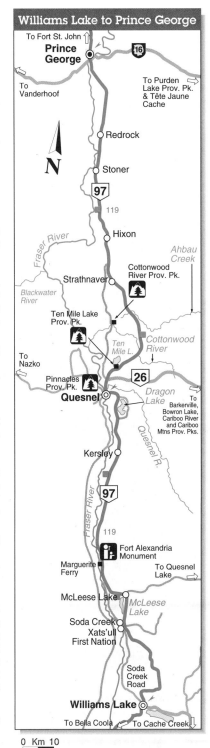

Williams Lake to Prince George

SIDE TRIP

to Barkerville

Area Information: Information centre at junction of Hwys 97 and 26. Mid-June to early Sept.

Cottonwood House Historic Park: 11ha. 28km east of Hwy 97 on Hwy 26. On the old Cariboo Wagon Rd. 250-

992-3997. Buildings open daily May-Sept. Grounds open year-round. Operated from 1874 to the 1950s by John and Janet Boyd and their children. Main house (from 1864), barns, sheds, animals, stagecoach ride. Excellent picnic site.

Blessing's Grave Historic Park: 1ha. 39km east of Hwy 97 on Hwy 26. (BC's smallest provincial historic site.) The melancholy tale is of Charles Morgan Blessing, from Ohio, lured to the Cariboo, like so many were, by gold. He wore a distinctive tiepin: a single gold nugget fashioned to the shape of a human head. In 1866, en route to Barkerville, he picked up two travelling companions. Delaney Moses, one of 600 black settlers to the new British colony, and a barber by trade, eventually went on ahead. Blessing's second companion, James Barry, arrived later in Barkerville, alone. Moses suspected foul play: the story is he noticed a prostitute wearing Blessing's tiepin, and asked where she got it. Moses alerted the authorities: Blessing was found, shot in the back of the head. He was only 30 years old. Barry was arrested, and later found guilty. Judge Matthew Baillie Begbie sentenced him to hang at Richfield. Moses, who took up a collection to give Blessing's grave a headstone, died in Barkerville. And there he was buried, in an unmarked grave.

Stanley Cemetery: About 65km east of Quesnel on Hwy 26, beside Stanley Rd, a short loop to the right. Historic grave markers from the gold-rush era, and the open pits of 36 former Chinese graves. The bones were dug up and shipped to China to find their final resting place in family plots. Relics of the ghost town of Stanley nearby.

Jack of Clubs Lake: Near outskirts of Wells. Rest area and picnic tables. Fishing and family boating on south side of Hwy 26. Some locals, concerned that the lake may contain either pollutants or a toxic concentration of minerals, are recommending the fish not be eaten. Others eat, heartily.

Wells: (Pop. 240). 80km east of Hwy 97 on Hwy 26. Dates from a gold rush, but not the Cariboo rush of the 1860s. In the 1930s, as depression set in and rumours abounded that the price of gold would soon rise, hundreds trekked to Wells. The Cariboo Gold Quartz Mining Co set up shop at the gold-bearing quartz vein found by Fred Wells. Then the company planned the town, and very carefully, so it would have staying power. According to Gordon R. Elliot, "The town was wheel shaped, with the hub on top of a knoll. Churches, banks, theatres, hospital, newspaper and recreation centres were located on the 'spokes' and 'rim.'"

The mining company continued operating until 1967, so Wells did become (and remained) a bright spot in dark days. Also integral to the community's development was the Island Mountain Mining Company. It closed 1967, too. Architecturally interesting, the wooden sidewalks, false-fronted stores, and romantic names recall an earlier era. The Wells Hotel, one of the first two buildings here,

1933-34 (the other was the hospital, now apartments), houses an impressive collection of archival photographs.

Wells/Barkerville Information: Contact Wells Museum, below, for brochures, maps and information. Also ask at local shops, such as Amazing Space Studio.

■ **Wells Museum:** On Pooley St (Wells' main street). Box 244, Wells, BC, V0K 2R0. 250-994-3422. Daily, 10-6, June-Sept.

■ **Island Mountain Gallery:** Pooley St. Features local and other BC artists.

■ **St George's Gallery:** Bowman Cr. In former Anglican church. 250-994-3492. June-Sept.

■ **Amazing Space Studio and Gallery:** Bowman Cr. In old Holy Rosary Catholic Church. 250-994-2332. June-Sept. By appointment in winter.

■ **Island Mountain Arts Summer School:** Late July to mid-Aug. 1-800-442-2787 or 250-994-3466. Celtic harp school in Aug. Public gallery, readings, concerts, coffeehouses.

Bowron Lakes Rd: North from Hwy 26, 6km east of Wells. Leads southeast to Cariboo Mountains and Cariboo River provincial parks; west to Bowron Lake Provincial Park.

Cariboo River Provincial Park: 3,211ha; no facilities. 250-398-4414. About 200m along Bowron Lakes Rd, turn onto logging road marked "3100." About 40km farther, road crosses the Cariboo River and transects park. Valley bottom wetlands and forests area an important winter range for moose.

Cariboo Mountains Provincial Park (Ghost Lake): 113,469ha; rustic camping only. Via "3100" logging road, about 67km from Bowron Lakes Rd. Watch for sign: turn left onto 2.5km road, cross the bridge, turn right up the hill, 0.5km to campground. This is the only easy road access to park linking Bowron Lake and Wells Gray provincial parks, creating 760,000ha of protected wilderness incorporating old-growth spruce, cedar and hemlock forest, steep valleys, rugged mountains, glaciers, and habitat for grizzlies, caribou, and moose. At Ghost Lake: hiking, canoeing, and fishing.

Bowron Lake Provincial Park: 123,117ha; 25 vehicle/tent campsites, 103 wilderness campsites. 32km from Wells; 28km north from Hwy 26 turnoff via Bowron Lakes Rd. 250-398-4414. One of the best canoe circuits in the province, 116km long, with portages between the six major lakes and other waterways in the chain. Trails, patrol cabins, and cooking shelters. Wildlife sanctuary. Allow a week or more for full canoe circuit; one- to four- day trips on west side. Moose, deer, caribou, mountain goats, grizzly bears, beavers. Reservations mandatory for groups of more than six, and advised for groups of six and fewer: 1-800-689-9025; from Lower Mainland or overseas, 604-689-9025. Accommodation, equipment and canoe rentals at Bowron Lake. Information available from BC Parks at 281 First Ave N, Williams Lake, BC, V2G 1Y7.

Bowron Lake Registration Centre: At park headquarters. May 15-Sept 30.

Barkerville Historic Town: 2km southeast of turnoff to Bowron Lake Park, 8km from Wells, and 88km from Hwy 97. Box 19, Barkerville, BC, V0K 1B0. 250-994-3332. Daily, year-round, historic programs mid-June to Labour Day.

This restored gold-rush town from the 1860s is one of BC's premiere attractions – well worth the side trip off Hwy 97. One could easily spend a full day here. In its prime, Barkerville seemed on its way to becoming the largest city west of Chicago and north of San Francisco. But the gold rush fizzled and Barkerville died. For about 75 years it was a ghost town.

Restoration of this significant site began in 1958. Today, there are more than 40 restored pre-1900 structures and a well-preserved cemetery. Businesses operate as they might have 120 years ago: bakery, restaurant, merchants, photographer, print shop. Also gold panning and Chinese restaurant. Events include excellent performances in historic costume at the **Theatre Royal** and 1860s-style Dominion Day celebrations. Off-season: slide shows at administration building. Cross-country ski trail from Barkerville's main street to Richfield, the gold-rush ghost town where the courthouse is located.

Barkerville Provincial Park: 55ha; 168 campsites at three campgrounds (reservations taken: call 1-800-689-9025; from the Lower Mainland or overseas, call 604-689-9025). Sani-station, showers. Adjacent historic town. 250-398-4414.

Return to Highway 97

Ten Mile Lake Provincial Park: 260ha; 141 campsites (reservations taken: call 1-800-689-9025; from the Lower Mainland or overseas, call 604-689-9025). 11km north of Quesnel. General info: 250-398-4414. Developed beach, boat ramp, hiking trails, cross-country ski trails, snowshoeing, ice fishing, interpretive programs.

Hush Lake Rest Area: 25km north of Quesnel. Boat launch.

Cottonwood River Provincial Park: 68ha; 15 campsites. 29km north of Quesnel on old **Prince George Rd**. (Left off Hwy 97 just past drive-in theatre on northern outskirts of Quesnel.) 250-398-4414. Fishing, picnicking, in quiet setting.

Strathnaver: (Pop. 21). 43km north of Quesnel, at Naver Creek. **Old Prince George Rd** returns to Hwy 97 here.

Hixon: (Pop. 191). 56.5km north of Quesnel. Tourist facilities.

Viewpoint: 62km north of Quesnel. About halfway up (down) the hill. Excellent view westward into infinity, over the tops of millions of spruce trees.

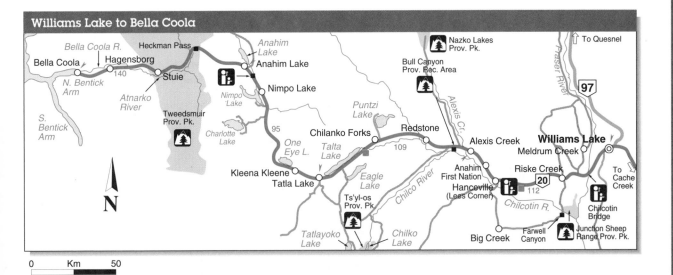

Bella Coola R. Heckman Pass Anahim Lake Nazko Lakes Prov. Pk. To Quesnel
Bella Coola Hagensborg Anahim Lake Bull Canyon Prov. Rec. Area
140 Stuie Nimpo Lake
N. Bentick Arm Atnarko River Nimpo Lake Puntzi Lake 97
S. Bentick Arm Tweedsmuir Prov. Pk. Charlotte Lake 95 Chilanko Forks Redstone Alexis Creek Williams Lake Meldrum Creek
One Eye L. Talta Lake 109 Riske Creek To Cache Creek
N Kleena Kleene Tatla Lake Eagle Lake Anahim First Nation 20 112
Ts'yl-os Prov. Pk. Chilco River Hanceville (Lees Corner) Chilcotin Bridge
Tatlayoko Lake Chilko Lake Big Creek Farwell Canyon Junction Sheep Range Prov. Pk.
Chilcotin R.
0 Km 50

Woodpecker Rest Area: 64.5km beyond Quesnel. Named for Woodpecker Landing, a sternwheeler dock once nearby.

Stoner: 76km beyond Quesnel. Small community.

Red Rock: About 88km beyond Quesnel. Another small community.

Prince George: (Pop. 75, 150) 119km beyond Quesnel. For details, see *Northern BC* p.263.

WILLIAMS LAKE TO BELLA COOLA

BELLA COOLA ROAD (Highway 20)

Highway 20 traverses the Chilcotin Plateau and the Coast Mountains from the Cariboo Hwy to the head of a Pacific Ocean fiord. This Bella Coola Rd – the Freedom Road – begins at Williams Lake, at Hwy 97, and runs west 456km to Bella Coola.

It is only relatively recently – 1953 – that the two ends of the road finally met. For years there was a 60km gap in the road, that wild section through the towering Coast Mountains. In 1950, tired of waiting for an unenthusiastic government that felt that the feat couldn't be done, or at least not without an outpouring of millions, settlers on both sides of the gap took matters into their own capable hands. In three backbreaking years, they completed the road themselves. They called it the Freedom Road because, at last, Bella Coolans could drive from their homes to the outside world, and the outside world could visit them.

Today Hwy 20 is still a challenge. More than half is paved now: all the way from Williams Lake to Tatla Lake; and two other portions, between Nimpo Lake and Anahim Lake, and east from Bella Coola into Tweedsmuir Provincial Park near Park

Headquarters. The rest is gravel. And then there's the Big Hill. Well, this is not a road for speed demons.

The eastern starting point of Hwy 20 is Williams Lake: turn west at the traffic lights just south of town. Note that you won't see another set of traffic lights from here to Bella Coola. The Chilcotin is the last western frontier for the pioneer rancher: limitations on freedom of movement are scarce. There are rolling vistas of plateau backed by long, fish-filled lakes. In the rugged Coast Mountains, where horses outnumber cars, it seems rules are things to be ignored. One of the earliest European imports was, in fact, the horse, and herds of wild horses, obeying no man's rules, still roam the Chilcotin.

The Tsilhqot'in people who give this region its name have long lived between the Fraser River and the Coast Mountains, trading with neighbouring Secwepemc, Dakelh (Carrier), and Nuxalk (Bella Coola) peoples.

In the history of BC, the Tsilhqot'in people distinguish themselves as having been strongly resistant to intrusion into their territories. They tolerated the presence of a Hudson's Bay Company fort at the forks of the Chilko and Chilanko rivers between 1829 and 1844. But in a series of events sometimes referred to now as the Chilcotin War, 1862-1864, they kept road developers from turning their ancient trails into a highway to Cariboo gold fields. For more see p. 253.

Just after this time, the first cattle ranchers trickled in, but the only non-native settlements to this day are the tiny unincorporated villages of Alexis Creek and Ahahim Lake named for Tsilhqot'in leaders of the previous century. Names of other wee settlements on Hwy 20 derive from early traders and shopkeepers: Tom Hance (Hanceville Post Office); L. W. Riskie, who shipped bacon and butter to Barkerville (Riske Creek); Norman Lee (Lees Corner).

The Tsilhqot'in people continue to protect their traditional territories and livelihood. In the early 1990s, the Xeni Gwet'in people of Nemiah, south of Hwy 20, were joined by their non-native neighbours in an effort to stop the unchecked logging of their traplines and

fishing grounds. That resulted in the creation of Ts'yl-os Provincial Park, where the Xeni Gwet'in continue to live as closely as possible to the old ways. Visitors are welcome to enjoy the land and its scenery.

Chilcotin back roads and trails crisscross the central Chilcotin and are the only access to many of area's most interesting places. However, roads are gravel or dirt, some challenging. Rain can turn roads to quagmires: check locally before setting out.

Williams Lake: (Pop. 10,472). At junction of Hwys 97 and 20. For details, see *Cache Creek to Williams Lake*, p.247.

Big Bar Rd: 2km beyond Williams Lake turn south off Hwy 20 for Dog Creek and Gang Ranch (70km). For details, see *Cache Creek to Williams Lake*, p.244.

Upper Fraser River Canyon: For the first 24km the road climbs sharply, then drops just as sharply into the upper Fraser Canyon. Use this section to test brakes and engine.

Viewpoint: 24.5km from Williams Lake, north of highway. Views of upper Fraser Canyon.

Chilcotin Bridge: Just beyond the viewpoint, 25km from Williams Lake, the highway crosses the Fraser River 500km from its mouth at the Fraser Delta.

Chilcotin Country: From the bridge, another long climb to the Chilcotin (or Fraser) Plateau. Boulder-strewn plains, distant snowy mountains, ranches, one-blink towns (blink and you miss it), crumbling log cabins, and the best general stores you'll ever find. Up on the plateau, watch for a flash of brilliant blue. That will be a bluebird. Nesting boxes are nailed to fence posts along the road. The birds eat crop-threatening grasshoppers.

Meldrum Creek Rd (or West Side Rd): 33.5km beyond Williams Lake. Gravel road leads north to Quesnel, travelling on the west side of the Fraser River. Details in *Williams Lake to Prince George*, p.248.

Loran C. Tower: 35km west of Williams Lake, north of highway. With others in Alaska and Washington, this huge tower is part of a long-range marine navigation system that can locate precise positions within a 4,000km range. Tours possible: 250-659-5611.

Farwell Canyon Rd: 44.5km beyond Williams Lake, south of highway on a 95km loop via Farwell Canyon, Big Creek, and Hanceville. Back to Hwy 20 at Hanceville/Lees Corner (46km west of Farwell Canyon Rd junction). Road is suitable for 4x4s only: can be slick when wet.

SIDE TRIP

to Farwell Canyon

Junction Sheep Range Provincial Park: 4,573ha; no facilities. Triangular plot at confluence of Chilcotin and Fraser rivers, 15km south of Hwy 20. Protects the habitat of some 100 California bighorn sheep. In the early 1900s, there were only 2,000 bighorns left in North America; today, thanks to a long-term (begun in 1954) transplant program from healthy herds here, there are more than 9,000 of these spectacular animals alive and well in most of the historic ranges of the continent.

There are more than 40 species of butterflies in the protected area. And Lewis woodpeckers and other cavity-nesting birds attracted by the giant snags. Black bears feast on rose hips and berries. Rubber boas come out after dark and enjoy lying on the warm road. They're gentle creatures. Drive carefully.

Farwell Canyon: 19km from Hwy 20 junction, road crosses the Chilcotin River at Farwell Canyon. A spectacular bridge over a spectacular canyon. The Chilcotin River cuts deeply through golden clay and limestone cliffs, forming groves of hoodoos on the rock walls. Active sand dune at top of cliffs changes form with wind currents. Early rock paintings can be seen on the overhang, south of the bridge. Under the bridge are fish ladders. Summer and fall, Tsilhqot'in fishermen dip-net from riverbanks, then rack salmon in the sun to dry.

River rafting, hiking trails. These are so-called badlands: note sagebrush, rabbit brush, and prickly pear cactus. Sit carefully.

Big Creek: Small settlement 41km west of Farwell Canyon. Along this side trip, Farwell Canyon Rd loops over the Chilcotin River twice, and Big Creek once. There are trout in the creeks, steelhead in the river. In fall, sockeye return, heading for Chilko Lake. Logging roads lead south from the community of Big Creek, tracing Big Creek south to northern reaches of **Big Creek Provincial Park**, a 65,982ha an undeveloped preserve for grizzly bears, bighorn sheep, and moose. Access is difficult; no signs or facilities.

Hanceville: (Pop. 68). 35km from Big Creek, just beyond second Chilcotin River bridge, near return to Hwy 20. Signs name the small community Hanceville, but it's always been called Lees Corner (see below). Hanceville was the post office at Tom Hance's (the "TH") ranch. Hance also had a trading post on the site as early as 1869. Certainly an historic settlement, once the area's largest.

Return to Highway 20

Riske Creek: (Pop. 181). 46.5km west of Williams Lake, 2km west of Farwell Canyon Rd junction. Farming in this open country may well be risky, but the name is for L.W. Riskie, a Polish farmer here in the 1870s. Drop in at the Riske Creek General Store.

Chilko Lake is the jewel of Ts'yl-os Provincial Park.

Point of Interest and Lees Corner Rest Area: 82km west of Williams Lake, south side of highway. Panoramic views over Chilcotin country, with first glimpses of Coast Mountains to the west. Plaque describes Norman Lee's ill-fated cattle drive to Dawson City in 1889. At least he survived, and set up shop at what is still known as Lees Corner.

Lees Corner (Hanceville): 90.5km west of Williams Lake, 44km west of Riske Creek. Site of historic Norman Lee Ranch (established 1893) and long-lived general store. Norman Lee himself ran the store until 1939. The current building is the fourth Lees Corner general store since opening day more than a century ago. Help yourself to an ever-ready Chilcotin coffee. The general store is truly general: post office, snack bar, laundromat, liquor store, rooms, fishing licences, cases of canned peas, and books on how to build a log cabin.

Chilcotin Lakes: Back roads from Lees Corner lead to a variety of lakes large and small; many are fishermen's favourites. Smaller lakes are often at ends of rough side roads, impassable except by 4x4 vehicles. The road to Nemiah leads south more than 100km to **Ts'yl-os Provincial Park**. The route is not well marked. Maps of roads and campgrounds are

available at local tourist offices or Ministry of Forests offices at 100 Mile House, Clinton, Quesnel, or Alexis Creek.

Ts'yl-os Provincial Park: 233,240ha; two campgrounds at Chilko Lake. 250-398-4414. Park can be reached from Hanceville on the Nemiah Valley Rd or from Tatla Lake on the Tatlayoko/Chilko Lake Rd (see p.253). A vast undeveloped wilderness the size of Prince Edward Island, embracing Chilko and Taseko lakes and the rivers where one-quarter of the Fraser River's salmon are born. Most of the park has been zoned for wilderness recreation.

Parklands, once threatened by logging, are within the traditional territories of the Xeni Gwet'in, or Nemiah people, of the Tsilhqot'in First Nation. The park takes its name from the mountain known to the Tsilhqot'in as Ts'yl-os (Mt Tatlow, 3,066m). Their stories say the mountain, once a man with a wife and six children, watches over the people, and when necessary, intervenes. A four- to six-day hiking trail leads through Yohetta Valley, Spectrum Pass, and Tchaikazan Valley. The Xeni Gwet'in offer round-trip boat shuttles to one of the trail's main access points.

Chilcotin Whitewater: Rafters, kayakers, and canoeists consider these rivers among the continent's best. Highest rated for rafters: the Chilko's Lava Canyon; for canoeists and kayakers, stretches of the Chilcotin and Taseko rivers. Check with local outfitters for info, rentals, and tours.

Taseko Lake Rd: South at Lees Corner, then southwest toward **Taseko Lake** and **Nemiah Valley** after crossing the Chilcotin River. Southeast fork is Farwell Canyon Rd, described above. Road from Lees Corner to **Konni Lake**, 100km, is all-weather gravel. Beyond this, the road continues to **Chilko Lake**, but is suitable only for 4x4 vehicles.

Chilko Lake stretches a spectacular 90km along a Coast Mountain valley; its blue glacier-fed waters are an important spawning area for sockeye, pink, and chinook salmon. The **Chilko River**, flowing out toward the Fraser, is a major river rafting destination. Many resorts, guest ranches, guiding operations in the area.

Chilko Lake can also be accessed from Tatla Lake (see p.253).

Anaham: (Pop. 750). 98km west of Williams Lake. This Tsilhqot'in community (not to be confused with Anahim Lake, below) is named for a prominent leader here in the 1860s. Community's Tsilhqot'in name is Tl'etinqox. Ask at band office for local guide-outfitters. 250-394-4212.

Alexis Creek: (Pop. 243). 112km west of Williams Lake, 21.5km west of Lees Corner. Service centre for eastern Chilcotin. Accommodation, Red Cross outpost hospital, RCMP station, gas, groceries, post office. BC Forest Service office is a good source of info.

Nazko Lakes Provincial Park: 7,919ha; rustic campgrounds at Loomis and Deerpelt lakes. 250-398-4414. Just west of

Alexis Creek, turn onto Alexis Lakes Forest Service Rd; 45km to road to Nazko Lake Canoe Route; 5km (past Loomis Lake) to road on left leading to Deerpelt Lake, staging area for canoe route. Short portages for three- to four-day canoe expeditions.

Bull Canyon Provincial Park: 123ha; 20 campsites. 250-398-4414. 9km west of Alexis Creek. Scenic spot by Chilcotin River, sheer rocks, caves. Site of an historic battle between the Tsilhqot'in and Secwepemc peoples. More recently a cattle round-up point.

Redstone: (Pop. 190). 54.5km west of Alexis Creek. Tsilhqot'in settlement also sometimes called Alexis Creek, not to be confused with non-native settlement, above. Alexis was a leader during the Chilcotin War. Winter cold spot: to -50 C.

Puntzi Lake Rd: 60.5km west of Alexis Creek. Road leads north 7km to Puntzi Lake. Stocked with trout and kokanee. White pelicans now feed and rest on the lake. Many lakeside resorts, campgrounds. Hiking, riding. Fishing derby last weekend in June.

Chilanko Forks: (Pop. 123). On Hwy 20, about 1km west of Puntzi Lake Rd junction, 61.5km west of Alexis Creek. Well-stocked traditional general store with accommodation, post office, crafts.

Chilanko Forks Wildlife Management Area: From Chilanko Forks take road to the airport. The marsh is on the south side of the road. View waterfowl, muskrats, and beavers.

Polywog Rest Area: 35.5km beyond Chilanko Forks, 97km west of Alexis Creek. Duck nesting ground.

Tatla Lake: (Pop. 52). 109km beyond Alexis Creek, 221km from Williams Lake. Considered a rough halfway mark on Hwy 20. Stop in at the Graham Inn, have a coffee and some homemade pie, and discuss the matter. This is the western edge of the Chilcotin Plateau, and a taking-off point for wilderness fly-ins, fishing/diving charters, and cross-country ski trails. Old buildings, home-style food, accommodation.

Tatla Lake Information: In West Chilcotin Trading. 250-476-1111. Maps, brochures, sani-dump, auto repairs, gas, dry goods, bank machine, ice cream.

Tatlayoko/Chilko Lake Rd: South at Tatla Lake for Tatlayoko Lake. Bear southwest at road fork for Horn and Bluff lakes; keep left at fork, 35km to Tatlayoko. Small community in dry-belt ranching country; basic services. Private campground. Turn right at Tatlayoko community hall for lake beyond town, in Coast Mountains. The Homathko River runs into Tatlayoko Lake, then drains directly into the salt water of Bute Inlet, only 80km away. The valley sits in the Coast Mountains, with distant views of Mt Waddington, at 4,016m the highest peak total-

ly within BC. This is also western access to Ts'yl-os Provincial Park: for **Chilko Lake**, go east at Tatlayoko community hall, past **Choelquoit Lake**, then south 25km along road, to Chilko River bridge. Just before the bridge, turn south, keeping to west side of Chilko River; Chilko Lake is 20km farther on. For **Tsuniah Lake**, cross the Chilko River bridge and follow signs to lake (20km).

Many ranches, resorts, and lodges. Local trail operators take visitors through the mountains to fishing lakes, ancient native sites, caves, fossils, and wildlife viewing (mountain goats, grizzlies, cougars). Also cross-country and alpine skiing in winter.

Ranger Station: On Hwy 20, at outskirts of Tatla Lake, marks beginning of the climb into the Coast Mountains. Open ranching country is replaced by pine forest and scattered lakes. Sadly, the lodgepole pines here have fallen prey to the pine beetle. Forest is pockmarked with red and black dying and dead trees.

Kleena Kleene: (Pop. 92). 31km west of Tatla Lake. "One-honk" settlement, post office, and general store. In the language of the coastal Kwakwaka'wakw people the name refers to eulachon grease. Near here, the eulachon-rich **Klinaklini River** flows into **One Eye Lake**. Wilderness and fly-in fishing resorts take visitors to truly remote spots.

Charlotte Lake Rd: 65.5km beyond Tatla Lake, leads southwest some 15km to Charlotte Lake. Big rainbow trout. Resort accommodation.

Nimpo Lake South Rd: 71km west of Tatla Lake. To Nimpo Lake's south end.

Nimpo Lake: (Pop. 164). 76.5km west of Tatla Lake. Scenic 12km lake, with Mt Kappan in background, is the "floatplane capital of BC" and centre for air charters to remote fly-in fishing spots. General store, motels, campgrounds. Resorts on the lake.

■ **Note: Highway is paved between Nimpo Lake and Anahim Lake!**

Chilcotin War: 81.5m west of Tatla Lake. Historic site marker. During the gold rush, in 1861, Victoria entrepreneur Alfred Waddington set about to build a road from Bute Inlet to Quesnel, crossing through territories of the Tsilhqot'in people. Fearing for their lands, terrified by the threat of smallpox, having endured hunger and mistreatment by white newcomers, a handful of Tsilhqot'in warriors, in the spring of 1864, undertook a series of attacks that left dead 18 road builders and packers, and the only white settler in Tsilhqot'in territories. This place marks the site of the final event in which three men and one woman were killed. The colonial governor dispatched troops, and Chief Alexis persuaded the war chief Lha tses'in to meet authorities for "peace talks." Five men, including Lha tses'in, were immediately arrested, then executed. The road was never finished. In 1993, more than a century later, a justice inquiry recommended

that the Tsilhqot'in who were executed be granted a posthumous pardon and be honoured with a memorial.

Waddington himself died in 1872 of smallpox, the white man's disease that had killed so many Tsilhqot'in.

Anahim Lake: (Pop. 522). 95km west of Tatla Lake, 316km west of Williams Lake. Largest settlement in the west Chilcotin. Expanded in the 1940s and 1950s, when Dakelh (Carrier) Ulkatcho native peoples gradually left remote villages and moved to town. The Anahim Lake Stampede happens here each July, a major social event and showcase for talent. Free coffee in the general store. Full tourist services; centre for outfitting, guides.

Anahim Lake Airport: Paved airport across highway from general store. Daily flights to Bella Coola and Vancouver. Fly-in charters to popular Dean River fishery.

Lessard Lake Rd: North at Anahim Lake, goes 18km to Lessard Lake and points north. Check road conditions first. Good gravel for 32km along Dean River (famed for its downstream steelhead fishery); fair gravel for another 32km. Only 4x4 vehicles or hiking beyond. Visible to the northeast: Far Mountain in the Itcha Ilgachuz Range, now embraced by the 109,063ha roadless wilderness of **Itcha Ilgachuz Provincial Park**. Popular with hikers, campers, snowmobilers, and cross-country skiers, the park protects critical foraging grounds for caribou, bighorn sheep, and grizzlies.

Farther north, running east to west, is the Nuxalk-Carrier Grease Trail (see p.248) and access to Southern Carrier (Dakelh) village sites, Iluak and Ulkatcho, no longer occupied.

Rainbow Range: About 30km from Anahim Lake, multicoloured 2,500m peaks are visible from several pullouts on north side of Hwy 20. Heavily dissected shield volcanoes, like Hawaiian peaks but with different vegetation; bare rock bluffs and scree slopes brightly coloured by purple, red, and yellow mineralization. Accessible by hiking and horseback trails.

Coast Mountains: From 30km west of Anahim Lake all the way to Bella Coola. The highway climbs steadily, then drops to the Pacific fiord. Steep-sided valleys, rugged peaks with icefields and glaciers.

Tweedsmuir Provincial Park and Recreation Area: 994, 246ha; 35 campsites; sani-station. 250-398-4414. Write BC Parks, 281 First Ave N, Williams Lake, BC, V2G 1Y7. 36km west of Anahim Lake, 352km west of Williams Lake. Hwy 20 enters BC's second largest provincial park. (It was BC's largest until Northern BC's 4.4 million-hectare **Muskwa-Kechika Special Management Area** was set aside in 1997; Tweedsmuir remains, however, the largest *contiguous* tract of parkland in the province). The highway transects the narrowing southern wedge of the park for 54km. **Park Headquarters are 28km west of the park's east entrance.** Although Hwy 20 through the park is open year-round, campgrounds and picnic areas close after the first snowfall. The park was established in 1938, and named for Baron Tweedsmuir of Elsfield, then Governor-General of Canada. Tweedsmuir is a wilderness park: bring suitable clothing, equipment, supplies, and maps. Exercise caution along the Dean and Atnarko rivers as bears frequent the park.

Bella Coola Rd Summit/Heckman Pass: Just beyond park entrance. Highway clears Heckman Pass, 1,524m.

Rainbow Range Trailhead and Picnic Ground: 6km west of east entrance, 42km west of Anahim, north side of highway. On East Branch Creek. Trails lead 20km to Rainbow Range. Snowmobile-designated area (not permitted elsewhere).

Descent to Valley – The Big Hill: Descent starts about 7km from east entrance, continues for 19km. Steepest part of the 1,400m descent is known as "The Hill." The road was finally completed in 1953, not by the government, but by locals themselves. (A plaque marked the spot where two bulldozers met – one from the east, one from the west – to complete the last link. The plaque was stolen, but the Bella Coola Valley Museum has a replica.) Bella Coolans had conquered a double rise and fall. Heading west, the road climbs to 1,600m, then drops to 1,000m at Young Creek, climbs back up to 1,300m, then makes its final precarious descent to 300m and the beginning of the Bella Coola Valley.

Young Creek Picnic Site: 26km west of east entrance, south side of highway. At the bottom of The Hill. No facilities.

Upper Atnarko Valley: From Young Creek picnic site, 4x4 tote road and trails head south along spectacular Upper Atnarko Valley. Hike to Hunlen Falls 29km from picnic site, one of the highest single-drop waterfalls in Canada (260m) with an overall cascade series of 366m. Falls are at start of Turner Lakes chain, unique subalpine canoe route above Atnarko Valley; wilderness resort and fishing. High alpine hiking on Ptarmigan Trail and Panorama Ridge above lakes. Lonesome Lake is 30km from picnic site; Monarch Icefield is 70km. In 1912, Ralph Edwards endured a harsh climate and isolation to create a homestead and farm in dense forest on the east side of Lonesome Lake. Members of his family still occupy the farm, where trumpeter swans winter. Contact John Edwards at Box 308, Bella Coola, BC, V0T 1C0. Edwards' story was made famous through the best-seller *Crusoe of Lonesome Lake*, by Leland Stowe.

Atnarko River Campground: 24 sites; sani-station. 1.5km west of Young Creek picnic site, 27.5km from east entrance. May-Oct.

Tweedsmuir Provincial Park Headquarters: 0.5km west of campground, 28km from park's east entrance (26km from park's west entrance). 250-398-4414. RV sani-station. Open May-Oct. Not staffed full-time.

Big Rock: 11km west of park headquarters, 39km from east entrance. Picnic site.

Stuie: Little settlement on the Atnarko River, 14km west of park headquarters, 42km from east entrance. Or, as locals put it, 16km west of the bottom of The Hill. Atnarko in Dakelh language means "river of strangers." The strangers were the coast natives, and here is the historic meeting place of coast and Interior peoples. Unexcavated smokehouse, burial grounds, pictographs.

■ **Tweedsmuir Lodge:** Established as the Stuie Lodge by nature lover Tommy Walker who, early this century, left a parade of "bowler hats bobbing across London Bridge" for the wilds of BC. He was instrumental in the creation of Tweedsmuir Park, announced in 1937 by Britain's Lord Tweedsmuir (for whom the historic lodge was also renamed). Tweedsmuir Lodge, rebuilt after a fire in 1950, continues to draw guests from around the world. It has become more of an ecotourism outpost than a hunting lodge, however, offering hiking, wildlife viewing, and fishing. It's not uncommon to see grizzly bears on the front lawn. Reservations: 250-982-2402.

Fisheries Pool: 16km west of park headquarters, 44km from east entrance. 14-site campground, boat launch, and picnic site.

Burnt Bridge: 26km west of park headquarters, at **Tweedsmuir Park West Entrance.** Picnic site south side of highway. Cairn commemorates federal-provincial agreement on the Mackenzie Grease Trail, or Nuxalk-Carrier Grease Trail (see below). Scenic hiking trail loop (one to two hours) leads north, offering a view of **Stupendous Mountain**. At 2,677m it is one of several massive mountains visible south of the highway. Mackenzie wrote: "Before us appeared a stupendous mountain, whose snow-capped summit was lost in clouds."

Tweedsmuir Provincial Park West Entrance: 26km west of park headquarters, 54km from east entrance, 90km west of Anahim. Or 51km east of Bella Coola.

Nuxalk-Carrier Grease Trail: Access from Burnt Bridge. For details on entire trail, see p.248. Trail descends from the north along Alexander Mackenzie's route on his historic trip in 1793. From here, the trail follows the Bella Coola Valley.

Summer Trail: 10.5km beyond park's west entrance, 40km east of Bella Coola. North from Hwy 20, one of several grease trails used up until the 20th century.

Hagensborg: (Pop. 1,217). 32km beyond west entrance to park, 18.5km east of Bella Coola. Non-native settlement of Bella Coola Valley began here in 1894, when Norwegians, attracted by the familiar settings of the fiords, moved here from their first settlements in Minnesota. Original settlement here centred around Hagen Christensen's store, hence the name. Today the square-timbered,

hand-adzed log barns and houses, as well as place names and surnames, reflect Norwegian heritage. About 1,000 descendants remain in the area.

Bella Coola Airstrip: At Hagensborg. Chilcotin and Vancouver flights.

Acwsalcta (Nuxalk Nation School): On the highway, just west of Hagensborg. This magnificent school, called Acwsalcta, "the place of learning," was built by the Nuxalk Nation.

Snootli Creek Hatchery: 4km beyond Hagensborg, 14.5km from Bella Coola. Established to enhance runs of chum and chinook salmon in the Bella Coola River system.

Thorsen Creek Petroglyphs: 10km beyond Hagensborg, 8km east of Bella Coola. A large petroglyph site, with more than 100 rock paintings. Ask at Bella Coola for a guide to the site.

Bella Coola: (Pop. 992). Hwy 20 ends here 456km west of Williams Lake. Bella Coola, the major port between Vancouver Island and Prince Rupert, and terminus of BC Ferries Discovery Coast Passage, sits at the head of North Bentinck Arm, an inlet of the Pacific.

The Nuxalk (or Bella Coola) aboriginal people who live here were visited in 1793 by British captain George Vancouver, who arrived by sea. A few weeks later, Alexander Mackenzie walked in on the Great Road. Nothing remains of the Hudson's Bay Company post established here in 1869. Now the Nuxalk share the valley with the descendants of Norwegian settlers who arrived in 1894, and later settlers seduced by the beauty of mountains and glaciers, the productivity of the valley and the sea, and the solitude of surrounding wilderness.

For years, Bella Coola was linked to the world beyond only by horse trail and by sea. It wasn't until 1953 that the Freedom Road was pushed through the Chilcotin. So completely did Bella Coolans adopt land travel that passenger service by sea was halted; the maiden voyage of BC Ferries' *Queen of Chilliwack* in 1996 was the first scheduled passenger run in some 20 years.

Beyond town are the docks where fishboats ride the milky turquoise waters of the Bella Coola River as it spills into the sea. Its waterfront offers an interesting collection of fishing boats, pleasure boats, sportfishing charters, cannery sites, tidal flats, log-storing facilities. Bella Coola offers a full range of tourist facilities. It also provides access to a wide world of maritime excitement (see *Side Trips to Coastal Points*, below).

Bella Coola Information: Information centre, Box 670, Bella Coola, BC, V0T 1C0. June-Sept. In Bella Coola Valley Museum. 1-888-863-1181 or 250-799-5767. Nuxalk "goodwill ambassador" Darren Edgar is often on hand to greet visitors.

■ **Bella Coola Valley Museum:** Town centre, in schoolhouse and surveyor's cabin dating from 1800s. Items brought from Norway by early settlers, Hudson's Bay Company relics. June-Sept.

■ **Eulachon Fishery:** In April, along the riverbank right in Bella Coola, visitors can witness the traditional harvest of these tiny, silvery smelt. They are prized by the Nuxalk for their arrival early in the season, after the long fast of winter, and for their oil or "grease," a favorite traditional source of nutrition, and an important trade commodity.

■ **Charters:** To Fiordland and Hakai provincial recreation areas. See Bella Bella, below, and ask at information centre.

SIDE TRIPS

to Coastal Points

The coastline is quiet and unpopulated, the domain of humpback whales and porpoises. The protected waters of the inside passage and these long fiords were once home to dozens of villages of Oweekeno, Heiltsuk, and Nuxalk First Nation peoples. In the last century, there were fur traders, and up until a few decades ago, canneries, floating logging camps, homesteaders. Mechanization and centralization took most of the newcomers away, leaving the coast again mostly to the original, aboriginal, inhabitants.

This spectacular archipelago melding land and sea is now being billed as an adventure getaway, offering comfortable lodges, luxury resorts and vessels, good meals, and fishing. There is sea kayaking, diving, wildlife viewing, and petroglyphs. Places with exotic names – Ocean Falls, Shearwater, Klemtu, Namu, Fiordland – can be reached by air or boat charter from Bella Coola. There is also BC Ferries **Discovery Coast Passage,** running from late May-September. Along the route, travellers can disembark to make short shoreside excursions: these may be as short as the one to four hours the ship is in port, or as long as you choose.

Tourist operators at Port Hardy, Shearwater, Klemtu, Ocean Falls, and Bella Coola offer two- to seven-day packages that include accommodation, food, and recreational activities. There is also a special cradle aboard the ferry that enables the crew to lower kayaks and paddlers into the water at any safe point en route, and pick them up at requested stops.

Many travellers make the round trip by ferry between Port Hardy and Bella Coola, others take their cars to Bella Coola and continue their journey overland from here. There are no staterooms for overnight passengers, but there are reclining chairs, and you can rent pillows and blankets. Hardy types are welcome to pitch their tents out on the bridge deck. You can get information and make shoreside reservations through BC Ferries, 1112 Fort St, Victoria, BC, V8V 4V2. 1-888-223-3779 (from within BC) or 250-386-3431.

Sir Alexander Mackenzie Provincial Park and Mackenzie Rock: 5ha. 60km west of Bella Coola on Dean Channel. No road access: ask at Info Centre about transportation. Western terminus of Alexander Mackenzie's voyage to the Pacific in 1793, and terminus of choice to many dedicated modern voyageurs, determined to finish the Nuxalk-Carrier Trail, who are flown in or come by boat charter from the trail's end at Bella Coola.

Bella Coola is at the end, or the beginning, of the road.

Alexander Mackenzie was brought here by the Nuxalk people, and this is the spot where, in Mackenzie's words, he "mixed some vermilion in melted grease, and inscribed in large characters on the south-east face of the rock on which we had slept last night, this brief memorial: **'Alexander Mackenzie, from Canada, by land, the twenty-second of July, one thousand, seven hundred and ninety-three.'"** The words have since been engraved into the rock.

Ocean Falls: (Pop. 160). Northwest of Bella Coola, at the head of Cousins Inlet. Former thriving pulp-mill town, almost abandoned after mill closure. Now it's a base for fishing and hunting, and is considered one of the few unspoiled spots on the globe: dolphins in the sea, eagles in the air. There's homemade soup and espresso-flake ice cream at Bernie Bashan's floating cafe.

Bella Bella (Waglisla): (Pop. 1,211). On Campbell Island, across Fitz Hugh Sound from Bella Coola. The contemporary headquarters of the Heiltsuk First Nation is often called Bella Bella, although its Heiltsuk name is Waglisla. In 1993 this was the setting for the first major gathering of coastal First Nations in more than a century. *Qatuwas,* "people gathered together in one place," drew some 3,000 people from 30 First Nations (nearly half of them arrived in canoes) and inspired a cultural revival in communities up and down the coast.

While hospitable, the Heiltsuk people are cautious of opening their doors too wide, too soon, to an influx of tourists, and for the time being, the band council has decided to restrict tourist activities to McLoughlin Bay, just south of the village. It may also be possible to visit the **Heiltsuk Cultural Education Centre.** For more information about these sites, and Heiltsuk charter operators, contact the band administration office.

Heiltsuk Information: Heiltsuk Band Administration, Box 880, Waglisla, BC, V0T 1Z0. 250-957-2381.

■ **McLoughlin Bay:** 3km south of Waglisla. During the fur-trade era, the Heiltsuk people coalesced around Fort McLoughlin, a Hudson's Bay Company fort open from 1833 to 1843.

After the turn of the century, the Heiltsuk made their new centre at Waglisla. Small longhouse and fish-packing plant. Possible tours.

Shearwater: (Pop. 50). Opposite Bella Bella, on Denny Island. In the Second World War, the Royal Canadian Air Force based flying boats here, patrolling the coast and watching for Japanese submarines. Today, there's a marina, restaurant, hotel, pub, charter fishing business, and ship and repair yard, the largest such facility between Port Hardy and Prince Rupert.

Klemtu: (Pop. 500). North of Bella Bella, on the east coast of Swindle Island. Home of the Kitasoo people of the Tsimshian First Nation. Moorage facilities, some accommodation, groceries, and post office.

Klemtu Information: General Delivery, Klemtu, BC, V0T 1L0. 250-839-1255.

Fiordland Recreation Area: 91,000ha embracing Mussel and Kynoch inlets, northeast of Klemtu. About four hours by boat north of Bella Bella. No development. Info from BC Parks in Williams Lake. 250-398-4414. Magnificent oceanscapes in one of the most scenic areas of the Pacific coast.

Hakai Recreation Area: 122,998ha straddling Hunter and Calvert islands. Four hours by boat south of Bella Bella. No road access. Accommodation. Info from BC Parks in Williams Lake. 250-398-4414. Myriad islands surrounding some of the world's finest salmon fishing.

Rivers Inlet: Southeast of Bella Bella, and east of Hakai Provincial Recreation Area. In traditional territories of the Oweekeno First Nation. Inlet is named for Baron Rivers, 18th-century English writer and politician, characterized by Horace Walpole as "brutal and half-mad." Captain George Vancouver must have been running out of good names by the time he reached the inlet: Baron Rivers was a relation of a midshipman in his crew. About 12 salmon canneries were located here in the days before refrigeration. Now there are fly-in fishing lodges – the inlet is a famed saltwater fishing locale with record-breaking tyee to 36kg. Spring salmon, steelhead, scenery, reefs, coves, sea life. Logging operations along the inlet have clearcut a lot of the scenery.

Great Bear Rainforest: Taking in BC's central coast from the northern reaches of Vancouver Island to Bella Bella; including Fiordland Recreation Areas and Kitlope Heritage Conservancy. An intense focal point for the divergent interests of environmentalists, timber companies, the government, and aboriginal peoples. Some are calling it the "last buffalo." Perhaps *the* evnironmental hotspot as we enter a new millennium. Do we log its old-growth rainforests? Or preserve them for the great grizzly bears that still roam here; the salmon that still return to unscathed rivers; the tourists shocked by clearcuts; and the residents who want it all – a livelihood now, and in the future?

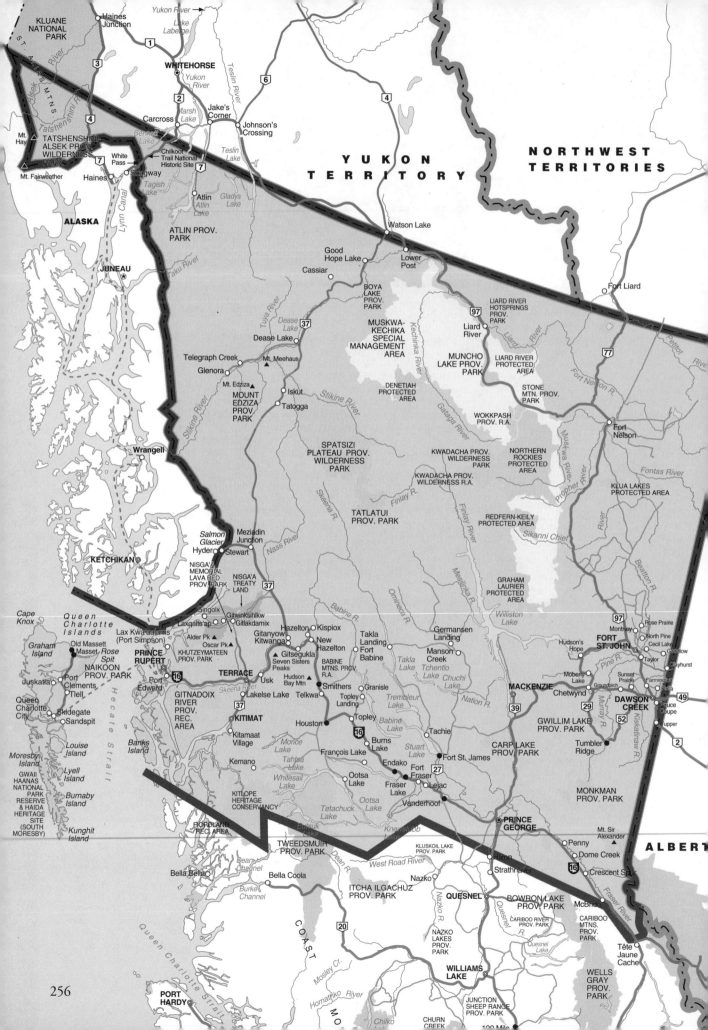

NORTHERN BRITISH COLUMBIA
ENDLESS LANDSCAPES, ROOM TO ROAM

For those who live in the southern parts of this province — i.e. most British Columbians — the thought of heading North is often accompanied by a frisson of excitement, perhaps even fear. Just tracing the region's features on a map can bring to mind a stampede of images: mile after mile of highway, desolation, wildness.

There's the sheer size of the North. Just look at it. The region comprises more than half the entire province — about 500,000 square kilometres. It is larger than California or Japan, twice the size of the United Kingdom. Its northern border, tracing the 60th degree of latitude, stretches more than 1,000 kilometres from Alberta to Alaska.

There is the mystique of the North: its remoteness, its dangerous vitality, its extremes of climate, terrain, and animal life. In the larger scheme of things, people and their works are barely discernible: where industrial man has dared to make his mark it is with the most mega of mega projects: giant dams, giant mines, giant highways. Despite, and because of these extremes, human travel is surprisingly possible in the North. Three main highways and many smaller ones knit together daunting distances. Half a dozen cities press up against its southern and eastern edges. And its inhabitants are a special breed. True northerners may be famous for their independence and self-sufficiency, but they surely know how to put out the welcome mat.

Flying over the North, one suspects there must be many countries here: an empire of lakes and rivers, a biological treasure trove of offshore islands, range after mighty range of mountains, astonishing swaths of rolling prairie. There are countries here with distinct geologies, animals and plants, and human cultures. To make better sense of this prodigious expanse, it's helpful to encounter it in three stages — first the coastal section including the Queen Charlotte Islands (known to its original inhabitants as Haida Gwaii), then the mountainous interior and, finally, the Peace River valley east of the Rocky Mountains.

Boreal forests, like this, near Lower Post at the BC/Yukon border, blanket the north.

The ragged, stormy archipelago, Haida Gwaii, its rocky scarps coated with cedar, hemlock, and spruce, is one of the world's marvels. To paddle or sail its shores is, for many, the dream of a lifetime. Scientists postulate, during the last ice age, which ended 9-13,000 years ago, these islands were not completely glaciated and hence, became an ecological refuge: rare species and subspecies, including the world's largest black bear, several birds and small mammals, and dozens of plants and invertebrates, still thrive in this Canadian Galapagos.

In the language of the archipelago's first human inhabitants, Haida means "the people," Gwaii means "islands," or "homeland." Their vibrant arts and history reflect their tenure here, and are in themselves a draw for visitors from around the world. Many Haida sites are protected in the 1,470-square-kilometre Gwaii Haanas National Park Reserve on south Moresby Island. Pre-eminent among them is Anthony Island (Sgung Gwaii) near the reserve's south tip, where a haunting assemblage of weathered poles marks former Red Cod Island Village, or Ninstints, protected since 1981 as a UNESCO world heritage site.

Across Hecate Strait from Haida Gwaii is the mainland, traditional territory of Tsimshian, Nisga'a, and Haisla First Nations. Fishermen and ferry captains skirt the huge, sparsely inhabited islands that buffer this stretch of coast, to converge on Prince Rupert, Canada's main north Pacific port. Born in 1906, when it was chosen as the Grand Trunk Pacific railway terminus, the port today marks the end of both VIA Rail (Grand Trunk's successor) and the Yellowhead Highway, which parallels the tracks for much of its length. Khutzeymateen Grizzly Bear Sanctuary, Canada's only grizzly bear reserve, lies northeast of Prince Rupert. To the southeast, the industrial town of Kitimat, producer of paper, methanol and aluminum, co-exists with Kitlope Heritage Conservancy, protecting the largest intact coastal temperate rainforest in the world.

The Yellowhead Highway (Highway 16) bisects BC, running from Haida Gwaii to the Alberta border near Yellowhead Pass, a distance of 1,075 kilometres. The North's only major east-west vehicle route, it links many of the region's smaller centres — like Smithers, with its fertile farms and ranches, and the logging towns of Terrace, Houston, Burns Lake, and Vanderhoof — tying them to Prince George in central BC, the province's northern capital and fourth most populous city with 77,000 inhabitants. A City in the Wild: the BC Government has recently set aside 250,000 hectares of nearby wilderness as protected areas.

The Yellowhead traces some of the North's principal rivers: the upper Fraser and the Skeena, and their respective tributaries, the Nechako and Bulkley rivers. Farther north, the Nass and Stikine power their way through the Skeena and Coast mountains to the Pacific, with the Stikine passing through a spectacular 90-kilometre Grand Canyon, home to intrepid mountain goats. In BC's northwest corner, a new wilderness park in the St Elias Mountains protects two of the continent's wildest rivers: the Alsek and Tatshenshini. Meanwhile, much of northeastern

At the Gitxsan village of Kispiox, Weeping Woman mourns her brother's death during a famine.

BC is drained by other important river systems, those of the Liard and the Peace, which flow east and north and eventually into the Arctic Ocean.

The Yellowhead hugs the relatively hospitable southern reaches of the vast North, shielding its network of towns and homesteads from the wild like a shepherd protecting his flock from wolves. And the far northern hinterland bordered by the Yellowhead, Stewart-Cassiar, and Alaska highways is wolf territory, certainly. Grizzly, moose, bighorn sheep and caribou territory, too. In the Omineca and Cassiar mountains, on Spatsizi Plateau and throughout Muskwa-Kechika, a recently designated, 4.4-million-hectare park and special management zone in the northern Rockies, large predators pursue large prey through a wilderness so prolific it is known as the Serengeti of the North.

It was the furs of the region's animals that attracted the first European traders to the North, two centuries ago now, to trade with the Dakelh (Carrier) people in north-central BC and the Dunne-za (Beaver), Sekani, Saulteux, Dene-thah (Slave), and Cree peoples in the northeast. Explorers Alexander Mackenzie and Simon Fraser helped establish fur-trading posts in the area; one in particular, Fort St James, has been reconstructed as an his-

toric park. Rare minerals drew other early visitors to the North. Once-vital gold-fever boom towns such as Atlin and Telegraph Creek now serve as difficult-to-reach hamlets of history. At Hazelton's 'Ksan museum, by contrast, and at Kispiox village, travellers will encounter the living culture of the Gitxsan, "people of the river of mists."

The foothills, prairies, and forested plateaus of the northeast have more in common with Alberta than with BC. The Peace River, impeded by two enormous hydroelectric dams, flows through one of Canada's most productive grain-growing regions. The farming town of Dawson Creek is Mile 0 of the amazing 2,400-kilometre Alaska Highway, built as a supply route during the Second World War. This now-paved swath carries travellers through the least-known corner of the province — a land of stunning mountain scenery, sudden hot springs and wildlife viewing around every turn — for the adventure of their lives. The adventures continue, as the Alaska Highway crosses from BC into the Yukon Territory: a modern-day route to the Klondike.

Heading North is indeed an audacious act. It's a chance to connect with an unmarred realm of geographic wonder and to reawaken the daring in one's own spirit.

INFORMATION

Northern British Columbia Tourism Association: Box 1030, #11-3167 Tatlow Rd, Smithers, BC, V0J 2N0. 250-847-5227 or 1-800-663-8843. Fax: 250-847-4321. E-mail: info@northernbctourism.bc.ca. Fort St John office: 250-785-2544. Addresses and telephone numbers of local information centres are in the *Log* with write-ups on each of the communities.

TRANSPORTATION

Northern BC is served by major and local airlines, railways, car and passenger ferries, and bus lines. There is also an extensive and well-maintained system of paved and secondary roads. Access to the vast hinterlands is usually by air. Northerners take to bush planes and helicopters the way southerners jump in a truck. That's why it's not difficult to find aircraft available for charter in the smallest whistle stops.

Roads

Most visitors drive into this vast region. Prince George is very much a gateway. Highways 16 and 97 intersect here, less than 800km from Edmonton, Calgary, or Vancouver. Residents think nothing of driving this distance in a day. It's an easy two-day drive for vacationers. The main access route from the east is the Yellowhead Hwy (Hwy 16).

Visitors from southern BC and the US can travel Hwy 5 to its intersection with the Yellowhead near Tête Jaune Cache, or via Hwys 1 and 97 to Prince George.

"Doing" the Alaska Hwy is an irresistible draw for urban pioneers worldwide. The highway is paved now, but distances are great, northern weather is unpredictable, and common sense should accompany every driver: little things like keeping the gas topped up, carrying serviceable spare tires, keeping headlights on at all times when driving, and remembering to turn them off when parked. Service stations aren't plentiful, but most stay open year-round.

Winter driving requires more preparation. Roads are well maintained, but vehicle and driver should be in good condition to adjust to rapidly changing driving conditions. Obviously the vehicle must have good winter tread tires and be thoroughly winterized with a block heater. Don't take anything for granted. Remember, this isn't downtown. It's wise to stow an emergency kit of items like first-aid supplies, shovel, axe, matches, candles, emergency food, spare clothes, and sleeping bag. Chances are good it won't be needed. But if it is, it could save your own or someone else's life.

The highway is always going to be under repair and reconstruction. Obey signs. Don't be afraid of gravel sections, but don't use them as speedways.

The Stewart-Cassiar Hwy (Hwys 37 and 37A) is the newest and shortest route to Alaska. It begins at the Yellowhead Hwy near Kitwanga, 243km east of Prince Rupert, and joins the Alaska Hwy 23km west of Watson Lake in the Yukon. The road is paved for 597km of its 721km length.

In addition to Hwy 37, there are four highways crossing from BC into the Yukon. The Alaska Hwy, crosses the border near Watson Lake; the Atlin Road (Hwy 7) leads 96km south to Atlin, BC. The South Klondike Hwy (Hwy 2) crosses a corner of BC to link the Yukon and Skagway, Alaska. The Haines Hwy, a 256km mainly paved road connects Haines, Alaska, a port on the ferry system, with Haines Junction in the Yukon. These highways offer breathtaking passage north, but drivers should be prepared. In winter, northbound and southbound travellers on both highways should check road conditions before leaving. These are heavy snowfall areas, and services are scant. International border stations are open 24 hours a day. Identification is required.

Hundreds of logging roads are open to the public unless otherwise posted. Of course, there are no gas stations on them, and some are not suitable for large RVs. They are built for industrial traffic, and care should be taken. Follow an empty logging truck: the driver can radio your location to other truckers. Or travel weekends, when most logging ceases. Check information centres, or Forest Service offices for exceptions.

Where are We?

Sometimes when driving the Alaska Highway it's hard to tell exactly where you are. The original wooden mileposts were traded in for kilometre posts, but because the highway has been improved and shortened since then, they no longer always reflect the true distances between points. Your *Travel Guide* has done its best to provide accurate distances.

Historic ties confuse the matter further. Towns are often referred to by their original milepost numbers. To many, Fort Nelson will forever be Mile 300.

In 1992, BC, the Yukon, and Alaska cooperated in an historic milepost project to commemorate the highway's 50th anniversary. They identified 183 sites with historic mileposts where significant construction-related events occurred. Some sites also have a sign, and 38 of the most important ones have an interpretive panel. These historic posts use original highway mileage, but may not have been restored in the exact location.

Sour Gas

The Peace River region is BC's oil patch. Oil and natural gas wells are in production, and exploration for new finds continues. Activity stretches from the Monkman area south of Tumbler Ridge into the Interior plains near Fort Nelson. At a few well sites, the danger of hydrogen sulphide gas exists. These sites are identified by signs, and warnings must be heeded. High-level exposure to the "rotten egg" smell of hydrogen sulphide gas can kill. For further information call the Ministry of Environment, Lands, and Parks in Fort St John, 250-787-3411.

Bus Lines

■ **Alaskan Express:** 403-668-3225. Whitehorse to Skagway.

■ **Farwest Bus Lines:** 250-624-6400 or 250-632-3333. Charter service between Prince Rupert, Terrace, and Kitimat.

■ **Greyhound Bus Lines:** Vancouver, 1-800-661-8747, or specific communities. Coaches stop daily at all communities along the Yellowhead Hwy from the Alberta border to Prince Rupert, Highway 97, and the Alaska Hwy.

■ **Northland Buslines:** 250-996-8421. Weekday service between Fort St James and Prince George.

■ **Peace Coaches Inc:** 250-785-5945 in Fort St John. Daily service between Fort St John, Hudson's Hope, and Chetwynd.

■ **Seaport Limousine:** 250-636-2622. Weekday service, Stewart to Terrace.

Six cities in the region operate transit services. For information call Prince George, 250-563-0011; Prince Rupert, 250-624-6400; Terrace, 250-635-2666; Kitimat, 250-632-3333; Dawson Creek, 250-782 4630; and Fort St John, 250-787-7433

Car and RV Rentals

Rental agencies are at airports and downtown locations. Some RV rentals. Check information centres for leads. Taxis available in all but the smallest communities. Phone early.

Railways

■ **BC Rail:** 1-800-663-8238 from within BC, 1-800-339-8752 from outside BC. Northern passenger terminus is Prince George. Leaves North Vancouver for Prince George Sun-Wed-Fri mornings, a leisurely 13-hour (745km) trip.

■ **VIA Rail:** Booked through travel agents, or by calling 1-800-561-8630 from Western Canada. The *Skeena* provides year-round service to communities across north-central BC. It runs 1,160km along Canadian National Railways lines from Jasper, Alberta, in the Rocky Mountains, to Prince Rupert.

Travelling only in daytime, it stops overnight in Prince George. Passengers should reserve summer accommodation as much as the winter before, especially in Jasper. The journey is about 19 hours – seven from Jasper to Prince George, 12 more to Prince Rupert. Trains leave Jasper at 1pm Mountain Time and Prince Rupert at 8am Pacific Time. They arrive in Prince George on Sun, Wed, and Fri evenings, and depart the next morning. In addition to coach class, a first-class service is offered May 15-Oct 15. Connections with BC Rail's passenger service to North Vancouver.

■ **White Pass and Yukon Route:** 1-800-343-7373 or 907-983-2217. This is a privately owned narrow-gauge (36") railway, built in 1898 to accommodate gold rushers, linking Skagway, Alaska, on the coast, with the Interior. Reservations required for summer-only service. Summit excursion (Skagway to Canadian border and return); Skagway to Whitehorse excursion; and Chilkoot Trail hikers shuttle.

Airlines

The largest airports are in Prince George, Smithers, Terrace-Kitimat, Prince Rupert, and Sandspit. All offer daily flights to and from Vancouver.

■ **Air BC:** 1-800-663-3721. Connects Prince George, Prince Rupert, Dawson Creek, Fort St John, and Vancouver with other Interior communities.

■ **Air North:** 867-668-2228. Scheduled and charter flights throughout the Yukon, Northwest Territories, Alaska.

■ **Alkan Air:** 867-668-2107. Charter service from Whitehorse to northern and Interior BC, and the far north.

■ **Alpine Aviation Ltd:** 867-668-7725. Northern charters.

■ **Canadian Airlines International:** 1-800-665-1177, or centres listed above. From Prince Rupert, Fort St John, and Whitehorse, to Vancouver.

■ **Canadian Regional Airlines:** 1-800-665-1177 or regionally in Sandspit, Prince Rupert, Smithers, Prince George Fort St John, and Fort Nelson.

■ **Canada 3000:** Call travel agents. Vancouver to Whitehorse and Anchorage.

■ **Central Mountain Air:** 1-800-663-3721. Serves Prince George, Smithers, Dawson Creek, Vancouver, Edmonton, and small communities in the northwest.

■ **Era Aviation:** 1-800-866-8394. Scheduled, Whitehorse to Anchorage.

■ **Harbour Air:** 250-627-1341 or 1-800-689-4234. Service to Port Simpson, Masset, Sandspit, Queen Charlotte City, Hartley Bay, Kitkatla, Gingolx (Kincolith), Laxqalts'ap (Greenville), Hunts Inlet, Oona River, Humpback Bay, and Porcher Island. Also flightseeing and charter service. Tours to Ketchikan, Alaska, Khutzeymateen Valley, and Haida Gwaii.

■ **Inland Air:** 250-624-2577. To Gingolx (Kincolith), Kitkatla, Port Simpson, Hartley Bay, ice fields, grizzly bears, and other destinations by reservation.

■ **Northern Thunderbird Air Ltd:** Prince George, 250-963-9611 or Mackenzie, 250-997-3247. Scheduled service between Prince George and Mackenzie, Quesnel, Williams Lake, Kamloops, Kelowna, Vancouver, Chetwynd, and points on Williston Lake.

■ **South Moresby Air Charters:** 250-559-4222. Tours to Gwaii Haanas area.

■ **Tutchone Air Inc:** 867-667-2488. Fly-in gold-mine tour in the Salmon River Valley. Day-long, week-long, cabin, meals, fishing, and hiking. Mid-May to Sept.

This is bush-plane country. Charter flights by fixed-wing plane and helicopter readily available. Most communities and some isolated work camps and resorts have small airstrips. Landings on grass, gravel, or water. Check with information centres. Local sporting-goods stores often provide leads.

Ferries

■ **BC Ferries:** In BC: 1-888-223-3779. In Victoria and outside BC, 250-386-3431. **Prince Rupert** is northern terminus for Inside Passage route from **Port Hardy** on Vancouver Island. *Queen of the North* runs year-round. 491km, 15 hrs. In winter, one sailing a week. In summer, ship leaves Port Hardy one day, Prince Rupert the next. Vehicle and cabin reservations essential.

Also reserve early for service between **Prince Rupert** and **Skidegate** on Graham Island in Haida Gwaii (the Queen Charlottes). 172km, eight hrs. Up to six sailings a week in summer, three in winter.

MV *Kwuna* connects Skidegate Landing to Alliford Bay on Moresby Island. 12 sailings a day, year-round, 20 minutes.

■ **The Alaska Marine Highway System:** 1-800-642-0066 from the US and Canada; in Canada, 907-465-3941. Or write Alaska Marine Highway System, 1591 Glacier Ave, Juneau, AK, USA, 99801. Prince Rupert is southern terminus of the Alaska Marine Highway System. Ferries call at Alaskan Panhandle communities and terminate in Skagway, 789km north of Prince Rupert. 36-hour trip. Vehicle reservations required.

Ferry leaves **Hyder**, Alaska weekly on Tues, June to mid-Sept, for **Ketchikan**. Hyder shares head of Portland Canal with Stewart, BC.

Inland Ferries

BC's transportation and highways ministry operates free car-and-passenger ferries to complement the road network.

■ **François Lake to Southbank:** Hwy 35, 29km south of Burns Lake. 20 daily sailings aboard MV *Omineca Princess*, 25-minute turnaround. 32 cars.

■ **Hwy 16 to Usk across Skeena:** 20km east of Terrace. On demand. Five minutes, two vehicles. Cable car only, in winter.

Stone's sheep are often encountered along northern BC's highways.

NORTHERN BRITISH COLUMBIA EVENTS

Atlin
- **Tarahne Day:** Aug, 1st Mon.
- **Bathtub Races:** July.

Burns Lake
- **Eagle Creek Stampede:** Early June.
- **Bluegrass Festival:** Early July.
- **Tweedsmuir Park Days:** Early July.

Chetwynd
- **Annual Rodeo:** April.
- **Moberly Lake Music Festival:** Early July.
- **Moberly Lake Bathtub Races:** Early Aug.
- **Pine Valley Country Days:** Aug/Sept. Fall Fair.

Dawson Creek
- **Mile Zero Celebrations:** Late May.
- **Summer Solstice:** June 21.
- **Fall Fair and Stampede:** Mid-Aug.
- **Downtown Light Up:** Late Nov.

Fort Nelson
- **Welcome Visitor Program:** June-July.
- **Rodeo:** Aug.
- **Canadian Open Dogsled Races:** Dec.

Fort St James
- **Al Baxter Memorial Rodeo:** Early Aug.

Fort St John
- **North Peace Rodeo:** Early July.

Fraser Lake
- **Mouse Mountain Days:** July 1st weekend.

Granisle
- **Granisle Days:** Mid-June.
- **Fishing Derby:** Early Aug.

Hazelton
- **Pioneer Day:** Early Aug.

Houston
- **Pleasant Valley Days:** May long weekend. Horse show, loggers' sports, rodeo, chuckwagon races.

Hudson's Hope
- **Rodeo and Parade:** Early June.

Kispiox
- **Kispiox Valley Rodeo:** Early June.
- **Kispiox Music Festival:** Late July.

Kitimat
- **July 1 Celebrations:** Parade, food festival, hill climb.

Mackenzie
- **Winter Carnival:** Feb.
- **Childrens Festival:** June.

McBride
- **Dunster Ice Cream Social:** July 1.

Manson Creek
- **Gold Rush Days:** July.

Pouce Coupe
- **Pouce Coupe Parade and Barbecue:** July 1.

Prince George
- **Canadian Northern Childrens Festival:** May.
- **Prince George Rodeo:** June.
- **Prince George Airshow:** Late July.
- **Sandblast:** Mid-Aug.
- **Prince George Exhibition:** Aug.

Prince Rupert
- **Sea Fest and Indian Cultural Days:** June, 2nd weekend.
- **Seashore Fishing Derby:** Early Aug.

Queen Charlotte City
- **Hospital Days:** Late June. Taking place for the better part of a century.

Skagway
- **Trail of '98 Sled Dog Race:** Late Jan. Three days along White Pass & Yukon Route line.
- **Buckwheat Ski Classic:** Late March. International event following the gold seekers route.
- **Windfest:** Late March. Marking spring's arrival.
- **Mini Folk Festival:** Late April.
- **Independence Day, Ducky Derby, Soapy Smith's Wake:** July 4 week. Soapy Smith rode at the head of the first parade, in 1898. Also softball tournament.
- **Klondike Road Relay:** Early Sept. 110km relay from Skagway to Whitehorse.
- **Yuletide Weekend:** Dec.

Skidegate
- **Singaay Laa Day:** Early June.

Smithers
- **Mid-summer Festival:** June.
- **Bulkley Valley Exhibition:** Late Aug.
- **Telkwa Barbecue:** Labour Day Weekend.

Stewart
- **Stewart/Hyder International Rodeo:** Early June.
- **Stewart/Hyder International Days:** July 1-4. Canada/US birthday celebrations.

Taylor
- **World Invitational Gold Panning Championships and Raft Race:** Aug, BC Day weekend.

Terrace
- **Riverboat Days:** Early Aug.
- **Skeena Valley Fall Fair:** Late Aug.

Treaty 8 Communities
- **Treaty Days Celebrations:** During the summer, several Treaty 8 First Nations communities, including West Moberly Lake, Saulteux, and Fort Nelson, host a weekend-long event drawing friends, relatives, and visitors from afar to honour the treaty's spirit and intent, and to feast, dance, and play traditional games. For more information see *Logs*, or call the Treaty 8 Tribal Association in Fort St John, 250-785-0612.

Tumbler Ridge
- **Tumbler Ridge Days:** 3rd weekend Aug. Fair and rodeo.
- **Grizzly Valley Days:** Aug.

Vanderhoof
- **Bull-A-Rama:** April. Bull riding championships.
- **Nechako Valley Summer School of the Arts:** July 24-Aug 5. Day- and week-long art courses. Box 1438, Vanderhoof, BC, V0J 3A0. 250-567-3030.

Watson Lake
- **Snowmobile Race:** Mid-Feb.

Whitehorse
- **Yukon Quest Dogsled Race:** Mid-Feb. 1,600km from Fairbanks, Alaska to Whitehorse.
- **Frostbite Music Fest:** Feb.
- **Yukon Sourdough Rendezvous:** Late Feb.
- **Yukon International Storytelling Festival:** Early to mid-June. Four days of tales spun by storytellers from around the world — a feast for the imagination.
- **Goldrush Bathtub Race:** Aug.

From the dark rainforest of Graham Island, the vibrant Haida culture emerged.

NORTHERN BRITISH COLUMBIA ROUTES AND HIGHLIGHTS

TRAVELLER'S LOGS

HIGHLIGHTS

PRINCE GEORGE

PRINCE GEORGE

BC'S NORTHERN CAPITAL

Prince George: (Pop. 75,150). Situated midway on Hwy 97, a 2,260km north-south artery connecting Osoyoos on the US border with Lower Post bordering the Yukon. Also roughly midpoint on the 1,073km Yellowhead Hwy (Hwy 16) connecting Prince Rupert on the central west coast with Jasper National Park on the BC/Alberta border. Prince George is 786km northeast of Vancouver. Two major transprovincial railways, BC Rail (south/north), and VIA Rail (east/west), intersect here as well.

Here, just 91km east of the province's geographical centre, two of BC's most important rivers converge. Prince George's downtown core has grown up in the bowl formed between the Nechako River gliding down from the west and the larger Fraser River flowing from the Rockies. The flat-bottomed basin was once the bed of a lake during the glacial period. Distinctive cutbanks have emerged from that evolutionary tumble. Sandy cliffs topped with evergreens enwrap the north shore of the Nechako and the east flank of the Fraser. The cutbanks contribute to the city's character.

For hundreds, even thousands, of years, native peoples – represented today by the Lheidli T'enneh Nation – have used the lands where the two rivers meet. The first Europeans arrived in June 1793. Alexander Mackenzie and his men, canoeing southward on the Fraser in early morning mists, didn't notice the outpouring of the Nechako. He left it to Simon Fraser, 14 years later, to recognize this important river junction and name it Fort George after King George III. Fraser actually wintered over in the area, 1807-08, and built the tiny outpost at the confluence of the rivers. With the arrival of spring, he embarked on his famous journey down the river now bearing his name.

Fort George remained little more than a trading post until a century later when the Grand Trunk Pacific Railway found, through the Fraser and Nechako valleys, a feasible route for its line to Prince Rupert on the coast (now part of the CNR system). A wild wave of speculation accompanied the line's completion in 1914, and Prince George was officially incorporated in 1915. The First World War brought this period of growth sharply to an end, and for two decades Prince George became a sleepy hollow again.

However, another destiny awaited the city so pivotally situated. Completion of the John Hart Hwy between Prince George and Dawson Creek in 1952 opened access to the Yukon. The same year, the Pacific Great Eastern (now BC Rail) finally extended its line from Quesnel to Prince George. (It reached the Peace River in 1958 and Fort Nelson in 1970.)

Then there was a big change in the forest industry. In the '40s and '50s, about 600 tiny portable "gypo" sawmills occupied the surrounding forests, producing rough-cut white spruce for lumber. Better use of the trees changed the economy and the city forever. Pulp was the factor. Lumber mills could turn their leftovers into pulp, and that could be converted into paper products. In 1964, Prince George Pulp and Paper's $80-million mill was started. It was followed by Northwood Pulp and Timber, and Intercontinental Pulp, and together the three mills triggered a population boom. Prince George exploded from a comfortable little place of 14,000 people in 1961 to 50,000 in 1971. It is now the province's fifth largest city (if the cities of Greater Vancouver are counted as one).

Prince George is no longer a rough-and-ready lumber town. At the heart of Canada's largest softwood lumber producing area, the city is home to some of the most sophisticated and efficient sawmills in the world. Silvicultural techniques to reestablish trees on logged areas and ways of managing forest lands for non-timber values have been pioneered here and continue to evolve.

Paralleling its industrial development, Prince George is emerging as a cosmopolitan city with everything visitors require. It has more art galleries than pulp mills, more municipal parks than warehouses. There is, of course, a daily newspaper, the *Prince George Citizen*. For all its government, service, distribution, and transportation functions, Prince George plays a corresponding role in offering cultural, entertainment, recreational, and educational opportunities for visitor and resident alike.

The new University of Northern British Columbia's main campus sits on Cranbrook Hill, overlooking the city. Canada's first autonomous university in more than two decades opened in 1994. The university's structure is based on programs of First Nations, environmental, international, northern, and women's studies. UNBC's impact has brought an influx of people with different talents and fresh dreams. The university's presence has helped spur downtown rejuvenation with construction of the new 1,880-seat **Prince George Civic Centre Complex** at 7th and Dominion, and a domed courthouse. New homes, shopping and recreational facilities, and cappuccino shops have sprung up throughout the city.

And yet just an hour's drive in any direction from the city are lakes and rivers where the harried traveller will only have to share space with loons, and the occasional moose.

Prince George Information: Tourism Prince George, 1198 Victoria St, Prince George, BC, V2L 2L2. Year-round. 250-562-3700. A seasonal Info Centre is located at Hwys 16/97 junction. May-Sept. 250-563-5493 or 1-800-668-7646.

Prince George Airport: 10km southeast of downtown Prince George. Take Hwy 97 south across Fraser Bridge. At Sintich Rd turn left, follow signs for 5km.

■ **Heritage River Trail System:** Peace and seclusion fringing downtown. Starts at Cameron St Bridge. Some 10km along Fraser and Nechako rivers, with viewpoints and signed nature trails. Check Info Centres or City Hall (250-561-7633) for details.

■ **Forests for the World Park:** 106ha. Atop Cranbrook Hill, an escarpment lying west of the city. The largest of the city's 117 parks, affording expansive views and containing a small lake with beavers and waterfowl. There are nature walks, hiking and cross-country skiing trails through mixed hardwood and softwood forests. Learn about forest management techniques, and plant tree seedlings in an unusual "Leave Your Roots in Prince George" program. BC Wildlife Watch viewing site.

■ **Cottonwood Island Nature Park:** 32ha. Off River Rd 2km northeast of downtown Prince George. A peaceful wooded sanctuary with trails skirting the Nechako River, close to junction of Fraser. Bring a bird identification book. BC Wildlife Watch viewing site.

■ **Prince George Railway and Forestry Museum:** 850 River Rd, adjacent Cottonwood Island Nature Park. 250-563-7351. Thurs-Mon, May-Sept. Steam Days twice each season. Revives the days of steam, including history of Grand Trunk Pacific Railway (now CNR) and Pacific Great Eastern (now BCR). On site: section house, 1914 Penny Station, Yalenka bunkhouse, BC Tel Pioneers building, and heritage fire hall. Rolling stock includes 1913 CPR working steam crane and 1903 Russell snow plow.

■ **Fort George Park:** At the end of 20th Ave, running between 17th and 20th, and overlooking the Fraser. Site of small outpost built by Simon Fraser for the North West Company in 1807. Now a popular picnic and meeting spot. Summer rides on a narrow-gauge steam locomotive, Canada's smallest official railway. Weekends and holidays, May-Sept. Nearly 1ha of the park is the ancestral burial ground for local Lheidli T'enneh First Nation.

■ **Fraser-Fort George Regional Museum:** In Fort George Park. 250-562-1612. History Hall, hands-on science centre, changing exhibits. Museum shop, archives. Daily, 10-5, summer; closed Mon, off-season.

■ **Connaught Hill Park:** Off Queensway on Connaught Dr. A plug of land rising above city hall, 360-degree views. Shady trees, flower gardens, and fresh air where downtowners come to "brown bag it."

■ **Prince George Art Gallery:** 2820-15th Ave. 250-563-6447. (Plans for new location adjacent civic centre complex at 7th and Dominion.) Daily in summer; off-season closed Mon. Regular exhibitions of local, regional, and provincial artists and craftspeople. Travelling exhibits or thematic displays.

■ **Studio 2880:** 2880-15th Ave. Year-round. 250-562-4526. Regular craft fairs. Ticket office.

■ **Native Art Gallery:** 1600 3rd Ave. Year-round. 250-564-3568. Coastal and Interior native art and crafts for sale.

■ **Tours:** Tourism Prince George offers scheduled and self-guided tours during summer. 1-800-668-7646 or 250-562-3700. Forest industry tours, including Northwood Pulp and Timber operations. Northwood's Tree Farm Licence is to become one of 10 Model Forest locations in Canada. Note: advance booking recommended.

■ **Huble Homestead:** 40km north of Prince George, 6km off Hwy 97 North, on Mitchell Rd. Daily late May-Labour Day. 250-960-4400. Living museum of trading post established 1905 at the Fraser River end of Giscome Portage, connecting Pacific and Arctic watersheds; declined 1919 when highway drew traffic away from river route. Guided tours.

■ **Golf: Aspen Grove**, on Mile 9, Hwy 97 S, right at Leno Rd. 250-963-9650. **Pine Valley**, 2.5km west on Hwy 16. 250-562-4811. **Prince George Golf and Curling Club**, at Hwys 16/97 junction. 250-563-0357. **Yellowhead Grove**, Hwy 16W, Leland Rd. 250-964-8313.

The Railway and Forestry Museum in Prince George.

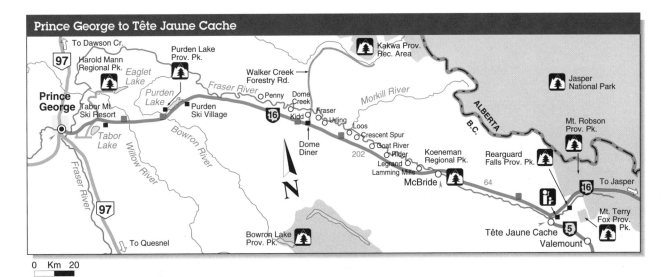

Prince George to Tête Jaune Cache

PRINCE GEORGE TO TÊTE JAUNE CACHE

YELLOWHEAD HIGHWAY (Highway 16)

The Yellowhead Hwy (Hwy 16) leaves Prince George east of the city centre on First Ave. Tête Jaune Cache is 266km from here. Leave "the Bowl" area of Prince George by crossing the Fraser River on the Yellowhead Hwy Bridge, 500m long and opened in 1987 to the relief of all Prince Georgians. Cause of relief is immediately upstream (north), a graceless but historic steel trestle bridge shared uncomfortably for 75 years by trains and two lanes of automobiles. There was no room for both cars and train, and the train had right-of-way. The bridge was completed by the Grand Trunk Pacific Railway (GTP) in 1914, and engineered with a movable centre span for sternwheelers to pass through. However, the railway killed river traffic, and the bridge was never raised in earnest. Strictly for rail traffic these days.

The highway curves up Airport Hill after crossing the river, offering views of city's three pulp mills. Distances are measured from the east end of the Yellowhead Hwy Bridge.

Tabor Lake: Turn south 4km from Yellowhead Hwy Bridge in Prince George. Follow old Cariboo Hwy and Giscome Rd 7km to small, weedy lake. Consistent producer of pan-sized rainbow trout. RV park, restaurant.

Harold Mann Regional Park: 13ha. 250-960-4400. On Fraser-Fort George Rd, 17km beyond Prince George. Turn north for 30.5km. Duck habitat, fishing and boating on Eaglet Lake. Named for the man who brought in the first two logging trucks in 1934, putting horse loggers out to pasture.

Tabor Mountain Ski Resort: Access road 20km beyond Prince George. 250-963-7542. Full-service ski hill. Triple chair, T-bar, lessons, lodge with solarium, restaurant. Vertical drop 244m.

Moose Viewing Area: About 29km beyond Prince George. A raised platform five minutes' walk from a pullout on north side of highway. Area burned in 1961 Grove Forest fire. Now good moose habitat. Please approach cautiously.

Willow River Rest Area and Demonstration Forest: 33km east of Prince George. Easy 2km, 45-minute walk through mixed hardwood and softwood forest. Memorial cairn for eight teenage boys who died May 10, 1974 canoeing an "impassable canyon just downstream."

Bowron River Rest Area: 55km east of Prince George. Day-use rest area, north side of highway. Upper Bowron River valley scene of intense salvage logging of trees killed or damaged by spruce bark beetle epidemics. Now the largest silviculture plantation in the world (53,000ha).

Purden Lake Provincial Park: 320ha; 78 campsites. 57km from Prince George. 250-565-6340. Large picnic area with sandy beach, rainbow trout. 7km of woodsy trails. Boat launching.

Purden Lake Resort is on south shore 3.5km from park. **Last gas service for about 145km.** Gas stations in small towns often close early.

Purden Ski Village: South off highway 60km from Prince George, drive short distance up a gravel road. Call mobile 250-565-7777. Full-service ski hill with two double chairs and T-bar. Vertical drop 335m.

From Purden Lake to McBride is the Yellowhead's loneliest stretch. The only settlements are the tiny Fraser River communities of Penny, Dome Creek (the largest with pop. 80), Kidd, Fraser, Urling, Loos, Crescent Spur, Goat River, Rider, Legrand, and Lamming Mills, located off the highway, and offering no travellers services. The highway crosses many streams and passes through dense wet-belt cedar and hemlock forests. The stark beauty made an indelible impression on Alexander Anderson, a young English Hudson's Bay Company clerk on his first assignment to the area. "Indeed, after leaving Fort Assiniboine in the winter of 1835, not the vestige of a human inhabitant was met with, save a few recluses at Jasper's, until we reached the neighbourhood of Fort George. The whole was one trackless waste, save where occasionally the footprints of wild animals disturbed the snow."

Sugarbowl Mountain Trail: About 77.5km from Prince George. Steep access to alpine and 1,836m peak of Sugarbowl Mountain. Five hours. For information write Caledonia Ramblers, Box 26, Station A, Prince George, BC, V2L 4R9.

Slim Creek Rest Area: 118km east of Prince George, south side of highway. Washroom with running water, parking and roadways accommodating over-length vehicles, children's play structure, picnic area, information kiosk, and creekside walkway.

Coffee Break: Dome Diner, about 121km from Prince George at junction of Hwy 16 and Bristow Rd. Home-cooked pies, muffins, tarts.

Kakwa Provincial Recreation Area: 127,690ha. 250-565-6340. A remote wilderness recreation area on BC/Alberta border, northwest of Mt Robson, along the Continental Divide. There is minimal road access on Walker Creek Forestry Rd, 133km from Prince George. It leads 87km north and is very rough. Travel is restricted by bridge washouts and high-water levels. There is also air-charter access. Visitors must be self-sufficient. Old guiding trails; some designated campsites. Grand open valleys and stunning mountain peaks; prime grizzly and black bear habitat, also caribou and moose. Park ranger headquarters at south end of Kakwa Lake. Elevations: Mt Sir Alexander, 3,270m, Mt Ida, 3,180m.

265

Goat River Rest Area: 166km east of Prince George. North side of highway.

McBride: (Pop. 740). 207km east of Prince George on fertile Fraser River benchlands. This was a railway boom town before the First World War, known as Railway Siding 39. Now named McBride after BC Premier Richard McBride (1903-15). Many of the 2,000 residents moved out with the construction crews. Those who stayed relied on farming or cutting cedar telegraph poles and posts. Agriculture and forestry are still the mainstays. McBride is a bustling little market town for a scattered population of about 2,500 who enjoy a laid-back rural lifestyle. It has all the basic tourist services, including good campsites. Back-country hiking and canoeing. A good place to get advice from locals before going into Kakwa Recreation Area (see above).

McBride Information: Info Centre, Railway caboose, Robson Square Shopping Centre. Box 519, McBride, BC, V0J 2E0. 250-569-3366. Off season: McBride Village Office, 250-569-2229.

Koeneman Regional Park: 7ha. About 1.5km beyond McBride. Drive or hike to Rainbow Falls and first of two lookouts on Dear Mountain. Views of Robson Valley and Cariboo Mountains. Named for homesteading family whose log house, built in 1939, is now used as theatre and special events gallery. In summer, call 250-960-4400.

Horseshoe Lake: About 2km beyond McBride. Waterfowl and muskrats.

Small River Rest Area: 253km beyond Prince George, south side of highway.

Highway 5: Leads south, just west of Tête Jaune Cache. 340km to Kamloops. Hwy 16 continues east from here, to Mt Robson Provincial Park and Jasper National Park. See *Thompson Okanagan*, p.180.

Tête Jaune Cache: (Pop. 143). 266km beyond Prince George. Turn south and cross one-way bridge over Fraser River. Tête Jaune, pronounced "Tea Jawn" by locals, is French for "Yellow Head," the nickname of a golden-haired, dark-skinned, mixed-blood Iroquois trapper, possibly named Pierre Hatsinaton. Man and legend have been brought to life in Howard O'Hagan's *Tay John*, a 1939 Canadian classic. A powerful story, not for the faint-hearted. Tête Jaune was reputed to have cached a fortune in furs somewhere between here and Yellowhead Pass in the early part of the 19th century.

Tête Jaune Cache, at the confluence of the Fraser and Robson rivers, was a major railway construction centre and head of navigation for sternwheelers on the Fraser. In its heyday early in the century, it was a booming shantytown of 5,000. Today, though remnants of boom days are all around, Tête Jaune's "downtown" is a loose cluster of buildings along the highway. The Tête Jaune Motel has two gas pumps, but don't bet on them. The Tête Jaune General Store and Deli serves "the best french fries in

the whole valley," according to some, and the Country Restaurant occupies one of the area's oldest buildings, constructed about 1913. Up the hill is the Rainbow Retreat Bed and Breakfast, where resident (but wild) elk roam the yard. About 200 hardy souls live in homesteads scattered throughout the woods.

Some 5.5km westward, down the Tête Jaune Cache Rd, there's a bend in the Fraser and remains of old pilings, a landing area for sternwheelers that hauled passengers and supplies up from Prince George. One wonders how boats so large – carrying 200 people and 200t of freight – could get this far upriver, where it's swift and narrow. Just upstream is a recreation site.

The river here is a beautiful green. As it broadens in its rampage to the coast, it becomes a silty yellow.

PRINCE GEORGE TO SMITHERS

YELLOWHEAD HIGHWAY (Highway 16)

This section of the Yellowhead Hwy runs west 371km from Prince George to Smithers. It crosses the rolling Interior Plateau and an ever-changing landscape. Ranches and farms in pleasant, open country blend with extensive spruce, pine, and fir forests, near some of the largest natural lakes in BC. The Hazelton Mountains come into view approaching Houston and form an impressive backdrop to Smithers. This section begins at the Prince George Info Centre, at Hwys 16/97 junction.

Prince George: (Pop. 75,150). For details, see p.263.

Blackwater Rd: 9.5km from Prince George.

SIDE TRIP

to Park and Canyon

West Lake Provincial Park: 256ha. 250-565-6340. On Blackwater Rd, 14km from Hwy 16 to park. Grassy picnic sites, sandy beaches, good swimming.

Fort George Canyon Trail: On West Lake Rd, 11km beyond park. 4.5km trail a naturalist's and photographer's delight. Some 56 species of flowers, almost as many shrubs. Trail ends where Fraser River boils in whirlpools and courses over jagged rocks through canyon. Small sternwheelers used to be winched up the canyon while passengers walked around. Cross-country skiing.

Return to Highway 16

Bednesti Lake: 39km from Blackwater Rd. Services and lake access.

Cluculz Lake: Several access routes south of highway, from 2.5km to 17km past Bednesti Lake Resort. Prince George cottage country. Rainbow trout and some big char, uncatchable, lurk in lake.

Cluculz Creek Rest Area: 13km beyond Bednesti Lake Resort, on the south side of the highway. Cluculz means "white fish site" in the Yinka Dene language of the Dakelh (Carrier) people whose villages line the Nechako River corridor. Until a generation ago, families from Sai-K'uz, or Stoney Creek, to the southwest, made camp here at first frost. A colourful three-panel sign introducing the history, place names, and culture of local Dakelh communities is the product of collaboration by the BC Ministry of Transportation and Highways, the Yinka Dene Language Institute in Vanderhoof, and the Carrier-Sekani Tribal Council in Prince George. Washroom with running water, parking, and picnic area.

Sob Lake Rd: 11.5km beyond rest area. Apparently named for an early homesteader who was, well ... cantankerous.

The Geographical Centre of BC: 16.5km west of rest area, 560m west of Blackwater Rd, look for trailer court, then cairn. Plaque says centre of BC is nearby, closer to the river.

Vanderhoof: (Pop. 4,401). 10km beyond Geographical Centre, 97km west of Prince George, 129km east of Burns Lake. On Nechako River. In the early 1900s, pioneer Herbert Vanderhoof, an American publicist working for the railway, had a recurring dream of a luxury riverside hotel amid spruce forests, a haven for writers and artists. (Writing was a vocation he pursued in his native Chicago.) The hotel was never built, and the writers were never rejuvenated. But Vanderhoof and district flourishes. Writers didn't stay, but ranchers did, lured by large and cheap acreages for raising beef and dairy cattle.

Vanderhoof today is a service centre for ranchers and loggers. Lots of cowboy boots and hard hats. Logging has provided access to many lakes, and resorts are plentiful. Fly in to remote locations. Check Info Centre for details.

Vanderhoof Information: Info Centre one block north of Hwy 16, on Burrard St. Year-round. 250-567-2124. Off-season, Vanderhoof and District Chamber of Commerce, Box 126, Vanderhoof, BC, V0J 3A0. 250-567-2124.

■ **Vanderhoof Heritage Village Museum and Information Centre:** On Hwy 16, West and Pine, on western perimeter of town. Daily May-Aug. 250-567-2991. 11 reconstructed 1920s buildings, including OK Cafe. Tours.

■ **Vanderhoof Bird Sanctuary (Riverside Park):** 200ha along 5km of Nechako riverbank. On north perimeter of town. Nechako Valley Sporting Association, Box 1077, Vanderhoof, BC, V0J 3A0. Each spring and fall, skies are filled with sights and sounds of 50,000 migrating birds. BC Wildlife Watch viewing site.

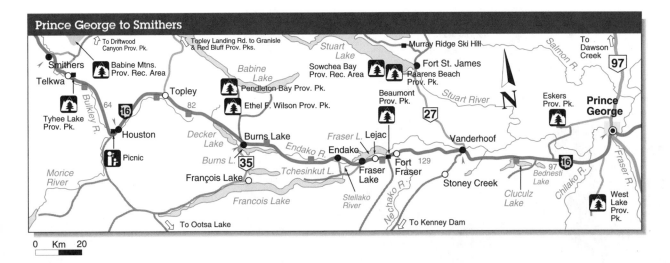

Prince George to Smithers

0　Km　20

■ **Sai-K'uz (Stoney Creek):** Dakelh village 11.5km south of Vanderhoof on Stoney Creek Rd. Potlatch House has arts and crafts; caters group feasts. Campground. Fishing derby on May long weekend.

■ **Kenney Dam/Cheslatta Falls:** Road from Vanderhoof leads 96km southwest. Dam, constructed in 1952, impounds Alcan reservoir – including Ootsa and Eutsuk lakes. Water from the spillway is directed over the Cheslatta Falls into the Nechako River. About one third of the Nechako's water is redirected west, through the Coast Mountains and a 16km tunnel through Mt Dubose, to spin turbines at Kemano and power the aluminum smelter at Kitimat. Forest Service recreation area provides camping and picnicking.

■ **Cross-country Ski Trails:** Three sets of maintained and tracked trails close to town – 6.5km Nechako Valley Sporting Association trail; 30km Water Lily Lake trail; 15km Mooney Pit trail. For details: Nechako Valley Sporting Association, Box 1077, Vanderhoof, BC, V0J 3A0.

■ **Omineca Golf Course:** 1.5km north of Vanderhoof on Hwy 27. 250-567-2920. Offers 18 holes.

Highway 27: Turn north off Hwy 16 in Vanderhoof for Fort St James, 62km away.

SIDE TRIP

to Fort St James

Paarens Beach Provincial Park: 43ha; 36 campsites. West off Hwy 27, 57km north of Vanderhoof, on Sowchea Rd. (15km west of Fort St James.) 250-565-6340. South end of 100km Stuart Lake. Fishing, boat launch, swimming, windsurfing. High winds and waves.

Sowchea Bay Provincial Recreation Area: 13ha; 30 campsites. On Sowchea Rd about 20km west of Fort St James, just past Paarens Beach. On Stuart Lake: boat launch, swimming, fishing. High winds and waves.

Fort St James: (Pop. 2,046). 62km north of Vanderhoof on Hwy 27. At site of Dakelh village, Nak'azdli. Fur-trade fort was established here in 1806, by explorer Simon Fraser, as headquarters of his "New Caledonia." Stunning lake and mountain setting, access to 300km chain of lakes and rivers. Not for neophyte navigators.

"The Fort" retains its pioneer feel. It's a busy, friendly little place with accommodation, stores, banks, and gas stations on the fringe of the great outdoors. Guiding, boat rentals. Nak'azdli Handicraft Shop is across from national historic park.

Fort St James Information: Info Centre on Hwy 27 entering village. Daily May-Sept. 250-996-7023 year-round. Or write Fort St James Chamber of Commerce, Box 1164, Fort St James, BC, V0J 1P0.

■ **Fort St James National Historic Park:** 4ha on Chief Kwah Rd. 250-996-7191. Mid-May to Sept 30. Splendid restoration of Hudson's Bay Company fur-trade post on Stuart Lake. The fur warehouse, fish cache, men's house, officer's dwelling house and trade store and office have been restored to 1896 appearance. Park staff in period costume explain fort life back then; a pair of oxen, Whitley and Davy, are on show daily. Visitor centre houses theatre, display room with artifacts, gift shop and administration offices. Audio tours in four languages available for rent.

■ **Lady of Good Hope Church:** On Lakeshore Drive. Built 1873. BC's third oldest (Catholic) church.

■ **Junkers W-34 Replica:** In Cottonwood Park, on lakeshore at edge of town (walking distance). Memorial to "fly by the pants" bush pilots and the region's pioneer aviation history. The little park by the lake is a locals' favourite for picnicking and swimming.

■ **Russ Baker Memorial:** On Lakeshore Dr just north of town, 0.5km beyond old Catholic Church. For Frank Russell ("Russ") Baker who died Nov 15, 1958. In the 1930s he was one of the area's first bush pilots. Before Second World War he founded Western Canada Airways here, and after the war, started BC Airways, later Pacific Western Airlines.

■ **Stuart Lake Golf Course:** Northwest of town on Stones Bay Rd, follow signs. Nine-hole course. Spectacular views of Stuart Lake.

■ **Mt Pope:** 5km northwest of town along Stones Bay Rd. Two- to four-hour hike up, half that coming down. 250-996-7023. An old forestry lookout building at the top offers great view of Stuart Lake and other lakes around mountain.

Murray Ridge Ski Hill: Follow main road about 1km north of Fort St James to Tachie Rd. Turn west and follow signs for 8km. 250-996-8513 or 1-888-229-1155. Longest T-bar in North America (1,981m). Vertical drop is 518m. 20km cross-country ski trails.

Tl'azt'en Nation: North of Fort St James, on Tachie Rd. Four Dakelh communities comprise the Tl'azt'en Nation living on the shores of the vast Stuart and Trembleur lakes. Binche is 52km northwest of Fort St James on Stuart Lake; Tache is 19km farther. K'uche (Grand Rapids) is to the north on the Tachie River. Dzitl'ainli sits at the mouth of the Middle River on Trembleur Lake. Tl'azt'en guides take visitors to traditional camps and fishing sites. For information call the Tl'azt'en Nation: 250-648-3212.

On **Takla Lake** at Takla Narrows, about 150km north of Fort St James, houseboating vacations, camping tenting, RV parking, and pub are at the Takla Rainbow Lodge, Box 1479, Fort St James, BC, V0J 1P0. Call 250-996-8892.

Back on main road, Hwy 27 becomes known as the Omineca Mining Access Rd. Goes to some rugged country. Don't expect fast-food franchises and gas bars here. Gravel road is generally good; side roads may be difficult. Logging, guiding, prospecting, trapping are main activities.

Manson Creek: (Pop. 0). 180km north of Fort St James. Was temporary home to thousands during Omineca gold rush of early 1880s. Until recently, Manson Creek offered private accommodation, gas and diesel. General Store was source of all local knowledge. Now, its small population has scattered hither and yon.

The late 1800s are brought to life at Fort St James National Historic Park.

Germansen Landing: (Pop. 44). 27km beyond Manson Creek. Bridge across Omineca River. Fishing for large Dolly Varden. Boating. Emerald-coloured water. Mining area. Large deposits of jade at nearby Ogden Mountain. Omineca Mining Rd continues 220km to private mine site in Toodoggone River area.

Return to Highway 16 in Vanderhoof

Alternate Rd to Fort St James: 7km west of Vanderhoof. Info sign.

Sawmill: 22km west of Vanderhoof on Hwy 16. Operated by Slocan Forest Products.

The Last Spike: 15km beyond sawmill. Plaque at south side of highway commemorates the last spike driven on the GTP, April 7, 1914.

Fort Fraser: (Pop. 370). Small community less than 1km from last spike. Named for trading post established by Simon Fraser in 1806 (situated in Beaumont Park, below).

Beaumont Provincial Park: 191ha; 49 campsites (reservations taken: call 1-800-689-9025; from the Lower Mainland or overseas, call 604-689-9025). Sani-station. On Fraser Lake, 4km west of Fort Fraser. General Info: 250-565-6340. Fine sandy beach. Saskatoons and huckleberries. Nautley River, north from park, flows less than 1km from lake to Nechako River. Important fishing site for nearby Nadleh Whut'en First Nation.

Drywilliam Lake Rest Area: 4.5km beyond park. On lake.

Lejac: 6.5km beyond rest area, north side of highway. Site of Catholic residential school on First Nations Nadleh Whut'en land. Former classroom building and cemetery remain.

Fraser Lake: (Pop. 1,344). 5km beyond Lejac. Attractive lakeside setting. Bedroom community for sawmill at Lejac and Canada's largest molybdenum mine located southwest of here. Cattle ranching, tourism.

Fraser Lake Information: Information centre on north side of highway. June-late Sept, hours vary. 250-699-8844. Off-season try Village Office, 250-699-6257, or write Box 430, Fraser Lake, BC, V0J 1S0.

■ **Museum:** At information centre. Tells the community's story.

■ **Lava Flows:** Flat top of Table Mountain, northwest of village. Remains of a volcanic cone 25 million years old. Lava gives hills their red tinge.

François Lake Rd: 4km west of Fraser Lake. Turn south down to resorts at east end of François Lake, 120km long, sometimes rough. Great lake views partly responsible for fairways missed at challenging **Moly Hills Golf Course:** 250-699-7761.

Stellako River: 4km from Fraser Lake. Premier fly-fishing stream for rainbow trout. Catch and release. Spectacular salmon spawning, Aug-Sept.

Endako Mine Rd: 9km beyond Stellako River. Leads to Endako molybdenum mine and alternate access to François Lake.

Endako: (Pop. 102). Just west of Endako Mine Rd. Divisional point on the GTP. During railway construction (1908-14), nearby tent town of Freeport housed 1,500 navvies, gamblers, and soiled doves.

Savory Rest Area: About 9km beyond Endako, north side of highway.

Tintagel Cairn and Rest Area: 43km beyond Endako, 11km east of Burns Lake. Contains a 45kg chunk of wall from King Arthur's Tintagel Castle in Cornwall, England. Symbolic tie to this tiny settlement of Tintagel. Wheelchair accessible washroom, information kiosk.

Burns Lake: (Area pop. 2,500). 129km west of Vanderhoof, 81km east of Houston. Far-flung populace of 10,000. Claim is: 5,000km of fishing in a 100km radius (17 or 18 lakes).

Building the GTP (1908-14) ushered in the stump farm and broadaxe era. Raising cattle in summer, cutting lodgepole-pine railway ties in winter.

A plethora of places to fish, camp, canoe, horseback ride, or explore, most within easy reach. Resorts for classic cross-country skiing, snowmobiling, and ice fishing.

Burns Lake is an access point to **Tweedsmuir Provincial Park:** 994,246ha. Call Smithers 250-847-7320 for information. This is BC's largest contiguous provincial park. Access only by boat (see *Side Trip to Ootsa Lake*, below), or floatplane. Visitors should be self-sufficient and wilderness-wise. Also see *Cariboo Country*, p.253.

Burns Lake Information: Info Centre on Hwy 16 opposite College of New Caledonia. Year-round: winter weekdays 9-4:30; summer extended hours. 250-692-3773. Or write Burns Lake and District Chamber of Commerce, Box 339, Burns Lake, BC, V0J 1E0.

■ **Heritage Centre:** Includes Lakes District Museum with 1920s operating room, and logging paraphernalia. Weekdays in winter, extended hours in summer. 250-692-3773. 1943 forestry building houses Info Centre as well as art shows during the summer. The "Bucket of Blood" is a fur trading office turned gambling den and scene of a gruesome shooting.

Highway 35: South off Hwy 16 at the eastern end of the village. Access to numerous lakes and ultimately, Ootsa Lake.

SIDE TRIP

to Ootsa Lake

Radley Park on Burns Lake: On Hwy 35, less than 1km from junction with Hwy 16. Small municipal park with playground, picnic tables, boat launch.

Eagle Creek Agate/Opal Beds: On Hwy 35, about 3km from junction. Turn right on Eagle Creek Rd. 45-minute hike each way. Rockhounders' delight. White and amber agates up to 5cm.

Tchesinkut Lake: On Hwy 35, 16km south of junction. Native name refers to crystal-clear water. Nice camping and fishing spot.

François Lake and Ferry: 23km south of junction. Free 20-minute ferry ride to Southbank. Washrooms and picnic tables at north- and south-shore terminals. The area is very popular for camping and fishing (access is provided to many lakes, such as Uncha and Takysie). For a scenic route, drive along the shore of François Lake and up to Houston. Ask at Burns Lake Info Centre.

Ootsa Lake: 42km from François Lake ferry on sign-posted gravel road. Ootsa Lake is part of Nechako reservoir and northern boundary of **Tweedsmuir Provincial Park**. Shoreline of drowned forest and floating debris creates dangerous boating conditions. Also visit the Skins Lake Spillway operated by Alcan.

Little Andrew's Bay Provincial Park: 102ha. 8 campsites. About 45km west of Ootsa Lake boat launch on Nechako Reservoir. 250-847-7320. Boat launch. Firewood not provided.

*Return to Highway 16
at Burns Lake*

Babine Lake Rd: Follow signs from junction of Hwy 16 and 8th Ave in Burns Lake. Turn north from Hwy 16 toward Babine Lake.

SIDE TRIP

to Babine Lake

Ethel F. Wilson Provincial Park: 29ha; 10 campsites. On Pinkut Lake, 24km from Hwy 16 on gravel road. 250-847-7320. Park named for Ethel Wilson, author of novel *Swamp Angel*, about a woman escaping a troubled marriage and travelling to a remote lake in northern BC.

Babine Lake: Side roads of varying lengths lead to resorts and residences on lake. Main road leads 12km to provincial park, below. This is the longest natural lake in BC, slicing 177km between mountain ridges. Creeks important for sockeye salmon spawning. Excellent summer lake fishing for char, trout, and kokanee.

Babine Lake Marine/Pendleton Bay Provincial Park: 16 campsites (user maintained). May-Sept. 12km from Ethel F. Wilson Park. 250-847-7320. Boat launch, swimming.

Pinkut Fisheries: About 50km from Burns Lake. Follow signs. Box 1180, Burns Lake, BC, V0J 1E0. 250-847-8132. Sockeye salmon spawning in Sept.

*Return to Highway 16
at Babine Lake Road*

Carnoustie Golf Course: 16km west of Babine Lake Rd. 250-698-7677. Open weather permitting. nine-hole course with fairways carved out of the bush. Course obstacles may include moose. Dining by reservation.

Palling Rest Area: 1km west of golf course, south side of highway. Wheelchair-accessible washroom, pay phone, picnic tables. Pet walking area.

Burns Lake Airport: 4km west of rest area. Landing strip adjacent highway.

Six Mile (China Nose Mountain) Summit: 20km beyond airport. El 1,423m. Gradual climb to highest point on Hwy 16. Offers splendid view of mountains and valley.

Topley: (Pop. 178). 10km down from Six Mile summit. Have a chin-wag with the locals in the cafe/store.

Topley Landing Rd (Hwy 118): Turn north in Topley for Granisle, 50km away.

SIDE TRIP

to Granisle

Good paved road, but drive with caution, as there is always the opportunity to spot moose, black bears, or coyotes.

Topley Landing: (Pop. 30). 40km north of Topley, right for 1km. A former Dakelh trapping and trading area, and base for Hudson's Bay Company warehouse and forest industry until the 1950s. Now, lakeside resorts and year-round residents. Our Lady Fatima Church, built 1948, has been restored: inside are antiques and a collage of angels; arts and crafts shop. The Fulton River flows into Babine Lake just north of Topley Landing. An easy 6.5km hike upstream takes you to Millionaires Pool, below Fulton Falls. Bob Hope has fly-fished there.

Fulton River Spawning Channels: 40km from Topley (just past turnoff to Topley Landing). 250-697-2314. Box 9, Granisle, BC, V0J 1W0. Considered the world's largest artificial sockeye spawning channel, producing up to half a million returning adults. Salmon return late Aug to mid-Oct.

Red Bluff Provincial Park: 148ha; 27 campsites. 45km north of Topley. 250-847-7320. Named for iron-stained cliffs of ruddy hue. Picnic area with sandy swimming beach. Nature trails, boat launch.

Granisle: (Pop. 446). 49km north of Topley. A quiet waterfront community and outdoor recreation centre for Babine Lake. Several nature trails to explore right in town. Fishing, camping, hiking. Museum displays replica bones of Columbian mammoth unearthed here in 1971 by workmen excavating in an open-pit copper mine on Newman Peninsula, just north of town. Radiocarbon dating indicates the mammoth died in a sticky pond deposit 34,000 years ago.

Granisle Information: Log building at entrance to town. May-Oct. 250-697-2428. Off-season, 250-697-2248, or write Granisle Visitor Information and Museum, Box 128, Granisle, BC, V0J 1W0.

From Granisle you may choose to return to the Hwy 16 via Hwy 118 to Topley, or you may travel a back road circle route that brings you to Hwy 16 just east of the town of Smithers.

Return to Topley on Highway 16

Topley Rest Area: 2km west of Topley, south side of highway. Information kiosk.

Houston: (Pop. 3,9346). 30km west of Topley, 64km south of Smithers. Started out in early 1900s as tie-cutting centre for the GTP. In the decades to follow, forest industry has kept Houston working.

But for play, there's the steelhead. Houston sports the world's largest fly-fishing rod, more than 18m long, with a reel 1m in diameter, a bright orange line, and 53cm long fly. A deft cast away from a nicely sculpted trout and salmon, suggesting scope of local angling.

Sitting in friendly clatter of a Houston coffee shop, talk is about clearcuts, cattle ranching, and probably fishing, breaking in new 4x4s and going to the lake for the weekend. Young families everywhere. 70 percent of Houston's population is under 35. Day-long forestry tours can be reserved mid-July to Aug. 250-845-7640. Houston is at Bulkley-Morice rivers' junction, names to bring a lump to any dedicated steelhead fisherman's throat. Aug-Nov is prime steelhead time. Sockeye salmon run in summer. Wilderness canoeing on Nanika-Kidprice lake system.

Wilderness and local accommodation, two golf courses, groomed and natural cross-country skiing, hiking, and mountain-bike trails.

Houston Information: Info Centre on north side of Hwy 16 opposite Houston Shopping Centre, and under shadow of huge fishing rod. Year-round. 250-845-7640. Houston and District Chamber of Commerce, Box 396, Houston, BC, V0J 1Z0. Forest interpretation centre on site.

Nadina River Salmon Project: 3km west of Houston turn onto Morice Forest Rd. Follow past Owen Lake to Nadina Lake turnoff (Tahtsa Rd); follow Tahtsa Rd for 30km almost to Nadina Lake; signs lead to project. Sockeye salmon. Spawning peaks mid-Sept.

Leaving Houston, Hwy 16 crosses the Bulkley River and heads north. Watch for moose on road, particularly at night.

Picnic Area: 5km west of Houston. Pit toilets. Maintained by Northwood Pulp.

Hungry Hill: 12km west of Houston. Roadside pullout with pit toilets and picnic tables. Spectacular view of valley. Important moose and deer wintering area.

Bulkley View Rest Area: 43km west of Houston. Good leg-stretching spot. Sign describes 1866 construction of Collins Overland Telegraph. It would have linked North America to Europe via the Bering Sea, but was superceded by the transatlantic cable. The telegraph's trail, however, opened this region to white settlement.

Telkwa: (Pop. 1,1948). On Hwy 16, some 49km beyond Houston. Picture-postcard village where the green Telkwa River meets the blue Bulkley. Telkwa made *Ripley's Believe It or Not* when it had three bridges crossing two rivers, all anchored to one rock. Pilings remain where the rivers meet at Riverside St. The community began in the 1860s with the arrival of Collins Overland Telegraph workers. It remained the Bulkley Valley's economic centre until 1913 when the railway diverted traffic. The river remains an attraction for its salmon and steelhead pools. Novice and intermediate canoe runs. Scenic drive up Telkwa River Rd past old coal-mine workings.

Telkwa Information: Year-round from the village office, 250-846-5212. Box 220, Telkwa, BC, V0J 2X0.

■ **St Stephen's Anglican Church:** On Hwy 16. Built in 1910. Roofed English gate.

■ **Telkwa Museum:** On Hwy 16 next to post office. In a 1920 heritage building. Mon-Sat through summer. 250-846-9656. Self-guided heritage walk; map of 31 historic sites available.

■ **Eddy Park:** On the Bulkley River, a pretty picnic spot.

Telkwa High Rd: About 1km west of village centre. Turn north and wind gently through farmlands of Glentanna and Driftwood on eastern benchlands of Bulkley River. Superb views of Hudson Bay Mountain. Rejoins Yellowhead at Moricetown, 35.5km north of Smithers.

Tyhee Lake Provincial Park: 33ha; 59 campsites (reservations taken: call 1-800-689-9025; from the Lower Mainland or overseas, call 604-689-9025); sani-station. 2km north of Telkwa off Telkwa High Rd. 250-847-7320. Long-lived pygmy whitefish. Family recreation. Marsh viewing platform to see common loons, red-necked grebes, ruffed grouse, beavers. Boat launch, swimming, hiking, wheelchair access.

Another Road to Babine Lake: Turn east off Hwy 16, 9km beyond Telkwa, for Driftwood Canyon Provincial Park and Babine Mountains Recreation Area.

SIDE TRIP

to Babine Mountains

Driftwood Canyon Provincial Park: 23ha. 11km from Yellowhead Hwy. 250-847-7320. Fossils, 40-70 million years old, exposed in creek beds and canyon walls. Fernlike metasequoia, poplar, cranberry leaves, occasional mosquito or fish fossils. Don't prospect in canyon walls, they are unstable. Removal of fossils prohibited.

Babine Mountains Recreation Area: 32,400ha. 4km beyond Driftwood Canyon Park. 250-847-7320. Telkwa High Rd also intersects this road to Babine Lake. Wilderness hiking and skiing into alpine country. Flowers at peak in Aug. ATVs restricted. Watch for mountain goats.

Smithers Landing Provincial Park: 158ha. On Babine Lake about 46km beyond Babine Mountains Provincial Recreation Area and 65km northeast of Smithers. 250-847-7320. New, undeveloped park with access to Babine Lake.

Babine River Fish Counting Fence/Fort Babine Salmon Enhancement: 120km northeast of Smithers. Write Fort Babine Enterprises, Box 2292, Smithers, BC, V0J 2N0. 250-847-8513. Sockeye, coho, pink, and chinook salmon. The **Babine River** flows 100km north and west from the north end of Babine Lake to the Skeena River near Hazelton. One of the few rivers in BC without development or bridge crossings, it is being recommended for Heritage River status, and for a 15,000ha provincial park, extending about 1km on each side of its length. Here are major sockeye salmon runs, excellent steelhead fishing, aboriginal village sites, and about 100 grizzly bears. The river can be explored by kayak or on commercial river rafting expeditions.

Return to Highway 16

About 11km beyond Telkwa, Hwy 16 crosses Bulkley River and enters Smithers. See *Smithers to Prince Rupert*, following.

SMITHERS TO PRINCE RUPERT

YELLOWHEAD HIGHWAY (Highway 16)

This section of the Yellowhead travels southwest, down into the valley of the Skeena River. The river's name is derived from Xsan or 'Ksan – in the language of the Gitxsan and Tsimshian peoples who have lived here for millennia, it means "river of mists." The Skeena and its tributaries form a massive whitewater system that drains more than 39,000 sq km of northwestern BC. The Gitxsan, of the river's middle and upper reaches, are the "people of the river of mists." The Tsimshian, downriver, below the canyons to the sea, are the people "going into the river of mists."

Perhaps it's the Skeena's misty, moody nature that has inspired the potent and still ascendant native culture here. The river has provided transportation and food. Cedar canoes 18m long once navigated between villages. Eulachon, coho, chinook, sockeye, pink, and chum salmon were and are still plentiful. The Kispiox River, a major tributary, is perhaps the world's most famous steelhead fishing stream.

In ancient Gitxsan villages along Hwy 16, between New Hazelton and Hwy 37, visitors are invited to witness both ancient and newly carved poles that stand singly or in clusters beside native homes. All that is asked is your respect.

The *Log* starts in Smithers from the Info Centre at the junction of Main St and Hwy

16. Smithers is halfway along the wide Bulkley River, the Skeena's major tributary. At Hazelton, the Bulkley adds its considerable volume to the Skeena, which then makes its way to the sea. The transition to lush cedar and hemlock forests indicates the influence of the Pacific Ocean. It is 354km to ferry terminals in Prince Rupert.

Smithers: (Pop. 5,794). 64km north of Houston, 68km south of New Hazelton. Centre of the Bulkley Valley. Smithers' atmosphere is set by the commanding presence of Hudson Bay Mountain. The 2,621m classically shaped peak appears etched upon the sky. The main street of Bavarianlike architecture, red brick sidewalks, and statue of a man playing an alpenhorn are efforts to reinforce the alpine atmosphere.

Like Prince Rupert (following) the history of Smithers is rooted in the GTP. In 1913, the railway selected this site and undertook plans to build a town that would serve as a major railway station.

Legends of the local aboriginal Wet'suwet'en (relatives of the Interior Dakelh) tell of a shallow swampy lake where Smithers is now, extending east 212km to Fraser Lake. Perhaps that accounts for the fertile soils of the Bulkley Valley. Agriculture, forestry, mining, and tourism are key industries. Ask at Info Centre about summer activities: hiking, rock climbing, horseback riding, canoeing, river rafting (whitewater and scenic), fishing and outdoor tennis, soccer, and baseball. Winter activities: alpine and cross-country skiing, curling, ice skating, and snowmobiling.

Smithers Information: 1411 Court St (behind Canadian National Railways parlour car on east side of Hwy 16). Sani-station. June-Aug. 250-847-5072 or 1-800-542-6673. Box 2379, Smithers, BC, V0J 2N0. Off-season, Smithers and District Chamber of Commerce, same location.

Smithers Airport: 5km west of Smithers, east off Hwy 16. Daily flights to Vancouver, Terrace, and Prince George.

■ **Riverside Recreation Centre:** On the Bulkley River. Full-service RV park, golf course, and restaurant.

■ **Central Park Building:** 1425 Main St. Municipal heritage structure built in 1925. Houses **Smithers Art Gallery** and the **Bulkley Valley Museum.** 250-847-5322. Year-round. Museum features development of Smithers and Surrounding communities.

■ **Ski Smithers:** Premier downhill skiing from 1,676m Hudson Bay Mountain. 18 runs, gentle to challenging. Triple chair, two T-bars, full services. Vertical drop 530m. Day lodges, rentals, child-minding, lessons. Season Nov-late April. Access road 22.5km from downtown Smithers. 250-847-2058 or toll-free in BC: 1-800-665-4299.

■ **Smithers Murals:** Local artist has illustrated aspects of life in the local area and around Northern BC. Brochure describing self-guided tour at Info Centre.

■ **Perimeter Trail:** Accessible from various points in Smithers. 9.5km walking and biking trail follows town perimeter. Info Centre has map.

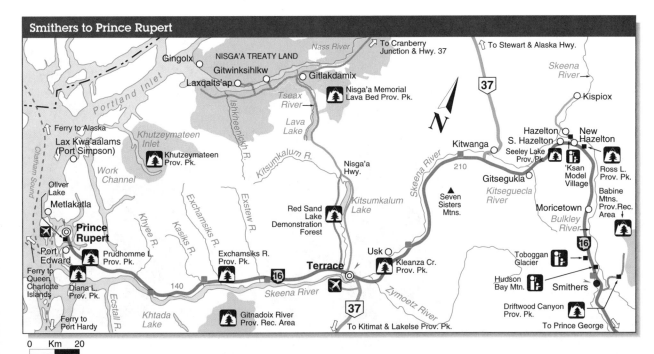

■ **Community Forest:** En route to ski hill. Interpretive nature trail makes for a pleasant afternoon walk. Winds through a variety of ecological habitats. Pine Creek (Cross Country Ski) Trails in same area, can also be enjoyed.

■ **Smithers Golf and Country Club**, 1km west of Smithers on Hwy 16 (Scotia Rd). 250-847-3591. 18 holes with views of Hudson Bay Mountain.

■ **Views:** From **Ski Hill Rd**, look out over the Bulkley Valley. It is also possible to access alpine meadows once ski area has been reached. From **Telkwa High Rd**, Look out to Kathlyn Glacier and pastoral farmlands.

Kathlyn Lake Rd: Turn west about 4km from Smithers.

SIDE TRIP

to Glacier and Falls

Glacier Gulch and Twin Falls: Follow signs on Kathlyn Lake Rd. 2km-wide gulch has twin waterfalls cascading 152m down canyon walls. Easy 0.5km trail leads to base of south falls. Difficult hike to 120m-thick Lake Kathlyn Glacier.

Return to Highway 16

Hudson Bay Rest Area: 3.5km beyond road to airport. Excellent view of Hudson Bay Glacier.

Adams' Igloo Wildlife Museum: Beside rest area. Mounted displays.

Moricetown: (Pop. 780). 31.5km beyond Smithers. Wet'suwet'en village named for Father A.G. Morice, missionary here 1885-1904. The Wet'suwet'en call it Kyah Wiget, "old village." The archaeological record puts people at this major fishing site for at least 4,000 years. The Bulkley River narrows here to 15m at the base of falls. Here, native fisherman still gaff fish, standing poised on rocks above milling salmon. A 57kg specimen was speared in the 1950s. Campground, handicrafts shop. Cultural Awareness Week in June offers visitors the opportunity to learn about Wet'suwet'en culture. Call Office of Wet'suwet'en Hereditary Chiefs, 250-847-3630.

■ **Moricetown-Cronin Trail:** Starts at Moricetown, and when complete will lead 40km around north side of Babine Mountains though ancient balsam fir forests, to the Cronin Mine, through Silverking, and back to Smithers. Trail was originally built in 1907, for horses and mule trains packing minerals from the high-elevation Cronin Mine to what is now the Moricetown Reserve.

Ross Lake Provincial Park: 307ha. 30km from Moricetown. Day-use park. Canoeing, swimming, fly-fishing, hiking. No powerboats.

New Hazelton: (Pop. 822). 67km northwest of Smithers. Dominated by Mt Rocher Déboulé, mountain of "rolling stone," named by the miners who explored its peak and were frequently threatened by landslides and large rolling boulders. The Gitxsan call the mountain Stii Kyo Din, "stands alone." They tell us the mountain stood at the heart of an ancient city state, Tam Lax Aamid, stretching for miles along the Skeena where the Kitwanga Back Rd is now. Here all tribes lived together as one until a series of events – including the massacre of men by supernatural one-horned goats – led to the abandonment of what may very well have been one of the continent's greatest societies.

New Hazelton, 1914. The scene of a gun-fight never matched in the Canadian West. Seven Russian anarchists, having once successfully stolen the railway's payroll, attempted to steal it again. Within two minutes of the hold-up, 200 bullets had zinged between townsfolk and thieves (police were nowhere). When all quieted down, three robbers were dead, three were wounded (later deported), and one escaped. *He* had the money.

Hazelton Area Information: At junction of Yellowhead Hwy and Hwy 62 north. Beside fibreglass statues of Jean Jacques Caux (Cataline, a legendary packer) and a generic miner and logger. Provides info for the three Hazeltons: New Hazelton, "Old Town" Hazelton, and South Hazelton. June-Sept. 250-842-6071. Off-season, write District of New Hazelton, Visitor Info Centre, Box 340, New Hazelton, BC, V0J 2J0. 250-842-6571.

Highway 62: Turn north off Yellowhead Hwy at Info Centre in New Hazelton. After about 2km, highway crosses Bulkley Canyon on one-lane Hagwilget suspension bridge, built in 1931. River is a dizzying 76m below. The Gitxsan and Wet'suwet'en used to sway across the gorge on a footbridge of poles lashed with cedar bark rope.

SIDE TRIP

to Hazelton and Kispiox

Hazelton: (Pop. 384). 6km northwest of New Hazelton on Hwy 62. Hazelton, at the junction of Bulkley and Skeena rivers, is the heart and soul of a vibrant Gitxsan culture. This is living, breathing stuff, past and present fused into the 'Ksan model village. Seven communal houses sit where villages have been for some 7,000 years.

White man is a new neighbour, arriving around 1866. Sternwheelers puffed up from the coast through misty Skeena shoals and canyons riverboat captains claimed were as capricious as a temperamental mistress. Initially boats carried supplies for the Collins

Overland Telegraph link with Europe via Bering Strait. In the end, what they did was open up the Skeena Valley for settlers and agriculture. By 1910 they were bringing supplies for the building of Canada's second transcontinental railway which, of course, ended the steamboat era. The road came through in 1944.

Old Town Hazelton could be a movie set with its Victorian buildings and the characters who once lived there. Cataline was a famed packer and guide with legendary stamina. Simon Gunanoot was an accused murderer whose bush craft let him elude RCMP for 13 years.

Hazelton Information: Village office, 250-842-6071, or write District of Hazelton, Visitor Info Centre, Box 340, New Hazelton, BC, V0J 2J0.

■ **'Ksan:** Model Gitxsan village and museum on High Level Rd. 250-842-5544. Northwest Coast Exhibition Centre also here, features local and international artists. Daily, mid-April to Sept; five days a week off-season. Gift shop, museum and carving school open year-round. 'Ksan dancers perform Fri evenings July-Aug. Idyllic riverside campground, good fishing.

■ **Hands of History Tour:** 113km loop tour between Hazelton and Kitwanga. About 14 information plaques along route.

■ **Walking Tour of Hazelton:** Original steam donkey, paddlewheelers, and 100-year-old St Peter's Anglican Church. Check with village office.

■ **Abandoned Gold and Silver Mines:** Ask at village office about hiking trails.

Kispiox Valley Rd leaves Hwy 62 just before Hazelton and continues on to Kispiox. About 5km from Hazelton, the road passes the quiet Gitxsan village of Glen Vowell. There are no carved poles here.

Kispiox: (Pop. 553). 13km north of Hazelton on Kispiox Valley Rd, at junction of Kispiox and Skeena rivers. Ancient Gitxsan village, home of Frog, Wolf, and Fireweed clans. Its name, given to village by Department of Indian Affairs, means "loud talkers." The community's traditional name is Anspayaxw, "the hidden place." In an enclosure by the river are 15 outstanding carved poles, records of the long history here. Also here, the Bent Box Gallery featuring inspired work of local artist Art Wilson, usually open 10-4. The Hidden Place Gallery is in the newer part of the village just across the bridge.

The Kispiox is world renowned as a steelhead river. Check Info Centre in New Hazelton for fishing camps, guiding, and rafting services. Steelhead run Sept-Nov; coho salmon Aug-Sept.

Return to New Hazelton on Highway 16

South Hazelton Access Rd: 3km west of New Hazelton. Turn north.

South Hazelton: (Pop. 654). Lodging, services. Road rejoins Hwy 16.

The Bulkley River plunges through the canyon at Moricetown.

Seeley Lake Provincial Park: 24ha; 20 campsites. 10km west of New Hazelton. 250-847-7320. Secluded campsites. Use binoculars to spot old mine workings on flanks of Mt Rocher Déboulé. Cutthroat and rainbow trout fishing. Birdwatching spring and summer.

Gitsegukla (Kitseguecla): (Pop. 506). 16km beyond Seeley Lake Park on Kitseguecla River straddling Hwy 16. Gitxsan community with fine carved poles. Elementary school is adorned with painted carvings representing clans.

Highway 37 North (Stewart-Cassiar Hwy): 16km beyond Gitsegukla, 91km northeast of Terrace, leads a short distance to communities of Gitwangak, Kitwanga, and Gitanyow. It's 721km to Yukon border. For details, see *Stewart-Cassiar Hwy*, p.280.

Seven Sisters Mountain Peaks: 6km past junction with Hwy 37.

Boulder Creek Rest Area: 9km west of Hwy 37 junction. Sign created by children from bilingual Gitxsanmx-English school at Gitwangak explains this is Lax Wii Tdin, "place where fish are caught in traps." Also, a forest information sign.

Skeena River Boat Passage: 33km west of Hwy 37 junction. Where steamboats churned up the Skeena as early as 1866.

Sanderson Point Rest Area: 60km beyond Hwy 37 junction. Riverside site with wheelchair-accessible washroom and picnic tables. Water pump.

Usk Ferry: On Hwy 16, 12km from rest area. On-demand reaction ferry crosses Skeena to small community of Usk. Note tiny Usk Pioneer Chapel east of highway.

Kleanza Creek Provincial Park: 269ha; 21 campsites. 4km from Usk Ferry Rd (10km east of Terrace). 250-847-7320. Kleanza comes from the Gitxsan word for gold. A 180g nugget was taken from creek in 1934. 4.5km Bornite Mountain trail starts in park. Canyon, waterfalls, fishing. Wheelchair access.

Highway 37 South: 15.5km beyond Kleanza Creek Park turnoff, at outskirts of Terrace. 57km paved road south to Kitimat. Lake and mountain views.

SIDE TRIP

to Kitimat and Kitamaat

Terrace-Kitimat Airport: Turn west on access road 5km south of Hwy 37/16 junction. Daily jet service to Vancouver, Prince Rupert, Smithers, and Prince George.

Lakelse Lake Provincial Park: 362ha; 156 campsites, plus group camping (reservations taken: call 1-800-689-9025; from the Lower Mainland or overseas, call 604-689-9025). Park headquarters 9km south of airport. Campground at Furlong Bay 4.5km beyond. 250-847-7320.

In Tsimshian language, Lakelse means freshwater mussel. Fishing is great. Natural beaches, mature forests. Twin Spruce self-guiding nature trail. Williams Creek is spawning stream for sockeye salmon end of Aug. Moose, wolves, and bears. Trumpeter swans winter over. Amphitheatre, visitor program, showers, boat launch, swimming, wheelchair access.

Mount Layton Hot Springs: A few kilometres beyond park headquarters. Odourless mineral hot springs. Nine very hot pools (42-72C). Most pools inaccessible, and too hot for bathing, but their water has been channeled into resorts here since 1910. Today's place to soak is **Mount Layton Hot Springs Resort**. Hotel complex with lounge, dining, and conference facilities. Hot pool, leisure pool, splashdown pool, childrens wading pool. 250-798-2214 or 1-800-663-3862 in BC.

Onion Lake: Turn west off Hwy 37 about 6km south of hot springs. 2km multiple-use trail with lovely lake views.

Kitimat River: 6km beyond Onion Lake. Good salmon and steelhead fishing in clean, green water.

Hirsch Creek Park: 22km south of Kitimat River Bridge. Municipal park, campsite, playground, trails.

Kitamaat Village Rd: Left off Hwy 37 just past Visitor Info Centre. Paved road winds 11km around Kitimat Arm of Douglas Channel to **Kitamaat Village** (pop. 553), headquarters of the now united Haisla and Henaaksiala First Nations. The original villages of the Henaaksiala people were farther south, along the Kitlope and Kemano rivers. The first Haisla village was at the mouth of the Kitimat River. One of several older Haisla villages sits below the present-day town of Kitimat, on the river's east bank. It was an important eulachon-oil processing site through to the 1970s, until industrial pollution destroyed the fishery central to their culture (the Kitimat Centennial Museum, below, has an excellent display). The people here now rely on fisheries on the Kitlope and Kemano rivers to the south. The Greater Kitlope Valley is also the source of much spiritual wealth. The Haisla and Henaaksiala people were very active in the 1994 campaign to save the valley from logging. It is now a provincial heritage conservancy, and Kitamaat Village is departure point for visits there (see below). Also in the village are four carved poles, a carving shop, and beautifully designed school.

Kitlope Heritage Conservancy (Huchsduwachsdu Nuyem Jees): 321,120ha; wilderness camping. South of Kitamaat by boat or air. Park established in 1995, jointly managed by the Haisla Nation and BC government. Or, contact BC Parks, 3790 Alfred Ave, Smithers, BC, V0J 2N0. Call 250-847-7320. For boat transportation to the Kitlope from Kitamaat Village, call the Nanakila Institute, 250-632-3308. For information on routes, guided eco-tours, and protocol: The Haisla Tribal Council, Box 1101 Kitamaat Village, BC, V0T 2B0. 250-639-9382. Park preserves the world's largest intact coastal temperate rainforest, and Kitimat and Kitlope watersheds, from which the Haisla people take the precious, oily fish called eulachon – a staple in their diet, and central to their culture. Throughout the park are ancient trails, culturally modified trees, and other sites the Haisla consider sacred. Says elder, Cecil Paul, instrumental in the valley's preservation: "I don't go to church, but I'm a spiritual man, and the Kitlope is my cathedral." A Rediscovery Camp inside the park brings elders

and youth together. Visitors who dare to venture here will see old-growth forest, waterfalls, mountain goats, bears, eagles and geese, and other birds.

Kitimat: (Pop. 11,136). 57km south of Yellowhead/Hwy 37 junction. At head of Douglas Channel, a 90km fiord reaching in from the Pacific. Visitors quickly notice the space and sense of order, even the street names. In one neighbourhood, streets are named after fish. In others, birds, rivers, and pioneers. Residential areas back onto buffers of trees and park. Industrial plants are tucked well away. Kitimat, a company town, is better planned than most weddings.

The Aluminum Company of Canada (Alcan) selected Kitimat for its aluminum smelter in 1948. Kitimat has a natural deep-sea harbour and ample room for development; Kemano, 75km southeast across the Coast Mountains, provides hydroelectricity.

Kitimat is a microcosmic Canada. Wander round the shops and listen to the accents. Alcan's and Kitimat's industrial partners, Eurocan Pulp and Paper and Methanex Corporation, have attracted workers from around the world.

People come from all over for the fishing, too. Salmon, trout, and steelhead are in the rivers. Radley Park, in the city, is a hot spot (well-used smokehouse in the campground attests to that). On Douglas Channel, there is great deep-sea fishing between snowcapped mountains. Troll for salmon, halibut the size of barn doors, and red snapper, or go for shrimp, crab, and abalone. Check Info Centre for boat charters and guides. Skippers know where hot springs are along Douglas Channel – there are several natural mineral hot springs in the area.

Fine hiking trails, up mountains and along Douglas Channel. Also a popular 18-hole golf course where foxes have been known to steal golf balls. And swimming in channel, or in area lakes.

Kitimat Information: Info Centre on south side of Hwy 37 near residential areas. Year-round. 250-632-6294 or 1-800-664-6554. Kitimat Chamber of Commerce, Box 214, Kitimat, BC, V8C 2G7.

■ **Kitimat Centennial Museum:** City centre. Mon-Sat, year-round. 250-632-7022. Haisla Nation and eulachon fishery, pioneer and natural history exhibits. Archives, art gallery, gift shop.

■ **Radley Municipal Campground:** Centre of town on Dike Rd. Hot showers, some electric hook-ups, picnic sites, smokehouse. Here is **BC's oldest Sitka spruce tree**, more than 11m in circumference, 50m tall, and 500 years old.

■ **Industrial Tours:** To register, call Info Centre or sites. Alcan Kitimat Works, one of the world's largest aluminum smelters, 250-639-8259. Eurocan Pulp and Paper, ultra-modern, Canada's number one exporter of unbleached packaging paper, 250-639-3597. Methanex Corporation, for methanol and ammonia, a building-block chemical for petro-chemicals and plastics, 250-639-9292.

■ **Kitimat River Hatchery:** 250-639-9888. Box 197, Kitimat, BC, V8G 2G7. Chum, coho, steelhead, cutthroat from Oct-Nov.

Juveniles, Feb-June. Tours May Sept. BC Wildlife Watch viewing site.
■ **Tamitik Pool and Sports Complex:** 250-632-7161. Swims, swirls, racquet sports. Also **Riverlodge Recreation Centre**, 250-632-3161.
■ **Golf: Hirsch Creek Golf Club**, 2000 Kingfisher Ave. 250-632-4653. 18 holes.

Return to Highway 16 at Highway 37

Ferry Island Municipal Campground and Park: 61ha; 68 campsites. 1km from Yellowhead/Hwy 37 junction, 3km east of Terrace, on island in Skeena. Good base camp for exploring Terrace area.

Terrace: (Pop. 12,779). Starts just beyond park. 210km southwest of Smithers, 140km east of Prince Rupert. Incorporated in 1927, a full-range service centre with a colourful history. Natural terraces cut by the Skeena River provide its name. Sternwheeler days are not forgotten. Nostalgia and period costumes are part of Riverboat Days in Aug. Farmer's market Sat mornings next to library. Fresh veggies, fireweed honey, crafts. Art of the local Tsimshian people is enjoying a renaissance.

Terrace is famous for fish and bears. The Skeena River is the mother of sportfishing streams. A 42kg rod-caught spring salmon was once landed about 6km from downtown Terrace, a world record. And then there's the Kermode bear (ker-mode), an exotic and distinct subspecies of the black bear. Its fur ranges from chestnut blonde to white. Hunting the legendary white Kermode is prohibited. It's unknown how many roam the mountainous terrain and lush forests around Terrace. Visitors are sure to see the bear's likeness on signs and vehicles. Terrace adopted the great animal for its municipal symbol.

Terrace Information: Info Centre on south side of Hwy 16 next to old logging spar, 1.5km from Hwy 16/37 junction. 250-635-2063. Fax: 250-635-2573. Year-round. Terrace and District Chamber of Commerce, 4511 Keith Ave, Terrace, BC, V8G 1K1.

Terrace-Kitimat Airport: See p.230 for details on location and service.

■ **Heritage Park:** On Kerby Rd, Late April-early Sept. Operated by Terrace Regional Museum Society, Box 246, Terrace, BC, V8G 4A6. 250-635-4546. A popular spot. Tours of nine original log buildings. Clap hands and keep time with down-home music of old-time fiddlers.

■ **Terrace Art Gallery:** On Park Ave, below library. 250-638-8884. Local arts and crafts.

■ **Historical Points of Interest Tour:** Map from Info Centre.

■ **House of Sim-Oi-Ghets:** Off highway just west of town. Showcase for the Kitsumkalum, the local Tsimshian people. Carvings, jewelry, prints, books.

■ **Deep Creek Salmon Hatchery:** 2km north of Terrace, past Northwest College, then follow signs. Write Terrace Salmon Enhancement Society, Box 21, Terrace, BC, V8G 4A2. 250-635-3471. Interpretive trail. Pink and chum salmon spawning late Aug-Sept. BC Wildlife Watch viewing site.

■ **Skeena Valley Golf and Country Club:** 3525 Golf Course Rd, Thornhill in Terrace. 250-635-2542 or 1-800-770-2542. Nine-hole course.

■ **Recreation Facilities:** Aquatic Centre, 250-635-9212. Also tennis courts in three locations, ask at Info Centre.

■ **Terrace Mountain Nature Trail:** Turn east at intersection of Kalum St and Halliwell Ave. Moderate grade trail, excellent views of city and valley. Three-hour round trip.

■ **Farmers Market:** For location, ask at Info Centre. Sat, 9-1; Wed 4-7, May-Oct.

Kalum Lake Rd/Nisga'a Hwy: 3km west of Info Centre. Turn north, about 85km to traditional territories of the Nisga'a people and **Nisga'a Memorial Lava Bed Park. Please note:** if you intend to camp at **Red Sand Lake Demonstration Forest campground** on your way up to Nisga'a Territories, **West Kalum Rd**, below, is the route to go.

SIDE TRIP

to Nisga'a Memorial Lava Bed Park

Finley Lake: 10.5km beyond junction, on Kalum Lake Rd. Little kettle lake, fun for canoeing.

Kitsumkalum Lake: 17.5km beyond Finley Lake. Offers golden beaches, good fishing.

Rosswood: (Pop. 181). 41km north of Hwy 16 junction, on north end of Kitsumkalum Lake. General store, gas. Good fishing on all area lakes and streams.

Lava Lake: 23km beyond Rosswood. The Nisga'a call it Sii T'axl, "new lake," created when lava poured out from Tseax Cone, the volcano Wil Ksi Baxl Mihl, "where the fire flowed from," more than two centuries ago, diverting the area's rivers. Lake marks entrance to **Nisga'a Memorial Lava Bed Park** (below).

Nisga'a Memorial Lava Bed Provincial Park: 17,683ha; basic camping beside Vetter Creek. Visitor Centre near Vetter Creek (follow signs), 250-683-9589. Provincial park managed jointly with Nisga'a government. Info: BC Parks, 250-847-7320, or Nisga'a Tribal Council, 250-633-2601. Entrance at south end of Lava Lake.

Scientists believe Tseax Cone erupted around 1775. It destroyed two Nisga'a villages, killed as many as 2,000 people, dammed waterways, and rerouted the Nass River. Now the reminder, a sparsely vegetated lava plain, stretches 10km along the Tseax, "new river," and Nass rivers. The Nisga'a tell us this was nature's lesson: the eruption followed a time when children amused themselves by watching salmon flit and dart after sticking smoldering bits of bark into their backs.

Some of the lava is rope-like in shape, some rough and jagged; there are also lava blocks. In some places it is 35m deep. Colourful lichens have colonized the mineral-rich matter. Their

chemical secretions are slowly breaking it down, providing precarious footholds for rock mosses, spotted saxifrage, and mountain parsley. In moist, shady pockets, where a little humus has built up, ferns trace elegant patterns; a few larger plants – birch, alder, cottonwood, and an occasional evergreen – have also found a niche.

Guided hikes to Lava Cone, weekends, and some Wednesdays, July-Oct, from Visitor Centre. Must reserve for this 3km, four-hour hike: call 250-638-9589. Although this is a Class A provincial park, the Nisga'a have retained hunting, fishing, trapping, and food-gathering rights. They also see the park as an opportunity to showcase their traditional customs and inform visitors about age-old sustainable land management practices. Visitor Centre displays history and is a performance space for dancers, drummers, and storytellers. Boat ramp and picnic site at north end of Lava Lake. A second boat launch is on the Nass near the Tseax River, a popular place for salmon and trout fishing.

New Aiyansh (Gitlakdamix): (Pop. 2,000). 2km northeast of road through park. Headquarters and easternmost of four Nisga'a villages. The "old village" is across the river: after years of flooding, the people moved here in 1961. Here are offices of the Nisga'a Tribal Council, B&B accommodation, gas, groceries. Information: 250-633-2601.

This is the heartland of 1,930 square kilometres of new Nisga'a treaty territories. In 1998, the Nisga'a people, with the governments of BC and Canada, signed a treaty they ardently sought for 111 years. The historic agreement, the first to be negotiated in this province, will give the Nisga'a title to land (about one-tenth of their traditional territories embracing the Nass River), some $250 million in cash and grants, control over their forests, and greater access to fisheries. They will have control over education and their own police force. Nisga'a names will be returned to important sites.

Nass Camp: (Pop. A dozen families plus guests). 250-633-2434. 11km east of Gitlakdamix along Nass Forest Service Rd. Says Canada's national newspaper, "an unconventional place housing an unconventional cast of characters" – a scene from the T.V. series *Northern Exposure*. William Young took over former logging camp in 1983, offering backwoods accommodation and gourmet fare to hunters, fishermen, mushroom pickers, and land-claims negotiators: here are the Tillicum Lodge (bunkhouses and tiny rooms offering fresh towels and thin walls), The Kitchen, and The Bar.

Canyon City (Gitwinksihlkw): (Pop. 231). About 9km west of Gitlakdamix on gravel road tracing the Nass River. Until 1995, boats, or the pedestrian bridge suspended 15m over the churning Nass, were this Nisga'a community's only link to the world beyond. A new 174m road bridge is adorned with four remarkable carved poles, recounting the histories of the four Nisga'a clans – Wolf, Eagle, Killer Whale, and Raven.

Greenville (Laxqalts'ap): (Pop. 600). 44km west of Gitlakdamix. Accessible by road since 1984. This Nisga'a community sits just above the tidal waters of Fishery Bay. There, the many Nisga'a villagers of times past, along with their Haida, Tsimshian, and Gitxsan friends, gathered to share in the bounty of oily eulachon that break winter's fast, arriving sometimes even before the ice has melted. Community offers B&B accommodation, arts and crafts, and is developing recreational opportunities for nearby Ishkheenickh River. Band office: 250-621-3213.

Beyond Laxqalts'ap, the road is being extended seaward 28km to the Nisga'a village of Kincolith (Gingolx), long accessible only by air, private boat, or ferry service from Prince Rupert. Ask at Laxqalts'ap or Gitlakdamix before attempting to proceed.

Kincolith (Gingolx): (Pop. 318). At the mouth of the Nass River. The "people of the place of skulls" long ago scared off invaders by posting old skulls on sticks. Today, this Nisga'a community welcomes visitors who come to fish for salmon and view sea life. Accommodation. Band office: 250-326-4212.

Visitors can leave the Nass Valley by returning south to Hwy 16 via the Nisga'a Hwy, or by following the unpaved Nass Forest Service Rd east from Gitlakdamix, 86km to Cranberry Junction and Hwy 37. See p.280 for connecting point.

Return to Highway 16 at Kalum Lake Road/ Nisga'a Highway Junction

West Kalum Rd: 3km west of Kalum Rd. North for **Red Sand Lake Demonstration Forest**.

Red Sand Lake Demonstration Forest: 40ha; three campgrounds – on Red Sand Lake (toilet and one of 14 campsites is wheelchair accessible), the Hart Farm on Kalum Lake, the Old Field (group camping) on road into main campground. 24km from Hwy 16 on gravel logging road. 250-638-5100. Formerly Kitsumkalum Provincial Park. Now managed by BC Ministry of Forests. Red sandy beach legacy of volcanic activity. Demonstration forest lies along trade trail used by Nisga'a and Kitsumkalum peoples. Some trees show evidence of native use: strips of bark have been taken for making baskets, clothing, and rope. There is also evidence of farmsteads, including Hart Farm, established early in this century. Three trails (1.6-3.8km) lead through managed and unmanaged stands of trees, to show effects of nature and man. One trail is wheelchair accessible. Wildlife includes moose, porcupines, even kermode bear; bald eagles, ospreys, swans, loons.

Shames Mountain Ski Corporation: 18km from West Kalum Rd, then 14km north on Shames Rd. 250-635-3773. Wed-Sun. Double chairlift, T-bar handle tow. Vertical drop 518m. Cafeteria. Summer hiking. Afternoon tea in the alpine.

Exstew Rest Area: 20km beyond Shames Mountain Ski Resort access. Lovely spot on misty Skeena, south of highway. Wheelchair accessible picnic table, hand pump for water.

Exchamsiks River Provincial Park: 18ha; 20 campsites beneath towering sitka spruce. 55km west of Terrace. 250-847-7320. Nature trail, boat launch; salmon fishing. In summer, scan nearby cliff for mountain goats.

Gitnadoix River Recreation Area: 58,000ha. 250-847-7320. Almost opposite Exchamsiks River Park on Hwy 16. Access by crossing the Skeena. Protects entire Gitnadoix drainage. Harbour seals swim 100km upstream to Alastair Lake in pursuit of spawning salmon. Lower reaches of twisting Gitnadoix River can be explored by canoe or boat. Look for mountain goats May to Oct.

Kasiks Rest Area: 60km west of Terrace. On the banks of the Kasiks River. Picnic tables, pit toilet, and boat launch.

Telegraph Point Rest Area: 85km west of Terrace. Wheelchair-accessible picnic table, pet walking area.

Basalt Creek Viewpoint: 33.5km beyond Telegraph Point Rest Area. Eulachon (silvery smelt) migrate upstream on the Lower Skeena to spawn, mid-March to early April. They attract harbour seals, Steller's sea lions, bald eagles, and many species of gulls, which can be seen here.

Prudhomme Lake Provincial Park: 7ha; 24 campsites. 27.5km west of rest area. 250-847-7320. Small forested lakefront park. Fishing, boat launch.

Diana Lake Provincial Park: 233ha. South 1.5km past Prudhomme Lake. Follow narrow gravel road for 2.5km. Dipping, windsurfing, kites, cutthroat trout. Small stream provides opportunities to observe several spawning fish species. In May, look for steelhead; sockeye salmon from mid-Aug to Sept; pink salmon from late Aug-early Sept; coho and chinook salmon from Sept to mid-Oct.

Skeena Dr: 8km beyond Diana Lake Park (8km from Prince Rupert). An old route to canneries and fish processing plants. Leads to historic North Pacific Cannery at Port Edward.

Port Edward: (Pop. 739). On Skeena Dr, 4km west of Hwy 16. A fishing village and service community for Skeena Cellulose Inc's Skeena Pulp operations: the pulp mill, a major employer for Prince Rupert, faces possible closure.

Viewpoint: On Skeena Dr, 5km west of Hwy 16. Industry as scenery: grain elevator on Ridley Island dominates skyline to the southwest. Sani-station.

Kitson Island Marine Park: 45ha – 25ha of ocean, 20ha of shoreline. Undeveloped park across from Port Edward. 250-847-7320.

Inverness Cannery: 8.5km from Hwy 16. A thinning of the forest and historic sites sign mark site of northern BC's first cannery, opened 1876, closed 1950.

North Pacific Cannery Village Museum: 1889 Skeena Dr (10.5km from Yellowhead Hwy). Programs May 1-Sept 30. Off-season open, but no programs; tours by appointment. Write North Pacific Cannery and Museum, 1889 Skeena Dr, Port Edward, BC, V0V 1G0. 250-628-3538.

BC's oldest surviving salmon cannery, dating from 1889. Declared a national historic site in 1985. Restoration is ongoing. This is the last of 19 canneries that operated at the mouth of the Skeena. Authentic glimpse of pioneer coastal lifestyle. Displays show how fish were caught and processed. Rope making and net mending demonstrated.

Galloway Rapids Rest Area: Just west of Skeena Dr. On west side of rapids and short bridge separating Mainland BC from Kaien Island, upon which Prince Rupert sits. Looks out to delightful maze of islets and waterways; map on sign helps you understand just where you are.

Ridley Island Access Rd: 3km beyond Skeena Dr and Hwy 16 intersection. 8km to terminal where grain and coal are transferred to ships bound for international markets. Viewpoint at 5.5km looks back to Skeena Cellulose pulp mill at Port Edward, and ahead to sky-high grain elevator. Prince Rupert Grain Ltd elevator is a big draw for Prairie farmers who come to see where their grain goes. Check with Prince Rupert Info Centre for tours. 250-624-5637.

Oliver Lake Park: 5ha. Less than 1km from Ridley Island Rd. 250-847-7320. Guided walks, May-Oct, 250-628-3298. Named for John Oliver, BC Premier 1918-1927. Boardwalks around small lake offer a rare chance to explore the stunted and unusual plants of the northern Canadian muskeg ecosystem. Sign describes what you will find: tiny sundew growing in the sphagnum moss are insect eaters; there are bog blueberries, bonsail-like shore pines, and if you're lucky, bald eagles, beavers, deer. Picnic tables.

Butze Rapids: 3km beyond Oliver Lake park. Rapids reverse with tides, confused water foams, particularly on falling tide.

Prince Rupert: (Pop. 16,714). Beyond rapids. 140km southwest of Terrace on Kaien Island, linked to Mainland BC by a very short bridge. Northwestern terminus for VIA Rail, BC Ferries' *Queen of the North* from north Vancouver Island; and the Alaska Marine Highway System. Terminal for cruise ships, and BC Ferries to Haida Gwaii.

Where city meets sea is a new, and still unnamed park, a people place, graced by a simple, evocative sculpture: killer whale and her calf. From just the right angle, they appear to be plunging into the depths before them – Prince Rupert's harbour, a source of life for many. From here we look out to the maze of

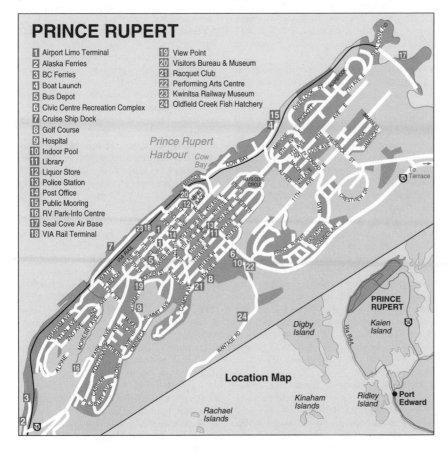

PRINCE RUPERT

1. Airport Limo Terminal
2. Alaska Ferries
3. BC Ferries
4. Boat Launch
5. Bus Depot
6. Civic Centre Recreation Complex
7. Cruise Ship Dock
8. Golf Course
9. Hospital
10. Indoor Pool
11. Library
12. Liquor Store
13. Police Station
14. Post Office
15. Public Mooring
16. RV Park-Info Centre
17. Seal Cove Air Base
18. VIA Rail Terminal
19. View Point
20. Visitors Bureau & Museum
21. Racquet Club
22. Performing Arts Centre
23. Kwinitsa Railway Museum
24. Oldfield Creek Fish Hatchery

Prince Rupert Harbour Cow Bay

Location Map

PRINCE RUPERT

Digby Island

Kaien Island

Kinaham Islands

Rachael Islands

Ridley Island

Port Edward

islands and passages that have given sustenance to the Tsimshian people for some 10,000 years. Tsimshian means "going into the river of mists"– the river we now call Skeena. In the late 1700s, 10 Tsimshian tribes – about 8,000 people – occupied 60 winter villages in Prince Rupert and Venn Passage. It may have been the largest concentration of people in North America, north of Mexico. Then came the fur trade, disease, alcohol, and depopulation. From the late 1800s, more than two dozen salmon canneries came and went from the river mouth, employing whole families of Tsimshian people, as well as other aboriginal, Chinese, and European peoples.

In those days, there was no Prince Rupert. Kaien Island, at the mouth of the river of mists, was a mountain of rock and muskeg, doused by rain (the annual average is 2,552mm a year – about twice what Vancouver gets).

But what Charles Hays saw when he arrived here in the early 1900s was the third deepest harbour in the world (after Buenos Aires, Argentina and Sydney, Australia). He saw a transcontinental railway delivering lumber, grain, and coal to waiting ships, and a city that would eclipse Vancouver in importance (being five days closer to Asian markets). Hays – president of the new Grand Trunk Pacific railway (GTP) – quietly purchased 4,000ha of land for a song, then began promoting his Vienna of the North.

Prince Rupert – named in a contest for European royalty, and designed by architects – was one of Canada's first planned cities (it still shows, with its wide boulevards, viewscapes, and a lack of strip-mall development). Hays was determined there should be a hotel grander than the Empress in Victoria, and called upon its architect, Francis Rattenbury, to design it. In 1912, on a fund-raising mission, Hays sailed to England: and in keeping with his style, undertook his return voyage aboard the grandest ship of all time, the RMS *Titanic*. Hays was among those lost at sea. The hotel was never built.

Two years later, and eight years after construction began, the first train rolled into Prince Rupert. The new city didn't fare well during the First World War. The GTP, too, fell on hard times, and in 1919 was taken over by the Canadian Pacific Railway.

Prince Rupert today is a "working man's town" – a shipping centre suffering the effects of the floundering fishing and forest industries. It's a city on a very human scale: visitors (300,000 a year) are greeted with small-town warmth. Prince Rupert's downtown, unlike most small cities in Canada, is quite walkable – a bonus for passengers off ferries and cruise ships. The airport bus terminal, B&Bs, hotels, restaurants, shops featuring native art, museums, parks and the bustling waterfront are all within a small radius. The ferry terminals are about 2km south of town, with the city-owned Park Ave Campground nearby.

Prince Rupert is more of a waypoint than an end point, explains Andree, of Andrees Bed and Breakfast. "Hardly anyone drives here on the Yellowhead and leaves the same way," she says, "except Prairie farmers who come to see where their grain goes." However one gets here, there is good reason to stay awhile. Here are fishing and diving charters; guided heritage tours; totem, nature, and whale-watching tours; grizzly-bear-watching tours, hot springs, and kayak tours and rentals. The Info Centre has a list of operators.

Prince Rupert Information: Information Centre at 1st and McBride (Yellowhead Hwy) in Museum of Northern BC. Year-round. 250-624-5637 or 1-800-667-1994. Write Prince Rupert Information Centre, Box 669, Prince Rupert, BC, V8J 3S1. Further seasonal information at Park Ave Campground, 1km from BC Ferries/Alaska Marine Highway System terminals.

BC Ferries Terminal: At end of Trans-Canada Hwy (16), about 2km from heart of downtown. *Queen of the North*, from Port Hardy. To Queen Charlotte Islands.

Alaska Marine Highway System: Adjacent BC Ferries Terminal. For details, see p.260.

VIA Rail: Below First Ave, on waterfront, via Bill Murray Way. 250-627-7589 or 1-800-561-8630. The *Skeena* provides Scenic daylight service between Jasper, Alberta and Prince Rupert, BC, with overnight stop in Prince George. Departs Wed, Fri, Sun year-round from both Jasper and Prince Rupert.

Prince Rupert Airport: On Digby Island west of Prince Rupert. The plane lands, passengers get in small buses and pay $11 (you have no choice, there is no other transportation to downtown Prince Rupert). Do not look for your luggage: it is being transported directly to the airport "terminal" in the Rupert Square Mall. No matter what car rental agencies have told you, Budget and Tilden are at the mall, not the airport. **For your flight out of Prince Rupert, check the airport bus schedule well ahead of time** – passengers have missed the bus, and hence, their plane.

■ **Park Ave Campground:** 1km from ferry terminals. Serviced and unserviced sites. Reservations recommended in summer: 1-800-667-1994 or 250-624-5861.

■ **Museum of Northern BC:** 1st Ave and McBride. In Chatham Village, dramatic longhouse-style building is also home to Northwestern BC Community College and Tsimshian Tribal Council. 250-624-3207 or 1-800-667-1994. Daily, in summer; Mon-Sat, in winter. One of BC's best community museums. Main focus is story of the Tsimshian, "people going into the river of mists." Their communities are along the coast, on outlying islands, and up the Skeena River as far as Kitselas Canyon above Terrace. Museum works with the Tsimshian people recording history, preparing databases, publishing books. Excellent bookstore, gift shop. Artists are often working at the **Carving Shed**, one block away. Regular programs include: *The Prince Rupert Story: an Evening of Drama*, a dramatization and slide show, and *Living Along the North Coast: Stories and Adventures*, with local authors.

■ **Archaeology Harbour Tours:** From museum. June-Sept. Three-hour tours with expert guides to petroglyphs, middens, and Tsimshian village sites past and present. Operated by the Museum of Northern BC and and the Metlakatla Development Corporation, 250-628-3201. First stop is **Metlakatla** (pop. 153), a Tsimshian village, 20 minutes by boat west of Prince Rupert (Metlakatla is actually on the Mainland; Prince Rupert on Kaien Island). The pretty village occupies an ancient site where a group of Tsimshian returned, in 1862, to establish a utopian Christian society under the guidance of missionary, William Duncan. Tour boats pass through Venn Passage, once the site of dozens of Tsimshian villages.

A separate five-hour tour is to nearby Laxspa'aws or **Pike Island**, site of three Tsimshian villages, one inhabited in the 1800s; two abandoned 18-20 centuries ago. Knowledgeable guides lead visitors along shores, highlighting some of more than 100 petroglyphs, and through the forest to house depressions where their ancestors lived millennia ago. Salmon lunch. **Metlakatla Ferry Service** office and docks are below the Museum of Northern BC. 250-624-3337.

■ **Self-guided Tour of Carved Poles:** Brochure at Info Centre. The book *Totem Poles of Prince Rupert* is at museum book shop.

■ **Downtown Walking Tour:** Info Centre has detailed booklet. 3km tour features historic harbour sites, courthouse and sunken gardens, and tales of how the city came to be. Also guided tours from museum.

■ **Performing Arts Centre:** 1100 McBride. Entertainment complex with 700-seat theatre. 250-627-7529 for attractions.

■ **Kwinitsa Station Railway Museum:** At Pacific Place, across from VIA Rail station, at First Ave and Bill Murray Way. 250-627-1915 or 250-627-3207. Daily mid-May to Sept. The station, built 1911, was originally located between Prince Rupert and Terrace.

■ **Prince Rupert Fire Museum Society:** 200-1st Ave W. 250-627-4475. Open full days, summer; winter by appointment. Displays a 1925 REO Speed-wagon fire truck and history of fire department 1908 to present.

■ **Pacific Mariners Memorial Park:** Adjacent Chatham Village Longhouse. A poignant stop overlooking harbour: statue of a mariner surrounded by Memorial Wall with names of souls lost at sea. Enshrined here, the small fishing boat of a Japanese fisherman. In 1987, two years after he failed to return home, it washed up the shores of Haida Gwaii; a search for identification led to Owase, Japan, Prince Rupert's sister city.

■ **Prince Rupert Salmonid Enhancement Project:** On Oldfield Creek. Past Performing Arts Theatre and left onto Wantage Rd for 1km. 250-624-6733. Pink salmon, coho. Picnic site. BC Wildlife Watch viewing site.

■ **Harbour Tours and Fishing Charters:** Prince Rupert Charter Operators, Box 1052, Prince Rupert, BC, V8J 4H5. 1-800-667-1994.

■ **Khutzeymateen Grizzly Bear Sanctuary:** 44,902ha. 250-847-7320. Wild coastal valley 45km north of Prince Rupert by air. Accessible only by air and sea: ask at Info Centre about charters (you *will* see grizzly bears). Rugged, densely forested terrain where the Khutzeymateen River flows down through the Kitimat Ranges of the Coast Mountains to the Khutzeymateen Inlet, a narrow 25km-long seaway joining Portland Inlet near the BC/Alaska border. Khutzeymateen or K'tzim-a-Deen in the Tsimshian language means "a long inlet in a steep valley."

Valley is home to about 60 grizzly bears, the largest known grizzly population on BC's coast. This is the only park in the world expressly preserved for grizzly bears, slowly disappearing from shrinking wilderness. Environmentalists want many more grizzly areas preserved before it is too late. Park is off-limits to hunting and logging, and jointly managed by the BC government and Tsimshian First Nation. BC Wildlife Watch viewing site.

■ **Prince Rupert Centennial Golf Club**, 523-9th Ave W. Three blocks from city centre. 250-624-2000. 18 holes.

■ **Cow Bay:** On Cow Bay Rd, walking distance from downtown. Named for city's first "dairy." In 1909, an entrepreneurial farmer had cows shipped here, and without a dock, they swam ashore. Dairy was short-lived, but today, mailboxes and garbage cans are adorned with Jersey spots. Cowpuccino's Coffee House, seafood, pub, shops, galleries, B&B, lots of boat watching.

HAIDA GWAII

THE QUEEN CHARLOTTE ISLANDS

Haida Gwaii, known in the last two centuries as the Queen Charlotte Islands, is a triangular archipelago of some 200 islands, most of them small and uninhabited, covering an area of 9,596 sq km, running 251km from south to north, and roughly 84km west to east. They are separated from the mainland by stormy Hecate Strait, ranging in width from 50km to 130km. The largest islands are Graham to the north, and Moresby, to the south.

The modern hub is the cluster of towns near the ports of entry. Skidegate Landing (BC Ferries terminal), Skidegate, and Queen Charlotte City are on southern Graham Island. Sandspit, and the airport, are on northern Moresby Island. A second airport, at Masset, now offers scheduled air service to Vancouver, May-Oct. The communities of Tlell and Port Clements are located along Hwy 16 (an extension of the Yellowhead) that runs north on Graham Island, 108km from Skidegate Landing to Masset. The only paved road on Moresby Island runs the 13km between the Alliford Bay ferry terminal and Sandspit. See *Transportation*, p.259.

Easy access to the islands, via BC Ferries, has only existed since 1980, yet Haida Gwaii has been drawing European travellers since the late 1700s. Before that, these islands were the sole domain of the Haida, the "people." The appeal of the islands comes in part from their isolated, storm-swept landscape. It also comes from the arts and culture of the people who have lived here since Raven set the islands down in what was a boundless expanse of sea and sky. The Haida are sometimes called

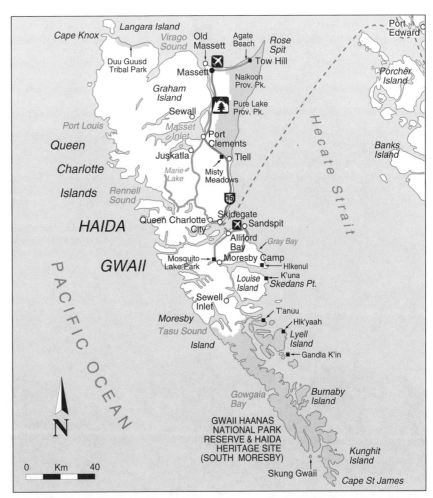

the Vikings of the Pacific Northwest for their sea-faring prowess; among them have been, and still are, artists of great renown.

The Haida tradition of precision and awareness (be it in carving, canoeing, trading, environmental appreciation) has been strong enough to survive even the holocaust of smallpox that followed the arrival of the first Europeans in the late 1700s. At that time the Haida population was an estimated at more than 7,000 people distributed throughout the islands, and some 1,700 more who had recently emigrated to southern Alaska. By 1915, the Haida population had dropped to less than 600. Today, Haida live throughout the archipelago with two main centres: Old Massett (pop. 650), and Skidegate (pop. 550).

The Haida make up almost half of the islands' total population: their influence is significant. They participate heavily in the islands' major industries, logging and fishing, and as stewards of the environment. They are also playing an important role in tourism.

Increasingly popular are opportunities to visit ancient Haida villages in **Gwaii Haanas National Park Reserve and Haida Heritage Site** (south Moresby Island) accessible only by air or watercraft, or guided tours (for reservations and registration information, see below). The Haida have also established **Duu Guusd Tribal Park** to protect villages on the northwest coast of Graham Island: visits may be possible with permission from the band office in Old Massett.

In 1787, some 13 years after Spanish explorer Juan Perez sailed to Haida Gwaii, British explorer Captain George Dixon named the islands Queen Charlotte for his ship and his queen. Many of the more recent travellers here have been artists and poets. Emily Carr, Sean Virgo, Susan Musgrave, Toni Onley, Roy Vickers and others have all brought images of the islands and their inhabitants to the outside world.

The isolation and climate make the islands distinctly different from the mainland. Unique subspecies thrive here, from the largest black bears to tiny saw-whet owls. A type of yellow daisy blooms only in the Charlottes. Wild rocky shorelines and coves characterize the west coast. Luxurious rainforests grow through the islands' heartland. Eastern beaches are deserted scimitars of sand and driftwood.

The Charlottes provide superlative wilderness adventures. Boating, camping, crabbing, beach walking, scuba diving, photography, and rainbow-watching opportunities are unlike any place else. There is excellent freshwater and saltwater fishing. Gwaii Haanas is a dream challenge for the experienced kayaker or sailor. Each storm washes in a whole new world for the beachcomber. There is excellent freshwater and and saltwater fishing.

Exploring Haida Gwaii involves driving some of the 2,000km of logging roads. Check with forest companies first and obey signs and procedures. Roads are narrow, loaded logging trucks are wide. Most logging roads on Graham Island are controlled by MacMillan Bloedel. Call Queen Charlotte City, 250-559-4224, or Juskatla, 250-557-4212. On Moresby Island check at the Sandspit information centre located at the Sandspit Airport May-Labour Day. The rest of the year, contact the TimberWest office in Sandspit, 250-637-5323.

Graham Island

Graham Island is the largest, most accessible, and most populated of the islands. Visitors come by ferry from Prince Rupert and dock at Skidegate, also terminal for the ferry to Moresby Island.

Highway 16: At Skidegate. Leads west to Queen Charlotte City. Leads north to Tlell, Port Clements, and Masset.

Balance Rock, north of Skidegate on Graham Island.

SIDE TRIP

to Queen Charlotte City

Queen Charlotte City: (Pop. 1,222). About 5km west of BC Ferries terminal at Skidegate. Though Queen Charlotte City, on Bearskin Bay, is administrative centre for the islands, there is very much a small, frontier-town feeling here. The people you'll most likely meet will be (Haida and non-Haida) loggers, fishermen, local services operators, and their families. Shops and excellent galleries display arts and crafts. Bus and nature tours and boat charters can be arranged here. There is a floatplane base, accommodation, restaurants, grocery stores, laundromat. Here also are headquarters for the Gwaii Haanas National Park Reserve and Haida Heritage Site: 250-559-8818.

Queen Charlotte City Information: Queen Charlotte Visitor Information Centre, 3220 Wharf St, Box 819, Queen Charlotte City, BC, V0T 1S0. 250-559-8316. Daily year-round.

■ **Haydn Turner Park:** Community park, 15 campsites, west end of town. Follow main street through town past pavement. Primitive camping at own risk: park's future uncertain.

■ **Skidegate Band Salmon Project:** On Honna River. 3km west of town on Honna Forest Service Rd. Write Skidegate Band Council, Box 1301, Queen Charlotte Islands, BC, V0T 1S1. 250-559-4496. Coho and chum, mid-Oct to June. BC Wildlife Watch viewing site.

■ **Kagan Bay Forest Service Campground:** Four beautiful user-maintained beachfront campsites. 5km west of town on Honna Forest Service Rd. Demonstration forest.

Rennell Sound: A deep inlet on west coast with access by logging road. Gravel beaches. Call MacMillan Bloedel (250-559-4224 or 250-557-4212), Forest Service office, or ask at information centre before travelling. Mainline logging road runs north to Km 22. Turn west on gravel road.

Rennell Sound Recreation Site: Two campgrounds, containing seven and three wilderness beach campsites respectively. 14km from logging main line on rough and exceedingly steep gravel road. Walking trails through virgin rainforest to sandy west-coast beaches. Look for Japanese fishing floats.

Return to Skidegate Landing

Hwy 16 starts from ferries terminal, follows coastline east then north to Skidegate.

Haida Gwaii Museum: At Qay'llnagaay. East off Hwy 16 at Second Beach, 1km from ferry terminal. 250-559-4643. June-late Aug, 10-5 weekdays. Afternoons most weekends. World's largest collection of carvings in argillite, a slate black rock found only in the Charlottes and only in one undisclosed location. Prized as carving medium by Haida artists. Videos to see, books to buy.

Haida Gwaii Watchmen and the Wave Eater: In longhouse-style office next to museum. Box 609, Skidegate, Haida Gwaii, V0T 1S0. 250-559-8225. Seasonal. In the 1970s, members of the Haida community took over the role of protecting from vandalism and theft the ancient villages of what is now **Gwaii Haanas National Park Reserve and Haida Heritage Site**. They became the first modern-day Haida Gwaii Watchmen. During summer, Watchmen live at the villages and act as guardians and a point of contact for visitors. Can ask here for information; also see *Gwaii Haanas*, below, for visitor protocol.

Adjacent the Watchmen's office is the canoe, *Loo Taas*, "Wave Eater." Launched at Vancouver during Expo '86, it was the first Haida canoe carved since 1909.

Skidegate: (Pop. 695). Haida community on Rooney Bay 2km north of Skidegate Landing ferry terminal. After a mission was established here in 1883, it became a focal point for the southern Haida. Gift shop; Haida Arts Coop and Carving Longhouse (at end of the village) display Haida art and souvenirs.

■ **Balance Rock:** Pull off highway about 1km north of Skidegate. Short trail leads to beach. An erratic glacial boulder (2m wide by 1.5m tall) dumped by ice on the beach appears to balance on the smaller beach stones. Best viewed during low tide.

■ **Spirit Lake Trail:** Across the highway from George Brown Recreation Hall in Skidegate. 1.5km gravel trail for joggers, hikers, mountain bikers leads through second-growth to old-growth forest revealing traditional Haida forest use, to two lakes used by eagles for bathing. Haida tradition tells of a sea monster (Wasko) who lived in the farther of the two lakes, and had a tunnel to Skidegate Inlet.

SIDE TRIP

to Moresby Island

Visitors arrive on Moresby by ferry from Skidegate Landing on Graham Island or by air.

Grassy Island Rest Area: 7km from Alliford Bay. Overlooks outcropping in Skidegate Inlet, which, during low tide, appears to be a grassy island.

Sandspit: (Pop. 702). About 13km from Alliford Bay, Moresby Island terminus for ferry sailings to Skidegate Landing on Graham Island. RV park on Alliford Bay Rd. Year-round birdwatching for loons, grebes, scoters and migrating shorebirds.

Sandspit Information: Sandspit Information centre, Airport Terminal Building, Alliford Bay Rd, Sandspit, BC. 250-637-5362. Fax: 250-637-2326. Daily, May-Sept.

Sandspit Airport: Main airport for Queen Charlotte Islands. Scheduled flights to Vancouver (Canadian Regional), and Prince Rupert (Harbour Air). Charter operators for visits to Gwaii Haanas.

Most logging roads on north Moresby are controlled by TimberWest. Before travelling check at the Sandspit Information Centre, Airport Terminal Building, Sandspit, 250-637-5362, May 1-Labour Day. Forest tours available.

Gray Bay: BC Forest Service/MacMillan Bloedel has 20 campsites about 21km southeast of Sandspit. Hard sand and gravel beaches. It really is peaceful.

Mosquito Lake Park: 11 rural camp-sites, about 44km southwest of Sandspit. Operated by Western Forest Products and BC Forest Service. Named for the Second World War mosquito bombers. Sitka spruce for building bombers was harvested from area, and is still treasured for making fine pianos and guitars.

Pallant Creek Hatchery: About 46km southwest of Sandspit. Write Box 225, Sandspit, BC, V0T 1T0. 250-559-8695. Chum, pink, coho, and steelhead. Spawning mid-Sept to Oct. See juvenile chum Feb-April, juvenile coho March-June.

Moresby Camp: 2km beyond Pallant Creek. 7 campsites and boat-launching for exploring Cumshewa Inlet and Moresby Islands. There are also two campsites just north of here at Sheldons Bay.

Gwaii Haanas

Gwaii Haanas (south Moresby Island), the much smaller islands of Lyell, Kunghit, and Sgung Gwaii (Anthony Island), and countless islets form the Gwaii Haanas National Park Reserve and Haida Heritage Site. This 90km-long archipelago was set aside in 1987. At 1,470 sq km, the park reserve forms about 15 percent of Haida Gwaii's land mass. This place of sumptuous wildlife, rare plants, and ancient forests was saved from clearcut logging following a decade of efforts and a final stand on Lyell Island in 1985 by members of the Haida Nation. In 1990, Ottawa signed an agreement with the Haida Nation to share the planning, operation, and management of a new park reserve. Haida land claims here are unresolved, but at least their ancient villages are protected.

It's all wilderness: **there are no roads** or shore facilities in the park reserve. Access is by boat and chartered floatplane only. The journey requires commitment: distances are great; it's expensive to get there. All visitors must make a reservation and participate in a mandatory orientation session before departing to the protected area.

For more information contact the Gwaii Haanas Office, Box 37, Queen Charlotte City, BC, V0T 1S0. 250-559-8818. Visit in person in Queen Charlotte City. Orientation sessions are held daily. For an up-to-date planning information package please call the office. Sea kayakers must be aware that the islands are subject to rapidly changing weather, major tidal variations, strong currents, and high winds. Be sure to obtain orientation, route and safety information prior to leaving home.

Ancient villages protected by the Haida Gwaii Watchmen:

■ **Skedans (K'una):** A day-trip from Moresby Camp, by motorized boat from Cumshewa Inlet to Louise Island.

■ **T'anuu:** Harder to reach, on the east shore of Tanu Island.

■ **Hotspring Island (Gandla K'in):** Healing springs south of T'anuu.

■ **Windy Bay (Hlk'yaah):** South of Gandla K'in. Focus of the struggle to save Gwaii Haanas.

■ **Anthony Island (Sgung Gwaii):** The very south end of Haida Gwaii. In the 1880s, after a series of smallpox epidemics, the last Kunghit Haida left the place they called Red Cod Island and Red Cod Island Village (known to white traders as Nunsting or Ninstints). Here is one of the world's most remarkable displays of carved poles: it was declared a UNESCO World Heritage Site in 1981.

Return to Skidegate

Hwy 16 hugs the coast north of Skidegate with views across Hecate Strait. Look for migrating grey whales breaking water late April-June. Rainbows are extraordinary.

Halibut Bight Rest Area: 26km north of Skidegate. Overlooking Hecate Strait.

Tlell: (Pop. 369). 36km north of Skidegate. Picturesque grassy estuary of Tlell River. First homesteaded by Mexican Tom in 1904. Here is the Richardson Ranch, the oldest working ranch on Haida Gwaii (1919). It's a place where artists gather: there's a gallery, cappuccino bar, arts and crafts, and a rock/jewelry shop. The sea is not far away — mile after mile of sand dunes and driftwood. See coho salmon, migrating shorebirds late summer. Several new B&B's have sprung up.

Naikoon Provincial Park: 73,325ha covering almost entire northeast corner of Graham Island. 41 campsites at Agate Beach Campground on the north end; 30 sites at Misty Meadows near Tlell. Wheelchair access. Also primitive campsites throughout park. 250-847-7320. Park headquarters at Tlell on Yellowhead Hwy. Access to southern end is at Tlell; to northern end 25km, mostly gravel, from Masset causeway.

A place sacred to the Haida, Naikoon, "point town," sits on Rose Spit, jutting 12km from the northeast tip of Graham Island, at the park's far north end. This is where some members of the Raven clan find their origins: they were lured out of a giant clamshell by a lonely Raven. Naikoon is an intriguing combination of low-lying bogs, stunted pine and cedar, lakes, sand dunes, beaches.

■ **East Beach Hike:** 94km of sand dunes, driftwood, and deer, from Tlell to Tow Hill. Takes four-six days. Limited water but no dangerous headlands. Some shelters.

■ **Pesuta** (or Pezuta): South-end access. Shipwreck in Naikoon Park is about 5km west of Tlell River bridge through forest and sand. Half-buried hull of 1928 log carrier.

■ **Rose Spit:** North-end access. 17km along beach from parking lot. An ecological reserve. BC Wildlife Watch viewing site.

■ **Tow Hill:** North-end access. Trail leads 15 minutes from parking lot through heavy rainforest to top of hill for views of mainland and Alaska. Site was largest of Haida villages within park boundaries. Tow Hill's 109m basalt cliff is the most prominent landmark on northeast coast. Visit nearby blowhole. Agates on beach.

Yellowhead Hwy swings abruptly northwest from the coast, leaving Tlell.

Port Clements: (Pop. 577). 21km northwest of Tlell on Masset Inlet, between the Kumdis and Yakoun rivers. Giant spruce trees made this an airplane building centre in the First World War. Logging still main industry. Bedroom community for MacMillan Bloedel's operations at Juskatla. Call 250-557-4212 before using logging roads.

Port Clements Information: Village of Port Clements, Box 198, Port Clements, BC, V0T 1R0.

■ **Port Clements Museum:** 45 Bayview Dr (main road into town). Open each afternoon except Mon, June-Sept. Winter hours depend on availability of volunteers. 250-557-4576.

■ **Golden Spruce Trail:** About 5.5km south of Port Clements on Juskatla Rd, then via a 10-minute walk to the river. For nearly three centuries visitors looked across the river to a spectacular spruce ablaze with golden needles. The scientific world was puzzled by this unusual 50m conifer affected by a genetic quirk causing the chloroform in its needles to break down under the sun. The Haida believe the tree held the spirit of a boy named Kiidkayyaas: he fled his village after a snowstorm came as punishment to his people; despite his grandfather's instructions, the boy looked back as he ran, and was transformed into the Golden Spruce. In early 1997 a vandal cut the sacred tree down. With cuttings, geneticists are frantically trying to create another Golden Spruce. Still worth walk in.

■ **Haida Canoe:** On east side of Juskatla Rd 8km from Golden Spruce trail marker. Short walk on trail. Cedar canoe abandoned before it was completed more than a century ago. Its carver may have died from smallpox. Not much left but one gets the idea. Bow of canoe points to stump of tree it was taken from. Largest Haida canoes were 23m long with a 2m beam and could carry 40 people.

■ **Marie Lake Salmon Hatchery:** 40km south of Port Clements on logging road. Write Old Massett Village Council, Box 189, Masset, BC, V0T 1M0. 250-626-5655. Chinook, coho, sockeye. BC Wildlife Watch viewing site.

Watch for black-tailed Sitka deer along roadside north of Port Clements.

Pure Lake Provincial Park: 130ha. North of Port Clements. Day use. Warm lake for swimming. Canoeing, fishing.

Masset: (Pop. 1,293). 40km north of Port Clements. Masset, on Masset Sound, is largest community in Haida Gwaii. At terminus of Hwy 16. Canadian Forces Station Masset, here, was an important search and rescue and information and communications base until the mid-1990s, when global politics shifted, and the Canadian government began downsizing Department of National Defence sites. Only a few military personnel remain, and many of the station's assets, including church, hospital, and recreation centre have been handed over for joint management and development by the Haida in Old Massett and non-natives in Masset. The houses are being sold to people from all over North America seeking nature, recreational fishing, and the area's hundreds of kilometres of sandy beach. All travellers services. RV park open year-round. Road access to north end of Naikoon Provincial Park on Tow Hill Rd. Fishing trips for salmon, halibut, and crab. Beachcombing. Restaurants, accommodation, groceries.

Masset Information: Travel infobooth, About 400m from the "Welcome to Masset" sign on the east side of the highway. 250-626-3982. Daily June-late Aug. In the off-season, Queen Charlotte Info Centre, Box 819, Queen Charlotte Islands, BC, V0T 1S0. 250-559-8316.

■ **Delkatla Wildlife Sanctuary:** 554ha in Masset. Haven for weary wings on Pacific flyway for migratory birds. Some 113 species identified. BC Wildlife Watch viewing site.

Old Massett: (Pop. 692). About 2km north of Masset on east shore of Masset Inlet. Three ancient Haida towns – Atewaas, Kayang, and Jaaguhl – were still here when Massett, the captain of a damaged European ship, landed during a storm to receive provisions and repairs. The people who live here now are descended from citizens of many northern Haida Gwaii villages. Old Massett is the administrative seat of the Council of the Haida Nation. Visitors are asked to be respectful when visiting the community, artists' galleries, and poles. The Old Massett Council, in the large hall on Eagle Rd, has information about local artists and attractions, and, possibly, permits for visiting Duu Guusd Tribal Park (see below): 250-626-3337.

■ **Jim Hart's Carving Shed:** Daily 1-4, for those who wish to view pole carving.

■ **Chief Edenshaw/Morris E. White Haida Canoe and Carving Shed:** Daily 1-4. Large groups please call ahead. 250-626-3985.

■ **Duu Guusd Tribal Park:** Northwest coast of Graham Island from Naden Harbour to Kiusta and south to Seal Inlet. Site of two village sites still in use. A base for Haida Gwaii Rediscovery Society, offering programs for children. Park may be open for limited use by tourists. Ask at Old Massett band office.

STEWART-CASSIAR HIGHWAY

HIGHWAY 37

The Stewart-Cassiar Hwy runs north 721km linking the Yellowhead Hwy 37 with the Alaska Hwy. It leaves the Yellowhead near Kitwanga, and joins the Alaska Hwy 23km west of Watson Lake, 432km east of Whitehorse. The early portion of the highway traces or parallels the Kitwancool Grease Trail that until the last century linked Gitxsan villages to eulachon fisheries on the Nass River.

Now, most of the highway is paved. 124km remains gravel and it is continuously being improved. Rough and broken pavement sections require that care be taken. Distances are great, communities and travellers services few. Keep the gas tank topped up and carry spare tires. Local people are friendly and informal. The Gitxsan communities of Gitwangak and Gitanyow offer glimpses of their culture.

The scenery is spectacular and varied. Wildlife is abundant. The highway, built in sections over many years and completed in 1972, is becoming increasingly popular as a destination in itself. The *Log* starts where Yellowhead Hwy 16 meets the Stewart-Cassiar Hwy 37, 35km west of Hazelton.

Hwy 37 crosses the Skeena River immediately north of its junction with the Yellowhead.

Gitwangak: (Pop. 481). East off Hwy 37, 0.5km north of Hwy 16 junction, then 2km along narrow road that loops to rejoin Hwy 37. Name means "place of rabbits." The three village clans are Eagle, Wolf, and Frog, each with a hereditary chief and its own traditional territories.

Visitors are encouraged to stroll through, take photographs of remarkable totems (at least one was erected as early as 1875), and ask questions. Drive carefully in village.

■ **St Paul's Anglican Church:** Opposite totems. Built 1893. 400-year-old stained-glass windows from England. Services held regularly, visitors welcome. Gitwangak tourist information may be available here.

The Gitwangak road rejoins Hwy 37 almost 4km from the Yellowhead Hwy.

Kitwanga: (Pop. 30). South-access road is 4km north of Yellowhead Hwy 16. Basic travellers services. Sawmilling is the main occupation in this pretty village offering great views of 2,900m Seven Sisters Mountains. School playground good vantage point for photographs. Try Mill Pond for swimming, Bard's Hole on Kitwanga River for fishing. Ask if local craftspeople have work for sale.

Kitwanga Information: Kitwanga Community and Association, Box 98, Kitwanga, BC, V0J 2A0.

Kitwanga Back Rd: 6.5km north of Hwy 37 unpaved road leads east. 1.5km east of Hwy 37, stop-of-interest sign suggests this is the Skeena-River site of the ancient Gitxsan capital, Tam Lax Aamid, that dissolved long ago after a series of catastrophic events. Kitwanga Back Rd joins the Kispiox Valley Rd just south of Glen Vowell.

Fort Kitwanga National Historic Site: Just north of Kitwanga Back Rd along Hwy 37. Call Gwaii Haanas National Park Reserve/Haida Heritage Site: 250-559-8818. Year-round. Known locally as Battle Hill, this 13m manmade hill was site of a Gitxsan fortress or *ta'awdzep*. Five houses here were protected by trap doors, wooden decoys, and great log rollers. About two centuries ago, it was base for the warrior Nekt who defended Gitxsan boundaries wearing armor that made him look like a grizzly bear. He was killed just before the arrival of Europeans to this area. Self-guiding trail.

Kitwanga Rd North: 2.5km north of south access. Alternate route to Kitwanga.

Gitanyow: (Pop. 408). 14km north of Kitwanga north access, just west of Hwy 37. Formerly Kitwancool, meaning "people of a small village." Depleted by disease and warfare over a century ago, Kitwancool has recently reclaimed its former name, Gitanyow, "awesome warrior people." Here are about 18 major poles, including the oldest, "Hole in the Ice" or "Hole in the Sky." This powerful totem, dramatically perforated with a large oval opening, is about 140 years old. Some poles may be removed for repairs. Carvers work in shop nearby. Visitors are encouraged to ask them about their work. New school has beautifully carved doors showing community's crests.

Gitanyow Information: Information centre, Gitanyow Band Council, Box 340, Kitwanga, BC, V0J 2A0. 250-849-5222. Centre in old school next to carving shed. Open late June-Sept.

Gitanyow Rd North: About 5km beyond south access. Alternate route to Gitanyow.

Moonlit Creek Rest Area: About 4.5km from Gitanyow north access. East side of highway. Sign with route map.

Kitwancool Lake: Access about 2km north of rest area and again about 8km. Lake, sometimes referred to as Kitwanga Lake, is off old highway to the west and below Hwy 37. Roads often in poor condition.

Cranberry Junction (Nass River Forest Service Rd): About 40km beyond Kitwancool Lake; 74km north of Hwy 37/16 junction, just before the second crossing of the Cranberry River. The Nass River or Cranberry Rd turns west off Hwy 37 leading 86km to Gitlakdamix. Active logging road: take care. Small Forest Service campground 45km from Hwy 37, at Dragon Lake. Good salmon fishing in Cranberry River. Watch for bears. This is a route to **Nisga'a Memorial Lava Bed Park**. See *Smithers to Prince Rupert*, p.274.

Cranberry River Rest Area: About 8km north of Cranberry Junction.

Kelly Lake Rest Area: About 25km north of Cranberry Junction.

Fasten Seat Belts: Highway becomes an airstrip about 47km beyond Cranberry Junction. Highway also doubles as an emergency airstrip about 27km north of 1st crossing of Bell-Irving River, see below. Aircraft have right-of-way.

Nass River Bridge: 65km north of Cranberry Junction; 138km north of Hwy 16. Rest area east side of highway. Crosses 122m-wide Nass River gorge. One-lane bridge, opened in 1972, was final link completing Hwy 37.

Meziadin Fish Ladders: Turn west about 300m beyond bridge. More than a quarter million salmon, mainly sockeye, use these ladders July to mid-Sept en route to spawning streams.

Meziadin Lake Provincial Park: 335ha; 62 campsites. 12km beyond Nass River bridge. 250-847-7320. Popular spot with boat launch, canoeing, wildlife viewing. Wheelchair access. Extremely busy July-Aug.

Meziadin Junction: (Pop. 7). 1.5km beyond road to park. From here it's 160km south to Hwy 16 and 570km north to the Alaska Hwy. Small community: accommodation, food, gas, repairs.

Meziadin Information: Information centre in log building on north side of highway at junction of Hwys 37 and 37A. Late June-Sept. No phone. Information boards year-round. Off-season write Stewart/Hyder Chamber of Commerce, Box 306, Stewart, BC, V0T 1W0, or call 250-636-9224.

Highway 37A: Paved road heads west 62km to Stewart. A "Will you look at that!" drive between walls of rock, forest, and ice.

SIDE TRIP

to Stewart and Hyder

Strohn Lake and Bear Glacier Rest Area: About 24km beyond Hwy 37A junction. Lake created by melting Bear Glacier, still retreating. It's grubby from glacial debris on top, but incredibly blue inside crevices. Glows at night. Rest area on south side of highway, 1km before glacier. Also pullouts for picture taking. Bring your sweater. It can be chilly even in summer.

Highway and glacial river plunge through narrow Bear Canyon, a year-round active slide zone. **No stopping.** When the road widens, scan the mountainsides for mountain goats.

Clements Lake: About 22km past Bear Glacier. Pretty Forest Service recreation site and hiking trail on south side of highway.

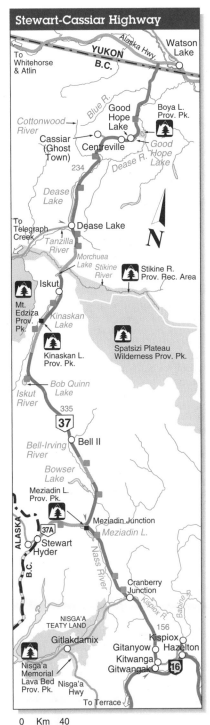

Stewart-Cassiar Highway

0 Km 40

Stewart: (Pop. 858). 62km southwest of Meziadin Junction, on the BC/Alaska border. Canada's most northerly ice-free port, at the head of the Portland Canal.

At the intersection of boundaries between Nisga'a and Gitxsan peoples to the south, the Tahltan to the north, the coastal Tlingit to the east, and the Tsesaut, an Interior people absorbed by their neighbours after a series of wars in the early 1900s. About the same time, in 1896, US Army Engineers entered the region to survey yet another boundary, that separating Canada from the US.

By the time the boundary was finalized in 1903, prospectors on the Klondike trail were searching here for riches, or a least a gateway to them. Among them were Robert, John, and James Stewart, brothers who envisioned for this dramatic setting a great mining centre and port. Robert Stewart, first postmaster of the new town bearing his name, became president of the Stewart Land Company in 1907. By 1910, some 10,000 people lived in a booming town built on pilings above tidal flats. Hard rock gold, silver, and copper were taken by railroad from mines to ships in the canal. Although pilings that supported the railroad along the old road to Hyder, Alaska are no longer visible, there are some pilings left from the little town of Hyder, BC that sat between Stewart and Hyder, Alaska from 1911-1920. Its row of houses, two hotels, and two beer parlours were occupied by Americans during prohibition.

When the mining boom ended, Stewart all but disappeared. A few miners hung on, and loggers moved in. Just like in the movies, something always turns up. Four major movies, including *The Iceman* and *The Thing*, have been set in the rugged mountains, limitless snow, and frontier atmosphere surrounding Stewart.

Visitors can tour old mine sites and movie locations. A highlight is a trip to **Salmon Glacier** (below). Excellent saltwater fishing in Portland Canal (but note that separate licences are required for Canadian and US waters). Boat rentals. Moderately difficult hiking trails, some rewarded by icefield panoramas. RV campground, accommodation, stores, restaurants, gas station.

Stewart Information: Info Centre at 222 5th Ave. Open June-Sept. 250-636-9224. Fax: 250-636-2199. Off-season, Chamber of Commerce, Box 306, Stewart, BC, V0T 1W0. Telephone as above.

■ **Stewart Museum:** In former fire hall at 6th and Columbia. Stewart Historical Society: 250-636-2568. Mining, logging, transportation, and wildlife exhibits.

■ **Salmon Glacier:** First views are about 90km from Stewart via gravel road that weaves across the border into the US and out again. Glacier spectacular and well worth the trip, but the road is unmarked and rough. Bus tours from Stewart.

Hyder, USA: (Pop. 70). 3km from Stewart. Border marked with stone storehouse built by US Army engineers surveying in 1896. 24-hour Canada Customs office. It was first called Portland City, and many of its first citizens were miners and prospectors en route to the Klondike. It was renamed for F.B. Hyder, a geologist. Hyder's claim to fame today is its two bars. Take a shot glass of pure grain alcohol in a gulp to become formally "Hyderized."

The Alaska Marine Highway System: 1-800-642-0066 from the US and Canada; in Canada, 907-465-3941. Or write Alaska Marine Highway System, 1591 Glacier Ave, Juneau, AK, USA, 99801. Ferry leaves Hyder, Alaska weekly on Tues, June to mid-Sept, for Ketchikan.

Return to Highway 37 at Meziadin Junction

The highway strikes north through wild country with the Coast Mountains to the west and the Skeena Mountains, to the east.

Bell-Irving River (Bell I) Rest Area: 31km north of Meziadin. Bear country. Pavement ends here.

Hodder Lake Rest Area: 57km beyond Bell-Irving (Bell I) crossing.

Bell-Irving River (Bell II): Highway crosses again, 3km beyond Hodder Lake rest area. First services in a while. Food, lodging, gas, minor repairs. Dominion Telegraph Line (1889-1901) ran along river's north side.

Ningunsaw Pass: 25km north of Bell-Irving River. Summit 466m. Divide between the drainages of the vast Nass and Stikine river systems. Try the deep bankside pools of the Ningunsaw River for Dolly Varden.

Bob Quinn Lake, Airport, and Rest Area: 22km north of Ningun-saw Summit. New landing strip, not shared with highway traffic. Just west is attractive, mountain-fringed Bob Quinn Lake.

Eastman Creek Rest Area: About 50km beyond Bob Quinn rest area.

Trail to Natadesleen Lake: About 12km from Eastman Creek rest area. 1km walk. Fishing for rainbow trout.

Kinaskan Lake Provincial Park: 1,800ha; 50 campsites. 8km from Natadesleen Lake trail. 250-847-7320. Camp at lake's south end. Easy boat launching, good rainbow trout fishing. June-Aug, look for spruce, willow, and white-tailed ptarmigan. Also seen are Arctic hare, coyote, and moose. Boat required to reach head of Mowdade Trail from Kinaskan Park. Trail leads northwest 24km into **Mount Edziza Provincial Park**. Not for the inexperienced. For access information, check with guides and outfitters in Iskut area, north about 56km. See continuation of *Log*. Full details on Mount Edziza Park in *Side Trip to Telegraph Creek*, below.

Todagin Mountain: On east side of Hwy 37, halfway along Kinaskan Lake. Stone sheep may be seen year-round.

Tatogga Lake: About 25km beyond Kinaskan Lake Park. Resort, gas, food, information. Tatogga Lake is a southern extension of Eddontenajon Lake.

Ealue Lake Rd: Turns northeast off Hwy 37 about 2km north of Tatogga Lake Resort. Follow past private campsite at

Ealue Lake. Road crosses the Klappan River and intercepts abandoned BC Rail bed 22km from Hwy 37. Turn southeast along bed. Parallels southwestern boundary of Spatsizi Plateau Wilderness Park for 60km. Bed is rough, narrow, and may be impassable in bad weather. Check before leaving Hwy 37. Access is only to trailheads leading into park. No direct road access.

SIDE TRIP

to Spatsizi Park

Spatsizi Plateau Wilderness Provincial Park: 656,785ha. No road access. Located 300km by air north of Smithers. 250-847-7320. Write BC Parks Skeena District Office, Bag 5000, 3790 Alfred Ave, Smithers, BC, V0J 2N0.

One of Canada's largest and most significant parks. Quintessential wilderness, Spatsizi encompasses rolling Spatsizi Plateau and glaciated Skeena Mountains. Only for experienced hikers and campers.

Large wildlife populations, including woodland caribou. Spatsizi, in the Dene language of the north, means "red goat," for the local goats' habit of rolling in iron oxide dust. Gladys Lake ecological reserve has been set aside here for the study of Stone's sheep and mountain goats. Also, more than 140 species of birds, including gyrfalcons.

"From the time of creation, slowly and inevitably this tiny segment of our world had heaved, erupted, and finally been scraped by the ice until it won its present glory. No wonder mountain people are moved to simple prayer in the natural cathedral of an unaltered wilderness," wrote Tommy Walker, one of the first to call for Spatsizi's protection.

Floatplanes can be chartered from Hwy 37 communities or Smithers and Terrace. Local guides and outfitters on Hwy 37 offer horseback trips. Air sightseeing tours. Eight cabins and cookhouse for public use at Cold Fish Lake; year-round, first-come, first-served basis; fee charged. Riverboat and canoe trips can also be arranged.

Tatlatui Provincial Park: 105,826ha. No road access. A magnificent wilderness that adjoins Spatsizi Park. Similar to Spatsizi in landscape and wildlife, great for anglers. Floatplanes most common access. 250-847-7320.

Return to Highway 37

Eddontenajon Lake Rest Area: About 4km north of Ealue Lake Rd. Boat launch here provides only access to lake.

Iskut: (Pop. 350). 9km from rest area; 15km beyond Tatogga Lake. Community is located along lakes bordering Hwy 37. Here are descendants of Sekani and Gitxsan aboriginal families that came together around Fort Connelly, southeast of

here, about a century ago. Some are still trappers.

Iskut Information: Iskut Band Administration Office (weekdays): Box 30, Iskut, BC, V0J 1K0. 250-234-3331. Stores, resorts, gas stations, and outfitters are also happy to provide information.

Morchuea Lake: Turn west about 20km beyond Iskut. Forest Service recreation site. Mt Edziza views. Canoe launch.

Stikine River Provincial Recreation Area: 217,000ha. 250-847-7320. Southern boundary nearly 4km beyond Morchuea Lake turnoff. A corridor on both sides of Stikine River from Spatsizi Park along the Grand Canyon to Telegraph Creek and border of Mount Edziza Park. No east-west road access.

Hwy 37 begins a switchbacking descent into Stikine River valley. Drivers: watch road, not scenery.

Stikine River: Highway crosses the "great river" about 12km from Morchuea Lake turnoff. It is a magnificent, wild river, with as many moods as twists and turns. Its name was given by the Coast Tlingit who traditionally occupied its lower reaches. The Interior Tahltan people inhabited the river along and above the Grand Canyon. Just downstream from the bridge, the Stikine enters this dangerously unnavigable 80km passage: waters surge between sedimentary and volcanic walls 305m high. BC Hydro has noted the potential here, and has pondered the construction of two dams and the creation of a 120km reservoir. Environmentalists fear for the mountain goats and caribou. Pullout for canoeing trips on the river starting in Spatsizi Park. Weather and water conditions can change rapidly.

Upper and Lower Gnat Lakes: 17km beyond northern boundary of Stikine River Recreation Area. Rest area is on Lower Gnat Lake.

Tanzilla River: 15km beyond Upper Gnat Lake. Former rest area converted to campsite. Sparkling Tanzilla River flows southeast toward, but never reaches, the community of Dease Lake. The Arctic-Pacific divide abruptly diverts the river's course southwest toward the Stikine.

Dease Lake: (Pop. 700). On the south end of Dease Lake, 9km from the rest area. About 490km north of Kitwanga on Hwy 16, 234km south of Alaska Hwy. Government supply centre for region. Scheduled air service to major BC cities. Full travellers services, guides and outfitters. Near site of Hudson's Bay Company fort and trading post, 1838-41. This was also a centre for the 1873 gold rush on Dease and Thibert creeks. Mining exploration continues. Sip a cool one in the Tanzilla pub.

Canada's most northerly ice-free port is Stewart, at the head of the Portland Canal.

Dease Lake Information: Dease Lake Information Centre, in south campus building of Northern Lights College. 250-771-3900. Mid-June to Sept. Off-season, write Dease Lake and Tahltan District Chamber of Commerce, Box 338, Dease Lake, BC, V0C 1L0.

Telegraph Creek Rd: Southwest off main road through Dease Lake. 113km to Telegraph Creek. Expect two-hour trip under ideal conditions. This all-weather route, punched through in 1922, twists like a serpent on a narrow roadbed with up to 20 percent grades. The scenery is spectacular through the Grand Canyon of the Stikine. Check with highways department for current road conditions.

SIDE TRIP

to Telegraph Creek

Road starts off benignly, traversing Tanzilla Plateau through an old burn punctuated by small creeks. Expansive view.

Mount Edziza: 63km beyond Dease Lake, volcanic cone visible to southeast.

Deep Breath Time: Road leaves plateau and enters canyon about 80km from Dease Lake. Switchback begins down to Tuya River. Passing oncoming vehicles requires cooperation. Be respectful of Tahltan First Nation fish camps.

Windy Point Rest Area and Viewpoint: 88km from Dease Lake by Stikine River. Expansive views, picnic tables at cliff's edge.

Lower Grand Canyon of the Stikine: 93km from Dease Lake. Breathtaking views from 15m-wide ridge of lava supporting the road. Drop-offs 122m either side. Road spirals down bare, sandy side cuts of adjoining canyon to swift, blue Tahltan River.

Telegraph Creek: (Pop. 450). 113km from Dease Lake, 260km upriver from Wrangell, Alaska. As the crow flies, less than 60km from Alaska's border. It's the only town on the 600km Stikine River. Today's Tahltan First Nation village sits atop the hill. Their ancestral village is upriver, where the salmon-rich Tahltan River pours into the Stikine. Around 1875 a community diminished by smallpox and the flu moved to a new site 2km downriver from there. Then in the early 1900s, after a devastating forest fire, they moved here. The non-native village is one terrace down, on the banks of the Stikine. A delightful spot.

Telegraph Creek has been continuously settled by non-native peoples since placer gold was found a few kilometres downriver in 1861. As the farthest navigable point on the Stikine for steamships, the community was well situated for such enterprises as Western Union's overland telegraph to link New York and Paris. Telegraph Creek may have been the Northwest's great communications centre by 1866 if the transatlantic

cable, completed the same year, had not made the overland line redundant. Less than a decade later, Telegraph Creek was rejuvenated as a gateway to the Cassiar gold rush and, in 1897, gateway to the Klondike. In 1901 another telegraph line, linking the Klondike with the south, was strung into Telegraph Creek, but brought few changes to the village. Benefits came after 1928 with improvements to the road east to Dease Lake, and during the Second World War, with construction of the Alaska Hwy.

More recently, the community has been, simply, a refuge for people who prefer fewer links with the world beyond. Another mini-boom is looming, though. Gold again, 100km south, between the Scud and Iskut rivers, and the mining companies are moving in.

Gas, food, and lodging (by reservation Oct-May). **RiverSong Cafe, Lodge, General Store & Outfitters** (250-235-3196) is where you'll meet nearly everyone in town at some point or another. Riverboat and aircraft charters. Guided river-raft trips. Limitless hiking. Take a gold pan. Sawmill Lake is a convenient camping spot. Enjoy locally grown vegetables and Stikine salmon.

Mount Edziza Provincial Park and Recreation Area: 232,702ha. Park begins across the Stikine from Telegraph Creek. 250-847-7320. Write BC Parks, Skeena District, Bag 5000, 3790 Alfred Ave, Smithers, BC, V0J 2N0. Call in advance to select suitable access. Guided hiking and packhorse trips arranged in Telegraph Creek, Dease Lake, and Iskut areas.

The eruptions creating Mt Edziza (el 2,787m) began four million years ago. Smaller eruptions only 1,300 years ago produced an eerie landscape of perfectly symmetrical cone and craters. Five major lakes in park and Spectrum Range with purple, yellow, and red rocks have been affected by lava flows. Look for Arctic ground squirrels and spruce, willow, and white-tailed ptarmigan June-Aug. Mountain goats year-round.

No road access or services. Trails difficult to follow, especially in bad weather. Edziza is not for the ill-equipped or inexperienced.

Forest Service Recreation Camping: Two pleasant sites between Telegraph Creek and Glenora. Watch closely for signs. Tahltan fish camps nearby.

Glenora: 19km beyond Telegraph Creek. First this was a Tahltan and Tlingit fishing camp. In 1874, the Hudson's Bay Company established a trading post here. During the Klondike gold rush, it became a thriving tent city for thousands of miners preparing for their trek north. The miners left, and after 1900, the HBC moved its headquarters to Telegraph Creek. Glenora is once again a Tahltan fishing camp.

Return to Highway 37

Hwy 37 continues north with views of Dease Lake.

Rabid Grizzly Rest Area: 28km beyond townsite, turn west for easy access to deep cold waters of Dease Lake. Big char.

Dease River Bridge: New structure 37km from Rabid Grizzly Rest Area. Grayling fishing. Convenient starting point for canoe trips.

Pine Tree Lake: About 9km beyond Dease River bridge. Series of narrow lakes and meandering Dease River.

Wildfire Sign: Burned areas start near Cotton Lake, just beyond Pine Tree Lake. Caused by abandoned campfire.

Cottonwood River Rest Areas: 7km beyond Wildfire Sign.

Simmons and Twin Lakes: 7km and 10.5km respectively from rest area. Small lakes deep in mountain folds, surrounded by spires of spruce.

Jade City: About 9.5km past Twin Lake. Locally mined jade. Souvenirs, rock cut to order.

Cassiar Junction: At Jade City. 116km north of Dease Lake, 119km south of Alaska Hwy. Road takes sharp west off Hwy 37. 14km paved road to Cassiar.

Cassiar: (Pop. 0).133km from Alaska Hwy, tucked into an impressive mountain valley. In 1992, this thriving community of 1,500 became another BC ghost town. Cassiar was created 40 years before to help satisfy the postwar need for asbestos. However, it became too costly to develop new underground mines and transport the asbestos to world markets. So, the townsite has been given back to the mountain sheep; mining equipment, houses, and other assets have been sold and moved. The site is now closed to visitors.

Centreville: (Pop. 2). About 14km north of Cassiar Junction on Hwy 37. In the mid-1870s, hundreds of miners working up and down McDame Creek clustered in this gold camp. A massive 2kg gold nugget was found nearby in 1877.

Good Hope Lake: (Pop. 150). 21km beyond Cassiar Junction. Attractive lake is home of the Dease River First Nation – Kaska people closely related to those at Lower Post (see p.296).

Boya Lake Provincial Park: 4,597ha; 45 campsites. Take access road 33km from Cassiar Junction; 13.5km beyond Good Hope Lake. Turn east 2.5km from Hwy 37. 250-847-7320. A landscape contoured eons ago by slow-grinding glaciers: the rolling lands around Boya Lake consist of drumlins, eskers, moraines, and glacier-gouged depressions occupied by shallow lakes. The exception is the Horseranch

Range, with its surprisingly prominent alpine peaks and amphitheatre-shaped cirques, directly facing the park campground. The rocks underlying this range are highly anomalous in northern BC. Once sedimentary, the rocks recrystallized and developed a high resistance to erosion through localized high pressure and metamorphic processes. Thus the range withstood the levelling action of the Pleistocene glaciers. Swimming, boat launching, canoeing. Fishing best on cloudy days when surface is ruffled. Water is clearer than a municipal swimming pool, and is chlorine free. Wheelchair access. There are park programs in summer.

Beaver Dam Rest Area: 11km from Boya Lake access road. Information sign.

Hwy 37 moves onto the Liard Plateau. Dry sandy soils and small pine trees. Horseranch Range on eastern horizon dates to pre-Cambrian era.

Blue Lakes: 46km beyond rest area. Little picnic spot for weary travellers, by clear blue waters.

60th Parallel: 22km from lakes. Boundary between BC and Canada's Yukon Territory. 4km to Alaska Hwy. **Road is now Yukon Hwy 16**.

Alaska Highway: 3.5km north of 60. 721km north of Hwy 16. Alaska Hwy goes east 23km to the town of Watson Lake. West to Atlin in BC, Whitehorse in the Yukon, and Alaska, US. For details, see *Watson Lake to Whitehorse*, p.296.

PRINCE GEORGE TO DAWSON CREEK

HART HIGHWAY (Highway 97)

The Hart Highway is an extension of Hwy 97 which starts near the US border at Osoyoos and traverses the Okanagan and Cariboo regions to Prince George. North of Dawson Creek it becomes the famous Alaska Highway.

This *Log* is measured from the John Hart bridge in Prince George, where Hwy 97 crosses the Nechako River. For details on Prince George, see p.263. The paved highway angles northeast 406km to Dawson Creek. Farmlands north of Prince George gradually give way to rolling forested terrain. The road climbs after crossing the Rocky Mountain Trench into the wild Hart Ranges of the Rockies. Once it has twisted its way through the mountains, the highway unwinds into attractive foothills country. By the time you get to Dawson Creek, it's a prairie landscape with grain elevators and expansive skies.

The highway is named for John Hart, BC premier, 1941-47.

Eskers Provincial Park: 1,603ha; day use. 250-565-6340. 10km north of John Hart bridge, west onto Chief Lake Rd for 28km, then north 1km to park featuring several lakes between glaciated ridges or eskers. Hiking, wildlife viewing, cross-country skiing. Some areas wheelchair accessible.

Salmon River: 23km beyond John Hart bridge. Refreshing swimming holes.

Giscome Portage Regional Park: 22ha; day use. 13km beyond Salmon River on unpaved road. East 4km to peaceful park on bench above Fraser River. 250-960-4400. Here, at the south end of Giscome Portage linking the Arctic and Pacific watersheds, Al Huble in 1905 established a trading post and transported goods across the portage for traders and settlers. Park features Huble Homestead restored log house, barn, and warehouse. Guided tours daily mid-May to early Oct. Hike or cross-country ski 8km of the Giscome Portage Trail.

Summit Lake: About 3.5km beyond Mitchell Rd. South and north access roads to community west of Hwy 97. Cottage country. Char and rainbow trout fishing. Here is the **Arctic-Pacific Divide**. Waters to north drain into the Arctic, those south to the Pacific. The Crooked River flows north from Summit Lake paralleling Hwy 97. Good for canoeing. Boats restricted to 10 horsepower motors. Lots of squawfish.

Crooked River Provincial Park: 873ha; 90 campsites (reservations taken: call 1-800-689-9025; from the Lower Mainland or overseas, call 604-689-9025). 20km beyond northern Summit Lake access road. Open year-round. Excellent sandy beaches at Bear Lake. Swimming and boating (no powerboats). Hart and Squaw lakes offer fine swimming and fishing for rainbow trout. Good fishing in the Crooked River as well. Hiking trails, including 9km route around Bear and Squaw lakes. Winter activities: cross-country skiing, snowshoeing. Paddle boats for rent.

Bear Lake: (Pop. 270). East side of Hwy 97, 2.5km from park. Services.

Tacheeda Lake Rd: 13km beyond Bear Lake, turn east on gravel road for rainbow trout fishing and Forest Service recreation sites. Watch for industrial traffic. Also route of BC Rail's 129km branch line to Tumbler Ridge, Canada's first electrified heavy freight railway. 99-unit coal train line electrified to eliminate ventilation of 9km and 6km tunnels through Rocky Mountains.

Crooked River Rest Area: 21.5km beyond Tacheeda Lake Rd. West side of highway. Trumpeter swan viewing close by.

Whiskers Point Provincial Park: 52ha; 69 campsites; sani-station. 250-565-6340. 15km from rest area on highway's west side. Pleasantly forested park with campground on McLeod Lake. Good swimming, fine sand and gravel beaches, play area. Rainbow trout, char, and grayling. Boat launch. Wonderful sunsets. Nature trail.

McLeod Lake: (Pop. 51). 11km beyond Whiskers Point Park. From here, local Tsek'ehne (Sekani) people traversed a trail to the Fort St James area. Simon Fraser established the Trout Lake Fort near here in 1805. This was the first European settlement west of the Rockies and is the longest continuously occupied European settlement in BC (see *Tsek'ehne Heritage Park*, below). McLeod Lake General Store is a source of supplies, fuel, and local info. Check out funky little motel here. You can't miss it.

Road to Carp Lake: West off highway. 300km north of McLeod Lake General Store. Gravel.

SIDE TRIP

to Carp Lake

Tsek'ehne Heritage Park: 300m past store, turn left off Hwy 97. It is 0.6km to McLeod Lake First Nation land and Heritage Park, site of the original store operated by the North West Company and then the Hudson's Bay Company until 1952. Buildings date from the 1920s and 1940s. Just beyond the adjacent Tsek'ehne cemetery, on a point of land covered with wild roses, clover, and fireweed, is the spot by the lake where Simon Fraser built the original trading post. Please be respectful of the site. Some information may be available at McLeod Lake Band office a short distance along Carp Lake Rd. 250-750-4415.

War Falls and Lake: In Carp Lake Provincial Park about 26km from McLeod Lake. Campground and small boat launch. War Falls tumble 18m in two cascades divided by 100m of white water. About 8km to Carp Lake and park headquarters.

Carp Lake Provincial Park: 19,344ha; 102 campsites and wilderness tenting campsites on five of Carp Lake's 20 islands. 250-565-6340. May-Oct. 32km from McLeod Lake on narrow road: can be rough, especially during spring break-up. Trout fishing is a big draw. Fish from here kept explorer Simon Fraser and his men alive in 1806. Swimming, canoeing, hiking including McLeod River Trail. Moose and black bears seen in park. Keep campsites clean.

Return to Highway 97

Tudyah Lake Provincial Park: 56ha; 36 campsites and group site. 250-565-6340. On Hwy 97, 8km beyond community of McLeod Lake. North of highway. Fishing, boating, and swimming. This park marks western edge of the **Rocky Mountain Trench**, between the Hart Ranges on the east and Nechako Plateau on the west.

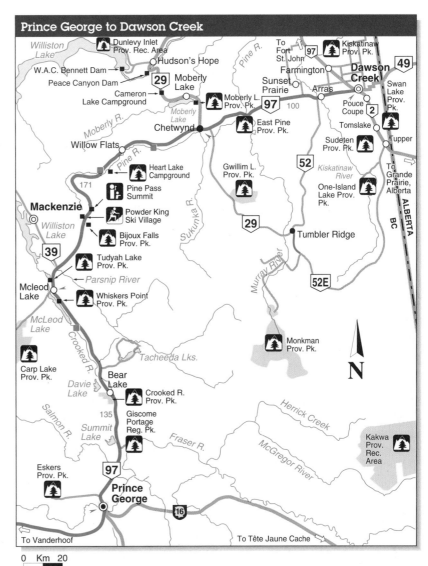

The steep-sided trench, probably formed by a combination of volcanic and glacial action, ranges from 3-16km wide. In Canada, it parallels the western edge of Rocky Mountains for more than 1,440km.

Parsnip River: Hwy 97 crosses river 7.5km beyond park. Named for the wild parsnips growing along its banks. Before the creation of Williston Lake, the Parsnip joined the Finlay River to form the Peace.

Highway 39 (Mackenzie Junction): 500m north of Parsnip River bridge. Summer Info Centre (details below).

SIDE TRIP

to Mackenzie

Hwy 39 provides access to Mackenzie, backcountry, and recreation on Williston Lake, one of the largest manmade reservoirs on the continent. At 164,600ha, it's also the most expansive body of freshwater in northern BC.

Mackenzie: (Pop. 5,997). North off Hwy 97. On paved Hwy 39, 29km from junction. Area was wilderness until 1965 when town was built near southern end of Williston Lake as a centre for pulp, paper, and lumber manufacturing.

Town is named for Alexander Mackenzie, who camped near here on his 1793 epic journey as the first white person to reach Canada's Pacific coast by land. Today, a centre for fishing, hiking, swimming, waterskiing, and wilderness adventure, Mackenzie has the amenities of a larger town. Logging roads fan out, offering year-round access to wilderness back-country camping. (Roads must be driven with care; keep lights on at all times.) For information on access and restrictions contact BC Forest Service, Mackenzie District Office, Bag 5000, 1 Cicada Rd, Mackenzie, BC, V0J 2E0. 250-997-2200.

Mackenzie Information: Travel Infocentre, Box 880, Mackenzie, BC, V0J 2C0. 750-4497. At Hwys 97 and 39 junction. Daily May-Sept. Chamber of Commerce open year-round. 250-997-5459.

✈ **Mackenzie Airport:** Mill Rd, short distance south of town. 1,555m runway. Scheduled service to Prince George.

✈ **Morfee Lake Float Plane Base:** 2km east of Mackenzie, on Centennial Dr.

■ **Mackenzie Museum:** In Community Centre next to John Dahl Park, downtown. 250-997-3021. July-Aug, Tues-Sat 9-5; Sept-June, Wed-Sat 1-5. Videos include *Before the Waters Came*, a trip up the Finlay River between Finlay Forks and Fort Ware before Lake Williston was formed. Park has hiking trails, picnic tables, view of Morfee Lake.

■ **World's Largest Tree Crusher:** On Mackenzie Boulevard. Weighs 178t. Cleared forested land for W.A.C Bennett Dam and creation of Williston Lake. "This is not exactly an inspiring site," notes *Beautiful British Columbia Magazine* editor, Bryan McGill. "Perhaps it was a worshipful icon in the '60s, when Progress was God, and dams were symbols of man triumphing over nature."

■ **Mackenzie Municipal RV Park:** 20 campsites, sani-station, showers. In town.

■ **Mackenzie Golf and Country Club:** Just south of town. 250-997-4004. May-Sept. Nine-holes.

■ **Recreation Complex:** In town. Pool, arena, curling rink, library.

■ **Demonstration Forest:** Along the 29km of Hwy 39 between Hwy 97 and Mackenzie. Signs to several trails through replanted forest.

■ **Forestry Tours:** In mill and forest. May-Sept. Fletcher Pulp, 250-997-2431. Finlay Forest Industries, 250-997-2775.

■ **Morfee Lake:** 2km east of town, on Centennial Dr. Swimming and boating.

■ **Morfee Mountain:** (1,817m). For an endless view of Williston Lake and the Rockies. Turn right about 3km north of town. Drive right up in midsummer.

Return to Highway 97

The Misinchinka River soon flows into view on east side of Hwy 97. Rugged valley views.

🌲 **Bijoux Falls Provincial Park:** 40ha; day use. About 31km beyond Hwy 39 junction. May-Oct. Park named for sparkling waterfall that spills 40m through the spruce forest. Bijoux means jewel in French. Don't feed the bears.

🎿 **Powder King Mountain Resort:** 6.5km beyond park. Box 22023, Pine Centre, Prince George, BC, V2L 4Z8. 250-563-9438. Dec-April. Fine powder skiing. 640m vertical drop, longest run 2,650m. 23 runs, one triple chair, two T-bars. RV hook-ups, on-mountain accommodation.

ℹ️ 🔭 **Pine Pass Summit and Viewpoint:** (El 933m). 2.5km from ski village. View of Azouzetta Lake. Its name means "flying grizzly bear" in local native language.

ℹ️ **Pine River:** Hwy 97 crosses the Pine for the first time about 3.5km beyond summit. Watch it gather strength from its tributaries as it flows through the Rocky Mountains to the rolling plains of the Peace River Valley.

ℹ️ **Time Zone:** On Hwy 97, about 10km beyond Pine Pass Summit. No changes in summer, when daylight-saving time is in effect elsewhere in BC. But from late Oct-April, set your time one hour ahead for **Mountain Standard Time**.

🏞 **West Pine Rest Area:** 30km beyond Pine Pass River bridge by railway underpass. Fishing on river.

🏕 **Heart Lake Campground:** Across highway from rest area. Take gravel road 3km east. Pretty spot. Forest Service recreation sites.

🏢 **Willow Flats:** About 29km from Heart Lake turnoff. Small rural community and access to Westcoast Energy's natural gas pumping station.

❓ **Peace Foothills Area Map:** 12km beyond Willow Flats, near Hassler Flats. View of the foothills and meandering, green Pine River.

In 1935 the provincial government sponsored a search for oil. The first producing well was drilled at Commotion Creek near here in 1940.

🏢 **Chetwynd:** (Pop. 2,980). 28km beyond foothills map. Once known as Little Prairie, the town changed its name in 1959 to honour the late Ralph Chetwynd, BC highways minister, son of an English baronet. Community depends on forestry, mining for oil and gas, farming, and tourism. At Chetwynd, BC Rail tracks divide: one line goes to Dawson Creek, the other to Fort St John. (Both are freight lines only. The passenger service from North Vancouver ends at

Prince George.) It's a bustling little place with poplar trees and two dozen chainsaw sculptures – from bears to birds to park benches – adorning parks, streets, and public and private buildings. Chetwynd has distinguished itself as the "Chainsaw Sculpture Capital of the World."

❓ **Chetwynd Information:** Info Centre, 1km west of Hwy 97 in log building. Box 1000, Chetwynd, BC, V0C 1J0. Year-round, daily July-Aug. 250-788-3345 or 250-788-3655.

✈ **Chetwynd Airport:** Charter service only. Also heli-pad.

■ **Little Prairie Heritage Museum:** 2km west of town, in old post office. Open June-Sept. 250-788-3358. Call 250-788-3345 year-round. Trapping and farming implements. Pioneer bedroom with antique quilt made by the residents, and caboose displaying railway artifacts. Adjacent museum is a statue of "the Little Giant of Big Peace," the town logo.

■ **Mt Baldy:** Within town. A gentle hike up. Benches to view community below.

■ **Forestry Tours:** Canfor, 250-788-2231. Late May-Aug. Mon, Wed, Fri. Also self-guided interpretive forest trail.

■ **Chetwynd Greenspace Hiking Trails:** An 80km network of trails linking Info Centre to Little Prairie Museum, the Mt Baldy trail system, and Demonstration Forest.

■ **Leisure Wave Pool:** Family oriented; depth from 0-25m; sauna, whirlpool, weight room.

🛣 **Highway 29 North:** In Chetwynd. North to **Moberly Lake, Moberly Lake Provincial Park, Spencer Tuck Park, Hudson's Hope, Peace Canyon Dam,** and **W.A.C. Bennett Dam.** Hwy 29 rejoins Hwy 97 (the Alaska Hwy) 13km north of Fort St John. See *Fort St John to Tumbler Ridge,* p.287.

🛣 **Highway 29 South:** 3km beyond Chetwynd. South to **Sukunka Falls, Gwillim Lake** Provincial Park. 90km to **Tumbler Ridge.** For details see *Fort St John to Tumbler Ridge,* p.289.

Hwy 97 travels through open country punctuated by broad ridges of deciduous trees. About 31km beyond Chetwynd, the road takes a broad sweep down the terraced valley of the Pine River.

🌲 **East Pine Provincial Park:** 14ha. South of highway at bridge. Year-round. At junction of East Pine and Murray rivers. Boat launching.

ℹ️ **Pine River:** At access to East Pine Provincial Park, Hwy 97 crosses Pine River bridge and BC Rail tracks.

❓ ℹ️ **Groundbirch Store:** About 21km beyond Pine River crossing. Source of local knowledge. Check the **Bruce Groner Memorial Museum**.

🛣 **Road to Sunset Prairie:** North about 10km from store. Gravel road to small rural community joins Hwy 97 north of Dawson Creek.

DAWSON CREEK (map)

1	Arena	8	Indoor Pool
2	Bus Depot	9	Kinsmen Park
3	Chamberlain Memorial Pioneer Park	10	Library
4	City Hall	11	Liquor Store
5	City Park	12	Northern Lights College
6	Fire Hall	13	Post Office
7	Hospital	14	RCMP
		15	Visitor Info Centre

Highway 52: About 13km beyond road to Sunset Prairie. This mostly paved Heritage Highway leads south 98km to Tumbler Ridge. See *Fort St John to Tumbler Ridge*, p.289.

Arras: Small community 2km beyond Hwy 52 junction.

Road to Farmington: 2km beyond Arras. Road, bypassing Dawson Creek, travels north to rejoin Hwy 97 (Alaska Hwy) at small town of Farmington.

Highway 97N (Alaska Hwy): 17km beyond Arras. Leads north 73km to Fort St John. See *Dawson Creek to Fort Nelson*, p.290.

Dawson Creek (Historic Mile 0): (Pop. 11,125). At crossroads of Alaska and Hart Hwys, and Hwys 49 and 2 to Alberta. Dawson Creek is 663m above sea level, and operates on Mountain Standard Time year-round. City boasts 125 frost-free days annually.

The town was named for George Mercer Dawson, of the Geological Survey of Canada, whose meticulous geological and natural history reports on this region, and much of Canada, have rarely been improved upon. The biggest surge of settlement here began just before the First World War, and continued in the following two decades.

Dawson Creek is the major transportation centre in the Peace River area, and serves an extensive agricultural area. There has been recent diversification into game farming: reindeer and plains bison (buffalo). Located on what was once called the Beaver Plains, community's grain elevators are a visual link with the prairie provinces.

Dawson Creek is a friendly, laid-back city with every visitor service. It's famous as Mile Zero of the legendary Alaska Hwy. A post to commemorate this is located in the heart of the city, a popular spot to be photographed before setting off on adventures north. Interpretive panels explain the town's role in highway construction.

The community is also the terminus of Northern Alberta Railways (NAR). The first passenger steam train arrived Jan 15, 1931, and the last steam train left Dawson Creek in 1974. The NAR Station, handsomely restored in its original location, received the Canada Built Heritage Award in 1984. Dawson Creek is still a railway town, served by BC Rail (freight only) and Canadian National Railways.

Dawson Creek Information: Dawson Creek Info Centre, 900 Alaska Ave, Dawson Creek, BC, V1G 4T6. 250-782-9595. In Northern Alberta Railway Park on Alaska Ave at 10th St. Daily, 8-7, May-Sept; Tues-Sat, 10-4, Oct-April.

Dawson Creek Airport: On Hwy 2, southeast of town. Scheduled and charter aircraft.

■ **Farmers Market:** Sat, May-Oct. NAR Park. See below.

■ **Northern Alberta Railways Station Park (NAR Park):** On Alaska Ave near traffic circle in centre of city. Site of several interesting

exhibits, including a turn-of-the-century rail car and restored 1949 grain elevator. Walking tours of Dawson Creek start here. Ask at Info Centre.

■ **The NAR Station Museum:** In restored NAR Station, in NAR Park. Daily May-Sept; Tues-Sat, Oct-April. 250-782-9595. Wildlife exhibits. Huge mammoth tusks. Dunne-za First Nations artifacts.

■ **Dawson Creek Art Gallery:** Housed in Alberta Wheat Pool Elevator Annex of NAR Park. Daily, 8-5, May-Aug. Tues-Sat, 10-5, Sept-May. 250-782-2601. Local arts and crafts.

■ **Walter Wright Pioneer Village:** At Hart/Alaska Hwys junction. 250-782-7144, June-Aug; off-season, 250-782-9595. Restored buildings commemorate 1940s.

■ **Forest Trails:** Self-guided forest interpretive trails and 25km of hiking/cross-country ski trails. 250-784-1205.

■ **Dawson Creek Golf and Country Club:** 250-782-7882. April-Oct. 18 holes.

■ **McQueen's Slough:** From town centre go east on Spirit River Road 3km, then turn north onto Rolla Rd, 3km to BC Wildlife Watch viewing site. Waterfowl, shorebirds, songbirds.

Dawson Creek is a jumping-off spot for the spectacular **Monkman Provincial Park** 130km to the southwest. Access is by air from Dawson Creek, or jet boat from Tumbler Ridge. Also, the north end of the park is accessible by a 35km two-lane Forest Service gravel road from the **Tumbler Ridge** mining site (60km south of town of Tumbler Ridge). Kinuseo Falls campground offers 42 campsites, picnic shelter, and special-needs facilities. Viewing platform for 60m falls. 24km hiking trail leads from campground to further backcountry explorations. 250-787-3407. Also see *Fort St John to Tumbler Ridge*, p.289.

Highway 49: To province of Alberta, 89km to Spirit River.

Highway 2: To Alberta via Pouce Coupe, Toms Lake, Tupper.

For continuation of Hwy 97 north to Fort Nelson, see *Dawson Creek to Fort Nelson*, p.290.

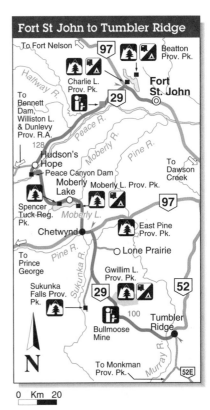

Fort St John to Tumbler Ridge

FORT ST JOHN TO TUMBLER RIDGE

HIGHWAY 29

Highway 29 from Fort St John south to Tumbler Ridge is one of BC's most scenically varied stretches. It parallels the Peace River for more than 70km, sliding through rolling hills and plains patchworked with farms and ranches. The drive's a treat any time of year. This area produces more grain, forage, seed, and honey than any other in the province, and is also the main sheep-farming valley.

Manmade marvels have also added to the attraction of the area. The W.A.C Bennett Dam represents an incredible engineering feat; building the Peace Canyon Dam involved re-routing part of the Peace River, which revealed dinosaur prints and the tracks of ancient birds in the canyon bedrock. Both dams have fasci-

nating visitor centres, and should not be missed.

South of Chetwynd, Hwy 29 moves into the Rocky Mountain Foothills scoured by deep valleys. Tumbler Ridge is attractively located away from the coal mines it serves.

Fort St John: (Pop. 15,021). On Hwy 97, 387km south of Fort Nelson; 73km north of Dawson Creek, 13km east of Hwy 29. Details in *Dawson Creek to Fort Nelson*, p.291.

Highway 29: Leads west 13km north of Fort St John, from Hwy 97 opposite turnoff to **Charlie Lake Provincial Park**. See *Dawson Creek to Fort Nelson*, for park and lake. Hudson's Hope is 75km beyond.

Lakepoint Golf and Country Club: At Charlie Lake. 250-785-5566. May-Oct. 18 holes overlooking lake.

About 12km beyond Hwy 97 junction, Hwy 29 switchbacks down Bear Hill's 10 percent grades. Lovely views for passengers. Below, the Peace River is studded with islands, a home for Canada geese.

The highway and Peace River now wind for about 63km through a serene mix of bottom lands and hills. Good chance to spot deer; bear and moose not uncommon.

Peace View Rest Area: 31km beyond junction. On a high bench overlooking the Peace River, silent from here, only the sound of the wind blowing and the smell of sweet summer grasses. Below are steep cutbanks, farmland, forested islands, distant mountains. To the southwest, the Halfway River flows into the Peace.

Halfway River: 35km beyond junction. Good fishing for rainbow trout, Dolly Varden, grayling, and whitefish from the bridge. River is about halfway between Fort St John and 1,429m Portage Mountain overlooking Hudson's Hope.

Hudson's Hope: (Pop. 1,115). On Hwy 29 some 75km beyond Hwy 97 junction. A charming little town perched 61m above the Peace River. A few kilometres west of where the town sits now – and about 15,000 years ago – the Peace River was blocked by earth and rock (terminal moraine) left by a slow-melting glacier. The mighty river carved for itself a new route, a sheer-walled canyon around Portage Mountain, and continued on its long and more gentle journey east.

For First Nations peoples and the white fur traders who followed them, the Peace River was the road in. But the treacherous waters of the canyons above Hudson's Hope marked a terminus for westbound travellers in canoes. In May 1793, Alexander Mackenzie was forced to make a portage here: "The river above us, as far as we could see, was one sheet of foaming water and it was really awful to behold with what infinite force the water drives against the rocks on one side, and with what impetuous strength it is repelled to the other." Simon Fraser, in Mackenzie's wake, chose this place as the site for his fur-trading post, Rocky Mountain Portage. Remains of the original settlement can still be seen, supporting the town's claim to be BC's third oldest community.

The town has been called Hudson's Hope or "The Hope of Hudson" from as early as the 1870s. However, the origin of the name is a mystery. In the early part of this century, the emerging town became the head of navigation for sternwheelers plying the Peace – the transportation link to the east. From Hudson's Hope to Vermilion Chutes in Alberta, 917km away, the fare was $52; this included use of bedding and bathroom.

From early in this century through the Depression and the Second World War, Hudson's Hope has been sustained by coal mining, guiding and outfitting, trapping, placer mining, and the hope of striking it rich. As it turned out, the mother lode turned out to be the river itself: in the 1960s, the town boomed during construction of the Bennett Dam at the top of the canyon (the far side of the portage, 24km west of town). BC Hydro continues to be a major employer.

Besides a must-visit to both the Bennett and Peace Canyon dams, there are excellent cross-country skiing and hiking trails around the community, and fishing in lakes and rivers. Maps and information at Info Centre. Ask about sightseeing and flight-seeing tours. Full range of visitor services.

Hudson's Hope Information: Information centre, in Beattie Park on Hwy 29. 250-783-9154. Daily 8-8, mid-May to Sept. Playground and picnic area. Or contact District of Hudson's Hope, Box 330, Hudson's Hope, BC, V0C 1V0. 250-783-9901.

Hudson's Hope Airport: About 5km beyond junction on Dam Access Rd. Charter service.

■ **Hudson's Hope Museum:** 10506-105th Ave, opposite information centre. Daily May-early Sept. By appointment, off season. 250-783-5735. On north bank of Peace River, overlooking where Simon Fraser wintered 1805-1806. Museum, in original Hudson's Bay Company store, is on the first parcel of land ever surveyed on the north side of the Peace, in 1899. Subject of displays range from dinosaurs to trappers. Also Peace gold-mining equipment, early pioneers. Gift shop.

■ **St Peter's Church:** Beautiful log church beside museum, built 1938. Open for viewing during museum hours. Sunday services.

■ **Alwin Holland Park:** 3km beyond town on banks of the Peace. Fantastic view. Also trout, grayling, whitefish.

■ **King Gething Park and Campground:** At edge of town. Mid-May to Sept. Sani-station, cook house, showers. By donation.

Dam Access Rd: West off Hwy 29, from downtown Hudson's Hope.

SIDE TRIP

to Bennett Dam

Viewpoint: About 2km along Dam Access Rd, informal pullout for view of the Peace Canyon Dam to the south.

Dunlevy Inlet Provincial Recreation Area: 110ha. West 15km on Dam Access Rd then northwest 23km on road along north side of Williston Lake. April-Oct. Pretty park on north shore of Williston Lake's Peace Reach. Boat launch. Good fishing, but watch for floating debris on lake. Wildlife viewing for elk, Stone's sheep, and caribou. Also Brewer's blackbirds, dark-eyed juncos, yellow-rumped warblers, black-capped chickadees, bald eagles, and hawks.

W.A.C. Bennett Dam, Visitor Centre, and Underground Tour: West 24km along Dam Access Rd. 250-783-5000. Visitor Centre open daily, May 24 weekend to early Oct; by appointment, off-season. Underground tours daily in summer; in winter, by appointment. On eastern tip of 362km Williston Lake, BC's largest reservoir and the 10th largest hydroelectric reservoir in the world: it took five years to fill. Powerhouse was the largest in the world when it went into operation in 1968.

The story less often heard here is that of the Tsay Keh Dene people, whose traditional territories, homes, burial grounds, and game were drowned as the waters rose before their eyes at the upper end of the reservoir. The dam that holds it all back is one of the largest earthfill structures in existence – 183m high and 2km across, constructed from 100 million tons of glacial moraine that blocked the Peace during the last ice age. Using the same fill, a 3.6m by 2.7m wall would stretch from sea to sea across Canada, linking Vancouver and Halifax. The dam was named for BC's premier at the time of construction, W.A.C. Bennett; the reservoir was named for Ray Williston, Minister of Lands, Forests, and Water Resources.

The Visitor Centre offers an introduction to electricity; a dated film, *Canyon of Destiny*, about the dam's construction; then a tour through the Gordon M. Shrum Generating Station Powerhouse, one of the world's largest underground powerhouses. Carved out of the bedrock below the dam, it's as long as three football fields, as wide as a four-lane highway, and as high as a 15-storey building. Power produced from 10 spinning turbines and generators is delivered via transmission lines to cities throughout BC. For more information, write BC Hydro, Corp and Environmental Affairs, 970 Burrard St, Vancouver, BC, V6Z 1Y3. Summer snack bar.

Return to Hudson's Hope

Peace Canyon Dam, Generating Station, and Visitor Centre: East side of Hwy 29, 7km beyond Hudson's Hope. Daily Mid-May to Sept, 8-4. Weekdays only in winter when tour reservations are necessary. 250-783-9943. Second hydroelectric project to harness the Peace River. This dam was constructed in 1976 at the bottom of the Peace River Canyon, 23km below the Bennett Dam. During its construction, a fossilized partial skeleton of a plesiosaur was found. This giant marine reptile, about 12m long, with a long neck and great paddles, swam here about 100 million years ago in what was an inland sea. Also found were footprints belonging to creatures that roamed the sea's shores: hadrosaurs (duck-billed dinosaurs), horned dinosaurs, ancestors of Tyrannosaurus Rex, and wee birds, only about 10cm tall. The Peace Canyon offers some of the only evidence on Earth of the existence of certain creatures. The canyon also offers a record of life forms here after the seas retreated – such as woolly mammoths, and humans. The Visitor Centre presents the history of the Peace Canyon from the time of the dinosaurs (there are life-sized models) to now. Behind the dam is a small reservoir, 800ha in size, 21km long, called Dinosaur Lake, that has flooded over part of the canyon.

Dinosaur Lake Campground: On Dinosaur Lake. By donation. Boat launch, hiking trails.

Peace River Bridge: 1km beyond turnoff to Peace Canyon Dam, highway crosses Peace River's only suspension bridge. Bull trout. Pullouts at each end for viewing unusual concrete totem poles.

Cameron Lake Campground: About 17km beyond Peace River bridge. Swimming and playground. No motorboats. By donation.

Moberly Lake: (Pop. 242). 28km south of Peace River bridge. This community on the north shore of Moberly Lake is named for Henry Moberly, trader, trapper, and prospector who lived on the lakeshore 1865-1868. On either side of the village are the Treaty 8 First Nations, **West Moberly Lake** and **Saulteux**, comprised of Dunne-za (Beaver)

The W.A.C. Bennett Dam on the Peace River has created Williston Lake, BC's largest body of freshwater.

people who have always lived in the region, Cree people who arrived during and after the fur trade, and descendants of Saulteux people who came from Manitoba after the Riel Rebellions. On separate weekends, usually late Aug, each hosts a celebration honouring "the spirit and intent" of Treaty 8. At **West Moberly Lake Days** and **Saulteux Pemmican Days**, visitors are heartily welcomed to join in the Friendship Feast, powwow dancing, the traditional hand game, and other sports, including the axe throw, bow-and-arrow contest, teepee-creeping contest, moose call, and canoe races. For dates call West Moberly Lake, 250-788-3663, or Saulteux, 250-788-3955. Basic camping on site and at nearby BC Parks campgrounds.

Spencer Tuck Regional Park: 4ha; day use. April-Oct. About 3km beyond town of Moberly Lake. Picnic spot on north shore of Moberly Lake. Good swimming, fishing.

Moberly Lake Provincial Park: 98ha; 109 campsites and group site (reservations taken: call 1-800-689-9025; from the Lower Mainland or overseas, call 604-689-9025). Sani-station. General info: 250-787-3407. May 1-Oct 30. South side of highway, 10km from community of Moberly Lake, then west 3km along gravel road to lake's south shore.

Chetwynd: (Pop. 2,980). About 20km beyond Moberly Lake. See *Prince George to Dawson Creek*, p.286.

Highway 97 (Hart Hwy): At Chetwynd. East 100km to Dawson Creek. Southwest 306km to Prince George. See *Prince George to Dawson Creek*, p.284.

For Hwy 29 south to Tumbler Ridge, head east on Hwy 97.

Highway 29S: South, 3km beyond Hwy 97 junction. Leads 90km southeast to Tumbler Ridge. (Highway 52 East is also a popular and scenic route to Tumbler Ridge, see below).

Sukunka River: 12km beyond Hwy 97, Hwy 29 crosses river. Bull trout; catch-and-release rainbow trout and grayling.

Gwillim Lake Provincial Park: 9,199ha; 49 campsites. 250-787-3407. 48km from Chetwynd, then east off Hwy 29. Paved access. Deep blue waters beneath Mt Meikle. Wooded campsites. Good boating but water choppy when windy. Viewpoint, trails, playground, horseshoe pits, picnicking.

Bullmoose (Coal) Mine: Access road 20km from Gwillim Lake Park. Tours mid-June to late Aug. 250-242-4702.

Tumbler Ridge: (Pop. 3,775). 37km south of Bullmoose Mine road. Incorporated in 1981; well planned in attempt to avoid the instant-town image and architecture. Home to the people who work at the two coal mines nearby. The Quintette mine is the world's largest computerized open-pit mine – it produces some 4.3 million tonnes of clean coal per year. Developing the mines and building Tumbler Ridge and its transportation infrastructure has been BC's largest industrial undertaking.

Facilities cluster around the town centre on Main St. Tumbler Ridge is an excellent centre for outdoor recreation year-round, offering easy access to fishing, hunting, cross-country skiing, and horseback riding. Hiking to several falls: ask at Info Centre. Snowmobiling is big in the area: there is snowmobile access right in the town centre. Nine-hole golf course, recre-

ation and aquatic centre, and RV park. Jet-boat charters to Monkman Provincial Park may be available.

Tumbler Ridge Information: Info Centre and Chamber of Commerce on Southgate and Front streets. Box 606, Tumbler Ridge, BC, V0C 2W0. Weekdays, year-round; weekends also July-Aug. 250-242-4702.

■ **Quintette and Bullmoose Mine Tours:** Ask at or call Info Centre. Tours in summer. Off-season by arrangement.

■ **Tumbler Point Bird Sanctuary:** Self-guided 3.5km hike, 250-242-4242. Picnic shelters. BC Wildlife Watch viewing site.

■ **Tumbler Ridge Golf and Country Club:** 250-242-3533. Nine holes.

Greg Duke Memorial Recreation Area: About 61km from Tumbler Ridge. Short trail leads from Murray River Forest Service Rd to series of small lakes called Kinuseo Lakes. The first on the trail is Irene Lake, stocked with eastern brook trout.

Monkman Provincial Park: 32,000ha; 42 campsites. 250-787-3407. **Kinuseo Falls Campground** is 63km from Tumbler Ridge on gravel-surfaced Murray River Forest Service road. Watch for industrial traffic. Viewing platform at falls is wheelchair accessible.

No road access to rest of park. Air, hiking, or horseback access only. Park is on eastern flank of Rockies in Hart Ranges. Fine wilderness hiking. Fascinating geological structures. Stirring alpine views and crystal-clear lakes. Prime grizzly habitat. Park named for Alex Monkman, trapper and homesteader who envisioned a route along old Indian trails to connect Peace River country to BC coast. Alas for Monkman, the Pine Pass route to the west was selected instead.

Return via Hwy 29 to Chetwynd. Hwys 52N and 52E are alternative routes back to Hwy 97.

Highway 52: East of Tumbler Ridge, Hwy 52N (Heritage Highway) winds 98km through foothill country to join Hwy 97 at Arras, 17km west of Dawson Creek.

A longer scenic route to Hwy 2 and Dawson Creek, or to the province of Alberta, is Hwy 52E, also known as Boundary Rd. The mainly gravel highway circles east, then north about 146km from Tumbler Ridge to join Hwy 2 at Tupper on BC/Alberta border.

SIDE TRIP

on Highway 52E

After turnoff to Quintette Mine, about 13.5km south of Tumbler Ridge, the paved highway is used by oil, gas, and forest industries. Lonely, wild country. See moose, deer, and bears. Respect sour-gas warnings on some side roads. Forest Service recreation sites at Flatbed Creek East (about 34km from Tumbler Ridge), Stoney Lake (56km), Red Willow (79km), and Thunder Creek (82km).

One Island Lake Provincial Park: 61ha; 30 campsites. 250-787-3407. Take One Island Lake Rd north off Hwy 52E about 136km beyond Tumbler Ridge, or from Hwy 2 south, 30km rough road access. In the gently undulating Rocky Mountain foothills. Chance of large rainbow, brook trout. Boat launch.

Highway 2: About 10km beyond Hwy 52E junction with One Island Park Rd. This *Log* travels northwest 36km to Dawson Creek via Pouce Coupe. Southeast leads 2km to Alberta.

Tupper: (Pop. 33). Off Hwy 2, 1km beyond junction with Hwy 52. Seeking refuge from Hitler, a group of Sudetens (ethnic Germans living in the mountainous Sudeten areas of the former Czechoslovakia), settled in this attractive area in the late 1930s. Services.

Swan Lake Provincial Park: 67ha; 42 campsites. 250-787-3407. East off highway about 2km beyond Tupper. Access on 3km gravel road. May-Oct. Attractive park with beautiful beach, excellent swimming and boating on 5km Swan Lake. Recently stocked, the lake offers good fishing for pike and some perch. Viewing of waterfowl, shorebirds, and eastern songbird species. This, the third oldest provincial park in BC, celebrated its 80th birthday in 1998. Baseball diamond, horseshoe pits, picnic shelter. Tupper River Fish Ladder at weir where Tupper Creek flows out of Swan Lake.

Sudeten Provincial Park: 5ha; 15 campsites. Day-use area in pastoral setting. 250-787-3407. West off Hwy 2, 3km beyond Swan Lake park. Facilities include picnic shelter, playing field.

Pouce Coupe: (Pop. 894). A serene little community overlooking the Pouce Coupe River, 20km beyond Sudeten Park. Locals pronounce it "Pouce Coopy." The words, in French, mean "thumb cut off." One story says a local Sekani trapper lost a thumb in a gun accident; another says it was an old French voyageur, and he lost his thumb skinning a buffalo. Another version says Pouce Coupe or Pooscapee was a Dunne-za (Beaver) chief. And yet another says the name is derived from a Dunne-za phrase: "An abandoned chief's lodge by a deserted beaver dam."

In any event, the first white settler in the area was Hector Tremblay, a French Canadian en route to the Yukon in 1898 seeking his fortune. He established a trading post here in 1908, and began work on a trail south to Grande Prairie and north to Fort St John. Most settlement occurred after 1911 and the completion of the Edson Trail from Edmonton.

The town calls itself Peace River country's pioneer capital – it was, in its early days, the seat of government for the region and "end of steel" for the Northern Alberta Railways. The first passenger train arrived in 1931, and ran until service ended in 1974. Dawson Creek and Fort St John have taken over as administrative and transportation centres.

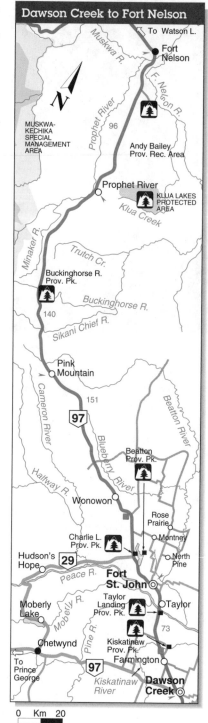

Dawson Creek to Fort Nelson

0   Km   20

Pouce Coupe Information: Village of Pouce Coupe, Box 190, Pouce Coupe, BC, V0C 2C0. Information centre on Main St, one block off Hwy 2. Daily mid-May to mid-Sept. 250-786-5555; off-season 250-786-5794.
■ **Pouce Coupe Museum:** On Main St, one block off Hwy 2. Daily May 15-Sept 15. 250-786-5555. Exhibits housed in former Northern Alberta Railways Station (1931).
■ **Pouce Coupe Regional Park:** East end of town.

Dawson Creek: (Pop. 11,125). 10km beyond Pouce Coupe, at Hwy 2/97 junction. See *Prince George to Dawson Creek*, p.287.

DAWSON CREEK TO FORT NELSON

THE ALASKA HIGHWAY (Highway 97)

Within the first year of its construction in 1942, the Alaska Highway had earned a reputation as an arduous drive. It was "a tortuous little trail barely wide enough to allow one vehicle to work its way through the trees," declared a 1943 issue of *National Geographic* magazine. "We drove through deeply rutted bogs which required the lowest gear and four-wheel drive...the major and I were thrown from side to side and beaten about as if we were in a small boat on a rough sea."

That same year, Canadian and American contractors began upgrading the supply road for year-round use. Bridges were built, stretches of road were straightened and widened, surfaces gravelled. On April 1, 1946, after the war, the Canadian government took over the highway in exchange for certain concessions, such as right-of-way.

Civilians were denied the rigours of travelling the Alaska Highway until 1948. Soon after its public opening, the journey's reputation as "tough and challenging" was upgraded, to "suicidal." The highway was closed. It re-opened again in 1949, but flat tires and empty gas tanks continued to plague persistent drivers.

Today, more than 300,000 people from around the world, lured by its legendary status, travel the Alaska Hwy from May-Sept (though it remains open year-round). An omniscient view reveals a black ribbon of pavement, now 2,288km, running just less than 1,000km through BC, more than that across the Yukon, and 320km in Alaska.

Still, this remains a road to adventure. The forests, the mountains, and all the encompassing wilderness stir the spirit and the adrenaline. The section from Dawson Creek slices 73km through rolling farmlands, crossing the Peace River at Taylor. Then it's on to Fort St John, and from there, 387km to Fort Nelson. The mood of the land becomes more rugged and wild, the views more camera-defying. To the west, the Rocky Mountains shimmer. They are a seductive prelude to what awaits.

Dawson Creek (Historic Mile 0): A junction point for Alaska/Hart/49/2 highways. For details on city, see *Prince George to Dawson Creek*, p.287.

Farmington: (Pop. 79). 19km beyond Dawson Creek (Alaska/Hart junction). A secondary highway from Farmington leads south, joining Hwy 97 at Arras, 17km west of Dawson Creek. East of Farmington, Sweetwater Rd leads to Rolla and Clayhurst.
■ **Farmington Fairways:** 250-843-7774. Nine holes, driving range, camping, RV sites.

Kiskatinaw Provincial Park: 58ha; 28 campsites. 250-787-3407. 2km beyond Farmington, turn east off Hwy 97 onto Rd 64 (a loop of the old Alaska Highway). 4km to well-treed riverside park. Just past park entrance, old highway crosses the **Old Kiskatinaw River Bridge at historic Mile 21 of the Alaska Hwy.** This three-span wooden trestle, 30m above the river, was built 1942-43 and is the only original timber bridge still in use on the highway. It curves a remarkable 9 degrees along its 162.5m length. The old highway loops around (a total of 10km) to rejoin the new Alaska Hwy.

Kiskatinaw Rest Area: 14km north of Kiskatinaw Park turnoff (Rd 64). View of bridge and river gorge.

Peace River Valley Viewpoint: On Hwy 97, 22km north of Kiskatinaw Park turnoff (Rd 64). From the top of the hill looking down to the Peace River Bridge and Taylor Flats where Alexander Mackenzie camped. There's also the Westcoast Energy Inc refinery and the Fibreco pulp mill.

Taylor Landing Provincial Park: 2ha. East side of highway, 5km from viewpoint, 25km beyond Kiskatinaw Park turnoff. Boat launch – boaters take care, the river here is downstream from Bennett and Peace Canyon dams; water levels here can fluctuate suddenly.

Peace Island Regional Park: 17.5ha; 20 campsites, four group sites (one with shelter). On the highway's west side, across from Taylor Landing Park, linked to south shore by a causeway. May-Sept, 250-789-9295. Off-season, 250-789-3392. Playground, nature trail, and chances to see beaver, geese, moose, deer. Home to World Gold Panning Championships, Aug.

Peace River Bridge: 500m beyond Peace Island Park. A cantilever and truss structure built 1960. Its predecessor, a suspension bridge known as Galloping Gerdie, was built in just nine months by the company that built the Niagara and Brooklyn bridges. It opened in 1943, and collapsed in 1957. Before that bridge, the way across was by ferry. On the highway's east side is the natural gas pipeline that looks like a bridge itself. From here to Fort St John, gas pipelines run beneath fields, and gas-processing plants are many.

Taylor (Historic Mile 35): (Pop. 1,031). Begins at Peace River bridge. Community is built on a broad plateau above the river. Alexander Mackenzie, describing the area in 1793, wrote: "The land above the spot where we are encamped, spreads into an extensive plain and stretches onto a very high ridge. The country is so crowded with animals as to have the appearance, in some places of a stall-yard from the state of the ground. The soil is black and light. We this day saw two grisly and hideous bears."

Town takes its name from Donald Herbert Taylor, in 1906 the area's first homesteader. He spoke English, French, and his native Cree, and was, before his arrival here, a Hudson's Bay Company factor at Hudson's Hope.

Taylor – its economy based on lumber, pulp, oil, and gas – is deep in the river valley, surrounded by lightly forested hills of poplar, cottonwood, and spruce. Fall colours are wonderful. Wildlife is plentiful, but Mackenzie's "hideous" bears are seldom seen. Try delicious sweet corn from local garden markets.

Taylor Information: Info Centre, May-late Aug. 250-789-9015. District of Taylor, Box 300, Taylor, BC, VOC 2KO. 250-789-3392.

■ **Historic Mile 35:** Interpretive panels describe the bridging of the Peace at Taylor.

■ **Church of the Good Shepherd:** Little 1932 structure was built as memorial by father of four daughters who drowned in a boating accident on the Peace.

■ **World's Largest Golf Ball:** Marks location of Lone Wolf Golf Club adjacent Alaska Hwy. 250-789-3711. Ball, once an old fuel tank, is 12.8m in diameter and weighs 37t. Club offers 18-hole championship course, restaurant and lounge. 3.5km walking/cross-country ski trail circles course.

Fort St John (Historic Mile 47): (Pop. 15,021). 19km beyond Taylor. A small town with big city dreams – wide streets, wide buildings, parking meters, cappuccino shops. There's still lots of room to grow – geography certainly sets no limits. Fort St John sits on prairie, near, but not up against, the riverbank where its stories begin. From the heart of downtown you can follow streets to roads that look down over the Peace River, where the original forts stood. There were six of them in this area between 1794 and 1925, and Fort St John can claim to be the oldest settlement in mainland BC.

But the human history of Fort St John begins much before this. In quiet obscurity on

FORT ST JOHN

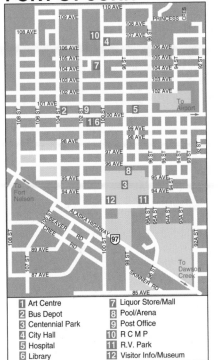

1 Art Centre	**7** Liquor Store/Mall
2 Bus Depot	**8** Pool/Arena
3 Centennial Park	**9** Post Office
4 City Hall	**10** R C M P
5 Hospital	**11** R.V. Park
6 Library	**12** Visitor Info/Museum

the northwest edge of town, near the east shore of Charlie Lake, behind a thin veil of trees – and visible from Hwy 97 if you knew what you were looking for – is what we might call the *first* Fort St John. Less than 5m wide and 6m deep – a perfect cave formed of round boulders. Eleven thousand years ago, this was someone's home. It looked out to a widening of the Peace River created by a glacial dam: "Peace Lake" covered what is now Fort St John and northern Alberta.

Here at today's Charlie Lake was a narrowing, a crossing place for animals (including some we might no longer recognize) and the people who hunted them. Archaeologists speculate, based on their findings in the Charlie Lake Cave, that at the end or even before the end of the ice age, a sophisticated society of people visited this site. Items found in the cave – a fluted-point stone spearhead, scrapers, and an ornamental bead – offer in some ways a more substantial record of human presence than the fur traders' forts.

In fact, historians until recently disputed the existence of the first fort, Rocky Mountain House, at the confluence of the Peace and Moberly rivers. They now tell us this North West Company depot opened in 1794, the year after Alexander Mackenzie passed through. For 10 years, traders, who often married into Dunne-za or Sekani families, arrived in the fall, stayed the winter, bought furs, and usually left in the spring with their cargo.

Rocky Mountain House closed in 1805 with the opening of two forts farther west, deeper within Sekani territories. (These were Rocky Mountain Portage House, at what is now Hudson's Hope, and the Trout Lake Fort at McLeod Lake.)

But just one year later, the North West Company of fur traders established a second fort here at the request of the local Dunne-za. Fort d'Epinette sat at the confluence of the Peace and Beatton rivers, just east of where Rocky Mountain House had stood.

Fourteen years later, in 1820, the rival Hudson's Bay Company appeared on the scene to open a competing depot on the former site of the old Rocky Mountain House. The two companies merged the following year to become the Hudson's Bay Company, and Fort d'Epinette became Fort St John.

Two years after that, the HBC decided to close Fort St John again in favour of a more westerly fort. The local Dunne-za, however, saw the closure as a threat to their very survival, a betrayal of an unwritten contract: the fort's clerk and four other employees were murdered. In retaliation, the HBC closed each and every one of its forts in the Peace River region. Many aboriginal people starved. Fort St John did not re-open until nearly 40 years later. (It sat for 12 years on the south bank of the Peace, opposite present-day Fort St John. Then, for the next half-century, until 1925, it sat on the north bank. Finally, it was shifted away from the riverbank altogether, closer to established homesteads.)

Gold seekers passed through Fort St John in the 1860s. They arrived again in 1898, en route to the Klondike, but this time were blocked by the Dunne-za and Sekani who saw their own hunting and trapping economy threatened. Their stance resulted in the drafting of Treaty 8, including Dunne-za, Sekani, Cree, Saulteux, and Dene-thah peoples living between Moberly Lake and Fort Nelson. The treaty, however, rather than protecting traditional aboriginal hunting grounds, opened the way for logging, settlement, and farming, and for the development of the rich gas and oil reserves.

Fort St John has become the Peace River capital, with government offices, headquarters of the Treaty 8 Tribal Association, the Northern Lights College, a daily newspaper, transportation and communications services. Because of oil and gas, the city is booming, brash, and materialistic: sometimes even experiencing a shortage of labour – contrary to life in much of the rest of BC.

Visitors can enjoy the lively North Peace Cultural Centre, hotels and motels, restaurants, cafes, and shopping.

Fort St John Information: Info Centre, Fort St John Chamber of Commerce, 9923-96th St, Fort St John, BC, V1J 1K9. 250-785-3033. Year-round.

Fort St John Airport: 8km southeast toward Taylor. Terminus for scheduled and charter airlines.

■ **Historic Mile 47:** Signs describe how Fort St John changed during the Alaska Highway construction.

■ **Centennial Park:** Adjacent museum complex, below. RV Park, campsites, picnic tables.

■ **Fort St John-North Peace Museum:** 93rd Ave and 100th St. 250-787-0430. Daily May-Sept, Mon-Sat rest of year. Reconstructed schoolhouse, pioneer artifacts, trapper's cabin, exhibit on Alaska Hwy. Gift shop and unique Peace River crafts.

■ **Monument to Alexander Mackenzie:** In Fort St John Centennial Park, Mackenzie St.

■ **North Peace Cultural Centre:** 100th and 100th. 250-785-1992. Houses library and theatre. Also **Peace Gallery North**, featuring the exciting work of local artists. Special exhibits of traditional and contemporary pieces by local First Nations artists. Excellent gift shop.

■ **Peace River Lookout:** South end of 100th St. Wonderful view of river valley. On the south bank, site of Fort St John, 1860-1872; on the north bank, site of Fort St John, 1872-1925.

■ **Fish Creek Community Forest:** 250-785-8906. 2km northeast of town, off 100th St. Guided or self-guided forest walks year-round. Also guided mill tours of Fort St John and Taylor operations, Mon-Fri. 250-785-8906.

■ **The Honey Place:** Mile 42, Alaska Hwy. 250-785-4808. Mon-Sat. World's largest glass beehive.

■ **Golf:** Lakepoint Golf and Country Club, right off Hwy 97 at Charlie Lake; 250-785-5566. 18 holes. **Links Golf Course**, 250-785-9995. Nine holes.

■ **North Peace Leisure Pool:** At 98th and 96th avenues. 250-787-8178. Waterslide, wave pool, sauna, cafe.

■ **Troy's Family Amusement Park:** Mile 45, Hwy 97. 250-785-8655. Driving range, mini-golf, RV park.

North of Fort St John, east of the Alaska Highway, straight roads lead through rolling, green countryside, yellow with canola in the summer. In the rich farmland between St John Creek and the Beatton River, are tiny communities that simply wish to be noted as you drive by: hello **North Pine**, **Montney**, **Murdale**, and **Rose Prairie**. (Montney, at Montney Corner, has a gas station).

Beatton Provincial Park: 312ha; 37 campsites (reservations taken: call 1-800-689-9025; from the Lower Mainland or overseas, call 604-689-9025). General info: 250-787-3407. 6km north of Fort St John. Year-round; camping May-Oct. Turn north off Hwy 97. 10km on paved road to park entrance, then turn west on gravel. Aspen-lined trails lead to 300m developed beach on Charlie Lake. Boating, hiking, walking trails. Fishing for walleye and northern pike. Playing field. Winter activities: cross-country skiing, ice fishing, snowshoeing.

Charlie Lake (Historic Mile 52): 7km north of Fort St John. Services. Was Mile 0 on Army Tote Road. Some locals insist this is the true beginning of Alaska Hwy construction. It was also here, on May 14, 1942, that a group of soldiers drowned when their cargo barge sank.

Highway 29: 13km north of Fort St John. Leads south 75km to Hudson's Hope, rejoining Hwy 97 at Chetwynd, 100km west of Dawson Creek. See *Fort St John to Tumbler Ridge*, p.287.

Charlie Lake Provincial Park: 92ha; 58 campsites (reservations taken: call 1-800-689-9025; from the Lower Mainland or overseas, call 604-689-9025). Sani-station. General info: 250-787-3407. At Hwys 29/97 junction. May-Oct. A destination for walleye anglers. Can also catch northern pike, burbot, and yellow perch. Boating and hiking. Heavily treed park, with berries in autumn. Snowshoe hare and ruffed grouse commonly seen. Playground, picnic shelter, boat launch.

Mile 80 Rest Area: 41km north of Hwy 29/97 junction. On highway's west side. Amenities include washroom with running water, parking and roadways accommodating over-length vehicles, children's play structure, picnic area, and information kiosk.

Wonowon (Historic Mile 101): (Pop. 84). 76km from Hwy 29/97 junction. Tourist facilities. Wonowon used to be known as Blueberry, for the Blueberry River that flows on the highway's east side. Was a 24-hour military checkpoint during the Second World War.

North of Wonowon the highway starts climbing through dense forests intersected by arrow-straight seismic lines. Enjoy 360-degree vistas as highway breaches ridges.

Pink Mountain (Historic Mile 143): (Pop. 19). 62km beyond Wonowon.

Services. Moose often seen, sometimes caribou, too. Highway has steadily climbed to 1,100m. Now, descends into the Beatton River valley.

Pink Mountain Wildlife Viewing Site (Historic Mile 147): Access to summit at Mile 147. Woodland caribou, moose, Rocky Mountain elk, plains bison, mule deer, and white-tailed deer.

Suicide Hill (Historic Mile 148): About 8km from Pink Mountain. Prepare to meet thy maker. "I rolled her along 'till I reached the drop they now call suicide hill. As I inched her down with squeaking brakes, it was a horrible thrill." Words of Gene Wilkinson who trucked perishables to work camps during Alaska Highway construction, and lived to write about it. Today, the hill's a breeze.

Time Zone: About 4km beyond Suicide Hill. No changes in summer, when daylight-saving time is in effect elsewhere in BC. But from late Oct-April, set your clock back one hour as you move from Mountain Standard to **Pacific Standard Time**.

Muskwa-Kechika Special Management Area: 4.4 million ha. As you approach the Sikanni Chief River, look west: the Alaska Hwy skirts the **Northern Rocky Mountains** right to the Yukon border. At Stone Mountain Provincial Park (see p.295), the road actually crosses into their domain, and exits again through Muncho Lake Provincial Park. The Northern Rockies is the heartland of the Muskwa-Kechika Special Management Area – an area larger than Switzerland, and a significant piece of precious North American wilderness. It has been called the Serengeti of North America because, wildlife ecology experts say, outside Africa, there is no place like this for large mammal diversity and intact ecosystems. The Muskwa-Kechika area is renowned internationally for wildlife "ecology values" that include bison, caribou, and Stone's sheep. And it has a high priority in BC for wildlife and habitat protection and management, including species such as elk, wolf, and grizzly bear.

The area was named for its two largest river valleys. The Kechika, at 2.2 million ha, is western North America's biggest wild watershed south of the Yukon. The few people who live near this wilderness are native and non-native trappers, hunters, and guide-outfitters. Meanwhile, loggers, miners, and oil and gas companies are interested in the mountains' resources. The new area includes 1.17 million ha of existing and new protected areas – provincial parks and recreation areas, river corridors, hot springs, rare habitats, and grassland ecosystems. In the surrounding 3.24 million ha, traditional economies, mining, logging, and oil and gas development will continue under "environmentally sensitive" management.

While the Northern Rockies' preservation represents BC's largest single designation of preserved wilderness, Tweedsmuir Provincial Park, at 994,246ha, remains BC's largest contiguous tract of parkland.

The Rocky Mountains of northern BC, hailed as "the Serengeti of the North," are now protected.

For those who would do more than skirt this Serengeti, a number of guide-outfitters offer horseback trips and expeditions. Contact: Northern BC Guides Association, Box 6370, Fort St John, BC, V1J 4K6 or ask at information centres.

Sikanni Chief River Bridge (Historic Mile 162): 21km from Suicide Hill. (30km from Pink Mountain.) 5km descent into valley to bridge. Reasonable summer fishing for pike, grayling, and whitefish.

Buckinghorse River Provincial Park (Historic Mile 173): 55ha; 33 campsites. 250-787-3407. 22.5km beyond Sikanni Chief River. Park at edge of Rocky Mountain foothills. Cast a fly at grayling. Moose wintering area. Services across the highway.

About 4km north of park, the highway was rerouted around Trutch Mountain in 1987. Heavy vehicles had problems climbing 1,260m summit. The military chose the high route rather than contend with muskeg at lower elevations. The new stretch of road follows the side hill of Minnaker River Valley.

This is a scenic stretch, with mountain and river valley views, and moose.

Prophet River (Mile 233): (Pop. 77). 84km Buckinghorse River Park. On highway's east side, First Nations community, school, little wooden church with tin roof and no bell. On west side, services.

Curve Cutting (Historic Mile 234): The Adsett Creek realignment project completed in 1992 removed 132 arm-aching curves from some 56km of highway. From here it's mile after mile of stubby forest, power poles, seismic lines cutting straight through the wilderness. Caribou are relatively abundant, as are moose, and a significant attraction from Mile 234 to Fort Nelson.

Andy Bailey Recreation Area (Historic Mile 265): 174ha; 6 campsites. 250-787-3407. Turn east 60.5km north of Prophet River, and 11km on dirt road. Named for pioneer who cut the original access road. May-Oct. Long sandy beach on Jackfish Lake. Because most northern beaches are rocky, sand has been imported. Good fishing for northern pike. Swimming, boat launch. The spruce forests here encourage insects. Marshy.

From here it's 25km to the lowest point on the Alaska Hwy, 307m, at the Muskwa River Bridge. Muskwa, we are told, is the Cree name for bear.

Fort Nelson (Historic Mile 300): (Pop. 4,401). 28km beyond road to Andy Bailey Recreation Area. Where the Muskwa and Prophet rivers flow into the Fort Nelson River, Dene-thah, Dunne-za, Sekani, Cree and European histories also meet. The first of five Fort Nelsons was established in the region by the North West Company in 1805. It was named for the British Lord Horatio Nelson who won the Battle of Trafalgar. The second fort is reported to have been destroyed in 1813 by a group of aboriginal people. Not until 1865 was the third fort established by the Hudson's Bay Company (since 1821 merged with the North West Company) on the west bank of the Nelson River near today's airport. After a flood in 1890, "Old Fort Nelson" was built across and up the river. Fort Nelson number five, 1942, was established midst an emerging community – today's town.

It was the same year that 2,000 troops made this their base for construction of the Alaska Hwy. For a time, this was Mile Zero, the start of roads north to Whitehorse and Fort Simpson.

The town now thrives on the oil and gas industry, forestry, and agriculture. North America's largest gas-processing plant, Westcoast Energy, is located here. A byproduct, sulphur, is shipped around the world. The surrounding area is heavily forested with marketable white spruce, lodgepole pine, and aspen, that supported the world's largest chopstick manufacturing plant until it recently closed. Fort Nelson's largest employer, the Slocan Group-Tackama Division, has an oriented strand board plant – the largest industrial building of its kind in BC. Here is the northern terminus of BC Rail's freight-only line.

Just south of town are the Dene-thah (Slave) and Sekani descendants of those who supplied the fur-trade forts nearly two centuries ago. The Eh-Cho Dene, "people among the big animals," still trap for furs, although the community also prospers from gas-sharing agreements with the province dating back to the 1980s, and from a number of industrial enterprises. Visitors are welcome to Fort Nelson Treaty Day Celebrations, usually the second weekend in August.

Fort Nelson is an especially friendly town. Here are a full range of services, including campgrounds and B&Bs. It also offers the easi-

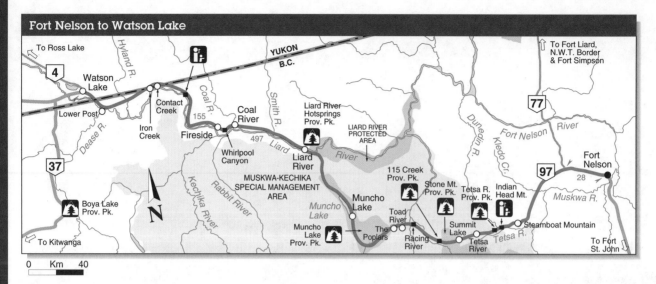

Fort Nelson to Watson Lake

est access into the Kwadacha Wilderness Park (see below), and is becoming a destination for adventure tourism.

? Fort Nelson Information: Info Centre, Fort Nelson-Liard Regional District, Bag Service 399, Fort Nelson, BC, V0C 1R0. 250-774-6400. Daily May-Aug. Off-season, call 250-774-2541.

✈ Fort Nelson Airport: 6km east of town. Airport Dr leads right from Hwy 97 in centre of town. Scheduled and charter.

■ Fort Nelson Heritage Museum: North end of town. Daily, 8:30-7:30, May-Aug. 250-774-3536. A presentation of fur-bearing animals: beaver, mink, red fox, lynx, a timber wolf, grizzly, and even a white moose cow. Display of a spruce canoe and how to make it; story of local hero Harry Rusk, the first North American native to perform at the Grand Olde Oprey.

■ Fort Nelson-Liard Native Friendship Centre: 250-774-2993. On 49th Ave, next to Anglican Church. High-quality local native crafts for sale: mukluks, moccasins, birch-bark baskets, and moosehair-tufted wall hangings.

■ Welcome Visitor Program: Phoenix Theatre. Mon-Thurs, 6:45pm, June-July. Evening stories, talks, and demonstrations by residents about anything and everything to do with the area, from flowers to native legends to horseback riding. Details at Info Centre.

■ Forest Eco-tours: Pamphlets describing the forest ecology and points of interest, and an interpretive trail guide are available at the Forest District Office, off Hwy 97 at north end of town. 250-744-3936.

■ BC's Most Northerly Grass Greens Golf Course: Poplar Hills Golf Club, Mile 304 Radar Rd. On highest point in Fort Nelson, the old DEW Line radar site. 9-hole course.

🏕⛺🔭 Kwadacha Wilderness Provincial Park: 158,475ha. 250-787-3407 for maps and information. Roughly 160km southwest of Fort Nelson. No road access. Most visitors fly in, but guided horseback riding or hiking access can be arranged. Open all year, wilderness campsites. Excellent climbing and hiking, but no marked trails. For wilderness-wise visitors only.

Kwadacha, the Sekani word for white water, describes the milky colour of the Kwadacha River, heavy with glacial debris leached from the Lloyd George Icefield, one of the most spectacular features of this rugged park. Kwadacha is carefully preserved as a truly total wilderness park. Hikers beware: grizzlies are common. Among the sky-reaching limestone peaks are thickly wooded valleys, flower-studded alpine meadows, and turquoise lakes. Here, too, are hoodoos – castellated rock sculpted by the elements. A great diversity of habitats is reflected in wildlife populations. Elk are abundant, as are bears, wolves, wolverines, mountain goats, and many smaller mammals. Park is also a bird refuge. More than 70 bird species have been identified, including peregrine falcons, golden eagles, and the red-throated loon.

For continuation of Alaska Hwy see *Fort Nelson to Watson Lake*, following.

🏛 Dawson Creek: (Pop. 11,125). 10km beyond Pouce Coupe, at Hwy 2/97 junction. See *Prince George to Dawson Creek*, p.287.

FORT NELSON TO WATSON LAKE

THE ALASKA HIGHWAY (Highway 97)

This section is everything the Alaska Hwy is supposed to be. A mountain lover's dream. The highway climbs and curls through 525km of the most diverse landscape imaginable. The rugged peaks of the northern Rocky Mountains with their convoluted rock formations present spectacular views at each twist of the road. Occasional remains of log cabins are a reminder of the prospectors, explorers, and trappers who lived in this splendid isolation. Some still do.

The region contains lakes of crystal clarity, but perhaps most unlikely of all are the relaxing waters of Liard River Hotsprings where moose munch algae and carnivorous plants await their prey. Visitors should take care as black and grizzly bears await their prey here as well.

The highway from Fort Nelson starts benignly enough through mixed forests and patches of muskeg. Then it winds up into the mountains. The stretch through Stone Mountain and Muncho Lake parks is arguably the most scenic in North America. After conquering the mountains, the highway follows the Liard River to the BC/Yukon border.

🏛 Fort Nelson (Historic Mile 300): (Pop. 4,401) On Alaska Hwy (97 North), 460km north of Fort St John. And 525km southeast of Watson Lake. See *Dawson Creek to Fort Nelson*, above.

🛣 Highway 77 (Liard Hwy): 27km beyond Fort Nelson. Leads north off Alaska Hwy, 137km to BC/NWT border. There it becomes Hwy 7. The first settlement north of the border is tiny **Fort Liard**, about 42km away. In all, the Liard Hwy travels nearly 400km through to its junction with the Mackenzie Hwy near **Fort Simpson**. This wilderness highway is very much like the old Alaska Hwy: it's a gravel road, with few facilities and travel should be undertaken with care. The Liard Hwy is also part of a 2,240km loop drive along the Alaska, Liard, and Mackenzie highways, passing through BC, Alberta, and the Northwest Territories.

🏕 Maxhamish Provincial Park: 520ha. West of Hwy 77 (Liard Hwy) near NWT border. No road access; fly in only. Sandy beaches and solitude.

🏛 Steamboat Mountain (Mile 351): (Pop. just 3). 57km beyond Liard Hwy junction. Road clings to valley side. Services. Locals call this "steamboat country." One story says it was named by a homesick Scot who, used to looking down on the loch steamboats from his hikes among Scottish hills, decided the mountain here resembled a steamboat. Accommodation, food, and gas.

🛣 Road to Vista: North off Hwy 97, 1km from community of Steamboat Mountain. A rough, narrow road leads up Steamboat Mountain, 1,067m. Views of the Rocky Mountains.

Indian Head Mountain: 14.5km from Steamboat. View of the mountain shaped, someone thought, like the classic native profile.

Teetering Rock: 2.5km beyond Indian Head, north side of highway. Rock visible from viewpoint, which is also start of 12.5km hiking trail to this glacial erratic.

Tetsa River Provincial Park: 115ha; 25 campsites. 250-787-3407. About 21.5km beyond Steamboat Mountain. 1km south off Hwy 97 on dirt road. April-Oct. Good fishing for grayling. Check fishing regulations. Pleasant, short hikes through poplar trees along river. Braided river channels. Pleasant, private campsites.

Tetsa River Services: 17km beyond Tetsa River Park. Gas, food, accommodation, camping, and jet-boat rides.

Stone Mountain Provincial Park: 25,691ha; 28 campsites. Boundary about 22km from Tetsa River Services; straddles highway for 14km. 250-787-3407. Park offers landscapes of extensive alpine tundra and long, U-shaped valleys beneath sweeping, bare mountain peaks. Dramatic stuff. Erosion pillars or hoodoos. Turquoise subalpine lakes and waterfalls. Park is home to mountain caribou and Stone's sheep. Also watch for elk, deer, bear, and moose. Stone Mountain offers limitless wilderness hiking. Much of it strictly for experienced backpackers as distances are great, terrain rugged, and marked trails few (see *Stone Mountain Trails*, below).

Summit Lake (Historic Mile 392): (Pop. 50). About 3km beyond park entrance. Summit Lake, 1,295m, is the highest point on the Alaska Hwy. The timberline, where spruce and dark firs give way to scrub willow and birch, is only a few hundred metres above the road. It can snow here at any time of year. Accommodation, gas, food.

Summit Lake Provincial Campground (Stone Mountain Park): 28 sites. 0.5km past Summit Lake services.

Stone Mountain Trails: Summit Lake campground is starting point for some great walks. Just west of campground, a 10-minute trail to two hoodoos; legend has it they are the heads of devils. Just north, an arduous 5km hike through spruce forests to alpine near **Summit Peak**. And just south of the campground, 4x4 trail leads to microwave tower and stunning views. **Flower Springs Lake Trail** leads 6km return trip to enchanting aquamarine tarn. Reasonably easy going. A memorable way to introduce children – or grandparents – to alpine country. But stay on the trail, as the land's as fragile as it is beautiful.

Wokkpash Provincial Park: 37,000ha; wilderness camping. No facilities. 250-787-3407. Adjoins southwestern boundary of Stone Mountain Park.

Access trail starts at Churchill Mine Rd, about 15km west of Summit Lake campground. The bridge is washed out. This 70km (five-to-seven-day) loop is recommended only for experienced hikers. Hikers can rejoin Alaska Hwy 8km west of Summit Lake campground near Rocky Mountain Lodge, or retrace steps, but it is strongly recommended the hike is completed at Buba Canyon trailhead in the MacDonald Valley bottom near Rocky Mountain Lodge, 8km west of Summit Lake. Flash flooding on MacDonald Creek – a braided stream up to 1km wide – can render the creek impassable, stranding hikers for several days.

Within this wilderness valley is the spectacular Wokkpash Gorge, also called Devils Gorge, 5km of which is lined on both sides with 30m hoodoos, or erosion pillars. Nearby Forlorn Gorge, is a miniature Grand Canyon, only 25m wide, but 150m deep, giving a rocky record of millions of years of the Earth's upheavals. Share wilderness with caribou, mountain goats, Stone's sheep, and moose.

Highway parallels MacDonald Creek and the next few kilometres offer views of the Stone Range to the northeast and the Muskwa Ranges of the Rockies to the west.

Deadly Mix: Graphic red signs depicting dead sheep and crumpled cars urge motorists to slow down in areas frequented by Stone's sheep. Pull well off road to photograph animals. It is illegal within a provincial park to feed wildlife: this creates a hazard for both wildlife and people. Respect caribou signs, these indicate where these animals usually cross the Alaska Hwy. Beware of both black bears and grizzly bears; they live and roam throughout the park.

Northern Boundary: End of Stone Mountain Provincial Park about 11km beyond Summit Lake campground.

115 Creek Provincial Campground: 51ha; eight campsites. 250-787-3407. South side of highway, 18km beyond Summit Lake campground. A series of big, old beaver dams and ponds are just two minutes' walk behind the park. Creek was named during construction of the pioneer road, for its distance from Fort Nelson. Trails.

From the summit, highway traces MacDonald Creek, descending deep into the mountain valley.

Racing River Wayside Area: Hwy 97 crosses bridge 25km from 115 Creek Park. Good fishing for grayling and Dolly Varden in late summer. River access is at south end of bridge.

Toad River (Historic Mile 422): (Pop 60). 5km from the Racing River bridge. Interpretive panel tells of Dennis and John Callison, who lead Public Roads Administration surveyors to the area in 1941, and stayed. Here are 4,580 hats, one for every mile of the highway from the southern US border to the Alaska border.

Lodge, gas, RV hook-ups, cafe, groceries, airstrip, school. Fishing for bull trout, grayling, and whitefish.

The Poplars (Historic Mile 426): (Pop. 4). 5km beyond Toad River. Motel, gas, cafe, gift shop.

Muncho Lake Provincial Park (Historic Mile 456): 88,420ha; 30 campsites (see Strawberry Flats and MacDonald, below). 250-787-3407. Southern boundary of park is 2km beyond The Poplars. Canada's northern Rocky Mountains at their spectacular best. Fortunately for today's visitors, they're on view because highway surveyors wanted to avoid the Grand Canyon of the Liard. They chose to route the highway 82km along the Toad and Trout river valleys. In between, the highway skirts the eastern shore of Muncho Lake. It looks longer than its 12km, probably because it pops up unexpectedly from the tight quarters of the mountains. And because these jade-green waters that change tone with the light have the visual impact of a sledgehammer. The colour originates from copper dioxides deep down in the lake's bedrock.

Wildlife loves the park, although several species are near the northern limit of their range. Watch for loons, grebes and mergansers in spring. Also, be careful along the highway in spring and summer. Stone sheep enter the park with their lambs and frequent the highway edges seeking the remaining salt used to control winter ice. Check locally for best photo opportunities. Serendipity helps.

Provincial campgrounds ahead may be full later in the day: private campgrounds, motels, and lodges in the area can often squeeze latecomers in.

Folded Mountain: 4km from southern boundary of Muncho Lake Park. A mountain with wrinkles. One of several peaks tortured by tectonic folding and faulting; pastel colours in exposed rock. Sign explains how, about 175 million years ago, the continent of North America began to move westward, causing land masses to collide and rock to fold.

Centennial Falls: 8km beyond Folded Mountain sign, a stop to view attractive waterfall.

Sawtooth Mountain: 16km beyond Centennial Falls, sign describes how slabs of dolomite rock were thrust up during "construction" of the Rockies.

Strawberry Flats Provincial Campground: 15 sites on gravel fan overlooking Muncho Lake. 13km from Sawtooth Mountain stop. Popular spot in summer, with imposing lake and mountain views. Admire but don't pick the wildflowers.

Muncho Lake: (Pop. 24). About 8km beyond Strawberry Flats. Services. One of the few Canadian towns inside a provincial park. Ask about lake tours June-Sept.

MacDonald Provincial Campground: 15 sites. 2km from Muncho Lake. Boat launch.

Muncho Lake Park Northern Boundary: 28km from MacDonald campground. Gradually, the highway leaves the Rockies behind and descends into the Liard River valley. Liard is French for "cottonwood tree."

Liard River (Historic Mile 496): About 25km beyond northern boundary of Muncho Lake Park. Lodging, gas, restaurants, limited groceries.

Liard River Hotsprings Provincial Park: 976ha; 53 campsites (reservations taken: call 1-800-689-9025; from the Lower Mainland or overseas, call 604-689-9025).General info: 250-787-3407. 2km beyond Liard River bridge. North off Hwy 97. Two hot, soothing, mineral water pools creating their own luxuriant microclimate. Access to Alpha and Beta pools by wooden boardwalk across warm water swamps. Look for tiny chub skittering about. Water temperatures range 38-49C. Using shampoo or soap in pools is not permitted. Nor is liquor. Prolonged lounging may not be safe for some medical conditions. Plan to stop early in day; it's a very popular spot in summer. Informative visitor programs, including nature walks. In winter, hot springs are transformed into a mystical oasis of steam and hoarfrost.

When homesteader John Smith lived here in the 1920s, word spread of a tropical valley in the northern wilderness – images of monkeys and parrots frolicking in banana groves. Well, not quite – but the hot springs proved a most welcome "discovery" to highway building crews in 1942, although women in the construction camps were granted the privilege of relaxing in them only once a week.

The hot springs increase humidity and raise temperatures about 2C from regional annual averages. That allows plants to grow here in profusion farther north than their normal range. Moose, bear, and many bird species share this haven.

A few kilometres beyond the hot springs is the southern boundary of a June 1982 forest fire. BC's second largest, it burned 182,725ha. Two separate fires, the Eg and Cran, were sparked by lightning and then joined. The area has an extensive fire history, and the single largest fire was the Tee fire in 1972, which was partially overlapped by the Eg and Cran fires. The worst of the burned area has been covered by low scrub and wildflowers.

Smith River Falls: About 27km beyond Liard River Hotsprings, 2km off Hwy 97. Pleasant picnic spot. Short walk to good fishing for Dolly Varden and grayling in river beneath falls.

Coal River (Historic Mile 533): (Pop. 8). About 30km north of road to Smith River Falls. Services. In wet weather before highway was paved, vehicles emerged from this section splattered in black from coal in the road's surface.

Whirlpool Canyon Rest Stop/Campground: Nearly 9km beyond Coal River. Sign misnames this site: here are actually the Mountain Portage Rapids, where the Liard River makes a sweeping turn between three rocky-rimmed channels. Whirlpool Canyon is downriver. Very rustic Forest Service campground.

Fireside (Historic Mile 543): (Pop. 4). 7km beyond Whirlpool Canyon. Stark reminders in all directions of devastation caused by the forest fires that give the community its name.

Lookout (Historic Mile 570): About 40km beyond Fireside. Great view of Liard River and Goat Mountain.

Contact Creek (Historic Mile 588): (Pop. 4). 27km beyond lookout. Alaska Hwy construction crews working from the north (Teslin) and south (Fort Nelson), met here September 24, 1942. Services 3km beyond. This is the Yukon. Highway flip-flops across the BC/Yukon border seven times before the official border about 63km away.

Iron Creek (Historic Mile 596): (Pop 4). 10km north of Contact Creek. South side of highway. Services.

Hyland River Bridge: Kilometre Post 1,000. About 14km from Iron Creek. Dolly Varden and grayling.

Lower Post Rd (Historic Mile 620): 21km beyond Hyland River bridge. South off Hwy 97. Road leads to Lower Post, or Den Kayah Kaka'ke, homeland of the Kaska Dena, on the banks of the Liard. No services for visitors now. Lower Post, a former Hudson's Bay Company post, derived its name from Upper Post on McDame Creek, a tributary of the Dease River. The Liard and Dease rivers meet here.

BC/Yukon Territory Border (Historic Mile 627): 17km beyond Lower Post junction. The Alaska Hwy crosses the 60th parallel as it enters the Yukon Territory.

WATSON LAKE TO WHITEHORSE

ALASKA HIGHWAY, THE ROAD TO ATLIN, AND THE SOUTH KLONDIKE HIGHWAY

At the BC/Yukon border, Alaska Hwy 97 becomes Alaska Hwy 1 slicing west across the bottom of the Yukon Territory. Four tendrils reach south to the remote northwest corner of BC. The Stewart-Cassiar Hwy (37) leads 721km to BC's Yellowhead Hwy (16). The other three routes traverse parts of BC only accessible from the Yukon: Hwy 7 to Atlin; Hwy 8 to Skagway, Alaska, and the Canada/US Chilkoot Trail; and Hwy 3, tracing the eastern boundaries of the Kluane

National Park to BC's Tatshenshini-Alsek Wilderness Park.

These are roads less travelled, but on them we will encounter most of the Yukon's population. Whitehorse, 551km from the BC/Yukon border, is the Yukon's capital, and home to 24,000 of the territory's total population of 31, 349. En route, Watson Lake and Carcross – small towns by southern standards – are important Yukon centres, as are Atlin in BC and Skagway in the US.

Northwest ho! Into the Land of the Midnight Sun. Should you arrive in Whitehorse at summer solstice, you'll have 21 hours of daylight for exploring (three hours of nighttime for sleeping); in mid-winter, there are just six hours of daylight. Our highways carry us through the stunted boreal forest, muskeg, and permafrost that characterize the North – the hunting, trapping, and fishing grounds of Athapaskan-speaking peoples that today make up one-quarter of the Yukon's population. This southern lip of the Yukon is home to Kaska, Tagish, and Taku or Inland Tlingit peoples. It was their northern cousins who named North America's fifth longest river – Yu-kun-ah, or Yukon, the "great river." On this journey we will meet the three vast bodies of water – Teslin Lake, Atlin Lake, and Tagish Lake – that are the Yukon's headwaters; we will travel alongside the first of its 3,185km to the Bering Sea; we may even walk across it, on a bridge suspended over Miles Canyon.

Along the banks of the great river, things are quiet now, more like they were before the Klondike – a place as well as an event. The Klondike is a river, a tributary of the Yukon, about 550km northwest of Whitehorse, near Dawson City. It was here, on August 16, 1896, that the glimmer of gold caught the eye of Tagish packer-prospectors, Skookum Jim and Dawson Charlie and their associate, George Carmack. It took 11 months for the news to get out, but when it did, the words "a ton of gold" stirred the souls of dreamers and fortune seekers around the world.

It would take the better part of another year for most of them – some 30,000 – to get here. (An estimated 100,000 started out). Those who could afford it took the "all water-route" – via the navigable waters of the Yukon River, from its mouth at the Bering Sea right to the new boom town of Dawson. A very few chose the "all-Canadian" options – bushwhacking from Telegraph Creek on the Stikine River to Atlin, or from Edmonton. Most sailed from Seattle, Washington or Victoria, BC to Skagway, then slogged over Coast Mountain passes – the Chilkoot and the White – to the Yukon's headwaters at Bennett Lake. From there, in anything that floated, they got as far north as Miles Canyon and the Whitehorse Rapids, then portaged around them to today's Yukon capital, Whitehorse. From there, the Yukon River carried stampeders to the gold fields. By the summer of 1898, almost as soon as they had arrived, the rush was over. In those two short years, it's believed miners gleaned $50 million from the Klondike – about what they spent on getting there.

Watson Lake to Whitehorse

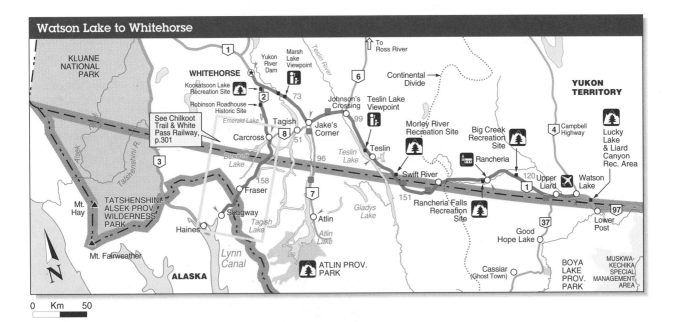

Whitehorse, Atlin, and Skagway each have their place in this story, and, though a full century has passed, modern-day travellers can't help but being swept up in it all over again. If it was the dream of riches, what is it now? Perhaps, it has always been, simply, the "Spell of the Yukon," as Robert Service wrote: "I wanted the gold, and I got it. Came out with a fortune last fall. Yet somehow life's not what I thought it. And somehow the gold isn't all."

BC/Yukon Territory Border (Historic Mile 627): 513km northwest of Fort Nelson.

Yukon Information: Yukon Territorial Government, Tourism Branch, Box 2703, White Horse, YT, Y1A 2C6. Offices and Visitor Reception Centre, 100 Hansen St, Whitehorse. 867-667-5340. For road conditions: Yukon Gold radio station, broadcast from Visitor Reception Centres at 96.1 FM, and radio stations close to major communities; or call 867-667-8215.

Yukon Government Campgrounds: Listed in the *Log* are government campgrounds offering a range of basic, roadside wilderness facilities, including tenting and RV sites, picnic tables, cold water, and outhouses. Fees posted at kiosks. General information: 867-667-5159.

Lucky Lake and Liard Canyon Recreation Area: 3km from the BC border. Small pine-fringed lake by the highway entering Watson Lake. Sandy beach, picnic tables, rodeo grounds, beach volleyball, horseshoe pits, waterslide into the lake. 2.2km trail descends to the Liard River canyon. Interpretive panels.

Watson Lake (Historic Mile 635): (Pop. 1,700). 9km north of BC border. Frank Watson, trapper and miner, was one of the few who arrived by the Edmonton Trail in '98: he

made his homestead on the shores of Fish Lake (now Watson Lake) near the present-day airport. In the 1930s, Grant McConachie, late president of Canadian Pacific Airlines, saw this outpost as a key air juncture for a "northwest passage to the Orient," and established Yukon Southern Air Transport.

During the Second World War, Watson Lake became a strategic link in the Northwest Staging Route, a series of airfields for fighter planes, safe from Japanese attack, connecting northwestern Canada with Alaska, Siberia, and China. Hence Watson Lake's place on the Alaska Highway, constructed in 1942, to link those airfields.

With a major airport, and its proximity to the Stewart-Cassiar Hwy, Watson Lake continues to thrive as a transportation centre for the southeast Yukon. (If you're not going to Whitehorse, but simply making a "mostly-BC" loop through the North, Watson Lake is the only town you'll encounter in the 1,289km between Fort Nelson and Hazelton on the Yellowhead Hwy. Other mainstays here: mining, logging, and outdoor recreation (fishing, camping, downhill skiing, golf). Accommodation and services.

Symbolizing Watson Lake's role as southern gateway to the Yukon is the **Sign Post Forest**, off Hwy 1 at the west end of town: this inspiring collection of more than 26,000 signs and licence plates from all over the world began with a carved sign of Danville, Illinois, posted during construction of the Alaska Hwy, by a homesick US army soldier.

Watson Lake Information and Interpretive Centre: Visitor Reception Centre, 104 Campbell Hwy (Hwy 1 and 4 junction). 867-536-7469 or Watson Lake Chamber of Commerce, 867-536-2240. Daily, May to mid-Sept. Focuses on Watson Lake as a transportation centre.

Watson Lake Airport: On Airport Rd, 10km north of town via Campbell Hwy. Terminal, built in 1942, is a heritage building. Base for private planes, floatplanes, and heliport.

Watson Lake Campground (Yukon Government): 55 RV/campsites. West side of town, right off highway. Trails, boat launch, swimming, fishing, playground.

Northern Lights Space and Science Centre: At Hwy 1 and Frank Trail, west end of town. 867-536-7827. New high-tech centre presents the science and mythology of the northern lights.

Wye Lake Park: North off Hwy 1. Sheltered picnicking, restrooms. Boardwalk trails for birdwatching.

Watson Lake Multi-Use Trail System: 867-536-7778. 18 walking/hiking/cross-country ski trails around town for a total of 80km. Beginner to advanced.

Watson Lake Ski Hill: 867-536-2258. 6km north of town on Campbell Hwy. Nine runs. Half pipe for snowboarders.

Upper Liard: 16km west of Watson Lake. Entering small Kaska native village. Highway crosses the Liard River.

Greenway's Greens Golf Course: 867-536-2477. Nine holes.

Highway 37: 23km west of Watson Lake. Nearest centre is Dease Lake, 234km; Hwy 16 junction is 721km. For route details, see p.280).

Rest Area: 24km west of Watson Lake. Pit toilets.

Big Creek Recreation Site (Yukon Government): 65km west of Watson Lake. Day-use area set in lodgepole pine forest by a big creek. Pit toilets.

Pullout: 107km west of Watson Lake. Highway traces the Rancheria River, headwaters of the Mackenzie River.

Rancheria Hotel/Motel (Historic Mile 710): 120km west of Watson Lake. Services.

■ **Historic Mile Sign:** Rancheria was among the first lodges to provide services for post-war highway travellers.

Rancheria Falls Recreation Site (Yukon Government): 134km west of Watson Lake. 500m trail to the falls,; wheelchair accessible. Signs introduce boreal forest.

Walker's Continental Divide Lodge: 140km west of Watson Lake. Homemade cookies and bread.

The Continental Divide: 141km west of Watson Lake. Height of land separates two of North America's largest watersheds – the Mackenzie River system flowing 4,241km to the Beaufort Sea, and the Yukon River system, flowing 3,185km to the Bering Sea. We leave behind the Rancheria River, and take up with the Swift River, a Yukon River tributary.

Swift River: 159km west of Watson Lake. Cafe, store, gas.

Rest Area: 175km northwest of Watson Lake. Pit toilets.

Rest Area: 219km northwest of Watson Lake. Pit toilets.

Morley River Recreation Site (Yukon Government): 226km west of Watson Lake. Day-use area. Good fishing.

Morley River Lodge: 227.5km west of Watson Lake. Gas, food, lodging.

Dawson Peaks Resort: 254km west of Watson Lake. Services.

Teslin (Historic Mile 804): (Pop 478). 264km west of Watson Lake. Just west of the Nisutlin Bay Bridge – at 575m, the longest bridge on the Alaska Hwy – crossing an arm of Teslin Lake. Teslin or Deisleen Aayi, in the Tlingit language, means "long narrow waters." This welcoming village is home to one of the Yukon's largest native communities. Excellent museum, trading post, outfitters, accommodation and services. Teslin Tlingit Woodcrafts sign advertises "fine snowshoes, freighter canoes, and traditional beaded garments" – in case your car breaks down?

■ **George Johnston Museum:** 867-390-2550. Celebrates local history and the Teslin Tlingit entrepreneur who chronicled the first half of this century in photographs. In 1928, Johnston brought in the region's first car, a Chevrolet now on display in the museum. This was before the Alaska Highway: his roads were frozen lakes and hand-cut trails.

■ **Historic Milepost Sign:** Describes the impact of the Alaska Hwy on northern native communities.

Teslin Lake Viewpoint: 271km west of Watson Lake. Shafts of light and rainbows dance over the Dawson Peaks, visible to the southwest. At the beginning of the world, these peaks helped support a giant hammock:

into it, Game Mother placed her newborn game animals, and rocked them to sleep. Interpretive panels describe Teslin Tlingit history and culture, and area wildlife.

Muckluck Annie's Salmon Bake: 278.5km west of Watson Lake. 867-667-1200. A commercial establishment offering salmon feasts, charter fishing.

Teslin Lake Campground (Yukon Government): 19 RV/tent sites. 281km west of Watson Lake. Boat launch, fishing.

Sign Post Forest at Watson Lake.

Johnson's Crossing Campground Services (Historic Mile 836): 300km west of Watson Lake. Hwy 6 leads north to Ross River, then the Northwest Territories. Camping, services.

■ **Historic Milepost Sign:** Another major Second World War development in the region was the Canol (Canada Oil) Pipeline Project, to supply airfields and highway. It consisted of oil fields in Norman Wells, 1,000km of pipeline, and an oil refinery in Whitehorse.

Rest Area: 344km northwest of Watson Lake. Pit toilets. Overlooks Squanga Lake.

Squanga Lake Campground (Yukon Government): 12 RV/tent sites. 345km northwest of Watson Lake. Swimming, fishing.

Jake's Corner/Highway 7: 370km west of Watson Lake. Hwy 7, mostly unpaved, leads south 96km to Atlin, BC. Who was Jake? Maybe Captain Jacobson, in charge of a highway construction camp here, in 1942; or maybe Jake Jackson, a Teslin Tlingit who travelled the area.

SIDE TRIP

to Atlin, British Columbia

Rest Area: 2km south of Hwy 1 at Jake's Corner. Pit toilets. Nice spot on Little Atlin Lake.

Snafu Lake Campground (Yukon Government): 4RV/tent sites. 25km south of Hwy 1. Boat launch, fishing.

Tarfu Lake Campground (Yukon Government): 4 RV/tent sites. 32km south of Hwy 1. Boat launch, fishing. Lake stocked with trout.

Yukon Territory/BC Border: 40km south of Hwy 1. Atlin Lake and daunting peaks of the Coast Mountains come into view.

Hitchcock Rest Area: 52km south of Hwy 1. Boat launch access to Atlin Lake.

Como Lake Forest Service Recreation Site: 88km south of Hwy 1. Boat launching on pretty Lake.

Atlin: (Pop. 506). 96km south of Hwy 1. Midway on the eastern shores of BC's largest natural lake – Atlin Lake covers 17,500ha and is 140km long.

This is BC's most northwesterly town. Not that people here make a big deal of that – their allegiances are more with the Yukon and Alberta than BC (Whitehorse and Edmonton are eminently more accessible than Vancouver, 2,500km by road). The only road link with BC died during the gold rush: a tortuous trail from Telegraph Creek on the Stikine River to the south end of Atlin Lake. Most who started out turned back.

Most, but not all. Until 1898, this area was the domain of the Taku River Tlingit who journeyed here from their salmon fisheries 60km south on the Taku River, to hunt, and later, trap furs for the Hudson's Bay Company. They called the lake A Tlen, "great water." Then, Klondike-bound prospectors found gold in the shallows of a small creek flowing into the "great water." Two cities emerged instantly and simultaneously: Discovery City on the banks of Pine Creek where the gold was found; Atlin City, 10km west via Discovery Road. In the heydays of 1899, there were 19 hotels in Atlin, the centre of commerce and culture. There were 10 hotels in Discovery, the working man's town. By 1902, there were only eight hotels in Atlin; six in Discovery.

Discovery died slowly, but Atlin flourished for the next 30 years, still a base for miners and a destination for tourists. They travelled via Skagway on the coast, taking the WP&YR railway to Carcross, a boat down Tagish Lake, another train 3km along the Atlino River to the west shore of Atlin Lake, and another boat to Atlin. Finally there, intrepid tourists boarded the MV *Tarahne* for luxury cruises to the awesome

Llewellyn Glacier, and to witness mountain goats, bears, moose, and loons. They golfed near the Warm Springs, drank from mineral springs, fished, enjoyed the orchestra, and purchased souvenirs (including works in silver by Taku Jack, chief of the Taku River Tlingit). The *Tarahne* carried 6,029 passengers in 1936. The following year, as the Depression sunk in, Atlin received only 57 visitors. The *Tarahne* never sailed again.

The road to Atlin opened in 1949 delivers travellers once again to this idyllic retreat. The Coast Mountains protect Atlin from the worst of Pacific storms. Summer is short, summer days are long (18 hours at solstice) and warm; evenings can be cool. Winter is long, and dark. Visitors quickly discover what residents prize, a magical quality of life that seems to evoke spiritual journeys and creative endeavours. Photographers, artists, naturalists, scientists, and Tom Sawyers gravitate to Atlin. Many stay.

Small houses and shops facing the lake date to the turn of the century. Panes and doors are dabbled with bright hues. Flowers erupt from a short growing season. From town you look across Atlin Lake to glaciers, mountains, subarctic forest, all part of Atlin Provincial Park surrounding the southern half of Atlin Lake.

There are air charters to see ice fields and glaciers; charter boats to secluded coves and islands; guided nature hikes; canoe and kayak expeditions; gold panning. There are hefty lake trout and grayling where streams enter the lake, and salmon to catch, 130km south in the Taku River country. Local accommodation includes lakeshore cottages, a hotel, motels, B&Bs, RV park with hookups, camping (there are also several Forest Service recreation sites in the area), and houseboat rentals. Atlin has a service station, groceries, hardware, craft and gift shops, liquor store, and limited banking facilities. Also, cappuccino in the old courthouse.

With mining at its roots, some in the community are supporting a scheme to reopen an abandoned mine southwest of here, near the Tulsequah River, a tributary of the Taku River: in the 1950s, minerals were barged out, now Vancouver-based Redfern Resources wants to build a 160km road linking Atlin and the Tulsequah Chief Mine. Opponents fear mining here would hurt the salmon fishery, and that the road, through virgin territory, would encourage more mining ventures.

Atlin Information: Info Centre, Atlin Visitors Association, Box 365, Atlin, BC, V0W 1A0. 250-651-7522 or in winter, 250-651-7470. Third and Trainor, in Atlin Museum. Daily mid-May to mid-Sept.

Aircraft Landing Strip: 1km east of town. For helicopters and fixed-wing planes.

■ **Atlin Museum:** Third and Trainor. 250-651-7522. Daily, Victoria Day weekend to mid-Sept. In 1902 schoolhouse. Exhibits and photos featuring the gold rush, settlement period, early transportation, and the Taku River Tlingit people. Walking tour of historic buildings.

Morning performs its magic on Palmer Lake near Atlin.

■ **Gold Panning:** Visitors can still pan for colour alongside modern-day miners at the provincial government placer lease on Spruce Creek, 8km from town. Info Centre has a map and rents pans and shovels, or buy your own at the general store.

■ **MV Tarahne:** On the lakeshore in front of town. Daily tours and slide shows; *Tarahne Tea*, July 1 weekend. Designed for sightseeing, this stately 24m gas-powered passenger boat was launched in 1918 and cruised through some of the most beautiful scenery in the world. She was lengthened to 36m in 1928. In 1937, a smaller vessel took her place. A restoration is planned.

■ **Discovery:** 10km east of Atlin on road to Surprise Lake. Mountains of gravel, a few old buildings.

■ **Atlin Pioneer Cemetery:** East of town on road to Surprise Lake. For those who died 1898-1948. Restored by Atlin Historical Society.

■ **Warm Springs:** 24km south of Atlin. Small undeveloped woodland pool, 29C, a pleasant summer stop, especially for kids. There is basic camping in surrounding meadow; no facilities.

■ **Taku Bar-B-Q:** At Friendship Corner, south end of Atlin, near Taku River Tlingit community. Serves salmon caught on the Taku River. The Taku is a relatively short river for migrating salmon, compared to the 3,185km Yukon River on this side of the divide. The fish are tastier and more nutritious, and fishermen who live in Atlin find it

worth their while to fly south to catch them.

■ **Atlin Centre for the Arts:** 3km from Atlin, on flank of Monarch Mountain. Box 207, Atlin, BC, V0W 1A0. 250-651-7659. Three-to four-week art, writing, and adventure programs.

■ **Llewellyn Glacier:** Viewpoint about 12km south of Atlin on Warm Bay Rd. One of the continent's largest ice fields, it reaches from the southwestern tip of Atlin Lake almost to the sea, at Juneau, Alaska. Charter flights are available for an even better view.

■ **Atlin Provincial Park:** 271,140ha; wilderness/walk-in campsites. 250-771-4591. No roads, access only by boat or plane. Total wilderness in Tagish Highlands of the Coast Mountains. One third of park is covered by glaciers and ice fields. Park also encompasses the southern half of Atlin Lake and includes 40km-long Theresa Island, crowned by Birch Mountain, 2,060m, the highest mountain on a lake island in the world. Outstanding wildlife photography, climbing, fishing, birdwatching. Consult area guides and outfitters. BC Wildlife Watch viewing site.

Return to Alaska Highway (1) at Jake's Corner

Highway 8 (Tagish Road): 2km beyond Jake's Corner. 372km west of Watson Lake. 54.5km route links Alaska Highway with Klondike Hwy (2) at Carcross.

SIDE TRIP

on Tagish Road

Tagish: (Pop 100). 21km southwest of Alaska Highway. On Tagish River linking the vast lakes, Tagish and Marsh lakes. Tagish is from *ta gizi*, "it [spring ice] is breaking up." Summer recreation area has services, accommodation, fishing and boating, houseboat tours. Just south of there was Northwest Mounted Police/Canadian customs post, Fort Sifton, established 1897, later named Tagish Post.

■ **Tagish Lake Campground (Yukon Government):** 28 RV/tent sites. Boat launch, fishing.

■ **Tagish Bridge Recreation Site (Yukon Government):** Picnicking, fishing.

Carcross: (Pop. about 300). 54.5km south of Hwy 1. Details, below.

Return to Highway 1

Lakeview Resort: 401km northwest of Watson Lake. On Marsh Lake.

Marsh Lake Viewpoint: 404.5km northwest of Watson Lake. Interpretive sign.

Marsh Lake Campground and Recreation Site (Yukon Government): 37 RV/tent sites; four tent only sites. 407km northwest of Watson Lake. Trails, swimming, fishing.

Yukon River Dam: 419km northwest of Watson Lake. Boat launch, viewpoint, interpretive panel.

Sourdough Country Campsite: 431.5km northwest of Watson Lake.

Highway 2 (South Klondike Highway): 433km northwest of Watson Lake. Leads south, 158km to Skagway, Alaska. Highway traces the gold-rush route between Skagway and Dawson City. Highway construction began in the 1950s; the section south to Skagway was not complete until the early 1980s.

SIDE TRIP

to Skagway, Alaska

Kookatsoon Lake Recreation Site (Yukon Government): 2km south of Hwy 1 on Hwy 2. Swimming, picnicking.

Robinson Roadhouse Historic Site: 18km south of Hwy 1. Remains of turn-of-the-century townsite.

Emerald Lake: 25.5km south of Hwy 1. Pullout overlooks pretty lake, also called Rainbow Lake.

Cinnamon Cache Bakery: 43km south of Hwy 1. Surprise! Sweet and sticky cinnamon buns and cappuccino.

Frontier Heritage Park/Wildlife Gallery: 49km south of Hwy 1. 867-667-1055. Daily, May-Sept. Live animals include Dall sheep and lynx. Petting farm, cafe, and gift shop.

Carcross Desert: 50km south of Hwy 1. The "smallest desert in the world" is actually the sandy bottom of a glacial lake. In these incessant southwesterly winds, vegetation can't take root.

Highway 8 (Tagish Road): 51km south of Hwy 1. Leads 54.5km to Jake's Corner on Hwy 1.

Carcross (Historic Mile 66): (Pop about 300). 51.5km south of Hwy 1, at a narrowing between Nares and Bennett lakes. Cariboo crossed here. And Tagish hunters, whose main community was at today's Tagish, had a seasonal camp. In their native Athapaskan language, they called this windy place Todezaane, "blowing all the time." In the the Tlingit language, this was Naataase Heen "water running through the narrows." Wind, water, caribou. People – in 1898, thousands floated by in boats and rafts of all sorts.

In 1902, an Anglican bishop, William Bompas, established St Saviour's Church at what was then being called Caribou Crossing. (The Chooutla Indian Residential School ran here until the 1960s.) But the bishop, tired of having his mail go to other towns named Cariboo Crossing, requested the abbreviation, Carcross.

Light rays reflect off Emerald Lake's shallow bottom to create rainbow colours.

It was here in 1904, that Skookum Jim (James Mason) – the strong-backed Tagish packer who helped trigger the gold rush – retired. He sold his claim and built himself a house. He died in 1916.

Today's Carcross is a pleasant, unassuming town of native and non-native people, century-old houses, and cabins set against a backdrop of big mountains and big lakes. It's well worth a meal and a wander. Here is the Caribou Hotel, a gift shop in the old police barracks and jail cell, and native crafts. The Matthew Watson General Store displays turn-of-the-century goods; gifts, snacks.

The Skookum Jim Dancers perform regularly near the Visitor Reception Centre. The Tagish community is concentrated on the south side of the bridge.

? Carcross Information: Visitor Reception Centre. In Old Train Depot (historic WP&YR) station. 403-821-4431. Mid-May to mid-Sept.

■ **Carcross Campground (Yukon Government):** 12 RV/tent sites. Adjacent Carcross.

■ **Historic Milepost Sign:** Carcross, on rail and waterways, played an important role in development of the Alaska Highway.

■ **Frontier Heritage Park/Wildlife Gallery:** 3km north of Carcross. See above.

■ **Carcross Cemetery:** Just south of Carcross. Here lie key gold-rush figures, James Mason (Skookum Jim), Dawson Charlie, Kate Carmack. Also Bishop Bompas.

Bove Island Viewpoint: 64km south of Hwy 1. Sign tells of American Lieutenant, Frederick Schwatka, who trekked over the Chilkoot Pass in 1883, and carried out a reconnaissance of the area, giving new names to places, despite existing names.

Venus Mill: 76km south of Hwy 1. In the early 1900s, this side of Montana Mountain was a gold and silver mine. Remains of ore-crushing mill and tramway are visible.

Yukon/BC Border: 79km south of Hwy 1. Rocky, barren hills, pools of glacial water trickling into small turquoise lakes: this is the birthplace of the Ya-kun-ah, the great river we call the Yukon. En route pull-outs offer views, photo-ops of the Coast Mountains. WP&YR tracks appear and disappear. Highways are rarely built to go where this one does.

Log Cabin: 116km south of Hwy 1. Highway and WP&YR tracks intersect here. (It's about 11km from the north end of the Chilkoot Trail. See Parks Canada, the Trail Centre, in Skagway, below). Log Cabin was a Northwest Mounted Police Customs House and police post during the gold rush. Access to Chilkoot Trail provided by WP&YR. Rest rooms.

Fraser: 125km south of Hwy 1. Signs provide area information and history of WP&YR construction. Canada customs is 1km south. Have ID ready and be prepared to stop. Information: 867-821-4111.

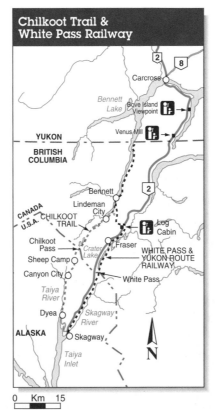

Chilkoot Trail & White Pass Railway

White Pass Summit: (El 1,003m.) 135km south of Hwy 1. This natural mountain boundary between coast and Interior is also a boundary between peoples. For millennia, the coastal Tlingit crossed back and forth over the White Pass and the Chilkoot Pass, exchanging goods with the Interior Athapaskans. There were other exchanges as well – they married each other; learned each other's languages, so much so that the Tagish peoples became fully speakers of Tlingit (that's why they are often referred to as Inland Tlingit people). The fur trade of the 19th century intensified these exchanges: the Russians trading with the Tlingit along the coast wanted Interior furs; the Tlingit, as middlemen, procured them from the Athapaskans. (The Athapaskans meanwhile maintained a direct trading relationship with the British Hudson's Bay Company).

These partnerships became the basis of the international boundaries we now acknowledge. In 1825, when the British and Russians came together to negotiate their respective shares of the New World, the British were granted the lands east of the Coast Mountains; the Russians, those to the west. In 1867, Russian interests were sold to the US as Alaska, and Britain's interests became Canada.

The Chilkoot Pass (el 1,140m) is in the next valley to the west. Klondikers, having reached Skagway, faced a difficult choice: the Chilkoot Pass or the White Pass. "Whichever way you go, you will wish you had gone the other," said one omniscient traveller. The White Pass was a horse-pack trail, though not a good one: in 1897, more than 3,000 horses died negotiating it; it is estimated only 500 of

5,000 trekkers actually got through on this route. On the Chilkoot Trail, men carried a year's supplies on their backs.

Canada/US Border: 135.5km south of Hwy 1. As the highway descends, reach out and touch glaciers. You are now leaving the Pacific Time Zone and entering the **Alaska Time Zone**, turn your watches back one hour.

US Port of Entry: 148km south of Hwy 1. Have ID ready and be prepared to stop. Information: 907-983-2325. If you arrive during unstaffed hours, report to the video camera.

Skagway: (Pop 806; triples in summer). 158km south of Hwy 1. Skagway sits at the head of a long fiord called Lynn Canal, its narrow streets lined by the false-fronted buildings that witnessed a gold rush. A cross between Barkerville and Banff, this town is a park – the Klondike Gold Rush National Historical Park. This park however, is just one component of the larger Klondike Gold Rush *International* Historical Park. Officially proclaimed in 1998, a century after the stampede, it is a park without boundaries, a gold-rush corridor, embracing a visitor centre in Seattle's Pioneer Square (Seattle was point of departure for most Klondikers), the Skagway Historic District, the Chilkoot and White Pass trails, the Thirty Mile Heritage River (a stretch of the Yukon River near Dawson), and historic sites in the city of Dawson. (This is Canada's sixth international park, but its first international *historical* park).

The lure is no longer gold, but gold-rush history. Tour buses from Whitehorse, ferries, cruise ships, and RVs disgorge passengers into Skagway's museums, vaudeville shows, souvenir shops. There are historic walking tours, mini-van tours, plane and helicopter tours, bicycle tours (up to the summit and back down again). It's only a relative few who skirt the inlet to Dyea, strap on their backpacks, and trek the Chilkoot Trail (see below).

Skagway was the domain of Tlingit people, a trickle of non-native traders and goldseekers, and a homesteader until 1897. In a gold rush, the real mother lode is the miners themselves, and suddenly, here were some 70 saloons, prostitutes, suppliers, and a certain lawless element.

Until mid-1898, however, Dyea, 14.5km around the inlet, was the busier place – the Chilkoot Pass being favoured over the White Pass as the route north. A landslide killing more than 60 miners on Palm Sunday, 1898, and construction of the WP&YR helped kill Dyea. Railroad construction from Skagway began in May 1898. It reached the White Pass summit by Feb 1899, and Whitehorse in the summer of 1900, but by then, the rush was over. Skagway's businesses moved to front onto the railway tracks, and this became a quiet rail and port town. There was a small boom during construction of the Alaska Highway. In 1982 the WP&YR closed: it started again in 1988, on a summer-only run.

Accommodation and services. Recreational opportunities include fishing, rafting, hiking on glaciers, horseback riding, sea kayaking.

? Skagway Information: Skagway Convention and Visitors Bureau Visitor

Centre, 5th St and Broadway. Write Box 415, Skagway, AK, 99840. 907-983-2854.

Alaska Marine Highway System: 1-800-642-0066 from the US and Canada; in Canada, 907-465-3941. Or write Alaska Marine Highway System, 1591 Glacier Ave, Juneau, AK, USA, 99801. Links Bellingham, Prince Rupert, Haines, and Skagway.

White Pass and Yukon Route Railway (WP&YR): 1-800-343-7373. Full and half-day excursions. To White Pass Summit, historic Bennett and end of Chilkoot Trail; bus and rail between Skagway and Whitehorse; Chilkoot Trail hikers service between Bennett, Fraser, and Skagway.

■ **Klondike Gold Rush National Historical Park Visitor Centre:** 2nd Ave and Broadway St. Daily, late May-Sept. Information, films, talks, tours, exhibits. Also visit **Mascot Saloon**, 3rd Ave and Broadway, replica of 1898 saloon.

■ **Parks Canada Trail Centre:** 907-983-3655.

■ **Trail of '98 – Skagway Museum:** 245 Broadway St. Daily, May-Sept. In winter, when ferry is in. Featuring Alaskan native heritage and the gold rush.

■ **Gold Rush Cemetery:** About 3km north of Skagway. 133 gravesites, occupied by such infamous characters as con man Soapy Smith, killed in a shootout. Visitor Centre has guide.

■ **Historic Walking Tour:** Visitor centre has guide to some 24 heritage buildings.

■ **Alaskan Wildlife Adventure:** 4th St and Spring St. 907-983-3600.

Road to the Chilkoot Trail: North out of Skagway. Scenic drive past glacial-green waters of the fiord. Look back to see how Skagway runs lengthwise to fit into the narrow valley.

Chilkoot Trail: 14.5km from Skagway to start of 53km trail ending at old Bennett townsite on Lake Bennett. Taxis and shuttle buses run from town.

Hikers come from around the world to experience the life of the stampeders – the trail is still strewn with well-preserved debris cast off when their feverish dreams encountered cold reality – muscle-wrenching climbs, mosquitoes, weather. To distract you: the dramatic scenery of coastal rainforest, lofty summits, high alpine lakes.

Trains used to run daily between Bennett and Skagway to pick up and drop off hikers, but the WP&YR has curtailed its service, with most trains now running only between Skagway and the White Pass Summit. Many backpackers hike the 13km out to the highway at Log Cabin and catch a bus or pick up a vehicle they have left in the parking lot. Chilkoot Water Charters (867-821-3209) offers pre-arranged boat transport from Bennett to Carcross; then, hikers can continue by bus to Whitehorse or Skagway.

Every person using the Chilkoot Trail requires a backcountry permit ($35 for adults, $17.50 for children under 15). Permits and maps can be obtained from Parks Canada in Whitehorse or at the Trail Centre in Skagway. Only 50 hikers may cross the summit each day. Reservations ($10 per person) recommended.

For information on preparedness, transportation, recommended reading, and regulations: Superintendent, Yukon National Historic Sites, Canadian Heritage, 205-300 Main St, Whitehorse, Yukon, Y1A 2B5. 867-667-3910.

Dyea: From Chilkoot Trailhead, continue across bridge to former townsite. National Parks staff offers guided tours: close your eyes and imagine: 8,000 people who once lived in Dyea. Here, Klondikers readied themselves for the gruelling trek ahead. Of those who started out, only half would make it. Some died, others turned back. Those who conquered the Chilkoot still faced a 1,000km trip to Dawson, mostly by water. Even in Dyea there were perils. The nearby **Slide Cemetery** is resting place of stampeders killed in an avalanche, April 1898. It's said the native people heard the mountain talking, and refused to travel the pass that day.

Return to Alaska Highway (1) at Highway 2 Junction

Wolf Creek Campground (Yukon Government): 29 RV/tent sites; 11 tent-only sites. 435.5km west of Watson Lake.

McRae (Historic Mile 910): 440.5km west of Watson Lake. McRae, a flagstop on the WP&YR, became a supply depot during construction of the Alaska Hwy.

Miles Canyon: 443.5km west of Watson Lake. 1km to suspension bridge above the Yukon River: water shoots through two million-year-old basalt canyon walls. Miles

WHITEHORSE

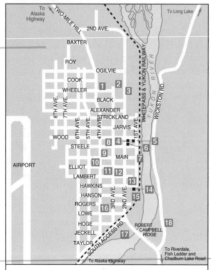

1 Quanlin Mall	**10** RCMP
2 Yukon Centre	**11** Old Log Church
3 Bus Depot	**12** Log Skyscrapers
4 Fire Hall	**13** Visitor Info Centre
5 MacBride Museum	**14** Public Library
6 City Hall	**15** Yukon Government Building
7 Train Depot	**16** Lion's Pool
8 Chamber of Commerce	**17** S.S. Klondike II
9 Federal Building	**18** Hospital

Canyon, and the Whitehorse Rapids that give the Yukon capital its name, were the final obstacles for Klondike-bound stampeders. Most portaged around the rapids (a few risked everything, and plunged through). In 1897, a horsedrawn tramway was built to carry goods and small boats around the rapids. At the head of the tramway, Canyon City emerged: here was a roadhouse and saloon, and an NWMP detachment under the redoubtable Sam Steele (see *BC Rockies*, p.200). At the other end of the tramway was the fledgling city of Whitehorse, and from here on, smooth sailing on river steamer to Dawson City. In 1900, the WP&YR from Skagway killed the tramway. Half a century later, the Whitehorse Dam killed the rapids, and created Schwatka Lake.

Canyon City Tours featuring gold-rush history and archaeology, depart from from bridge, daily, in summer. Road continues for 3km along river, past Whitehorse Dam, connecting with the South Access Rd into Whitehorse.

Whitehorse: (Pop 20,000). About 551km west of Watson Lake to downtown Whitehorse. Head of navigation on the Yukon River, 600km southeast of Dawson. This may be capital of the Yukon, but it's a frontier town, too: wide, rather than high: no skyscrapers to compete with the mountains. Whitehorse's official area is 421 square km, making it one of Canada's largest metropolitan areas. Wild, yet cultured, the city has cappuccino shops and bars for the season of long nights; its own CBC (Canadian Broadcasting Corporation) station, two newspapers (the *Yukon News* and *Whitehorse Star*), *Up Here Magazine*, the Yukon Arts Centre and Yukon College (Ayamdigut Campus), the Yukon Olympic Centre, and lots of art galleries representing the Yukon's disproportionate number of artists.

Whitehorse is where Canadians go when they've had enough (smog, crime, snooty neighbours). Residents hibernate, or at least slow down, in winter, play in the summer. When the days are long, the city is a base for canoe trips to Dawson; rafting expeditions to the Tatshenshini-Alsek rivers; trail riding, hiking, fishing. It's made easy for visitors: there's good tourist info, guided expeditions and nature walks, river cruises, books on hikes and bikes in the area, rentals. The gold-rush is tastefully and playfully presented at Miles Canyon, the MacBride Museum, in vaudeville performances featuring the Frantic Follies and stories by Robert Service. (For winter activities, see below).

The story of Whitehorse, as Whitehorse tells it, is not one of man's conquest over nature. Nature is big, humans are small. A full-size model of a wooly mammoth is on display at the Beringia Interpretive Centre. Here, and at the MacBride Museum, we learn of Beringia – the vast region encompassing the Yukon, Alaska, and Siberia, that remained unglaciated during the last ice-age. This wild and grassy prairie was home to camels, scimitar cats, beavers the size of black bears, and their diminutive human hunters. We also learn of the volcanic eruption, near the head of the Kluktan Glacier, 24km west of the Yukon-Alaska border: 1,500 years ago it left a telltale layer of dust over everything. The aboriginal people whose oral histories described the event are still here now.

The gold rush was, by comparison, a flash in the pan. The city of Whitehorse was born, and has persisted quietly since then. During the Second World War, Whitehorse was a hub for Alaska Highway construction, and a supply centre for the Canol pipeline project. It became a capital city in 1953, when the Yukon Territory was established.

? **Whitehorse/Yukon Information:** Yukon Visitor Information Centre, 100 Hanson St. Write Yukon Tourism, Box 2703, Whitehorse, YT, Y1A 2C6. 867-667-3084. Daily, mid-May to mid-Sept. Call year-round.

✕ **Whitehorse International Airport:** Off Hwy 1, at southeast end of Whitehorse. World's largest weather vane here, is a Douglas DC-3 plane that flew 1946-1970. Sits on a rotating pedestal, nose to the wind.

■ **Beringia Interpretive Centre:** Adjacent Whitehorse Airport, southeast of Whitehorse off Hwy 1. 867-667-8855. Mid-May to mid-Sept. Features the Yukon during the ice age.

■ **MacBride Museum:** First Ave and Wood St. 867-667-2709. Daily, late May-Labour Day. Gold Street Theatre, songs and skits about Yukon gold. Gold panning, rocker-box demos, wildlife, and geology exhibits, the history of Whitehorse, and the Sam McGee Fact and Fiction program. Excellent exhibit of mammals of the Pleistocene. Gift shop.

■ **Whitehorse Rapids Fishway:** At end of Nisutlin Dr. 867-633-5965. Late May-early Sept. Longest wooden fish ladder in the world (2m deep, 400m long), built 1959, allows Yukon River chinook to bypass the Whitehorse Dam and return to spawning grounds in the southern Yukon. Seven years before their arrival here, these remarkable salmon were spawned in Michie Creek, a tributary of the M'Clintok River, and made their way more than 2,800km north to the sea. Returning to their birthplace, they stop feeding for their three-month upriver migration. Best viewing is July-Aug. Underwater windows bring people nose to nose with fish. The dam, to power Whitehorse, was built 1957-58, with turbines added in 1968 and 1985.

■ **SS Klondike:** Southern entrance to town, near Robert Campbell Bridge. 867-667-3970. Mid-May to mid-Sept. From 1930 to the 1950s, this steamer carried passengers between Whitehorse and Dawson City. Film, tours.

■ **Yukon Transportation Museum:** Adjacent airport. 867-668-4792. Daily, mid-May to mid-Sept. From dogsleds to monoplanes and highways. Giant murals, replicas, models.

■ **Old Log Church Museum:** On Elliot at Third St. Built 1900, now an historic site, featuring pioneer missions.

■ **Historic Walking Tours:** Kiosk at 3rd Ave between Steele and Wood streets. Informative guides take you back to the gold rush, several times daily, July-Aug. For self-guided tours, pick up *A Walking Tour of Yukon's Capital*.

■ **Guided Nature Hikes:** 867-668-5678. Yukon Conservation Society. One- to six-hour hikes, easy to challenging. Interpretive programs at Canyon City.

■ **Miles Canyon:** See above. Tours, raft trips, July-Aug.

Along the South Klondike Highway, the roof of the world.

■ **Winter Activities:** The Yukon Quest Thousand-Mile International Sled Dog Race, in February, draws enthusiasts from around the world. Dogsledding tours available, Dec-March. There are about 300km of groomed trails in the Whitehorse area for snowmobiling, and lots of cross-country skiing. In addition to a lively arts and cultural scene, there are major events, including the Sourdough Rendezvous and International Storytelling festivals. See Events, p. 261.

■ **Mt Sima Downhill Ski Area:** South of Whitehorse, turn right just before Fraser Rd. 867-668-4557. Chairlift, rope tow, warming hut, rentals, services.

■ **Rockhounding and Mining:** Information at the **Yukon Rock Shop**, Hwy 1 and Carcross Rd, 867-668-2772. Also **Murdoch's Gem Shop** on Main St, and the **Whitehorse Gem and Mineral Club**, 26 Sunset Dr N, Whitehorse, YT, Y1A 4M8.

■ **Yukon Wildlife Preserve:** 867-668-3225. Tours, daily, mid-May to mid-Sept. 283ha preserve of indigenous northern animals.

■ **Mountain View Public Golf Course:** Take Porter Creek exit off Hwy 1. 18-holes.

■ **Boat Tours:** MV *Youcon Kat*, across from MacBride Museum, 2.5-hour trips down Yukon River. River raft, *Emerald Mae*, four-hour trips. *MV Schwatka*, tours of Miles Canyon. May be others too. Ask at Visitor Reception Centre.

■ **Takhini Hot Springs:** Northwest from Whitehorse, 6km on North Klondike Hwy, then 10km on Takhini Hot Springs Rd. 867-633-2706. Year-round; reduced winter schedule. B&B, camping, cafe, trail rides, cross-country skiing in winter.

The Alaska Hwy continues northwest from Whitehorse, 943km to Fairbanks, Alaska. At Haines Junction, 124km from Whitehorse, Hwy 3 leads south, tracing a portion of the gold-rush Dalton Trail, 256km to Haines, Alaska. The highway's Yukon section provides access to Kluane National Park. 101km from Haines Junction Hwy 3 crosses the Yukon/BC

border and skirts the western boundary of BC's provincial Tatshenshini-Alsek Wilderness Park (below).

SIDE TRIP

to Tatshenshini-Alsek Provincial Park

From Haines Junction, the first 65km stretch of Hwy 3 climbs from lush coastal valley to Canada Custom's Pleasant Camp. For the next 74km the highway flanks the St Elias Mountains in glorious open alpine country. The highest point in BC is in the St Elias Mountains. Mt Fairweather, el 4,663m, is tucked away in range's southwest on the BC/Alaska border. From the Chilkat Pass, el 1,065m, the highway gradually descends into interior valleys of the Yukon basin.

▲ 👁 **Tatshenshini-Alsek Wilderness Provincial Park:** 958,000ha. BC Parks, 800 Johnson St, Victoria, BC, V8W 1X4. 250-387-5002. For those who think, "So that was the Chilkoot Trail, what's next?" The "Tat," by raft. The 193km Tatshenshini River, with its headwaters in the northern Coast Mountains, flows through the Haines Triangle in northwestern BC to the Alsek River, which runs 370km from the Yukon's Kluane National Park, to the ocean at Alaska's Glacier Bay National Park. The 260km rafting journey starting from **Dalton Post**, in the Yukon, is for serious adventurers only. The Tat traverses a vast new wilderness park in the knob of BC northwest of the Chilkoot, separating Alaska from the Yukon. The area is known as the Haines Triangle for the highway forming its eastern boundary. Midst the St Elias Mountains – North America's highest peaks, ranging 3,000-4,000m, and among some 350 glaciers forming part of the largest non-polar icecap on Earth – this has been called a Lost Horizon, a rare, unspoiled place. (It has been pointed out, however, that with 1,100 and more wilderness river rafters a year, enthusiasm for beauty is already putting some pressure on this not-so-Lost Horizon.)

The Tatshenshini-Alsek watershed was spared in the early 1990s from the greater threat of a mining scheme that would have converted the peak of Windy Craggy Mountain into a gigantic open pit. Conservationists declared the Tat "the wildest river on the continent" and, until the Class A – no development, ever – park was proposed, they said it was "the second most endangered [river], after the Colorado."

The region supports a valuable salmon fishery and a rare diversity of wildlife, including half of BC's population of Dall's sheep, grizzlies, and what may be Canada's only glacier bears.

Linked up with Kluane National Park and Alaska's Wrangell-St Elias and Glacier Bay national parks, this becomes the largest international protected area in the world – 8.5 million hectares. It has been designated a UNESCO World Heritage Site.